[redacted]

THEOLOGICAL DICTIONARY
OF THE
OLD TESTAMENT

THEOLOGICAL DICTIONARY

OF THE

OLD TESTAMENT

EDITED BY

G. JOHANNES BOTTERWECK,
HELMER RINGGREN,
AND
HEINZ-JOSEF FABRY

Translated by

DAVID E. GREEN

Volume VII

כְּ - ליץ

k^e – **lyṣ*

WILLIAM B. EERDMANS PUBLISHING COMPANY
GRAND RAPIDS, MICHIGAN

THEOLOGICAL DICTIONARY OF THE OLD TESTAMENT
Volume 7
Translated from
THEOLOGISCHES WÖRTERBUCH ZUM ALTEN TESTAMENT
Band IV, Lieferungen 1-5
Published 1982-1984 by
Verlag W. Kohlhammer GmbH, Stuttgart, Germany

255 Jefferson Ave. S.E., Grand Rapids, Michigan 49503

Printed in the United States of America

05 04 03 02 01 00 99 98 97 96 95 7 6 5 4 3 2 1

Library of Congress Cataloging-in-Publication Data

Botterweck, G. Johannes
Theological dictionary of the Old Testament
Translation of Theologisches Wörterbuch zum Alten Testament.
Translated by David E. Green
Includes rev. ed. of v. 1-2.
Includes bibliographical references.
1. Bible. O.T. — Dictionaries — Hebrew. 2. Hebrew language — Dictionaries — English.
I. Ringgren, Helmer, 1917 — joint author. BS440.B5713 221.4′4 73-76170
ISBN 0-8028-2338-6 (set)

Volume VII ISBN 0-8028-2331-9

CONSULTING EDITORS

George W. Anderson
Henri Cazelles
David Noel Freedman
Shemaryahu Talmon
Gerhard Wallis

CONTRIBUTORS

G. André, Uppsala
†C. Barth, Basel
A. Baumann, Wolfsburg
J. Bergman, Linköping
K.-M. Beyse, Halle am Salle
†G. J. Botterweck, Bonn (Editor)
R. E. Clements, Cambridge
J. Conrad, Leipzig
C. Dohmen, Bonn
W. Dommershausen, Davos
†H. Eising, Münster
H.-J. Fabry, Bonn (Editor)
D. N. Freedman, Ann Arbor / San Diego
J. Gamberoni, Paderborn
M. Görg, Bamberg
H. Haag, Lucerne
†G. F. Hasel, Berrien Springs
J. Hausmann, Neuendettelsau
F. J. Helfmeyer, Cologne
A. S. Kapelrud, Oslo
D. Kellermann, Tübingen
K. Koch, Hamburg
B. Lang, Mainz
E. Lipiński, Louvain
N. Lohfink, Frankfurt am Main
G. Mayer, Zornheim
R. Mosis, Eichstätt
H.-P. Müller, Halstenbek
†M. J. Mulder, Badhoevedorp
M. P. O'Connor, Ann Arbor
E. B. Oikonomou, Athens
H. D. Preuss, Neuendettelsau
†J. Reindl, Erfurt
H. Ringgren, Uppsala (Editor)
J. Schüpphaus, Königswinter
K.-D. Schunck, Rostock
K. Seybold, Basel
P. Stenmans, Würzburg
A. Stiglmair, Bressanone
S. Wagner, Leipzig
G. Warmuth, Kiel
M. Weinfeld, Jerusalem
H.-J. Zobel, Greifswald

CONTENTS

EDITORS' PREFACE TO VOLUME VII

The original plan for the *Theological Dictionary of the Old Testament* provided for the completion of this multivolume work over the span of approximately a decade. Almost immediately such a swift realization proved to be utopian. The abundant influx of new insights in exegesis (e.g., pressing discussions concerning the Pentateuch, the Deuteronomistic history, the prophetic books, etc.), lexicography and semantics, comparative linguistics, ancient Near Eastern studies, and certainly not least archaeology with the discovery of new cultures (e.g., Tell Mardikh-Ebla) again and again forced to a standstill the otherwise unimpeded flow of work on the Dictionary. Many entries that had already been completed had to be reedited. Rightly so, several contributors and subscribers expressed their displeasure.

In the midst of this persistent grappling our venture encountered a serious blow. On April 15, 1981, Professor Gerhard Johannes Botterweck died. His profound knowledge of the Old Testament and its milieu, his vast experience in all practical matters associated with book production, his organizational skills, and above all his theological foresightedness had come to be of inestimable value to our undertaking. All this will be missing in the future. All colleagues acknowledge with gratitude the value of his accomplishments. R.I.P.

Dr. Heinz-Josef Fabry, a student of Professor Botterweck and an editorial colleague since 1971, has become the new co-editor. This should guarantee a continuity in the editorial work in keeping with the established principles.

Deliberation over fundamental matters is therefore unnecessary. The principal goal of the project remains the same (see the Preface to Volume I), to analyze the Hebrew words semantically. The presentation of the fundamental concepts intended by the respective words and terms, the traditions in which they occur, and the different nuances of meaning they have in each tradition stand at the focus of this analytical work, so that in the end one might ultimately bring together the individual building blocks of an Old Testament theology.

Helmer Ringgren/Heinz-Josef Fabry

ABBREVIATIONS

AANLR	*Atti dell' Academia Nazionale dei Lincei, Rendiconti,* Rome
AASOR	*Annual of the American Schools of Oriental Research,* New Haven, Ann Arbor, Philadelphia
AAWLM.G	*Abhandlungen der Akademie der Wissenschaften und der Literatur in Mainz,* Geistes- und sozialwissenschaftliche Klasse, Wiesbaden
AB	*The Anchor Bible,* ed. W. F. Albright-D. N. Freedman, Garden City
ABAW	*Abhandlungen der bayerischen Akademie der Wissenschaften,* Munich
ABL	R. F. Harper, *Assyrian and Babylonian Letters,* 14 vols. (Chicago, 1892-1914)
ABR	*Australian Biblical Review,* Melbourne
ABRT	J. A. Craig, *Assyrian and Babylonian Religious Texts,* 2 vols. (Leipzig, 1895-97)
abs.	absolute
acc.	accusative
ACLingSém-Cham	*Actes du premier congrès internationale de linguistique sémitique et chamito-sémitique,* Paris, 16-19 July, 1969. *Janua linguarum,* 159 (Hague, 1974)
AcOr	*Acta orientalia,* Copenhagen, Leiden
act.	active
AcThD	*Acta theologica danica,* Århus, Copenhagen
ADAI.Ä	*Abhandlungen des Deutschen Archäologischen Instituts in Kairo.* Ägyptologische Reihe, Glückstadt
ADAW	*Abhandlungen des Deutschen Akademie der Wissenschaften,* Berlin
adj.	adjective
adv.	adverb
AfO	*Archiv für Orientforschung,* Graz
ÄgAbh	*Ägyptologische Abhandlungen,* Wiesbaden
AHDO	*Archives d'histoire du droit oriental,* Brussels
AHw	W. von Soden, *Akkadisches Handwörterbuch,* 3 vols. (Wiesbaden, 1965-1981)
AION	*Annali dell'Istituto Universitario Orientali di Napoli*
AIPH	*Annuaire de l'Institut de Philologie et d'Histoire Orientales et Slaves,* Brussels
AJBI	*Annual of the Japanese Biblical Institute* (*Seisho-gaku ronshū*), Tokyo
AJSL	*The American Journal of Semitic Languages and Literatures,* Chicago
AJT	*American Journal of Theology,* Chicago
Akk.	Akkadian
AKM	*Abhandlungen für die Kunde des Morgenlandes,* Leipzig, Wiesbaden, Hildesheim
Amhar.	Amharic
Amor.	Amorite
AN	J. J. Stamm, *Die akkadische Namengebung. MVÄG,* 44 (1939, ^{2}1968)
AnAcScFen	*Annales Academiae Scientarum Fennicae,* ser. B, Helsinki
AnBibl	*Analecta biblica,* Rome
AncIsr	R. de Vaux, *Ancient Israel: Its Life and Institutions* (Eng. trans., New York, 1961, ^{2}1965)
ANEP	*The Ancient Near East in Pictures,* ed. J. B. Pritchard (Princeton, 1954, ^{2}1969)
ANET	*Ancient Near Eastern Texts Relating to the OT,* ed. J. B. Pritchard (Princeton, ^{2}1955, ^{3}1969)

AnOr	*Analecta orientalia,* Rome
AO	*Der Alte Orient,* Leipzig
AOAT	*Alter Orient und AT,* Kevelaer, Neukirchen-Vluyn
AOB	*Altorientalische Bilder zum AT,* ed. H. Gressmann (Berlin, ^{2}1927)
AO Beihefte	*Beiheft zum AO,* Leipzig
AOS	*American Oriental Series,* New Haven
AOT	*Altorientalische Texte zum AT,* ed. H. Gressmann (Berlin, ^{2}1926, repr. 1953)
AP	A. E. Cowley, *Aramaic Papyri of the Fifth Century B.C.* (1923, repr. Osnabruck, 1976)
APN	*K. Tallqvist, Assyrian Personal Names. ASSF,* 43/1 (1914, repr. 1966)
APNM	H. B. Huffmon, *Amorite Personal Names in the Mari Texts* (Baltimore, 1965)
Arab.	Arabic
ARAB	D. D. Luckenbill, *Ancient Records of Assyria and Babylonia,* 2 vols. (Chicago, 1926-27)
Aram.	Aramaic
ArbT	*Arbeiten zur Theologie,* Stuttgart
ARM	*Archives royales de Mari. Textes cunéiformes,* Paris
ArOr	*Archiv orientální,* Prague
ARW	*Archiv für Religionswissenschaft,* Freiburg, Leipzig, Berlin
AS	*Assyriological Studies,* Chicago
ASAE	*Annales du Service des Antiquités de l'Égypte,* Cairo
Ash.	Tablet in the Ashmolean Museum
ASSF	*Acta Societatis Scientiarum Fennicae,* Helsinki
Assyr.	Assyrian
ASTI	*Annual of the Swedish Theological Institute in Jerusalem,* Leiden
AT	Altes Testament, Ancien Testament, etc.
ATA	*Alttestamentliche Abhandlungen,* Münster
ATD	*Das AT Deutsch,* ed. V. Herntrich-A. Weiser, Göttingen
AThANT	*Abhandlungen zur Theologie des Alten und Neuen Testaments,* Zurich
ATR	*Anglican Theological Review,* Evanston
Aug.	*Augustinianum,* Rome
AUM	*Andrews University Monographs,* Berrien Springs
AuS	G. Dalman, *Arbeit und Sitte in Palästina,* 7 vols. (1928-1942, repr. Hildesheim, 1964)
AUSS	*Andrews University Seminary Studies,* Berrien Springs
AWEAT	*Archiv für wissenschaftliche Erforschung des ATs,* ed. E. O. A. Merx, 2 vols. (Halle, 1869-1872)
BA	*The Biblical Archaeologist,* New Haven, Ann Arbor, Philadelphia, Atlanta
Bab.	Babylonian, Babylonian Talmud
BAfO	*Beiheft zur AfO*
BAR	*Biblical Archaeology Review,* Washington
BA Reader	*Biblical Archaeologist Reader,* ed. D. N. Freedman, *et al.,* 3 vols. (Garden City, 1961-1970)
BASOR	*Bulletin of the American Schools of Oriental Research,* New Haven, Ann Arbor, Philadelphia, Baltimore
BASS	*Beiträge zur Assyriologie und semitischen Sprachwissenschaft,* Leipzig, Baltimore
BBB	*Bonner biblische Beiträge*
BBET	*Beiträge zur biblischen Exegese und Theologie,* Frankfurt, Las Vegas
BBLAK	*Beiträge zur biblischen Landes- und Altertumskunde. ZDPV,* 68 (1949-1951)
BBR	H. Zimmern, *Beiträge zur Kenntnis der babylonischen Religion. Assyriologische Bibliothek,* 12 (Leipzig, 1901)

BDB	F. Brown-S. R. Driver-C. A. Briggs, *A Hebrew and English Lexicon of the OT* (Oxford, 1907; Peabody, Mass., ²1979)
BDBAT	*Beiheft zur Dielheimer Blätter zum AT*
BdÉ	*Bibliothèque d'études,* Paris
Benz	F. L. Benz, *Personal Names in the Phoenician and Punic Inscriptions. StPohl,* 8 (1972)
BeO	*Bibbia e oriente,* Milan
BER	*Babylonian Expedition of the University of Pennsylvania, Researches* I
BethM	*Beth mikra,* Jerusalem
BETL	*Bibliotheca ephemeridum theologicarum Lovaniensium,* Paris, Gembloux
BEvTh	*Beiträge zur evangelische Theologie,* Munich
BFChTh	*Beiträge zur Förderung christliches Theologie,* Gütersloh
BHHW	*Biblisch-historisches Handwörterbuch,* ed. L. Rost-B. Reicke, 4 vols. (Göttingen, 1962-1966; index and maps, 1979)
BHK	*Biblia hebraica,* ed. R. Kittel (Stuttgart, ³1929)
BHS	*Biblia hebraica stuttgartensia,* ed. K. Elliger-W. Rudolph (Stuttgart, 1966-1977)
BHTh	*Beiträge zur historischen Theologie,* Tübingen
BibB	*Biblische Beiträge,* Fribourg
Bibl	*Biblica,* Rome
bibliog.	bibliography
BIES	*Bulletin of the Israel Exploration Society,* Jerusalem (= *Yediot*)
BietOr	*Biblica et orientalia,* Rome
BiLe	*Bibel und Leben,* Düsseldorf
BIN	*Babylonian Inscriptions in the Collection of James B. Nies* (New Haven, 1918–)
BiOr	*Bibliotheca orientalis,* Leiden
BJRL	*Bulletin of the John Rylands Library,* Manchester
BK	*Biblischer Kommentar AT,* ed. M. Noth-H. W. Wolff, Neukirchen-Vluyn
BL	*Bibel-Lexikon,* ed. H. Haag (Einsiedeln, 1951, ²1968)
BLe	H. Bauer-P. Leander, *Historische Grammatik der hebräischen Sprache des ATs* (1918-1922, repr. Hildesheim, 1991)
BM	Tablet in the collections of the British Museum
BMAP	E. G. Kraeling, *The Brooklyn Museum Aramaic Papyri* (New Haven, 1953)
BMB	*Bulletin du musée de Beyrouth*
BN	Biblische Notizien, Bamberg
BRL	K. Galling, *Biblisches Reallexikon. HAT* (1937, ²1977)
BS	*Bibliotheca sacra,* Dallas
BSAW	*Berichte über die Verhandlungen der Sächsischen Akademie der Wissenschaften zu Leipzig*
BSOAS	Bulletin of the School of Oriental and African Studies, London
BSt	*Biblische Studien,* Neukirchen-Vluyn
BT	*The Bible Translator,* London
BTAVO	*Beiheft zum TAVO,* Wiesbaden
BuA	B. Meissner, *Babylonien und Assyrien,* 2 vols. (Heidelberg, 1920-25)
de Buck	A. de Buck, *The Egyptian Coffin Texts,* 7 vols. OIP (1935-1961)
BVC	*Bible et vie chrétienne,* Paris
BWA(N)T	*Beiträge zur Wissenschaft vom Alten (und Neuen) Testament,* Leipzig, Stuttgart
BWL	W. G. Lambert, *Babylonian Wisdom Literature* (Oxford, 1960)
BZ	*Biblische Zeitschrift,* Paderborn
BZAW	*Beihefte zur ZAW,* Berlin
BZNW	*Beihefte zur ZNW,* Berlin
ca.	*circa,* about

CAD	*The Assyrian Dictionary of the Oriental Institute of the University of Chicago* (1956–)
CAH[3]	*Cambridge Ancient History,* ed. I. E. S. Edwards, *et al.* (Cambridge, 1970–)
CahB	*Cahiers de Byrsa,* Paris
CahTh	*Cahiers théologiques,* Neuchâtel
Can.	Canaanite
CB	*Coniectanea biblica, OT Series,* Lund
CBQ	*Catholic Biblical Quarterly,* Washington
CCT	*Cuneiform Texts from Cappodician Tablets in the British Museum* (London, 1921–)
CD A,B	Damascus document, manuscript A, B
cf.	compare, see
ch(s).	chapter(s)
CH	Code of Hammurabi
ChrÉg	*Chronique d'Égypte,* Brussels
ChW	J. Levy, *Chaldäisches Wörterbuch über die Targumim und einen grossen Theil des rabbinischen Schriftthums,* 2 vols. (Leipzig, 1867-68, repr. 1959)
CIH	*Corpus inscriptionum himyariticarum* (= *CIS,* IV)
CIS	*Corpus inscriptionum semiticarum* (Paris, 1881–)
CJT	*Canadian Journal of Theology,* Toronto
CML	G. R. Driver, *Canaanite Myths and Legends* (Edinburgh, 1956; [2]1977, ed. J. C. L. Gibson)
comm(s).	commentary(ies)
conj.	conjecture
ContiRossini	K. Conti Rossini, *Chrestomathia arabica meridionalis ephigraphica* (Rome, 1931)
Copt.	Coptic
CSD	R. Payne Smith, *A Compendious Syriac Dictionary* (Oxford, 1903, repr. 1976)
CT	*Cuneiform Texts from Babylonian Tablets in the British Museum* (London, 1896–)
CTA	A. Herdner, *Corpus des tablettes en cunéiformes alphabétiques découvertes à Ras Shamra-Ugarit,* 2 vols. (Paris, 1963)
d.	died
DAWB	Deutsch Akademie der Wissenschaft zu Berlin. *Schriften der Sektion für Altertumswissenschaft*
DAWW	Denschriften der (kaiserlichen) Akademie der Wissenschaften in Wien
DB	*Dictionnaire de la Bible,* ed. F. Vigouroux (Paris, 1895-1912)
DBS	*Dictionnaire de la Bible, Supplement,* ed. L. Pirot, et al. (Paris, 1926–)
DISO	J. F. Jean-J. Hoftijzer, *Dictionnaire des inscriptions sémitiques de l'ouest* (Leiden, 1965)
diss.	dissertation
DJD	*Discoveries in the Judean Desert* (Oxford, 1955–)
DMOA	*Documenta et monumenta orientis antiqui,* Leiden
DN	Deity name
DtrN	nomistic Deuteronomistic source
DTT	*Dansk teologisk Tidsskrift,* Copenhagen
E	Elohistic source
EA	Tell el-Amarna tablets
EAEHL	*Encyclopedia of Archaeological Excavations in the Holy Land,* ed. M. Avi-Yonah-E. Stern, 4 vols. (Englewood Cliffs, N.J., 1975-78)
EB	*Die Heilige Schrift in deutscher Übersetzung. Echter-Bibel,* Würzburg

EDNT — *Exegetical Dictionary of the NT,* ed. H. Balz-G. Schneider, 3 vols. (Eng. trans. Grand Rapids, 1990-93)
Egyp. — Egyptian
EH — *Europäische Hochschulschriften,* Frankfurt, Bern
EHAT — *Exegetisches Handbuch zum AT,* Münster
Einl. — Einleitung
EMiqr — *Enṣiqlōpedyā miqrāʿit* (*Encyclopedia Biblica*), (Jerusalem, 1950–)
EncBib — *Encyclopaedia Biblica,* ed. T. K. Cheyne, 4 vols. (London, 1800-1903, repr. 1958)
EncJud — *Encyclopaedia judaica,* 16 vols. (Jerusalem, New York, 1971-72)
EnEl — Enuma Elish
Eng. — English
ERE — *Encyclopedia of Religion and Ethics,* ed. J. Hastings, 13 vols. (New York, 1913-1927)
ErfThSt — *Erfurter theologische Studien,* Leipzig
Erg. — Ergänzungsreihe
ErIsr — *Eretz-Israel,* Jerusalem
ErJb — *Eranos-Jahrbuch,* Zurich
esp. — especially
ÉtB — *Études bibliques,* Paris
Eth. — Ethiopic
EvQ — *Evangelical Quarterly,* London
EvTh — *Evangelische Theologie,* Munich
ExpT — *Expository Times,* Edinburgh
FARG — *Forschungen zur Anthropologie und Religionsgeschichte,* Saarbrucken
fem. — feminine
fig. — figure
fr. — fragment
FreibThSt — *Freiburger theologische Studien,* Freiburg
FRLANT — *Forschungen zur Religion und Literatur des Alten und Neuen Testaments,* Göttingen
FuF — *Forschungen und Fortschritte,* Berlin
FzB — *Forschung zur Bibel,* Würzburg
GaG — W. von Soden, *Grundriss der akkadischen Grammatik. AnOr,* 33 (1952, ^{2}1969 [with *Ergänzungsheft. AnOr,* 47])
Ger. — German
GesB — W. Gesenius-F. Buhl, *Hebräisches und aramäisches Handwörterbuch über das AT* (Berlin, ^{17}1921, ^{18}1987–)
GesTh — W. Gesenius, *Thesaurus philologicus criticus linguae hebraecae et chaldaeae Veteris Testamenti,* 3 vols. (Leipzig, 1829-1858)
GGM — C. Müller, *Geographici Graeci minores* (Paris, 1855)
Gilg. — Gilgamesh epic
Gk. — Greek
GK — W. Gesenius-E. Kautsch, *Hebräische Grammatik* (Halle, ^{28}1909) (= Kautsch-A. E. Cowley, *Gesenius' Hebrew Grammar* [Oxford, ^{2}1910])
Gl — Number of OSA inscription in the Glaser collection
GLECS — *Comptes rendus du Groupe Linguistique d'Études Chamito-Sémitiques,* Paris
GSAT — *Gesammelte Studien zum AT,* Munich
GThT — *Gereformeerd theologisch Tijdschrift,* Aalten, Kampen
GTTOT — J. J. Simons, *The Geographical and Topographical Texts of the OT. StFS,* 2 (1959)
H — Holiness Code

HAT	*Handbuch zum AT,* ser. 1, ed. O. Eissfeldt, Tübingen
HAW	*Handbuch der Altertumswissenschaft,* ed. W. Otto (Munich, 1923–)
HDB	*Dictionary of the Bible,* ed. J. Hastings, 4 vols. (Edinburgh, 1898-1902; sup 1904; New York, ²1963)
Heb.	Hebrew
Herm	*Hermeneia,* Philadelphia, Minneapolis
HeyJ	*Heythrop Journal,* Oxford
Hitt.	Hittite
HKAT	*Handkommentar zum AT,* ed. W. Nowack, Göttingen
HO	*Handbuch der Orientalistik,* Leiden
HS	*Die Heilige Schrift des AT,* ed. F. Feldmann-H. Herkenne, Bonn
HSAT	*Die Heilige Schrift des ATs,* ed. E. Kautsch-A. Bertholet (Tübingen, ⁴1922/23)
HTC	*Herders Theological Commentary on the NT,* New York
HThR	*Harvard Theological Review,* Cambridge, Mass.
HUCA	*Hebrew Union College Annual,* Cincinnati
Hurr.	Hurrian
ICC	*The International Critical Commentary,* Edinburgh
IDAM	Israel Department of Antiquities and Museums
IDB	*The Interpreter's Dictionary of the Bible,* ed. G. A. Buttrick, 4 vols. (Nashville, 1962); *Sup,* ed. K. Crim (Nashville, 1976)
IEJ	*Israel Exploration Journal,* Jerusalem
ILC	J. Pedersen, *Israel: Its Life and Culture,* 4 vols. in 2 (Eng. trans., Oxford, 1926-1940, ⁵1963)
impf.	imperfect
impv.	imperative
inf.	infinitive
in loc.	on this passage
Intro(s).	*Introduction(s) (to the)*
IPN	M. Noth, *Die israelitischen Personennamen im Rahmen der gemeinsemitischen Namengebung. BWANT,* 46[3/10] (1928, repr. 1980)
J	Yahwist source
JA	*Journal asiatique,* Paris
JAC	*Jahrbuch für Antike und Christentum,* Münster
JANES	*Journal of the Ancient Near Eastern Society of Columbia University,* New York
JAOS	*Journal of the American Oriental Society,* Baltimore, Boston, New Haven
Jastrow	M. Jastrow, *A Dictionary of the Targumim, the Talmud Babli and Yerushalmi, and the Midrashic Literature* (1903; repr. 2 vols. in 1, Brooklyn, 1975)
JBL	*Journal of Biblical Literature,* Philadelphia, Missoula, Chico, Atlanta
JCS	*Journal of Cuneiform Studies,* New Haven, Cambridge, Mass., Philadelphia, Baltimore
JDAISup	*Jahrbuch des Deutschen Archäologischen Instituts, Supplement,* Berlin
JE	Yahwist-Elohist source
JEA	*Journal of Egyptian Archaeology,* London
Jer.	Jerusalem (Palestinian) Talmud
JHS	*Journal of Hellenic Studies,* London
JJS	*Journal of Jewish Studies,* London
JMOS	*Journal of the Manchester Oriental Society,* Manchester
JNES	*Journal of Near Eastern Studies,* Chicago
JNSL	*Journal of Northwest Semitic Languages,* Stellenbosch
Joüon	P. Joüon, *A Grammar of Biblical Hebrew,* 2 vols. *SPIB.B, biblica,* 14/1 (Eng. trans, Rome, 1991)
JP	*Journal of Philology,* London

JPOS	*Journal of the Palestine Oriental Society,* Jerusalem
JQR	*Jewish Quarterly Review,* Philadelphia
JRAS	*Journal of the Royal Asiatic Society,* London
JSJ	*Journal for the Study of Judaism in the Persian, Hellenistic and Roman Period,* Leiden
JSOR	*Journal of the Society of Oriental Research,* Toronto
JSOT	*Journal for the Study of the OT,* Sheffield
JSS	*Journal of Semitic Studies,* Manchester
JTS	*Journal of Theological Studies,* Oxford
Jud	*Judaica,* Zurich
K	*Kethibh*
K.	Tablet in the Kuyunjik collection of the British Museum
KAH	*Keilschrifttexte aus Assur historischen Inhalts.* I, ed. L. Messerschmidt. *WVDOG,* 16 (1911); II, ed. O. Schroeder. *WVDOG,* 37 (1922)
KAI	H. Donner-W. Röllig, *Kanaanäische und aramäische Inschriften,* 3 vols. (Wiesbaden, ^{2}1966-69, ^{3}1971-76)
KAR	*Keilschrifttexte aus Assur religiösen Inhalts,* ed. E. Ebeling. *WVDOG,* 28 (1919); 34 (1923)
KAT	*Kommentar zum AT,* ed. E. Sellin-J. Herrmann, Leipzig, Gütersloh
KBANT	*Kommentare und Beiträge zum Alten und Neuen Testament,* Düsseldorf
KBL	L. Koehler-W. Baumgartner, *Lexicon in Veteris Testamenti Libros* (Leiden, ^{1}1953, ^{2}1958, ^{3}1967–)
KBo	*Keilschrifttexte aus Boghazköy. WVDOG* (1916–)
KD	C. F. Keil and F. J. Delitzsch, *Comm. on the OT,* 10 vols. (Eng. trans., repr. Grand Rapids, 1954)
KDVS	*Kongelige Danske Videnskabernes Selskab,* Hist.-phil. Kl., Copenhagen
KEHAT	*Kurzgefasstes exegetisches Handbuch zum AT,* ed. O. F. Fridelin (Leipzig, 1812-1896)
KHC	*Kurzer Hand-Commentar zum AT,* ed. K. Marti, Tübingen, Leipzig
KHS	*Kleinkommentar zur Heiligen Schrift,* Düsseldorf
KlPauly	*Der Kleine Pauly. Lexikon der Antike,* ed. K. Ziegler-W. Sontheimer, 5 vols. (Stuttgart, 1964-1975)
KlSchr	*Kleine Schriften* (A. Alt [Munich, 1953-59, ^{3}1964]; O. Eissfeldt [Tübingen, 1962-1979]; K. Elliger [*ThB,* 32 (1966)]; E. Meyer [Halle, 1910-1924])
KTU	*Die keilalphabetischen Texte aus Ugarit,* I, ed. M. Dietrich-O. Loretz-J. Sanmartín. *AOAT,* 24 (1976)
KuD	*Kerygma und Dogma,* Göttingen
Kuhn	K. G. Kuhn, *Konkordanz zu den Qumrantexten* (Göttingen, 1960); Nachträge, *RevQ,* 4 (1963-64), 163-234
l(l).	line(s)
Lane	E. W. Lane, *An Arabic-English Lexicon,* 8 vols. (London, 1863-1893, repr. 1968)
LAPO	*Littératures anciennes du Proche-Orient,* Paris
Lat.	Latin
LB	*Linguistica biblica,* Bonn
LCP	*Latinitas Christianorum primaeva,* Utrecht
LD	*Lectio divina,* Paris
Leslau, *Contributions*	W. Leslau, *Ethiopic and South Arabic Contributions to the Hebrew Lexicon* (Los Angeles, 1958)
LexÄg	W. Helck-E. Otto, *Lexikon der Ägyptologie* (Wiesbaden, 1975–)
LexHebAram	F. Zorrell, *Lexicon hebraicum et aramaicum Veteris Testamenti* (Rome, 1958, repr. 1968)
LexLingAeth	A. Dillmann, *Lexicon linguae aethiopicae* (Leipzig, 1865)

LexLingAram	E. Vogt, *Lexicon linguae aramaicae Veteris Testamenti documentis antiquis illustratum* (Rome, 1971)
LexSyr	C. Brockelmann, *Lexicon syriacum* (Halle, 1928, ^{2}1968)
Lic.	Licentiate
LidzNE	M. Lidzbarski, *Handbuch der nordsemitischen Epigraphik* (Weimar, 1898)
Lisowsky	G. Lisowsky, *Konkordanz zum hebräischen AT* (Stuttgart, 1958, ^{2}1966)
lit.	literally
LO	*Lex orandi,* Paris
LSS	*Leipziger semitische Studien*
LThK	*Lexikon für Theologie und Kirche,* ed. M. Buchberger, 10 vols. (Freiburg, 1930-38); ed. J. Höfer-K. Rahner, 10 vols. with index, 3 sups. (^{2}1957-1968, ^{3}1966-68)
LTP	*Laval théologique et philosophique,* Quebec
LUÅ	*Lunds Universitets Årsskrift*
LXX	Septuagint (LXX^{A}, Codex Alexandrinus; LXX^{B}, Codex Vaticanus; LXX^{R}, Lucianic recension; LXX$^{S[1,2]}$, Codex Sinaiticus, correctors 1, 2, etc.)
MAD	*Materials for the Assyrian Dictionary,* Chicago
Mand.	Mandaic
MAOG	*Mitteilungen der Altorientalistischen Gesellschaft,* Leipzig
MÄSt	*Münchener Ägyptologische Studien,* Berlin
masc.	masculine
MDAI.K	*Mitteilungen des Deutschen Archäologischen Instituts. Abteilung Kairo,* Munich
MdD	E. S. Drower-R. Macuch, *Mandaic Dictionary* (Oxford, 1963)
MEE	*Materiali Epigrafica di Ebla,* ser. maior, Naples
MGWJ	*Monatsschrift für Geschichte und Wissenschaft des Judentums,* Breslau
Midr.	Midrash
MIO	*Mitteilungen des Instituts für Orientforschung,* Berlin
Mm	Masora magna
Moab.	Moabite
Mon.	Monograph
MPG	J. P. Migne, *Patrologia graeca,* 167 vols. (Paris, 1857-1866); index, 2 vols. (1928-1936)
MPL	J. P. Migne, *Patrologia latina,* 221 vols. (Paris, 1841-1864); sup, 5 vols. (1958-1970)
MRS	*Mission de Ras Shamra,* Paris
ms(s).	manuscript(s)
MSL	*Materialen zum sumerischen Lexikon,* Rome
MT	Masoretic Text
Mus	*Muséon,* Louvain
MUSJ	*Mélanges de l'Université St.-Joseph,* Beirut
MVÄG	*Mitteilungen der Vorderasiatisch-Ägyptischen Gesellschaft* (Berlin), Leipzig
n(n).	note(s)
N	name
NEB	*Die Neue Echter-Bibel,* Würzburg
NedThT	*Nederlands theologisch Tijdschrift,* Wageningen
NICOT	*The New International Commentary on the OT,* Grand Rapids
NJPS	*The New Jewish Publication Society of America Translations of the Holy Scriptures* (Philadelphia, 1962-1978)
NKZ	*Neue Kirkliche Zeitschrift,* Erlangen, Leipzig
no(s).	number(s)
NRSV	*New Revised Standard Version* (New York, 1989)
NRTh	*Nouvelle Revue Théologique,* Louvain, Paris

N.S.	New Series
NT	New Testament, Neues Testament, etc.
NTS	*New Testament Studies,* Cambridge
NTT	*Norsk teologisk Tidsskrift,* Oslo
OBO	*Orbis biblicus et orientalis,* Fribourg, Göttingen
obv.	obverse of a papyrus or tablet
OIP	*Oriental Institute Publications,* Chicago
OLZ	*Orientalistische Literaturzeitung,* Leipzig, Berlin
Or	*Orientalia,* Rome
OrAnt	*Oriens antiquus,* Rome
OrBibLov	*Orientalia et biblica Lovaniensia,* Louvain
OSA	Old South Arabic
OT	Old Testament, Oude Testament, etc.
OTL	*The Old Testament Library,* Philadelphia, Louisville
OTS	*Oudtestamentische Studiën,* Leiden
p(p).	page(s)
P	Priestly source (P^G, Priestly *Grundschrift* ["basic material"])
PÄ	*Probleme der Ägyptologie,* Leiden
Pahl.	Pahlavi
par.	parallel/and parallel passages
pass.	passive
PBS	*Publications of the Babylonian Section of the University Museum,* Philadelphia
PEQ	*Palestine Exploration Quarterly,* London
perf.	perfect
Pers.	Persian
Phil.-hist. Kl.	Philosophische-historische Klasse
Phoen.	Phoenician
PIASH	*Proceedings of the Israel Academy of Sciences and Humanities,* Jerusalem
PJ	*Palästinajahrbuch,* Berlin
pl(s).	plate(s)
pl.	plural
PN	Personal name
PNPI	J. K. Stark, *Personal Names in Palmyrene Inscriptions* (Oxford, 1971)
PNU	F. Grondähl, *Die Personennamen der Texte aus Ugarit. StPohl,* 1 (1967)
POS	*Pretoria Oriental Series,* Leiden
PredOT	*De Prediking van het OT,* Nijkerk
prep.	preposition
PRU	*Le Palais royal d'Ugarit,* ed. C. F.-A. Schaeffer-J. Nougayrol. *MRS*
PSBA	Proceedings of the Society of Biblical Archaeology, Bloomsbury
ptcp.	participle
Pun.	Punic
PW	A. Pauly-G. Wissowa, *Real-Encyclopädie der classischen Altertumswissenschaft,* 6 vols. (Stuttgart, 1839-1852); sup., 11 vols. (1903-1956); ser. 2, 10 vols. (1914-1948)
Q	*Qere*
Q	Qumran scroll (preceded by arabic numeral designating cave)
QuaestDisp	*Quaestiones disputatae,* ed. K. Rahner-H. Schlier (Eng. ed., New York, 1961–)
R (preceded by roman numeral)	text in H. C. Rawlinson, *The Cuneiform Inscriptions of Western Asia,* 5 vols. (London, 1861-1884)
R^D	Deuteronomistic redactor
RA	*Revue d'assyriologie et d'archéologie orientale,* Paris

RAC	*Reallexikon für Antike und Christentum,* ed. T. Klauser (Stuttgart, 1950–)
RAcc	F. Thureau-Dangin, *Rituels accadiens* (Paris, 1921)
RÄR	H. Bonnet, *Reallexikon der ägyptischen Religionsgeschichte* (Berlin, 1952, ²1971)
RB	*Revue biblique,* Paris
RdM	*Die Religionen der Menschheit,* ed. C. M. Schröder, Stuttgart
RE	*Real-Enzyklopädie für protestantische Theologie und Kirche,* ed. A. Hauck, 24 vols. (Leipzig, 1896-1913)
RechBib	*Recherches bibliques,* Paris
repr.	reprint, reprinted
Répr. géogr.	*Répertoires géograpique des textes cunéiformes,* ed. W. Röllig. *BTAVO,* B, 7 (1974–)
RÉS (with number of text)	*Répertoire d'épigraphie sémitique* (Paris, 1900–)
RÉS (with vol. number)	*Revue des études sémitiques,* Paris
rev.	revised, revision
RevQ	*Revue de Qumrân,* Paris
RGG	*Die Religion in Geschichte und Gegenwart* (Tübingen, ²1927-1931, ed. H. Gunkel-L. Zscharnack, 5 vols. ³(1957-1965, ed. K. Galling, 6 vols.)
RHPR	*Revue d'histoire et de philosophie religieuses,* Strasbourg, Paris
RHR	*Revue de l'histoire des religions,* Paris
RivBibl	*Rivista biblica,* Rome
RLA	*Reallexikon der Assyriologie,* ed. E. Ebeling-B. Meissner (Berlin, 1932–)
RLV	*Reallexikon der Vorgeschichte,* ed. M. Ebert, 15 vols. (Berlin, 1924-1932)
RS	Ras Shamra text
RScR	*Recherches de science religieuse,* Paris
RSO	*Rivista degli studi orientali,* Rome
RSP	*Ras Shamra Parallels: The Texts from Ugarit and the Hebrew Bible,* ed. L. R. Fisher, *et al.,* I, *AnOr,* 49 (1972); II, *AnOr,* 50 (1975); III, *AnOr,* 51 (1981)
RSV	*Revised Standard Version* (New York, 1946, 1952)
rto.	recto, on the obverse of a papyrus or tablet
RyNP	G. Ryckmans, *Les noms propres sud-sémitiques,* 3 vols. *Bibliothèque de muséon,* 2 (Louvain, 1934-35)
SAHG	A. Falkenstein and W. von Soden, *Sumerische und akkadische Hymnen und Gebeten* (Zurich, 1953)
Sam.	Samaritan
SAW	*Sitzungsberichte der Óesterreichischen Akademie der Wissenschaften in Wien,* Vienna
SB	*Sources bibliques,* Paris
SBL	Society of Biblical Literature
SBM	*Stuttgarter biblische Monographien*
SBS	Stuttgarter Bibel-Studien
SBT	Studies in Biblical Theology, London, Naperville
ScrHier	*Scripta Hierosolymitana,* Jerusalem
SDAW	*Sitzungsberichte der Deutschen Akademie der Wissenschaften zu Berlin*
SEÅ	Svensk exegetisk Årsbok, Lund
Sef.	*Sefarad,* Madrid
Sem.	Semitic
Sem	*Semitica,* Paris
ser.	series

Seux	J. M. Seux, *Epithètes royales akkadiens et sumériennes* (Paris, 1967)
sg.	singular
SGKA	*Studien zur Geschichte und Kultur des Altertums,* Paderborn
SHAW	*Sitzungsberichte der Heidelberger Akademie der Wissenschaften*
ShnatMikr	Shenaton le-mikra ule-ḥeker ha-mizraḥ ha-kadum (*Shnationian Annual for Biblical and Ancient Near Eastern Studies*), Jerusalem
SJT	*Scottish Journal of Theology,* Edinburgh
SKG.G	*Schriften der Königsberger Gelehrten Gesellschaft,* Geisteswissenschaftliche Klasse, Halle
ŠL	A. Deimel, *Šumerisches Lexikon* (Rome, 1925-1937, repr. 1961)
SMEA	*Studi Milani ed Egeo-Anatolici,* Rome
SNumen	*Sup to Numen,* Leiden
Sond	Sonderband, Sonderheft
Soq.	Soqoṭri
SPAW	*Sitzungsberichte der Preussischen Akademie der Wissenschaften,* Berlin
SPIB	*Scripta Pontificii Instituti Biblici,* Rome
SPIB.B	*Subsidia bibliographica,* Rome
SSAOI	*Sacra scriptura antiquitatibus orientalibus illustrata,* Rome
SSAW	*Sitzungsberichte der Sächsischen Akademie der Wissenschaften zu Leipzig,* Phil.-hist. Kl.
SSN	*Studia semitica neerlandica,* Assen
StANT	*Studien zum Alten und Neuen Testament,* Munich
St.-B.	H. L. Strack-P. Billerbeck, *Kommentar zum NT aus Talmud und Midrasch,* 6 vols. (Munich, 1922-1961)
StBTh	*Studia biblica et theologica,* Pasadena, New Haven
StDI	*Studia et documenta ad iura orientis antiqui pertinentia,* Leiden
StFS	*Studia Francisci Scholten memoriae dicata,* Leiden
StJLA	*Studies in Judaism in Late Antiquity,* Leiden
STLI	*Studies and Texts.* Philip W. Lown Institute of Advanced Judaic Studies, Brandeis University, Cambridge, Mass.
StOr	*Studia orientalia,* Helsinki
StPb	*Studia Postbiblica,* Leiden
StPohl	*Studia Pohl,* Rome
StR	*Studies in Religion/Sciences religieuses,* Toronto
StSem	*Studi semitici,* Rome
StT	*Studi e testi,* Rome
STT	*The Sultantepe Tablets,* I, ed. O. R. Gurney-J. J. Finkelstein (London, 1957); II, ed. Gurney and P. Hulin (1964)
StTh	*Studia theologica,* Lund, Århus
StudGen	*Studium generale,* Berlin
StUNT	*Studien zur Umwelt des NTs,* Göttingen
subj.	subject
subst.	substantive
suf.	suffix
Sum.	Sumerian
Sup	Supplement(s) (to)
s.v.	*sub voce* (*vocibus*), under the word(s)
SVT	*Supplements to VT,* Leiden
syn.	synonym(ous)
Synt	C. Brockelmann, *Hebräische Syntax* (Neukirchen-Vluyn, 1956)
Syr.	Syriac

Syr	*Syria. Revue d'art oriental et d'archéologie,* Paris
SZ	*Kurzgefasster Kommentar zu den heiligen Schriften Alten und Neuen Testamentes,* ed. H. L. Strack-O. Zöckler (Nordlingen, 1886-1898)
TAik	*Teologinen aikakauskirja,* Helsinki
Tanḥ.B	*Tanḥuma* (ed. Buber)
TAPhS	*Transactions of the American Philosophical Society,* Philadelphia
Targ.	Targum
TAVO	*Tübinger Atlas des Vorderen Orients,* Wiesbaden
TCL	*Textes cunéiformes du Musée du Louvre,* 31 vols. (Paris, 1910-1967)
TCS	*Texts from Cuneiform Sources,* Locust Valley, N.Y.
TDNT	*Theological Dictionary of the NT,* ed. G. Kittel-G. Friedrich, 10 vols. plus index (Eng. trans., Grand Rapids, 1964-1976)
TDOT	*Theological Dictionary of the OT,* ed. G. J. Botterweck–H. Ringgren–H.-J. Fabry (Eng. trans., Grand Rapids, 1974–)
TGI	K. Galling, *Textbuch zur Geschichte Israels* (Tübingen, 1950, ²1968)
Tham.	Thamudic
THAT	*Theologisches Handwörterbuch zum AT,* ed. E. Jenni-C. Westermann, 2 vols. (Munich, 1971-79)
ThB	*Theologische Bücherei,* Munich
ThEH	*Theologische Existenz heute,* Munich
ThLZ	*Theologische Literaturzeitung,* Leipzig, Berlin
ThQ	*Theologische Quartalschrift,* Tübingen, Stuttgart
ThR	*Theologische Rundschau,* Tübingen
ThSt	*Theologische Studien,* Zurich
ThStKr	*Theologische Studien und Kritiken,* Hamburg, Gotha, Leipzig
ThZ	*Theologische Zeitschrift,* Basel
Tigr.	Tigriña
TigrWb	E. Littmann-M. Höfner, *Wörterbuch der Tigre-Sprache* (Wiesbaden, 1962)
TOTC	*Tyndale Old Testament Commentaries,* London, Downers Grove
trans.	translation, translated by
TRE	*Theologische Realenzyklopädie,* ed. G. Krause–G. Müller–H. R. Balz, 22 vols. (Berlin, 1977-1992)
TrThSt	*Trierer theologische Studien*
TrThZ	*Trierer theologische Zeitschrift*
UET	Joint Expedition of the British Museum and of the Museum of the University of Pennsylvania to Mesopotamia, *Ur Excavations: Texts* (London, 1928–)
UF	*Ugarit-Forschungen,* Neukirchen-Vluyn
Ugar.	Ugaritic
Univ.	University
Urk.	*Urkunden des ägyptischen Altertums,* ed. G. Steindorff (Leipzig, Berlin, 1903–)
UT	C. H. Gordon, *Ugaritic Textbook. AnOr,* 38 (1965, ²1967)
UUÅ	*Uppsala universitets êrsskrift*
v(v).	verse(s)
VAB	*Vorderasiatische Bibliothek,* 7 vols. (Leipzig, 1907-1916)
VAS	*Vorderasiatische Schriftdenkmäler der königlichen Museen,* Berlin
VD	*Verbum domini,* Rome
VG	C. Brockelmann, *Grundriss der vergleichenden Grammatik der semitischen Sprachen,* 2 vols. (1908-1913, repr. Hildesheim, 1961)
vo.	verso, on the reverse of a papyrus or tablet
vs(s).	version(s)
VT	*Vetus Testamentum,* Leiden

Vulg.	Vulgate
VVAW.L	*Verhandelingen van de Koninklijke Vlaamse Academie voor Wetenschappen, Letteren en Schone Kunsten van België,* Klasse der letteren, Brussels
WbÄS	A. Erman-H. Grapow, *Wörterbuch der ägyptischen Sprache,* 6 vols. (Leipzig, 1926-1931, repr. 1963)
WbMyth	*Wörterbuch der Mythologie,* ed. H. W. Haussig (Stuttgart, 1965–)
WdF	*Wege der Forschung,* Darmstadt
Wehr	H. Wehr, *A Dictionary of Modern Written Arabic,* ed. J. M. Cowan (Ithaca, 1961, ^{3}1971)
Whitaker	R. E. Whitaker, *A Concordance of the Ugaritic Language* (Cambridge, Mass., 1972)
WKÄS	*Wörterbuch der klassischen arabischen Sprache,* ed. M. Ullmann (Wiesbaden, 1970–)
WMANT	*Wissenschaftliche Monographien zum Alten und Neuen Testament,* Neukirchen-Vluyn
WO	*Die Welt des Orients,* Göttingen
WTJ	*Westminster Theological Journal,* Philadelphia
WTM	J. Levy, *Wörterbuch über die Talmudim und Midraschim,* 4 vols. (Leipzig, ^{2}1924, repr. 1963)
WuD	*Wort und Dienst,* Bielefeld
WUNT	*Wissenschaftliche Untersuchungen zum NT,* Tübingen
WUS	J. Aistleitner, *Wörterbuch der ugaritischen Sprache. BSAW,* Phil.-hist. Kl., 106/3 (1963, ^{4}1974)
WVDOG	*Wissenschaftliche Veröffentlichungen der deutschen Orient-Gesellschaft,* Leipzig, Berlin
WZ Halle	*Wissenschaftliche Zeitschrift der Martin-Luther-Universität Halle-Wittenberg,* Halle
WZ Leipzig	*Wissenschaftliche Zeitschrift der Karl-Marx-Universität Leizpig*
WZKM	Wiener Zeitschrift für die Kunde des Morgenlandes, Vienna
YNER	*Yale Near Eastern Researches,* New Haven
YOSBT	*Yale Oriental Series: Babylonian Texts,* New Haven
YOSR	*Yale Oriental Series: Researches,* New Haven
ZA	*Zeitschrift für Assyriologie,* Leipzig, Berlin
ZÄS	*Zeitschrift für ägyptische Sprache und Altertumskunde,* Leipzig, Berlin
ZAW	*Zeitschrift für die alttestamentliche Wissenschaft,* Giessen, Berlin
ZBK	*Zürcher Bibelkommentare,* Zurich, Stuttgart
ZDMG	*Zeitschrift der Deutschen Morgenländischen Gesellschaft,* Leipzig, Wiesbaden
ZDPV	*Zeitschrift des Deutschen Palästina-Vereins,* Leipzig, Stuttgart, Wiesbaden
ZE	*Zeitschrift für Ethnologie,* Braunschweig
ZKTh	*Zeitschrift für katholische Theologie,* Innsbruck
ZMR	*Zeitschrift für Missionskunde und Religionswissenschaft,* Berlin
ZNW	*Zeitschrift für die neutestamentliche Wissenschaft,* Giessen, Berlin
ZRGG	*Zeitschrift für Religions- und Geistesgeschichte,* Cologne
ZS	*Zeitschrift für Semitistik und verwandte Gebiete,* Leipzig
ZThK	*Zeitschrift für Theologie und Kirche,* Tübingen
→	cross-reference within this Dictionary
<	derived from
>	whence derived, to
*	theoretical form

TRANSLITERATION

VOWELS

◌ַ	a
◌ֲ	^{a}
◌ָ	ā
◌ָה	â
◌ָיו	āw
◌ַי	ay
◌ָי	āy
◌ֶ	e
◌ֱ	^{e}
◌ֶי	ey
◌ֵ	ē
◌ֵי	ê
◌ְ	^{e}
◌ִ	i
◌ִי	î
◌ׇ	o
◌ֳ	^{o}
◌ֹ	ō
◌וֹ	ô
◌ֻ	u, ū
◌וּ	û

CONSONANTS

א	ʾ
בּ	b
ב	ḇ
גּ	g
ג	ḡ
דּ	d
ד	ḏ
ה, הּ	h
ו	w
ז	z
ח	ḥ
ט	ṭ
י	y
כּ, ךּ	k
כ, ך	ḵ
ל	l
מ, ם	m
נ, ן	n
ס	s
ע	ʿ
פּ	p
פ, ף	p̄
צ, ץ	ṣ
ק	q
ר	r
שׂ	ś
שׁ	š
תּ	t
ת	ṯ

כְּ k^e; כְּמוֹ $k^em\hat{o}$; כַּאֲשֶׁר $ka'^a\check{s}er$

Contents: I. Etymology and Function. II. Syntax. III. Theological Usage: 1. Common Contexts; 2. Individual Passages.

I. Etymology and Function. The proclitic particle *k^e* probably derives from the common Semitic morpheme *ka.*[1] It is usually considered a primitive linguistic gesture, an "elementary demonstrative sound," and a "primary element of linguistic structure"[2] in the sense of a "deictic interjection."[3] The proposed derivation from a noun meaning "amount, quantity, identity"[4] is unlikely. There is more to recommend König's view that *k^e* "originated as an expression of the impulse toward parallelism," and in the course of linguistic development gradually took on more specific functions as adverb, preposition, and conjunction (cf. the suffixed forms, as well as *k^emô* [< *kamā*] and *ka'^ašer*).

As a functional particle, *k^e* can represent all kinds of parallelism. It introduces a kind of "side glance"[5] at something similar or comparable. The context may involve persons, things, or phenomena, when *k^e* precedes a noun, as well as actions or events, where it precedes a verb. In the latter case, *k^e* + infinitive or *ka'^ašer* often expresses simultaneity. The particle *k^e* combines a deictic element (pointing to something comparable) with an associative element (linking comparable entities), thus conveying the fundamental thought process of comparison from visualization through metaphor to identification of correspondence and analogy in conceptual judgment. This process finds verbal expression (both with and without *k^e*) primarily in → דָּמָה *dāmâ* (*dāmāh*), "resemble"; → מָשַׁל *māšal* I niphal, "become identical"; עָמַם *ʿāmam,* "be common"; → ערך *ʿāraḵ,* "equate"; → שָׁוָה *šāwâ,* "be identical or similar."[6]

The syntactic function of parallelizing dominates all the usages of *k^e* as preposition, adverb, and conjunction.

---

k^e. K. Aartun, "Einige besondere Wortstrukturen im Jüdisch-Aramäischen," *ZDMG,* 130 (1980), 1-14; E. Jenni, "דמה *dmh* gleichen," *THAT,* I, 451-56, esp. 453; G. Johannes, *Unvergleichlichkeitsformulierungen im AT* (Mainz, 1968); E. König, *Historisch-kritisches Lehrgebäude der hebräischen Sprache,* II/1 (Leipzig, 1895), esp. 179-287; C. J. Labuschagne, *The Incomparability of Yahweh in the OT. POS,* 5 (1966); C. H. Scheele, *Commentatio grammatica-exegetica de hebraea particula* כ (diss., Halle, 1832); E. Schwabe, כּ *nach seinem Wesen und Gebrauche im alttestamentlichen Kanon gewürdigt* (diss., Halle, 1883), 1-44; → דָּמָה *dāmâ* (*dāmāh*).

1. *KBL.*
2. König, Schwabe.
3. *Synt,* §109a.
4. Cf. *GesB.*
5. König.
6. Jenni; H. D. Preuss, "דָּמָה *dāmâ* (*dāmāh*)," *TDOT,* III, 250-260.

II. Syntax. The statistics of the more than 3000 (about 3030) occurrences of k^e in the OT will be found elsewhere.[7] Organizing this wealth of occurrences syntactically and contextually reveals certain typical usages.

1. The use of correlative k^e — k^e (also *kēn*) to mean "as . . . so" in direct address (e.g., Gen. 44:18: "just as Pharaoh, so are you"; reverse word order in Hebrew) still preserves some of the deictic force and gestural overtones (nodding or looking toward someone) inherent in the particle (cf. 1 K. 22:14).

2. Apart from a few occurrences with a suffix, the expanded form *k^emô* (about 120 occurrences) appears only in poetic texts (Psalms, Job), obviously because it appeared more primitive and also better served the intended deixis rhythmically (e.g., Job 19:22: "Why do you, like God [*k^emô-'ēl*], pursue me?").

3. The particle appears frequently with infinitives (about 250 occurrences), usually to establish that actions or events are simultaneous. Here the parallelizing function of the particle comes into full play. "And it happened, when Abraham entered Egypt, the Egyptians saw . . ." (Gen. 12:14). At a certain point in the chain of events, a new action begins. Parallelism between clauses is expressed by *ka'ašer,* as in Gen. 7:5: "And Noah did just as Yahweh had commanded him (*k^ekōl 'ašer-ṣiwwāhû*],"[8] while adverbial k^e establishes parallelism between modes of action: "Should he toward our sister as toward a harlot (*k^ezônâ*)?" (Gen. 34:31; cf. Jgs. 9:16).

4. The particle is joined most frequently to nouns; in these cases, the import of the noun determines the meaning. Identity, similarity, correspondence, indeed any kind of parallelism can be expressed, usually in such a way that the familiar phenomenon cited for comparison is ascribed normative force.[9] The nature and position of the noun determine whether the correlation is made sufficiently clear. Naturally the import of the comparison is greatest in noun clauses, e.g., "The first [child] came forth red, just like a hairy mantle" (Gen. 25:25), or "Like a child upon me, [so] is my soul" (Ps. 131:2).

The line between this usage and metaphor (without k^e) is fluid. The so-called k^e *veritatis* of the older grammarians illustrates the transition: "He was *k^e'îš 'emet* (= 'something like a man of constancy,' or = 'such as only a . . . can be')" (Neh. 7:2); "There is but a step (*k^epeśa'*, = 'something like a step') between me and death" (1 S. 20:3). The similes with k^e in Cant. 4:1ff., which are introduced by a metaphor in the form of a noun clause, are similar: "Your eyes are doves . . . , your hair is like a flock of goats . . . , your teeth are like a flock of shorn [ewes] . . . ; like a scarlet thread are your lips . . ." (cf. 7:2f.[Eng. vv. 1f.]).

---

7. Jenni, 452ff.
8. See III.1.f. below.
9. Schwabe.

5. Jenni has noted that k^e appears more often with nouns of general or abstract meaning than with concrete substantives. This would mean that k^e serves more frequently to associate and integrate individual phenomena in a rational structure than to introduce an illustrative parallel.

6. There is a certain imprecision inherent in a parallel relationship introduced by k^e; it can express at most an approximate identity, more often only a partial similarity, which is also dependent on the subjective judgment of the speaker. One result of vague general parallelism is the way prepositions can be left implicit when k^e is used, e.g., *kaḥ^{a}lôm,* "as [in] a dream" (Isa. 29:7). Comparative estimation with respect to a scale of known values also lies behind many vague approximations: *k^{e}ḏereḵ yôm,* "about a day's journey" (Nu. 11:31); *k^e'eśer šānîm,* "about ten years" (Ruth 1:4); *k^e'êp̄â,* "about an ephah" (Ruth 2:17).

7. The OT contains frequent combinations that illustrate common usage that is becoming idiomatic or formulaic, such as the statement (probably proverbial) that the "wicked" are *k^{e}mōṣ,* "like chaff" (8 times), or the topos "[flaky] like snow" used 3 times of *ṣāra'aṯ* (so-called "leprosy"). Wax is used as a simile 4 times (Mic. 1:4; Ps. 22:15[14]; 68:3[2]; 97:5). Animals appear relatively often in similes (e.g., Ps. 11:1; 42:2[1]; 59:7,15[6,14]; 102:8[7]; 124:7[10]), as do persons ("like David," "like Daniel") and places ("like Lebanon").[11]

8. Among the rhetorical forms of the OT, k^e is associated particularly with the individual lament, especially the sections describing the petitioner's distress, which, aided by the particle, serve the function of self-presentation and role identification (e.g., Ps. 38:14f.[13f.]; 88:6[5]; 102:4ff.[3ff.]; Nu. 12:10,12; Job 6:15; 10:19,22; 19:22; 30:19; also Isa. 53:3,7). By use of a simile (e.g., Ps. 11:1), the speaker seeks a fundamental orientation and often conformity to a particular paradigm of behavior. The analogy curse in Ps. 58 represents a special case, using 5 repetitions of *k^{e}mô* in an almost magical coercion of roles and images.[12]

9. Another context where the particle appears frequently is wisdom discourse — aphorisms (e.g., Ps. 32:9; 90:9; Prov. 23:7), didactic wisdom psalms (e.g., Ps. 1:3,4; 49:13,21[12,20]; 133:2f.), or other forms of Wisdom Literature (Job 28:5; 38:14; 40:17ff.; 41:16[24]). The teacher seeks to illustrate new knowledge and associate it didactically with what is already known. The particle k^e can serve in many ways as a means of association (cf. Isa. 55:10f.).

---

10. See II.8 below.

11. Jenni, 453; on usage of k^e with the divine name, see III.1 below.

12. See K. Seybold, "Psalm LVIII: Ein Lösungsversuch," *VT,* 30 (1980), 53-66. On similar formulas in so-called "incantations," which closely resemble sympathetic magic, see W. Mayer, *Untersuchungen zur Formensprache der babylonischen "Gebetsbeschwörungen." StPohl,* Ser. maior, 5/16 (1976), 362-373.

10. The particle is a standard element of the so-called descriptive song, a poetic genre (Arab. *waṣf*) found in Cant. 4:1-7; 5:10-16; 7:2-10[1-9]).[13] Here the vivid simile, usually introduced by k^e, serves to identify the figure of the beloved with the ideal of beauty recorded in the pictorial arts, especially those drawing on Egyptian tradition. The preferred stylistic features of this form of poetry are the noun clause of identity and the noun clause with a predicate introduced by k^e (compare Cant. 5:10ff. with 4:1ff.).

III. Theological Usage.

1. *Common Contexts.* The particle k^e that indicates parallelism does not play any additional role in religious discourse. Nevertheless, in certain contexts it provides a special theological accent, above all when associated directly with divine appellatives. The mode of expression introduced by k^e makes contrapuntal comparisons, going beyond the parallel course that it sometimes follows; this language touches on the fundamental theological problem of divine incomparability.

a. Personal names such as *mîḵāyāhû* or *mîḵā'ēl* that derive from an interrogative clause — "Who is like Yahweh/God/El?" — are formulas expressing the incomparability of Yahweh. The question, which implies a negative answer, presupposes an individual's realization that the "side-glance" at something comparable, generally possible under all circumstances, is impossible here. As a confession of faith asking for assent, such statements are probably rooted less in religious polemic[14] than in an overwhelming experience of the divine associated with the birth of a child.

b. This conclusion is supported by the instances of explicit incomparability formulas, including both the interrogative *mî ḵ*^{e} and the statement *'ên* k^e. The majority of occurrences are in hymnic doxological contexts (e.g., Ex. 15:11; Ps. 89:7ff.[6ff.]; 35:10; 71:19; 77:14[13]; 113:5; Mic. 7:18; cf. Dt. 33:26; 1 S. 2:2; Ps. 86:8). The motivation in each case shows that the assertion of incomparability is rooted in a specific experience of salvation that the worshipper has had or hopes to have. An example is the Song of Hannah: "My heart exults in Yahweh . . . , because I rejoice in thy salvation. There is none holy like Yahweh, there is none besides thee; there is no rock like our God" (1 S. 2:1f.). A late variant is found in one of Elihu's speeches: "Behold, God is exalted in his power [described in the creation hymn, Job 36:24ff.]; who is a teacher (*môreh*) like him?" (v. 22).[15] This idiom was incorporated as a standard topos in the repertoire of official liturgical language (cf. 2 S. 7:22; Ps. 89:7ff.[6ff.]; 1 K. 8:23).

c. In only 4 passages is k^e combined directly with the name of Yahweh (Ex. 8:6; Dt. 4:7; 1 S. 2:2; Ps. 113:5) — a sign that the assertion of divine incomparability was taken seriously. In these passages, the impossibility of comparison is extended to deities worshipped by Israel's neighbors (cf. Dt. 4:32ff.). In a different vein, although theoretical comparison of humanity to God may be possible (Ps. 8:6[5]), the human claim to

---

13. G. Gerleman, *Das Hohelied. BK,* XVIII (1965), 58ff.
14. Labuschagne, 21f., 126-28; cf. Johannes, 92ff.
15. Cf. Labuschagne, 22, 112f.; Jenni, 455.

be like God as expressed by the serpent's words in Gen. 3:5 ("to be like God [*kē'lōhîm*], knowing good and evil") proves to be impossible; cf. the related statement in Ezk. 28:2,6: ". . . you said, I am a god (*'ēl*) . . . , and claimed your heart to be like the heart of a god (*'ᵉlōhîm*)." The attempt fails in the face of the divine "No!" The claim to be like God in the sense of identification (*kᵉ*) runs counter to the anthropological axiom "You are dust . . ." (Gen. 3:19) or "You are but a man, and no god (*'ēl*)" (Ezk. 28:2,6). But note the theological opposite: "Like them [the dead idols] be those who make them" (Ps. 135:18). The comparison particle stands at the center of the theological struggle with the mythological view of humanity (cf. the echo in Job 40:9). Also of interest in this context is the comparison *kᵉ'āḏām* ("you shall die like men") in the judgment pronounced upon the gods in Ps. 82:7 (cf. Hos. 6:7; Job 31:33).

d. The particle is naturally obligatory in the context of the imagery used by texts that record visions; adequate description of what has been seen is achieved most simply by a series of similes introduced by *kᵉ*. Thus the dazzling description in Nu. 24:3ff. gives the oracle a theological dimension: "How fair are your tents, O Jacob, your encampments, O Israel! Like valleys that stretch afar, like gardens beside a river, like oaks that Yahweh has planted, like cedars beside the waters. . . !" Similar language appears in 1 K. 22:17: "I [Micaiah] saw all Israel scattered upon the mountains, like sheep that have no shepherd." An extreme example is Joel's vision of the plague of locusts on the day of Yahweh (Joel 2:1-11), with 11 occurrences of *kᵉ* (cf. also Zec. 4:1; 5:9; etc.). Finally, the particle is an essential stylistic feature in the visions recorded in Ezekiel and Daniel, e.g., in the vision of the son of man in Dnl. 7:4ff.[16]

A parallel usage occurs in theophanies, in which Yahweh's appearance is represented by comparisons designed to emphasize Yahweh's ineffability and incomparability. The *locus classicus* is found in the Sinai tradition: "And they saw the God of Israel; and there was under his feet [something] like the form (*kᵉma'ᵃśēh*) of a *sappîr* tile, like the very heaven (*kᵉ'eṣem haššāmayim*) for clearness" (Ex. 24:10). The elliptical language — there is no explicit subject — shows that we are dealing with formulaic discourse. Cf. also Isa. 30:27ff.; Ps. 29:6; 18:43[42]; also Ezk. 1ff.; 8ff.; 40ff.; and the 3 occurrences of the topos "like wax" (Mic. 1:4; Ps. 68:3[2]; 97:5).

e. Noteworthy is the relatively frequent use of *kᵉ* in prophetic oracles to cite analogies from the realm of sacred history. The particle is the simplest and most direct means of expressing a correspondence — in this case usually the correspondence of divine acts of salvation in the future to past events in God's history with Israel. Examples include Isa. 28:21: "For Yahweh will rise up as on Mount Perazim, he will be wroth as in the valley of Gibeon"; Hos. 12:10(9): "I am Yahweh your God from the land of Egypt; I will again make you dwell in tents, as in the days of the distant past"; also Isa. 1:9,26; 9:3(4); 23:5; Am. 9:11; Hos. 2:5,17(3,15); Ob. 16; Isa. 31:4; Hag. 2:3; etc. The frequent occurrence of *kᵉ* in Hos. 14:5ff.(4ff.) is striking: speaking in the 1st person, Yahweh likens himself to the "dew" (v. 6[5]) and the "evergreen cypress" (v. 9[8]) and likens

16. See III.2 below.

Israel to various trees, flowers, and natural phenomena, so that the beautiful and serene world of nature becomes the image and likeness of the salvation to come.

f. As an expression of normative correspondence, *kᵉ* plays a role in theological phraseology. It may indicate that an action conforms to existing norms or authorities: divine authority (Ex. 7:20; 29:35), the law (Dt. 4:8; cf. 2 K. 17:13; Nu. 9:3,12), the prescriptions of the law (2 Ch. 30:18). It may also state the factors that will govern Yahweh's own actions: his steadfast love (Ps. 106:45; 109:26), his righteousness (Ps. 35:24), his wrath (Ezk. 25:14), his wisdom (Ezr. 7:25). This normative usage expresses the "criterion of an action"[17] and thus becomes an ethical theologoumenon.[18]

2. *Individual Passages.* Certain passages in which *kᵉ* makes a contribution to specifically theological conceptions deserve special mention.

In the second term of the "image of God" passage (Gen. 1:26 [P]), *kᵉ* is joined with the abstract noun *dᵉmûṯ*[19] to define more precisely the more general first term *bᵉṣalmēnû:*[20] "Let us make man as our image, just like us." The adverbial *kiḏᵉmûṯēnû* expresses more precisely the aspect of similarity between humanity and God, already implicit in the notion of an "image," as a leitmotif of creation (v. 27), preventing an erroneous interpretation of what is meant by "image." It speaks explicitly of a deliberate, intentional analogy in form and function (v. 26b) — in other words, likeness. In supporting the two terms "image" and "likeness," the particle *kᵉ* has, as it were, the task of expressing the reciprocal motion of the comparison.

If the proposed emendation of the MT is correct, Gen. 5:3 states that Adam begot a son "like an image of himself" (*kᵉṣalmô*), so that once again *kᵉ* comes to the aid of likeness terminology by providing its own deictic force.[21] Gen. 2:18,20 (J), too, in recording the decision of the creator Yahweh Elohim to create a helper for the man so that he would not be alone, uses the comparative particle *kᵉ* to describe the project in more detail: "a help, [but] like a counterpart to him (*kᵉnegdô*[22])." Here *kᵉ* refers once again to the model of creation, this time in the sense of a leitmotif and background idea, standing in some tension to the abstract concept "help" and lending it a personal form in the sense of comparability and partnership ("counterpart"). The comparison introduced by *kᵉ* thus establishes the norm of the planned work of creation.

The law of love in the Holiness Code (Lev. 19:18), "And you shall love[23] your neighbor as yourself," formulates a parallelism between love of one's neighbor and love of self (cf. the correspondence in 1 S. 18:1 between love of a friend and love of self [*'hb kᵉnapšô*]) and postulates an equilibrium. The given love of self is taken as the

17. Schwabe, 33.
18. See II.8 above.
19. → דמה *dāmâ* (*dāmāh*).
20. → צלם *ṣlm.*
21. Cf. T. N. D. Mettinger, "Abbild oder Urbild? 'Imago Dei' in traditionsgeschichtlicher Sicht," *ZAW,* 86 (1974), 403-424.
22. → נגד *ngd.*
23. → אהב *'āhaḇ* (*'āhabh*).

norm and also as a counterpoise, which requires constant balancing against the love of one's neighbor as required by the Holiness Code. Once again, *kᵉ* establishes a norm.[24]

In the series of *kᵉ*-similes in the vision of Ezk. 1, vv. 26f. constitute the climax: the gaze is now lifted to behold the deity in person: a firmament shining like crystal (v. 22), and above it "something that looked like a *sappîr* stone, something like a throne; and upon what looked like a throne *dᵉmûṯ kᵉmar'ēh 'āḏām* (= something that looked like a human being)" (v. 26). The language resembles that of Gen. 1:26; Ex. 24:10. Despite the daring theme of this passage, the description is extremely guarded. Double indirection robs the account of any explicit visual element. The already vague term *dᵉmûṯ* is further relativized by the cautious *kᵉmar'ēh:* "it looked like." The inadequacy of the description is strongly emphasized.

The frequent use of *kᵉ* in Daniel shows that the particle with its comparative and interpretative function became a stylistic feature of vision accounts, intended simultaneously to explain and conceal the meaning of the vision. It constantly transports the listener and reader into the figurative world of apocalyptic visions. The high point of the vision in Dnl. 7 is a simile: "With the clouds of heaven there came one (who looked) like a son of man" (*kᵉḇar 'ᵉnāš,* i.e., "a human individual"; v. 13), a figure standing in visual and thematic contrast to the fantastic animals just described (cf. 7:4: *ke'ᵉnāš*).

Seybold

---

24. Cf. III.1.f above.

כאב *k'b;* כְּאֵב *kᵉ'ēḇ;* מַכְאֹב *maḵ'ōḇ*

Contents: I. General: 1. Other Languages; 2. Statistics; 3. Basic Meaning. II. Biblical Usage: 1. Verb; 2. Nouns. III. Theological Usage: 1. Suffering as Discipline; 2. Suffering and Sin; 3. Unexplained Suffering; 4. The "Man of Sorrows." IV. LXX.

I. General.

1. *Other Languages.* Besides Hebrew, the root *k'b/kyb* appears in Arabic,[1] in the Aramaic of the Elephantine papyri,[2] in Judeo-Aramaic,[3] in Syriac, and in Mandaic.[4] The Targum often uses Aram. *k'b* to render Heb. *ḥlh* (e.g., in 1 S. 22:8; Ezk. 34:4; Am.

---

k'b. J. Scharbert, *Der Schmerz im AT. BBB,* 8 (1955), 41-47, 55-58; K. Seybold, *Das Gebet des Kranken im AT. BWANT,* 99[5/19] (1973), 24f. For additional bibliog. see → חלה *ḥālâ* (*chālāh*).

1. *WKAS,* I, 11f.
2. Cf. *DISO,* 118.
3. *WTM, s.v. k'b* and *k'b'.*
4. *MdD, s.v. kib* and *kiba.*

6:6b). So far the root is not attested in Ugaritic, and it is not found in Akkadian.[5] Thus *k'b/kyb* is restricted to the West Semitic languages. In other languages, as in Hebrew, the root appears both as a verb and in various substantival forms.

2. *Statistics.* In the OT, the root *k'b* appears in substantival forms and as a verb, but not as an adjective. The verb is found 8 times in the OT, plus 2 occurrences in Sirach (4:3; 13:5). There is a conjectural occurrence in Ezk. 13:22aα, where *hak̠'ôt̠* is probably a mistake for *hak̠'îb̠*[6] (cf. Ezk. 28:24). In Prov. 3:12, *k^e'āb̠* is probably a scribal error for *(w^e)yak̠'ib̠* (cf. LXX = He. 12:6; the Vulg. has a different reading). The MT of Ps. 41:4(Eng. v. 3) should probably be retained.[7] Of the 12 occurrences, 5 are in the qal (including Sir. 13:5) and 7 in the hiphil (including Sir. 4:3; Ezk. 13:22aα conj.; Prov. 3:12 conj.). The piel, pual, hophal, and hithpael are not found.[8]

The noun *k^e'ēb̠* appears 6 times in the MT plus 4 times in Sirach (4:6; 30:17a,b; 34:29; not cited in *KBL*³), always in the singular. The noun *mak̠'ōb̠* appears 16 times in the MT plus 3 times in Sirach (3:27; 34:20; 38:7; *KBL*³ notes only 3:27). Six of these occurrences (including Sir. 3:27) are in the plural, mostly with *-îm* but once with *-ôt̠* (Isa. 53:3: *'îš mak̠'ōb̠ôt̠*). The frequency of the verb and noun in Wisdom Literature (Proverbs, Job, Sirach) and in laments (Psalms, Lamentations, Jeremiah) is striking.[9]

3. *Basic Meaning.* The lexica generally render *k'b* as "suffer(ing)," "(feel) pain."[10] Discussion concerning the basic meaning of the root is largely dominated by the question as to whether *k'b* denotes primarily or exclusively an objective diminution and injury or a subjective perception of pain.[11] But this strict distinction between objective fact and subjective experience is clearly in error. In some passages the objective element of "suffering" can stand in the foreground, in others the subjective element; but *k'b* always denotes simultaneously and without distinction the injury that exists as an objective fact and is also suffered and felt as such. In all the languages where it appears and in all its forms, the root is used almost exclusively with human subjects; this is its primary domain. This observation prohibits the theory that *k'b* inherently denotes only objective injury and that the element of subjectively perceived suffering is merely a secondary accretion in passages where *k'b* is used of a sentient being. The rare usage of *k'b* with inanimate and therefore insentient objects (e.g., farmland [2 K. 3:19]) is a metaphorical transfer of the notion from the human to the nonhuman realm, a phenomenon often observed in related concepts.[12]

---

5. Cf. *AHw* and *CAD*; contra Scharbert, 42.
6. E.g., W. Zimmerli, *Ezekiel 1. Herm* (Eng. trans. 1979), 289.
7. Cf., e.g., H.-J. Kraus, *Psalms 1–59* (Eng. trans., Minneapolis, 1988), 430, contra *KBL*³, *s.v. mak̠'ōb̠*.
8. See I.3 below.
9. See III below.
10. E.g., *GesB, KBL*³, *s.v.*
11. See Scharbert, *passim.*
12. Cf. E. König, *Stilistik, Rhetorik, Poetik* (Leipzig, 1900), 105-7.

The fact that the verb *k'b* appears only in the qal and hiphil in the OT shows that in verbal usage the root never describes an isolated timeless state, statically conceived, but always depicts an event or action in a temporal nexus.[13] This conclusion is reinforced by the absence of adjectival formations, which would denote a static state. The root *k'b* thus refers to an injury that objectively damages the vital force of a sentient being, causing subjective suffering.

II. Biblical Usage.

1. *Verb.* a. *qal.* In Gen. 34:25, the qal participle of *k'b* denotes pain that afflicted the Shechemites three days after their circumcision and rendered them helpless to defend themselves against Simeon and Levi. In Ps. 69:30(29), the qal participle stands in parallel with → ענה *ʿnî* (cf. Ex. 3:7), describing the helpless and defenseless situation brought before God in the petitioner's lament. According to Prov. 14:13, the heart may be sad (*k'b* qal, par. *tûgâ,* "grief"[14]) even in the midst of joy and laughter.

In these passages, the qal of *k'b* is used absolutely. Job 14:22, however, states the cause of the pain that is felt (*ʿal* with a reflexive pronominal suffix; the only occurrence of the qal of *k'b* with *ʿal*). The man whose face God has disfigured, whom he has "dismissed," can no longer share in the fortune, good or ill, of his own children, because he is already consigned to death. His "flesh"[15] and "soul,"[16] i.e., his total bodily existence, during his own lifetime are already and totally (*'aḵ*) dominated by sorrow for his own fate (*ʿālāyw yiḵ'āḇ* par. *'bl ʿālāyw*).[17] Here the qal of *k'b* denotes the pain occasioned by a sense of one's own imminent and certain end, which leaves no room for any other human emotion. In Sir. 13:5 (the only occurrence of *k'b l*ᵉ), the qal of *k'b* is used impersonally with an attentuated meaning: conduct that has injured another party "makes one sorry."

In all 5 passages, the qal of *k'b* denotes the suffering that diminishes a person's vital force, restricting him and causing him pain.

b. *hiphil.* In the emended text of Ezk. 13:22aα,β, the hiphil of *k'b* contrasts with "strengthen the hands."[18] It refers to the conduct of women who are false prophets, accusing them of supporting the wicked in their actions, thereby preventing their repentance, while disquieting the hearts of the righteous and doing them injury (*k'b* hiphil) through falsehood[19] by perverting the norms established by Yahweh (cf. Lam. 2:14; Isa. 5:20). In Sir. 4:3, the sage exhorts the reader to show mercy especially to the humble and not to injure (*k'b* hiphil) the "soul" of the oppressed (*ʿānî*). The metaphor

---

13. Cf. E. Jenni, *Das hebräische Piʿel* (Zurich, 1968), 59, 87f., etc.
14. → יגה *yāgâ.*
15. → בשׂר *bāśār.*
16. → נפשׁ *nepeš.*
17. For a similar interpretation, see G. Fohrer, *Das Buch Hiob. KAT,* XVI (1963), 260f.; for different views, see Scharbert, 55-58; also F. Horst, *Hiob. BK,* XVI/1 (1968), 179, 213f.; A. Weiser, *Das Buch Hiob. ATD,* XIII (⁵1968), 89, 109; etc.
18. → חזק *ḥzq;* → יד *yāḏ.*
19. → שׁקר *šeqer.*

in Ezk. 28:24 describes the hostile neighbors of the house of Israel as vicious briers (*sillôn mam'îr*) and painful, injurious thorns (*qôṣ mak̲'ib̲*). In 2 K. 3:19, the hiphil of *k'b* metaphorically describes how the good farmland (*ḥelqâ ṭôb̲â*) of a conquered territory is ruined by stones (cf. v. 25).

Finally, Job 5:17f. describes the reproof (→ יכח *ykḥ*) of God and the chastening of the Almighty (*mûsar*[20] *šadday*): he wounds (*k'b* hiphil) and smites (→ מחץ *mḥṣ*), but also binds up (→ חבש *ḥbš*) and heals (→ רפא *rp'*). And according to Prov. 3:12 (as emended), God brings pain (*k'b* hiphil, par. *ykḥ*) to the man in whom he delights (→ רצה *rṣh*, par. *'hb*).[21]

2. *Nouns.* a. *ke'ēb̲*. According to Ps. 39:3(2), the painful distress of the psalmist is *ke'ēb̲* to the wicked in his presence (cf. v. 2[1]), remote and "taboo" (*'kr* niphal),[22] as long as he remains silent concerning the blow (*nega'*[23]) God has dealt him (cf. v. 11[10]). In Job 16:6, *k'b* refers to Job's suffering, which cannot be assuaged even if he speaks of it. According to Job 2:13, Job's suffering (*ke'ēb̲*) is so great (*gdl* qal) that his friends cannot find words to address it. Isa. 65:14 speaks of "pain of heart" (*ke'ēb̲ lēb̲*) in parallel with "anguish (*šeb̲er,* lit., 'breaking') of spirit" and in contrast to "gladness (*ṭûb̲*[24]) of heart." Sir. 5:6 similarly speaks of suffering of the soul (*ke'ēb̲ nepeš*[25]) in parallel with "bitterness of spirit" (*mar rûaḥ*; compare also *ke'ēb̲* with *merôrîm* in 1QH 8:28). In Jer. 15:18, the prophet laments that his suffering is unceasing pain (*ke'ēb̲ neṣaḥ,* par. *makkâ 'anûšâ,* "incurable wound"). Isa. 17:11, too, speaks of "incurable pain" (*ke'ēb̲ 'ānûš*); the same phrase appears also in 1QH 5:28; 8:28 (cf. Jer. 30:15: *'ānûš mak̲'ōb̲ēk̲*).[26] According to Sir. 30:17a,b, suffering can be so "unremitting" (*ne'emān*[27]) and "constant" (*'ômēd̲*) that it makes life a calamity, worse than death. In Sir. 34:29, too, *ke'ēb̲ rō'š* in parallel with *qālôn,* "contempt," and in antithetical parallelism with *śimḥat̲ lēb̲,* "joy of heart," in v. 28 probably denotes a pain deeper than just the headache that follows immoderate consumption of wine.

Thus *ke'ēb̲* almost always (except possibly in Sir. 34:29) denotes pain or suffering that afflicts the very heart of life, bringing the sufferer close to his final end and damaging or destroying his ties with the circle of the living.

b. *mak̲'ôb̲*. In Jer. 45:3, unending pain (*mak̲'ôb̲* with *yāgôn*) evokes a cry of distress (*'ôy-nā' lî*[28]): pain so afflicts the prophet's companion that it seems impossible to go on living (cf. v. 5b). In Ps. 38:18(17), a lament, *mak̲'ôb̲* clearly refers to a disease (cf.

---

20. → יסר *ysr.*
21. See III.1 below.
22. Cf. *KBL*³ *s.v.*, contra *GesB, s.v.*; *KBL*³ *s.v. ke'ēb̲*; H. Gunkel, *Die Psalmen. HKAT,* II/2 (⁵1968 = ⁴1926), 166; and most transls. and comms.
23. → נגע *ng'.*
24. → טוב *ṭôb̲,* V, 307.
25. → נפש *npš.*
26. See II.2.b below.
27. → אמן *'mn.*
28. → הוי *hôy.*

vv. 4, 6, 8f.[3, 5, 7f.]) that has brought the psalmist close to death and alienated him from his closest friends (cf. v. 12[11]). In Ps. 69:27(26), also a lament, the psalmist is afflicted with pain and suffering (*mak̲'ôb̲*); he is facing death and isolated from those around him. A similar total and profound devastation of life is denoted by *mak̲'ôb̲* (together with *ḥ^olî*) in Isa. 53:3f.

In Job 33:19, *mak̲'ôb̲* refers to pain inflicted by Yahweh that consigns the sufferer to a sickbed, i.e., a bodily disease. In 2 Ch. 6:29, *mak̲'ôb̲* in conjunction with *rā'āb̲,*[29] "famine," → דבר *deb̲er* (*debher*) "plague," *maḥ^alâ,*[30] "sickness," etc. denotes the physical devastation of human life. In Sir. 34:20, *mak̲'ôb̲* refers to the pain occasioned by immoderate eating and drinking; in 38:7, it denotes a disease to be treated by a physician.

In some passages, the "pain and suffering" (*mak̲'ôb̲*) that inherently can afflict only individuals is transferred metaphorically to the nation as a whole or a destroyed city. Jer. 51:8 states that there is no balm to heal the disease (*mak̲'ôb̲*) that has afflicted Babylon. According to Lam. 1:12,18, the suffering Yahweh has inflicted upon the city of Jerusalem is incomparably severe; Jer. 30:15 calls it incurable (*'ānûš* par. *šeb̲er*). Ex. 3:7 uses *mak̲'ôb̲* for the suffering of Yahweh's people in Egypt.

According to Ps. 32:10, a wisdom aphorism, the pangs (*mak̲'ôb̲*) of the wicked are many, whereas Yahweh surrounds those who trust in him with steadfast love. In Sir. 3:27, similarly, *mak̲'ôb̲* refers to the suffering brought on by a "rebellious heart." According to Eccl. 1:18; 2:23, however, suffering (*mak̲'ôb̲*) is not brought on by specific circumstances; it is a fundamental and inevitable element of human life, the human "portion" (*'inyān*). Even wisdom is incapable of healing such injury.

The noun *mak̲'ôb̲* thus denotes a generally severe injury afflicting the life of individuals, cities, or entire nations; it consigns them to the sphere of death or brings them close to it. Sometimes it denotes the kind of suffering that inevitably characterizes all human existence.

III. Theological Usage.

1. *Suffering as Discipline.* The suffering denoted by *k'b* represents an unmitigated threat; those who experience such suffering or see it in others cannot initially see any positive sense in it. In the view of Israel's "earlier wisdom," however, pain and sickness can become means by which God may discipline people, aiding and healing them. It is even an exemplary mark of God's care and favor: "The very one whom Yahweh loves" (emphasis through inversion!), who is as a son to him, in whom Yahweh delights — that one it is whom Yahweh reproves through affliction (Prov. 3:12). This is true above all when the defect to be remedied through suffering is the result of human error and transgression. Those God reproves are called blessed because the sickness and suffering he brings upon them lead to healing: God binds up the wounds he inflicts (Job 5:17f.; cf. 1 S. 2:6f.; Dt. 32:39). Through sickness, God brings people near to

---

29. → רעב *r'b.*
30. → חלה *ḥlh.*

death in order to deliver them from unrighteousness, to "bring them back from the Pit" and restore them fully to life (Job 33:19-30).[31]

2. *Suffering and Sin.* Pain and sickness or destruction and devastation are often looked upon as a consequence of sin or a punishment from God. Suffering is the lot of the wicked (Ps. 32:10). The day on which Damascus and the northern kingdom of Israel are judged will be for them a day of grief and incurable sickness (Isa. 17:11; cf. Jer. 51:8, which uses similar language of Babylon). The sin of Israel or Jerusalem also brings pain and sickness (Lam. 1:12,18; Jer. 30:15; cf. also Ezk. 28:24). The suffering described in the psalmist's prayer to God is also the basis of his plea for help, even though the suffering is basically the result of his own transgression (Ps. 38:18[17]; 39:3[2]; 69:30[29]).

3. *Unexplained Suffering.* Several passages simply speak of sickness and pain with no attempt to trace them to an underlying cause or find in them a positive purpose. Pain is simply given as a harsh, unexplained fact of life. This holds true of the grief the wise understand everyone must bear (Prov. 14:13; Eccl. 1:18; 2:23; Sir. 30:17a,b), but also of the additional pain and sickness that afflicts certain individuals. The claim of Eliphaz and Elihu that Job's torments are a means of divine reproof[32] is not accepted. His pain and suffering remain inexplicable, even though — or perhaps precisely because — they come from God (Job 2:13; 14:22; 16:6). Particularly mysterious is the suffering inflicted on those entrusted by Yahweh with a special commission (Jer. 15:18; 45:3).

4. *The "Man of Sorrows."* The various semantic elements associated with the root *k'b* and the various traditions of which it is typical are joined in Isa. 52:13–53:12. The sufferings inflicted on the "man of sorrows" are mortal (53:8). They alienate him from all human associations (vv. 3, 12), even after his death (vv. 8f., 12). At the same time, however, in a more profound sense his sufferings associate him with the multitude: it is not "his" sickness that causes his suffering and death but that of others (vv. 4, 10-12). The mortal illness of others that he suffers is a consequence of their sin (v. 5); it brings about in turn victory over their sin and death (v. 5).[33]

IV. LXX.

The LXX renders *k'b* with *algeín* (3 times), *achreioún,* and *diastrépsein,* as well as *pónos* (3 times) and *lýpē*. The nouns *kᵉ'ēḇ* and *maḵ'ôḇ* are rendered by *álgos, álgēma, malakía, pónos,* and *plēgḗ*.

Mosis

---

31. Cf. G. von Rad, *Wisdom in Israel* (Eng. trans., Nashville, 1972), 200-202.

32. See III.1 above.

33. → דכא *dk'* III.3.f, with bibliog.; →חלה *ḥlh,* III.3, with bibliog.

כָּבֵד *kāḇēḏ* I; כָּבֵד *kāḇēḏ* II; כֹּבֶד *kōḇeḏ*; כְּבוּדָּה *kᵉḇûddâ*; כְּבֵדֻת *kᵉḇēḏuṯ*

Contents: I. 1. Etymology; 2. Meaning; 3. Personal Names; 4. OT; 5. LXX. II. 1. Weight; 2. Approbation; 3. Theological Usage; 4. Wisdom Literature. III. *kāḇēḏ* II. IV. Nouns. V. Dead Sea Scrolls.

I. 1. *Etymology.* The root *kbd* (West Semitic) or *kbt* (East Semitic)[1] is found in all the Semitic languages with the meaning "be heavy," figuratively "be important": Akk. *kabātu,*[2] Amor. *kbd,*[3] Ugar. *kbd* I/III,[4] Arab. *kabada,*[5] Eth. *kabda,*[6] OSA *kbd,*[7] Tigr. *käbdä,*[8] Amhar. *käbbädä,*[9] Phoen./Pun. *kbd.*[10] Instead of *kbd,* Aramaic usually uses → יקר *yāqār,* "be heavy," "be precious,"[11] which may have entered Hebrew as an Aramaic loanwoard.[12]

The same group of consonants is also found in most Semitic languages as a noun with the meaning "liver," "interior," "soul," etc.[13] It is hard to decide whether the two roots are etymologically associated, either because the liver is considered the "weightiest" or "most important" organ (for extispicy)[14] or because the various mean-

---

kāḇēḏ. W. Caspari, *Studien zur Lehre von der Herrlichkeit Gottes im AT* (diss., Leipzig, 1907); M. Dahood, "Hebrew-Ugaritic Lexicography III," *Bibl,* 46 (1965), 326; É. P. Dhorme, *L'Emploi métaphorique des noms de parties du corps en hébreu et en akkadien* (Paris, 1923, repr. 1963), 128-133; F. Hesse, *Das Verstockungsproblem im AT. BZAW,* 74 (1955); E. Jenni, *Das hebräische Piʿel* (Zurich, 1968); J. S. Kselman, "*RB // KBD:* A New Hebrew-Akkadian Formulaic Pair," *VT,* 29 (1979), 110-14; M. Liverani, "*kbd* nei testi administrativi ugaritici," *UF,* 2 (1970), 89-108; L. Rost, "Der Leberlappen," *ZAW,* 79 (1967), 35-41; C. Westermann, "כבד *kbd* schwer sein," *THAT,* I, 794-812.

1. The assimilation *d/t* is discussed by *VG,* I, 152; W. von Soden, *Ergänzungsheft zum GaG. AnOr,* 47 (1969), 8**.

2. *AHw,* I (1965), 416f.; *CAD,* VIII (1971), 14-18.

3. I. J. Gelb, *Computer-Aided Analysis of Amorite. AS,* 21 (1980), 22.

4. *WUS,* no. 1274.

5. Lane, 2584; *WKAS,* I, 18.

6. *LexLingAeth,* 849.

7. ContiRossini, 166.

8. *TigrWB,* 411f.

9. W. Leslau, *Concise Amharic Dictionary* (Berkeley, 1976), 161.

10. *DISO,* 114.

11. *DISO,* 110.

12. Cf. M. Wagner, *Die lexikalischen und grammatikalischen Aramaismen im Alttestamentlichen Hebräisch. BZAW,* 96 (1966), 62f.

13. Cf. P. Fronzaroli, "Studi sul lessico comune semitico. II: Anatomia e Fisiologia," *AANLR,* VIII/19 (1964), 257f., 272, 279; also W. Leslau, *Lexique soqotri* (Paris, 1938), 410; *idem, Contributions,* 25.

14. *GesB, KBL*³, Westermann.

ings of *kbd* and its derivatives can be derived from the meaning "liver."[15] If there is in fact a connection, *kāḇēḏ,* "liver," must derive from *kbd,* "be heavy," since *kbd* is a stative verb, not a denominative.

Also controversial is the derivation of the root *kbd* with its various verbal and nominal derivatives from a Proto-Semitic biliteral root **kb* with a semantic range including "slay, (op)press, burden, be heavy" (cf. Arab. *kabba* and *kabā,* possibly also Akk. *kâpu* or *kepû*). Biliteral roots are not found among the stative verbs.

2. *Meaning.* The Semitic root *kbd/t* is not semantically independent, since there are instances of semantic overlap with Semitic *kbr.* Arab. *kabura,* "be/become large,"[16] for example, is closer semantically to *kbd/t* in other Semitic languages than to Arab. *kabada*; and the meaning of Heb. *kbh,* "extinguish,"[17] is associated in Akkadian with the G and D stems of *kabātu.*[18] In almost all the Semitic languages, however, the semantic element "be heavy" (and by extension "honor") is constant.

The wide range of usage (especially in Akkadian and Hebrew) that draws on the various meanings of the root is also found in Egyptian, where *wdn*[19] and its derivative *dnś,*[20] "be heavy, burden," are used not only of physical weight but also figuratively of an illness that burdens parts of the body, the oppressive power of the king, good and bad qualities, and (with the meaning "weighty") names and reputations. The homonymous root *wdn,* "sacrifice,"[21] may be associated with *wdn,* "be heavy," as meaning "make heavy," "consider weighty," "honor (with offerings)," "worship," as in the case of Semitic *kbd/t.*[22]

The root *kbd/t* does not, however, convey this double sense of heaviness as both physical weight and "weightiness" in all the Semitic languages: Arab. *kabada,* for example, is limited to the negative meaning "oppress," III "endure";[23] contrariwise, Ugar. *kbd* I means only "honor" in the D stem and "be weighty, honored" in the N stem.[24]

In administrative texts from Ugarit, the adj. *kbd* III[25] appears in descriptive apposition to the shekel (*ṯql*) stating quantities of metals, wool, and textiles, as well as to the cubic measures *dd, kd,* etc.[26] It designates a heavier weight in contrast to the

---

15. K. Vollers, "Die solare Seite des alttestamentlichen Gottesbegriffes," *ARW,* 9 (1906), 176-184.

16. *WKAS,* I, 21; Lane, 2585.

17. *KBL*^{3}, 435f.

18. *AHw,* I, 416; *CAD,* VIII, 18.

19. *WbÄS,* I, 390; cf. Arab. *wadana.*

20. *WbÄS,* V, 468; cf. E. Edel, *Altägyptische Grammatik,* I. *AnOr,* 34 (1955), §444.

21. *WbÄS,* I, 391.

22. Cf. *AHw,* I, 416f.; Dahood, 326.

23. *WKAS,* I, 18.

24. *WUS,* no. 1274; *UT,* no. 1187.

25. *WUS,* no. 1274.

26. See esp. Liverani.

normal lighter weight, indicating simultaneous use of different systems of weights and measures.[27]

The noun from the root *kbd/t*[28] also encompasses a wide semantic range in Semitic. First, it can denote the liver as an organ. The importance of the liver in extispicy is attested by many texts[29] as well as by liver models[30] unearthed by excavations in Mesopotamia,[31] Syria, and Palestine.[32] It can also denote the interior of the body;[33] in this sense it resembles the heart[34] and the other internal organs, which are of fundamental importance for Semitic psychology,[35] since they were considered the seat of the human will and emotions.[36] In Akkadian, *kabattu* denotes the realm of "violent emotions" and "blind passions," just as *libbu* denotes the realm of "sentiments" and "manifestations of the moral and intellectual life."[37] In Ugaritic, too, *kbd* — often in parallel with *lb* — denotes the seat of feelings and emotions: " 'Her liver' swells with laughter, her heart is filled with joy, Anat's 'liver' with victory."[38] This semantic development then led to the use of the word for the interior or middle of anything (e.g., the earth or the heavens), especially in Arabic.

3. *Personal Names.* The root *kbd/t* appears as a constituent of personal names in many Semitic languages. In the concrete sense of "heavy," it is found in names referring to physical features: *kabittu, kabbutum, kubbutum,* "the heavy one."[39] It also appears in "occasional"[40] names such as *is-sú-ka-bi-it,* "his strength is weighty,"[41] which expresses a lament to a deity. In the sense of "honor," it appears in names that allude to human society: *kab-ta-at a-na-ḫa-wi-ri-ša,* "she is honored by her spouse." In this sense, the root is especially common in divine epithets: *ka-bit arallî,* "prince of the underworld"; *kab-tu kat-tu,* "mighty in build."[42]

---

27. Cf. M. Dietrich and O. Loretz, "Der Vertrag zwichen Šuppiluliuma und Niqmandu," *WO,* 3 (1966), 219-223.

28. See I.1 above.

29. Cf. M. Jastrow, *Die Religion Babyloniens und Assyriens,* II/1 (Giessen, 1912), 213-415; *BuA,* II, 267-275.

30. Cf. A. Jeremias, *Handbuch der altorientalischen Geisteskultur* (Leipzig, ²1929), 259f.

31. *ANEP,* nos. 594, 595.

32. The details of the inscribed liver models from Ugarit are described by M. Dietrich and O. Loretz, "Beschriftete Lungen- und Lebermodelle aus Ugarit," *Ugaritica,* 6. *MRS,* 17 (1969), 172-79.

33. → קרב *qereḇ.*

34. → לב *lēḇ.* The relationship between heart and liver in sacrificial practice is discussed by F. Blome, *Die Opfermaterie in Babylonien und Israel,* I. *SSAOI,* 4 (1934), nos. 174-180.

35. Dhorme, 109.

36. *Ibid.,* 109-137.

37. See R. Labat, "Herz," *RLA,* IV (1972-75), 367.

38. *KTU* 1.3 II, 25ff.; the text is discussed by M. Dahood, "Ugaritic-Hebrew Syntax and Style," *UF,* 1 (1969), 23.

39. *AN,* 267.

40. *AN,* 237.

41. *AN,* 17f.

42. See K. Tallqvist, *Akkadische Götterepitheta. StOr,* 7 (1938, repr. 1974), 107.

Similar names with *kbd* as an element are found at Ugarit,[43] among the Canaanites,[44] and in South Semitic.[45]

In the OT, we find *'î-kāḇôḏ* (lit., "infamous") with a popular etymology in 1 S. 4:21;[46] Ex. 6:20; Nu. 26:59 in the disputed form *yôḵeḇeḏ*.[47]

4. *OT.* In the OT, the root *kbd* encompasses a wide range of meanings, which can be derived primarily from the basic meaning "be heavy." "Weight" is often felt to be a burden,[48] so that *kbd* is often best translated by a transitive verb such as "burden," "weigh down," or "impede" (cf. "onus"). A further group of meanings of *kbd* suggests the comparative "heavier."[49] Although no specific point of comparison is stated, these passages suggest something added, an excess (image of a balance?). Here the best translation is often "too/very heavy/difficult." This usage of *kbd* is especially common in declarative statements.

There are 114 occurrences of the verb in the OT, plus 26 in Sirach. All the stems but the hophal are attested. The qal appears 23 times; it stands closest to the basic meaning. There is no passage in which it means "be heavy" in the concrete physical sense, but this sense can explain the meanings "impede," "burden," "oppress," "be onerous." Twice (Ex. 9:7; Isa. 59:1) the qal is used with "heart" or "ear" to express stubbornness.[50] The hiphil (17 occurrences, plus 2 in Sirach) functions primarily as the causative of the qal, so that its meanings are closely related to those of the qal: "make something difficult or burdensome for someone," etc., and "make someone's heart/ear stubborn." In the sense of "honor," the hiphil is found with the purely causative meaning "cause to be held in honor" in Isa. 8:23(9:1); Jer. 30:19.[51] In the majority of cases, the piel (38 occurrences, plus 6 in Sirach) has declarative or estimative meaning:[52] "honor, approve." The secondary meaning deriving from the basic meaning "be heavy" has a broader range than the abstract English term "honor": it extends from simple "recognize, respect" through "esteem, consider competent or expert (in something)" to "honor, venerate." With respect to Yahweh, in the sense of "revere," it denotes a concrete religious attitude (often par. → ירא *yārē'*). In the sense "make stubborn," the piel (in contrast to the hiphil) refers to a casual action.[53] The niphal (30 occurrences, plus 11 in Sirach) is especially common with a human subject as the

43. Cf. *PNU,* 148.
44. Benz, 330.
45. *RyNP,* I, 112.
46. See J. J. Stamm, "Hebräische Ersatznamen," *Festschrift B. Landsberger. AS,* 16 (1965), 416.
47. See J. J. Stamm, "Hebräischen Frauennamen,"*Hebräische Wortforschung. Festschrift F. Baumgartner. SVT,* 16 (1967), 315; *IPN,* 111.
48. Westermann, 795.
49. Caspari, 14.
50. See II.3.d below.
51. Jenni, 105.
52. *Ibid.,* 40ff.
53. *Ibid.,* 105.

passive equivalent of the piel: "be(come) recognized or honored." With Yahweh as subject, it takes on the reflexive sense "show oneself to be weighty or important."[54] Like the niphal, the pual (3 occurrences) functions as the passive of the piel: "be honored" or (from the piel meaning "reward") "become rich."[55] The hithpael (3 occurrences, plus 3 in Sirach) functions semantically as the reflexive or passive[56] of the piel.

The adjective (40 occurrences, plus 5 in Sirach) corresponds in meaning to the qal: "heavy, burdensome, oppressive, stubborn"; also "much, many."

5. *LXX.* The wide range of meanings conveyed by the verb *kbd* is also evident in the 23 equivalents used by the LXX. The qal is rendered by *barýnein* (11), *barýs* (5), *katabarýnein* (2), and *baryōpeín, doxázein, katischýein, mégas, polýs* (1 each); the niphal by *éndoxos* (13), *doxázein* (7), *endoxázesthai* (6), *éntimos* (2); the piel by *doxázein* (21), *timán* (10), *eulogeín* (2), *barýnein, entímōs, dóxa* (1 each); the pual by *barýnein, doxázein,* and *timán* (1 each); the hiphil by *barýnein* (13), *barýs, akoúein baréōs, pleonázein, sklērýnein* (1 each); and the hithpael by *barýnein* and *peritithénai* (1 each).

The LXX generally renders the adj. *kāḇēḏ* by *barýs* (16), *polýs* (5), or *euischýein.* For the subst. *kāḇēḏ,* the LXX uses *hḗpar* 9 times, *sklērós* 3 times, and *hēpatoskopeísthai* and *plḗthos* once each.

Dohmen

II. 1. *Weight.*

a. *Physical Weight.* The basic meaning "be heavy" is most apparent in those passages that speak of something that (figuratively) weighs upon or oppresses someone; the frequent use of the prep. *ʿal* in these cases makes the concrete conception of the burden especially clear. Many of the passages in question speak of the heavy yoke[57] (1 K. 12:11 par. 2 Ch. 10:11; 1 K. 12:4 par. 2 Ch. 10:4; Sir. 40:1; etc.) that rulers "make heavy" upon the people (*kbd* hiphil; 1 K. 12:10 par. 2 Ch. 10:10; 1 K. 12:14 par. 2 Ch. 10:14; Isa. 47:6; Neh. 5:15 [either following *BHS* in supplying an *ʿōl* omitted by haplography or reading *ʿōl* for the *ʿal* of the text]).

In similar fashion, forced labor can be considered burdensome (qal: Ex. 5:9; Neh. 5:18), and extremely harsh imprisonment can be described by the image of heavy chains (hiphil: Lam. 3:7). In these passages, the weight is a physical burden on the body. There are also instances of psychological pressure, e.g., through words (Job 33:7). The verb *kbd* may be applied to anything that weighs down human life; guilt and sin, misfortune and disaster can burden people and oppress them (Ps. 38:5[4]; Job 6:3; Gen. 18:20;

---

54. Cf. *GK,* §51c; on a possible tolerative meaning of the niphal of *kbd,* see J. H. Eaton, "Some Misunderstood Hebrew Words for God's Self-Revelation," *BT,* 25 (1974), 337f.

55. Cf. S. Gevirtz, "West-Semitic Curses and the Problem of the Origins of Hebrew Law," *VT,* 11 (1961), 141f.

56. *BLe,* §291j.

57. → על *ʿōl.*

Isa. 24:20; Prov. 27:3). Theological language speaks of the heavy hand[58] of Yahweh (Job 23:2; Ps. 32:4; 1 S. 5:6,11) to illustrate the distress and lament of the oppressed.

b. *Size and Quantity.* The element of size and quantity is especially evident where *kbd* is used of famine (*rā'āḇ*); the common expression *kî-ḵāḇēḏ hārā'āḇ bā'āreṣ* describes a terrible famine that weighs heavily upon the land (Gen. 12:10; 47:4,13; etc.). The vexatious aspect of quantity is particularly clear in the exodus tradition, where *kbd* describes such plagues as flies (Ex. 8:20[24]), locusts (10:14), hail (9:18,24), and disease (9:3). The same expression can describe a task that is too burdensome (Ex. 18:18; Nu. 11:14). Size and strength appear together in passages where *kbd* describes military forces (Gen. 50:9; Nu. 20:20; 2 K. 6:14; 18:17; 2 Ch. 9:1; Isa. 36:2). The phrase *ḥayil kāḇēḏ,* however, can denote not only a mighty army but also an imposing entourage, as in the entrance of the queen of Sheba into Jerusalem (1 K. 10:2).

In addition, *kbd* can be synonymous with *raḇ,* referring to quantity in the literal sense — for example, in Prov. 8:24;[59] Sir. 16:17; or Nah. 3:15, where it actually stands in direct parallelism with → רב *raḇ.*[60]

The aspect of wealth is found not only in passages where the piel of *kbd* means "enrich, reward" (Nu. 22:17,37; 24:11) but also in Hab. 2:6, where the greedy man enriches (RSV "loads") himself with pledges (*kbd* hiphil).

c. *Difficult, Burdensome.* Something heavy can also be difficult or burdensome. For example, the weight of Absalom's hair (two hundred shekels) became burdensome, and so he had it cut (2 S. 14:26). A large number of guests can likewise be a burden to a host (2 S. 13:25). The statement that Moses' hands grew heavy (Ex. 17:12) refers to weariness resulting from the posture of prayer, which makes one's hands feel like lead. The meaning "difficult, complex" lies behind 1 K. 3:9, which thinks of Israel as both a chosen and a stubborn people (Dt. 9:6,13):[61] "For who is able to govern this difficult people?"

d. *Battle.* An especially interesting aspect of the usage of *kbd* appears in 4 passages where the qal describes a battle. When a battle (*milḥāmâ*; also *yaḏ bêṯ-yôsēp̄* in Jgs. 1:35) grows "heavy," it means that the decisive moment is at hand (not noticed by the Benjaminites in Jgs. 20:34), the defeat of the side on which the battle presses (1 S. 31:3 *'el-šā'ûl* par. 1 Ch. 10:3 *'al-šā'ûl*; cf. also *kōḇeḏ milḥāmâ* in Isa. 21:15).

e. *Physical and Mental Disability.* When *kbd* is used of a part of the body, it indicates that the organ or member cannot carry out its normal function. Sir. 3:26,27, for example, describes a fool as having a *lēḇ kāḇēḏ*; Ex. 4:10 ascribes Moses' lack of eloquence to *k^{e}ḇaḏ-peh ûḵ^{e}ḇaḏ lāšôn.*[62] Zimmerli is probably right in interpreting the gloss in Ezk.

---

58. → יד *yāḏ.*

59. The text is discussed by G. M. Landes, "The Fountain of Jazer," *BASOR,* 144 (1956), 32f.

60. Cf. Kselman, *passim.*

61. Cf. E. Würthwein, *Die Bücher der Könige. ATD,* XI/1 (1976), 35.

62. Cf. J. H. Tigay, " 'Heavy of Mouth' and 'Heavy of Tongue': On Moses' Speech Difficulty," *BASOR,* 231 (1978), 57-67.

3:5,6 from this perspective.[63] Gen. 48:10 differs from the passages describing stubbornness[64] in giving the reason (*mizzōqen*) for Israel's poor eyesight. Just as *kbd* can denote the unhealthy state of a particular part of the body, it can also indicate the general debility of someone who is old and sick (1 S. 4:18; cf. *ʿênāyw qāmû,* v. 15).

2. *Approbation.*

a. *Social Status.* Several passages use the piel of *kbd* to mean "make someone heavy, consider someone important" in the sense of the acceptance, respect, or recognition accorded people with a certain social or political status. Within the family, the piel of *kbd* can express recognition of parental authority (Ex. 20:12 par. Dt. 5:16; Mal. 1:6); in the diplomatic realm, it can describe recognition of dynastic succession by demonstrations of sovereignty (2 S. 10:3 par. 1 Ch. 19:3). Cf. also Saul's request that Samuel confirm him as king in the presence of the people (1 S. 15:30). In a perversion of this basic code of conduct, Eli honors his sons more than Yahweh (1 S. 2:29).

b. *Individuals.* The niphal of *kbd* can express the recognition due someone who displays special abilities not shared by others. This precedence is justified on the grounds of demonstrated competence. Benaiah and Abishai, for example, are honored because — as the context makes clear — they have shown themselves to be stronger and braver than others (2 S. 23:19,23 par. 1 Ch. 11:21,25). David is honored for many qualities, including his faithfulness (1 S. 22:14). The respect Shechem enjoys (Gen. 34:19) is illustrated by the acceptance of his far-reaching decision. Finally, Eli, the man of God, was honored because his words had often proved true (1 S. 9:6). This contrasts with the conduct of Amaziah, who strives for even greater honor after achieving victory (2 K. 14:10 par. 2 Ch. 25:19 conj. [*lᵉhikkāḇēḏ*]).

The subjective aspect of honor and recognition is especially clear in 2 S. 6:20,22, where opposing views clash: Michal despises the honor David enjoys and longs for. The nominalized niphal participle embodies this usage, denoting individuals honored or considered important by others. The listing of such persons along with kings (*meleḵ*), princes (*śar*), etc. shows that they belong to an upper stratum of society (Isa. 23:8; Ps. 149:8; Nu. 22:15; Nah. 3:10).

3. *Theological Usage.*

a. *The Honor Due Yahweh.* The piel of *kbd* can express religious honor. This honor is conceived in much broader terms, however, than its secular equivalent; it denotes the total human response to Yahweh's love and favor. This response ranges from the personal prayer of the individual (Ps. 86:9; Isa. 25:3) through observance of the laws and commandments (Dt. 28:58; Isa. 58:13) to the sacrificial cult (Ps. 50:23; Prov. 3:9). This human response in concrete acts and conduct has its source in the demonstration of Yahweh's → חסד *ḥesed*; the close connection is illustrated by Ps. 50:15: "Call upon me in the day of trouble; I will deliver you, and you shall glorify me." Acknowledgment of God's steadfast

63. W. Zimmerli, *Ezekiel 1. Herm* (Eng. trans. 1979), 93.

64. See II.3.d below.

love goes beyond mere words (Isa. 29:13; 43:23): it takes concrete form in the life of the community. Those who despise the wicked but honor those who fear Yahweh (Ps. 15:4), those who are kind to the needy (Prov. 14:31) — they honor Yahweh. Human beings (Ps. 22:24[23]; 86:12), animals (Isa. 43:20), indeed the whole circle of the earth (Ps. 86:9; Isa. 24:15) can and do honor Yahweh as they should (Ps. 86:12).

Only Dnl. 11:38 uses *kbd* for religious worship in general. This late passage — other gods, not Yahweh, are the object of *kbd* — should probably be understood as reflecting Hellenistic influence.[65]

b. *Yahweh's Steadfast Love.* In 1 S. 2:30, we read: "Those who honor (*m^e^ḵabb^e^ḏay*) me [Yahweh] I will honor (*'^a^ḵabbēḏ*)." This verse, too, reflects the connection between divine action and human response (discussed from the opposite perspective in II.3.a above); the antonyms → בזה *bāzâ* (*bāzāh*), "despise," and → קלל *qālal*, "be unimportant," in the second member of the antithetical parallelism show how concretely and broadly Yahweh's action is to be understood. Yahweh loves people and defends them (Isa. 43:4). He delivers those who are in need and honors them (Ps. 91:15). The overtones of protection and enablement are clear from the context. When Yahweh honors people by making them important (*kbd* hiphil), this can mean de facto — as the parallel *rbh kbd* shows[66] — that he makes them increase and prosper (Jer. 30:19), i.e., makes them happy. When the servant of God is honored (*'ekkāḇēḏ*) in the eyes of Yahweh, then Yahweh is his strength (Isa. 49:5). Yahweh's steadfast love also finds expression in the importance he gives to his land (Isa. 8:23[9:1] [niphal]) or the temple, the place of his feet (*m^e^qôm raḡlay,*[67] Isa. 60:13).

c. *Demonstration of Yahweh's Power.* Semantically, the passages in which the niphal appears with Yahweh as subject have a special position. Yahweh shows his "weightiness" by demonstrating his power (to affect the course of history). When Yahweh acts upon (*b^e^*) Pharaoh and his host (Ex. 14:4,18), those who approach him (Lev. 10:3), or Sidon (Ezk. 28:22), the emphasis is on what Yahweh does[68] to make himself known. The "knowledge formula" *yd' kî-'^a^nî YHWH,*[69] which has roots in the traditions of the exodus (Ex. 14:4,17f. [P]) and of the wars of Yahweh (Ezk. 39:13; Isa. 26:15), suggests that the niphal of *kbd* has more to do with a demonstration of Yahweh's power than with "God's own responsibility for seeing that he is duly honored."[70] When Yahweh demonstrates his power, his faithful rejoice (Isa. 66:5 conj.).

d. *Stubbornness.* Extending the use of *kbd* to denote physical and mental disability,[71] theological language describes the heart and ear as "heavy," i.e., unresponsive, depicting "a phenomenon in the religious sphere."[72] But *kbd* is just one of the terms used

---

65. See O. Plöger, *Das Buch Daniel. KAT,* XVIII (1965), *in loc.*
66. See Kselman, *passim.*
67. H.-J. Fabry, הֲדוֹם *h^a^ḏōm* (*h^a^dhōm*)," *TDOT,* III, 331f.
68. Cf. W. Zimmerli, *Ezekiel 2. Herm* (Eng. trans. 1983), 98.
69. → ידע *yāḏa'.*
70. Westermann, 801.
71. See II.1.e above.
72. Hesse, 7.

to describe the phenomenon of stubbornness.[73] While E and P use → חזק ḥāzaq (chāzaq) in this context, J prefers *kbd* (Ex. 7:14; 8:11,28[15,32]; 9:7,34) with *lēḇ* as its object. The verbal adjective (Ex. 7:14) and the qal (Ex. 9:7) express the state of stubbornness; the hiphil (Ex. 8:11,28[15,32]; 9:34) describes Pharaoh's stubborn reaction. In Ex. 10:1, however, it is Yahweh who hardens Pharaoh's heart; and in Isa. 6:10,[74] the prophet is commanded to harden the heart of the people.[75] The use of the root in 1 S. 6:6 (twice) is unique in suggesting that the Philistines may harden their hearts (*kibbēḏ*) with respect to the Israelites; the piel here[76] points to the accidental nature of the action.

4. *Wisdom Literature.* In texts reflecting wisdom influence, *kbd* usually means "honor, esteem" (piel, niphal, hithpael). In antithesis to terms associated with the semantic field of inferiority,[77] in discussions of conduct and reward (Prov. 4:8; 13:18; 27:18; Sir. 3:6,8; etc.) the root depicts the honor and esteem that follow when one does what is right and good. It is also used (esp. the niphal ptcp. *nikḇāḏîm*) in texts describing the vanity of those who are honored (Sir. 10:26,27; 11:6; 48:6; Prov. 12:9)[78] in contrast to those who fear God (Sir. 10:19,20,24).

III. *kāḇēḏ* II. In the light of the important role played by the liver in hepatoscopy elsewhere in the ancient Near East,[79] the comparative rarity of the noun *kāḇēḏ* in the OT (14 occurrences) is unusual. Thirteen texts mention the liver of an animal: a bull (Ex. 29:13; Lev. 3:4; 4:9; 8:16; 9:10,19), a sheep (Ex. 29:22; Lev. 3:10; 8:25; 9:19), a goat (Lev. 3:15), a stag (Prov. 7:23), or an animal in general (Lev. 7:4; Ezk. 21:26[21]). In 11 passages, *kāḇēḏ* appears in conjunction with *yōṯereṯ,* "appendage of the liver," as a sacrificial element; the various syntactic combinations show that the reference is to something closely connected with the liver: *yōṯereṯ hakkāḇēḏ* (Ex. 29:22; Lev. 8:16,25; 9:19), *yōṯereṯ ʿal-hakkāḇēḏ* (Ex. 29:13; Lev. 3:4,10,15; 4:9; 7:4), *yōṯereṯ min-hakkāḇēḏ* (Lev. 9:10).[80] In 2 passages (Lam. 2:11; Prov. 7:23), *kāḇēḏ* means the interior of the body, i.e., life itself. In this context we also find the only passage that speaks of the human liver (Lam. 2:11). Ezk. 21:26(21) explicitly attacks the hepatoscopy of the Babylonians, which is also probably implicitly forbidden by Dt. 18:9-12. Perhaps hostility toward such practices helps explain why the OT rarely speaks of the liver.

---

73. The whole subject is discussed by Hesse, *passim.*

74. Cf. Chung Hsin Chi, *The Concept of "Hardening the Heart" in the OT with Special Refernce to Isaiah 6* (diss., South East Asia Graduate School of Theology, 1974); R. Kilian, "Der Verstockungsauftrag Jesajas," *Bausteine biblischer Theologie. Festschrift G. J. Botterweck. BBB,* 50 (1977), 209-225.

75. The LXX makes the people harden their own heart; cf. H. Wildberger, *Isaiah 1–12* (Eng. trans., Minneapolis, 1991), *in loc.*

76. Cf. Jenni, 105.

77. → קלל *qālal*; cf. C. A. Keller, "קלל *qll* leicht sein," *THAT,* II, 641-47.

78. On *kbd* with the meaning "celebrate, honor with a banquet," see Dahood, 326.

79. See I.2 above.

80. Cf. Rost, *passim*; → יתר *yāṯar* I.

In 6 passages (Gen. 49:6; Ps. 7:6[5]; 16:9; 30:13[12]; 57:9[8]; 108:2[1]), *kāḇôḏ* should not be translated "soul" but emended to *kāḇēḏ,* understood as the seat of the emotions, as in Akkadian.[81]

IV. Nouns. There are three rare noun forms, of no particular importance: *kōḇeḏ* (4 occurrences), *kᵉḇûddâ* (3), and *kᵉḇēḏuṯ* (1).

The text of Isa. 30:27 is uncertain. It is preferable to read the adj. *kāḇēḏ* instead of *kōḇeḏ,* following Hans Wildberger,[82] Otto Kaiser,[83] and others. Walther Zimmerli[84] assumes that *kᵉḇûddâ* in Ezk. 23:41 is a scribal error involving *resh* and *kaph,* translating "a bed that has been made ready" (cf. Prov. 7:16).

While *kᵉḇûddâ* (Ps. 45:14[13]; Jgs. 18:21), like → כבוד *kāḇôḏ,* means "wealth, richness," *kōḇeḏ* stands closer to the basic meaning; it denotes the weight of a stone (Prov. 27:3) or the press of battle (Isa. 21:15), and in parallel with *rōḇ* refers to a large quantity.[85] The hapax legomenon *kᵉḇēḏuṯ* (Ex. 14:25), used of chariot wheels, suggests sluggishness.

V. Dead Sea Scrolls. The use of *kbd* in the Dead Sea scrolls closely follows biblical usage. Of 30 occurrences, the niphal participle ("those who are honored, aristocrats") accounts for the largest number (13); an additional 10 involve the meaning "honor, esteem." In 11QT 49:11, however, we find the postbiblical meaning[86] "sweep up, clean."

Stenmans

---

81. Cf. F. Nötscher, "Heisst *kābōd* auch 'Seele,' " *VT,* 2 (1957), 358-362 = *Vom Alten zum NT. BBB,* 17 (1962), 237-241; → כבוד *kāḇôḏ* I.1.
82. *Jesaja. BK,* X/3 (1982), *in loc.*
83. O. Kaiser, *Isaiah 13–39. OTL* (Eng. trans. 1974), *in loc.*
84. Zimmerli, *Ezekiel 1,* 478.
85. Cf. Kselman, *passim.*
86. *WTM,* II, 284f.

כָּבוֹד *kāḇôḏ*

Contents: I. 1. Etymology and Meaning; 2. Distribution; 3. LXX. II. 1. Substance, Quantity, Power; 2. Honor and Dignity. III. 1. Glory; 2. Synonyms. IV. Glorified Objects. V. Divine Glory in the Ancient Near East. VI. *kᵉḇôḏ YHWH* in P and Ezekiel. VII. Manifestation of *kᵉḇôḏ YHWH* at the Revelation of a Message. VIII. Future Revelation of the *kᵉḇôḏ YHWH*; Eschatology. IX. *kᵉḇôḏ YHWH* and *šem YHWH.* X. Qumran Scrolls.

---

kāḇôḏ. G. J. Botterweck, "Klage und Zuversicht der Bedrängten," *BiLe,* 3 (1962), 184-193, esp. 187; W. Caspari, *Die Bedeutung der Wortsippe "kabida" im Hebräischen* (Leipzig,

I. 1. *Etymology and Meaning.* The noun *kāḇôḏ* derives from *kbd,* which denotes "heaviness" in the physical sense as well as "gravity" and "importance" in the spiritual sense — i.e., "honor" and "respect." As an antonym of *kbd, qll* similarly expresses "lightness" in the physical sense as well as "slightness" or "insignificance" in the figurative sense — i.e., "lack of honor or respect." The antithesis *kbd/qll* is illustrated by 1 S. 2:30; 2 S. 6:22; Isa. 23:9; cf. also the antonyms *kāḇôḏ/qālôn* in Isa. 22:18; Hos. 4:7; Hab. 2:16; Prov. 3:35. The Aramaic equivalent of *kāḇôḏ,* → יקר *yᵉqār,* has the same dual connotation of "heavy, difficult" and "respected, honored." Thus *millᵉṯā' yaqqîrâ* (Dnl. 2:11), like *dāḇār kāḇēḏ* (Ex. 18:18), means a "heavy matter," a difficult task, whereas *yᵉqār malkûṯ* (Dnl. 4:33[Eng. v. 36]), like Heb. *kᵉḇôḏ malkûṯ,* means "royal majesty" (cf. Akk. *melam šarrūti*).

The noun → כבד *kāḇēḏ,* "liver," is also derived from the root *kbd,* "heavy" (physically and spiritually). Together with the heart,[1] the liver was considered the most important bodily organ; in Akkadian, Ugaritic, and possibly Hebrew, the words *libbu* ("heart") and *kabattu* ("liver") are interchangeable. Akkadian and Ugaritic expressions such as "gladness of heart and happiness of liver (= 'mind')" are especially instructive in this regard. Cf. Akk. *ḫud libbi, nummur kabatti,*[2] and Ugar. *tġdd kbdh bṣḥq yml'u*

1908); E. Cassin, *La splendeur divine* (Hague, 1968); H. Frankfort, *Kingship and the Gods* (Chicago, 1948); A. von Gall, *Die Herrlichkeit Gottes* (Giessen, 1900); H. L. Ginsberg, "The Arm of YHWH in Isaiah 51–63 and the Text of Isa 53:10-11," *JBL,* 77 (1958), 152-56; *idem,* "Gleanings in First Isaiah," *Mordecai M. Kaplan: Jubilee Volume* (New York, 1953), 245-260; M. Haran, "The nature of the ''Ōhel Môʿēdh' in Pentateuchal sources," *JSS,* 5 (1960), 50-65; H. Hegermann, "δόξα," *EDNT,* I (1990), 344-48; H. Kittel, *Die Herrlichkeit Gottes. BZNW,* 16 (1934); S. E. Loewenstamm, "Notes on the History of Biblical Phraeology," *Comparative Studies in Biblical and Ancient Oriental Literature,* AOAT (Band 204, 1980), 214-16; T. A. Meyer, *The Notion for Divine Glory in the Hebrew Bible* (diss., Louvain, 1965); C. Newsome, *Songs of the Sabbath Sacrifice, A Critical Edition,* HSS 27 (1985); F. Nötscher, "Heisst *kābōd* auch 'Seele,' " *VT,* 2 (1952), 358-362 (= *Vom Alten zum NT. BBB,* 17 [1962], 237-241) (cf. J. van der Ploeg, "Prov. xxv 23," *VT,* 3 [1953], 192); A. L. Oppenheim, "Akkadian *pul(u)ḫ(t)u* and *melammu,*" *JAOS,* 63 (1943), 31-34; *idem,* "The Golden Garments of the Gods," *JNES,* 8 (1949), 172-193; G. von Rad, "כָּבוֹד in the OT," *TDNT,* II, 238-242; W. H. P. Römer, "Beiträge zum Lexikon des Sumerischen," *BiOr,* 32 (1975), 145-162, 296-308; B. Stein, *Der Begriff Kᵉbod Jahweh und seine Bedeutung für die alttestamentliche Gotteserkenntnis* (Emsdetten, 1939); M. Weinfeld, *Deuteronomy and the Deuteronomic School* (1972, repr. Winona Lake, 1992), 191-209; *idem,* "Presence, Divine," *EncJud,* XIII, 1015-1020; *idem,* "Divine Intervention in War in Ancient Israel and in the Ancient Near East," *History, Historiography and Interpretation, Studies in Biblical and Cuneiform Literature,* ed. H. Taolmor and M. Weinfeld (Jerusalem 1982), 121-147; C. Westermann, "Die Herrlichkeit Gottes in der Priesterschrift," *Wort-Gebot-Glaube. Festschrift W. Eichrodt. AThANT,* 59 (1970), 227-249; *idem,* "כבד *kbd* schwer sein," *THAT,* I, 794-812; W. Zimmerli, *Ezekiel 1. Herm* (Eng. trans. 1979), 123f.; *idem, Ezekiel 2. Herm* (Eng. trans. 1983), 414f.

1. → לב *lēḇ.*

2. R. Borger, *Die Inschriften Asarhaddons, Königs von Assyrien. BAfO,* 9 (²1967), 64, VI, 55.

lbh bšmḫt,[3] "her liver grows (= becomes large) from laughter, her heart is filled with joy."

On the basis of such Akkadian and Ugaritic evidence, scholars have suggested reading *kāḇēḏ* instead of *kāḇôḏ* in Ps. 16:9: *śāmaḥ libbî wayyāgel k^eḇēḏî,* "my heart rejoiced and my liver (= 'mind') exulted."[4] Caution is necessary, however. The noun *kāḇôḏ* itself can mean "substance, being"; and, since Ps. 16:9 uses *bāśār,* "flesh, body," as a parallel term (*'ap-b^eśārî yiškōn lāḇeṭaḥ,* "my body dwells secure"), the interpretation of *kāḇôḏ* here as meaning "substance" or "whole being"[5] is highly plausible and emendation of the MT is unnecessary. A similar parallel *kāḇôḏ* par. *bāśār* (and *nep̱eš*) is found in Isa. 10:18.[6] Furthermore, Akk. *kabattu* can also mean the "inward" aspects of the person — thought, emotion, spirit — so that the translation "liver" is not always correct.[7]

The other passages where *kāḇôḏ* might be emended to *kāḇēḏ* are Gen. 49:6; Ps. 108:2(1) (cf. 57:8f.[7f.]; 7:6[5]). In Gen. 49:6, *k^eḇōḏî* is written defectively; the LXX translates "my liver" *(tá hḗpatá mou);* in Ps. 108:2(1), *k^eḇôḏî* stands in parallel to *libbî* (cf. Ps. 16:9). Here *k^eḇôḏî* means "body" or "mind." In Gen. 49:6, *nep̱eš* and *kāḇôḏ* stand in parallel; both can mean "inner being." The emendation to *kāḇēḏ* in Ps. 7:6(5) is highly uncertain; here *k^eḇôḏî* stands in parallel to *ḥayyîm,* "life," a parallelism found elsewhere (cf. Prov. 21:21; 22:4).[8]

There is undoubtedly a connection between *kāḇēḏ* and *kāḇôḏ,* since both mean "gravity" or "importance" (= "weightiness"); this may well have led to confusion between them. In all the passages listed, however, the MT should be retained.

2. *Distribution.* The noun *kāḇôḏ* appears 199 times in the OT (200 according to Westermann). There are 24 occurrences in the Pentateuch (13 in P), 7 in the Deuteronomistic history, and 18 in the Chronicler's history. It is especially frequent in the prophets Isaiah (38) and Ezekiel (19), and is found occasionally in Jeremiah and the Minor Prophets. The 51 occurrences in the Psalms and 16 in Proverbs illustrate the fondness these books have for the term, although the Psalms speak primarily of the *k^eḇôḏ YHWH,* whereas Proverbs speaks more of human *kāḇôḏ.*

3. *LXX.* The translation of the LXX is unequivocal: *dóxa* is used 177 times, along with the related *éndoxos* (3), *doxázein* (2), and *dóxis* (1). There are 7 occurrences of *timḗ.* More specific interpretations are illustrated by *ploútos* (2), *kalós,* and *dýnamis* (1 each). The rendering *glṓssa* in Ps. 16:9 (LXX 15:9) is probably similar. Hegermann

3. *KTU* 1.3 II, 25ff.; cf. 1.12 I, 12f.
4. Cf. Nötscher, 358f.; Loewenstamm, 214f.; M. Dahood, *Psalms I. AB* XVI (1965), *in loc.*
5. Cf. NJPS.
6. See below.
7. Cf. *CAD,* VIII (1971), *s.v. kabattu.*
8. Cf. *ILC,* I-II, 239.

has shown[9] that the Greek equivalent *dóxa* has incorporated the whole range of meanings of OT *kāḇôḏ*. The meaning "opinion" often associated with *dóxa* outside the Bible is not found in either the OT or the NT.

II. 1. *Substance, Quantity, Power.* The noun *kāḇôḏ* appears frequently with the meaning "body," "substance," "mass,"[10] hence "power" or "might." In Isa. 5:13, for example, *k^eḇôḏô* stands in parallel with *h^amônô* and means "multitude"[11] (cf. Isa. 16:14). A similar connotation is implied by Isa. 8:7, which speaks of the *kāḇôḏ* of Assyria that rises over its banks in the context of the mighty waters of the Euphrates; here "might" is clearly implied. In Isa. 10:16; 17:4, *kāḇôḏ* is synonymous with "fatness"; in 10:18, similarly, the *kāḇôḏ* of the forest that will be destroyed stands in parallel to soul and body (*minnep̄eš w^eʿaḏ-bāśār*). The context of Hos. 9:11 ("Ephraim — his *kāḇôḏ* shall fly away like a bird") speaks of a multitude of children of whom the parents will be bereft. The noun *k^eḇûddâ* in Jgs. 18:21, where it is associated with *ṭap,* "children," and *miqneh,* "cattle," has almost the same meaning; Prov. 23:5 also uses the metaphor "fly away" for the vanishing of wealth and power.[12]

As we have already indicated, "quantity" implies "power"; in Ps. 145:11f. and the Dead Sea scrolls (1QH 5:20; 10:11), *kāḇôḏ* actually appears in conjunction with *g^eḇûrâ,* "strength." The meaning "strength" for *kāḇôḏ* is attested in Job 29:20 ("My *kāḇôḏ* is fresh within me, my bow always in my grasp") and Ps. 3:4(3) ("Thou . . . art a shield about me, my *kāḇôḏ,* that lifts my head high"); bow and shield are symbols of strength and power. Isa. 21:16f. speaks of *kāḇôḏ* in conjunction with bows and warriors: "Within a year, according to the years of a hireling, all the *kāḇôḏ* of Kedar will come to an end; only a few bows of the warriors of Kedar will be left."[13] Cf. also Isa. 16:14: "In three years, like the years of a hireling, the *kāḇôḏ* (= 'power') of Moab will be brought into contempt with all his great multitude (*hāmôn*). Only a remnant will survive."

It has been proposed[14] that *kāḇôḏ* also means "strength" (*g^eḇûrâ*) in the parallel divine epithets of Ps. 24:8: *meleḵ hakkāḇôḏ,* "king of glory," and *ʿizzûz w^egibbôr,* "mighty and valiant."[15]

Another meaning of *kāḇôḏ* is "wealth," e.g., in Gen. 31:1: "From what was our father's he has gained all this *kāḇôḏ* (= 'wealth')." Similarly, Isa. 10:3 ("Where will you leave your *kāḇôḏ?*") refers to the wealth the aristocrats have amassed by exploiting

---

9. P. 345.
10. Ginsberg, *Festschrift M. Kaplan,* 246f.
11. Cf. NJPS.
12. For further discussion, see Westermann, *THAT,* I,798f.
13. Cf. A. B. Ehrlich, *Randglossen zur hebräischen Bibel* (repr. Hildesheim, 1968), *in loc.*: "Here *kāḇôḏ* does not mean "glory" but "multitude," "military might."
14. R. Weiss, משוט במקרא (Jerusalem, 1976), 299 [Heb.].
15. See below on *ʿōz* and *kāḇôḏ* as synonyms.

the poor; in Isa. 22:24, "all the *kāḇôḏ* of his father's house" refers to "vessels, cups, and flagons." In Nah. 2:10(9), *kāḇôḏ* includes the supplies and valuables to be taken from the Assyrians in Nineveh: "Plunder the silver, plunder the gold! There is no end of treasure, or *kāḇôḏ* ("a hoard, or wealth") of every precious thing."[16]

The noun *kāḇôḏ* often appears in conjunction and parallelism with *ʿōšer,* "wealth"; cf. 1 K. 3:13; Prov. 3:16; 8:18; 22:4; etc.; and especially Ps. 49:17(16): "Do not be afraid when one becomes rich, when the *kāḇôḏ* of his house [i.e., his household goods] increases." In Isa. 61:6, *kāḇôḏ* stands in parallel to *ḥayil,* "riches"; and in Isa. 66:12, *keḇôḏ gôyim* means "wealth of the nations."

2. *Honor and Dignity.* It is fitting that God, the king, and persons of high status and authority should receive *kāḇôḏ,* "honor." God is honored above all others. He is the "God of *kāḇôḏ*" (*'ēl-hakkāḇôḏ,* Ps. 29:3), the "King of *kāḇôḏ*" (*meleḵ hakkāḇôḏ,* Ps. 24:7,9,10).[17] His kingdom is a kingdom of *kāḇôḏ* and *hāḏār,* "splendor" (*keḇôḏ malkûṯ* par. *keḇôḏ haḏar malkûṯ,* Ps. 145:11f.; cf. Akk. *melam šarrūti,* "splendor of kingship," discussed below), unsurpassed by the *kāḇôḏ* of anyone else: "My *kāḇôḏ* I give to no other, nor my praise (*tehillāṯî*) to graven images" (Isa. 42:8; cf. 48:11). This explains Jeremiah's lament: "Has a nation ever changed its gods . . . , but my people have changed their *kāḇôḏ*" (Jer. 2:11; cf. Ps. 106:20). Cf. Mal. 1:6: "If I am a father, where is the *kāḇôḏ* [that I deserve]?" God above all deserves the respect shown in hymns and anthems: he must receive *kāḇôḏ.* Even divine beings offer him *kāḇôḏ* (Ps. 29:1f.). In Ps. 96:7f. (cf. 1 Chr. 16:28f.) it is the "families of the people" who ascribe to the Lord *kāḇôḏ* and strength (*ʿōz*). According to Ps. 66:1f., the whole earth is to sing the *kāḇôḏ* of his name and praise him by offering *kāḇôḏ* (*śîm kāḇôḏ*); cf. the similar statement in Isa. 42:12: "Let them [the inhabitants of the whole earth] give *kāḇôḏ* to the Lord, and declare his praise in the coastlands."

"To give *kāḇôḏ*" is often tantamount to a confession. Therefore when Achan transgresses the requirements of *ḥerem* and is called upon to confess his sins, Joshua says to him: "My son, give *kāḇôḏ* to Yahweh, the God of Israel, and confess it to him" (Josh. 7:19). When the Philistines set about to return the ark of the covenant, they must make reparation to the God of Israel. This act of reparation is called "giving *kāḇôḏ*" (1 S. 6:5). Honor through confession is also implied by Jer. 13:16: "Give *kāḇôḏ* to Yahweh your God before he brings darkness, before your feet stumble."[18]

Biblical prayers often request God to deliver Israel for the sake of God's *kāḇôḏ,* i.e., for the sake of his reputation among the nations: "Help us, O God of our salvation, for the *kāḇôḏ* of thy name. . . . Why should the nations say, 'Where is their God?' " (Ps. 79:9f.). "Not to us, O Yahweh, not to us, but to thy name give *kāḇôḏ*. . . . Why should the nations say, 'Where is their God?' " (Ps. 115:1f.). A positive statement of

16. Cf. Westermann, *THAT,* I, 798f.

17. On *meleḵ hakkāḇôḏ* as an allusion to the Jerusalem temple cult, see J. Maier, *Das altisraelitische Ladeheiligtum. BZAW,* 93 (1965), 77; on the possibility of Canaanite influence, see Westermann, *THAT,* I, 804f.

18. Cf. A. B. Ehrlich, *Mikra Ki-Peshuto* (1969), *in loc.*

God's honor among the nations is found in Isa. 66:18f.: "They [the nations] shall come and shall see my *kāḇôḏ.* I will set a sign among them and send them . . . and they shall declare my *kāḇôḏ* among the nations."

Kings (Isa. 14:18; Ps. 21:6[5]; Prov. 25:2), priests (Ex. 28:2,40), and sages (Prov. 3:35) are also due *kāḇôḏ,* but never fools (Prov. 26:1,8). It is likewise proper that parents and the masters of slaves receive *kāḇôḏ*; cf. Mal. 1:6: "A son should honor his father, and a slave his master. If then I am a father, where is the honor due me (*k*ᵉ*ḇôḏî*)? And if I am a master, where is the fear of me (*môrā'î*)?" The parallelism of *kāḇôḏ* and *môrā'* is discussed below.

The term *kāḇôḏ* can also denote personal honor and dignity, which can be attained through proper conduct, restraint, generosity, and humility: "It is a man's *kāḇôḏ* to keep aloof from strife; but every fool will be quarreling" (Prov. 20:3); "a gracious woman gets *kāḇôḏ*" (Prov. 11:16); "[whoever] has distributed freely . . . to the poor . . . his horn is exalted in *kāḇôḏ*" (Ps. 112:9); "humility goes before *kāḇôḏ*" (Prov. 15:33).

III. 1. *Glory.* When it means "glory" or "splendor," *kāḇôḏ* usually refers to God, his sanctuary, his city, or other sacred paraphernalia.[19] P uses the term in connection with God's appearance in the tabernacle (Ex. 29:43; 40:34f.; Lev. 9:6,23; Nu. 14:10; 16:19; 17:7[16:42]; 20:6). Here *kāḇôḏ* takes the form of a consuming fire surrounded by a cloud (Ex. 24:16ff.; cf. 16:10; Nu. 17:7[16:42]). Only Moses, who was privileged to converse with God face to face (Ex. 33:11; Nu. 12:8; Dt. 34:10) could enter this cloud (Ex. 24:18). Contact with the radiance of the deity caused his face to shine, and therefore he used a mask to hide his face and enable the people to come near him (Ex. 34:29ff.).[20]

As we shall see below, in the ancient Near East the divine glory was embodied in the crown of the deity or hero; this holds true of Heb. *kāḇôḏ* as well. In Job 19:9, we read: "He has stripped from me my *kāḇôḏ,* and taken the crown from my head"; cf. also Ps. 8:6(5): "Thou hast made him a little less than God, and dost crown him with *kāḇôḏ* and honor." In the Jewish liturgy (the Amidah on the morning of the Sabbath), the radiance of Moses is described as a crown of glory (*k*ᵉ*lîl tip'ereṯ*), given him by God.[21]

Ezekiel, whose imagery is closely allied to that of P, transfers his concept of *kāḇôḏ* to the Jerusalem temple. Here *kāḇôḏ* is depicted as a phenomenon of radiant splendor (Ezk. 10:4; 43:2) that moves, rises, and comes near (9:3; 10:18; 11:23; 43:4). Like P, Ezekiel describes the *kāḇôḏ* as a blazing fire surrounded by radiance and a great cloud (1:4; 8:2).

Deutero-Isaiah and Trito-Isaiah describe God's return to Zion as the revelation (*gālâ*) of his *kāḇôḏ* (Isa. 40:5; cf. Ps. 97:6; 102:17[16]) and his shining over Jerusalem (Isa. 60:1; cf. below).

---

19. See IV below.

20. See J. Morgenstern, "Moses with the Shining Face," *HUCA,* 2 (1925), 1-27; A. Jirku, "Die Gesichtsmaske des Mose," *ZDPV,* 67 (1944-45), 43-45; F. Dumermuth, "Moses strahlendes Gesicht," *ThZ,* 17 (1961), 241-48; → קרן *qāran.*

21. S. Singer, *SPIB* (1943), 200.

2. *Synonyms.* In the sense of "glory," "beauty," etc., *kāḇôḏ* is conjoined with a whole series of terms such as *ʿōz* (Ps. 29:1; 63:3[2]) that, like *kāḇôḏ*, can also mean "power": *hāḏār, hôḏ*, "splendor" (Ps. 8:6[5]; 21:6[5]; etc.); *tip̱ʾereṯ*, "ornament" (Ex. 28:2,40); *ṣᵉḇî*, "beauty"; and *gēʾûṯ/gāʾôn*, "pride" (Isa. 4:2). Like Akk. *melammu* and its derivatives,[22] all these can be understood as describing a crown[23] or a splendid garment, especially when used of God or the king. Thus Ps. 104:1f. says that God is "clothed with honor and majesty (*hôḏ wᵉhāḏār*)," covering himself "with light as with a garment." Ps. 21:6(5) says of the king: "His *kāḇôḏ* is great . . . , splendor and majesty (*hôḏ wᵉhāḏār*) thou dost bestow upon him." According to Ps. 8, which describes humanity as being a little less than divine, it is crowned with *kāḇôḏ* and *hāḏār* (v. 6[5]). The terms *gāʾôn, ṣᵉḇî*, and *tip̱ʾereṯ*, conjoined with *kāḇôḏ* in Isa. 4:2, are associated in Isa. 28:1-5 with a crown of pride: "Woe to the crown of pride (*gēʾûṯ*) of the drunkards of Ephraim, and to the fading flower (*ṣîṣ*) of its glorious beauty (*ṣᵉḇî tip̱ʾartô*). . . . In that day Yahweh of hosts himself will be a crown of beauty, (*ṣᵉḇî*) and a diadem of glory (*tip̱ʾereṯ*) to the remnant of his people." Similarly, *gēʾûṯ, ʿōz*, and *hāḏār, hôḏ* can be conceived as garments; e.g., Ps. 93:1: "The Lord reigns as king; he is robed in majesty (*gēʾûṯ*) . . . , he is girded with strength (*ʿōz*)"; Isa. 52:1: "Put on your strength (*ʿōz*), O Zion, put on your garments of beauty (*tip̱ʾereṯ*)"; Job 40:10: "Deck yourself with majesty and dignity (*gāʾôn wᵉgōḇāh*); clothe yourself with *hôḏ wᵉhāḏār*."

Akk. *melammu*, "terrifying radiance," has a similar wealth of synonyms: *namrirru*, "radiance"; *šalummatu*, "brilliance"; *šarūru*, "brightness"; *baštu/baltu*, "dignity"; etc.[24] As in the Bible, people may be clothed, girded, and crowned with them; cf. the inscription of Esarhaddon: "This crown clothed with terrifying radiance (*melammu*), surrounded with dignity (*baltu*), surrounded with brilliance (*šalummatu*), wrapped in radiance (*namrirru*)."[25] Kings and gods are clothed and girded with *melammu, namrirru, šalummatu*, etc.[26]

IV. Glorified Objects. Not just the deity but all kinds of special religious objects may be endowed with *kāḇôḏ*, e.g., the throne (→ כסא *kissēʾ*; 1 S. 2:8; Isa. 22:23; Jer. 14:21; 17:12), the temple (Hag. 2:9; cf. Ps. 29:9), holy garments (Ex. 28:2,40), and above all crowns (Job 19:9; Ps. 8:6[5]). The same holds true of Akk. *melammu* and its synonyms. Temples,[27] crowns, sacred weapons, and garments[28] are surrounded by *melammu*. The glory of a city and its temple are likewise depicted in the same terms as in the OT. Thus the Nebuchadnezzar inscription describes the palace at Babylon: "This palace . . . I filled with plenty (*lulû*), so that all the people could see it; its sides were encompassed by dignity (*baltu*) . . . with the awesome majesty (*puluḫti melammi*;

22. See below.
23. See above.
24. Cf. Cassin; Oppenheim, *JAOS*, 63 (1943), 31f.; Römer, 145ff.
25. Borger, 83, 34.
26. Cf. Cassin; Römer, 307, with citations of relevant passages.
27. *CAD*, X/2 (1978), *s.v. melammu*, 1.d.
28. Oppenheim, *JNES*, 8 (1949), 172ff.

see below) of my kingship. Neither evil nor wicked persons may enter it."[29] Rebuilt Jerusalem is described in similar terms: "Awake, awake, put on your strength (*ʿōz*), O Zion; put on your garments of majesty (*tip'ereṯ*), O Jerusalem, the holy city; for there shall no more come into you the uncircumcised and the unclean" (Isa. 52:1).

This splendor extends to encompass or fill entire regions. We are told that God's *kāḇôḏ* fills the whole earth (Nu. 14:21; Ps. 72:19; Isa. 6:3); his glory covers the heavens and fills the earth (Hab. 3:3). In Mesopotamia, too, the splendor (*melammu*) of gods and kings covers (*katāmu, saḫāpu*) heaven and earth or fills (*malû*) the whole earth.[30] This notion is especially common in the narratives describing the dedication of the tabernacle and temple. The entrance of the Lord into his divine dwelling place is indicated by the statement that his *kāḇôḏ* fills (*mālē'*) the tabernacle (Ex. 40:34f.) or the temple (1 K. 8:11; Ezk. 10:4; 43:5; 44:4). The glory (*kāḇôḏ*) of God reaches the heavens: "His *kāḇôḏ* is high (*rām*) above the heavens" (Ps. 113:4); cf. Ps. 57:6,12(5,11) (par. 108:6[5]): "Be exalted (*rûmâ*), O God, above the heavens! Let thy *kāḇôḏ* be over all the earth." Mesopotamian texts state similarly that the glory and splendor (ní-melam) of the gods reach the heavens.[31]

Glory also covers the forests of Lebanon and Carmel: "It shall blossom abundantly. . . . The *kāḇôḏ* of Lebanon shall be given to it, the majesty (*hāḏār*) of Carmel and Sharon" (Isa. 35:2; cf. 60:13). The trees of the garden of God in Eden were likewise clothed with glory: "Who can be likened to you in *kāḇôḏ* and in greatness?" (Ezk. 31:18; cf. vv. 8f.). In Mesopotamia, too, cedars and cedar forests were considered sacred and filled with glory.[32]

V. Divine Glory in the Ancient Near East. In the ancient Near East, gods and kings were described as being surrounded with glory; their headdress or crown in particular is adorned with glory and majesty. The Egyptian crown was endowed with power and represented something like a gleaming fiery diadem (*nsr.t* [cf. Heb. *nēzer*], *3ḫt*). It was deified as a goddess[33] and considered a source of awe and of the terror that overthrows the enemy.[34]

In Assyria, similarly, "awe" and "terrible splendor" (*pulḫu melammu* [Sum. ní-melam]) are associated with the tiara.[35] As already noted,[36] Heb. *kāḇôḏ* and *hôḏ wᵉhāḏār* are likewise connected with the crown.

The Greek epics also associate divine radiance with the head of the god. We are told, for example,[37] that Athena crowned the head of Achilles with a cloud of fiery

29. S. H. Langdon, *Die neubabylonischen Königsinschriften. VAB,* 4 (1912), 118, 52f.; 138, 29f.

30. For examples, see *CAD,* X/2, 10f.

31. Cf. Römer, 149, no. 16.

32. Cassin, 62ff.

33. Frankfort, 107f.

34. See below.

35. Cf. EnEl I, 68; Oppenheim, *JAOS,* 63 (1943), 31ff.; Cassin, 9ff.; Römer, 308f.

36. See IV above.

37. *Iliad* xviii.20.

power that terrified the Trojans. Zeus himself was shrouded in a cloud of incense,[38] which recalls the God of Israel, who is also pictured in a cloud of smoke (*'ᵃnan haqqᵉṭōreṯ*) above the ark (Lev. 16:2,13). In the Sinai narratives, the *kᵉḇôḏ YHWH* is depicted as a cloud (Ex. 16:10; Nu. 17:7[16:42]).

Majestic glory evokes both reverence and fear. This is especially clear in Akkadian terminology. The phrase *pulḫu melammu* (Sum. ní-melam) is an hendiadys; its components mean, literally, "fear, glory," but in fact the phrase means "majesty." The expression is used of deities, kings, and other awesome sacred objects,[39] and is itself an object of reverence and fear. The fear (*pulḫu*) and glory (*melammu*) of the Assyrian god or king overcome (*isḫupšunūti*) the enemy in battle.[40] The fiery diadem (*3ḫt, nsr.t*) of Egyptian gods and kings[41] likewise spreads fear (*nrw*) and terror (*śnḏ*) that vanquish the enemy in battle.[42] In this respect, the terrifying aspect of the divine manifestation of Inanna in Mesopotamian literature is quite striking; cf. the Sumerian hymn of Enheduanna (the daughter of Sargon I) to Inanna:[43] "O my Lady, the Anunna, the great gods,/Fluttering like bats fly off from before you to the clefts [in the rock],/They who dare not walk [?] in your terrible glance (igi-ḫuš),/who dare not proceed before your terrible countenance (sag-ki-ḫuš)."[44] The "terrible countenance" is that of the goddess; it beams forth radiance and splendor like that of the god Nanna, "whose face is full of radiance (sag-ki-bi me-lám-gál-la-gim)."[45] This imagery recalls the blazing head of Achilles[46] and the radiant face of Moses (Ex. 34:29f.).

The terrifying glory of Inanna, before which the Anunna deities flee to the rocky clefts like bats, recalls Isaiah's prophecy concerning the "terror and glory" (*paḥaḏ wᵉhāḏār*) of the Lord, before which the nations flee like bats to the clefts of the cliffs: "In that day men will cast forth their idols of silver . . . to the bats, to enter the caverns of the rocks and the clefts of the cliffs, from before the terror (*paḥaḏ*) of Yahweh, and from the glory of his majesty (*hᵃḏar gᵉ'ônô*), when he rises to terrify the earth" (Isa. 2:20f.).

Hiding in the rocks from the *kāḇôḏ* of Yahweh is mentioned in Ex. 33:21f. (cf. 1 K. 19:11ff.). In Job 40:10ff. Job is challenged to deck himself with majesty and dignity, glory and splendor (*hôḏ wᵉhāḏār*) like God — which is naturally impossible — and tread down the wicked so that they hide in the dust.

The terrifying aspect of Yahweh's *kāḇôḏ* is especially prominent in the revelation at Sinai. The people are alarmed at seeing the *kāḇôḏ* of the Lord (Dt. 5:24; cf. Ex. 20:18), and they are afraid of being consumed by the great fire that blazes forth from

38. *Iliad* xv.153.
39. Oppenheim, *JAOS*, 63 (1943), 31ff.; Cassin.
40. For examples, see *CAD, s.v. melammu.*
41. See above.
42. Weinfeld, *ErIsr,* "Divine Intervention etc.," 126, nn. 27-28.
43. W. W. Hallo and J. J. A. van Dijk, *The Exaltation of Inanna. YNER,* 3 (1968), 18f., ll. 34f.
44. Cf. *ANET*³, 579ff.
45. Cf. S. N. Kramer, *Enmerkar and the Lord of Aratta* (1952), 22, l. 273.
46. See above.

the *kāḇôḏ* (Dt. 5:25). The parallel in Ex. 20:18 states that the people present at the theophany shrank back and kept their distance.

The fire that issues from the *kāḇôḏ* appears also in the context of the dedication of the tabernacle (Lev. 9:23f.) and the dedication of Solomon's temple (2 Ch. 7:1ff.), at which the people witnessed the descent of the fire and of Yahweh's *kāḇôḏ* upon the temple. The fire that consumed the sacrificial gifts was taken as evidence that God had accepted the dedication; the people rejoiced with praise and thanksgiving (Lev. 9:24; 2 Ch. 7:3). The same phenomenon is recorded in 1 K. 18, when Elijah consecrates the altar on Mt. Carmel. When Yahweh's fire came down and consumed the sacrificial offerings, the people fell upon their faces and cried out: "Yahweh alone is God . . ." (1 K. 18:39).

The fire of the *kāḇôḏ* can also be dangerous. It consumes not only the sacrificial gifts but also Aaron's sons Nadab and Abihu, who offered unholy fire and transgressed God's commandment (Lev. 10:1f.).

The divine flames strike the enemy so that "fire goes before [the Lord], and burns up his adversaries round about," and all behold his *kāḇôḏ* (Ps. 97:3f.).

The dangerous aspect of Yahweh's *kāḇôḏ* is especially clear in the narratives of Israel in the desert. Here the *kāḇôḏ* of Yahweh threatens the Israelites if they murmur against him (Ex. 16:7,10; Nu. 14:10; 16:19; 17:7[16:42]; 20:6). On one occasion the "fire of Yahweh" — understood as a manifestation of his *kāḇôḏ* — is kindled against the Israelites and their rebellion (Nu. 11:1).

The manifestation of Yahweh's *kāḇôḏ* is accompanied by signs of reverence such as proskynesis, praise, and acclamation. Lev. 9:24 states that "when all the people saw it [the *kāḇôḏ* and the fire], they shouted and fell on their faces." Ezekiel, too, saw the *kāḇôḏ* and fell upon his face (Ezk. 1:28; 3:23). Cf. also the ceremony at the dedication of the temple in 2 Ch. 7: "When all the Israelites saw the fire come down and the *kāḇôḏ* of Yahweh upon the temple, they bowed down with their faces to the earth . . . and gave thanks" (v. 3; cf. also 1 K. 18:38).

Besides the phrase *paḥaḏ wᵉhāḏār* (in Isa. 2:10,19,21), the polarity of fear and reverence is suggested by the compound expressions *gōḇah wᵉyir'â,* "majesty and fear" (Ezk. 1:18; cf. the discussion of *gōḇah* and *gā'ôn* above), *nôrā' tᵉhillōṯ,* "terrible in glorious deeds" (Ex. 15:11), and *nôrā' hôḏ,* "terrible majesty" (Job 37:22); cf. also *môrā'* par. *kāḇôḏ* in the context of the reverence due a father and master (Mal. 1:6).

VI. *kᵉḇôḏ YHWH* in P and Ezekiel. In P and Ezekiel, the *kāḇôḏ* of Yahweh is conceived as a blazing fire surrounded by a cloud (Ex. 24:16f.; cf. 16:10; 40:34f.; Nu. 17:7[16:42]; Ezk. 1:4; 10:4). The cloud is an indispensable element of a theophany. It serves as a cloak to protect against the mortal danger of viewing the deity. Only Moses, who can look upon God face to face (cf. Nu. 12:8; Dt. 34:10), may enter this cloud (Ex. 24:18). To the other Israelites God reveals himself only wrapped in clouds. Unlike Moses, they see only the flames that blaze within the cloud (Ex. 24:17). Only once, at the consecration of the tabernacle (Lev. 9:23), does God reveal himself to Israel without such protection — an event parallel in importance to the Sinai revelation in the other Pentateuchal sources.

When the *kāḇôḏ* enters the tabernacle, the cloud surrounds the holy of holies; Moses cannot enter the tabernacle while the *kāḇôḏ* of Yahweh is present (Ex. 40:34f.).[47] According to Ezekiel, the *kāḇôḏ* departs from the temple at the time of the exile: "The *kāḇôḏ* of Yahweh went up from the cherubim. . . . The temple was filled with the cloud, and the court was full of the brightness (*nōḡah*) of the *kāḇôḏ* of Yahweh" (Ezk. 10:4). Isaiah, too, sees the temple filled with smoke in his vision of the *kāḇôḏ* of Yahweh (Isa. 6:3f.). The deity dwells in the thick darkness of the holy of holies (1 K. 8:12), but this does not suffice to keep it from being gazed upon by mortals. When the high priest Aaron enters the holy of holies each year, he must first fill it with a cloud of incense (Lev. 16:13), "for I will appear in the cloud upon the *kappōreṯ*" (v. 2). This cloud of smoke produced by Aaron is therefore not the same as the cloud in which the *kāḇôḏ* is revealed. If a cloud constantly shrouded the seat of the deity between the cherubim, Aaron did not need to produce an artificial cloud. The phrase "lest he die" (Lev. 16:2, 13) shows that the cloud of incense was intended to conceal the image of God and thus protect the high priest from the death he would suffer if he looked upon the deity.

This conception of the *kāḇôḏ* associated with the tabernacle and temple was obviously developed by the Jerusalem priesthood. The other source strata see the revelation of the deity differently: here cloud and fire are not a constant manifestation of the divine presence but are accompanying phenomena (Ps. 97:2f.; cf. Ex. 19:16ff.; Dt. 4:11; 5:22); they are instruments of God's protection and power. Cloud and fire serve to guide (Ex. 13:21; Nu. 10:34; Dt. 1:33) and protect (Ex. 14:19ff.; cf. Ps. 105:39) the people; they are divine agents to destroy the enemy (Ex. 14:24; Ps. 97:2f.; Hab. 3:5) and provide the vehicle for God's descent to earth (Ex. 34:5; Nu. 11:25; 12:5; Dt. 31:15). According to P, however, God does not descend (*yāraḏ*) in the cloud; his *kāḇôḏ* dwells perpetually in the tabernacle. Its presence is manifested to the Israelites by the cloud that covers the tabernacle (Nu. 17:7[16:42]). Although the *kāḇôḏ* of Yahweh has its own form of representation in P, the notion of the *kāḇôḏ* of the deity is very ancient and is associated with the notion of God's dwelling place.[48] Thus Ps. 29, which revolves around the *kāḇôḏ* attributed to God (vv. 1-3), reaches its climax in the statement: "In his temple all cry, '*kāḇôḏ*'" (v. 9). Other psalms mention the temple explicitly: "the place where thy *kāḇôḏ* dwells" (Ps. 26:8).

In later Jewish literature, the *kāḇôḏ* is replaced by the *šᵉḵînâ*.[49] The notion of the divine chariot throne (*merkāḇâ*), first found in Ezekiel's visions, acquired similar significance.[50]

---

47. The assignment to particular source strata of the various aspects associated with the *kᵉḇôḏ YHWH* is discussed by M. Görg, *Das Zelt der Begegnung. BBB,* 27 (1967), 59-66. On Yahweh's presence in the temple and the signs associated with it, see R. E. Clements, *God and Temple* (Philadelphia, 1965), *passim.*

48. On the various conceptions and descriptions of theophany, see Jörg Jeremias, *Theophanie. WMANT,* 10 (²1977), 100-112.

49. → שׁכן *škn,* "dwell."

50. See J. Maier, *Vom Kultus zur Gnosis. Kairos,* 1 (Salzburg, 1964), esp. 119f., 144ff.; J. Neusner, "The Development of the *Merkavah* Tradition," *JSJ,* 2 (1971), 149-160; G. Scholem, "Merkabah Mysticism," *EncJud,* XI, 1386-88; more recently J. Marböck, "Henoch — Adam — Der Thronwagen," *BZ,* N.S. 25 (1981), 103-111.

Rolf Rendtorff[51] has described *kāḇôḏ* as "that aspect of the activity of Jahweh that could be perceived by men and in which he himself is revealed in his power." This *kāḇôḏ* represents the divine majesty in the broad sense; it often alternates with God's face (*pānîm*), goodness (*ṭûḇ*), power (*ʿōz),* beauty (*nōʿam*), steadfast love (*ḥeseḏ*), salvation (*yēšaʿ*), etc. This is especially clear in Ex. 33:18ff. Moses asks permission to see God's *kāḇôḏ,* and God answers: "I will make all my goodness pass before you" (v. 19; cf. also v. 22). The verses that follow then speak of the revelation of God's face (*pānîm*). According to von Rad,[52] this passage reflects a cultic etiology (of which traces also appear in the Psalms) that associates God's dwelling in his house with the experience of a theophany.

The Psalms often express a yearning for the temple as God's domain: "O God . . . I seek thee, my soul thirsts for thee. . . . I have looked upon thee in the sanctuary, beholding thy power (*ʿōz*) and glory (*kāḇôḏ*). Because thy steadfast love (*ḥeseḏ*) is better than life. . ." (Ps. 63:2-4[1-3]). A similar enthusiasm is found in Ps. 65:5(4), where the psalmist yearns for the goodness of God's house (*ṭûḇ bêṯᵉḵā*). Cf. also Ps. 73:16ff., where *kāḇôḏ* refers to God's majesty in a future life; here we find the expression "receive behind the *kāḇôḏ,*" i.e., bring the soul to God in an assumption (v. 25[24]; RSV "receive me to glory"; cf. Gen. 5:24; 2 K. 2:3,5,9; also Ps. 49:16[15]: "But God will ransom my soul from *šᵉʾôl,* will snatch me away").

Interpretations of the expression *wᵉʾaḥar kāḇôḏ tiqqāḥēnî* (Ps. 73:24b) vary widely. Most exegetes agree that the verse refers to a future life (H. H. Rowley, Victor Maag, Friedrich Nötscher, Artur Weiser, etc.). Others see a specific parallel to the assumption of Enoch (Martin Buber, Han-Joachim Kraus, Gerhard von Rad, etc.). Still others find no allusion to a future life but rather a promise to the faithful of happiness and success in this life (Edward J. Kissane, Sigmund Mowinckel, Hermann Gunkel, Raymond-J. Tournay, etc.). Sidney Jellicoe sees an allusion to acceptance into Yahweh's presence as the result of a theophany.[53] C. B. Hansen suggests an ecstatic experience,[54] while Helmer Ringgren conjectures an event "somehow connected with the cultic manifestation of the *kāḇôḏ* at the New Year's Festival."[55] Finally, Armin Schmitt[56] suggests an assumption like that of Elijah or Enoch, in which the worshipper is received into God's presence after death, so that he does not fall into *šᵉʾôl.*

Thus union with the *kāḇôḏ* means entrance into God's possession in life after death, in deliverance from *šᵉʾôl,* and in the joy of beholding God's countenance (cf. Ps. 16:10f.; 17:15). In Ps. 62:7f.(6f.), *kāḇôḏ* is used in parallel with *yēšaʿ* ("salvation") and *ʿōz*: "He only is my rock and my salvation. . . . I trust in God, my salvation (*yēšaʿ*) and my *kāḇôḏ,* the rock of my strength (*ʿōz*)."

---

51. R. Rendtorff, in W. Pannenberg, Rendtorff, and U. Wilckens, eds., *Revelation as History* (Eng. trans., New York, 1968), 37.

52. G. von Rad, " 'Righteousness' and 'Life' in the Cultic Language of the Psalms," in *The Problem of the Hexateuch* (Eng. trans. 1966, repr. London, 1984), 258.

53. "The Interpretation of Psalm lxxiii. 24," *ExpT,* 67 (1955/56), 210.

54. "Bagefter herlighet, et bidrag til forstêelsen af psalme 73," *DTT,* 13 (1950), 84f.

55. "Einige Bemerkungen zum LXXIII Psalm," *VT,* 3 (1953), 270f.

56. A. Schmitt, *Entrückung — Aufnahme — Himmelfahrt. FzB,* 10 (1973), 302.

VII. Manifestation of *k*ᵉ*ḇôḏ YHWH* at the Revelation of a Message. During Israel's wanderings in the desert, the *kāḇôḏ* is revealed to inform the Israelites of God's will,[57] usually immediately after their revolt or rebellion against their leaders (Ex. 16:10; Nu. 14:10; 16:19; 17:7[16:42]; 20:6).[58] God intervenes by manifesting his *kāḇôḏ*; there follows a divine message to Moses in the tent of meeting (*'ōhel mô'ēḏ*). The tent of meeting is understood as the central sanctuary, from which God addresses Moses (cf. Ex. 40:34–Lev. 1:1). After the tent is consecrated, it is filled with the *kāḇôḏ* of Yahweh and covered by the cloud. God calls to Moses from the tent of meeting and conveys to him the laws governing sacrifice. For P, the tent or tabernacle sanctified by God's *kāḇôḏ* (Ex. 29:43) is the place where God meets Moses to speak to him and give him the law for the Israelites (Ex. 25:22; 29:42-45; Nu. 7:89).

The tent of meeting as the place where God makes his decisions known is not an invention of the Priestly writer. In the early source of Ex. 33:7-11, too, the tent is an oracular sanctuary Moses enters to meet with God, who descends in the pillar of cloud and stands at the entrance to the tent. There is clearly an enormous difference between the notion of the tent of meeting in this early tradition (JE) and that of P. In the JE traditions, the tent of meeting stands outside the camp (Ex. 33:7; Nu. 11:26; 12:5); God stands outside the tent, not within it.[59] In P, however, the tent of meeting stands in the center of the camp and God speaks from within it. According to P, furthermore, God does not descend in a cloud to speak with Moses at the entrance to the tent, as the JE tradition provided. The tent is God's permanent dwelling place (Ex. 25:8; 29:45), from which he declares his will. In P, the tent actually functions as the central sanctuary in the midst of the camp.

If, however, we focus our attention on the prophetic function of the tent, we see that both traditions share a common basis. Both in the early lay sources (JE) and in P, God appears in the tent to admonish and to speak to Moses. According to Nu. 12:5f., God descended in the cloud to reprove Aaron and Miriam for their slander; and according to Nu. 11:25, he descended similarly to speak to Moses concerning the appointment of the elders. Dt. 31:15 (E) states that God revealed himself in the pillar of cloud at the tent of meeting to inaugurate Joshua in his new office.

According to all three sources, the revelation of God's presence is marked by signs of honor and respect (Ex. 33:10). In Ezekiel, too, the manifestation of Yahweh's *kāḇôḏ* is accompanied by the transmission of a message: in Ezk. 1:28; 3:12,23, it inaugurates the prophet's mission; the occurrences of *kāḇôḏ* in 8:2f.; 10:4,18; 11:23 are connected with censure of Jerusalem, in consequence of which the *kāḇôḏ* departs from the city.

VIII. Future Revelation of the *k*ᵉ*ḇôḏ YHWH;* Eschatology. In the prophets and Psalms, the future deliverance of the people in Zion is depicted as a new revelation of

57. Westermann, *Festschrift W. Eichrodt.*
58. See above.
59. Cf. Haran, 50ff.

the *kāḇôḏ*. In the future, the Lord will reveal his glory once again, as in the days of old when he led Israel out of Egypt. Isa. 4:5 says that the Lord will create over Zion "a cloud by day, and smoke and the shining of a flaming fire by night"; "over all the *kāḇôḏ* there will be a canopy and a pavilion." This imagery recalls the pillars of cloud and fire of the Exodus Narrative.

Isa. 24:23 speaks of the future kingdom of God upon Mt. Zion, when "before his elders he will manifest his glory." This expression is to be understood against the background of Ex. 24:9f., which describes God's revelation of himself to the "elders of Israel." Just as God the King revealed himself to the elders of the people at Sinai, so he will reveal himself once more to the elders when he inaugurates his reign on Mt. Zion. Isa. 25:6ff.[60] describes a feast on Zion as the direct consequence of the revelation of the *kāḇôḏ* to the elders. This association of a feast with God's revelation also recalls Ex. 24:11.

In postexilic texts, the future revelation of the *kāḇôḏ* takes on universal dimensions. Not just the Israelites but the whole world will behold the glory and splendor of God: "The *kāḇôḏ* of Yahweh shall be revealed (*wᵉniglâ*), and all flesh shall see it together" (Isa. 40:5). The LXX renders the second part of this verse as: ". . . and all flesh shall see the salvation of God." Cf. Isa. 52:10, where all the ends of the earth will see the salvation (*yᵉšûʿâ*) accomplished by the arm of Yahweh. According to Ginsberg,[61] the term *zᵉrôaʿ*, "arm," serves in Deutero-Isaiah as a metaphor for revelation and salvation (cf. 51:5; 52:10; 53:1), which may explain the phrase *zᵉrôaʿ tipʾartô*, "arm of his glory," in 63:12. It is interesting that Deutero-Isaiah speaks in similar terms of the revelation of Yahweh's *kāḇôḏ* (40:5) and of his arm (53:1). In fact, Isa. 40–66 and the Psalms treat *kāḇôḏ*, God's righteousness, and salvation as synonyms (cf. Isa. 58:8; 62:1f.). Righteousness (*ṣeḏeq*), salvation (*yᵉšûʿâ*), and *kāḇôḏ* overlap: "For Zion's sake I will not keep silent . . . until her righteousness (RSV 'vindication') goes forth as brightness (*nōgah*), and her salvation (*yᵉšûʿâ*) as a burning torch. The nations shall see your righteousness (*ṣeḏeq*), and all the kings your glory (*kāḇôḏ*)" (62:1f.). This *kāḇôḏ* of Jerusalem is nothing less than the *kāḇôḏ* of Yahweh, which rests upon the city (cf. Isa. 60:1-3); the manifestation of Yahweh's *kāḇôḏ* (*kᵉḇôḏô yērāʾeh)* is associated with his light (*ʾôr*), his coming (*bāʾ*), his brilliance (*zāraḥ*), and his shining (*nōgah*). We are dealing here with a revival of conventional theophany terminology from ancient Israelite texts (cf. Dt. 33:2 [*bāʾ, zāraḥ, hôpîaʿ*]; cf. also Hab. 3:3f. [*yāḇōʾ, hôḏô, nōgah, kāʾôr, ʿōz*]). The cliche *nirʾâ kāḇôḏ* (Isa. 60:2) also appears already in the Exodus Narrative (see above).

There is nevertheless a significant difference between the function of the *kāḇôḏ* in the theophany descriptions of Deuteronomy and Habakkuk and its function in Isa. 40–66. According to Dt. 33:2 and Hab. 3:3f., the *kāḇôḏ* is the glory of the God of Israel, who appears to his people to give them the law (Dt. 33:4) or to deliver them from their enemies (Hab. 3:6f.). According to Isa. 40–66, the *kāḇôḏ* of Yahweh is delegated to his people and

60. Cf. H. Wildberger, *Jesaja. BK*, X/2 (1978), 899f., 960.
61. *JBL*, 77 (1958), 152-56.

to Jerusalem; its purpose is to attract other nations and guide them in their darkness. In the postexilic Psalms, the *kābôḏ* has a similarly universal function. The restoration of Zion and the reestablishment of Yahweh's *kābôḏ* upon it move the nations and their kings to pay homage to the God of Israel: "The nations will fear the name of Yahweh, and all the kings of the earth thy *kābôḏ*. For the Lord will build up Zion, and will appear in his *kābôḏ* (*nir'â bikḇôḏô*)" (Ps. 102:16f.[15f.]; cf. 97:6f.). The same idea appears in Isa. 2, where the idolaters discard their idols and retreat into caves out of fear of God's majesty (vv. 10, 18, 20f.; cf. above).

This universal extension of Yahweh's *kābôḏ* is also implicit in the idea that it "fills the whole earth" (Isa. 6:3; Nu. 14:21; Hab. 2:14; Ps. 72:19). This expression is based on the notion that the whole human race will be subject to God's sovereignty, an idea that already lies behind Isaiah's prophecy of the day of Yahweh (Isa. 2). Here the human race acknowledges Yahweh's sovereignty by following his radiance and glory (cf. above), which spread through the entire universe. The eschatological function of the earth's being "filled with Yahweh's glory" is clear from a comparison of Isa. 11:9 with Hab. 2:14. In the latter, Isaiah's notion of the knowledge of Yahweh that fills the earth (11:9) is linked with the idea that Yahweh's *kābôḏ* fills the earth: "For the earth will be filled with the knowledge of the *kābôḏ* of Yahweh, as the waters cover the sea." This *kābôḏ* fills the earth as universal salvation (cf. Nu. 14:21; Ps. 72:19).

Psalm 72:19 constitutes a doxology concluding the second book of the Psalter. Here the filling of the earth with *kābôḏ* has an eschatological function, like the verses speaking of the ingathering of the exiles at the end of the fourth book (Ps. 106:47). The eschatological function of Yahweh's *kābôḏ* is especially clear in the Amidah prayer of the Jewish New Year's liturgy: "O God, the God of our fathers, mayest thou rule over the whole earth in thy glory (*yᵉqār*) and appear in the radiance of thy majestic greatness (*bahᵃḏar gᵉ'ôn 'uzzᵉkā*) before all the inhabitants of the world and of the earth, so that all creatures may know that thou hast made them . . . and that all those who have breath may say: The Lord, the God of Israel, is king; his kingdom holds sway over all things."[62]

IX. *kᵉḇôḏ YHWH* and the Name of Yahweh. The *kābôḏ* of Yahweh thus has both a concrete meaning (a fiery phenomenon from which radiance shines forth) and an abstract meaning (honor, dignity, majesty). In the latter meaning, *kābôḏ* recalls → **שֵׁם** *šēm,* which has similar connotations. The noun *šēm* occurs in parallel with *tᵉhillâ* and *tip'ereṯ* (Dt. 26:19; Jer. 13:11; Isa. 63:14; 1 Ch. 29:13), which are synonymous with *kābôḏ* (see above). It also occurs in parallel with *kābôḏ* (cf. Isa. 48:9; Ps. 102:16[15]; also Isa. 42:8; 43:7; Jer. 14:21; Ps. 113:3f.); for the parallel *šēm* par. *tᵉhillâ,* cf. Ps. 102:22(21); 106:47; 145:21. And *šēm,* like *kābôḏ,* was associated with the dwelling place of Yahweh (see above). Deuteronomy and the Deuteronomistic

62. See M. Weinfeld, "'The Day of the Lord': Aspirations for the Kingdom of God in the Bible and in Jewish Liturgy," *Studies in Bible* (ed. S. Japhet), *ScrHier* 31 (1986), 341ff.

literature in particular use *šēm* to speak of the divine presence in the temple: "the place that Yahweh will choose to cause his name to dwell (*l^eyakken/lāśûm š^emô*) there" (Dt. 12:5,11; etc.).[63] In this usage, the temple was built for the name of Yahweh (2 S. 7:13; 1 K. 5:19[5]; 8:18; etc.) or dedicated (*qdš* hiphil) to it (1 K. 9:7). The Priestly and Deuteronomistic schools thus use different terminology for the divine presence in the temple: P uses *kāḇôḏ,* while Deuteronomy and the Deuteronomistic literature use *šēm.* The difference in terminology reflects a conceptual difference. P thought of God in a more corporeal way: God dwells in a tent, which is his *miškān* (Ex. 25:8; 29:45; Lev. 26:11f.). Deuteronomy thinks of God more abstractly: God himself dwells in heaven (Dt. 4:36); only his name is associated with the sanctuary. The author of Deuteronomy is very conscientious about this distinction. In contrast to the earlier sources, which still speak of building a house for Yahweh's dwelling place (*l^ešiḇtô*; 2 S. 7:5,7) or for God himself (1 K. 6:1f.; 8:13), the Deuteronomist speaks with absolute consistency of the dwelling of God's name or building a house for his name.[64]

We must admit, however, that both *šēm* and *kāḇôḏ* express semantically the majesty of sovereign divine power. "Establishment of a name" means glory and honor (Gen. 11:4; 2 S. 7:9,23; 8:13; Isa. 63:12), and the proclamation of God's name throughout the world (Ex. 9:16) is identical with the proclamation of God's *kāḇôḏ* among the nations (Isa. 66:19). In Ps. 102:22(21), we find the proclamation of God's name in Zion in parallel with the proclamation of his praise (*t^ehillâ*) in Jerusalem. Like *šēm* and *hôḏ* ("splendor"), *šēm* and *kāḇôḏ* are used in parallel (cf. Ps. 8:2[1]; 148:13). This observation might account for the construct phrase *k^eḇôḏ š^emô* (cf. Ps. 29:2; 66:2; 79:9; 96:8; the OT frequently uses word pairs in construct phrases[65]). The reverse combination *šēm k^eḇôḏô* is found in late texts (Ps. 72:19; Neh. 9:5); it may reflect liturgical usage in the period of the Second Temple (cf. Mishnah *Yoma* vi.2: *bārûḵ šēm k^eḇôḏ malkûṯô l^eʿôlām wāʿeḏ*).

X. Qumran Scrolls. According to Kuhn,[66] *kāḇôḏ* occurs 112 times in the Qumran scrolls (plus 2 occurrences of *kybwd*). Almost half of the occurrences (51) are in 1QH; there follow 1QM (16), 1QS (10), 1QSa and 1QSb (4 each), and CD (3). Of special importance are the 6 occurrences in 4QŠîrŠab, which extend the notion of *kāḇôḏ* found in Ezekiel.[67] In the Manual of Discipline, *kāḇôḏ* is rare in the regulatory passages (cf. 1QSa 2:14-21, which states that the seating arrangement depends on the *kāḇôḏ* of the individual); most occurrences are in the hymnic sections, where God is extolled as the height of *kāḇôḏ* (1QS 10:12; cf. CD 3:20; 20:26). This *k^eḇôḏ ʾēl* will not be revealed fully until the eschaton (1QM 1:9; 12:7). The semantic richness of *kāḇôḏ* in the OT Psalms continues in the Hodayoth. The meanings "victory," "strength," and "army"

---

63. See esp. A. S. van der Woude, "שֵׁם *šem* Name," *THAT,* II, 935-963, esp. 955.
64. Weinfeld, *Deuteronomy and the Deuteronomic School,* 191-209.
65. Cf. Y. Avishur, *Construct State of Synonyms in Biblical Rhetoric* (1977), 49 [Heb.].
66. Kuhn, 96f.; Nachträge, 200.
67. Newsome, *Songs of the Sabbath Sacrifices, HSS* 27 (1985).

proposed by Menahem Mansoor,[68] however, are dubious, since they are based on the parallelism with *ḥayil* and *g^e^ḇûrâ* found in the OT. God is *meleḵ kāḇôḏ* (1QM 12:8; 19:1) and *'îš kāḇôḏ* (1QM 12:10; 19:3); his is *'^e^meṯ kāḇôḏ* (1QH 3:34f.); his *kāḇôḏ* is beyond measure (5:20; 9:17) and is vouchsafed to his faithful followers at Qumran (6:12f., etc.). Their community is established *l^e^ḵāḇôḏ* of God (8:5,20), just as the meaning of each individual's life is *l^e^ḵāḇôḏ* of God (1:10; 10:11f.).

Weinfeld

---

68. M. Mansoor, "The Thanksgiving Hymns and the Massoretic Text (Part II)," *RevQ,* 3 (1961/62), 387-394, esp. 387ff.

כָּבָה *kāḇâ*

Contents: I. Meaning and Occurrences. II. Literal Usage. III. Figurative Usage: 1. Extinguishing of Life; 2. Judgment; 3. Everlasting Fire.

I. Meaning and Occurrences. The root *kbh* is found only in Hebrew and its immediate neighbors; it has the same meaning in Middle Hebrew, Jewish Aramaic, and possibly Egyptian Aramaic. It is also related to Arab. *kabā,* "glow," "hide fire under ashes."

The basic meaning refers to flames that die out or are extinguished. This meaning is clear from the nouns with which the verb is used: → אשׁ *'ēš* (Lev. 6:5,6[Eng. vv. 12,13]; Isa. 66:24; Jer. 4:4; 17:27; 21:12; Ezk. 21:3[20:47]; Am. 5:6; Prov. 26:20; Cant. 8:6f.), → נר *nēr* (1 S. 3:3; Prov. 31:18; 2 Ch. 29:7), *gaheleṯ* (2 S. 14:7), *zepeṯ* (Isa. 34:9f.); *laheḇeṯ šalheḇeṯ* (Ezk. 21:3[20:47]; cf. Cant. 8:6f.), as well as → חמה *ḥēmâ* (2 K. 22:17; Jer. 4:4; 7:20; 21:12; 2 Ch. 34:25). Besides the synonym *d'k* (Isa. 43:17), the semantic field includes primarily verbs that refer to fire that is kindled (*b'r* [Isa. 1:31; 34:9f.; Jer. 4:4; 7:20; Ezk. 21:4(20:48)], *yṣt* [2 K. 22:17; Jer. 17:27; Ezk. 21:3(20:47)], *yqd* [Lev. 6:5,6(12,13)], *yṣ'* [Jer. 4:4; 21:12]) or consumes (*ṣrb* [Ezk. 21:3(20:47)], → אכל *'āḵal* [Jer. 17:27; Ezk. 21:3(20:47); Am. 5:6]). Most of the references do not suggest active extinguishing. Only Cant. 8:7 — an obviously exaggerated metaphor — speaks of water as an extinguishing agent, probably because the climate of Palestine generally does not provide enough water to extinguish fires. Usually, then, the verb refers to a fire that dies for lack of fuel (cf. Prov. 26:20: a fire goes out for lack of wood) or a lamp that goes out for lack of oil (cf. Mt. 25:8).

The root appears 24 times in the OT; 14 occurrences are in the qal, 10 in the piel (although Ezk. 32:7 should probably be read as a qal). There is no great difference in meaning: the qal means "go out" or "extinguish," the piel means "put out." Of the

---

kāḇâ. F. Lang, "σβέννυμι," *TDNT,* VII, 165-68.

occurrences, 2 K. 22:17 par. 2 Ch. 34:25 and Jer. 4:4 par. 21:12 are doublets. The root appears only as a verb and is found only in Leviticus, 1 Samuel, 2 Samuel, 2 Kings, 2 Chronicles, Isaiah, Jeremiah, Ezekiel, Amos, Proverbs, and Song of Songs. It does not appear in the Psalms or Job, where the synonym *d'k* is used instead. It exhibits a clear affinity with Deuteronomistic and prophetic language.

The LXX renders *kbh* 22 times with *sbénnymi* and its derivatives, using other words in only 2 passages.

II. Literal Usage. The OT does not use the verb in its literal, basic sense, although the praise of the good wife in Prov. 31 includes the statement that her lamp does not go out at night (v. 18), i.e., that she keeps it burning. Lev. 6:5f.(12f.) deals with the fire on the altar before the temple; 1 S. 3:3; 2 Ch. 29:7 deal with the lamp inside the temple. Jer. 17:27; Ezk. 21:3f.(20:47f.) speak of kindling a fire. In all these passages, however, the fire that is extinguished or kept burning has symbolic significance. In Prov. 26:20, the fire that goes out for lack of wood reflects the observation that a slanderer's absence puts a quarrel to rest.

III. Figurative Usage.

1. *Extinguishing of Life.* The basic meaning of *kbh* makes it well suited to describing the cessation of life. The "glowing wick" (Isa. 42:3; 43:17) of a lamp that has run out of oil and will go out entirely if not refilled reflects the very point of death. The quenching of a coal (2 S. 14:7) similarly describes the utmost peril to the survival of a family. The extinguishing of the lights of heaven (Ezk. 32:7) symbolizes the utter debility of Pharaoh and Egypt. Contrariwise, the fire upon the altar (Lev. 6:5f.[12f.]) and David as the "lamp of Israel" (2 S. 21:17) — as long as they do not go out — symbolize vitality and permanence; when the lamps in the temple go out (1 S. 3:3; 2 Ch. 29:7), it is a sign of defeat. The irresistible power of love is shown by the fact that it cannot be quenced by floods of water (Cant. 8:7).

2. *Judgment.* The prophets' messages of judgment against their own nation as well as other nations repeatedly state that a fire (Isa. 1:31; 34:10; Jer. 17:27; Ezk. 21:3f.[20:47f.]; Am. 5:6) or God's flaming wrath (2 K. 22:17; Jer. 4:4; 7:20; 21:12; 2 Ch. 34:25) will be ignited, which no one will be able to put out. This statement uses both the qal (*lō' tiḵbeh*) and the piel (*'ên meḵabbeh*). The emphasis is not on active attempts to extinguish the flames but on the unquenchable violence and duration of God's judgment. The qal proclaims the inescapable coming of this judgment, while the piel warns against it (with *pen* in Jer. 4:4; 21:12; Am. 5:6; without *pen* in Isa. 1:31).

3. *Everlasting Fire.* The last verse of Isaiah (66:24), dating from the late postexilic period, associates the notion of the unquenchable violence and duration of God's judgment with the fate of individuals who have rebelled against Yahweh and with their bodies. This verse is the point of departure for the notion of the flames of hell. The impression made by the passage is shown by Sir. 7:17; Jth. 6f.; and Mk. 9:44.

Baumann

כָּבַס kāḇas

Contents: I. Etymology, Semantic Field, Occurrences. II. Washing of Garments: 1. Literal Usage; 2. Figurative Usage. III. The Fuller's Field. IV. LXX. V. Dead Sea Scrolls.

I. Etymology, Semantic Field, Occurrences. The root *kbs,* "wash," "full (cloth)," appears with the same meaning in Ugaritic: *kbs/śm,* "fullers guild."[1] It has a similar meaning in Akk. *kabāsu,* "tread (out),"[2] and Arab. *kabasa,* "press."[3] Its semantic field includes → רחץ *rāḥaṣ,* "wash"; → טהר *ṭhr,* "be clean"; → טמא *ṭm',* "be unclean"; and → קדשׁ *qdš* piel, "sanctify."

The qal occurs 3 times in the OT, the piel 44 times (once in Genesis, twice in Exodus, 27 times in Leviticus, 8 times in Numbers, once in 2 Samuel, twice in Jeremiah, once in Malachi, and twice in Psalms), and the pual and hothpael twice each (all in Leviticus).

II. Washing of Garments.

1. *Literal Usage.* The OT uses the piel of *kbs* for the most part to mean the literal washing of garments to make them clean. Figuratively, the word can refer to cleansing from sin (Jer. 2:22; 4:14; Ps. 51:4,9[Eng. vv. 2,7]) and the metaphorical washing of garments (Gen. 49:11; Mal. 3:2).

The washing of garments is intended to remove various kinds of uncleanness: (a) primary uncleanness, such as blood from the sin offering (Lev. 6:20[27]), a "diseased" spot (Lev. 13:54-56,58), a spot of semen on any garment or skin (Lev. 15:17); (b) secondary uncleanness, such as affects the garments of someone who has come in contact with an unclean animal or the scapegoat (Lev. 11:25,28,40 [twice]; 16:26,28; 17:15,16; Nu. 19:7f.,10,21), leprosy (Lev. 14:8f.,47 [twice]) or suspected leprosy (Lev. 13:6,34), male emission or female bleeding (Lev. 15:5-8,10f.,13, 21f.,27), a corpse (Nu. 19:19), or battle (Nu. 31:24; cf. 1QM 14:2). The clothes of the Levites are washed during their consecration (Nu. 8:7), but the source of the uncleanness is not specified.

The expression *yeḵabbēs* (or *weḵibbes*) *beḡāḏāyw weṭāmē'* (*yiṭmā'*) *'aḏ-hā'āreḇ* (Lev. 11:25,28,40 [twice]; Nu. 19:10,21) indicates that *kbs* begins a lengthy process of cleansing. The garments are washed with water (Lev. 15:17; Nu. 19:8; for Lev. 14:47, cf. v. 46). Those who are unclean must also wash their bodies (*rāḥaṣ*: Lev. 15:5-8,10f.,21f.,27; 17:15; *beśārô*: Nu. 19:8). After seven days, they are to wash their

---

kāḇas. G. Brunet, "Le terrain aux foulons,"*RB,* 71 (1964), 230-39; M. Burrows, "The Conduit of the Upper Pool," *ZAW,* 70 (1958), 221-27; G. Dalman, *AuS,*V (1937), 145-159.

1. *WUS,* no. 1281.
2. *AHw,* I (1965), 415f.
3. *WKAS,* I, 28f.

garments again in order to be clean (*wᵉḵibbes bᵉgāḏāyw wᵉṭāhēr*: Lev. 13:6,34,58; Nu. 8:7; 31:24). This time, too, they must wash themselves with water (*rāḥaṣ*: Lev. 14:8f.; 15:13; Nu. 19:19). In addition, those who are cleansed from leprosy must cut off their hair (→ גלח *gillaḥ*: Lev. 14:8f.). The words *ṭhr* and *ṭm'* are not always used explicitly (Lev. 6:20[27]; 16:26,28; 17:16; Nu. 8:21; 19:7). Those who do not wash their clothing and bathe their flesh bear their iniquity (*nāśā' ʿāwōn*: Lev. 17:16).

Failure to wash one's clothes is mentioned by 2 S. 19:25(24) as a sign of mourning, along with other examples of carelessness about personal hygiene.

The washing is done outside the camp (Lev. 14:8f.; 16:26,28; Nu. 19:7; 31:24) at a holy place (Lev. 6:20[27]), a place where there is running water (*mayim ḥayyîm*: Lev. 15:13). In preparation for the theophany at Sinai, Moses sanctified (*qdš* piel) the people for two days; they washed their clothes and admonished to keep ready (*nāḵôn*) for the third day (Ex. 19:10,14f.).

The poetic statement of Gen. 49:11 that Judah washes his garments in wine and his vesture in the blood of grapes is usually interpreted as a reference to paradisal abundance and luxury in the messianic age to come; the mention of colors in v. 12, however, raises the possibility that the red color of the wine had some kind of symbolic significance.

2. *Figurative Usage*. The piel of *kbs* is used figuratively with personal objects. Jerusalem is to wash its heart of wickedness in order to be saved (Jer. 4:14); Jeremiah also says, however, that literal washing with lye and soap does not remove guilt before God (2:22). It is also possible to liken Yahweh's appearance to the purification and cleansing of the Levites with a refiner's fire and a fuller's (*mᵉḵabbēs*) lye (Mal. 3:2). The psalmist prays to Yahweh to wash him thoroughly from his transgressions and cleanse (*ṭhr* piel) him from his sin (Ps. 51:4[2]). He also prays to Yahweh to purge (*ḥṭ'* piel) him with hyssop so as to cleanse him and to wash him so that he will be whiter than snow (v. 9[7]). Here we find a spiritualization of what was originally understood as cultic purity: sin is identified with uncleanness and forgiveness of sins with cleansing.[4] These verses probably allude to purification ceremonies.[5]

III. The Fuller's Field. The 3 occurrences of *kbs* in the qal all involve the fixed expression *tᵉʿālaṯ habbᵉrēḵâ hāʿelyônâ bᵉl'el-mᵉsillaṯ śᵉḏēh kôḇēs* (2 K. 18:17; Isa. 7:3; 36:2), usually translated "the conduit of the upper pool, which is on the highway to the Fuller's Field."

"Fulling" is today the process of kneading newly woven wool in warm soapy water in order to mat it into cloth. Dalman, however, notes that he never observed such fulling in the Near East. What he did see was the sizing and burnishing of silken material, which was then pressed (Arab. *kabas*) in a wooden press (*makbas*); a vertical screw, advanced by means of an attached crank, pressed the material between two horizontal

4. See → טמא *ṭāmē'*; → טהר *ṭāhar.*
5. H. Ringgren, *Die Psalmen. Urban Taschenbücher,* 120 (Stuttgart, 1971), 81.

boards.[6] The "Fuller's Field" would thus be a field where fulled cloth was spread out to dry and bleach.[7] Eissfeldt disagrees, suggesting instead that the *śᵉḏēh kôḇēs* was a field belonging to the guild of fullers.[8]

It is important in this context to note the difference between the qal and the piel of *kbs*. According to Jenni,[9] *kôḇēs,* "fuller," refers to the regular process of trampling and kneading, whereas *mᵉḵabbēs,* "washer," suggests the cleansed product that results from the activity, just as in other contexts *kbs* piel, "wash, cleanse," focuses on the final condition of the object ("make clean"). Alternatively, *kôḇēs* and *mᵉḵabbēs* could be more or less synonymous; the "Fuller's Field" would then be a place for the ritual cleansing of garments, the holy place outside the camp[10] where water emerges from the conduit of the upper pool and carries away the uncleanness that has been removed.

The site of the upper pool and the Fuller's Field is disputed. Gustav Dalman[11] and Hans Kosmala[12] locate it west of the northwest corner of the modern Old City (around the pool of Mamilla), at the head of the valley that continues as the Valley of Hinnom. J. J. Simons[13] locates it on the northern edge of Jerusalem; Millar Burrows suggests the lower Kidron Valley: there is enough water there for the fullers, and this was also the location of the "Fuller's Spring" (*ʿên rōḡēl*).

IV. LXX. The LXX usually uses *plýein* to translate *kbs*; the same verb also renders the hiphil of *dwḥ* (Ezk. 40:38) and occasionally *rāḥaṣ* (Ex. 29:17; Lev. 1:9,13; 8:21; 9:14; 2 Ch. 4:6). In Jer. 2:22; 4:14, the figurative sense of *kbs* is translated by *apoplýein.* The translation of *śᵉḏēh kôḇēs* is *ho ágros toú gnaphéōs.*

V. Dead Sea Scrolls. In the Dead Sea scrolls, *kbs* appears 3 times. The soldiers are to purify their clothing on the morning before they return to camp, cleansing it of the blood of the iniquitous corpses (1QM 14:2; cf. Nu. 31:24: "on the seventh day"). On the Sabbath, no one is to wear dirty (*ṣôʾîm*) clothes or garments that have been stored in their chamber unless they have been washed (*kbs* pual) with water or scoured with incense (CD 11:4). No one in a state of uncleanness that requires washing (*ṭᵉmēʾ kibbûs*) may enter a house of prayer (CD 11:22).

André

---

6. Dalman, 145f.

7. F. Nötscher, *Biblische Altertumskunde. HSAT,* Sup. 3 (1940), 213; V. Maag, in H. Schmökel, ed., *Kulturgeschichte des Alten Orients* (Stuttgart, 1961), 692.

8. O. Eissfeldt, "The Alphabetical Cuneiform Texts from Ras Shamra Published in 'Le Palais Royal d'Ugarit' Vol. II, 1957," *JSS,* 5 (1960), 37 = *KlSchr,* II (1963), 405.

9. E. Jenni, *Das hebräische Piʿel* (Zurich, 1968), 163.

10. See above.

11. P. 152.

12. "Jerusalem," *BHHW,* II (1964), 826f.

13. J. Simons, *Jerusalem in the OT. StFS,* 1 (1952), 334ff.

כֶּבֶשׂ *keḇeś*; כֶּשֶׂב *keśeḇ*; כִּבְשָׂה *kiḇśâ*; כִּשְׂבָּה *kiśbâ*; שֶׂה *śeh*

Contents: I. Etymology and Meaning: 1. *keḇeś*; 2. *śeh*; 3. Personal Names. II. Ancient Near East: 1. Domestic Animals; 2. Cult and Sacrifice; 3. Mythology. III. Occurrences: 1. Distribution; 2. Compound Phrases; 3. LXX. IV. OT: 1. Domestic Animals; 2. Legal Texts; 3. Metaphorical Usage; 4. Sacrifice. V. Dead Sea Scrolls.

I. Etymology and Meaning.

1. *keḇeś*. With Heb. *keḇeś* belongs the lexical variant *keśeḇ*, a product of consonantal metathesis[1] (cf. the variants cited in *BHS* at Ex. 12:5; Lev. 3:7; 4:32; Nu. 15:11). Among the corresponding feminine forms, besides *kiḇśâ* and the hapax legomenon *kiśbâ* (Lev. 5:6), we find in Lev. 14:10 and Nu. 6:14 the earlier form *kaḇśâ*.[2] The root *kbs/š* with the meaning "sheep, lamb" is found in East Semitic and Southwest Semitic languages, e.g., Akk. *kabsu*, "young ram";[3] Amor. *kabś(ān)um*; *kaśb(ān)um*;[4] Arab. *kabš*.[5] Hebrew is unique among the Northwest Semitic languages as the only one in which *kabs/š* with the meaning "sheep" is attested. The others use *'immēr* II,[6] cognate with Akk. *immeru*,[7] which appears in the OT (apart from the Aramaic sections [Ezr. 6:9,17; 7:17]) only in proper names (Jer. 20:1; Ezr. 2:59; Neh. 3:29; 7:40, 61; 11:13; 1 Ch. 9:12; 24:14). Later isolated forms include Syr. *kēḇšā*[8] and Soq. *kobš*.[9] Heb. *keḇeś* is related to the common Semitic verb *kbš*, "overthrow," and *kbs*, "roll," derived from Akk. *kabāsu*, "tread (down)."[10] The semantics of *kabsu* may be explained by the early use of sheep to tread seed into the ground or to tread out grain on the threshing floor;[11] this etymology is supported by the Egyptian parallels *sḥ* and *sḥ.t*.[12]

---

keḇeś. F. Blome, *Die Opfermaterie in Babylonien und Israel. SSAOI,* 4 (1934); F. S. Bodenheimer, *Animal Life in Palestine* (Jerusalem, 1935); G. Dalman, *AuS,* VI (1939), 180-287; H. Kees, *Der Götterglaube im alten Ägypten. MVÄG,* 45 (⁵1983); W. Nagel, "Frühe Tierwelt in Südwestasien," *ZA,* N.S. 21[55] (1962), 169-236; R. Rendtorff, *Studien zur Geschichte des Opfers im alten Israel. WMANT,* 24 (1967); I. Seibert, *Hirt, Herde, König. DAWB,* 53 (1969); E. D. Van Buren, *The Fauna of Ancient Mesopotamia as Represented in Art. AnOr,* 18 (1939); E. Werth, "Die afrikanischen Schafrassen und die Herkunft des Ammonkultes," *ZE,* 73 (1941[1944]), 307-321.

1. *GK*, §19n.
2. *BLe*, §75g.
3. *AHw*, I (1965), 418; *CAD*, VIII (1971), 23.
4. I. J. Gelb, *Computer-aided Analysis of Amorite. AS*, 21 (1980), 22.
5. *WKAS*, I, 30.
6. Cf. *KBL³, s.v.*
7. *AHw*, I, 378.
8. *LexSyr*, 317.
9. Leslau, *Contributions*, 214.
10. *AHw*, I, 415f.
11. See II.1 below.
12. *WbÄS*, III, 464.

Heb. *keḇeś,* originally (as in Akkadian) a term meaning "young ram," is also used by the OT for the entire species (*ovis*) (Dt. 14:4, etc.).

2. *śeh.* Heb. *śeh* has cognates in most Semitic languages: Akk. *šūm* III, *šu'u* I; Assyr. *śūbu;*[13] Arab. *šāt;*[14] Ugar. *š;*[15] Aram. *š'h.*[16] The proposed connection with Copt. *esou*[17] and Egyp. *s3,*[18] "son," is to be rejected. Friedrich Schulthess[19] has attempted unsuccessfully to derive *śeh* from an animal cry on the basis of a connection with *t't'.*[20] Heb. *śeh* is derived from a base **śai;*[21] its original form is **si'ya* or **wisay.*[22]

In both Aramaic and the OT, *š'h* is used in the phrase *š'h wšwrh*[23] as a collective term for small livestock (sheep and goats).[24] Like the generic term → צאן *ṣō'n, śeh* functions as a *nomen unitatis*; it can designate, regardless of gender or age, a single animal from the flock,[25] sheep as well as goats. By that reckoning, it designates also the ram (*'ayil*), the ewe (*rāḥēl,* Gen. 31:38; 32:15[14]; Isa. 53:7; Cant. 6:6), the newborn lamb (*ṭāleh,* Isa. 40:11; 65:25; *ṭ*^e^*lēh ḥālāḇ,* 1 S. 7:9; Sir. 46:16), the young lamb (*keḇeś/kiḇśâ*), and the fatted lamb (*kār*).

3. *Personal Names.* In Semitic personal names, an animal name (*kbś/š,* etc.) may be found as a nickname or pet name: *kabšat,*[26] *kabsatum* (fem.), "lamb,"[27] *immerum,* "sheep."[28] In particular, diminutive forms are used as terms of endearment: *immeriya,* "my little sheep";[29] *ḫurāpum,* "little lamb."[30] Theophorous names are found that parallel the *māru* names, such as *immer-ilī,* "sheep of the gods," or possibly "Immer is my god."[31] These suggest the special care and protection of the deity for the person bearing the name. William F. Albright[32] explains the name "Ben-kosbah" as "Son of an Ewe Lamb."

---

13. *AHw,* III (1981), 1255.
14. Wehr, 449; Lane, I/4, 204f.
15. *WUS,* no. 2561.
16. *DISO,* 286.
17. W. Spiegelberg, *Koptisches Handwörterbuch* (Heidelberg, 1921), 29.
18. *KBL*², *GesB,* etc.
19. F. Schulthess, "Noch einige Zurufe an Tiere," *ZS,* 2 (1924), 15.
20. Cf. *DISO,* 286, *s.v. s'h* II; also H. Y. Priebatsch, "*š* and *ṯ* in Ugarit und das Amoritische," *UF,* 7 (1975), 389-394.
21. Joüon, §98e; *BLe,* §61u.
22. Cf. *GK,* §96.
23. See III.2 below.
24. Cf. R. A. Brauner, *A Comparative Lexicon of Old Aramaic* (Philadelphia, 1974), 562.
25. Joüon, §135b4.
26. *RyNP,* I, 112f.
27. *APNM,* 152.
28. *AN,* §35.5.
29. *AN,* §3.11.
30. *AN,* §35.5.
31. *AN,* §37.2.
32. W. F. Albright, "An Ostracon from Calah and the North-Israelite Diaspora," *BASOR,* 149 (1958), 34, n. 13.

II. Ancient Near East.

1. *Domestic Animals.* The domestic sheep (*Ovis aries*) is found depicted, especially in pictographs and glyptography, from the seventh millennium on; skeletal remains from this period have also been found.[33] With the dog and the goat, it is among the earliest domesticated animals. The varieties found in the ancient Near East are descended for the most part from the argali (*Ovis ammon*) and mouflon (*Ovis musimon*).

In contrast to Mesopotamia, where representatives of both species are already attested in the Early Sumerian and Proto-Elamite period,[34] only the Dinka sheep, with its almost horizontal spiral horns, is found in Egypt during the Old Kingdom (also as a hieroglyph). Sheep of the mouflon type, with circular horns, do not appear until the Twelfth Dynasty.[35] In the course of time, the broad-tailed sheep (*Ovis laticaudata*), possibly a descendant of the wild sheep (*Ovis vignei*),[36] came to dominate.[37] The tail of the broad-tailed sheep, a product of mutation, may weigh from 5 to 10 kilograms (10-25 lb.), depending on the sex of the animal. Comparable to the camel's hump, it enabled this species of sheep to adapt exceptionally well to the climate of the Near East.[38] Hermann Kees[39] has suggested that the sheep with circular horns attested in the cult of Amon (and Khnum) from the Middle Kingdom onward were broad-tailed, but E. Werth[40] disputes this identification, preferring to see in them the Fezzan sheep depicted in Neolithic petroglyphs from northwest Africa. The earliest representations of sheep, from both Mesopotamia[41] and Egypt,[42] depict hairy sheep, which indicates that the dense coat of wool is a mark of domestication.

Since the earliest period, sheep were used to trample seed into the soil[43] and to tread out harvested grain on the threshing floor;[44] their primary use, of course, was as a source of meat and milk. The ox probably replaced the sheep early on for plowing and carrying loads.[45] When a sheep was slaughtered, the pelt[46] may well have supplied the familiar "shaggy cloak," but tendons and skin were also processed for other uses. Before shears made their appearance, the wool was probably plucked loose to be spun,

---

33. R. Berger and R. Protsch, "The Domestication of Plants and Animals in Europe and the Near East," *Or,* 42 (1973), 214-227.
34. Nagel, 184.
35. Werth, 317.
36. Bodenheimer, 122.
37. For pictorial representations from the Assyrian period, see *ANEP,* nos. 366, 367; also van Buren, fig. 62.
38. Bodenheimer, 123.
39. P. 80.
40. Pp. 311-17.
41. E. Strommenger and M. Hirmer, *Fünf Jahrtausende Mesopotamien* (Munich, 1962), nos. 19, 23.
42. K. Lange and M. Hirmer, *Egypt: Architecture, Sculpture and Painting in Three Thousand Years* (Eng. trans., London, [4]1968), no. 3.
43. Cf. L. Störck, "Aussaat," *LexÄg,* I (1975), 576.
44. *BuA,* I, 196; cf. CH §§268-270.
45. B. Brentjes, *Die Haustierwerdung im Orient* (Wittenberg, 1965), 31.
46. See *BuA,* I, fig. 63.

woven, and dyed.[47] Besides distiguishing sheep providing wool from those used for food, Sumerian and Akkadian had a series of different terms to indicate the variety, sex, and age of the animals.[48] As in the ancient Near Eastern system of farming out cattle, attested in legal documents,[49] sheep were put under the care of a shepherd for grazing.[50] Mythological overtones (Tammuz) then caused "shepherd" to become a royal epithet.

2. *Cult and Sacrifice.* Sheep appear throughout the ancient Near East in representations or symbols of the gods. Since the Old Babylonian period, a staff with a ram's head symbolized the god Ea,[51] and the Hittites depicted the sun-god with a flock of sheep.[52] In Egypt, however, certain gods were themselves represented with the head of a ram and a human body. Among the many Egyptian ram cults,[53] that of Khnum (and of Amon from the Middle Kingdom on) is unique both in its historical development and in its iconography. Khnum was depicted with spiral horns during the Old Kingdom but with circular horns during the Middle Kingdom. During the New Kingdom, representations with both types of horns appear simultaneously, with the striking addition of a sun disc between the horns, as in the northwest African petroglyphs mentioned above.[54] All the Egyptian ram cults focus on the fertility of the ram in procreation.[55]

The sacrificial system of the two great civilizations of Egypt and Mesopotamia also reflects the same difference. In Mesopotamia, the sheep was a popular sacrificial animal; in Egypt, with a few exceptions, it was never so used, probably because an animal representing a deity was inappropriate for sacrifice. This notion is confirmed by the observation that after the Dinka sheep became extinct at Mendes, a goat with spiral horns was worshipped and sheep were sacrificed.[56] In Mesopotamia, there was great variation among the individual sacrifices, since certain animals could be not used for certain sacrifices.[57] Sheep and goats, and more rarely cattle, were the usual sacrificial offerings. The sex, age, number, and condition of the victims lent each sacrifice its particular emphasis. Young male animals were preferred; according to Herodotus,[58] a special golden altar for very young animals stood in front of the temple at Babylon.

47. *BuA,* I, 217, 254f.
48. Cf. B. Landsberger, "Studien zu den Urkunden aus der Zeit des Ninurta-tukul-Aššur," *AfO,* 10 (1935/36), 152-57.
49. Cf. R. Haase, *Die keilschriftlichen Rechtssammlungen in deutscher Fassung* (Wiesbaden, ²1979).
50. CH, §§265-67.
51. U. Seidl, "Göttersymbole und Attribute,"*RLA,* III (1971), 488f.; *AOB,* 329.
52. O. R. Gurney, *Some Aspects of Hittite Religion* (Oxford, 1977), 13.
53. Kees, 78-81.
54. Cf. Werth, 317f.
55. Kees, 81.
56. Kees, 80f.
57. Cf. Blome, 151f.
58. *Hist.* i.183.

The value of the sacrificial animals was measured by their normal utility, just as in certain sacrifices the portions preferred for human consumption (such as thigh or tail) were offered.[59]

The same sacrifices were offered by the surrounding nations that were the economic and cultural equals of Mesopotamia.[60] Sheep and goats were sacrificed throughout the whole Fertile Crescent.[61] Apart from the idea that it provided food for the deity, rooted in anthropomorphic conceptions of the gods, the purpose of animal sacrifice was primarily to show honor and reverence, as the sacrifice of one's own possessions makes clear. The notion of substitutionary sacrifice, common throughout the ancient Near East, deserves special mention;[62] in it an animal dies in place of a human being. Akkadian texts speak vividly of such sacrifice: "The head of the lamb he shall give for his head, the neck of the lamb for his neck. . . ."[63] Citing as evidence Punic votive stelae that represent Baʿal Hammon with a sheep, Gese[64] interprets the OT term *mlk* as denoting the substitution of a lamb for a human sacrifice. Sheep were also used in Mesopotamia for divination[65] and rites of exorcism.

3. *Mythology.* Sumerian cosmologies describe the world prior to creation in negative terms, by listing what was not present.[66] The listing of cattle, sheep, and goats, which as yet bear no names and do not yet procreate, together with the crops that are mentioned, points to an early stage of domestication. Myths like Enki and Ninhursag,[67] however, describe the world in its primal state as a paradise where all antagonisms are reconciled: "the wolf does not attack the lamb." The crops and domestic animals also appear together in the myth of Laḫar, the god of cattle, and his sister Ashnan, the goddess of grain.[68] Many of these myths reflect new advances of civilization. In the mourning rites following the death of Baʿal, ʿAnat offers to the dead god an enormous sacrifice: seventy each of wild oxen, cattle, sheep, etc.[69]

A widespread mythological motif is the dying and rising fertility-god Tammuz (Dumuzi), usually depicted as a shepherd with his flock.[70] This motif appears on innumerable cylinder seals as well as in literary texts,[71] and was also common in

---

59. Blome, 137, 161.
60. *ANET,* 350; Gurney, 27; H. Gese, M. Höfner, and K. Rudolph, *Die Religionen Altsyriens, Altarabiens und der Mandäer. RdM,* 10/2 (1970), 174f.
61. *ANEP,* 600, 612-18; M. Riemschneider, *Die Welt der Hethiter* (Stuttgart, 1954), pl. 79.
62. Cf. Gurney, 52f.
63. Cf. Blome, 49.
64. Pp. 176f.
65. M. Jastrow, *Die Religion Babyloniens und Assyriens,* II (Giessen, 1912), 813-884.
66. Cf. M. Lambert, "Sumerische Schöpfungsmythen," in E. Klein, ed., *Schöpfungsmythen* (1964), 108ff.
67. *ANET,* 37-41.
68. S. N. Kramer, *Sumerian Mythology* (New York, ²1961), 53f.
69. *KTU* 1.6 I, 18ff.
70. Cf. A. Moortgat, *Tammuz* (Berlin, 1949).
71. W. Heimpel, *Tierbilder in der sumerischen Literatur. St.Pohl,* 2 (1968), 214-226.

Egypt.[72] In Mesopotamia, it developed into the official title of the king.[73] Besides being represented in flocks symbolizing protection and guidance, from the Jemdet-naṣr period on the sheep as source of life (on account of its milk, flesh, and fleece) appears frequently (along with the goat) in representations of the tree of life.[74]

III. Occurrences.

1. *Distribution.* Of the 130 occurrences of *ke̲beś* (including 8 of *ki/ab̲śâ,* 13 of *keśeb̲,* and 1 of *kiśbâ*), 112 are in sacrificial contexts. Of these, 6 are in Exodus, 22 in Leviticus, 70 in Numbers, 7 in Ezekiel, 4 in 2 Chronicles, and 1 each in 1 Chronicles, Ezra, and Isaiah. Of the 18 occurrences in secular contexts, 7 are in Genesis, 3 in 2 Samuel, 2 in Isaiah, and 1 each in Deuteronomy, Job, Proverbs, Sirach, Jeremiah, and Hosea. Of the 43 occurrences of *śeh,* 18 are in secular contexts; of the 25 in cultic contexts, 19 involve sacrificial terminology. Apart from a passage in Ezekiel that is related to P, all these occurrences are in the Pentateuch.

2. *Compound Phrases.* In 12 passages, *śeh* and *šôr*[75] (used as *pars pro toto*) are combined to form a phrase synonymous with *ṣō'n ûb̲āqār.*[76] In this form, it refers to the totality of gregarious livestock; it can be extended to encompass all domestic animals (in the context of the ban, for example) by the inclusion of camels (*gāmāl*) or asses (*ḥ^{a}môr*) (Josh. 6:21; 1 S. 15:3; 22:19). The meaning of *šôr w^{e}śeh* (Ex. 34:19; Lev. 22:23,28; Dt. 17:1; etc.) can be further specified by dividing the second element into *ke̲beś* and *'ēz.* In Lev. 17:3; 22:27; Nu. 18:17, this combination (with *keśeb̲*) is used as an inclusive term for sacrificial animals. Previously mentioned sacrificial animals are cited without distinction in secondary Leviticus texts: in Lev. 5:7, for example, *dê śeh* refers to a young female sheep or goat sacrificed as a sin offering; in 12:8, it denotes a male lamb sacrificed as a burnt offering.[77] The summary language in Lev. 22:28[78] shows that it, too, is secondary; the reading *w^{e}śeh* (Sam., LXX) here is exactly parallel to the secondary addition in 22:23.

Besides the substitution of *ke̲beś* and *'ēz* for *śeh,* we also find phrases combining *śeh* with one or both of them; *ke̲beś* and *'ēz* are appended epexegetically to *śeh* either in a construct phrase (Dt. 14:4) or with *b^{e}* (Gen. 30:32; Nu. 15:11) or *min* (Ex. 12:5). The combination means: "one of the livestock, a sheep or a goat." The use of these same phrases with the compound *ṣō'n ûb̲āqār* (e.g., 2 Ch. 35:7; Lev. 22:21) supports the conclusion that these expressions, as well as *šôr w^{e}śeh,* are synonymous. The sequence *šôr, ke̲beś,* and *'ēz* or *śeh,* found primarily in Leviticus, differs from the

72. Cf. D. Müller, "Der gute Hirte," *ZÄS,* 86 (1961), 126-144.
73. Cf. Seibert.
74. Cf. H. Schmökel, "Ziegen am Lebensbaum," *AfO,* 18 (1957-58), 373-78; Nagel (p. 170) has identified some of the animals as sheep.
75. Cf. R. Péter, *"Par* et *Sōr," VT,* 25 (1975), 486-496.
76. → בקר, 210f.
77. Cf. K. Elliger, *Leviticus. HAT,* IV (1966), *in loc.*
78. Ascribed by Elliger, 295, to Ph[4].

dominant sequence in the sacrificial regulations of Numbers (esp. Nu. 7:15-88; 28:11-30): *pār* (*ben-bāqār*), *'ayil,* and *keḇeś* (*'ēz*). In the construction with *lᵉ*, the sacrificial animals are listed once more along with the accompanying sacrifices. When the animals are described, *ben-šᵉnāṯô* is added to *keḇeś,* etc.;[79] the singular always has the suffix (*ben-šᵉnāṯô*: Lev. 23:12; Nu. 6:12,14; 7:15,21,27; Ezk. 46:13; etc.), the plural never (*bᵉnê-šānâ*: Ex. 29:38; Lev. 9:3; 23:18; Nu. 7:17,23,35; etc.). F. Blome[80] is wrong in suggesting a difference in meaning. The only exception (*ben-šānâ* in Ex. 12:5) points up the special character of the word *śeh,* singular in form but thought of collectively; only here it is required to be a year old.

3. *LXX.* The LXX renders *keḇeś* 82 times by *amnós,* 18 times by *amnás,* 9 times by *arnós,* 4 times by *próbaton,* and once by *arníon.* For the fem. *ki/aḇśâ,* it uses *amnás* 6 times and *próbaton* once. Although the LXX renders *keśeḇ* 8 times by *próbaton* and only 4 times by *arnós* and once by *amnós,* and the corresponding fem. *kiśbâ* by *amnás,* in contrast to the regular use of *amnós* for *keḇeś,* there is no discernible difference in meaning. For *śeh,* the LXX uses *próbaton* 36 times, *amnós* 3 times, *kriós* twice, and *poímnion* and *chímaros* once each. The LXX also uses *amnós* for *qᵉśîṭâ,* an obscure ancient monetary unit that appears only in Gen. 33:19; Josh. 24:32; Job 42:11.

IV. OT.

1. *Domestic Animals.* For Israel, as for its neighbors, the sheep was always the most important and the most common domestic animal. Among the Israelites, however, it was forbidden to castrate these animals for any reason, including fattening, or to acquire castrated animals from other nations (Lev. 22:24f.).[81] Many OT narratives and images reflect the frequent use of sheep.[82] The story of Jacob and Laban (Gen. 30:25-43), for example, depends on the assumption of familiarity with the natural coloration of the animals; the use of branches to influence the color of the offspring may reflect ancient magical ideas,[83] illustrated also on Assyrian cylinder seals.[84] Abraham offers Abimelech the gift of seven female lambs from his flock; by accepting them, Abimelech acknowledges Abraham's rights to the well (Gen. 21:27-30).

2. *Legal Texts.* In sacred and secular law, sheep and goats appear primarily in three contexts: (1) the sacrifice of the first-born, including both the first-born of the animal itself (Ex. 34:19) and the redemption of the first-born of human beings and asses, which could not be sacrificed (Ex. 34:20); (2) the ban[85] in the holy war; and (3) restitution for stolen (Ex. 21:37[22:1]; 22:3[4]) or misappropriated (Ex. 22:8f.[9f.]) livestock.

---

79. See IV.4 below.
80. Pp. 147f.
81. Cf. Elliger, 300.
82. Cf. K. Galling, "Viehwirtschaft," *BRL*², 351f.
83. C. Westermann, *Genesis 12–36* (Eng. trans., Minneapolis, 1985), 483.
84. Siebert, 59.
85. → חרם *ḥāram.*

3. *Metaphorical Usage.* The shepherd/flock motif provides a common metaphor, reflecting the intimate bond between human and beast (2 S. 12:3) as well as the strength and courage of the shepherd (a widespread theme of Near Eastern glyptography), to which David appeals before his fight with Goliath (1 S. 17:34). Ezk. 34:1-31 draws upon this motif; an "old form of speech traditional in the Near East"[86] frequently employs "shepherd"[87] as a divine and royal epithet, while representing the people as a flock.[88] Yahweh is the shepherd of his people (Ps. 23); he feeds Israel like a flock (Isa. 40:11). Hos. 4:16 uses this image to admonish Israel, described as a "stubborn heifer" for its devotion to the cult of Baʿal. Jer. 50:17 likewise compares Israel to a sheep (*śeh*) pursued by lions, without a shepherd and separated from its flock.

It is not just Israel as a nation that can be likened to a sheep; the fate of an individual may be compared to that of a sheep gone astray (Ps. 119:176) or a lamb led unknowingly to the slaughter (Jer. 11:19). Above all, the patient suffering of the Servant of God (Isa. 53:7) finds expression in the image of a sheep that remains silent before being sheared and slaughtered.[89] In an oracle of judgment, Isaiah threatens that the settled areas will become pasture for sheep (Isa. 7:25; 5:17).[90] In the coming peaceful kingdom, by contrast, the lamb and the wolf will lie down together (Isa. 11:6). On the textual problem of *kebeś* in connection with the royal throne (2 Ch. 9:18; 1 K. 10:19), see → כסא *kissēʾ* III.3.

4. *Sacrifice.* In Israel and Mesopotamia, sheep (esp. young males) were by far the most common sacrificial animals. Besides lambs (*kebeś*), both rams (*ʾayil*) and, more rarely, female lambs (*kibśâ*) are mentioned as sacrificial offerings. The use of an animal for sacrifice usually presupposes a certain quality, expressed by the attributes *zāḵār, tāmîm,* and *ben-šᵉnāṯô* (Ex. 12:5; Lev. 1:10; 9:3; Nu. 28:3; Ezk. 46:13; etc.). These attributes need not be explicit: P uses *kebeś* in the sense of a perfect male sacrificial lamb one year old. The common use of "sheep" to translate *kebeś* fails to observe the distinction between *kebeś* and an adult ram (*ʾayil*), which may also be sacrificed. The omission of *zāḵār* or the use of a masculine plural form that includes both males and females does not mean that both male and female animals might be sacrificed without distinction,[91] since the sacrifice of a female animal is always mentioned explicitly, as the mention of both male and female animals in Lev. 14:10 and Nu. 6:14 shows. Only 4 passages that deal with a special kind of sin offering explicitly require a female lamb (*kiśbâ/kabśâ*: Lev. 5:6; 14:10; Nu. 6:14; *kebeś nᵉqēbâ*: Lev. 4:32). The reason for the unusual sacrifice of a female animal is not apparent, especially since Israel, without

86. W. Zimmerli, *Ezekiel 2. Herm* (Eng. trans. 1983), 213.
87. → רעה *rōʿeh.*
88. Cf. Seibert, 7-22.
89. On the NT application of this passage to Jesus, see Joachim Jeremias, "αμνός," *TDNT,* I, 338-341. Besides the borrowing of the motif itself, Jeremias finds an allusion to the double meaning of Aram. *ṭalyāʾ* "lamb," "servant" = *ʿeḇeḏ.* Cf. B. Gärtner, "*ṭaljāʾ* als Messiasbezeichnung," *SEÅ,* 18f. (1953-54), 98-108; G. Dautzenberg, "αμνός," *EWNT,* I, 168-172.
90. Cf. H. Wildberger, *Isaiah 1–12* (Eng. trans., Minneapolis, 1991), *in loc.*
91. Blome, 156.

the pantheon of Egypt and the rest of the ancient Near East, did not have the opportunity to choose the sex of sacrificial animals according to the sex of the deity honored. The general preference for male animals is based in part on the notion of their strength, exhibited especially in their virility. All the *keḇeś* sacrifices are also required to be one year old (*ben-šᵉnāṯô*); this must mean "at most a year," since lambing took place twice a year[92] and the daily *tāmîḏ* offering (Ex. 29:38; Nu. 28:3f.; Ezk. 46:13; etc.) would otherwise have been impossible (cf. the requirement of Lev. 22:27 that a new-born animal not be sacrificed until eight days old). Blome's hypothesis[93] that considerations of "sexual integrity and purity" account for the choice of young animals is not convincing, since it is contradicted by the use of adult rams (*'ayil*). The preference for young animals is determined by their normal value, even if they were set aside for religious purposes (cf. Dt. 15:19). Since the flock could be maintained if only a tenth of the animals were males,[94] male lambs were preferred for consumption and therefore also for sacrifice.

All sacrificial animals had to be clean (Lev. 11:1-30), i.e., fit for sacrifice, and *tāmîm*; this requirement is stated explicitly for private sacrifices and is undoubtedly implicit for public sacrifices (Lev. 22:17-25). The antithetical expression *'ᵃšer-bô mûm* (22:20) refers to the list of physical disabilities in 22:22-24 that render an animal unsuitable for sacrifice (cf. Mal. 1:14). In contrast to Canaanite practice, the sacrifice of a wether was strictly forbidden in Israel.[95] The animal must be *tāmîm* not only for the sacrifice but also for those offering it (Ex. 12:5; Nu. 28:19,31).[96]

When several different animals are to be sacrificed, the lamb is usually mentioned last, especially in the sacrificial lists of Nu. 28:11-30 (*par ben-bāqār, 'ayil, kᵉḇāśîm*). The primary basis for this sequence is not the relative value of the various animals: inclusion of those making up a smaller proportion of the livestock emphasized the special nature of a sacrifice or feast, at which greater numbers of the usual sacrificial animal (*keḇeś*) were also offered (Nu. 29:2,20).

The primary use of lambs was in the → עולה *'ôlâ*; besides the daily *tāmîḏ* offering of two lambs, they are listed with bullocks and rams for all burnt offerings. Rolf Rendtorff[97] attempts to identify from these lists a "priestly schema" in which lambs were associated specifically with the *'ôlâ* of an individual. Lev. 9:3, however, diverges from this schema in requiring an *'ēgel* and a *keḇeś* for the *'ôlâ* of the Israelites. In texts that do not depend on P, the choice of sacrificial animals appears to be free: sheep and goats (*śeh*: Gen. 22:7,8; Jer. 43:23) may be offered in an *'ôlâ*, and Samuel even offers a "sucking lamb" (1 S. 7:9; Sir. 46:16). The difference between these texts and those of P is noteworthy.[98]

---

92. *AuS*, VI, 192.
93. P. 150.
94. *AuS*, VI, 192f.
95. Cf. Elliger, 299f.
96. Cf. K. Koch, "טמם *tmm* vollständig sein," *THAT*, II, 1048.
97. Pp. 115f.
98. *Ibid.*, 117f.

Although the animal offered in a *zeḇaḥ* is seldom mentioned, domestic animals in general (*ṣō'n ûḇāqār*) are referred to for the *zeḇaḥ šᵉlāmîm*. For "technical reasons,"[99] *ṣō'n* is further specified (*keḇeś, 'ēz*), since the fat tail of the lamb receives special treatment as belonging to Yahweh (Lev. 3:6-11).[100] For a *ḥaṭṭā't*, in which we can recognize a dependence of the sacrificial victim on the individual offering the sacrifice,[101] a female lamb or a goat might be offered. For a purification offering in the originally independent → אשׁם *'āšām* ritual,[102] a male lamb (*keḇeś hā'āšām*: Lev. 14:24; Nu. 6:12 [secondary?]) was required. For the Passover sacrifice, the sources differ: Ex. 12:5 stipulates a lamb or a kid, while Dt. 16:2 and 2 Ch. 35:7 include cattle.

Prophetic criticism of the cult (Isa. 1:11; 43:23; 66:3) forcefully attacked decadent forms of sacrifice, even equating them with the unlawful sacrifices of nations.[103]

V. Dead Sea Scrolls. Except for quotations from the Pentateuch in the Temple scroll, the words *keḇeś* and *śeh* do not occur in the Dead Sea scrolls.

Dohmen

---

99. *Ibid.*, 161.
100. See → חלב *ḥēleḇ*.
101. Rendtorff, 228.
102. *Ibid.*, 227f.
103. → חזיר *ḥᵃzîr* (*chᵃzîr*), 299.

כָּבַשׁ *kāḇaš*; כֶּבֶשׁ *keḇeš*; כִּבְשָׁן *kiḇšān*

Contents: I. Root, Meaning, Occurrences. II. OT Usage. III. Summary. IV. Derivatives. V. Dead Sea Scrolls and LXX.

I. Root, Meaning, Occurrences. The root *kbš* is a common Semitic root, appearing in most Semitic languages: Akkadian (*kabāsu*), Canaanite (El Amarna), Arabic, Samaritan, Jewish Aramaic, Christian Palestinian Aramaic, Egyptian Aramaic, Syriac, Mandaic, and Middle Hebrew. Its meaning corresponds almost without exception to that of Hebrew. In the OT, there are 14 occurrences in various stems (qal, niphal, piel [1 time]; 1 instance of the qal is attested only as *Q*; *K* presupposes a hiphil). The meaning can always be rendered by "subdue";[1] it does not vary in the different stems.

---

kāḇaš. P. Gössmann, " 'Scabellum Pedum Tuorum,' " *Divinitas*, 11 (1967), 30-53; L. Kopf, "Arabische Etymologien und Parallelen zum Bibelwörterbuch," *VT*, 8 (1958), 161-215, esp. 174-75 = *Studies in Arabic and Hebrew Lexicography* (Jerusalem, 1976), 133ff.

1. Cf. *KBL*³.

The OT also contains a single occurrence of the derivative *keḇeš* ("footstool") and 4 occurrences of the noun *kiḇšān,* likewise taken to derive from *kāḇaš.* The semantic relationship of the latter, which means "furnace," to the basic root is not immediately apparent. Earlier exegesis conjectured another occurrence of *kāḇaš* in Am. 8:4[2] and of *kiḇšān* in Ps. 68:23 (Eng. v. 22).[3]

II. OT Usage. It is not a simple matter to distinguish early and late passages within the OT and define a particular usage of *kāḇaš* as being primary. It is hard, for example, to assign the texts in Nu. 32 concerning the conquest of the land to a literary source.[4] The tribes east of the Jordan are to (or possibly wish to — there is a certain ambiguity in Nu. 32) help the tribes west of the Jordan subdue their territories and then return to their own settlements (or to be allotted them). Nu. 32:22 reads: *wᵉnikḇᵉšâ hāʼāreṣ lip̄nê YHWH* (cf. v. 29: *lip̄nêḵem*), ". . . when the land is subdued before Yahweh" (v. 29: "before you"); then the Reubenites and Gadites are free to conduct their own affairs. In this traditio-historically complex chapter, we may have the earliest occurrences of *kāḇaš.* The statements are formulated as passives (niphal), but the logical object of *kāḇaš* is in fact *hāʼāreṣ* (here meaning the settled territory west of the Jordan; the logical subject is the other Israelite tribes, assisted by the tribes east of the Jordan. The expression *lip̄nê* followed by a noun or pronominal suffix seems to go with the term *kāḇaš* with *hāʼāreṣ* or some other object. The land is subdued "before" someone (i.e., "in the presence of"; some exegetes prefer "for, on behalf of"), so that those who subdue it can enter and take possession of it. This can be said with reference both to Yahweh and to Yahweh's people. Here we sense theological overtones connected with the gift (or occupation) of the land. This is also clear in v. 29.

Josh. 18:1 is a summary verse from the hand of a priestly redactor, inserted just before the account of Joshua's further division of the land, which precedes the description of Benjamin's borders (vv. 11ff.); it uses the same formula: *wᵉhāʼāreṣ nikḇᵉšâ lip̄nêhem,* "and the land was subdued before them." The very late date of this verse argues against the antiquity of the passages in Numbers.

The "formula" appears once more in the Chronicler's history (1 Ch. 22:18), in the context of a theological interpretation of David's battles (vv. 17-19) appended to the account of his concern for building the temple.[5] This verse states that it was Yahweh who gave the inhabitants of the land into David's hand, *wᵉnikḇᵉšâ hāʼāreṣ lip̄nê YHWH wᵉlip̄nê ʻammô,* "and the land is subdued before Yahweh and his people." The theological interpretation of David's battle is set in the framework of the theology of the gift of the land and its occupation (cf. the context). The urging to build the temple of Solomon, which the Chronicler puts in David's mouth, is thus grounded in sacred

2. Cf. the apparatus in *BHK*³; rejected by *BHS*.

3. Cf. the apparatus in *BHK*³; not included in *BHS*.

4. See M. Noth, *A History of Pentateuchal Traditions* (Eng. trans. 1972, repr. Chico, Calif., 1981); *Numbers. OTL* (Eng. trans. 1968), *in loc.*

5. Cf. K. Galling, *Die Bücher der Chronik. ATD,* XII (1959), *in loc.*; W. Rudolph, *Chronikbücher. HAT,* XXI (1955), 151f.

history. In all these passages, of course, the "land" is not to be thought of in literal (e.g., agrarian) terms, but as the whole territory shaped by human habitation, as an historical entity. To "subdue" it means primarily to conquer and subdue its previous population, but also to make use of all the economic and cultural potential associated with the concept of "land."

The concept of *hā'āreṣ* receives its broadest semantic extension in Gen. 1:28 (P's Creation account), where God blesses the man and woman and commands them to subdue *hā'āreṣ* after it has been filled (or possibly by filling it) through human fertility (*p^e^rû ûr^e^ḇû ûmil'û 'eṯ-hā'āreṣ w^e^ḵiḇšuhā*). If the imperative that follows (*r^e^ḏû*, "tread down," "have dominion over") is intended to explicate *w^e^ḵiḇšuhā,* it would mean that the human race is to rule over the animal kingdom (cf. v. 26b); but probably the command is more fundamental and comprehensive, with *hā'āreṣ* denoting the whole inhabited world without territorial or geographic limitation.[6] This understanding would at least not run counter to common priestly usage, which embodies statements of principle in specific terminology. It may be asked whether this meaning of *hā'āreṣ* suggests the dominion of some human beings over others; the answer is that Gen. 1:28 (like the entire text of vv. 26-28) does not envision such dominion. Instead, it supports the utopian anthropological maxim that every human individual is a "ruler" of the world.

Most of the remaining *kāḇaš* passages in the OT show that human beings can be spoken of directly as the object of *kāḇaš* (not just indirectly as in the *kāḇaš hā'āreṣ* passages discussed above, with the exception of Gen. 1:28). In 2 S. 8:11, we have another summary statement (probably Deuteronomistic[7]), this time concerning the tribute and booty David dedicated to the temple, which he had obtained from the lands he subdued: *mikkol-haggôyîm 'ašer kibbēš* (the only occurrences of the piel), "from all the nations that he had subdued." Here *gôy* and *'ereṣ* are interchangeable.

In two areas, the direct reference to people is significant: sexual assault and enslavement. The verb is used in the sense of assault on a woman in Est. 7:8, where Haman's plea for his life before Queen Esther is misunderstood as importunity. To make his petition, Haman falls before the queen as she is reclining on her couch (*nōp̄ēl ʿal-hammiṭṭâ 'ašer 'estēr ʿāleyhā*[8]). When the king sees this, he cries out: *h^a^gam liḵbôš 'eṯ-hammalkâ ʿimmî babbāyiṯ,* "Will he even assault the queen in my presence, in my own house?" In Neh. 5:5, *kāḇaš* (niphal) has the same overtones. The citizens, burdened economically by heavy taxes, complain that Nehemiah's program has forced them to pledge not only their property but also their sons and daughters as security for loans and that some of their daughters have already been taken by force: *w^e^hinnēh 'anaḥnû kōḇšîm 'eṯ-bānênû w^e^'eṯ-b^e^nōṯênû laʿaḇāḏîm w^e^yēš mibb^e^nōṯênû niḵbāšôṯ,* "And behold, we are forcing our sons and our daughters to be slaves, and some of our daughters have already been assaulted." "Force to be slaves" is literally "subdue as slaves."[9]

6. Cf. C. Westermann, *Genesis 1–11* (Eng. trans., Minneapolis, 1984), *in loc.*
7. Cf. M. Noth, *Überlieferungsgeschichtliche Studien* (Tübingen, ³1967), 65.
8. H. Bardtke, *Esther. KAT,* XVII/5 (1963), *in loc.,* proposes emending *ʿal* to *'el.*
9. Galling, *in loc.*

While the qal already has the sense of "assault" in Est. 7:8, only the niphal has this meaning in Neh. 5:5; the qal is used for the imminent or actual situation in which people force others to be slaves.

This specialized use of the qal is also found in Jer. 34:11,16; 2 Ch. 28:10. In Jeremiah, it appears in the motivation for a prophecy of disaster in the period of Zedekiah, while the Babylonians are laying siege to Jerusalem and other cities of Judah. During this critical period, there had been a solemn agreement to release all who had been enslaved for debt; afterwards, when the emergency was over, the agreement had been renounced. This behavior amounted to treachery toward Yahweh. Jer. 34:11 reads: *wayyaḵbîšûm* (*K*; *Q* reads *wayyiḵbᵉšûm*) *laʿᵃḇāḏîm wᵉlišpāḥôṯ,* "and they subdued them as male and female slaves"; v. 16 uses the same idiom, but in the 2nd person: *wattiḵbᵉšû ʾōṯām lāḵem,* "but you forced them to be your slaves." The text is composite, but it incorporates genuine Jeremiah material.[10] Whether the verses with *kāḇaš* are authentic is hard to say. The direct allusion to Ex. 21:2ff.; Dt. 15:12; Lev. 25:39f. does not argue against their genuineness; the idiom *kāḇaš* + object + *laʿᵃḇāḏîm* used in Jeremiah is not found in these passages. It is possible that this formula in Jeremiah preserves the earliest examples illustrating this usage of *kāḇaš*. The same idiom appears once more in 2 Ch. 28:10, in the Chronicler's account of the so-called Syro-Ephraimite War; in this version, the outcome was unfortunate for Ahaz, so that men and women of Judah were taken captive and forced to go to Samaria as slaves. In the face of this event, a prophet (named Oded; cf. vv. 9-15) comes forward in Samaria and threatens the Israelites for having enslaved their "kinsfolk" (v. 11), demanding the release of the Judahites (none of this is mentioned in 2 K. 15). The motivation for Oded's threat is stated in 2 Ch. 28:10: "And, as to the Judahites and Jerusalem, you intend to subdue them, male and female, as your slaves (*ʾattem ʾōmᵉrîm liḵbōš laʿᵃḇāḏîm wᵉlišpāḥôṯ lāḵem*); but are you not burdened with sins of your own against Yahweh your God?"[11]

If Jer. 34:16 is authentic, then this idiom in 2 Ch. 28:10 (as in Neh. 5:5) would be dependent on Jeremiah. In this case, Jer. 34:11, the prose account of the release, would also have borrowed the expression from v. 16. But it is also possible to argue in the other direction, concluding that the idiom found its way into the Jeremiah from the later texts.

Unfortunately, the final two occurrences do not help resolve the debate. Mic. 7:19 clearly belongs to a late hymnic passage that exalts Yahweh's readiness to forgive.[12] The highly abstract usage of *kāḇaš* is noteworthy: *yiḵbōš ʿᵃwōnōṯênû* (with *ʾēl* as subj.; cf. v. 18), "God will subdue our iniquities" ("tread under foot" [cf. Artur Weiser];

10. Cf. G. Fohrer, *Intro. OT* (Eng. trans., Nashville, 1968), 394f.; W. Rudolph, *Jeremia. HAT,* XII (³1968), *in loc.*

11. Cf. Galling, 150f.

12. Exegetes differ in their analyses: T. H. Robinson (*Die zwölf kleinen Propheten: Hosea bis Micha. HAT,* XIV [³1964], 151f.) treats vv. 14-20 as a prayer for forgiveness and restoration; A. Weiser (*Das Buch der zwölf kleinen Propheten, I: Micha. ATD,* XXIV [1949], 287, 289) calls vv. 18-20 a hymn.

Theodore H. Robinson unnecessarily emends the text). In other words, God himself subdues, subjugates, and rules over human sin (more precisely, the sin of the chosen people), thus establishing salvation (cf. the context). Most exegetes reject the appearance of *kāḇaš* in Zec. 9:15, considering the text corrupt and (also or therefore) glossed. The noun *bāśār* is usually substituted for *wᵉḵāḇᵉšû*. V. 15 stands in the larger context of vv. 11-17, a section that Karl Elliger calls a "prophetic promise discourse."[13] Friedrich Horst sees in vv. 14-16 a short "eschatological hymn" celebrating Yahweh's victory over the enemies of his people, which paves the way for their final restoration and salvation.[14] Yahweh appears to help his people as in a devastating theophany and a holy war. Lightning, whirlwind, and stones (clearly associated with volcanic eruptions) do their devastating work. In this context, the *'aḇnê-qelaʿ* are mentioned; the predicate is *kāḇᵉšû* along with a series of other verbs (*'āḵᵉlû, šāṯû, mālᵉ'û*). The literal translation would be: "And they shall devour and tread down [subdue] slingstones and drink their blood[15] like wine. . . ." The imagery clearly reveals the devastating function of the hurled stones, but the details remain conjectural. If *kāḇaš* is in fact the correct reading, its occurrence in Deutero-Zechariah is also very late (cf. the mention of the Greeks in v. 13, perhaps not by chance) and its usage obscure.

III. Summary. The Hebrew verb *kāḇaš* is one of several that express the exercise of force. The meaning of *kāḇaš* can be realized in various contexts: in military hostilities, when whole territories and their populations are subdued, in the conquest of established kingdoms, but also in individual cases, when someone is enslaved, or in the sexual realm when a woman or girl is importuned and assaulted. The verb always presupposes a stronger party as subject and a weaker party as object. In a few instances, the verb may lose its concrete personal associations so that its object can be an abstraction: for example, in P's fundamental anthropological statement that every person is a "ruler of the world," or in the hymnic celebration of the fact that God "subdues" human iniquity (Mic. 7:19).[16] Every exercise of force expressed by *kāḇaš* is ultimately sent or at least permitted by God. Occasionally God even exercises force himself through human agency. In the realm of slavery, God tolerates it within certain limits and subject to certain rules; but punishment ensues when the limits are transgressed and the rules broken.

"Secular" usage is apparently found only in Est. 7:8, probably only on account of the "secular" character of the entire book. Neh. 5 sees sexual assault not only as a

13. K. Elliger, *Das Buch der zwölf kleinen Propheten, II: Sacharja. ATD,* XXV (^{7}1975), 152; cf. also 151.

14. F. Horst, *Die zwölf kleinen Propheten: Nahum bis Maleachi. HAT,* XIV (^{3}1964), 248; cf. also 246.

15. The word following "drink" is another verb, *hāmû* (from *hāmâ*), which is probably an error. Modern exegesis follows the reading of some LXX versions, reading *dāmām,* "their blood," for *hāmû*; cf. the apparatus in *BHS*.

16. Contra W. Rudolph, *Micha. KAT,* XIII/3 (1975), *in loc.,* who emends the text to read the piel of *kbs,* "wash clean."

human problem but also as a serious question concerning the conduct toward God of all who belong to God's community. Most of the occurrences are in late texts; the few possibly early passages in Numbers and Jeremiah therefore occasion the suspicion that at least the expressions using *kāḇaš* are of a later date.

IV. Derivatives. The derived noun *keḇeš* appears only once in the OT, in the Chronicler's description of the precious throne that Solomon made of ivory overlaid with gold (2 Ch. 9:18; cf. vv. 17-19). This throne also had a footstool "in gold" (*wᵉḵeḇeš bazzāhāḇ lakkissē'*).[17] The meaning is easily derived from the basic meaning of the root, with emphasis on the concrete notion of treading underfoot.[18]

The other derivative, *kiḇšān,* "(smelting) furnace,"[19] is hard to associate with the meaning of *kāḇaš*; at best, one must appeal to the association with metallurgy, in which the metal is "subdued" and "trodden." Twice in the OT a smoking furnace is used as a simile to describe other phenomena: Sinai with its smoke and fire at Yahweh's appearance (Ex. 19:18 [J]) and the smoking region Abraham looks back on after Yahweh's judgment upon Sodom and Gomorrah (Gen. 19:28 [J]). The word also appears twice in a P passage within the long narrative about the "plagues of Egypt" (Ex. 9:8,10). Yahweh commands Moses and Aaron to take handfuls of soot from the furnace and throw them toward heaven in the sight of Pharaoh so that they will spread over all the land of Egypt and descend on man and beast, causing boils.[20] At least the 2 occurrences in J of this derivative of our root are early, but only with a highly specialized meaning.

V. Dead Sea Scrolls and LXX. In the Dead Sea scrolls, *kiḇšān* is found only as a metaphor in 1QH 9:5: the speaker of the lament likens his eyes to a moth in the furnace and his tears to streams of water.

The LXX uses a wide variety of translations for *kāḇaš*: *katakyrieúein, katadynasteúein* (3 times), *krataioún* and *krateín, biázesthai,* and *ekbiázein* (once each).

For *keḇeš* in 2 Ch. 9:18, the LXX has *protomaí móschōn,* clearly reading *kebeś.* The regular translations of *kiḇšān* are *káminos* and *kaminaíos.*

Wagner

17. See *BHK*³, the different description in 1 K. 10:18-20, and the reconstructions proposed by Rudolph (*HAT,* XXI, 224: "The throne had six steps, and the throne had a footstool, both overlaid with gold") and Galling (p. 96: "The throne had six steps, and behind the throne were bulls' heads of gold").

18. See → כסא *kissē'*; also F. Canciani and G. Pettinato, "Salomos Thron, philologische und archäologische Erwägungen," *ZDPV,* 81 (1965), 88-108; → כבשׂ *keḇeś.*

19. See also *KBL*³.

20. Cf. G. von Rad, *Genesis. OTL* (Eng. trans. ²1972), *in loc.*; M. Noth, *Exodus. OTL* (Eng. trans. 1962), *in loc.* On the archaeological background, see M. Kellermann, "Ofen," *BRL*², 240f.; *AuS,* VII (1942), 26, 209; R. J. Forbes, *Metallurgy in Antiquity* (Leiden, 1950); *idem, Studies in Ancient Technology,* VI (Leiden, 1958); C. Baldauf, *Läutern und Prüfen im AT* (diss., Greifswald, 1970), with bibliog.

כָּהָה kāhâ; כֵּהֶה kēheh; כֵּהָה kēhâ

Contents: I. 1. Etymology, Occurrences; 2. Meaning. II. OT Usage: 1. Physical Weakness; 2. Psychological Weakness. III. Theological Contexts: 1. Legal Texts; 2. Prophets; 3. Job.

I. 1. *Etymology, Occurrences.* The root *khh* is found with two basic meanings in the OT: "grow weak" and "reprimand." With the meaning "grow weak," the root also appears in Middle Hebrew, Jewish Aramaic, and Mandaic texts; it has Semitic cognates in Arab. *kahiya* IV, "despair," and Eth. *hakaya,* "be loose," Tigre *hakka,* "grow tired." Its use with the meaning "reprimand" (only in 1 S. 3:13) is connected with Syr. *k'',* Arab. *k'y* and *kwy,* and Mand. *kh'* (with the same meaning);[1] in this sense, *khh* is probably only a by-form of *k'h.*[2] Besides its use as a verb (qal and piel), the root appears in the derived adj. *kēheh,* and possibly also as a noun in another derivative, *kēhâ.*[3]

2. *Meaning.* With the basic meaning "grow weak" as a starting point (Isa. 42:4), the group of words based on *khh* developed four secondary meanings: (1) "(grow) dim" (Lev. 13:6,21); (2) "(dimly) glowing" (Isa. 42:3); (3) "(become) blind" (Gen. 27:1; 1 S. 3:2; Zec. 11:17); (4) "lose courage" (Ezk. 21:12[Eng. v. 7]; Isa. 61:3; RSV "faint"). A further meaning, "alleviate," associated only with the hapax legomenon *kēhâ* in Nah. 3:19,[4] is uncertain, since the LXX suggests the reading *gēhâ.*

II. OT Usage. All 15 occurrences of the word group with its whole range of meanings illustrate secular usage. Only the context — albeit in most cases — establishes an association with cultic acts or theological statements.

1. *Physical Weakness.* The root usually expresses physical weakening, which can affect the entire body (Isa. 42:4), the eyes (Gen. 27:1; Dt. 34:7; 1 S. 3:2; Zec. 11:17; Job 17:7), or the visible manifestations of a skin disease (Lev. 13:6,21,26,28,39). This meaning can also be applied to any physical object, such as spots on clothing (Lev. 13:56) or the wick of a lamp (Isa. 42:3).

2. *Psychological Weakness.* In addition, *kāhâ* and *kēhâ* can denote psychological

---

kāhâ. E. Jenni, *Das hebräische Piʿel* (Zurich, 1968); P. Joüon, "Notes de lexicographie hébraique. III. Racine חתח," *MUSJ,* 5 (1911/12), 432-36.

1. *KBL*³, 440.
2. H. J. Stoebe, *Das erste Buch Samuelis. KAT,* VIII/1 (1973), 122.
3. See I.2 below.
4. W. Rudolph, *Nahum. KAT,* XIII/3 (1975), 181; *GesB,* 335; *KBL*³, 440.

weakness. This can been seen from their use with the noun *rûaḥ* (Ezk. 21:12[7]; Isa. 61:3), although an analogous association with *lēḇ* or *nepeš* is not found in the OT.

III. Theological Contexts.

1. *Legal Texts.* In the section of the purity laws that deals with leprosy, *kāhâ* and *kēhâ* denote the dimming or dim appearance of suspicious spots on the skin of the human body (Lev. 13:6,21,26,28,39) or on clothing (Lev. 13:56). Here the dimness of these spots is a sign that leprosy is either unlikely (vv. 21, 26) or clearly not present, implying that the person concerned is clean (vv. 6, 28, 39).

2. *Prophets.* Among the prophets, only Deutero-Isaiah, Ezekiel, and the authors of Zec. 11 and Isa. 60f. (and possibly Nahum[5]) use this group of words. It appears in statements that are theologically very different or even contradictory. In Deutero-Isaiah, it is used in the image of a dimly glowing wick that the servant of Yahweh will not quench, to express the promise that his work will not lead to the destruction of the oppressed who are on the point of perishing. It then expresses the promise to the servant himself that he will not collapse under the burden of his mission (Isa. 42:3,4). Ezekiel, by contrast, uses the verb *kāhâ* in association with the noun *rûaḥ* to express the discouragement that will afflict the people when they hear the prophet's message of disaster (Ezk. 21:12[7]). The anonymous prophet in Isa. 61 then uses the same combination (the adj. *kēheh* in conjunction with *rûaḥ*) to denote the very state the prophet's message is meant to overcome (Isa. 61:3). The preexilic prophet of Zec. 11, likewise anonymous,[6] uses the association of the root with eyes (already found in Gen. 27:1; Dt. 34:7; 1 S. 3:2) to denote blindness: by threatening the worthless shepherd (Zedekiah?[7]) with total blindness in his right eye, the prophet seeks to show that the shepherd's power and very existence are subject to Yahweh's judgment (Zec. 11:17).

If the reading *kēhâ* in Nah. 3:19 is correct, then Nahum, too, associates the root *khh* with a prophecy of judgment: the collapse of the empire of the Assyrian king will be unmitigated.

3. *Job.* Like Zec. 11:17, Job 17:7 uses the association of *kāhâ* with *ʿayin.* The blinding of one of Job's eyes here symbolizes the severity of the disasters that have befallen him.

Schunck

5. Cf. I.2 above.
6. B. Otzen, *Studien über Deuterosacharja. AcThD,* 6 (1964), 162.
7. *Ibid.,* 161.

כֹּהֵן kōhēn

Contents: I. Ancient Near East: 1. Egypt; 2. Mesopotamia; 3. Western Semites. II. 1. Etymology; 2. LXX. III. Functions: 1. Guarding the Sanctuary; 2. Dispensing Oracles; 3. Teaching; 4. Cultic Duties. IV. Status and Support. V. The High Priest. VI. Qumran. VII. Priest, King, and Prophet. VIII. Summary.

---

kōhēn. S. Amsler, "Les ministères de l'ancienne Alliance: rois, prètres et prophètes," *Verbum Caro,* 18 (1964), 29-41; E. Auerbach, "Der Aufstieg der Priesterschaft zur Macht im AT," *Congress Volume, Bonn 1962. SVT,* 9 (1963), 236-249; J. W. Bailey, "The Usage in the Post Restoration Period of Terms Descriptive of the Priest and High Priest," *JBL,* 70 (1951), 217-225; W. Baudissin, *Die Geschichte des alttestamentlichen Priesterthums* (1889, repr. Osnabrück, 1967); R. Beaudet, "Le Sacerdoce et les Prophètes," *LTP,* 15 (1959), 127-138; J. Begrich, "Die priesterliche Tora," *BZAW,* 66 (1936), 63-88 = *GSAT. ThB,* 21 (1964), 232-260; A. Bentzen, "Zur Geschichte der Ṣadoḳiden," *ZAW,* 51 (1933), 173-76; O. Betz, "Le ministère cultuel dans la secte de Qumran et dans le christianisme primitif," *RechBib,* 4 (1959), 162-202; H. Cazelles, "Sainteté et pureté du sacerdoce," *Populus Dei. Festschrift A. Ottaviani,* I: *Israel. Communio,* 10 (1969), 169-174; A. Cody, *A History of OT Priesthood. AnBibl,* 35 (1969); M. A. Cohen, "The Role of Shilonite Priesthood in the United Monarchy of Ancient Israel," *HUCA,* 36 (1965), 59-98; J. Coppens, *Sacerdoce et célibat. BETL,* 28 (1971), 5-21; A. Deissler, *et al., Der priesterliche Dienst. QuaestDisp,* 46 (1970), 9-80; M. Delcor, "Le sacerdoce, les lieux de culte, les rites et les fêtes dans les documents de Qumrân," *RHR,* 144 (1953), 5-41; W. Eichrodt, *Theology of the OT,* I. *OTL* (Eng. trans. 1961), 392-436; J. A. Emerton, "Priests and Levites in Deuteronomy," *VT,* 12 (1962), 129-138; G. Fohrer, "Priester und Prophet — Amt und Charisma?" *KuD,* 17 (1971), 15-27; J. de Fraine, "Peut-on parler d'un véritable sacerdoce du roi en Israël?" *Sacra Pagina,* I. *BETL,* 12f. (1959), 537-547; J. Gabriel, *Untersuchungen über das alttestamentliche Hohepriestertum* (1933); A. Gelin, "Le sacerdoce de l'ancienne alliance," in R. Fourrey, *et al., La tradition sacerdotale* (LePuy, 1959), 27-60; A. Gonzalez, *Profetismo y Sacerdocio* (1969); G. B. Gray, *Sacrifice in the OT* (1925, repr. New York 1971), 179-270; A. H. J. Gunneweg, *Leviten und Priester. FRLANT,* 89 (1965); E. Haag, "Priestertum und AT: Ezechiel als Prophet und Priester," *TrThZ,* 80 (1971), 20-42; H. Haag, "Das liturgische Leben der Qumrangemeinde," *Archiv für Liturgiewissenschaft,* 10/1 (1967), 78-109; C. Hauret, "Moïse était-il prêtre?" *Bibl,* 40 (1959), 509-521; *idem,* "*Lewy* et *Kohen,*" *RScR,* 44 (1970), 85-100; H. J. Katzenstein, "Some Remarks on the Lists of the Chief Priests of the Temple of Solomon," *JBL,* 81 (1962), 377-384; H. J. Kraus, *Worship in Israel* (Eng. trans., Richmond, 1966); L. Leloir, "Valeurs permanentes du sacerdoce lévitique," *NRTh,* 92 (1970), 246-266; M. Noth, "Office and Vocation in the OT," *Laws in the Pentateuch* (Eng. trans. 1967, repr. London, 1984), 229-249; J. Pedersen, *ILC,* III-IV, 150-198; A. Penna, "Riflessioni sul sacerdozio dell' AT," *RivBibl,* 18 (1970), 105-129; O. Plöger, "Priester und Prophet," *ZAW,* 63 (1951), 157-192; R. Rendtorff, *Die Gesetze in der Priesterschrift. FRLANT,* 62 ([2]1963); L. Rost, "Der Status des Priesters in der Königszeit," *Wort und Geschichte. Festschrift K. Elliger. AOAT,* 18 (1973), 151-56; L. Sabourin, *Priesthood: A Comparative Study. NumenSup,* 25 (1973); J. Salguero, "Sacerdocio levítico y sacerdocio real en el AT," *La Ciencia Tomista,* 93 (1966), 341-366; J. Scharbert, *Heilsmittler im AT und im alten Orient. QuaestDisp,* 23/24 (1964); O. Schilling,

I. Ancient Near East.

1. *Egypt.* a. The basic Egyptian word for "priest" is *wʿb,* "pure man."[1] Another common title, denoting higher rank, is *ḥm-nṯr,* "servant of the deity,"[2] usually translated "prophet." As a collective term for the priesthood, we find "the *wnw.t* of the house of the deity";[3] this expression may, however, refer to a particular institution such as the horary priests. The feminine forms *wʿb.t* and *ḥm.t-nṯr* are common. From very early times there were special titles for the highest officers of the great temples; these were later used as titles of honor, e.g., "Supreme Master of the Artists" for the high priest of Ptah at Memphis, "The Greatest of Those Who Behold" (probably originally "He Who Beholds the Great One") for the high priest of Re at Heliopolis, etc. "Reciting priest" (*ẖry-ḥb*) denotes a ritual priest. Especially in the late period there came to be many special titles, often local, the exact meaning of which is uncertain.[4]

b. As to the organization of the local priesthood, the lower priesthood (i.e., the "pure men," the reciting priests, assistants of various kinds, and a variety of female cultic attendants) was organized into four divisions or "phyla."[5] The phyla served a month at a time in regular rotation; the members of the active phylum were called

---

"'Nicht schwindet vom Priester die Weisung'," *Christuszeugnis der Kirche. Festschrift F. Hengsbach* (Essen, 1970), 11-37; W. H. Schmidt, "Prophetisches Zukunftswort und priesterliche Weisung," *Kairos,* 12 (1970), 289-308; R. J. Sklba, *The Teaching Function of the Pre-exilic Israelite Priesthood* (diss., Rome, 1965); L. A. Snijders, "Knechten en bedienden," *NedThT,* 16 (1961/62), 344-360; R. de Vaux, *AncIsr,* 312-357; *idem,* "Le sacerdoce en Israël," *Festschrift A. Ottaviani,* I, 113-168; P. P. Zerafa, "Il sacerdozio nell' AT," *Sacra Doctrina,* 15 (1970), 621-658.

I.1. A. M. Blackman, "On the Position of Women in the Ancient Egyptian Hierarchy," *JEA,* 7 (1921), 8-30; H. Gauthier, *Le personnel du dieu Min* (Cairo, 1931); H. Kees, *Das Priestertum im ägyptischen Staat vom neuen Reiches bis zur Spätzeit. Probleme der Ägyptologie,* 1 (Leiden, 1953, indexes and sup, 1958); G. Lefèbvre, *Histoire des grands-prêtres d'Amon de Karnak jusqu'a la XXI*^e^ *dyn.* (Paris, 1929); M. I. Moursi, *Die Hohenpriester des Sonnengottes von der Frühzeit Ägyptens bis zum Ende des Neuen Reiches. MÄSt,* 26 (1972); S. Sauneron, *The Priests of Ancient Egypt* (Eng. trans., New York, 1960).

I.2. E. Dhorme, "Quelques prêtres assyriens d'aprèes leur correspondance," *RHR,* 113 (1936), 125-148; 116 (1937), 5-25; *idem, Les religions de Babylonie et d'Assyrie. Mana,* I/2 (Paris, 1945), 198-219; C. Frank, *Studien zur babylonischen Religion* (Strasbourg, 1911), 1-37; C. F. Jean, *La religion sumérienne, d'après les documents sumériens antérieurs à la dynastie d'Isin* (Paris, 1931), 197-212; B. Meissner, *BuA,* II, 52-72; J. Renger, "Untersuchungen zum Priestertum in der altbabylonischen Zeit," *ZA,* N.S. 24[58] (1967), 110-188; 25[59] (1969), 104-230; H. W. F. Saggs, *The Greatness That Was Babylon* (New York, 1962), 345-351.

1. *WbÄS,* I, 282f.
2. *Ibid.,* III, 88.
3. *Ibid.,* I, 317.
4. See *ibid.,* VI, 119f., *s.v.* "Priester."
5. *Ibid.,* VI, 120.

ỉmy ỉbd.f, "monthly servers." This organization should be thought of primarily as a lay institution.

The *wʿb* was originally a lay office in which all able-bodied full citizens of the nome participated. This lay ministry continued to predominate through the Old and Middle Kingdoms. The nomarch could be called "overseer of the prophets," and many priestly benefices were gradually given by the king to members of the royal family and other nobles as awards to honor. It is therefore impossible to separate political office from religious and cultic office.

c. Theoretically, the king was the only legitimate priest who could enter into ritual association with the gods. Cultic scenes on the temple walls depict him alone as a cultic functionary. In reality, however, the king appointed priests to serve as his delegates. "It is the king who sends me to look upon the deity."[6] Therefore priests also bear royal titles.

Priestly office was not meant to be hereditary: "offices do not have children," says the Instruction of Ani. Often, however, it was passed from father to son, as is suggested, for example, by the common idiom "a pure man, son of a pure man." This tendency increased with the passage of time, and Herodotus[7] considers it the normal rule for a priest to appoint his son as his successor. Long genealogies of priestly families confirm the practice. Examination for physical deformities, verification of lineage, and testing for familiarity with the rituals kept in the "house of life" (temple archives) preceded consecration to higher priestly rank. The preparation also included circumcision, which is depicted in funerary scenes from the fourth dynasty on. The terminology of priestly consecration parallels to some extent that of royal enthronement. When performing cultic functions, priests were subject to strict regulations governing purity and abstinence. An insight into how priests lived is given by the Instruction for Merikare 33f.: "Perform your monthly priestly service, wear white sandals. Go to the temple, unveil what is secret, enter the holy of holies, and eat bread in the house of the god." Two long inscriptions by the main entrance to the temple at Edfu illustrate both the requirements imposed on the priests and the promises associated with proper performance of their office.[8]

d. Female priests played an important role in Egypt. Not only "pure women," priestesses of minor rank, but also "handmaidens of the deity" or "prophetesses" are attested at an early date, especially in the cults of goddesses. Female singers, dancers, and musicians were recruited from the noblest families. Thus the temple came to include a "harem" (*ẖnr*). The high priestess of the temple was "chief of the harem." At Thebes, the queen was referred to from the eighteenth dynasty on as the consort of the god Amon, a title intended to emphasize the divine sonship of the king.

---

6. Ritual of Amon, IV, 2, 5f.
7. *Hist.* ii.37.
8. For extracts, see H. Ringgren, *Die Religionen des Alten Orients. ATDSond* (1979), 36f.

e. Special priests were involved in the funerary cult. The earliest attested title is *sẖnw 3ḫ,* "he who seeks [or 'embraces'?] the *akh.*" It was soon replaced by *ḥm k3,* "servant of the *ka.*" From the New Kingdom on, temple priests were often appointed contractually as funerary priests. In the same period there appeared the "water pourers" (*w3ḥ mw*; Gk. *choachytes*), a new professional funerary priesthood; they cared for the mummies and tombs. The work of the funerary priests was explained mythologically by references to the myth of Osiris.

Bergman

2. *Mesopotamia.* Cultic ministers with various types of specialized knowledge were employed in the Sumerian temples, but we know very little about their duties. There is no evidence of a general term for "priest"; we know only the names of the various classes of priests. There was no sharp distinction between political and priestly office. The kings boast that they are priests of various deities. The highest spiritual dignitary was the *en*; the *sanga* had administrative duties. The *išib* appears to have dealt with libations and purification rituals; the *gala* seems to have been a singer and poet. There were other classes of priests called *guda, maḫ,* and *nin-dingir,* but their functions are hard to discover.

In the temple of Inanna, there were eunuchs and prostitutes for the cult of the love-goddess. Early pictorial representations show that the priests were often naked when performing their duties.

Akkadian, too, lacks a word for "priest" in general. The closest approximation is *šangu,* "priest, temple administrator."[9] The term *ērib bîti,* literally, "the one who enters the temple," denotes someone authorized to enter all parts of the temple at any time. From the Old Babylonian period on, his function was to perform minor cultic duties; later, however, the term was occasionally applied to all the cultic functionaries.[10] The Aramaic loanword *kiništu,* often translated "college of priests,"[11] is not attested until late and appears in fact to denote a group of minor cultic ministers.[12]

Theoretically, the king was the chief minister of the cult and bore a priestly title. In practice, of course, he had to delegate these functions to the priests.

The priests were specialists; various groups of experts formed a kind of guild or college. Such groups occasionally traced their origin back to mythical ancestors, but the extent to which hereditary priesthood was the rule is unclear. We know that fathers transmitted their priestly wisdom to their sons and that there were families made up of priests for many generations; in other cases, however, understanding and ability appear to have been decisive. We know that the *kalû* priests claimed a secret knowledge they

9. *AHw,* III (1981), 1163.
10. *CAD,* IV (1958), 290ff.; *AHw,* I (1965), 240.
11. *AHw.*
12. *CAD,* VIII (1971), 386.

were forbidden to impart to the uninitiated. The specialized groups did not constitute an organized hierarchy.

Our knowledge of the various priestly ranks is unfortunately imperfect; Johannes Renger's study is limited to the Old Babylonian period. The highest ranks, *ēnu* (Sum. *en*) and *šangû* (Sum. *sanga*), were assigned originally to priestly princes or kings; later, however, they were given to other high priests. The *ēnu* was obviously the chief priest of a temple, while the *šangû* held the highest administrative office.

The *āšipu* and *mašmašu* were in charge of exorcism and purification ceremonies. Divination devolved upon the *bārû* and *šāl'ilu* ("seer" and "inquirer"); there was also the *maḫḫû*, someone "possessed by the deity." This latter category has become well known through the example of ecstatic prophecy at Mari.[13] There were also musicians (*nāru*) and singers (*zammeru*), as well as female functionaries: *qadištu* (cf. Heb. *qᵉḏēšâ*), *nadîtu*, etc.

The priests undoubtedly wore distinctive vestments. Linen garments of different colors were used.

A ritual for the consecration of a priest of Enlil provides an interesting picture of the requirements imposed on the priests:[14]

> If his body is as pure as a statue of gold, and fear of god and humility are present in his body, he may enter the temple of Enlil and Ninlil. . . . A man stained with blood, someone who has been caught in the act of theft or robbery [?], a condemned criminal who has been caned or whipped, . . . someone afflicted with birthmark [?] — he may not enter the temple of Enlil and Ninlil.

3. *Western Semites.* Ugaritic documents mention *khnm*, "priests," almost exclusively in lists and similar texts. They appear together with *nqdm* ("shepherds"?[15]) and *qdšm* ("hierodules"[16]), as well as merchants, smiths, etc.[17] A damaged letter to a *rb khnm* ("high priest")[18] does not contribute anything significant to our understanding of *khn*. In the colophon of *KTU*, 1.6, we learn that *'tn prln*, who dictated the text, was a *rb khnm* and *rb nqdm*, but this is more relevant to the discussion about the meaning of *nōqēḏ* than to our understanding of the priesthood.

Phoenician, Punic, and Aramaic inscriptions unfortunately have little to say about the priesthood. Usually only a title is involved. In an inscription from Kition,[19] for example, we learn that a certain *bd'* is a priest of Resheph; an inscription from Lapethos[20] calls *ytn-b'l* "priest of the lord of kings," i.e., Ptolemy I Soter. A bilingual

---

13. See → נביא *nāḇî'*.

14. R. Borger, "Die Weihe eines Enlil-Priesters," *BiOr*, 30 (1973), 163-176; citation from p. 172.

15. See → נוקד *nōqēḏ*.

16. See → קדש *qdš*.

17. *KTU*, 4.29; 4.38; 4.68, 71-75; 4.126, 5-9.

18. *KTU*, 2.4.

19. *KAI*, 32.

20. *KAI*, 43, 5.

inscription (Greek and Phoenician) speaks of a high priest (*rb khnm*) of Nergal. Kings are often styled priests: *ʿz-bʿl* is priest of Baʿalat;[21] Tabnit and his father were priests of Astarte.[22]

Sacrificial tariffs often define precisely which portions of various sacrifices belong to the priests.[23] This shows that administration of the sacrificial system was in the hands of the priests and that they derived part of their income from it.

One passage[24] speaks of a man who is both suffete and priest; several texts[25] mention high priests (*rb khnm*). A Neo-Punic inscription from Altiburus[26] mentions the *kmr*[27] of a goddess (Neith?) and a *khn* of Baʿal Hammon.

Priestesses (*khnt*) are mentioned frequently, either by title alone[28] or with the name of the deity added (e.g., Lady Astarte).[29]

In Aramaic inscriptions, the priestly title is *kmr,* a word usually associated with the root *kmr,* "be excited."[30] There is in fact evidence in the Mari texts that a *kumrum* was an ecstatic. One of the Amarna letters[31] speaks of a *kāmiru.* Albright[32] proposes the meaning "eunuch" for *kumru* in northern Syria.

These Aramaic inscriptions, too, have little to contribute. We are told of a priest of *šhr,*[33] priests in a temple,[34] priests of Atargatis,[35] and priests of the "the great [god]," i.e., Baʿal-shamem.[36] The details of their function, however, remain unknown.

The OT occasionally uses the word *kōmer* for idolatrous priests. For example, 2 K. 23:5 speaks of such priests who offer sacrifice on the *bāmôṯ* and worship Baʿal, the sun, the moon, and the constellations. Hos. 10:5 excoriates the priests of the king, alluding to their lamentation for dead Baʿal; Zeph. 1:4 prophesies the destruction of the *kᵉmārîm* and the priests (*kōhᵃnîm),* clearly because they worship Baʿal.

Ringgren

---

21. *KAI,* 11.
22. *KAI,* 13, 1f.
23. *KAI,* 69 (Marseille), 9 occurrences; *KAI,* 74, 6 occurrences; *KAI,* 75.
24. *KAI,* 93, 3f.
25. *KAI,* 65, 10f.; 81, 8f.; 95, 1; 96, 8; see W. Huss, "Die Stellung des *rb* im Karthagischen Staat," *ZDMG,* 129 (1970), 217-232.
26. *KAI,* 159.
27. See below.
28. *KAI,* 93, 1; 140, 2; 145, 45.
29. *KAI,* 14, 15; 70, 1.
30. W. Mowinckel, "כמר, כֹּמֶר," *ZAW,* 36 (1916), 238f.
31. EA 1, 15, 33.
32. W. F. Albright, *From the Stone Age to Christianity* (Garden City, 1957), 234f.
33. *KAI,* 225, 1; 226, 1.
34. *KAI,* 228 A, 23; 228 B, 2.
35. *KAI,* 239, 3.
36. *KAI,* 246, 1.

II. 1. *Etymology.* The noun *kōhēn* appears 740 times in the OT; it is the only term used for priests of Yahweh, but it is also used for priests of foreign gods (the Phoenician Baʿal [2 K. 10:19; 11:18], the Philistine Dagon [1 S. 5:5], the Moabite Chemosh [Jer. 48:7], the Ammonite Milcom [Jer. 49:3]), priests of the high places (1 K. 12:32), a priest of the Egyptian city On (Gen. 41:45), a priest of the Midianites (Ex. 3:1), and Melchizedek, the priest of El Elyon (Gen. 14:18). Some biblical authors also use the term *kōmer* for idolatrous priests (2 K. 23:5; Hos. 10:5; Zeph. 1:4).[37] Hauret[38] suggests that the early Hebrews called their cultic ministers → לוי *lēwî.* The denominative verb *kihēn* means "function as a priest" (Ex. 31:10; Lev. 7:35; Nu. 3:3f.; Dt. 10:6; Ezk. 44:13; Hos. 4:6; 1 Ch. 5:36[Eng. 6:10]; etc.). The noun *keʰunnâ* denotes the priests of a sanctuary (1 S. 2:36) and the priesthood in general (Ex. 29:9; Nu. 3:10; etc.).

The etymology of *kōhēn* is obscure, although the word appears in Ugaritic, Phoenician, Aramaic, and Nabatean with the meaning "priest." Arab. *kāhin,* "seer," "soothsayer," is a specialized development of the common basic meaning and denotes part of the priestly ministry. Several cognates have been suggested: (1) Akk. *kânu,* which in the Š stem means "bow down, worship";[39] (2) Syr. *kahhēn,* which, in addition to "be a priest," also means "bring abundance, make happy" (cf. *kahhinûṯā',* "abundance");[40] (3) Heb. *kûn,* "stand (before God)," "serve" (cf. Dt. 10:8), also transitively "lay down, set forth (a sacrifice)" (cf. Job 31:15).[41]

2. *LXX.* The LXX translates *kōhēn* more than 700 times with *hiereús* or one of its derivatives: *hierateúein* (22 times), *hieráteuma* (Ex. 19:6), *hierōsýnē,* and *hierateía.* The LXX recognizes the sense of specifically cultic activity in the translations *archiereús* (Lev. 4:3; Josh. 22:13; 1 K. 1:25; 1 Ch. 15:14) and *aulárchēs* (2 S. 8:17), which differ significantly from the original understanding of the priesthood.[42] The translation *leitourgeín* (2 Ch. 11:14) also places the major emphasis on cultic ministry. The *peritithénai* of Isa. 61:10 reflects the uncertainty of the MT.

III. Functions.

1. *Guarding the Sanctuary.* The development of the priestly office is relatively transparent. During the patriarchal period, there was as yet no explicit priesthood. As among all nomads and seminomads, the heads of families or tribal elders performed ritual functions (animal sacrifice, offering of the first-born).

With permanent settlement came sanctuaries, which a specific group of people was appointed to "guard" or "keep" (*šāmar, mišmereṯ*; cf. Nu. 1:53; 3:28,32). The first priests were thus charged with guardianship of the sacred precincts and what went on there. Sacrifices are offered by the worshippers themselves, but the priests are permitted

37. Cf. I.3 above.
38. *Bibl,* 40 (1959), 520.
39. Zerafa, 624.
40. Cody, 28.
41. B. Reicke, "Priester," *BHHW,* III (1966), 1486.
42. Cf. G. Schrenk, "ἱερεύς," *TDNT,* III, 260f.

to take a portion of the offerings for their sustenance. Micah, for example, establishes a sanctuary in the hill country of Ephraim and employs a Levite to serve as priest (Jgs. 17); priests are installed similarly for the "graven image" of the Danites (Jgs. 18:30). Eli and his sons serve as priests at Shiloh; the sons are censured for taking the portions due them prematurely (1 S. 2:16f.). Abimelech, the priest of Nob, gives David some of the bread of the Presence because he does not have any ordinary bread (1 S. 21). David names Zadok, Abiathar, and several of his sons as priests in Zion (2 S. 8:17f.); and Jeroboam appoints priests in the temple at Bethel (1 K. 12:32).

2. *Dispensing Oracles.* In the early period, the primary function of the priests was oracular. Whenever a difficult decision has to be made, the people (or individual Israelites) ask the priest as official mediator for a divine oracle. The Danites, for example, turn to Micah the priest with the words: "Inquire of God, that we may know whether the journey on which we are setting out will succeed" (Jgs. 18:5). In the course of his conflict with the Philistines, David twice asks for an oracle from Yahweh (1 S. 23:2; 30:7f.). "Yes or no" questions are answered by the sacral technique of casting lots.[43] Oracular techniques included Urim and Thummim, ephod, and teraphim (cf. Nu. 27:21; Jgs. 17:5; Hos. 3:4). Urim and Thummim disappeared from the priestly repertory at an early date, probably before the First Temple. Saul and David still seek oracles from the priestly ephod; in similar situations, Ahab and Jehoshaphat seek counsel from a "seer" or "prophet" (1 K. 20:13f.; 22:6; 2 K. 3:11). According to Ezr. 2:63 par. Neh. 7:65, in postexilic Jerusalem there were no longer any priests capable of using Urim and Thummim, although it is likely that in individual cases priests answered inquiries in God's name, although without using special methods of divination (cf. Mal. 2:7).

3. *Teaching.* From the time of the monarchy on, the priests function as teachers. In Hos. 4:4ff., the prophet castigates the priests of the northern kingdom — *kōhēn* is to be understood collectively — for rejecting knowledge (*daʿaṯ*) and forgetting the law (*tôrâ*) of God. Hosea also speaks of written *tôrôṯ* (Hos. 8:12), so that the priests' fault consists in deliberate neglect of their traditions and instructional duties. These duties they have "despised" and "forgotten," i.e., they have not attached sufficient importance to them. After the fall of Samaria, the prophet Micah similarly attacks the corruption of the whole Jerusalem aristocracy (Mic. 3:11). He accuses the priests of teaching (*hôrâ*)[44] for hire. The noun *tôrâ* derives from *hôrâ.* Here we learn that priestly torah is no longer given freely, as in the past, but for a price: the thoroughness of the instruction depends on how much is paid. Jeremiah, too, attacks the priests, "shepherds," and prophets (Jer. 2:8). The priests, he says, are guardians of the *tôrâ*; but they refuse to learn from Yahweh and therefore cannot tell the people Yahweh's will. The priests, sages, and prophets seek to get rid of Jeremiah because he prophesies that *tôrâ* will perish from the priests, counsel from the wise, and revelations from the

---

43. → גורל *gôrāl.*
44. See → ירה *yrh.*

prophets (18:18). Ezk. 7:26 repeats Jeremiah's words about *tôrâ* perishing, applying them to the day of judgment against Jerusalem. When Isaiah has the pilgrims approaching Zion say, "May Yahweh teach (*hôrâ*) us his ways," and speaks of the law (*tôrâ*) going forth from Zion (Isa. 2:3), he is referring to priestly instruction. We may see an ancient tradition in the Chronicler's statement that King Jehoshaphat (868-851 B.C.) sent priests as well as laypeople to instruct the people (2 Ch. 17:8f.). We are also told that they took the book of Yahweh's law (*tôrâ*) with them. In Mal. 2:7, it is the duty of the priests to guard knowledge (*daʿaṯ*) and proclaim *tôrâ* as messengers of Yahweh Sebaoth. Acording to Dt. 31:9, Moses entrusts the law (*tôrâ*) to the priests; they are to recite it publicly every seven years at the Feast of Booths so that the people may learn to keep all the words of this law. The practice of reciting the law at a cultic festival is undoubtedly ancient. The blessing of Levi (Dt. 33:10) also speaks of the law (*tôrâ*) and ordinances (*mišpāṭîm*) that the Levites are to teach (*hôrâ*) the people.

We may conclude that *tôrâ, daʿaṯ,* and *mišpāṭîm* are technical terms for priestly instruction. The nature of this instruction is suggested by Ezk. 44:23: "They [the priests] shall teach (*hôrâ*) my people the difference between the holy and the common, and show them how to distinguish between the unclean and the clean" (cf. 22:16). According to 2 K. 17:27, the king of Assyria sends priests back to the conquered northern kingdom to instruct the new settlers in the proper worship (*mišpāṭ*) of the god of the land. There is thus priestly professional lore (*daʿaṯ*) that is to be communicated to the laity. It includes not only knowledge of God and proper worship, but also proclamation of God's will, which presses the human will to act. The parallel term "law" (*tôrâ*) makes this even clearer: it denotes priestly instruction concerning what accords with Yahweh's will in specific cases.[45]

Hag. 2:11ff. furnishes an example of specific priestly instruction concerning what is holy and what is unclean. The prophet asks whether other food becomes holy when someone brings it into contact with the flesh of a sacrificial meal and whether everything is unclean that is touched by someone who has become unclean through contact with a corpse. The priests answer the first question negatively, the second affirmatively. The distinction between "holy" and "profane," between "unclean" and "clean," affects both the cult and everyday life. The holiness of the cult demands clear knowledge of the requirements for the various types of sacrifice (e.g., Lev. 7:12ff.; Nu. 6:10). The priest must know the conditions for admission to the cult and how deficiencies in them can be remedied (e.g., Lev. 15:28; Nu. 6:9). When payment is made in lieu of a votive offering, the priest often functions as assessor and appraiser (Lev. 27:8, 12, 18). Uncleanness has its locus outside the cult; it infects everything that is dead, sexuality, and certain illnesses. The dangers posed by contact with uncleanness require information about how to distinguish what is clean from what is unclean in daily life — in diet (Lev. 11), "leprosy" (Lev. 13), and sexual intercourse (Lev. 12).

Form-critical analysis also underlines the instructional function of the priesthood. Several forms or genres are of priestly origin: the declaratory formulas that state divine

---

45. W. Rudolph, *Hosea. KAT,* XIII/1 (1966), 103.

acceptance of a sacrifice or a state of cleanness or uncleanness (e.g., *minḥâ hîʾ* [Lev. 2:6]; *ṣāraʿaṯ hîʾ* [Lev. 13:8]);[46] the oracle of favor that follows a lament;[47] the entrance liturgy with criteria determining the uprightness of the pilgrims (Ps. 15; 24:3-5); certain apodictic laws (e.g., Lev. 7:23b,26); the ritual laws (e.g., Lev. 1–5); cultic recitation as a special form of instruction (Dt. 31:9-13). Dt. 20:2-4 preserves in summary the words of a priest before battle. The war sermon appears to have been an ancient institution in Israel.

Closely related to the teaching function of the priesthood is its role in jurisprudence. In disputed cases (lawsuits, manslaughter, bodily injury) they and the secular judges are to arrive at a ruling together (Dt. 17:8-13; 21:5). In 2 Ch. 19:8, we are told explicitly that King Jehoshaphat appointed Levites, priests, and heads of families to decide disputed cases in Jerusalem.

4. *Cultic Duties.* During the monarchy, the cultic ministry of the priesthood took concrete shape. Especially on festal occasions, both David and Solomon offered sacrifice as leaders of the people. We may assume that they were assisted by priests. Later all sacral acts through which sacrifice was brought into the immediate presence of God came to be reserved to the priesthood. King Uzziah (748-740) is rebuked on this account: "It is not for you, Uzziah, to burn incense to Yahweh, but for the priests" (2 Ch. 26:18). The deeper reason for reserving this function was probably the greater holiness of the priests. "Come near to God" (Ex. 19:22; Lev. 21:17), "enter into God's presence" (Ex. 28:35), "minister" (Ex. 28:35,43; Nu. 18:7), and "ascend the altar" (1 S. 2:28) are technical terms for this priestly function.

The priestly ministry is thus primarily an altar ministry. When animals are sacrificed — except for birds, which the priest is required to kill upon the altar — the priest himself does not slay the victim. His real role begins with the blood, which he sprinkles around the burnt offering or pours out at the foot of the altar (Lev. 1–3). When a burnt offering is made, he brings the individual portions to the altar to be burned. He is responsible for seeing that the fire upon the altar never goes out and that the ashes are always removed. When a *šᵉlāmîm* sacrifice is offered, the priest receives as his portion the breast and right hind leg of the victim; he consigns the fat to the flames as Yahweh's portion. He likewise must burn a portion of each cereal offering with incense on the altar and pour out the wine of a drink offering at the foot of the altar or sprinkle it on the animal to be sacrificed (Nu. 15:7). For an incense offering, the priest takes a scoop of glowing coals from the altar, pours incense on them, and carries the censer to the altar of incense (Lev. 16:12). Some sacrifices are offered symbolically to Yahweh by being "lifted" or "waved" toward the altar by the priest, to whom they then belong (Lev. 7:14,30). As part of the ritual of firstfruits, the priest greets the worshipper, hears his confession of faith, and places his basket of produce as an offering before the altar (Dt. 26:1-10).

The duties of priests at the central sanctuary also include replacing the bread of the Presence on the Sabbath (Lev. 24:8), dressing the lamps in the holy place (Ex. 30:7), maintaining all the temple appurtenances, sounding the festal trumpets (Nu. 10:8,10),

---

46. Cf. Rendtorff, 74ff.
47. Begrich, *GSAT,* 239.

and "blessing in the name of Yahweh" (Dt. 10:8; 21:5; 1 Ch. 23:13). This last function is singled out liturgically — probably after the exile — by the "Aaronic blessing," an especially solemn formula reserved to the priesthood (Nu. 6:22-27).

During the period of the monarchy, most sacrifices were probably offered in connection with thanksgiving, vows, or adoration. Atonement sacrifice probably did not become customary until the time of the Second Temple: when the exile was interpreted as a judgment upon the sins of the people, a ritual was developed for sin and guilt offerings. When a sin offering is made for a prince or a private individual, the priest catches the blood, rubs some of it on the horns of the altar, and pours out the rest at the foot of the altar. All the fat is burned on the altar; the flesh, being extremely holy, is consumed by the priests alone to effect atonement before Yahweh.

Together with this priestly office of reconciliation and atonement, special rituals of lustration took on great importance: the so-called jealousy offering when a woman has committed adultery (Nu. 5:11-31), the sprinkling with water mixed with the ashes of a red heifer for purification after contact with a human corpse (Nu. 19), and the declaration of innocence when a murder has been committed by an unknown hand (Dt. 21:1-9). Priestly intercession is also mentioned more frequently. In agreement with common postexilic practice, the priest formulates such intercession in the 1st person plural, including himself among the people (Ezr. 6:10; 9:6-15; 1 Mc. 12:11).[48]

The various priestly duties share the common basis of mediation: in oracles and instruction, the priest represents God to the people; in sacrifice and intercession, he represents the people to God.

IV. Status and Support. According to P, constant holiness and purity are important requirements for the priesthood (Lev. 21:6ff.). Before the priests approach the altar, they are to wash their hands and feet (Ex. 30:17-21). They are to abstain from wine on days when they serve at the altar (Ezk. 44:21). Only those without physical blemish may enter the sanctuary (Lev. 21:17-21). Priests must not defile themselves by touching a corpse (except for a close family member) or wear tokens of mourning (Lev. 21:1-5). They must not marry prostitutes or divorced women (Lev. 21:7). The priesthood in Israel is not a vocation but a profession; like most professions in the ancient Near East, it is hereditary. "Consecrate" (Ex. 29:44) and "fill the hands" (Jgs. 17:12; RSV "install") are technical terms for the assumption of priestly office; without any specific ordination, the priest enters the sphere of the sacred and receives rights to the sacrificial offerings. Rupprecht, however, is of the opinion that "filling the hands" actually is a rite of ordination, even if the liturgical details are borrowed from other rituals.[49] There is no evidence that the solemn ordination of Aaron and his sons by Moses (Ex. 29; Lev. 8) was ever repeated.[50]

---

48. Cf. Scharbert, 276f.

49. K. Rupprecht, "Quisquilien zu der Wendung מלא (את) יד פלוני u z Terminus מלאים," *Sefer Rendtorff. Festschrift K. Rendtorff. BDBAT,* 1 (1975), 73-93, esp. 91.

50. See → מלא *mālē'*.

Holiness and purity also require a priest to wear sacral vestments while performing his cultic duties. The earliest such vestment is apparently the *'ēpôḏ bāḏ* (1 S. 2:18), a simple loincloth that later developed into knee-length trousers. Over it the priest wears a long full garment of white linen, probably with sleeves and cinched with a brightly colored sash. His head is covered with a kind of turban, also of white linen. He must remove his sandals to enter the sanctuary.

Generally speaking, the income of the priesthood comprises portions of the sacrifices and other temple offerings. Certain sources of income are mentioned specifically: the firstfruits of tree and field, the redemption of the first-born, and the tithe (Ex. 22:29[30]; Dt. 26; Nu. 18; Dt. 14:22-29). The nature and extent of these payments differed in various periods.

V. The High Priest. During the monarchy, the priests were royal officials, headed by a leader usually called simply *hakkōhēn,* e.g., Azariah (1 K. 4:2), Jehoiada (2 K. 11:9; 12:8[7]); Uriah (2 K. 16:10f.), and Hilkiah (2 K. 22:10,12,14). Other passages call this "chief priest" *kōhēn hārō'š,* e.g., Seraiah (2 K. 25:18), Amariah (2 Ch. 19:11), and Azariah (2 Ch. 26:20; 31:10). The chief priest represents and supervises the entire priesthood; he is responsible in turn to the king (cf. 2 K. 12:8[7]). According to 2 K. 11:12, the chief priest Jehoiada anoints the young Joash to be king. Besides the *kōhēn hārō'š,* 2 K. 25:18 refers to Zephaniah as *kōhēn mišneh.* Jer. 29:26 refers to this same priest as being in charge of the house of Yahweh, probably meaning that he is chief of the temple police.

Among the higher ranks of the priesthood, the *ziqnê hakkōh*^{a}*nîm,* "senior priests," play an important role. As heads of the priestly families, they are called upon to perform special duties: King Hezekiah sends them with other officials to the prophet Isaiah to seek counsel in the face of the Assyrian threat (2 K. 19:1-7); the prophet Jeremiah uses them as witnesses of his prophecy of disaster against Jerusalem (Jer. 19:1-15).

The office of "high priest" (*hakkōhēn haggāḏôl*) did not develop until the postexilic period. Zerubbabel's contemporary Joshua was the first to bear this title (Hag. 1:1,12,14; 2:2,4; Zec. 3:1,8; 6:11). The high priest Eliashib leads the list of those rebuilding Jerusalem's walls (Neh. 3:1,20). Neh. 13:28 chastises one of his grandsons for marrying the daughter of a non-Jewish governor of Samaria. Finally, Sir. 50:1-21 is an effusive paean of praise to the high priest Simon II (225-192 B.C.). When this title is given preexilic priests, we are dealing with retrojection or redaction (2 Ch. 34:9; Nu. 35:25,28,32). One of the Elephantine papyri (408 B.C.) uses the Aramaic equivalent *kāhnā' rabbā'* for the high priest Johanan of Jerusalem. The Mishnah and Talmud often speak of the *kōhēn gāḏôl* or *kāhnā rabbā.* Other postexilic documents, including P, use additional terms as synonyms of "high priest": *hakkōhēn hammāšîaḥ* ("the anointed priest"; Lev. 4:3,5,16); "the chief officer (*nāgîḏ*) of the house of God" (1 Ch. 9:11; 2 Ch. 31:13; Neh. 11:11); "prince" (Dnl. 9:25); and "prince of the covenant" (Dnl. 11:22).

P describes the rights and duties of the high priest in the figure of Aaron. Once a year, on the great Day of Atonement, he alone is permitted to enter the holy of holies to make atonement for the temple and people through a blood ritual (Lev. 16). Once a year he is also to make atonement upon the horns of the incense altar (Ex. 30:10). If he himself or the entire community has transgressed, he is to offer a young bull as a sin offering. He lays his hands (or the elders lay their hands) on the animal's head when it is killed; then he takes some of the blood into the sanctuary and sprinkles it seven times on the veil that separates the sanctuary from the holy of holies. Dipping his finger in the blood, he puts it on the horns of the incense altar. Finally he pours out the rest of the blood at the foot of the altar of burnt offering. He is not permitted to eat any of the flesh; it is burned on the ashes outside the sanctuary (Lev. 4:3-21).

Except on the great Day of Atonement, the high priest may wear special vestments when performing his liturgical functions. These include the ephod (a shoulder cape), a breastplate with twelve precious stones, and a headband with a golden plate at the forehead (Ex. 28,39; Sir. 45:6-13).

The office of high priest is hereditary (Nu. 20:26ff.) within the family of the Zadokites. He must marry a virgin and must not defile himself by touching a corpse (Lev. 21:10-15). The death of the high priest effects atonement for those who have committed manslaughter and found asylum in the cities of refuge (Nu. 35:25ff.). The special position of the high priest in the cult is also expressed by his anointing, a ceremony that probably dates from the end of the Persian period.[51] From the early Hellenistic period on, the high priest increasingly becomes also the political head of the Jewish community. Under Antiochus IV Epiphanes, Menelaus, who was not even a priest, was installed as high priest. From 152 B.C. on, the Hasmoneans filled this office.

VI. Qumran. Under the Zadokite high priests, a portion of the priesthood was expelled from Jerusalem. Some retreated to Egypt (Leontopolis); others joined sects like the Qumran community. The founder of this latter group, the "Teacher of Righteousness," was a priest. In 1QS 2:19-21, its membership is described as comprising priests, Levites, and "all the people" (i.e., the laity). The priests have a preeminent position and are in charge of the groups of ten into which the community is divided. Their duties include instructing the people in the law and seeing that it is observed, serving as judges in disputes, supervising the ministry of the Levites and other officials, pronouncing the blessing at meals, and leading liturgical rituals, above all at the yearly renewal of the covenant and at the reception of new members (1QS 1:18–2:23). The schism with the Jerusalem priesthood and the temple leads to a spiritualization of the notion of sacrifice: atonement is not effected by sacrifice but by prayer and moral conduct (1QS 9:3-6). Before the eschatological battle of the sons of light against Belial, a priest exhorts the army; and the chief priest even establishes the order of battle after he has spoken a prayer before the fighters. The priests themselves do not take an active part in the battle, but sound the signal trumpets, encourage the men to fight, and celebrate a liturgy of thanksgiving after the enemy camp has been put to the ban (1QM).

---

51. De Vaux, *Festschrift A. Ottaviani,* I, 128.

Finally, the Qumran texts speak of a priestly as well as a royal messiah; the latter is subordinate to the former (1QSa 2:2ff.).[52]

VII. Priest, King, and Prophet. In the course of time, the priesthood came to have a special relationship to the other spritual leaders, the kings and prophets. The interaction between the kings and the priesthood is one of the outstanding features of Israel's history; in Israel — unlike the rest of the ancient Near East — the king himself never claimed to be a priest (with the possible exception of Ps. 110:4). Israel's priesthood antedates the monarchy, but it was the monarchy that created the possibility of an extensive priesthood. The relationship of priest to king is that of a servant. King David brings in the ark, dances before it, and appoints priests (2 S. 6:12ff.; 8:17f.). Solomon builds the temple and offers sacrifice; he blesses the people and incorporates the priests into his bureaucracy (1 K. 4:2; 8). The temple belongs to the king and its treasures are his to use as he wills. The king has "his" priests (2 K. 10:11). Joash orders the priests to repair damage to the temple (2 K. 12:5-17[4-16]). Ahaz commissions the priest Uriah to build an altar and establishes cultic ordinances to be observed by the priests (2 K. 16:10-18).

With the help of the priesthood, holiness and spiritual power are mediated to the king. The king, anointed by a priest, is not only a sacral person but also himself a mediator empowered by Yahweh. The faithful kings bring blessings upon their people. Probably the king also depended on the priesthood in his role as supreme judge. The royal program of cultic centralization, however, also strengthened the priesthood and made it more independent. According to P and Ezk. 40–48, the king (or "prince") no longer has the right to offer sacrifice himself; all he has is the "privilege" of being present within the forecourt of the temple when sacrifice is offered. The proximity of the temple to the king's palace and the royal tombs in fact renders it unclean. When the monarchy finally falls, priesthood and temple can exist without it and the priestly hierarchy can commence.

When we turn to the relationship between priest and prophet, we must remember that prophecy in Israel is not a homogeneous entity like the priesthood. From the period of the monarchy on, there were undoubtedly professional prophets. Besides the unorganized prophets who wander through the countryside, we find prophets who function as "information specialists" at the sanctuaries and the royal court (cultic and court prophets). Like the priests, they work for pay and their profession is hereditary. As mediators between God and the people, cult prophets provide oracles and represent the people before God through intercession. They often act spontaneously and in a state of ecstasy, whereas the priests rely more on casting lots. The prophets also are not incorporated so tightly into the sanctuary personnel as are the priests. Jeremiah often speaks of priest and prophet in the same breath (e.g., Jer. 26:7f.,11,16), but the group

52. A. S. Kapelrud, "Die aktuellen und die eschatologischen Behörden der Qumrān-gemeinde," in H. Bardtke, ed., *Qumran-Probleme, DAWB,* 42 (1963), 259-268; A. Caquot, *Le messianisme qumranien. BETL,* 46 (1978), 231-247.

of prophets at the Jerusalem temple is subordinate to a chief priest (29:26). In the postexilic period, these cultic prophets lost their importance and were absorbed into the minor clergy (temple singers). We also hear occasionally of female prophets (2 K. 22:14; Neh. 6:14), whereas there were never any female priests in Israel.

Besides these professional prophets, there is a group of individual prophets ("writing prophets"), few in number but of outstanding importance. They perform their ministry by virtue of a special call and are not members of a special class; they are neither cultic nor royal officials. They are often at odds with the priests and professional prophets, whom they attack and condemn both individually and as a group. Amos comes into conflict with Amaziah, the chief priest of Bethel (Am. 7:10-17). Hosea castigates the syncretistic cult of the priests of the northern kingdom and their contempt for God's law (Hos. 4:4-14; 5:1). Isaiah charges the priests and prophets of Jerusalem with drunkenness at religious meals (Isa. 28:7-13). Micah accuses the priests of corruption (Mic. 3:11); Zephaniah charges that they "profane what is sacred and do violence to the law" (Zeph. 3:4). In Ezekiel (Ezk. 22:26) this charge is expanded: the priests do not distinguish sacred from profane, clean from unclean, and they violate the Sabbath. Jeremiah, himself the son of a priest, sees desire for popular favor and greed as the reasons why every one of the prophets and priests deals falsely (Jer. 6:13). Because of his prophecy of disaster against the city and temple, he is threatened with death by "the priests and prophets" (Jer. 26:11). Malachi extends the criticism of the preexilic prophets to his own day; above all he charges that the priests are accepting for sacrifice blind and crippled animals unfit for other purposes.

We must include the sage or wisdom instructor along with priest and prophet (cf. Jer. 18:18). Under Solomon, there emerged from among the "scribal clerks" a group of professional "wisdom instructors," for whom Yahweh's instruction is also the most fertile source of wisdom. In the postexilic period, these wisdom instructors are gradually replaced by the scribes. At first, the priests shared with them their instructional duties; later, however, they relinquished most of these duties entirely in favor of the scribes.

VIII. Summary. It would be difficult to overstress the importance of the priesthood for OT religion. The priests represent Israel's relationship with God; in a sense, they are mediators of the covenant. The high priest, bearing the names of the twelve tribes on his breastplate, represents as it were the entire nation. The priests actualize Yahweh's presence in the words of their many liturgical functions. The holiness worship demands is symbolized in the priesthood, which makes a visible statement that Yahweh is the lord and master of the nation.

Priestly theology is documented above all in P. God's immutability, his ontic and ethical holiness, his work in creation and history, his covenants with the human race, and the enduring presence of his name in Israel are the major themes of the written priestly traditions. Through the preservation and transmission of laws, rituals, and hymns, the priests function as faithful servants of this tradition. It is this tradition on which their authority is grounded, not the theological acumen and gifts of the individual. The intellectual structure of the priesthood is fundamentally static. P, for example, leaves the other source documents of the Pentateuch intact, and does not edit out the critical texts of the prophets. Priestly concern for cultic forms guards and preserves the faith; it also cultivates ethical conduct and an alert conscience. The priesthood exerts a major influence on poetry and historiography, jurisprudence and politics. The post-exilic temple state is governed internally by a priestly regime; Ezra, a priest, promotes learning and the rise of the lay scribes. Once a year, the high priest must make atonement for the people.

It cannot be gainsaid, of course, that the priestly zeal for the true faith also involved dangers, exemplified by the emphasis on cultic externals inveighed against by the prophets, the clericalizing retrojection of the postexilic cult into the early history of the people, and a reluctance to include the gentile nations within the domain of salvation.

In conclusion, we may state that the ministry of the priests brings blessing and salvation to the entire nation and that the failures of the priesthood hardly influence the fate of the people.

Dommershausen

כּוֹכָב *kôḵāḇ*

Contents I. 1. Etymology; 2. Occurrences; 3. Religious Background. II. OT: 1. Astronomy; 2. Creation; 3. Figurative Usage; 4. Unusual Phenomena; 5. Illicit Worship; 6. Special Examples. III. LXX. IV. Dead Sea Scrolls.

---

kôḵāḇ. M. A. Beek and B. Reicke, "Stern," "Sternbild," "Sterndeutung," "Sternkunde," *BHHW,* III (1966), 1865-68; K.-H. Bernhardt, "Chiun," *BHHW,* I (1962), 300; *idem,* "Sikkuth," *BHHW,* III, 1792f.; F. M. T. de Liagre Böhl, "Babylonien. II. Babylonische und assyrische Religion," *RGG*³, I (1957), 812-822; F. J. Boll, *Kleine Schriften zur Sternkunde des Altertums* (Leipzig, 1950); W. Brueggemann, "Arcturus," *IDB,* I, 216; *idem,* "Orion," *IDB,* III, 609; *idem,* "Pleiades," *IDB,* III, 826; E. P. Dhorme, *Les religions de Babylonie et d'Assyrie. Mana,* I/1 (Paris, ²1949), 53-82, 282-89; M. J. Dresden, "Science," *IDB,* IV, 236-244, esp. 241f.; G. R. Driver, "Two Astronomical Passages in the OT," *JTS,* N.S. 4 (1953), 208-212; 7 (1956), 1-11; H. Gressmann, *Die hellenistische Gestirnreligion des alten Orient. AO Beihefte,* 5 (1925); W. Gundel, *Sternglaube, Sternreligion und Sternorakel* (Heidelberg, ²1959); J. Henninger, "Über Sternkunde und Sternkult in Nord- und Zentralarabien," *ZE,* 79 (1954), 82-117; J. J. Hess, "Die Sternbilder in Hiob 9,9 und 38,31," *Festschrift G. Jacob* (Leipzig, 1932), 94-99; F. X. Kugler, *Entwicklung der babylonischen Planetenkunde von ihren Anfängen bis auf Christus* (Münster, 1907); *idem, Sternkunde und Sterndienst in Babel,* I-III (Münster, 1907-1924); J. W. MacKay, *Religion in Judah under the Assyrians 732-609 B.C. SBT,* N.S. 26 (1973); E. W. Maunder, *The Astronomy of the Bible* (London, ⁴1935); S. Mowinckel, *Die Sternnamen im AT. NTTSup,* 5 (1928); O. Neugebauer, *An Astronomical Almanac for the Year 348/9. KDVS,* 36/4 (1956); *idem, Astronomical Cuneiform Texts,* I-III (Princeton, 1955); *idem, The Astronomical Treatise P. Ryl. 27. KDVS,* 32/2 (1949); *idem, Commentary on the Astronomical Treatise Per. gr. 2425* (Brussels, 1969); *idem, The Exact Sciences in Antiquity* (Princeton, ¹1957; New York, ²1969); *idem, Hypsicles die Anfangszeiten der Gestirne* (1966); M. P. Nilsson, "Die astrale Unsterblichkeit und die kosmische Mystik," *Numen,* 1 (1954), 106-119;

I. 1. *Etymology.* Heb. *kôkāb* has cognates in all the Semitic languages, all with the same basic meaning of "star," "heavenly body (planet)": Ugar. *kbkb,* once *kkb*;[1] Phoen. *hkkbm*; Akk. *kakkabu*;[2] Amor. *kakkabum*;[3] Syr. *kawkᵉbā'*; Arab. *kaukab*; Eth. *kokab.* The noun represents a reduplicated form[4] of the element *kb*; *kabkab* developed into *kawkab,* which in turn became *kôkāb.* The precise meaning of this verbal root in Proto-Semitic must remain conjectural. The most likely basic meaning is "burn brightly."[5]

2. *Occurrences.* The noun *kôkāb* occurs 37 times in the OT. Only 2 occurrences are in the singular; the rest are in the plural. In 9 passages the noun is associated directly with the heavens.[6] A few other passages mention the stars in conjunction with the sun[7] and moon[8] as luminaries of the heavens. In most cases, the stars are not considered divine beings; neither do they represent such deities or have a life of their own. An important exception is Job 38:7, which says that at the creation of the world all the stars sang God's praise. But the OT does bear witness to a widespread popular worship of the stars as divine beings, both individually and collectively as the "hosts[9] of heaven" (Dt. 4:19; 2 K. 23:5). This phrase is the most common term for the stars. The "queen (*malkâ*)[10] of heaven," the Babylonian

---

F. Normann, *Mythen der Sterne* (Gotha, 1925); U. Oldenburg, "Above the Stars of El: El in Ancient South Arabic Religion," *ZAW,* 82 (1970), 187-208; T. G. Pinches and J. N. Strassmaier, *Late Babylonian Astronomical and Related Texts* (Providence, 1955); H. D. Preuss, *Verspottung fremder Religionen im AT. BWANT,* 92[5/12] (1971); C. Ptolemaeus, *Handbuch der Astronomie* (Leipzig, 1963); O. Rühle–C.-M. Edsman, "Astralreligion," *RGG*³, I (1957), 662-64; J. Schaumberger, "Drei planetarische Hilfstafeln," *AnOr,* 6 (1933), 3-12; T. F. von Scheffer, *Die Legende der Sterne im Umkreis der Antiken Welt* (Stuttgart, 1940); G. Schiaparelli, *Astronomy in the OT* (Eng. trans., Oxford, 1905); H. J. Schoeps, *Astrologie* (1950); F. Strunz–C.-M. Edsman, "Astrologie," *RGG*³, I (1957), 664-66; A. E. Thierens, *Astrology in Mesopotamian Culture* (Leiden, 1935); B. L. van der Waerden, "Babylonian Astronomy. II: The Thirty-Six Stars," *JNES,* 8 (1949), 6-26; *idem,* "Babylonian Astronomy. III: The Earliest Astronomical Computations," *JNES,* 10 (1951), 20-34; E. J. Webb, *The Names of the Stars* (1952); E. F. Weidner, "Die astrologische Serie Enûma Anu Enlil," *AfO,* 14 (1941-44), 308-318; 17 (1954-56), 71-89; *idem,* "Ein babylonisches Kompendium der Himmelskunde," *AJSL,* 40 (1923/24), 186-208; *idem, Handbuch der babylonischen Astronomie,* I (Leipzig, 1915); E. Zinner, *Sternglaube und Sternforschung* (Munich, 1953).

1. *UT,* no. 1189; *WUS,* no. 1277.
2. *AHw,* I (1965), 421b.
3. *APNM,* 220.
4. Cf. *BLe,* §61d.
5. Cf. *KBL*³, 441f. (contra *BDB,* 456): "journey, circle"; cf. Arab. *kabba,* "turn around."
6. See → שמים *šāmayim.*
7. → שמש *šemeš.*
8. → ירח *yārēaḥ.*
9. → צבא *ṣābā'.*
10. → מלך *melek.*

goddess Ishtar, plays a special role, being identified with the planet Venus, the morning star. The OT does not distinguish planets from stars; only the word *mazzārôṯ* in Job 38:32 can be understood as "constellations."[11] It is likewise uncertain whether the constellations of the zodiac, especially the signs of the solar zodiac, are singled out by the OT text.[12] The OT mentions several individual stars and constellations.[13] One of the clearest witnesses to religious and mythological interpretation of the stars and planets is Isa. 14:12, which speaks of the "Day Star, son of Dawn" (*hêlēl ben-šaḥar*), alluding to a fragmentary myth.[14]

3. *Religious Background.*

a. *Mesopotamia.* The stars occupy an important place in the intellectual and religious development of the human race, since they evoke the complex and impressive image of an ordered creation. Awe and reverence for the heavens, coupled with a desire to comprehend them rationally, is nowhere more evident than in ancient Mesopotamia. The roots of astronomy as a mathematical science, of astral religion as a dimension of religious speculation, and of astrology as a popular pseudoscience all can be traced to this origin. Above all, we must admire the role played by the observations and calculations of the Sumerians — and the even more impressive work of the later Babylonians — in developing a true science of astronomy. The outlines of the stellar constellations, the regularity of their rising and setting in the night sky, and the harmony of their movements together with the movements of the sun and moon laid an important groundwork for human understanding of the physical universe; it is the foundation of modern astronomy.[15]

Alongside this scientific observation and calculation there existed a more popular and mythological understanding of the stars and their motions. Here we find the basis of astrology, which invaded the classical world from Babylon, influenced both Judaism and Christianity, and achieved enormous popularity in the Middle Ages. It interprets the movements of the stars as obeying the will of various divine powers; noting such movements, a human observer can determine in advance the occurrence of favorable or unfavorable days and obtain oracular knowledge of the future so as to predict human success or failure. Beginning with the fifth century B.C., such prognostication became intimately connected with the twelve signs of the zodiac, which served to delineate the months along the ecliptics of the sun and moon. Each phase was represented by a specific symbolic configuration; the names of these individual figures clearly antedate the system as a whole. In the Greek and Roman period, this Babylonian system

---

11. See II.1 below.
12. See II.1 below on *mazzālôṯ* in 2 K. 23:5.
13. See II.1 below.
14. See II.6 below.
15. Cf. Neugebauer, *The Exact Sciences in Antiquity,* 97-144.

increasingly penetrated the Mediterranean world as well as Judaism. In many respects, the signs of the zodiac served to incorporate the popular features of Babylonian astral mythology and religion into a relatively simple system, which remained popular long after the religion had vanished as a cultic reality. As a result, the "star-gazers" of Babylon (cf. Isa. 47:13) enjoyed a lasting fame in the intellectual history of humanity, long after the scientific details of the Babylonians' astronomical observations were forgotten.

The fundamental connection between the two aspects of Mesopotamian interest in the stars is apparent in Babylonian religion, which exhibits prominent astral features.[16] The astral god *kakkab* was already worshipped at Ebla.[17] Along with the moon-god Sin and the sun-god Šamaš, a number of stars and planets enjoyed enough importance to be identified with specific deities. The most important was the goddess Ishtar (Sum. Inanna), whose sign was the planet Venus. She appears in Canaanite and Phoenician religion as Astarte or Ashtaroth, and in the OT as the queen of heaven. As a goddess, her primary role was to serve as patron of love and war. The star Sirius likewise enjoyed great reverence as the embodiment of the god Ninurta (Nimrod), patron of the hunt. Other stars and planets were associated with other deities; among them we may mention Mars, identified with the god Nergal, lord of the underworld, and Saturn, associated primarily with maintenance of justice and law. The Pleiades were worshipped as a constellation of seven stars. Babylonian observation clearly distinguished the fixed stars from the planets, a distinction not maintained so consistently by the OT.

b. *Ugarit.* Whitaker[18] counts 21 occurrences of the noun *kbkb* in Ugaritic, all but 5 in the plural. There is also 1 occurrence of *kbkbn.* To the extent that their context makes their meaning clear, all these passages refer to the luminaries of the night sky. Traces of religious overtones are nevertheless evident. In *KTU,* 1.5 II, 2f., the stars are called the highest part of the universe in contrast to the deepest part, the jaws of Mot. The mythological allusion is even clearer in *KTU,* 1.19 IV, 25, 31, where we find a reference to sacrifices offered to the stars; this implies recognition of their divine status. At the least, they are clearly equated with specific deities, even though the texts in question do not provide further detail. Elsewhere the stars are simply considered nocturnal luminaries of the heavens, evoking special attention because of their brightness.

II. OT.

1. *Astronomy.* Beside the observations, identifications, and calculations of the Babylonians, the extent of astronomical knowledge in the OT seems relatively limited. The interest of the OT focuses on the uncountable number of the stars, their brightness, and

16. Cf. Dhorme, 53-82.

17. Cf. G. Pettinato, "Polytheismus und Henotheismus in der Religion von Ebla," in O. Keel, ed., *Monotheismus im AT und seiner Umwelt. BibB,* 14 (1980), 31-48, esp. 36.

18. Whitaker, 343.

their regular motion. There is less interest in the appearance of individual stars and constellations and the proper motions of the major planets. The extent of OT familiarity with the developed mythology associated with the twelve signs of the zodiac is still subject to debate.

Our knowledge of Israelite astronomy depends almost entirely on 3 passages that refer to specific stars and constellations: Am. 5:8; Job 9:9; 38:31f. Am. 5:8 is part of a hymnic doxology, one which (4:13; 5:8f.; 9:5f.) does not derive from the prophet Amos himself.[19] Our knowledge relates to *kîmâ* and *k^esîl,* which there is good reason to identify respectively with the Pleiades and Orion. The LXX translates *kîmâ* as "all things"; but this rendering is clearly due to the translator, who was seeking to avoid any reference to a heavenly constellation associated with pagan mythology. Etymologically, the meaning "bunch (of stars)" is supported by Arab. *kaum,* "herd of camels," and *kauma,* "pile of dirt." This is an appropriate term for the Pleiades, identified since time immemorial with a constellation of seven stars. The noun *k^esîl,* from a root meaning "fat, gross, stupid," has been identified with Orion since the Vulg (cf. the LXX of Job 38:31). The name might suggest that the star was associated with the figure of a giant. In Babylonian religion, it was identified with Ninurta, the prototype of the mighty hunter Nimrod. In Job 9:9, the LXX translates the name as *Hésperos,* the evening star. Isa. 13:10 uses a plural form in the more inclusive sense of "constellation." Sirius, the Dog Star, has been proposed as an alternative.[20]

None of the 3 passages where these names appear contains any explicit reference to mythology. It is more likely that interest in these stars stems from their seasonal movements. The early rising of the Pleiades marks the beginning of summer; similarly, the appearance of Orion's dog (Sirius) heralds the heat of midsummer.[21] The text of Am. 5:8 is corrupt, the first hemistich having been lost;[22] but the religious interest of the passage focuses on the statement that the cycle of the seasons heralded by the movement of the stars reveals God's power over creation, as does the alternation of day and night. G. R. Driver,[23] following G. Hoffmann,[24] emends Am. 5:9 so as to find references to Sirius, Procyon, and the twins Castor and Pollux: this chain of constellations ("the Navigator's Line"), he claims, constitutes the "raised arm" mentioned in the verse (cf. Job 38:15).

Job 9:9 exhibits comparable interest in the identity of individual stars as witnessing to the beauty and elegance of God's power. Here, besides references to *kîmâ* and *k^esîl,* just discussed, we find *ʿāš,* "the Bear," and *ḥaḏrê tēmān,* "the chambers of the south." The LXX and Syr reverse the series of constellations, clearly influenced by Job 38:31f. and Am. 5:8; the sequence of the MT is therefore probably correct. The noun *ʿāš* clearly

---

19. H. W. Wolff, *Joel and Amos. Herm* (Eng. trans. 1977), 240f.
20. *AuS,* I (1928), 497ff., 501.
21. *Ibid.,* 501.
22. Cf. *BHS.*
23. *JTS,* N.S. 4 (1953), 208-212.
24. G. Hoffmann, "Versuche zu Amos," *ZAW,* 3 (1883), 110f.

denotes the same constellation as *ʿayiš* in Job 38:32. Driver[25] disputes the identification with Ursa Major, which goes back at least to Saadia and Ibn Ezra; following Giovanni Schiaparelli, he proposes identification with Aldebaran. The Syr *ʿayûṯāʾ* appears to vacillate among Orion, Aries, and Aldebaran (the "eye of Taurus").[26] The Vulg identifies it with Arcturus, which the LXX uses to translate *kᵉsîl.* If *ʿāš/ʿayiš* is Ursa Major, the "little ones" of Job 38:32 would be Ursa Minor; Driver, however, prefers to identify them with the Hyades. The "chambers of the south" cannot be identified precisely in the ancient versions, which preferred paraphrase. Édouard P. Dhorme and Schiaparelli identify them with Argo, the Centaur, and the Southern Cross.

Job 38:31 refers to the "chains (*maʿᵃḏannôṯ*) of the Pleiades"; the popular mind thought of chains holding the stars together to form a constellation. The reference to the "cords (*mōšᵉḵôṯ*) of Orion," however, requires a different explanation: they may be envisioned as binding the giant. V. 32 speaks of *massārôṯ*; since Theodotion, this term has often been identified with the *mazzālôṯ* of 2 K. 23:5, a hapax legomenon whose meaning can be derived with reasonable certainty from Akk. *manzaltu,* "location, position": "constellation, position of the stars." Jewish tradition also finds the meaning in 2 K. 23:5, but it is probably too narrow for our passage. Driver[27] has suggested either the signs of the zodiac or the five planets; the latter is more likely. From its association with the signs of the zodiac (cf. Aram. *mazzālāʾ* and Middle Heb. *mazzāl,* "sign of the zodiac"), the term takes on the sense of "fortune" in Late Hebrew and Aramaic.

The *mazzārôṯ* of Job 38:32 are clearly not the same objects, and the two should not be confused; neither are they related to the *mᵉzārîm,* "scattering winds," of Job 37:9. The LXX simply transliterates (*masourōth*), but seems to refer to a specific group of stars. Here, too, Driver[28] suggests the signs of the zodiac; Dhorme, following J. D. Michaelis, identifies them with the Corona Borealis.[29]

In comparison to Mesopotamian material, the extent of astronomical terminology and observation attested in the OT is not very great. There is nevertheless enough evidence for us to say that it represents only a small fraction of the astronomical interest and its concomitant mythology that the ancient Israelites shared with their Mesopotamian neighbors. The way the references are introduced shows that identification of individual stars and knowledge of their motions in association with the months and seasons was a familiar subject of popular learning and speculation. Like the moon, the stars must have played a part in calculating times and seasons, although for the OT this must remain largely hypothetical.

2. *Creation.* In P's creation account, the creation of the stars along with the sun and moon is assigned to the fourth day (Gen. 1:16). The casual way they are introduced

---

25. *JTS,* N.S. 7 (1956), 1-11.
26. Cf. E. Dhorme, *A Commentary on the Book of Job* (Eng. trans. 1967, repr. Nashville, 1984), *in loc.*
27. *JTS,* N.S. 7 (1956), 7.
28. *Ibid.,* 8.
29. Dhorme, 59, citing Michaelis, *Adnotationes in Hagiographos* (1720), *in loc.*

shows surprising disregard for their importance in the scientific reckoning of time. Undoubtedly this reflects an effort to play down the popular religious and mythological connotations associated extensively with the courses of the stars. This effort removes the stars from the immediate realm of religion (cf. Mesopotamia).

Further evidence of OT resistance to speculation about the influence of the stars on human fate is discussed in II.5 below. In the OT, the stars are looked upon mostly as signs of Yahweh's exalted power in and over creation. Their countless number, their brightness in the clear night sky, and the ordered regularity of the movements inspired awe, demonstrating the wisdom and power of their creator. Besides the references to specific stars or constellations discussed above, there are many other passages that develop this theme.

We shall first consider references to the countless number of the stars. Ps. 147:4 says that Yahweh determines their number and gives them all their names. Such an immense number overwhelms human comprehension and points to a higher mind, which alone can comprehend and understand such quantity (cf. Isa. 40:26; 45:12). The belief that Yahweh gave them their names may indicate that the psalmist was no longer familiar with the basis of their alien and largely mythological nature, since he ascribes their naming exclusively to God. It is also clear that awe at the brightness and number of the stars provides motivation for praise, as in Ps. 8:4(Eng. v. 3) and 136:9, where the stars are associated with the moon and sun; cf. also Ps. 148:3. Analogous interest in the "fixed order" (*ḥuqqōṯ*; reading *ḥōqēq* with *BHS*) of the moon and stars is found in Jer. 31:35, which stresses the unalterable nature of God's will. The appearance of the stars at evening marks the end of the working day, as Neh. 4:15(21) makes clear. In Job 22:12, the reference to the "highest stars" reflects the assumption that the sky is hemispherical, so that the pole star and those closest to it are higher than the others. Since God is even higher than they, he can see everything that happens on earth.

The idea that the stars stand high above the earth is also reflected in Ob. 4, which uses an exaggerated metaphor: Edom is like an eagle that builds its nest "among the stars." Job 38:7 alludes to the dawn of creation, when the "morning stars" (cf. the "dawn star" of Job 3:9) sang together, praising God for all that he had made. The reference to the "sons of God" (*bᵉnê ᵓᵉlōhîm*) in the parallel hemistich shows that we have here an echo of the ancient mythology in which the stars were divine beings of second rank. With this reference to the existence of the stars, the author seeks to indicate and emphasize the greatness and majesty of their creator. That the Creator is greater than his works is also shown by the reference to the stars in Job 25:5, which states that from God's perspective the moon cannot be considered bright nor the stars clean in comparison to God. How much the less can mortals be considered clean before him!

In Dnl. 12:3, the brightness of the stars provides the basis for a figure of speech illustrating the joy and happiness after death that awaits those who have been faithful to the Torah during the time of persecution. This passage refers primarily to the Jews who, during the Maccabean revolt, suffered martyrdom rather than betray their ancient faith. Their reward after death is depicted in the image of "shining like stars." Here it is clear how the stars as images of brightness take on increasingly complex metaphorical meaning, the connotations of which are hard to define precisely.

The most striking characteristic of the stars is their countless number, which also evoked the most extensive literary deposit in the OT. The fact that the stars cannot be counted makes them an effective point of comparison for an infinite number. Ps. 147:4 (cf. Isa. 40:26) already shows that only God can have determined their number, because God alone can count so many. The most extensive development of this literary device of countless stars appears in the context of God's promise to Abraham and to his descendants that they would be a great nation. Their number will grow so great that they will be comparable to the number of the stars in the night sky. This promise first appears in Yahweh's words to Abraham in Gen. 15:5 (E?). Later, the stars frequently represent the greatness and might of the Israelite nation as foreseen in God's promise (Gen. 22:17 [E]; 26:4 [J]; Ex. 32:13 [R^D]; Dt. 1:10; 10:22; 28:62; 1 Ch. 27:23; Neh. 9:23).

In Nah. 3:16, the point of comparison is the great number of the Ninevite merchants, which the prophet uses to indicate the extent of the imminent disaster awaiting the city.

3. *Figurative Usage.* The metaphor of the brightness of the stars gives rise to another meaning of the stars in the OT. Dnl. 12:3 uses the "shining of the stars" to describe the life after death awaiting faithful Jews. As a striking visible image of the created order, the stars by synecdoche can embody all creation. In Jgs. 5:20, the Song of Deborah describes a battle of Yahweh in which all the stars fight against Sisera, Israel's foe. The conceptual background of this ancient poem is strongly influenced by the institution of the holy war, in which victory in battle is seen as a mighty act on the part of Yawheh. Participation of the stars in this battle thus expresses the idea that all the elements of the created world stand at Yahweh's disposal and can be used to achieve victory. A totally different metaphorical use of the stars appears in the account of Joseph's dream in Gen. 37:9ff. (J): the sun and moon represent Joseph's father and mother, eleven stars his brothers. The differing brightness of the heavenly luminaries makes them ideally suited to represent a human family.

A similar albeit less obvious image appears in Balaam's oracle in Nu. 24:15-19 (J): in v. 17, the "star" out of Israel that crushes Moab and Edom undoubtedly represents the historical David and the period of his rule of Israel. The LXX and the ancient Syriac version explain the image by reading "man" and "leader," respectively; Targum Onkelos interprets the star as the coming Messiah. Since stars were appropriate symbols for rulers or leaders, they were incorporated into the apocalyptic imagery of Dnl. 8:10. Speaking of a little horn, which must stand for Antiochus Epiphanes, this verse says that it grew great, even reaching the host of heaven, and cast some of the host of stars down to the ground. This may allude to Antiochus's military victories, but the vision narrative with its mythological overtones also clearly suggests the arrogance of the Syrian ruler. It is also clear that we have here a conscious echo of the language of Isa. 14:12ff.[30]

4. *Unusual Phenomena.* The great brightness of the stars in the clear night sky lent support to the conviction that a great catastrophe was imminent when the stars grew

30. See II.6 below.

or ceased totally to shine. In some cases, physical phenomena are mentioned, e.g., the experience of seeing the stars obscured by dark, heavy storm clouds; in traditional theophanic language, these clouds lent a note of special solemnity and significance to such darkness. The naturalness and regular appearance of starlight was perceived as part of the natural order. Its disappearance thus meant the loss of a fundamental feature of existence. Job can therefore think of the day of his birth as a day of darkness: "Let the stars of its dawn be dark" (Job 3:9). The power of the creator God over creation manifests itself in the ability to change what has been made. The author of Job includes God's power to "seal up"[31] the stars (Job 9:7); i.e., it is in God's power, if he wills, to cause the stars to cease shining.

The darkening of the stars that cease to shine means loss of a basic manifestation of the natural order. This finds expression in the difficult allegory of old age in Eccl. 12:2-6. The signs of winter — a cloudy sky and the dimming of the sun, moon, and stars — are used to evoke the image of life's "winter." This boundary between literal and metaphorical treatment of the stars is fluid. Ezk. 32:7, in a divine judgment against the Egyptian pharaoh, announces his imminent death. But this event has greater significance than usual, because it is meant to signal a special punishment sent by God; it is accompanied by an extraordinary darkening of the stars and "the bright lights[32] of heaven" (Ezk. 32:7f.).

This image of dimming stars as a phenomenon accompanying a strikingly gloomy event on earth leads to the eschatological darkening of the stars as a feature of the coming day of Yahweh.[33] This darkening includes the sun and moon (Isa. 13:10; Joel 2:10; 4:15[3:15]) and evokes a vivid description of the tumult and confusion that will reign when Yahweh's judgment strikes the world. The extinction of the starlight shows how the totality of creation, whose fixed order expresses God's salvation and blessing, is dissolved in the judgment that Yahweh will carry out on that day.

5. *Illicit Worship.* Most other OT references to the stars concern their association with religion and mythological forms felt to be hostile and detrimental to the basic tradition of Yahwism. A clear example appears in Isa. 47:13, where the prophet brutally mocks the respect enjoyed by the Babylonian astrologers. All the skill of the Babylonian experts in magic, sorcery, and interpretation of the movements of the stars will not avail Babylon to deliver it from the coming judgment of Yahweh. A similarly harsh and direct expression of hostility toward worship of the stars, sun, and moon is found in many texts of the Deuteronomistic school. A fundamental statement along these lines appears in Dt. 4:19, which speaks of the sun, moon, stars, and all the host of heaven as potential objects of idolatrous worship. Josiah's destruction of various cultic objects associated with such astral worship is recorded in 2 K. 23:4, together with the deposition of the priests involved (2 K. 23:5). Here the stars, the "hosts" of heaven, are also called

31. → חתם *ḥāṯam.*
32. → אור *'ôr.*
33. → יום *yôm.*

"constellations" (*mazzālôṯ*). A later tradition identified these with the individual signs of the zodiac. A particular target of the Deuteronomistic writer was worship of the queen of heaven, the Babylonian Ishtar. Her characteristic sign was the planet Venus, so that her cult, together with its Canaanite equivalents, constituted a prominent expression of the illicit cult (cf. Jer. 7:18) associated with the stars; the women of Jerusalem are charged with having baked cakes for the queen of heaven. Jer. 19:13; 44:17,25 condemn burning incense and offering libations in her honor. Undoubtedly this extremely bitter attack of the Deuteronomistic writer on astral worship in Judah during the seventh century B.C. is a direct result of Assyrian influence on Judah and Israel during the preceding century. Some of this found its way into Israel when the Assyrians settled foreign population elements in the northern kingdom after 722. This conclusion is disputed by J. W. MacKay, who prefers to trace such elements of astral religion to the Canaanite and Phoenician environment. The date and nature of the events, however, point unmistakably to Mesopotamian influence on Judah.

A writer with Deuteronomistic affinities seems to be responsible for the condemnation of astral deities in Am. 5:26. While some commentators[34] ascribe part of the text to Amos, Wilhelm Rudolph[35] considers v. 26b a Judahite gloss opposing the astral religion of the mixed population of the northern kingdom after 722. Others[36] consider vv. 25f. the work of a Deuteronomistic redactor. This latter theory is the most likely, since it makes it possible to read v. 26 as a continuation of v. 25 and identify it as a rhetorical question.[37] It is a charge that Israel has transgressed by taking refuge in the worship of foreign gods, not a threat against future devotion to so useless a religion. The passage speaks of Sakkuth and Kaiwan (Akk. *kayyamānu*[38]), two Assyro-Babylonian deities identified with the planet Saturn. Expansion of these names with the appositive "your star-god" must therefore be considered a gloss,[39] correctly identifying the alien astral nature of the deities in question. The entire addition appears to date from the sixth century, when Israel was no longer so familiar with Babylonian religion.

6. *Special Examples.* Astral mythology appears most clearly in the OT in a fragmentary myth preserved in Isa. 14:12ff. William F. Albright[40] was the first to identify its dependence on an extended myth of Canaanite and Phoenician provenance. This myth describes the fall of the "Day Star, son of Dawn" (*hêlēl ben-šaḥar*). After attempting to set up his dwelling "among the stars of El," he is condemned for his hybris and banished to the underworld of Sheol. This fragment is cited in a satirical

---

34. Sellin, Weiser, Haag, Amsler.

35. W. Rudolph, *Amos. KAT,* XIII/2 (1971), 208.

36. W. H. Schmidt, "Die deuteronomistiche Redaktion des Amosbuches," *ZAW,* 77 (1965), 188ff.; Wolff, 2-4.

37. Cf. S. Erlandsson, "Amos 5:25-27, ett crux interpretum," *SEÅ,* 33 (1968), 76ff.

38. *AHw,* I, 420.

39. *BHS.*

40. W. F. Albright, review of S. H. Hooke, ed., *Myth and Ritual* (London, 1933), *JPOS,* 14 (1934), 156.

dirge for the Babylonian king (Isa. 14:1-21), which most commentators[41] do not consider authentic, although some have defended an Isaianic nucleus within the poem.[42] The identity of the person condemned by the myth is clear, since it must refer to the planet Venus. The text nevertheless rules out any association with the goddess Ishtar. A connection with the Canaanite god ʿAthtar is suggested by the parallel in the Ugaritic Baʿal-ʿAnat cycle, which describes ʿAthtar's unsuccessful attempt to capture Baʿal's throne.[43] Marvin Pope finds a connection with an ancient myth about the fall of the god El.[44] Fritz Stolz[45] comes up with a myth of the fall of the deity Šaḥar, citing Isa. 8:19f. and Job 38:12 as further evidence for this god; he also sees in Ps. 22:1(Eng. superscription) a cryptic reference to Šaḥar. The name Hêlel (cf. Ugar. *hll*) means simply "the bright one," and must be derived from its application to the planet Venus.

On the basis of such a mythological background, supported by Isa. 14:12ff., further traces of astral mythology have been detected in Ezk. 28:12b-19. The points of contact, however, scarcely suffice to reconstruct a coherent astral mythology. There is, however, enough evidence to show that such points of contact existed in Canaan and Phoenicia and deeply influenced Israelite religion.

III. LXX. The LXX uses *astḗr* and *ástron* equally to render *kôḵāḇ*.

IV. Dead Sea Scrolls. In the Dead Sea scrolls, *kôḵāḇ* occurs only 4 times (1QM 11:6; CD 7:18,19; 1QH 1:12); its usage follows that in the OT.

Clements

---

41. Kaiser, Schoors, Wildberger.
42. Gottwald; S. Erlandsson, *The Burden of Babylon. CB,* 4 (1970).
43. *KTU,* 1.6 I, 48ff.; cf. M. Dietrich and O. Loretz, "Ein Spottlied auf ʿAṯtar [KTU 1.6 I 50-52]," *UF,* 9 (1977), 330f.
44. M. Pope, *El in the Ugaritic Texts. SVT,* 2 (1955), 27ff.; cf. Oldenburg.
45. F. Stolz, *Strukturen und Figuren im Kult von Jerusalem. BZAW,* 118 (1970), 210ff.

כול *kwl*

Contents: I. 1. Etymology; 2. Meaning, Occurrences. II. Literal Usage: 1. Holding. 2. Provisioning. III. Figurative Usage: 1. Comprehension; 2. Endurance; 3. Keeping on Course.

I. 1. *Etymology.* The root *kwl* is found in a range of Semitic languages, albeit with characteristic differences of meaning. In West Semitic, the dominant meaning is "measure" (Jewish Aramaic,[1] Mandaic, Palmyrene,[2] Syr. *'akkēl,* Arab. *kyl*; cf. OSA *kltn,* Aram. *kaylā',* "measure," Middle Heb. *kayyāl,* "surveyor"); Akk. *kullu* and Assyr. *ka''ulu,* however, have a range of meanings centering on "hold fast." Both meanings have apparently influenced the Hebrew root, as can be seen in both Middle and Modern Hebrew. It is also likely that similar Hebrew roots like *ykl* (with the meaning "grasp, endure") and *kl'* (with the meaning "hold back") have influenced the semantic development of *kwl.*

2. *Meaning, Occurrences.* Originally, the Hebrew root *kwl* probably denoted an activity having to do with measuring and enclosing a space or quantity. This basic meaning can be detected in the majority of its biblical occurrences. The various shades of meaning all have to do with "holding" (cf. the noun *kᵉlî,* "container," which is probably related).

The root *kwl* appears 38 times in the Hebrew OT; it occurs once in the qal (Isa. 40:12), 12 times in the hiphil, 24 times in the pilpel, and once in the pulpal (1 K. 20:27). Conjectural emendation adds a possible pilpel in Ps. 68:11(Eng. v. 10). There are also 4 occurrences (pilpel or hithpalpel) in Sirach (Sir. 6:20; 12:15; 43:3; 49:4) and 4 (pilpel or hiphil) in the Dead Sea scrolls (1QS 3:17; 11:20; 1QH 9:34,36). The root appears with some frequency in certain literary contexts such as the story of Joseph and the Elijah narratives; it is especially common in late texts.

In the LXX, only the pilpel forms with the meaning "provide for" are translated with some consistency: the most frequent equivalents are *diatréphō* (10 out of 17 OT occurrences), *ektréphō,* or *tréphō* and *chōréō* (3 out of 6 occurrences) or *chorēgéō* (all 3 occurrences in the Hebrew OT).

II. Literal Usage.

1. *Holding.* The only instance of the qal (Isa. 40:12) uses *kwl* in parallel with other verbs of measuring (*mdd, tkn, šql*) in a series of rhetorical questions citing various ways of measuring water, air, dust, and rock; their purpose is to bring out the immensity of creation.[3] The root *kwl* serves to describe the measuring of dust with the aid of a cubic measure called a "third" (*šālîš*). It is here that we probably see the original meaning of *kwl* most clearly.

In a few passages, *kwl* denotes the capacity of containers. In 1 K. 7:26(f.?[4]), it refers to the contents of the bronze sea in the temple; in 1 K. 7:38 par. 2 Ch. 4:5, it refers to the contents of the lavers. In both cases, the unit involved is the *baṯ.* In 1 K. 8:64 par. 2 Ch. 7:7, we are told that the bronze altar of the temple was too small to hold the

---

1. On Pahl. *kylwn,* "measure," see E. Ebeling, *Das aramäisch-mittlepersische Glossar Frahang-i-pahlavik im Lichte der assyriologischen Forschung. MAOG,* 14/1 (1941, repr. 1972), 42, and his comparison with Akk. *kadāru,* "delimit"; cf. *AHw,* I (1965), 419; *CAD,* VIII (1971), 30.

2. *DISO,* 116.

3. Cf. III.1 below.

4. M. Noth, *Könige. BK,* IX/1 (1968), 155f.

burnt offerings, the cereal offerings, and the fat portions of the *šᵉlāmîm* offerings. We may conclude that there were depressions in the surface of this altar so that it could be treated like a container.

In Hebrew inscriptions (Gezer calendar,[5] ostracon from Yabneh-Yam[6]), *kwl* appears in the context of the harvest, between reaping (*qṣr*) and storing (*'sm*). The word probably denotes not just measuring the grain, as suggested by *KAI,* but also packing it in containers for transport to storage.

In all these occurrences, *kwl* appears in the context of measuring solids or liquids with the aid of a measuring vessel. It is not limited, however, to measuring in the narrow sense; it can also be used in an extended sense: the basic meaning "hold, contain" can be discerned in most of these cases. This is especially true in Jer. 2:13, where God, the source of "living" (i.e., fresh running) water, is contrasted with the cisterns the people have made for themselves, which leak because they have cracks and therefore cannot "hold" the water that runs into them. Ezk. 23:32 speaks similarly of a cup that holds an unusually large amount, from which the southern kingdom will have to drink its share of judgment like the northern kingdom before it.

2. *Provisioning.* The pilpel and pulpal of *kwl* underwent a specialized semantic development in the many passages where it means "provision." Here, in accordance with the iterative nature of the pilpel, the emphasis is on regular preparation of a specific quantity of provisions. In this sense, the verb often is used absolutely, clearly as a technical term: Gen. 45:11; 50:21; 2 S. 19:33f.(Eng. vv. 32f.); 20:3; 1 K. 4:7; 5:7(4:27); Ps. 55:23(22); Sir. 25:22; 45:24; possibly also Ps. 68:11(10) conj.[7] In 1 K. 4:7; 5:7(4:27), the word describes the function of Solomon's stewards; the latter passage explains in more detail that they are to provision the "table of the king," i.e., furnish food. In the story of Joseph, *kilkal* in Gen. 47:12 is further defined as provisioning with bread.[8] In the Elijah narratives, *kilkal* is always defined more specifically. The context of 1 K. 17:4 mentions bread, meat, and water; the context of 17:9 speaks of water, bread, and oil; 18:4,13 speaks of bread and water. Zec. 11:16 also uses *'kl,* "eat," in the immediate context. Neh. 9:21 — a recollection of the period in the desert — mentions clothes and shoes in the same context; these can therefore be included among "provisions" in the extended sense. In 1 K. 20:27, the only passage that uses the pulpal, the word appears in the context of a military campaign as a technical term for the provisioning of the army. In Sir. 45:24, it is used for the provisioning of the sanctuary. Sir. 25:22 means support in general when it says that it is a disgrace for a woman to "maintain" her husband.

In Ruth 4:15, *kilkal* has a different meaning. Here it refers to old age support of one's grandparents' generation. The corresponding duty on the part of the elderly person

---

5. *KAI,* 182, 5.
6. *KAI,* 200, 5.
7. Cf. *KBL*³, 442; also 1QS 3:17; 1QH 9:34.
8. → לחם *leḥem.*

is to undertake to nurture the infant child and take it in her bosom. In 1QH 9:36, which likewise uses both *ḥêq,* "bosom," and *'ômēn,* "nurse," the same notion is applied to God. Quite generally, there is an increasing tendency to associate *kilkal* in the sense of "provide for" with God's work. The association is implicit in the miraculous supplying of Elijah's needs by the ravens (1 K. 17:4) and the widow (17:9); it is explicit in Ps. 55:23(22) (cf. Ps. 68:11[10] conj.), Neh. 9:21, and the passages from the Dead Sea scrolls.

III. Figurative Usage.

1. *Comprehension.* The root is used figuratively especially to speak of God's incomprehensibility. Isa. 40:12[9] expresses this attribute by means of rhetorical questions that bring out the immensity of creation. In the same vein are the statements in Solomon's prayer at the dedication of the temple (1 K. 8:27 par. 2 Ch. 6:18; cf. 2 Ch. 2:5), which apply this notion to God himself: God is so great that neither "heaven" nor the whole heavenly realm[10] constitutes a vessel large enough to contain him. He is in the truest sense of the word incomprehensible, beyond measure or definition. Elsewhere, too, rhetorical questions (like the one beginning with *mî,* "who?" in Isa. 40:12) serve to underscore the incomprehensible immensity of God, his day[11] (Joel 2:11; Mal. 3:2), or his glory[12] (1QS 11:20).

2. *Endurance.* In these last passages, however, the meaning of *kwl* (possibly influenced by *kl'*) tends in the direction of "withstand, endure." Even here, though, a spatial element is still present, especially when we recall that the coming of the *yôm YHWH* or Yahweh's *kāḇôḏ* is experienced as an inward shock. According to Jer. 10:10, for example, Jeremiah is filled to the bursting point with the wrath[13] of God, which is likened to an earthquake; he also strives in vain to hold in the wrath[14] of Yahweh (Jer. 6:11). Jer. 20:9 describes the prophet's attempt to forget and repress his prophetic calling: the words entrusted to him are like fire within him and he cannot hold them in. Here, too, we have a futile effort[15] on the part of the prophet to "contain" himself. When such contexts use the pilpel, the reference is probably to a repeated experience; Prov. 18:14 speaks similarly of repeated endurance of sickness.

The basic notion of physical capacity is also present in Am. 7:10. The land is pictured as an enormous container in danger of bursting asunder with the rebellious words of Amos. It can no longer endure the pressure; the measure is full.[16]

---

9. See II.1 above.
10. → שמים *šāmayim.*
11. → יום *yôm.*
12. → כבוד *kāḇôḏ.*
13. → זעם *z'm.*
14. → חמה *ḥēmâ* (*chēmāh*).
15. → לאה *l'h.*
16. Cf. H. W. Wolff, *Joel and Amos. Herm* (Eng. trans. 1977), 306, 310.

3. *Keeping on Course.* Finally, *kwl* is used in a much weaker sense in Ps. 112:5, which appears to deal with keeping to the straight path. The same reduction of human capacity to a constant appears in Sir. 6:20; 12:15; 43:3; 49:9.

Ezk. 21:33(28) cannot be explained on the basis of the basic meaning of *kwl* discussed above or its derived meanings. It is reasonable to assume textual corruption.[17]

Baumann

---

17. Cf. W. Zimmerli, *Ezekiel 1. Herm* (Eng. trans. 1979), 439.

כּוּן *kûn*; כֵּן *kēn*; מָכוֹן *māḵôn*; מְכוֹנָה *m^eḵônâ*; תְּכוּנָה *t^eḵûnâ*

Contents: I. Frequency and Distribution: 1. Verb; 2. Nouns; 3. *kēn*; 4. Special Problems. II. Semitic Context: 1. Distribution; 2. South Semitic; 3. Akkadian; 4. Northwest Semitic. III. Common Usage. IV. Technical Usage in the Cult. V. Anthropological Usage: 1. Psalms and Wisdom Literature; 2. Dead Sea Scrolls. VI. Creation: 1. Psalter and Late Wisdom; 2. Temple of Solomon. VII. Throne and Kingdom: 1. Davidic Kingship; 2. Divine Kingship.

I. Frequency and Distribution. The root *kwn* appears more than 280 times in the OT, not counting the occurrences of the particle *kēn,* whose connection with the root is uncertain.

1. *Verb.* There are 270 passages that use the verb, primarily in the factitive and causative stems: the hiphil appears 110 times, the polel 30 (including Ps. 37:23 as repointed). Yahweh is frequently the subject, a sign that the verb denotes an exceptionally effectual act. The basic meaning of both forms is defined as "prepare, make ready" by *KBL*[3], but greater weight is ascribed to the polel, which may mean "establish, make permanent," while the specific sense of the hiphil is rendered as "determine" or "be determined" (in the psychological sense). For *THAT,* too, the hiphil is "broad and vague in meaning" compared to the polel, which often has concrete physical associations. When both stems are used in the same context, however, the polel refers to preparations and the hiphil denotes the result. Ps. 7:13f.(Eng. vv. 12f.) provides an example: "The

---

kûn. H. Brongers, "Weltschöpfungsgedanken in Alt-Israel. 5. (כון) כּוֹנֵן, הֵכִין) (*kün*), *kônēn,* *hēkîn* 'aufstellen, errichten,' " *Persica,* 7 (1975-78), 117-123; M. Dietrich, O. Loretz, J. Sanmartín, "*KUN-Š* und *ŠKN* im Ugaritischen," *UF,* 6 (1974), 47-53; E. Gerstenberger, "כון *kūn* ni. feststehen," *THAT,* I, 812-17; W. Grundmann, "ἕτοιμος," *TDNT,* II, 704-6; M. J. Mulder, "Die Partikel כֵּן im AT," *Remembering All the Way . . . Festschrift Outdtestamentisch Werkgezelschap in Nederland. OTS,* 21 (1981), 201-227; E. Talstra, "The Use of כֵּן in Biblical Hebrew," *OTS,* 21 (1981), 228-239; G. J. Thierry, "Notes on Hebrew Grammar and Etymology," *OTS,* 9 (1951), 3-5.

wicked man makes ready (*yᵉḵônēn,* "spans") his bow . . . , he prepares (*hēḵîn*) his instruments of death" (cf. also Ps. 68:10f.[9f.]). It is accordingly more common for God to be the subject of the hiphil than of the polel.

The purely passive stems are rarely used: there is 1 occurrence of the polal (Ezk. 28:13), 4 of the hithpolel, and 6 of the hophal. The niphal, which appears 66 times, describes "fixed" entities like "full daylight" (*nᵉḵôn hayyôm*: Prov. 4:18) or a woman's firm breasts (Ezk. 16:7), but refers more often to the result of an action generally denoted by the hiphil or polel; it thus functions as a passive with nouns like *zeraʿ*, "descendants" (Ps. 102:29[28]; cf. 89:5[4]); *kissēʾ*, "throne" (Ps. 93:2; cf. 103:19); and *lēḇ,* "heart" (Ps. 57:8[7]; cf. 10:17). The niphal can also denote preparations for a future event, especially a cultic encounter with God: *wᵉhāyû nᵉḵônîm lᵉ*, "make yourselves ready for" (Ex. 19:11,15; cf. 34:2; Josh. 8:4); *hikkôn* (Am. 4:12; cf. Ezk. 38:7).

2. *Nouns.* Nominal derivatives of the root are rare. There are 17 occurrences of *māḵôn,* translated variously as "place, location"[1] or "position, support."[2] In the singular, it is restricted to holy places, the place of Yahweh's presence (his throne: Ps. 89:15[14]; 97:2). The plural is found only once, in Ps. 104:5, where it refers to the foundations of the earth, firmly established by God. "Secular" usage first appears in Sir. 41:1; 44:6, where it may mean "dwelling place" or "security." The feminine form *mᵉḵônâ* is used twice for a holy place (for the woman who personifies wickedness in Zec. 5:11; for the altar in Ezr. 3:3). In 23 other passages, it denotes the wheeled lavers (RSV "stands") that were important objects in the temple of Solomon. In Neh. 11:28, finally, *mᵉḵônâ* is the name of a city. The substantives with a *mem* preformative often show that what is established is the result of a *kûn* action (Zec. 5:11; Ezr. 3:3); in other words, they are not used of things that subsist independently. The noun *tᵉḵûnâ* appears 3 times: it denotes the place from which Yahweh gives help (Job 23:3), the arrangement of the Jerusalem temple (Ezk. 43:11), and the quantity of silver and gold amassed at Nineveh (Nah. 2:10[9]).

A special problem is associated with *yāḵîn* (*yāḵûn* in several LXX manuscripts), the name of one of the temple pillars in 1 K. 7:15ff. The entrance to Solomon's temple was flanked by two bronze pillars nearly 9 meters (30 ft.) tall, topped by capitals with botanical ornamentation. One was named *yāḵîl/ûn,* the other *bōʿaz.* Much ink has been spilled over the purpose and names of these pillars.[3] Did they echo Canaanite massebahs, standards at the entrance to Mesopotamian temples,[4] or Egyptian *djed* pillars?[5] It is generally agreed that the name *yāḵîn* is a catchword beginning an oracle or prayer and is therefore a verbal form (not a noun with a *yodh* preformative). It clearly refers

1. *GesB.*

2. *KBL*³.

3. For a survey, see W. Kornfeld, "Der Symbolismus der Tempelsäulen," *ZAW,* 74 (1962), 50-57; M. Noth, *Könige. BK,* IX/1 (1968), 152-55.

4. T. A. Busink, *Der Tempel von Jerusalem,* I: *Der Tempel Salomos. StFS,* 3 (1970), 317.

5. Kornfeld.

to the God of the temple; but what is it that this God "prepares"? Might the object of the verb be the temple or the royal palace?

3. *kēn.* The OT form *kēn* exhibits a variety of meanings. Its relationship to the root *kûn* is not clear.

a. *Particle.* It is disputed whether the particle *kēn* (sometimes written *ken-*), usually translated "so," derives from *kûn*[6] or from a demonstrative *k.*[7] The particle frequently emphasizes (anaphorically or otherwise) that what is said truly represents the facts of the situation or the fulfillment of a prediction (122 out of 344 occurrences, according to *KBL*), and therefore sometimes plays a significant role in religious texts.[8]

b. *Conjunction (lāḵēn).* The conjunction *lāḵēn* introduces a result clause and often correlates with *yaʿan* (*ʾᵃšer/kî*), "it is the case that"; in OT prophecy, it plays a key role in the transition from description (invective) to prophecy (threat).[9] It is unclear whether this conjunction is related to the particle and/or the root *kûn.* The translation "therefore"[10] is probably too weak; a better rendering would be "in view of which, on my word of honor."[11]

c. *Noun, "Right."* There is clearly a noun *kēn*[12] that derives from the root *kûn.*[13] According to *GesB,* it means "(what is) right"; according to *KBL,* it also means "(what is) firm, upright, true." It is often hard to distinguish the noun from the particle. The noun is found by *GesB* in 16 (19) passages, by *KBL*² in 20, and by *KBL*³ in 24. Different passages are included by each authority. The distinction between the particle and the noun is significant, for example, in Am. 4:5, where the prophet concludes his attack on a wealth of sacrifices coupled with a lack of social conscience with the words *kî kēn ʾᵃhaḇtem.* Is he speaking ironically ("you [claim to] love what is right"[14]) or merely summing up his charge ("for so you love to do")? The admonition in Am. 5:14 is equally obscure to the modern reader: "Seek good, and not evil, that you may live, *wayᵉhî ḵēn.*" Does this mean "thus what is right will come to pass,"[15] or does the last syntagma go with the following clause: "thus Yahweh . . . will be with you?"[16]

---

6. *KBL*²·³ under *kēn* II.

7. Cf. *GesB., s.v. kēn* I.

8. Mulder; Talstra; on *wayᵉhî-ḵēn* in Gen. 1:7ff., see O. H. Steck, *Der Schöpfungsbericht der Priesterschrift. FRLANT,* 115 (²1981), 97f.

9. K. Koch, *The Growth of the Biblical Tradition* (Eng. trans., New York, ²1975), 212.

10. *GesB, KBL.*

11. F. J. Goldbaum, "Two Hebrew Quasi-Adverbs: לכן and אכן," *JNES,* 23 (1964), 132-35; see also V. Maag, *Text, Wortschatz und Begriffswelt des Buches Amos* (Leiden, 1951), 82, 111f.; F. Nötscher, "Zum emphatischen Lamed," *VT,* 3 (1953), 375f.

12. I, *GesB* = II, *KBL*³.

13. *BLe,* §61c‴.

14. Maag.

15. *Ibid.*

16. The interpretation of most exegetes; see K. Koch, *Amos. AOAT,* 30 (1976), I, 142, 172; II, 37.

d. *Noun, "Base, Office."* There is another noun *kēn* III, which appears as *kann-* before suffixes and therefore derives from a by-form *knn.*[17] In 8 (or 9?) passages (including 1 K. 7:31?), it refers to the bronze pedestal of a priestly laver in the tent of meeting. P may substitute this term for the wheeled laver (*m*ᵉ*ḵônâ*) of Solomon's temple, which has a mythological ring.[18] In 1 passage, *kēn* denotes the crossbeam that supports the mast on the deck of a ship (Isa. 33:23). In 6 passages,[19] it refers to the institutionalized office of the royal butler (Gen. 40:13; 41:13) or that of the reigning king (Dnl. 11:7,20f.,38).

4. *Special Problems.*

a. *The Root knn as a Possible By-form.* Ps. 80:16(15) appeals to Yahweh: "*w*ᵉ*ḵānnâ* that which thy right hand has planted [= the vine of Israel]." Here *GesB* finds the qal imperfect of a root meaning "cover, protect"; so probably does Mitchell Dahood,[20] who translates "take care of." Following the Targ., Ferdinand Hitzig (and also *KBL*³) interprets *w*ᵉ*ḵānnâ* as a suffixed form and translates "his shoot," a meaning not otherwise attested for *kēn.* On the basis of the LXX, Julius Wellhausen proposes the conj. *w*ᵉ*ḵôn*ᵉ*nâ* (polel); other exegetes have accepted his emendation, and there have been still other suggestions. Nevertheless, personal names like *k*ᵉ*nanya(hu), k*ᵉ*nani* (Neh. 9:4, if it does not mean "someone born in the month *kanūnu*"[21]), and *y*ᵉ*konyahu* ("may Yahweh establish him"?) suggest that the word may represent a qal of *knn.*[22]

b. *Personal Names.* Other personal names demonstrate that the polel and hiphil of *kûn* with a divine subject signify a crucial numinous occasion in human life: *kônanyāhû, y(*ᵉ*h)ôyāḵîn*; also the niphal form *nāḵōn.* Personal names based on the root *kn* plus a theophorous element are common in Akkadian,[23] at Mari,[24] in Ugaritic,[25] and in Phoenician.[26]

c. *'āḵēn.* Thierry[27] considers the asseverative *'āḵēn* a fossilized hiphil; most scholars (most recently *KBL*³) reject the association with *kûn.*

d. *A Star kywn?* In 5:26, Amos accuses Israel of "carrying about the *sikkûṯ* (of?) your king and the *kiyyûn* (of) your image, the star of your god." The Masoretes vocalized both nouns to suggest the reading *šiqqûṣ,* "abomination." The ancient versions indicate that the first colon used the word *sukkâ,* "(festal) booth" (or possibly

---

17. *GesB;* cf. *BLe,* §71x.
18. K. Koch, *Die Priesterschrift von Exodus 25 bis Leviticus 16. FRLANT,* N.S. 53[71] (1959), 34f.
19. *KBL*³: *kēn* IV.
20. M. Dahood, *Psalms II. AB,* XVII (³1979), 259.
21. *KBL*³.
22. *IPN,* 179, n. 2; 202, n. 1; *KBL*³, 461.
23. *AN,* 356b.
24. *APNM,* 221f.
25. *PNU,* 153.
26. Z. S. Harris, *A Grammar of the Phoenician Language. AOS,* 8 (1936), 110.
27. P. 4.

"image"; cf. Ugar. *sknt,* Akk. *šukkuttu*) and that the second used Akk. *kayyamānu*[28] in the aramaized form *kêwān,* "the constant one," an epithet of the planet Saturn. As the heavenly patron of kings, Saturn sees to the preservation of law and order on earth. The context (Am. 5:21ff., esp. v. 24) shows that the people castigated by the prophet expected that such rites, in conjunction with *zeḇaḥ* sacrifice, would bring divine *ṣᵉḏāqâ* to the cultic community and ensure their security in the land. For Amos, however, such an idolatrous cult achieves the very opposite.[29]

This initial survey of the lexical material, necessarily provisional, points to a lexeme denoting energetic, purposeful action, aimed at forming useful enduring places and institutions, with a secondary element asserting the reliability of statements.

II. Semitic Context. 1. *Distribution.* The biliteral root *kn* with a long medial vowel is widespread through all the Semitic languages. It has a broad range of meanings, from the everyday sense of "belonging to" (with the prep. *la/li/lᵉ*) to religious dicta concerning the endurance of the cult and of creation. It can even express ontological conceptions such as nature, becoming, and being. The root appears primarily as a verb, but (except in Arabic) factitive and causative stems are noticeably more common than the simple stem. Nominal derivatives are likewise attested everywhere in a variety of forms. In the absence of semantic studies, a general semantic plane can only be conjectured. A "basic meaning" of "upright" is proposed by *GesB* and G. J. Thierry, "be firm, straight" by *KBL*³; it must be noted, however, that the focus in most texts is not on a state but rather on making or becoming. What is emphasized is not stability but permanence and utility. If we try to reduce the various usages to a single common denominator, it would be: "call something into being in such a way that it fulfills its function (in the life of an individual, in society, or in the cosmos) independently and permanently."

2. *South Semitic.* In the South Semitic languages, the meaning appears to have broadened to "being" or "becoming" in general; on occasion, Arab. *kāna* can even be a mere copula (with a predicate).[30] In Ethiopic, we find not only *kōna,* "take place, become, exist," but also the theologically significant reduplicated form *kʷanana,* which can mean both "judge" and "rule."[31]

3. *Akkadian.* The range of meanings in Akkadian was probably narrower.[32] The simple stem *kânu,* "be or become permanent, trustworthy," can refer to the foundations of buildings as well as to testimony and laws. The D stem, "make permanent, stabilize, organize," is frequently used in "political" and cultic texts to describe the kingship,

---

28. *AHw,* II (1972), 420.
29. See the discussion in Koch, *Amos,* I, 182f.; II, 40f.
30. *WKAS,* I, 451-473.
31. *LexLingAeth,* 854-57, 861-65.
32. *AHw,* II, 438-440; *CAD,* VIII (1971), 159-171. The latter, however, treats *kânu* B separately as a West Semitic loanword.

throne, and scepter; in other contexts, it is used for the salutary intent of the human heart (*libbu*) or the success of outstanding human deeds. Such contexts suggest Hebrew usage,[33] as does the technical use of the D stem to mean "prepare for cultic use." As a nominal derivative, *kittu*(*m*),[34] "constancy, truth, faithfulness," is noteworthy; in many ways it is analogous to Heb. *mišpāṭ,* denoting the meaningful permanence of salubrious entities as well as the truth of statements and omens. Along with *mī/ēšaru*(*m*), "righteousness,"[35] *kittum,* the feminine of the adj. *kīnu*(*m*), "constant," represents the power of an ordered and orderly reality; it is conceived as an invisible entity and practically deified.[36]

4. *Northwest Semitic.* Understandably, the Northwest Semitic languages exhibit even greater affinity with the OT.

a. *Phoenician and Punic.* An impv. *kuṇa* appears as a Canaanite gloss in EA 147, 36; it refers to the appointment of a commander of the army. In Phoenician and Punic,[37] the verb is commonly used in the sense of "come into being, exist" or "belong to" (with *l*ᵉ); in this usage, *kn* occasionally takes the place of Heb. *hāyâ,* which is not found in Phoenician or Punic. It is also used specifically of institutions and "ideal" entities important for the stability of society. In corresponding syntagmemes, *kn* may mean the appearance of "evil in the land," but more often the good bestowed by the gods, primarily a plentiful supply of food but also offspring or "a good name for ever."[38] Also noteworthy is its use in royal ideology to express the endurance of a beneficent reign.[39] In Punic, it is also used for the office of temple overseers and market foremen.[40] With respect to the OT, its use (as a technical cultic term?) for the fulfillment of a vow should be mentioned.[41]

b. *Ugaritic.* In Ugaritic, too, the lexica translate *kn* as "be."[42] A survey of the texts, however, hardly supports so broad a translation. All the contexts are more restricted: *kn* refers to the absolute desire for an enduring line of descendants.[43] The longer form *knn* describes either the creation[44] or installation[45] of the gods Baʿal and ʿAnat by the high god El.[46] We also find a causative stem *škn,* probably meaning "make ready, create," which must be distinguished from *škn,* "dwell."[47] A nominal derivative *knt,*

33. See below.
34. *AHw,* II, 494f.; *CAD,* VIII, 468-472.
35. → יָשַׁר *yšr;* → צדק *ṣdq.*
36. H. Ringgren, *Word and Wisdom* (Lund, 1947), 53ff.
37. *DISO,* 117.
38. *KAI,* 26 A, I, 9, 14; I, 5, 15; *KAI,* 43, 15; 13, 17; 14, 8-11; 19, 10; 18, 6.
39. *KAI,* 11; 26 A, I, 16, 19.
40. *KAI,* 80, 1; 130, 3; 137, 2.
41. *KAI,* 40, 5.
42. *WUS,* no. 1335; *UT,* no. 1213.
43. *KTU,* 1.17 I, 25, 42; 1.14, 15; 1.14, 11, with the noun *mknt.*
44. *WUS; UT.*
45. *CML,* 145.
46. *KTU,* 1.3 V, 36; 1.4 IV, 48; 1.10 III, 6.
47. Dietrich-Loretz-Sanmartín.

which *WUS* is probably correct in translating "appointed sacrifice," appears in two texts.[48] In the second, Otto Eissfeldt translates it "permanence."[49]

c. *Aramaic*. Old Aramaic appears to have used the root infrequently. In later Jewish Aramaic, only the reduplicated stems are used, the pael in the sense of "keep straight," used of concrete objects like the walls of a building as well as thoughts and ideas. Nominal derivatives like *kêwān,* "that which is upright," and *kawwān(ûṯ)ā',* "intention," are more common.[50] Usage becomes more nuanced later in Syriac, where derivatives of the root range in meaning from "righteous(ness)" (*kē'nā, kē'nûṯā*) to "natural" or "nature" (*kēyānāyā, kēyānā*).[51] The wide range of usage in Mandaic[52] may have been influenced by Akkadian.

III. Common Usage. The OT uses *kûn* relatively infrequently in the language of everyday life, and then only in specific circumstances. The polel and the corresponding hithpolel are used of building a city to dwell in (Nu. 21:27; Hab. 2:12; Ps. 107:36; Prov. 24:3) or spanning a bow to shoot (Ps. 7:13[12]; 11:2; 21:13[12]), and in general of preparing means to destroy an enemy (Isa. 51:13; Ps. 59:5[4]). Wisdom also uses these forms when it appears necessary to reassert the certainty of something (Job 8:8).[53] The hiphil and hophal refer to preparation of a specific meal or of food in general (Gen. 43:16; Prov. 6:8; 24:27; 30:25), preparations for war with weapons, troops, and strategy (Jer. 46:14; 51:12; Ezk. 7:14; 38:7; Nah. 2:4[3]; Prov. 21:31), and preparation of an ambush in a private dispute (Ps. 57:7[6]; Job 15:35). They are also used to assert that a statement (1 S. 23:22) or pronunciation (Jgs. 12:6) is correct. In the postexilic period, the polel falls into almost total disuse and the hiphil appears to take over its usage; the ratio of polel to hiphil is 1 (2?) to 7 in Job, 1 to 45 in the Chronicler. Now *hēḵîn* is also used with objects such as clothing (Job 27:16f.), seats in the marketplace (Job 29:7), or even a gallows (Est. 6:4; 7:9f.). The niphal appears in similar contexts: it is used of a solid house (Jgs. 16:29) and preparations for war (Ezk. 38:7), but also of a true word (Gen. 41:32; Dt. 13:15[14]; 17:4). The fem. ptcp. *n^eḵônâ* becomes an independent substantive denoting the trustworthiness of someone's words (Ps. 5:10[9]; Job 42:7f.).

In summary, we may state that in common usage *kûn* is limited to securing the basic necessities of life, preparations for war, and asserting the truth of statements. The appropriateness of categorizing the third usage as "secondary"[54] is dubious. For the Hebrews, the reliability of certain statements and traditions may have been as important as the solidity of their houses and the security of their cities, so that the use of *kûn* in both contexts may well be primary.

---

48. *KTU,* 1.23, 54; 1.65, 17.
49. O. Eissfeldt, *El im ugaritischen Pantheon. BSAW,* 98/4 (1951), 60, n. 3.
50. *WTM,* II, 306-7; Jastrow, 622, 631.
51. *LexSyr,* 321f.
52. *MdD,* 207f.
53. M. Dahood, "Hebrew-Ugaritic Lexicography III," *Bibl,* 46 (1965), 329.
54. *THAT.*

IV. Technical Usage in the Cult. From the earliest occurrences in the historical books (Nu. 23:1,29; Josh. 3:17; 4:3f.) to the latest, the hiphil and hophal (never the polel!) are used for ritually correct preparation of sacrifices, cultic sites, holy persons, and sacred rites (Dt. 19:3; 1 K. 5:32[18]; 6:19; Ezk. 40:43) required of all the devout. Yahweh himself can *hēḵîn* a cultic or sacrificial site (Ex. 23:20; Isa. 14:21; 30:33; Zeph. 1:7). The sinful cult of an idol is also described in these terms (Isa. 40:20; Zec. 5:11). Some 50 out of the 110 occurrences of the hiphil are of this nature; 30 of these are in 1 and 2 Chronicles, primarily in the context of David's preparations for building the temple and Solomon's completion of the project (1 Ch. 22,29; 2 Ch. 1–3).

In such contexts, the niphal is used either reflexively to describe the subject's own preparations for a cultic encounter with God (Ex. 19:11,15; 34:2; Am. 4:12) or passively for the mountain of God, prepared by God as the cultic center of the world (Isa. 2:2; Mic. 4:1). The cultic association is even stronger in the nominal derivatives *māḵôn, mᵉḵônâ, tᵉḵûnâ,* and *yāḵîn.*[55] It is noteworthy that there is no trace of this usage in the Psalter except for the reference to prayer in Ps. 141:2.

The cultic usage of this lexeme, found also in other Semitic languages,[56] derives from the conviction that cultic acts are the source of all life and prosperity for those who share the cult. Therefore creative, purposeful preparation is necessary, on the part of God as well the worshipper, to guarantee the success of the rite.

V. Anthropological Usage. 1. *Psalms and Wisdom Literature.* The hiphil and polel of *kûn* are used in the Psalms (frequently) and Wisdom (less often) for the way the condition of an individual or group is affected by conduct that promotes or impugns the well-being of the community; this usage reflects the Hebrew notion that actions carry their own consequences. Since right actions presuppose right thoughts and understanding, *kûn* can also be used for the conscious intention of one's own intellect (*lēḇ*).

According to wisdom teaching, those who are *ṣaddîq* by their conduct establish (Prov. 21:19 [hiphil]; 4:26 [niphal]) their way.[57] The same point can be made without an expressed object: the honest "endure for ever" (Prov. 12:29); through them their posterity is also established (Ps. 102:29[28]; Job 21:8). The wicked, however, who bend (polel) the bow against the innocent thereby prepare (hiphil) the weapon for their own death (Ps. 7:13f.[12f.]; cf. 57:7[6]). In their hearts they prepare a *mirmâ* that returns to destroy the doer (Job 15:35); they prepare their day of darkness through their own hand (Job 15:23; cf. 18:12). It is therefore possible, using the verb absolutely, to say that the wicked are not established or are unable to establish themselves (Ps. 140:12[11]; the niphal may be either passive or reflexive). What they gain through their labors they unwittingly prepare for those who are *ṣaddîq* (Job 27:16f.). The preparation of the intellect and will (*lēḇ*) necessary for doing what is right consists in attending to the counsel of the wise (Prov. 8:5;[58] 20:18; 22:18). Heedless slanderers, however, will not endure (Ps. 140:12[11]).

55. See I above.
56. See II above.
57. → דרך *dereḵ,* III, 286-88.
58. See *BHS.*

What wisdom treats as an immanent nexus of cause and effect the Psalter associates with God. The "heart" is rightly ordered when the *rûaḥ* is faithful (*ne'emān*) to God (Ps. 78:8; cf. v. 37; 112:7; 1 S. 7:3; Job 11:13). The Chronicler, too, associates steadfastness of *lēḇ* with "seeking Yahweh" (*dāraš*: 2 Ch. 12:14; 19:3; 30:19; cf. 20:33; 1 Ch. 29:18; Ezr. 7:10). One's own way is accordingly ordered "before Yahweh" by right actions (2 Ch. 27:6). On the other hand, one can also say that Yahweh, understood as the ultimate cause of human actions, strengthens the *lēḇ* (Ps. 10:17; cf. 57:8[7]; Prov. 16:3) and orders the steps of mortals (Ps. 37:23; 40:3[2]; 119:133), making their *dereḵ* steadfast (Ps. 119:5). He thus brings to fruition what the *lēḇ* has conceived (Prov. 16:9) and establishes "the work of our hands" (Ps. 90:17). It is therefore a good idea to commit one's work to Yahweh (Prov. 16:3). Conversely, he prepares judgment for scoffers (Prov. 19:29). Since divine power encompasses human actions from the moment they are conceived by the mind to the time they yield their fruit, Yahweh is addressed as the one who brings the evil of the wicked to fruition (*gmr*), just as he establishes the righteous (polel: Ps. 7:10[9]).

The anthropological usage of this lexeme thus provides an eloquent illustration of the Hebrew conviction that actions are linked inescapably with their consequences as well as of the "panentheistic" notion that human existence is set within the domain of Yahweh's governance.

2. *Dead Sea Scrolls.* In the Dead Sea scrolls, this tendency is heightened to belief in the predestination of human actions, a notion often expressed by the hiphil of *kûn*. The lexeme becomes the key concept for the relationship between mortals and God. "A man's way is not his to control, nor can he make his footsteps endure" (hiphil: 1QH 15:13; 1QS 11:10). Of their own accord, mortal subjects cannot do what is good and thus ensure a corresponding fate: "How could dust establish its steps?" (1QH 15:21). As creator, God not only frames the purpose of the *lēḇ* but also controls the resulting steps (1QH 7:13); cf. 1QH 1:28. "Thou hast formed (*yṣr*) my *rûaḥ* and shaped (*kûn* hiphil) its works" (1QH 15:22). Even in the womb, those who are *ṣaddîq* are prepared (hiphil) for the day of God's pleasure (1QH 15:15; cf. 1:19; 2:17; etc.); they go in the way of the divine *lēḇ* and are therefore established (niphal: 1QH 4:22; cf. 1QS 3:9). Even the wicked, who cannot refrain from evil, are predestined (1QH 15:19). Such "preparation" apparently comprehends everything that is, transcending the realm of human existence (1QS 3:15; 11:11).

VI. Creation. 1. *Psalter and Late Wisdom.* Hymnic sections of the Psalter and late wisdom praise Yahweh for what he establishes in creation, usually employing the hiphil, rarely the polel, and hardly ever the passive niphal. The verb *hēḵîn* is never used of creation as a whole but of extraordinary works that bring beneficent order to the rest of creation, such as the heavens (Ps. 89:3[2]; Prov. 3:19; 8:27), the light of sun and moon (Ps. 8:4[3]; 74:16), the mountains (Ps. 65:7[6]), and above all the earth as *tēḇēl*, arable land moistened by rainfall (Ps. 24:2; 68:10[9]; Jer. 10:12; etc.). Strictly speaking, *heḵîn* does not denote an act of creation as such but the shaping and establishing of an entity already present. Thus Yahweh made the earth in order (*l*^{e} + inf.) to form and establish it (hiphil: Jer. 33:2). The making of the *'ereṣ* is followed by the *hēḵîn* of the *tēbēl* (Jer. 51:15). The consequential and purposeful nature of divine *kûn* is clear in Isa. 45:18:

[Yahweh] . . . who formed (*yṣr*) the earth and made (*ʿśh*) it,
who established (*kônēn*) it.
He did not create (*brʾ*) it a *tōhû;*
he formed it to be inhabited.

The statement of purpose ("formed for habitation") in the second line probably parallels *kônēn* in the first. The positive aspect of *kûn* (hiphil and polel), implying the preservation and enhancement of life, explains why the passages under discussion often cite the myth of God's battle with the primeval sea in antithesis to God's *hēkîn*. God established the earth above the tumultuous seas (Ps. 24:1f.; cf. Jer. 10:12f. par. 51:15f.). Having slain Leviathan and related monsters, Yahweh established light and the sun as forces of order (Ps. 74:12-16) or the mountains to maintain the cosmos (Ps. 65:7f.[6f.]). He brought into being *ṣedeq* and *mišpāṭ* as "guarantors" (*māḵôn*) of his throne (Ps. 89:10-15[9-14]).

Its functional sense of purpose explains why the usage of *hēkîn* combines primeval and present-day acts of creation, the governance of the seasons, and (less often) the governance of sacred history. Like the fruitful earth, Yahweh first made (*ʿśh*) Israel and then established (*kwn* hiphil) it as his own people (Dt. 32:6; 2 S. 7:24); the same usage describes his establishment of Zion as the site of his cultic presence upon earth (Ps. 48:9[8]; 87:5; this usage is closely related to the cultic usage discussed in IV above). Just as God prepared the fruitful earth in the beginning, so in the present he prepares rain (Ps. 147:8), grain and food (Ps. 65:10[9]; 78:20; Job 38:41), and shelter (Ps. 107:36). And he shapes every human being in the womb as an individual (Job 31:15 [reading the polel]; Ps. 119:73). The creative establishment of vital cosmic and historical phenomena is ascribed more particularly to attributes of Yahweh such as his strength (Ps. 65:7[6]), his *ṭôḇâ* (Ps. 68:11[10]), or his *ʾᵉmûnâ* (Ps. 89:3[2]; 119:90); in Wisdom Literature, they are also ascribed to *ḥoḵmâ* (Prov. 3:19; 8:27; cf. Jer. 10:12 par. 51:15; 1QH 1:14, 19). On the other hand, such entitities can themselves be looked upon as creatures established by God, e.g., *ḥoḵmâ* (Job 28:27) and *mêšārîm* (Ps. 99:4).[59]

The creative aspect of the lexeme, already noted in Ugaritic,[60] does not arise from an authentically Israelite idea; it was borrowed from the Canaanites. It is nevertheless noteworthy that the Psalms associate it with God's battle against the chaotic sea. This association is not found at Ugarit, where Baal's battle with the sea has nothing to do with creation; *kn* is used instead for acts of creation by the peaceful patriarchal god El.

2. *Temple of Solomon.* The ten *mᵉḵônôṯ* in the temple of Solomon present a special problem. The word is usually translated "wheeled lavers"[61] (RSV "stands"), a meaning that has nothing to do with the root *kûn.* Each of these objects was a metal box roughly 2 meters (6 ft.) on a side and 1 meter (3 ft.) high, decorated with lions, oxen, and

---

59. On the star *kêwān* as mediator of *ṣᵉdāqâ,* see I.4.d above.
60. See II above.
61. Most recently by *KBL*³.

cherubim, supporting a laver with a capacity of about 920 liters (240 gals.)[62] or 1575 liters (415 gal.)[63] and mounted on four wheels (1 K. 7:27-39). Since each must have weighed at least two and a half tons,[64] it is debatable whether the ten objects were actually moved within the temple or the wheels merely symbolized movement.

According to 2 K. 16:17, these objects were stripped of their mythological trimmings by Ahaz; the Chronicler reduces them to basins in which the sacrificial animals were washed (2 Ch. 4:6,14). Excavations on Cyprus[65] and at Megiddo[66] have unearthed smaller and simpler parallels, showing that such "vehicles" played a role in Canaanite religion. On Zion, there were five along each of the long walls of the temple; together with the altar and *m*ᵉ*nôrâ,* they were the most striking furnishings of the Solomonic temple and most therefore have played an important role in the cult. Undoubtedly they are earthly likenesses of heavenly entities (clouds? constellations?) responsible for rain.[67] But why were there so many in the temple? It seems that Sigmund Mowinckel[68] has hit upon the only plausible explanation: during the autumn festival at Jerusalem, creation as an actualization of the mythological battle with the primeval sea was regularly celebrated in symbolic dramatic presentations, which included such rain-chariots accompanying the arrival of the deity. Since in the context of divine creation *hēḵîn* is associated with Yahweh's battle with the sea,[69] the term *m*ᵉ*ḵônâ* is best explained as involving a *mem* prefix with instrumental meaning: "that which prepares [the rain and earth]." Ps. 65, a "harvest thanksgiving," supports this interpretation, citing first Yahweh's victory over the sea and then his beneficent visitation of the earth (vv. 10b, 12[9b, 11]):

The canal of God is full of water.
Thou preparest (*kûn* hiphil) their grain, for permanently [or "so" (*kēn*)] thou dost
prepare it [the earth: *t*ᵉ*ḵîneḥâ*; polel?]. . . .
Thou crownest the year of thy bounty;
the tracks of thy chariot drip with fatness.

VII. Throne and Kingdom. 1. *Davidic Kingship.* At certain high points in the history of David and Solomon, the historical books state that with this or that event God established, prepared, or secured the Davidic kingship — however one wishes to translate the hiphil or polel of *kûn.* Thus we read in the heart of Nathan's prophecy (2 S. 7:12f.):

When your [David's] days are fulfilled,
you will lie down with your fathers.
And I will raise up (*hēqîm*) your seed after you . . .
and I will establish (*hēḵîn*) his kingdom.

---

62. E. Würthwein, *Die Bücher der Könige. ATD,* XI/1 (1977), *in loc.*
63. Noth, *in loc.*
64. Busink, 349.
65. *AOB,* 505f.
66. *ANEP,* no. 587.
67. Noth, 162 translates: "rainbearers."
68. S. Mowinckel, *Psalmenstudien,* II: *Das Thronbesteigungsfest Jahwäs und der Ursprung der Eschatologie* (1922, repr. Amsterdam, 1961).
69. See above.

He shall build a house 'for me,'
and I will establish (*kônēn*) the throne of his kingdom for ever.

As elsewhere, the polel denotes an action that accompanies the purpose stated by the hiphil; the permanence of the throne establishes the kingship. The necessary condition is the guarantee of succession promised by Yahweh. This theme is taken up once more by the conclusion of the Court History of David (1 K. 2:12): "So Solomon [finally and conclusively] sat upon the throne of David his father; and his kingdom was firmly established (*tikkôn me'ōḏ*)." It is also taken up by the second conclusion (v. 46): "So the kingship was established (*nāḵôn*) in the power of Solomon" (cf. Solomon's own words in v. 24). The account of David's rise to power appears also to have ended with such an historico-theological summary (2 S. 5:12): "And David perceived that Yahweh had established [hiphil] him as king over Israel and that his kingship had been exalted (*niśśē'*) for the sake of [Yahweh's] people Israel." It is noteworthy that David does not perceive this when he is anointed (v. 3) but only after he has captured Jerusalem for his residence and built his palace (vv. 6ff.!). In the case of Saul, too, 1 S. 13:13 (cf. 20:31) presupposes that the divine establishment of *mamlāḵâ* was not the result of anointing but would take place in a subsequent reaffirmation.

Possession of the city of Jerusalem, dynastic continuity, and an enduring throne appear to go together for these traditions, which probably derive from the environment of the court. But their association also has a profound religious significance; it is the result of a specific creative act on the part of Yahweh. It is therefore a theme of prayer and praise in the royal psalms (Ps. 89:3,38[2,37]) and can even be thought of as the substance of the Davidic covenant (v. 5[4]).

Wisdom Literature and the Prophets treat this association somewhat differently. A king who is true to his people, who rejects the wicked and supports the poor, by his actions and their inevitable consequences establishes his throne forever (*yikkôn lā'aḏ*: Prov. 29:14; 16:12; 25:5; Isa. 9:6[7]; 16:5).

2. *Divine Kingship.* The establishment of the Israelite kingship through an enduring throne upon earth has its parallel in the enduring divine kingship in heaven. There Yahweh established his throne in the beginning (*nāḵôn mē'āz,* "from then on," usually mistranslated "from the first"!); its endurance reflects that of the fruitful earth below (Ps. 93:2; 96:10; 1 Ch. 16:30) and makes it possible for him to vouchsafe *ṣeḏāqâ* to his worshippers on earth (Ps. 9:8[7]; 103:17-19). The entities *ṣeḏeq* and *mišpāṭ* are even called the enduring foundations (*māḵôn*) of the divine throne (Ps. 89:15[14]; 97:2).[70]

Yahweh's kingship, which he establishes permanently for his own sake and the sake of his creation, is associated (in the preexilic period) both with primeval creation and with the contemporary cult on Mt. Zion. This is attested by Solomon's prayer at the dedication of the Temple (1 K. 8:12f.) in its ancient form, preserved in LXX^{L}:

---

70. On the Egyptian origin of the throne structure, see H. Brunner, "Gerechtigkeit als Fundament des Thrones," *VT,* 8 (1958), 426-28; on Akkadian parallels, see G. Ahlström, *Psalm 89* (Lund, 1959), 53-55.

Yahweh has established (*hēḵîn*) the sun in the heavens.
He has said that he would dwell in thick darkness.
[And so] I have built a house of dominion (*z*ᵉ*ḇul*) for thee,
an enduring foundation (*māḵôn*) for thy throne for ever.

The *māḵôn* of the divine throne above Zion can hardly be distinguished from *ṣeḏeq* and *mišpāṭ,* its buttresses or guarantees of permanence,[71] especially since the psalms in question link both entities with God's enthronement on Zion (Ps. 97:1-8; 89:15f.[14f.]). The language that speaks of the *hēḵîn* of Yahweh as king lends Zion and its cult a mediating role and hence cosmic significance. Even the sun and dark clouds are so established as to serve Yahweh's sovereignty through the rites of the Jerusalem temple, whence they "maintain" the earth and the human race. Thus faith in Yahweh's kingship as a dynamic force closes the circle initiated by *hēḵîn* whenever the lexeme is used with a divine subject.

Koch

71. See above.

כּוֹס *kôs*

Contents: I. Etymology, Occurrences, Meaning. II. The Object. III. Usage: 1. Secular; 2. Religious; 3. Origin of Religious Usage.

kôs. H. Bardtke and B. Reicke, "Becher," *BHHW,* I (1962), 208f.; A.-G. Barrois, *Manuel d'archéologie biblique,* I (Paris, 1939); Z. Ben-Hayyi, *The Literary and Oral Traditions of Hebrew and Aramaic amongst the Samaritans,* II (Jerusalem, 1957); W. Beyerlin, *Die Rettung der Bedrängten in den Feindpsalmen der Einzelnen auf institutionelle Zusammenhänge untersucht. FRLANT,* N.S. 81[99](1970); Y. Brand, *Ceramics in Talmudic Literature* (Jerusalem, 1953) [Heb.]; H. A. Brongers, "Der Zornesbecher," *OTS,* 15 (1969), 177-192; G. H. Dalman, *AuS,* IV (1935), 390f.; VII (1942), 227-29; *idem, Jesus-Jeschua* (1922, repr. Darmstadt, 1967); J. G. Davies, "The Cup of Wrath and the Cup of Blessing," *Theology,* 51 (1948), 178-180; M. Dietrich and O. Loretz, "Der Vertag zwischen Šuppiluliuma and Niqmandu," *WO,* 3 (1966), 232-39; S. Fraenkel, *Die aramäischen Fremdwörter im Arabischen* (Leiden, 1886); L. Goppelt, "ποτήριον," *TDNT,* VI, 148-158; H. Gressmann, "Der Festbecher," in *Beiträge zur Religionsgeschichte und Archäologie Palästinas. Festschrift E. Sellin* (1927), 55-62; *idem,* "Η κοινωνια των δαιμονιων," *ZNW,* 20 (1921), 224-230; *idem, Der Ursprung der israelitisch-jüdischen Eschatologie. FRLANT,* 6 (1905); M. Haran, "The Reliefs on the Sides of the Sarcophagus of Ahiram King of Byblos," *BIES,* 19 (1955), 56-65 [Heb.], II-III [Eng. summary]; A. M. Honeyman, "The Pottery Vessels of the OT," *PEQ,* 71 (1939), 76-90; H. Jahnow, *Das hebräische Leichenlied im Rahmen der Volkerdichtung. BZAW,* 36 (1923); J. L. Kelso, *The Ceramic Vocabulary of the OT. BASORSup,* 5f. (1948); T. Klauser and S. Grün, "Becher," *RAC,* II (1954), 37-62; E. W. Klimowsky, "Symbols on Ancient Jewish Coins," *The Dating and Meaning of Ancient Jewish Coins and Symbols. Numismatic Studies and Researches,* 2 (1958), 81-97; W. Lotz, "Das Sinnbild des Bechers," *NKZ,* 28 (1917), 396-407; R. Otto, *The*

I. Etymology, Occurrences, Meaning. The noun *kôs* appears 31 times in the MT of the OT with the meaning "cup, goblet." It has cognates in many Semitic languages (Ugar. *ks,* Akk. *kāsu(m)*, Aram. *ks* (*kās*), Syr. and Mand. *kāsā,* Arab. *ka'su,* Tigre *kas*). The LXX always translates the word with *potḗrion.* It also interprets the *k*^e^*lê zāhāḇ* of Est. 1:7 as *potḗria chrysá kaí argyrá.* The *potḗrion* of Lam. 2:13 is probably due to an error confusing *kym* and *kws,* which resemble each other in some scripts.

II. The Object. The noun *kôs* denotes a drinking vessel, variable in size (Ezk. 23:32), for wine (Jer. 35:5; Prov. 23:31) or water (2 S. 12:3); such vessels were used by rich (Gen. 40:11,13,21) and poor (2 S. 12:3). They might therefore be executed with high artistry in gold (Jer. 51:7) or simply made of clay (Ezk. 23:33f.[?]). One possible form, a lotus blossom, is mentioned in 1 K. 7:26 par. 2 Ch. 4:5. This information is in part confirmed and in part supplemented by extrabiblical and postbiblical texts. As in the Bible, the materials mentioned include gold[1] and clay,[2] but also silver,[3] copper or bronze,[4] and stone.[5] Although there was a normal size, the weights listed by Manfred Dietrich and Otto Loretz[6] suggest considerable variation. Although the assignment of particular forms to the various terms is not absolutely certain, archaeological evidence supplements the textual record. The noun *kôs* includes both bowl-shaped and stemmed vessels.[7] Cups of a material other than clay are very rare in Israel and Palestine.[8] There are Egyptian faience goblets shaped like lotus blossoms.[9]

III. Usage. 1. *Secular.* As a rule, an individual would drink wine or water from a *kôs*; this does not rule out the possibility of using it for other purposes such as giving animals something to drink (2 S. 12:3).[10] A special role was played by the cup of

---

Kingdom of God and the Son of Man (Eng. trans., Boston, ²1957); J. L. Palache, *Semantic Notes on the Hebrew Lexicon* (Eng. trans., Leiden, 1959); L. J. Rachmani, "כּוֹס," *EMiqr,* IV (1962), 50f.; A. Reifenberg, *Ancient Jewish Coins* (Jerusalem, ⁴1965); H. Ringgren, "Vredens kalk," *SEÅ,* 17 (1952), 19-30; D. Ruiz-Baxdanelli, *Le symbolisme de la coupe dans la bible* (Lic., Fribourg, 1971); E. D. Van Buren, *The Flowing Vase and the God with Streams* (Berlin, 1933).

1. Dietrich-Loretz, 235; *AHw,* II (1972), 454b; cf. Est. 1:7 LXX; Mishnah *Tamid* iii.4; *Me'il.* v. 1, 3.
2. Dietrich-Loretz, 235.
3. Dietrich-Loretz, 235; *KTU,* 3.1, 31; *AHw,* II, 454b; *AP,* 61, 4.
4. Dietrich-Loretz, 235; *AHw,* II, 454b; *AP,* 51, 12; 61, 1.
5. Mishnah *Para* iii.2.
6. Pp. 235f.
7. Kelso, 19.
8. *BRL*², index, *s.v.* "Becher."
9. H. Schäfer, *Die ägyptischen Prunkgefässe mit aufgesetzten Randverzierungen* (Leipzig, 1903), 13.
10. Cf. Dietrich-Loretz, 235; Mishnah *Tamid* iii.4.

consolation given to mourners (Jer. 16:7) as part of the meal that played an important role in rites of condolence (Jer. 16:7; Ezk. 24:17,22; Hos. 9:4).[11]

2. *Religious.* Prophetic texts from the period just before the exile and from the exilic period use the image of a cup that must be drained to describe the judgment that awaits Judah and the nations (Jer. 25:15-29), Nebuchadnezzar (Hab. 2:16), Judah (Ezk. 23:31-34), Edom (Jer. 49:12; Lam. 4:21), or has already befallen the nations (Jer. 51:7) and Judah (Isa. 51:17-23). In the hand of the person who is to drink from the cup, its contents, which come from Yahweh's hand (Jer. 25:15,17; 51:7; Hab. 2:16; Ezk. 23:31; Isa. 51:17), may be literal (wine: Jer. 25:15; 51:7) or figurative (wrath: Jer. 25:15; Isa. 51:17,22). Those who drink of it lose their senses. Being drunk (Jer. 25:27; Ezk. 23:33; Isa. 51:21; Lam. 4:21), they stagger (*gāʿaš*: Jer. 25:16), reel (*rāʿal*: Hab. 2:16;[12] *tarʿēlâ*: Isa. 51:17,22), act as though crazed (*hll*: Jer. 25:16; 51:7), strip themselves bare (*ʿrh*: Lam. 4:21), vomit, fall, and rise no more (Jer. 25:27) — clearly degrading behavior, as Hab. 2:16 says directly. Here, too, interpretation can color the imagery: this drunkenness evokes horror and desolation (Ezk. 23:33). Although they do not use the word *kôs,* the threats against Nineveh (Nah. 3:11), Judah (Jer. 13:13), and the nations (Ob. 16) reflect the same idea. The liturgy of Ps. 75, however, describes in great detail how the cult prophet proclaims judgment against the wicked in the land:[13] from the cup in Yahweh's hand they must drain the foaming wine to the dregs (v. 9[8]). Such a prophecy of judgment has probably been turned into a declaration of confidence in Ps. 11, a prayer. Here again we note that the contents of the cup are interpreted rather than described (v. 6). In the other passages (Ps. 16:5; 23:5; 116:13), the cup plays a positive role. Although they are far less colorful than the texts describing judgment, they show that the psalmist drinks salvation from the cup. It is reasonable to assume that we are dealing with the same cup, which brings judgment to the *rāšāʿ* and deliverance to the *ṣaddîq,* especially since the first two passages appear in hymnic prayers and Ps. 116:13 also speaks of the psalmist's assurance of salvation.

3. *Origin of Religious Usage.* Apart from the commonplace of the deity with a cup, H. A. Brongers has shown that caution is in order in the use of extrabiblical parallels to explain biblical usage. He is wrong, however, in his pessimistic conclusion that the cup is nothing more than a metaphor. It is noteworthy that this image appears only in a restricted environment. We find it in texts of the late preexilic and exilic periods (subject to the difficulty of dating certain Psalms), on which its use in texts outside the OT is clearly dependent (1QpHab 11:14f.: Hab. 2:16; Ps.Sol. 8:14f.: Jer. 32:15 LXX; Rev. 14:18: Jer. 51:7; Rev. 14:10: Jer. 25:15; Rev. 16:19: Isa. 51:17; Rev. 17:4: Jer.

11. Cf. Jahnow, 7, 31.

12. *BHS*; given a different meaning by W. Rudolph, *Habakkuk. KAT,* XIII/3 (1975), 221.

13. Jörg Jeremias, *Kultprophetie und Gerichtsverkündigung in der späten Königszeit Israels. WMANT,* 35 (1970), 118f.

51:7; Rev. 18:3: Jer. 25:15). Furthermore, all these texts have some relationship to the cult. The association of the Psalms and Lam. 4:21 with worship is evident. As priests, Jeremiah and Ezekiel were clearly familiar with the professional lore of the priesthood. Scholars have identified Habakkuk, Nahum, and Obadiah as cult prophets. Deutero-Isaiah uses the genre of the cultic lament (Isa. 51:17-23).

Of the cups in the Second Temple,[14] one must have played a particularly important role; otherwise it would not have been honored by representation on the Arch of Titus.[15] There is no reason not to see in it the prototype of the cup that symbolizes the theocratic state on many coins from the period of the first Judaeo-Roman War (65-70 A.D.).[16] Not only do Pss. 11, 16, 23, 75, and 116 speak of drinking in the temple, but so does Ob. 16; it is reasonable, therefore, to assume that this metaphor derives from the language of the cult. Beyerlin has established that Pss. 11 and 23 have to do with the divine judgment to which those who are wrongly accused appeal. Drinking from the cup determines guilt or innocence; it means salvation or condemnation. This is where we must look for the concrete situation to which these texts allude.[17]

G. Mayer

14. Mishnah *Tamid* iii.4; *Meʿil.* v. 1; cf. Josephus *BJ* vi.388.
15. *AOB,* no. 509.
16. Y. Meshorer, *Jewish Coins of the Second Temple Period* (Eng. trans., Tel Aviv, 1976), nos. 148, 151, 152, 154, 155, 158, 159, 163, 164; cf. Klimowsky, 87f.
17. See also I. Engnell, *Studies in Divine Kingship in the Ancient Near East* (Uppsala, 1943), 210; Ringgren.

כזב *kzb* I; כָּזָב *kāzāḇ*; אַכְזָב *ʾakzāḇ*; כִּדְבָה *kiḏbâ*; כָּזְבִּי *kozbî*; אַכְזִיב *ʾakzîḇ*; כְּזִיב *keziḇ*; כּוֹזֵבָא *kôzēḇāʾ*

Contents: I. General: 1. Cognates; 2. Proper Names; 3. Statistics and Syntax; 4. Basic Meaning; 5. LXX. II. OT Usage: 1. Verb; 2. Nouns. III. Theology: 1. Inherent Falsehood; 2. Avoidable Falsehood.

I. General.

1. *Cognates.* The lexica generally translate the root *kzb* as "lie" (verb and noun), "lying," "liar." It is distinct from the root *kzb* II,[1] "be abundant, magnificent."[2] The

kzb. M. A. Klopfenstein, *Die Lüge nach dem AT* (Zurich, 1964), esp. 176-254; *idem,* "כזב *kzb* lügen," *THAT,* I, 817-823; H. Conzelmann, "ψεῦδος," *TDNT,* IX, 594-603, esp. 597-99.

1. Equivalent to *kazābu* I in *AHw,* II (1972), 467.
2. The roots are still lumped together by *GesTh,* 674; *GesB, s.v.*

root *kzb* I is common in Arabic (*kaḏaba*).[3] It is found in Imperial Aramaic (*kdb* II, *kdbh, kzb*)[4] and is very common in Jewish Aramaic (*k^e^ḏaḇ, kîḏbā', kaddāḇā', kazbānā', kāzāḇ*),[5] as well as Syriac[6] and Mandaic.[7] It is not attested in Ugaritic; the Ugaritic name *bn kzbn*[8] is discussed below. It appears as a foreign word in the El Amarna tablets,[9] but is otherwise unknown in Akkadian. It may also appear in Hebrew in Lachish ostracon VIII (reading uncertain) and once in Biblical Aramaic (Dnl. 2:9).[10] The root is therefore restricted to West Semitic, where it is very common in various substantival and verbal forms.

2. *Proper Names.* Nu. 25:15,18 mention a Midianite woman named *kozbî* (Sam. *kzbyt*). *GesTh* (*s.v. kozbî*) and *GesB* (*s.v. kzb*) still derive this personal name from *kzb* I, "lie." The homonymous root *kzb* II (= *AHw kazābu* I), "be abundant, magnificent," however, is common in Akkadian personal names.[11] The Ugaritic personal name (*bn*) *kzbn*[12] also derives from *kzb* II.[13] The epithet *bn kzb'* (with orthographic variants) applied to Bar Kokhba probably also derives from *kzb* II ("the magnificent")[14] and was later reinterpreted in the sense of *kzb* I ("liar"). Most scholars today therefore derive the feminine name *kozbî* from *kzb* II.[15]

The situation is different in the case of the various toponyms based on *kzb* (6 occurrences in the MT), which are usually considered to be of pre-Israelite Canaanite origin. Mic. 1:14 mentions *'aḵzîḇ,* a city in southern Judah identical with the *'aḵzîḇ* of Josh. 15:44. Josh. 19:29 and Jgs. 1:31 speak of a city bearing the same name in the territory of Asher. The Judahite *'aḵzîḇ* may also appear in one of the Lachish ostraca;[16] the northern *'aḵzîḇ* is clearly mentioned in the Sennacherib prism.[17] The town of *k^e^zîḇ* in Gen. 38:5 is identified with the southern *'aḵzîḇ,* as is (*'anšê*) *kōzēḇā'* in 1 Ch. 4:22. These toponyms are generally derived from *kzb* I, "lie," with the meaning "[place by the] deceptive [i.e., dry] watercourse,"[18] and are associated with the noun *'aḵzāḇ*.

For several reasons, however, the possibility of deriving (some of?) these toponyms

---

3. *WKAS,* 90ff.
4. *DISO,* 115, 117.
5. *WTM, s.v.*
6. See *LexSyr, s.v.*
7. See *MdD, s.v. kdb* I.
8. *UT,* no. 1214.
9. Cf. *AHw,* II, 467, *s.v. kazābu* II; *kazbūtu.*
10. See II.2.c below.
11. Cf. *AHw, s.v. kazbum*; *AN,* 249.
12. *UT,* no. 1214.
13. Cf. *KBL*³, *s.v. kzb* II; *PNU,* 29.152.
14. Cf. F. Nötscher, "Bar Kochba, Bar Kosba: der Sternsohn, der Prächtige," *VT,* 11 (1961), 449-451.
15. Cf. *KBL*³, *s.v. kozbî* and *kzb* II.
16. Lachish ostracon VIII, vol. 1 (*'kzb*); but cf. Klopfenstein, *Die Lüge nach dem AT,* nn. 770, 1208.
17. II, 40; *ANET,* 287.
18. See, e.g., M. Noth, *Das Buch Josua. HAT,* VII (²1953), 142.

from *kzb* II, "be abundant," should not be ruled out totally. Even if it should turn out to be true that the noun *'akzāb* always and invariably refers to a (deceitful) watercourse (but cf. II.2.b below), the association of the toponyms with this noun is by no means as direct as is commonly assumed, as we can see from the forms *kᵉzîḇ* (Gen. 38:5) and *kōzēḇā'* (1 Ch. 4:22). In Josh. 15:44, LXX^B reads *Kezib* for *'akzîḇ,* and in Josh. 19:29 *Echozob*; it appears therefore not to reflect the pronunciation *'akzîḇ* in either passage.

At many sites in Palestine, it is very common for a wadi to flow only in the rainy season and to be dry at other times. It is highly unlikely that such a common and unremarkable phenomenon should account for the names of several individual villages, presumably from the time of their original foundation.

Finally, it should be noted that in the Copper scroll from Qumran (3Q*15* 7:14,15) we find *hkwsb'* as the name of a village in Wadi el-Qelt; it clearly survives in the Greek name of the present-day monastery of St. George: *Chōlouziba*.[19] The accent was probably on the first syllable; cf. *swdm* for Sodom in 1QIs^a 1:9,10; 3:9. The name is clearly associated with the spring ʿAin el-Qelt, which has a permanent and substantial flow; it cannot derive from a wadi flowing only in the rainy season. Furthermore, the two references to water in Wadi el-Qelt are so different in nature that the name *hkwzb',* which must be associated with the appearance of water, cannot possibly refer both to the spring and to a wadi that flows only during the rainy season.[20] In the face of the real situation, the Arabic legend that ʿAin el-Qelt or possibly some other spring is intermittent and can therefore be called "deceitful"[21] cannot have led to a name based on *kzb* I, "lie." It is therefore highly likely that *hkwzb'* in 3Q*15* 7:14,15 derives from *kzb* II, "be abundant."

Like the personal names *kozbî* and *ben kôzîḇā',* therefore, the (Canaanite) toponyms in the OT may derive not from *kzb* I, "lie," but from *kzb* II, "be abundant." Even if the customary derivation of these toponyms from *kzb* I should be correct, they have no bearing on the meaning and especially the theological usage of *kzb* I and will therefore be ignored in the discussion that follows.

3. *Statistics and Syntax.* The root *kzb* I appears in the OT both as a verb and in a variety of noun forms. Of the 56 occurrences (including Sirach and Dnl. 2:9 but not proper names), the great majority — roughly two thirds — involve nouns.

a. *Verb.* The verb appears 17 times (including Sir. 16:21[22]). The qal is represented only by the act. ptcp. *kōzēḇ* in Ps. 116:11, where it clearly functions as a noun, being the predicate of a noun clause. The niphal appears twice (Job 41:9[Eng. v. 1]; Prov. 30:6), the hiphil only once (Job 24:25). The remaining 13 occurrences (including Sir. 16:21) all involve the piel. The piel, however, does not focus on an action or event but

---

19. M. Baillet, J. Tadeusz, and R. de Vaux, *Les 'petites grottes' de Qumrân. DJD,* III (1962), 231, no. 15c; 242, no. 52; 260, no. 20; 265, no. 20, with bibliog.

20. Contra *DJD,* III, 231, no. 15c.

21. *DJD,* III, 242, no. 52.

22. Verses as counted in D. Barthélemy and O. Rickenbacher, *Konkordanz zum Hebräischen Sirach* (Göttingen, 1973).

on its result; it refers to the generation of the the condition or "thing" denoted by nouns from the same root.[23] Thus 14 of the 17 occurrences of the verb, including the qal participle, have a clear affinity with the substantival use of the root. The same holds true for the 2 occurrences of the niphal. This observation must be kept in mind when we discuss the basic meaning of the root *kzb* I.[24]

In Job 24:25, the hiphil has a pronominal "object," but this object is itself the subject of the *kzb* that is brought about. In Mic. 2:11, *šeqer* is not really the transitive object of *kzb* piel; it is used adverbially to modify and intensify the verb. The verb *kzb* is not found with any other "objects." It has in itself a meaning that does not need to be amplified by further reference to an "object." We therefore do not have any "objects" of *kzb* I to help us determine its basic meaning or specify various shades of this meaning. Here we are helped by the nature of its various "subjects."[25]

In 5 passages, a prepositional phrase associates the action denoted by *kzb* piel with persons (*l^e^*: Ezk. 13:19; Ps. 78:36; 89:36[35]; *b^e^*: 2 K. 4:16; *ʿal-p^e^nê*: Job 6:28[26]). The action thus takes place in the context of communication involving one or more persons, an element that is probably also consistently present in the other passages.[27]

It is noteworthy that no (negative) imperatives are found; neither are there negative imperatives of other verbs with the noun *kāzāḇ* as object. Although *kzb* I is clearly evaluated negatively, it appears neither in "apodictic" instructions to refrain from dealing falsely nor in "casuistic" laws as a punishable offense. This striking observation must also be kept in mind in determining the basic meaning.[28]

b. *Nouns.* Substantival forms of *kzb* I are much more common than the verb. The noun *kāzāḇ* occurs 31 times in the MT, plus 5 in Sirach (Sir. 15:8 [ms. A]; 15:20; 31:1; 36:24 [text?]; 51:2). Of these occurrences, 12 involve the plural in *-îm*;[29] the rest involve the singular. Twice we find the (nominalized) adj. *ʾaḵzāḇ* (Jer. 15:18; Mic. 1:14) and once the Aramaic subst.[30] *kiḏbâ* (Dnl. 2:9).

Only once is the plural of *kāzāḇ* used as the subject of a clause (Am. 2:4, metaphorically for idols). The singular appears once in a double accusative construction (depending on → שׂים *śîm*), corresponding to the subject of a noun clause (Isa. 28:15). In 16 passages, the singular or plural of *kāzāḇ* depends on a noun or participle (functioning as a noun) in the construct, serving attributively to describe persons or objects. It serves the same function as predicate of a noun clause in Ps. 62:10(9) and in the use of Aram. *kiḏbâ* in apposition to *millâ*. In its 2 occurrences, (*k^e^mô*) *ʾaḵzāḇ* is the predicate of a noun clause, likewise being used as a noun to denote something that is present.

---

23. Cf. E. Jenni, *Das hebräische Piʿel* (Zurich, 1968), *passim.*
24. See I.4 below.
25. See I.4 below.
26. Cf. EA 62, 39f., 43f.; 138, 119: *ana pan.*
27. See I.4 below.
28. See I.4 below.
29. Cf. D. Michel, *Grundlegung einer hebräischen Syntax* (Neukirchen-Vluyn, 1977), 40, 45, 59, etc.
30. See II.2.c below.

Although the stock phrase *yāpîaḥ* (*kᵉzāḇîm*), found 5 times (Prov. 6:19; 14:5,25; 19:5,9), does not involve a construct, more likely representing a finite form of the verb,[31] *kᵉzāḇîm* has ceased to function as an object. In conjunction with *ʿēḏ,* this plural (like *šeqer*/*šᵉqārîm* or *ʾᵉmûnîm*/*ʾᵉmeṯ*) describes the character of a witness in court; it is therefore a kind of adverbial accusative, so that even here *kāzāḇ* characterizes a person by describing how he or she has come to act habitually.

In the remaining 12 passages, *kāzāḇ* is an accusative object: twice of a participal in the absolute functioning as a verb (Ezk. 13:9; 22:28), once of an infinitive (Ezk. 21:34[29]), and 9 times of a finite verb (*dbr* piel: Jgs. 16:10,13; Hos. 7:13; Zeph. 3:13; Dnl. 11:27; *rbh* piel: Hos. 12:2[1]; *ḥzh*: Ezk. 13:8; *bqš* piel: Ps. 4:3[2]; *rṣh*: Ps. 62:5[4]). But the participles and probably also the infinitive are used in apposition to characterize persons; and often the verbal clause with *kāzāḇ* as object must be construed as the predicate (clause) of a (compound) noun clause,[32] so that even as accusative object of a finite verb *kāzāḇ* often describes a noun denoting a person or thing.

In the great majority of passages, therefore, the nouns *kāzāḇ, ʾaḵzāḇ,* and *kiḏbâ* refer not to actions or events but to the character of persons or things involved. It is likewise clear that the character described is related to persons with the power of perception. The syntactic usage of the nouns thus largely parallels the usage of the verb.[33]

4. *Basic Meaning.* The basic meaning of *kzb* I is often given as "speak lies," "say what is untrue." The use of the root with things rather than persons must then be understood as secondary and metaphorical. The use of *kzb* I to describe persons must similarly represent a metonymy that shifts the meaning from the act of lying to the person who speaks the lies.[34] This view is based primarily on the observation that some two thirds of the OT passages using *kzb* I involve references to speaking or hearing.

In modern European languages, in conformity with the European tradition of philosophical ethics, "lie" in the sense of "speak lies" is defined as "saying what the speaker knows to be untrue." Three major elements determine the precise meaning of such "lying": its predominant or exclusive association with the use of language to convey information, its primary emphasis on the act of communication, and its stress on the subject of the action. "Lying" in this sense refers primarily to the discrepancy between what the speaker knows and says. It means the deliberate statement of something known to be untrue and thus belongs in the realm of ethics.

A series of observations makes it clear that identification of *kzb* I with "lie" or its equivalent in modern European languages is misleading if not actually wrong. These observations suggest instead[35] that the primary meaning of *kzb* I is "(objectively) deceptive, false, untrustworthy, false, worthless." In this interpretation, in the act of

31. But cf. *THAT,* I, 818, with bibliog.

32. See II.2.a below.

33. See I.3.a above.

34. Cf. Klopfenstein, *Die Lüge nach dem AT,* 177, 209f., 211; etc.; *THAT,* I, 818.

35. With J. L. Palache, *Semantic Notes on the Hebrew Lexicon* (Eng. trans., Leiden, 1959), 41.

communication that is indisputably the setting of *kzb* I, the reference of *kzb* I to the subject that brings forth what is untrustworthy is of secondary importance if it is present at all; the primary focus is on those who encounter what *kzb* I conveys, its "addressees." The fact that *kzb* I is frequently associated with speaking or hearing is easily explained by this basic meaning: in an act of communication, spoken or written language is the "thing" that most frequently raises the question of objective trustworthiness for those addressed.

In support of "(objectively) untrustworthy, false, worthless" as the basic meaning of *kzb* I, we may cite first the fact that this meaning predominates in its historically and linguistically earliest occurrences. This is especially true in Arabic, where *kaḏaba* means primarily "delude, disappoint, run dry," and only secondarily "lie, speak falsely."[36]

The same is true in the scattered occurrences of the root in Imperial Aramaic. A deed of gift from Elephantine takes the precaution of stating that any contrary document cited to impugn the validity of the gift is not genuine and therefore invalid: "That document is a 'lie' (*kdb*), I did not write it, it is not accepted by the court."[37] A similar statement appears in another legal document from Elephantine: if a document other than the document in question is produced, "that document is a 'lie' (*kdb*) . . . , but this one is trustworthy (*yṣb*)."[38] In both documents, *kdb* (in contrast to *yṣb*) describes a document that is not genuine and therefore worthless; it neither establishes nor documents a claim. The few occurrences of *kdb* in Ahikar[39] all have to do with speaking and hearing; but they, too, favor understanding *kdb* in the sense of "delusion, untrustworthiness." Ahikar 132 states that a man's respect depends on his trustworthiness (*hymtwh ʾmn*), his oppobrium on the untrustworthiness or "lie" of his lips (*kdbt śpwth*). Here, too, as a human attribute opposite to *ʾmn, kdb* probably means primarily objective untrustworthiness. The third of the three similes that follow is especially significant: "A liar (*mkdb*) is . . . like a man who practices magic without the aid of the gods." Here *kdb* is like a magical charm that remains ineffectual because the gods do not support it; it denotes the untrustworthiness of the speaker and the futility of his words, not an intention to convey false information.

Of the 4 occurrences of the Canaanite loanword in the Amarna letters, at least one points in the same direction. Rib-Addi of Gubla writes to the pharoah: "When you wrote saying, 'Soldiers have set forth,' you spoke a 'lie' (*kazbūtu*): there are no troops."[40] Rib-Addi can hardly be accusing the pharaoh of a subjective intent to deceive; he points instead to the vacuity and untrustworthiness of the message: there is no reality behind what Pharaoh has written.

What is more important, OT usage itself shows that "(objectively) false, untrustworthy" is the basic meaning of *kzb* I. In the first place, we should note the semantic

36. Cf. *WKAS,* I, 90ff.; also Klopfenstein, *Die Lüge nach dem AT,* 179.
37. *AP,* 8, 16.
38. *BMAP,* 10, 16f.
39. *AP,* 204ff.
40. EA 129, 37.

field in which *kzb* I appears. As antonyms we find words and metaphors that describe something (objectively) reliable and trustworthy: *'mn, kwn, ysd* ("foundation"), etc. As synonyms we find words and metaphors describing something worthless and untrustworthy, e.g., *šāw', šeqer, tarmîṯ, heḇel.*[41]

In synonymous expressions, *kzb* I can be replaced with other words for worthlessness and delusion without any apparent change in meaning. This is true above all in the contexts of (false) prophecy and forensic testimony, both of which involve speech. The predominantly substantival usage of *kzb* I, in conjunction with the almost exclusive focus on the result of the action in verbal usage,[42] likewise supports the interpretation of *kzb* I as meaning "(objectively) untrustworthy, worthless."

Finally, about a third of the occurrences are in passages that have nothing to do with speech and language. Such usage is much easier to account for if we do not have to posit a metaphorical extension of a basic meaning "lying words" but can assume instead that *kzb* I inherently means something "objectively worthless, untrustworthy," encountered above all in the context of speech.

We may therefore posit "falsehood, untrustworthiness, worthlessness" as the basic meaning of *kzb* I. This primary meaning does not belong in the first instance to the domain of responsible action, i.e., ethics; it serves to describe something as it is, and thus belongs to the domain of "ontology." Even when *kzb* I is used of a speaker or spoken words, the primary focus is not on the (ethically dubious) untruthfulness of the speaker, but on the objective untrustworthiness of the speaker or the message. The falsehood, untrustworthiness, or worthlessness always affects a second party. The root *kzb* I thus denotes a relational attribute of some entity with respect to a person addressed.

5. *LXX.* The LXX usually employs derivatives of the stem *pseud-* to render *kzb* I. In 3 passages we find *kenós* (Hos. 12:2[1]; Mic. 1:14; Hab. 2:3), in 7 *mátaios* (Ezk. 13:6,7,8,9,19; Am. 2:4; Zeph. 3:13), in 1 *adíkōs* (Prov. 19:5), in 1 *kakía* (Prov. 19:9), and in 1 *ekleípein* (Isa. 58:11, of water). It is noteworthy that in Zeph. 3:13 *kāzāḇ* is translated *mátaia* even though it depends on a verb that denotes speaking. It is also noteworthy that in Ezk. 13:6,7,8,9,19 it is translated *mátaios,* while the parallel *šāw'* is translated *pseúdos.* In Prov. 19:5,9, similarly, *'ēḏ š^{e}qārîm* is translated *mártys pseudḗs,* while the parallel *yap̄îaḥ k^{e}zāḇîm* is rendered by *enkalṓn adíkōs* (v. 5) and *ekkaúsē kakían* (v. 9). In Ezk. 13:6,7,8, one might suggest that the translator exchanged the objects of the parallel verbs in order to produce an onomatopoetic assonance (*manteúesthai mátaia* [v. 6]; *manteíai mátaiai* [vv. 7,8]). This explanation cannot apply to Ezk. 13:9,19; Prov. 19:5,9, however, so that for the LXX even in the context of speaking and hearing the basic meaning of *kzb* I as "objectively worthless" sometimes prevailed over the usual translation using *pseud-*. The LXX of Jer. 15:18 and Mic. 1:14 are discussed in II.2.b below.

---

41. For the details, see II below.
42. See I.3 above.

II. OT Usage. 1. *Verb.* a. *Piel.* Unlike a man (*'îš*) or human being (*ben 'āḏām*), God does not "lie" (*kzb* piel: Nu. 23:19). This would be the case if he were to "repent" (→ נחם *nḥm* niphal) of what he has determined, i.e., if God's words were not followed by the promised action. In Ps. 89:36(35), similarly, Yawheh swears that he did not give David a "lying" (*kzb* piel) promise; the promise once spoken by him will remain unchanged (cf. the piel of *šnh* in v. 35[34]) — in other words, it will become reality.

Hab. 2:3 describes a vision (*ḥāzôn*) as not "lying" (*kzb* piel). Here, as in many other passages, *ḥāzôn* denotes the prophetic message stated in words, even written words (cf. v. 2).[43] In this instance "not lying" means that the (written) prophetic word is not empty and worthless; it echoes a reality that it both declares and foretells. In 2 K. 4:16, Elisha promises a barren woman that she will have a son within the year. She rejects the promise (cf. Gen. 18:12): "Do not deceive (*kzb* piel, with *bᵉ*) your maidservant," i.e., do not make her a promise that will not be fulfilled.

Ezk. 13:19 describes as "lying" (*kzb* piel) the activity of the false prophetesses, who delude their clients by consigning them to life or death without good reason. Here the piel of *kzb* means to utter a judgment that is not justified by reality. These prophetesses, however, are merely doing what the people, who listen to "lies" (*kāzāḇ*), expect.[44] Mic. 2:11 also uses the piel of *kzb* for false prophecy. Here it appears with the adverbial acc. *šeqer,* "delusion," and stands in parallel with *hlk rûaḥ* (*rûaḥ* is an adverbial acc. with *hlk,* not with *kzb*[45]). Like *kzb* piel by itself in Ezk. 13:19, *kzb* piel with *šeqer* here characterizes the activity of the false prophets (cf. → נטף *nṭp* in v. 11b), who preach what the people want to hear.

Prov. 14:5 states that a "trustworthy witness" (*'ēḏ 'ᵉmûnîm*) does not "lie" (*kzb* piel), whereas one who "breathes out lies" (*yāp̄îaḥ kᵉzāḇîm*)[46] is a "false witness" (*'ēḏ šeqer*). Here the piel of *kzb* means giving objectively inaccurate testimony and characterizes an untrustworthy witness (predicate clause in a compound noun clause). In Job 6:28, too, we may assume that the language reflects the courtroom. Job assures his friends that he has not "lied" (*kzb* piel) in maintaining his innocence. His words are consonant with reality.

In Isa. 58:11, an oracle of salvation, the people are likened to a watered garden (*gan rāweh*) and a spring of water (*môṣā' mayim*) whose waters will never "lie," i.e., fail (*lô'-yᵉḵazzᵉḇû mêmayw*). Here the piel of *kzb* means the drying up of a spring; it "lies" and deceives in that it no longer fulfills the expectations it engendered while it furnished water. It denotes failure to meet a justified expectation. (This verse is incorporated in 1QH 8:4f., 16f.; 1QSb 1:3-6.)

In Ps. 78:36, the piel of *kzb* stands in parallel with the piel of *pth.* Previous generations are said to have made a fool of God with their mouths and brought forth

---

43. → חזה *ḥāzâ.*
44. See II.2.a below.
45. Cf. H. W. Wolff, *Micah* (Eng. trans., Minneapolis, 1990), 75f., with bibliog.
46. See II.2.a below.

"lies" (*kzb* piel) for him (*lô*) with their tongues. Verse 37 elaborates on this statement: their heart[47] was not steadfast[48] toward him and they did not trust faithfully[49] in his covenant.[50] Here the piel of *kzb* means to use words of prayer — a confession of faith or a solemn vow — to convey the impression that one stands on God's side even though this impression does not correspond to the reality of one's own life. In Isa. 57:11, too, the piel of *kzb* denotes the conduct of Israel or Jerusalem toward God. Here it appears in antithetical parallelism with "remembering"[51] God, taking God seriously in the way one lives (*śîm ʿal-lēḇ*): conduct that again gives the impression of standing on God's side, an impression that is not grounded in reality. Sir. 16:21 claims that such conduct is possible *bᵉḵol seṯer,* "in total secrecy." Here the piel of *kzb* stands in parallel with → חטא *ḥṭʾ*, "go astray, sin," and characterizes sin as a worthless and vacuous act. Since the sinner's notion that he can sin "in total secrecy" is wrong (cf. Sir. 16:17, 23), here, too, the piel of *kzb* involves an attentive addressee — God.

The piel of *kzb* in Job 34:6 is hard to interpret. Elihu is summing up (without actually quoting) the charge Job has brought against God (vv. 5f.), a charge Elihu sharply denies in vv. 7ff. Exegetes have attempted to interpret the *ʾᵃḵazzēḇ* of the MT in Job's quoted accusation as meaning that Job claims to have brought forth a "lie" in his declaration of innocence, in that this declaration contradicts the clear fact that disaster has befallen him; according to wisdom tradition, such suffering necessarily presupposes guilt. Since Job himself, however, is convinced that his declaration of innocence is true, this interpretation involves a kind of oxymoron: "Although I am in the right (*ʿal-mišpāṭî*), I stand here as a liar (*ʾᵃḵazzēḇ*)."

This interpretation of the verb, however, would normally lead us to expect a niphal, as in Job 41:1; Prov. 30:6.[52] Bernard Duhm[53] accordingly reads the niphal *ʾekkāzēḇ*. An intransitive use of the piel in the sense of "prove to be a liar" would be totally unparalleled, both with respect to the general function of the piel[54] and with respect to the usage of *kzb* piel elsewhere. The LXX reads *epseúsato,* representing the 3rd person singular piel of *kzb,* making God the subject not only of the perf. *hēsîr* in Job 34:5b but also of the impf. *kzb* piel in v. 6a.

There are several reasons for thinking that the LXX bears witness to the original text. The syntactic structure of the three clauses in Job 34:5aβ, 5b, and 6a suggests God as the subject in v. 6a. The perfective "I am innocent" (*ṣāḏaqtî*) in v. 5aβ stands in antithesis to the perfective statement in v. 5b: "But [inversion!] God has taken away my right" (*wᵉʾēl hēsîr mišpāṭî*). The piel imperfect of *kzb* in v. 6a denotes a result

47. → לב *lēḇ*.
48. → כון *kwn*.
49. → אמן *ʾmn* niphal.
50. → ברית *bᵉrîṯ*.
51. → זכר *zāḵar*.
52. See II.1.b below.
53. B. Duhm, *Das Buch Hiob. KHC,* XVI (1897), *in loc.*
54. See I.3.a above.

dependent upon the preceding perf. *hēsîr.*[55] The *mišpāṭî* at the end of v. 5b is also repeated at the beginning of v. 6a. The intimate syntactic and semantic connection between the two clauses in vv. 5b and 6a makes it appropriate for both to have the same subject. Furthermore, the denial in vv. 7ff. presupposes that the cited accusation against God is very serious (cf. esp. vv. 10, 12). This is all the more true if God is the subject not only of *hēsîr* (*mišpāṭî*) but also of *kzb* piel. It is also not surprising that Elihu should exaggerate Job's accusation, which he rejects, and that he should therefore quote Job as charging God with "lying," although such an accusation does not actually appear in Job's words. Finally, the reading of the LXX is by far the more difficult; it is easy to understand how an offensive statement making God out to be a "liar" was eliminated by changing its subject. As a parallel, we may cite the LXX and Vulg. as well as the Targ.'s paraphrase of Jer. 15:18.[56] Following the LXX, therefore, we read the 3rd person *yᵉḵazzēb* in Job 34:6.[57]

So read, the passage means that, by "taking away" Job's right and inflicting undeserved suffering upon him despite his innocence, God himself creates an appearance that denies the reality of Job's innocence, thus bringing forth a "lie" (*kzb* piel).

In all its occurrences, therefore, the piel of *kzb* denotes the creation of an empty appearance that does not reflect any reality. This can be done through words, but not uncommonly also by silent actions and conduct. Intent to deceive may well be present; it may even be implicit in certain passages. The focus, however, is not the the subjective intent of the person who is the subject of *kzb* piel but on the objective untrustworthiness and worthlessness of the resulting situation. The worthless appearance is always associated clearly with an observer to whom the words or actions are addressed.

b. *Niphal.* The wisdom aphorism in Prov. 30:6 cautions against adding anything to God's words. God might well "rebuke"[58] someone who did so. Here, as in many other passages, the use of a perfect following an imperfect denotes a consequent result:[59] the person would be shown up as a "liar" (*kzb* niphal) by such a rebuke, i.e., shown to be someone who without justification deceives others by falsely claiming certain words to be from God. Job 41:1(9) speaks of the "hope" (*tôḥeleṯ*) that a human being could win a battle with a crocodile. The mere sight of the beast proves that this hope is "deceptive" (*kzb* niphal). In both passages, the niphal of *kzb* means that a deceptive appearance is revealed for what it is.

c. *Hiphil.* In Job 24:25a, Job uses a rhetorical question to reject as impossible the notion that anyone might make him out to be a "liar" (*kzb* hiphil), i.e., prove that his words were worthless and meaningless (v. 25b: *yāśēm lᵉʿal millāṯî*). His assertion of his own innocence is correct, and therefore no one can cause him to be proved a "liar,"

---

55. Cf. D. Michel, *Tempora und Satzstellung in den Psalmen. Abhandlungen zur evangelischen Theologie,* 1 (Bonn, 1960), 128ff.

56. See II.2.b below.

57. G. Hölscher, *Das Buch Hiob. HAT,* XVII (²1952), *in loc.,* contra Klopfenstein, *Die Lüge nach dem AT,* n. 795, and most commentators.

58. → יכח *ykḥ.*

59. Michel, *Tempora und Satzstellung in den Psalmen,* 95-98.

which he is not. Here, then, the hiphil of *kzb* means to bring to light deceptive conduct and character that are objectively present and to treat the person involved as a deceiver.[60]

d. *Qal.* In contrast to the piel, the qal ptcp. *kōzēḇ* in Ps. 116:11 denotes not the production of a specific deceitful utterance or situation but a deceitful nature, a deeply rooted, habitual tendency to produce worthless delusion and disappoint hopes.[61] In place of the qal participle, the similar statement in Ps. 62:10(9) uses the noun *kāzāḇ*.[62] Thus Ps. 116:11 really belongs in the context of the substantival occurrences of *kzb* I.

2. *Nouns.* a. *kāzāḇ*. Isa. 28:15,17 states that "scoffers" (v. 14) make "lies" — i.e., "untrustworthy delusion" — their refuge (v. 15), which turns out to be a "deceptive refuge" (v. 17: *maḥᵃsēh kāzāḇ*). Here *kāzāḇ* stands in parallel with *šᵉʾôl* ("the netherworld"), *māweṯ* ("death"), and *šeqer* ("falsehood"); it is contrasted with the unshakable "foundation" that gives enduring stability to those who trust in it.[63] In Ps. 40:5(4), "trust"[64] in Yahweh is the opposite of turning to those who "ensnare themselves in lies" (*śāṭê kāzāḇ*; the same expression appears in Sir. 51:2). Ps. 62:10(9) states that the "sons of Adam" are a "deluding source of help" (*kāzāḇ*, par. *heḇel,* "mere breath"; cf. also Ps. 116:11), while Yahweh is a refuge in which one can trust (*bṭḥ*). The worthless futility of idols, often expressed by *heḇel* in the language of the Deuteronomistic school and Jeremiah (e.g., Jer. 2:5; 2 K. 17:15; cf. 1 S. 12:21),[65] is characterized as *kᵉzāḇîm* in Am. 2:4. The use of *kᵉzāḇîm* as a term for idols expresses their fundamental inability to help or deliver. In Ps. 4:3(2), *bqš* piel *kāzāḇ* appears in parallel with *ʾhb rîq*. Instead of seeking "delusion" and loving "emptiness," those addressed should "trust" (*bṭḥ,* v. 6b[5b]) in Yahweh, like the psalmist (cf. v. 9b[8b]). Then Yahweh, who is the "glory" of the psalmist (*kᵉḇôḏî,* v. 3a[2a]; cf. Jer. 2:11; Hos. 4:7; Ps. 106:20; also Rom. 1:23),[66] will no longer suffer shame (*kᵉlimmâ*). In Prov. 19:22, the phrase *ʾîš kāzāḇ* describes a person who acts deceitfully in commerce. In Prov. 23:3, *leḥem kᵉzāḇîm* ("bread of delusion") serves as a metaphor for table fellowship with the ruler of v. 1, in that it does not guarantee his benevolence which it appears to reflect. In Hos. 12:2c(1c), a gloss,[67] *kāzāḇ* and *šōḏ,* "violence," describe the deceitful and worthless conduct of Ephraim. In Ps. 62:5(4), "taking pleasure in falsehood" (*rṣh kāzāḇ*) is a hypocritical pretense of benevolent solidarity that conceals one's true attitude (v. 5b[4b]).

Hos. 7:13 says that Ephraim speaks "lies" (*dbr* piel *kāzāḇ*) against Yahweh. This expression is expanded upon in v. 14: it means "not crying to Yahweh from the heart."

---

60. This function of the hiphil is discussed by Jenni, *Das hebräische Piʿel,* 44ff.

61. This use of the qal participle of verbs found primarily in the piel is discussed in the treatment of the qal participle of *dbr* ("דבר *dāḇar* [*dābhar*]," III, 96f.), with bibliog.

62. See II.2.a below.

63. → אמן *ʾmn;* → יסד *ysd.*

64. → בטח *bṭḥ.*

65. Cf. also → יעל *yʿl.*

66. Contra Klopfenstein, *Die Lüge nach dem AT,* 224; H.-J. Kraus, *Psalms 1–59* (Eng. trans., Minneapolis, 1988), 144f., 148; and most comms.

67. See, e.g., H. W. Wolff, *Hosea. Herm* (Eng. trans. 1974), 206.

The noun *kāzāḇ* probably refers to insincere expressions of repentance like those cited in Hos. 6:1-3. Thus *kāzāḇ* describes these expressions as empty and insincere because they do not reflect real penitence (cf. Ps. 78:36).[68]

Prov. 21:28 contrasts the *ʿēḏ-keząḇîm* with the *ʾîš šômēaʿ*. Unlike someone who was in fact a witness to the event (*šômēaʿ*) and can therefore be a reliable witness in court, the *ʿēḏ-kezāḇîm* is someone who testifies concerning something that he has neither seen nor heard. The word *kezāḇîm* thus characterizes the witness and his testimony as objectively untrustworthy. In Prov. 19:5,9, *yāp̄îaḥ kezāḇîm* stands in parallel with *ʿēḏ šeqārîm*; in 14:5, it stands in (chiastic) parallelism with (*lôʾ*) *yeḵazzēḇ*. Here this expression is a predicate noun with *ʿēḏ šeqer,* which in turn stands in antithetical parallelism with *ʿēḏ ʾemûnîm,* "trustworthy witness." Prov. 14:25 uses *ʿēḏ ʾemeṯ* in parallel with *yāp̄îaḥ kezāḇîm,* with the ptcp. *merammeh* (text emended), "betrayer," added as a predicate noun. In Prov. 6:19, *ʿēḏ šeqer* stands in explanatory apposition to *yāp̄îaḥ kezāḇîm.* As in Prov. 21:28, where it is associated with *ʿēḏ,* the pl. *kezāḇîm* in the phrase *yāp̄îaḥ kezāḇîm* (5 occurrences) probably means primarily the objective error and untrustworthiness of a witness who testifies despite his lack of competence and is therefore a "lying" witness.

In Ezk. 13:19b, *šômēaʿ kāzāḇ* appears in apposition to "people" (namely of Yahweh: *ʿammî*). They listen to "lies," to which they are in bondage (cf. Mic. 2:11). Here *kāzāḇ* characterizes the oracles of the false prophets, spoken without Yahweh's authorization and therefore having nothing to do with reality. In Ezk. 13:6(conj.[69]),9; 21:34(29); 22:28, *kāzāḇ* is dependent on the verb *qsm,* "utter an oracle"; in Ezk. 13:7, it modifies the noun *miqsām,* "oracle"; and in Ezk. 13:8, it is dependent on the verb *ḥzh,* "describe a prophetic vision." In these 6 passages, *kāzāḇ* stands in parallel with *šāwʾ,* "something worthless"; as in Ezk. 13:19b, it describes a prophetic message that is false because it does not correspond to reality. Thus *kāzāḇ* plays for Ezekiel the same role that *šeqer* does for Jeremiah (cf. Jer. 5:31; 14:14; 20:6; 23:26,32; 27:15; 29:9,23; etc.).

Prov. 30:8aα requests God to remove "worthlessness" (*šāwʾ*) and "lying" (*deḇar kāzāḇ*) from the speaker. The mention of "two" requests in v. 7 probably referred originally to vv. 8aβ and 8b; v. 8aα may therefore be a secondary addition (possibly occasioned by v. 6), to be understood in isolation. In parallel with *šāwʾ*,[70] *deḇar kāzāḇ* refers to words that are objectively worthless, devoid of reality, conveying falsehood even though spoken in (subjectively) good faith.

In Jgs. 16:10,13, *dbr* piel *kezāḇîm* stands in parallel with the hiphil of *tll,* "deceive." Here, as in Dnl. 11:27, it denotes words that are deliberately and consciously false.

In Ps. 5:7(6), *dōḇrê ḵāzāḇ,* "those who speak lies," is used in parallel with *rešaʿ,* "wickedness," *rāʿ,* "evil" (v. 5[4]), *hôlelîm,* "boastful," *pōʿalê ʾāwen,* "evildoers" (v. 6[5]), and *ʾîš-dāmîm ûmirmâ,* "bloodthirsty and deceitful men" (v. 7b[6b]). The *dōḇrê ḵāzāḇ* are those in whose mouths is found no truth (*neḵônâ*: v. 10a[9a]). In Ps.

---

68. See II.1.a above.
69. W. Zimmerli, *Ezekiel 1. Herm* (Eng. trans. 1979), 286, etc.
70. See the discussion of Ezk. 13 above.

58:4(3), *dōḇrê ḵāzāḇ* stands in parallel with *rᵉšāʿîm,* "wicked." In both passages, *kāzāḇ* refers to words that have no basis in reality; it characterizes the enemies of the speaker. Similarly, *dbr* piel *kāzāḇ* stands in parallel with *ʿśh ʿawlâ* in Zeph. 3:13, where it is further characterized by the phrase "tongue of deceit" (*lᵉšôn tarmîṯ*).

Sir. 15:8b uses *ʾanšê ḵāzāḇ,* "men of deceit," in a series that includes *mᵉṯê šāwʾ,* "men of worthlessness" (v. 7a), *ʾanšê zāḏôn,* "men of arrogance" (v. 7b), and *lēṣîm,* "scoffers" (v. 8a). The same expression appears again in Sir. 15:20b alongside *ḥṭʾ,* "sin." Here *kāzāḇ,* like the piel of *kzb* in Sir. 16:21,[71] is almost synonymous with sin, something contrary to God's will that strays from the right way and therefore from God's community. This passage probably connects with the usage of *kāzāḇ* in the Dead Sea scrolls, where 1QpHab 2:2; 5:11; 10:9; 11:1 (?); CD 1:15; 8:13; 19:26; 20:15; 1Q14 10:2 (?) speak of a "man [or 'preacher'] of lies." Here *kāzāḇ* characterizes a specific historical individual (note the definite article!) who was an enemy of the community.[72]

b. *ʾaḵzāḇ.* The word *ʾaḵzāḇ* appears only twice (Jer. 15:18; Mic. 1:14); the lexica translate it as "deceitful"[73] or "something deceitful."[74] In both passages it is understood (metaphorically) as a technical term for a "deceitful brook," a watercourse that flows only during the rainy season but is dry in summer.[75]

This raises the question whether the semantic element "brook" or "watercourse" is in fact implicit in *ʾaḵzāḇ.* It is commonly claimed that *ʾêṯān,* "enduring, permanent," hence "permanent watercourse," is an antonym of *ʾaḵzāḇ.* It is not impossible that *ʾêṯān* inherently includes the semantic element "flowing water, brook," or the like. (In *KBL*³, the basic meaning of *ʾêṯān* is given as "permanently flowing"; the meaning "permanent, enduring" is said to be a metaphorical extension. But it is also possible that in the case of *ʾêṯān,* too, a basic meaning of "permanent" was extended secondarily and metaphorically to brooks and water.) There is no text, however, in which *ʾaḵzāḇ* and *ʾêṯān* appear together; since the two words never appear in opposition, the assumed presence of the semantic component "brook" in *ʾêṯān* cannot serve to justify the same assumption in the case of *ʾaḵzāḇ.*

Job 6:15-21 is often cited for understanding the meaning of *ʾaḵzāḇ*; but this description of a dried-up brook does not use the word *ʾaḵzāḇ* (or *ʾêṯān!*). Isa. 58:11 uses the piel of *kzb* to describe a spring; here, too, however, we find neither the noun *ʾaḵzāḇ* nor the noun *ʾêṯān.* The piel of *kzb,* used to characterize other things elsewhere, is used here to describe water. This does not imply that *ʾaḵzāḇ* must be understood as a technical term for a dry watercourse. Such toponyms as *ʾaḵzîḇ* contribute nothing to the question of *ʾaḵzāḇ*'s meaning, since their interpretation is itself derived from the presumed meaning of *ʾaḵzāḇ* (possibly wrongly[76]) and the argument is circular.

---

71. See II.1.a above.

72. For a discussion of the "man of lies" at Qumran, see G. Jeremias, *Der Lehrer der Gerechtigkeit. StUNT,* 2 (1963), 79-126, with bibliog.

73. *KBL*³, *s.v.*

74. *LexHebAram, s.v.*

75. Cf. also the comms. *in loc.*

76. See I.2 above.

Finally, the 2 occurrences of *'akzāb* can be interpreted quite easily without assuming that the meaning "flowing water, brook" is inherent in the word or that *'akzāb* is a technical term for a dry wadi. This is obvious in the case of Mic. 1:14: the play on words *'akzîb/'akzāb* makes good sense (in fact better sense!) if the city *'akzîb* is not called a "deceitful brook" but is simply described as being a "deeply disappointing delusion"; the rare adjective form appears to express an intensification of the root meaning.[77]

In parallel with *'akzāb* Jer. 15:18b speaks of *mayim lō' ne'emānû,* "water that cannot be trusted." This parallelism suggests the meaning "brook, (untrustworthy) watercourse" for *'akzāb* as well. But 2 other passages in Jeremiah (Jer. 2:13; 17:13) also use water metaphorically in association with God. The metaphorical description of God as "water that cannot be trusted" in 15:18b could therefore be derived from the metaphor in 2:13; 17:13, so that in 15:18b the meaning "untrustworthiness" alone would constitute the parallel to *(mayim) lō' ne'emānû* without the component "brook, water." Verse 18bαβ would then be an instance of "synthetic" rather than "synonymous" parallelism. In Jer. 15:18, therefore, *'akzāb* can be understood without the semantic component "water, brook"; as in Mic. 1:14, it can mean "deeply disappointing delusion." So interpreted, the accusation against God from the mouth of Jeremiah is almost intolerably bitter.[78]

The theory advanced here, that *'akzāb* includes only the semantic component "(especially heinous) delusion," not the component "watercourse," is supported by the ancient versions. In Mic. 1:14, the LXX renders *bātê 'akzîb le'akzāb lemalkê yiśrā'ēl* as *oíkous mataíous eis kená egéneto toís basileúsin toú Israḗl,* the Vulg. as *domus Mendacii in deceptionem regibus Israhel.* Neither makes any reference here to any kind of watercourse. In Jer. 15:18, for *hāyô tihyeh lî kemô 'akzāb* the LXX reads *ginoménē egenḗthē* (3rd person!) *moi hōs hýdōr pseudés ouk échon pístin.* Here *hýdor* represents the *mayim* of the MT; *'akzāb* is treated as an attributive adjective and translated *pseudés.*[79] The Vulg. is similar: *facta est* (3rd person!) *mihi quasi mendacium aquarum infidelium.* Both versions avoid the repugnant association of Yahweh with *'akzāb* by making it refer to the wound mentioned just before. The Targ. paraphrases in a different manner, but for the same reason.[80] Neither the LXX nor the Vulg. takes *'akzāb* in Jer. 15:18 in the sense of "watercourse" or "brook."

c. *The Aramaic Noun kidbâ.* In Dnl. 2:9, the king demands that his counselors not only interpret his dream but divine the nature of the dream itself. Since they cannot do so, he declares: *ûmillâ kidbâ ûšeḥîtâ hizmintûn lemē'mar qodāmay.* The syntax of the nouns depending on the verb *mē'mar* is difficult. The noun *kidbâ* is sometimes interpreted as an attributive adjective, "lying," along with the adjectival ptcp. *šeḥîtâ,* "corrupt."[81] Now *šeḥîtâ* appears in Dnl. 6:5(4) with the two nouns *'illâ,* "ground for

77. Cf. Klopfenstein, *Die Lüge nach dem AT,* 243-48, with bibliog.

78. See III.1 below.

79. Contra Klopfenstein, *Die Lüge nach dem AT,* 251.

80. Cf. the discussion of Job 34:6 in II.1.1 above.

81. E. König, *Hebräisches und aramäisches Wörterbuch zum AT* (Leipzig, 1910), *s.v. kedab'* also *GesTh,* II, 660; and *LexLingAram, s.v.* The latter two also note the possibility of treating *kidbâ* as a noun.

complaint," and *šālû,* "fault." In Dnl. 6:5(4), therefore, as in Sir. 30:11, *šᵉḥîṯâ* is a noun (nominalized adj. or ptcp.). It is therefore likely also to be a noun in Dnl. 2:9. But the same assumption must then also apply to *kiḏbâ.* Furthermore, there is an adj. *kaddāḇ(ā')* derived from Aram. *kdb,*[82] so that another adjective formation is unlikely. Above all, the plural of *kiḏbâ* appears in 1QapGen 2:6,7 as a noun (*bkdbyn*),[83] and elsewhere as well.[84] With *KBL*², therefore, we must recognize *kiḏbâ* as a noun. The noun *millâ* in Dnl. 2:9 thus has two substantives in direct apposition: "You have agreed to speak something [that is] deception, [something] corrupt." Like Heb. *kāzāḇ, kiḏbâ* here denotes not the act of speaking but its result. It can therefore not really describe the deceitful intention of the speaking subject; it characterizes the substance of what is said as untrustworthy and flawed.

III. Theology. When speaking of "delusion" and "worthlessness," OT thought makes a clear distinction between the human realm on the one hand and the divine realm — God's words and actions — on the other. The difference is stated classically in Nu. 23:19. A theological analysis of the OT usage of *kzb* I that does justice to the thought of the OT must be grounded on the radical separation of the realms in which *kzb* I can be used.

There is a second distinction in the semantic perspective conveyed by *kzb* I; the OT does not state this distinction so clearly and directly, but it is no less important for a theological understanding of the meaning of *kzb* I. The "delusion" referred to always reflects the expectations and perceptions of the persons for whom the "delusion," "worthlessness," "falsehood," and "untrustworthiness" becomes a reality.[85] The expectation of "trustworthiness" and "truth" that the "addressee" of *kzb* I has with respect to the "agent" or "sender" may be justified or unjustified. Accordingly, the "delusion" and "disappointment" of the addressee expressed by *kzb* I, as well as the justification for his expectations, may be judged theologically to be necessary and inevitable (if the expectation of "truth" and "trustworthiness" is unjustified) or to be avoidable and inappropriate (if the expectation of "truth" and "trustworthiness" is justified). The OT occurrences of *kzb* I easily show that this second distinction is fundamental for the theological understanding of *kzb* I in both the human and the divine realm.

Finally, there is a third element important for a theological understanding of the situation denoted by *kzb* I. The root conveys a negative concept; it denotes a defect, which may or may not be necessary. At the same time, it implies censure and negative criticism. This criticism, however, is not always aimed at the "agent" or "sender" of *kzb* I. It can also be aimed at the "addressee" who is deceived. This is the case when the "addressee" is not justified in expecting "trustworthiness" and "truth" from the

---

82. Cf. G. H. Dalman, *Aramäisch-neuhebräisches Handwörterbuch zu Targum, Talmud und Midrasch* (1938, repr. Hildesheim, 1967); *WTM, s.v.*

83. Cf. J. A. Fitzmyer, *The Genesis Apocryphon of Qumran Cave I. BietOr,* 18A (²1971), 85.

84. Ahikar 132, 133; Behistun inscription 51 (cf. *AP,* 217, 253; Targum (e.g., Jgs. 16:10; Isa. 57:11; Hos. 7:13; Ezk 13:19).

85. See I.3,4 above.

"agent" or "sender." Then it is not the "deceiver" but the disappointed "dupe" who is criticized and blamed.

1. *Inherent Falsehood.*

a. *God.* Calling on Balak to pay attention (Nu. 23:18b) and thus underlining the importance of what is to follow, Balaam introduces his promise of blessing by citing the unfailing, immutable trustworthiness of God and God's promise: "God is not man, that he should lie [*kzb* piel], or a son of man, that he should repent" (v. 19a). God guarantees that he will do what he says and will fulfill what he has spoken (v. 19b; cf. Ezk. 17:24; 22:14; 36:36: "I Yahweh have spoken, and I will do it"; cf. also Ezk. 5:15,17; 6:10; 21:22[17]; 23:34; 24:14; 37:14; 26:5,14; 28:10; 30:12; 34:24). God and God's word are such that "delusion" and "untrustworthiness" are simply out of the question. The situation here expressed by the negated piel of *kzb* is expressed elsewhere by the ascription of *'ᵉmeṯ* ("fidelity, trustworthiness")[86] to God as an inherent attribute. The inviolability that Nu. 23:19 associates with God himself is associated by Hab. 2:3 with the prophetic message as well. The prophetic oracle, too, because it comes from God, is inherently incapable of deceiving (negated piel of *kzb*).

Ps. 89 begins as a hymn praising the steadfast love and faithfulness of Yahweh. The word *'ᵉmûnâ* appears 7 times (vv. 2[1], 3[2], 6[5], 9[8], 25[24], 34[33], 50[49]); there is also 1 occurrence of *'ᵉmeṯ* (v. 15[14]) and 2 of the niphal of *'mn* (vv. 29[28], 38[37]). The "faithfulness" of Yahweh is here extolled with reference to his promises to David (cf. Ps. 132:11). The statement that Yahweh does not lie (*kzb* piel: Ps. 89:36[35]) says negatively what is said positively by attribution of *'ᵉmûnâ* to Yahweh. The hymn in vv. 2-38(1-37), however, turns unexpectedly into a lament in vv. 39-52(38-51). This section laments that everything described in the hymn no longer obtains. It does not go so far as to assert "untrustworthiness" and "deception" on God's part. It does, however, ask where Yahweh's *'ᵉmûnâ* is, thus calling it into question. The possibility is raised that God might "deceive." The psalm ends (vv. 50f.[49f.]) with a very muted prayer, formulated indirectly, that God will prove faithful as of old. Thus Ps. 89, while affirming and praising God's faithfulness, which does not deceive, recognizes at the same time that this faithfulness does not absolutely fulfill the expectations of the psalmist. The "confidence" with which the worshipper feels secure (*bṭḥ*) in Yahweh and his faithfulness has here lost the support of direct confirmation.

Jeremiah associates *kzb* with God in a similar fashion. For him, Yahweh is like water that cannot be trusted (*lô' ne'ᵉmānû*): "Thou hast become to me like a great deception (*'aḵzāḇ*)" (Jer. 15:18).[87] The complaint is barely mitigated by the inclusion of *kᵉmô,* "like." Jeremiah contests in his own case the general affirmation that Yahweh is "faithful" and "trustworthy." For his own part, he is forced to say, Yahweh has turned into treacherous footing. Yahweh's response does not solve the problem by promising

86. → אמן *'āman,* I, 313-16.

87. See II.2.b above.

an immediate experience confirming God's faithfulness, which Jeremiah had expected and missed, but by censuring Jeremiah for speaking in error and promising him help and support if he "returns" from this error (Jer. 15:19-21; cf. Jer. 45, where Baruch receives a similarly reserved answer).

The absolute impossibility of God's "deceiving" (*kzb*) is thus affirmed by Nu. 23:19 and maintained even in Ps. 89; Jer. 15:18. The expectations of the person to whom God should be "faithful" may nevertheless be disappointed. God's unfailing faithfulness does not necessarily mean what the person concerned understands by it; it does not necessarily bring to pass its expected consequences.

b. *Human Beings.* In contrast to God, who is the "rock," "fortress," and "refuge" in which the psalmist can find security (Ps. 62:3,7-9[2,6-8]), the sons of Adam are *heḇel,* "a mere breath" (cf. Ps. 39:6,12[5,11]), and *kāzāḇ,* "a delusion" (Ps. 62:10[9]). Every human being (*kol-hā'āḏām*) is "deceptive" (*kōzēḇ*: Ps. 116:11) by nature. According to these two passages, *kzb* inherently characterizes human beings: every individual, all things human, must inevitably disappoint all expectations of total security and ultimate deliverance. These expectations are therefore always vain and without support. The inherent element of human nature expressed here by *kzb* is expressed by *šāw'* in Ps. 60:13(11); 108:13(12): "Vain is human help" (*šāw' tešû'aṯ 'āḏām*); cf. also Ps. 146:3 and 118:8: it is right and proper to take refuge in Yahweh, but not in mankind.[88]

The OT, however, often speaks of attempts to find security in something other than Yahweh. Such refuge is necessarily "treacherous" (*kzb*). This describes the idols behind which the people parade; these idols themselves can therefore be called "lies" or "delusion" (*kezāḇîm*: Am. 2:4). It also describes the refuge the people seek in addition to or instead of the refuge Yahweh provides upon Mt. Zion. Such refuge is necessarily a "treacherous refuge" (Isa. 28:15,17).

These passages use *kzb* I as an inherent attribute of human beings and the human world primarily in the context of hope for ultimate security. When such hope depends on other human beings, it will always be disappointed.

Not only the "addressee" but also the "sender" of what is characterized by *kzb* can claim something to be divine and therefore trustworthy even though it is not God and does not come from him. Like everything human, however, it is necessarily a "delusion" (*kzb*). A prophet who has not been sent by Yahweh but nevertheless proclaims an oracle proclaims "delusion" and "worthlessness" (Ezk. 13:6,7,8,9,19; 21:34[29]; 22:28; Mic. 2:11). The appearance of trustworthiness that the prophets lend their words by claiming they are the word of Yahweh is reinforced by their listeners' desire to accept this appearance as reality. They hearken to "delusion" (Ezk. 13:19). Such prophets fulfill the people's expectations with their message (Mic. 2:11). Like "idols" and "treacherous refuge," the words of the false prophets convey only what is human. The prophets and the people lend it an appearance of divine origin and therefore of ultimate trustworthiness, while in fact it remains "delusion."

---

88. → בטח *bāṭaḥ* [*bāṭach*], III.2, *TDOT,* II, 90-92.

2. *Avoidable Falsehood.*

a. *In Court.* Some passages where *kzb* I has the meaning "lying words" do not convey any hint of censure. The fact that Samson has "lied" to Delilah (Jgs. 16:10,13) appears to be reported more with a sense of satisfaction over Samson's sagacity. The situation is different when "lying" and "deception" are practiced in a situation whose very nature requires "trustworthiness" and "truth," where the addressee has a right to expect trustworthy, true, and accurate words. This is the case when a meal is shared. It is outrageous and reprehensible for people to sit at the same table and speak lies (Dnl. 11:27). On the other hand, a subordinate has no right to interpret a ruler's invitation as a token of the latter's good will; the bread he eats may be "bread of delusion," and he has his own foolishness to blame if he takes it as an assurance of favor (Prov. 23:3).

Above all, however, there must be no *kzb* in words spoken in court. Here statement and response must elucidate the situation to be decided if the stability of the community is to be secured. Untrustworthy and inaccurate testimony — either because the speaker has no knowledge of the question at issue or because he wants to create a false impression — is wrong and is condemned. The evil that a false witness represents and can bring about through his testimony is described primarily in wisdom aphorisms. We are also told, however, that a false witness and his testimony will not endure (Prov. 6:19; 14:5,25; 19:5,9; 21:28). In this context, too, belong Job's assurances that he is not "lying" in his argument, which is placed in a forensic setting (Job 6:28; 24:25). The same situation is described in other passages, without any apparent difference in meaning, by *šeqer,* "deception" (cf. Ex. 20:16, etc.) or *šāw',* "worthlessness" (cf. Dt. 5:20).

b. *Term of General Opprobrium.* In some Psalms and wisdom aphorisms, *kzb* serves to characterize sinners. The psalmist's enemies are called "speakers of lies" (Ps. 5:7[6]; 58:4[3]), people who "seek after deception" (Ps. 4:3[2]), who curse in their hearts while blessing with their mouths and therefore love "deception" (Ps. 62:5[4]). "Men of deception" are quite generally those who "go astray" (Sir. 15:20; cf. 16:21b); they are called "scoffers" (Sir. 15:8). Like "violence" (*šōḏ*), "deception" (*kāzāḇ*) is a general term for false conduct (Hos. 12:2[1]). The worshipper therefore prays to be preserved from it (Prov. 30:8). In the coming day of salvation, no one will speak "lies" (*kāzāḇ*) in Israel; a "deceitful tongue" will not be found (Zeph. 3:13; cf. Isa. 58:11).

In these passages, *kzb* refers to the untrustworthiness and uncertainty that sin, and especially deceptive speech, introduces into the structure of society, because it impugns and destroys the community.

c. *"Deceiving" God.* Two passages speak of Israel's "deceiving" God. Ps. 78:34-37 says that the Israelites, suffering under God's judgment, remembered that he was their "rock" and "redeemer" and sought him again. Their repentance, however, was only verbal and not from the heart; they therefore "lied" (*kzb* piel) to God with their tongues. Hos. 7:13f. states that the Israelites (Ephraim) called to God in their distress, but did not do so from the heart and therefore spoke "lies" (*k^e^zāḇîm*) to Yahweh.

Mosis

כֹּחַ kōaḥ

Contents: I. 1. Etymology; 2. Occurrences. II. OT Usage: 1. Meaning; 2. Human Strength; 3. God's Power. III. 1. LXX; 2. Dead Sea Scrolls.

I. 1. *Etymology.* Apart from Hebrew, the word *kōaḥ* is found only in the Aramaic of the Targumim, where it is probably a Hebrew loanword. Mandaic also has a word *kahuta,* "strength," and a verb *khw.*[1] More distant cognates have been suggested[2] in Arab. *wakaḥa,* "stamp firm," *'awkaḥ,* "hard soil," and *kwḥ* I, II, "subject," III, "fight."[3] Eth. *kʷakʷeḥ* and Tigr. *kauḥ,* "rock," are more likely related to Arab. *kīḥ,* "rock wall."[4]

2. *Occurrences.* The noun *kōaḥ* occurs 124 times in the OT: 21 times in Job alone, 13 times in the Pentateuch, 18 times in the Deuteronomistic history, 8 times in Deutero-Isaiah, and 11 times in the Psalms. The remaining occurrences are distributed roughly equally in various books.

II. OT Usage.

1. *Meaning.* The noun *kōaḥ* belongs to the semantic realm of power and strength. It is used in association or in parallel with various words for "strength." Parallels include: (1) *'ôn,* "might": God is great (*raḇ*) in *'ônîm* and strong (*'ammîṣ*) in *kōaḥ* (Isa. 40:26); Reuben is "my *kōaḥ,* and the first fruits of my *'ôn*" (Gen. 49:3); Behemoth possesses *kōaḥ* and *'ôn* (Job 40:16); God gives the faint *kōaḥ* and him who is without *'ôn* strength (*'oṣmâ*) (Isa. 40:29); (2) *gbr*: God has established the mountains by his *kōaḥ* and is girded with *geḇûrâ* (Ps. 65:7[Eng. v. 6]); the angels are *gibbōrê kōaḥ* (Ps. 103:20); in God's hand there is *kōaḥ ûgeḇûrâ* (1 Ch. 29:12; 2 Ch. 20:6; (3) *ḥayil*: human *ḥayil* and *kōaḥ* are of no avail, unlike the *rûaḥ* of God (Zec. 4:6); a king is not helped by his *ḥayil,* a warrior (*gibbōr*) by his *kōaḥ* (Ps. 33:16); possibly also 1 Ch. 26:8: *'îš-ḥayil bakkōaḥ la'aḇōḏâ,* "able men qualified for the service"; (4) *'mṣ*: Job 9:4; Isa. 40:26 (*'ammîṣ kōaḥ*); Prov. 24:5

---

kōaḥ. E. Beaucamp, "Riflessioni sull'idea di 'forza' nella Bibbia," *BeO,* 4 (1962), 81-83; P. Biard, *La Puissance de Dieu dans la Bible. Travaux de le'Institut catholique de Paris,* 7 (1960); A. Caquot, "Israelite Perceptions of Wisdom and Strength in the Light of the Ras Shamra Texts," *Israelite Wisdom. Festschrift S. Terrien* (Missoula, 1978), 25-33; H. Fredriksson, *Jahwe als Krieger* (Lund, 1945); W. Grundmann, "δύναμαι," *TDNT,* II, 284-317; W. Spiegelberg, "Die ägyptische Gottheit 'der Gotteskraft'," *ZÄS,* 57 (1922), 145f.; A. S. van der Woude, "כֹּחַ *kōaḥ* Kraft," *THAT,* I, 823-25; → גָּבַר *gāḇar* [*gābhar*]; → חַיִל *ḥayil* [*chayil*].

1. *MdD,* 195b, 295a.
2. *KBL*³, 447a.
3. *WKAS,* I, 421.
4. *WKAS,* I, 482a.

(*mᵉʾammeṣ-kōaḥ*; text?[5]); (5) *ḥzq*: "the strong (*ḥāzāq*) shall not retain his *kōaḥ*" (Am. 2:14); with great *kōaḥ,* with a mighty (*ḥāzāq*) hand (Ex. 32:11); (6) *ʿzz*: *lōʾ-kōaḥ* par. *lōʾ-ʿōz* (Job 26:2); (7) *ʿṣm*: Isa. 40:29;[6] *kōḥî wᵉʿōṣem yāḏî* (Dt. 8:17); (8) *yāḏ* and *zᵉrôaʿ* as terms for strength (Ex. 32:11;[7] Dt. 9:29; 2 K. 17:36 ["with great *kōaḥ* and an outstretched arm," referring to the exodus]; Jer. 27:5; 32:17 [the same phrase referring to creation]). Wisdom is associated with *kōaḥ* suprisingly often (Prov. 24:5; Isa. 10:13; Jer. 10:12 par. 51:15; Job 9:4; cf. Job 36:5 [*kabbîr kōaḥ lēḇ*]).

The noun *kōaḥ* denotes human strength, e.g., the physical strength of Samson (Jgs. 16:5,6,9,15,17,19,30) or the power that someone thinks enables him to acquire wealth (*ḥayil*) (Dt. 8:17 [with *ʿōṣem yāḏî*; cf. 1 Ch. 29:2: David provided gold "to the best of his ability"]). Someone who has nothing to eat loses *kōaḥ* (1 S. 28:20); eating restores strength (1 S. 28:22; cf. 1 K. 19:8, where the "strength" Elijah receives from the food enables him to continue on to Horeb). In a similar vein, Lam. 1:6 laments that the princes of Zion, like harts without pasture, have lost the "strength" to flee their pursuers. According to 1 S. 30:4, David and his people weep until they have no more "strength" to weep. In 2 K. 19:3 (par. Isa. 37:3), Hezekiah laments that the women no longer have "strength" to give birth (*kōaḥ lᵉlēḏâ*). In 1 Ch. 26:8; Dnl. 1:4, *kōaḥ* is the ability to serve as gatekeeper of the temple or page in the king's court.

Strength wanes with age (Ps. 71:9; cf. Prov. 20:29, which contrasts the strength of youth with the gray hair of old age). The strength to withstand attacks is also called *kōaḥ* (Dnl. 8:7). In a struggle between the mighty (*raḇ*) and the weak (*ʾên kōaḥ*), only God can help (2 Ch. 14:10[11]).

The noun can also refer to the strength or power of nations (Josh. 17:17: Joseph was a numerous [*raḇ*] people and had great power [*kōaḥ gāḏôl*]) or animals (wild ox [Job 39:11]; horse [Job 39:21]; Behemoth [Job 40:16]; ox [Prov. 14:4]; ram [Dnl. 8:7]).

This survey suggests a basic meaning of "vital energy" for *kōaḥ*. Job 3:17 accordingly refers to the dead in Sheol as *yᵉgîʿê kōaḥ,* "exhausted of strength." Vital energy is manifested in the ability to beget (cf. Gen. 49:3: Jacob calls Reuben his *kōaḥ*) or bear children (2 K. 19:3[8]) and act with vigor. Late texts (Chronicles, Daniel) use *kōaḥ* in the sense of ability to perform a function.[9]

Vital energy can also be manifested in other ways. The *kōaḥ* of the earth is its bounty. The curse on Cain in Gen. 4:12 threatens that the ground shall not yield its *kōaḥ* despite all his labor; Lev. 26:20 (H) states the consequences of disobedience: the land shall not yield its *kōaḥ* and the trees shall not yield their fruit. Job asks (Job 31:39) whether he has eaten the *kōaḥ* of his land without paying (*bᵉlî-kesep*), so that it might cry out (*zāʿaq*) against him (v. 38). On the other hand, when he asks his friends (Job 6:22) whether he has summoned them to offer a bribe for him out of their *kōaḥ,* we are dealing with money or

---

5. See II.2 below.
6. See above.
7. See above.
8. See above.
9. See above.

wealth, as the adjacent verses show (*hāḇû,* "give"; *šiḥ*ᵃ*ḏû,* "give a bribe"; *pāḏâ,* "redeem"). Vital energy thus also manifests itself in wealth. The same is true in Prov. 5:10: ". . . lest strangers (*zārîm*) take their fill of your *kōaḥ* (par. *ʿāṣāḇ,* 'labors')." Hos. 7:9 says: "Aliens devour his [Ephraim's] 'strength.' " This refers to the weakness of the land caused by enemy incursions; *kōaḥ* can mean the economic and military resources of the people as well as their strength in general. Ezr. 2:69 records that the returnees gave of their *kōaḥ* for the rebuilding; the result is stated as a sum of money.

There is a distant similarity between the *kōaḥ* concept of Hebrew as described and Egyp. *ka* (*k3*). On the one hand, *ka* denotes the vital energy of an individual, comprising honor, service, action, wealth, splendor, victory, strength, etc.;[10] on the other, *ka* is manifested *in food and provisions.[11] The Hebrew concept, however, lacks the other overtones of the Egyptian *ka,* such as the soul as the indestructible double of an individual.

2. *Human Strength.* Someone can be said quite objectively to possess physical strength, as in the case of Samson (Jgs. 16[12]) or when Caleb says (Josh. 14:11): "I am still as strong (*ḥāzāq*) to this day as I was in the day that Moses sent me; I still have the 'strength' to fight," or when Isa. 44:12 says that the arm of the smith who manufactures idols possesses *kōaḥ,* or when 1 Ch. 26:8; Dnl. 1:4[13] say that someone is "able" to do something. More often, however, the emphasis is on lack of strength or the insufficiency of human strength in comparison to God.

In the Psalms of Lament, the psalmist accordingly complains that his strength has vanished: "My strength is dried up like a potsherd" (Ps. 22:16[15]; or should we read *ḥikkî,* "my gums," instead of *kōḥî?*); "My strength fails (*kāšal*) because of my misery (reading *boʿ*ᵒ*nî* for *baʿ*ᵃ*wōnî*), and my bones waste away (*ʿāšēšû*)" (31:11[10]); "My strength fails (*ʿāzaḇ*) me; the light of my eyes has gone from me" (38:11[10]); ". . . in the time of old age, . . . when my strength is spent (*kālâ*)" (71:9); "He [God] has broken (*ʿinnâ*) my strength, he has shortened my days" (102:24[23]). The same terminology may appear in a communal lament: "The princes of Zion have lost their 'strength'; like harts that find no pasture, their majesty (*hāḏār*) has vanished" (Lam. 1:6); "My transgressions weigh like a yoke[14] upon my neck; they have broken (*kšl* hiphil) my strength" (1:14). Jer. 48:45 is similar: the fugitives at Hebron are without strength (*mikkōaḥ*; Theodotion and Vulg. read *mippaḥ*). The failure of human strength can become a cliche, as in 1 S. 2:9: *lōʾ b*ᵉ*ḵōaḥ yigbar-ʾîš,* "a man shall not prevail by his own strength"; the context indicates clearly that what matters is God's help. The words addressed to Zerubbabel in Zec. 4:6 are usually translated: "Not by military might (*ḥayil*). nor by [human] strength (*kōaḥ*), but by my spirit (*rûaḥ*), says Yahweh of hosts." This would mean that Zerubbabel must not rely on human aid but can expect

---

10. H. Ringgren, *Word and Wisdom* (Lund, 1947), 38ff.

11. H. Kees, *Totenglauben und Jenseitsvorstellungen der alten Ägypter* (Berlin, ⁵1983), 304; *RÄR,* 360.

12. See above.

13. See above.

14. Conj.; see *BHS.*

to succeed only with God's help.[15] A different idea is expressed in Ps. 33:16: "A king is not victorious (or 'saved'; *nôšāʿ*) by great might (*roḇ-ḥāyil*); a warrior is not delivered by great strength (*roḇ-kōaḥ*)" — as vv. 18f. show, deliverance can be expected only through God's *ḥeseḏ*. Conversely, a mighty man's strength does him no good when he is struck by God's judgment (Am. 2:14).

Mic. 3:8 is a special case. The prophet says: "I am filled with 'strength,' with the spirit of Yahweh, and with justice and might," to declare Israel's transgressions. The phrase *'eṯ-rûaḥ YHWH* should probably be taken as a gloss on *kōaḥ*. We then have *kōaḥ, mišpāṭ,* and *gᵉḇûrâ* with the purpose of declaring (*lᵉhaggîḏ*) to Israel its *pešaʿ* and *ḥaṭṭāʾṯ*. In other words, *kōaḥ* is part of the prophet's equipment, which is correctly interpreted by the gloss as "the spirit of Yahweh."

Mortals, however, think that they have strength in themselves. The king of Assyria says in his pride: "By the 'strength' of my hand I have done it," while in fact he is a tool in the hand of Yahweh (Isa. 10:13). And according to the prologue of Deuteronomy, Israel will say in times of prosperity: "My 'strength' and the might (*ʿōṣem*) of my hand have gotten me this wealth (*ḥayil*)" (Dt. 8:17). In reality, however, it is God who gives the power to obtain wealth (Dt. 8:18). It is therefore the ultimate hubris when the Chaldeans "make their own 'strength' their god" by scoffing at all resistance (Hab. 1:11). When attacked by the enemy, Jehoshaphat accordingly prays: "Wilt thou not execute judgment upon them? For we are powerless (*'ên bānû kōaḥ*) against this great multitude. . . . We do not know what to do, but our eyes are upon thee" (2 Ch. 20:12). Positively, Gideon receives the divine command: "Go in this 'strength' of yours" (Jgs. 6:14), i.e., from the context, in the strength given him by God. Jgs. 6:16 shows that it is God's presence that gives him this strength. Deutero-Isaiah emphasizes that God can give strength to the weary (Isa. 40:29) and that those who wait for Yahweh will constantly receive new strength (*yaḥᵃlîpû kōaḥ*: v. 31; the repetition of this clause with reference to the nations in 41:1 may represent a corrupt text). And when the Servant of Yahweh thinks that he has spent his 'strength' for nothing, he nevertheless has his recompense with God (Isa. 49:4).

Prov. 24:5 is problematic. The MT says that "a wise man is in might (*bāʿôz*), and a man of knowledge (*'îš-daʿaṯ*) increases his strength (*mᵉ'ammēṣ-kōaḥ*)." A minor emendation yields the following translation: "A wise man is mightier than a strong man (*gāḇar ḥāḵām mēʿāz*), and a man of knowledge than he who has strength (*mē'ammîṣ-kōaḥ*)." Wisdom and strength appear together elsewhere,[16] and so the MT may be correct; on the other hand, the emendation agrees with the texts just discussed.

Several passages in the book of Job measure human strength against God's strength in a kind of contest. In his suffering, Job asks: "What is my 'strength,' that I should wait? . . . Is my 'strength' the 'strength' of stones, or is my flesh bronze?" (Job 6:11f.). He can no longer endure waiting, for he is only a mortal, whose strength is limited.

---

15. For a different interpretation, see B. Hartmann, " 'Es gibt keine Kraft und keine Macht ausser bei Gott,' " כח *1940-1965. OTS,* 14 (1965), 115-121; contra W. Rudolph, *Sacharja 1–8. KAT,* XIII/4 (1976), *in loc.*

16. See II.1 above.

God attacks him, never leaving him in peace, and he says (9:19): "If it is a contest of strength, behold him (i.e., 'he is victorious'; reading *hinnēhû* for *hinnēh*)! If it is a matter of justice, who can summon him (reading *yôʿîḏennû* for *yôʿîḏēnî,* contra *BHS*)?" Job acknowledges his inferiority. If we keep the MT and interpret *hinnēh* as *hinnēnî,* we have instead a challenge to God: "I am ready." This interpretation might find support in Job 23:6, where Job confidently offers to go to court: "Would he contend (*rîḇ*) with me with great might (*roḇ-kōaḥ*), would that he would give heed to me [for then I would be vindicated]!" In 24:22, Job lodges a complaint against God: "He upholds tyrants (*'abbîrîm*) by his power (*kōaḥ*)." In his answer to Bildad's third speech, Job says ironically: "How you have helped him who has no power (*lō'-kōaḥ*) and have saved the arm that has no strength (*lō'-ʿōz*)!" (26:2).[17] At the beginning of his concluding discourse (30:2), he stresses the impotence of his human friends: "What could I gain from the strength of their hands, men whose vigor (*kelaḥ*) is gone?" Further on, he says: "With violence (*rob-kōaḥ*) my garment is disfigured" — i.e., God has gotten the upper hand (30:18). Elihu states that Job's cry of distress cannot prevail against God, "nor all the force of your strength (*kol ma'ᵃmaṣṣê-kōaḥ*)" (36:19).

By contrast, God is "wise in heart and mighty in strength"[18] (Job 9:4); before him no mortal can be just (v. 2). At the dawn of time God stilled the sea by his power (*kōaḥ*) and by his understanding (*tᵉḇûnâ*) smote Rahab (26:12) — another association of wisdom with strength. Elihu says that God is *kabbîr kōaḥ lēḇ,* "mighty in strength of heart," i.e. (probably), "very wise" (36:5), and does great things (*yaśgîḇ*) in his power (*kōaḥ*) (36:22). He concludes his speech by stating that God is great in power (*śaggî'-kōaḥ*) and rich in justice, and will not violate righteousness (37:23). There is no mention of *kōaḥ* in God's response.

3. *God's Power.* There is frequent mention of God's power in general. In the Song of the Sea (Ex. 15), v. 6 says: "Thy right hand, O Yahweh, glorious in power (*ne'dārî bakkōaḥ*) . . . shatters the enemy." Isa. 40:26 emphasizes that as a result of Yahweh's greatness of might (*raḇ 'ônîm*) and strength of power (*'ammîṣ kōaḥ*) none of the stars is missing when he calls them by name; here *'ônîm* and *kōaḥ* denote the power of the ruler of the universe. Isa. 50:2 speaks of his power to save (*lᵉhaṣṣîl*). Nah. 1:3 states in quite general terms that Yahweh is slow to anger and *gᵉḏol-kōaḥ,* letting no one go unpunished (should *ḥeseḏ* be read for *kōaḥ?*). Ps. 147:5 once again combines strength and wisdom: "Great is our Lord and abundant in power (*raḇ-kōaḥ*), his understanding (*tᵉḇûnâ*) is beyond measure." Verse 4 speaks of numbering the stars and v. 6 of lifting up the downtrodden and casting the wicked to the ground.

Two hymnic passages in Chronicles treat the same theme: "Thou art ruler over all (*môšēl bakkōl*). In thy hand are power (*kōaḥ*) and might; and in thy hand it is to make great and to give strength (*lᵉgaddēl ûlᵉḥazzēq*) to all" (1 Ch. 29:12); ". . . Art thou not God in heaven? Dost thou not rule (*môšēl*) over all the kingdoms of the nations? In

17. See II.3 below.
18. *GesB,* 610b.

thy hand are power (*kōaḥ*) and might (*g*ᵉ*ḇûrâ*), so that none is able to withstand (*hiṯyaṣṣēḇ*) thee" (2 Ch. 20:6). And in 2 Ch. 25:8, a man of God says to Amaziah: ". . . in God is power to help as well as to cast down (*laʿzôr ûl*ᵉ*hakšîl*)."

Elsewhere God's *kōaḥ* is usually associated with creation or the deliverance from Egypt. According to Job 26:12,[19] Yahweh has shown his power in his victory over the sea. The same idea may be present in Ps. 65:7(6). After a reference to Yahweh's *nôrā'ôṯ* in *ṣeḏeq,* which have made him the hope of all the ends of the earth (v. 6[5]), we read: ". . . who by [his] 'strength' establishes the mountains, being girded with might (*g*ᵉ*ḇûrâ*)." The following verse goes on to speak of stilling the roaring of the sea. Jer. 10:12[20] par. 51:15 (Jer. 51:15-19 echoing 10:12-16 word for word) simply state that Yahweh made (*ʿāśâ*) the earth by his power (*kōaḥ*) and established (*hēḵîn*) the world (*tēḇēl*) by his wisdom (*ḥoḵmâ*). Jer. 27:5; 32:17[21] use the formula "with great power and an outstretched arm," which normally appears in the context of the exodus, to refer to creation. There are several variants of this formula associated with the deliverance from Egypt: "with great power and with an outstretched arm" (Dt. 9:29; 2 K. 17:36); "with great power and with a mighty hand" (Ex. 32:11); "in thy might" (Nu. 14:13); "by his great power" (Dt. 4:37). In Ex. 9:16, Pharaoh is told that God has spared him to show his 'power.' God's acts both in creation and in history are thus an expression of his power. Thus Ps. 111:6 states that Yahweh has shown the power of his works by giving his people the land.

Finally, in Isa. 63, the Song of Edom, *kōaḥ* denotes the power of Yahweh's wrath: he comes from Edom in crimsoned garments and in the greatness of his power (*b*ᵉ*rōḇ kōḥô*; v. 1).

III. 1. *LXX.* In the LXX, *kōaḥ* is usually translated by *ischýs* (112 times + 7 in Sirach) and *ischýein* (3 times) or *dýnamis* (8 times). A few other translations also appear: *astheneín, dynatṓs, katischýein,* and *cheír* (once each).

2. *Dead Sea Scrolls.* There are numerous occurrences of *kōaḥ* in the Dead Sea scrolls. It turns out that the sense of "ability," frequently attested in the late texts of the OT, appears only rarely, in fact just once: 1QSa 1:19 states that anyone who joins the community is to be assigned a function according to his *kōaḥ.* There are also passages in the Manual of Discipline that state that new members are to bring to the community all their knowledge (*daʿaṯ*), strength (*kōaḥ*), and possessions (*hôn*) (1QS 1:11). The meaning of *kōaḥ* here is not entirely clear. The word appears between *daʿaṯ,* which denotes mental ability, and *hôn,* which clearly means worldly possessions. "Strength" might be either physical strength or, as often in the OT, personal property. The statement of purpose that follows contributes little to an understanding of the word *kōaḥ*: the strength is "to be employed according to the perfection of his [God's] ways." A similar

19. See above.
20. Late; see W. Rudolph, *Jeremia. HAT,* XII (^{3}1967), 71f.
21. Both genuine according to Rudolph, *HAT,* XII, 173f., 211-13.

expression occurs in CD 13:11: new members are to be examined "with respect to their works, their understanding, their strength, their power, and their possessions." Negatively, 1QS 3:2 states that the knowledge, strength, and possessions of the unworthy must not be brought into the community.

In one passage, a rhetorical question states that a human being, made of clay, is devoid of strength (*mah kōaḥ lî*: 1QH 3:24; cf. 1QH 10:11: "Which among thy works might have the power to stand before thy glory?"). Otherwise, the reference is almost always to the power of God or the strength he vouchsafes to mortals. God created the earth through his power (1QH 1:13; as in the OT, the parallel speaks of "wisdom"). With him are knowledge, power, and glory (1QH 11:8). His power destroys the foe (1QM 11:1). The words of 1QM 11:5 are typical: "Neither our strength (*kōaḥ*) nor the might (*ʿiṣṣûm*) of our hands has demonstrated power (*ʿāśâ ḥayil*), but it is through thy power (*kōaḥ*) and the strength (*ʿōz*) of thy great might (*ḥayil*)." "Apart from thee there is no one, and no one is like unto thee in power" (1QH 10:9f.; cf. 1QM 13:13: "Who is like unto thee in power?").

In his power, God appears to the psalmist "as perfect light (?)" (1QH 4:23). Although the experience of inadequacy "shatters" (*tmm* hiphil) human strength (1QH 5:29,36; 8:31), God gives strength to endure (1QH 2:8; cf. 8:35). God's power goes hand in hand with mercy (1QH 4:32,35). Thus mortals learn to know his glory and power (1QH 15:20) and to see that there is hope in his mercy and power (1QH 9:14). Thanksgiving is therefore due God "according to the greatness of his power and the fulness of his wonders" (1QH 14:23). These and other passages stand fully in the tradition of OT hymnody.

Finally, we may note that the angels are often called *gibbôrê kôaḥ*. In one passage (1QH 8:11), they deny outsiders admittance to God's plantation (cf. Gen. 3:24); another passage speaks of God's acts of judgment upon "the warriors of strength" and "the host of the holy one" (1QH 10:34f.).

Ringgren

כחד *kḥd*

Contents: I. Etymology. II. Piel: "Conceal." III. Hiphil: "Destroy." IV. The Omniscient God Who Punishes. V. God's Knowledge and Creation?

---

kḥd. H. Conzelmann, "ψεῦδος," *TDNT,* IX, 594-603; A. Guillaume, "Hebrew and Arabic Lexicography: A Comparative Study, II," *Abr-Nahrain,* 2 (1960/61), 5-35, esp. 18; M. A. Klopfenstein, *Die Lüge nach dem AT* (Zurich, 1964), 258-260; A. Oepke, "κρύπτω," *TDNT,* III, 957-978; G. Wehmeyer, "סתר *str* hi. verbergen," *THAT,* II, 173-181.

I. Etymology. The cognates of *khḍ* have a wide semantic range: Aram. ithpael, "be annihilated"; Syr. qal and ithpael, "be disgraced, fear"; Eth. *kĕḥda,* "deny one's faith"; Mehri and Tigré *ģēḥad,* "quarrel"; Arab. *ģaḥada,* "deny, lie."[1]

II. Piel: "Conceal." The root *khḍ* occurs 32 times in the OT. It merits attention both because of its wide range of meanings ("hide, conceal, be hidden," "destroy, be destroyed") and because of its use to describe both divine and human actions.

The qal is not attested. The piel occurs 15 times with the "resultative"[2] meaning "keep something hidden." It always appears negated in commands to reveal something. Except in Gen. 47:18, it is always coupled with a verb of speaking, most often the hiphil of *ngd* (Josh. 7:19; 1 S. 3:18; Isa. 3:9; Jer. 38:25; 50:2; Job 15:18). Jer. 50:2 also uses *'āmar* and a repeated hiphil of *šāma'*; Isa. 3:9 even includes a woe formula. The verb *'āmar* also appears in Ps. 40:11(Eng. v. 10), the piel of *spr* in Ps. 78:4, and the hiphil of *yārâ* III in Job 27:11. The message to be declared and not kept hidden sometimes belongs to the human world. In 2 S. 14:18, Solomon asks the woman from Tekoa who instigated her to intercede for Absalom. In Jer. 38:24, Zedekiah demands that Jeremiah keep their conversation secret upon pain of death. The matter is always something important. Job 15:18 makes the transition to the religious realm: the fathers have not hidden God's will for the wicked from their sons. In their insolence, the wicked do not even conceal their sins (Isa. 3:9). Since God's word must be obeyed, the king urges Jeremiah not to conceal it from him (Jer. 38:14). The wisdom instructor teaches concerning God's work and his plan to deal with the wicked (Job 27:11). The prophet knows of the fall of Babylon and must proclaim it to the people as imminent deliverance (Jer. 50:2). Whoever has experienced a personal demonstration of God's righteousness must praise God and not remain silent (Ps. 40:11[10]); God's glorious deeds must not remain concealed from generation to generation (Ps. 78:4).

Job 6:10, which uses the piel of *khḍ,* is probably an interpolation.[3] Here *khḍ* is often translated "deny."[4] Friedrich Horst[5] points out, however, that *khḍ* never means "deny": "It always denotes an act of concealment that seeks deliberately to keep something hidden; its opposite is always an act of speaking, proclaiming, informing, or teaching." In Job 6:10, therefore, the sufferer is innocent of remaining silent concerning God's works. The Hebrew word for "deny" is the piel of → כחשׁ *khš*; unlike *khḍ,* it is never constructed with *min,*[6] which appears in 10 of the 15 instances of *khḍ* piel.

The LXX renders the piel of *khḍ* 11 times with *krýptō,* "hide," a word that represents a variety of semantically related words in the OT.[7] In 4 passages, the LXX uses a

1. Cf. *MdD,* 205a; *TigrWb,* 393; W. Leslau, *Lexique soqotri* (Paris, 1938), 107.
2. E. Jenni, *Das hebräische Pi'el* (Zurich, 1968), 250.
3. G. Fohrer, *Das Buch Hiob. KAT,* XVI (1963), 161.
4. Cf. K. Budde, *Das Buch Hiob. HKAT,* II/1 (^{2}1913), 27.
5. F. Horst, *Hiob. BK,* XVI/1 (1968), 105.
6. Klopfenstein, 259.
7. Cf. Oepke, 967.

different word. Isa. 3:9 employs *emphanízō,* "make invisible"; Job 6:10; 27:11 use a negated form of *pseúdō,* "lie." The LXX changes the meaning of Gen. 47:18, using *ektríbō,* "destroy," which will be discussed below in the context of the niphal and hiphil. Instead of the MT "We cannot hide from my lord . . . ," the Greek text reads: "We would not be destroyed by (Gk. *apó* for Heb. *min*) our lord." Here *min* was probably taken as introducing the logical subject of the passive,[8] just as *apó* is commonly used for *hypó* in later Greek.[9] It is unlikely that the text means simply "before our lord," as suggested by the translation *enantíon* in vv. 18 and 19.

III. Hiphil: "Destroy." The hiphil of *kḥd* occurs 6 times. The lexica suggest the meaning "destroy" in 5 cases, but translate "hide" in Job 20:12 on the basis of the piel (cf. LXX *krýptō*). What the wicked man "hides" under his tongue is evil. "With his malicious schemes and plans, the wicked man is depicted as enjoying the luxury of self-indulgence — he is like a child with a piece of candy."[10] This interpretation is supported by Job 20:13, where we find *ḥāmal,* "hold onto," *lōʾ ʿāzab̲,* "not let go," and *mānaʿ,* "keep." Recalling the usage of the piel, Ps. 83:5(4) uses *zāk̲ar* (negated) in parallel with the hiphil of *kḥd.* Israel's annihilated enemies are to be remembered no more; the same idea is expressed in the LXX by *exolothreúō,* "destroy" (LXX 82:5). In Zec. 11:8a (probably a late interpolation[11]), the meaning of *kḥd* hiphil has been the subject of much discussion; it can mean either "destroy" or "remove."[12] Apart from the context, the *exaírō,* "take as booty," of the LXX argues for the latter.

Just as the "shepherd" in Zec. 11:8 actually represents God, so God is the explicit subject who "destroys" in 1 K. 13:34; Ex. 23:23. In the former, we may note the par. *šāmad̲,* "cut off," and the LXX *egéneto . . . eis aphanismón* in the sense of "vanish," which is similar in meaning to "keep hidden." It is also appropriate that God should wish the peoples of Canaan to vanish from before (*min*) the Israelites (Ex. 23:23), while in 2 Ch. 32:21 the angel of Yahweh destroys the Assyrians. In both passages, the LXX uses *ektríbō,* "destroy."

IV. The Omniscient God who Punishes. The 10 instances of the niphal constitute the passive to both the piel and the hiphil. Reflecting the usage of the piel, the former means that something is not "concealed"; God's omniscience is further emphasized by the use of *yād̲aʿ.* As in the piel construction, *min* appears in 2 S. 18:13; Ps. 69:6(5); 139:15. In the Samuel passage, it is the king from whom nothing is concealed; in the Psalms, it is God. In the last two passages, the LXX uses *krýptō*; in the first, it paraphrases with *lanthánō,* "hide." The reference is always to the omniscient God. Ps. 69:6(5) acknowledges that God knows the psalmist's misdeeds. In Ps. 139:15, the psalmist knows that his frame is not hidden from God even in the depths of the earth.

---

8. *KBL*^{3}, 566.

9. Cf. W. Pape, *Handwörterbuch der griechischen Sprache,* I (Braunschweig, 1842), 295; W. Bauer, *A Greek-English Lexicon of the NT* (Eng. trans., Chicago, ^{2}1979), 88.

10. Fohrer, 330.

11. W. Rudolph, *Sacharja 9–14. KAT,* XIII/4 (1976), 206.

12. *Ibid.*

Hos. 5:3 (LXX *ouk ápestin,* "is not absent") also belongs in this context: God insists that he know Ephraim well, that nothing can be concealed from him. But 2 S. 18:13 also contains an indirect statement about God, for 2 S. 14:17 likens the king to God: "My lord the king is like the angel of God, who knows (*yāḏaʿ*) good and evil." We may conclude that "the OT takes God's omnipresence and omniscience more seriously than any religion."[13] All of Ps. 139, not just v. 15, makes the same point: God has foreknowledge of every individual, before each person is formed in his mother's womb (vv. 15f.). God knows all the thoughts, deeds, ways of the psalmist (vv. 3f., 23), for whom God's nature and works are unfathomable (vv. 6, 17f.). Not even darkness can hide anyone from God (v. 12); there is no place to flee from God (vv. 7-12). Ps. 69:6(5); Hos. 5:3 add that God also knows human transgressions; thus in Ps. 139 the psalmist feels not so much at God's mercy as under God's protection (vv. 5,10,14,16,18).

The other 6 passages, where the niphal represents the passive of the hiphil, speak rather differently of God. Here *kḥd* has "markedly negative overtones."[14] Eliphaz's words in Job 4:7 are based on the conviction that the fate of each individual is dependent on God, which makes it appear impossible that the upright might be destroyed, an interpretation supported by the par. *'āḇaḏ* and the LXX *apóllymi,* "destroy." In Job 22:20, also, the righteous see the wicked destroyed (LXX *aphanízō,* "make invisible, annihilate"). Job 15:28 states that the wicked live in "uninhabitable houses," so that our parallel verb must refer to "desolate cities" (LXX *póleis erḗmous*). In contrast to the punishment of the wicked, the righteous is confident of God's help and protection. The remaining passages (Zec. 11:9,16) are in the "shepherd vision," in which the prophet describes first a "true" shepherd and then a "false" shepherd.[15] Here, too, the niphal of *kḥd* has a negative sense, denoting a punishment. In v. 9, the parallel is "What is to die, let it die," so that *hanniḵḥeḏeṯ* means "what is to be missing, let it be missing," the exact sense of LXX *to ekleípon ekleipétō.* With the same meaning, v. 16 has *eklimpánō*: the "false shepherd" does not care for "what is missing" (par. *nišbereṯ,* "what is broken").

V. God's Knowledge and Creation? God's benevolent omniscience stands in contrast to his destructive might; both are expressed by forms of *kḥd.* Would it therefore be correct to claim that his knowledge creates and his disregard destroys? This would chime with the notion that God creates through his word (Gen. 1; Sir. 42:15; Ps. 33:6) but destroys by turning away his face (Ps. 30:8[7]; 104:29). Ps. 1:6 states such an antithesis: God knows (*yāḏaʿ*) the way of the righteous, but the way of the wicked perishes (*'āḇaḏ*). Ps. 139 associates God's omniscience with the creation of each person (vv. 13f., 15). Jer. 1:5 expresses a similar idea: "Before I formed you in the womb I knew (*yāḏaʿ*) you." Sir. 23:20 says of God: "Before anything comes to pass, it is already known to him." God's knowledge is thus conceptually close to God's creative act, but the former is never described as being efficacious.

---

13. Oepke, 967.
14. Wehmeyer, 177.
15. Rudolph, *KAT,* XIII/4, 204.

We might also address our question to statements about God's wisdom in relationship to his creation. His works are shaped by wisdom (Ps. 104:24), and through his knowledge (*da'aṯ*) the waters of the deep spring forth (Prov. 3:20). These passages use the prep. *bᵉ*, which can introduce an "accompanying circumstance" but also a "means."[16] We must probably opt for the former, because, in the passages where Wisdom is personified (e.g., Prov. 8:22-31), she herself is created by God.[17] The closest association of Wisdom with God's knowledge and works is in Wis. 8:4: "For she is initiated into God's knowledge, and it is she who chooses his works." This probably means that "Wisdom's knowledge is the same as God's knowledge" and that "God and Wisdom know and will in the same act."[18]

Eising†

---

16. *KBL*³, 101.
17. Cf. G. Fohrer, "σοφία," *TDNT*, VII, 491; also Wis. 9:9.
18. Cf. P. Heinisch, *Das Buch der Weisheit. EHAT*, XXIV (1912), 160.

כָּחַשׁ *kāḥaš*; כַּחַשׁ *kaḥaš*; כֶּחָשׁ *keḥāš*

Contents: I. 1. Occurrences, Etymology; 2. Meaning; 3. LXX. II. Secular Usage: 1. Verb; 2. Noun. III. Theological Usage: 1. Denial of God; 2. Concealment; 3. Prophetic Dissimulation; 4. Dead Sea Scrolls.

I. 1. *Occurrences, Etymology.* The OT probably distinguishes two distinct roots *kḥš*,[1] one meaning "waste away," the other meaning "deny." The former appears only once in the qal (Ps. 109:24) and in the noun *kaḥaš* (Job 16:8, contra LXX, Aquila, and Vulg.). The root meaning "deny" appears 21 times as a verb (19 times in the piel, once each in the niphal and hithpael); it also appears 5 times in the noun *kaḥaš* and once in the adj. *keḥāš*. This root also appears 3 times as a verb or noun in Sirach (Sir. 41:17).

---

kāḥaš. J. Blau, "Über homonyme und angeblich homonyme Wurzeln II," *VT*, 7 (1957), 98-102; E. Jenni, *Das hebräische Pi'el* (Zurich, 1968); Jörg Jeremias, *Kultprophetie und Gerichtsverkündigung in der späten Königszeit Israels. WMANT*, 35 (1970), 31ff.; M. A. Klopfenstein, *Das Lüge nach dem AT* (Zurich, 1964); *idem*, "כחשׁ *kḥš pi.* leugnen," *THAT*, I, 825-28; J. L. Palache, *Semantic Notes on the Hebrew Lexicon* (Eng. trans., Leiden, 1959); G. Quell, *Wahre und falsche Propheten. BFChTh*, 46/1 (1952).

1. Cf. W. J. Gerber, *Die hebräischen Verba denominativa* (Leipzig, 1896), 26f.; E. Ben Yehuda, *Thesaurus totius hebraitatis* (1908-1959, repr. New York, 1960); G. Dalman, *Aramäisches-neuhebräisches Wörterbuch* (Frankfurt, 1897), 196; *LexHebAram*, 352; Klopfenstein, *THAT*, I, 825.

Both roots appear in Middle Hebrew as well as in Jewish Aramaic. It is uncertain whether the root meaning "waste away" is also found in Ethiopic texts[2] and whether there is any connection with Ugar. *ṯkḥ*.[3] S. Rin[4] associates *kḥš* with Ugar. *kḥṯ*, "throne," understanding it to mean "worship"; this would be relevant to the interpretation of Ps. 18:45(Eng. v. 44); Dt. 33:29.

2. *Meaning.* If we leave aside the meaning "waste away," we find an ambivalent meaning basic to the semantic content of the word group; the ambivalence can usually be expressed by the two translations "say [or 'bring about'] that something is not" and "not say [or 'bring about'] that something is."[5] Both meanings probably coexisted from the beginning as inversive functions. From them developed more specific meanings: (1) "deny (the truth of something)" (Gen. 18:15; Lev. 5:21,22[6:2,3]; Jer. 5:12; Job 8:18; Prov. 30:9); (2) "deny, be false to" (Job 31:28; Josh. 24:27; Isa. 30:9; 59:13; Hos. 9:2; 10:13; 12:1[11:12]; Hab. 3:17); (3) "conceal" (Lev. 19:11; Josh. 7:11; Hos. 4:2); (4) "dissemble" (1 K. 13:18; Zec. 13:4; Hos. 7:3; Nah. 3:1; Ps. 59:13[12]); (5) "flatter" (Dt. 33:29; 2 S. 22:45; Ps. 18:45[44]; 66:3; 81:16[15]).

In contrast to → כזב *kzb* and → שׁקר *šqr*, *kḥš* denotes the disguising, concealment, or denial of a given situation contrary to better knowledge; it thus also represents a deliberate accountable act.

3. *LXX.* The LXX translates the root meaning "waste away" with *alloioústhai* (Ps. 109:24[LXX 108:24]) but interprets the noun in Job 16:8 as meaning "lie" and translates it *pseúdos*. It renders all the forms based on the root meaning "deny" by a form of the root *pseud-*; only in Gen. 18:15 does it use the more precise *arneísthai* (cf. Aquila's *arnētḗs* in Isa. 30:9).

II. Secular Usage. All five specific meanings of the root appear in secular usage, which accounts for two thirds of all its occurrences. The meanings deriving from the sense "not say that" predominate.

1. *Verb.* a. Usage in the sense "not say that," i.e., "conceal," is typically associated with the legal realm. Thus the verb is used by Lev. 19:11 in a prohibition against stealing belonging to an ancient decalogue; Hos. 4:2 uses it in an oracle of judgment to describe a transgression that stands under Yahweh's judgment.

b. On the other hand, the meaning "cause to go unnoticed that," i.e., "dissemble," is associated with the everyday phenomenon of concealing one's true purpose in some area of human endeavor. This meaning can be applied to prophets who consciously conceal their intentions from others by deceptive words or actions. In 1 K. 13:18, for

---

2. Leslau, *Contributions,* 26.

3. W. F. Albright, "Are the Ephod and the Teraphim Mentioned in Ugaritic Literature?" *BASOR,* 83 (1941), 40, n. 7.

4. Svi Rin and Shifra Rin, "Ugaritic-OT Affinities II," *BZ,* N.S. 11 (1968), 174-192, esp. 182.

5. Klopfenstein, *Das Lüge nach dem AT,* 255f.

example, a *nābî'* misrepresents himself before another man of God in order to deceive him.

c. The meaning "flatter" can be understood as a special development of the meaning "dissemble." Usage of the verb to describe the conduct of enemies forced into subjection gave the piel (3 occurrences) as well as the niphal and hithpael the special nuance of dissimulation through a show of servility. The object of this hypocritical conduct on the part of Israel's enemies or foreigners (Ps. 18:45f.[44f.] par. 2 S. 22:45f.) may be Yahweh (Ps. 66:3; 81:16[15]), Israel (Dt. 33:29), or the Israelite king (Ps. 18:45f.[44f.] par. 2 S. 22:45f.).

d. Secular usage of the verb in the sense "say that . . . not," i.e., "deny," is found in Gen. 18:15; Lev. 5:21,22[6:2,3] as well as Job 8:18. In Gen. 18:15, Sarah denies the accusation that she laughed disbelievingly by asserting the contrary. Lev. 5:21,22(6:2,3) has to do with a situation in which someone deceives his neighbor concerning property taken as security or stolen or extorted, denying that he has found what is missing. In a similar but figurative usage, a garden can be described as denying the godless who has been pulled up like a luxuriant and deeply rooted plant (Job 8:18).

e. Parallel to this meaning there developed the meaning "cause that . . . not," i.e., "deny, abandon." The root is used figuratively in this sense in Hos. 9:2 as well as Hab. 3:17: the vine or olive tree shall abandon its owner, refusing to yield its fruit.

2. *Noun.* Like the verb, the noun exhibits semantic ambiguity. In secular usage, however, the meaning "lie, pretense" predominates. In Hos. 7:3, for example, *kaḥaš* refers to political chicanery on the part of wire-pullers at the king's court in Samaria. Nah. 3:1, in an invective against Nineveh, also concerns political tricks played on small neighboring states by rulers in the capital of the Assyrian Empire. In Ps. 59:13(12), a psalmist who is faithful to Yahweh laments the distortion of the true situation by false accusers; here again we are dealing with the everyday phenomenon of one person deceiving another.

III. Theological Usage.

1. *Denial of God.* In the religious realm, the group of words serves primarily to express denial or rejection of Yahweh. The denying subject — the house of Israel (Jer. 5:12) or someone wealthy who is full and self-satisfied (Prov. 30:9) — may use specific words that imply corresponding conduct. Primarily, however, denial of Yahweh finds expression in actions. This is true for the verb in Josh. 24:27; Isa. 59:13; Job 31:28, as well as for the noun in Hos. 10:13; 12:1(11:12) and the adjective in Isa. 30:9. The word group here characterizes conduct in its totality, including one's fundamental attitude. In practice, to deny Yahweh is to embrace alien cults (Josh. 24:27; Job 31:28; Hos. 12:1[11:12]), to refuse to listen to Yahweh's instruction (Isa. 30:9), or to transgress against his law, i.e., to break his covenant (Isa. 59:13; Hos. 10:13).

2. *Concealment.* The counterpart to denial by words or actions is concealment of a situation. In Josh. 7:11, what is concealed is the theft of things that had been devoted by ban, so that *kḥš* here refers more precisely to an infringement of sacral law, once again a transgression of Yahweh's covenant.

3. *Prophetic Dissimulation.* A theological usage of the root with the meaning "deceive" is found in Zec. 13:4. As in 1 K. 13:18,[6] prophets are the subject. In contrast to 1 K. 13:18, however, *kḥš* here does not mean ordinary concealment of one's true intentions but actual appearance in the guise of a prophet.[7] At the awaited eschaton, the syncretistically-minded prophets of the exilic period[8] will no longer don the hairy mantle of a prophet in order to pretend to communicate Yahweh's word to the people.

4. *Dead Sea Scrolls.* The root *kḥš* appears only 3 times in the Dead Sea scrolls. Here *kḥš* serves to characterize the spirit of wickedness, in conjunction with greed, sloth, wickedness, lying (*šqr*), arrogance, pride, deception (*rᵉmîyâ*), cruelty, and godlessness (1QS 4:9). The righteous must reject this spirit (10:12). In 4QpNah 2:2, the "bloody city" (Nineveh) of Nah. 3:1 is identified with the "city of Ephraim" (Jerusalem?) that will walk in *kḥš* and *šqr* at the end of days.

Schunck

---

6. See II.1 above.
7. Klopfenstein, *Das Lüge nach dem AT,* 279.
8. Cf. B. Otzen, *Studien über Deuterosacharja. AcThD,* 6 (1964), 194-98.

כֹּל *kōl*

Contents: I. Etymology. II. Meaning; OT Usage. III. Stylistic and Theological Considerations: 1. Style; 2. Theologically Significant Examples. IV. LXX, Dead Sea Scrolls.

I. Etymology. The word *kōl* *kull(u) is common Semitic: Ugar. *kl,*[1] Phoen. *kl,*[2] Aram. *kl, kōl,* determined *kōllā'* (Syr. *kul*), Arab. *kull,*[3] OSA *kl,*[4] Eth. *kʷĕll.* In Akkadian, we find both *kalû*[5] and *kullatu.*[6] There is also a noun *gimru,* "totality."[7]

---

kōl. P. P. Boccaccio, "I termini contrari come espressioni della totalità in ebraico (I)," *Bibl,* 33 (1952), 173-190; J. A. Fitzmyer, "The Syntax of *kl, kl',* 'All' in the Aramaic Texts from Egypt and in Biblical Aramaic," *Bibl,* 38 (1957), 170-184 = *A Wandering Aramean. SBL Mon,* 25 (1979), 205-217; H. Ringgren, "The Omitting of *kol* in Hebrew Parallelism," *VT,* 32 (1982), 99-103; G. Sauer, "כֹּל *kōl* Gesamtheit," *THAT,* I, 828-830; R. R. Stieglitz, "Minoan and Biblical Totals," *SMEA,* 14 (1971), 217f.

1. *WUS,* no. 1320.
2. *DISO,* 118ff.
3. *WKAS,* I, 292ff.
4. ContiRossini, 168.
5. *AHw,* I (1965), 427.
6. *Ibid.,* 501.
7. *Ibid.,* 289.

The root is *kll,* "be complete," factitive "make complete"; cf. Ugar. *kll* D, "make complete,"[8] the shaphel or aphel in various Aramaic dialects meaning "make complete," Akk. *šuklulu,* "make complete." Contrast Akk. *kullulu,* "conceal"; cf. Arab. *kll* V, "surround," OSA *kll,* "surround,"[9] Eth. *kallala,* "surround, protect," a meaning attested from the peal in several Aramaic dialects. Akk. *kalû* appears to be related to two roots, *kll* and *kly.*[10]

II. Meaning; OT Usage. Literally, *kōl* means something like "totality"; but it is rarely used absolutely in the sense of "everything, the whole" (e.g., Eccl. 1:2; 11:5; Isa. 29:11; Jer. 10:16 par. 51:19; Isa. 44:24; Job 13:1). It usually appears in the construct (generally written *kol*) and means: (1) "whole," when preceding a determined noun in the singular (*kol-hā'āreṣ,* "the whole earth" [Gen. 9:19; Isa. 6:3; Ps. 47:8(Eng. v. 7); 72:19; etc.]; *kol-ʿammî,* "all my people" [Gen. 41:40]); (2) "all," when preceding a determined noun in the plural (*kol-haggôyim,* "all the nations" [Isa. 2:2; 43:9; Ps. 67:3(2); 118:10]; cf. *kol-hāʿammîm* [Ps. 97:6; etc.]; cf. the collective *kol(-hā)'āḏām,* "all humankind" [Gen. 7:21; Ps. 64:10(9); etc.]); (3) "every," when preceding an undetermined noun in the singular (*kol-ʿām,* "every people" [Est. 3:8]; *kol-bayiṯ,* "every house" [Isa. 24:10]); also "any" (*kol-dāḇār,* "anything" [Ruth 4:7]) or "all kinds of" (*kol-ṭûḇ,* "all kinds of precious things" [Gen. 24:10]; *kol-ʿēṣ,* "all kinds of trees" [Lev. 19:23]); (4) "no," in the context of negation (*kol-mᵉlā'ḵâ lō'-yēʿāśeh bāhem,* "no work shall be done on those [days]" [Ex. 12:16; cf. 20:10: *lō'-taʿᵃśeh kol-mᵉlā'ḵâ*]; *kol-ṭumʿâ 'al-tō'ḵal,* "eat nothing unclean" [Jgs. 13:14]). For specialized usages, the lexica should be consulted.[11]

III. Stylistic and Theological Considerations. There would be hardly any point to cataloging all the occurrences. Here we shall merely point out certain examples of particular stylistic or theological interest.

1. *Style.* Stylistically, we may note that the OT writers often omit *kōl* when it is already clear that a totality is meant: even without *kōl,* "the nations of the earth" means "all the nations of the earth." But there is a whole series of parallelisms in which one member uses *kōl* while the other does not, although both clearly have the same sense of totality. Examples from the Psalms include: "All his ordinances were before me, and his statutes I did not put away from me" (18:23[22]); "Hide thy face from my sins, and blot out all my iniquities" (51:11[9]); "Let the peoples praise thee, O God; let all the nations (*'ammîm kullām*) praise thee" (67:4,6[3,5]; perhaps an augmentation); "I will meditate (*hāgâ*) on all thy work, and muse on thy mighty deeds" (77:13[12]; cf. 143:5); "all our days" par. "our years" (90:9); "The nations will fear the name of

8. *WUS,* no. 1320.
9. ContiRossini, 169.
10. → כליל *kālîl;* → כלה *kālâ.*
11. *KBL*[3], 451f.

Yahweh, and all the kings of the earth thy glory" (102:16[15]); "All thy works shall give thanks to thee, and thy saints shall bless thee" (145:10).

Prophetic examples include: "All you inhabitants of the world, you who dwell on the earth" (Isa. 18:3); "Every valley shall be lifted up, and every mountain and hill shall be made low; the uneven ground shall become level, and the rough places a plain" (Isa. 40:4); "Behold, all who are incensed against you [cf. 45:24] shall be put to shame and confounded; those who strive against you shall be as nothing and shall perish" (Isa. 41:11; cf. Ps. 35:26, with *yaḥdāw* instead of *kōl*); "The nations shall see your vindication, and all the kings your glory" (Isa. 62:2); "I will recount the steadfast love of Yahweh, the praises of Yahweh, according to all that Yahweh has granted us" (Isa. 63:7); "The wind shall shepherd all your shepherds, and your lovers shall go into captivity" (Jer. 22:22); "For I will satisfy the weary soul, and every languishing soul I will replenish" (Jer. 31:25; cf. Isa. 40:29, without *kōl*).

2. *Theologically Significant Examples.* The distribution of *kōl* is fairly even, but its frequency varies in different books. Certain genres have a predilection for expressions using *kōl.* There are significantly more occurrences in Jeremiah than in Ezekiel. The Enthronement Psalms and Ecclesiastes are full of *kōl* phrases. In large part, of course, this is due to the themes treated by the texts in question, as the following discussion will show.

a. *Creation and God's Universal Dominion.* Yahweh's creation of the entire world rarely finds expression in statements using *kōl.* Jer. 10:16 (par. 51:19), however, states that he formed "everything" (*yôṣēr hakkōl hû'*). Therefore his kingdom encompasses everything (*malkûṯô bakkol māšālâ*: Ps. 103:19). These two passages use the absolute form *hakkōl,* "everything." "He made heaven and earth, the sea, and all that is in them," says Ps. 146:6 (although Ps. 24:1, e.g., says the same thing without using *kōl*). In the Enthronement Psalms, *kōl* is frequently used to describe the universal dominion of Yahweh. "All the earth" is to praise him (Ps. 96:1) and tremble before him (v. 9); his marvelous works are to be declared among all the peoples (v. 3); he is more powerful that all gods (v. 4; 95:3; 97:9); the field and everything in it is to exult, and all the trees of the wood are to sing with joy (96:12). He is Lord of the whole earth (*'ᵃḏôn kol-hā'āreṣ*) (Ps. 97:5); all peoples (*kol-ha'ammîm*) behold his glory (*kāḇôḏ*) (97:6). All worshippers of images are put to shame, and all gods bow down before him (v. 7). All the ends of the earth see his victory (*yᵉšû'â*) (Ps. 98:3). God's blessing causes all nations (*gôyîm*) to know his saving power (Ps. 67:3[2]), so that all nations may praise him (vv. 4,6[3,5]). Isa. 6:3, in a context that also speaks of Yahweh as king, states that Yahweh's *kāḇôḏ* fills the whole earth.

Similar universalistic ideas are found in other psalms. Ps. 100:1 calls upon all the lands to praise Yahweh. The nations and all the kings of the earth will fear Yahweh when he restores Zion, thus demonstrating his power (Ps. 102:16[15]). Ps. 108:6(5) asks Yahweh to show his glory over all the earth; 113:4 states that he is high above all nations. Yahweh is above all gods; he does everything that he pleases in heaven and on earth (Ps. 135:5f.; cf. Isa. 46:10), a statement that is then justified by a reference to his power in nature and in history.

Deutero-Isaiah, who is strongly influenced by the language of the Psalms in other respects, uses *kōl* with surprising infrequency in passages dealing with creation and God's omnipotence (cf. Isa. 40:13,15,22f.; 41:5; 42:5, where one might have expected *kōl*). As examples using *kōl,* we may cite several passages. Isa. 44:23 calls on the heavens, the depths of the earth, the mountains (all without *kōl*), and all the trees of the forest to rejoice. According to 40:5; 49:26, all flesh — i.e., all humanity — will see and know the glory and mighty deeds of Yahweh. According to 52:10, all the nations (*gôyîm*) and all the ends of the earth shall see the salvation of Yahweh. Every knee shall bow before him, and every tongue swear fealty to him (45:23). All who were incensed against him will be ashamed (45:24), and all the offspring (*zeraʿ*) of Israel will triumph in his salvation (v. 25). A statement concerning creation appears in 45:12: Yahweh made the earth together with the human race, and the heavens with all their host. Of fundamental importance is 45:7: "I form light and create darkness, I make weal and create woe, I Yahweh do all these things (*ʿōśeh kol-ʾēlleh*)." Here everything that takes place, for better or worse, is ascribed to Yahweh in a way that excludes any type of dualism (cf. 1 S. 2:6f.). It is noteworthy that such creation texts never use *kōl* as a cosmological term meaning "the universe."[12]

b. *P's Creation Account.* The Creation account of P is quite restrained in its use of *kōl.* Quite naturally, the word does not appear at all in the words of creation; but it is found occasionally (and clearly on no systematic principle) in the subsequent descriptions: every winged bird (Gen. 1:21), everything that creeps upon the ground (vv. 25f.; cf. v. 28). Every plant upon the face of all the earth is given to the human race for food (vv. 29f.). Then God sees that everything he has made is good (v. 31). Finally, we are told that heaven and earth "with all their host" were finished (*wayᵉḵullû,* 2:1); God finished (*wayᵉḵal*) his work and rested from all the work that he had done (2:2b,3). The concluding words thus express the aspect of totality by using both *kōl* and the verb *kālâ.*

c. *The Flood.* The aspect of totality also appears in the story of the Flood. Every imagination of the human race was evil (Gen. 6:5); all flesh had corrupted their way upon the earth (v. 12).[13] God therefore determines to make an end of all flesh (6:13,17): everything that is on earth shall die (v. 17). Noah, however, is to save two of every sort of animal (6:19). Everything perishes (7:21-23 [6 occurrences]). After the Flood, everything comes forth once more (8:17,19), and God promises never again to destroy every living creature (v. 21). Now every animal alive is given to the human race for food (9:3). P's concluding account of the covenant (9:8-17) contains 12 occurrences of *kōl.*

d. *Patriarchal Narratives.* In the patriarchal narratives, *kōl* occasionally plays an important role. At the end of the primal history, the story of the Tower of Babel emphasizes that the whole earth once had the same language (Gen. 11:1; cf. v. 6); but

---

12. Cf. C. R. North, *The Second Isaiah* (London, 1964), 145f.; → עולם *ʿôlām.*

13. Cf. A. R. Hulst, "*Kol bāśar in der priesterlichen Fluterzählung,*" *Studies on the Book of Genesis. OTS,* 12 (1958), 28-68.

after the unsuccessful attempt to become like God (cf. v. 6: "everything they undertake"), the human race is scattered over the face of all the earth (vv. 8f.). This lays the groundwork for the election of Abraham, that in him "all the families of the earth" may be blessed (or bless themselves;[14] 12:3).

Also of interest is the statement that God caused Joseph to prosper (*ṣlḥ* hiphil) in all that he did (Gen. 39:3). As Ps. 1:3 shows, this is a wisdom motif. That Joseph subsequently gathered up all the food (Gen. 41:48), that there was famine in all the lands (v. 54), that finally even all of Egypt was famished (vv. 55f.) and that Joseph fed the people of all the land from all the storehouses (vv. 56f.) follows naturally.

e. *Exodus.* The exodus event is triggered by Pharaoh's order that every Hebrew baby born is to be thrown into the Nile (Ex. 1:22). Later Moses receives the commission to tell Pharaoh everything that Yahweh says to him (6:28f.; 7:2). The plagues strike "all the land of Egypt" (*kol-'ereṣ miṣrayim* [7:19,21; 8:12f.,20(16f.,24); 9:9,22,24; 10:14f.,22]), "all Egypt" (7:24), "all the country" (7:27[8:2]) (but just "the land of Egypt" [without *kōl*] in 8:2f.[6f.]; 9:22f.; 10:12,21[15]), all the servants of Pharaoh (7:29[8:4]; 10:6), all the people and animals in the field (9:19), "everything that was in the field, both man and beast, every plant and every tree" (9:25), and finally all the first-born (11:5; 12:29; cf. Ps. 105:36). Finally, we are also told that the entire army of Pharaoh perished in the sea (Ex. 14:28).

f. *Deuteronomy.* Statements using *kōl* often have a theological function in Deuteronomy. To Yahweh belong heaven and earth with all that is in it (Dt. 10:14), but Yahweh chose Israel out of all the peoples (7:6f.,14,16; 10:15; cf. also Ex. 19:5 [". . . you shall be my own possession among all peoples; for all the earth is mine"]; Am. 3:2). Israel is told to love Yahweh "with all your heart, and with all your soul, and with all your might" (Dt. 6:5; cf. 10:12) and keep all his commandments (11:8,22; 28:15; cf. Ezk. 18:21).

g. *God/Humankind.* The two aspects of the relationship between God and humankind are often characterized by statements using *kōl.* God knows everything, knows all the ways of the psalmist (Ps. 139:3), shapes all his days in advance (v. 16). He can do whatever he pleases (*kōl 'ᵃšer-ḥāp̱ēṣ 'āśâ* [Ps. 115:3; 135:6]; *kōl tûḵal* [Job 42:2]; *kol-ḥep̱ṣî 'e'ᵉśeh* [Isa. 46:10]). "All souls are mine," says Yahweh (Ezk. 18:4). Therefore all wait upon him (Ps. 104:27; 145:15); he satisfies everything that lives with *ḥesed̲* (Ps. 145:16). He is just in all his ways, and kind in all his doings (Ps. 145:17); he is near to all who call upon him (v. 18) and preserves all who love him (v. 20); therefore all flesh, i.e., all humankind, shall praise him (v. 21). All his work (*ma'ᵃśeh*) is done in faithfulness (Ps. 33:4); all his paths are steadfast love and faithfulness (Ps. 25:10).

On the other hand, God claims the faithful totally. The psalmist thanks God with all his heart (Ps. 86:12; cf. 111:1; 138:1). Joel exhorts: "Return *beḵol-lᵉḇaḇkem*" (Joel 2:12); Zephaniah says: "Rejoice *bᵉḵol-lēḇ*" (Zeph. 3:14). The psalmist calls on all that is within him (*kol-qᵉrāḇay*) to praise Yahweh (Ps. 103:1). Ps. 119:2 calls those blessed

---

14. → ברך *brk,* II, 297.

15. Cf. S. Ö. Steingrimsson, *Vom Zeichen zur Geschichte. CB,* 14 (1979), 185, 191.

who seek God with their whole heart. In Ps. 18:23(22), the psalmist boasts that he has kept all God's precepts before his eyes. Through his angels, God similarly protects all the ways of the faithful (Ps. 91:11).

h. *Psalms.* Laments often use *kōl* to describe suffering: "all my enemies" (*'ôyeḇay* [Ps. 6:11(10)]; *ṣôreray* [31:12(11)]; cf. also *kol-śōne'ay,* "all who hate me" [41:8(7)]); "all who see me mock me" (22:8[7]); "all my bones," i.e., my entire being, will acknowledge you to be a God who delivers (35:10); "deliver me from all my sins" (39:9[8]; cf. 51:11[9]); "all thy waves have gone over me" (42:8[7]; cf. Jon. 2:4[3]); "all my longing is known to thee" (Ps. 38:10[9]). A great concentration appears in Ps. 89:41-43(40-42): "Thou hast breached all his walls . . . , all that pass by despoil him . . . , thou hast made all his enemies rejoice." The psalmist gives thanks for deliverance from all his fear (34:5[4]), from every trouble (54:9[7]); he will tell all God's works (73:28) or meditate on them (77:13[12]; 143:5); he will tell of all his wonderful works (105:2). All who hope in Yahweh can take courage (31:25[24]); everyone who is godly prays to him in distress (32:6; cf. "all the godly" in 148:14; 149:9); all who seek him will rejoice (70:5[4]). "All who fear Yahweh" are called blessed (128:1; cf. 66:16). "The godly" and "those who fear God" probably refer primarily to members of the cultic community, who are called upon in Ps. 148:9-13 to praise God together with all of nature (5 occurrences of *kōl* in vv. 9-11).

i. *Prophets.* The prophetic books use *kōl* in a great variety of contexts. With the exception of a few stereotyped idioms, however, we do not find any usage that might be called especially typical.

The prophetic message is universal: all the people are to know it (Isa. 9:8[9]); "All you inhabitants of the world . . . , hear!" (Isa. 18:3); "Hear, you peoples, all of you!" (Mic. 1:2); cf. "Ho, every one who thirsts . . ." (Isa. 55:1).

The prophet is to proclaim the message in its entirety: "To all to whom I send you you shall go, and all that I command you you shall speak" (Jer. 1:7); "Then Yahweh said to me, 'Proclaim all these words in the cities of Judah" (11:6); cf. what is said of Jeremiah: "Now when he had finished speaking all that Yahweh had commanded him to speak to all the people . . ." (26:8).

The universal corruption of sin described in Ps. 14:3 par. 53:4(3) ("They have all [*hakkōl*] gone astray [*sār*], all alike [*yaḥdāw*] are corrupt") is also declared by the prophets, who make use of various expressions including *kōl.* Jer. 6:28 resembles the statement in Psalms most closely: "They are all stubbornly rebellious (*sārê sôrerîm*), going about with slanders (*hōleḵê rāḵîl*); all of them are bronze and iron, they act corruptly"; furthermore, "They are all adulterers, a company of treacherous men. . . . Let every one (*'îš*) beware of his neighbor . . . , for every (*kōl*) brother is a supplanter, and every neighbor (*kol-rēa'*) is a deceiver" (Jer. 9:1,3[2,4]). Additional examples include: "Every one loves a bribe" (Isa. 1:23); "From the least to the greatest of them, every one (*kullô*) is greedy for unjust gain; and from prophet to priest, every one (*kullô*) deals falsely" (Jer. 6:13 par. 8:10); "Every one (*kullōh*) turns to his own course" (Jer. 8:6); "All are estranged from me through their idols" (Ezk. 14:5); "When your transgressions are uncovered, so that in all your doings your sins appear . . ." (Ezk. 21:29[24]); "They all lie in wait for blood" (Mic. 7:2); "They do not consider that I remember all their evil works. . . . All of them are hot as an oven" (Hos. 7:2,7). Cf. also: "We have all become unclean and all our righteous deeds are like a polluted garment" (Isa. 64:5[6]); "All we like sheep have gone astray" (Isa. 53:6; cf. 56:11). Here, too, we may cite the stereotyped expression "on every high hill and under every green tree," a formula that probably derives from Hos. 4:13 (without *kōl*); with minor variants, it serves to describe the fertility cult (Jer. 2:20; 3:6; Isa. 30:25; 57:5; Ezk. 6:13; cf. Dt. 12:2; 1 K. 14:23; 2 K. 17:10).[16]

Total corruption is met by equally total punishment. Here we can cite only a few examples. A concentration of such statements is found in Jer. 25: "You have neither listened nor inclined your ears to hear, although Yahweh persistently sent to you all his servants the prophets [v. 4]. . . . Therefore I will send for all the tribes of the north . . . and I will bring them against this land . . . and against all these nations round about [v. 9]. . . . This whole land shall become a ruin and a waste [v. 11]. . . . Then I will bring upon that land all the words which I have uttered against it, everything written in this book, . . . against all the nations [v. 13]." Then comes the section describing the cup of wrath: "Take from my hand this cup of the wine of wrath, and make all the nations to whom I send you drink it [v. 15]. . . . So I took the cup . . . and made all the nations to whom Yahweh sent me drink it [v. 17]." There follow 14 additional occurrences in verses specifying those to whom the cup of wrath is given (vv. 19-26).

A similar concentration appears in the description of the day of Yahweh in Isa. 2:12ff.: A day of Yahweh comes "against all that is proud and lofty, against all that is lifted up and high," etc. There are 10 occurrences of *kōl* between vv. 12 and 16. Further examples include: "The whole head is sick, and the whole heart faint" (Isa. 1:5); "Yahweh is taking away . . . the whole stay of bread, and the whole stay of water" (3:1); "They come . . . to destroy the whole earth" (13:5); "Therefore all hands will be feeble [cf. Ezk. 7:17; 21:12(7)], and every man's heart will melt" (Isa. 13:7); "I have heard a decree of destruction . . . upon the whole land" (28:22); "The wind will carry them all off" (57:13); "I will punish all those who are circumcised but yet uncircumcised. . . . For all these nations are uncircumcised, and all the house of Israel is uncircumcised in heart" (Jer. 9:25f.[26f.]);[17] "Upon all the bare heights in the desert destroyers have come; . . . no flesh has peace" (12:12); "I will fill with drunkenness all the inhabitants of this land: the kings, . . . and all the inhabitants of Jerusalem" (13:13); "All your treasures I will give for spoil" (17:3); "Why has every face turned pale?" (30:6); "I will kindle a fire in you, and it shall devour every green tree in you and every dry tree; . . . all faces from south to north shall be scorched by it. All flesh shall see that I Yahweh have kindled it" (Ezk. 21:3f.[20:47f.]); "They are all slain, fallen by the sword," etc. (32:23-26); "I will put an end to all her mirth . . . and to all

---

16. The history of this formula is discussed by W. L. Holladay, " 'On Every High Hill and Under Every Green Tree'," *VT,* 11 (1961), 170-76.

17. Cf. J. W. Flanagan, "The Deuteronomic Meaning of the Phrase *'kol yiśrā'ēl,'* " *StR,* 6 (1976/77), 159-168.

her appointed feasts" (Hos. 2:13[11]); "In all the squares there shall be wailing; and in all the streets they shall say, 'Alas! Alas!' . . . In all vineyards there shall be wailing" (Am. 5:16f.); "I will turn your feasts into mourning, and all your songs into lamentation; I will bring sackcloth upon all loins" (8:10); cf. also Mic. 1:7; 5:8(9); Nah. 3:10,12. The reaction of the onlookers is described in formulaic terms: "Every one who passes by [or the like] is horrified (*šmm*)" (Jer. 18:16; 19:8; 50:13; Ezk. 27:35; 28:19; cf. also Nah. 3:19).

On the other hand, positive statements also frequently have to do with the aspect of totality. The expression "assemble [or the like] out of all the countries [nations, places] where they have been scattered" became a cliche (Jer. 16:15; 23:3; 29:14; 30:11; 46:28; Ezk. 34:12; 37:23; 36:24; without *kōl*: Ezk. 11:17; 34:13). Elsewhere, too, *kōl* appears in oracles of favor: "They shall feed along the ways, on all bare heights shall be their pasture. . . . I will make all my mountains a way, and my highways shall be raised up" (Isa. 49:9,11); "Yahweh will comfort Zion; he will comfort all her waste places" (51:3); "All who mourn will be comforted" (61:2); "The Lord God will wipe away tears from all faces, and the reproach of his people he will take away from all the earth" (25:8); "All nations (*gôyîm*) will flow to it [the mountain of Yahweh]" (2:2 [par. Mic. 4:1 without *kōl*]; cf. "many peoples" in Isa. 2:3; similarly Jer. 3:17); "Every languishing soul I will replenish" (Jer. 31:25); "And the whole valley . . . and all the fields as far as the brook Kidron . . . shall be sacred to Yahweh" (31:40); "I will cleanse them from all guilt . . . and forgive all the guilt of their sin" (33:8); "I will pour out my spirit on all flesh. . . . All who call upon the name of Yahweh shall be delivered" (Joel 3:1,5[2:28,32]).

j. *Ecclesiastes.* There are also many occurrences of *kōl* in Ecclesiastes. The author clearly intends to provide an overall survey of human existence and make statements that are universally true. He has searched out and studied everything that is done under the sun (Eccl. 1:13f.; 8:9). He observes all oppressions (4:1), all toil and all skill (v. 4); he sees how all streams run to the sea, how all things are full of weariness (1:7f.). He finds that for everything there is a season (3:1; cf. vv. 11,17), that everything God does endures forever (v. 14), that everything has the same end, that everything comes from dust and turns to dust (v. 20), that people have no profit from all their toil and strain (2:22), that all their days are full of pain and vexation (v. 23). In short, all is vanity[18] (1:2,14; 2:11,17; 11:8). Everything, both love and hate, may await each person (9:1); the same fate awaits all, the righteous and the wicked (v. 2). In all that is done under the sun, one fate comes to all (v. 3). Nevertheless, God will bring every deed into judgment (11:9).

IV. LXX, Dead Sea Scrolls. The LXX uses more than 30 words to render *kōl*. The real equivalent is *pás* (4701 occurrences); we also find *hápas* (51 occurrences), *sýmpas* (26 occurrences), *hólos* (173 occurrences), and *hósos* (57 occurrences).

In the Dead Sea scrolls, *kwl* appears well over 1000 times (1QpHab, 1QS/Sa/Sb,

---

18. → הבל *heḇel* (*hebhel*).

1QM, 1QH, 4QpPs[a] 37:4, 4QS *šîrôṯ ʿôlaṯ haššabbaṯ,* 4QDibHam, 11QT [*ca.* 230 occurrences]); defective orthography (*kl*) is used in 1QH and CD.[19] There are also numerous occurrences in the Aramaic texts from Qumran.[20] The range of usage agrees entirely with that in the OT.

Ringgren

---

19. Kuhn, 99f., 102f.; Nachträge, 200f.
20. Cf. J. A. Fitzmyer and D. J. Harrington, *A Manual of Palestinian Aramaic Texts. BietOr,* 34 (1978), 323.

כָּלָא *kālā'*; כֶּלֶא *kele'*; כְּלִיא *k[e]lî'*; מִכְלָה *miḵlâ*

Contents: I. Occurrences, Meaning. II. Literal Usage: 1. Noun; 2. Verb. III. Metaphorical Usage: 1. Noun; 2. Verb.

I. Occurrences, Meaning. The root *kl'* and its derivatives, found also in other Semitic languages,[1] appears in the OT as both a noun (15 times) and a verb (12 times in the qal, once in the piel, 3 times in the niphal). Both semantically and formally there is a close connection between *kālā'* and → כלה *kālâ.*[2] While *klh* has more the sense of "coming to an end" temporally, *kl'* has more to do with "restraining" spatially. Ugaritic makes a similar distinction between the roots *kl'* and *kly*; as in the OT, the latter is more common. Akk. *kalû* is discussed under → כלה *kālâ.* The nouns formed from the root have the meaning "prison" (*kele', k[e]lî'* [*k[e]lû'* (*Q*)]) or "pen" (*miḵlâ*). There may be a Moabite cognate for the latter.[3]

In the Dead Sea scrolls, *kl'* appears only as a verb in 1QH 5:38, which describes oppression by others as being like imprisonment.

It is hardly possible to distinguish between secular and theological use of *kl',* since even what is basically secular usage has theological overtones. It is more productive to distinguish between literal and metaphorical usage.

II. Literal Usage.

1. *Noun.* The noun appears only in late narrative texts. The most common use of *kele'* is in the construct phrase *bêṯ* (*hak*)*kele',* "prison." The persons imprisoned are always individuals such as prophets (Micaiah ben Imlah [1 K. 22:27; 2 Ch. 18:26], Jeremiah [Jer. 37:4,15,18]) or kings (Hoshea [2 K. 17:4]; Jehoiachin [2 K. 25:27; Jer. 52:31]). The phrase *bigḏê kil'ô* (2 K. 25:29; Jer. 52:33) also refers to Jehoiachin. In all

---

1. *KBL*[3], *s.v.*
2. Cf. G. Gerlemann, "כלה *klh* zu Endesein," *THAT,* I, 831-33.
3. Cf. *KAI,* 181, 23.

its occurrences, prison is a form of punishment. This interpretation is attested in Israel only from the period of the monarchy onward.[4] There is an equivalent to *bêṯ kele'* in Neo-Babylonian *bît killi/kîli* or *bît ṣibitti,* in a period contemporaneous with the OT occurrences of the noun.[5] The Neo-Babylonian texts also understand prison as a place of punishment.

On the other hand, the noun *miḵlâ* (Ps. 50:9; 78:70; Hab. 3:17) has a neutral if not positive sense, denoting the fold or pen that sets a (secure) area apart for domestic animals. In Hab. 3:17, however, there are overtones of the punishment theme, since the fold without a flock appears as a sign of judgment in a judgment oracle.

2. *Verb.* When used literally, the verb also appears primarily in narrative texts, 4 of which refer to an act of restraining others. In Ex. 36:6, Moses restrains the people in the camp from bringing more offerings to the sanctuary. In Nu. 11:28, Joshua asks Moses — in vain — to restrain two ecstatics. Disaster is averted in 1 S. 25:33: Abigail restrains David from an act that would involve bloodguilt. Out of reverence for Yahweh, the psalmist in Ps. 119:101 restrains his feet from every evil way. There is a protective aspect associated with *kl'* in these texts.

In 1 S. 6:10, *kl'* denotes the separation of young calves from the cows that have been suckling them. This action, which is negative from the perspective of the animals, nevertheless serves a positive function: it permits recovery of the ark. In Gen. 23:6, it is an open question whether the root is *kl'* or *klh.* If *yiḵleh* is read as an imperfect from *kl',*[6] this would be the only instance of the negated verb in a narrative text; the negation yields a positive meaning: no one will refuse Abraham the purchase of a sepulchre for Sarah. Eccl. 8:8 emphasizes human impotence in the face of death. No one has the power to hold back the wind or to prevent death. Jer. 32:2f., which speaks of Jeremiah's coming imprisonment, recalls the use of the noun.

III. Metaphorical Usage.

1. *Noun.* In 2 passages, both in Deutero-Isaiah, the noun is used metaphorically. Isa. 42:7 speaks of prison as a place from which the servant of God (Cyrus?) will bring people out. This passage does not refer to physical prison; *kl'* is to be understood as a code for the situation of exile (as in Isa. 42:22). The metaphorical nature of *kl'* is indicated by the subjects with whom it is associated: they are not individual prisoners, but an entire group. Isa. 42:22 describes Israel as having fallen into the hands of other nations. The mention of prison interprets Israel's situation and characterizes the exile as a punishment. The use of *kl'* in words spoken by Yahweh supports intepretation of the exile as a punishment willed by Yahweh. Isa. 42:7 points beyond the situation of imprisonment to Yahweh's deliverance through the servant of God (?). The punishment

---

4. Cf. T. Lohmann, "Gefängnis," *BHHW,* I (1962), 530f.; A. van den Born, "Gefängnis," *BL*², 527.

5. Cf. E. Ebeling, "Gefangener, Gefängnis," *RLA,* III (1957-1972), 181f.

6. *GK* §75qq.

of exile is not the last word. The root *kl'* implies the notion of divine judgment, but remains open to a positive future brought about by Yahweh — open to deliverance from prison, open to new salvation after judgment.

2. *Verb.* The aspects of judgment and salvation are also present in the metaphorical use of the verb. In Ezk. 31:15, these aspects are associated with a description of Pharaoh's arrival in the realm of the dead. As a token of his death, Yahweh restrains the "great waters"[7] as a sign of mourning among the forces of nature. Here *kl'* stands for judgment against Egypt, but for Israel it symbolizes the salvation brought about by the fall of the oppressor. Hag. 1:10 is also associated with Yahweh's act of judgment. Yahweh causes the heavens to withhold their rain and the earth its produce to punish the people for neglect in rebuilding the temple. The association of *kl'* with water[8] is also found in Gen. 8:2. Yahweh restrains the rains of the Deluge, thus bringing his punishment to an end. In the context of an oracle of salvation, Isa. 43:6 describes God's command to Israel's oppressors no longer to keep his people from their homeland. The piel form (?) in Dnl. 9:24 speaks of the apocalyptic end of Israel's sin. Ps. 40:10, 12 (9, 10) describe the reaction of an individual to deliverance. Verse 10(9) asserts that the psalmist does not restrain his lips, i.e., does not shut them, when telling of his deliverance. Verse 12(11) expresses confidence that Yahweh will not withhold his mercy in the future. Ps. 88:9(8) likens disease to imprisonment. This passage recalls Babylonian lament texts that use the metaphor of loosing someone's bonds to describe healing of a disease.[9] More negative is the conjectural emendation *k^elu'â* (for MT *kallēh*) in Ps. 74:11. The question here involves Yahweh's refusal to help.

In sum, we have identified two basic aspects of *kl'*: it can be used both positively and negatively. It is associated not only with acts of punishment on the part of Yahweh, but also with acts of deliverance. The relatively late appearance of the root (apart from Gen. 8:2) may also be traced to contacts with the Babylonian world, especially since the nexus of judgment and salvation took on great importance for Israel with the experience of the exile.

Hausmann

---

7. → מים *mayim.*
8. Cf. also *AHw,* I (1965), 428.
9. Cf. H. J. Kraus, *Psalms 60–150* (Eng. trans., Minneapolis, 1989), 194.

כֶּלֶב keleḇ

Contents: I. Etymology. II. Ancient Near East: 1. Egypt; 2. Mesopotamia; 3. Ugarit; 4. Aramaic and Phoenician Texts; 5. Personal Names. III. OT: 1. Occurrences; 2. The Animal; 3. Uncleanness; 4. Term of Opprobrium; 5. Mythological and Cultic Associations; 6. Figurative Usage. IV. 1. LXX; 2. Dead Sea Scrolls.

I. Etymology. The root *klb* is found in almost all Semitic languages and dialects; its etymology in uncertain. Some[1] derive Heb. *keleḇ* as an agent noun **kalib* from a verbal root like that in Arab. *kaliba,* "seize,"[2] "be greedy."[3] Probably, however, *kalb* is a noun designating an object, without verbal etymology.

The derivation from a verb *klb* is also contradicted by the absence of such a verb in Akkadian and Ugaritic, although the former has many instances of *kalbu,* "dog," *kalbatu,* "bitch," and *kalbānu,* "pack of dogs,"[4] and the latter of *klb, klby,* and *klbt,* "dog," etc.[5] On the other hand, Arab. *kaliba* can be interpreted as a denominative with the meaning "behave like a dog."[6]

---

keleḇ. W. Beltz, *Die Kaleb-Traditionen im AT. BWANT,* 98[5/18] (1974), 116-134; F. S. Bodenheimer, *Animal Life in Palestine* (Jerusalem, 1935), 128f.; *idem, Animal and Man in Bible Lands* (Eng. trans., Leiden, 1960); G. Cansdale, *Animals of Bible Lands* (Exeter, 1970); J. Feliks, *The Animal World of the Bible* (Eng. trans., Tel Aviv, 1962), 34; F. C. Fensham, "The Dog in Ex. XI,7," *VT,* 16 (1966), 504-7; H. G. Fischer, "Hunde," *LexÄg,* III (1980), 77-81; A. Hantart, "Les chiens dans l'ancienne Égypte," *ChrÉg,* 9 (1933/34), 28-34; W. Heimpel, *Tierbilder in der sumerischen Literatur. St.Pohl,* 2 (1968); *idem* and U. Seidl, "Hund," *RLA,* IV (1972-75), 494-97; H. Kees, "Der Gau von Kynopolis und seine Gottheit," *MIO,* 6 (1958), 157-175; *idem, Der Götterglaube im alten Ägypten. MVÄG,* 45 (^{3}1977), 26-32; O. Keller, "Hunderassen im Altertum," *Jahrbuch des Österreichischen Archäologischen Instituts* (1905), 242-269; M. Landmann, *Das Tier in der jüdischen Weisung* (Heidelberg, 1959); B. Meissner, "Apotropäische Hunde," *OLZ,* 25 (1922), 201f.; *idem,* "Magische Hunde," *ZDMG,* 73 (1919), 176-182; O. Michel, "κύων," *TDNT,* III, 1101-4; P. Mouterde, "La faune du Proche-Orient dans l'antiquité," *MUSJ,* 45 (1969), 445-462; M. Noth, "Kaleb," *RGG*^{3}, III (1959), 1100; F. Orth, "Hund," *PW,* VIII/2, 2540-2582; S. Reinach, "Les chiens dans la culte d'Esculape et les *kelabim* des stèles peintes de Citium," *RA* (1884), 129-135; L. Röhrich, "Hund, Pferd, Kröte und Schlange als symbolische Leitgestalten in Volksglauben und Sage," *ZRGG,* 3 (1951), 69-76; D. W. Thomas, "*Kelebh* 'Dog': its Origin and Some Usages of it in the OT," *VT,* 10 (1960), 410-427; E. D. Van Buren, *The Fauna of Ancient Mesopotamia as Represented in Art. AnOr,* 18 (1939); *idem, Symbols of the Gods in Mesopotamian Art. AnOr,* 23 (1945), 144; F. E. Zeuner, "Dog and Cat in the Neolithic of Jericho," *PEQ,* 90 (1958), 52-55.

1. *KBL*^{3}, 453; H. Bauer, "Die hebräischen Eigennamen als sprachliche Erkenntnisquelle," *ZAW,* 48 (1930), 79f.
2. *GesB,* 346.
3. *WKAS,* I, 306f.
4. *AHw,* I (1965), 424f.; *CAD,* VII (1971), 67-73.
5. *WUS,* no. 1313-15; *UT,* no. 1233.
6. *KBL*^{3}; Lane; cf. also Thomas, esp. 412f.; on Syr. *k*^{e}*lēḇ,* cf. also *CSD,* 215: "behave like a dog, be rabid."

Ever since the Middle Ages, there have been attempts to interpret *klb* as a crasis combining two independent morphemes: *keleḇ* from *k^e lēḇ*, "like the heart, faithful," or *kol-lēḇ*, "whole heart," or *k^e-laḇî*, "like a lion."[7] An equally long tradition lies behind the attempt of D. Winton Thomas[8] to derive *keleḇ* from an onomatopoeic root *kālaḇ*,[9] no longer attested, after the model of Eng. "yelp" or Ger. "kläffen."[10]

Besides Akkadian, Ugaritic, Arabic, Syriac, and Mandaic,[11] *klb* appears also in Aramaic inscriptions from Ashur[12] and Hatra[13] as well as Egyptian Aramaic papyri from Elephantine.[14] In the Lachish letters, we already find *klb* in a stereotyped phrase expressing humility; a similar expression occurs in the Amarna letters.[15] The Kilamuwa inscription (ca. 825 B.C.)[16] contains the only certain Phoenician occurrence. The occurrences in the late Phoenician administrative list from Kition (3rd or 4th century B.C.)[17] are unclear, but may cast light on the "wages of a dog" mentioned in Dt. 23:19(Eng. v. 18). In Old South Arabic, *klb* appears only as a proper name.[18] In Ethiopic, Tigre, and Tigriña we find *kal^eb, kalbī*.

II. Ancient Near East.

1. *Egypt.* In the Old Kingdom, *ṯsm*[19] was the common term for "hunting dog." During the Middle Kingdom, we find several terms for "dog": *ỉw, ỉwỉw,*[20] onomatopoetic words for "howler." In the late period we also find *bḥn* (cf. *bḥn,* "bark"),[21] *ỉshb, ỉš,*[22] *wnš* (cf. *wnš,* "lament, howl"), and *ktkt šry* (cf. *ktkt,* "tremble"), "little dog, whelp."[23] Very late we also find *bfn.*[24]

Representations of (hunting) dogs with little variation in form are found as early as the First Dynasty at Saqqara and Naqada. Not until the Eleventh Dynasty (the Dog stela of

---

7. Cf. already S. Bochart, *Hierozoicon sive de animalibus sacrae scripturae,* I (London, 1663), 662 (= [1793], 759), who himself derives *keleḇ* from Arab. *kullāb,* "iron hook, spur, tongs" [Lane, I/7, 2627], in the sense of "animal with jaws like tongs."

8. Pp. 413f.

9. Cf. already F. J. V. D. Maurer, *Commentarius Grammaticus Historicus in Psalmos* (Leipzig, 1838).

10. *GesTh,* 684.

11. *MdD,* 197.

12. *KAI,* 233, 7.

13. *KAI,* 255.

14. *AP,* 30, 16 = 31, 15.

15. See II.2 below.

16. *KAI,* 24, 10.

17. *KAI,* 37 B, 7, 10; "temple pederast (?)."

18. Cf. ContiRossini, 168; as the name of a tribe in *RÉS,* VIII (1968), 185; cf. also W. W. Müller, "Altsüdarabische Beiträge zum hebräischen Lexicon," *ZAW,* 75 (1963), 311.

19. *WbÄS,* V, 409.

20. *WbÄS,* I, 48, 50.

21. *WbÄS,* I, 468.

22. *Ibid.,* 132, 134.

23. *WbÄS,* V, 146.

24. *WbÄS,* I, 456.

Intef II) do representations exhibit more variety, so that we can recognize several different species, some of which were introduced from Libya and Nubia. Among the canids depicted, however, it is not possible to distinguish precisely which are dogs, which are wolves, and which are jackals. This confusion creates serious problems in interpreting the animal symbols of the deities.[25] In contrast to Mesopotamia, the hunting dog plays the dominant role in Egyptian depictions; there is also evidence for the use of dogs in battle.[26] The important role of dogs in the palace of Pharaoh is illustrated by the appearance of many "dog keepers" (*mnyw ṯsmw*) at court. Dogs are often depicted in domestic settings; literary texts also refer to pet dogs with all kinds of affectionate names. Such dogs are therefore frequently depicted on cosmetic implements, household objects, etc.[27] Janssen[28] cites the remarkable custom of Egyptians' naming dogs after themselves.

Despite this popularity, the dog often served as a metaphor for "slave" or "servant," as in Mesopotamian epistolary literature.

Until well into the late period, dogs were mummified and buried, either because the master's favorite animal should accompany him into the tomb or because the dog was identified at an early date with Anubis and Wepwawet. The (crouching) watchdog (or jackal) was probably identified with Khenti-Amentiu and Anubis, the gods of the dead,[29] because it roamed about the necropolis and its howling was associated with the souls of the departed. Figures of Anubis as symbols of watchfulness then came to be used frequently on sarcophagi. Similarly, the war dog (standing erect) symbolized the war-god Wepwawet. These observations help explain the existence of dog cults (especially at Cynopolis in Upper Egypt[30]), such as are depicted in the late New Kingdom.[31] In mythology, the bark of the sun-god is drawn by a dog. In Egyptian astronomy (as still today), finally, Sirius/Sothis was the Dog Star.[32]

2. *Mesopotamia.* Together with *mirānu,* "young dog, whelp," Akk. *kalbu* and *kalbatu*[33] are the common terms for "dog" and "bitch." These words correspond to Sum. UR and UR.GI$_7$, which, however, can also be used collectively to include "lion" (UR.MAḪ). The dog (*Canis familiaris*), which probably is descended from the wolf (*Canis lupus*),[34] should probably be considered the earliest domestic animal, having been domesticated during the Mesolithic period.[35]

---

25. Cf. *RÄR,* 674f.; for further discussion, see below.
26. Cf. R. Anthes, "Eine Polizeistreife des Mitteleren Reiches in die wetliche Oase," *ZÄS,* 65 (1930), 108-114.
27. See Fischer, 79.
28. J. M. A. Janssen, "Über Hundenamen im pharaonischen Ägypten," *MDAI.K,* 16 (1958), 176-182.
29. Cf. Kees, *Der Götterglaube im alten Ägypten,* esp. 28: Anubis referred to as "puppy."
30. Kees, *MIO,* 6 (1958), 157-175.
31. *RÄR,* 675.
32. Cf. R. Clarke, *Myth and Symbol in Ancient Egypt* (London, 1960), 188.
33. *CAD,* VII, 67-72; *AHw,* I, 424f.
34. Van Buren, *Fauna,* 14.
35. Mouterde, 447.

In Mesopotamian glyptography, greyhounds are depicted on seals as early as the Ubaid (Tepe Gawra), Uruk IV, and Jemdet Naṣr periods.[36] Pet dogs appear on clay reliefs from the Larsa period, and powerful watchdogs are depicted on cylinder seals of the Kassite period. Finally, the Late Babylonian murals of the royal palace at Nineveh include the hunting dogs of Ashurbanipal. People defended themselves against free-roaming dogs by throwing clods of earth (*kirbānu*) at them, because a dog's bite was considered poisonous.[37] Rabies was probably familiar.[38] Normally, dogs were kept around house and stable as watchdogs[39] or with flocks of sheep and goats to help herd them.[40] Since hunting was reserved to the highest strata of society, hunting dogs were correspondingly rare; there is no clear mention of them in any inscription, unlike the situation in Egypt.[41]

Dogs played an important role in keeping human settlements clean, since they ate carrion, garbage, and unburied corpses (cf. 2 K. 9); the murderous rage of Inanna was compared to this gruesome scene.[42]

Figures of dogs guarded gates and doors against the incursion of demons. Small earthenware dogs dating from the Neo-Assyrian and Late Babylonian periods, some painted with magical colors and inscribed with names, have been found at Kuyunjik.[43] According to van Buren,[44] this practice of burying figures of dogs near a gate goes back to the period of Gudea of Lagash. The practice is also mentioned in an inscription,[45] with an incantation in the same context.

Omen texts use the behavior of free-ranging dogs to determine the fate of individuals and cities;[46] there soon arose rituals based on sympathetic magic, such as the inclusion of dough figurines in dogs' food[47] or the use of dog hair to make amulets for adjurations of Lamaštu.[48]

In the religious realm, the dog symbolized the two goddesses of healing, Gula of Isin and Ninkarrak of Sippar.[49] Whether this association is due to a supposed healing effect of being licked by a dog[50] can no longer be determined. The dog of Gula was itself deified: anyone who touched it was considered clean.[51] In Old Babylonian

---

36. Van Buren, *Fauna,* 14ff.
37. *MSL,* IX, 78, 97ff.
38. Laws of Eshnunna, §56.
39. *BWL,* 216, 21-25.
40. *BWL,* 192, 19f.; cf. also the sheep-dogs in the Etana scene cited by van Buren, *Fauna,* 16.
41. Cf. II.1 above.
42. Heimpel, 362.
43. Cf. Meissner, *OLZ,* 25 (1922), 202.
44. *Fauna,* 18.
45. *KAR,* 298 r.17-22.
46. For citations, see *CAD,* VII, 69f.
47. D. W. Myhrman, *Babylonian Hymns and Prayers. PBS,* I/1 (1911), 13, 21.
48. IV R 58, II, 11.
49. *KAR,* 71, 6.
50. As suggested by T. Jacobsen; cf. Heimpel.
51. *CT,* 39.

documents, this dog appears as a witness to and guarantor of oaths.[52] Dogs are also associated with Ninkillim and Lamaštu (and more rarely with Enlil, Ea, and Damkina). The four dogs of Marduk are even named. Figurines of dogs made of gold, silver, and copper as votive offerings to Gula have been found. The evidence of buried dog skeletons suggests also that dogs were sacrificed to the goddess.[53]

The noun *kalbu* is often used figuratively and metaphorically in Mesopotamian literature: to chase someone away like a dog, to beg like a dog, to crawl about on all fours, to lie in filth, to die.[54] At Mari, *kalbu* is used as a term of abuse,[55] e.g., for a wayward son.[56] This probably led to the use of *kalbu* in epistolary style as a formula expressing humility; it is especially frequent in the Amarna letters.[57] In these expressions of modesty addressed to Pharaoh, his vassals refer to themselves as *kalbu,* "dog"; *ardu,* "slave"; *epru ša šêpēka,* "dust of your feet"; *ṭīṭu ša kapāšika,* "clay on which you step"; and *kartappu,* "groom." The extensive use of such humility formulas in the Amarna letters makes it almost impossible to consider *klb* in the similar formulas of the Lachish letters[58] a personal name, as suggested by Jepsen.[59] Cf. also the self-deprecation of Hazael before Elisha (2 K. 8:13; Lucianic recension: *ho kýōn ho tethnēkṓs*[60]).[61] A further exaggeration of such self-deprecation is found in Neo-Babylonian letters: *kalbu mītu,* "dead dog."[62] Cf. 1 S. 24:15(14) (David before Saul); 2 S. 9:8 (Meribbaal before David); 16:9.

3. *Ugarit.* The root *klb*[63] appears some 28 times at Ugarit (3 occurrences representing the PN *klb* and 13 the PN *klby*). This includes 3 highly unlikely conjectures[64] as well as 2 passages not noted by Richard Whitaker.[65] The dog does not play any identifiable role in the everyday life of Ugarit. The few relevant texts[66] cannot be interpreted with

52. Cf. *BIN,* VII, 176, 4, 7.
53. Cf. Heimpel-Seidl, 497.
54. For citations, see *CAD,* VII, 70.
55. G. Dossin, *Correspondence de Šamî-Addu et de ses fils. ARM,* I (1949, repr. 1978), 27, 28.
56. Heimpel, 356.
57. EA 60, 6f.; 61, 2f.; 201, 15; 202, 13; 247, 15; cf. also 320, 22; 322, 17; 319, 19.
58. *KAI,* 192, 4; 195, 4; 196, 3.
59. A. Jepsen, "Kleine Bemerkungen zu drei westsemitischen Inschriften," *MIO,* 15 (1969), 1-4, esp. 4.
60. Cf. Thomas, 416.
61. Cf. H. P. Müller, "Notizen zu althebräischen Inschriften I," *UF,* 2 (1970), 229-242, esp. 234f.
62. *ABL,* 521, 6; 721, 5; 831, 5; 1285, 12; *CAD,* VII, 72.
63. *UT,* no. 1233; *WUS,* no. 1313ff.
64. *KTU,* 1.41, 52; 1.114, 5, 29; 4, 357, 16.
65. *KTU,* 1.19 I, 10, 13; cf. B. Margalit, "Studia Ugaritica II: 'Studies in *Krt* and *Aqht,*' " *UF,* 8 (1976), 170.
66. *KTU,* 1.41, 52 (sacrificial list!); 4.54, 4.

certainty. The dogs in question are probably hunting dogs (*klb ṣpr*),[67] by means of whose barking King Keret wishes to wear out King Pabil in order to save his daughter.[68] Elsewhere the dog appears in negative metaphors.

In *KTU,* 1.16 I, 2, 15; II, 38, the metaphor of a dog probably serves to express the mortality and vulnerability of human existence in contrast to the immortality of the gods. The dog (*klb* par. *ỉnr,* "cur"[69]) here symbolizes a short life-span.[70] At the same time, the random straying and howling of dogs probably suggests human helplessness and sadness when facing the problem of mortality.[71]

In *KTU,* 1.114, 5, 12 (and the uncertain ritual use in 29), in a description of a banquet given by El, the drunken moon-god is compared to a *klb* that runs about on all fours under the tables.[72]

Marvin H. Pope[73] points out the role of dogs in Near Eastern sexual rites and funeral ceremonies.

In *KTU,* 1.3 III, 45, *klbt ỉlm,* identified with *ỉšt,* "flame," stands for the "bitch of the gods," who, along with other mythical monsters such as Tannin, stood on the side of Yam in his battle with Baʿal and is now slain by ʿAnat. We also find a *klb ʒlnm* mentioned in *KTU,* 1.19 I, 10, 13; it obviously serves as a watchdog guarding the underworld.[74] The function of the dog in guarding the underworld and accompanying the dead explains why dogs are often depicted in ancient representations of burial.

No association of dogs with sexual fertility rites has been demonstrated at Ugarit. There is accordingly no justification for translating the apparent pl. *klbm* (l. 4) in a list of names constituting a specialized detachment (*mḏrǵlm*[75]) as "male prostitutes."[76] Possibly the phrase *ṯlṯ klbm* refers to three dogs trained for battle accompanying the

67. Contra W. G. C. Watson, "Ugaritic and Mesopotamian Literary Texts," *UF,* 9 (1977), 279: "sheepdog."

68. *KTU,* 1.14 III, 19; V, 11.

69. Contra J. C. de Moor, "Studies in the New Alphabetic Texts from Ras Shamra I," *UF,* 1 (1969), 171: < Hitt. *inarrā,* "on one's own account"; also A. Sauren and G. Kestemont, "Keret, roi de Ḫubur," *UF,* 3 (1971), 209: pl. (?) of *nr,* "fire"; but cf. most recently Margalit, 147; L. Delekat, "Zum Ugaritischen Verbum," *UF,* 4 (1972), 20.

70. Cf. D. Pardee, "A Note on the Root *ʿtq* in CTA 16 I 2,5 (UT 125, KRT II)," *UF,* 5 (1973), 229-234.

71. Cf. Margalit.

72. Cf. S. E. Loewenstamm, "Eine lehrhafte ugaritische Trinkburleske," *UF,* 1 (1969), 73ff.; B. Margulis, "A New Ugaritic Farce (RŠ 24. 258)," *UF,* 2 (1970), 132ff.; M. Dietrich, O. Loretz, and J. Sanmartín, "Der stichometrische Aufbau von RS 24.258 (= Ug. 5, S. 545 Nr.1)," *UF,* 7 (1975), 109f.; for another interpretation, see de Moor, 170ff.

73. M. H. Pope, "A Divine Banquet at Ugarit," *The Use of the OT in the New. Festschrift W. F. Stinespring* (Durham, N.C., 1972), 170-203, esp. 183-89.

74. Cf. Margalit, 169f.

75. *KTU,* 4.54, 1.

76. *WUS,* no. 1313; followed by Beltz, 121.

detachment; such use of dogs was especially common among the ancient Greeks.[77] Or the reference may be to hunting dogs, whose existence in Palestine is attested at the beginning of the second millennium B.C. by the story of Sinuhe.[78]

4. *Aramaic and Phoenician Texts.* In Aramaic and Phoenician texts there are only scattered occurrences, and the interpretation of these is disputed. A seventh-century Aramaic inscription from Ashur[79] describes the Assyrian practice of locking prisoners up in dog cages. In a very late inscription from Hatra,[80] Nergal is called "dog" or "lord of the dogs."[81] At Elephantine,[82] *klby'* is probably used as a term of invective against the Egyptian governor who ordered the destruction of the temple of Yahweh at Elephantine. As a mark of degradation, his *kbl'*, "foot buckles" (a token of high office?), are taken away.[83]

Only 2 occurrences are known in Phoenician inscriptions: *KAI,* 37 B, 10,[84] and the Kilamuwa inscription.[85] In the latter, *klb* is used figuratively to describe the angry growling of the populace (*mškbym*) against their oppressive kings.[86]

5. *Personal Names.* Among the Amorite personal names in the Mari letters we already find a *ka-al-ba-an,* "dog."[87] In Old Akkadian, the word is used only rarely as part of a name, e.g., in combination with a theophorous element in *Kalab-Nannari* (*UR-ᵈŠEŠ.ki*) on the clay tablets from Nineveh[88] and in *Kalbi-ukūa,*[89] along with the short forms *Kalbi* and *Kalbu,* "dog, servant."[90] According to Stamm,[91] names taken from the animal world should generally be interpreted as terms of endearment; this category includes two proper names with theophorous elements, *Kalab-ᵈBāu* and *Mūrān-ᵈGula,* which use the dogs dedicated to the healing-goddess Gula as the basis for a term of endearment. The names *Kalab-ᵈŠamaš*[92] and *Kalab-ᵈMarduk*[93] imply that

77. For citations, see Orth, 2566f.
78. *AOT,* 57.
79. *KAI,* 233, 7.
80. *KAI,* 255.
81. Cf. also A. Caquot, "Nouvelles inscriptions araméenes de Hatra (IV)," *Syr,* 32 (1955), 269, no. 72.
82. *AP,* 30, 16 = 31, 15.
83. See P. Grelot, *Documents Araméens d'Égypte. LAPO* 5 (1972), 410.
84. See above.
85. *KAI,* 24, 10.
86. Cf. M. P. O'Connor, "The Rhetoric of the Kilamuwa Inscription," *BASOR,* 226 (1977), 15-29, esp. 19; cf. also Ps. 59:7(6).
87. *APNM,* 152, 221.
88. W. Lambert, "A Catalogue of Texts and Authors," *JCS,* 16 (1962), 66, VI, 14.
89. M. Dietrich, "Neue Quellen zur Geschichte Babyloniens (II)," *WO,* 4 (1967/68), 193.
90. *APN,* 111, 289.
91. *AN,* 11f.
92. *Ibid.,* 12, n. 2.
93. *Ibid.,* 261.

their bearers are dedicated to the god in question, as a token of either thanksgiving or petition. The Neo-Babylonian name *Kalbâ* is a hypocoristic form of such a name.

At Ugarit, the personal name *Klb* (*Kalbu*) appears 3 times and *Klby* (*Kalbe/iya*) 13 times.[94] According to *KTU,* 4.75 III, 5, this Kalbu was the son of a rich entrepreneur and administrator who served several Ugaritic kings. The name Kalbeya appears frequently in payrolls[95] and lists of royal servants.[96]

In Aramaic personal names, the noun appears as *klb'* or *klby,* with the meaning "dog" (i.e., "servant").[97] Phoenician and Punic inscriptions contain the personal names *Klb', Klb'lm, Klby,* and *Klbl'.*[98] Here *klb* is synonymous with *'bd*; when a theophorous element is present, it indicates dependence of the named person on the deity.[99] In the Hebrew world, *Klb'* and *Klby* are well attested,[100] as well as their Greek transcriptions *Chalbás, Chalbḗs, Chálēb,* and *Chelbḗs.*

III. OT.

1. *Occurrences.* The noun *keleḇ* appears 32 times in the Hebrew OT: 3 times in the Pentateuch, 16 times in the Deuteronomistic history, 3 times in Trito-Isaiah, once in Jeremiah, 15 times in the Psalms, twice in Proverbs, and once each in Job and Ecclesiastes.

2. *The Animal.* Dogs were common in Palestine from the eighth century on; soon after having been domesticated, they were used as watchdogs (Isa. 56:10) and hunting dogs; later they were used to help herd other domestic animals (cf. Job 30:1).

Among the various kinds of dogs, the OT singles out only the sheep dog (*kalḇê ṣō'n*: Job 30:1). Several portions of canine anatomy are mentioned, sometimes as insults: *rō'š keleḇ,* "dog's head" (2 S. 3:8); *lᵉšôn kᵉlāḇîm,* "dog's tongue" (Ps. 68:24[23]); *'oznê-keleḇ,* "dog's ears" (Prov. 26:17). The term *'ōrēp̄ keleḇ,* "dog throttler" (Isa. 66:3), is particularly opprobrious, as is the term *mᵉḥîr keleḇ,* "wages of a dog" (par. *'eṯnan zônâ,* "hire of a harlot"), used in Dt. 23:19(18) for payment to hierodules.

Dogs bark, howl, growl (*hāmâ*: Ps. 59:7,15[6,14]), run around (*'āḇar*: Prov. 26:17), circle their prey (*sāḇaḇ*: Ps. 22:17[16]), stick out their tongues in greed (*ḥāraṣ lāšôn*: Ex. 11:7), and slink away (*sāḥaḇ*: Jer. 15:3). They lick up (*yālaq*) water (Jgs. 7:5) and blood (1 K. 21:19; 22:38). It became a proverbial commonplace that dogs devour (*'āḵal*) corpses in the city (1 K. 14:11; 16:4; 21:24; cf. 21:23; Ex. 22:30[31]) and in the open

94. *PNU,* 28, 150, 395.
95. *KTU,* 4.69; 4.103.
96. *KTU,* 4.370; 4.609.
97. Contra W. Kornfeld, *Onomastica Aramaica aus Ägypten. SAW,* Phil.-hist. Kl., 333 (1978), 56.
98. Cf. Benz, 331.
99. Cf. *KAI,* II, 10; see the comments of W. F. Albright, "Two Letters from Ugarit (Ras Shamrah)," *BASOR,* 82 (1941), 47, n. 26.
100. *PNPI,* 92.

countryside (2 K. 9:10, 36). Prov. 26:11 alludes to the disgusting habit dogs have of returning (*šûḇ*) to their vomit (*qēʾ*).

3. *Uncleanness.* Because dogs ate garbage, carrion, and corpses, they were counted among the unclean and loathsome animals to which unclean flesh might be tossed (Ex. 22:30[31]). They were therefore also not allowed to enter houses.[101] On the other hand, there are no laws forbidding the keeping of dogs. Almost all OT passages (except Eccl. 9:4; Tob. 5:16; 6:1 [LXX^S]; 11:4[102]) illustrate the loathing that devout Israelites felt toward dogs. They also knew well how to make use of dogs to signalize and manifest their loathing for others. The death penalty imposed on Jezebel, for example, was made worse by throwing her body to the dogs for food (1 K. 21:23; 2 K. 9:10,36). According to 1 K. 22:38, dogs licked the blood of Ahab from his chariot.

4. *Term of Opprobrium.* The noun *keleḇ* appears in a variety of phrases. A living dog (*keleḇ ḥay*), despite its relative insignificance, is better than a dead lion (*ʾaryēh mēṯ*; Eccl. 9:4); it stands in contrast to a worthless "dead dog" (*keleḇ mēṯ*), found as a term of opprobrium in 1 S. 24:15(14); 2 S. 9:8; 16:9. "Dumb dogs" (*kᵉlāḇîm ʾillᵉmîm*) proverbially represent incompetent people (Isa. 56:10); self-seeking and insatiable statesmen are called *kᵉlāḇîm ʿazzê-nep̄eš,* "greedy dogs" (v. 11).

When Abishai berates Shimei as a "dead dog," it represents a severe personal insult (2 S. 16:9). It is all the more disgraceful for Job to be mocked by those whom, on account of their low social origin,[103] he would formerly not even have compared to his sheep dogs (Job 30:1). The contempt and humiliation expressed in the term *keleḇ* aroused bitter anger in the person addressed (2 S. 3:8; cf. 1 S. 17:43; 24:15[14]). The mere manner of David's approach shows the Philistine how much he despises him (1 S. 17:43). David feels like a dog pursued by Saul (1 S. 24:15[14]).

Finally, Abner does not want to be kept under petty control like a "dog's head of Judah" (2 S. 3:8). Thomas,[104] following Margoliouth, sees in *rōʾš keleḇ* a reference to the dog-faced baboon, a proverbial figure in the role of a knave throughout the Near East. Insults directed at the enemy before battle evoked a violent reaction; they are part of the psychological preparations for war.

Self-abasement in the form of a rhetorical question asked by the sender of a letter is common in the Near Eastern epistolary formulary; it appears also in the mouth of Meribbaal when he is addressing David (2 S. 9:8) and when Hazael meets Elisha (2 K. 8:13).

This self-abasement may also be found in a prayer in which David refers to himself as the *ʿeḇeḏ* and *keleḇ* of Yahweh (1 Ch. 17:19 par. 2 S. 7:21; reading *kalbᵉḵā*[105] for

---

101. S. Krauss, *Talmudische Archäologie,* II (1911, repr. Hildesheim, 1966), 120.
102. Cf. F. Zimmermann, *The Book of Tobit* (New York, 1958), 9ff.
103. Contra G. Fohrer, *Das Buch Hiob. KAT,* XVI (1963), 416.
104. Pp. 418ff.
105. Tur-Sinai and *BHS.*

k^elibb^eḵā). Thomas[106] cites a Babylonian prayer in which the worshipper refers to himself as a dog that follows after Marduk.[107]

In the threat to slay all the first-born in Egypt (Ex. 11:4-8 [J]), a secondary interpolation adds a promise of protection to Israel: "No dog will point his tongue against them" (v. 7).[108]

In Jeremiah's threat against the people of Israel, Jer. 15:3 uses a traditional series to express total annihilation: the sword to slay, the dogs to drag off, the birds of the air to devour, and the beasts of the earth to destroy.

Except for these passages, *keleḇ* appears only in threats pronounced by the preliterary prophets, using almost identical formulas modified slightly to fit the circumstances: 1 K. 14:11 (Ahijah against Jeroboam), 1 K. 16:4 (Jehu against Baasha), and finally 1 K. 21:23,24; 2 K. 9:10,36 (Elijah against Jezebel). The threat that "the dogs shall eat . . ." refers to the shameful manner in which the reprobates addressed will lose their lives; the primary emphasis, however, is on the much greater humiliation involved in not being buried.

In another threat of Elijah against Ahab (1 K. 21:19), the dogs will lick up Ahab's blood, just as they licked up the blood of Naboth, who had been wickedly murdered.[109]

5. *Mythological and Cultic Associations.* While Egypt enjoyed a religious use of dogs in the cult of Anubis and Wepwawet, and Mesopotamia in the cult of Gula, among the Hebrews the dog was removed from the realm of the legitimate cult.

In the cultic polemic of Isa. 66:3, sacrifice of dogs appears among four pagan cultic rituals that are contrasted with four legitimate sacrificial acts. On the interpretation of legitimate and illegitimate sacrifice, see → חזיר *ḥ^azîr* (*ch^azîr*): "He who sacrifices a lamb is like him who breaks a dog's neck." The polemic does not attack an unnamed temple (the rebuilt Jerusalem temple?) and the hopes for salvation associated with it, but simultaneous engagement in both legitimate and pagan cults and thus every form of cultic syncretism.

The law against bringing "the hire of a harlot" and "the wages of a dog" into the temple (Dt. 23:19a[18a]) condemns cultic prostitution, both male and female; vv. 18(17) and 19b(18b) frame and reinforce v. 19a(18a).

In Ps. 68, a victory hymn, a divine oracle (vv. 23f.[22f.]) voices the assurance that Yahweh will vanquish all his enemies. "I will bring them back from Bashan, bring them back from the depths of the sea, that you may bathe your feet in blood, that the tongues of your dogs may have their portion from the foe." It is unclear to whom the 2nd person singular refers: Israel[110] or God himself.[111] The similarity of this motif to

---

106. P. 424.
107. J. Hahn, *BASS,* 5 (1906), 359.
108. The covenant terminology in this text is discussed by Fensham, 504-7.
109. Cf. R. Bohlen, *Der Fall Naboth. TrThSt,* 35 (1978), 74, 82.
110. Gunkel, and others.
111. Dahood.

the Ugaritic goddess ʿAnat, who wades in blood,[112] as well as to the dogs of Marduk is striking; in both cases, we are probably dealing with mythologoumena associated with a theophany.[113]

The reference to *KAI,* 37 B, 7, 10[114] is also not persuasive, since this very obscure passage is usually explained from the perspective of Dt. 23:19(18). Probably *meḥîr keleḇ* here refers to the "love wages" of sacral male prostitutes, an interpretation supported by the par. *'eṯnan zônâ.*[115]

6. *Figurative Usage.* Figurative usage of *keleḇ* in the OT is naturally influenced by the observable behavior of dogs. In an especially vivid image, the proverbial wisdom of the later monarchy describes the fool: "Like a dog that returns to his vomit is a fool that repeats his folly" (Prov. 26:11). Such fools are incorrigible, irresponsible, and devoid of all sense of values; association with them is disgusting.

Prov. 26:17 points out the danger of becoming involved in other people's affairs. It is like grabbing a passing dog by the ears without realizing that one might be bitten. Quiet self-control and restraint are the quintessence of proper conduct.

Jgs. 7:5ff. describes a very strange process of selecting a special group for battle. Only those soldiers who lap the water of the spring like dogs are to be picked by Gideon for the coming battle with the Midianites. It is hardly likely that this manner of drinking reflects some kind of outstanding skill; the reduction of the troop of three hundred is instead meant to show that it is God's will to grant a great victory by means of so small an army.

Figurative usage also associates *keleḇ* with the great questions of life. The ironic *ṭôḇ*-saying of Eccl. 9:4, "A living dog is better than a dead lion," illustrates Qoheleth's whole skeptical attitude toward human existence. Nevertheless — in contrast to Eccl. 4:2 — this existence is preferable to death, in that it can be enjoyed (vv. 7ff.).

In the Psalms, the *kelāḇîm* represent the enemies who oppress the individual worshipper. They, the band of the wicked (sometimes with demonic overtones), surround the faithful psalmist and rob him of all chance for life (Ps. 22:17[16]). Like a pack of howling dogs on the prowl ("an image of disgusting, selfish, hateful activity"[116]), making the streets of the city unsafe, they greedily beset the psalmist (59:7,15[6,14]), who nevertheless finds his only help in God (22:21[20]; 59:9f.[8f.]). This confidence allows him to speak a prayer of thanksgiving. God drives the pack asunder and proves to be a deliverer (59:12[11]).

---

112. *KTU,* 1.3 II, 13f., 17-28.
113. Cf. M. Dahood, *Psalms II. AB,* XVII ([2]1973), 146.
114. See above.
115. For a discussion of the whole subject, see D. Arnaud, "La prostitution sacrée en Mésopotamie," *RHR,* 183 (1973), 111-15; J. P. Asmussen, "Bemerkungen zur sakralen Prostitution im AT," *StTh,* 11 (1957[1958]), 167-192, esp. 176ff.; E. M. Yamauchi, "Cultic Prostitution: A Case Study in Cultural Diffusion," *Orient and Occident. Festschrift C. H. Gordon. AOAT,* 22 (1973), 213-222, esp. 218.
116. F. Nötscher, *Das Buch der Psalmen. EB,* IV (1962), 129.

Apart from Jer. 15:3, Trito-Isaiah is the only prophet who uses the word *keleḇ.* It appears in the context of a prophetic oracle of judgment (Isa. 56:9-12) based on contrast against the leaders of the people (*ṣōp̄îm* and *rōʿîm*), who neglect their office like blind watchmen and like dumb dogs fail to sound the alarm in the face of impending danger (Isa. 56:10). V. 11 expands the metaphor by introducing the question of guilt: they are *kᵉlāḇîm ʿazzê-nepeš,* "greedy dogs, who never have enough." Human weakness and failure to live up to one's calling are eliminated as grounds for judgment. At the same time, Trito-Isaiah includes in this formula a personal invective against the contemporary administration by using the metaphor of the universally despised unclean dog together with extremely pejorative epithets.

IV. 1. *LXX.* The LXX uses *kýōn* for all 32 occurrences, as well as in Tob. 5:16 [$LXX^{B,A}$]; 6:1 [LXX^{S}]; 11:4; Jth. 11:19; Sir. 13:18.

2. *Dead Sea Scrolls.* In the Qumran literature, *klb* is found only once, in 11QtgJob 15:5, where it is an Aramaic translation of Job 30:1b.

Botterweck†

כָּלָה *kālâ*

Contents: I. 1. Ancient Near East; 2. LXX; 3. Dead Sea Scrolls; 4. *kālâ* and *kālāʾ.* II. 1. Be Decided; 2. Perish; 3. Destroy; 4. Finish; 5. Languish; 6. Synonyms.

I. 1. *Ancient Near East.* Many of the meanings associated with Akk. *kalû* in the sense of "restrain"[1] correspond to Heb. → כלא *kālāʾ.* In addition, *kalû* also means "bring to an end, cease"; these meanings correspond to Heb. *kālâ.* An association between the two meanings may exist in the case of a premature end (cf. the command: "Bring life to an end"[2]), especially since *kalû* can also denote interruption of an activity.[3] It is therefore dubious whether Heb. *kālâ* is equivalent to Akk. *kalû*; *kālāʾ* seems more likely. On the other hand, Ugar. *kly,* "be at an end, make an end, destroy, exhaust,"[4] does correspond to Heb. *kālâ.* The Ugaritic verb can mean that bread and

kālâ. M. Dahood, "Hebrew-Ugaritic Lexicography III," *Bibl* 46 (1965), 311-332, esp. 328; G. Gerlemann, "כלה *klh* zu Ende sein," *THAT,* I, 831-33; L. Kopf, "Arabische Etymologien und Parallelen zum Bibelwörterbuch," *VT,* 9 (1959), 247-287, esp. 284.

1. Cf. *CAD,* VIII (1971), 95; *AHw,* I (1965), 428f.
2. *AHw,* I, 429.
3. Cf. *CAD,* VIII, 95.
4. *WUS,* no. 1317; cf. L. Milano, "KLY nel lessico amministrativo del semitico di nord-ovest," *Vicino oriente,* 1 (1978), 85-89; F. C. Fensham, "The Semantic Field of *kly* in Ugaritic," *JNSL,* 7 (1979), 27-30.

wine are exhausted, that the river-god has been destroyed. In *KAI,* 200, 6, 8, too, *klh* means "complete" (the harvest).[5]

2. *LXX.* The LXX usually translates *kālâ* by means of *ekleípein, paúein, synteleín/syntéleia,* or (*ex*)*analískein.* These verbs reflect the sense of Heb. *kālâ*: come to an end, complete, consume.

3. *Dead Sea Scrolls.* The Dead Sea scrolls use the verb primarily in the sense of "destroy." On the day of judgment, God destroys all who worship idols (1QpHab 13:3), the sons of darkness (1QM 3:9; cf. 1QM 13:16; 1:10,16), sin (1QM 11:11), the wicked priest (1QpHab 12:6; 12:5; 9:11), the men of Belial's lot (1QS 2:6; cf. 2:15; 1QM 15:4), the wicked (1QS 4:13), every worthless nation (1QM 4:12; cf. 1QM 15:2), the army of the nations (1QM 14:5), the enemy (1QM 18:12), those who do not keep the covenant (CD 8:2). This survey already shows that this destruction is merited by the conduct of its "objects" (cf. also 1QH 6:19,32). This is stated explicitly in 1QpHab 12:5f.: God will condemn the wicked priest to destruction, just as he had planned to destroy (*kālâ*) the poor. In addition, *kālâ* can mean "cease" (1QS 6:10; 1QM 8:1; 4QTestim 21; cf. 22:1,2) and can denote the longing of eyes for rest (1QH 9:5).

4. *kālâ and kālā'.* The verb *kālâ* denotes an action that brings something to an end or a process in which something is brought to an end. In either case, the objects or subjects named attain or seek an appropriate or imputed goal. The close relationship that has been suggested[6] between *kālâ* and *kālā'* is therefore dubious, since the force of *kālâ* is not so much retarding as progressive. Even if the two verbs can hardly be distinguished morphologically,[7] great caution is necessary in analyzing the semantic consequences.

Phonetic considerations that can only be touched upon here may further the discussion. If the root *kl* can be assumed to lie behind both *kālâ* and *kālā',* then they both express something that involves *kōl* (totality, all, everything of the sort named). A final suffixed *aleph* was no longer pronounced ("passed over in pronunciation"[8]) or was represented by a lengthened vowel, signaling a phonetic break.[9] This leaves the question whether a final *he* was merely an orthographic convention, not representing a sound,[10] or whether it stood for some kind of lengthening.[11] If so, *kālā'* would denote cessation and *kālâ* the extension of *kālā'*; something is held back (*kālā'*) or continued to its end (*kālâ*). In this case, the connection between *kālâ* and *kālā'* would be merely morpho-

---

5. *KAI,* 145, 11 is probably an error.
6. E.g., by Gerlemann.
7. Gerlemann.
8. *KBL*³, 1.
9. On final aleph as a glottal stop, see G. Beer and R. Meyer, *Hebräische Grammatik,* I (Berlin, 1952), 27; A. Bertsch, *Kurzgefasste Hebräische Sprachlehre* (Stuttgart, ²1961), 25.
10. *KBL*³, 221.
11. Cf. Bertsch, 25: "aspirated termination."

logical, not semantic.[12] The emphasis in the case of *kālâ* is not on "stopping" an action or process but on bringing it to a conclusion.

II. 1. *Be Decided.* It is clear that *killâ l^e* denotes the end or conclusion of an action, but *kālâ* refers not only to the end but to what leads up to it. For example, the expression *killâ l^eḏabbēr,* "finish speaking" (Ex. 31:18; Nu. 16:31; Jgs. 15:17; 1 S. 18:1), indicates that someone has the intended goal in sight. Several passages illustrate the point: Gen. 17:22 mentions the conclusion of God's command to circumcise all the males born to Abraham and his descendants, which achieves its goal, the circumcision of Abraham's household, in vv. 23ff.; Gen. 24:15 speaks of the conclusion of a prayer that finds fulfillment in vv. 15ff.; 1 S. 24:17-22(16-21) describes the reaction on the part of Saul that David wished to achieve by speaking to him. It is not so much that a person "finishes" speaking[13] as that he brings his words to their conclusion, i.e., their goal.

Something that is firmly decided also represents the conclusion of a process of decision. Saul determines evil against David (1 S. 20:7,9,33), David against Nabal (1 S. 25:17), the king against Haman (Est. 7:7). In each case, a groundwork has been laid for the evil that is decided: in the first case, by Saul's anger over David's military successes (1 S. 18:6-15; cf. vv. 28f.), Saul's declaration of his will to kill David (19:1), and his attempts to lay hands on David (vv. 8ff.) and to pin David to the wall with his spear (vv. 10f.). Saul's feelings toward David and his attempts on David's life culminate in the firm decision to do him evil. With this decision, Saul brings disgrace upon David (20:34[14]), i.e., he seeks to destroy him by placing a curse upon him. (On *klm,* cf. Isa. 41:11 par. *k^e'ayin, 'āḇāḏ*; also Ps. 35:4f.; 44:10[9], where *klm* denotes the grounds for the catastrophe described in vv. 11-17[10-16]; Job 19:3 [cf. v. 2: "break in pieces with words"].) The evil David determines against Nabal likewise constitutes the conclusion of a process (cf. 1 S. 25:13,21f.); the same is true of the evil the king determines against Haman (on Est. 7:7, cf. 6:10,13).

2. *Perish.* Those who perish deserve to do so: those who forsake Yahweh (Isa. 1:28), the destroyer (Isa. 16:4), the scoffer (Isa. 29:20), the psalmist's accusers (Ps. 71:13), false prophets (Ezk. 13:14), the wicked (Ps. 37:20; Job 4:9), the Egyptians, who are only mortals even though Israel trusts in them (Isa. 31:3). This form of expression is found in an announcement of judgment (Isa. 1:28[15]), a "description of salvation" (Isa. 29:20[16]; cf. 16:4[17]), a threat (Isa. 31:3[18]), a "collection of proverbs" (Ps. 37:20[19]), and

12. Contra Gerlemann, 831.
13. Gerlemann, 832.
14. Contra H. W. Hertzberg, *I & II Samuel. OTL* (Eng. trans. 1964), 170.
15. Cf. H. Wildberger, *Isaiah 1–12* (Eng. trans., Minneapolis, 1991), *in loc.*
16. Cf. O. Kaiser, *Isaiah 13–39. OTL* (Eng. trans. 1974), 279.
17. *Ibid.,* 70.
18. *Ibid.,* 311.
19. A. Weiser, *Psalms. OTL* (Eng. trans. 1962), 315.

a popular wisdom aphorism (Job 4:9[20]). The language of prophecy and wisdom speaks of the "end" of the wicked. The "end" marks the conclusion befitting their actions; they receive the reward of their deeds.

The psalmist, however, also laments that he is perishing (Ps. 31:11[10]; 39:11[10]; 71:9; 73:26; 90:7; 102:4[3]; 143:7; cf. Job 33:21). We must not assume automatically that he, too, thus finds his proper end; but it is worth noting that the context speaks of sin and guilt (Ps. 31:11[10]; 39:12[11]; 73:21f.; 90:8; 143:2). The psalmist nevertheless affirms his innocence (73:13), his faithfulness (31:7[6]; 71:6), and his trust in God (31:15[14]); he calls himself Yahweh's servant (cf. 31:17[16]; 90:13,16) and righteous one (31:19[18]). The context of 71:9 does not mention any sin on the part of the psalmist. It is therefore conceivable that he should perish without cause; in other words, the imminent end does not invariably reflect previous negative actions.

A closer look at the psalmist's enemies and the literary form in question may point toward a possible solution. The psalmist describes his opponents as the "wicked" (Ps. 31:18[17]; 39:2[1]; 71:4; 73:3,12), who question God's knowledge (73:11) — obviously in contrast to those who fear Yahweh and take refuge in him (31:24[23]), who wait patiently for him (31:25[24]). The psalmist's enemies are thus also the enemies of Yahweh, those who are far from him (73:27). It is in fact the enemies who should perish (cf. 31:18,24[17,23]; 73:27); now, however, destruction threatens the psalmist. This cannot be Yahweh's intent, and so the psalmist laments; apart from Ps. 73, all the texts in question appear in laments. This lament is a kind of challenge, a charge brought against God himself to move him to intervene on behalf of the psalmist. It is quite natural that the psalmist should use a garish palette to describe his plight in furtherance of this purpose. The psalmist's fear of his enemies and his realization that he is actually challenging God justify his talk of "perishing." This language may not always reflect his actual condition, but it is evoked by the machinations of the enemy, who speak (31:19[18]; 71:10) and counsel (31:14[13]; 71:10) against the psalmist in calumny (31:12[11]; 73:8) — acts of verbal aggression that should probably be understood as curses (cf. above all 73:8f.). The psalmist is afraid that these words will strike home and that he will perish. Here, too, therefore, *kālâ* may have the meaning "attain the appropriate goal."

3. *Destroy.* Whoever destroys a person or a thing achieves his purpose and brings his corresponding efforts to their goal, which need not always be total destruction (cf. Jer. 5:3 in its context). When the text speaks of Yahweh's destroying Israel by sword, famine, and pestilence (Jer. 14:12; cf. 9:15[16]) and through his wrath (cf. Ezk. 20:13; 22:31), the question of Yahweh's motivation is of interest: Israel is a stiff-necked people (Ex. 33:5); they make for themselves a molten calf (Ex. 32:12; cf. v. 8), they can grow disobedient and forsake Yahweh (Dt. 28:21; cf. vv. 15, 20), they may worship other gods (Josh. 24:20), they are disobedient and go after the baʿals (Jer. 9:15[16]; cf. vv.

---

20. Cf. F. Horst, *Hiob. BK,* XVI/1 ([4]1983), 63; cf. G. Hölscher, *Das Buch Hiob. HAT,* XVII ([2]1952), 21: "proverbial wisdom."

12f.[13f.]), they vacillate between Yahweh and other gods (Jer. 14:12; cf. v. 10), they practice social injustice and religious perversion (Ezk. 22:31; cf. vv. 25-29). Above all, turning away from Yahweh to worship other gods is a reason for the (potential) destruction of Israel. These passages clearly speak of Yahweh's intervention, but this divine act is a reaction appropriate to the conduct-reward nexus: "Their way have I requited upon their heads" (Ezk. 22:31). Israel's conduct and Yahweh's corresponding reaction both attain their goal (except in Job 9:22: "He destroys both the blameless and the wicked"). The (potential) destruction of Israel serves to evoke return (Jer. 5:3; Ezk. 43:8) so that "I will dwell in their midst for ever" (Ezk. 43:9). Here it is already clear that the text refers not so much to the total destruction of Israel as to an act of Yahweh that attains its goal.

Yahweh "destroys" (or does not destroy: Ex. 33:3; Lev. 26:44; Nu. 25:11) not only Israel, but also arrogant and overbearing Assyria or some other world power (Isa. 10:18; cf. vv. 7, 12f., 15[21]) and the Elamites through the sword (Jer. 49:37). He will also destroy the wicked (Ps. 59:14[13]) and the enemy (Ps. 74:11). (The emendation of *kālâ* to *kālā'* in Ps. 74:11[22] is unnecessary if the impv. *kallēh* in v. 10 refers to the enemy or is connected with v. 12[23].) Here, too, Yahweh "requites their way upon their heads" (cf. Ezk. 22:31). The affliction they have brought upon Israel against Yahweh's will attains its appropriate goal. Something that begins with the actions of the people in question runs its course and attains its goal, just as the word of a prophet is fulfilled, a curse takes effect, and a house is destroyed (Zec. 5:4). The piel of *klh* in the sense of "destroy" does not merely denote the end of something; it takes into account the way that leads to this end and describes the goal attained.

"Destruction" carried out by Yahweh may be the subject of a threat (Jer. 9:15[16];[24] Ezk. 20:13;[25] Isa. 10:18[26]) that sets a chain of events in motion and expresses its goal. A lament may also speak of Yahweh's "destruction" (Jer. 14:12;[27] Ps. 59:14[13];[28] 74:11[29]). The lament is explicitly (Ps. 59:14[13]; 74:11) or by virtue of its context (Jer. 14:12; cf. vv. 19-22) conceived of as a prayer. Here, too, a chain of events is set in motion.

In the phrase *'āśâ kālâ* (Isa. 10:22: *killāyôn*), the noun *kālâ* also means "destruction, end." Yahweh will not make a full end of Israel (Jer. 5:18; 30:11; 46:28; Ezk. 20:17; Neh. 9:31), so that the people may understand their sin (Jer. 5:18; cf. v. 19), because Israel is "his" people and for the sake of David (Jer. 30:9; 46:27f.) or for the sake of his name and out of pity (Ezk. 20:14,17; Neh. 9:31). Here Yahweh's purpose and

---

21. Cf. Wildberger, *in loc.*
22. H. Gunkel, *Die Psalmen. HKAT,* II/2 (^{6}1986); H.-J. Kraus, *Psalms 60–150* (Eng. trans., Minneapolis, 1989), 96.
23. M. Dahood, *Psalms II. AB,* XVII (^{2}1973), 198, 204.
24. Cf. A. Weiser, *Das Buch Jeremia 1–25,14. ATD,* XX (^{8}1981), 82.
25. W. Zimmerli, *Ezekiel 1. Herm* (Eng. trans. 1979), 410.
26. Cf. Wildberger, 429f.
27. Cf. Weiser, *ATD,* XX, 122.
28. H.-J. Kraus, *Psalms 1–59* (Eng. trans., Minneapolis, 1988), 542f.
29. Cf. Kraus, *Psalms 60–150,* 96.

conduct with respect to Israel, his relationship with Israel, attain their goal. He acts accordingly, and refuses to make a full end of Israel.

Other passages, however, speak of Yahweh's destroying Israel or the land (Israel: Isa. 10:22; Ezk. 11:13 [in a question]; the land: Jer. 4:27) because Israel places its trust in Assyria (Isa. 10:20) and has been unfaithful to Yahweh (Jer. 4:14,17,18,22). Jer. 4:28 shows that Yahweh acts (*ʿāśâ kālâ,* v. 27) according to a plan that is now put into effect and attains its goal; Israel's wicked actions receive their corresponding reward.

The same holds true for Yahweh's "destruction" of the nations (Jer. 30:11; 46:28), the enemy (Nah. 1:8f.), or the whole earth (Isa. 10:23; Zeph. 1:18). They have oppressed Israel (Jer. 30:11; cf. v. 8; 46:28; cf. v. 27), they practice idolatry (Nah. 1:8f.; cf. v. 14), they — like Assyria — have offended against Yahweh through their arrogance (Isa. 10:23; cf. vv. 12f., 15) and have sinned against him (Zeph. 1:18; cf. v. 17).

4. *Finish.* Both God and human beings may bring something to completion, to an end or goal corresponding to their purpose and actions.

Following Gen. 2:1 (the completion of heaven and earth), v. 2a states that God finished his work. We are then told (v. 2b) that he rested — a statement that illuminates the meaning of "finish," especially since Gen. 2:2f. is "dominated totally by the language of the Sabbath commandment."[30] God's finishing of creation and resting are "not simply the negative sign of its end"[31] but characterize creation as an act open to the future, an act without limit, since the concluding formula ("it was evening and it was morning") is absent. Here something — God's work — is brought not to its end or conclusion, but to its goal: God's resting. God brings his work to its goal and through his resting establishes a goal: the Sabbath, for which the groundwork has been laid in the approbation formula (Gen. 1:4,10, etc.). Steck[32] on the contrary interprets *kālâ* in Gen. 2:1 as meaning "bring to a conclusion," after which a continuation of the work of creation is inconceivable; he argues that there follows in *šbt* (v. 2a) the totally different creative act of resting, "which as such is no longer a work in which God produces works of creation."[33]

Ex. 39:32-43 (P) contains a few parallels to Gen. 1:31; 2:1f. which suggest that P is attempting to find a relationship or even correspondence between the construction of the tent of meeting and the work of creation.[34]

Human beings finish buildings. Solomon finished the temple (1 K. 7:1; 9:1; 2 Ch. 7:11), the palace (1 K. 3:1; 9:1; 2 Ch. 7:11), and the city walls of Jerusalem (1 K. 3:1; cf. Neh. 3:34[4:2]). The work for the temple worship is also finished (1 Ch. 28:20), as are the temple furnishings (1 K. 7:40; 2 Ch. 4:11). The same is said — by analogy — of the tent of meeting (Ex. 39:32; 40:33). The temple and its furnishings were finished

---

30. W. H. Schmidt, *Die Schöpfungsgeschichte der Priesterschrift. WMANT,* 17 (³1973), 157.
31. G. von Rad, *Genesis. OTL* (Eng. trans. 1961), 60.
32. H. O. Steck, *Der Schöpfungsbericht der Priesterschrift. FRLANT,* 115 (²1981), 178-199, esp. 186ff.
33. *Ibid.,* 187.
34. Cf. Schmidt, 156, esp. n. 3.

"as it had been planned" (1 K. 6:38): the finishing is described as the realization of a plan, the goal of a course of action. This chimes with the description of 1 K. 6 as "a plan for the building of the temple reduced to words."[35]

Noah finishes the ark to the cubit (Gen. 6:16) — a description whose precision is typical of P, also found in the description of how the tent of meeting was constructed (Ex. 25ff.).[36] A deliberate intent to associate the finishing of creation, the tent of meeting, the temple, and possibly also the ark cannot be ruled out.

Human beings may also finish a project (Ruth 3:18), a job (Ex. 5:13; e.g., the division of the land: Josh. 19:49,51); measuring (Ezk. 42:15); a census (1 Ch. 27:24 [negated]); something evil (Prov. 16:30), a period of time (Ezk. 4:6), or a period of days (Ezk. 43:27; Job 36:11). In every case, an action (intended or begun) is brought to its goal.

God may bring his anger to completion (*'ap̱*: Ezk. 5:13; 7:8; 20:8,21; *ḥēmâ*: Ezk. 6:12; 13:15; Lam. 4:11). His anger can also blaze forth or rise up (Isa. 5:25; 2 K. 22:13,17; Ezk. 38:18); God sends it forth (Ezk. 7:3) or pours it out (Ps. 79:6; Lam. 2:4). "Bringing to completion" has a different sense: God's anger does not blaze forth or rise up, nor is it sent forth or poured out; instead it attains its goal, bringing God's plan to fruition (cf. Ps. 106:23). It is a fundamental characteristic of God's anger to "respond to human acts that impugn the nature and the commandments of this God."[37] The texts in question make this quite clear: God's anger is a reaction to Israel's sin (Ezk. 5:13; cf. v. 7; 6:12; cf. v. 11; 7:8; 20:8,21; Lam. 4:11; cf. vv. 6, 13). Besides this motif, the "knowledge formula"[38] expresses the purpose of God's anger: Israel is to know that Yahweh has spoken in his jealousy (Ezk. 5:13), that he is Yahweh (6:13), that it is he who smites (7:9) — a clear sign that Israel is not destroyed totally when Yahweh brings his anger to completion. God's anger finds expression in particular acts of punishment, which are "transient."[39] This is reflected in the form of the prophetic demonstration oracle (Ezk. 5:13; 6:12; 7:8[40]), which speaks of the completion of God's anger.

5. *Languish.* The meaning "languish, pine away" is associated with *kālâ* in texts that speak of an agonized decline born of passionate desire.[41] This idiom is used primarily of the eyes, sometimes also of the "soul" (Ps. 84:3[2]; 119:81: *nep̱eš*) or "kidneys" (Job 19:27: *kᵉlāyôṯ*). The purpose of the eyes is to see something; they are therefore mentioned in language that describes emotions, especially desire or longing.[42] The objects of this longing are varied: God's promise (Ps. 119:82), God's help and

---

35. M. Noth, *Könige 1–16. BK*, IX/1 (1968), 104.
36. Cf. H. Gunkel, *Genesis. HKAT*, I/1 (⁹1977), 142.
37. Gerlemann, 223; cf. W. Eichrodt, *Theology of the OT*, I. *OTL* (Eng. trans. 1961), 259f., 263f.
38. → ידע *yāḏa'*.
39. Eichrodt, 266.
40. Cf. Zimmerli, 176, 184, 202.
41. Cf. Gerlemann, 832.
42. Cf. E. Jenni, "עַיִן *'ajin* Auge," *THAT*, II, 261, 264.

righteous promises (Ps. 119:123), help (Lam. 4:17), sons and daughters taken into exile (Dt. 28:32). Other texts mention the psalmist's God (Ps. 69:4[3]), a place of refuge (Job 11:20), a share (of an inheritance) (Job 17:5), the harvest (Lev. 26:16), food (Job 31:16; cf. v. 17; also Jer. 14:6), and long life for one's sons (1 S. 2:33). In such contexts, *kālâ* does not so much denote "damage to the eyes"[43] as suggest an emotion.[44] The eyes perish out of longing for the objects in question, which constitute the goal of the longing.

The *nep̱eš* also languishes out of yearning for the courts of Yahweh (Ps. 84:3[2]) and God's help, a typical description of *nep̱eš*.[45] In Job 19:27, the kidneys, organs "of most delicate sensibility,"[46] are the subject of *kālâ*. Job's confidence that he will see God with his own eyes makes it clear that in this passage *kālâ* does not mean "shrivel"[47] but denotes intense yearning.[48] Almost all the texts that speak of such longing on the part of the eyes, the soul, or the kidneys appear in laments (cf. Ps. 69:4[3]; Job 17:5; 19:27; Lam. 4:17). Since lamentation is not performed for its own sake but in order to achieve a purpose, it is closely allied with petition — an indication that *kālâ* denotes attainment of a goal, even if only prospective.

6. *Synonyms.* Attainment of a goal by *kālâ* may also be expressed by various synonyms, of which some may be listed here: "perish" (*'āḇaḏ*: Ps. 37:20; Job 4:9), "cut off" (*kāraṯ*: Isa. 29:20; Ps. 37:20; cf. vv. 9, 22, 28, 38), "be destroyed" (*nišmaḏ*: Dt. 28:20; cf. v. 24; 2 S. 21:5; Ps. 37:20; cf. vv. 38, 28 [conj.]), "slay" (*hārag*: Ex. 32:12; Ps. 78:33; cf. v. 34), "die" (*mûṯ*: Ezk. 5:12), "fall" (*nāpal*: Isa. 31:3; Ezk. 5:12), "devour" (*'āḵal*: Jer. 10:25), "smite" (*nkh* hiphil: Dt. 28:21; cf. v. 22; Jer. 5:3), "cease to exist" (*'ênennû*: Ps. 37:20; cf. vv. 10, 36; 59:14[13]).

Helfmeyer

43. Gerlemann, 261f.
44. *Ibid.*, 264.
45. Cf. W. H. Schmidt, "Anthropologische Begriffe im AT," *EvTh*, 24 (1964), 380.
46. H. W. Wolff, *Anthropology of the OT* (Eng. trans., Philadelphia, 1974), 65.
47. Horst, 278.
48. Cf. A. Weiser, *Das Buch Hiob. ATD*, XIII (⁷1980), 141f.

כַּלָּה *kallâ*

Contents: I. 1. Distribution and Etymology; 2. Meaning. II. 1. Bride; 2. Daughter-in-Law.

kallâ. J. Conrad, *Der junge Generation im AT. ArbT*, 1/42 (1970); K. Elliger, "Das Gesetz Leviticus 18," *ZAW*, 67 (1955), 1-25; A. Goetze, "Short or Long *a*? (Notes on Some Akkadian

I. 1. *Distribution and Etymology.* The noun *kallâ* appears 34 times in the OT (plus a probable emendation in 2 S. 17:3[1]). It means both "bride" and "daughter-in-law." Parallel nouns are found in most Semitic languages. We may mention in particular Akk. *kallatu, kallutu,* "daughter-in-law, bride," also "sister-in-law";[2] Ugar. *klt,* "bride";[3] and later Hebrew and Aramaic.[4] The corresponding word in Arabic is *kannat(t),* "daughter-in-law, sister-in-law."[5] There are also South Arabic and Ethiopic equivalents.[6] A derivative of *kallâ* found only in Jer. 2:2 is the abstract pl. *k^elûlôt,* which means "bridal state" (cf. the Akkadian abstract noun *kallūtu, kallatūtu,* "status as daughter-in-law or bride"[7]).

The etymology of *kallâ* is obscure. It may be derived from a root *kll,* "conceal, veil (the face or head)," a reference to a bride's appearance[8] (cf. Akk. *kullulu;*[9] also Gen. 24:65). Another etymology traces the noun to a verb meaning "crown"[10] (cf. again Akk. *kullulu,* as well as the noun *kulūlu* or *kilīlu;*[11] Aram. *k^elīlā;*[12] Arab. *iklīl*[13]). It is unlikely, however, that *kallâ* derives from a verbal root.

The LXX consistently uses *nýmphē* to translate *kallâ;*[14] *k^elûlôt* is rendered by *teleíōsis,* "puberty."[15]

2. *Meaning.* The noun *kallâ* is ambiguous in two respects. It denotes the relationship of a young woman to her (future) husband ("bride") as well as her relationship toward her husband's father or mother ("daughter-in-law"). In addition, in the first sense it can designate a woman entering into marriage and, in the second, a woman who is already married, sometimes even a widow (Gen. 38:6-10; Ruth 1:4f.).

This double ambiguity is explained by the family structure of ancient Israel and of

---

Words)," *Or,* 16 (1947), 239-250; A. Hermann, *Altägyptische Liebesdichtung* (Wiesbaden, 1959); L. Rost, "Erwägungen zu Hosea 4,13f.," *Festschrift A. Bertholet* (Tübingen, 1950), 451-460; H. Schmökel, *Heilige Hochzeit und Hoheslied. AKM,* 32/1 (1956); R. de Vaux, *AncIsr;* E. Würthwein, "Zum Verständnis des Hohenliedes," *ThR,* 32 (1967), 177-212.

1. See II.1 below.
2. *CAD,* VIII (1971), 79-82; *AHw,* I (1965), 426. In many legal documents, the word appears to denote also a legally dependent woman without a marital relationship; cf. *CAD,* VIII, 86.
3. *WUS,* no. 1321; *UT,* no. 1241; sometimes also with the meaning "daughter-in-law."
4. Cf. *WTM,* II, 331f.; *LexSyr*², 326f.; *MdD,* 197.
5. *WKAS,* I, 372f.
6. *KBL*³, 455.
7. *CAD,* VIII, 85f.; *AHw,* I, 426.
8. *KBL*³, 455.
9. *CAD,* VIII, 518f.; *AHw,* I, 503.
10. *BLe,* §454; Goetze, 243f.
11. *CAD,* VIII, 358, 527f.; *AHw,* I, 476, 505.
12. *WTM,* II, 338f.; *LexSyr*², 327.
13. *WKAS,* I, 299f.
14. Cf. Joachim Jeremias, "νύμφη," *TDNT,* IV, 1099.
15. K. Weiss, "φέρω," *TDNT,* VIII, 85.

the ancient Near East in general.[16] When a woman marries, she generally becomes a member of her husband's family, in which his father exercises supreme authority as *paterfamilias*; the father's wife is likewise in charge of the housekeeping. In the great majority of cases, the *paterfamilias* had only one wife, who was thus the true mother-in-law of the young bride.[17] The bride's new status is thus defined both by her relationship to her husband and by her relationship to the head of the extended family and his wife.[18] Both relations are accordingly represented by the same word; cf. the double meaning of → חתן *ḥāṯān*. We must also note that under these circumstances the decisive turning point in the woman's life is not marriage but the birth of the first male child. Only by bearing her own son does she contribute to the preservation of the family, fulfilling her true vocation. Only thus does she become a full person.[19] It is therefore no accident that the two extended narratives concerning a *kallâ* end with the birth of a child (Gen. 38; Ruth; cf. 1 S. 4:19f.). In this respect, there is no substantial difference between a bride and a married woman without children or a widow. Cf. the analogous meaning of → עלמה *'almâ*.

II. 1. *Bride.* In the sense of "bride," *kallâ* is used primarily for its emotional content. In the prophets, it serves — usually in conjunction with *ḥāṯān*[20] — to describe events in sacred history. It is used in stereotyped expressions to symbolize the ultimate in joy and celebration, such as Yahweh will bestow in the time of salvation (Jer. 33:11) or deny when he brings disaster as punishment (Jer. 7:34; 16:9; 25:10). Israel's restored position of honor in the time of salvation is compared to a bride adorning herself (Isa. 49:18; 61:10). On the other hand, the premature summoning of bride and bridegroom from the wedding chamber is a sign that Yahweh is about to bring a terrible calamity, which demands immediate repentance (Joel 2:16). In addition, the loving relationship between bride and bridegroom symbolizes the original relationship between Yahweh and Israel (*kᵉlûlôt*: Jer. 2:2), which will be restored in the time of salvation (Isa. 62:5). The contrasting image of a bride, who would never forget her wonderful wedding attire, serves also to illustrate the incomprehensible alienation of Israel from Yahweh (Jer. 2:32). In this context we may also cite 2 S. 17:3, which compares the hope that the people will support the usurper Absalom to the attraction between a bride and her future husband.[21]

Three passages in the Song of Songs also illustrate this usage. As is true throughout the entire book, the emphasis is on intimate love between bride and bridegroom. The presence of the bride and the erotic pleasure she provides enchant her beloved (Cant.

16. For a discussion of the extended family in ancient Israel, see Elliger, 6-12; also *idem, Leviticus. HAT,* IV (1966), 238f.

17. Cf. de Vaux, 25f.

18. Rost, 452-55.

19. Cf. Conrad, 21-23.

20. → חתן *ḥāṯān,* II.1.a.

21. On the textual problems of the passage, see *BHK, BHS,* and the comms.; the proposal of *KBL*[2,3] that *kallâ* has a special meaning ("newly-married woman") in this passage is unnecessary.

4:9-11).[22] Up to now, the bride has remained inviolate; now she shares with her beloved all the delights of love (4:12–5:1).[23] With her, her beloved can escape all dangers and uncertainties (4:8).[24] The intimacy of the relationship is further emphasized by the device of calling the bride "sister" (4:9f.,12; 5:1).[25] In short, union with the bride means unlimited fulfillment of true and total erotic desire.

It is nevertheless surprising that the Song of Songs uses *kallâ* only in these 3 passages. Elsewhere the female partner is addressed as *raʿyâ,* "friend, (be)love(ed)"[26] (together with "sister" in Cant. 5:2). This usage corresponds to the use of *dôḏ* ("beloved") to designate the male partner, who is never called "bridegroom" (*ḥāṯān,* even in 4:12–5:1, where he is called *dôḏ* in v. 16). It has accordingly been suggested that the text does not refer to a bridal couple but to partners in a relationship of free love outside legal or familial constraints, and that *kallâ* can therefore be interpreted in the extended sense of "beloved."[27] It is doubtful, however, whether such a dichotomy between free love and married love can be maintained within the context of Israel.[28] It is much more likely that the text refers to the power of a love within legal and familiar constraints, which nevertheless allows bride and bridegroom to encounter each other on a free and equal basis within these constraints. The point is the fundamental experience of the bride as the bridegroom's beloved: despite her socially inferior status as a woman, she can play an equal role and is thus entitled to be called "friend" (*raʿyâ*) or "sister."

Another theory associates the Song of Songs with the domain of cultic mythology.[29] In other words, the partners are in fact deities whose marriage or love is recreated in the cult. The participants in the cult thus share in an experience of divine love that transcends their own erotic experience. This background might represent the origin of the notion of Israel as Yahweh's bride.[30] The particulars of this theory, however, are highly problematical.[31]

2. *Daughter-in-Law.* When *kallâ* means "daughter-in-law," the concern is her position within the family of the husband. The primary emphasis is on legal obliga-

---

22. For *dôḏîm* in the sense of "erotic pleasure," see → דוד *dôḏ* (*dôdh*), II.3.d.

23. For the garden as a *topos* of love poetry, see → דוד *dôḏ* (*dôdh*), II.3.d.

24. See the comms. on the problems presented by this difficult verse.

25. → אח *ʾāḥ* (*ʾāch*), II; on the description of the beloved as "sister" in Egyptian love poetry, see Hermann, 75-78.

26. → רע *rēaʿ*.

27. G. Gerleman, *Das Hohelied. BK,* XVIII (²1981), 153, 155; cf. also the discussion in → דוד *dôḏ* (*dôdh*), III.2.

28. See esp. E. Würthwein, *Die fünf Megilloth: Das Hohelied. HAT,* XVIII (²1969), 28f., 31-35, and *passim*; also (somewhat more cautiously), W. Rudolph, *Das Hohelied. KAT,* XVII/2 (1962), 100-109.

29. Schmökel; H. Ringgren, *Das Hohe Lied. ATD,* XVI/2 (1962); cf. Würthwein, *ThR,* 32 (1967), 196-201.

30. Ringgren, 260.

31. → דוד *dôḏ* (*dôdh*), III.1,

tions. Laws explicitly govern the sexual realm. The father-in-law in particular, as representative of the family, is obligated to respect the sexual integrity of the young wife and see that strict order is maintained within the family (Lev. 18:15; 20:12; cf. Ezk. 22:11).[32] This requirement is further amplified by Hosea, who harshly accuses the heads of families of having sexual relations with cult prostitutes after the manner of the Canaanites. They set their daughters and daughters-in-law a poor example, so that the latter are tempted into adultery and fornication (Hos. 4:13f.). The conduct of the young brides is hardly limited to sexual relations during cultic ceremonies or in an isolated initiation rite;[33] the prophet aims to show that the cultic misconduct of the influential men has disastrous consequences for the total life of the family and nation.

As daughter-in-law, the young bride is primarily a dependent individual needing protection, which is the responsibility of her husband's family and especially its head. She must, of course, deserve this protection — that is, she must in turn avoid unchastity. Otherwise she, like the transgressing father-in-law, is subject to capital punishment (Lev. 20:12; cf. Gen. 38:24). (In Hos. 4:13f., Yahweh himself refuses to carry out the punishment. This special case is intended to show clearly who the guilty parties really are; the demands of the law are not abrogated.) In addition, the bride must adapt to her husband's family and respect her mother-in-law as the wife of the head of the family;[34] otherwise she would contribute to the disruption of the family's life (Mic. 7:6; cf. Mt. 10:35; Lk. 12:53).

In extreme cases, she can even be expected to take an active role in maintaining her relationship with her new family. This is illustrated by the example of two women, whose husbands have died without offspring, who have hardly any chance of bearing such offspring through levirate marriage (Gen. 38; Ruth).[35] The first of these, who has already survived two husbands and has been returned in humiliation to her father's family (Gen. 38:6-11,14b), exhibits extraordinary acumen and determination in her campaign to recover a place of honor in the family of her in-laws (Gen. 38:12-26). (Even during her time with her father's family, however, she appears still to belong to her husband's family, since its head exercises jurisdiction over her [v. 24]; this may be related to the charge that she was sent back only temporarily [v. 11].) She thus becomes paradigmatic of a woman who acts with a sense of independent superiority even in a position of degradation and dependence.

The other woman, for whom continued residence with her widowed mother-in-law promises economic insecurity, not protection (Ruth 1:1-13; cf. 2:1-18), neverthess holds fast to these ties with exemplary love and devotion (1:14-17). In her case, this also makes her absolutely dependent on an alien people and an alien God (1:16; 2:11). The daughter-in-law symbolizes the ultimate in fidelity: faithfulness (→ **חסד** *ḥesed*) to

32. See Elliger, *ZAW,* 67 (1955), 8; *idem, HAT,* IV, 239.

33. Rost, 455-59.

34. See I.2 above.

35. For a discussion of widowhood and levirate marriage, see → **אלמנה** *'almānâ* (*'almānāh*); → **יבם** *ybm*; → **גאל** *gā'al*.

another human being who is in fact an alien with little to offer, but has been acknowledged as next of kin (3:10).[36] Since this also represents faithfulness to the other person's God, she also becomes an outstanding witness to faith in the God of Israel, who does not let her conduct go unrewarded: she finally attains security and can contribute to the preservation of her new family (2:19–4:17; cf. 2:12).

Conrad

---

36. Cf. also Würthwein, *HAT,* XVIII, 5f.

כְּלִי *k*

Contents: I. 1. Occurrences; 2. Etymology and Usage. II. Secular Usage: 1. Containers; 2. Furnishings; 3. Tools; 4. Weapons; 5. Art Objects; 6. Clothing; 7. Baggage, Cargo; 8. Ships. III. Cultic Usage: 1. Cultic Paraphernalia; 2. Musical Instruments.

I. 1. *Occurrences.* The masculine noun *k*ᵉ*lî* occurs some 320 times in the OT. It is not found in the Aramaic passages of the OT, but Dalman and *WTM* record its use in Jewish Aramaic with a range of meanings that corresponds approximately to OT usage. The same holds true for the Mishnah tractate *Kelim,* which deals with questions concerning the ritual cleanness of various common objects subsumed by the OT under the category of *k*ᵉ*lî.*[1] The Dead Sea scrolls also use *k*ᵉ*lî,* primarily in the sense of "weapons."[2]

The term is common throughout the ancient Near East (except at Ugarit), but only with a very limited meaning, which may reflect its original sense.[3] In Akkadian, *kallu*[4] denotes a kind of bowl; the etymological equivalent in various Arabic dialects always

---

*k*ᵉ*lî.* K. Albrecht, "Das Geschlecht der hebräischen Hauptwörter," *ZAW,* 16 (1896), 41-121, esp. 87f.; J. Barth, "Vergleichende Studien," *ZDMG,* 41 (1887), 603-641, esp. 604; M. Buttenwieser, "בִּכְלֵי עֹז לַיהוָה 2 Chronicles 30 $_{21}$," *JBL,* 45 (1926), 156-58; G. R. Driver, "Babylonian and Hebrew Notes," *WO,* 2 (1954), 19-26, esp. 24f. on Ezr. 8:27; S. Fraenkel, *Die aramäischen Fremdwörter im Arabischen* (Leiden, 1886), 204; M. D. Goldman, "Lexicographical Notes on Exegesis (4)," *ABR,* 3 (1958), 44-51, esp. 48; H. Grimme, "Südarabische Tempelstrafgesetze," *OLZ,* 9 (1906), 256-262, esp. 261; C. Maurer, "σκεῦος," *TDNT,* VII, 358-367, esp. 358-362; K. Vollers, review of C. Reinhardt, *Ein arabischer Dialekt, gesprochen in ʿOmān und Zanzibar* (Stuttgart, 1894), *ZDMG,* 49 (1895), 484-515, esp. 514.

1. Cf. H. L. Strack, *Introduction to the Talmud and Midrash* (Eng. trans. 1931, repr. New York, 1978), 59f.
2. See II.4 below.
3. See I.2 below.
4. *AHw,* I (1965), 426.

denotes a container or measure of capacity.[5] The word $k^e l\hat{\imath}$ must have had a similar meaning in Palmyrene during the first centuries of the Common Era.[6]

2. *Etymology and Usage.* Wilhelm Gesenius[7] derived the noun $k^e l\hat{\imath}$ (reflecting an original unattested *kēleh*) from a verb *kālâ*; he gives the basic meaning as "something made, like Ger. *Zeug* from *zeugen.*" He therefore adds corresponding German equivalents to his Latin translations: "*vestes* (*Zeug*); *navigium* (Fahr*zeug*); *instrumentum* (Werk*zeug*); *arma* (Rüst*zeug*)." He also relates the verb *klh* to the roots *kl'* and *kll.*[8] Appealing as this etymology is, the development of the broad meaning must be accounted for differently. The noun $k^e l\hat{\imath}$ is derived by *GesB* from a verbal root *klh* II, whose meaning is not defined.[9] In *KBL*³,[10] the root is given as *klh* III = *kwl,*[11] with the meaning "contain" in the qal, "surround" in the pilpel; this etymology would easily account for the use of $k^e l\hat{\imath}$ to denote all kinds of vessels. This meaning was retained in most languages,[12] while the extension to a much broader range of meanings is attested only for Hebrew and Aramaic, where the noun is used for vessels and household objects, tools and weapons, pieces of jewelry and musical instruments. The late Jewish usage of $k^e l\hat{\imath}$ as a euphemism for a woman[13] does not occur in the OT.

II. Secular Usage. The following paragraphs will attempt to describe the various meanings of $k^e l\hat{\imath}$ denoting objects not used in the cult. No attempt will be made to list all the relevant passages; such a list would be impossible, because many texts do not yield a precise definition of what $k^e l\hat{\imath}$ refers to. Our presentation of the noun's range of meanings takes as its point of departure the basic verbal meaning "contain, surround"[14] and then goes on to examine the extensions of this meaning.

1. *Containers.* The object that does the containing may be any kind of vessel, made of any kind of material for any purpose. Such a vessel is therefore appropriate for everyday use.

a. *Vessels, Pots.* In this sense, the noun denotes primarily an earthenware vessel for daily household use (2 S. 17:28; Isa. 22:24; also Nu. 19:15); its manufacture is described in Jer. 18:4. It may hold water (Lev. 14:5; 1 K. 17:10; Jer. 14:3; Ruth 2:9), oil (2 K. 4:3ff.), wine (Jer. 48:11f.), or food (Isa. 65:4; cf. 66:20, with reference to a cereal offering). It may serve as a baking pan (Ezk. 4:9) or as a container for a scroll (Jer.

---

5. Grimme, Fraenkel, Vollers.
6. *DISO,* 120; cf. H. Ingholt, H. Seyrig, J. Starcky, and A. Caquot, *Recueil des Tessères de Palmyre* (Paris, 1955), no. 280, 867.
7. *GesTh.*
8. *Ibid.,* 685ff.
9. P. 348.
10. P. 456.
11. → כול *kwl.*
12. See I.1 above.
13. Cf. Maurer.
14. See I.2 above.

32:14); the latter usage is illustrated by the scrolls discovered at Qumran. The fragility of earthenware vessels played an important role in the language of the OT as a symbol of punishment (Jer. 19:11; 25:34 [?]; Ps. 2:9; cf. also the symbolism of emptying in Jer. 48:12; 51:34), but there were also vessels made of wood (Lev. 15:12). Vessels of bronze (Lev. 6:21[Eng. v. 28]; Ezr. 8:27) also found employment in the cult.[15] At the royal court and among the wealthy upper classes there were drinking vessels made of gold (1 K. 10:21 par. 2 Ch. 9:20; Est. 1:7). When the text speaks of precious objects of gold or silver taken as booty (2 Ch. 20:25; 32:27) or given as tokens of friendship (2 S. 8:10; 1 K. 10:25), the reference is undoubtedly to cups, tankards, and similar vessels used for drinking, as well as other household objects,[16] even though a precise definition is not always possible.

Nu. 7:85 mentions silver vessels as dedication offerings. Quite generally, vessels play an important role in the legal sections of the OT. Objects related specifically to the cult will be discussed later,[17] but we may note here that containers were subject to especially stringent regulations governing ritual purity (cf. Lev. 6:21[28]; 11:32f.; 15:12; Nu. 19:15; 31:20).

Identification of the various OT terms for vessels with specific archaeological types is extremely difficult, since the scanty information in the text usually does not refer to the form of the vessel but to its function.[18]

b. *Containers (in General).* The function of an object denoted by *kᵉlî* is not limited to pots; the word can be used for various types of container.

The noun *kᵉlî* denotes the sack in which Saul and his servant carry their food (1 S. 9:7). Probably similar is the shepherd's bag into which David puts the stones he will use to slay Goliath; it may also hold his sling (1 S. 17:40,49; cf. Zec. 11:15). Larger sacks may also be called *kᵉlî*: Gen. 42:25 uses the word for the sacks in which Jacob's sons bring grain back from Egypt (cf. Gen. 43:11); in Dt. 23:25(24); Jer. 40:10, *kᵉlî* is a container for fruit that is harvested.

2. *Furnishings.* Containers (II.1.a), sacks, and bags (1.b) are common household furnishings. It is therefore easy to understand how *kᵉlî* can denote such furnishings in general.

The text can speak of objects that are usable (Lev. 11:32) or worthless (Jer. 22:28; Hos. 8:8). Some passages indicate material and function: Lev. 15:4,6,22f.,26 discuss the uncleanness of objects on which one sits or lies; Lev. 11:32; Nu. 31:20 mention household objects of wood that must be made clean if they have become unclean. It is impossible to make a sharp distinction between such objects and tools (II.3). Besides wood, furnishings may be made of metal (copper or iron; cf. Josh. 6:19,24; Ezk. 27:13). Precious metals (silver and gold) are also mentioned (given into safekeeping like

15. See III.1 below.
16. See II.2 below.
17. See III.1 below.
18. U. Müller, "Keramik," *BRL*², 183.

money: Ex. 22:6[7]; given as a token of friendship: 2 S. 8:10; given as an offering: Ezr. 1:6 [MT]). The plural of *kᵉlî* is used in the collective sense of "household effects" (Gen. 31:37; 45:20; Nu. 19:18; 1 K. 10:21 par. 2 Ch. 9:20; Jer. 49:29; Neh. 13:8f.).

3. *Tools.* Besides its use to denote a household object or household effects in general, *kᵉlî* can be used specifically in the sense of "tool, implement."

This meaning is clear in 2 S. 24:22; 1 K. 19:21, where *kᵉlî* refers to a wooden yoke, and Zec. 11:15, which speaks of the implements of a shepherd; the word is thus associated with agriculture. In 1 K. 6:7; Jer. 22:7, a *kᵉlî* is used by particular kinds of worker — stonecarvers and woodcutters. In texts that speak figuratively of Yahweh's anger, the concept of a tool — usually a hammer — is used to represent the weapons of Israel's foes (Isa. 13:5; 54:16f.; Jer. 51:20; Ezk. 9:1f.). The line between a craftsman's tools and household objects is often fluid: texts mention objects by which someone may be killed accidentally (Nu. 35:16,18,22), which must be made clean if the house is unclean (Lev. 11:32; Nu. 31:20), or which are gladly taken as booty (Josh. 6:19,24). The usage of *kᵉlî* in Isa. 32:7 is especially ambiguous; the best translation is: "The devices of the deceiver are evil."

4. *Weapons.* With the exception of Gen. 27:3, which speaks of the arrows, bow, and quiver needed for hunting, *kᵉlî* (often in the phrase *kᵉlî milḥāmâ*) in the sense of "weapon" denotes weapons of war (Dt. 1:41; Jgs. 18:11; Jer. 21:4; 1 Ch. 12:34; etc.).

Such weapons must be made for the king (1 S. 8:12); they are kept in a storehouse (2 K. 20:13), assembled before an attack (Isa. 10:28), taken as booty following a defeat (2 K. 7:15), and displayed as trophies of victory (1 S. 31:9f.; cf. 17:54). Warriors are buried and go to the netherworld with their weapons (Ezk. 32:27). Weapons are employed in regular warfare, in which the armor-bearer of the commander plays an important role (Jgs. 9:54; 1 S. 14:1; 31:4; etc.), but also in insurrections (2 K. 11:8; 2 Ch. 23:7; cf. 1 S. 21:9[8]). Weapons include swords (1 S. 21:9[8]), arrows (with bow and quiver: 1 S. 20:40), and chariot (1 S. 8:12). The weapons of Israel's enemies, by which they are to carry out Yahweh's judgment against Israel, are referred to in the figurative language of the prophets as "weapons of wrath."[19] Ps. 7:14(13) specifies the nature of the enemies' weapons: they are flaming arrows. In some cases, the translation "weapon" for *kᵉlî* is disputed: 2 S. 1:27,[20] 1 S. 21:6(5),[21] and Eccl. 9:18;[22] in all these passages, however, this translation is probably correct.

5. *Art Objects.* The usage of *kᵉlî* is not limited to common everyday objects such as household effects, tools, and weapons; the noun can also refer to what might be

---

19. Cf. II.3 above.
20. Cf. J. C. Matthes, "Miscellen," *ZAW*, 23 (1903), 120-27.
21. Cf. H. J. Stoebe, *Das erste Buch Samuelis. KAT,* VIII/1 (1973), 393.
22. Cf. MT.

called "cultural objects," including jewelry, art objects, and musical instruments. The last are discussed below,[23] because they are mentioned only in cultic contexts.

In Isa. 61:10; Ezk. 16:17 and elsewhere, *k*ᵉ*lî* clearly refers to women's jewelry. Such jewelry may be listed in detail (Ex. 35:22; Nu. 31:50); its nature is clear from its usage in parallel with clothing (Gen. 24:53) and pearls (Prov. 20:15).[24] Elsewhere the interpretation of gold or silver objects denoted by *k*ᵉ*lî* is is not simple. The reference might be to jewelry or works of art, but equally well to everyday objects, like cups, goblets, and bowls of precious metal or bronze for the court or cult, or used as gifts (Nu. 7:85; 2 K. 14:14; Ezr. 8:27; 1 K. 10:25 [with aromatic material]; 2 Ch. 32:27 [with precious stones]). We learn more about the origin of these precious objects, which are mentioned as tokens of friendship (2 S. 8:10 par. 1 Ch. 18:10; 1 K. 10:25 par. 2 Ch. 9:24) and as offerings for the sanctuary of Yahweh (1 K. 7:51; 15:15; Ezr. 8:25-28; 2 Ch. 15:18). From the royal palace or the temple treasury, they are coveted objects for booty or tribute (2 K. 14:14; Hos. 13:15; Nah. 2:10[9]; 2 Ch. 36:19; cf. also Dnl. 11:8).

The golden guilt offering of the Philistines mentioned in 1 S. 6:8,15 is of a special nature. Here *k*ᵉ*lî* refers collectively to artfully formed likenesses of mice and boils symbolizing the plague the Philistines had brought upon themselves as Yahweh's punishment for stealing the ark. Such objects may also have been included among the tokens of friendship and offerings mentioned above.

Articles made of pure gold would hardly have been put to everyday use, as the parallel with glass in the MT of Job 28:17 might suggest. Here, as in other wisdom passages, art objects of precious metal are used figuratively to describe wisdom (Prov. 20:15).

6. *Clothing.* Only in legal texts does *k*ᵉ*lî* refer to articles of clothing, which should probably be thought of as household effects (II.2) rather than art objects (II.5).

Dt. 22:5 forbids women to wear male clothing, in parallel with the law forbidding men to wear female clothing. Lev. 13:52f.,57ff. treats problems of uncleanness caused by leprosy, which also affects clothing. Here in the context of various textiles we find the phrase *k*ᵉ*lî ʿôr,* which probably refers to clothing made of skins or leather, or possibly leather household objects such as skins to hold water or wine, as is probably the case in Nu. 31:20.

7. *Baggage, Cargo.* Baggage can be understood as a special kind of container (II.2); it can vary in extent.

According to 1 S. 9:7, Saul and his servant carry their provisions in a *k*ᵉ*lî* (cf. also 1 S. 17:22, where David's baggage includes food for his brothers who are fighting against the Philistines). The baggage of Jacob's sons on their journey to Egypt is more extensive: they are bringing with them some of the produce of the land (Gen. 43:11). Jer. 46:19; Ezk. 12:3f.,7 speak of the baggage of those going into exile. From this

23. See III.2.
24. For a more general discussion, see H. Weippert, "Schmuck," *BRL*², 282-89.

meaning, it is but a small step to the baggage train of an army (1 S. 17:22; 25:13; 30:24; similarly 10:22). In Jon. 1:5, the crew of the ship throw their *kēlîm* into the sea; this might refer to the "cargo," but undoubtedly includes all kinds of other objects (II.2) as well.

8. *Ships.* In 1 passage (Isa. 18:2), *kᵉlî* is used in a construct phrase with the material from which the object referred to is made — *gōme'*, "reeds" — to mean the papyrus boat in which the inhabitants of Cush sail on the Nile.[25] This usage suggests emending the first words of Isa. 60:9, *kî-lî*, to *kᵉlî*, which would parallel *'ᵒniyyâ* in the second hemistich.

III. Cultic Usage. Theological usage of *kᵉlî* involves the frequent appearance of the word in legal texts and historical traditions of the OT that speak of the cult and objects employed in it.

1. *Cultic Paraphernalia.*[26] The tradition of P dates the manufacture of the cultic paraphernalia used in the cult of the Jerusalem temple back to the time of God's revelation at Sinai (Ex. 25:1–31:11; 35–40). Yahweh commands Moses to have all the necessary objects made by Bezalel and Oholiab (Ex. 31:1-11) according to the revealed design (25:9); they are to use finery collected from the Israelites (35:4-9,20-29). These objects include the "sacred tent" (25:10-16), the altar of burnt offering (27:1-8), the seven-branched lampstand (25:31-39), and the table for the bread of the Presence (25:23-30), together with the furnishings needed for each (25:29; 25:38ff.; 27:3; Nu. 3:36; 4:32). These come under the heading of "vessels" (II.1.1) or "tools" (II.3), but by virtue of their material (copper: Ex. 27:19; 38:3,30; gold: 37:16,24) exhibit some relationship to the art objects discussed under II.5. There can hardly be any doubt that the articles in question were not manufactured until the temple was built. According to 1 K. 7:40-45, Hiram, a Tyrian brazier, made many objects, including some mentioned in Ex. 27:3; 38:3, during the reign of Solomon; and according to 1 Ch. 23:26; 28:13f., David gave precise instructions for both the building of the temple and the manufacture of its cultic furnishings. The subsequent fate of these objects in the Jerusalem temple is described variously in the books of Kings and Chronicles (cf. 2 K. 14:14 par. 2 Ch. 25:24; 2 Ch. 28:24; 29:18f.). Several passages describe the Babylonians' seizure of the cultic furnishings under the last kings of Judah (2 K. 24:13; 25:14,16; Dnl. 1:2), as well as their return following Cyrus's decree (Ezr. 1:7,9ff.; cf. 6:3-5). The use of cult objects in the rebuilt temple is described in Ezk. 40:42. Anticipating these events, Deutero-Isaiah ordered the exiles to return with the temple vessels (Isa. 52:11). A single passage (2 K. 23:4) uses *kᵉlî* for the cultic paraphernalia of Ba'al and Asherah, which Josiah removed from the temple and destroyed.

25. Cf. H. Weippert, "Schaufel," *BRL*², 276.
26. Cf. A. Reichert, "Kultgeräte," *BRL*², 189-194.

2. *Musical Instruments.*[27] Finally, there is a highly specialized use of *k^elî* in the phrase *k^elê šîr,* "musical instrument." It appears only in connection with cultic music: worship in the temple (1 Ch. 16:42; 2 Ch. 5:13; etc.) and Nehemiah's consecration of the rebuilt city wall (Neh. 12:36). Two texts (Ps. 71:22; 1 Ch. 16:5 [MT]) specify the kind of instrument: *k^elî neḇel/n^ebālîm,* "stringed instrument." Elsewhere *k^elê šîr* appears with other instruments (1 Ch. 15:16; 2 Ch. 5:13 [trumpet, cymbals, harp, lyre]). In 2 Ch. 29:26f., *k^elê dāwîḏ* is specified by the instruments mentioned in v. 25.

Emendation of 1 Ch. 23:5 is unnecessary: unmodified *k^elî* is explained by its purpose (*l^ehallēl*). In 2 Ch. 30:21, however, the understanding of *k^elê-ʿōz l^eYHWH* as "instruments for the praise of Yahweh" depends on the interpretation of *ʿōz* as "glorification, praise."[28] Buttenwieser's translation of *k^elê-šîr* in Am. 6:5 as "melody"[29] is hardly convincing.

Beyse

27. Cf. H. P. Rüger, "Musikinstrumente," *BRL*², 234-36.
28. *GesB,* 575.
29. Buttenwieser, 157.

כְּלָיוֹת *k^elāyôt*

Contents: I. Root: 1. Etymology; 2. Occurrences. II. Ancient Near East: 1. Egypt; 2. Mesopotamia. III. OT: 1. Animals; 2. Human Beings; 3. *ṭuḥôṯ.* IV. Versions.

I. Root. 1. *Etymology.* Heb. **kilyâ,* "kidney," corresponds to Akk. *kalītu,*[1] Arab. *kulya,*[2] Eth. *k^welīt;*[3] cf. also Tigre *k^el'ot,*[4] Amhar. *k^{we}lalit,* Harari *kulay,* East Gurage **k^elayo,* Aram.

k^elāyôt. N. P. Bratsiotis, " Ἡ θέσις τοῦ ἀτόμου ἦν τῇ Παλαιᾷ Διαθήκῃ," Θεολογία, 37 (1966), 44-46; M. A. Canney, " 'Heart and Reins': Further Notes on Hebrew Idioms," *JMOS,* 1911, 93f.; É. P. Dhorme, "L'Emploi métaphorique des noms de parties du corps en hébreu et en akkadien," *RB,* 29-32 (1920-1923, repr. 1963), esp. 32 [1923], 511-13 (repr. 1963, 131-33); T. Durant, "The 'Kidneys,' Organs of Discernment," *Eternity,* 22/1 (1971), 17f.; J. G. Frazer, " 'Heart and Reins' and Ideas of Uncultured Races," *JMOS,* 1911, 107f.; H. W. Hogg, " 'Heart and Reins' in the Ancient Literatures of the Nearer East," *JMOS,* 1911, 49-91; L. W. King, " 'Heart and Reins' in Relation to Babylonian Liver Divination," *JMOS,* 1911, 95-98; J. Luyten, "Hart en nieren," *Schrift,* 57 (1978), 89-93; H. Preisker, "νεφρός," *TDNT,* IV, 911; G. E. Smith, " 'Heart and Reins' in Mummification," *JMOS,* 1911, 41-48; H. W. Wolff, *Anthropology of the OT* (Eng. trans., Philadelphia, 1974), 65f.

1. *AHw,* I (1965), 425; *CAD,* VIII (1971), 74-76.
2. *WKAS,* I, 337-39.
3. *LexLingAeth,* 882; cf. also W. Leslau, *Hebrew Cognates in Amharic* (Wiesbaden, 1969), 48, 95.
4. *TigrWB,* 392a.

and Syr. *kūlyā'*,[5] Mand. *kulai(a)*[6], Middle Heb. and Jewish Aram. *kūlyā'*. The single Ugaritic occurrence,[7] *klyth wlbh,* shows only that in Ugaritic as well as Hebrew "kidneys" (*klyth* = fem. pl. with pronominal suf.) can be used in parallel with "heart." The verb has been lost in the text, so that nothing more can be concluded.

The Coptic word for "kidney," *ǵloote,*[8] is often associated with the consonants *kl* of the Semitic root, although Adolf Erman[9] already considered this identification impossible or at least highly improbable. Wolf Leslau[10] proposes to see the Cushite words for "kidney" — Somali *keli,* Galla *kali,* Agau *ᵉnkʷᵉlaliti* — as loanwords from the Semitic languages of Ethiopia. This is true for Agau (from Amharic) and possibly for Bilin *kil'ot* (from Tigre). On the other hand, Marcel Cohen[11] considers both Somali *keli* and Galla *kali* to be originally Cushite words; A. B. Dolgopol'skii[12] identifies a Cushitic form **(ṃ)kʷAllA(')*, which is supported by such forms as Beḍauye *'onkʷel'a.*

The question as to the root from which Heb. **kilyâ* derives has found a variety of answers. Paul Haupt[13] suggests a root *kl,* "hold," and arrives at the meaning "capsuled, inclosed, referring to the capsules of the kidneys as well as to the fat in which the kidneys are embedded." Linus Brunner[14] arrives at a similar basic meaning when he associates *kilyâ* with Indoeuropean *kel(ə)*, "protect, hide." A root *klh* III with unknown meaning is found necessary by *GesB* and *BDB,* which is no more help than Harri Holma's statement[15] that the root is uncertain. Jacob Levy[16] suggests a root *kly* synonymous with *kll*; with the basic meaning "something round," this etymology accounts for the double meaning of Middle Heb. *kūlyâ,* which means both "testicle" and "kidney."

For the etymology of *kilyâ,* we should start with a root *kl,*[17] an originally onoma-

---

5. R. P. Smith, ed., *Thesaurus Syriacus* (1879, repr. Oxford, 1981), 1740; *LexSyr,* 329b.
6. *MdD,* 207a.
7. *KTU,* 1.82, 3.
8. W. E. Crum, *A Coptic Dictionary* (Oxford, 1939), 813.
9. A. Erman, "Das Verhältniss des Aegyptischen zu den semitischen Sprachen," *ZDMG,* 46 (1892), 121.
10. W. Leslau, *Etymological Dictionary of Harari* (Berkeley, 1969), 92.
11. M. Cohen, *Essai comparatif sur le vocabulaire et la phonétique du chamito-sémitique* (Paris, 1947), 116 (no. 191).
12. A. B. Dolgopol'skii, *Sravnitel'no-istoričeskaya fonetika kušitiskich yazykov* (Moscow, 1973), 195f.
13. P. Haupt, "Semitic Verbs Derived from Particles," *AJSL,* 22 (1905/6), 257; also "The Hebrew Stem Nahal, to Rest," *AJSL,* 22 (1905/6), 205.
14. L. Brunner, *Die gemeinsamen Wurzeln des semitischen und indogermanischen Wortschatzes* (Munich, 1969), 35 (no. 137).
15. H. Holma, *Die Namen der Körperteile im Assyrisch-Babylonischen. AnAcScFen,* 7/1 (1911), 80.
16. *WTM,* II, 334.
17. Cf. G. J. Botterweck, *Der Triliteralismus im Semitischen erläutert an den Wurzeln GL KL ḲL. BBB,* 3 (1952).

topoetic root that refers "both to the sound of rolling as well as to the act that causes this sound: '(make a noise >) roll,' which produces something 'round'."[18] Wilhelm Eilers[19] arrives at the same conclusion by a different route. The Semitic term for "kidneys" thus reflects their appearance and form.

2. *Occurrences.* The OT mentions kidneys 31 times, always in the pl. *k^e lāyôṯ,* reflecting by the normal rules of morphology a hypothetical sg. **kilyâ.* The word is used 16 times by P (in the laws governing sacrifice in Lev. 3–9, plus 2 occurrences in Ex. 29) for the organs of sacrificial animals (cattle, sheep, goats). It is used figuratively in Isa. 34:6. It also appears in Dt. 32:14, where the present text speaks of the "fat of the kidneys of the wheat." The remaining 13 passages speak of human kidneys. The noun appears 5 times in the Psalms, 4 in Jeremiah, 2 in Job, and once each in Prov. 23:16; Lam. 3:13.

Like most Semitic languages, Hebrew does not use a dual form for "kidneys." This may be due to the easy confusion of the hypothetical dual with *kilayim,* "pair." (Pierre Lacau[20] suggests that the dual "kidneys" may have contributed to the origin of the word for "pair" or vice versa. We may note that Enno Littmann and M. Höfner[21] list the word for "two" and the noun "kidney" [*k^e l'ot*] under the same lemma.) It may also be due to the knowledge that animals could live with only a single kidney as well as with a third, accessory kidney.[22] The fact that only the pl. *k^e lāyôṯ* is attested may also be because anatomical knowledge of the lobed kidneys of cattle gained from cutting up sacrificial animals and possibly from wounds inflicted in battle (cf. 2 S. 20:10) led to erroneous conclusions concerning the appearance of human kidneys, as in the case of Pliny.[23]

II. Ancient Near East. 1. *Egypt.* To date, no Egyptian word with the clear meaning "kidney" has been found.[24] This is the more surprising in view of the advanced state of medical knowledge in Egypt, attested not only by Herodotus[25] but by the extant Egyptian medical literature, and because it can be shown that the ancient Egyptians knew about the kidney. Diodorus Siculus,[26] for example, reports that in the course of embalming the Egyptians removed all the internal organs "except for the kidneys and heart," a statement confirmed by examination of mummies.[27] The kidneys of animals

18. *Ibid.,* 37.
19. W. Eilers, *Die vergleichend-semasiologische Methode in der Orientalistik. AAWLM.G,* 10 (1973), 8, with n. 7.
20. P. Lacau, *Les noms des parties du corps en Égyptien et en Sémitique* (Paris, 1970), 95, §247.
21. *TigrWB,* 392a.
22. Cf. the debate between R. Yohanan and R. Hiyya, Bab. *Ber.* 39a.
23. Pliny *Hist. nat.* xi.81 ("composed of many kidneys").
24. Hogg, 53f., 76ff.; H. Grapow, *Grundriss der Medizin der Alten Ägypter,* I (Berlin, 1954), 53.
25. *Hist.* ii.84.
26. *Library of History* i.91.5.
27. Smith, 41ff.; K. Sethe, *Zur Geschichte der Einbalsamierung bei den Ägyptern und einiger damit verbundener Bräuche. SPAW,* 1934/3, 236.

were also esteemed as food, as we learn from a menu preserved in a second dynasty tomb[28] and from an inventory of the meat needed each month by a cook,[29] which includes six pairs of kidneys. Clearly, however, the kidneys did not play any special role in the metaphorical language of the ancient Egyptians.

2. *Mesopotamia.* Akk. *kalītu(m)*, "kidney," denoting both the human and animal organ, is found from the Old Babylonian period on. Particular diseases of the kidneys[30] were known; there is also mention of a "kidney attack" (*miḫiṣ kalīti*) without further detail. Extispicy attached great importance to the kidneys (albeit nowhere near as much as hepatoscopy using the liver), seeing omens in their outward appearance. A distinction was made between the left and right kidneys.[31] Attention was paid not only to pathological changes in the appearance of animal kidneys (red, black, covered with bright spots or white streaks, enlarged) but also to anomalies (one kidney with two others upon it, the right kidney "riding" on the left kidney). It is by no means certain that the kidneys and kidney fat of sacrificial animals played a role in Babylonia similar to their role in OT ritual.[32] Specialized meanings are also found, e.g., *kalīt ᵈEa,* "waxing (kidney-shaped) moon." Once again, there is no evidence of special metaphorical usage associated with the kidneys in Akkadian.

III. OT. 1. *Animals.* Only P speaks of the two kidneys (*šᵉtê hakkᵉlāyōṯ*) in almost identical lists (Ex. 29:13,22; Lev. 3:4,10,15; 4:9; 7:4; 8:16,25; cf. 9:10,19; cf. also Jub. 21:8) of the parts of the sacrificial animal — besides the blood — that belong to Yahweh and must be burned upon the altar along with the fat portions[33] as part of the *šᵉlāmîm* sacrifice. The list includes the following: (1) "the fat covering the entrails," i.e., the caul fat or omentum; (2) "all the fat that is on the entrails"; (3) "the two kidneys"; (4) "the fat that is on them [the kidneys]," i.e., the renal capsule, further described as the fat "at the loins"; (5) "the appendage to the liver" (*hayyōṯereṯ ʿal hakkāḇēḏ*), i.e., the *lobus caudatus.* When a sheep is sacrificed, the fat tail is also included with the portions that belong to Yahweh. Rost[34] has shown that the directive to burn the appendage to the liver as part of the sacrifice was added after the Israelites came into contact with Mesopotamian hepatoscopy; its purpose was to rule out the possibility of practicing hepatoscopy. Originally, then, the portion of the animal sacrificed for a communal meal (*zeḇaḥ*) that was to be burned consisted "solely of the two kidneys with their fat and the caul."[35] The reason is probably not so much that the kidneys,

---

28. Cf. E. Brunner-Traut, *Die alten Ägypter* (Stuttgart, 1974), 152f.
29. Oxyrhynchus papyrus 108, second or third century A.D.
30. Cf. R. Labat, *Traité akkadien de diagnostics et pronostics médicaux,* I (Paris, 1951), no. 12, 100ff.
31. Cf. esp. *KAR,* 152.
32. M. I. Hussey, "Anatomical Nomenclature in an Akkadian Omen Text," *JCS,* 2 (1948), 31.
33. → חלב *ḥēleḇ* (*chēlebh*).
34. L. Rost, "Der Leberlappen," *ZAW,* 79 (1967), 35-41.
35. *Ibid.,* 40.

"because of their color and density,"[36] were regarded in a special sense as the seat of life,[37] as that they were considered (erroneously) to be genital organs, "which people were unwilling to touch."[38] (We may note Philo,[39] who assumes a connection between the genital organs and the production of semen; the Syrohexaplaric version of Sir. 47:19, which translates "loins" in the sense of "reproductive organs" as *byt kwlyt,* exhibits a similar understanding.)

The kidneys appear in a poetic metaphor in Isa. 34:5-7: Yahweh's judgment against Edom, which ends in annihilation, is described as a sacrificial banquet presided over by Yahweh. Yahweh's sword, which takes the place of the sacrificial knife, is sated with the blood and gorged with the fat of the sacrificial animals, especially the kidney fat of rams (*mēḥēleḇ kilyôṯ 'êlîm*). The Song of Moses (Dt. 32) also speaks of kidneys metaphorically. The section comprising vv. 7(8)-14, which recounts Yahweh's saving acts, speaks of honey, oil, curds (?) (*ḥem'aṯ bāqār*), milk from the flock (*ḥ^a^lēḇ ṣōn*), the fat of lambs and rams, herds of Bashan, and goats. It then adds: "with the fat of the kidneys of the wheat" (*'im-ḥēleḇ kilyôṯ ḥiṭṭâ*). This passage was already interpreted by Targ. Jonathan as a reference to the world to come, when grains of wheat will be as large as the kidneys of oxen.[40]

2. *Human Beings.*

a. *Diseases.* Some passages that mention the kidneys indicate a knowledge of certain diseases. Ps. 16:7 suggests kidney pains that come especially during the night and are felt more intensely in the lonely darkness (cf. also the Latin version of 2 Esd. 5:34: *torquent enim me renes mei per omnem horam,* "my reins torment me at every hour"). Job 16:13 says that Yahweh's arrows surround Job and slash open his kidneys without mercy; this verse, like Lam. 3:13 ("he drove into my kidneys the sons of his quiver"), speaks figuratively of agonizing pains of renal colic brought on by kidney stones. Ps. 73:21f. reflects similar symptoms, when the psalmist confesses: "When my heart was embittered, when my kidneys were pricked (*'eštônān*), I was stupid and ignorant, I was a beast before thee." In Job 19:27, the statement *kālû ḵilyōṯay b^e^ḥēqî,* "my kidneys faint in my bosom," may indicate cirrhosis, knowledge of which must be assumed in the talmudic period (cf. Bab. *Ḥul.* 55b: "if the kidney is shriveled [*šhqṭynh*], in the case of a sheep or goat to the size of a bean, in the case of cattle to the size of a medium grape").

b. *Figurative Usage.* Of all human organs, the OT associates the kidneys in particular with a variety of emotions. The range of usage is very wide; the kidneys are looked upon as the seat of emotions from joy to deepest agony. In Prov. 23:15f., for example, the father rejoices over his sensible son: "My son, if your heart is wise, my heart (*lēḇ*) too will be glad. My kidneys will rejoice (*'lz*) when your lips speak what is right." At the other extreme, the psalmist confesses in Ps. 73:21 that cares and bitterness not only embitter his

36. R. C. Dentan, "Kidneys," *IDB,* III, 10.
37. For parallels outside Israel, see *JP,* 19 (1891), 46f.
38. Rost, 40, with reservations.
39. *De spec. leg.* i.216.
40. Cf. also Bab. *Ketub.* 111b.

heart but pierce his liver (*šnn* hithpael). The deepest agony of soul, evoked by meditation on the unfathomable hiddenness of God, has its seat in the kidneys. The suffering which God sends makes him appear like an enemy archer who shoots his arrows into the kidneys with deadly effect (Job 16:13; Lam. 3:13; cf. Prov. 7:23, which speaks of an arrow piercing the liver). In Ps. 139, the psalmist singles out his kidneys as having been created by God when he recounts his "personal creation story"[41] in vv. 13f.: "For thou didst form my kidneys, thou didst knit me together in my mother's womb." Possibly the poet was moved to speak only of his kidneys because he was picturing an embryo (explicitly mentioned in v. 16 [*gōlem]), which resembles a kidney in form. In addition, he mentions the kidneys because, in the context of God's testing, he is thinking of the organ associated with pangs of conscience (cf. 1 En. 68:3, where the word of judgment disquiets the kidneys).

Early Christian tradition interpreted in two ways the fact that the kidneys symbolized the hidden interior of a human being. On the one hand, as organs associated with reproduction, they were considered the seat of desire (*concupiscentia*).[42] On the other hand, they were seen as the locus of the most secret thoughts and therefore of the emotions aroused by conscience.[43]

The image in Ps. 16:7 of the kidneys as nocturnal instructors is without parallel in the OT. Jewish exegetical tradition associates the verse with Abraham, who had neither a father nor a teacher to teach him the Torah. Therefore God gave him two kidneys that poured out wisdom and knowledge upon him by night.[44] According to Bab. *Ber.* 61a, the right kidney counsels what is good, the left kidney what is evil. The pain that results from anger can also be associated with the kidneys. We are told by 1 Mc. 2:24, for example, that Mattathias became angry and "his kidneys trembled" when he saw how an apostate Jew engaged in pagan sacrifice. T.Nap. 2:8 says that the kidneys are the seat of cunning (*panourgía*).

In contrast to the importance ascribed to the kidneys by the OT, which saw in them the seat of the innermost human emotions, we find the view recorded in Mishnah *Ḥul.* iii.2 that an animal can live even if both kidneys are removed (*nyṭlw*). This seems to reflect a notion similar to that of the followers of the physician Asclepiades of Bithynia (d. *ca.* 30 B.C.), that the kidneys, like several other organs, were created by nature without purpose (*mátēn*).[45]

3. *Trying the Heart and Kidneys.* "Trying the heart and the kidneys" is an OT idiom. On 3 occasions, Jeremiah describes Yahweh as "trying (*bḥn*) kidneys and heart" (Jer. 11:20) or "searching (*ḥqr*)" these organs and "trying (*bḥn*) the kidneys" (17:10). This image may be due to Jeremiah himself. Ps. 7:10(Eng. v. 9) also describes God as trying (*bḥn*) the heart and kidneys. In Ps. 26:2, the psalmist appeals to Yahweh: "Prove (*bḥn*)

---

41. Wolff, 96.

42. Cf. Theodoret's comm. on Ex. 29:13 (*MPG,* 80, 287ff.): when the priest offers the kidneys of the victim, he also offers *tás hypogastríous hēdonás.*

43. Cf. G. Q. A. Meershoek, *Le latin biblique d'après Saint Jérôme. LCP,* 20 (1966), 177-181.

44. Cf. *Midr. Ps.* on Ps. 16:7 and 1:13.

45. Cf. Galen *De nat. fac.* i, xiii.

me and try (*nsh*) me; purify (*ṣrp*) my kidneys and my heart." The mention of heart and kidneys together is presumably meant to characterize the total person by referring to an especially important organ in each of the two major portions of the body: the heart in the chest cavity above the diaphragm and the kidneys representing the abdominal cavity extending below the diaphragm. In addition, this expression combines the most profound feelings of the emotional life, conceived of as being localized in the kidneys, with the thoughts of the "heart" (*lēḇ*), in the majority of cases associated more with the rational faculties. Both together represent the total person, who is being tested by Yahweh. Thus Wis. 1:6 can speak of God as the witness of the kidneys, a true observer of the heart, and hearer of the tongue. Finally, Rev. 2:23 draws on the meaning of Jer. 11:20.

3. *ṭuḥôṯ*. The word *ṭuḥôṯ* appears only in Job 38:36; Ps. 51:8(6). Jewish tradition and the exegetes (such as Franz Delitzsch) who follow it interpret this word as a synonym of *kᵉlāyôṯ*. This is illustrated not only by the translation of both passages in the Targ. but also *Nu. Rab.* x.208, which states expressly that *ṭuḥôṯ* in Job 38:36 refers to the kidneys (*hakkᵉlāyôṯ*), which are "pressed" (< *ṭwḥ*) in the body. This interpretation has more recently lost support. The absence of a convincing answer to the question why the OT should use two totally different terms for the kidneys raises the suspicion that this interpretation represents an attempt to explain a word whose meaning had been forgotten on the basis of its context.

Job 38:1–40:14 is a divine discourse based on the technique of listing that is characteristic of didactic wisdom. Job 38:22-38 speaks of God's governance of the word; vv. 35-38 in particular describe God's power as expressed in thunderstorms. Verse 35 asks whether Job can send forth lightnings; v. 36 continues: "Who has put wisdom *baṭṭuḥôṯ,* or given understanding to the cock?" If *śeḵwî* refers to the cock as weather prophet (cf. Vulg., e.g.), it would be reasonable on grounds of parallelism to see also in *ṭuḥôṯ* the name of an animal reputed to be especially wise. Following Édouard P. Dhorme,[46] therefore, most exegetes interpret *ṭuḥôṯ* as referring to the ibis, the sacred bird of the Egyptian deity Thoth (Egyp. *ḏḥwty*). It was thought that the appearance of the ibis signaled the rising of the Nile. If this interpretation is correct, the poet refers here to the cock and ibis as weather prophets announcing an approaching storm.[47] It cannot be denied that this reading appears to do justice to the context.

This interpretation would be confirmed if the proposed translation "ibis" also made good sense in Ps. 51:8(6), the other passage where the word appears. Unfortunately, this is not the case. Ps. 51:8(6) reads: "Behold, thou desirest truth *baṭṭuḥôṯ,* and in secret dost thou teach me wisdom." Here *baṭṭuḥôṯ* stands in parallel with *bᵉsāṯum,* "in secret."[48] For our purposes, it is sufficient to say that there is little reason to see in

---

46. É. P. Dhorme, *A Comm. on the Book of Job* (Eng. trans. 1967, repr. Nashville, 1984), 591f.

47. For a different interpretation, see, e.g., A. Weiser, *Das Buch Hiob. ATD,* XIII (⁷1980), *in loc.*

48. For a survey of proposed interpretations, see E. R. Dalglish, *Psalm Fifty-one in the Light of Ancient Near Eastern Patternism* (Leiden, 1962), 67-69, 123ff.

ṭuḥôṯ a term for "kidneys." The Jewish interpretation of Ps. 51:8(6) is easily explained on the basis of the similarity to Ps. 16:7 and its exegesis. It therefore does not represent an independent tradition but the interpretation of an unknown word on the basis of a passage with parallel content. Whatever *ṭuḥôṯ* in Ps. 51:8(6) may originally have denoted, the psalmist is not referring to kidneys. And Job 38:36 certainly has nothing to do with kidneys; the translation of the Targ. is dependent on the Targ. version of Ps. 51:8(6).

IV. Versions. The LXX regularly translates *kᵉlāyôṯ* with *nephroí*; the Syr. and Targ. use the equivalent *kūlyāṯāʾ*. Recent translations of the Bible exhibit a tendency in figurative contexts to speak of the "heart" or "soul" rather than the traditional "reins" in such passages as Jer. 12:2; Ps. 16:7; Job 19:27; Prov. 23:16. The reverse tendency can be observed in the Vulg., which uses *"renes"* not only for *kᵉlāyôṯ* but also for *ḥᵃlāṣayim* ("loins") (1 K. 8:19; Isa. 5:27; 11:5; Dnl. 5:6 [Aram. *ḥarṣēh*]) and *moṯnayim* ("hips"; RSV "loins") (Ex. 12:11; 28:42; 2 K. 1:8; Ezk. 9:2; 23:15; 29:7; 47:4[Vulg. v. 5]; Nah. 2:11[10]; Job 12:18; Dnl. 10:5; Neh. 4:12[18]).

Kellermann

כָּלִיל *kālîl*

Contents: 1. Etymology and Meaning; 2. Ancient Near East; 3. Secular Usage; 4. Sacrifice; 5. LXX; 6. Dead Sea Scrolls.

---

kālîl. G. A. Cooke, *A Text-Book of North-Semitic Inscriptions* (Oxford, 1903); R. Dussaud, *Les origines cananéenes du sacrifice israélite* (Paris, 1921, repr. 1941); J.-G. Février, "Remarques sur le grand tarif dit de Marseille," *CahB,* 8 (1958/59), 35-43; G. Furlani, *Il sacrificio nella religione dei Semiti di Babilonia e Assiria* (Rome, 1932); H. Gese, M. Höfner, and K. Rudolph, *Die Religion Altsyriens, Altarabiens, und der Mandäer. RdM,* 10/2 (1970), esp. 174; H. L. Ginsberg, "A Punic Note צועה," *AJSL,* 47 (1930/1931), 52f.; G. B. Gray, *Sacrifice in the OT* (1925, repr. New York, 1971); J. Gray, *The Legacy of Canaan. SVT,* 5 (²1965), 192-209; A. de Guglielmo, "Sacrifice in the Ugaritic Texts," *Festschrift E. V. O'Hara. CBQ,* 17/2 (1955), 76-96 (196-216); A. M. Habermann, *The Scrolls from the Judean Desert* (Tel Aviv, 1959) [Heb.]; B. Janowski, "Erwägungen zur Vorgeschichte des israelitischen *šᵉlamîm*-Opfers," *UF,* 12 (1980), 231-259, esp. 254ff.; S. Langdon, "The History and Significance of Carthaginian Sacrifice," *JBL,* 23 (1904), 79-93; L. Moraldi, "Terminologia cultuale israelitica," *RSO,* 32 (1957), 321-337; W. O. E. Oesterley, *Sacrifices in Ancient Israel* (London, 1937); R. Rendtorff, *Studien zur Geschichte des Opfers im alten Israel. WMANT,* 24 (1967); L. Rost, "Erwägungen zum israelitischen Brandopfer," *Von Ugarit nach Qumran. Festschrift O. Eissfeldt. BZAW,* 77 (1958), 177-183 = *Das kleine Credo* (Heidelberg, 1965), 112-19; N. H. Snaith, "Sacrifices in the OT," *VT,* 7 (1957), 308-314; D. M. L. Urie, "Sacrifice among the West Semites," *PEQ,* 81 (1949), 67-82; R. de Vaux, *Studies in OT Sacrifice* (Eng. trans., Cardiff, 1964); A. Wendel, *Das Opfer in der altisraelitischen Religion* (Leipzig, 1927).

1. *Etymology and Meaning.* The word *kālîl* is derived from the root *kll,* "bring to completion." Since the *qāṭîl* noun formation in Hebrew is used to form both attributive adjectives and action nouns,[1] the meaning in the first case is "entire, whole," and in the latter "whole burnt offering," which in fact refers to the burning of the entire sacrifice.

2. *Ancient Near East.* The verb *kll* and its derivatives are also found in Akkadian, albeit not with the meaning "whole burnt offering." In Egyptian, we find *ḳrr,* "burnt offering,"[2] and in Coptic, *glil.* In Ugaritic, a word in the form *kll* with the meaning "totality, all" is attested,[3] e.g., *'mny kll mʒd šlm,* "everything is well with us [or 'me']."[4] especially in letters.

The closest parallels are found in Punic inscriptions from the end of the third century B.C. In the sacrificial tariff from Marseilles,[5] probably originally from Carthage, *kll* occurs 11 times, primarily with the meaning "whole burnt offering," but 5 times in the phrase *šlm kll,* which is translated "surrogate offering" in *KAI.*[6] This translation is based — after the analogy of Heb. *zeḇaḥ šᵉlāmîm* — on the interpretation of *šlm* as a piel. Still other translations have been proposed for *šlm kll*: "concluding offering" and "complete whole offering."[7]

The word also occurs in the plural in a third-century Punic inscription from Carthage.[8] Here, instead of the unusual *šlm kll,* we find *kllm,* which from the context clearly means "whole offering."

According to the Marseilles inscription, for the whole burnt offering the priests were to receive silver and a portion of meat; the person offering the sacrifice received nothing. The regulations are unclear, however, since several kinds of sacrifice are mentioned together. A poor person who could only offer a bird as *šlm kll* paid the priests three quarters of a shekel of silver and received the meat. The Carthaginian inscription states that the skin was given to the priests and that a portion (unspecified) of the whole burnt offering was given to the person offering sacrifice. Someone poor in cattle did not have to give the priests anything. The regulations of the Marseilles and Carthage inscriptions are not identical with those in Leviticus, nor can one say with certainty that the terms refer to the same kinds of sacrifice.

3. *Secular Usage.* In secular usage, the connection of *kālîl* with the verb *kll,* "complete," is clear. Isa. 2:18 speaks of the total disappearance of the idols; here

1. Joüon, §88Eb.
2. *WbÄS,* V, 61. The existence of burnt offerings in Egypt, however, is hard to demonstrate; cf. A. Eggebrecht, "Brandopfer," *LexÄg,* I (1975), 848f.
3. *WUS,* no. 1320.
4. *KTU,* 2.11, 10-12; 2.13, 9f.; 2.16, 14f.; 2.34, 7; 2.39, 3f.
5. *KAI,* 69.
6. Cooke: "whole thank-offering."
7. *ANET*³, 656.
8. *KAI,* 74.

kālîl means "totally, utterly," as in Sir. 37:18 (and possibly 45:8). When describing the color (possibly purple or violet) of the ephod, *kālîl* means "totally" (Ex. 28:31; 39:22; cf. Nu. 4:6).[9] In the phrase *kᵉlîl-hāʿîr* (Jgs. 20:40), *kālîl* means the whole of the city that was burned. This passage of course involves a play on words, suggesting "whole burnt offering." Ezekiel uses the word when he wants to describe perfect beauty; here the emphasis is not on totality but on perfection (Ezk. 16:14; 27:3). Thus Lam. 2:15 also uses *kālîl* for the perfect beauty of Jerusalem, the joy of all the earth; cf. the related form *miḵlal* in Ps. 50:2, which also has to do with the perfect beauty of Zion.

The meaning "garland, crown" has been proposed for Sir. 45:12 (like Aram. *kᵉlîlā'*; cf. Akk. *kilīlu,* "garland"; Arab. *'iklīl,* "crown." This meaning is reflected in the LXX translation *stéphanos.*[10]

4. *Sacrifice.* The noun *kālîl* appears to be an ancient term for "whole burnt offering," which in the opinion of many scholars was replaced at an early date by → עולה *ʿōlâ.*[11] But the sacificial regulations of Lev. 6:15f.(Eng. vv. 22f.) say only that the cereal offering of the priests is to be wholly (*kālîl* burned: "it shall be a *kālîl* [whole burnt offering]; nothing shall be eaten."[12] Little else is said concerning the *kālîl* offering. Dt. 33:10, in what is probably an early poem, lists the offering of the *kālîl* upon the altar of Yahweh as one of the tasks of Levi. Sir. 45:14 alludes to the regulations of Lev. 6:15f.(22f.): "His [Aaron's] cereal offering goes up wholly in smoke."

Roland de Vaux[13] interprets *kālîl* in 1 S. 7:9 as being in apposition with *ʿōlâ*; others consider the word in this passage to be a gloss.[14] The reference is to a sacrifice offered by Samuel when Israel is in dire straits. The next verse, however, merely calls the same sacrifice an *ʿōlâ.* In Ps. 51:21(19), generally considered a concluding gloss, the two words appear in coordination: *ʿōlâ wᵉkālîl.* De Vaux concludes that the two terms were not entirely synonymous. Such a conclusion, however, should not be drawn on the basis of so specialized a passage. The glossator was not acquainted with the historical development of these terms; his purpose was solely to preserve the honor of the cult. De Vaux points out that the Carthagian *šlm kll* may have been a "whole burnt offering," with *kll* being a different kind of offering. In the context of the psalm gloss, however, this parallel is totally irrelevant.

As may be suggested by Jgs. 20:40,[15] *kālîl* can also be used figuratively in the sense of "whole burnt offering, holocaust." Dt. 13:17(16) requires that a city in which foreign

---

9. Contra G. R. Driver, "Technical terms in the Pentateuch," *WO,* 2 (1954-59), 259: "woven in one piece."

10. See 5 below.

11. *KBL*³, 457.

12. See K. Elliger, *Leviticus. HAT,* IV (1966), 98; Rendtorff, 177.

13. P. 31.

14. E.g., L. Köhler, *OT Theology* (Eng. trans., Philadelphia, 1957), 183.

15. See 3 above.

gods have been worshipped be captured and devoted to destruction (*hrm* hiphil): the city and all the spoil taken from it are to be burned as a "whole burnt offering" for Yahweh, and it must never be rebuilt.

5. *LXX.* The LXX uses a wide variety of words to translate *kālîl*: *pás, hólos* (3 times each), *hápas* (once), but also (as a sacrificial term) *holókaustos, holokaútōma.* We also find *stéphanos* (Ezk. 28:12; Lam. 2:15) and *syntéleia, synteleín* (Jgs. 20:40; Ezk. 16:14).

6. *Dead Sea Scrolls.* The Dead Sea scrolls use *kālîl* with the meaning "perfect" in the phrase *k^elîl kāḇôḏ,* "perfect glory," denoting the divine glory in which the members of the community walk, having received the good spirit (1QS 4:7f.). Amid the hardships of daily life, too, one might experience such perfect glory (1QH 9:25).

Kapelrud

כלם *klm*; כְּלִמָּה *k^elimmâ*; כְּלִמּוּת *k^elimmûṯ*

Contents: I. Etymology and Basic Meaning. II. Occurrences and Usage. III. Secular Usage. IV. Theological Usage: 1. Psalms; 2. Prophets. V. LXX.

I. Etymology and Basic Meaning. Although the root *klm* has not yet been found in Ugaritic, it does appear in Akkadian (*kullumu*)[1] with the meaning "cause to see, show." In the other Semitic languages, the meaning is closer to that in OT Hebrew. In Middle Hebrew and Jewish Aramaic (aphel) the verb is used to mean "put to shame"; in modern Syriac it means "rob," in Arabic "injure," and in Old South Arabic "wrong." Whether Arabic allows us to assume "be injured" as the basic meaning[2] may be left an open question. M. A. Klopfenstein[3] finds the original locus of *klm* in legal terminology (procedural, criminal, and sacral), and proposes translating the various forms of the root with "charge, countercharge, denounce, expose, accuse," ignoring the fact that the usage of the term seems to have strayed from its original setting.

---

klm. R. Bultmann, "αἰσχύνω," *TDNT,* I, 189-191; O. Garcia de la Fuente, "Sobre la idea de contrición en el AT," *Sacra Pagina,* I. *BETL,* 12f. (1959), 559-579; M. Klopfenstein, *Scham und Schande nach dem AT. AThANT,* 62 (1972); L. Kopf, "Arabische Etymologien und Parallelen zum Bibelwörterbuch," *VT,* 8 (1958), 161-215 = *Studies in Arabic and Hebrew Lexicography* (Jerusalem, 1976), 133-288; F. Stolz, "בוש *bôš* zuschanden werden," *THAT,* I, 269-272; → בוש *bôš* (*bôsh*); → חפר *ḥāp̄ār*II; → חרף *ḥrp* II.

1. *AHw,* I (1965), 503f.
2. Kopf, 179.
3. Pp. 137f.

In the Hebrew OT, the meaning of *klm* appears to stay within the realm of "disaster" and "disgrace," both active and passive. The root conveys the notion of disintegration. A person to whom *klm* is applied is degraded both subjectively and objectively. That person is isolated within his previous world, and his own sense of worth is impugned. He becomes subject to scorn, insult, and mockery, and is cut off from communication. A person can be actively put in such a situation, so that the semantic domain of *klm* must include "put to shame." It must be noted that "shame" and "disgrace" denote the consequence, conscious or unconscious (and possibly brought to light by prophetic revelation), of antisocial conduct on the part of the person described by *klm*; they characterize and interpret such conduct. Description and consequence can in fact be identical: Israel's exile is a disaster brought upon Israel by Yahweh; subjectively, it is perceived and described from Israel's perspective as a disgrace. Israel's faithlessness toward Yahweh (foreign alliances, idolatry, etc.) are both a disgrace for Israel (the significative meaning of *klm*) and an objective profanation of Yahweh (the negative communicative meaning of *klm*). Synonyms in the same context often include substantival and verbal forms of the root → בוש *bôš*[4] and → חפר *ḥpr* II. The root → כבד *kbd* is an antonym.[5]

II. Occurrences and Usage. The root *klm* appears in the OT as both verb and noun. As a verb, it is found 38 times, plus 1 occurrence in Sirach. There is an additional occurrence if one follows *BHS* in Ps. 71:13, emending *yiḵlû* to *yᵉkkāllᵉmû*. The majority of occurrences are in the niphal, with the meaning "be put to shame, disgraced, ruined" (26 times, not counting the proposed emendation of hiphil to niphal in Jer. 6:15 and the emendation in Ps. 71:13 described above); 10 passages use the hiphil, with the meaning "damage, disgrace"; 2 use the hophal, with the meaning "suffer disgrace."[6] There are two substantival forms: *kᵉlimmâ,* "disgrace" (31 occurrences, including Prov. 9:13 LXX), and *kᵉlimmûṯ* (1 occurrence, with the same meaning). In Mic. 2:6, *BHK*³ proposes reading the sg. *kᵉlimmûṯ* instead of the pl. *kᵉlimmôṯ*; this conjecture has been dropped by *BHS.* It is noteworthy that most of the occurrences are in Ezekiel, followed by the Psalms, Jeremiah, and Deutero-Isaiah. But it would be wrong to conclude that *klm* is a term used only in the immediately preexilic, exilic, and postexilic period. Certain passages where it appears are clearly early. Apart from Nu. 12:14; Isa. 30:3, *klm* does not appear in either the Pentateuch or Isaiah. Neither is it found in Joshua, Judges, Kings, Daniel, or the Minor Prophets (except for Mic. 2:6). Ruth 2:15 is its only instance in the Five Scrolls. Its general use in secular contexts must be noted as well as its theological usage. Only rarely is God the subject of an action expressed by *klm.* The lamentations of the Psalms entreat God not to let his people be put to shame.

---

4. Cf. also Stolz, 269ff.
5. Cf. C. Westermann, "כבד *kbd* schwer sein," *THAT,* I, 794-812.
6. *KBL*³, 457f.

III. Secular Usage. The secular usage of *klm* is illustrated in early narratives of the OT and in wisdom aphorisms — for example, the familiar story of Nabal, Abigail, and David (1 S. 25). The messengers David sends to Nabal make it clear that David and his people have been guarding Nabal's shepherds and their flocks in the wilderness (v. 21); now, at the festival of shearing, David expects recognition of this protection. The text states (v. 7) that David's men have not "harmed" (*klm* hiphil) Nabal's shepherds; the parallel clause ("and they missed nothing") shows that this means that David did not rob them, that he did not take or kill anything that was Nabal's property. This interpretation is confirmed in the presence of Nabal's wife Abigail ("we suffered no harm" [*klm* hophal], v. 15), so that she may satisfy David's expectations instead of the recalcitrant Nabal and thus avert disaster.

In like fashion, the court history of David tells of the friendship between Saul's son Jonathan and David and recounts how Jonathan was grieved for David because his father had disgraced him (*kî hiḵlimô 'āḇîw*: 1 S. 20:34). Saul's "disgracing" acts involve a wide range of specific actions meant to eliminate David as a rival; they range from insults through threats to physical violence. These are all comprehended under the heading of *klm*.

Another well-known story recounts how the Ammonites put David's representatives to shame. In addition to the personal disgrace — the men had half their beards shaved off and their clothing cut in half — the narrative indicates that this act symbolized an insult to David and his kingdom. The men were greatly ashamed (*hā'ᵃnāšîm niḵlāmîm mᵉ'ōḏ,* 2 S. 10:5; 1 Ch. 19:5). The court history also records that David's impassioned lament for Absalom disgraced (*bôš* hiphil, 2 S. 19:6[Eng. v. 5]) David's victorious followers, so that they would have stolen away from the grieving king like an army that feels disgraced because it has fled from the enemy in battle (*hā'ām hanniḵlāmîm,* v. 4[3]). Flight documents the military loss and implies disgrace. To flee before the enemy is a disgrace.

The early traditions of the OT include two further examples, one quite concrete and the other more general, illustrating the meaning of *klm.* First, the traditions centering on Miriam's leprosy bear witness to a concrete form of disgrace (somewhat incomprehensible to the modern reader) in which a father spat in his daughter's face, after which she was shamed (*tikkālēm,* Nu. 12:14) for seven days, during which she had to remain outside the camp. The more general statement, which concerns the tribe of Dan and its wandering, appears in the appendices to the book of Judges: Jgs. 18:7 states that the inhabitants of Laish dwelt in security after the manner of the Sidonians and that there was no one who detracted from them (*wᵉ'ên-maḵlîm dāḇār*), i.e., no one who was willing to do them any injury. In the Numbers passage (from a secondary stratum of J or E?[7]), the occasion for the "punishment" is no longer clear. The description has been interwoven with regulations governing cultic purity in cases of leprosy (Lev. 13), but both the original occasion of the punishment and its meaning in its present context are obscure. In Jgs. 18:7, scholars have attempted to omit suspected glosses or proposed

7. Cf. M. Noth, *Numbers. OTL* (Eng. trans. 1968), *in loc.*

other emendations.[8] The verse does in fact appear to be overloaded. The general statement spoken of above nevertheless reflects accurately the intended state of affairs.

"Detraction" is also involved when widows, orphans, and resident aliens are prevented from gleaning after the harvest. Despite Lev. 19:9f.; 23:22; Dt. 24:17ff., this seems to have happened frequently (cf. Ruth 2:8,9,15,16,22); it brought disgrace (*klm* hiphil, Ruth 2:15) to the one wanting to glean. This disgrace consisted concretely in rebukes (Ruth 2:16) and molestation (vv. 9, 22), especially when the gleaner was a woman.

The empirical wisdom of the Solomonic book of Proverbs deals with the incidence and prevention of shame and disgrace. Someone who answers before listening is exposed to the danger of being in the wrong: the result is folly (*'iwwelet̠*) and shame (*k^elimmâ*) (Prov. 18:13). Prov. 25:8 (together with the relative clause ending v. 7) is another injunction on the same theme: do not be too quick to speak your mind, lest you finally be put to shame by your neighbor. Not everything that one has seen should quickly be brought to the attention of all (the text reads *lārîb̠,* "bring before the court"; Symmachus probably read *lārōb̠*[9]), lest someone else show that the true situation is different.[10] Wisdom precepts repeatedly urge a son or disciple to heed the instruction of a father or teacher; but someone who, against his father's counsel, keeps company with gluttons eventually shames (*klm* hiphil) his father (28:7). The LXX of 9:13 describes folly as a wanton woman who knows no shame (. . . *ûb̠bal-yād̠^eʿâ k^elimmâ* [instead of *mâ*]); she entices men to disaster. In this passage, *k^elimmâ* reaches into the sexual sphere: it denotes the sense of modesty that folly lacks. Sir. 41:16 appears in a lengthy discourse concerning the true nature of shame (41:14–42:8).

The book of Job is also Wisdom Literature. It uses forms of *klm* in two speeches of Zophar and one of Job. In Job 11:3, Zophar complains that Job is allowed to mock and scoff without being punished (or "rebuked, refuted": *w^e'ên mak̠lim*) or shamed for his wicked words. In Zophar's second speech (20:3), Job's statements are taken more personally as "insulting censure" (*mûsar k^elimmāt̠î*; the suffix is an objective genitive). In Job's fifth reply (if Job 3 is taken as an introductory monologue and not counted[11]), he accuses his friends (19:3) of "wronging" him (*tak̠lîmûnî* par. *hkr,* a hapax legomenon). In all three passages, *klm* has the verbal sense of "rebuke, revile." It is debatable whether the book of Job uses the word in its general or its theological sense. The boundary is fluid. Job's accusation of God shames his friends; their inability to understand him shames Job.

IV. Theological Usage.

1. *Psalms.* The semantic content of *klm* plays a significant role in petitions and expressions of trust in individual laments. Ps. 4:3(2) uses a contrast between *klm* and

---

8. See *BHS.*

9. See *BHS.*

10. On the basis of the context, B. Gemser, *Sprüche Salomos. HAT,* XVI (^{2}1963), 91, suggests a court setting.

11. Cf. F. Hesse, *Hiob. ZBK,* XIV (1978), *in loc.*

kbd in apostrophizing a group of people who turn the psalmist's honor into shame (*liklimmâ*). They use lies (slander), but past experience gives the psalmist confidence in Yahweh's help. Ps. 35 is clearly an individual lament,[12] even though its present discursive form creates problems. The psalmist feels persecuted (accused) and prays that his enemies may be put to shame (*yikkālᵉmû,* 35:4), probably above all in their plans to seek his life (*mᵉbaqᵉšê napšî*) and bring evil upon him (*ḥōšᵉbê rā'āṯî*). Here the meaning of *klm* is developed by a wealth of parallel terms and figures of speech (e.g., *bôš, ḥāpar*; cf. the context). (Almost the identical words appear in petitions against the psalmist's enemies in 70:3[2] and 40:15[14]; Ps. 70 is an individual lament that repeats 40:14-18[13-17] with minor differences.) Later in the lament (35:26), the same situation is expressed by means of the noun: "Let them be clothed with shame and dishonor" (*yilbᵉšû-bōšeṯ ûklimmâ*) who magnify themselves against the psalmist. Ps. 71:13 (again in the context of an individual lament) uses both the verb and the noun; the form of expression closely resembles that just discussed (with *ḥerpâ* par. *kᵉlimmâ*). Those who seek the psalmist's hurt are themselves to be covered (*'āṭâ*) with scorn and disgrace (the verbal form *yiklû* in the first clause is usually emended to *yikkālᵉmû*;[13] *klm* is frequently used in parallel with *bôš*). Finally, we may cite Ps. 109:29 (cf. Jer. 20:11). In Ps. 109:1-5 + 21ff. we clearly have an individual lament;[14] the enemies are described by a form of *śṭn* ("my accusers"). Here, too, the oppressed psalmist prays that his accusers may be clothed with dishonor and wrapped with shame (*bōšeṯ, kᵉlimmâ, 'āṭâ, lābaš*) — in other words, that Yahweh will not let them achieve their purpose and thus reveal their disgraceful actions (cf. 109:27, 28, 31).

A new aspect comes to light in the complaint that by granting success to the enemy Yahweh has abased his own people, as we hear in a communal lament (Ps. 44:10,16[9,15]; cf. the context). The concrete occasion is a lost battle and flight before the enemy (v. 11[10]; cf. 2 S. 19:4[3]); Yahweh has made his people "sheep for the slaughter" and scattered them among the nations. Israel therefore suffers shame and disgrace in the eyes of its neighbors and the nations (Ps. 44:16[15]: "all day long" is *kᵉlimmāṯî negdî*). We find the familiar parallel terms *bōšeṯ* and *ḥerpâ,* along with others that underline the taunts and mockery Israel must suffer, such as *māšāl* (become a byword) and *lā'ag*. Noteworthy in this context is the use of the active: *zānaḥtā wattaklîmēnû* (v. 10[9]: "thou hast cast us off and abased us"). This idea leads directly to the prayer of another communal lament (Ps. 74:21) that Yahweh will not let the downtrodden (*dak*) continue to be put to shame, although the words *'al-yāšōb dak niklām* are hard to render precisely (cf. Hans-Joachim Kraus:[15] "Do not let the downtrodden depart in shame").

Two further variations in the use of *klm* in laments are found in Ps. 69. In praying

12. Cf. H. Gunkel and J. Begrich, *Einl. in die Psalmen* (Göttingen, 1933, ⁴1985); H.-J. Kraus, *Psalms 1–59* (Eng. trans., Minneapolis, 1988), *in loc.*

13. Cf. *BHS,* on the basis of several mss.

14. On the intervening curses, see H.-J. Kraus, *Psalms 60–150* (Eng. trans., Minneapolis, 1989), *in loc.*

15. *Idem.*

for help in affliction, the believer expresses fear that his affliction may bring shame and disgrace (*bôš* and *klm* niphal; disappointment = disgrace) to others who hope in Yahweh and seek after him (*qāwâ* and *biqqēš*). It would appear (cf. vv. 8-13[7-12]) that the hostility of the enemies is due to the psalmist's unusual devotion (v. 10[9]); as a consequence, he feels that he bears his *k^e^limmâ* for Yahweh's sake (*ʿāleyḵā nāśā'ṯî ḥerpâ,* "for thy sake I have borne reproach": v. 8[7]). It is probably theological overinterpretation to read the text as suggesting innocent vicarious suffering.[16] In this individual lament, the prayer for deliverance is based on the psalmist's claim that his affliction and disgrace could disgrace Yahweh. This argument underlines the urgency of his petition. He is confident that Yahweh is aware of his reproach (*ḥerpâ,* v. 20[19]; the text of the verse is corrupt; usually *boštî ûḵ^e^limmaṯî* is read with v. 21[20]: "my shame and disgrace cannot be healed,"[17] so that *negd^e^ḵā* in v. 20[19] refers to *kol-ṣôr^e^rāy*: "before thee all are my foes"). In laments, then, a variety of inward and outward afflictions are interpreted as shame and disgrace and designated as such by means of several terms, including *klm.*

2. *Prophets.* A good half of all the occurrences of *klm* are found in prophetic traditions — almost exclusively in the traditions of Jeremiah, Ezekiel, and Deutero-Isaiah.

a. *Jeremiah.* In justification for a prophecy of disaster, Jer. 3:3 likens Israel's faithlessness toward Yahweh to the actions of a harlot who refuses to be ashamed. Priests and prophets appease the people by preaching *šālôm* where there is no peace. They should be ashamed (*bôš*) of their refusal to repent, but they have forgotten how to be ashamed (6:15; in the light of 8:12, an almost identical text, it is better to read *gam-hikkālēm lō' yāḏāʿû* as a niphal instead of the MT hiphil[18]). The people are expected to repent and confess their sins; this may be the burden of the vision Jeremiah communicates to his listeners in 3:19–4:4. Even if Deuteronomistic parenesis has reshaped this passage, it has developed a theme of Jeremiah's message. Jer. 3:25 belongs to a confession of sin: "Let us lie down [probably 'to die'] in our shame (*bōšeṯ*); and let our dishonor (*k^e^limmâ*) cover (*kissâ*) us; for we have sinned against Yahweh our God."

The book of comfort for Ephraim speaks of Ephraim's repentance and lament (31:18f.). "Being ashamed" is once more part of the penitential ritual: v. 19 speaks of turning, repentance, instruction and knowledge, smiting upon one's thigh, *bōšeṯ,* and "I was confounded (*w^e^gam-niḵlamtî*), because I bore the disgrace (= sin, *ḥerpâ*) of my youth." The slightly different readings of the LXX and Symmachus do not alter the meaning.

Between the oracles concerning Jehoiakim and Jehoiachin stands a prophecy of disaster (22:20-23) using the feminine imperative; it can only be addressed to Jerusalem,

---

16. As does Kraus, *idem.*
17. Cf. *BHS.*
18. See *BHS.*

and appears to reflect the situation between 597 and 587 B.C. As a result of judgment upon the leaders of the people ("the wind shall shepherd all your shepherds" [objective gen.: "those who shepherd you"]), Jerusalem will be ashamed and confounded (*kî 'āz tēḇōšî wᵉniḵlamt,* v. 22) because of all its wickedness — here probably not as the first step to repentance but as an expression of the judgment itself. This meaning is reflected in a late interpretative prophecy of disaster appended to the genuine (albeit misunderstood) pun of Jeremiah in 23:33, elaborated in the verses that follow (vv. 34-40): "And I will bring upon you everlasting reproach and *kᵉlimmûṯ 'ôlām,* which shall not be forgotten" (v. 40). For our purposes, the problems associated with the secondary text are unimportant; all that matters is that reproach and disgrace can represent the substance of a prophecy of disaster. The preceding statement speaks concretely of rejection by Yahweh (*mē'al pānay*).

The climax of the (undoubtedly late) oracles concerning the fall of Babylon and the salvation to come for Judah and Jerusalem, including return from exile, appears in 51:51, a quotation from those who have experienced the catastrophe of God's judgment; again shame is a consequence of judgment, specifically shame that aliens have entered the sanctuary of Jerusalem. The usual parallel terms are used; the quotation is given in the 1st person plural and gives the impression of deriving from a lament or possibly even from a penitential ceremony ("we are put to shame, for we have heard reproach; dishonor has covered our face"). The similarity to Deutero-Isaiah is unmistakable. Here again the accent is on formulaic discourse.

In yet another passage (14:1-6), which is genuine, shame is an element of judgment: the absence of water during a terrible drought brings shame to those who vainly seek water from an empty cistern. They are therefore ashamed and confounded (*klm* hophal) and cover their heads (*bōšû wᵉhoḵlᵉmû wᵉḥāpû rō'šām* in v. 3, absent from the LXX,[19] is frequently connected with v. 4b). Disappointment over unfulfilled expectations results in a sense of shame. Jeremiah uses this association, typical also of everyday contexts, to describe the drought brought by God's judgment.

There can be no doubt that Jeremiah used stereotyped expressions from laments, thanksgivings, and hymns in his confessions. In 20:11-13, *kᵉlimmaṯ 'ôlām,* "eternal shame" that is never forgotten, is wished upon his enemies (v. 11; cf. Ps. 109:29; but also Jer. 23:40).

b. *Ezekiel.* The traditions associated with the prophet Ezekiel use *klm* with some frequency. Not all the texts go back to the prophet himself; they do, however, reflect his message and develop its ideas. This is the case in ch. 16, a clumsy allegory of a faithless and adulterous wife, in which the prophet castigates the faithlessness of Jerusalem (and in this "corporative personality" the apostasy of the chosen people) as in a legal indictment.[20] The nucleus in vv. 1-43 itself includes many interpretative additions; it is followed by two appendices (vv. 44-58 and 59-63) that are clearly later than 587 B.C.; they no longer speak of judgment but of confession of sin, of willing

19. See *BHS.*
20. See W. Zimmerli, *Ezekiel 1. Herm* (Eng. trans. 1979), *in loc.*

acceptance of judgment and shame, and astonishing restoration and deliverance through Yahweh — clearly an attempt to come to terms theologically with the exilic situation. Jerusalem is compared to Samaria and Sodom: the disgraceful acts for which they were punished pale before those of Jerusalem. Jerusalem's faithless harlotry actually gives these sinful cities a kind of grotesque justification by virtue of their being more righteous than Jerusalem. In the light of this situation, Jerusalem must accept her shame and disgrace (v. 52). The phrase *nāśā' k^e^limmâ* is used twice; as Walther Zimmerli rightly emphasizes,[21] it echoes the formula used in declaring guilt (*nāśā' ʿāwôn*). Yahweh's deliverance, which will also include Jerusalem's more righteous "sisters" Sodom and Samaria (v. 53), serves (*l^e^maʿan*: purpose clause) to make Jerusalem bear her *k^e^limmâ* and be ashamed (*w^e^niklamt*) of all that she has done (v. 54). Yahweh's mercy is meant to effect repentance. In addition, the covenant Yahweh will make because he remembers (*zākar*) his act of election ("my covenant with you in the days of your youth"), an eternal covenant, is also meant to make Jerusalem "ashamed" of her "evil ways" (v. 61). The *zākar b^e^rîṯ* on Yahweh's part evokes on the part of Jerusalem a corresponding awareness or remembrance of her misdeeds (cf. 36:32 and the context of vv. 29-32). Covenant and forgiveness (16:62f.) bring forth (again a purpose clause with *l^e^maʿan* [v. 63]!) "remembrance," "shame," and finally as a climax "never opening your mouth again because of your *k^e^limmâ*" ("when I forgive [*kpr* piel] you all that you have done"). This theme of God's forgiveness and act of deliverance on behalf of his people as the basis of their repentance and return derives not just from the school of Ezekiel but from the prophet himself, as we see from 36:32 in the context of 36:29-32: "Be ashamed and confounded for your ways, O house of Israel" (*bôš* + *klm* niphal) as a consequence of Yahweh's mercy toward his people (cf. also 36:23).

Ezk. 16:27 is a somewhat obscure verse that also interrupts the continuity, anticipating punishments that are not announced until vv. 35ff. It is probably meant simply to emphasize the repugnance at Jerusalem's harlotry felt even by the pagan Philistines. They, not Jerusalem, are ashamed on account of her lewd behavior (fem. pl. niphal ptcp.).

The prophecies of salvation among the Ezekiel traditions, some of which are certainly the product of the school of Ezekiel, announce that Israel will no longer have to suffer the reproach of the nations (34:29; 36:6). Ezk. 34:29 belongs to an extensive post-Ezekiel prophecy of salvation (vv. 25-31), which proclaims not only wondrous fertility of the land and peace within the animal kingdom but also the breaking of the bars of the yoke with which Israel was enslaved (v. 27), obviously a concrete symbol representing the *k^e^limmaṯ gôyîm*. Probably 36:6 + 7 also belongs to one of the secondary strata of the larger unit 35:1–36:15, which develops the contrast between disaster prophesied against Mt. Seir (Edom) and salvation prophesied for the mountains of Israel. If it goes back to Ezekiel himself, it must date from the late period of his prophetic ministry. Because the mountains, hills, ravines, and valleys have suffered the "reproach

21. *Ibid.*, 350.

of the nations," Yahweh has spoken (against them) in his jealous wrath (36:6) and sworn that the nations round about Israel shall themselves suffer reproach (v. 7). If we take the context into account, this means that the neighbors who suffered no harm in the catastrophe that struck Judah and Jerusalem in 587 B.C. and the years following, which brought disgrace, must now bear their own reproach as Yahweh's punishment: salvation for the people of Yahweh through disaster inflicted on the nation oppressing them (Edom, although the text speaks only of *gôyim* [v. 6] and *haggôyim ʾ^{a}šer lāḵem missāḇîḇ* [v. 7]; on mockery of the nations, cf. v. 3). A different kind of reproach appears to be mentioned in 36:13-15: the fact that the land (a feminine figure is addressed) has devoured its children (in all the historical catastrophes brought on by its sin; cf. Nu. 13:32; Lev. 18:25,28).[22] In the time of salvation to come, the disgrace of childlessness will be removed from the people dwelling in the land, and the land itself will no longer have to hear the reproach (*k^{e}limmâ*) of the nations and bear the disgrace (*ḥerpâ*) of the peoples (Ezk. 36:15). The covenant (39:25-29) once again emphasizes the repentance of the people associated with Yahweh's restoration of Israel (v. 26, reading *w^{e}nāś^{e}ʾû ʾeṯ-k^{e}limmāṯām* with the versions and a few mss. instead of the emendation *w^{e}nāšû,* "and they shall forget," favored by many exegetes[23]). The parallel noun is *maʿal,* "treachery."

The lament in Ezk. 32:17-32 over the descent into the netherworld by Egypt, formerly glorious and powerful, develops the notion that Israel's former oppressors are themselves overtaken by the disgraceful fate of death and descent into the pit, where others who "spread terror" already suffer the disgraceful existence of shades (Assyria, Elam, Meshech-Tubal, Edom, and [secondarily] the kings of the north). The passage draws on the contrast between former greatness and present impotence (not conceived as natural biological death), as they are forced to lie in a dishonorable grave (contrast the honorable burial described in v. 27) with those slain by the sword and the uncircumcised. They must bear their shame (Elam: vv. 24f.; *n^{e}sîḵê ṣāpôn*: v. 30 [secondary]). In this context, *k^{e}limmâ* denotes disgraceful death followed by dishonorable burial — both understood as Yahweh's judgment (*yrd* hiphil).

In Ezekiel's plan for the restored temple, *klm* appears once more, albeit in a specific and typical sense. The rebuilding of the temple is a saving act on the part of Yahweh. The message of salvation (43:10,11) is intended once more to effect the sense of shame found elsewhere in the book of Ezekiel. It is reserved to the proclamation of salvation rather than the prophecy of judgment to effect repentance.

The regulations governing the Levites (which clearly do not go back to Ezekiel) are based on an historical schema (cf. 44:10: "when Israel went astray") according to which the Levites had forsaken Yahweh and gone after idols. They must now bear their punishment (*nāśāʾ ʿāwôn*). They may perform priestly functions, but not in the holy of holies and in Yahweh's immediate presence (44:13), clearly having only minor duties (v. 14). Thus they must bear their shame and atone for their abominations (v. 13). Here

---

22. Cf. W. Zimmerli, *Ezekiel 2. Herm* (Eng. trans. 1983), *in loc.*
23. See *BHS* and Zimmerli, *Ezekiel 2, in loc.*

k^elimmâ takes on the sense of punishment imposed by sacral law. This passage may possibly represent a theological interpretation of some state of affairs following the Josianic reform. It need not concern us further, since it has to do with the use of the term in sacral laws.[24]

Because it is related to this usage, we shall mention here the usage of *klm* in the Chronicler's history, where it appears to denote a ceremonial act performed by the priests and Levites when killing the passover lamb for sacrifice: "they were ashamed and sanctified themselves" (*nikl^emû wayyitqadd^ešû* [2 Ch. 30:15]; see the comms. for a discussion of the problems associated with "Hezekiah's passover" and textual questions; there seems to be no reason to delete the copula between "priests" and "Levites," as proposed by *BHS*). Whether the formula introducing the penitential prayer in Ezr. 9:6ff. is original and represents liturgical usage can no longer be determined: "O my God, I am ashamed and blush to lift my face to thee, my God, for our iniquities have risen higher than our heads . . ." (v. 6, using verbs such as *bôš* and *klm* niphal). If these texts are late, they document the use of *klm* in cultic penitential rites.

c. *Deutero-Isaiah.* For his prophecies of salvation, Deutero-Isaiah draws on a rhetorical form embodying the assurance of salvation pronounced in the sanctuary after a lament, the so-called priestly oracle of salvation.[25] Isa. 41:8-13 represents such an oracle, giving assurance of Yahweh's favor and help. V. 11 includes promises that Israel's foes will be as nothing, that they will be put to shame and confounded (*'ābad* par. *bôš* par. *k^e'ayin,* "as nothing"; cf. also the variety of terms for "enemy";[26] Westermann points out the striking parallels between lament and oracle of salvation, including formal details). A brief statement in 45:16f. contrasts the idol-makers, who are put to shame and confounded (*bôš* and *klm* niphal) and perish in disgrace (*k^elimmâ*), to Israel, which has its everlasting salvation in Yahweh and will therefore never be put to shame or confounded. Unfortunately, the context of this fragment is missing; exegetes frequently deny its authenticity. Its words proclaim a timeless truth of faith.[27]

The image of the barren woman who will rejoice over a multitude of descendants makes use of *klm* in 54:4. This verse is part of a skillfully organized hymn of praise based on an assurance of deliverance and salvation (54:1-10). It also incorporates the motif of the widow and the young woman who has been jilted — a triple disgrace, which Yahweh himself will reverse as (new) husband, creator, redeemer, and Lord (54:4 + 5ff.). Verse 4 uses the whole range of familiar Hebrew verbs and nouns that denote shame and disgrace (including *klm* niphal).

A kind of climax is reached in the so-called third Servant Song (50:4-9). It speaks of the prophet (preacher) who willingly accepts affliction and thus the shame of affliction, but is confident nonetheless of Yahweh's help and affirms that he will not

---

24. Cf. A. H. J. Gunneweg, *Leviten und Priester. FRLANT,* 89 (1965), 192ff.

25. Begrich.

26. See K. Elliger, *Deuterojesaja 40,1–45,7. BK,* XI/1 (1978); and C. Westermann, *Isaiah 40–66. OTL* (Eng. trans. 1969), *in loc.*

27. For a discussion of this passage and similar statements in Deutero-Isaiah, esp. 44:9-20, see Westermann, *Isaiah 40–66, in loc.*

be put to shame (vv. 6f.). In v. 6, *k^e^limmôṯ* refers to the suffering experienced in hostility and contempt, in being struck and spat upon. In v. 7, however, *ʿal-kēn lōʾ niḵlāmtî* means the Servant's assurance that he will not perish; here *klm* refers to existential destruction. This astonishing tension within abuse that is a palpable, suffered reality which cannot be assuaged and yet cannot achieve its goal of rendering existence impossible is grounded solely in the relationship between Yahweh and the Servant. Both aspects are experienced simultaneously, and thus the "world" is overcome! This is a unique note within the OT.[28]

Finally, we shall cite Isa. 61:7, from Trito-Isaiah, which occurs within an unconditional promise of salvation and exhibits clear affinities with Deutero-Isaiah. Instead of a double portion of shame and dishonor there will be a double heritage in Israel's own land (cf. 40:2; in 61:7aβ, *wārōq* should probably be read instead of *yārōnnû,* so that shame and smiting are mentioned together; in addition, *bōštām* should be read in v. 7aα[29]). This form of expression may recall 50:6. Here *k^e^limmâ* means the catastrophe ending in exile at the beginning of the sixth century B.C.

d. *Other Prophets.* Isa. 30:1-7 is a woe oracle from the last known phase of Isaiah's prophetic ministry. In it the prophet repeatedly attacks the disastrous policy that led the kings of Judah (in this case Hezekiah) to enter into alliances and coalitions. Apart from the fact that such alliances are contrary to Yahweh's will and signal lack of confidence in his trustworthiness (cf. v. 1: "rebellious children" who "add sin to sin"), reliance on Pharaoh's protection turns to shame, and trust in the shelter of Egypt turns to humiliation (v. 3). Egypt is called "a people that cannot profit" (vv. 5f.). Everyone who has tried to rely upon Egypt has been disappointed and disgraced (v. 5, with the familiar parallels to *klm*). Unmet expectations constitute shame and disgrace, above all when they have ignored their proper subject in favor of someone else.[30]

Mic. 2:6 occurs in a debate between Micah and his listeners (2:6-11), in which the rich citizens Micah threatens with disaster on account of their social injustice (vv. 1-5) dispute the accuracy of the prophet's threats. In doing so, they appeal to a more merciful God whom they claim to know (vv. 6 + 7). They demand that the prophet and his allies (possibly other prophets such as Isaiah) stop preaching prophetically (*ntp* hiphil), or at least in these terms; for "the *k^e^limmôṯ* of the prophet will not overtake us." It is impossible to decide whether *k^e^limmâ* refers to the prophecy or the substance of judgment; it may well include both (v. 6 is textually dubious; many exegetes emend *yissaḡ* to *yaśśiḡēnû*). Behind the oracle of Micah stands a whole train of thought: the prophet's words envision disaster (judgment), which will bring disgrace to those it strikes. They, however, maintain: "The [prophesied] disgrace will never afflict us!"

V. LXX. The LXX exhibits a wide range of variations in translating *klm.* Among the verbs, we find *entrépein* (13 times), *atimázein* (4 times), *atimoún, kataischýnein* (3

28. Cf. also Westermann, *Isaiah 40–66, in loc.*
29. See *BHS.*
30. Cf. G. Fohrer, *Das Buch Jesaja,* III. *ZBK* XIX/3 (1964), *in loc.*

times), as well as *aischýnein* with compounds, etc. In rendering the hiphil, it prefers *oneidízein, kataischýnein,* and *atimázein,* as well as *apokōlýein* (also for the hophal). As nouns we find *atimía* and *kólasis*.

The LXX translates *k^e^limmâ* by *atimía* (9 times), *entropḗ* (7 times), *básanos* (4 times), *oneidós* (3 times), as well as *aischýnē* and *oneidismós*. It translates *k^e^limmûṯ* by *atimía*.

Wagner

כֵּן *kēn* → כּוּן *kûn*

כנה *knh*

In Middle Hebrew, the piel of the root *kny* means "paraphrase, express in veiled language." Arab. *kana,* "speak allusively,"[1] has the same meaning. In the first and second stems, however, it also means "give a name of honor (*kunya*)": a father calls himself *abū* ("father") + the name of his eldest son.[2] The root is also attested in Phoenician,[3] Jewish Aramaic, Syriac ("give a nickname, name"), and Mandaic. Akk. *kanû*[4] has a different meaning.

The only occurrence in Phoenician appears in an inscription from A.D. 96, which states that "the community (*gw*) is designated (*lknt,* clearly a D-stem inf.) security for this stela."

In the Hebrew OT, the piel of *knh* occurs 4 times; there are 4 additional occurrences in Sirach. The LXX obviously had problems with this term, translating each of its occurrences with a different word: *boán, entrépein, thaumázein,* and *aineín*.

Isa. 44:5 says of those who will embrace Yahwism: "This one will say, 'I am Yahweh's,' another will call himself by the name of Jacob, and another will write on his hand, 'Yahweh's,' and give himself the name of honor (*y^e^ḵanneh*) Israel." It is an honor for them to belong to God's people and their God, and "Israel" is a name of honor. Isa. 45:4 says of Cyrus: "Therefore I call you by your name, I give you a name of honor (*'^a^ḵann^e^ḵa*), though you do not know me." Cyrus is thus honored by Yahweh and given a commission, even though he does not know Yahweh; this is repeated for emphasis in v. 5b.[5]

---

1. *WKAS,* I, 399f.

2. See I. Goldziher, *Muslim Studies,* I (1889/1890; Eng. trans. 1966, repr. Albany, 1977), 267; *idem,* "Gesetzliche Bestimmungen über Kunja-Namen im Islam," *ZDMG,* 51 (1897), 256-266; A. Spitaler, "Beiträge zur Kenntnis der Kunya-Namengebung," *Festschrift W. Caskel* (1968), 336-350.

3. See below.

4. *AHw,* I (1965), 440f.

5. C. Westermann, *Isaiah 40–66. OTL* (Eng. trans. 1969), 160f.

In the Elihu speeches of the book of Job, Elihu says at the end of his introduction: "I will not show partiality to any person or give any person a name of honor. For I do not know how to give names . . ." (Job 32:21f.). "Give a name of honor" is here equivalent to "flatter." Elihu will speak without partiality or flattery, calling everything by its right name.

The passages in Sirach are in part textually problematical. In the context of a prayer for the people of Israel, Sir. 36:12/17 says: "Have mercy, O Lord, upon the people called by thy name, upon Israel, whom thou didst call thy first-born (*b^eḵôr kinnîṯā*)." Israel thus bears the name of honor "first-born of God." Sir. 44:23 says of Jacob/Israel: *wykwnnhw bbrkh,* "he acknowledged him with a blessing." The LXX reads the same; the Syr. instead reads *b^erāḵâ* or *b^eḵōrâ,* "primogeniture." It is clear that *KBL*[3] follows 36:17: "He called him his first-born." Sir. 45:2 is also uncertain. The text is corrupt, but refers in any case to Moses, whom God "honored" like a deity or with the name of honor "man of God." Finally, 47:6 says of David that "the daughters sang his praises and honored him with [the appellation] ten thousand (*wyknwhw brbbh*)" — clearly an allusion to 1 S. 18:6-8.

Ringgren

כִּנּוֹר *kinnôr*

Contents: I. Etymology: 1. Ancient Near East; 2. Toponym; 3. Divine Name. II. Form and Function: 1. Sumer; 2. Egypt; 3. Palestine. III. OT: 1. Players; 2. Apotropaic Use; 3. Symbolism. IV. LXX. V. Dead Sea Scrolls.

---

kinnôr. N. Avigad, "The King's Daughter and the Lyre," *IEJ,* 28 (1978), 146-151; *idem,* "The King's Daughter and the Lyre," *Qadmoniot,* 12 (1979), 61f. [Heb.]; B. Bayer, *The Material Relics of Music in Ancient Palestine and its Environs* (Tel Aviv, 1963); F. Ellermeier, "Beiträge zur Frühgeschichte altorientalischer Saiteninstrumente," *Archäologie und AT. Festschrift K. Galling* (Tübingen, 1970), 75-90; V. Fritz, "Kinneret und Ginnosar," *ZDPV,* 94 (1978), 32-45; K. Galling, "Musik (und Musikinstrumente)," *BRL,* 389-394; M. Görg, "Die Königstochter und die Leier," *BN,* 14 (1981), 7-10; H. Gressmann, *Musik und Musikinstrumente im AT* (Giessen, 1903); E. Hickmann, "Leier," *LexÄg,* III (1980), 996-99; H. Hickmann, *Ägypten. Musikgeschichte in Bildern,* II/1 (1961); *idem,* "Altägyptische Musik," *Orientalische Musik. HO,* I, sup. 4 (1970), 135-170; *idem,* "Leier," *Die Musik in Geschichte und Gegenwart,* VIII (1960), 517-528; *idem, Die Rolle des Vorderen Orients in der abendländischen Musikgeschichte* (1957); *idem,* "Vorderasien und Ägypten im musikalischen Austausch," *ZDMG,* 111 (1961), 23-41; A. Jirku, "Gab es eine palästinisch-syrische Gottheit Kinneret?" *ZAW,* 72 (1960), 69; *idem,* "Der kyprische Heros Kinyras und der syrische Gott [il iš]Kinaru(m)," *FuF,* 37 (1960), 211; E. Kolari, *Musikinstrumente und ihre Verwendung im AT* (Helsinki, 1947); L. Manniche, *Ancient Egyptian Musical Instruments. MÄSt,* 34 (1975); R. North, "The Cain Music," *JBL,* 83 (1964), 373-389; A. F. Pfeiffer, *Über die Musik der alten Hebräer* (Erlangen, 1779); J. Rimmer, *Ancient Musical Instruments of Western Asia in the Department of Western Asiatic Antiquities, The British Museum, London* (London, 1969);

I. Etymology.

1. *Ancient Near East.* The earliest known reference to the musical instrument called *kinnôr* in Hebrew is the form ^{giš}*kinnarātim,* the plural of ^{giš}*kinnaru,* in a letter of Mukannišum to Zimri-Lim from the archives at Mari.[1] At Alalakh we find the Hurrian word *kinnaruḫli,* "lyre player."[2] Called *knr* in alphabetic Ugaritic texts,[3] the instrument name itself appears also in Old Aramaic[4] and Phoenician.[5] With the exception of Ethiopic, the word is also found in the later Semitic dialects.[6]

As a Semitic loanword in Egyptian, we find the term written *knynywrw* (= *knwrw*).[7] While this occurrence uses only the determinative for "wood,"[8] a lyre determinative is clearly recognizable in a fanciful late writing from Karnak, dating from the Ptolemaic period (cited as *gn.* in *WbÄS,*[9] but probably read more accurately by Osing[10] as *gn-yry*). The loanword then appears in Coptic in the Sahidic forms *ginēra* and *genēre.*[11]

H. P. Rüger, "Musikinstrumente," *BRL*², 234-36; C. Sachs, *Die Musik des Altertums* (Breslau, 1924); *idem,* "Die Namen der altägyptischen Musikinstrumente," *Zeitschrift für Musikwissenschaft,* 1 (1918/19), 265-68; H. Sachsse, "Palästinensische Musikinstrumente," *ZDPV,* 50 (1927), 19-66; O. R. Sellers, "Musical Instruments of Israel," *BA,* 4 (1941), 33-47; A. Sendrey, *Music in Ancient Israel* (New York, 1969); W. Stauder, *Die Harfen und Leiern der Sumerer* (Frankfurt am Main, 1957); *idem, Die Harfen und Leiern Vorderasiens, in babylonischer und assyrischer Zeit* (Frankfurt, 1961); *idem,* "Die Musik der Sumerer, Babylonier und Assyrer," *HO,* I, sup. 4 (1970), 171-243; *idem,* "Sumerischbabylonische Musik," *Die Musik in Geschichte und Gegenwart,* XII (1965), 1737-1752; G. Wallis, "Musik, Musikinstrumente," *BHHW,* II, 1258-1262; M. Wegner, *Die Musikinstrumente des alten Orients* (Münster, 1950); D. Wohlenberg, *Kultmusik in Israel* (diss., Hamburg, 1967); S. Yeivin, "On 'The King's Daughter and the Lyre' by N. Avigad," *Qadmoniot,* 13 (1980), 56 [Heb.].

On Egyptian music, see E. Hickmann, "Musik," "Musiker," "Musikinstrumente," "Musikleben," "Musik, Militär-," "Musizierpraxis," *LexÄg,* IV (1982), 230-243.

1. J. Bottéro, "Lettres de Mukannišum." *Textes Divers. Festschrift A. Parrot. ARM,* XIII (1964), 20, 5, 7, 11, 16; Ellermeier, 77; *CAD,* VIII (1971), 387b; *AHw,* I (1965), 480b.
2. *AHw,* II (1972), 1568.
3. M. Dahood, "Hebrew-Ugaritic Lexicography III," *Bibl,* 46 (1965), 329; cf. *KTU,* 1.19 I, 8; 1.101, 16; 1.108, 4; 1.148, 9.
4. *KAI,* 222 A, 19.
5. Cf. Z. S. Harris, *A Grammar of the Phoenician Language. AOS,* 8 (1936), 112; cf. *DISO,* 123.
6. Cf. *KBL*³, 460f.
7. Papyrus Anastasi IV, 12.2; cf. M. Burchardt, *Die altkanaanäischen Fremdworte und Eigennamen im Ägyptischen,* II (1910), no. 990; *WbÄS,* V, 132, 4; W. F. Albright, *The Vocalization of the Egyptian Syllabic Orthography. AOS,* 5 (1934), 47, C6; R. A. Caminos, *Late-Egyptian Miscellanies* (Oxford, 1954), 187; W. Helck, *Die Beziehungen Ägyptens zu Vorderasien im 3. und 2. Jahrtausend v. Chr. ÄgAbh,* 5 (²1971), 523, no. 253; Manniche, 91.
8. Cf. also Ellermeier, 76f.
9. V, 173, 1.
10. J. Osing, *Die Nominalbildung des Ägyptischen* (1976), 462.
11. Cf. Albright, 17, with n. 72; Osing, 462; W. Westendorf, *Koptisches Handwörterbuch* (1965, repr. Heidelberg, 1977), 459.

The term also appears in Hitt. *lúkinirtalla*[12] and Sanskrit *kinnarī,*[13] and above all in the Greek forms *kinýra* and *kinnýra,*[14] for which derivation from Phoen. **kinnūr* can be supported.[15] Although the word is found in eastern Indo-European (Sanskrit), an origin in this area cannot be supported convincingly;[16] a Semitic or at least Near Eastern origin is therefore open to consideration.[17] Another possibility is that the term comes from the vocabulary of "invading non-Semitic peoples such as the Hurrians,"[18] but no firm conclusion is possible. There can be no doubt that we are dealing with a cultural term of unknown origin that transcends geographic and linguistic boundaries.[19]

2. *Toponym.* In the realm of toponyms, the name inventory from the great Palestine list of Thutmose III of Karnak contains the form *kn-nꜣ-r'-tw* (= *knnrt*) together with the variant *k-nꜣ-tw* (= *knt*).[20] We also find[21] the form *kn-(n)ꜣ-r'tw* (= *knnrt*),[22] which may be identified phonologically and topographically with the *kinnereṯ* (modern Tell el-ʿOreimeh[23]) mentioned by Josh. 19:35 in a topographical list of the tribe of Naphtali. Since the toponym denotes both the lake and the adjacent region (cf. Nu. 34:11; Dt. 3:17; Josh. 11:2; 12:3; 13:27; 1 K. 15:20), the name *kinnereṯ* cannot be derived from the oval shape of the lake.[24] Neither can the present form of the hill be cited in explanation of the toponym.[25] More serious consideration should be given to the theory that the place name may be connected with the name of a Canaanite deity.[26]

---

12. *KBo,* I, 52, I, 15f.; cf. J. Friedrich, *Hethitisches Wörterbuch* (Heidelberg, 1952-54), 110a, with bibliog.

13. Cf. W. Baumgartner, *Zum AT und seiner Umwelt* (Leiden, 1959), 231f., n. 51; *KBL*³, 461.

14. Cf. H. Lewy, *Die semitischen Fremdwörter im Griechischen* (Berlin, 1895), 164; M. L. Mayer, "Gli imprestiti Semitici in Greco," *Rendiconti del Istituto Lombardo di scienze e lettere Milano,* 94 (1960), 328; *KBL*³, 461.

15. Cf. Albright, 47, C 6.

16. Ellermeier, 76.

17. Cf. already Pfeiffer, 28; J. Barth, *Die Nominalbildung in den semitischen Sprachen* (1889, repr. Hildesheim, 1967), 65, n. 2; T. Nöldeke, *Mandäische Grammatik* (1875, repr. Darmstadt, 1964), 122, with qualifications.

18. M. Ellenbogen, *Foreign Words in the OT* (London, 1962), 87.

19. Cf. also Friedrich, 110a.

20. J. Simons, *Handbook for the Study of Egyptian Topographical Lists Relating to Western Asia* (Leiden, 1937), 111, List I, 35a/b/c; see S. Yeivin, "The Third District in Thutmosis III's List of Palestino-Syrian Towns," *JEA,* 36 (1950), 54.

21. P. Petersburg 1116A.

22. Cf. W. M. Müller, "Ein ägyptischer Beitrag zur Geschichte Palästinas um 1500 v. Chr.," *OLZ,* 17 (1914), 103-5; C. Epstein, "A New Appraisal of Some Lines from a Well-Known Papyrus," *JEA,* 49 (1963), 49-56.

23. Cf. Fritz, 32ff.

24. *Ibid.,* 42f.

25. Contra W. F. Albright, "The Jordan Valley in the Bronze Age," *AASOR,* 6 (1926), 26, with Fritz, 43.

26. Cf. I.3 below.

In the arsenal of Ugaritic toponyms, neither *knr*[27] nor *knrt*[28] is certain. Instead of the ostensible *krn,* the correct reading in one text[29] is *snr*; another text[30] has only the questionable *k*nk*/r*t.*[31]

3. *Divine Name.* In the Ugaritic pantheon, one list of deities[32] (like its Akkadian parallel[33]) includes a god *d.giš kinarum.*[34] This divine name is probably also found in the legendary Cypriote figure *kinýras.*[35] The debate over the existence of a female counterpart *knrt,* a possible source of the toponym, remains unresolved.[36] The primary argument against the existence of a deity *knrt* is the supposed lack of evidence.

One possible occurrence may be cited, albeit with caution. Stela BM 646 of the British Museum[37] contains the name of a female deity written *knt.* Scholars have called this an "obvious mistake"[38] and, following Wolfgang Helck,[39] emended it to the more familiar divine name *qdš* ("Qadšu"). While there seems to be no evidence supporting this emendation,[40] the almost canonical illustration of the deity Qadšu[41] hardly suggests any other divine name than *qdš.* It is difficult to see, however, how the form *knt* could be confused with *qdš.* It is more reasonable to suppose that *knt* might stand for *knrt,* like the toponym in the Palestine list of Thutmose III,[42] which is written both with and without the *r.*[43] Furthermore, the name *qdš* appears on a similar stela in conjunction with the divine names ʿAnat and Aštart,[44] so that we cannot rule out representation of another Palestinian goddess in the same manner as Qadšu.

---

27. *UT,* no. 1274.
28. E. Ullendorf, "Ugaritic Marginalia II," *JSS,* 7 (1962), 342.
29. *KTU,* 4.341, 35.
30. *KTU,* 1.19 III, 41.
31. Both texts are discussed by Fritz, 43, n. 35.
32. *KTU,* 1.47, 32.
33. RS 20.24, 31.
34. Cf. J. Nougayrol, "Textes Suméro-accadiens des archives et bibliothèques privées d'Ugarit. III, a: Textes religieux (*18-19*)," *Ugaritica,* 5. *MRS,* 16 (1968), 45, 59.
35. Cf. Jirku, *FuF,* 37 (1960), 211; also Z. J. Kapera, "Kinyras and the Son of Mygdalion," *Folia Orientalia,* 13 (1971), 131-142.
36. For: Jirku, *ZAW,* 72 (1960), 69; *idem, FuF,* 37 (1960), 211. Against: Fritz, 43, with n. 35.
37. T. G. H. James, *Hieroglyphic Texts from Egyptian Stelae etc. in the British Museum* (London, 1970), pl. XXXIX.
38. R. Stadelmann, *Syrisch-palästinische Gottheiten in Ägypten. PÄ,* 5 (1967), 119, with n. 3.
39. W. Helck, "Beiträge zu Syrien und Palästina in altägyptischer Zeit," *AfO,* 22 (1968/69), 23.
40. Cf. James, 47, n. 3.
41. See Helck, *Beziehungen,* 463ff.
42. Simons, I, 34.
43. See I.2 above.
44. Cf. I. E. S. Edwards, "A Relief of Qudschu-Astarte-Anath in the Winchester College Collection," *JNES,* 14 (1955), 49-51, with pl. III.

II. Form and Function. The term *kinnôr* and its phonetic equivalents denote the "West Semitic lyre,"[45] which includes several variant forms.

1. *Sumer.* An early precursor of the "West Semitic lyre" was the Sumerian lyre, the various forms of which can be described genetically as ranging from "a large standing lyre to a smaller portable lyre" on the basis of seal impressions from the Jemdet Naṣr period to the Ur I period, as well as fragments preserved in the royal tombs of Ur.[46] The Sumerian lyre is characteristically associated with the bull, depicted either naturalistically or in stylized form, as a fertility symbol. The development of the lyre involves a change from a four-stringed instrument to an eleven-stringed instrument; the so-called "golden" and "silver" lyres from Ur I are especially valuable sources of information.[47] The Sumerian lyre apparently disappears toward the end of the first dynasty of Ur. According to Friedrich Ellermeier,[48] it was replaced by "the West Semitic lyre on the one hand and the mountain lyre on the other." The latter, a "simple, rectangular box-lyre played vertically," differed markedly from the "West Semitic lyre with its curved arms"; it came increasingly to be held obliquely and played with a plectrum.[49]

2. *Egypt.* The earliest evidence for the use of an imported "West Semitic lyre" in Egypt is found on the wall of a tomb at Beni-Hasan (*ca.* 1900 B.C.); the nomadic origin of this new instrument is also apparent.[50] Its initial simplicity of construction was replaced in Egypt by increasing complexity. In contrast to Palestine and Mesopotamia, where use of the lyre was reserved to males, in Egypt it became the preferred instrument for women to play.[51] It is likely that this Egyptian practice then influenced Israelite usage in Palestine.[52] The lyre underwent further modifications in Egypt.[53]

3. *Palestine.* To all appearances, lyres of various types were used in Palestine.[54] The extant representations nevertheless exhibit structural continuity.[55] The earliest appear to be petroglyphs at Megiddo and in the Negeb.[56] A Late Bronze ivory carving from Megiddo depicts a woman playing a lyre, possibly betraying Egyptian influ-

---

45. Cf. Ellermeier, 75ff.
46. Stauder, 181.
47. Cf. *ibid.,* 181.
48. P. 76.
49. Cf. also H. Hickmann, *Rolle,* 186ff.
50. *Ibid.,* 187.
51. Cf. E. Hickmann, 998.
52. Cf. II.3 below.
53. E. Hickmann, 997f.
54. Ellermeier, 76.
55. Cf. the sequence of illustrations in Avigad, *IEJ,* 28 (1978), 148.
56. Cf. Rüger, 234b.

ence.[57] Of Philistine provenience is the representation of a lyre on a cultic pedestal from Ashdod,[58] where a singular earthenware figure holding a lyre was also found.[59] Phoenician influence is evidenced by an eighth-century ivory pyx from Nimrud, which depicts a lyre being played.[60] The Assyrian relief from Nineveh documenting Sennacherib's conquest of Lachish depicts three Judahites playing lyres as they go into captivity.[61] A drawing on one of the ninth-century pithoi found at Kuntillat ʿAjrud shows a woman playing a lyre.[62] The context of the other decorations on these jars suggests association of the lyre with apotropaic rituals.[63] The seals depicting lyres[64] may also be interpreted in this sense, especially the picture of a lyre on a scaraboid (seventh century?) inscribed: "Belonging to *maʿadanâ,* the king's daughter."[65] The reason for the illustration is probably not so much to describe the princess as "an ardent lyre-player"[66] as to ward off potential danger through the symbolism of the lyre.[67] It is even possible that the Bar Kokhba coins with illustrations of lyres[68] can be interpreted in this sense.[69]

III. OT.

1. *Players.* According to Gen. 4:21 (late[70]), Jubal[71] was the "father of all those who play the lyre and pipe" — not as the "inventor of a skill" but as the ancestor of "those who possess a particular skill."[72] Postexilic literature singles out musicians, including lyrists, as participants in worship (cf. 1 Ch. 15:16,21; 16:5; 25:1,3,6; 2 Ch. 5:12; 29:25); the ministry of the levitical instrumentalists (esp. the family of Jeduthun) can be associated terminologically with prophecy (1 Ch. 25:1-3[73]). In any event, we must assume that prophetic ecstasy is connected with musical expression; *kinnôr* music, for

---

57. Cf. the illustrations in H. Weippert, "Elfenbein," *BRL*², 70.
58. Avigad, *IEJ,* 28 (1978), fig. 5.
59. *Ibid.,* fig. 6.
60. *Ibid.,* fig. 9.
61. *Ibid.,* fig. 11.
62. Cf. Z. Meshel, *Kuntellet ʿAjrud, a Religious Centre from the Time of the Judean Monarchy on the Border of Sinai. Exhibition Catalogue of the Israel Museum,* 175 (Jerusalem, 1978), fig. 12; see also V. Fritz, "Kadesch in Geschichte und Überlieferung," *BN,* 9 (1979), 49f.
63. Cf. Görg, 7ff.
64. Cf. Avigad, *IEJ,* 28 (1978), 148, fig. 12, 13.
65. *Ibid.,* 146ff.; *idem, Qadmoniot,* 61f.; Yeivin, 56.
66. Avigad, *IEJ,* 28 (1978), 151.
67. See Görg, 7ff.
68. Avigad, *IEJ,* 28 (1978), 148, fig. 15, 16.
69. The depiction of lyres on seals and elsewhere is discussed further by O. Keel in *Tell Keisan (1971-1976). OBO,* ser. arch. 1 (1980), 279, 294 (nn. 322-24).
70. Cf. P. Weimar, *Untersuchungen zur Redaktionsgeschichte des Pentateuch. BZAW,* 146 (1977), 137.
71. On the paronomasia involving Jabal, Jubal, and Tubal, see J. Ebach, *Weltentstehung und Kulturentwicklung bei Philo von Byblos. BWANT,* 108[6/8] (1979), 340ff.
72. *Ibid.,* 347.
73. Cf. A. Jepsen, *Nabi* (Munich, 1934), 236.

example, serves as a "means for inducing prophetic inspiration"[74] (cf. 1 S. 10:5). Wisdom poems as well as prophetic oracles appear to have been sung to the accompaniment of the lyre (Ps. 49:5[Eng. v. 4][75]). Power is clearly ascribed to instrumental accompaniment of words, power that can alter consciousness and conduct. This takes place because the authority of the good spirit can be felt in the playing, which can also overcome the effects of the "evil spirit from God" (cf. 1 S. 16:16,23). David's playing the lyre before Saul exhibits the "apotropaic" efficacy illustrated by the seal with the picture of a lyre.[76] Thus lyre music proves to be a medium of divine influence on a wide range of important functions. No wonder the instrument was especially esteemed in the temple precincts (e.g., 1 K. 10:12 par. 2 Ch. 9:11)!

2. *Apotropaic Use.* The lyre was a standard element in cultic processions (2 S. 6:5 par. 1 Ch. 13:8; Isa. 30:32); above all, to judge from most of the occurrences in the Psalms, it played a prominent role in the glorification of Yahweh (Ps. 33:2; 43:4; 57:9[8]; 71:22; 81:3[2]; 92:4[3]; 98:5; 108:3[2]; 147:7; 149:3; 150:3). It was also played at banquets (cf. Isa. 5:12) and during secular festivities (cf. Gen. 31:27). It appears dubious that evidence supports a fundamental distinction between secular and sacred *kinnôr* music, not least because the apotropaic function of the instrument affects both realms. Both in liturgical contexts and elsewhere, the lyre — like Egyptian instrumental music in general — can counter chaotic disharmony. Of course this understanding can itself present a problem, as when Job reflects on the success of the wicked in playing the lyre (Job 21:12).[77] The prophet's criticism of complacent enjoyment of the lyre (Isa. 5:12) takes up this existentially pessimistic point of view; in the last analysis, it is probably also to be understood as criticizing open defiance of Yahweh.

3. *Symbolism.* Because of its basic nature, lyre music can be a symbol of rejoicing.[78] This lends even more force to the taunting comparison of Tyre to a lyre-playing harlot trying to escape oblivion (Isa. 23:16) and to the harsh prophecy (Ezk. 26:13) that the sound of its lyres will no longer be heard, that is, that its position of dominance will vanish. The Isaiah apocalypse uses the stilling of the *kinnôr* as a sign of the final judgment (Isa. 24:8). When it is no longer played, the instrument becomes a sign of lost vitality and a hopeless future (Ps. 137:2). The primary role of the *kinnôr* is obviously to elevate human life and establish a sense of security; this function can be turned on its head when the lyre plays a dirge (Job 30:31), signifying total hopelessness. Thus the lyre also plays a critical role in the realm of symbolism.

Görg

---

74. C. Westermann, "נֶפֶשׁ *nāᵆfᵆš* Seele," *THAT,* II, 71.
75. Cf. H.-J. Kraus, *Psalms 1/-59* (Eng. trans., Minneapolis, 1988), 482.
76. Cf. II.3 above.
77. Cf. M. Dahood, "Northwest Semitic Philology and Job," *The Bible in Current Catholic Thought. M. J. Gruenthaner Memorial Volume. St. Mary's Theology Studies,* 1 (New York, 1962), 65.
78. This usage was already discussed by Pfeiffer, 28f.

IV. LXX. For the LXX, *kinnôr* clearly designated a variety of musical instruments. It is translated as *kithára* (19 occurrences, primarily in Psalms and Isaiah), *kinýra* (17 occurrences, only in the Deuteronomistic history and the Chronicler's history), *psaltḗrion* (5 occurrences), and *órganon* (1 occurrence).

V. Dead Sea Scrolls. The Qumran Essenes used instrumental music to show reverence to the *kᵉḇôḏ 'ēl* and his Torah (1QS 10:9; 11QPs[a] 28:4). The present is the age of the "mourning lyre" (*kinnôr qînâ*: 1QH 11:22), but the end of wickedness will be marked by the sound of the "lyre of salvation" (*kinnôr yᵉšû'ôṯ* par. *nēḇel śimḥâ,* "harp of rejoicing," and *ḥᵃlîl tᵉhillâ,* "flute of praise"). In a lament, the worshipper describes the exhausting effect of the mob persecuting him: "they made tumult upon the lyre of my controversy" (*kinnôr rîḇî*: 1QH 5:30).

Botterweck†

כנע *kn'*

Contents: I. Occurrences and General Meaning. II. Theological Usage: 1. Political Humiliation; 2. Reflexive; 3. Other Usages. III. LXX. IV. Dead Sea Scrolls.

I. Occurrences and General Meaning. Besides the MT of the Hebrew OT, the root *kn'* appears in the Dead Sea scrolls, Judaeo-Aramaic, Samaritan, and Arabic. It is not found in Biblical Aramaic, and there are no known occurrences in the earlier Semitic languages. The basic meaning of the verb is "humble"; it may be active, reflexive, or passive. Sometimes it can mean "subdue" or "suppress," referring not only to outward, concrete events but also to inward experiences rooted in the mind, spirit, and emotions. Often both aspects are interwoven. The verb does not denote a punctiliar action but a process or its result.

The root appears 36 times in the OT, always in the niphal (with passive or reflexive meaning) or hiphil (with transitive active meaning). The same usage is found in the Dead Sea scrolls. The OT passages in which forms of this root appear are all late or very late. There seems to be a preference for stereotyped expressions. There is no evidence for a developed "secular" usage. One passage, 2 Ch. 30:11, describes how some people from Asher, Manasseh, and Zebulun accepted the invitation of Hezekiah, king of Judah, to celebrate the Passover in Jerusalem. Their response was understood in their own territories as "humbling themselves"; this passage might represent a "secular usage." Theological usage predominates, however.

---

kn'. O. Garcia de la Fuente, "Sobre la idea de contrición en el AT," *Sacra Pagina,* I. *BETL,* 12f. (1959), 559-579, esp. 567-571.

II. Theological Usage.

1. *Political Humiliation.* The Deuteronomistic conclusions to the individual narratives concerning the deliverer judges,[1] which probably originally followed a stereotyped pattern, contain an expression using *kn'*. Even though the form is not strictly preserved in each instance, the meaning is the same. In Jgs. 3:30, for example, at the conclusion of the story of Ehud, we are told that through Ehud's deeds "Moab was humbled (*wattikkāna'*) (or 'subdued') under the hand of Israel," so that Israel had eighty years of pest. Undoubtedly the saving acts of Gideon were originally summed up in the same way in the Deuteronomistic account (Jgs. 8:28): "So Midian was humbled before the people of Israel . . ." (*wayyikkāna' miḏyān lipnê ḇᵉnê yiśrā'ēl*), except that the formula has been modified slightly. The feature of the rest that followed has likewise been brought out in the very same words. The fact that further information follows concerning Gideon himself as well as his death and burial is due to the complex traditio-historical situation of the Gideon and Abimelech traditions. In the Jephthah traditions, this concluding formula has shrunk to a brief comment (Jgs. 11:33: "So the Ammonites were humbled before (*mippᵉnê*) the people of Israel"), which has the effect of an aside, to be followed in Jgs. 12:7 by the statement concerning Jephthah's death and burial, which constitutes the conclusion in the present context. The formula is even more abbreviated — consisting simply of *wayyikkānᵉ'û happᵉlištîm* — in 1 S. 7:13, a late Deuteronomistic passage. Here, too, however, the motif of subsequent rest finds expression, albeit in different words. The situation is the same as on previous occasions: the Philistine threat is countered by a successful defensive action of the Israelites, with crucial intervention on the part of Samuel, here clearly pictured as a figure like the deliverer judges. The life and work of this figure is interpreted explicitly as meaning that "the hand of Yahweh was against the Philistines" (*wattᵉhî yaḏ-YHWH bappᵉlištîm*). There is a clear theological element behind all these acts of deliverance. In the last analysis, the *môšî'îm* ("deliverers") Ehud (Jgs. 3:15), Gideon (6:11ff., esp. v. 34), and Jephthah (11:29) were helpers sent by Yahweh in Israel's hour of need. It is not surprising, therefore, that the formula can also be expressed in the active voice (*kn'* hiphil) with God as subject: "On that day God humbled (*wayyaḵna' 'ᵉlōhîm*) Jabin the king of Canaan before (*lipnê*) the people of Israel."

Despite the variations in the conclusion formula, its constitutive elements are easy to define. The preceding narrative is summarized in a niphal or hiphil form of *kn'* introduced by a *waw*-consecutive. Then the person affected by *kn'* is introduced — as subject of the niphal or object of the hiphil. There can also be a temporal statement, either general ("at that time," "on that day") or specific ("in the days of Samuel"). Then comes the statement that Israel had "rest" from its enemies. Further details of the subduing may be included. Usually a prepositional phrase modifies *kn'*: "humbled *before* the Israelites" or "under the hand of Israel" (*lipnê, mippᵉnê, taḥaṯ yaḏ*). The verb *kn'* thus summarizes the entire process of defense against the enemy, from the

1. Cf. W. Richter, *Traditionsgeschichtliche Untersuchungen zum Richterbuch. BBB,* 18 (²1966); *idem, Die Bearbeitungen des "Retterbuches" in der deuteronomischen Epoche. BBB,* 21 (1964).

call of the charismatic military leader and his actions to the defeat and subjection of Israel's foe. This denotes not only the process leading up to the act of subjection but also the shame, dishonor, and loss of prestige brought about by defeat, the humiliation associated with the entire complex of events. The meaning encompasses not only the event itself but also its interpretation and appreciation.

This state of affairs can also have a human subject like David, whose military exploits are occasionally summarized by *kn'* as well as other verbs (2 S. 8:1). Here the hiphil of → נכה *nkh* stands in parallel with the hiphil of *kn'*; as the discussion above makes clear, the latter is the more inclusive term. The chapter lists annalistically David's battles with various peoples. Should one be tempted to see this as a secular history, v. 6 shows that David, too, is only a tool in the hands of Yahweh.

The Chronicler's history borrows this formulation in 1 Ch. 18:1 (cf. 20:4, where *wayyikkānē'û* must refer to *pelištîm* in the first half of the sentence; the comment does not appear in 2 S. 21:18). The same preference of the Chronicler (in contrast to the Deuteronomistic historian) for the hiphil of *kn'* can be observed in the tradition of Nathan's prophecy to David (1 Ch. 17:10; cf. 2 S. 7:11), where the personal assurance spoken to David in the name of Yahweh promises that Yahweh will "humble" (*wehiḵna'tî*) all David's enemies. The Chronicler for the most part incorporates the account of 2 S. 7 in its final literary stage with its traditio-historically complex text; the associated problems are irrelevant here. In the Chronicler's version, *kn'* represents "giving rest from all your enemies" in 2 S. 7:11 (Deuteronomistic). In both cases (1 Ch. 17:8; 2 S. 7:9), the expression is interpreted by a preceding hiphil of → כרת *krt* ("I will cut off all your enemies from before you").

Yahweh's humiliation of Israel's enemies (*'aḵnîa'* par. *'al ṣārêhem 'āšîḇ yāḏî*) is promised in a liturgical prophecy (Ps. 81:15[14]); the sole condition is that Israel listens to Yahweh's voice and walks in his ways (v. 14[13]). This psalm appears (at least in part) to be a liturgical adaptation of Deuteronomistic ideas.

In a Chronistic historical retrospect (Neh. 9:24), the hiphil of *kn'* describes the occupation of the land in strictly theological terms. In the course of a great liturgical prayer, the postexilic community confesses its faith: "Thou didst humble before them (*wattaḵna' lipnêhem*) the inhabitants of the land . . . and didst give them into their hand (*beyāḏām*)." The same idea reappears in Deuteronomic (or Deuteronomistic?) historical parenesis in Dt. 9:3 (cf. the context beginning with v. 1), where we find once more the characteristic *kn'* hiphil with God (*hû'*) as subject and *lepāneyḵā*.

The notion that even God's own people might be subject to Yahweh's anger as a consequence of disobedience, apostasy, and wickedness is not unknown to either the Deuteronomistic theology of history or that of the Chronicler, but it seldom finds expression in *kn'* with Israel as its object. In fact, Ps. 106:42 is the only instance. This post-Deuteronomistic historical psalm does not hesitate to use *kn'* for the result of Yahweh's anger against Israel. The ongoing train of events is depicted in the preceding verses: Yahweh's anger and abhorrence (v. 40), his surrender of Israel into the hand of the nations (*wayyittenēm beyaḏ-gôyîm,* v. 41), Israel's oppression under its enemies, and finally the brief conclusion: "Thus they were humbled under their (i.e., the nations') power" (v. 42).

Two further passages in the Chronicler's history say the same thing, albeit without the fundamental theological balance of Ps. 106 but with primary reference to a specific historical situation. For example, 2 Ch. 13:18 cites (the Chronicler's account of) Judah's victory (under Abijah) over Israel (under Jeroboam). The conclusion uses the same formula, but now with reference to Israel: "Thus the Israelites were subdued at that time." The otherwise common qualification "before" or "under the hand of" someone is expressed in other terms, namely in the statement that the men of Judah prevailed. This victory and its theological background are not mentioned in the Deuteronomistic parallel, which has little to say — and that little not nearly so favorable — about the reign of Abijah (1 K. 15:1-8). In the Chronicler's account, Judah's victory over Israel is due to the Judahites' reliance on Yahweh, in contrast to the Israelites' apostasy from the true faith.

A similarly limited situation is described by the Chronicler (or possibly by an even later narrator) in a unique account of the historical and theological situation during the reign of Ahaz, whose troubles (especially the incursions of the Edomites and Philistines) must ultimately be understood as "humiliations" (*kn'* hiphil) brought about by Yahweh for his transgressions (2 Ch. 28:19).[2] The account in 2 K. 16 differs from this version.

In conclusion, we may cite the subjectivizing tendency of Ps. 107 (v. 12) in describing the same situation. This postexilic thanksgiving liturgy tells how at certain times rejection of the *'imrê-'ēl* by certain groups or their contempt for the *'aṣaṯ 'elyôn* (v. 11) caused the Most High to "humble" (*kn'* hiphil) the hearts of the wicked *be'āmāl* ("with hard labor, distress"), so that they fell down with none to help. Not until they cried out to God did he come to their aid (v. 13). There is good reason to follow the LXX's reading of a niphal instead of a hiphil. In this context, *libbām* ("their hearts") does indeed stand by synecdoche for the whole person; there may nevertheless be a sense in which the humiliation is felt with special force in the very heart of the individual, the seat of sensation and response, where it might evoke repentance and return.

2. *Reflexive.* In this section, we shall discuss all the occurrences of *kn'* in the niphal with reflexive meaning: "humble oneself." Used in this sense, the term belongs to the theology and preaching of repentance. In the majority of cases, the subject is an individual.

Our first passage is Lev. 26:41, in the conclusion to the Holiness Code; it is a conditional assurance of deliverance in the context of the usual blessing and curse formulas. Unfortunately, the passage is difficult to date; indeed, the traditio-historical background of the whole chapter constitutes a difficult problem. According to Elliger,[3] v. 41 belongs to a secondary stratum. It would certainly not be wrong to assume that P is a terminus ad quem, since it promotes the idea in question. The passage states that,

2. Cf. K. Galling, *Die Bücher der Chronik. ATD,* 12 (1954), *in loc.*

3. K. Elliger, *Leviticus. HAT,* IV (1966), *in loc.*

if the uncircumcised heart humbles itself — defined more precisely in the parallel clause by "and if they pay off (*rsh*) their *ʿawôn*" — then Yahweh will remember (*zkr*) his covenant, and the historical situation of oppression will be altered. This is the meaning of the conditional assurance of deliverance. What is at issue is the people's fundamental attitude toward Yahweh, which is vital; the niphal of *kn*ʿ is the term that denotes turning to Yahweh.

The description of Solomon's dedication of the temple contains texts that recount prayers and God's response. The Chronicler's version of one such response likewise includes a conditional assurance of deliverance (2 Ch. 7:14). The schema is the same: the people's evil ways (*dereḵ*) have prompted Yahweh to inflict special punishments, in this case natural disasters (cf. v. 13). If, however, the people humble themselves (*kn*ʿ niphal), pray to Yahweh, seek Yahweh (in the sanctuary, i.e., inquire concerning his will), and turn (*šûḇ*) from their wicked way, then Yahweh will hear them, fogive their sin, and heal their land. In this context, *kn*ʿ takes on cultic and ethical overtones. The substance of this passage is also recorded in 1 K. 8:33,35 (albeit in a different sequence), but instead of *kn*ʿ we find the hiphil of *ʿnh,* "oppress," used transitively to denote God's punishment.[4]

Following the story of Naboth's vineyard and the account of Yahweh's prediction of disaster through the mouth of Elijah, we are told that, in response to Elijah's words, Abah felt remorse and did penance (1 K. 21:17-29). In a new revelation from Yahweh, Elijah learns that Yahweh has decided to defer the punishment until the next generation. This change is based explicitly on God's observation that Ahab has humbled himself (v. 29: "Have you seen *kî-niḵaʿ ʾaḥāḇ millᵉpānāy?*"). Deferral of the punishment is introduced by *yaʿan kî-niḵnaʿ mippānay,* which is not found in the LXX and may therefore be considered a case of homoioteleuton.[5] The nature of *kn*ʿ is defined by the Ahab's acts of penitence and fasting described in v. 27: rending his garments, putting sackcloth on his bare flesh, fasting, and sleeping in penitential garments, as well as a corresponding disposition (*wayᵉhallēḵ ʾaṭ,* "going about dejectedly"). Here *kn*ʿ suggests ceremonial repentance. It is dubious that this passage was part of the original tradition. It is more likely a *vaticinium ex eventu,* whose content reflects the Deuteronomistic theological program.

Huldah the prophetess also promises King Josiah a peaceful end because he humbled himself before Yahweh in response to the reading of the law (2 K. 22:19). Here, too, *kn*ʿ is defined as hearing Yahweh's word, taking it to heart (*raḵ-lᵉḇāḇᵉḵā*), rending garments, and weeping before Yahweh. The Chronicler's version generally adopts the Deuteronomistic idea and language (2 Ch. 34:27). Here, too, therefore, *kn*ʿ is a cultic term associated with penance, introduced by the Deuteronomistic redactor.

The Chronicler's account of the Egyptian campaign against Rehoboam (in contrast to the Deuteronomistic variant in 1 K. 14) likewise tells how the king and his court

---

4. M. Noth, *Könige 1–16. BK,* IX/1 (1968), 170: "Yahweh humbles"; cf. also E. Würthwein, *Die Bücher der Könige. ATD,* XI/1 (1977), *in loc.* The LXX and the Vulg. read the piel; cf. *BHS.*

5. Cf. *BHS.*

humbled themselves in response to a prophetic oracle; as a consequence, Yahweh's punishment, proclaimed by the same prophet Shemaiah, was mitigated (2 Ch. 12:6,7[twice],12). The passage bears a striking similarity to the account of Ahab's penance discussed above. The other accounts of repentance and return in the Chronicler's history add almost nothing to the picture. In Hezekeiah's penance, pride of heart (*gbh libbô,* 2 Ch. 32:25) played a role; on account of it the king humbled himself (v. 26). We merely note in passing that this account also differs from 2 K. 20. In the story of King Manasseh's penance (2 Ch. 33:12,19; not mentioned in 2 K. 21), *kn'* is amplified by *m*^{e}*'ōd*: Manasseh "humbled himself greatly." The text goes on to speak of Manasseh's prayer (2 Ch. 33:13) and says that he "softened (*hlh* piel) the face of his God" (v. 12), i.e., that he performed certain acts of penance and prayer. Manasseh's son Amon did not humble himself before Yahweh as his father had done, as 2 Ch. 33:23 (*kn'* twice) states explicitly. The same failure is recounted in the case of Zedekiah (2 Ch. 36:12), but with the minor difference that Zedekiah did not humble himself before Jeremiah — who is described immediately, however, as *hannāḇî mippî YHWH.* It was clearly possible to perform such an act of penance before a prophet, who represented Yahweh.

Of the 17 occurrences of *kn'* niphal with reflexive meaning, 13 are in the Chronicler's history, so that *kn'* almost appears to be a typically Chronistic term. The cultic and ceremonial associations of *kn'* are striking.

3. *Other Usages.* There are three further usages of *kn'* that do not fall readily into either of the categories discussed.

God's second speech to Job (Job 40:6ff.) describes God's incomparable power, which Job must find irresistible. God's mighty demonstrations of power in nature and history include the power to bring low the proud, apparently by fixing his gaze on them (*r*^{e}*'ēh kol-gē'eh haḵnî'ēhû,* v. 12). Parallel to the hiphil of *kn'* we find in this context *špl* hiphil, *hdk* (a hapax legomenon), and *ṭmm* (cf. vv. 11, 13). Here *kn'* clearly denotes a punctiliar event, not a process. In the "moment" God looks at the proud, it is all over. The usage of *kn'* hiphil in the thanksgiving hymn Isa. 25:1-5 (specifically v. 5) in the so-called small apocalypse of Isaiah points in the same direction. This hymn extols Yahweh's mighty powers, with which he can subdue (*kn'*) the tumult of the aliens and still (*'nh*) the (victory) song of the ruthless. Probably *zēḏîm* should be read for *zārîm* and *'nh* should be read as a niphal.[6] The poetic description of Yahweh's saving greatness, which he employs on behalf of the poor and afflicted, ultimately means subjugation of the oppressors, the proud, and the mighty.

For the people of the battered northern tribes left behind in Israel after the Assyrian deportation, it must have been ignominious to heed Hezekiah's call to celebrate a passover at Jerusalem. Some men from Asher, Manasseh, and Zebulun nevertheless did come; the Chronicler's tradition says that they "humbled themselves" (*kn'* niphal) and came to Jerusalem (2 Ch. 30:11). Here *kn'* denotes an act of submission to the

6. Cf. the LXX; *BHS.*

claims of Judah (Jerusalem); it might be a secular political term. The context (vv. 6ff.), however, makes it quite possible that the passage ultimately has in mind something like an act of penance on the part of the remnant of Israel. If so, even here *kn'* would stay within the context of its ordinary theological usage.

III. LXX. The LXX does not translate *kn'* uniformly. The most frequent equivalent is *tapeinoún* (10 times for the niphal, 5 for the hiphil). Also found are: *ektríbein* (qal); *katanýssesthai, systéllein, trépein* (niphal); and *apostréphein, ektríbein, tropoún, exaírein* (hiphil).

IV. Dead Sea Scrolls. Of the 10 known occurrences of *kn'* (niphal and hiphil) in the Dead Sea scrolls, 5 are in the War scroll (1QM). Even if this document is not entirely of a piece, its intellectual milieu can be considered relatively uniform, at least in the passages where *kn'* appears. In the war between the "sons of light" and the "sons of darkness," the point is repeatedly made that God's decisive intervention will bring "humiliation" and subjection to evil, to wickedness, to Belial, however many may stand on the side of these entities (the sons of Ashur, the Kittim: 1:6; Belial himself and the angels of his dominion: 1:14f.; the army of the foe: 6:5f.; the prince of the power of evil: 17:5f.). The vision of sacred history assures confidence in the power of Israel's God, who gave David victory over Goliath of Gath and enabled him to "humiliate" the Philistines (11:3; cf. 1f.). The instruments of victory are God's "great hand," "judgment," or "name," which subjugate the foe. In all these instances, *kn'* reflects the "politico-theological" usage of the OT.[7]

The *niknā'îm* ("humble") are mentioned in 1QS 10:26 — those deserving of the special love and kindness of the devout worshipper within the community defined by the Rule. They stand in parallel to the disheartened, the erring spirits, and the dissatisfied (11:1). This nuance of *kn'* is something new. The hiphil of *kn'* in 1QSa 1:21 and 1QSb 3:18, however, remains in the semantic realm of "subjugate." In the latter passage God is the subject, in the former the devout man, albeit only under certain conditions (he must not be an *'îš pôṯeh* [conj.]) that are ultimately dependent on God. The context of *wtkn'* in 1QH fr. 9:6 is unfortunately missing. Finally, we may cite 4QDibHam 6:5, which uses *kn'* niphal reflexively with *lēḇ* to denote the "self-humbling" of the heart and the atonement for sin that will be followed by God's deliverance and favor toward the penitent.[8] This passage, too, stays within the familiar OT context.

Wagner

---

7. See II.1 above.
8. Cf. II.2 above; also Lev. 26:41.

כְּנַעַן $k^ena'an$; כְּנַעֲנִי $k^ena'^an\hat{i}$

Contents: I. 1. Occurrences; 2. LXX; 3. Etymology; 4. Meaning. II. Canaan: 1. Boundaries; 2. Appraisal. III. Canaanites: 1. Civilization; 2. Religion; 3. Appraisal.

---

kena'an. Y. Aharoni, *The Land of the Bible* (Eng. trans., Philadelphia, ²1979), 67-77; W. F. Albright, "Palestine in the Earliest Historical Period," *JPOS,* 15 (1935), 193-234; *idem, Archaeology and the Religion of Israel* (Garden City, ⁵1968); *idem,* "The Rôle of the Canaanites in the History of Civilization," *Studies in the History of Culture. Festschrift W. H. Leland* (1942, repr. Freeport, N.Y., 1969), 11-50 (= *The Bible and the Ancient Near East. Festschrift W. F. Albright* [1961, repr. Winona Lake, 1979], 438-487); *idem, Yahweh and the Gods of Canaan* (1968, repr. Winona Lake, 1978); A. Alt, "The Formation of the Israelite State in Palestine," *Essays on OT History and Religion* (Eng. trans., Garden City, 1966), 171-237 = *KlSchr,* II, 1-65 [Ger.]; *idem, "Völker und Staaten Syriens im frühen Altertum," AO,* 34/4 (1936) = *KlSchr,* III, 20-48; M. C. Astour, "The Origin of the Terms 'Canaan,' 'Phoenician,' and 'Purple,' " *JNES,* 24 (1965), 346-350; F. M. T. de Liagre Böhl, *Kanaanäer und Hebräer. BWAT,* 9 (1911); M. du Buit, *Géographie de la Terre Sainte* (Paris, 1958); A. Caquot, *Les songes et leur interprétation selon Canaan et Israel. Sources orientales,* 2 (Paris, 1959), 99-124; G. Contenau, "Phoenicia," in E. Drioton, Contenau, and J. Duchesne-Guillemin, *Religions of the Ancient Near East* (Eng. trans., New York, 1959), 74-81; E. Cortese, *La Terra di Canaan nella storia sacerdotale del Pentateuco. RivBiblSup,* 5 (1972); A. D. Crown, "Some Factors Relating to Settlement and Urbanization in Ancient Canaan in the Second and First Millennia B.C.," *Abr-Nahrain,* 11 (1971), 22-41; M. J. Dahood, "Ancient Semitic Deities in Syria and Palestine," in S. Moscati, ed., *Le antiche divinità semitiche. StSem,* 1 (1958), 65-94; É. P. Dhorme, "Les pays bibliques au temps d'el-Amarna d'après la nouvelle publication des lettres," *RB,* N.S. 5 (1908), 500-519; 6 (1909), 50-73; W. Dietrich, *Israel und Kanaan. SBS,* 94 (1979); H. Donner, *Einführung in die biblische Landes- und Altertumskunde* (1976), §8; R. Dussaud, *Les origines cananéens du sacrifice israélite* (Paris, 1921, repr. 1941); *idem,* "Phéniciens," *Les religions de Babylonie et d'Assyrie. Mana,* I/II (²1947), 355-388; *idem, Le sacrifice en Israël et chez les Phéniciens* (Paris, 1914); O. Eissfeldt, "The Hebrew Kingdom," *CAH*³, II/2, 537-605; *idem,* "Die israelitisch-jüdische Religion," *Saeculum Weltgeschichte,* 2 (1966), 217-260; *idem,* "Kanaanäisch-ugaritische Religion," *HO,* I/VIII, 1/1 (1964), 76-91; *idem,* "Palestine in the Time of the Nineteenth Dynasty. (a) The Exodus and Wanderings," *CAH*³, II/2, XXVI(a) 307-330; G. Fohrer, "Israels Haltung gegenüber den Kanaanäern und anderen Völkern," *JSS,* 13 (1968), 64-75; *idem,* "Die wiederentdeckte kanaanäisch Religion," *ThLZ,* 78 (1953), 193-200; T. H. Gaster, "The Religion of the Canaanites," in V. T. A. Ferm, ed., *Forgotten Religions* (New York, 1950), 111-143; J. Gray, *The Canaanites. Ancient Peoples and Places,* 38 (London, ²1965); *idem,* "The God *Yw* in the Religion of Canaan," *JNES,* 12 (1953), 278-283; *idem, The Legacy of Canaan. SVT,* 5 (1957, ²1965); E. Herzfeld, "Archäologische Parerga," *OLZ,* 22 (1919), 212-14; F. Hommel, *Ethnologie und Geographie des alten Orients. HAW,* III/1, 1 (Munich, 1926); K. Jaroš, *Die Stellung des Elohisten zur kanaanäischen Religion. OBO,* 4 (1974); Z. Kallai, "The Boundaries of Canaan and the Land of Israel in the Bible," *N. Glueck Memorial Volume. ErIsr,* 12 (1975), 27-34 [Heb.]; K. M. Kenyon, *Amorites and Canaanites* (New York, 1966); H. Klengel, *Geschichte Syriens im 2. Jahrtausend v.u.Z.,* 3 vols. *DAWB,* 40 (1965-1970); S. Landersdorfer, *Sumerisches Sprachgut im AT. BWANT,* 21 (1916); J. Lewy, "Influences ḫurrites sur Israël," *RÉS,* 21 (1938), 49-75; F. Løkkegaard, "The Canaanite Divine Wetnurses," *StTh,* 10 (1957), 53-64; V. Maag, "Syrien-Palästina," in

I. 1. *Occurrences.* The proper noun *kᵉna'an* occurs 94 times in the Hebrew OT; the various derived gentilic forms occur a total of 74 times. In addition to several passages in the Apocrypha and Pseudepigrapha (e.g., Jth. 5:3,9,10,16; Bar. 3:22; 1 Mc. 9:37) that mention Canaan and Canaanites, there is substantial extrabiblical material. The earliest is a text from Mari that mentions *ˡᵘki-na-aḫ-numᵐᵉˢ̌*.[1] A somewhat later occurrence appears in the autobiography of Idrimi of Alalakh, where ll. 20ff. speak of *māt kin'āni.* The same phrase occurs 3 more times in the Alalakh texts, and the word *kinaḫḫu* appears frequently in the Nuzi texts.[2] The texts from Ḫattusas are almost as early.[3] Shortly thereafter come the Amarna letters, with 12 instances of *ki-na-aḫ-ḫi, ki-na-aḫ-ni,* or *ki-na-aḫ-na,*[4] and occurrences in Egyptian and Ugaritic texts. An Ugaritic list of workers contains the name *y'l.kn'ny,* "Ja'al the Canaanite,"[5] and RS 20.182ᴬ⁽⁺⁾ᴮ uses the phrase *mârîᴹ ᴹᴬᵀki-na-ḫi,* "men of the land of Canaan." The earliest Egyptian occurrence (cf. also the mention of Canaanite captives in the inscription of Amenhotep II[6]) appears in an inscription of Seti I, which speaks of *pꜣ*

H. Schmökel, ed., *Kulturgeschichte des Alten Orients* (Stuttgart, 1961), 447-604; A. Malamat, "Syrien-Palästina in der zweiten Hälfte des 2. Jahrtausends," *Fischer-Weltgeschichte,* 2 (Frankfurt, 1966), 177-221; B. Mazar (Maisler), "Canaan and the Canaanites," *BASOR,* 102 (1946), 7-12; *idem, Untersuchungen zur alten Geschichte und Ethnographie Syriens und Palästinas,* I (Giessen, 1930); S. Moscati, *I predecessori d'Israel. Studi orientali,* 4 (1956); *idem,* "Sulla storia del nome Canaan," *AnBibl,* 12 (1959), 266-69; M. Noth, "Mari und Israel: Eine Personennamenstudie," *Geschichte und AT. Festschrift A. Alt. BHTh,* 16 (1958), 127-152 = *Aufsätze zur biblischen Landes- und Altertumskunde* (Neukirchen-Vluyn, 1971), II, 212-233; *idem,* "Die syrisch-palästinische Bevölkerung des zweiten Jahrtausends v.Chr. im Lichte neuer Quellen," *ZDPV,* 65 (1942), 9-67; *idem, The OT World* (Eng. trans., Philadelphia, 1966); J. Pedersen, "Kana'anæsk Religion," *Illustreret Religionshistorie* (Copenhagen, 1948), 191-212; F. E. Peiser, "Zum ältesten Namen Kana'ans," *OLZ,* 22 (1919), 5-8; G. von Rad, "The Promised Land and Yahweh's Land in the Hexateuch," *The Problem of the Hexateuch* (Eng. trans. 1966, repr., London, 1984), 79-93; A. F. Rainey, "A Canaanite at Ugarit," *IEJ,* 13 (1963), 43-45; *idem,* "The Kingdom of Ugarit," *BA,* 28 (1965), 102-125; *idem,* "Ugarit and the Canaanites Again," *IEJ,* 14 (1964), 101; L. Rost, "Noah der Weinbauer," *Geschichte und AT. Festschrift A. Alt. BHTh,* 16 (1953), 169-178 = *Das kleine Credo* (Heidelberg, 1965), 44-53; G. Schmitt, *Du sollst keinen Frieden schliessen mit den Bewohnern des Landes. BWANT,* 91[5/11] (1970); A. van Selms, "The Canaanites in the Book of Genesis," *Studies on the Book of Genesis. OTS,* 12 (1958), 182-213; J. Simons, *GTTOT*; E. A. Speiser, "The Name Phoinikes," *Oriental and Biblical Studies* (Philadelphia, 1967), 324-331; F. Stähelin, "Der Name Kanaan," *Festschrift J. Wackernagel* (Göttingen, 1923), 150-53; R. de Vaux, *The Early History of Israel* (Eng. trans., Philadelphia, 1978); *idem,* "Le pays de Canaan," *JAOS,* 88 (1968), 23-30.

1. G. Dossin, "Une mention de Cananéens dans une lettre de Mari," *Syria,* 50 (1973), 299f.
2. Cf. Speiser, 328f.
3. See *Rép. géogr.,* IV, with bibliog.
4. See the index in J. A. Knudtzon, *Die El-Amarna-Tafeln. VAB,* 2 (1915, ²1964), 1577; and A. F. Rainey, *El Amarna Tablets 359-379.* AOAT, 8 (²1978), 92.
5. 311 = 120, 7.
6. *ANET,* 246.

knʿn, "the Canaan," and mentions a "city of Canaan" in the caption to an illustration.[7] The so-called Israel stela (Merneptah inscription) likewise mentions the land of Canaan;[8] an inscription of Rameses III[9] speaks of building the "house of Rameses . . . in Canaan." While the occurrences in Papyrus Anastasi III and IV are obscure,[10] a basalt statue of an Egyptian from the period of the twenty-second dynasty bears an inscription reading: "Envoy of the Canaan and of Palestine."[11] Among Phoenician and Greek texts, the outstanding instance is a passage in which Philo Byblius says that *Chná,* the eponymous ancestor of the Canaanites, was also the first to bear the name *Phoínix.*[12] A coin from the Hellenistic period calls the city of Laodicea (= Berytos) the "mother in Canaan."[13] Josephus uses *Chananaía*[14] as an indeclinable noun denoting Canaan. The NT uses *Chanáan* (Acts 7:11; 13:19) and the adj. *Chananaía* (Mt. 15:22). Finally, Augustine of Hippo uses "Canaan" as the term by which the Punic peasants refer to themselves.[15]

2. *LXX.* The LXX regularly renders the noun with *Chanaan* (90 times) and the adjective with *chananaíos* and its derivatives (64 times). We also find the forms *Chananís* (Nu. 21:1,3; 33:40; Ezr. 9:1), *Chananítis* (Gen. 46:10; Isa. 19:18), and *Chanaanítis* (1 Ch. 2:3). It is noteworthy that in Ex. 6:15 the LXX describes the mother of one of Simeon's sons as *Phoiníssa,* "a Phoenician woman," while translating the same expression in Gen. 46:10 as *tḗs Chananítidos.* The statement in Ex. 16:35 that the Israelites ate the manna "till they came to the border of the land of Canaan" is translated by the LXX as *eis méros tḗs Phoiníkēs.* Josh. 5:1 mentions besides the "kings of the Amorites that were beyond the Jordan" "all the kings of the Canaanites that were by the sea," which the LXX renders as *hoi basileís tḗs Phoiníkēs hoi pará tḗn thálassan.* Alluding to Ex. 16:35, Josh. 5:12 says that from the day after celebrating the Passover the Israelites no longer ate manna but instead "ate of the fruit of the land of Canaan," which the LXX renders as *hē chṓra tṓn Phoiníkōn.* Finally, Job 40:30(Eng. 41:6) speaks of the *Phoiníkōn génē.*

3. *Etymology.* The etymology of the name "Canaan" is not clear. By and large, there are two schools of opinion. One considers *kᵉnaʿan* to be a non-Semitic loanword; the other thinks the word is Semitic or, more precisely, West Semitic. The

---

7. *ANET,* 254.
8. *ANET,* 378.
9. Papyrus Harris I, IX, 1-3.
10. Böhl, 4.
11. *ANET,* 264.
12. Eusebius *Praep. ev.* i.10.39.
13. Böhl, 5.
14. Cf. *Ant.* 1.186.
15. Mazar, *Untersuchungen,* 59.

first group includes several earlier scholars whose theories are no longer tenable. Fritz Hommel[16] derived "Canaan" from Bab. *kingin,* "lowland,"[17] and theorized that the "Canaanites" migrated from Babylonia to Palestine, taking with them this name, which is known to have been applied to the region of Arabia bordering on Babylonia. Simon Landersdorfer[18] proposed Sum. *kanaga,* "land"; and E. Herzfeld[19] explained the ending *-na* in *kinaḫna* as a suffix used to form names of lands and peoples. This theory was modified slightly by F. Stähelin,[20] who derived this *-na* from Anatolian *-ḗnē.*[21] Albrecht Alt[22] still spoke of the "clearly non-Semitic origin of the name."

The others took as their starting point the assumption that "Canaan" is a Semitic name. Rosenmüller[23] and above all Wilhelm Gesenius[24] attempted to derive the name from the verb *knʿ,* associated with Canaan in Neh. 9:24 (possibly by popular etymology), suggesting that it means "lowland" (in contrast to *ʾārām,* "highland"). Redslob[25] interpreted "Canaan" as a descriptive name meaning "subjugated." As Benjamin Mazar explicitly states,[26] the noun is made up of *knʿ* and the Semitic ending *-an/-ōn*; the *n* therefore is not part of the root.[27] This etymology gained much support in the recent past. Benjamin Mazar, for example,[28] considers the meaning "lowland" to be "not unlikely." F. M. Abel takes the same position.[29] Michael C. Astour,[30] too, derives our noun from the root *knʿ* and assigns it the meaning "Occident," the "Land of the Sunset" or "Westland." Sabatino Moscati[31] likewise supports the meaning "lowland," albeit with a question mark.

A new element entered the discussion when it was discovered that in the Nuzi texts *kinaḫḫu* means "purple." Since this dye comes from Phoenicia, the land where it comes from was called "the land of purple," i.e., Canaan.[32] Many scholars have accepted this

---

16. P. 158; cf. also *Grundriss der Geschichte und Geographie des Alten Orients* (Munich, ²1904), 148, n. 1, cited by Böhl, 1, n. 3.
17. An etymology also accepted by Peiser, 5-8.
18. P. 23.
19. P. 212.
20. Pp. 150ff.
21. For additional suggestions, see Böhl, 1; Landersdorfer, 23; Mazar, *Untersuchungen,* 54f.
22. *KlSchr,* III, 37.
23. See Böhl, 1.
24. *GesTh,* 696.
25. Cf. Böhl, 1.
26. *Untersuchungen,* 55.
27. This analysis is also supported (with reservations) by *BLe,* §61 li, p. 504.
28. *Untersuchungen,* 55, n. 3.
29. F. M. Abel, *Geographie de la Palestine,* I (Paris, 1933), 254, 318.
30. P. 348.
31. *AnBibl,* 12 (1959), 266-69.
32. E. A. Speiser, "The Name *Phoinikes,*" *Language,* 12 (1936), 121-26; *idem, Oriental and Biblical Studies,* 328f., but with the comment (327, n. 12) that this does not entirely solve the problem of the origin and etymology of *kᵉnaʿan.*

etymology.[33] William F. Albright[34] believed that the name "Canaan" is Hurrian and means "belonging to [the land of] Purple," with the following etymology: Akk. *uknû* became Can. *'iqna'u,* which in Hurrian became **ikna, iknaggi* or *knaggi,* which the Akkadian of Nuzi turned into *kinaḫḫi*; with the determinative suf. *-ni,* this became **knággini,* Akk. *kinaḫni,* Heb. *kᵉnaʿan.*

Objections have also been raised against these etymologies. Mazar[35] emphasizes the difficulty of explaining the origin of *knaʿ* and *kinaḫ(ḫ)i.* Moscati[36] points out that *kinaḫnu* (*kinaḫḫu*) is derived from *knʿn,* not the reverse. Because of the *ʿayin* and also because the word occurs in the Idrimi inscription and the Alalakh texts, Roland de Vaux[37] maintains that *kᵉnaʿan* is clearly West Semitic. He also points out that in western Palestine and in Canaan itself other words were used for purple. These observations opened the way for a new interpretation of "Canaan."

Mazar[38] had already pointed out that "Canaan" was originally an appellative: in both Egyptian and the Greek of Philo Byblius, it is used with the definite article. According to Mazar,[39] the further observation that an inscription of Rameses II speaks of "640 captured *kynʿnw*" (= *kinʿanu*) between *maryana* and "sons of princes" suggests that the word denotes here some kind of "noble caste," "merchants," specifically "Phoenician merchants."[40] He concludes that the land was called "Canaan" because of the merchants that came from it.[41] Taking the same basic meaning as their point of departure but with differences in detail, Moscati[42] and de Vaux[43] have proposed the opposite development, namely that merchants were called "Canaanites" because they came from the land of Canaan, so that the term "merchant" was derived from the name of the land. In the present state of our knowledge, these theories appear to be the most likely, especially because the OT uses *kᵉnaʿan* 8 times in the sense of "merchant." Furthermore, this etymology does not rule out the possibility of a secondary association between "purple," a major commercial product around the middle of the second millennium, and the name "Canaan," "the land of the purple-merchants." The identification of Chna, the eponymous ancestor of the Canaanites, with Phoinix, the ancestor of the Phoenicians, points in the same direction, since *phoínix* also means "purple."

---

33. Gray, *The Canaanites,* 15, 47f.; Noth, *The OT World,* 56; Kenyon, 59; Malamat, 181; Aharoni, 61f.
34. *Festschrift W. F. Albright,* 450 and 477f., n. 50.
35. *BASOR,* 102 (1946), 8.
36. *AnBibl,* 12 (1959), 266-69.
37. *JAOS,* 88 (1968), 24 = *Early History,* I, 126.
38. *Untersuchungen,* 55.
39. *BASOR,* 102 (1946), 9.
40. Cf. the inscription of Amen-hotep II discussed above.
41. Cf. also *GTTOT,* 16.
42. *AnBibl,* 12 (1959), 266-69.
43. *JAOS,* 88 (1968), 25 = *Early History,* I, 126.

4. *Meaning.* The first occurrences of "Canaan" in Gen. 9:22,25-27 understand it as the name of an individual, speaking of his father (v. 22) and brothers (v. 25). (The words "and Ham, that is, the father of Canaan" [v. 18] and "Ham, the father" [v. 22] are redactional additions to harmonize the group of sons implicit in these sayings with the group of brothers listed by J in v. 18 and the Table of Nations.[44]) The individualized interpretation is found also in J's Table of Nations: Canaan is the father of Sidon and Heth (Gen. 10:15 par. 1 Ch. 1:13).[45] V. 19 defines the territory of the Canaanites (gentilic + article). P also individualizes, introducing Canaan as the fourth son of Ham (Gen. 10:6 par. 1 Ch. 1:8).

This form of expression is based on an abstract genealogy in which an eponymous ancestor stands for a group bearing the same name. Thus the "people" of the Canaanites is present in the patriarch Canaan. This is clearly the meaning of the words spoken by Noah in Gen. 9:25-27.[46] According to Hans-Jürgen Zobel,[47] these words represent the genre of "national adage."[48] Their primary theme is the dominance of one group over the others. The word *ʿbd* (and specifically the noun *ʿeḇeḏ*) is a technical term for political subordination. Gen. 9:25 is thus intended to express the total subjection and subservience of the Canaanites.

These observations make it clear that the word "Canaan" can be synonymous with "Canaanites." Additional examples of this usage, however, are few. In Gen. 28:1,6,8; 36:2 (P), we find the phrase "daughters of Canaan," i.e., Canaanite women. Isa. 19:18 speaks of "the language of Canaan" with reference to the Jewish diaspora in Egypt. Hos. 12:8(7) castigates Canaan for holding false balances in his hand; the reference may be to the Canaanites or to "merchants" in general.[49] Finally, it is possible that in the phrase "the idols (*ʿᵃṣabbê*) of Canaan" (Ps. 106:38) the proper name may denote the Canaanites who worship these idols.

As a rule, the gentilic noun is used for "Canaanites" (74 times). This indicates that at least in the OT the word *kᵉnaʿan* was inherently a geographical term denoting the land of Canaan.[50] Construct phrases such as *yōšᵉḇê kᵉnaʿan* (Ex. 15:15), *meleḵ-kᵉnaʿan* (sg. and pl.: Jgs. 4:2,23,24), *milḥᵃmôṯ kᵉnaʿan* (Jgs. 3:1), and *mamlᵉḵôṯ kᵉnaʿan* (Ps. 135:11) presuppose this interpretation; the common expression "land of Canaan" (64 times) confirms it. Although the latter phrase is typical of P's style (30 times in the

---

44. First suggested by J. Wellhausen, *Die Composition des Hexateuchs und der historischen Buches des ATs* (Berlin, ⁴1963), 12f.; a different theory was proposed by Mazar, *Untersuchungen,* 63, and most recently by C. Westermann, *Genesis 1–11* (Eng. trans., Minneapolis, 1984), 482-86; for discussion, see H.-J. Zobel, *Israel und die Völker* (inaugural diss., Halle, 1967), 4f.

45. On Gen. 10:16-18a as a secondary addition, see the comms.

46. Rost, 46.

47. *Israel und die Völker.*

48. Mazar, *Untersuchungen,* 64, already calls them "political poetry of the early monarchy."

49. H. W. Wolff, *Hosea. Herm* (Eng. trans. 1974), 207ff.

50. Böhl, 6-11; also Alt, *KlSchr,* III, 37f.; Noth, *The OT World,* 53f.; Rost, 46, n. 10 (p. 52); etc.

Pentateuch alone),[51] it is also found in E (Gen. 42:5,13,29,32; 45:17,25) and J (Gen. 42:7; 44:8; 46:31; 47:1,4,13-15; 50:5; Ex. 16:35), as well as the Holiness Code (Lev. 18:3; 25:38) and 1 Ch. 16:18 (par. Ps. 105:11). This distribution indicates an early date for the expression and use over a long period of time.

The use of k^{e}*na'an* to denote both a territory and the pre-Israelite population of Palestine requires an historical explanation. The proper noun was inherently a geographical term; it came to be associated with "the bearers and artifacts of a culture which was present in the area which the Israelite tribes settled before they occupied it, and which continued to maintain itself there."[52] As a result, "Canaan" finally could become a general term for all the pre-Israelite elements in Israel's territory.[53]

In extrabiblical texts, "Canaan" is clearly a geographical term. It appears as the name of a region in the cuneiform and Egyptian texts discussed above, and again in the legends of Phoenician coins. This usage is also consonant with the observation that the Idrimi inscription appears to use "Canaan" for a large, politically fragmented region,[54] probably centering on the city of Ammia.[55] In the Amarna letters, by contrast, where "Canaan" is the name of an Egyptian province, it appears to be more a political term.[56]

II. Canaan.

1. *Boundaries.* The extrabiblical evidence for the extent of Canaan is difficult to interpret, because there is a strange inconsistency in the assignment of certain territories to Canaan. According to de Vaux,[57] the Canaan of the Idrimi inscription comprised the Phoenician coastland north of Byblos. The term seems to include a rather larger territory in the early Egyptian inscriptions we have discussed, referring to Phoenicia as a whole. In the Amarna letters, however, "Canaan" is the name of a third Egyptian province, distinct from the northern province of Amurru (central Syria) and the province of Upe (with Kumidi as its capital); Canaan lay to the south of these, had Gaza as its capital, and was later expanded by the inclusion of Upe. The extent of Canaan in the Ugaritic texts is probably about the same, except that Ugarit itself does not appear to have been included.[58] In the late Hellenistic period, finally, "Canaan" is once more identical with Phoenicia.[59]

---

51. Cf. M. Noth, *Numbers. OTL* (Eng. trans. 1968), 239; and esp. Cortese.
52. Noth, *The OT World,* 53f.
53. *Ibid.;* cf. Rost, 46, n. 10.
54. Cf. A. Goetze, review of S. Smith, *The Statue of Idri-mi* (London, 1949), *JCS,* 4 (1950), 230f.; I. J. Gelb, "The Early History of the West Semitic Peoples," *JCS,* 15 (1961), 42; cited by Klengel, I (1965), 187.
55. On the location of this city, see Klengel, I, 187, n. 9; III (1970), 14.
56. *Ibid.,* II, 245f.
57. *JAOS,* 88 (1968), 25ff. = *Early History,* I, 127f.
58. Klengel, II (1969), 329f.; Rainey, *BA,* 28 (1965), 105f.
59. Böhl, 5; Mazar, *Untersuchungen,* 58f.; etc.

If we ask about the extent of Canaan in the OT,[60] we find the same variation. Of primary importance are several statements to the effect that certain places are "in the land of Canaan": Shiloh (Josh. 21:2; 22:9; Jgs. 21:12), Hebron (Gen. 23:2,19), Shechem (Gen. 33:18), and Luz (Gen. 35:6; 48:3), as well as the field of Machpelah (Gen. 23:19; 50:13) and the king of Arad, who dwelt in the Negeb in the land of Canaan (Nu. 33:40; cf. 21:1,3). Because all the cities lie more or less west of the Jordan and the Dead Sea, it is easy to see how the Jordan can constitute the eastern boundary of Canaan in other texts. When one crosses the river from the east, one arrives in Canaan (Nu. 33:51; 35:10,14; also Nu. 32:30,32; Josh. 22:32).

This information helps define the *g^elîlôṯ* (RSV "region") of the Jordan geographically. According to Josh. 22:11, they are opposite the land of Canaan, and according to v. 10, they lie within this land. It follows that the *g^elîlôṯ* are to be found on both sides of the Jordan.[61] The situation is similar in the case of Gen. 13:12, which says that Abraham stayed in the land of Canaan, whereas Lot settled among the cities of the valley.

This definition of Canaan is consonant with the statements that the patriarchs dwelt in Canaan (Gen. 11:31; 12:5; 16:3; 17:8; 31:18; 36:5,6; 37:1; 42:5; etc.) and that Israel wished to be buried there (50:5). It also agrees with the information that the site of Rachel's death was west of the Jordan (Gen. 48:7), where Er and Onan also died (Gen. 46:12; Nu. 26:19), that the portions assigned by Joshua all lay west of the Jordan (Josh. 14:1ff.), and that the boundaries of the land of Canaan as defined by Nu. 34:3-12 did not include territory east of the Jordan, even though to the south (wilderness of Zin and Kadesh) and to the north (Mt. Hor and the entrance of Hamath) they extended beyond the actual territory west of the Jordan.

This also agrees with the evidence of the gentilic noun, although the lists of the peoples dwelling in the land before the Israelites (Gen. 15:21; 34:30; Ex. 3:8,17; etc.)[62] frequently do not indicate the precise limits of the territory of the Canaanites. The terms "Canaan" and "Canaanites" nevertheless coincide, as is shown, for example, by the fact that the phrase *b^enôṯ k^ena'an* (Gen. 28:1,6,8; cf. 36:2) is synonymous with *b^enôṯ hakk^ena'^anî* (24:3,37; cf. 38:2). Similarly, Jgs. 1:9,10,17 speak of Canaanites as the indigenous population of greater Judah; the so-called negative occupation list mentions a number of cities that remained in the hands of the Canaanites until Israel became strong enough to change the situation in its favor (Jgs. 1:27-30,32f.; cf. Josh. 16:10; 17:12,13,16,18). Dt. 11:30 says that Ebal and Gerizim lie within the land of Canaan; according to 1 K. 9:16, Canaanites dwelt in Gezer.

As we have seen, all the evidence points exclusively to the territory west of the Jordan (cf. also Dt. 1:7). But this is precisely the situation reflected by the composition of the blessing of Noah (Gen. 9:25-27). Canaan is cursed: he must be the servant of Shem and Japheth. We have already seen that "Canaan" stands for the Canaanites; it

---

60. Cf. esp. Aharoni.

61. Contra M. Noth, *Das Buch Josua. HAT,* VII (1938, ^{3}1971), 134; *idem, The OT World,* 58ff.

62. Cf. the summary in Böhl, 63-67.

is also likely that "Japheth" refers to the Philistines who settled in Palestine. The appearance of the name "Yahweh" in Gen. 9:26 means that "Shem" must be identified with Israel or at least a portion thereof (greater Judah?). These three sons of Noah thus represent three peoples of Palestine; Canaan comprises just this territory, which does not include Phoenicia (Jgs. 3:3). Julius Wellhausen's classic statement that "Palestine extends the length of the Jordan"[63] reflects this definition.

Only Gen. 50:11 might be interpreted to mean that the Canaanites witnessing the mourning for Jacob had to dwell east of the Jordan because that is the locus of the ancient burial tradition; this argument, however, is far from persuasive.[64]

There exists also a different conception, according to which the Canaanites did not inhabit the entire territory west of the Jordan. Nu. 13:29 assigns the Amalekites to the Negeb, locates the Hittites, Jebusites, and Amorites in the hill country, and has the Canaanites dwelling by the sea and along the Jordan (cf. also Nu. 14:25). The list in Josh. 11:3 (with secondary expansions) includes the statement, "possibly based on special knowledge,"[65] that Jabin of Hazor sent to several kings and peoples, including the Canaanites in the east and by the sea. According to this tradition, the Canaanites were located "in the plains by the sea and along the Jordan,"[66] as Nu. 13:29 also states. Josh. 5:1 presupposes a similar location, speaking of "the kings of the Amorites that were beyond the Jordan to the west" and "all the kings of the Canaanites that were by the sea." Again we find the Canaanites in the coastal plain by the Mediterranean, although it is not entirely clear whether this plain lies to the west of the Amorites, who would then inhabit only the mountains west of the Jordan,[67] or whether the Amorites also possessed the coastal region, so that the Canaanites dwelt only in the coastal strip to the north (cf. LXX "Phoenicia"). Josh. 13:3 states that the territory of the Philistines is reckoned as Canaanite; in Zeph. 2:5, too, "Canaan" appears to be identical with "land of the Philistines." It cannot be denied that this tradition reflects historical reality: a distinction between the peoples occupying the valleys and plains on the one hand and the inhabitants of the hill country and mountains on the other resembles the early period of Israel's occupation in differentiating between the Canaanites, who dominated the plains with their iron chariots, and the Israelites, whose foothold was largely restricted to the hills and mountains (cf. Josh. 17:16; Jgs. 4:2; 5:19).

Finally, we may mention the tradition that identifies Canaan with Phoenicia. The oracle against Tyre in Isa. 23:11 threatens the "strongholds of Canaan," referring to the Phoenician seaside strongholds, including Sidon and Tyre. A similar conception appears to lie behind 2 S. 24:7: the route taken by the men numbering the people goes

---

63. J. Wellhausen, *Prolegomena to the History of Israel* (Eng. trans. 1885, repr. Magnolia, Mass., 1977), 1.

64. Cf. G. von Rad, *Genesis. OTL* (Eng. trans. 1961), 426; Noth, *The OT World,* 53f.; *GTTOT,* 35, 222; de Vaux, *Early History,* 128f.

65. Noth, *HAT,* VII, 68.

66. *Idem.*

67. *Ibid.,* 39.

through Gilead to Kadesh (LXX) on the Orontes, then to Dan, the vicinity of Sidon (v. 6), and the fortress of Tyre. The text continues: ". . . and to all the cities of the Hivites and Canaanites." Only then does the route proceed to the Negeb of Judah and Beer-sheba.

This notion, however, contradicts the view that Phoenicia is part of Canaan. This conception of a "greater Canaan" is expressed in J's genealogy by the statement that Sidon was the first-born of Canaan, followed by his brother Heth (Gen. 10:15 par. 1 Ch. 1:13) and by the definition of Canaanite territory as extending roughly to Sidon in the north, Gaza in the south, and Lasha (?) in the east (v. 19). In Ex. 16:35 ("the people of Israel ate the manna . . . till they came to a habitable land . . . to the border of the land of Canaan") and Josh. 5:12 ("the people of Israel . . . ate of the fruit of the land of Canaan that year"), the LXX renders the proper name as "Phoenicia," a translation also based on the conception that greater Canaan is simply Phoenicia extended to the south.

Whether these various conceptions can be correlated with specific historical situations[68] or whether we should assume that the territory of Canaan expanded with the passage of time, possibly through colonization,[69] is disputed.[70] What is clear is that the term "Canaan" was borrowed by Israel[71] and that at least in J's Table of Nations it has the same inclusiveness as the Egyptian province of Canaan after the merger with the province of Upe. But it is also accurate to use "Canaan" in the much more common sense of the region west of the Jordan as the name of Israel's dwelling place, because this usage corresponds to the notion of the promised land. When the text speaks in an even more limited sense of the Canaanites dwelling in certain plains and identifies Canaan with Phoenicia, the emphasis is on the cultural meaning of Canaan rather than its geographic or ethnic meaning.[72]

2. *Appraisal.* Within the Pentateuch, we hear the first description of the land of Canaan from the mouth of the spies: "It flows with milk and honey, and this is its fruit" (Nu. 13:27): an enormous cluster of grapes, together with some pomegranates and figs (v. 23). In word and deed, the spies thus confirm the description (first found in Ex. 3:8) of the promised land as "a good and broad land, a land flowing with milk and honey." The phrase "a land flowing with milk and honey" appears 18 more times in the OT (J: Ex. 3:17; 13:5; 33:3; Nu. 14:8; 16:13,14; then later: Lev. 20:24; Dt. 6:3; 11:9; 26:9,15; 27:3; 31:20; Josh. 5:6; Jer. 11:5; 32:22; Ezk. 20:6,15). As the two words

---

68. Cf. esp. Kallai.

69. Mazar, *Untersuchungen,* 66-74; *idem, BASOR,* 102 (1946), 11; Noth, *The OT World,* 53-56; Gray, *The Canaanites,* 15-48; cf. W. F. Albright, "Syrien, Phönizien, und Palästina vom Beginn der Sesshaftigkeit bis zur Eroberung durch die Achämeniden," in F. Kern, ed., *Historia Mundi,* II (Bern, 1953), 356.

70. Cf. de Vaux, *Early History,* I, 130-32.

71. O. Eissfeldt–A. Kuschke, "Kanaan. I. Geographisch," *RGG*^{3}, III (1959), 1106; de Vaux, *Early History,* I, 130f.

72. Cf. Noth, *The OT World,* 53f.

ḥālāḇ ("curds") and *dᵉḇaš* ("[wild] honey") show, the expression reflects a (semi)nomadic world[73] and is therefore very ancient.

Ex. 3:8 (J) associates with the words "a land flowing with milk and honey" the phrase "a good and broad land," into which Yahweh will bring Israel. In Nu. 14:7, P has the spies say that the land is "exceedingly good." These words probably represent an intensification of the characteristic Deuteronomic description of the land as "good" (Dt. 1:25,35; 3:25; 4:21,22; 6:18; 8:7,10; 9:6; 11:17), also found outside Deuteronomy in Josh. 23:16; 1 Ch. 28:8. Its meaning is expanded in Dt. 8:7-9: "A land of brooks of water, fountains and springs . . . , a land of wheat and barley, of vines and fig trees and pomegranates, a land of olive trees and honey, a land . . . in which you will lack nothing, a land whose stones are iron, and out of whose hills you can dig copper." The longest description appears in Dt. 11:9-15, which first compares Canaan with Egypt, the land of the Nile, mentioning its hills and valleys, but above all extolling Canaan for its rain, which furnishes the water necessary for the increase of the human and animal population and always provides plenty of food for Israel.

These descriptions strain reality if they do not already exaggerate conditions in Palestine. Some OT poetry at least gives this impression. The third oracle of Balaam, for example, begins by extolling the land of Israel (Nu. 24:5-7) before going on to praise the might of its monarchy and the majesty of its God:

How fair are your tents, O Jacob,
'and' your encampments, O Israel!
Like valleys that 'Yahweh stretches out,'
like gardens beside a river,
like aloes that Yahweh has planted,
like cedar trees beside the waters.
From its buckets flow water in abundance,
and its water in plenty.

Dt. 33:26-29, another hymn extolling Israel, describes Israel's dwelling place as "full of grain and wine, whose heavens drop down dew" (v. 28); and the Blessing of Isaac (Gen. 27:28 [E]) promises: "Elohim will give you of the dew of heaven, and of the fatness of the earth, and plenty of grain and wine" (cf. v. 39). Similar images appear in Ps. 65:10-14(9-13), a passage with hymnic features in a thanksgiving song: it speaks of Yahweh's blessing as providing the land's plenty, the abundance of its waters from the river of God and rain, its wealth of grain, fat, and flocks (cf. also such other passages as Dt. 33:13-16).

This description of Canaan, limited primarily to its natural beauty and fertility, is already augmented in the report of the spies by a reference to a "strong people" dwelling in the land, with cities that are "fortified and very large" (Nu. 13:28 [J]), words that are taken up in Dt. 1:28; 9:1f. and developed in Dt. 6:10f. into an expansive promise: "Great and goodly cities, which you did not build, and houses full of all

73. Contra (most recently) A. Caquot, "דְּבַשׁ *dᵉḇaš* (*dᵉbhash*)," *TDOT,* III, 130f.; for a discussion of the Ugaritic material cited by Caquot, see H.-J. Zobel, "Der bildliche Gebrauch von šmn in Ugaritischen Hebräischen," *ZAW,* 82 (1970), 210-12.

good things, which you did not fill, and cisterns hewn out, which you did not hew, and vineyards and olive trees, which you did not plant" — all these Yahweh will give Israel.

These descriptions of Canaan's extent and beauty, wealth and abundance, border on paradisal opulence. Behind them stands, if only implicitly, Israel's conviction that the land is a gracious gift bestowed by Yahweh on his beloved people.

Already in the patriarchal narratives the theme of the "promised land" occupies a central place.[74] The one who made these promises was inherently the Canaanite deity El; we may also assume that the promises went hand in hand with imminent fulfillment. In the present structure of the Hexateuch, however, the patriarchs merely hear the promises; the fulfillment of the promises is experienced only by their descendants, the Israelites. This led P to coin the phrase "land of sojourning" for Canaan (Gen. 17:8; 28:4; 36:7; 37:1; Ex. 6:4; cf. Ezk. 20:38). This association of the promise to the patriarchs with the promise to Moses was made possible by the fact that the theme of the promised land also played an important role in the theophany of Yahweh at Sinai (cf. Ex. 3:8,17 [J]; 6:8 [P]; 13:5,11 [J?]; etc.).[75]

It is noteworthy, however, that in comparison to the promise to the fathers, Yahweh's promise to Moses with its assurance of Yahweh's active aid in driving out the Canaanites reveals a new feature, which reflects the dynamism of Israel's Yahwism. Following an emphatic reference to the promise — or better the "oath" — to the father, J repeatedly adds the assurance that Yahweh or his *mal'āḵ* will "drive out" (*grš* qal or piel) the inhabitants of the land and bring Israel into the land (Ex. 33:2; 34:11; cf. Josh. 3:10; 24:12,18; also Ex. 23:28-31 [J+E]). Clearly the notion that the Canaanites would be driven out by Yahweh was always linked with the notion that they would be driven out by the Israelites. The antiquity of these convictions, which may even belong to the nucleus of the Yahweh theophany, is evident from the so-called negative occupation list (Jgs. 1:27-30,32f.; cf. Josh. 16:10; 17:12,13,18), which always states that such-and-such a tribe was unable to drive out (*yrš* hiphil) the Canaanites from such-and-such a city. The reality of the occupation, which often enjoyed limited success, was measured against the preexisting postulate that the Canaanites should have been driven out totally because Israel had been promised the land by its God. Because this idea concerns itself with history while interpreting this history theologically, von Rad calls it the "historical conception of the land of Canaan."

Gen. 9:27 shows that Israel sensed this tension between expansive promise and partial fulfillment and tried to resolve the problem. Philistine possession of part of the promised land, which belonged by rights to the people of Yahweh, was explained as the result of Noah's prayer that God would give a broad territory to the ancestor of the Philistines, so that he might even dwell in the tents of Shem; the presence of the Philistines in Canaan is thus ultimately ascribed to God himself. The explanations in Jgs. 2:20–3:5 point in a different direction. On the one hand, Yahweh lets the Philistines

74. Cf. von Rad, *The Problem of the Hexateuch*, 79.
75. Cf. also Fohrer, *JSS*, 113 (1968), 65.

and Canaanites remain in the land to test Israel's faith; on the other hand, the Israelites are to learn the art of war from these peoples.

Alongside this historical conception of the land of Canaan, limited primarily to the Hexateuch, von Rad has identified another conception, which he labels "cultic." It looks upon Canaan as "Yahweh's land," in which the Israelites can be only "strangers and sojourners with Yahweh" (Lev. 25:23). This idea is associated with the conception of the land of Canaan as Yahweh's *naᵃlâ* (Dt. 4:21,38; 12:9; 15:4; 19:10; 20:16; 21:23; 24:4; 25:19; 1 S. 26:19; 2 S. 14:16; Jer. 2:7; 16:18; 50:11; Ps. 68:10[9]; 79:1; 105:11 [par. 1 Ch. 16:18]; Ps. 135:11f.) or *'ᵃḥuzzâ* (Josh. 22:19; cf. Lev. 14:34; Dt. 32:49). Gerhard von Rad rightly assigns "the laws concerning firstlings, tenths, the leaving of gleanings, and so on," "the proscriptions of any kind of cultic defilement of the land," including the details of the Jubilee Year, to this cultic conception.[76] The question whether the cultic conception, "as against the historical conception, which is undoubtedly an ancient Yahwistic one," is of Canaanite origin von Rad rightly answers in the negative.[77] It is true that for Canaanite religion Baʿal is the proprietor of the land — or, more precisely, of the earth. This feature of Baʿalism, however, had universalistic features; it was never limited to a single people, like the notion that the land of Canaan is Yahweh's property. Besides this contrast between the universalism of the Canaanite idea and the particularism of the Israelite idea, there is a further difference: the so-called cultic conception presupposes the occupation of the land by Yahweh, for the land had to become Yahweh's property before he could give it to Israel as an inheritance.

The two clusters of ideas are linked in such passages as Dt. 1:8, where Yahweh gives the land to Israel, thus treating it as his own possession, while at the same time commanding Israel to enter the land and take possession of it according to the oath to the fathers.

The last question we shall discuss in this context is whether these differing conceptions can be associated with different boundaries of the promised land. We have already seen that P identifies Canaan with the territory west of the Jordan; Ezekiel follows the same line (Ezk. 48). Deuteronomy, too, shares this interpretation, even though it is noteworthy that Dt. 12:20; 19:8 look forward to an expansion of the land of Israel. It remains dubious whether this expectation is connected with the historical situation of, say, the time of Josiah or is purely hypothetical, possibly reflecting earlier notions, and whether the territory east of the Jordan is included in either case. Such early conceptions might include above all the ideology of J. The Jacob narratives, which are set in Gilead, locate the definition of the boundary between Jacob and Laban here, as well as the solemn renaming of Jacob as Israel; Gilead becomes Israel's land, although there is no promise of land to Jacob/Israel associated with Penuel. Even if there were, this would not decide the question of whether the territory east of the Jordan is also part of Canaan. Even if the text of Josh. 22 is based on an ancient narrative concerning the exclusive claims of the sanctuary at Shiloh (even in the territory east of the Jordan), or a narrative recounting the efforts of the

76. Pp. 87-89.
77. P. 88.

people living there to be recognized as worshippers of Yahweh and thus be accounted full members of Israel,[78] this would not merely indicate tensions between the people to the east and to the west of the Jordan — which are known from other sources — but would also suggest that the question whether the territory east of the Jordan constituted part of Israel was decided only over the course of history, so that originally the promised land was limited to the west bank of the Jordan and was consequently identical with Canaan. If so, this core of Josh. 22 probably antedates J. Since the so-called cultic conception is evident in Josh. 22, identification of Canaan with the promised land west of the Jordan would be associated with this conception, while the historical conception would be associated with the historical schema of J.

III. Canaanites.

1. *Civilization.* The appraisal of the land of Canaan in the various strata of the OT speaks not only of its fertility — the result of rain and groundwater — but also of cities, houses, cisterns, fortresses, and household goods that came into Israelite possession from the hands of the Canaanites. Such statements should make us aware that cultural achievements constitute an essential characteristic of the concept of Canaan.[79] This is the more remarkable in view of the general political fragmentation and ethnic variety of the Canaanite population, who dwelt in more or less independent city-states.[80] The complex situation is reflected in the lists that include other population groups along with the Canaanites. The unifying element holding this politically and ethnically diverse entity together was, in the broadest, a common culture, which can be called a settled urban culture based primarily on agriculture and trade. In its most characteristic form, it remained limited to western Palestine and the Phoenician coast and never included the interior of Syria, so that from around the beginning of the second millennium we can speak of an independent Canaanite cultural domain.[81]

The elements defining this civilization include on the one hand a language with common syntactic, stylistic, and metrical features (cf. Isa. 19:18; also 2 K. 18:26,28; Isa. 36:11,13; Neh. 13:24; 2 Ch. 32:18), the independence of which was underscored by the development of the alphabet at Ugarit and the spread of this alphabet to Palestine, and on the other a socio-political structure that might be described as feudal, within which the monarchy and senate of nobles constituted the ruling class and the populace, including slaves, constituted the subject class, held together less by bonds of blood and family than by the special interests of each group.[82] Not the least important expression

---

78. Josh. 22 is discussed by C. Steuernagel, "Jahwe, der Gott Israels," *Studien zur semitischen Philologie und Religionsgeschichte. Festschrift J. Wellhausen. BZAW,* 27 (1914), 329-349, esp. 346f.; Aharoni, 76; most recently, O. Eissfeldt, "Monopol-Ansprüche des Heiligtums von Silo," *OLZ,* 68 (1973), 327-333.

79. Cf. most recently Dietrich.

80. Already noted by Böhl, 97f.

81. Cf. Alt, *KlSchr,* III, 31, 37; Fohrer, *ThLZ,*78 (1953), 196; Noth, *Aufsätze,* II, 231f.; Gray, *The Canaanites,* 16; above all Kenyon, 3-5, 33-35, 51f.

82. Gray, *The Canaanites,* 139-183; Eissfeldt, *CAH*^{3}, II/2, 540ff.; de Vaux, *Early History,* I, 139-143.

of this society is its law, which Alt has accurately described as casuistic law on the basis of formal and substantial criteria.

2. *Religion.* A major element of Canaanite civilization was their unique religion, which the texts from Ugarit have made known to us in a way that previous generations could never have imagined. This religion is defined on the one hand by the deities of its pantheon, including above all the male deities El, Baʿal, Dagon, and Yam, and the female deities Asherah, ʿAnat, and Astarte. On the other hand, this religion is shaped by the cult practiced at the sanctuaries with their temples and cultic installations during the great annual festivals and on other appropriate occasions and reflected in a variety of ceremonies.[83] The fundamental core of this polytheistic popular religion was the renewal of life and the guaranteeing of fertility,[84] although moral and ethical considerations were not entirely foreign to it[85] and there were even trends in the direction of a practical monotheism.[86]

3. *Appraisal.* When we come to the Israelites' attitude toward the Canaanites, we shall first mention a few passages that are simple statements of fact. Gen. 12:6; 13:7, for example, tell the reader with historical accuracy that in the time of Abraham and even afterwards "the Canaanites were in the land" or were "the inhabitants of the land" (Gen. 24:3,37; 50:11). Nu. 14:43 states that the Amalekites and Canaanites were the previous possessors of Hormah. Nothing in the narratives of the Hexateuch suggests that the land of Canaan was not settled. Indeed, it is striking how the narratives in Genesis[87] describe the patriarchs as respecting the Canaanites as possessors of the land and avoiding (or at least attempting to avoid) any action that would have disturbed this peaceful coexistence (cf. Gen. 34:30); all land, for example, was acquired solely by purchase (cf. Gen. 23:3-20; 33:19).

This cautious relationship between the patriarchs and the Canaanites made it possible and easy for the new arrivals to adopt Canaanite civilization, thus beginning a process that lasted well into the history of Israel and was never completely finished, although Israel sensed the difference between nomadic life and settlement as long as it dwelt in Palestine. Canaanite civilization showed itself to be so strong that it was able to absorb the new influences, as it had done already in the case of the Hurrians and Hyksos, and was to do again in the case of the Philistines. In particular, this means that the Israelites adopted the agriculture and urban civilization of Canaan as rapidly as its language and forms of expression; the Hebrew of the OT represents a hybrid combining Canaanite with the language of the immigrants. Examples from the legal realm include a portion

---

83. Cf. Albright, *From the Stone Age to Christianity* (Garden City, 1957), 175-79; *Yahweh,* 104-132; Eissfeldt, *HO,* I/VIII, 1/1; Gray, *The Canaanites,* 66-89, 119-138; Fohrer, "Religion"; de Vaux, *Early History,* I, 139-152.

84. Fohrer, *ThLZ,* 78 (1953), 196.

85. Gray, *The Canaanites,* 135-38.

86. O. Eissfeldt, *El im ugaritischen Pantheon. BSAW,* 98/4 (1951), 60-70.

87. Cf. esp. van Selms, 202-212.

of the Covenant Code (Ex. 20:22–23:13) and the instructions in Lev. 19:23-25. In the artistic realm, we might cite the ivories from Samaria, which resemble in many respects the Canaanite ivories from Megiddo.[88]

In the religious and cultic realm, the situation is not basically different. According to the Genesis narratives, the patriarchs participated in the indigenous cult of the various local sanctuaries, and Abraham paid due reverence to the God of Melchizedek at Jerusalem. Later the Israelites borrowed the temple cult with its priestly hierarchy, music, sacrificial system, and calendar of feasts.[89] This broad acceptance of Canaanite civilization and religion was for the most part felt to be quite natural; it is therefore all the more remarkable that the patriarchal narratives insist so emphatically that Isaac and Jacob must under no circumstances take wives from among the Canaanite women (Gen. 24:3,37; 28:1,6,8; contrast Esau: 36:2). The patriarchs could enjoy commercial relations with the Canaanites, but not intermarriage.

No reason is stated for this prohibition. We might conclude that it grew out of hostility toward the Canaanite fertility cult, arguing that the wife, standing in special need of the blessing bestowed by the deities responsible for a multitude of offspring, was much more vulnerable than her husband to the danger of slipping into worship of these Canaanite gods. That this did indeed take place is suggested by archaeological excavations that have discovered amulets of female deities in early Israelite strata. We must nevertheless remember that the sociological barriers separating the patriarchs as well as the later Israelites from the Canaanites never disappeared fully, despite all cordial relations. In contrast to the feudal society of the Canaanites, Israel always retained a lively sense of the "interrelationship of the tribes and of their alienation from their other neighbors,"[90] even if its intensity varied. In later Israel, this fundamental awareness was based on such religio-historical institutions as the covenant with Yahweh: it therefore represents an outgrowth of Yahwism. A similar situation may have obtained in the pre-Palestinian period of the patriarchs, characterized by the worship of the "God of the fathers," which later coalesced with the El cult of Canaan. Its basic feature was the bond between clan and deity. Blood relationship was of preeminent significance for the religion of the patriarchs. It is therefore probably right to see in the religious convictions of the patriarchal period the ultimate basis for the prohibition against intermarriage with the Canaanites, whether or not one thinks in terms of Baʿal and Astarte figures.

Both Judah and Simeon appear to have fallen victim to the temptation of being "canaanized," if only to a limited extent, at least in the early period. An ancient narrative in Gen. 38 says (v. 2) that Judah married a Canaanite woman named Shua (cf. 1 Ch. 2:3). Gen. 46:10; Ex. 6:15 indicate that the mother of one of Simeon's sons was a Canaanite woman (cf. also Nu. 25:14). This establishes a genealogical rela-

---

88. Cf. Eissfeldt, *CAH*³, II, XXXIV, 25, 27f.

89. Cf. Albright, *Yahweh and the Gods of Canaan,* 169-171; Eissfeldt, *CAH*³, II, XXXIV, 28f.; *idem,* "Israelitisch-jüdische Religion," 233-35; Fohrer, "Israels Haltung," 65-75.

90. Alt, *Essays,* 233.

tionship with Canaanite civilization on the part of two of the groups constituting greater Judah — the most important two, because they became part of the twelve-tribe system.

In the time of the patriarchs, then, relationships between the indigenous population and the new element were cordial, at least to some degree. In greater Judah, early Israelite groups lived side by side with the Canaanites; intermarriage was not ruled out in principle. But when we come to the Yahweh theophany in the setting of the exodus, we find categorical statements that the Canaanites are to be fought, driven out, put to the ban, or enslaved, and that there must be no ties between them and the Israelites. Jgs. 1:1,3,5 speak of fighting against the Canaanites; 5:19 (cf. Ps. 135:11) speaks of fighting "the kings of Canaan." We are told that fear and trembling seized "all the inhabitants of Canaan" (Ex. 15:15) or "all the kings of the Canaanites" (Josh. 5:1). Yahweh is described as driving out the Canaanites in Ex. 23:28,29f.; 33:2 (*grš* piel); 34:11 (*grš* qal); Dt. 7:1 (*nšl*); Josh. 3:10 (*yrš* hiphil). Israel is the subject of *yrš* hiphil in Nu. 33:52 and of the negated verb (with occasional reference to later servitude) in Josh. 16:10; 17:12f.; Jgs. 1:27-33 (cf. Gen. 9:25-27; Neh. 9:24). Dt. 7:2; 20:17 (cf. Nu. 21:2; Josh. 11:11) are convinced that the Canaanites must be "utterly destroyed." Josh. 17:18 blames the iron chariots of the Canaanites for the failure[91] of the Israelite tribes to drive them out (*yrš*) of the cities. In Ex. 23:29f. (*grš* piel), the Canaanites are driven out over the course of many years, lest the land become desolate and turn into the playground of wild beasts (cf. Jgs. 2:22–3:2, discussed above). In the same spirit, Josh. 2 seeks to account for the survival of the clan of Rahab the harlot (Josh. 6:17) and Josh. 9 explains the survival of the Gibeonites. The attitude of the Israelites toward the Canaanites finds its most emphatic expression in the repeated prohibition against any kind of participation in the Canaanite cult.[92] In J, we read: "You shall not bow down to their gods, not serve them, nor do as they do" (Ex. 23:24). Ex. 34:12-16 elaborates on this basic prohibition: the Israelites must not make a covenant with the inhabitants of the land, because such a covenant obviously means participation in the alien Canaanite religion and adoption of Canaanite cultic practices as well as intermarriage, implying recognition of the Canaanites as equal partners. Instead, their cultic sites (altars, pillars, Asherim) are to be destroyed.

E likewise stresses that Israel must make no covenant with the Canaanites and their deities (Ex. 23:32). In the language of Dt. 7:2-5, the command to destroy the Canaanites reads: "You shall carry out the ban against them." In particular, this means: (1) making no covenant with them, which would protect them (v. 2); (2) refusing to make marriages with them, because this would mean recognizing their deities (vv. 3f.); and (3) destroying their altars, pillars, Asherim, and graven images (v. 5). P, finally, merely orders the destruction of their *maśkiyyôṯ, ṣalmê massēḵôṯ,* and *bāmôṯ* (Nu. 33:52).

---

91. Cf. *BHS*.
92. Cf. Jaroš.

The core of these prohibitions is the irreconcilable conflict between Israel's worship of Yahweh and the Canaanite fertility cult — in short, between Yahweh and Baʿal. The stages of this struggle between Yahwism and the Canaanite theology of divine immanence are marked by Nu. 25; Jgs. 6:25-32; 1 K. 18; and Hosea. Extensive periods in the history of Israel's religion bear the stamp of this interplay. Despite Israel's radical rejection of the Canaanites' immanent conception of the deity, many elements of Canaanite religion infiltrated the concept of Yahweh and enriched the faith of Israel.[93]

Ps. 106:38 speaks of "the blood of their sons and daughters, whom they sacrificed to the idols of Canaan," probably an explanatory gloss to v. 38a. In the Holiness Code, the parenetic introduction to the laws governing marriage and virginity singles out as abominations to be shunned by the Israelites not only the customs of Egypt but above all "the practice of the land of Canaan" (Lev. 18:3); the section concludes with a long-winded passage castigating "the defilement of the pagans," whom Yahweh will cast out before Israel, and "all these abominations" practiced by the inhabitants of the land (vv. 24-30). This passage may have led exegetes to read Gen. 9:20-27 in the same sense, seeing in the heinous transgression of Noah's youngest son Canaan an example of "immodesty," and in "the sexual depravity of the Canaanites"[94] "aetiologically the true reason for their defeat before the invading Israelites." It is true that the curse on Canaan reflects the political subjection of the Canaanites to the Israelites,[95] but it is incorrect to interpret that narrative basis of the curse literally (cf. Gen. 34; 35:21f. + 49:3f.,5-7; also Gen. 38).

None of these observations alters the fact that the Canaanites are also judged negatively elsewhere in the OT. Jerusalem is chastised for her origin "from the land of the Canaanites" (Ezk. 16:3), on which Walther Zimmerli comments: "For the religious consciousness of Israel, what was 'Canaanite' bore a strongly negative emphasis, indicating that which was rejected by Yahweh and indeed was even cursed."[96] In Hos. 12:8(7), the Canaanites are proverbial for their false balances and love of oppression. Later texts continue the derogatory usage: "land of Canaan" can mean "land of mercenaries" (Ezk. 16:29; 17:4), and "Canaanite" can mean "merchant" (Job 40:30[41:6]; Prov. 31:24; Isa. 23:8; Zec. 14:21). The very late text Isa. 19:18, however, describes five cities in Egypt as "swearing allegiance to Yahweh" and "speaking the language of Canaan."

Zobel

---

93. Cf., e.g., O. Eissfeldt, "Jahve und Baal," *KlSchr,* I (1962), 1-12.

94. Von Rad, *Genesis,* 132-34.

95. Mazar, *Untersuchungen,* 63-65; Rost, 46; for a different interpretation, see most recently Westermann, 485.

96. W. Zimmerli, *Ezekiel I. Herm* (Eng. trans. 1979), 337, citing Gen. 9:25.

כָּנָף *kānāp̱*

Contents: I. Etymology. II. Birds and Other Living Creatures. III. Symbolism. IV. Specialized Meanings. V. Dead Sea Scrolls. VI. LXX.

I. Etymology. The root *knp* is common Semitic.[1] Besides "wing," it can also mean "corner of a garment,"[2] "extreme edge" (Old South Arabic), "side, region" (Arabic), and "lap" (Judaeo-Aramaic). Isa. 30:20 contains the niphal of the denominative verb with the meaning "hide oneself" (cf. Arab. *kanafa,* "surround, protect").

II. Birds and Other Living Creatures. The noun *kānāp̱* appears in the singular, plural, and dual in the Pentateuch, the Prophets, and the Writings. Literally it means "wing" or, in phrases like *ʿôp̱/ṣippôr/baʿal kānāp̱,* "fowl" (e.g., Gen. 1:21; Ps. 148:10; Prov. 1:17). Particular mention is made of the wings of the eagle, ostrich, hawk, stork, falcon, and dove (e.g., Jer. 48:40; Job 39:13,26; Ps. 68:14[Eng. v. 13]). A bird may spread or beat its wings or have them torn off (Jer. 49:22; Isa. 10:14; Lev. 1:17). Synonyms include *'eḇrâ* (Dt. 32:11; Ps. 68:14[13]; 91:4; Job 39:13), *'ēḇer* (Ezk. 17:3), and Aram. *gap̱* (Dnl. 7:4,6). Isa. 18:1 uses "whirring wings" for the insect swarms of Ethiopia. Nebuchadnezzar and the Egyptian pharaoh are likened to eagles with "great wings" (Ezk. 17:3,7), as is the spreading devastation of the Moabites and Edomites (Jer. 48:40; 49:22). The silver and gold taken in battle make Israel gleam like the wings of a dove (Ps. 68:14[13]); dishonorable wealth, however, takes to itself wings and flies away like an eagle (Prov. 23:5). The cities ravaged by the Assyrians did not venture to defend themselves as a bird defends its nest by beating its wings (Isa. 10:14). In the day of salvation, Yahweh will once more enlarge the Davidic kingdom: it will be like a cedar under which "birds of every sort" (lit., "birds of every wing") will find peace and security (Ezk. 17:23).

"Winged" cherubim[3] stood in the holy of holies of the temple of Solomon; they were wooden figures some ten cubits tall, probably covered in part with gold leaf. They stood

---

kānāp̱. O. Eissfeldt, "Die Flügelsonne als künsterliches Motiv und als religiöses Symbol," *KlSchr,* II (1963), 416-19; F. C. Fensham, "Winged Gods and Goddesses in the Ugaritic Tablets," *OrAnt,* 5 (1966), 157-164; R. Gradwohl, *Die Farben im AT. BZAW,* 83 (1963); P. Joüon, " 'כָּנָף,' 'aile', employé figurément," *Bibl,* 16 (1935), 201-4; R. de Vaux, "Les chérubins et l'arche d'alliance, les sphinx gardiens et les trônes divins dans l'Ancien Orient," *Festschrift R. Monterde,* I. *MUSJ,* 37 (1960/61), 91-124 = *Bible et Orient* (Paris, 1967), 231-259; P. Welten, "Mischwesen," *BRL*², 224-27; A. S. van der Woude, "כָּנָף *kānāf* Flügel," *THAT,* I, 833-36.

1. P. Fronzaroli, "Studi sul lessico comune semitico. II:Anatomia e Fisiologia,"*AANLR,* N.S. 19 (1964), 274, 279; 23 (1968), 283.

2. *DISO,* 123.

3. → כרוב *kᵉrûḇ.*

side by side with their faces toward the entrance, wings outstretched (1 K. 6:23-27; 8:6f.; 2 Ch. 3:10-13; 5:7f.). No further details are given, but we may conjecture two erect "winged sphinxes," possibly with the body of an animal (lion?), two wings, and a human head.[4] They acted as guardians and protectors of the ark, which was situated beneath their wings (cf. *hassôḵēḵ* describing the cherub in Ezk. 28:14,16). Ex. 25:18ff.; 37:7ff. associate two small gilded cherubim with the cover (RSV "mercy seat") of the ark; they faced each other and spread their wings upward to protect the ark.

Ezk. 1 speaks of winged creatures having human form, which Ezk. 10 interprets as cherubim. Four such creatures bear God's throne. Each of them has four faces and four wings. With two wings they cover their entire body, while the other two are spread out above and touch the wings of the others (1:11). The noise of the wings is heard (1:24), and they can be seen rising and falling (10:16). A secondary passage (1:10; cf. 10:14) says that the four faces are those of a human being, a lion, an ox, and an eagle; the redactor conceives of the cherubim as hybrid creatures. The statement in v. 12 that their backs, hands, and wings are covered with eyes likewise comes from a later hand.

In the vision of Isaiah's call (Isa. 6:2), seraphim hover above the throne of God; the author conceives of them as a kind of royal household, spirits standing in the service of Yahweh. They should probably be pictured as six-winged serpents with human faces and hands.[5] Of their three pairs of wings, they use only one to fly; with the other two they show respect by covering their faces and "feet" (i.e., genitals). This description is clearly meant to emphasize the disparity between these creatures and the holy Lord. A "flying seraph" (RSV "serpent") is spoken of in parallel with *nāḥāš* (Isa. 14:29) and in conjunction with lion, lioness, and viper (30:6). The emblem of Nehushtan, worshipped in the Jerusalem temple, is also called a "seraph" (RSV "serpent") (Nu. 21:8). The six-winged guardian spirit of Tell Halaf carries two serpents in its hands, probably symbolizing its earlier animal form.[6] Borrowing the common fairy-tale motif of traveling through the air, the vision of Zec. 5:9 describes the ephah containing the sin and wickedness of Israel as being carried through the air to Babylon by two women with the wings of a stork. This motif appears also in Ex. 19:4 describing the steadfast love with which Yahweh bears Israel.

III. Symbolism. Ps. 18:8-16(7-15) par. 2 S. 22:8-16 is a powerful description of a theophany: earthquake, thunder and lightning, hail, and tempest herald the appearance of Yahweh. "Wings" symbolize the speed and violence of the onrushing storm. The "wings of the wind" stand in parallel with a winged "cherub" (Ps. 18:11[10] par. 2 S. 22:11; Ps. 104:3). The "wind with its wings" will seize and destroy idolatrous Ephraim (Hos. 4:19). No one can escape God's omnipresence, even by taking the wings of the dawn and flying from the extreme east to the west where the sun sets (Ps. 139:9). The

---

4. Cf. de Vaux, pls. 2ff.

5. Cf. G. R. Driver, "Isaiah 6:1: his train filled the temple," in H. Goedicke, ed., *Near Eastern Studies in Honor of W. F. Albright* (Baltimore, 1971), 87-96.

6. *ANEP,* no. 655.

winged sun-disk was a common conception in the ancient world:[7] from its wings (i.e., 'rays') comes healing (Mal. 3:20[4:2]). The text of Dnl. 9:27 ("on the wing of abomination shall come one who makes desolate") does not need to be emended; it suggests the sudden and unusually terrifying appearance of the destroyer. Hiding "in the shadow of God's wings" or "under (the shelter of) his wings" is a topos in individual laments as well as in confessions of faith and petitions (Ps. 17:8; 57:2[1]; 36:8[7]; 63:8[7]; 61:5[4]; 91:4; Ruth 2:12). God's wings protect the land and the people (Isa. 8:8; Dt. 32:11). The image undoubtedly derives from the way a bird protects its young; it also found expression in the conception of the winged deity.[8]

IV. Specialized Meanings. The typical biblical garment is a rectangular piece of cloth, which can be used and worn in various ways. Its corners are referred to as "wings." These corners may be grasped (1 S. 15:27;[9] Zec. 8:23), used to carry flesh or hair (Hag. 2:12; Ezk. 5:3), smeared with blood during a murder (Jer. 2:34), or cut off, as David did to Saul (1 S. 24:5,6,12[4,5,11]). The Israelites are to wear bluish-white tassels on the four corners of their outer garment (Nu. 15:38; Dt. 22:12).[10] The original apotropaic function of these tassels was given an artificial Yahwistic interpretation: the sight of these tassels is to remind Israel of Yahweh's commandments. To spread the corner of one's garment over a woman chosen as bride means to cover her nakedness, to marry her (Ruth 3:9; Ezk. 16:8). To uncover a man's garment means to interfere in his marriage. Dt. 23:1(22:30); 27:20 prohibit intercourse with the wife of a man's father (i.e., the man's stepmother), because to do so would "uncover the father's garment," i.e., desecrate his father's marriage. In a construct phrase with *hā'āreṣ, kānāp̱* means the (four) ends (Isa. 11:12; Ezk. 7:2; Job 37:3; 38:13) or edges of the earth (Isa. 24:16).

V. Dead Sea Scrolls. The Dead Sea scrolls speak of the *b^e^nê/'ôp̱ k̲ānāp̱* as well as the "wings of the wind" (1QM 10:14; 1QH 8:9; fr. 19:3). A new usage is represented by the "advancing spearheads and wings at both ends of the line of battle" (1QM 9:11; cf. Lat. *ala,* "wing [of an army]"). The Temple scroll uses *knp* 5 times, all of which reflect OT usage: "wings of the cherub" (11QT 7:11; cf. Ex. 25:20); five kinds of insects with "wings" that may be eaten (11QT 48:5, an expanded version of Lev. 11:21); "corners of a garment" (11QT 66:12f.; cf. Lev. 20:21; Dt. 23:1[22:30]); and 11QT 65:1, where the text is probably corrupt.

VI. LXX. In translating *kānāp̱,* the LXX clearly prefers *ptéryx* (66 times) and *pterýgion* (11 times); we also found the derivatives *pterōtós* (5 times) and *megaloptérygos* (twice).

Dommershausen

---

7. Eissfeldt, 416; *AOB,* 307-311, 331-33; P. Welten, "Siegel und Stempel," *BRL*², 300-303.

8. *AOB,* 35, 197, 258; Fensham, 157ff.

9. On the magical significance of the hem of a garment, see D. Conrad, "Samuel und die Mari-'Propheten'," *XVII. Deutscher Orientalistentag, Vorträge. ZDMG Sup.,* 1 (1969), I, 273-280; R. A. Brauner, " 'To Grasp the Hem' and 1 Sam 17:27," *JANES,* 6 (1974), 35-38.

10. Gradwohl, 71f.

כִּסֵּא *kissē'*

Contents: I. 1. Etymology and Distribution; 2. Mesopotamia; 3. Ugarit; 4. Egypt; 5. Aram and Phoenicia. II. OT: 1. Distribution; 2. Related Words; 3. LXX. III. 1. Everyday Life; 2. The Throne of David; 3. The Throne of Solomon; 4. Righteousness as the Foundation of the Throne; 5. Thrones of Kings and Princes; 6. Priestly Throne? 7. Enthronement Ceremonial. IV. Yahweh's Throne: 1. Ark; 2. Temple; 3. Zion/Jerusalem; 4. Heaven; 5. Chariot Throne. V. Metaphorical Usage: 1. Enthronement; 2. Deposition; 3. Exaltation; 4. Mourning; 5. Harlot's Throne. VI. Dead Sea Scrolls.

I. 1. *Etymology and Distribution.* The root *ks'* is amply attested in almost all the Semitic languages, where it represents two groups of meanings: "full moon"[1] and "throne." Like the Sumerian loanword GU.ZA,[2] "seat," *kissē'* in the sense of "throne" goes back to Old Akk. *kussû (kussiu),* "chair, throne," also "saddle" and "part of the liver,"[3] which may derive from a root **ksī,* "tie (reeds) together." The root appears in Ugaritic as *ksu̇, ksi,* and *ks',* "throne, seat, saddle."[4] Also ancient are the Phoenician occurrences of *ks'* in the sarcophagus inscriptions of Aḥiram from Byblos (*ca.* 1000

---

kissē'. H. S. Baker, *Furniture in the Ancient World* (London, 1966); O. R. Blosser, *A Study of "the Throne of David" Motif in the Hebrew Bible* (diss., Univ. of Wisconsin, 1975); H. Brunner, "Gerechtigkeit als Fundament des Thrones," *VT,* 8 (1958), 426-28; F. Canciani and G. Pettinato, "Salomos Thron, philologische und archäologische Erwägungen," *ZDPV,* 81 (1965), 88-108; F. Gössmann, " 'Scabellum Pedum Tuorum,' " *Divinitas,* 11 (1967), 31-53; M. Haran, "The Ark and the Cherubim," *IEJ,* 9 (1959), 30-38, 89-94; A. Hug, "Thron," *PW,* VI A, 613-18; J. J. Jackson, "David's Throne: Patterns in the Succession Story," *CJT,* 11 (1965), 183-195; W. Krebs, "Der sitzende Gott," *ThZ,* 30 (1974), 1-10; K. P. Kuhlmann, *Der Thron im Alten Ägypten. ADAI.Ä,* 10 (1977); H. Kyrieleis, *Throne und Klinen. JDAISup,* 24 (1969); M. Metzger, "Himmlische und irdische Wohnstatt Jahwes," *UF,* 2 (1970), 139-158; *idem, Königsthron und Gottesthron. AOAT,* 15 (1985); A. Salonen, *Die Möbel des Alten Mesopotamien nach sumerisch-akkadischen Quellen. AnAcScFen,* 127 (1963); H. H. Schmidt, "Kerubenthron und Lade," Εὐχαριστήριον. *Festschrift H. Gunkel,* I. *FRLANT,* 19[36] (1923), 120-144; O. Schmitz, "θρόνος," *TDNT,* III, 160-67; A. van Selms, "A Guest-Room for Ilu and its Furniture," *UF,* 7 (1975), 469-476; H. Seyrig, "Thrônes phéniciens flanqués de sphinx," *Antiquités syriennes. Syr,* 36 (1959), 38-89, esp. 51f.; H. Weippert, "Möbel. 4," *BRL*², 231f.; P. Welten, "Lade — Tempel — Jerusalem," *Textgemäss. Festschrift E. Würthwein* (Göttingen, 1979), 169-183.

1. Cf. M. Dahood, "Hebrew-Ugaritic Lexicography III," *Bibl,* 46 (1965), 330; also F. Vattioni, "Miscellanea Biblica," *Aug,* 8 (1968), 382ff.

2. *ŠL,* 52. M. Ellenbogen notes the Sumerian verb GUZ, "to cower, to squat, to be lowered"; *Foreign Words in the OT* (London, 1962), 89.

3. Cf. I. J. Gelb, *Glossary of Old Akkadian. MAD,* III (1957), 152; *AHw,* I (1965), 5-15; *CAD,* VIII (1971), 587-593; on *u* > *i,* see V. Christian, *Untersuchungen zur Laut- und Formenlehre des Hebräischen. SAW,* Phil.-hist. Kl., 228/2 (1953), 15.

4. *WUS,* no. 1351; *UT,* no. 1277.

B.C.),[5] of Kilamuwa from Zinjirli (*ca.* 825)[6] and of Azitawadda from Karatepe (*ca.* 720).[7] Neo-Punic *ks'h* is found in inscription no. 28 from Tripoli.[8]

In the Aramaic language group, dissimilation of the geminated sibilant *ss* resulting in the consonant sequence *rs*[9] led to the morpheme *krs.* Fraenkel[10] rejects treating the medial *r* as secondary, preferring to treat it as an original element of the root. The proposed relationship between this morpheme and Akk. *kurṣu,* "fetter,"[11] is ruled out by the differing spirants.

The earliest occurrences in Old Aramaic (*krs'*) are found in the third Sefire stela (prior to 740)[12] and the stela of Barrākib from Sam'al (*ca.* 730).[13] The word also appears in Imperial Aramaic, Egyptian Aramaic,[14] Jewish Aramaic, and Biblical Aramaic;[15] and we find *kissē',* "seat, chair, throne," in Middle Hebrew.[16] The term *g/ksy',* "throne," is found in the Aramaic and Middle Persian *Frahang i-pahlavik,* where it appears in parallel with *'ršy,* "bed, divan."[17] Whether Phoen. *krsy*[18] is related to our root is hotly debated.

Syr. *kûrs^{e}yā'* means "throne, head of a region," specifically "episcopal see";[19] a similar meaning is found in Christian Palestinian Aramaic. Mand. *kursia,* also miswritten *kurṣia,* can mean both "throne" and "cathedra."[20] In Arabic, *kursî* denotes the "throne, seat, chair" of God, the ruler, or a bride, but also an "academic chair" and (by metonymy) "(royal) residence."[21]

In South Semitic, Tigre *kursî* means "small bed, seat." Tigr. *kōras,*[22] Mehri *karsī,* Shauri *kersí,* and Soq. *korsiy* all mean "throne."[23] Harari *kursi* means "chair, stand on which the Koran is placed while one recites it."[24]

---

5. *KAI,* 1.2.
6. *KAI,* 24.9.
7. *KAI,* 26.11.
8. Cf. G. Levi della Vida, "Die iscrizioni imperiali neo-puniche di Leptis Magna," *Africa Italiana,* 6 (1935), 1-29.
9. Cf. H. Bauer and P. Leander, *Grammatik des Biblisch-Aramäischen* (1927, repr. Hildesheim, 1962), §§13f.; *VG,* I, 243ff.
10. M. Fraenkel, "Bemerkungen zum hebräischen Wortschatz," *HUCA,* 31 (1960), 78f.
11. *AHw,* I, 512; cf. *LexLingAram,* 86.
12. *KAI,* 224, 17.
13. *KAI,* 216, 7.
14. Cf. *AP,* 6, 2; Ahikar 133.
15. *DISO,* 127; *LexLingAram,* 86f.; *WTM,* II, 412.
16. *WTM,* II, 361f.
17. Cf. E. Ebeling, *Das aramäisch-mittelpersische Glossar Frahang-i-pahlavik im Lichte der assyriologischen Forschung. MAOG,* 14/1 (1941, repr. 1972), 10.
18. *CIS,* I, 22; 44, 2; 88, 3, 5, 6.
19. *LexSyr,* 348.
20. *MdD,* 209.
21. *WKAS,* I, 126f.
22. *TigrWb,* 399a.
23. W. Leslau, *Lexique soqotri* (Paris, 1938), 226.
24. W. Leslau, *Etymological Dictionary of Harari* (Berkeley, 1969), 94.

2. *Mesopotamia.* In Mesopotamia, stools, chairs, and thrones are attested in great numbers in every era, especially in pictorial representations. The parallel influence of Egypt in the Amarna period makes it highly likely that the Mesopotamian artifacts resembled their Egyptian counterparts. Besides *kussû,* we find *durgarû,* "chair of state" (of a king or deity), *gišgallu* and *mūšabu,* "seat, throne," *kibsu,* "stool," *littu* and *matqanu,* "footstool," and *dakkannu,* "bench."[25]

a. *Form.* Mesopotamian art illustrates the broad outlines of typological development. In the prehistoric period, people sat without distinction on the ground or on mats. Later, when thrones were introduced, those seated higher were accorded higher social status. As early as the Jemdet Naṣr period, bundles of reeds served as the earliest form of stool. Beginning with the Ur III period, we find the first cubical wooden stools.[26] Later, the stool developed typologically into a chair through the addition of a high back; armrests led to the development of the armchair (*kussû nēmedi*). This completed the formal development of the object; subsequently, variations appear only in the choice of materials, ornamentation, and the addition of a base.

Even in the Old Babylonian period, more than thirty native kinds of wood (*eṣṣu*) are mentioned as materials (esp. *ušû,* "ebony"), besides precious varieties that had to be imported. Later we find reeds, rushes, and palm fiber.[27] Thrones included pads and cushions made of skin or leather, as well as fabric covers. They might be painted, overlaid with precious metals, or decorated with gems or ivory. The legs terminated in "feet" — in Mesopotamia usually in the form of an ox's hoof instead of the lion's paw common in Egypt.[28] We sometimes find precise theriomorphic differentiation between forelegs and hind legs; this distinction shows that the person seated upon the throne was conceived of as being borne by a strong animal, attesting to his power and guarding him against enemies.

The legs of Assyrian thrones terminated in stylized pine cones, which played an important role in blessing rituals. The legs of Sumerian, Babylonian, Urartian, and Egyptian thrones, however, came at an early date to be shaped like the feet of lions or other animals, symbolically intensifying the exaltation provided by the throne. In the eighth century, we find human figures supporting the armrests; cf. the personification of conquered nations in the registers of Achaemenid throne architecture.

b. *Terminology.* Chairs or thrones belonged to the category of "household furnishings" (Sum. *nig-ga,* Akk. *makkūru, unūtu*), which included chairs, stools, beds, tables, jars, and spoons.[29] Like the king (*šarru*), judges, armorers, and mariners had their appointed seats. The right to a seat could be granted (e.g., to a high military rank[30]) or

25. Cf. Salonen.
26. *ANEP,* 637.
27. *ANEP,* 24.
28. Salonen, 87.
29. Salonen, 16ff.
30. J.-R. Kupper, *Correspondance de Baḫdilim. ARM,* VI (1953), 69 r.10.

taken away (e.g., from a judge[31]). Highly ornate were the *kussî puḫri,* "chair of the judicial council," and the *kussî pitḫurti,* "chair of the assembly," which sometimes were decorated with gold and covered with fabric.

c. *Magic.* In some cases, magical notions were associated with chairs and thrones.[32] A *kussû eṭemmē,* "chair of the departed spirit," might be set up for a dead member of the family,[33] and a concubine would place the chair of a childless wife in the temple.[34] A *kussû* could also serve as witness to an oath.[35]

d. *Royal Ceremonial.* The *kussû* naturally played its most important role in Mesopotamian royal ceremonial. The year of accession constituted a chronological baseline (cf. Est. 1:2).[36] The "king's throne" (*kussî šarri*) or "throne of royalty" (*kussî šarrūti*) together with tiara (*agû*) and scepter (*ḫaṭṭu*) constituted the royal regalia.[37] The king received the acclamation of his subjects while seated on his throne.[38] Sennacherib had his throne set up before Lachish to review the spoils taken from the city.[39] Sargon's throne, likewise, was set up before the city gate so that he could witness the battle;[40] seated on his golden throne, he is described as being "like a god."[41] During military expeditions, the king was carried to the battlefield in a "litter" (*kussû ša ḫarrāni, kussî serdê, šadittu*). The throne and above all sitting upon it were thus symbols of power. In Egypt, this symbolism took concrete form in the design of the footstool; in Mesopotamia, however, the throne itself retained the symbolic associations: the throne of Darius, for example, was borne by twenty-eight representatives of conquered nations.[42]

"Place someone on the throne" (*wašābu* Š) means "give power to"; "ascend the throne" (*elû, erēbu, ṣabātu*), "possess the throne" (*kullu* II[43]), and "sit upon the throne" (*wašābu*; Assyr. also *kammu*) mean "have power." Contrariwise, "topple someone from the throne" (*ubbuku*) means the end of power (also with respect to deities). In dynastic succession, the father "places" (*ašābu*[44]) his son upon the throne; the son,

---

31. CH §5, 24.
32. Šurpu, II, 101; *CT,* 28, 5.
33. Salonen, 65.
34. R. Harris, "The Case of Three Babylonian Marriage Contracts," *JNES,* 33 (1974), 365 and n. 2.
35. Cf. Šurpu, III, 147.
36. E. Weidner, *Die Inscriften Tukulti-Ninurtas I. und seiner Nachfolger. BAfO,* 12 (1959), 26, 30.
37. Cf. G. Dossin, *Correspondance féminine. ARM,* X (1978), 10.14; also *CAD,* VIII (1971), 591f.
38. *MVAG,* 41, 3, II, 4.
39. Salonen, 84.
40. EA 359, r. 10; cf. Jer. 1:15; A. F. Rainey, *El Amarna Tablets 359-379.* AOAT, 8 (1970), 77.
41. EA 359, r. 14.
42. Salonen, 285.
43. I. J. Gelb, "Two Assyrian King Lists," *JNES,* 13 (1954), 218, 36.
44. A. Goetze, *Old Babylonian Omen Texts. YOSBT,* 10 (1947), 31, 9, etc.; *CAD,* VIII, 591.

conversely, "receives" (*ṣabātu*[45]) the throne from his father. But possession of the throne became a subject of conflict even in the Old Babylonian period.[46] In a series of Late Babylonian prophecies, the present occupant of the throne is threatened with such a change of throne (power).[47] Kingship is manifested in the throne, so that *kussû* can be synonymous with "power, dominion." When the king has shed blood, his throne is defiled (*lā taqnat,* lit., "it is not in order") (cf. 2 S. 14:9).[48] Kings were aware of the divine origin of their kingship, and Sargon could say: He [= the deity] gave me *ḫaṭṭu, kussû,* and *agû.*"[49] Possibly the ritual of placing the tiara of Marduk upon the throne during the Neo-Assyrian coronation ritual was intended to reflect the sovereignty of the gods.[50] At Mari, the god Hadad says: "I possess the throne, the lands, and the city."[51] In many Neo-Assyrian and Neo-Babylonian blessing formulas, the gods are asked to grant the king eternal dominion[52] or secure the continuance of his throne.[53] We also find the opposite: "May the gods take scepter and throne away from him (Sennacherib)!"[54]

e. *Cult.* The phrases *kussû elletu,* "holy chair," and *kussû parṣi* or *kussû ša qīšti,* "cultic chair," suggest a cultic function, as does the association of *kussû* with the name of a deity.[55] Such thrones for gods were set up in temples. Precious thrones of lapis lazuli, gold, silver, or ivory are found as votive offerings.[56] One text[57] describes the ritual construction of three thrones (for Ea, Šamaš, and Marduk) and their "investiture" with purple and linen. The erection of such a divine throne — "establishment of the foundation of the divine throne"[58] — clearly exhibits the features of a cultic institution (cf. Jer. 49:38). Sacrifices were offered to such thrones; they were anointed, sprinkled with holy water, and consecrated.[59]

The deity was expected to be present with the throne, even though there might also be a throne "set up in the gleaming heaven."[60] A Neo-Babylonian document from

---

45. *AHw,* III (1981), 1067.
46. Goetze, 31, I, 53.
47. Šumma izbu, XVIII, 63, etc.
48. *CCT,* 4, 30a, 14.
49. H. W. F. Saggs, "Historical Texts and Fragments of Sargon II of Assyria. I: The 'Aššur Charter,'" *Iraq,* 37 (1975), 14, 35; cf. A. W. Sjoberg, "in-nin šà-gur$_4$-ra: A Hymn to the Goddess Inanna by the en-Priestess Enḫeduanna," *ZA,* N.S. 31[65] (1975), 192, 142, of Ishtar.
50. *MVAG,* 41/3, 10, II, 16.
51. Citations from A. Lods, "Une tablette inédite de Mari," *Studies in OT Prophecy. Festschrift T. H. Robinson* (New York, 1950), 103-110.
52. *CAD,* VIII, 592.
53. *ABRT,* 1, 9, 7.
54. D. D. Luckenbill, *The Annals of Sennarcherib. OIP,* 2 (1924), 131, VI, 82.
55. *ARM,* X, 52, 12.
56. M. L. Burke, *Textes Administratifs de la Salle 111 du Palais. ARM,* XI (1963), 57, 7.
57. *BBR,* 31-37, II, 20.
58. Gudea E, VIII, 2f.; Salonen, 75.
59. J. Læssøe, "A Prayer to Ea, Shamash, and Marduk, from Hama," *Iraq,* 18 (1956), 62, 20.
60. E. G. Perry, *Hymnen und Gebete an Sin. LSS,* 2/4 (1907), no. 5a, 2.

Sippar concerning the building of a temple[61] graphically identifies the god's throne in the temple with his heavenly throne.[62] Thrones were depicted iconographically as temples from the earliest Sumerian period onward.[63]

Several figurines apparently represent enthroned deities:[64] pegs on the bottom of the figurines or linen cords running over their knees[65] suggest that they were associated with thrones.[66] The worship of empty thrones at the same time points to a certain degree of abstraction in the notion of divine presence.[67]

3. *Ugarit.*

a. *Terminology.* In Ugaritic we find alongside *ksʾ,* "throne, chair,"[68] the synonyms *nḫt,* "cushion" (par. *ksʾ*),[69] *kḥṯ,* "chair" (with *ksʾ*),[70] and *ʾlt,* "piece of furniture for sitting (?)."[71]

b. *Divine Thrones.* The noun *ksʾ,* "throne," appears 30 times in the Ugaritic corpus (plus 9 occurrences in reconstructed texts). The battle among the gods Baʿal, Yam, and Mot for sovereignty over all the gods is a struggle for the *ksʾ mlk,* "throne of kingship,"[72] and *kḥt drk,* "seat of sovereignty."[73] The throne is the ruler's center of power; here he pronounces his threats against rivals.[74] To "occupy" (*ywḫd ksʾ*) this throne,[75] "ascend" (*yrd*) it,[76] or "sit upon" it (*yṯb*)[77] is synonymous with "being king." The weaker contender is "driven" (*grš*) from the throne;[78] he must "depart" from the throne (*mr lksʾ*).[79] In this scenario of divine battle, the radical termination of a particular regime is described by a

61. *AOB,* 322.
62. Cf. Metzger, *UF,* 2 (1970), 141f.
63. *Ibid.,* 149, n. 31.
64. *ANEP,* 497.
65. *ANEP,* 826.
66. Cf. P. Welten, "Götterbild, männliches," *BRL*², 105; *idem,* "Göttergruppe," *BRL*², 122.
67. Cf. O. Keel, *Jahwe-Visionen und Siegelkunst. SBS,*84/85 (1977), 37-45.
68. *UT,* no. 1277; *WUS,* no. 1351.
69. *KTU,* 1.1 IV, 24; 1.6 V, 5; 1.22 I, 18; cf. S. Rin, "Ugaritic — OT Affinities," *BZ,* N.S. 7 (1963), 24f.
70. *KTU,* 1.1 IV, 24; 1.2 IV, 12, 20; 1.6 V, 5; 1.22 I, 18; cf. esp. H. Donner, "Ugaritismen in der Psalmenforschung," *ZAW,* 79 (1967), 349, who cites *kaḫšu* in apposition with *kussû* in EA 120, 18.
71. *KTU,* 1.6 VI, 27f.; J. C. de Moor, *The Seasonal Pattern in the Ugaritic Myth of Baʿlu. AOAT,* 16 (1971), 236. See below for further discussion.
72. For parallels, see M. C. Astour, "Place Names," *RSP,* II, 299.
73. *KTU,* 1.1 IV, 24; 1.3 IV, 2; 1.6 V, 5; 1.6 VI, 33; 1.10 III, 13.
74. *KTU,* 1.2 IV, 7.
75. *KTU,* 1.22 I, 17; this reading follows *CTA*; cf. also J. Sanmartín Ascaso, "Semantisches über 'MR/'Sehen' und 'MR/'Sagen' im Ugaritischen," *UF,* 5 (1973), 269.
76. *KTU,* 1.2 III, 14; cf. G. Del Olmo Lete, "Notes on Ugaritic Semantics III," *UF,* 9 (1977), 46.
77. *KTU,* 1.6 V, 5; 1.10 III, 13.
78. *KTU,* 1.2 IV, 12 (Yam); 1.1 IV, 24; 1.3 IV, 2 (Baʿal).
79. *KTU,* 1.2 IV, 20 (Yam).

trio of phrases: "break down the door posts of the palace" (*ys' 'lt ṯbt*), "overturn the royal throne" (*hpk ks' mlk*), and "break the scepter of rule" (*yṯbr ḫṭ mṯpṭ*).[80] This parallelism is universally Semitic.[81] El can intervene in the struggle and place Ba'al on the throne as the clear victor over Mot.[82]

The dimensions of a throne also reflect on its occupant; it is felt to be a terrible humiliation that 'Athtar is too small for Ba'al's throne (*kḥṯ*): his head does not come up to the back and his feet do not reach the footstool.[83] When El comes down (*yrd*) from his throne[84] to sit on the footstool (*hdm*) and then on the ground, he is using a sign of mourning to signify his grief over the death of Ba'al (cf. v. 4) and an interruption of his sovereignty.

After recovering from a deadly disease, Keret ascends the throne[85] and resumes the tasks of government.

In myths, *ks' ṯbt* can stand for "palace" and "dominion," as in the case of Kothar the smith god[86] and above all Mot, god of the underworld, whose throne is the underworld itself (*hmry*).[87]

c. *Furniture.* The adj. *ʒl* describes the grandiose dimensions of a chair.[88] Normal household furnishings include tables, chairs (*ks't*), and footstools;[89] cf. also the furnishing of a room for El to rest in.[90] When the gods come to the feast celebrating the dedication of Ba'al's new palace, they bring lambs, oxen, heifers, thrones (*kḥṯ*), chairs (*ks'*), amphoras and skins of wine, etc.,[91] a scene that recalls ancient Near Eastern tribute offerings.[92]

d. *Ritual.* Finally, *ks'* appears also in religious texts and sacrificial lists.[93] One ritual[94] consecrates a throne to the dead king in order to provide a better position for him in the underworld.[95]

---

80. *KTU,* 1.2 III, 18; 1.6 VI, 28.

81. Cf. *KAI,* 1, 2; J. Friedrich, "Kleine Bemerkungen zu Texten aus Ras Schamra und zu phönizischen Inschriften," *AfO,* 10 (1935-36), 81f.; for Akkadian, see Y. Avishur, "Word Pairs Common to Phoenician and Biblical Hebrew," *UF,* 7 (1975), 36f.

82. *KTU,* 1.6 VI, 33.

83. *KTU,* 1.6 I, 58ff.; cf. de Moor, 202-6.

84. *KTU,* 1.5 VI, 12.

85. *KTU,* 1.16 VI, 23.

86. *KTU,* 1.1 III, 1; cf. Caphtor: *KTU,* 1.3 VI, 15; 1.4 VIII, 12.

87. *KTU,* 1.4 VIII, 12; 1.5 II, 15; cf. Isa. 47:1 and *RSP,* II, 297.

88. Cf. *KTU,* 1.12 I, 18; D. W. Thomas, "A Consideration of Some Unusual Ways of Expressing the Superlative in Hebrew," *VT,* 3 (1953), 209-224, contra van Selms, 470.

89. *KTU,* 1.3 II, 21, 36.

90. *KTU,* 1.4 I, 30-44; R. Heyer, "Ein archäologischer Beitrag zum Text KTU 1.4 I 23-43," *UF,* 10 (1978), 93-109.

91. *KTU,* 1.4 VI, 52.

92. Cf. the annals of Ashurbanipal, 67.

93. *KTU,* 1.50, 2; 1.53, 7; 1.57, 4.

94. *KTU,* 1.161.

95. Cf. J. F. Healey, "Ritual Text KTU 1.161 — Translation and Notes," *UF,* 10 (1978), 83-88; cf. Gilg., VIII, III, 2f.; Death of Ur-Nammu, 135 (S. N. Kramer, "The Death of Ur-Nammu and his Descent to the Netherworld," *Festschrift A. Goetze. JCS,* 21 [1967], 115, 119).

4. *Egypt.*

a. *Terminology.* The Egyptian language signalizes graphically the sociological significance of enthronement, since the hieroglyph for "noble" (*špśś/špś.w*) is an empty chair or a man seated upon a throne.[96] The significance of the throne is also illustrated by the Egyptian use of eighteen words or phrases meaning "throne": *ḫndw, wṯs.t, sm3(y)t,*[97] *tpy-rdww, sʿnḫyt m3ʿt, mn by.t, yśb.t, ḥmr, sp3, hdmw, bḥdw, bkr, bdy, śk3, śyt, nś.t, śrḫ,* and the late word *py.*

The terminology itself reveals an organic connection between the notion of the pharaoh's throne, the primeval hill, and the concept of *m3ʿt.* The estrade or platform of the throne symbolizes the primeval hill, but also appears in the orthography of *m3ʿt.* There is thus an equivalence between the "foundation of the throne" and "cosmic order, truth, righteousness."[98] "The semantic similarity of the spiritual 'foundation' on which the Egyptians thought the world had been established by the deity at creation to a physical foundation may have encouraged the transfer of meaning."[99] The cubiform throne representing the *bnbn* stone is a variant of the primeval hill.[100]

b. *Badge of Royalty.* There were two types of throne in Egypt: union throne and lion throne. The union throne (*ḥwt* < *ḥwy,* "include, comprise") is decorated with horizontal lines of feathers, arranged individually or in groups, symbolizing the divine sphere; it frequently symbolizes the union of the two lands.[101] The *srḫ* union throne is adorned with the facade of a palace.[102] It symbolizes political unity, the dependence of the kingdom on the ruler, the divinity of Pharaoh and his successful reign, as well as the union of all things living and the *m3ʿt* of the entire world.[103] The lion throne symbolizes secular dominion. Its back is decorated with the heads of lions; on the arm rests, a sphinx (cf. the Israelite cherubim throne) symbolizes Pharaoh victorious over his enemies.[104] According to Kuhlmann,[105] the association of king and lion is a survival of a totemistic culture; it symbolizes mutual protection while simultaneously depicting Pharaoh in his terrifying aspect.

The primary aspect of the Egyptian throne concept is associated with the term *ś.t* (< **śy,* "rest"). The phrase *ś.t wrr.t,* "high throne," also "high chamber," documents linguistically the parallelism between the place where Pharaoh appears on his throne and the place where the deity appears in the sanctuary. The highest position was

96. *WbÄS,* IV, 445-453.

97. The throne unifying Upper and Lower Egypt.

98. Cf. Kuhlmann, 93; Brunner, 426ff.

99. Kuhlmann, following W. Helck; cf. also *KAI,* 26 A, I, 10.

100. Cf. Metzger, *Königsthron und Gottesthron,* 22f.; O. Keel, "Der Bogen als Herrschaftssymbol," *ZDPV,* 93 (1977), 160.

101. Cf. *ANEP,* 422, 545; Kuhlmann, pl. 1.

102. Cf. K. Lange and M. Hirmer, *Egypt: Architecture, Sculpture and Painting in Three Thousand Years* (Eng. trans., London, [4]1968), pl. 6.

103. Kuhlmann, 82.

104. The symbolism of the lion throne is discussed by M. Pongracz, "Löwendarstellungen an Podesten der Königsthrone," *MDAI.K,* 15 (1975), 213ff.

105. Pp. 87f.

accorded originally to the deity; the exaltation of the king was therefore something like an act of deification. The terraced elevation of the divine sanctuary (signifying the primeval hill) is repeated in the throne estrade: the throne of the ruler and the throne of the gods are identical.[106] The throne of Pharaoh is therefore called "throne of Horus," "throne of Re," "throne of Amon," etc., but especially "throne of his father Aten"[107] (cf. esp. the testamentary formula relating to the throne). The father-son relationship stated here between the god and Pharaoh designates the ruler as the legitimate successor and heir to the throne. This shows "that the royal throne of Egypt, inherited from generation to generation, was considered a link with the 'age of the gods' (*rky-nṯrw*); in the earthly kingship, it manifested the facets of the sovereignty of all the gods who had preceded the pharaoh on the throne."[108] The complexity of this throne theology is also illustrated by the fact that the pharaoh likewise represents all the divine kings, sitting on the thrones of Geb and exercising the office of the Atum like Re.[109] As throne heir of the sun-god, Pharaoh, "appearing in glory on the Horus throne like Re," daily reactivates the process by which the world was created and guarantees the *mꜣʿt* of the world. According to K. P. Kuhlmann,[110] the throne here reveals its true relevance as one of the insignia of state: "Egypt considered the endurance of its god-given political order dependent on the earthly ruler's continued inheritance of the throne from the sun-god and the divine kings succeeding him; this inheritance guaranteed the continuance of the mythological rule of the earth by the sun and the associated creation of an ordered world." More than scepter, staff, mace, weapon, or crown, the throne is the principle of official authority and succession, in the dual a sign of dominion over Upper and Lower Egypt, in the plural a sign of dominion over all the deities of the nomes.

c. *Deification.* The throne of Pharaoh was deified at an early date[111] in a development comparable to the deification of the "throne seat" (*ḫalmašuit*) in the Old Hittite period of Boghazköy.[112] The same hieroglyph represented both the throne and the goddess Isis.

The so-called identity theory[113] holds that Isis as the personification of the ruler's throne represents the personified power of the throne. Jürgen Osing[114] and Kuhlmann,[115] however, reject any etymological, morphophonemic, or semantic connection between

---

106. *Ibid.,* 40.
107. *Urk.,* IV, 2003.
108. Kuhlmann, 42.
109. Cf. F. A. F. Mariette, *Abydos,* I (Paris, 1869), pl. 51, ll. 31f., 40-47, cited by Kuhlmann.
110. P. 41.
111. E. Otto, "Die Religion der alten Ägypter," *Ägyptologie, HO,* I/VIII, 1/1 (1952), 19.
112. Cf. H. Otten, "Die Religionen des alten Kleinasien," *Ägyptologie, HO,* I/VIII, 1/1 (1952), 97f.; M. Popko, *Kultobjekte in der hethitischen Religion nach Keilschriftlichen Quellen* (Warsaw, 1978), 59-65; and esp. F. Starke, "Ḫalmašuit im Anitta-Text und die hethitische Ideologie vom Königtum," *ZA,* 69 (1979), 47-120, esp. 72f., 111.
113. K. Sethe, Otto, Helck, H. Bonnet, and H. Kees.
114. J. Osing, "Isis und Osiris," *MDAI.K,* 30/1 (1974), 91-113, esp. 91ff.
115. Pp. 96f.

ś.t, "throne," and *3śt,* "Isis," on the grounds that the name of the goddess derives from the root *w3s* (< **3s*) and means "the one who has sovereign power, powerful influence." The throne symbol depicted on Isis's head represents merely a graphic aid to identification, although even the Greek Isis aretalogies already interpreted this symbol as identifying the throne and Isis.[116]

d. *Cult.* The throne is mentioned occasionally in cultic contexts: it is censed, and it can play the role of a *ḥtp* altar, holding sacrificial offerings;[117] this usage might lie behind the "cult of the empty throne."[118]

5. *Aram and Phoenicia.*

a. *Archaeology.* Ugaritic thrones betray Egyptian influence (lion legs, high curved back, high foot supports),[119] but their geometric decoration already illustrates the uniqueness of Phoenician throne architecture. In addition to Egyptian influence (cf. the Phoenician stela of Yeḥimilk from Byblos[120]), Hittite influence[121] can be seen in the lion sphinx that supports the throne of Aḥiram[122] and in two ivories from Megiddo.[123] This is the predominant throne type.[124] The throne of Barrākib[125] suggests Mesopotamian influence.

Especially in Phoenicia, the "empty throne"[126] is a familiar object of devotion from the eighth century until the Roman period. Othmar Keel[127] notes the remarkable spread of such aniconic cults among the Urartean, Anatolian, Iranian, and Old Arabic peripheral cultures during the second and first millennia. In Phoenicia, the deity is conceived of as truly present not only on the throne but also through the placement of sacred stones (baitylia) upon the throne (cf. the Punic cippus from Carthage [*ca.* 6th century] in the form of a throne seat with a double baitylion[128]).

b. *Inscriptions.* In Phoenician epigraphy, *ks'* is found in the inscription of Aḥiram[129] in a threat against potential grave robbers: "may the scepter of his rule be defoliated [= 'broken'?[130]], his throne overturned."[131] With the formula "I sit upon the throne of

---

116. Cf. J. Bergman, *Ich bin Isis* (Uppsala, 1968); also *idem,* "Isis," *LexÄg,* III (1980), 186-203.

117. For citations, see Kuhlmann, 101.

118. See I.2.e above.

119. Cf. A. Parrot, *Les Phéniciens* (Paris, 1975), 11; *ANEP,* 493.

120. Parrot, 56.

121. *Ibid.,* 78.

122. *ANET,* 458.

123. Cf. Keel, *Jahwe-Visionen und Siegelkunst,* 18ff.

124. Cf. Parrot, 100, 111, 201, 271; other examples in Seyrig, 51f.

125. *ANEP,* 460.

126. Cf. R. de Vaux, "Les chérubins et l'arche d'alliance, les sphinx gardiens et les trônes divins dans l'Ancien Orient," *Bible et Orient* (Paris, 1967), 250ff. = *MUSJ,* 37 (1960/61), 104ff.

127. Keel, *Jahwe-Visionen und Siegelkunst,* 40.

128. Parrot, 271.

129. *KAI,* 1, 2.

130. Friedrich, 81f.

131. Cf. *KTU,* 1.6 VI, 28f.

my father," Kilamuwa of Zinjirli[132] and Azitawadda[133] announce their accession; the latter describes his accession as a restoration of the high ideals of *nʿm lb,* "kindness of heart," *ḥkmh,* "wisdom," and *ṣdq,* "righteousness," which he describes as the "roots of my rule" (*šrš 'dny*).[134]

"Sitting upon the *krs' 'by*" is understood as referring to dynastic succession.[135] In Ahikar 133, *krs'* stands metaphorically for outwardly visible "permanence," for the endurance and apparent security that outwardly characterize the liar but ultimately turn against him out of inner necessity.

II. OT.

1. *Distribution.* The noun *kissē'* is found 135 times in the OT, Aram. *korsē'* 3 times. The word appears most frequently in the Deuteronomistic history (50 times, of which 20 are in 1-2 Kings), Psalms (18 times), Jeremiah (17 times), and the Chronicler's history (16 times). Elsewhere it appears only sporadically (8 times in Isaiah, 6 in Proverbs, 5 in Ezekiel, 4 in the Pentateuch, 3 in Esther, twice each in Zechariah and Job, and once each in Jonah, Haggai, and Lamentations).

2. *Related Words.* Almost two thirds of the occurrences of *kissē'* are in prose, the rest in poetry. It appears 23 times absolutely, 61 times with a suffix (46 of which refer to the king, 15 to Yahweh).

a. *Nouns.* Very early we find *kissē'-dîn* (Prov. 20:8) and *kissē' lᵉmišpāṭ* (Ps. 122:5), the "throne of judgment" in the "throne hall" (*'ûlām hakkissē'*, 1 K. 7:7), turned by the depravity of its occupant into a "throne of wickedness" (*kissē' hawwôṯ,* Ps. 94:20 [RSV "wicked rulers"]). The phrase *kissē' kāḇôḏ,* "throne of honor," serves as a metaphor for Jerusalem (Jer. 14:21), the invisible throne of Yahweh above the ark (Jer. 17:12), and the throne of David (Isa. 22:23).

Apart from its use with suffixes, *kissē'* appears in the construct almost exclusively in combination with personal entities. These phrases, however, soon turn into a stereotyped and abstract terminology.

1. What is probably the earliest phrase, *kissē' lᵉḇêṯ dāwiḏ,* "throne for David's house" (Ps. 122:5) — in parallel with *kissē' lᵉmišpāṭ* — could go back to the earliest period of the Israelite monarchy, when the office of judge was transferred to the king. The basic stratum of the court history of David uses the phrase *kissē' 'ᵃḏōnî-hammeleḵ* (*dāwiḏ*), "throne of my lord and king (David)," but only in submissive terms of address spoken by Bathsheba, Nathan, and Benaiah (1 K. 1:20,27,37). The *kissē' dāwiḏ* represents the royal seat of the Davidic dynasty in Jerusalem (2 S. 3:10; 1 K. 2:45; Jer. 13:13; 17:25; 22:2,4,30; 29:16; 36:30). The phrase also appears in a messianic prophecy (Isa. 9:6[Eng. v. 7]).

---

132. *KAI,* 24, 9.

133. *KAI,* 26 A, I, 11.

134. L. 10; cf. III, 4.

135. *KAI,* 216, 7; 219, 5; 224, 17 (*khs'*!); for Akkadian parallels, see I.2 above. On accession to the throne as a fixed date for determining chronology, cf. also *AP,* 6, 2.

2. The dynastic element is emphasized by the Deuteronomistic phrase *kissē' 'āḇîw,* "throne of his father" (cf. 1 K. 2:12, with reference to David; 2 K. 10:3, with reference to Ahab), expanded to *kissē' dāwiḏ 'āḇî* (1 K. 2:24).[136]

3. A first stage of abstraction from personal references appears in the phrase *kissē' mamlāḵâ,* "throne of the kingdom," first in the law of the king (Dt. 17:18 [secondary?]), then in the dynastically oriented Deuteronomistic redaction of 2 S. 7:13; 1 K. 9:5 (Chronicles reads *kissē' hammalḵûṯ*), and finally in connection with the enthronement of Joash (2 Ch. 23:20); it is synonymous with *kissē' hammᵉlûḵâ* (1 K. 1:46 [Deuteronomistic]). On the other hand, *kissē' hammᵉlāḵîm* (2 K. 25:28; Jer. 52:32) refers to a real plurality of kings in Babylon, but can also mean the royal throne of Jerusalem (2 K. 11:19; 2 Ch. 23:20 has *kissē' hammamlᵉḵâ*). The phrase *kissē' malḵûṯ* is used only by late texts for the throne of Solomon (1 Ch. 22:10; 2 Ch. 7:18, corresponding to Deuteronomistic *kissē' mamlāḵâ*), as well as for the throne of Ahasuerus in Susa (Est. 1:2; 5:1). In Hag. 2:22, the phrase *kissē' malḵôṯ,* an internal plural suggesting power politics, probably refers to the central government of the Persian empire, imposed upon many nations,[137] and the struggles for power following the reign of Cambyses.[138]

4. The Deuteronomistic expression *kissē' yiśrā'ēl* appears 4 times in the formula of continuity "there shall not fail you a descendant on the throne of Israel" (1 K. 2:4; 8:25 par. 2 Ch. 6:16; 1 K. 9:5; the late passage Jer. 33:17 uses *kissē' bêṯ-yiśrā'ēl*; Jer. 33:21 uses *kissē'* with a suffix). In 1 K. 8:20 par. 2 Ch. 6:10; 1 K. 10:9, Solomon occupies this throne, which 2 Ch. 9:8 theologizes into the *kissē' YHWH,* proving that in this expression "Israel" is a theological term (in contrast to 2 K. 10:30; 15:12). There is no occurrence of **kissē' yᵉhûḏâ.*

5. The explicit formula *kissē' YHWH* is Deuteronomistic at the earliest (earlier with the suffix). In 1 Ch. 29:23, it refers to the throne of David (cf. 1 K. 1:46); the same is true of 1 Ch. 28:5, which, however, uses *kissē' malḵûṯ YHWH.* These passages illustrate the Chronicler's intention of linking the earthly monarchy more closely with Yahweh.[139]

By and large, these phrases appear to be essentially synonymous. Their semantic development, however, moves from the concrete physical throne to a more generalized concept, divorced from personal references of the throne as representing sovereignty, especially in dynastic contexts.[140] The early development of a stereotyped terminology, initiated primarily by the Deuteronomistic history, stood in the way of further personal compounds. Despite the importance of Solomon and the extensive Deuteronomistic reworking of the story of David and Solomon in Solomon's favor,[141] we never find the phrase **kissē' šᵉlāmōh* ("throne of Solomon"). Even the dynastic principle in the

---

136. Cf. F. Langlamet, "Pour ou contre Salomon?" *RB,* 83 (1976), 321-379; 481-528.

137. Elliger.

138. W. Rudolph.

139. Cf. T. Willi, *Die Chronik als Auslegung. FRLANT,* 106 (1972), 131; Welten, *Festschrift E. Würthwein,* 178.

140. Cf. T. Veijola, *Die ewige Dynastie. AnAcScFen,*193 (1975), 26f., 60, 75.

141. Cf. Veijola; Langlamet; for a different view, see F. Crüsemann, *Der Widerstand gegen das Königtum. WMANT,* 49 (1978), 129, n. 5.

northern kingdom, more highly developed than previously realized,[142] did not lead to the development of an independent throne terminology associated with the northern kingdom.

b. *Verbs.* With few exceptions, *kissē'* appears in verbal clauses. In the sense of "set up a throne," it is the object of *nāṯan* (Jer. 1:15; 52:32; 2 K. 25:28), *hēqîm* (2 S. 3:10; 1 K. 9:5; 2 Ch. 7:18), *hērîm* (Isa. 14:13), *śîm* (1 K. 2:19; Ps. 89:30[29]; Jer. 43:10; 49:38), and *hēḵîn* (2 S. 7:13,16; Ps. 103:19). The sense of physical construction is suggested by *'āśâ* (1 K. 10:18; 2 Ch. 9:17); cf. also *ṣāpâ* (1 K. 10:18; 2 Ch. 9:17). Dynastic prolongation is expressed by *bānâ* (Ps. 89:5[4]) and *sā'aḏ* (Prov. 20:28). A throne is "set" (*yāšaḇ,* Ps. 122:5) or "established" (*kûn,* Prov. 16:12; 25:5; 29:14; Ps. 93:2; 1 K. 2:45); antonyms are *hāpaḵ* (Hag. 2:22) and *miggar* (Ps. 89:45[44]), "overturn."

The semantic field of enthronement includes "placing someone on the throne" (*hôšîḇ l^e* [Job 36:7], *hôšîḇ 'al* [1 K. 2:24; 2 Ch. 23:20], *nāṯan 'al* [1 K. 5:19(5); 10:9; 2 Ch. 9:8], *śîm 'al* [2 K. 10:3], and *šîṯ l^e* [Ps. 132:11]); the opposite is *hēqîm mikkissē',* "raise from the throne" (Isa. 14:9) or *nḥt,* "be deposed" (Dnl. 5:20). Related is "sit upon the throne" (*yāšaḇ l^e* [Ps. 9:5(4); 132:12], *yāšaḇ 'al* [Ex. 11:5; 12:29; 1 K. 1:13,17,20,24,27,30,35; 22:10; Est. 1:2; 2 Ch. 18:9], *hāyâ* [Zec. 6:13(?)], *māšal* [Zec. 6:13], and *mālaḵ* [Jer. 33:21]), with the antonyms "fall" or "rise" from the throne (*nāpal* [1 S. 4:18], *yāraḏ* [Ezk. 26:16], *qûm* [Jgs. 3:20; Jon. 3:6]) and "sit in the dust without a throne" (*'ên-kissē'* [Isa. 47:1]).

Comparison is expressed by the phrases *raq kissē' gāḏal,* "be greater only as regards the throne" (Gen. 41:40, the pharaoh with respect to Joseph), *giddēl kissē' min,* "make the throne greater than" (1 K. 1:37,47), and *śîm 'eṯ-kissē' mē'al,* "set the throne above" (Est. 3:1).[143]

Certain unique expressions are also found, always with figurative meaning: *hinḥîl kissē',* "inherit a throne" (1 S. 2:8), *nibbēl kissē',* "dishonor a throne" (Jer. 14:21), *'āḥaz p^enê-kissē',* "cover the face of the throne" (Job 26:9), and *naqqēh kissē',* "declare the throne guiltless" (2 S. 14:9).

The *kissē'* is personified when we are told that someone belongs to the throne (*l^ekissē',* Neh. 3:7), i.e., is under its jurisdiction, or can become a throne of honor (*hāyâ l^ekissē' kāḇôḏ,* Isa. 22:23). The statement that the throne can "frame mischief" (*yāṣar 'āmāl,* Ps. 94:20) also involves personification.

c. *Synonyms.* There are no precise synonyms for *kissē'* in the sense of "seat." The nouns → הדם *h^aḏōm* (*h^adhōm*) and → כבשׁ *keḇeš* mean "(foot)stool," while *môšāḇ,* "seat," is a more general term used for anything on which one can sit. When *kissē'* is used in the sense of "(royal) throne," words like *mamlāḵâ* meaning "kingship" are commonly used as synonyms and can be used interchangeably (cf. *sā'aḏ kissē'* [Prov. 20:28] and *sā'aḏ mamlāḵâ* [Isa. 9:6]). In theological usage, God's *kissē'* is identical with the "place where he is enthroned" (*m^eḵôn-šiḇtô,* Ps. 33:14; cf. 1 K. 8:13]), his "seat" (*môšāḇ*) upon Zion (Ps. 132:13f.), and his "resting place" (*m^enûḥâ,* Ps. 132:8).

---

142. Cf. T. Ishida, *The Royal Dynasties in Ancient Israel. BZAW,* 142 (1977), 183-86.
143. Cf. also the Assyrian examples in G. Rinaldi, *"Nota: kissē'," BeO,* 9 (1967), 207f.

3. *LXX.* The LXX uses *thrónos* to translate *kissēʾ* (130 times); in Esther (except for Est. 5:1), however, it uses verbal forms: *enthronízesthai, thronízein* (1:2, of Ahasuerus), *prōtobathreín* (3:1). The LXX limits *thrónos* to the royal throne of Israel. Six passages use *díphros,* "stool" (the priestly seat of Eli [1 S. 1:9; 4:13,18], the chair of Elisha [2 K. 4:10], the throne of Lady Folly [Prov. 9:14], and in the law of kings the royal throne of Israel [Dt. 17:18]).

The use of *anḗr hēgoúmenos* to paraphrase *ʾîš mēʿal kissēʾ* (1 K. 9:5) conveys the meaning accurately. In Sirach, *kissēʾ* is found 4 times; in 3 cases (Sir. 10:14; 40:3; 47:11) the LXX uses *thrónos*, in 1 case (11:5) *edaphos,* "floor."

III. 1. *Everyday Life.* By its very nature, the OT pays almost no attention to Israelite furniture; there is scarcely any mention of chairs or thrones in everyday secular life. Eli the priest sat on his chair by the doorpost of the temple of Yahweh at Shiloh (1 S. 1:9), where he functioned as guardian of the peace. Here *kissēʾ* probably denotes a simple, portable folding chair, such as is common throughout the Near East.[144] Sitting on his chair by the city gate[145] or by the road,[146] he waited for the messenger bearing news of the battle at Aphek (1 S. 4:13). In 2 K. 4:10, the Shunemite woman prepares a room for Elisha, for which she needs a bed, table, chair, and lamp.

2. *The Throne of David.* Despite the unambiguous terminology, a concrete "throne of David" is hard to find in the text of the story of David's rise to power (1 S. 16:14–2 S. 5:10). The primary narrative does not use the word *kissēʾ*; the earliest reference (2 S. 3:10: Abner's proclamation that the throne of David will be set up over Israel *and* Judah [Deuteronomistic]) already understands the phrase *kissēʾ dāwīḏ* politically as David's sovereignty over both kingdoms. The descriptions of the anointing of David as king over Judah (2 S. 2:4) and Israel (5:3) do not speak of an enthronement, and there is no mention at all of any throne symbol before the monarchy was established at Jerusalem. We find *kissēʾ* for the first time in the Deuteronomistic redaction of Nathan's prophecy (2 S. 7:13,16),[147] where it appears in parallel with *bayiṯ,* "house, dynasty," with which it is generally synonymous, emphasizing the dynastic continuity of the monarchy.

The noun appears a number of times in the court history of David,[148] but again without reference to an actual throne. The passages in question — mostly Deuteronomistic — speak of the throne of David in the sense of the Davidic dynasty (1 K. 1:13,17,30,35,37,46,47,48; 2:4,12,24,33).[149] In the primary text, 1 K. 1:20,24,27

144. *AuS,* VII (1942), 177.

145. Hertzberg.

146. Stoebe.

147. Cf. Veijola, 72, 75f., contra L. Rost, *The Succession to the Throne of David. Historical Texts and Interpreters,* 1 (Eng. trans., Sheffield, 1982), 44, who assigns v. 16 to the earliest stratum of the promise.

148. Cf. now G. Garbini, " 'Narrativa della succession' o 'storia dei re'?" *Henoch,* 1 (1979), 19-41.

149. Cf. Jackson.

(Bathsheba's asking David who will sit on the throne after him and Nathan's reference to Adonijah's designation of himself) also already understand *kissē'* in the dynastic sense. The first mention of a physical throne in the basic text is associated with Solomon (1 K. 2:19: the king's mother is specially honored by sitting on a throne on the right hand of the king's throne). In the enthronement described in 1 K. 1:35, therefore, the Deuteronomistic historian may possibly be thinking not only of a transfer of power but also of Solomon's sitting on the physical throne of David.[150] Thus even if the text never speaks explicitly of the physical throne of David, such a throne must at least be postulated as the basis for the metaphorical language.

The *kissē' dāwīḏ* thus embodies the divinely established kingship of David and the Davidic line in Jerusalem (cf. Jer. 13:13; 17:25; 22:2,4,30; 29:16). In this throne is realized the kingship of Yahweh upon earth (1 Ch. 28:5); it is therefore promised continuity and endurance forever (2 S. 7:13,16 par. 1 Ch. 17:12,14; Ps. 132:11). Because David is granted a successor to sit upon his throne, he knows Yahweh has heard his prayer and delivered him (1 K. 1:30,48); he designates his son Solomon as his successor, king, and *nāgîḏ* (v. 35). In the throne of David are manifested righteousness and justice (Jer. 33:17; cf. v. 16), the existential foundation of Israel. Keeping of the covenant guarantees continuation of the dynasty (1 K. 2:4; 8:25; 9:5; 2 K. 10:30; 2 Ch. 6:16; 7:18; Ps. 132:12), while absence of a successor is a significant manifestation that the covenant has been broken (Jer. 33:21 [Deuteronomistic revision]). The phrase *kissē' dāwīḏ* becomes a technical term associated with the Davidic dynasty. The continuous repetition of the dynastic promise to the line of David (Ps. 132:11; Jer. 33:17), David (2 S. 7:13,16 par. 1 Ch. 17:12,14), Solomon (1 K. 9:5; 1 Ch. 22:10), and Jehu (2 K. 10:30; 15:12) documents God's salvific work. Ps. 89 probably reflects an associated liturgy[151] in which the ancient dynastic promise was cultically reactualized for the king — originally in times of need, later probably in the setting of an annual festival (vv. 5,30,37[4,29,36]).[152] A basic element of this "oracle of the king"[153] was the promise that the throne would endure forever. This promise attracted further motifs: the promise of help and protection (Ps. 89:23[22]ff.), a mighty name (v. 25[24]), the declaration that the king is the universal victor over chaos (v. 26[25]) and ruler of the world, his adoption as God's son (vv. 27f.[26f.]; cf. 1 Ch. 22:10), sometimes indeed something like "divinization" (cf. Ps. 45:7[6]). In times of peril, this led to a theologization of the king as messiah; the throne of David becomes the focus of hope, because David's line sits upon the "throne of Yahweh" (1 Ch. 28:5; 29:23 [David]; 2 Ch. 9:8 [Solo-

---

150. M. Noth, *Könige 1–16. BK,* IX/1 (1968), 24f.; for a different interpretation, see K. Homburg, "Psalm 110_1 im Rahmen des judäischen Krönungszeremoniells," *ZAW,* 84 (1972), 243-46: the enthronement of the king at the right hand of Yahweh (Ps. 110:1) refers to the location of his palace just south of the temple.

151. S. Mowinckel, *Psalmenstudien,* III: *Kultprophetie und prophetische Psalmen* (Amsterdam, 1924, repr. 1961), 34ff.

152. H.-J. Kraus, *Psalms 60–150* (Eng. trans., Minneapolis, 1989), 203.

153. *Ibid.,* 208; its cosmic extension is discussed by G. W. Ahlström, *Psalm 89* (Lund, 1959), 53ff., 118ff., 130.

mon]),[154] the "throne of the kingdom of Yahweh over Israel" (1 Ch. 28:5) and as such is the source of divine deliverance and fulfillment of the promises. The king reigns "for Yahweh" (2 Ch. 9:8), exercising Yahweh's mandate. The messianic dimension of the Davidic kingship[155] is reflected in the history of the tradition recorded in Isa. 16:5. The prophecy of the end of this dynasty (Jer. 36:30) was thus simultaneously the abrupt termination of all hope, a punishment upon the present and the future.

3. *The Throne of Solomon.* After building the temple, the royal palace, and the House of the Forest of Lebanon, Solomon made a throne (1 K. 10:18-20 par. 2 Ch. 9:17-19) of proverbial magnificence, which later became a feature of Semitic and Byzantine legend[156] and a symbol of world dominion.[157] This throne was made of rare wood inlaid with ivory and overlaid with gold. In form it was a chair with sides and a back, set upon an estrade having six steps.

The complex textual history of 1 K. 10:19b shows that the details of this form soon became a matter of debate. V. 19b reads: *wᵉrōʾš-ʿāg̱ōl lakkissēh mēʾaḥᵃrāyw* (MT), "the upper part of the throne was round in back." The LXX misread *ʿag̱ōl* as *ʿēg̱el,* "calf," and understood the text to mean that the back (!) was decorated with protomas of calves.[158] There is no evidence for such a throne in the ancient Near East; not even the elaborate Old Assyrian footstool with protomas of bulls[159] is comparable. Many scholars[160] nevertheless consider LXX *rāʾšê ʿᵃgālîm* to be the original reading and suggest that it was reshaped to eliminate all reminiscences of bull worship. The parallel hemistich in 2 Ch. 9:18b involves similar problems: *wᵉk̲eb̲eš bazzāhāb̲ lakkissēʾ moʾᵒḥāzîm,* "and the throne had a footstool of gold attached." Only Lucian translated the text in this way. The repointing of *keb̲eš,* "footstool," as *keb̲eś,* "lamb," proposed by the Editio Bombergiana to explain the ox heads in the parallel is without foundation.

According to the MT, the throne with its rounded back points typologically to Phoenicia and Egypt, as does the theriomorphic form (lions) of the armrests. The six steps (each with a lion) of the estrade together with the footstool[161] constitute a substructure with seven levels. The theory of some scholars[162] that this base is com-

---

154. Cf. K.-H. Bernhardt, *Das Problem der altorientalischen Königsideologie im AT. SVT,* 8 (1961), 86f.

155. Cf. → דוד *dāwiḏ* (*dāvidh*); M. Rehm, *Der königliche Messias im Licht der Immanuel-Weissagungen des Buches Jesaja* (Kevalaer, 1968), 256f.; and esp. T. N. D. Mettinger, *King and Messiah. CB,* 8 (1976), 259-274.

156. Cf. G. Salzberger, *Salomos Tempelbau und Thron in der semitischen Sagenliteratur* (Berlin, 1912).

157. Cf. F. Wormald, "The Throne of Solomon and St. Edward's Chair," *Festschrift E. Panofsky* (New York, 1961), 532-541.

158. Similarly Josephus *Ant.* viii.5.2.

159. *BuA,* I, 248.

160. Kautzsch, de Vaux, North, etc.

161. → הדם *hᵃḏōm* (*hᵃdhōm*).

162. Noth, 231, contra E. Würthwein, *Die Bücher der Könige,* I. *ATD,* XI/1 (1977), 125; cf. also Bernhardt, 86, n. 5.

parable to the Babylonian ziggurat with the dwelling of the deity at its top (symbolizing the world mountain) is unlikely; it resembles more the typical Egyptian throne estrade, which symbolizes *mꜣʿt,* cosmic order and wisdom. The lions symbolize the power and majesty of the king.[163]

The court history of David makes Solomon's throne the direct successor to the throne of David (1 K. 1:46; 2:12). On this dynastic succession Solomon bases his claim to exclude Adonijah (1 K. 2:24) and Joab (v. 33) and to build the temple (5:19[5]; 8:20; 2 Ch. 6:10). He uses the dynastic promise given to David as a reason why his own prayer for wisdom should be granted (1 K. 3:6).

The splendor of Solomon's throne is seen also in the homage of Benaiah (1 K. 1:37) and the courtiers (v. 47), who call the throne of Solomon greater than the throne of David (*gāḏal* piel). These words reflect the rapidly developing splendor of the consolidated Jerusalem monarchy.

4. *Righteousness as the Foundation of the Throne.* Hellmut Brunner cites Egyptian parallels to account for the notion (which Ze'ev W. Falk[164] considers indigenous to Israel) that righteousness is the foundation of the throne.[165] Brunner's argument may be accepted if one is prepared to find in Heb. *ṣᵉḏāqâ*[166] the element of "cosmic order" found in Egyp. *mꜣʿt,*[167] although it is a relatively minor factor in the total range of meaning of the two terms.[168] The phrase *ṣeḏeq ûmišpāṭ* as the foundation of the throne of Yahweh (Ps. 89:15[14]; 97:2) and of the king (Prov. 16:12; 20:18; 25:5; 29:14) indicates the original judicial function of the monarch in Israel.[169] The theologoumena of God as king and judge were basic, and at a very early date (perhaps even by the beginning of the first millennium[170]) the devout Israelite affirmed: "*mišpāṭ* and *ṣᵉḏāqâ* are the foundation of thy throne; *ḥeseḏ* and *'ᵉmeṯ* go before thee" (Ps. 89:15[14]). The language reflects Mesopotamian mythology, in which the pair of deities *kittu* ("truth") and *mîšaru* ("righteousness") flank the sun-god when he acts as judge.[171] Ps. 97:2 (postexilic), too, uses archaizing language to express the same pre-Israelite tradition: "Clouds and thick darkness are round about him; righteousness and justice are the foundation of his throne." Kraus[172] maintains that interpretation must go beyond the ultimately static notion of

163. Cf. Canciano-Pettinato, 107.

164. Z. W. Falk, "Two Symbols of Justice," *VT,* 10 (1960), 72-74.

165. Cf. I.4.a above.

166. → צדק *sdq.*

167. A. Jepsen, "צדק und צדקה im AT," *Gottes Wort und Gottes Land. Festschrift W. Hertzberg* (Göttingen, 1965), 78-89 = *Der Herr ist Gott* (Berlin, 1978), 221-29; H. H. Schmid, *Gerechtigkeit als Weltordnung. BHTh,* 40 (1968), 46-60 and *passim.*

168. Cf. K. Koch, "צדק *ṣdq* gemeinschaftstreu/heilvoll sein," *THAT,* II, 510, 516.

169. Cf. G. C. Macholz, "Die Stellung des Königs in der israelitischen Gerichtsverfassung," *ZAW,* 84 (1972), 157-182.

170. Albright; cf. Kraus, *Psalms 60–150,* 203.

171. *SAHG,* 222, 230, 334; H. Ringgren, *Word and Wisdom* (Lund, 1947), 53ff., 83ff.; cf. also Schmid, *Gerechtigkeit als Weltordnung,* 79f.

172. *In loc.*

"cosmic order"[173] as the foundation of the throne, since *ṣᵉḏāqâ* implies all the dynamism of God's creation and governance. In Ps. 9:5(4) (not datable), too, the psalmist thanks God for his role in human justice. The ancient theophany formula that Kraus[174] claims to find behind *yāšaḇtā lᵉkissē'* is not all that evident. Despite the inclusion of the eschatological judgment of the nations in Ps. 9:7(6),[175] the major theme of this psalm is God's help for an individual before the bar of justice.

As the meaning of → שׁפט *šāp̱aṭ* shifted from "judge" to "rule,"[176] more and more emphasis was placed on the obligation of the "ruler" to observe the Torah. The Deuteronomic law of the king accordingly makes the monarch subject to the Torah; an amendment (Dt. 17:18) even requires him to have the Torah ready to hand when he sits upon his throne.[177] This markedly judicial role of the king finds expression in Ps. 122, which probably goes back to the time of David: in vv. 5ff., there is synonymous parallelism between *kiss'ôṯ lᵉmišpāṭ* and *kiss'ôṯ lᵉḇêṯ dāwiḏ*. Along with *šālôm* ("general well-being"), this notion was extended to characterize the city of Jerusalem. It was embodied architecturally in Solomon's building of the palace: he gave the *'ûlām hakkissē'* the function of an *'ûlām hammišpāṭ — 'ᵃšer yišpoṭ-šām,* "in order to pronounce judgment there" (1 K. 7:7).

This royal ideology of the ancient Near East (primarily Mesopotamia — in Egypt, administration of justice was in the hands of the vizier[178]) is reflected in Ps. 45:7f.(6f.), a preexilic hymn of praise to the king: "Your throne, O divine one, endures for ever and ever. Your royal scepter is a scepter of equity; you love righteousness and hate wickedness." This thetic formulation makes divine election and righteousness the twin requirements for an enduring reign.[179] According to Ps. 72:1ff., God appoints the king his mandated representative by giving him *mišpāṭîm* and *ṣᵉḏāqâ.* In their inclusive function, they comprehend the primary realms for which the king is responsible: law, truth, nature, battle, and cult.[180] They constitute the foundation of the dynasty (1 K. 3:5f.).[181] If he fails in this regard, he loses his mandate (cf. the prophetic admonition to the king in Jer. 22:3,13,15-17).

The ancient proverbial wisdom of the early monarchy already made it clear that endurance of the king's throne depended on his righteousness, placing the maxim "If a king judges the poor with equity his throne will be established for ever" (Prov. 29:14) in the very center of the rules of conduct for princes[182] (cf. also 20:8,28). Because

---

173. Schmid.

174. H.-J. Kraus, *Psalms 1–59* (Eng. trans., Minneapolis, 1988), 194.

175. F. Nötscher, *Das Buch der Psalmen. EB,* IV (1959), in loc.

176. Cf. G. Liedke, *Gestalt und Bezeichnung alttestamentlicher Rechtsätze. WMANT,* 39 (1971), 70ff.

177. Cf. Bernhardt, 137f.

178. E. Otto, "Prolegomena zur Frage der Gesetzgebung und Rechtsprechung in Ägypten," *MDAI.K,* 14 (1956), 150-59, esp. 156.

179. Cf. A. Neuwirth, כסאך אלהים *"Dein Thron, o Gott"* (diss., Graz, 1964).

180. Schmid, *Gerechtigkeit als Weltordnung,* 23.

181. *Ibid.,* 85f.

182. U. Skladny, *Die ältesten Spruchsammlungen in Israel* (Göttingen, 1962).

flatterers and evildoers are always lurking in the wings (Prov. 25:5), righteousness and justice — that is, endurance of the throne — can be achieved only by radical elimination of these elements (cf. also 16:12). Perversion of justice and acts of violence turn the *kissē' l^e^mišpāṭ* into a *kissē' hawwôṯ,* "a throne of wickedness that works mischief against the law" (Ps. 94:20), embodied in antisocial treatment of widows, sojourners, and orphans (v. 6) as well as condemnation of the innocent (v. 21).

The notion that justice and righteousness constitute the foundation of the throne is a fundamental element of the Davidic tradition[183] and therefore also of the messianic hope shaped by this tradition. The true line of succession between the throne of David and the throne of the Messiah is traced through *mišpāṭ* and *ṣ^e^ḏāqâ.* The promise of the royal messiah in Isa. 9:1-6(2-7) (*ca.* 733) recalls the conferment of royalty upon the unborn son of the pharaoh:[184] "Great will be his government and peace will have no end over the throne of David and over his kingdom, since he establishes it and upholds it [the fem. suffixes show that the verbs refer to *mamlāḵâ,* contrary to the reading of 1QIs[a][185]] with justice and righteousness from this time forth and for evermore" (v. 6[7]). The Messiah totally fulfills the will of God, for God himself acts (*'āśâ,* v. 6[7]) in the Messiah. Thus the throne of David is likewise the locus and vehicle of God's salvation for his people through the Messiah.

Isa. 16:5 addresses the judicial office of the Messiah. Here his work *baḥeseḏ* and *be'^e^meṯ* is not associated primarily with the *kissē'* (contrary to Jer. 33:15ff.); it is localized *b^e^'ōhel dāwiḏ,* an archaizing feature. Isaiah sees in the messianic ruler a new embodiment of the authentic Davidic kingship, now extended to be universal.[186] As a postexilic ideal of the one who will rule in the age of salvation, the *kissē'* also is associated with *dāraš mišpāṭ,* the scriptural expertise of the scribes.

5. *Thrones of Kings and Princes.* The royal symbol of the "throne" is associated primarily with the Davidic dynasty: David, Solomon, Jehoshaphat (1 K. 22:10; 2 Ch. 18:9), Joash (2 K. 11:19; 13:13; 2 Ch. 23:20), Jehoiachim (Jer. 36:30), Zedekiah (Jer. 22:2), and Jehoiachin (metaphorically: 2 K. 25:28; Jer. 52:32).

Succession to the throne in the northern kingdom was not primarily dynastic, being based rather on the "ideal of charismatic kingship."[187] De facto, it followed the principle of "might makes right."[188] Zimri usurped the throne of Elah (1 K. 16:11), forestalling the establishment of a dynasty analogous to the royal house of Judah. Jehu prevented the enthronement of one of Ahab's sons after the murder of Jezebel

---

183. K. Seybold, *Das davidische Königtum im Zeugnis der Propheten. FRLANT,* 107 (1972), 85ff., 104, 116-132.

184. *AOT,* 47f.; *ANET,* 445f.; cf. also J. de Savignac, "Théologie pharaonique et messianisme d'Israël," *VT,* 7 (1957), 82-90.

185. Cf. the apparatus of *BHK.*

186. → אהל *'ōhel.*

187. A. Alt, "The Monarchy in the Kingdoms of Israel and Judah," *Essays on OT History and Religion* (Eng. trans., Garden City, 1966), 315ff.

188. Cf. Ishida, 171ff.

(2 K. 10:3) and seized power himself after a bloodbath. The other coups d'état and usurpations in the northern kingdom are recounted without mention of the *kissē'*, as are the few short-lived dynasties, so that *kissē'* in the sense of dynastic succession remained limited to the Davidic dynasty. Only when the throne was occupied by the "charismatic" Jeroboam II (2 K. 13:13) do we find the word *kissē'* once more. This observation suggests that in the Deuteronomistic history the term has positive moral connotations.

Finally, the OT speaks of thrones of kings and princes outside Israel. In Egypt, the throne is peculiar to Pharaoh: it is in regard to the throne that he is greater than Joseph, his grand vizier (Gen. 41:40).[189] According to the Egyptian law of succession, the first-born son of Pharaoh succeeds to this throne, so that the slaying of all the first-born (Ex. 11:5; 12:29) strikes the vital nerve of the dynasty. Other occupants of thrones include Eglon of Moab (Jgs. 3:20), Nebuchadnezzar (Dnl. 5:20), the king of Nineveh (Jon. 3:6), the enemy kings of the north (Jer. 1:15), the princes of the sea (Ezk. 26:16), Ahasuerus (Est. 1:2; 5:1), as well as the prince Haman (Est. 3:1) and the satrap of the province Beyond the River (Neh. 3:7).

The kings exiled to Babylon also clearly have thrones as a mark of their rank (2 K. 25:28; Jer. 52:32); cf. the picture of a ruler of Judah toward the end of the monarchy found at Ramat Raḥel.[190] Even in the underworld, a *kissē'* is a mark of the princes of the earth and the kings of the nations (Isa. 14:9).

As part of the ceremonial accompanying military campaigns, kings had their thrones set up before the gates of besieged cities: the kings of the north before Jerusalem (Jer. 1:15), Nebuchadnezzar before Tahpanhes, which Jeremiah uses stones to represent in a symbolic action (Jer. 43:10); cf. the parallels of Sennacherib and Sargon outside of Israel.[191] The kings of Israel and Judah likewise sit upon their thrones when planning their campaign against the Arameans (1 K. 22:10; 2 Ch. 18:9); cf. also the description of Yahweh as a warlord in Jer. 49:38.[192]

Despite all the power and magnificence surrounding kings and their thrones, it is God who sets them there (Job 36:7; 2 Ch. 9:8) and bestows their sovereignty upon them: they are all kings by the grace of God. If they contravene his commandments and make themselves his equals, God topples them from their thrones for their arrogance (Dnl. 5:20; Isa. 14:13). The Davidic king is no exception (Ps. 89:45[44]). Yahweh has the power to overthrow even the "throne of kingdoms" (Hag. 2:22)[193] in far-off Persia.

6. *Priestly Throne?* Only Zec. 6:13b, a passage with serious textual problems,[194] mentions the throne of the high priest: "And he [Zerubbabel] shall build the temple of Yahweh, and shall bear royal honor, and shall sit and rule upon his throne; and he

---

189. Cf. G. von Rad, *Genesis. OTL* (Eng. trans. 1961), 353.
190. Y. Aharoni, "Excavations at Ramat Raḥel," *BA*, 24 (1961), 108.
191. See I.2.d above.
192. See IV.1 below.
193. On the text, see W. Rudolph, *Haggai. KAT*, XIII/4 (1976), 52f.; cf. II.2.a.3 above.
194. See the comms.

[probably Joshua] shall be a priest upon his throne (*w^e hāyâ kōhēn ʿal-kis^e'ô*), and peaceful understanding shall be between them both."

a. Earlier scholars such as Knabenbauer and Wellhausen favored the LXX text,[195] according to which the high priest exercised his office in concert with the reigning descendant of David "at his right hand" (*ʿal-ye mînô*) without any disagreement over their spheres of authority.[196] In this view, a later (post-LXX) revision of the Hebrew text adapted it to the contemporary situation, with the high priest ruling as a quasi-monarch. Elliger[197] suggests a concentration of the divided messianic role in Zechariah in a single figure, "king and priest" (cf. Ps. 110). Brunner[198] ascribes high-priestly authority to the king on his throne. Chary[199] thinks in terms of a close cooperation between king and high priest, already attested for the exilic period, and sees the development of the text as reflecting the transition from monarchy to theocracy. The MT, according to this theory, bears witness to the final preeminence of the priesthood.[200]

b. Other scholars give priority to the MT.[201] A. Petitjean finds in it the realization of a "bicephalous authority," and holds that the LXX restored the importance of the Davidic kingship by downgrading the authority of the priesthood.

c. Wilhelm Rudolph[202] takes a harmonizing position, claiming that the "enthronement" of the high priest represented his de facto occupation of the throne of David in a theocratic form of government; there is no trace of any theologizing "throne of Yahweh."[203] From this time forward, this concentration of authority shaped the messianic hopes of Judaism. Despite the variety attested in the figure of the Messiah, a division into two messiahs is found only in the extracanonical literature.[204]

7. *Enthronement Ceremonial.* The enthronement ritual of Solomon (1 K. 1:32-48) and Joash (2 K. 11:11-20) is alluded to by Pss. 2, 72, 110, 132. It consisted of two major elements: (a) a procession to the sanctuary, where the king was invested with the royal symbols of the *nēzer* ("diadem") and *ʿēḏûṯ* ("royal protocol"; RSV "testimony"), anointed by the priest or people, and acclaimed by the people; and (b) a

---

195. Cf. also G. Wallis, "Erwägungen zu Sacharja VI 9-15," *Congress Volume, Uppsala 1971. SVT,* 22 (1972), 235-37, etc.

196. K. Elliger, *Das Buch der zwölf kleinen Propheten, II. ATD,* XXV (^{8}1982), *in loc.*

197. *Ibid.,* 130f.

198. R. Brunner, *Sacharja. ZBK* (1960), 89f.

199. T. Chary, *Aggée-Zacharie, Malachie. SB* (1969), 114.

200. N. Poulssen, *König und Tempel im Glaubenszeugnis des ATs. SBM,* 3 (1967), 151.

201. Lars G. Rignell, A. Petitjean, Rudolph; B. A. Mastin, "A Note on Zechariah VI 13," *VT,* 26 (1976), 113-15, etc., occasionally citing the *kissē'* (= "chair"!) of Eli the priest (1 S. 1:9; 4:13,18); cf. *BDB.*

202. Rudolph, 127f.

203. As suggested by E. König, *Die messianischen Weissagungen des ATs* (Stuttgart, 1923), 270f.

204. Cf. K. Schubert, "Der alttestamentliche Hintergrund der Vorstellung von den beiden Mesiassen im Schrifttum von Chirbet Qumran," *Jud,* 12 (1956), 24-28; A. S. van der Woude, *Die messianischen Vorstellungen der Gemeinde von Qumrân. SSN,* 3 (1957), 226-247.

procession to the palace, where the king ascended the throne and received the homage of the court.[205]

IV. Yahweh's Throne. The question of Yahweh's throne — referred to explicitly in 22 passages by means of the term *kissē'*[206] — goes hand in hand with the question of Yahweh's kingship. This kingship is borrowed from Canaanite tradition[207] and is probably to be explained as an amalgamation of the royal titles borne by El and Ba'al in Ugaritic. The use of the title "king" for Yahweh can hardly antedate the formation of the Israelite state, but is probably premonarchic.[208] It therefore does not represent a polemic reaction against the political monarchy.[209] The notion of Yahweh's throne clearly illustrates the development of royal terminology as applied to Yahweh.[210]

1. *Ark.* Yahweh was probably revered as an enthroned king at an early date, since the epithet *YHWH ṣᵉḇā'ôṯ yôšēḇ hakkᵉrūḇîm* was already applied to him at Shiloh (e.g., 1 S. 4:4).[211] In a continuation of the desert tent tradition (Nu. 10:35ff.; esp. the sacred tabernacle),[212] the throne idea here became associated with the ark,[213] although the actual word *kissē'* is not used. Even the terminology, then, militates against citing as analogous the "empty throne" found elsewhere in the ancient Near East,[214] a notion that overemphasizes the later role of the ark in the Solomonic temple. Gerhard von Rad,[215] too, suggests that an earlier function of the ark as a container was superseded by its function as a throne. At this

---

205. On the details, see R. de Vaux, *AncIsr,* 100-107; G. von Rad, "The Royal Ritual in Judah," *The Problem of the Hexateuch* (Eng. trans. 1966, repr. London, 1984), 222-231; E. Lipiński, *La royauté de Yahwé. VVAW.L,* 27/55 (1965), 336-391; H.-J. Kraus, *The Theology of the Psalms* (Eng. trans., Minneapolis, 1986), 120ff.; on divine adoption or legitimation of the new king as an important theological element of his enthronement, see H. Donner, "Adoption oder Legitimation?" *OrAnt,* 8 (1969), 87-119; on the king's throne name, see K. D. Schunck, "Der fünfte Thronname des Messias (Jes. IX 5-6)," *VT,* 23 (1973), 108ff.; H. Wildberger, *Isaiah 1–12* (Eng. trans., Minneapolis, 1991), 389-409; on the festival of Yahweh's enthronement, see J. A. Soggin, "מֶלֶךְ *mǣlǣk* könig," *THAT,* I, 914f.; → מלך *mlk.*

206. Cf., however → ישב *yāšaḇ*; → מלך *mlk.*

207. W. H. Schmidt, *Königtum Gottes in Ugarit und Israel. BZAW,* 80 ([2]1966), 91.

208. Alt; but cf. L. Rost, "Königsherrschaft Jahwes in vorköniglicher Zeit?" *ThLZ,* 85 (1960), 721-24, who dates the usage in the early period of the monarchy.

209. Cf. H.-J. Kraus, *Die Königsherrschaft Gottes im AT. BHTh,* 13 (1951), 94, and already H. Gressmann.

210. For bibliog., see Soggin, I, 914f.

211. See → צבאות *sᵉḇā'ôṯ*; → ישב *yāšaḇ*; → כרוב *kᵉrûḇ*.

212. O. Eissfeldt, "Kultzelt und Tempel," *Wort und Geschichte. Festschrift K. Elliger. AOAT,* 18 (1973), 51-55 = *KlSchr,* VI (1979), 1-7.

213. → ארון *'ᵃrôn,* I, 368.

214. H. Gunkel, "Die Lade Jahwes als Thronsitz," *ZMR,* 21 (1906), 33-42; E. Nielsen, "Some Reflections on the History of the Ark," *Congress Volume, Oxford 1959. SVT,* 7 (1960), 64ff.; still accepted by Albright, Barrois, and Bright; for additional bibliog., see J. Maier, *Vom Kultus zur Gnosis. Kairos,* 1 (Salzburg, 1964), 59, n. 59; *idem, Das altisraelitische Ladeheiligtum. BZAW,* 93 (1965), 54ff.

215. G. von Rad, "The Tent and the Ark," *The Problem of the Hexateuch,* 103-124, esp. 112.

late stage of its development, the ark with the two cherubim in the *d^e^bîr* of the temple (according to P, resting upon the *kappōreṯ*[216]) does indeed give the impression of an outsize cherubim throne (well attested in the ancient Near East);[217] this conception, however, never became standard in the OT. Thus the ark-throne theory is contradicted by the notorious absence of *kissē'* terminology, by the rapid application of → הדם *h^a^ḏōm* terminology[218] to the ark to emphasize Yahweh's transcendence, and finally by the gross disproportion between the ark and the cherubim.[219] At most, therefore, this throne theory might be the by-product of a theophanic motif closely associated with the ark.[220]

The passages that use *kissē'* for the ark as the throne of Yahweh in the temple are themselves disputed (cf. esp. Isa. 6:1; Job 26:9) and should be read solely as indicating Yahweh's presence and epiphany in the temple.[221] It is highly unlikely that *kissē' kāḇôḏ* in Jer. 14:21; 17:12 (secondary) refers to the ark.[222] In the figurative hymnic language in which Yahweh is here addressed, extension of the term to the whole temple mountain, Jerusalem, or even all Israel is by no means impossible.

Identification of an altar with a throne, a common religious concept,[223] may lie behind Ex. 17:16, a textually difficult verse. The etiology in Ex. 17:8-16 of the altar built by Moses at Rephidim, *YHWH nissî,* associates its construction with the Amalekite wars. The MT, Vulg., Sam. Pentateuch, Syr., and Targ. derive the name of the altar ("Yahweh my standard") from the strange expression *yaḏ kēs yāh* ("the hand of the throne of Yahweh"), clearly some kind of battle cry. The LXX no longer understood the text, interpreting it on the basis of *ksh,* "hidden."[224] J. Clericus (17th century), followed by many others, emended the text to *nēs-yāh* ("banner, military standard of Yahweh").[225] Other proposed emendations deserve no support.[226] The MT as it stands

---

216. → כפר *kpr.*

217. De Vaux, *MUSJ,* 37 (1960/61), 96f., 118; Maier, *Vom Kultus zur Gnosis,* 72f.; *idem, Das altisraelitische Ladeheiligtum,* 67f.

218. On the ark as God's footstool, see esp. Haran, esp. 89; J. Schreiner, *Sion-Jerusalem Jahwehs Königssitz. StANT,* 7 (1963), 24; Gössmann, esp. 34, following H. Tur-Sinai, H. Schmidt, F. Nötscher, and Y. Congar.

219. Maier, *Vom Kultus zur Gnosis,* 78f.

220. Cf. J. Dus, "Herabfahrung Jahwes auf die Lade und Entziehung der Feuerwolke," *VT,* 19 (1969), 290-311.

221. Cf. W. Zimmerli, "Das Bilderverbot in der Geschichte des alten Israel," *Studien zur alttestamentlichen Theologie und Prophetie. Gesammelte Aufsätze,* 2. *ThB,* 51 (1974), 247-260; Wildberger, 261.

222. G. Fohrer, review of Maier, *Das altisraelitisch Ladeheiligtum, ZAW,* 77 (1965), 360.

223. C. H. Ratschow, "Altar. I. Religionsgeschichtlich," *RGG*^{3}, I (1957), 251-53.

224. Cf. also D. N. Freedman and M. P. O'Connor, "יהוה *YHWH,*" *TDOT,* V, 500-521; A. R. Müller, "Ex 17,15f in der Septuaginta," *BN,* 12 (1980), 20-23.

225. A. Clamer; Noth; B. S. Childs; Eissfeldt; R. Gradwohl, "Zum Verständnis von Ex. XVII 15f.," *VT,* 12 (1962), 491-94 (institution of a votive hand?); F. Stolz, *Jahwes und Israels Kriege. AThANT,* 60 (1972), 99 (a kind of ark of Yahweh); M. Görg, "Nēs — ein Herrschaftsemblem?" *BN,* 14 (1981), 11-17 (emblem of sovereignty); → נס *nēs.*

226. U. Cassuto: from *kss,* "plan" (the altar as a "memorial pillar" for God's plans) (*A Comm. on the Book of Exodus* [Eng. trans., Jerusalem, 1967], *in loc.*); Nielsen: *kese',* "(full) moon" (a relic of Arabian moon worship in the Moses tradition).

is accepted by many.[227] Werner Fuss suggests a traditional practice (a priest's laying his hand on the massebah of Rephidim during the battle) analogous to E's concept of Moses' staff. It seems more realistic, however, to accept Georg Beer's theory, which sees in the altar a throne of the warlord Yahweh.[228] In Jer. 49:38, too, Yahweh appears as a warlord, setting up his throne before Elam to destroy kings and princes.

2. *Temple.* With the decline of the immanent and anthropomorphic concept of God, the *kissē'* of Yahweh soon was extended to refer to the temple (mountain) of Jerusalem, especially in the psalms of Yahweh's enthronement.[229] Here we find clear echoes of the Canaanite myths of Ba'al's battle with chaos and enthronement, in which Ba'al's throne on Mt. Saphon constitutes the focal point of the action (cf. Ps. 93:2; Jer. 17:12). The mythological language, however, does not make a convincing case for such a localization.[230] The situation is clearer in the identification of *m^{e}qôm kis^e'î* with *m^{e}qôm kappôṯ raglay* (cf. Ezk. 43:7; Isa. 60:13; and esp. Ex. 15:17f.),[231] although the latter is also associated with the ark (Ps. 132:7; cf. also 1 Ch. 28:2; Ps. 99:5; Lam. 2:1). The identification is not made explicit, however, either in Ezekiel or in the Psalms.

3. *Zion/Jerusalem.* Zion and Jerusalem were also looked upon as Yahweh's throne (Jer. 3:17).[232] The original limited notion of Yahweh's throne was further expanded and extended geographically. Here, finally, the notion of Yahweh's special presence in Zion clearly drew on the throne concept with the deliberate polemic intention of setting itself apart from earlier notions (ark = throne [Jer. 3:16]). Jeremiah (or one of his epigoni) wishes to call into question the historically grounded assurance of salvation associated with the presence of the ark. This passage reflects the controversy over Yahweh's presence with the ark,[233] especially following its loss. Like Jer. 17:12, Jer. 14:21[234] speaks of Jerusalem as the throne of Yahweh.[235] This usage may have given rise to the epithet *yôšēḇ ṣiyyôn,* "enthroned upon Zion" (Ps. 9:12[11]; cf. Isa. 8:18). Here we find echoes of the ancient Near Eastern notion of the sacred mountain as the place where the divine ruler of the universe has his throne,[236] the source of constant new creation and the blessing that upholds the world (cf. Isa. 8:18; 31:4; Joel 2:1; Jer. 8:19; 17:12;

---

227. A. Dillmann; O. Procksch; G. Beer, *Exodus. HAT,* III (1939); J. de Fraine, "La royauté de Yahvé dans les textes concernant l'arche," *Volume du Congrès, Genève 1965. SVT,* 15 (1966), 134-149, esp. 147f.; H. H. Schmid, *Mose. BZAW,* 110 (1968), 63f.; W. Fuss, *Die deuteronomistische Pentateuchredaktion in Exodus 3–17. BZAW,* 126 (1972), 360f.

228. Cf. I.2.d; III.5 above.

229. Cf. Lipiński, 117f.

230. Cf. Kraus, *Psalms 60–150,* 234f.

231. Metzger, *UF,* 2 (1970), 147.

232. Cf. M. Noth, *The History of Israel* (Eng. trans., New York, ^{2}1960), 101; de Vaux, *MUSJ,* 37 (1960/61), 97; A. Weiser, *Das Buch Jeremia 1–25,14. ATD,* XX (^{5}1966), 31.

233. Weiser, 29.

234. See above.

235. W. Rudolph, *Jeremia. HAT,* XII (^{3}1968), *in loc.*

236. Cf. R. L. Cohn, *The Sacred Mountain in Ancient Israel* (diss., Stanford, 1974), 123-203.

Ps. 9; 43:3; 48; 68:17-19[16-18]; 74:2; 132:13f.; God's mountain throne also appears in 1 En. 18:8; 24:3; 25:3).[237]

4. *Heaven.* The ultimate extension is explicit in Isa. 66:1, a messenger speech in which Yahweh calls heaven his throne and the earth his footstool. Here Trito-Isaiah takes up the Deuteronomistic criticism of a superficial understanding of the temple (2 S. 7:6f.), sketching the picture of a God beyond all earthly limitations, removed from the ready access of mortals. He sits enthroned in heaven (Ps. 2:4; 11:4; 123:1) while his name[238] dwells in the temple (1 K. 8:29f.,38f.,44f.):[239] "With Yahweh's throne, the heavenly world invades the sanctuary; with the divine throne resting on its base in the sanctuary and soaring into the heavens, the heavenly realm is present."[240] A heavenly throne is reserved for Yahweh alone. The arrogant attempt of the king of Babylon to equal him and set up his throne above the stars of El ends in his fall (Isa. 14:13ff.). Micaiah ben Imlah describes Yahweh's sitting in majesty on his throne, thus legitimating himself before Jehoshaphat and Ahab (1 K. 22:19 par. 2 Ch. 18:18; cf. Isa. 6). Yahweh is king over the nations; they celebrate his sovereignty. He reigns through all eternity, but in its cultic reenactment his reign takes on new actuality for present and future (Ps. 47:8f.[7f.]). He sits enthroned forever — a ground of hope and confidence for the oppressed, since it guarantees justice forever (Ps. 9:8[7]). His sovereignty is unaffected by the loss of temple and ark (Lam. 5:19), which only a superficial faith could think of as guaranteeing the power of God's presence. According to 2 Ch. 9:8, Yahweh's power is also manifested through the king's throne on earth; the eternity of Yahweh, however, does not depend on the endurance of this throne.

Thus the idea of Yahweh's throne displays a clear line of development. In the early period, Yahweh dwelt in the midst of his people as he journeyed with them; the ark symbolized his presence. The nascent conception of Yahweh's kingship led to identification of the ark with his throne. By the time of the Solomonic empire, this concept was transferred to the temple. Because popular faith made God's existence dependent on the existence of the temple (and not the reverse!), this causal nexus was shattered by Deuteronomy and the Deuteronomistic school. This change was facilitated by the existing association of Zion with the mountain of God, a "cosmic mystery"[241] that made the throne concept independent of the temple. Heaven became the throne of Yahweh, a development that laid the theological foundation for overcoming the catastrophe of 587. The "interchangeability of mountain, sanctuary, throne, and footstool"[242] is based on more than a "mythological sense of space";[243] it reflects a progressive revelation.

---

237. Maier, *Vom Kultus zur Gnosis,* 97-101.
238. → שׁם *šēm.*
239. Cf. A. S. van der Woude, "שֵׁם *šēm* Name," *THAT,* II, 954f.
240. Metzger, *UF,* 2 (1970), 145.
241. Maier, *Vom Kultus zur Gnosis,* 102.
242. Metzger, *UF,* 2 (1970), 156.
243. Maier, *Vom Kultus zur Gnosis,* 105f.

5. *Chariot Throne.* In the context of Ezekiel's prophecies, we find mention of Yahweh's chariot throne. Ezk. 1:26; 10:1 speak of a *d^emûṯ kissē',* "something like a throne," resting on a chariot of cherubim. The terminology rules out any association of this chariot with the portable stand on which the ark rested. Furthermore, references to the chariot throne in conjunction with the ark are later than Ezekiel: 1 Ch. 28:18 (*taḇnîṯ hammerkāḇâ*), Dnl. 7:9 (Aramaic) (a throne [*korsē'*] with wheels [*galg^elîn*]). In 4QŠirŠab 40:24, the phrase *tbnyt ks' mrkbh* already reflects a complex formulation of incipient Jewish *merkāḇâ* mysticism.[244]

The nature and significance of the chariot throne have been the subject of much debate. The description in Ezekiel (largely secondary) probably represents a technological transposition of the ancient Israelite tradition of Yahweh's appearance in a windstorm.[245] There may be parallels to Mesopotamian processional shrines[246] or possibly the chariot of the sun-god (2 K. 23:11). Johann Maier[247] sees in the chariot throne a transformation of the cultic expression *yōšēḇ hakk^eruḇîm* into cosmic mythology, deliberately dissociating it from the temple. The chariot throne of Ezekiel is developed further in Dnl. 7:9ff., 1 (Eth.) En. 46f.,[248] and numerous texts of the Dead Sea scrolls. In 4QŠirŠab 40:24, we have the liturgical formulary of a *merkāḇâ* ritual, one performed only in the holy of holies, invisible to the people.

V. Metaphorical Usage. The metaphorical usage of *kissē'* can be divided into five categories.

1. *Enthronement.* To "set up one's throne" always expresses a seizure of power through superior force (esp. Jer. 1:15; 43:10; cf. Isa. 14:13); to "sit upon the throne" usually signalizes dynastic succession (1 K. 1; 2:12; 22:10; etc.). Sitting upon the throne is taken as a sign of uncontested sovereignty (Ps. 9:5[4]; 132:12; Jer. 33:21; Zec. 6:13).

2. *Deposition.* The violent end of a reign is described by "being toppled from the throne" (Hag. 2:22; Ps. 89:45[44]; Dnl. 5:20) or "falling from the throne" (1 S. 4:18; Isa. 14:12 [with mythological hyperbole]).

3. *Exaltation.* Honor or disgrace may be expressed by the raising or lowering of a throne. This concept first appears during the Israelite sojourn in Egypt: Joseph is made vizier by Pharaoh and is inferior to him only with respect to the throne (Gen. 41:10). During the enthronement ceremony, the king is wished a greater throne than his predecessors (1 K. 1:37,47), symbolizing the extent of his domain. Exaltation of a

244. Cf. J. Neusner, "The Development of the Merkavah Tradition," *JSJ,* 2 (1971), 149-160.

245. W. Zimmerli, *Ezekiel I. Herm* (Eng. trans. 1979), 42f.

246. H. Schrade, *Die verborgene Gott: Gottesbild und Gottesvorstellung in Israel und im alten Orient* (Stuttgart, 1949).

247. *Vom Kultus zur Gnosis,* 120, following Procksch.

248. Cf. J. Marböck, "Henoch–Adam–Der Thronwagen," *BZ,* N.S. 25 (1981), 103-111.

throne was a mark of special honor. It is recorded only in the setting of foreign courts (2 K. 25:28 par. Jer. 52:32; Est. 3:1), where it served to symbolize the rehabilitation of subject monarchs. Hannah uses this motif in her hymn when she praises Yahweh as the God who raises the poor and needy from the dust, giving them a *môšāḇ* with princes and a *kissē' kāḇôḏ* (1 S. 2:8). The phrase *kissē' kāḇôḏ* reflects the extraordinary degree of this exaltation: in Jer. 14:21; 17:12, it clearly refers to the throne of Yahweh; and in Isa. 22:23 (secondary), describing the throne of honor of the Davidic king Eliakim, it refers to the throne of David as the focus of hope for the future.

4. *Mourning.* "Coming down from one's throne" — a custom also attested at Ugarit — was a sign of penitence or mourning. It undoubtedly signalized a voluntary (or forced: Isa. 14:12f.) act of self-degradation. The *kāḇôḏ* thus released was offered to the deity in hopes for a change of fortune. At an early date, however, the primary purpose of this ceremony shifted to a manifestation of grief and the absence of joy. It is odd that the OT mentions this ceremony only in the case of foreign monarchs (Isa. 47:1; Ezk. 26:16; Jon. 3:6).[249] Traces of it, however, may also be discerned in Israel (2 S. 12:16-19; 19:1-3[18:33–19:2]; 1 K. 21:27; 2 K. 19:1).[250]

5. *Harlot's Throne.* Sitting on a throne or seat before the gate means putting oneself on display — the seductive conduct of a harlot. In Prov. 9:14, personified Folly sits on a seat before the gate to entice the unwary.[251] Sitting on a chair before the gate[252] is here intended to feign elegance, rank, and *kāḇôḏ,* since only those who were noble (Isa. 47:1)[253] or rich (cf. Jas. 2:3) commonly sat on chairs. This pretense is designed to seduce those with no notion of true values. The facade is deceptive, however: just as the loose woman leaves a taste like wormwood in the mouth of the man she seduces, ultimately bringing him to the kingdom of death (Prov. 5:4f.), so Folly conceals that behind her "dwell only the shades, that her guests are in the depths of Sheol" (Prov. 9:18).[254]

VI. Dead Sea Scrolls. The noun *ks'* occurs only 8 times in the Dead Sea scrolls (3 times in the Temple scroll, but not in any of the other major scrolls). Three passages speak of the throne of David. The outline of sacred history in 4QDibHam recalls the election of the tribe of Judah and its shepherd David, who will sit upon the "throne of

---

249. Cf. N. Lohfink, "Enthielten die im AT bezeugten Klageriten eine Phase des Schweigens?," *VT,* 12 (1962), 269-273.

250. Cf. E. Kutsch, *"Trauerbräuche" und "Selbstminderungsbräuche" im AT. ThSt,* 78 (1965), 25-42; → הדם *h^a^ḏōm* (*h^a^dhōm*), 333.

251. Cf. H. Ringgren, *Sprüche. ATD,* XVI (1962), 43; G. Boström (*Proverbiastudien. LUÅ.* 30/3 [1935]) erroneously thinks the passage refers to cultic prostitution.

252. For Akkadian parallels, see *BuA,* II, 436; cf. also Lat. *prosedae,* "those who sit in front [of a bordello]" (Plautus *Poenulus* 266).

253. *ANEP,* 537.

254. Cf. also B. Lang, *Wisdom and the Book of Proverbs* (Eng. trans., New York, 1986), 97-101.

Israel" (*ks' yśr'l*) in the sight of God forever (4QDibHam 4:7). How this can be applied to the contemporary eschatological situation of the community is illustrated by 4QFlor (4Q174): in the manner of the Qumran pesharim, Nathan's prophecy concerning the endurance of David's dynasty and throne is applied to the present. The eternal throne (*ks' mmlkwt*) promised to David is now transferred to the messiah of the Davidic line (4QFlor 1:10f.). According to 4QpIs[a] 8-10,19 (interpreting Isa. 11:1-5), this Messiah will rise up at the end of days and sit upon the *ks' kbwd* (cf. 1 En. 45:3), wearing the "holy diadem" (*nzr qdwš*) and bright garments (*bgdy rwqmwt*) of the ruler. In 11QT 56:20 (citing Dt. 17:18) and 59:14,17 (a cento of 1 K. 2:4; 8:25; 9:5; Jer. 33:17), obedience to the torah is emphasized as a guarantee that the dynasty will endure. In 4QŠirŠab. there is a description of the heavenly chariot throne; it largely follows the text of Ezk. 1.[255] The statement in 11QPs[a] 26:11 that "righteousness and justice and truth are the foundations of his [God's] throne" has its precursors in Ps. 89:15(14); 97:2.[256] This expansion of the OT formula *mišpāṭ* and *ṣeḏeq* by the addition of *'ᵉmeṯ* is due to the popularity of this term at Qumran, but is also intended to motivate the Essenes of the community to practice this fundamental virtue. Almost all the Aramaic texts of 4Q refer to the chariot throne vision: 4QEn[c] fr. 1 7:18; 8:18 (cf. 8QEn[c] fr. 1 8:27); the throne of God is also mentioned in 4QEn[b] fr. 1 3:15 and 4Q246 fr. 1 1 (cf. 1 En. 14:18-20). In 11QtgJob 27:1 we find an interpretation of Job 36:7 saying that "kings on their thrones" (*mlkyn ytby kwrsyhwn*) are under God's protection only if they practice righteousness (cf. 11QPs[a] cited above).[257]

Fabry

255. Cf. IV.5 above; → רכב *rkb*.
256. Cf. I.4.a; III.4 above.
257. J. A. Fitzmyer and D. J. Harrington, *A Manual of Palestinian Aramaic Texts. BietOr,* 34 (1978), 35.

כָּסָה *kāsâ*; כָּסוּי *kāsûy*; כְּסוּת *kᵉsûṯ*; מִכְסֶה *mikseh*; מְכַסֶּה *mᵉḵasseh*

Contents: I. 1. Etymology; 2. Occurrences; 3. LXX. II. OT: 1. Literal Usage; 2. Covering the Land; 3. Covering the Face; 4. Cultic Usage; 5. Water; 6. Protection; 7. Earth; 8. Sins; 9. Concealment. III. Nouns.

I. 1. *Etymology.* The root *ksy* is attested in most Semitic languages. The verb occurs frequently in Ugaritic with the meaning "cover" in the context of words for clothing (*mʒzrt*);[1] we also find the derived nouns *kst,* "outer garment,"[2] and *mks,* "covering,

1. *KTU,* 1.5 VI, 16, 31; also 1.10 III, 24 (damaged).
2. *KTU,* 1.19 I, 36, 47; 1.17 VI, 15; 2.3, 12; 4.206, 5.

clothing."[3] In Phoenician, the verb is found in the Kilamuwa inscription:[4] "The one who had seen no linen from his youth in these my days was 'clothed' with byssus." The root is also found in most Aramaic dialects, in Old South Arabic (*ksw*), and in Arabic (*kasā*[*w*], "clothe").[5] It is uncertain whether the root is related to Akk. *kašû,* "cover up"; Akk. *kasû* means "tie."

2. *Occurrences.* The verb appears 3 times in the qal, twice in the niphal, 129 times in the piel with fairly even distribution, 7 times in the pual, and 9 times in the hithpael. Of the derived nouns, *kāsûy* appears twice, *k*ᵉ*sûṯ* 8 times, *mikseh* 12 times, and *m*ᵉ*kasseh* 4 times; all mean "covering."

3. *LXX.* In the vast majority of cases, the LXX translates with *kalýptein* or its compounds (*epikalýptein, katakalýptein, synkalýptein*); we also find *krýptein, peribállein, skepázein, stégein,* etc.

II. OT.

1. *Literal Usage.* The primary meaning of *kāsâ* is "cover," either to render invisible what is covered or to protect it or keep it warm. Jael covers the fugitive Sisera with a rug (*ś*ᵉ*mîḵâ*) to hide him (Jgs. 4:18f.). Michal covers a *t*ᵉ*rāp̄îm* image with a garment (*beged*) to make David's pursuers think that he is lying sick in bed (1 S. 19:13). The aging David is covered with clothes (*b*ᵉ*gāḏîm*) to keep him warm (1 K. 1:1). The tabernacle is covered with curtains (Ex. 26:13). When the Israelites break camp during their wandering in the desert, Aaron and his sons are to cover the ark and the other sacred objects with cloths (Nu. 4:5,8,9,15). Ezekiel reproves the inhabitants of Jerusalem for covering their idols with embroidered garments and worshipping them (Ezk. 16:18).[6] The sacrificial laws frequently speak expressly of the fat "that covers the entrails" (Ex. 29:13,22; Lev. 3:3,9,14; 4:8; 7:3). Clouds cover the heavens or the sun so that they cannot be seen (Ezk. 32:7; Ps. 147:8). Frogs covered "the land of Egypt" and locusts covered "the whole surface of the land, so that the ground could not be seen" (Ex. 8:2[Eng. v. 6]; 10:5,15). We are told similarly that the quails "covered the camp" (Ex. 16:13). The field of the sluggard is covered with nettles (Prov. 24:31). Leprosy can cover the whole body (Lev. 13:12f.); rot covers the dead in the dust (Job 21:26). Mal. 2:13 uses figurative language: "You cover Yahweh's altar with tears, with weeping and groaning because he no longer regards the offering or accepts it with favor at your hand."

2. *Covering the Land.* Balak tells Balaam how the people of Israel came out of Egypt and covered the whole land (Nu. 22:5; cf. Ps. 80:11[10], where the figurative

3. *KTU,* 1.4 II, 5.
4. *KAI,* 24, 12f.
5. *WKAS,* I, 196ff.
6. The adornment of idols is discussed by W. Zimmerli, *Ezekiel 1. Herm* (Eng. trans. 1979), 344.

language of the psalmist describes the shade of the vine of Israel covering the mountains of the land). Jer. 46:8 pictures the Egyptian assault upon Babylon as the flood of the Nile: Egypt says, "I will rise, I will cover the earth, I will destroy cities and their inhabitants." According to Ezk. 26:10, the dust of the enemy horses will cover Tyre. In Ezk. 30:18, a cloud covers the city of Tehaphnehes in Egypt and its inhabitants go into exile; in Ezk. 38:9, Gog and his hordes cover the land like a cloud. Isa. 60:1-7 contains two occurrences that may constitute a deliberate pun: "Darkness shall cover the earth, and thick darkness the peoples" (v. 2); but when the light of Yahweh rises over Israel, camels and dromedaries (bearing pilgrims or offerings) will cover the land of Israel (v. 6).

3. *Covering the Face.* In Isa. 6:2, the seraphim cover their faces with two wings to protect themselves from the sight of the Holy One; with two others they cover their "feet," i.e., their genitals, which must not be uncovered in God's presence (cf. Ezk. 12:6,12, where the face is covered to prevent seeing the land). The cherubim and "creatures" of Ezk. 1 cover their bodies (*g^ewiyyōṯ*) with their wings (vv. 11, 23). The covering of "nakedness" (*'erwâ*) is mentioned in Ex. 28:42 (the high priest's); Gen. 9:23 (Noah's, by his sons); Ezk. 16:8 (that of personified Israel, by God); Hos. 2:11(9) (with flax given by God). The root *ksh* is also used of ordinary clothing and thus becomes a synonym of → לבשׁ *lāḇēš,* "clothe." Dt. 22:12 (hithpael) speaks of a cloak "with which you clothe yourself"; cf. also 1 K. 11:29. Isa. 58:7 urges the "clothing" of the naked (cf. Ezk. 18:7,16). According to Ezk. 16:10, Yahweh clothes the foundling Israel with fancy garments. In a similar way, *ksh* can be used for clothing oneself in mourning (2 K. 19:1f. par. Isa. 37:1f.; Jon. 3:6,8; 1 Ch. 21:16) or putting on a veil (Gen. 24:65; 38:14 [hithpael]).

4. *Cultic Usage.* According to Ex. 24:15f. (P), a cloud covered Mt. Sinai for six days before Yahweh appeared to Moses; here the cloud is associated with the → כבוד *kāḇôḏ* of Yahweh. The cloud likewise covered the tabernacle or tent of meeting (*'ōhel mô'ēḏ*), signalizing that "the *kāḇôḏ* of Yahweh filled the dwelling place (*miškān*)" (Ex. 40:34; v. 35 states that the cloud "abode" [*šāḵan*] upon the tent). During the entire period of the wilderness wanderings, a cloud covered the tent by day (Nu. 9:15f.) and a fire by night. This is restated emphatically after the destruction of Korah and his company (Nu. 17:7[16:42]): the cloud covered the tent and the *kāḇôḏ* appeared — in other words, "Yahweh appeared in the manner typical of P."[7] The cloud was clearly intended to symbolize the presence of the holy God and to conceal him from the gaze of the people.

The latter function is explicit in the poetic theophany of Hab. 3:2ff. Yahweh's majesty (*hôḏ*) covers the heavens, while his praise (*t^ehillâ*) fills the earth (v. 3). This passage goes on to say that his power was veiled by his glory. This cloud of incense on the Day of Atonement plays a similar role: it covers the *kappōreṯ* lest the high priest perish (Lev. 16:13).

---

7. M. Noth, *Numbers. OTL* (Eng. trans. 1968), *in loc.*

5. *Water.* The waters of the Sea of Reeds covered the Egyptian army, leading to their destruction (Ex. 14:28; 15:5,10; Ps. 78:53; 106:11; cf. the allusion to the exodus in Josh. 24:7).

In Israelite cosmogony, the primal deep (*t^ehôm*) covered the earth as with a concealing garment (Ps. 104:6); but the waters will never again cover the earth, because Yahweh has set them a bound (v. 9). It therefore signals the return of chaos[8] when the waters once more cover the earth (Gen. 7:19f.). Ezk. 26:19 uses *t^ehôm* and its waters as an image for the destruction of the enemy (cf. Jer. 51:42). The same figurative motif appears in Job 22:11: "Your light is darkened,[9] so that you cannot see, and a flood of waters (*šip̱ʿâ*) covers you." Water and darkness are the standard images representing death and the underworld. Job 22:11b is repeated in 38:34b, where it seems intrusive.[10] A similar use of the motif appears in Ps. 44:20(19): ". . . that thou shouldst have . . . covered us with deep darkness."

Other passages use the water "that covers the sea" in similes: in Hab. 2:14, the knowledge of the *kāḇôḏ* of Yahweh will fill the world as the waters cover the sea (cf. Isa. 11:9).

6. *Protection.* Covering clearly serves as protection in 2 Ch. 5:8: the cherubim spread their wings over the place where the ark stood in order to cover it. Instead of *ksh,* the parallel passage 1 K. 8:7 uses the verb *skk,* which has a similar meaning. In Isa. 51:16, Yahweh hides ("covers") Israel in this shadow of his hand, to protect Israel as his own people.

7. *Earth.* The earth quite literally covers Korah and his followers (Nu. 16:33; Ps. 106:17). When the blood of an animal is poured out, it must be covered with earth lest some other living creature accidentally ingest it;[11] according to Karl Elliger,[12] this is an ancient apotropaic custom. But when Joseph's brothers seek to cover their brother's blood, they are trying to conceal a crime (Gen. 37:26). According to Isa. 26:21, at the eschaton the earth will disclose (*gillâ*) all the blood that has been shed and will no longer cover (*kissâ*) the slain — in other words, all blood guilt will be revealed. A similar idea lies behind Ezk. 24:7f.: blood is poured out on the bare rock so that it will lie exposed to provoke God's wrath. Job therefore prays: "O earth, cover not my blood, and let my cry find no resting place!" (Job 16:18).

8. *Sins.* The verb *ksh* is also used for "covering" — i.e., forgiving — sins. One should not place too much weight on the fact that if sin is "covered" it is still really present, even though hidden; for Ps. 32:1 uses the qal of *ksh* in parallel with *nśh* (= *nāśāʾ*), "take away, remove," and Ps. 85:3(2) says: "Thou didst forgive (*nāśāʾṯā*)

8. → מבול *mabbûl.*
9. Cf. *BHS.*
10. Cf. *BHS.*
11. Noth, *in loc.*
12. K. Elliger, *Leviticus. HAT,* IV (1966), *in loc.*

the iniquity of thy people; thou didst cover (*kissîṯā*) all their sin." Neh. 3:37(4:5) uses the piel of *ksh* in parallel with *māḥâ,* "blot out."

A totally different usage is present, however, in passages that speak of concealing or hiding sin. In Ps. 32:5, for example, the psalmist says that he does not hide his iniquity but acknowledges it (*yd*ʿ hiphil + *ydh* hiphil); the result is God's forgiveness (*nāśāʾ*). In Job 31:33, Job says that he has not concealed his transgressions or hidden (*ṭmm*) his iniquity in his bosom. Prov. 28:13 says: "He who conceals his transgressions will not prosper, but he who confesses (*ydh* hiphil) and forsakes (*ʿāzaḇ*) them will obtain mercy." In other words, "cover" (in the sense of "conceal") and "confess" are antonyms.

9. *Concealment.* There are other passages, too, where *ksh* means "conceal" or "keep secret." Proverbial wisdom teaches that one should "cover" secrets, i.e., keep them to oneself (Prov. 11:13); one should not show anger, but rather "ignore" an insult (12:16). The prudent "cover" their knowledge, i.e., keep it under wraps, while fools proclaim their folly (Prov. 12:23). According to 10:18, "upright lips conceal hatred," and according to v. 12, love covers all offenses; cf. 17:9: "he who conceals an offense seeks love, but he who repeats a matter alienates a friend." In Gen. 18:17, Yahweh says that he will not hide what he is about to do from Abraham; and in Ps. 40:11(10), the psalmist says that he has not hid (*ksh* piel) God's righteousness, but has always spoken (*ʾāmar*) of his faithful deliverance and not concealed (*kḥd*) his steadfast love and faithfulness. Prov. 10:11 makes a slightly different point: "The mouth of the wicked conceals violence."

A different metaphorical meaning is present when feelings or emotions "cover" or overwhelm someone. Subjects include *k*ᵉ*limmâ,* "dishonor" (Jer. 3:25; 51:51; Ps. 69:8[7]), *bûšâ* or *bōšeṯ,* "shame" (Ob. 10; Mic. 7:10; Ps. 44:16[15]), and *pallaṣûṯ,* "terror" (Ezk. 7:18; Ps. 55:6[5]). Cf. also *ʿāmāl* in Ps. 140:10(9) and *ṣalmāweṯ* in Ps. 44:20(19).

III. Nouns. Among the nominal derivatives of *ksh, k*ᵉ*sûṯ* is the most important. It means "covering, clothing," and appears in the first instance in its concrete meaning. In Gen. 49:11, the Samaritan Pentateuch uses *k*ᵉ*sûṯ* for MT *sûṯ*; it the latter is the correct reading, it must also mean something like "garment": Judah washes his garments in wine. In Ex. 22:26(27), it refers to the mantle (*śalmâ* = *śimlâ*) that must not be kept overnight if taken in pledge; Dt. 24:11ff. uses only the general word *ʿ*ᵃ*ḇôṭ,* "pledge." Dt. 22:12 speaks of tassels on the four corners of the cloak (*k*ᵉ*sûṯ*) "with which you cover (*ksh* piel) yourself." Ex. 21:10 decrees that if a man marries a slave and then takes another wife, he shall not diminish the food, clothing (*k*ᵉ*sûṯ*), or marital rights of the former. Twice in the book of Job we find the parallelism *mibb*ᵉ*lî l*ᵉ*ḇûš* par. *ʾên k*ᵉ*sûṯ* (24:7; 31:19), clearly referring to clothing in the literal sense.

The noun is used figuratively in Isa. 50:3 (God makes sackcloth [*śaq*] to cover the heavens in mourning); Job 26:6 (Sheol is naked [*ʿārôm*] and without covering before God — in other words, everything there is clearly known to him). Gen. 20:16, finally, uses the phrase *k*ᵉ*sûṯ ʿênayim,* "eye covering," for the gifts Abimelech gives Abraham in compensation for Sarah's honor. The expression probably comes from the legal realm and refers to a gift intended to avert mistrustful glances.[13]

The noun *mik̲seh* means "covering"; it denotes the roof of Noah's ark (Gen. 8:13), the roof of the tabernacle (Ex. 26:14; 35:11; 36:19; 40:19; Nu. 3:25) and the covering made of hides to cover the ark (Nu. 4:8,10-12; cf. Ex. 39:34). In Nu. 4:6,14, *kāsûy* has the same meaning. Finally, *meḵasseh* means both a "covering" in general (worms as the "covering" of people in Sheol [Isa. 14:11]; fine clothing [Isa. 23:18]) and the deck of a ship [Ezk. 27:7; RSV "awning"]).

Ringgren

13. Cf. G. von Rad, *Genesis. OTL* (Eng. trans. 1961), *in loc.*

כסל *ksl*; כְּסִיל *k^esîl*; כְּסִילוּת *k^esîlûṯ*; כֶּסֶל *kesel*; כִּסְלָה *kislâ*

Contents: 1. Etymology, Meaning; 2. OT Usage; 3. Theological Context; 4. LXX.

1. *Etymology, Meaning.* Despite differences in meaning, the occurrences of *ksl,* including those in the OT, suggest derivation from a single root with the basic meaning "fat, dull, clumsy."[1] Very close to this basic meaning is Heb. *kesel* I, "flanks," which is associated with physical fat: it actually denotes the fat musculature of the lumbar region in the vicinity of the kidneys or the fat of the loins, and hence by synecdoche the flanks or loins themselves; cf. Ugar. *ksl,* "loins," also "back";[2] Akk. *kislum, kaslu,*

ksl. G. Boström, *Proverbiastudien: die Weisheit und das fremde Weib in Spr 1–9. LUÅ,* 30/3 (1935); W. Caspari, "Über den biblischen Begriff der Torheit," *NKZ,* 39 (1928), 668-695; É. P. Dhorme, *L'emploi métaphorique des noms de parties du corps en hébreu et en akkadien* (Paris, 1923, repr. 1963); T. Donald, "The Semantic Field of 'Folly' in Proverbs, Job, Psalms, and Ecclesiastes," *VT,* 13 (1963), 285-292; G. R. Driver, "Two Astronomical Passages in the OT," *JTS,* N.S. 7 (1956), 1-11; M. Held, "Studies in Comparative Semitic Lexicography," *Studies in Honor of Benno Landsberger. AS,* 16 (1965), 395-406; J. J. Hess, "Die Sternbilder in Hiob 9.9 und 38,31f., *Festschrift G. Jacob* (Leipzig, 1932), 94-99; S. A Mandry, *There is No God! A Study of the Fool in the OT* (diss., Rome, 1972); S. Mowinckel, *Die Sternnamen im AT. NTTSup,* 5 (1928), 36ff.; G. von Rad, *Wisdom in Israel* (Eng. trans., Nashville, 1972); H. N. Richardson, "Some Notes on ליץ and its Derivatives," *VT,* 5 (1955), 163-179; W. M. W. Roth, "NBL," *VT,* 10 (1960), 394-409; M. Sæbø, "כְּסִיל *k^esīl* Tor," *THAT,* I, 836ff.; R. B. Y. Scott, "Wise and Foolish, Righteous and Wicked," *Studies in the Religion of Ancient Israel. SVT,* 23 (1972), 146-165; U. Skladny, *Die ältesten Spruchsammlungen in Israel* (Göttingen, 1962); U. Wilckens, *Weisheit und Torheit. BHTh,* 26 (1959), 160-196.

1. Cf. the lexica and *THAT,* I, 836.
2. *WUS,* no. 1357; *UT,* no. 1280.

"loins."[3] Details may be found elsewhere.[4] Cf. also the toponym *k^e^sālôn* (Josh. 15:10), "(upon the) back."[5]

(It is also possible that *kesel/kislu* is a primary noun distinct from the other words associated with *ksl.*[6])

Distinct from *kesel* I is the noun *kesel* II;[7] it means figuratively "dull, dogged, slow," both in the negative sense of "stupidity" and in the positive sense of "trust" or "confidence." The latter meaning, however, can itself take on negative overtones of "false hope."[8] The derived noun *kislâ* has the corresponding positive sense of "confidence," and the noun *k^e^sîlûṯ* has the negative sense of "stupidity."[9]

The Hebrew verb *ksl* and the nouns *k^e^sîl* I and II are likewise used in the figurative sense of "be fat, dull, sluggish," always with negative overtones; cf. also the personal name *kislôn* (Nu. 34:21) with the meaning "dull."[10] The verb *ksl* exhibits the meaning "be stupid"; cf. Arab. *kasila,* "be dull";[11] Akk. (metathesized) *saklu,* "stupid."[12] The constellation of Orion is denoted by *k^e^sîl* II, which clearly means "foolish," since Orion was thought to be "foolish and violent."[13] The plural means the stars of Orion with or without the associated constellations. Used as either a substantive or an adjective, *k^e^sîl* II means "fool" or "foolish, stupid." The theory that *k^e^sîl* is a loanword[14] or an aramaism[15] is therefore unnecessary and unconvincing.[16]

2. *OT Usage.* It is noteworthy that the OT occurrences of *ksl* appear for the most part in Wisdom Literature and to a lesser degree in cultic and priestly texts. In the sense of "loins," *kesel* I (7 occurrences: Lev. 3:4,10,15; 4:9; 7:4; Ps. 38:8[Eng. v. 7]; Job 15:27; cf. also Sir. 47:19)[17] is found primarily in the context of the sacrificial ritual detailed in Lev. 3, where it defines more precisely certain pieces of fat near the

---

3. *AHw,* I (1965), 486f.
4. Dhorme, 132f.; Held, 395ff.; *KBL*³, 466.
5. *IPN,* 146; *KBL*³, 466.
6. *AHw,* I, 486f.
7. But cf. Held, 395ff.
8. *KBL*³, 466.
9. *THAT,* I, 836; *KBL*³, 466.
10. *IPN,* 227; *KBL*³, 466.
11. Which L. Kopf, "Arabische Etymologien und Parallelen zum Bibelwörterbuch," *VT,* 8 (1958), 179f., would associate instead with *kšl* (= *Studies in Arabic and Hebrew Lexicography* [Jerusalem, 1976]).
12. *AHw,* II (1972), 1012; Held, 406f.; *KBL*³, 466.
13. Cf. Mowinckel, 36ff.; Hess, 97ff.; *AuS,* I (1928), 497ff.; M. A. Beek, "Sternbild," *BHHW,* 1867; Driver, 1ff.; for further bibliog., cf. G. Fohrer, *Das Buch Hiob. KAT,* XVI (1963), 198.
14. Cf. *BLe,* §471.
15. G. Beer–R. Meyer, *Hebräische Grammatik,* II (Berlin, ³1969), 28.
16. Cf. *GK,* §84a⁰; *THAT,* I, 836.
17. Cf. *KBL*³, 466.

kidneys of the sacrificial animal, which are among the portions to be burned for Yahweh.[18]

The noun *kesel* II in the positive metaphorical sense of "confidence" appears twice in the book of Job (Job 8:14; 31:24) and once each in Psalms (Ps. 78:7) and Proverbs (Prov. 3:26).[19] In these latter passages, *kesel* describes a positive relationship with Yahweh: remembering his works, trusting[20] in him, being constant in mind (Ps. 78:7), or refusing to fear (confident in God's salvation) when faced with the sudden destruction of the wicked (Prov. 3:26).[21] In Job, however, *kesel* appears in negative contexts, being likened (as the attitude of those who forget God) to an insubstantial spiderweb that breaks asunder or a house that collapses (Job 8:14), or being rejected (as trust in wealth) as conduct out of the question for the faithful (31:24).

The derived noun *kislâ* appears 3 times: Job 4:6; Ps. 85:9(8); 84:6(5) (*kislôṯ* [conj.]); possibly also Ps. 143:9 (conj.). In Job 4:6, it stands in parallel with "hope" (*tiqwâ*), being grounded in a God-fearing life; in Ps. 84:6(5), it stands in parallel with "refuge, strength" (*ʿōz*). It thus denotes a hope shared by the oppressed faithful because Yahweh's help is near (Ps. 85:9[8]) or because Yahweh can rescue them from their enemies (Ps. 143:9 [?]).

The verb *ksl* appears only once: Jer. 10:8 uses it in the qal with the negative metaphorical meaning "be stupid," describing the worthless and impotent idols that need not be feared. The context clearly exhibits wisdom influence: the idols are so stupid that instruction (*mûsār*) cannot be expected of them.

The noun *kesel* II likewise appears twice in a negative sense. It describes the stupidity of those who delight in their own words, refusing to take seriously the transitoriness of human life (Ps. 49:14[13]). Eccl. 7:25 uses it in parallel with "folly,"[22] "madness," and "wickedness."[23] The noun *kᵉsîlûṯ* appears only once, in Prov. 9:13, where it serves to personify stupidity and folly as "Lady Folly," who in contrast to "Lady Wisdom" lacks all knowledge[24] but nevertheless seeks with passion to lead the simple[25] astray from the right way.[26]

Most common are the inherently negative nouns *kᵉsîl* I and II. The latter occurs only 4 times (Am. 5:8; Isa. 13:10; Job 9:9; 38:31). As a term for Orion or the constellations associated with Orion, it conveys the deliberately negative sense of "foolish," because elsewhere in the ancient Near East the stars[27] were worshipped as deities who foolishly called Yahweh's power into question. In Israel, therefore, it was constantly necessary

18. → חלצים *ḥᵃlāṣayim* (*chᵃātsayim*), VI.
19. But cf. M. Dahood, "Hebrew-Ugaritic Lexicography III," *Bibl*, 46 (1965), 330, who follows the Vulg. in reading *kesel* I in Prov. 3:26.
20. → בטח *bāṭaḥ* (*bāṭach*).
21. For a different interpretation, cf. F. Vattioni, "Proverbi 3_{26}," *Aug*, 6 (1966), 324f.
22. → סכל *skl*.
23. → רשע *ršʿ*.
24. → ידע *ydʿ*.
25. → פתי *petî*.
26. Cf. B. Lang, *Wisdom and the Book of Proverbs* (Eng. trans., New York, 1986), 102-9.
27. → כוכב *kôḵāḇ*.

to describe them as having been created by Yahweh's creative power and being subordinate to his sovereign authority.

There are 70 occurrences of *k^e^sîl* I, almost all of which appear in Proverbs (49 in all: 4 in Prov. 1–9, 30 in the collection 10:1–22:16, and 11 in 26:1-12, the "guidelines for fools") and Ecclesiastes (18 in all). There are 3 occurrences in the Psalms (Ps. 49:11[10]; 92:7[6]; 94:8). The observation that over the course of time *k^e^sîl* comes increasingly to be used as a noun instead of an adjective suggests that it denoted initially a specific human trait and only later developed into a term for a specific type of person.[28] The characteristic of "slowness" (in the metaphorical sense) seems to have constituted the starting point of this development.

This basic meaning of *k^e^sîl* can still be found in the sections of Proverbs incorporating mostly early material. In Prov. 26:1-12, for example, the *k^e^sîl* is a foolish individual who will not learn and can be kept in line only by use of the rod (v. 3; cf. also 19:29), but nevertheless considers himself wise (26:5, 12). Wisdom is fundamentally alien to the mouth of the fool; he does not know how to employ it (vv. 7, 9). He merely repeats his folly like a dog returning to its vomit (v. 11). It is therefore unwise and dangerous to entrust one's affairs to a fool (vv. 6, 10). One should not even answer a fool except to put him and his supposed wisdom to shame (vv. 4f.).

The general description seems to fit a young person for whom all attempts at education and training have failed; he acts injudiciously, proves himself foolish and incompetent, and must therefore be disciplined. He is thus also the kind of person who causes his parents grief and worry (Prov. 17:21,25; 10:1) and despises his father and mother (15:20; cf. Eccl. 4:13).

It thus became easy to see a *k^e^sîl*[29] in anyone who lacks understanding (Prov. 8:5; 17:16; Ps. 92:7[6]; 94:8), despises wisdom (Prov. 23:9), and takes no pleasure in understanding (18:2). A *k^e^sîl* flaunts his folly[30] (Prov. 13:16), wastes what is precious (21:20), and has no concrete goal (17:24). Thus the *k^e^sîl* comes to be the primary antithesis of the one who is "wise" (cf. Ps. 49:11[10]; Prov. 3:35; 10:1; 13:20; 14:16,24; 15:2,7,20; 21:20; 26:5; 29:11; Eccl. 2:14f.,16; 4:13; 6:8; 7:4f.; 9:17; 10:2,12).[31] Other antonyms to *k^e^sîl* include *nāḇôn,* "judicious" (Prov. 14:33; 15:14), and *mēḇîn,*[32] "astute" (17:10,24), as well as *ʿārûm,* "prudent" (12:23; 13:16; 14:8). Synonyms include → **בער** *baʿar,* "brutish, dumb" (Jer. 10:8; Ps. 49:11[10]; 92:7[6]; 94:8), → **פתי** *peṯî,* "simple" (Prov. 1:22,32; 8:5), → **ליץ** *lyṣ,* "scoffer" (1:22; 19:29),[33] → **אויל** *'^e^wîl,* "fool" (10:8,10,21; 14:3; 17:28), and finally → **נבל** *nāḇāl,* "fool" (17:21).[34] Unlike the wise, a fool never deserves honor (Prov. 26:1,8); his folly is his only garland (14:24), and it is not fitting for him to live in luxury (19:10).

28. Cf. *THAT,* I, 837.
29. For a general discussion, cf. *ibid.*
30. → **אויל** *'^e^wîl.*
31. → **חכם**; cf. Skladny, 12, 21f., 33ff., 50f., 60f.; Donald, 285ff.
32. → **בין** *bîn.*
33. Cf. Richardson.
34. Cf. Roth.

His own stupidity makes such a fool complacent (Prov. 1:32); he feels totally secure (14:16). Nothing can make any impression on him, not even rebukes and blows (Prov. 17:10). Hand in hand with his foolishness goes his lack of restraint, so that he flares up easily and gives vent to his anger (Prov. 29:11; cf. 14:17; Eccl. 7:9). His folly thus finds expression above all in what he says: he lays his heart bare (Prov. 18:2), his heart and mouth proclaim folly (12:23; 15:2; also 13:16), his mouth feeds on folly (15:14). He speaks at length or loudly and without judicious lips (Prov. 29:20; Eccl. 5:2[3]; 9:17).

With an explicit theological accent, the fool shows himself to be one who hates knowledge (Prov. 1:22) or suppresses wisdom (14:33), trusting instead in his own mind (28:26). His heart is false and wicked (cf. Prov. 15:7; 19:1); his heart (= mind) inclines toward the left (Eccl. 10:2), the side of ill omen. The fool walks in darkness (Eccl. 2:14).

He thus mistakes the serious purpose of life (Eccl. 7:5ff.), delights in evil (Prov. 13:19; cf. 14:16; Eccl. 4:17[5:1]), and takes pleasure in wrongdoing (Prov. 10:23).

His folly proves deceptive (Prov. 14:8); he is recognized as one who speaks with perverse lips (19:1) and utters slander in the gate (10:18). His lips bring strife (Prov. 18:6) and he does not do what he has promised (Eccl. 5:3[4]).

Not only does he heap disgrace on disgrace (Prov. 3:35), but he is also a snare to himself, bringing about his own ruin (18:7; Eccl. 4:5; 10:12) and that of others (Prov. 13:20; 19:13). He is so great a danger to others that it is better to meet an enraged bear than a fool (Prov. 17:12).

3. *Theological Context.* When *ksl* is used in the context of theological wisdom to express an attitude or action related to Yahweh or Yahweh's works, his help and deliverance, the fundamental semantic element of "heaviness, endurance" serves to describe a perseverance and strength, a hope and trust, an act of confidence that arrives at length at its goal (cf. Ps. 78:7; 84:6[5]; 85:9[8]; 143:9 [?]; Prov. 3:26; Job 4:6). Such conduct is characteristic of someone who is faithful and fears God, who grounds his life in Yahweh and endures through trial and tribulation.

When the root, however, is used of reliance on what is worthless, deceptive, and ephemeral, it describes a stubborn, defiant, and obstinate persistence in a presumptuous false sense of security and perilous stupidity (cf. Ps. 49:14[13]; Eccl. 7:25; Job 8:14; 31:24). Such conduct is typical of the godless, who do not set their hope upon Yahweh.

This aspect is further developed in the personal noun *k^{e}sîl* when the stupidity of the fool is understood as conduct reflecting an incorrect attitude toward Yahweh and his ordering of the world. The primarily intellectual "slowness" of the fool is thus interpreted theologically as malice, as a deliberate rejection of the divine reality, as trust in one's own judgment (cf. Prov. 1:22; 13:19; 15:7; 19:1; 28:26; Eccl. 2:14; 4:17[5:1]). The fool's consequent actions are then characterized morally as deliberate malfeasance.[35] This malice and wickedness find expression primarily in the fool's decep-

35. → דבה *dibbâ* (*dibbāh*), IV.1.

tive, lying, slanderous words, deliberately stirring up strife with the intent to injure others and bring disaster upon them (cf. Prov. 10:18; 13:20; 14:8; 18:6; 19:1,13; Eccl. 5:3[4]), which however also brings the fool to destruction (cf. Prov. 17:12; 18:7; Eccl. 4:5). In this context, then, the fool is the antithesis not only to the "sage"[36] but to the one who is "righteous"; "foolish" thus becomes synonymous with "wicked" (cf. Prov. 10:23 and 15:7 in context).[37]

In the context of a skeptical wisdom theology like that of Ecclesiastes, who rejects an optimistic, all-embracing rational wisdom by emphasizing that the divine order is ultimately beyond human ken, that Yahweh transcends any comprehensible order, the fool can stand, in a sense, in the company of the sage. It can be pointed out that the sage has scarcely any advantage over the fool because even the sage cannot comprehend the order that governs the world and human life (Eccl. 8:17). All human efforts must remain ultimately vain and meaningless. The same fate awaits both the sage and the fool: both must die, even in the memory of future generations (Eccl. 2:15). Sage and fool thus draw very close to each other.

There remains, nonetheless, an essential difference. The enduring advantage of the sage over the fool is like the advantage of light over darkness, so that the fool is like one who gropes about blindly while the sage sees (Eccl. 2:12ff.). While the true sage demonstrates a realistic sense of life, considering its course and end, taking it seriously just as it is and enjoying the pleasures of the moment vouchsafed by God, the fool does not do justice to this reality, living thoughtlessly and superficially, out of contact with reality (cf. Eccl. 7:5ff.).

Since both wisdom and folly are conceived as powers influencing and controlling human life, both can be thought of as mutually hostile principles and personified as Lady Wisdom[38] and Lady Folly (cf. Prov. 9:13ff.; 6:20ff.). Lady Folly, as the antithesis to the soteriological figure of Lady Wisdom, appears as a wicked and treacherous power, passionately and seductively attracting the unsuspecting into her power and then administering deadly poison.[39]

4. *LXX.* The LXX interprets the various derivatives of the root with some uniformity, translating *k^esîl* with *áphrōn* (57 times), *asebḗs* (5 times), and *apaídeutos* (twice). For *kiṣlâ* it uses *aphrosýnē*; for *k^esîlûṯ, áphrōn.* In translating *kesel,* it varies between *mēríon* (4 times) on the one hand and *aphrosýnē, skándalon,* and *elpís* on the other.

Schüpphaus

36. → חכם *ḥaḵam* (*chākham*).
37. On the antonyms "righteous" and "wicked," cf. → צדק *ṣdq,* → רשע *rš'.*
38. → חכם *ḥāḵām* (*chākham*), V.1.
39. Cf. Bostrom, 15ff.; von Rad, 166ff.; Lang, 97-109.

כֶּסֶף kesep

Contents: I. General: 1. Occurrences, Etymology; 2. Meaning; 3. LXX. II. Production. III. Usage: 1. Secular; 2. Cultic. IV. Appraisal: 1. General; 2. Prophets; 3. Deuteronomy; 4. Wisdom. V. Figurative Usage. VI. Dead Sea Scrolls.

I. General.

1. *Occurrences, Etymology.* The noun *kesep* occurs some 400 times in the Hebrew portion of the OT and 13 times in the Aramaic portion. Apart from the Hebrew and Aramaic language group, it is attested also in Akkadian (*kaspu*). The noun might be derived from either *ksp* I, "break off," or *ksp* II, "grow pale"; the basic meaning would

---

kesep. S. Abramski, " 'Slag' and 'Tin' in the First Chapter of Isaiah," *ErIsr,* 5 (1958), 105-7 [Heb.], 89* [Eng. summary]; M. Avi-Yonah and J. Liver, "מטבע," *EMiqr,* IV (1962), 816-825; J. Babelon, "Monnaie," *DBS,* V (1957), 1346-1375; W. G. Barnes, *Business in the Bible* (Philadelphia, 1926); A.-G. Barrois, *Manuel d'archéologie biblique,* I (Paris, 1939), 3732-73; II (Paris, 1953), 228-243, 258-273; H. Blümner, "Silber," *PW,* III A/1 (1927), 13-23; R. Bogaert, "Geld (Geldwirtschaft)," *RAC,* IX (1976), 797-907; A. E. Crawley, "Metals and Minerals," *ERE,* VIII (1958), 588-593; P. Einzig, *Primitive Money in Its Ethnological, Historical and Economic Aspects* (London, 1949); R. J. Forbes, "Extracting, Smelting, and Alloying," in C. Singer, *et al.,* eds., *A History of Technology* (Oxford, [3]1956), I, 572-599; *idem, Metallurgy in Antiquity* (Leiden, 1950); *idem, Studies in Ancient Technology,* VII (Leiden, [2]1966), 130f.; VIII (Leiden, [2]1971), 193-259; W. Frerichs, "Silber," *BHHW,* III (1966), 1793f.; K. Galling, "Münze," *BRL*[2], 233f.; A. Guillaume, "Metallurgy in the OT," *PEQ,* 94 (1962), 129-132; P. Haupt, "The Hebrew Terms for Gold and Silver," *JAOS,* 43 (1923), 116-127; E. W. Heaton, "Metal Workers," *Everyday Life in OT Times* (New York, 1956), 125-29; L. Köhler, "Alttestamentliche Wortforschung: Sīg, sīgīm = Bleiglätte," *ThZ,* 3 (1947), 232-34; R. Loewe, "The Earliest Biblical Allusion to Coined Money?" *PEQ,* 87 (1955), 141-150; O. Loretz, " 'Verworfenes Silber' (Jer 6,27-30)," *Wort, Lied, und Gottespruch. Festschrift J. Ziegler,* II. *FzB,* 2 (1972), 231f.; A. Lucas, "Silver in Ancient Times," *JEA,* 14 (1928), 313-19; F. W. Madden, *History of Jewish Coinage, and Money in the Old and New Testament* (1864, repr. San Diego, 1967); Y. Meshorer, *Jewish Coins of the Second Temple Period* (Eng. trans., Tel Aviv, 1967); K. Regling, "Silberprägung und Silberwährung," *PW,* III A/1, 23-34; B. Reicke, "Geld," *BHHW,* I (1962), 540f.; A. Reifenberg, *Ancient Jewish Coins* (Jerusalem, [2]1947); C. Sauer, "Metalle," *BHHW,* II (1964), 1206-8; D. Schlumberger, *L'argent grec dans l'empire achéménide* (Paris, 1953); W. Schwabacher, "Geldumlauf und Münzprägung in Syrien im 6. und 5. Jahrh. v. Chr.," *Opuscula archaeologica,* 6 (Lund, 1948), 139-149; E. Stern, "[ה]כסף," *EMiqr,* V (1963), 668-671; E. L. Sukenik, "More About the Oldest Coins of Judaea," *JPOS,* 15 (1935), 341-43; *idem,* "Paralipomena Palæstinensia: I. The Oldest Coins of Judaea," *JPOS,* 14 (1934), 178-182; P. Thomsen, "Silber," *RLV,* XII, 161-64; F. R. Walton, "Metalle," *RGG*[3], IV (1960), 908; H. Weippert, "Geld," *BRL*[2], 88-90; *idem,* "Schmuck," *BRL*[2], 282-89; M. Weippert, "Metall und Metallbearbeitung," *BRL*[2], 219-224.

then be either "something broken off" or "white metal."[1] Von Soden,[2] however, instead of deriving *ksp* from a verbal root, considers it a non-Semitic intrusion. Outside the OT, *ksp* occurs frequently in Phoenician,[3] Punic,[4] Old Aramaic,[5] Ya'udic,[6] Egyptian Aramaic,[7] Jewish Aramaic,[8] Nabatean,[9] and Palmyrene[10] inscriptions. It is also clearly used as a monetary unit in an Ammonite ostracon.[11] In most cases there is hardly enough evidence for a semantic distinction between "silver" and "coin." As the nature of the extant inscriptions would lead us to expect, *ksp* can denote many things: a monetary price, a fine, interest, a bride-price, etc. The precise meaning of *ksp ṣryp* at Elephantine is discussed by Porten.[12]

2. *Meaning.* As a material, *kesep̱* means "silver"; as money, it means "(silver) coin." Until well into the Persian period, of course, the metal itself served as a medium of exchange; an appropriate amount would be weighed out on a balance as necessary (Isa. 46:6; Jer. 32:10). One's supply was carried about in a bag (Prov. 7:20). Often, as in general statements of a person's wealth, it is impossible to draw a sharp distinction between the two meanings. The monetary units were therefore identical with weights. The basic unit was the shekel, weighing roughly 11.4 grams (.4 oz.);[13] it may be understood when no unit is stated (Gen. 20:16; 1 K. 10:29; Isa. 7:23; etc.). Higher values were expressed in terms of talents (*kikkār,* 1 K. 20:39; 2 K. 5:5; 2 Ch. 36:3; etc.). P uses a talent of 3,000 shekels (Ex. 38:25); a shekel in turn comprised 20 gerahs (30:13). Ezr. 2:69; Neh. 7:70 reckon silver in minas (*māneh*); the relationship between the mina and the shekel is not clear. At Ugarit, 50 shekels constituted a mina; in Mesopotamia, it was 60, in harmony with the dominant sexagesimal system.[14] The *'ᵃg̱ôrâ* (RSV "piece of silver") of 1 S. 2:36 was probably a small unit of weight; the LXX translation *obolós* is anachronistic. The shekel in Neh. 5:15 and third of a shekel in 10:33(Eng. v. 32) probably represent the first actual coinage. The silver coins that have been discovered from the province "Yehud" date from the fourth century.[15] Archaeological evidence indicates, how-

---

1. *KBL*³, 467a.
2. *AHw, s.v.*
3. *KAI,* 3, 2; 13, 4; 24, 12; 43, 14; 50, 3, 5; 51 vo. 4; 60, 6.
4. *KAI,* 74, 7; 89, 4, 6; 191 B, 1; Marseilles sacrificial tariff: *KAI,* 69, 3, 5, 7, 9, 11, 12.
5. *KAI,* 216, 10f.
6. *KAI,* 215, 11.
7. *AP,* 1, 7; 2, 15; 5, 10, 13; 10, 7, 11, 12, 18; etc.; *BMAP,* 1, 3, 7; 1, 6; etc.
8. *DISO,* 124; *LexLingAram,* 85.
9. *CIS,* II, 200, 7, 8; 206, 7; etc.
10. *CIS,* II, 3902, 1; 3945, 4; 3951, 5; etc.
11. F. M. Cross, "Ammonite Ostraca from Heshbon," *AUSS,* 13 (1975), 1-20.
12. B. Porten, *Archives from Elephantine* (Berkeley, 1968), 305ff.
13. H. Weippert, "Gewicht," *BRL*², 93b.
14. *Idem.*
15. Meshorer, 38.

ever, that foreign coins were already in use in the sixth century.[16] Adolf Reifenberg's interpretation[17] of coin 1A as the earliest Jewish coin, dating from the fifth century, is not generally accepted.[18]

The use of the word in conjunction with gold and in lists is discussed elsewhere,[19] as is the monetary use of silver at Ugarit.[20]

3. *LXX.* The LXX usually translates *kesep* with *argýrion*; for construct phrases, it can use the adj. *argyroús.* When the metal itself is meant, we sometimes find *árgyros* (Isa. 60:9; Ezk. 22:20; Prov. 10:20; 17:3; 27:21; Dnl. 2:35,45; Ezr. 1:11). Instead of the adjective we also found the participial expressions *periērgyrōménos* (Isa. 30:22; Ps. 68:14[13][LXX 67:14]), *periērgyrōménos argýrō* (Ex. 27:11) or *argyríō* (Ex. 38:17,19[LXX 37:15,17]), and *katērgyrōménos argyríō* (Ex. 27:17). For *miqnaṯ-kesep,* we find *argyrṓnētos* (Gen. 17:12,13,23; Ex. 12:44). All other translations are interpretative, aiming only to convey the meaning (*lýtra* [Nu. 3:51]; *chrḗmata* [Job 27:17]; *timḗ* [Job 31:39]; *hormískos sardíou* [Prov. 25:11]) or referring anachronistically to coinage (*argyroí* [Zec. 11:12,13]; *chrysoí* [!] [Gen. 37:28; 45:22]; *dídrachma* [Gen. 20:16]; *síkloi* [Dt. 22:19; Isa. 7:23]; *tálanta* [Est. 4:7]).

II. Production. It is clear from metaphors and similes that the Israelites knew how to produce silver in the preexilic period. The process common in antiquity was based on the silver content of galena (PbS). First the sulfur was removed; then the lead was separated from the silver by a process of oxidation.[21] The process made use of a smelting furnace (*kûr,* Ezk. 22:18; etc.) and crucible (*maṣrēp̱,* Prov. 17:3; 27:21).[22] The hapax legomenon *ʿalîl* in Ps. 12:7(6) is interpreted by the Targ. as a smelting furnace. The precise stages in the process denoted by the verbs *ṣrp,* "purify," *bḥn,* "test," *ntk,* "melt," *ṭhr,* "purify," and *zqq,* "filter," are not completely clear. Educated circles were also aware that the needed ore had to be mined (Job 28:1).[23] The scarcity of domestic ore made it necessary to meet the demand by importation; the import of Spanish silver, brought by the Phoenicians, was apparently well known (1 K. 10:22; Jer. 10:9; Ezk. 27:12). The noun *sîgîm* probably refers to the dross, yellow lead oxide (PbO) (Isa. 1:22,25; Prov. 25:4; 26:23),[24] also called "refuse silver" (Jer. 6:30).[25]

---

16. *Ibid.,* 35.
17. Pp. 1-8.
18. Meshorer, 39f.
19. → זהב *zāhāḇ* (*zāhābh*), IV, 2.
20. Cf. *UT,* no. 1284.
21. Köhler, Forbes.
22. M. Weippert, 221f.
23. Forbes, *Studies in Ancient Technology,* VII, 130f.
24. Köhler, Forbes.
25. Abramski.

III. Usage.

1. *Secular.* a. *Economics.*

(1) Commerce. Commercial prices were quoted in silver shekels. Various articles of merchandise are named: grain (the Joseph story; 2 K. 7:1,16; Job 31:39f.), wine (Isa. 55:1; Cant. 8:11), milk (Isa. 55:1), cattle (Ex. 21:35), slaves (Gen. 37:28; Hos. 3:2; Isa. 52:3),[26] and chariots and horses (1 K. 10:28f. par. 2 Ch. 1:16f.). The stated value of a slave varies: Gen. 37:28 gives 20 shekels; Ex. 21:32, 30 shekels; and for a female slave Hosea paid 15 shekels and a homer and a half of barley (Hos. 3:2). The Egyptian export price for a horse was 150 shekels, for a chariot 600 shekels (1 K. 10:29 par. 1 Chr. 1:17). In times of distress, prices for things which in better times would never be regarded as foodstuffs reached staggering heights: in beleaguered Samaria, an ass's head cost 80 shekels (2 K. 6:25). Even water and wood had to be purchased (Lam. 5:4). On the other hand, the offer willingly to purchase even water could proclaim peaceful intentions (Dt. 2:6,28). Buyers and sellers were usually private individuals, but we also hear of professional traders (Zeph. 1:11). The king derived part of his income from sale of the produce of the crown lands and payments in kind (the Joseph story; Cant. 8:11); Solomon in fact carried on what amounted to a state export-import trade (1 K. 10:28f.).

(2) Wages. Craftsmen and other workers received their wages in kind, but also in cash as *kesep* (2 K. 12:12f.[11f.]; 22:5-9; Ezr. 3:7). The statement in Zec. 11:4-14 that the good shepherd received 30 shekels of silver is not a reference to actual wages; it expresses contempt for his labor.[27] Prophets, too, originally took payment to defray their living expenses (1 S. 9:8; cf. Am. 7:12); at an early date, however, such conduct became suspect as a mark of venality (Nu. 22:18; 24:13; Mic. 3:11).

(3) Loans and Interest. Only at a time when interest-free loans as the only form of lending were a thing of the past does the law prohibiting interest (Ex. 22:24[25]; Lev. 25:35-37) make sense; such loans had been based on a social solidarity idealized in Dt. 23:20(19). Loans at interest between Jews are documented at Elephantine.[28] It became a mark of piety to refuse any kind of interest (Ps. 15:5). But even loans made only against security could lead to loss of property; in 445, Nehemiah enforced a cancellation of all debts (Neh. 5:1-13).

(4) Taxes. During the monarchy, it is only in exceptional instances that we hear of tribute in the form of silver and gold (2 K. 15:19f.; 23:33ff.).[29] The Persian regime collected taxes on a regular basis (Neh. 5:4). For bread and wine alone, Nehemiah's predecessors are said to have collected 40 shekels of silver per day (Neh. 5:15). Taxes in the Jerusalem temple state are discussed elsewhere.[30]

---

26. Cf. also III.1.b(1)(b) below.
27. E. Lipiński, "Recherches sur le livre de Zacharie," *VT,* 20 (1970), 53-55.
28. E. Neufeld, "The Prohibitions against Loans at Interest in Ancient Hebrew Laws," *HUCA,* 26 (1955), 355-412; R. de Vaux, *LO,* I, 274f.
29. Cf. III.1.c below.
30. Cf. III.2.b below.

b. *Law.* (1) Property.

(a) Personal Property. The property law of the Covenant Code speaks explicitly of *kesep* as something that can be given into safekeeping (Ex. 22:6[7]).

Damages could also be paid in *kesep*. If an ox or ass should die by falling into a cistern that had carelessly been left uncovered, the owner had to be compensated in full, while the dead animal became the property of the one responsible (Ex. 21:33f.). If, however, an ox should die from a wound inflicted by another ox, the owner was compensated only to the extent of half the market value of the live animal. The owner of the animal at fault was clearly responsible only to the extent of ordinary liability for endangerment (Ex. 21:35).

(b) Slaves. Despite the existence of a law concerning slaves, a slave counted as property with monetary value (Ex. 21:20f.,32). Female slaves, however, could achieve higher status on the basis of laws similar to those governing marriage. A slave who became a concubine acquired the right to support and sexual relations; if her owner denied her these rights, he must set her free without payment (Ex. 21:10f.). Dt. 21:10-14 lays down similar stipulations governing the marriage and divorce of women taken as prisoners of war. If such a woman is divorced, she does not lose her freedom.

Among those who were not free, the common distinction between those bought from foreigners for money and those born in their owner's house (e.g., Gen. 17:12,13,23,27) was the result of a social and legal development; it does not just illustrate, as is often claimed, the special trustworthiness of the latter. The legal texts define a slave acquired by purchase[31] as being a member of the family; the mention of those born in the house (whose status should be self-evident) is a systematizing addition (compare Ex. 12:44 with Lev. 22:11). Since Eccl. 2:7 suggests that *y^elîḏê bayiṯ* and *b^enê bayiṯ* are synonymous, we may conclude from Gen. 15:3 that the *ben bayiṯ* enjoyed more rights (cf. also Gen. 14:14).[32]

When an Israelite debtor became the slave of a resident alien, the Holiness Code envisions the possibility of his redemption by the debtor himself or one of his kinsmen. The price of redemption amounted to the difference between the sale price reflecting the years of servitude remaining until the next year of release and the years already worked. The calculations were made on the basis of a free laborer's wages (Lev. 25:47-55). The legal institution of enslavement for debt knew no mercy (Am. 2:6; 8:6).

(c) Real Property. According to Israelite law, hereditary real property could not be alienated.[33] When Jeremiah bought Hanamel's field at Anathoth for 17 shekels as a sign of salvation to come (Jer. 32:6-16), he followed Babylonian usage;[34] but he was merely anticipating the opportunity for redemption offered the nearest kinsman.[35] The

31. Cf. III.1.a(1) above.
32. Cf. F. Willesen, "The Yālīḏ in Hebrew Society," *StTh,* 12 (1958), 192-210.
33. Cf. also III.2.b below.
34. A. Jirku, *Altorientalischer Kommentar zum AT* (Leipzig, 1923), 206f.
35. Cf. → גאל *gā'al,* II, 352.

sale of the "threshing floor of Araunah" to David as a site for his temple and palace (2 S. 24:20-25) and of the hill of Samaria to Omri (886/85–875/74)[36] for his capital (1 K. 16:24)[37] was based on Canaanite law. The same is true of Abraham's purchase of his burial site; P's account in Gen. 23 reflects the formulary of Neo-Babylonian two-party documents.[38] Whether the prices (50 shekels, 2 S. 24:24; 2 talents, 1 K. 16:24; 400 shekels, Gen. 23:15f.; to glorify David and the temple, 1 Ch. 21:25 turns the 50 shekels of silver for the purchase of the threshing floor into 600 shekels of gold) reflect contemporary reality or are artificially inflated must remain an open question. The story of Naboth's vineyard (1 Kgs. 21)[39] reflects a fundamental conflict between Israelite and Canaanite law. The point at issue was in fact the conflict between a traditional interpretation and a legal development based on Canaanite law that excepted improvements, especially vineyards (Isa. 7:23) and orchards, from the *naḥ^a^lâ*.[40]

(2) Family Law. The pre-Deuteronomic law in Dt. 22:13-21 serves the ends of legal certainty, but is intended primarily to protect the woman's reputation.[41] If a husband slanders his wife by accusing her falsely of not having been a virgin, he suffers corporal punishment, pays a fine of 100 shekels, and may never divorce her. We may conjecture a similar legal principle behind Gen. 20:16 (E), except that the narrator has exaggerated the fine (here paid voluntarily) to the fabulous sum of 1,000 shekels.

In Ex. 22:15f.(16f.), the Covenant Code includes the seduction of a virgin who is still under the authority of her father among property offenses, leaving her still under her father's authority but granting him compensation equivalent to the bride-price (*mōhar*) he has lost. Dt. 22:28f., however, thinks in personal categories, seeking in the same circumstances to protect the woman, whom the seducer is forced to marry and may not divorce. Instead of the *mōhar* (the amount of which is negotiable) or the equivalent compensation, the law imposes a set fine of 50 shekels.[42]

In the complaint of Rachel and Leah (Gen. 31:15), *kesep* refers to the → מהר *mōhar*, of which the father enjoys only the usufruct or a portion of the capital. They are robbed of this property by Laban, who has been "paying out" their *mōhar* as wages.[43]

---

36. S. Herrmann, *A History of Israel in OT Times* (Eng. trans., Philadelphia, ²1981), 206, 217.

37. Cf. A. Alt, "Der Stadtstaat Samaria," *BSAW*, 101/5 (1954) = *KlSchr*, III (1959), 258-302.

38. R. de Vaux, *The Early History of Israel* (Eng. trans., Philadelphia, 1978), I, 254-56.

39. K. Baltzer, "Naboths Weinberg (1 Kön 21)," *WuD*, N.S. 8 (1965), 73-88; F. I. Andersen, "The Socio-Juridical Background of the Naboth Incident," *JBL*, 85 (1966), 46-57; P. Welten, "Naboths Weinberg (1. Könige 21)," *EvTh*, 33 (1973), 18-32; H. Seebass, "Der Fall Naboth in 1 Reg. XXI," *VT*, 24 (1974), 474-488; R. Bohlen, *Der Fall Naboth. TrThSt*, 35 (1978), esp. 320-349.

40. A. Alt, "Der Anteil des Königtums an der sozialen Entwicklung in den Reichen Israel und Juda," *KlSchr*, III, 351; cf. also *KlSchr*, III, 265, n. 1.

41. M. Weinfeld, *Deuteronomy and the Deuteronomistic School* (Oxford, 1972), 293.

42. *Ibid.*, 284-87.

43. M. Burrows, "The Complaint of Laban's Daughters," *JAOS*, 57 (1937), 259-276; E. Speiser, *Genesis. AB*, I (1964), 245.

Gifts of silver to compensate princes who are not in the line of succession are probably based on the law of inheritance (2 Ch. 21:3; cf. 11:22f.).

c. *Military and Political Contexts.* The first time we hear of the use of silver or money for military or political purposes is the account of Abimelech's recruiting supporters in his attempt to establish a monarchy at Shechem (Jgs. 9:4).[44] The hiring of troops by Hanun and the Ammonites against David (1 Ch. 19:6f.) and by Amaziah for a campaign against the Edomites (2 Ch. 25:6) probably represents a retrojection of Persian and Hellenistic practice into the period of the monarchy. From the period of the occupation on, it was self-evident that *kesep̱* (silver or money) was highly esteemed as booty (Jgs. 5:19; Nu. 31:21-24; Josh. 22:8; 2 K. 14:14; 2 Ch. 25:24; Ezk. 38:13; Nah. 2:10[9]; Ps. 68:31[30]; Dnl. 11:43).[45] By paying enormous sums, Asa, the king of Judah (914/13–874/73),[46] persuaded Ben-hadad of Damascus to break his treaty with the northern kingdom (1 K. 15:18f.). And when Hezekiah led the representatives of Merodach-baladan of Babylon (reigned 722-711, 703) through the treasury and storehouse (2 K. 20:12-19 par. Isa. 39:1-8), it was to recruit their lord to join a coalition against Sennacherib.

In all periods, tribute paid to acknowledge the hegemony of a foreign sovereign probably included silver. Toi, the king of Hamath on the Orontes, sent David "gifts" (2 S. 8:9f.). According to 2 Ch. 17:11, the Philistines paid tribute to Jehoshaphat, king of Judah (874/73–850/49). Usually, however, it was Israel and Judah that were tributary to the empires of Assyria and Egypt. In 738,[47] Menachem of Israel paid Pul (Tiglath-pileser III) 1,000 talents, which he exacted from all the free property owners subject to military duty, each of whom had to pay 50 shekels (2 K. 15:19f.). In 733, Ahaz, king of Judah, accepted the sovereignty of Tiglath-pileser (2 K. 16:7-9). In 701, Hezekiah sent 300 talents of silver (along with 30 talents of gold) to Sennacherib; some of this he had to take from the temple (2 K. 18:13-16). In 609, Pharaoh Necho deposed Jehoahaz of Judah and extorted 100 talents of silver (together with 10 talents of gold) from Eliakim, whom he had set up to succeed Jehoahaz; he was able to raise this sum only by imposing a special tax based on wealth (2 K. 23:33-35). If we leave aside for the moment the brutal conduct of the Egyptians, these payments served to maintain political stability. The conduct of Ahaz, king of Judah, is typical. As is clear from 1 K. 20:1-9, a ruler seeking an occasion for war had to press his demands above and beyond the usual tribute of precious metal in order to achieve his goal.

d. *Material.* Ownership of silver objects (*k^elê-ḵesep̱*) was a mark of prosperity. Together with other items of value, therefore, they made suitable gifts for securing the political favor of those in power (2 S. 8:9f. par. 1 Ch. 18:9f.; 1 K. 10:25 par. 2 Ch. 9:24). Joseph's cup (Gen. 44:2) should be pictured as chased silver;[48] so probably should the *maśkîṯ* (bowl?) referred to in Prov. 25:11. Sections of furniture

44. Herrmann, 122f.; A. Alt, *Grundfragen der Geschichte Israels* (Munich, 1970), 139, 263f.
45. Cf. also IV.1 below.
46. Herrmann, 200f.
47. *Ibid.*, 245.
48. M. Weippert, 222b and fig. 74_3.

were manufactured by casting. The metal portions of the frame were usually bronze,[49] but the couches (*miṭṭôṯ*) at the Persian court were made of gold and silver (Est. 1:6). The rings (*g^e lîlîm*)[50] on the covering for the garden court were of the same material (Est. 1:6). Whether palanquins[51] like the one described in Cant. 3:9f. really existed cannot be determined. There may have been silver cords, i.e., cords that included silver threads; in Eccl. 12:6, however, silver is mentioned only for the sake of the metaphor.

In Gen. 24:53; Ex. 3:22; 11:2; 12:35 (cf. Ps. 105:37), the context of *k^e lê-ḵesep* suggests the meaning "jewelry." Ezk. 16:13 speaks of jewelry made of gold and silver. Of the various kinds of jewelry attested archaeologically (earrings, nose rings, armlets, anklets, toe rings, finger rings, diadems),[52] in conjunction with *kesep* the OT mentions only "ornaments of gold with silver pearls" (Cant. 1:11), most likely a reference to earrings with silver pendants,[53] and the crown worn by a bride (Cant. 8:9).[54]

2. *Cultic.*

a. *Temple.* In the premonarchic period, the silver in the treasury of the sanctuary was augmented by a share in the spoils of battle (Josh. 6:19; cf. 7:21-24). After the temple was built, its treasure, considered the legal successor to the "treasure of Yahweh" (Josh. 6:24; 2 S. 8:11; 1 K. 7:51), was increased by royal donations (1 K. 15:15 par. 2 Ch. 15:18: Asa). The gifts of the people were added to the income of the priesthood, which was drawn on to keep the temple in repair (2 K. 12:5-7[4-6]). The reign of Joash (836/35–797/96)[55] saw the establishment of a temple repair fund supported by general subscription, from which the laborers were paid (2 K. 12:8-16[7-15]; cf. 22:3-7,9; 2 Ch. 34:8-14,17). In the postexilic period down to the time of the Maccabees, those in power took the place of the Davidic kings (Ezr. 6:3-12; 7:11-22); for the most part, however, most of the support for the temple was contributed by wealthy families and individuals, together with the general populace (Neh. 7:70f.; Ezr. 2:69; 7:16; 8:24-34; Zec. 6:9-14; 11:13). Even contributions by Gentiles were considered acceptable (Ezr. 7:15f.). The change from the time of the monarchy to the situation after the exile can also be observed in Chronicles. David is described as making detailed preparations for the construction and furnishing of the temple (calculated in astronomical sums, because the structure alone is intended to put everything previously existing in the shade), thus as it were making David responsible for the temple (1 Ch. 22:14-16; 29:1-5). The exclusive patronage of the monarch is also eliminated (1 Ch. 29:6-8), a change especially evident in the Chronicler's treatment of

---

49. M. Weippert, "Möbel," *BRL*², 229 and fig. 55.

50. G. Gerleman, *Esther. BK,* XXI (²1981), 46, 58: "poles."

51. F. Rundgren, "אפריון 'Tragsessel, Sänfte,' " *ZAW,* 74 (1962), 70-72, and most modern exegetes; G. Gerleman, *Das Hohelied. BK,* XVIII (²1981), 139-142: "throne room."

52. H. Weippert, *BRL*², 282-89.

53. *Ibid.,* 286, fig. 75.

54. E. Würthwein, *Die fünf Megilloth: Das Hohelied. HAT,* XVIII (²1969), 70.

55. Herrmann, 228.

2 K. 12:14(13): now the surplus silver is made into utensils for the cult (2 Ch. 24:14).[56] P and its additions likewise speak of the offerings of the people (Ex. 25:3; 35:5,24; 38:25). Contributions to foreign sanctuaries, even when made by foreigners like Antiochus IV Epiphanes, were considered betrayal of the traditional religion and as such were bitterly castigated (Dnl. 11:38).

A substantial portion of the temple treasure was made up of the utensils used in the cult. In the summer of 586, when Nebuzaradan, the special representative of Nebuchadnezzar, destroyed the royal palace and the temple some four weeks after the capture of Jerusalem,[57] he had the furnishings of the temple brought to Babylon. While 2 K. 25:15 lists only pans (*maḥtôṯ*) and bowls (*mizrāqôṯ*) made of gold or silver, the parallel account in Jer. 52:19 is much fuller, mentioning (besides the pans and bowls) basins (*sippîm*), pots (*sîrôṯ*), lampstands (*m^e^nōrôṯ*), a small vessel called a *kap̱,* and libation bowls (*m^e^naqiyôṯ*). As 2 K. 12:14(13) shows, this is the list of cultic utensils traditionally made of precious metal. Thanks to an edict issued by Cyrus, these utensils were restored to the temple (Ezr. 6:3-5; cf. 5:13-15). In contrast to 2 K. 25:15; Jer. 52:19, the documentation that lists the items to be returned speaks specifically only for *ʾ^a^garṭālîm* and *k^e^p̱ôrîm,* usually translated "basins" and "bowls," subsuming all the other utensils under the term *kēlîm* (Ezr. 1:7-11). Unfortunately, the numbers associated with the gold and silver utensils are confused and cannot all be reconstructed. The grand total probably amounted to 5,499 objects.[58] According to the evidence of 1 Ch. 28:14-17 and especially the terminology of the Mishnah, the document of return did not affect the nomenclature of the cult utensils, to which 2 K. 12:14(13) adds silver knives (*m^e^zamm^e^rôṯ*) and trumpets (*ḥ^a^ṣōṣ^e^rôṯ*) and 1 Ch. 28:16 tables (*šulḥ^a^nôṯ*) of silver.

The Bible has little to say about the use of these objects. The *mizrāq* was employed at the altar (Ex. 27:3), the *maḥtâ* with incense (Nu. 16:6), the *kap̱* for cereal offerings (Nu. 7:14), the *m^e^naqqîṯ* for libations (Ex. 25:29), and the *sîr* to remove ashes (Ex. 27:3). Only the use of the silver trumpets, sounded in pairs, is described in greater detail in Nu. 10:1-10, a composite of theory and practice. According to the Mishnah, they played a specific role in various liturgical ceremonies (*Tamid* vii.3; *Sukk.* v.4f.; *Roš Haš.* iii.4). Their enormous symbolic value (which is probably reflected in 1 Mc. 3:54; 4:40; 5:33; 7:45; etc.) is due to their representation on the arch of Titus[59] and the coins of Simon bar Kokhba.[60] The Mishnah also speaks of a *maḥtâ* and table of silver. The priest performing the daily burnt offering used the former to take the coals for the incense altar from the altar of burnt offering (*Tamid* i.4); on the latter he placed the implements used to dismember the sacrificial animal (*Šeqal.* vi.4).

Undoubtedly the terms do not always refer to the identical utensils. We must reckon

---

56. The question of support for the temple is discussed by K. Galling, "Königliche und nichtkönigliche Stifter beim Tempel von Jerusalem," *BBLAK* (= *ZDPV*), 68 (1951), 134-142.

57. Herrmann, 284.

58. K. Galling, "Das Protokoll über die Rückgabe der Tempelgeräte," *Studien zur Geschichte Israels in persischer Zeitalter* (1964), 78-88.

59. *AOB,* no. 509.

60. Reifenberg, no. 186.

with repairs and modifications (cf., e.g., 2 K. 12:14[13]; Ezr. 8:26). Removal by authorized individuals (cf. 2 K. 16:8; 2 Mc. 4:32ff.) and looting like that of Antiochus IV Epiphanes in the fall of 169 B.C. (1 Mc. 1:20-24)[61] repeatedly depleted the stock. Special workshops were set aside for such repairs and replacements (2 K. 12:14f.[13f.]; 2 Ch. 24:14; cf. Ex. 31:4; 35:32). Also kept in the temple was the diadem of silver and gold with which the high priest Joshua[62] had been crowned after the exile (Zec. 6:9-14).

P's programmatic[63] plan for the "dwelling place" or tabernacle of Yahweh in Ex. 25–27 specifies silver as the material for the bases of the wall frames (26:19-21,25), the four pillars holding the veil protecting the holy of holies (26:32), and the hooks and fillets supporting the hangings of the forecourt (27:10,11,17). The secondary account of the tabernacle's construction in Ex. 36–38 repeats these specifications and adds a silver overlay for the capitals of the pillars of the forecourt (38:17). With the help of Nu. 1:46, this account calculates that 100 talents and 1,775 shekels of silver were used, relating the bill of materials to the temple tax (Ex. 38:25-28). This interest in "precise" numbers resurfaces in Nu. 7:84-88, which states that 12 silver plates (*qᵉʿārôṯ*) each weighing 130 shekels and an equal number of basins each weighing 70 shekels were contributed to the sanctuary by the twelve representatives of the tribes, for a total of 2,400 shekels (v. 85).

No difference was probably perceived between these furnishings and those of foreign temples. Ptolemy III Euergetes carried off to Egypt idols and cultic utensils of silver and gold from the territory of his rival Seleucus II (Dnl. 11:8).

b. *Regular Income.* Isa. 43:24 casts a retrospective spotlight on the extravagance of the sacrificial system. Welcome as contributions and occasional offerings were, they were insufficient to cover the expense, especially since the priests' living costs had to be defrayed. There was need for constant sources of income, the existence of which is documented primarily for the postexilic period. The most important was the temple tax in the amount of half a shekel (Ex. 30:11-16; 2 Ch. 24:6-9), to be paid annually by every Israelite who had reached the age of twenty. Neh. 10:33(32) sets this tax at a third of a shekel; a possible explanation, if we do not assume that this was a temporary expedient, is that the passage refers to a different monetary unit.[64] Also significant was the use of money to redeem or replace offerings in kind (Nu. 18:16; Lev. 27:27f.: the first-born of unclean animals) and as a substitute for a person, animal, or object promised by vow. This substitution is regulated in detail by Lev. 27, an appendix to the Holiness Code. The replacement price of a person is based on his or her value as a laborer, varying from 3 to 50 shekels; special provision is made for those who are poor (Lev. 27:2-8). Unclean animals must be replaced, because they cannot be sacrificed; clean animals can only be redeemed (Lev. 27:12f.). The cost of redemption was 20 percent more than the valuation of the animal (interpreted by the rabbis as 25% on

61. Herrmann, 357, 366.

62. *Ibid.*, 305, following the MT; other scholars emend the text to read Zerubbabel. Cf. Galling, *Studien*, 121-23.

63. K. Koch, "Stiftshütte," *BHHW*, III (1966), 1872; *idem*, → אהל, I, 127f.

64. W. Rudolph, *Esra und Nehemia. HAT*, XX (1949), 178.

the grounds that the 20% is based on the sum paid). The cost of replacing a house was estimated; the cost of replacing a field (which as a rule would revert to its owner in the year of release) was calculated precisely on the basis of its remaining term of possession and its area at the rate of 50 shekels per 1.8 hectares (4.5 a.) (Lev. 27:16-24).[65] The option of either redeeming or replacing a house or field shows that when something was replaced, only the right of possession was transferred to the temple; the owner retained ownership, and by paying the 20 percent surcharge could recover possession. It is quite possible that these regulations also aimed at protection against creditors.[66] During the period of the judges, a priest could be given a fixed income (Jgs. 17:10). Payment of priests is reflected in 1 S. 2:36. There must also have been single occasions when payment was made to the priests (Nu. 3:40-51). Josiah's centralizing reform of the cult transformed the tithe, which had been payment in kind, into a sum representing the cost of a sacrificial meal in Jerusalem, of which it is safe to assume that the priests received their portion (Dt. 14:22-26). Rabbinic tradition considers this text the Torah authority for the so-called "second tithe."[67] The income of the priesthood in the period of the Second Temple included also the monetary fines that in certain cases had replaced sin offerings and guilt offerings (Lev. 5:14-16; 2 K. 12:17[16]).[68]

c. *Idols.* It was not merely foreign peoples who had cultic images (Dt. 7:25; 29:16[17]; Ps. 115:4; 135:15; Jer. 10:4; Dnl. 5:4; etc.); they were also widespread in Israel. In the time of the judges, Dan was the location of a tribal sanctuary whose silver idol had come from the private sanctuary of a certain Micah (Jgs. 17f.).[69] With Hosea there began a wave of criticism that lasted into the exilic and postexilic period (Ex. 20:23; Isa. 2:20; 30:22; 31:7; 40:19; 46:6; Ezk. 16:17; Hos. 8:4; 9:6; 13:2; Hab. 2:19). In Jgs. 17:4; Hos. 13:2, they represent Yahweh himself; elsewhere (e.g., Ex. 20:23) they surround him with a pantheon. Except for the sanctuaries at Dan and Bethel (1 K. 12:26-30), they had their locus in the private chapels of the wealthy (Isa. 46:6). It is possible that they were also used as amulets. What they looked like can be determined with some assurance only from Hos. 13:2; 8:4f. Hosea denounced the public and private bull images, which we may conceive of as theriomorphic pedestals for Yahweh, on the grounds that they contravened the prohibition of images.[70] Many scholars interpret the "male images" (*ṣalmê zāḵār*) of Ezk. 16:17 as phallic images.[71] The "dove" in Ps. 68:14(13) probably refers to a winged sun.[72]

Cultic images could be cast of silver (cf. probably Jgs. 17:4). As a rule, however,

---

65. *AuS,* II (1932), 50f.

66. K. Elliger, *Leviticus. HAT,* IV (1966), 388f.

67. See the tractate *Ma'aser Šeni* in the Mishnah and Tosefta.

68. M. Noth, *Leviticus. OTL* (Eng. trans. 1965), 47f.

69. M. Noth, "The Background of Judges 17–18" (Eng. trans.), *Israel's Prophetic Heritage. Festschrift J. Muilenburg* (New York, 1962), 68-85.

70. W. Zimmerli, "Das Bilderverbot in der Geschichte des alten Israel," *Studien zur alttestamentlichen Theologie und Prophetie. Gesammelte Aufsätze,* II. *ThB,* 51 (1974), 247-260.

71. W. Zimmerli, *Ezekiel 1. Herm* (Eng. trans. 1979), 343f.

72. K. Galling, *BRL*², 353; cf. fig. $78_{29\text{-}31}$; for a different view, cf. H.-J. Kraus, *Psalms 60–150* (Eng. trans., Minneapolis, 1989), 52.

they had a core of wood and probably also bronze, as is attested literarily (Isa. 40:19) and archaeologically[73] in the case of gold, overlaid with silver (Isa. 30:22; Jer. 10:4). The silver might also be used simply for decoration (Isa. 40:19). The fact that the extant examples are quite small[74] agrees with the weight (200 shekels) given in Jgs. 17:4).

IV. Appraisal.

1. *General.* The attractiveness of silver as a sign of wealth (among other things) and the possibility of using it when necessary to achieve specific goals[75] made it a welcome gift (Gen. 45:22; 2 K. 5:5; Ezr. 1:4,6). Of course it also had its dark side. It could entice people into dishonesty (2 K. 5:19-27) and theft (Josh. 7; Jgs. 17:2f.; 2 K. 7:8). By promising Delilah a horrendous sum, the Philistines persuaded her to betray Samson's secret (Jgs. 16:4-21). Joab would have paid richly for the murder of Absalom (2 S. 18:11f.). A price can be set on a human life (1 K. 20:39). According to the author of the book of Esther, Haman even thought that the king of Persia could not resist the temptation of handing over the Jews in return for ten thousand talents (Est. 3:8-11; 4:7). God chose the Medes (or Persians) as his instruments because they were immune to the temptations of silver and gold (Isa. 13:17). The naive view (expressed by J, e.g.) that possession of silver (and other forms of wealth) expressed God's blessing (Gen. 24:35), not surprisingly, was soon countered by critical voices.

2. *Prophets.* The prophets rebuked the people for casually forgetting that it was God who gave them their bounty (Hos. 2:10[8]; Ezk. 16:13f.). They castigated the ruthlessness born of avarice (Am. 2:6; 8:6; Joel 4:5[3:5]). They unmasked the luxury of Israel and foreign nations as a source of arrogance (Isa. 2:7; Ezk. 28:4). There can be no reliance on silver and gold (Ezk. 7:19; Zeph. 1:18; Zec. 9:3f.), but only on Yahweh (Isa. 55:1f.).

In the salvation oracles of postexilic prophets, perversion of wealth is canceled; silver and gold are returned to their true owners (Isa. 60:9; Hag. 2:8; Zec. 14:14; cf. also Isa. 60:17).

3. *Deuteronomy.* Deuteronomy considers the wealth that is manifested in silver and other forms a possible source of alienation between Yahweh and his people, against which they must be warned (Dt. 8:13). The king was thought to be especially vulnerable — probably on the basis of experience (17:14-20).[76]

4. *Wisdom.* Wisdom heartily endorses the value of silver. This attitude is illustrated by the use of silver to reflect the value of immaterial goods such as wisdom itself (Prov. 2:4), intelligent speech (10:20), and divine instruction (Job 22:25; cf. Ps. 12:7[6]).

---

73. P. Welten, "Götterbild, männliches," *BRL*², 104.
74. *Ibid.*, 99-111.
75. Cf. also III.1.c above.
76. A. Alt, "Die Heimat des Deuteronomiums," *KlSchr,* II (1953), 264f.

Qoheleth can even state quite neutrally that everything can be had for money (Eccl. 10:19). Wisdom can also maintain the point of view expressed by J in Gen. 24:35. Much more often, however, it states that silver or money is not the most precious thing in the world. It is surpassed by popular favor (Prov. 22:1), the Torah (Ps. 119:72), and especially by wisdom (Job 28:15; Prov. 3:14; 8:10,19; 16:16). The meaning of life is not to be found in money (Eccl. 2:8; 5:9[10]; 7:12).

V. Figurative Usage. The smelting process is a common image for the purification God imposes upon his people, certain groups, or an individual (Ps. 66:10; Prov. 17:3; Isa. 1:25; 48:10; Zec. 13:9; Mal. 3:2b-4). Jeremiah uses this metaphor to describe his own ministry, with a negative outcome: all that is left is dross (Jer. 6:27-30).[77] Ezekiel, too, uses this image, but only with reference to judgment by fire (Ezk. 22:18-22).

VI. Dead Sea Scrolls. The use of the word in the Dead Sea scrolls follows the usage of the Bible; cf. especially the 10 occurrences in the Temple scroll (11QT), mostly OT quotations. Together with gold, precious stones, and cattle, *kesep̱* denotes the wealth (cf. Gen. 13:2) bestowed as God's gift (1QM 12:11f.; 19:5). The shields (1QM 5:5), lances (5:8), and sword handles (5:14) of the sons of light are adorned with gold, silver, and precious stones. Following Ex. 30:12, 4QOrd 2:6,11 speak of a "ransom." The nations will come to Zion with silver, gold, and precious stones (4QDibHam 4:10).[78] The poor man is purified like silver (1QH 5:16).[79] In the Copper scroll (3Q*15*), *ksp* appears more than 20 times. The goods hidden throughout the land according to this document (the temple treasure or the wealth of the Qumran Essenes?[80]) amounted to 2,286 talents and 14 bars of silver,[81] as well as great quantities of gold, precious stones, precious spices, and books.

G. Mayer

77. Loretz.
78. Cf. IV.2 above.
79. Cf. V above.
80. Cf. H. Bardtke, "Qumrān und seine Probleme," *ThR,* N.S. 33 (1968), 185-204.
81. Cf. J. T. Milik, *Les 'petites grottes' de Qumrân. DJD,* III (1962), 282.

כָּעַס *kāʿas;* כַּעַס *kaʿas*

Contents: I. 1. Etymology; 2. OT Usage; 3. Meaning. II. Theological Usage: 1. Pre-Deuteronomistic; 2. Deuteronomistic; 3. Later. III. LXX, Dead Sea Scrolls.

kāʿas. E. Cortese, "Lo schema deuteronomistico per i re di Giuda e d'Israele," *Bibl,* 56 (1975), 37-52, esp. 46f.; W. Dietrich, *Prophetie und Geschichte. FRLANT,* 108 (1972), 90f.; J. Scharbert, *Der Schmerz im AT. BBB,* 8 (1955), 32-34; W. H. Simpson, *Divine Wrath in the Eighth Century Prophets* (diss., Boston, 1968); F. Stolz, "כעס *kʿs* sich ärgern," *THAT,* I, 838-842; W. Thiel, *Die*

I. 1. *Etymology.* The root *k'sl/ś,* "be discontent, angry," is attested only in Northwest Semitic. The earliest occurrence is Aramaic:]*štb' k's mn lḥm*[.[1] The Punic occurrence (*k's lp'l*) in the Latin and Neo-Punic bilingual Tripolitana 31[2] is the direct equivalent of *faciendum curavit.*[3] The semantic distance from the Hebrew meaning cannot be due to an internal Semitic shift, but must be connected with the wider range of meanings associated with Lat. *curare.* Later Aramaic and Middle Hebrew occurrences of the root are analogous in meaning to the occurrences in the Hebrew Bible. Jakob Barth[4] connects *k's* etymologically with Arab. *kaša'a,* "fear." If this is true, the spelling *kā'aś,* found in all the occurrences in Job, could indicate the earlier pronunciation.

2. *OT Usage.* The noun *ka'as/ś* occurs 25 times in the OT (plus 1 occurrence in Sir. 34:29ᴮ). The occurrences are concentrated in Wisdom Literature (14) and Psalms (4). The remaining 8 passages include 4 where the noun functions as a cognate accusative with a piel (1 S. 1:6) or hiphil (1 K. 15:30; 21:22; 2 K. 23:26).

The qal of the verb is uncommon (6 occurrences). The very rare piel appears to represent merely a stylistically motivated variant to a nearby hiphil (Dt. 32:21a [cf. v. 21b]; 1 S. 1:6 [cf. v. 7]).[5] The hiphil, however, appears 46 times (plus Sir. 3:16ᴬ; contrast 3:16ᶜ). Most of the occurrences are in the Deuteronomistic history (24), Jeremiah (11), and other texts exhibiting Deuteronomistic influence (probably 9). It is in this setting that the theological usage of the root is concentrated. God is the explicit object in 38 occurrences, the implicit object in 5 or 6. In Dt. 32:21a, God is the object of the piel; in Ezk. 16:42 — with the equivalent meaning — he is the subject of the qal. In Dt. 32:21b; Ezk. 32:9, God is the subject of the hiphil.

The root does not appear in Genesis–Numbers, Isaiah (except Isa. 65:3), the Minor Prophets (except Hos. 12:15[Eng. v. 14]), or the Five Scrolls outside Ecclesiastes. The occurrences in Ezk. 8:17; 20:28 were absent from the text used by the LXX. They therefore represent a very late addition to the text, in both cases reflecting dependence on Deuteronomistic ideas.

Before the root entered the theological language of sacral history, it was used not only in proverbial wisdom and laments (where it is well attested) but undoubtedly also

---

deuteronomistische Redaktion von Jeremia 1–25. WMANT, 41 (1973), 120; M. Weinfeld, *Deuteronomy and the Deuteronomistic School* (1972, repr. Winona Lake, 1992), 323f.; H. Weippert, "Die 'deuteronomistischen' Beurteilungen der Könige von Israel und Juda und das Problem der Redaktion der Königsbücher," *Bibl,* 53 (1972), 301-339, esp. 323-333; *idem, Die Prosareden des Jeremiabuches. BZAW,* 132 (1973), 222-27.

1. Ahikar 189.
2. *KAI,* 124, 4.
3. G. Levi della Vida, review of *KAI,* I-II, *RSO,* 39 (1964), 307f.; M. Dahood, "Hebrew and Ugaritic Lexicography III," *Bible,* 46 (1965), 330, citing the translation of *kā'as* as *in curis* in the Vulg. of Eccl. 5:16.
4. J. Barth, *Wurzeluntersuchungen zum hebräischen und aramäischen Lexikon* (Leipzig, 1902), 27.
5. E. Jenni, *Das hebräische Pi'el* (Zurich, 1968), 68f.

(despite the paucity of evidence) in everyday language concerning personal well-being and interpersonal reactions (cf. 1 S. 1:6f.,16; 2 Ch. 16:10; Neh. 3:33,37[4:1,5]).

Was there an expression "provoke anger" (possibly of cultic origin) that referred to divine displeasure without mentioning God explicitly? Such a usage may appear in 1 K. 21:22; 2 K. 21:6; 23:19; Hos. 12:15[14]; Ps. 106:29; and possibly Neh. 3:37[4:5]. Since each passage involves a lectio difficilior, there is no reason to normalize any of these texts. Hos. 12:15(14) is the earliest "theological" usage that can be dated with certainty. This observation would support the theory of formulaic language. Here, however, stylistic considerations may account for the absence of an explicit divine object. The word *'ᵃḏōnāyw* at the end of the verse is strongly accented and may function not only as the emphatically delayed subject of the second and third lines but also as the object of the first line. If so, the later passages without an explicit object may merely be echoing this verse. In Neh. 3:37(4:5), the object may also be introduced by *lᵉneḡeḏ*; this analysis would accord better with 3:33(4:1).[6]

3. *Meaning.* The root always denotes "a sense of exasperation, a bad temper,"[7] a "very intense emotion."[8] Almost always — most of the exceptions being in Ecclesiastes — there is an interpersonal context: *kaʿas* is evoked by others and leads to a reaction against them. Within this broad meaning, however, the root can take on a variety of nuances, especially in the case of the noun.

We see from 1 S. 1:7; Ps. 6:8(7); 31:10(9); 112:10; Job 17:7 that *kʿs* refers to the general psychosomatic process that Collins calls the "physiology of tears."[9] It ends with decomposure of the belly, throat, and eye (cf. Ps. 6:8[7]; 31:10[9]; 112:10). The seat of *kaʿas* is the heart, midway between the belly and the throat, when tears are produced (cf. 1 S. 1:8; Eccl. 7:9). In conjunction with *kʿs* we find words denoting sadness of heart (1 S. 1:8), anxiety (1 S. 1:16), sorrow (Ps. 31:11[10]), and sighing (Ps. 6:7[6]; 31:11[10]). Sighing comes from the throat, where *kaʿas* produces a bitter taste and is therefore associated with words for bitterness (Hos. 12:15[14]; Prov. 17:25; Sir. 34:29). In Ecclesiastes, we find words for pain and sickness associated with *kʿs* (Eccl. 1:18; 2:23; 5:16[17]; 11:10); in Ezk. 32:9, it is associated with trembling. In many of the passages cited, the best translation would be something like "grief, sorrow, displeasure."

Ps. 112:10, however, uses *kʿs* in conjunction with the gnashing of teeth, the symbol of "unbridled rage";[10] Eccl. 5:16(17) associates it with *qeṣep̱,* "anger." This usage suggests a semantic nuance that is characteristic of all the occurrences of the qal (with the exception of Eccl. 7:9) and was incorporated into the theological usage of the root (i.e., in almost all occurrences of the hiphil): anger at others. Physiologically, this anger manifests itself as heat (Neh. 3:33[4:1]; cf. the image in Dt. 32:21f.). Various words for anger appear in the context of Dt. 9:18; 32:19(?); Jgs. 2:12; 2 K. 22:17; 23:19; 2 Ch. 16:10; 34:25; Eccl.

---

6. W. Rudolph, *Esra und Nehemia. HAT,* XX (1949), *in loc.*
7. Scharbert, 32.
8. Stolz, 839.
9. T. Collins, "The Physiology of Tears in the OT: Part II," *CBQ,* 33 (1971), 186f.
10. H.-J. Kraus, *Psalms 60–150* (Eng. trans., Minneapolis, 1989), *in loc.*

5:16(17); Jer. 7:18; 32:29-32; Ezk. 8:17; 16:42.[11] In Ezk. 16:42, we find the antonym *šqṭ*, "be calm." Another important root often found in the context of *kʿs* is → קנא *qnʾ*, which denotes passionate jealousy (on the part of another human being [Job 5:2] or God [Dt. 4:24f.; 32:16,21; Ps. 78:58; Ezk. 16:42); Ezk. 16:26 uses *znh* similarly. The LXX understood *kʿs* primarily in this sense and translated accordingly.[12]

Wisdom appears to have used *kʿs* in yet another sense: excitement, confusion, and discomfiture. According to Prov. 12:16; Job 5:2; Eccl. 7:9 (probably to be interpreted as a quotation from traditional wisdom), this reaction is characteristic of fools (cf. also Sir. 34:29). These passages may mean simply that the wise can control themselves and suppress sudden surges of emotion, but they may also suggest an ideal of inward balance and composure. In the latter case, feelings of *kaʿas* would never even arise in the wise.

A sense of *kaʿas* can be provoked by what one sees (Dt. 32:19; Ps. 112:10) or even hears of at second hand (Ezk. 32:9; Ps. 78:58f.; Neh. 3:33[4:1]). The mockery of others has an even more immediate effect (Dt. 32:19[?]; Hos. 12:15[14]; 1 S. 1:6f.; Job 17:6f.; Prov. 12:16). The cause can also be one's own misfortune: in Job 6:2, Job calls for his own *kaʿaś* (which Eliphaz has charged him with in 5:2) to be weighed against his calamity, to determine which is heavier in the scales. Above all, however, *kaʿas* is provoked by the faithlessness of someone with whom one has close ties. This is the basis for the theological usage of the Deuteronomistic school.

The noun can also denote the action or object that provokes *kaʿas*: Dt. 32:19(?),27(?); 1 K. 15:30; 21:22; 2 K. 23:26; Ezk. 20:28; Prov. 17:25; 27:3; 21:19.[13]

The common translation "offend, offense" can suggest misleading associations with impugning someone's honor, a semantic field that is only tangential to that of *kʿs*. This translation is therefore better avoided.

II. Theological Usage.

1. *Pre-Deuteronomistic*. Theological usage appears primarily in Deuteronomistic texts, but is also attested in earlier texts independent of this tradition. In Hos. 12:15(14), which concludes the original unit comprising 12:3-7,12-15(2-6,11-14),[14] Yahweh has been affronted by Israel's bloody deeds; he is therefore in bitter *kaʿas* and advances for vengeance. This passage is not Deuteronomistic; neither can it simply be the basis for the Deuteronomistic theologoumenon of Yahweh's wrath, which always describes "the effect upon Yahweh when Israel worships foreign idols or shares in the cultic practices of the nations."[15]

Theological usage of the hiphil in the prophets apart from the Deuteronomistic tradition may also be found in 1 K. 14:9,15; 2 K. 22:17; Isa. 65:3; Jer. 7:18f.; 8:19. It can be argued, however, that all these passages are Deuteronomistic in origin or exhibit Deuteronomistic

---

11. → אנף *ʾānap* (*ʾānaph*).
12. O. Grether and J. Fichtner, "ὀργή, C," *TDNT,* V, 412.
13. Other roots with similar meanings are discussed by Scharbert.
14. R. Kümpel, *Die Berufung Israels* (diss., Bonn, 1973), 61-70.
15. Weippert, *Die Prosareden des Jeremiabuches,* 222.

influence.[16] Ezk. 32:9 is unique: here Yahweh is the subject rather than the object of the hiphil. Dt. 32:21 shows how such statements can arise spontaneously.

The root *kʿs* does not appear in the text of Deuteronomy proper. The basis for Deuteronomistic usage may be found in the Song of Moses (Dt. 32:1-43), where *kʿs* is a leitmotif formulating the double peripeteia of the history described by the song: Israel provokes Yahweh (vv. 16, 19, 21a); Yahweh provokes Israel by summoning other nations against it (v. 21b); because, however, these other nations, instruments of Yahweh's wrath, anger him in turn, he finally comes to Israel's aid (v. 27). The cause of Yahweh's anger is Israel's apostasy from worshipping him alone (vv. 15-19). The cause of Yahweh's anger against the other nations is their self-aggrandizement for their success against Israel (vv. 27-30). Ps. 78, which in many ways resembles the Song of Moses,[17] uses the hiphil of *kʿs* in conjunction with *qn'* to interpret the period of the judges, in which Yahweh's anger is provoked by the *bāmôṯ* and *peṣîlîm* (v. 58).

2. *Deuteronomistic*. The hiphil of *kʿs* with Yahweh as its object is used by the internal Deuteronomistic framework of the Song of Moses (Dt. 31:29) to interpret Israel's sin; it appears with the phrases *ʿāśâ + hāraʿ beʿênê YHWH* and *bemaʿaśēh yāḏayim.* In the retelling of the golden calf story, which is likewise Deuteronomistic and exhibits other similarities to Dt. 32 (cf. Israel as Yahweh's *naḥalâ* in 32:9 and 9:26,29, but not in the prototype [Ex. 32:11]), the original interpretation from Ex. 32:30f. (*ḥaṭā'â* as cognate acc. with *ḥṭ'*; cf. v. 21) is expanded in Dt. 9:18 by the addition of the hiphil of *kʿs,* the catchword from Dt. 32.

Here, then, we have the double basis on which the Deuteronomistic history and the Deuteronomistic sections of Jeremiah developed the two typical cliche combinations using the hiphil of *kʿs.* In the one case, "the hiphil of *kʿs* appears with the phrase *ʿśh + hāraʿ* (*beʿênê YHWH*) and/or *maʿaśēh yad*"; in the other, "the hiphil of *kʿs* is expanded by the use of the noun *kaʿas* as a cognate accusative and/or associated with a cognate accusative from the root *ḥṭ',*" with a regular preference for the *ḥaṭṭā'ṯ* as in Dt. 9:18.[18] The cognate accusative with *kʿs* may have been suggested by 1 S. 1:6 (or 2 K. 23:26) in the source material used by the Deuteronomistic history. All the passages with *ḥṭ'* refer in one way or another to the "sin of Jeroboam." This association shows that the choice of formula was determined by the subject matter and that the combination with *ḥṭ'* alludes consciously to (Ex. 32 and) Dt. 9. The Deuteronomistic prose of Jeremiah, which belongs to Weippert's first group, makes the freest use of the cliches in combination, like the oracle of Huldah in 2 K. 22:17, which may have served as a source. In the majority of cases, the hiphil of *kʿs* is appended to the preceding statement as an infinitive introduced by *le*. This syntax is at least consecutive in meaning. In the light of the fundamental text in Dt. 32, however, we are justified in asking whether it is not

---

16. On the Jeremiah passages, cf. Thiel and Weinfeld.

17. O. Eissfeldt, *Das Lied Moses Deuteronomium 32,1-43 und das Lehrgedicht Asaphs Psalm 78 samt einer Analyse der Umgebung des Mose-Liedes. BSAW,* 104/5 (1958), 26-43.

18. Quotations from Weippert, *Die Prosareden des Jeremiabuches,* 223, with a convenient tabulation of the texts.

in fact meant to express purpose: Israel deliberately provoked Yahweh to anger. In more than half the passages, the immediate context speaks either of Yahweh's anger or of his punishment.

In the books of Kings, the combined formula appears primarily in the redactional judgments on the individual kings and in prophetic oracles formulated more or less in Deuteronomistic style. It is not found in the central section from Jehoshaphat and Ahaz of Judah to Joram and Hosea of Israel. This (together with other considerations) leads Weippert[19] to posit a preliminary Hezekian stage of the Deuteronomistic history, which attained its full extent later under Josiah. Weippert's analysis has its weaknesses and is rejected by Cortese; the arguments of the latter, however, are also open to criticism. In any case, the theological *kʿs* passages appear first in the Josianic redaction and exilic revisions of the Deuteronomistic history, including a possible redaction that is fond of introducing prophets.[20] For the kings of the northern kingdom, the Josianic redaction almost always uses the formula based on Dt. 9:18, which mentions the "sins of Jeroboam" (1 K. 15:30; 16:2,13[with an allusion to the prophecy of Jehu in v. 2!],26; 21:22; 22:54[53]); cf. the absence of *ḥṭʾ* in 2 K. 23:19, the source used by this redaction. The basic exilic redaction of the Deuteronomistic history, which blames the exile primarily on the sins of Manasseh of Judah, uses in its crucial passages the already standard formula that speaks of "Yahweh's anger" (2 K. 21:6; 23:26). The same is true when it summarizes the sins of Israel and Judah (cf. 2 K. 17:13) as well as when it mentions the sins of Manasseh (v. 17).

The Jeremiah passages take what is said in very stereotyped language in Kings and bring it to life. Jer. 7:18f., for example, describes what the people do to provoke Yahweh to anger and then asks: "Is it I whom they provoke? Is it not themselves, to their own harm?" The last phrase is echoed in 25:6f. ("to your own harm"); 44:8 ("you cut yourselves off"). The notion that ultimately it is not Yahweh but Israel itself that is provoked was already expressed in Dt. 32:21, but the primary narrative of the Deuteronomistic history did not take up this idea.

In Jer. 32:29-32, with expansive rhetoric, the formula is repeated thrice. The immediately following verse might account for the late introduction of the formula in Ezk. 8:17. According to Jer. 32:33, the Israelites turned their backs and not their faces to Yahweh (cf. 2:27; 7:24, but without reference to *kʿs*). In Ezk. 8:17,[21] the interpolated formula refers not to the *ḥāmās* but to cultic worship of the sun, which involved turning to the east, away from the altar of Yahweh. This provoked Yahweh's anger.

3. *Later.* In later texts, only Ezk. 16:26; Sir. 3:16 dissolve the close association of the Deuteronomistic cliche with the primary sin of worshipping other gods. In Ezk. 16:26,[22] the hiphil of *kʿs* refers to the alliance with Egypt; in Sir. 3:16, it refers to

19. *Bibl,* 53 (1972), 301-339.
20. Dietrich.
21. Contra Stolz, 841.
22. Contra *idem.*

transgression of the commandment to honor one's father and mother. In the latter, the name of Yahweh is replaced by the term "creator." The LXX interprets this passage somewhat differently, along the lines of Prov. 17:25; 27:3, thus avoiding this extension of the theological usage.

III. LXX, Dead Sea Scrolls. The preferred LXX translation of *kāʿas* is *par/orgízein* (37 times); *para/ek/pikraínein* (7), *thymoún,* etc. (5), and *paroxýnein* (3) are also found. The noun *kaʿas* is translated by *thymós* (8 times), *orgḗ* (5), and *athymía* (2). For *kaʿaś, orgḗ* is always used (4 times).

In the literature of the Qumran Essenes, the noun *kaʿas* appears only twice. In 1QpHab 11:5, in conjunction with *ḥēmâ,* it denotes the terrible wrath of the Wicked Priest when persecuting the Teacher of Righteousness. In 1QH 5:34, *kaʿas* causes the eyes of the worshipper to grow dim (cf. Ps. 6:8[7]; 31:10[9]).

Lohfink

כַּף → יָד

כִּפֶּר *kipper*; כַּפֹּרֶת *kappōreṯ*; כֹּפֶר *kōp̱er*; כִּפֻּרִים *kippurîm*

Contents: I. 1. Etymology; 2. Syntax; 3. LXX. II. Basic Concept: 1. Non-Priestly Texts; 2. Priestly Texts; 3. Lines of Interpretation. III. Interpersonal Reconciliation. IV. Cultic Atonement: 1. The Altar; 2. Communal Sin Offering; 3. Day of Atonement; 4. *kippurîm*; 5. Extended Usage; 6. Non-Priestly Literature. V. Divine Atonement. VI. *kōp̱er.* VII. Dead Sea Scrolls.

---

kipper. Y. Avishur, "Biblical Words and Phrases in the Light of Accadian Parallels," *ShnatMikr,* 2 (1977), 11-19 [Heb.], IX-X [Eng. summary]; J. Barr, "Expiation," *Dictionary of the Bible* ([3]1963), 280-83; H. C. Brichto, "On Slaughter and Sacrifice, Blood and Atonement," *HUCA,* 47 (1976), 19-55; C. H. Dodd, "ἱλάσκεσθαι, Its Cognates, Derivatives, and Synonyms in the Septuagint," *JTS,* 32 (1931), 352-360 = "Atonement," *The Bible and the Greeks* (London, 1935), 82-95; K. Elliger, *Leviticus. HAT,* IV (1966); E. E. Evans-Pritchard, *The Nuer* (Oxford, 1940); *idem, Nuer Religion* (Oxford, 1956); N. Füglister, "Sühne durch Blut — Zur Bedeutung von Leviticus 17,11," *Studien zum Pentateuch. Festschrift W. Kornfeld* (Vienna, 1977), 143-164; P. Garnet, "Atonement Constructions in the OT and the Qumran Scrolls," *EvQ,* 46 (1974), 131-163; *idem, Salvation and Atonement in the Qumran Scrolls. WUNT,* II/3 (1977); T. H. Gaster, *Myth, Legend, and Custom in the OT* (New York, 1969), no. 146; M. J. Geller, "The Šurpu Incantations and Lev. V.1-5," *JSS,* 25 (1980), 181-192; G. Gerleman, "Die Wurzel kpr im Hebräischen," *Studien zur alttestamentlichen Theologie* (Heidelberg, 1980), 11-23; H. Gese, "Die Sühne," *Zur biblischen Theologie. BEvT,* 78 (1977), 85-106; M. Görg, "Die Lade als Thronsockel," *BN,* 1 (1976), 29f.; *idem,* "Nachtrag zu

I. 1. *Etymology.* The lexica of the nineteenth century associated Heb. *kipper* with Arab. *kafara,* "cover," describing the act of atonement as the covering of guilt. Since Heinrich Zimmern's reference to Bab. *kuppuru,* the two etymologies agree.

In the Koran, Arab. *kaffara,* "absolve" (with God as subject), is a term borrowed from Judaism but given a new semantic structure: atonement is an act of the merciful God, without the need for any sacrifice.[1] Arabic lexicographers derive the word from *kafara,* "cover," so that *kaffara* may have overtones of "atone (by covering)." It is nevertheless difficult to link this idea with the OT concept of atonement. The closest point of contact is Jer. 18:23: *'al-teḵappēr,* "do not forgive (their iniquity)," which is echoed in Neh. 3:37(Eng. 4:5) by *'al-teḵas,* "do not forgive (their guilt)." The piel of *ksh* can also mean "cover"; but since it often means "forgive (guilt or sin)" (Ps. 32:1; 85:3[2]), it is unlikely that Neh. 3:37(4:5) involves a consciously etymologizing vari-

---

כַּפֹּרֶת," *BN,* 5 (1978), 12; *idem,* "Eine neue Deutung für *kăpporæt,*" *ZAW,* 89 (1977), 115-18; K. Grayston, "'Ιλάσκεσθαι and Related Words in LXX," *NTS,* 27 (1981), 640-656; Y. M. Grintz, "Archaic Terms in the Priestly Code," *Lešonénu,* 39 (1974/75), 163-67 [Heb.]; R. Hanhart, "Die jahwefeindliche Stadt," *Beiträge zur alttestamentlichen Theologie. Festschrift W. Zimmerli* (Göttingen, 1977), 152-163; M. J. L. Hardy, *Blood Feuds and the Payment of Blood Money in the Middle East* (Beirut, 1963); B. Janowski, "Auslösung des verwirkten Lebens," *ZThK,* 79 (1982), 25-59; *idem, Sühne als Heilsgeschehen. WMANT,* 55 (1982); *idem* and H. Lichtenberger, "Enderwartung und Reinheitsidee: Zur eschatologischen Deutung von Reinheit und Sühne in der Qumrangemeinde," *JJS,* 34 (1983) [Qumran]; K. Koch, "Sünde und Sündenvergebung um die Wende von der exilischen zur nachexilischen Zeit," *EvTh,* 26 (1966), 217-239; J. Z. Lauterbach, *Rabbinic Essays* (Cincinnati, 1951), 354-376; B. A. Levine, *In the Presence of the Lord. StJLA,* 5 (1974); R. G. Lienhardt, *Divinity and Experience* (Oxford, 1961); F. Maass, "כפר *kpr* pi. sühnen," *THAT,* I, 842-857; J. Milgrom, "Israel's Sanctuary," *RB,* 83 (1976), 390-99; *idem,* "A Prolegomenon to Leviticus 17:11," *JBL,* 90 (1971), 149-156; *idem,* "Sin-Offering or Purification-Offering?" *VT,* 21 (1971), 237-39; *idem,* "Two Kinds of *ḥaṭṭā't,*" *VT,* 26 (1976), 333-37; L. Morris, "The Use of ἱλάσκεσθαι etc. in Biblical Greek," *ExpT,* 62 (1950/51), 227-233; R. R. Nicole, "C. H. Dodd and the Doctrine of Propitiation," *WTJ,* 17 (1955), 117-157; R. Péter, "L'imposition des mains dans l'AT," *VT,* 27 (1977), 48-55; R. Rendtorff, *Studien zur Geschichte des Opfers im Alten Israel. WMANT,* 24 (1967); J. Scheftelowitz, *Alt-palästinensischer Bauernglaube in religionsvergleichender Beleuchtung* (Hannover, 1925), 47-51; A. Schenker, "*kōper* et expiation," *Bibl,* 63 (1982), 32-46; *idem, Versöhnung und Sühne* (Fribourg, 1981); K. Seybold, *Das Gebet des Kranken im AT. BWANT,* 99[5/10] (1973); E. A. Speiser, "Census and Ritual Expiation in Mari and Israel," *BASOR,* 149 (1958), 17-25 = *Oriental and Biblical Studies* (Philadelphia, 1967), 171-186; J. J. Stamm, *Erlösen und Vergeben im AT* (Bern, 1940); F. Thureau-Dangin, *RAcc*; H. Thyen, *Studien zur Sündenvergebung im NT und seinen alttestamentlichen und jüdischen Voraussetzungen. FRLANT,* N.S. 78[96] (1970); S. Wefing, *Untersuchungen zum Entsühnungsritual am grossen Versöhnungstag* (diss., Bonn, 1978); J. Weismann, "Talion und öffentliche Strafe im mosaischen Rechte," in K. Koch, ed., *Um das Prinzip der Vergeltung in Religion und Recht des ATs. WdF,* 125 (1972), 325-406; N. H. Young, "C. H. Dodd, 'Hilaskesthai' and his critics," *EvQ,* 48 (1976), 67-78; H. Zimmern, *Akkadische Fremdwörter als Beweis für babylonischen Kultureinfluss* (Leipzig, ²1917).

1. Koran, Sura 5:12; 8:29; etc.

ant.[2] The use of Aram. *k^esāyā'*, "cover," to translate *kappōreṯ* in 4Q156[3] presupposes a specific concept of the sacral object called *kappōreṯ*; it is not an etymological conjecture. The interpretation of *kipper* as "cover" on the basis of Arabic, most recently supported by Stamm, is fraught with problems.

Babylonian incantation and ritual texts, especially from the first half of the first millennium, use the term *kuppuru* (D stem of *kapāru*)[4] with the meaning "purify cultically"; it refers to acts performed by an incantation priest. The purpose is to restore a sick individual to health; typical instructions read: "Wipe him off (*tu-kap-pár-šu*) seven times with seven pieces of dry bread"[5] or "[Mix?] flour with water from the cistern and wipe off (*tu-kap-pár*) the person's body."[6] During the Babylonian New Year Festival, cultic ceremonies were carried out to purify houses, temples, cities, and the countryside; as an example of the instructions, we find: "The incantation priest shall purify (*u-kap-par*) the temple with the cadaver of a sheep."[7] In contrast to the Bible, the Mesopotamian cult knows nothing of sin offering or guilt offering; the *kuppuru* rituals have nothing to do with any sacrificial cult; and finally, blood does not play an essential role in either the Babylonian sacrificial system or the *kuppuru* rituals. Despite these differences, discussed by Janowski, both he and Levine suggest an historical relationship between Akk. *kuppuru* and Heb. *kipper*.

2. *Syntax*. The verb *kipper* (piel) can take a direct object: *y^eḵappēr ʿāwōn*, "he forgave the iniquity" (Ps. 78:38); *w^eḵipper 'eṯ-miqdaš haqqōḏeš*, "he shall purify the sanctuary" (Lev. 16:33). Its use with prepositions is highly varied, with many semantic nuances:

a. *l^e*: *kappēr l^eʿamm^eḵā*, "forgive thy people" (Dt. 21:8); *b^eḵapp^erî-lāḵ l^eḵol-'^ašer ʿāśîṯ*, "when I forgive you all that you have done" (Ezk. 16:63).

b. *b^e*: *b^ezō'ṯ y^eḵuppar ʿāwōn*, "by this the guilt will be expiated" (Isa. 27:9); *bammâ '^aḵappēr*, "How shall I make expiation?" (2 S. 21:3); *hakkōhēn y^eḵappēr ʿālāyw b^e'êl hā'āšām*, "the priest shall make atonement for him with the *'āšām* ram" (Lev. 5:16).

c. *ʿal* (single or repeated): *w^eḵipper ʿālāyw hakkōhēn*, "the priest shall make atonement for him" (Lev. 5:26[6:7]); *'al-t^eḵappēr ʿal-ʿ^awōnām*, "do not forgive them their iniquity" (Jer. 18:23); *w^eḵipper ʿālāyw hakkōhēn ʿal-ḥaṭṭā'ṯô*, "the priest shall make atonement for him for his sin" (Lev. 4:35).

d. *min*: *w^eḵipper ʿālāyw hakkōhēn lip̱nê YHWH mizzôḇô*, "the priest shall make atonement for him before Yahweh for his discharge" (Lev. 15:15).

---

2. Levine, 57f.
3. J. T. Milik, "Tefillin, Mezuzot, Targums," *Qumrân Grotte 4*, II. *DJD*, VI (1977), 87.
4. *AHw*, I (1965), 442f.
5. *CAD*, VIII (1971), 179a = G. Meier, "Ein akkadisches Heilungsritual aus Boğazköy," *ZA*, 45 (1939), l. II.20.
6. R. Caplice, "Namburbi Texts in the British Museum III," *Or*, 36 (1967), 274-77.
7. *CAD*, VIII, 179b = *RAcc*, 141, l. 354.

e. *b^{e}ʿaḏ*: *ʾ^{a}ḵapp^{e}râ b^{e}ʿaḏ ḥaṭṭaʾṯ^{e}ḵem,* "I will make atonement for your sin" (Ex. 32:30); *l^{e}ḵappēr b^{e}ʿaḏ bêṯ-yiśrāʾēl,* "to make atonement for the house of Israel" (Ezk. 45:17). According to Garnet,[8] the use of the prep. *b^{e}ʿaḏ* is intended to give these an especially solemn tone.

In some texts, it is hard to translate *kipper*: Lev. 17:11:[9] "For the life of the flesh is in the blood; and I [God] myself have given it for you upon/for the altar, that it may make atonement for you personally (*l^{e}ḵappēr ʿal-nap̱šōṯêḵem*); for it is the blood that makes atonement by virtue of the life (*bannep̱eš y^{e}ḵappēr*) [that is in it]. Dt. 21:8: The translation "cover" used by some versions is inappropriate, being based on Arab. *kafara.* Dt. 32:43: Avishur suggests "he wipes away (*w^{e}ḵipper*) the tears of his people"; neither the reference to Akk. *kapāru,* "wipe off," nor the emendation of MT *ʾdmtw,* "his land," to **ʾdmʿt,* "tears," however, is convincing. Isa. 28:18: "And your covenant with [the god of] death will be forgiven" is emended by many exegetes. The reading *w^{e}ṯupar,* "and will be broken" (hophal of *prr*), has long been suggested on the basis of the Targ.; but emendation is probably unnecessary (cf. Isa. 6:7). Or does the text involve a form of *kāp̱ar,* "cover," as in Gen. 6:14?[10] Isa. 47:11: "You cannot avert it [calamity] by an act of atonement (*kapp^{e}rāh*)."

3. *LXX.* In the LXX, words based on the root *kpr* are translated consistently by derivatives of *hiláskomai,* "propitiate, appease." The regular equivalent of *kipper* is *exiláskomai*; the Day of Atonement is translated *hēméra exilasmoú* (Lev. 23:27f.); the sacral object termed *kappōreṯ* is translated *hilastḗrion*; *kōp̱er* is translated *exílasma* (1 S. 12:3; Ps. 49:8[7][LXX 48:8]).

a. The construction of the verb *exiláskomai* carefully imitates that of *kipper,* especially in the use of prepositions: *exilásetai perí autoú ho hiereús en tṓ kriṓ* (Lev. 19:22); *exilásetai perí autoú ho hiereús apó tḗs hamartías* (Lev. 4:26).

b. The usage just described is a semitism; it does not agree with the common Greek idiom, in which a human being is the active subject and God is the object. In Zec. 7:2 (cf. 8:22; Mal. 1:9), *exilásasthai tón kýrion* means "propitiate the Lord"; this is the normal Greek syntax, which can be used when *exiláskomai* is not being used to translate *kipper*.

c. Contrary to a popularly accepted theory, certain other translations of *kipper* — in particular, *apokathaírō* (Prov. 16:6[LXX 15:27a]) and *apaleíphō* (Dnl. 9:24, possibly a double translation in conjunction with *exiláskomai*[11]), "wipe away" — cannot be cited in support of a basic meaning of "cover" for *kipper.*

d. The variety of translations used for *kōp̱er* is noteworthy. Besides *exílasma,* "means

8. *Salvation,* 66, nn. 1 and 101.
9. Following Janowski.
10. Schenker, *Versöhnung und Sühne,* n. 109.
11. Nicole, 155ff.

of atonement," we find *állagma* (Isa. 43:3; pl. in Am. 5:12), "means of deception"; *dṓra* (Job 36:18), "gifts"; *lýtron* (Prov. 6:35; 13:8; pl. in Ex. 21:30; 30:12; Nu. 35:31f.), "ransom"; and *perikátharma* (Prov. 21:18), "means of purification."

II. Basic Concept. Most of the occurrences of the verb *kipper* are found in P and related texts, above all in the books of Leviticus, Numbers, and Ezekiel (81 out of 101 instances[12]). It is therefore useful to examine the occurrences in the Priestly literature separately from the rest in order to determine the basic meaning.

1. *Non-Priestly Texts.* The basic concept in the non-Priestly texts may be summarized as follows: When a positive or neutral relationship between two groups or parties is broken by a crime, transgression, or sin, tension is produced. This tension must be neutralized and relieved by an act of atonement in order to restore the original order. When the parties involved are humans, one may speak of "appeasing the face" or "assuaging wrath" (Gen. 32:21[20]; Prov. 16:14), but the notion of an angry God who must be appeased is not expressed directly in these texts. The deity is *never* propitiated or appeased. The tension to be neutralized between human beings, but also between a human being and God, is perceived not emotionally as displeasure or discord but rather legally as a grievance that must be satisfied by specific acts. Acts of atonement frequently refer to bloodguilt (*dām*: Nu. 35:33; Dt. 21:8b; 2 S. 21:1,3), but more general expressions are found as well: sin (*ḥaṭṭā'ṯ*: Ex. 32:30; Ps. 79:9), guilt (*'āwôn*: 1 S. 3:14; Isa. 22:14; 27:9; Jer. 18:23; Dnl. 9:24; Ps. 78:38; Prov. 16:6).

The act of atonement can be initiated either by the person or by God; in the latter case, *kipper* means "forgive" (if God is not "purifying" an object such as the land [Dt. 32:43]). If God "forgives," he ceases from his anger (Ps. 78:38); if not, he gives free rein to his anger (Jer. 18:23).

2. *Priestly Texts.* The fundamental structure of atonement in Priestly practice finds full expression in Lev. 19:22: "With this ram the priest shall make atonement before Yahweh for the sin which he has committed." A sin — in this case sleeping with a female slave betrothed to someone else as a concubine — creates tension between the sinner and the deity. As in the non-Priestly texts, the emphasis is not on God's anger, which is mentioned only in special cases (Nu. 17:11[16:46]; 25:11,13). The priest acts as a mediator, removing the tension through a sacrifice, provided by the guilty party and sacrificed by the priest. Frequently the text mentions where the act of atonement takes place: "before Yahweh," i.e., in the temple. It is the priest who performs the act of atonement — generally on behalf of others, but also on behalf of himself and his family (Lev. 16:6,11; etc.). Besides objects like the altar, the sanctuary, the temple (Lev. 16:20,33; Ezk. 43:20; 45:20), a house (Lev. 14:53), or the land (Nu. 35:33), atonement

12. Janowski.

is made primarily for human beings, both individuals (e.g., Lev. 5:26[6:7]; 19:22, cited above) and groups: the congregation (Nu. 15:25), the Levites (Nu. 8:12), the entire nation (Nu. 17:12[16:47]; 25:13; Neh. 10:34[33]). In the case of the altar and the temple, no reason is stated for the act of atonement; the house is atoned for when it is restored to use after being cleansed of efflorescence or mildew; atonement must be made for the land "on account of" bloodguilt. When atonement is made for human beings, the text often cites the reason for the rite: atonement must be made for someone who is "cleansed" after the healing of a skin disease (Lev. 14:31), who has sinned inadvertently (Lev. 5:18; Nu. 15:28), or whom contact with a corpse has made unclean (Nu. 6:11). There are still other grounds: atonement is made "on account of" a discharge (*min*: Lev. 15:15,30), uncleanness (Lev. 14:19), and above all sin (*min*: Lev. 4:26; 5:6,10; *ʿal*: 4:35; 5:13; etc.). Often the means of atonement is stated: atonement is made "by means of" a ram (*bᵉ*: Lev. 5:16; 7:7; 19:22; Nu. 5:8; Ex. 29:33).

3. *Lines of Interpretation.* Earlier debate about the precise meaning of *kipper* centered on C. H. Dodd's article, published in 1931, in which he claimed that the Israelites had no notion of "propitiation" — they spoke instead of "expiation," a human act performed for the purpose of being freed by God from the burden of sin. According to this view, atonement (expiation) is a theocentric act, an interpretation preserved by the LXX with its semitizing use of *exiláskomai.* Critics such as Leon Morris and James Barr replied that Dodd downplayed the notion of divine wrath and that in fact there is less difference between "propitiation" and "expiation" than Dodd admitted. Other scholars may represent more recent discussion. Their interpretations of atonement may be categorized as follows: redemption through substitution or purification of the sanctuary (Jacob Milgrom), symbolic offering or redemption of forfeited life (Hartmut Gese, Bernd Janowski), and commutation of punishment with settlement between the offender and the injured party (Adrien Schenker).

a. Milgrom distinguishes two basic understandings of atonement: in one, *kipper* means "purify (ritually)"; in the other, it means "redeem." When used in the latter sense, the purpose of the *kipper* act is to avert God's wrath, which would strike innocent and guilty alike. This is the understanding behind the scapegoat (Lev. 16) and the ritual described in Dt. 21:1-9. In both cases, "redemption" involves the ritual "substitution" of an animal for a human being. In this usage, *kipper* derives from *kōper,* "ransom," as may be seen from the collection of "atonement money" as a kind of head tax (Ex. 30:16) and the prohibition against ransoming someone guilty of murder (Nu. 35:31-33). When the idea of averting God's wrath is involved, the verb *kipper* is to be interpreted as deriving from *kōper*: innocent life is protected by the substitution of the guilty party or an equivalent ransom or sacrificial offering. Although "ransom" in substitution for a murderer is forbidden, a homicide is "ransomed" by the natural death of the high priest. In like manner, the head tax ransoms everyone who is counted in the census. The Levites "substitute" for any Israelite who comes too near the sanctuary (Nu. 1:53; 8:19; 18:22f.).

A small group of texts (Lev. 15:31; 16:19; Nu. 19:13, 20; cf. Jer. 17:1) constitutes the evidence for understanding the Priestly conception of atonement associated with the verb *kipper* in the sense of "purify" or "cleanse." These texts do not specify how the altar and sanctuary have been affected by the "uncleannesses of the people of Israel"; Milgrom theorizes that whenever someone sins, the sin is attracted as it were magnetically to the sanctuary, where it accumulates almost like a physical substance. Finally the deity, no longer able to endure its presence, departs from the temple and leaves the people to suffer the consequences of their sin. The accumulation of individual sins leads without fail to the "departure" of the deity and therefore the destruction of the community, which can live only in communion with its God. It is therefore incumbent upon Israel, through its priests, to "cleanse" (*kipper*) the sanctuary regularly of all uncleannesses. In this view, there is no evil that escapes God's attention, even if the individual offender eludes the inevitable punishment. The evil accumulates in the sanctuary; it not only defiles the altar outside, but penetrates within the holy of holies as far as the ark. On the Day of Atonement, therefore, the whole temple complex must be ritually purified.

We may ask whether this theory does not err by trying to combine several individually correct ideas into a uniform system. Of value for the theology of the cult may be Henri Frankfort's "multiplicity of approaches."[13]

b. In his analysis, Janowski distinguishes two groups of texts involving *kipper* and *kōp̱er*: one group comprises the texts in P and the Priestly tradition in Ezk. 40–48 and the Chronicler's history, the other comprises the texts outside the complex. In the latter group, *kipper* and *kōp̱er* refer to interpersonal reconciliation and compensation (Gen. 32:21[20]; 2 S. 21:3; Prov. 16:6,14), Yahweh's act of expiation (Dt. 21:8a; 32:43; 1 S. 3:14; etc.), the act of atonement of an intercessory mediator (Ex. 32:30; Nu. 17:11f.[16:46f.]; 25:13), and redemption of a forfeited life through the offering of an equivalent (*kōp̱er*: Ex. 21:30; 30:12; Nu. 35:31f.; 1 S. 12:3; Isa. 43:3; etc.). In marginal situations, when the life of an individual or the people is forfeit on account of a legal, moral, or religious offense, deliverance from death is accomplished by an act of atonement. The verb *kipper* never refers to "propitiation" of God. Even when a human person (Ex. 32:30; Nu. 17:11f.[16:46f.]; 25:13) or an angel (Job 33:24; 36:18) is the subject of the action, *kipper* (or the offering of a *kōp̱er*: Job 33:24; 36:18) denotes the action of a substitutionary mediator, effecting forgiveness of sin (Ex. 32:30,32), withdrawal of wrath (Nu. 25:11), or cessation of a plague (Nu. 17:13,15[16:48,50]).

In the Priestly texts, by contrast, a priest is always the subject of the action denoted by *kipper*; God's response is indicated by the recurring formula "thus the priest shall make atonement (*wᵉḵipper*) for him, and he shall be forgiven [by God]" (Lev. 4:31; cf. vv. 20,26,35; etc.). The classic Priestly *kipper* ritual is the sin offering (*ḥaṭṭā'ṯ*),[14] in which the person providing the sacrifice lays a hand on the animal whose blood is to be applied to the altar by the priest or — on special occasions — carried into the

---

13. H. Frankfort, *Ancient Egyptian Religion* (New York, 1948, repr. 1961), 4.
14. → חטא *ḥāṭā'* (*chāṭā'*).

holy of holies in the temple. The hand laid on the animal (Lev. 1:4; 3:2,8,13; etc.) identifies the sinner with the sacrificial victim to be slain and symbolizes the offering of his own life. The treatment of the blood (Lev. 4:25,30,34; 16:14f.; Ezk. 43:20; etc.) completes the symbolism: by applying the blood to the altar, the priest carries out the symbolic surrender of the worshipper's own life to the sanctuary and thus to the deity.

c. Schenker develops his interpretation of the act of atonement on the basis of Ex. 21:28-32: if someone is killed by a goring ox, the ox's owner can avoid being put to death by paying a "propitiatory offering" (*kōp̄er*) to any injured party. The essence of atonement is thus mitigation of punishment, freely conceded by the injured party, who agrees to a settlement instead of insisting ruthlessly on justice. This structure can be seen not only in Gen. 32:21(20); Nu. 35:31; 2 S. 21:3; Prov. 16:14, but also in texts referring to God and in cultic texts. When God "forgives" our sins (*wᵉḵappēr ʿal-ḥaṭṭōʾṯênû,* Ps. 79:9), it means that he does not insist on full punishment but mitigates it — in the extreme case, not requiring any act of penance on the part of the sinner. Atonement, therefore, is based on God's willingness to compromise and be conciliatory. Mediation plays a role in the act of atonement: Yahweh himself arbitrates between Israel and its enemies (Dt. 32:43); Moses mediates as advocate between God and his people (Ex. 32:30); Yahweh refrains from further punishment because of Phinehas's "zeal" (Nu. 25:13). In the cult, Yahweh declares himself satisfied with offerings of his own choosing instead of demanding punishment in full; the cult with animal blood as its most important form of sacrifice is God's own offer of reconciliation. Although God is "propitiated" by the sacrifice, there is a theocentric element in the divine establishment of the cult: forgiveness is not purchased by the sinner but made possible by God's preemptive offer.

III. Interpersonal Reconciliation. The verb *kipper* is comparatively rare in the sense of interpersonal reconciliation. Two passages allude to the impossibility of legal atonement of bloodguilt. Because Saul had killed some of the Gibeonites, the relationship between Israel and Gibeon was burdened by bloodguilt. "How shall I make atonement (*ʾᵃḵappēr*)?" David asks (2 S. 21:3). The answer — "we want neither silver nor gold from Saul and his house" (v. 4) — makes it clear that David's question is to be understood as an offer of a material gift, a *kōp̄er* payment. The Gibeonites demand that seven of Saul's sons be handed over to be put to death. The basic principle is enunciated with absolute clarity in Nu. 35:33: "No atonement can be made (*lōʾ-yᵉḵuppar*) for the land, for the blood that is shed in it, except by the blood of him who shed it." The figurative usage of the verb in this statement should be noted: "atonement" in fact denotes compensation through a material gift; understood literally, the slaying of the murderer as an act of blood vengeance effects purification but not "atonement."

Two other texts use *kipper* for the attempt of someone in a weak position to "appease" someone powerful in order to avoid the latter's punishment or vengeance — for example, by wise counsel (Prov. 16:14) or a gift (Gen. 32:21[20]). In the Genesis passage, Jacob, who has defrauded his brother Esau, succeeds in averting the latter's threatened revenge, so that we see once more the same basic structure as in 2 S. 21:3: tension that has arisen between two parties is relaxed by an act of appeasement on the part of the weaker. The noun *kōp̱er* is related to the use of *kipper* for the resolution of interpersonal conflict.[15]

IV. Cultic Atonement.

1. *The Altar.* According to Ezk. 43:18-26, the rebuilt altar of burnt offering in the Jerusalem temple cannot be put to use until after a complex seven-day ritual comprising a series of sin offerings (*ḥaṭṭā'ṯ*) and burnt offerings (*'ôlâ*). The crucial role is played by the sin offering, whose central feature is a blood rite for which precise instructions are given: the blood of the sacrificial animal (on the first day a bull, on succeeding days a goat) is put on the four horns of the altar, the four corners of the middle step, and the wall surrounding the altar. In this way the whole altar — like the former victim of a skin disease in Lev. 14:14 — is included in the ceremony. Thus the altar is cleansed of sin (*ḥāṭā'* piel), atoned for (*kipper*), purified (*ṭhr* piel), and consecrated (*qiddēš*); the first three verbs are probably meant to be taken as synonyms describing the same process, while the "consecration" probably involves an additional rite of anointing (Ex. 29:36). Ezk. 45:18,20 requires a somewhat abbreviated version of this ceremony to be repeated annually on the first and seventh days of the first month; the blood rite is extended to include various gates of the temple, which are sprinkled with blood. Analogous regulations concerning the consecration of the altar and an annually repeated consecration of the altar of incense are found in Ex. 29:36f.; 30:10. The consecration of the altar is also repeated before a newly consecrated priest performs his first sacrifice and on the Day of Atonement (Lev. 8:15; 16:16ff.,20,33). The regulations concerning the Day of Atonement extend the blood rite to the holy of holies. Lev. 16:19 (cf. Ezk. 45:20) emphasizes the lustral character of the blood rite: by means of the blood, the priest is to cleanse the altar "and hallow it from the uncleannesses of the people of Israel."

2. *Communal Sin Offering.* A sin offering (*ḥaṭṭā'ṯ*)[16] is necessary when the whole congregation has unwittingly "sinned and done something forbidden by Yahweh" (Lev. 4:13). The ritual described in Lev. 4:14-21 involves five phases: the elders of the congregation lay their hands on the head of the sacrificial animal (a bull); the animal is killed; the priest takes some of the blood and performs a ceremony within the temple; the priest puts blood on the horns of the altar of burnt offering in the courtyard; the fat from the animal is burned upon the altar. The text does not state which is the central action that performs the atoning function mentioned in v. 20, but it can be identified. Many exegetes think that the laying on of hands transfers the sin like a material substance to the sacrificial animal; this substance is then destroyed with the animal.[17] It is more likely that the laying on of hands — possibly a relic of the elders' participation

15. See VI below.
16. → חטא *ḥāṭā'* (*chāṭā'*).
17. Rendtorff, 216.

in the ritual slaying — is meant to indicate that the animal is now to be sacrificed. The action may also be understood as a symbolic identification with the sacrificial animal, as ethnological parallels suggest.[18] Such an interpretation could well reflect the close "communion" between the herdsman and his flock. The laying on of hands is completed by the two blood rites. These represent a symbolic sacrifice of life to the deity;[19] for the life is in the blood, and the altar and sanctuary represent the deity. The atoning power of the blood is emphasized in Lev. 17:11 and, with even more explicit reference to the sin offering, in 2 Ch. 29:24. Especially significant is the formula "he makes atonement — they are forgiven" found in Lev. 4:20 and elsewhere: it relates the action of the priest to the action of the deity (Lev. 4:20,26,31,35; 5:10,13,16,18,26[6:7]; 19:22; Nu. 15:25,28). An analogous formula is found in Lev. 12:7,8; 14:20,53: "he [the priest] makes atonement — he/she [the lay person] is made clean [by the deity]."

Atonement rituals of the type found in Lev. 4:13-21 are prescribed under many circumstances; they are used to make atonement for individuals or groups that have deliberately or unwittingly come to bear the burden of sin. Most of the pertinent regulations are found within the complex Lev. 4:1–5:26(6:7). The regulations in Lev. 12:1–15:33 refer to atonement rites required for the purification of a woman after childbirth (Lev. 12:7f.) or the resocialization of someone who has had a skin disease (Lev. 14:18,20,31). It is especially noteworthy in the latter case that the lay person offering the sacrifice comes in contact with the sacrificial blood and oil before they are offered (Lev. 14:14-18): he or she is to be involved in the sacrifice from head to toe.

3. *Day of Atonement.* The present text of the Day of Atonement ritual (Lev. 16) combines three different rituals to constitute a single whole. (a) The high priest sacrifices an ox as a sin offering for himself and his family, then a goat for the people. He takes some of the blood from the animals and carries it into the holy of holies, where he sprinkles it on a sacral object made of gold called the *kappōreṯ* ("atonement piece"). This blood rite has atoning power for both the priest and the people (vv. 16f.), as does the subsequent burning of the fat portions of the sacrificial animal (vv. 24f.). (b) The altar in the courtyard is also sprinkled with the blood and thus "atoned for," i.e., "cleansed" and "hallowed" (vv. 18f.). (c) The priest lays his hands on a second goat while confessing the sins of the Israelites and then has it sent away into the desert. V. 10 states that the goat destined "for Azazel" is presented before Yahweh *lᵉḵappēr ʿālāyw,* which may mean "to make expiation with it,"[20] "to serve for the sin"[21] "to transfer sin to it,"[22] or "to perform rites of expiation beside it,"[23] if the text is not in fact corrupt.[24]

---

18. Evans-Pritchard, *Nuer Religion,* 279f.
19. Gese, 95ff.; Péter.
20. NJPS.
21. The standard German translation.
22. J. Milgrom, review of Levine, *JBL,* 95 (1976), 292.
23. Levine, 80.
24. Elliger, *s.v.*

According to Karl Elliger's literary analysis, two originally independent rituals have been combined here: a ceremony of atonement for the priests and people, including the rite of the scapegoat, and a ceremony of atonement for the sanctuary and altar. Elliger says: "In the course of the first centuries after the exile, the communal atonement ceremony of the preexilic period came to incorporate a ceremony of purification for the temple, whether the latter merely represents a theoretical requirement (originating during the exile) or a ceremony that was actually carried out, possibly even during the monarchy."[25] Sabina Wefing explains the development somewhat differently: At the outset there was an atonement ritual performed by the high priest solely for himself and his family (Lev. 16:3, 6, 11b, 14). This came to be associated with a communal sin offering in which the rite of the scapegoat played a role (vv. 5, 7-10, 15-17). Thus a comprehensive ritual was forged that was later rounded out by a ceremony of atonement for the sanctuary (vv. 18f.).

Unlike many exegetes, Gese and Janowski do not think of the *kappōreṯ* as the "cover" of the ark. According to Janowksi,[26] "beyond any superficial materiality, it is the locus of God's presence in Israel, conceived of as a 'pure plane.' The critical feature of the *kappōreṯ* is neither its outward form nor its precise structural description nor its position 'above the ark,' which appears to qualify it as a 'cover,' but its symbolic representation of a theological reality: the sign marking the boundary of the transcendent realm and therefore the site of God's condescension." The focal point of Lev. 16, according to Gese and Janowski, is the sprinkling of blood on the *kappōreṯ* as a meeting between the God who reveals himself and the human agent who offers himself; this action can be understood as a type of the original event at Sinai in Ex. 24:15ff.

The proverbial "scapegoat" could no longer be sacrificed after the destruction of the Jerusalem temple. During the seventh century, we learn of an alternative practice, probably much older, that is still in use: on the day before the atonement festival, as well as after the birth of a male child, a hen is sacrificed. This hen is called a *kappārâ* ("atonement") hen. The archaizing ritual of laying on hands and removing the entrails is attested.[27]

Other interpretations of *kappōreṯ,* not involving the root *kpr,* have been proposed by Manfred Görg and Y. M. Grintz. Görg cites the Egyptian phrase *kp* (*n*) *rdwy,* "sole of the foot," which contracts to *kappōreṯ,* denoting the place where the feet of the divine throne or of the enthroned deity himself are conceived as resting. Grintz suggests an etymology based on Egyp. *k3pt,* "roof," which would be appropriate for the "cover" of the ark. Gillis Gerlemann, assuming that *kipper* actually means "stroke, wipe, polish," thinks of the *kappōreṯ* as a polished mirror.

4. *kippurîm.* Several phrases using the noun *kippurîm,* "atonement," are found: *ḥaṭṭā'ṯ hakkippurîm,* "sin offering of atonement" (Ex. 30:10; Nu. 29:11); *kesep hak-*

25. *Ibid.,* 210.
26. Janowski, *Sühne als Heilsgeschehen,* 347.
27. Scheftelowitz, Lauterbach.

kippurîm, "atonement money" (Ex. 30:16); *yôm (hak)kippurîm,* "Day of Atonement" (Lev. 23:27f.; 25:9); *'êl hakkippurîm,* "ram of atonement" (Nu. 5:8); *par ḥaṭṭā'ṯ . . . 'al-hakkippurîm,* "bull (for) the sin offering of atonement" (Ex. 29:36). Priestly language uses the abstract noun *kippurîm* to describe anything immediately associated with atonement: the festival, the sacrificial animal, the sacrifice, and — extending the notion of atonement — the temple tax. It is noteworthy that the expression "Day of Atonement" does not appear in the detailed description of the ritual in Lev. 16 but only in the festival calendar of Lev. 23 and the regulations concerning the year of release in Lev. 25.

5. *Extended Usage.* The classical cultic acts that make atonement for Israel or an individual are the sin offering (*ḥaṭṭā'ṯ*)[28] and the guilt offering (*'āšām*).[29] In texts from the exilic and postexilic period, however, all the major kinds of sacrifice, that is, the whole sacrificial system, serve to make atonement. The only exceptions are *zeḇaḥ* and *zeḇaḥ šᵉlāmîm,*[30] which are never associated with atonement. Lev. 1:4, for example, speaks of the burnt offering[31] as making atonement. Characteristic of this usage are series comprising various types of sacrifice; atonement is associated with the group as a whole. Examples include:

Lev. 9: *ḥaṭṭā'ṯ, 'ôlâ, minḥâ, šᵉlāmîm*;
Lev. 14:10-20: *'āšām, ḥaṭṭā'ṯ, 'ôlâ, minḥâ*;
Nu. 15:24: *'ôlâ, minḥâ, neseḵ, ḥaṭṭā'ṯ*;
Ezk. 45:15: *minḥâ, 'ôlâ, šᵉlāmîm*;
Ezk. 45:17: *ḥaṭṭā'ṯ, minḥâ, 'ôlâ, šᵉlāmîm*;
Sir. 45:16 (Heb.): *'ôlâ, ḥᵃlāḇîm, 'azkārâ*;
1QM 2:5: *'ôlôṯ, zᵉḇāḥîm, miqṭereṯ*.

The Priestly texts of the Pentateuch also reinterpret other traditions, turning them into acts of atonement. For example, the notion of atonement becomes central to the sacrifices offered at the ordination of priests (*millu'îm*: Lev. 8:33; Ex. 29:34), the half shekel to be paid as *kōp̄er* when a census of Israel is taken (Ex. 30:11-16; Nu. 31:48-54), and the intercession of the Levities, Aaron, and Phinehas (Nu. 8:19; 17:11f.[16:46f.]; 25:13). In Lev. 14:53, a rite involving a bird makes atonement for a house that has been cleansed of efflorescence and mildew.

6. *Non-Priestly Literature.* Texts outside the Priestly corpus make only scattered reference to rites and ceremonies involving atonement. When the golden calf in the desert has been destroyed and those guilty of worshipping it put to death, atonement must still be made for the sin of idolatry (Ex. 32:30); Moses makes atonement through

28. → חטא *ḥāṭā'* (*chāṭā'*).
29. → אשׁם *'ā\chām* (*'āšām*).
30. → זבח *zāḇaḥ* (*zābhach*); → שׁלמים *šᵉlāmîm.*
31. → עולה *'ôlâ.*

an intercessory prayer in which he brings his own personal influence to bear. When someone is found slain by an unknown hand, a heifer is taken to a stream and its neck broken; an accompanying prayer calls on Yahweh to "make atonement for" the blood and "forgive" the bloodguilt (Dt. 21:8). Just as in Ex. 32 the slaying of the guilty precedes the prayer of atonement, so here an animal must be ritually slain before the act of atonement proper, which consists in the prayer.

When Isaiah is called, his sin must be "forgiven" by God; the touching of his lips with a burning coal carried by an angelic being (Isa. 6:7) is a heavenly (and therefore extraordinary) rite of purification, but not an act of atonement.

Offenses against God for which no cultic act of atonement is prescribed are atoned for through demonstrations of loyalty and faithfulness toward others (Prov. 16:6) or acts of charity (Sir. 3:30).

V. Divine Atonement. In texts belonging to the Priestly tradition, a priest is invariably the subject of *kipper* as a (cultic) act of atonement; there are other texts, however, in which the deity himself is the subject of *kipper*: Dt. 21:8a; 32:43; 2 Ch. 30:18; Ps. 65:4(3); 78:38; 79:9; Jer. 18:23; Ezk. 16:63. There are also passages in which God is the logical subject of *kipper*; these use the piel infinitive (Dnl. 9:24) or the passive hithpael (1 S. 3:14) or pual (Isa. 6:7; 22:14; 27:9; 28:18). The active use of *kipper* with God as subject is associated primarily with the language of prayer (Dt. 21:8a; 2 Ch. 30:18; Ps. 65:4[3]; 79:9; Jer. 18:23).

The text of Isa. 27:9 does not indicate precisely what the relationship is between "atonement for the guilt of Jacob" and destruction of the altars: is it Yahweh himself who has the altars destroyed,[32] or does atonement depend on Israel's prior destruction of them?[33] Dt. 32:43 likewise poses a riddle: does Yahweh forgive the shedding of the Israelites' blood through an act of vengeance that makes atonement?[34] Or does Yahweh, in an act of loyal solidarity, intervene on behalf of his people and "bring relief to the land of his people" by driving out the enemy?[35]

Whatever the answer, all these texts "share a fundamental problem that bears on the nature of human existence *coram Deo*: since these texts all deal with situations in which — on account of legal, moral, or religious guilt — the life of the individual or the group is forfeit, God's act of atonement (prayed for, vouchsafed, or refused) relates in each instance to an exceptionally critical situation in which not simply some aspect of human life but its very existence is at stake."[36] This relationship to the human situation of life and death can be observed in the individual texts: if forgiveness is not refused (Isa. 22:14; 1 S. 3:14), it means deliverance from death (Isa. 6:7), restoration of God's presence (Ps. 65:3ff.[2ff.]), preservation of life (Ps. 78:38; 79:8f.), healing (2 Ch. 30:18ff.), and God's vengeance against the life-threatening enemy (Dt. 32:43;

32. Hanhart.
33. Schenker.
34. Janowski.
35. Schenker.
36. Janowski, *Sühne als Heilsgeschehen,* 134f.

Ps. 79:6-12; cf. Jer. 18:19-23). As in cultic atonement, standing "between the dead and the living" (Nu. 17:12f.[16:47f.]) is the symbolic location of the act.

VI. *kōp̱er.* The noun *kōp̱er* is a legal term. It denotes the material gift that establishes an amicable settlement between an injured party and the offending party. The fullest detail relates to the case of a man whose ox, known to be vicious, kills someone. The ox's owner gives to the family or clan injured by the loss of its member whatever *kōp̱er* it requires (Ex. 21:30). The injured family may insist that the owner be put to death, but may also accept the payment of *kōp̱er* as an agreed settlement. The same rule obtains in pre-Islamic and early Islamic law.[37] The agreement may reflect "extenuating circumstances": the ox's owner may be considered guilty only of "reckless endangerment" rather than murder. Settlement by *kōp̱er* is also suggested in cases of accidental homicide, but is forbidden in cases of murder (Nu. 35:31f.). According to Prov. 6:35, a deceived husband will accept no *kōp̱er* from his wife's "friend" — the adulterer has forfeited his life. These examples illustrate the various aspects of *kōp̱er*: for the recipient, it is represents compensation, reparation, indemnification; from the perspective of the offender, it represents a ransom (cf. Ex. 21:30: *piḏyōn napšô,* "redemption of his life") for his own life, which is forfeit, a gift to propitiate the enraged injured party.

According to Job 36:18; Prov. 13:8, the rich can escape the death penalty (and other forms of punishment?) by payment of a *kōp̱er.* In all these cases, the gift is given to the injured party. There are also texts, however, which speak of a *kōp̱er* used to bribe a judge (1 S. 12:3 [cf. Sir. 46:19]; Am. 5:12). In these cases, *kōp̱er* takes on the meaning "bribe." This usage may reflect the fact that the judge mediating between the parties in cases of a proper *kōp̱er* settlement did not go away empty-handed and that the fee paid the judge was also called *kōp̱er,* although there is no evidence to support this theory. There are ethnological parallels for having the guilty party pay the mediator.[38]

In sacral law, the postexilic half-shekel head tax paid to support the Jerusalem cult is also called *kōp̱er* (Ex. 30:12). Ex. 30:11-16 combines two reasons for this usage. According to v. 16, the money is used to pay for the regular cult of atonement, i.e., *kipper*; according to v. 12, the half shekel averts the deadly peril consequent upon census and conscription (cf. 2 S. 24:10-17; Nu. 31:50). Treatment of a census as a religious offense presupposes that at one time it was prohibited entirely. The census was clearly felt to mark the beginning of the state's encroachment upon the individual (Jgs. 8:14; 1 S. 8:11ff.), who had previously found protection within family, clan, and village, in a sacred order beyond the reach of human calculations. This encroachment put the individual at the service of the state, eliminated intermediate social structures, and moved in the direction of the later census lists, which reflect a highly developed state bureaucracy and extensive control (Jer. 22:30; Ezk. 13:9; Ezr. 2:62; Neh. 7:5). Atonement for those counted in the census is based on the sacral nature of the social order that preceded the organized state. Hostility against counting the human and animal

---

37. Hardy, 22, 28.
38. *Ibid.,* 83, 86, 91; Evans-Pritchard, *The Nuer,* 154, 163; Lienhardt, 288.

population is familiar from ethnology;[39] at Mari, too, military conscription was associated with cultic purification.[40]

The payment of *kōp̱er* also plays a role in figurative religious language. No one can ransom his life from death by paying a *kōp̱er* to God (Ps. 49:8[7]); God's clutches here are cruel. Prov. 21:18 is probably to be understood as meaning that God accepts the misfortunes of the wicked as *kōp̱er* for the righteous, who therefore do not feel God's wrath for minor offenses. God accepts as a *kōp̱er* the act of penance performed by someone sick and restores him to health (Job 33:24); it is unclear from the text whether it is an angel[41] or a priest who acts as mediator here between the sufferer and God. According to Isa. 43:3, Yahweh himself pays *kōp̱er* in the form of lands to the Persian king to gain the release of exiled Israel.

VII. Dead Sea Scrolls. The members of the Qumran community created a spiritual and moral substitute to compensate for the ritual impoverishment caused by their distance from the temple: "atonement is made (*ykwprw*) for human ways through the spirit of God's true counsel" (1QS 3:6); those who join the community "will find favor before God through pleasing rites of atonement (*bkpwry nyḥwḥ*)" (1QS 3:11), which do not involve ritual actions. The human role is passive, for God vouchsafes atonement; its means are therefore God's saving power (*ṣdqh*), God's holy spirit, the spirit of God's true counsel, long-suffering and plentiful forgiveness (on the part of God), the riches of his grace, his wonderful mysteries (1QH 4:37; fr. 2:13; 1QS 3:6; 11:14; CD 2:4f.; 3:18).

The interpretation of certain ablutions and water rites at Qumran as rites of atonement might be suggested by 1QS 3:4-12; nowhere, however, are they explicitly so described, and the possibility seems unlikely. Material atonement sacrifices appear to be impugned in a prayer that states: "Thou dost not take indemnification (*kwpr*) for deeds of wickedness" (1QH 15:24). The community observed the Day of Atonement (*ywm hkpwrym*: 1QpHab 11:7), also called the Day of Fasting (CD 6:19; 1QpHab 11:8), with fasting and communal prayer. In 1Q34*bis* 2:6,[42] we have the title of a "prayer of the Day of Atonement" (*tplh lywm kpwrym*) whose text is not preserved; 11QPs*a* DavComp extols David as the writer of hymns, including some for the Day of Atonement.[43]

The logical or grammatical subject of the *kipper* act varies. (a) Usually, as the absence of outward rites of atonement would suggest, the subject is God (1QS 2:8; 11:14; 1QH 4:37; 17:12; fr. 2:13; CD 2:4f.; 3:18; 4:6f.,9f.; 20:34). According to 1QS 2:8f., God will be angry with the "men of the party of Belial" and will not make atonement for their transgressions. (b) The community may also be the subject. By its very existence, it makes atonement for its members as a group (1QS 5:6 [?]). Especially by attacking and condemning the wicked, those who are not members, it also makes atonement for the land

39. Cf. the references in Gaster and the interpretation given by Lienhardt, 22f.
40. Speiser.
41. Seybold, 61.
42. D. Barthélemy and J. T. Milik, *Qumran Cave I. DJD*, I (1955), 153.
43. J. A. Sanders, *The Psalms Scroll of Qumrân Cave 11 (11 Q Psa)*. *DJD*, IV (1965), 92.

— an echo of Dt. 32:43 (1QS 8:6,10; 1QSa 1:3). Disciplinary measures taken within the community likewise contribute to atonement for the land (1QS 9:4). (c) Finally, the priesthood may be the subject. In the time of the great final battle, sacrifices of atonement will again be offered in the Jerusalem temple (1QM 2:5). The Priestly messiah will also make atonement for sin through sacrifice (CD 14:19). The Temple scroll (11QT) contains detailed regulations for ritual atonement, but only the instructions for the Day of Atonement are relatively well preserved and legible (11QT 25:10–27:10): on this day, the high priest "shall make atonement with it [the ox of the sin offering] for all the people of the community" (*wkpr bw ʿl kwl ʿm hqhl*: 11QT 26:7).

Lang

כָּרָה *kārâ*; כֵּרָה *kērâ*; כְּרִית *k^erîṯ*; מִכְרֶה *mikreh*

Contents: I. 1. Roots, Occurrences; 2. Etymology; 3. Specialized Meanings. II. Secular Usage: 1. Dig; 2. Trade; 3. Make a Feast; 4. Tie. III. Religious Usage: 1. Dig; 2. Trade. IV. LXX, Dead Sea Scrolls.

I. 1. *Roots, Occurrences.* In the OT, we must distinguish several — probably four — distinct roots *krh*[1] with the basic meanings "dig," "trade," "make a feast," and "tie together." Of these, the root with the meaning "dig" is the most common; it appears as a verb in the qal (12 times, omitting Prov. 16:27, where the probable reading is *kûr*) and niphal (twice, including Sir. 50:3), as well as in the nouns *k^erîṯ* (twice) and *mik̲reh* (once). The root with the meaning "trade," of which *nkr* is probably a variant (Hos. 3:2),[2] appears only as a verb in the qal (5 times) and niphal (once [*weniḵrû*:[3] Neh. 5:8]). The root meaning "make a feast" occurs once as a verb in the qal and once as the noun *k^erâ.* The fourth root, with the meaning "tie together," appears only in a conjectural emendation of Ps. 22:17(Eng. v. 16), reading *kārû* on the basis of several manuscripts and Symmachus[4] and comparing 2 S. 3:34; John 11:44.[5]

---

kārâ. G. Dalman, *AuS,* VI (1939), 334f.; K. Koch, "Gibt es ein Vergeltungsdogma im AT?" *ZThK,* 52 (1955), 1-42, repr. *Um das Prinzip der Vergeltung in Religion und Recht des ATs. WdF,* 125 (1972), 130-180; A. Schwarzenbach, *Die geographische Terminologie im Hebräischen des ATs* (Leiden, 1954); A. D. Tushingham, "A Reconsideration of Hosea, Chapters 1–3," *JNES,* 12 (1953), 150-59, esp. 153f.

1. Cf. *KBL*³, 472f.

2. Cf. Tushingham, 153f.; W. Rudolph, *Hosea. KAT,* XIII/1 (1966), 84f.

3. Following W. Rudolph, *Esra und Nehemia. HAT,* XX (1949), 130.

4. Cf. the apparatus in *BHS.*

5. Cf. G. R. Driver, "Mistranslations," *ExpT,* 57 (1945/46), 193; S. Mowinckel, *Det Gamle Testamente. Skriftene,* I (Oslo, 1938, repr. 1955), 62; H.-J. Kraus, *Psalms 1–59* (Eng. trans., Minneapolis, 1988), 292, j; *KBL*³, 473.

2. *Etymology.* All four roots are found in other Semitic languages besides Hebrew. The root meaning "dig" appears in Middle Heb. *k^e^riyyâ,* "trench," OSA *krw,* "cave,"[6] Arab. *karā^w^,* "dig," as well as Eth. *karaya*; it is also found in Punic, Jewish Aramaic, and Mandaic texts. The root meaning "trade" corresponds to Middle Heb. *kîrâ,* "purchase," and Arab. *kry,* "rent." The root meaning "make a feast" is probably not related to Assyr. *qerītu,* "banquet" (< *qerû,* "invite"), but has a parallel in OSA *krwm,* "festal or cultic meal."[7] For the root with the meaning "tie together," Arab. *kwr,* "wind a turban," provides an etymological parallel.

3. *Specialized Meanings.* In the case of two of the roots, we can note the development of specialized meanings alongside the basic meaning. The basic meaning "dig" gives rise to the more specific meaning "hew out" (Ex. 21:33; Ps. 7:16[15]; 2 Ch. 16:14; Sir. 50:3) as well as the figurative meaning "prepare" (Gen. 50:5; Ps. 40:7[6]; possibly also 2 Ch. 16:14). In a similar fashion, the root with basic meaning "trade" has evolved the specialized meanings "purchase" (Dt. 2:6; Isa. 57:8, reading *wattik̲rî*;[8] Neh. 5:8, reading *w^e^nik̲rû*[9]) and "bargain" (Job 6:27; 40:30[41:6]).

II. Secular Usage. All four roots appear in the OT in the context of everyday statements and acts, which constitute the majority of all occurrences.

1. *Dig.* The use of the verb representing the root from the word group "dig" is characterized by an association with the nouns "pit," "well," "cistern," "collecting basin," and "tomb" (13 of 14 occurrences). The noun *mik̲reh* (Zeph. 2:9) derived from this root likewise means "pit,"[10] and the root also appears in *k^e^rîṯ,* the name ("Trench") of a wadi leading to the Jordan that has been carved deeply into the East Jordanian massif (1 K. 17:3,5).[11]

The basic meaning "dig" is present when the verb is used with nouns meaning "pit" (*šûḥâ, šîḥâ, šaḥaṯ*) or "well" (*b^e^'ēr*); here *kārâ* denotes either the physical action of digging out a hole or cavity in the earth (Ps. 94:13; Gen. 26:25; Nu. 21:18) or an attitude symbolized by such an action; in the latter case, the familiar image of a pit used as a snare in hunting is in the background (Prov. 26:27; Ps. 57:7[6]; 119:85; Jer. 18:20,22). Analogously, the specialized meaning "hew out," present when the verb is used with the nouns "cistern" (*bôr*), "collecting basin" (*miqwâ*), or "tomb" (*qeb̲er*), refers to the labor of chipping a hole out of rocky ground (Ex. 21:33; Sir. 50:3; 2 Ch.

6. ContiRossini, 170.

7. See *KBL*³, 473; cf. J. Barr, *Comparative Philology and the Text of the OT* (1968, repr. Winona Lake, 1987), 102f.

8. B. Duhm, *Jesaja. HKAT,* III/1 (⁵1968), 428f.

9. Rudolph, *HAT,* XX, 130.

10. Cf. W. Rudolph, *Zephanja. KAT,* XIII/3 (1975), 277, contra G. Gerleman, *Zephanja* (Lund, 1942), 37.

11. Cf. Schwarzenbach, 203; F. M. Abel, *Géographie de la Palestine,* I (Paris, 1933), 484f.; *GTTOT,* §898.

16:14); this action, too, can be used as the basis of a figurative statement (Ps. 7:16[15]). The figurative meaning "make ready" is already suggested by the use of *kārâ* with the noun *qeḇer*, "tomb" (cf. Gen. 50:5; also 2 Ch. 16:14). It is clearly present in Ps. 40:7(6), where *kārâ* is used with *'ōzen*, "ear"; this idiom (cf. LXX *katartízō*) is then used to mean "open one's ears," "listen to," "be obedient."[12]

2. *Trade.* All the passages in which the root meaning "trade" occur have to do with a secular act or use such an act as the basis for making a religious statement. For example, Dt. 2:6 uses the verb in the specific sense of "acquire" or "buy" to denote the totally secular purchase of water for money; in Hos. 3:2, an adulterous woman is the object of such a purchase; Isa. 57:8 speaks of the purchase of sexual favors[13] or the payment made for them.[14] Even Neh. 5:8, which in fact deals with the redemption of Jewish compatriots who have been sold into slavery,[15] is based, like Hos. 3:2, on the common practice of treating human beings as property to be bought and sold. Similarly, the passages in which *kārâ* has the additional specialized meaning "bargain" refer to a totally secular act; in Job 6:27 a friend is bargained over, in 40:30(41:6) a crocodile.

3. *Make a Feast.* The root that generates the word group meaning "make a feast" is used only in secular contexts. The verb in the qal and the related noun *kᵉrâ* appear only in 2 K. 6:23, where they are linked grammatically. The passage describes a substantial but quite ordinary meal, consisting solely of bread and water, which the Israelite king provides for the Syrian prisoners of war before he releases them to return to their homes. Wolfram von Soden,[16] we may note, disputes this meaning, claiming that the meaning "buy" adequately fits the context.

4. *Tie.* The only occurrence of the root *kārâ* in the sense of "tie together" (Ps. 22:17[16] conj.) also denotes an everyday action. It was customary to tie the hands and feet of prisoners (cf. 2 S. 3:34) and, as a reflection of this practice, the hands and feet of the dead (cf. John 11:44); the passage describes the same thing being done to the persecuted speaker, who is mortally ill.[17]

Raymond-J. Tournay,[18] followed by Mitchell Dahood,[19] reads *ke'ᵉrô* and derives *'ᵉrô* from *'ārâ*, "pluck," "gather," in the sense of "pick to pieces": "as though to pick the flesh from my hands and feet." J. J. M. Roberts[20] reads *kārû* and relates the verb

12. Kraus, 426.
13. Duhm, 429.
14. C. Westermann, *Isaiah 40–66. OTL* (Eng. trans. 1966), 323.
15. Cf. Vulg. and Rudolph, *HAT,* XX, 130.
16. W. von Soden, "Zum hebräischen Wörterbuch," *UF,* 13 (1981), 162.
17. Kraus, 297.
18. R.-J. Tournay, "Note sur le Psaume XXII 17," *VT,* 23 (1973), 111f.
19. M. Dahood, "The Verb *'Ārāh,* 'To Pick Clean', in Ps. XXII 17," *VT,* 24 (1974), 370f.
20. J. J. M. Roberts, "A New Root for an Old Crux, Ps. XXII 17c," *VT,* 23 (1973), 247-252.

to Akk. *karû,* "be short,"[21] in the sense of "shrivel": "my hands and my feet are shriveled."

III. Religious Usage. Only two of these roots are associated with religious statements or cultic acts: the root meaning "dig" and the root meaning "trade."

1. *Dig.* Building on the familiar image of the pit trap, the OT uses the root meaning "dig" in two types of religio-theological statement. First, it associates the digging of pits with the conduct of the wicked (Ps. 119:85) — the enemies of the devout Israelite or the enemies of a prophet like Jeremiah (Jer. 18:20,22). Digging a pit here symbolizes plans and actions that aim to destroy the devout. Second, this image can also express the general conviction that evil deeds return upon the heads of those who do them. Someone who digs a pit to trap others will fall into it himself (Prov. 26:27). The psalmists in turn take this general principle enunciated by wisdom and apply it specifically to the relationship of the devout to their enemies and persecutors (Ps. 7:16[15]; 57:7[6]).

The use of the root in the figurative sense of "make ready" leads into cultic contexts. Preparation of a tomb to receive a dead body (Gen. 50:5; also 2 Ch. 16:14) already borders on cultic usage; the contrast between ears that have been made ready by Yahweh (= "obedience") and various types of sacrifice (Ps. 40:7[6]) makes a clear reference to the cultic sphere.

2. *Trade.* The root *kārâ* in the sense of "trade" appears in religious or cultic contexts only with the specialized meaning "acquire," "buy." When the prophet Hosea purchases an adulterous woman in an ordinary business transaction (Hos. 3:2), this purchase serves as a symbolic action representing the unmerited love with which Yahweh yearns to receive back his people Israel, who have turned aside from him to worship other gods. Isa. 57:8 is likewise concerned with Israel's rejection of Yahweh. The people practice the Canaanite fertility cult, characterized as adultery and fornication, upon the high places: unfaithful Israel purchases her lover for money or the fruits of the earth[22] or pays the price of a lover.[23]

IV. LXX, Dead Sea Scrolls. The LXX translates *kārâ* 8 times with *orýssein* and twice with *latomeín*; it translates *kᵉrâ* with *paráthesis* and interprets *kᵉrîṯ* as the toponym *Chorrath.*

At Qumran *krh* occurs only in CD 6:3,9, with the meaning "excavate." In parallel with *ḥāpar,* the verb denotes the work of "well diggers," a metaphor the Torah students of the Community use for themselves.

Schunck

---

21. *AHw,* I (1965), 452.
22. Duhm, 428f.
23. Westermann, 323.

כְּרוּב *kᵉrûḇ*

Contents: I. 1. Orthography; 2. Etymology. II. OT: 1. Living Beings; 2. Representations; 3. Divine Epithets; 4. Summary. III. Extrabiblical Parallels. IV. Concluding Remarks.

I. 1. *Orthography.* The singular form *kᵉrûḇ* is always written plene. In the plural, we find 35 plene spellings as opposed to 29 defective forms; all 15 occurrences in the Pentateuch and 11 of the 12 occurrences in the Writings are spelled defectively, whereas in the Prophets there are 13 defective spellings and 24 plene.[1]

---

kᵉrûḇ. W. F. Albright, "What Were the Cherubim?" *BA,* 1 (1938), 1-3; J. P. Brown, "Literary Contexts of the Common Hebrew-Greek Vocabulary," *JSS,* 13 (1968), 184-88; R. L. Cleveland, "Cherubs and the 'Tree of Life' in Ancient South Arabia," *BASOR,* 172 (1963), 55-60; H. Demisch, *Die Sphinx* (Stuttgart, 1977); É. Dhorme, "Les chérubins. I: Le nom," *RB,* 35 (1926), 328-339 = *Recueil Édouard Dhorme* (Paris, 1951), 671-683; H. J. van Dijk, *Ezekiel's Prophecy on Tyre (Ez. 26,1–28,19). BietOr,* 20 (1968); W. Eichrodt, *Ezekiel. OTL* (Eng. trans. 1970); J. Flagge, *Untersuchungen zur Bedeutung des Greifen* (Sankt Augustin, 1975); T. C. Foote, "The Cherubim and the Ark," *JAOS,* 25 (1904), 279-286; H. Frankfort, *The Art and Architecture of the Ancient Orient* (1970, repr. New York, 1977); T. H. Gaster, "Ezekiel and the Mysteries," *JBL,* 60 (1941), 289-310; M. Görg, "Keruben in Jerusalem," *BN,* 4 (1977), 13-24; P. Grelot, "Sur une pointe de flèche à inscription Phénicienne," *Or,* 26 (1957), 273-79; M. Haran, "The Ark and the Cherubim," *IEJ,* 9 (1959), 30-38, 89-94; A. Jacoby, "Zur Erklärung der Cherube," *ARW,* 22 (1924), 257-265; L. Kákosy, "Mischgestalt," *LexÄg,* IV (1982), 145-48; A. S. Kapelrud, "The Gates of Hell and the Guardian Angels of Paradise," *JAOS,* 70 (1950), 151-56; O. Keel, *Jahwe-Visionen und Siegelkunst. SBS,* 84/85 (1977); *idem, The Symbolism of the Biblical World* (Eng. trans., New York, 1978); M. Kmoskó, "Kerub und Kurib," *BZ,* 11 (1913), 225-234; H. Krüger, *Die Kerubim: Geschichte einer Vorstellung* (diss., Halle-Wittenberg, 1968); S. Landersdorfer, *Der* ΒΑΑΛ ΤΕΤΡΑΜΟΡΦΟΣ *und die Kerube des Ezechiel. SGKA,* 9/3 (1918); F. Landsberger, "The Origin of the Winged Angel in Jewish Art," *HUCA,* 20 (1947), 227-254; J. Maier, *Das altisraelitische Ladeheiligtum. BZAW,* 93 (1965); G. E. Mendenhall, *The Tenth Generation* (Baltimore, 1973); T. N. D. Mettinger, *The Dethronement of Sabaoth. CB,* 18 (1982); G. von Rad, "The Tent and the Ark," *The Problem of the Pentateuch* (Eng. trans., 1966, repr. London, 1984), 103-124; G. Rinaldi, "Nota: kᵉrûb," *BibO,* 9 (1967), 211f.; A. Rosenvasser, "Kerub and Sphinx: More on the Phoenician Paradise," *Milla wa-Milla,* 12 (1971), 28-38; H. Schmidt, "Kerubenthron und Lade," *Eucharisterion. Festschrift H. Gunkel, I. FRLANT,* 19[36] (1923), 120-144; J. Trinquet, "Kerub, Kerubim," *DBS,* V (1957), 161-186; E. Tsoref, "Die Keruben in der Altertumskunde und nach Y. Kaufmann," *BethM,* 11 (1965/66), 59-88; E. Unger, "Mischwesen," *RLV,* VIII, 195-215; R. de Vaux, "Les chérubins et l'arche d'alliance, les sphinx gardiens et es trônes divins dans l'Ancien Orient," *MUSJ,* 37 (1960/61), 91-124 = *Bibel et Orient* (Paris, 1967), 231-259; L. H. Vincent, "Les chérubins. II: Le concept plastique," *RB,* 35 (1926), 340-358, 481-495; P. Welten, "Mischwesen," *BRL*^{2}, 224-27.

1. On the significance of such orthographic variation, cf. D. N. Freedman, "Orthographic Peculiarities in the Book of Job," *Festschrift W. F. Albright. ErIsr,* 9 (1969), 35-44.

2. *Etymology.* a. The root *krb* is not otherwise attested in Biblical Hebrew; it is found, however, in Akk. *karābu,* "bless," in Old South Arabian, and in Ethiopic derivatives. The common West Semitic root *brk,* "bless," is generally thought to be related.[2] Some scholars also cite *rkb,* "ride" (in the context of 2 S. 22:11 par. Ps. 18:11[Eng. v. 10]; cf. Ps. 104:3). Such metatheses, however, should be rejected. None of the six possible permutations of the consonants *k, r,* and *b* is convincingly related in meaning to any of the others. The closest are *krb* and *brk,* "bless," already mentioned.

b. Akk. *karābu* means "pray, bless, greet (persons), worship (deities and persons), promise or offer a sacrifice." The verb is common in Assyrian epistolary salutations: "To the king, my lord, your servant NN. . . . May Nabu and Marduk bless the king [*likrubū̆*]."[3] Derivatives of special interest include *kāribu, kāribtu,* "one who blesses,"[4] and the diminutive *kurību,*[5] which describe cultic images, the former often, the latter always. Since these words are associated with other words applied to cultic images (*lamassu* and *laḫmu*), they have been interpreted as terms denoting such images and identified erroneously with cultic images attested elsewhere.[6] Since, however, there are no cultic images actually called *kāribu, kurību, lamassu,* or *laḫmu,* the words cannot be associated convincingly with any types of cultic images. The form *kāribu* is an active participle describing any person or image in a position of blessing.[7] A text from Elam[8] uses *kāribtu* in conjunction with *lamassu*; this text is quite untypical of Assyrian usage, and mentions other cultic images and practices not attested elsewhere. The diminutive *kurību* appears in lists of cultic images in several building inscriptions of Esarhaddon where lions, *anzû* birds, dolphins (?), *laḫmu,* and *kurību* are mentioned.[9] These images differ widely in nature, permitting no conclusions about the appearance of the *kurību.* One Neo-Assyrian letter[10] even associates *kurību* with royal images. Nonhuman features are suggested by a vision of the underworld seen by an Assyrian crown prince, which describes the first of fifteen monsters as a hybrid creature having the head of a *kurību* but human hands and feet.[11]

---

2. Rinaldi, 211; Dhorme, *Recueil,* 672.

3. *ABL,* 773 = S. Parpola, *Letters from Assyrian Scholars to the Kings Esarhaddon und Ashurbanipal. AOAT,* 5/1 (1970), no. 113, 1-7; additional examples in Seux, 176, 235.

4. *AHW,* I (1965), 449.

5. *Ibid.,* 510.

6. De Vaux, *MUSJ,* 99; Dhorme, *Recueil,* 678, 681; G. A. Cooke, *Ezekiel. ICC* (1936, repr. 1951), 112; Vincent, 341f.

7. *CAD,* VIII (1991), 216.

8. E. Reiner, "Inscription from a Royal Elamite Tomb," *AfO,* 24 (1973), 87-102, esp. 95f.

9. Cited in *CAD,* VIII, 559; cf. Seux, 147; for similar lists associated with the *takultu* festival, see *CAD, ibid.*

10. *AL,* 1194, 13; cited in *CAD,* VIII, 559.

11. W. von Soden, "Die Unterweltsvision eines assyrischen Kronprinzen," *ZA,* N.S. 9[43] (1936), 16, l. 43; *ANET,* 109.

The "blessing images" *lamassu* and *laḫmu* do not belong in this context. The *laḫmu* are mentioned primarily in mythological contexts; in Enuma Elish, for example, they fight against Tiamat. Only later are they described as guards; how they were pictured remains obscure.[12] The words *laḫmu, lamassu, kāribu,* and *kurību* have in common only their use to describe cultic images.

These facts have led certain scholars to assume a connection between Heb. *k*ᵉ*rûḇ* and one of the Akkadian words, either by direct borrowing[13] or indirectly through one of the other West Semitic languages.[14] There is no evidence, however, to support such a conclusion.

There are also traces of a root *krb* meaning "plow," e.g., in *nukaribbu,* "gardener,"[15] which is usually derived from Sum. *nu-kiri.*[16]

c. In Old South Arabic, we find the verb *krb,* "vow, consecrate, offer sacrifice," and the nouns *krb,* "sacrifice, temple offering," and *krbt,* "blessing."[17] The root is extremely common in Old South Arabic onomastics.[18] So far the facts agree with the East Semitic material.

Especially characteristic of the South Arabic area, however, is the technical term *mkrb,* used in the early period for the rulers of Saba, Qataban, and Hadramaut but more or less replaced by *mlk* around the middle of the first millennium B.C. The word is usually understood as meaning "offerer" in the sense of "priest-king." The texts, however, do not assign him any priestly functions, although he clearly had exclusive jurisdiction over religiously established offices. On the basis of South Semitic lexicographical evidence for the root *krb,* "come near," Albert Jamme has proposed[19] interpreting *mkrb* as "one who brings near," i.e., "unifier."

In Ethiopic, we find *m*ᵉ*k*ʷᵉ*rab,* "temple, sanctuary,"[20] and *k*ʷᵉ*rbat,* "amulet";[21] cf. also *karabō,* "basket."

In Classical Arabic, the root *krb* usually has the meaning "be near, approach"; the meaning "plow, prepare for sowing" is also attested.[22] The noun *karab,* "leaf stalk," is an Aramaic loanword.

---

12. *CAD,* IX (1973), 41f.; Dhorme, *Recueil,* 683; Vincent, 344.
13. Rinaldi, 212; Dhorme, *Recueil,* 682.
14. De Vaux, *MUSJ,* 98.
15. *AHw,* II (1972), 802.
16. See S. A. Kaufman, *The Akkadian Influences on Aramaic and the Development of the Aramaic Dialects. AS,* 19 (1974), 85, n. 275; contra A. Salonen, "Notes on the Stem R-K-B in Akkadian," *ArOr,* 17 (1949), 321f.
17. ContiRossini, 170; A. Jamme, *Sabaean Inscriptions from Maḥram Bilqîs (Mârib)* (Baltimore, 1962), 346, 49f., 186.
18. G. L. Harding, *An Index and Concordance of Pre-Islamic Arabian Names and Inscriptions* (Toronto, 1971), lists more than forty names.
19. A. Jamme, "Inscriptions des alentours de Mareb (Yemen)," *CahB,* 5 (1955), 265-281, esp. 271f.
20. *LexLingAeth,* 836f.; Leslau, *Contributions,* 27.
21. *LexLingAeth,* 837.
22. *WKAS,* I, 110f.

There is thus little evidence for a South Semitic *krb* meaning "bless." Instead we find the meanings "plow" and "be near," and in derivatives traces of a meaning "twist together."

d. The root is not definitely attested in Ugaritic. The reading *k.krb.b*[23] is no longer confirmed. Another occurrence is also dubious:[24] the correct reading is *bk rb ʿẓm,* "a large and strong container." The formant does seem to occur in Ugaritic onomasticon.[25]

An occurrence of *krb,* "dedicate," in Phoenician[26] is likewise dubious.[27] A Punic text from Sainte-Monique,[28] unfortunately damaged, almost certainly contains the word *k^erûḇîm* (*w t krbm ʿl,* "and the cherubim above . . .").

Aramaic occurrences are in part dependent on biblical tradition. The verb *krb,* "plow," occurs in all the late East Aramaic dialects.[29] A verb *krb,* "plait," is also attested in Syriac;[30] cf. Jewish Aram. *aph,* "tie, plait."

e. In short, there seem to be three roots *krb*: I, "bless" (Akkadian, possibly South Semitic); II, "plow" (Aramaic, South Semitic); and III, "bring near," "plait," "unite" (Aramaic, Arabic, South Semitic). Either of the first two might furnish the etymology of *k^erûḇ,* but they might also represent a single root.

II. OT. The biblical cherubim appear either as mounts for the deity or in association with sacred vegetation. They are rarely found as living beings: the majority of the 91 occurrences either refer to representations of cherubim or belong to divine epithets. Apart from the latter usage, cherubim appear only in the primeval history or in technical descriptions of God's throne in P, the Deuteronomistic history, and Ezekiel.[31]

1. *Living Beings.* Cherubim appear twice in the context of vegetation, each time associated with a garden of God.[32]

They are mentioned at the conclusion of the Paradise narrative (Gen. 3:24). Adam and Eve are driven out of Eden; the rest of the text appears to be corrupt. The MT reads: "East of the garden of Eden God placed the cherubim, and a flaming sword which turned every way, to guard the way to the tree of life." The LXX reflects a

23. *CTA* [II K], I, 2; *KTU,* 1.16 I, 2.
24. *KTU,* 1.3 I, 12.
25. *PNU,* 151.
26. Grelot, 273ff.
27. J. T. Milik, "Flèches à inscriptions phéniciennes au Musée National Libanais," *BMB,* 16 (1961), 105f.; S. Yeivin, "Sur une pointe de flèche inscrite provenant de la Beqaa (Liban)," *RB,* 65 (1958), 585-89.
28. *KAI,* 96, 2.
29. G. H. Dalman, *Aramäisches-neuhebräisches Wörterbuch* (Frankfurt, 1897), 206; Jastrow, 663f.; *MdD,* 223a.
30. *LexSyr,* 343.
31. → כִּסֵּא *kissēʾ.*
32. De Vaux, *MUSJ,* 101ff.; Mendenhall, 88.

longer text: "God placed him [the man] and placed [*ntn*] the cherubim. . . ." As always in the primeval history, it is important to see what the text does *not* say. The cherubim guard neither the tree of life nor the gates of the garden, but the way. They do not appear in pairs, nor are there just two of them. They neither hold nor wield the sword, nor do they drive Adam and Eve out. They are not described as being either good or evil. They do not act independently of God. There is no suggestion that they were originally alien to the garden; like the serpent, they even seem to have been among its original inhabitants. We may therefore theorize that they, too, belong to the animal world, although this is not stated explicitly. It is even possible that they are inanimate, like the whirling flaming sword in the parallel tradition.[33]

A cherub appears once more in the obscure words concerning the king of Tyre in Ezk. 28:14-16:[34]

> You [reading *'attâ*], O guardian cherub,
> I appointed you, O anointed one [reading *mamšûaḥ*].
> You were the holy one on the mountain of God.
> You walked in the midst of the stones of fire.
> You were blameless in your ways
> from the day of your creation
> till iniquity was found in you.
> In the abundance of your trade you sinned,
> your inward heart was filled with violence.
> I cast you down from the mountain of God,
> I destroyed you, O cherub,
> O guardian, from the midst of the stones of fire.

Although the setting is the garden of God, nothing suggests that the king of Tyre is the first human being. Instead, he is a creature who once inhabited the garden; the text does not say that he guarded the mountain of God. The cherub of Ezk. 28 dwells in a garden on a height adorned with precious stones; he is a "guardian" and is identified with the king of Tyre, but this does not necessarily mean that he had human form. Ezekiel's own contribution to the description is hard to determine; it is likely, however, that he is referring to the figure of the king in general rather than to a specific king, and that the text is based on the Tyrian royal ideology. Since the cherub is probably to be identified with the sphinx on royal and divine thrones, the king is referred to by metonymy as a major cultic symbol or what it represents. Finally, the Tyrian cherub appears alone.[35]

b. In two or three instances, cherubim serve to bear the deity in flight. Joseph

---

33. For further discussion see C. Westermann, *Genesis 1-11* (Eng. trans., Minneapolis, 1984), *in loc.*; Görg, 22ff.

34. Textual emendations that distinguish the figure of the king from that of the cherub and transform the king into an Adamic figure are rejected, following van Dijk, 113ff.

35. On the difference between the Genesis account and Ezk. 28, see G. von Rad, *OT Theology,* I (Eng. trans., New York, 1962), 442; II (1964), 180.

Needham[36] divides mythological flight into three categories: (a) flying vehicles; (b) (vehicles drawn by) one or more winged creatures; and (c) the deity in actual flight.[37] Most biblical descriptions belong to the second group: creatures (cherubim) draw the divine chariot throne.[38] The first type may be present when Yahweh rides on the clouds, since the cherubim may be involved even though they are not mentioned (Dt. 33:26; Isa. 19:1; Ps. 68:5,34[4,33]; 104:3). The third type is uncertain, since references to Yahweh's wings can be explained in other ways (Ps. 17:8; 36:8[7]; 57:2[1]; 61:5[4]; 91:4; like the wings of an eagle: Ex. 19:4; Dt. 32:11).

The most important example of Yahweh's riding upon winged creatures is 2 S. 22:11 par. Ps. 18:11(10): "He mounted upon a cherub, and flew; he hovered upon its wings through the wind [*rûaḥ*]." The antiquity of the psalm shows that the cherub belongs to one of the earliest strata of tradition. Yahweh rides directly upon the cherub. The latter cannot be identical with the wings of the wind, for the text says that Yahweh mounts the creature and then flies through the air.

The other texts presuppose that the cherubim are drawing a vehicle. God's chariot throne in Ezk. 1 and 9–11 is a very complex phenomenon, which has stirred the imaginations of later ages (*merkāḇâ* mysticism, etc.).[39] The descriptions in the two passages have influenced each other (Ezk. 10:15,20, e.g., refer to the first vision), and it is generally believed that little of this material derives from the prophet himself.[40] However that may be, the description must be taken seriously. Vague terminology, obscurity, and diffuse description are not so inappropriate to a divine vision as to demand rejection of Ezekiel's authorship.[41]

God's throne was movable; it had wheels and was drawn by living creatures (Ezk. 1) referred to in Ezk. 10 (vv. 15, 20) as *kᵉrûḇîm.* There is no reason to reject the identification of the *ḥayyôṯ* of ch. 1 with the *kᵉrûḇîm* of ch. 15.[42] The "living creatures" are described only as having the "likeness" (*dᵉmûṯ*) of animals.

In describing the creatures that support the divine throne, Ezekiel mentions a great many details. Their basic features are the following: (a) human form (*dᵉmûṯ 'āḏām*: Ezk. 1:5), usually interpreted as meaning upright bipeds; (b) four faces (1:6; 10:21) that are immobile (1:9), a human face and the face of a lion to the right, the face of an ox (or cherub: 10:14) and the face of an eagle to the left (1:10; 10:14); (c) four wings (1:6), in a sense immobile, two being extended and touching, two folded and covering their bodies (v. 11); (d) straight legs with the hoofs of calves (1:7); (e) human hands (1:8; 10:8,21); (f) an appearance resembling glowing coals (1:13) and movements

36. J. Needham, *Science and Civilization in China,* vol. 4: *Physics and Physical Technology,* pt. 2: *Mechanical Engineering* (Cambridge, 1965), 568-573.

37. On the Ugaritic material, see F. C. Fensham, "Winged Gods and Goddesses in the Ugaritic Tablets," *OrAnt,* 5 (1966), 157-164.

38. DeVaux, *MUSJ,* 106ff.

39. See J. Marböck, "Henoch–Adam–Der Thronwagen," *BZ,* N.S. 25 (1981), 103-111.

40. Eichrodt, 42f., 112-18; W. Zimmerli, *Ezekiel 1. Herm* (Eng. trans. 1979), 108ff., 234ff.

41. Cf. G. A. Cooke, *Ezekiel. ICC* (1936), xxvii.

42. Cf. de Vaux, *MUSJ,* 94f.; Eichrodt, 70; Zimmerli, 120.

like lightning (vv. 13,14). The cherubim are surrounded by wheels and support the throne. There are two forms of cherub here: just as Ezekiel speaks of fire within fire and wheels within wheels, he describes a cherub with a single face within one having four faces. Identification of the cherub face in 10:14 with the face of an ox in 1:10 provides a clue for understanding the figures: the word *kᵉrûḇ* could denote a hybrid creature with the face of an ox as well as a hybrid creature with several faces. The large cherub has wings, a calf's hoofs, and human hands; it has four faces, obviously on a single head. If the two lists are harmonized, the head can be pictured like this:

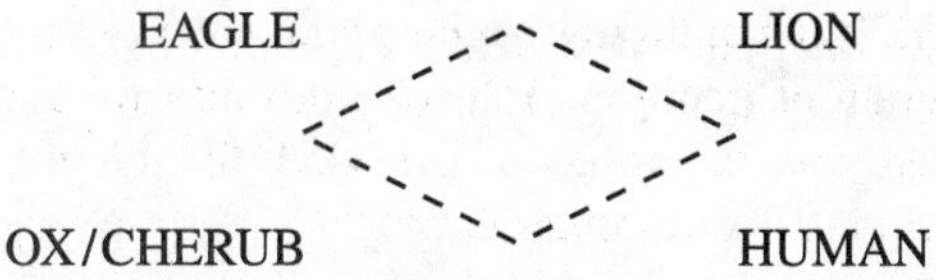

In the first list, the prophet sees the base of the figure and describes each side, from right to left and from front to back. In the second, he goes counterclockwise around the head. When the first passage is also understood correctly as describing a biped, Ezekiel's picture of the large cherub is complete.

2. *Representations.* The majority of OT passages mentioning cherubim refer to representations associated with the cult of the tabernacle or temple. In general, the free-standing sculptures are associated with transport, the relief figures with sacred vegetation.

a. The cherubim in the holy of holies of P's tabernacle are two small figures of hammered work (*miqšâ*) associated with the *kappōreṯ*[43] above the ark (Ex. 25:18-22 [7 occurrences]; 37:7-9 [execution of the design, 6 occurrences][44]). The only specific feature of the cherubim mentioned is their wings, which are extended to form Yahweh's throne,[45] and faces, which face each other and the *kappōreṯ*. The cherubim in the holy of holies of Solomon's temple are likewise two in number; the reference is to large figures carved from olive wood, overlaid with gold (1 K. 6:23-28 [11 occurrences], abbreviated in 2 Ch. 3:10-13 [6 occurrences];[46] 1 K. 8:6f. [2 occurrences] par. 2 Ch. 5:7f.). Only the wings of the cherubim are mentioned; there is no mention of their faces. The temple of Ezekiel has no parallels to these cherubim.

In David's final instructions to Solomon concerning the building of the temple, a model (*taḇnîṯ*) of the cherubim chariot (*merkāḇâ*) is developed in 1 Ch. 28:18. The text stands in total isolation, and so its conjectured dependence on Ezekiel cannot be proved.

---

43. → כפר *kpr.*

44. Nu. 7:89 may also be intended as an execution of Ex. 25:22; cf. M. Noth, *Numbers. OTL* (Eng. trans. 1968), 65.

45. Cf. de Vaux, *MUSJ,* 91, 96.

46. On *ṣaʿᵉṣuʿîm,* see J. M. Myers, *II Chronicles. AB* XIII (1965), 15, 18.

b. The curtains and veil of the tabernacle are adorned with cherubim (commanded: Ex. 26:1,31; carried out: 36:8,35). No details are given, and there is no visible association with vegetation. The walls and doors of Solomon's temple are decorated with carvings of cherubim, palm trees, and rosettes (*pᵉṭûrê ṣiṣṣîm*) (1 K. 6:29-35 [4 occurrences]; abbreviated in 2 Ch. 3:7). The veil of the tabernacle has no counterpart in 1 Kings; 2 Chronicles, however, mentions a veil with cherubim (2 Ch. 3:14). The absence of the veil in Kings is probably due to textual corruption. The kettle chariots ("stands") of the Solomonic temple bore reliefs of lions, bulls, and cherubim (1 K. 7:29,36).[47] The walls and doors of Ezekiel's temple are decorated with two-faced cherubim between palms (Ezk. 41:18-25 [6 occurrences]); the faces are human and leonine, corresponding to the right side of the cherubim in Ezk. 1. The rosettes of the Solomonic temple are not mentioned.

3. *Divine Epithets.* Among the appellations given to the God of Israel we often find *yōšēḇ (hak)kᵉrûḇîm,* "enthroned upon the cherubim." The expression is a title of El from the Canaanite cult; it is associated primarily with the ark (1 S. 4:4; 2 S. 6:2 par. 1 Ch. 13:6) but is also found in other contexts (2 K. 19:15 par. Isa. 37:16 [cf. the mention of chariots in 2 K. 19:23]; Ps. 80:2[1]; 99:1). These passages provide no information about the cherubim; the epithet does not indicate whether a chariot is involved.[48]

4. *Summary.* In short, cherubim are associated both with vegetation and with movement of the deity. The latter function is easier to define; it is more difficult to conceive precisely what the guarding of sacred vegetation involves. There is no connection between the two ideas.

As to the appearance of the cherubim, only one point is clear: they have wings. The descriptions of their faces are most contradictory: the cherubim of the ark almost certainly have only a single face, like the small cherub of Ezk. 10:14; the cherubim in Ezekiel's temple have two faces, those in his vision, four. The faces are both human and theriomorphic. There is no passage that paints a clear picture of the whole entity. If the expression *dᵉmûṯ 'āḏām* implies two legs, Ezk. 1 and 10 speak of bipeds. On the one hand, the analogy in Ezk. 28:14,16 seems also to suggest a biped. On the other hand, 2 S. 22:11 appears to suggest a quadruped or bird. If the lions and bulls of the kettle chariots are analogous, the cherubim would be quadrupeds. The evidence indicates that the word *kᵉrûḇ* does not denote a single type of creature like that represented on certain monuments but refers rather to a variety of winged creatures associated with a sacred landscape. In the majority of cases, the text suggests hybrid creatures, none of which can be considered "typical."

III. Extrabiblical Parallels. Examination of the relevant extrabiblical evidence presupposes that the monumental cherubim of the ancient Near East can be identified

---

47. Cf. J. A. Montgomery and H. S. Gehman, *The Books of Kings. ICC* (1951), 174-181.
48. → ישׁב *yāšaḇ* III.3.

with the biblical cherubim. This presupposition is actually erroneous, since the Israelite tradition fundamentally includes no graphic representations, although archaeology has uncovered some isolated exceptions.

At first, study of the extrabiblical material focused on Mesopotamia. On account of their hybrid nature, the cherubim were identified with the Neo-Assyrian colossi.[49] This assumption was reinforced by the fact that the colossi were associated with *lamassu, šēdu,* and other tutelary spirits, as well as by the (erroneous[50]) identification of Akk. *kurību* with Heb. *k^erûḇ.* Although this explanation implied lexicographic identity, it did not yield a unified interpretation. L. H. Vincent argued for the Mesopotamian origin of the term, but was unable to associate a particular form with the Mesopotamian concept and proposed a fluid identification of the biblical figure. He believed that on both sides the word originally denoted human figures and later came to denote hybrid beings.[51] This explanation, which is based on naive evolutionary presuppositions, is unsatisfactory.

Since the cherubim first appear in the context of the ark, which many scholars trace back to Canaan through the cult at Shiloh,[52] William F. Albright and Roland de Vaux look for the origin of the cherubim in Canaanite ideas and consider the winged sphinx the immediate prototype.[53] They do not reckon with the evidence that the biblical term does not refer to a single uniform figure. Albright assumes Mesopotamian origin, citing a painting in the palace of Zimri-Lim that depicts two cherubim (sphinxes) next to a sacred tree; de Vaux considers the Levant (including Syria, with Mari) the center from which the sphinx figure spread and ascribes the Mesopotamian *kurību* to Levantine influences, although he finds the origin of the term in Akkadian.

A further feature that supports the identification of the cherubim with Levantine quadrupeds is the similarity of their function to that of the gold calf, which was not worshipped but served as a platform for the deity.

The problem with this identification is that it cannot explain the variety of the biblical data and there is no reason to prefer the sphinx to the griffin or genius, for example. Nor does identification with the sphinx do justice to all the biblical data. Since, however, many biblical passages refer to concrete representations, the extrabiblical evidence can at least supply important comparative material.

We start with the fact that the cherubim are hybrid creatures that can have wings. The ancient Near Eastern material provides only four possible candidates: bipeds, quadrupeds, birds, and serpents. Nothing in the biblical descriptions suggests a serpent. An avian monster has so far not been proposed, but must be considered possible. We must therefore examine the first three categories.

First and foremost among avian monsters is the winged sun-disk,[54] plentifully

49. Vincent, 340.
50. See above.
51. Vincent, 344ff., 493ff.
52. Contra → ארון *'^arôn* III.3.
53. Albright, 93ff.; de Vaux, *MUSJ,* 98.
54. Mendenhall, 32-68.

attested in northern Mesopotamia and the Levant.[55] It is also found in Egypt, in Hittite Anatolia, and in Achaemenid Iran. A different kind of avian creature is the lion-headed eagle found in Mesopotamia in the third millennium.[56] A Jewish graffito from Medā'in-Ṣaliḥ in the Hejaz appears to depict the ark with cherubim in the form of large birds; but, since the picture is damaged and also late, its value as evidence is hard to judge.[57]

Hybrid quadrupeds exhibit a great variety of forms. In Mesopotamia, hybrids with the body of a lion may have the head of a lion and wings,[58] a human head with or without wings,[59] the head of a serpent and wings,[60] the head of an eagle or falcon and wings,[61] the head of a goat and wings,[62] or the head of a bull and wings.[63] The body of a bull with a human head appears both with and without wings.[64] The body of a horse with wings appears with the head of a horse[65] and the head of a bull.[66] Less well-defined quadrupeds occur,[67] including at least one centaur form having the body of a lion and a human head.[68]

In the Levant, quadrupeds with the body of a lion and a human head are common; most have wings.[69] Of particular interest is the rock drawing in the royal caves of Jerusalem, which de Vaux dates in the period of Solomon; his verdict that it represents "the most authentic picture of a biblical cherub"[70] is exaggerated. Winged figures (griffins) with the body of a lion and the head of an eagle or falcon are known,[71] as are winged lions with the head of a ram[72] or a bull.[73] Some examples depict a winged lion with a human head above the lion's head.[74]

Egyptian art depicts wingless[75] and winged sphinxes[76] and griffins.[77] Hittite monu-

---

55. For Mesopotamia, see, e.g., *ANEP*, 705, 440, 442-44, 447ff., 453, 534-36, 628, 658; for the Levant, see *ANEP*, 650, 493, 332, 477, 486, 630, 855, 653, 809a-c.
56. *ANEP*, 695.
57. Vincent, fig. 10.
58. *ANEP*, 651.
59. *ANEP*, 966, 649.
60. *ANEP*, 520, 671, 658, 760f.
61. Griffin type: *ANEP*, 682, 520, 860.
62. Mendenhall, fig. 6.
63. *ANEP*, 534.
64. *ANEP*, 192, 647.
65. Pegasus: Frankfort, 158.
66. *Ibid.*, 227.
67. *Ibid.*, 28, 164.
68. *Ibid.*, 163.
69. *ANEP*, 650, 128, 332, 648f., 662, 458; cf. de Vaux, *MUSJ*, 110f.; Cleveland; also Frankfort, 373, 274.
70. De Vaux, *MUSJ*, 117.
71. Frankfort, 301, 304, 341, 381.
72. *Ibid.*, 379.
73. *Ibid.*, 296.
74. *Ibid.*, 335; *ANEP*, 644.
75. *ANEP*, 765, 386, 393; cf. de Vaux, *MUSJ*, 98f.
76. *ANEP*, 415-17.
77. *ANEP*, 310.

ments include winged and wingless sphinxes.[78] An Urartian figurine has the winged body of a horse with a human head.[79] Winged sphinxes and griffins are found on Cyprus.[80] A great variety of forms is found in the region of Iran: a lion with wings and a lion's head,[81] with a human head but without wings,[82] with wings and the head of an eagle or falcon,[83] and with the head of a dragon or stag.[84] Bodies of bulls with human heads are known,[85] as are winged ibexes and stags.[86]

In the biped group, the genius, a human figure with wings, predominates;[87] it sometimes has the head of an eagle.[88] In early periods, we find human bodies with the legs of bulls[89] or scorpions[90] or having feathers and the legs of birds.[91] Winged "demons" have the form of serpents with human or leonine heads.[92] In the Levant, the most common form is the winged human figure.[93] The human figure with an eagle's head may be winged[94] or wingless.[95] Bull men are found,[96] as are wingless scorpion men.[97] A human figure with a dog's head also appears.[98]

Egyptian biped figures embody deities; few have wings.[99] There are winged Hittite bipeds with human heads[100] and lion heads.[101] The winged genius is found on Cyprus and in Iran.[102] In Iran we also find human figures with theriomorphic heads[103] and some with the legs of bulls.[104]

---

78. *ANEP,* 666; Frankfort, 249.
79. Frankfort, 398.
80. *Ibid.,* 393, 306.
81. *Ibid.,* 401, 411.
82. *Ibid.,* 402D.
83. *Ibid.,* 431, 443, 444.
84. *Ibid.,* 401, 438; 401.
85. *Ibid.,* 415, 426.
86. *Ibid.,* 402A, 445.
87. *ANEP,* 526, 685, 705, 614, 656, 651, 609.
88. Frankfort, 150C, 187.
89. Bull men: *ANEP,* 678, 681, 696.
90. Scorpion men: *ANEP,* 192, 519; Frankfort, 228.
91. Bird men: *ANEP,* 687; cf. P. Amiet, "L'homme-oiseau dans l'art mésopotamien," *Or,* 21 (1952), 149-167; E. D. van Buren, "An Investigation of a New Theory Concerning the Bird-Man," *Or,* 22 (1953), 47-58.
92. Frankfort, 119, 141; *ANEP,* 658, 857, 659; Frankfort, 22f., 25C; *ANEP,* 657, 658, 660, 665, 857.
93. *ANEP,* 829, 663, 652, 654, 854, 655.
94. *ANEP,* 645, 855.
95. Frankfort, 274.
96. *ANEP,* 653.
97. Frankfort, 342.
98. *Ibid.,* 274.
99. *ANEP,* 266, 542, 553, 558, 565, 567, 569, 572, 573, 649, 650.
100. *ANEP,* 611.
101. Frankfort, 263.
102. *Ibid.,* 393; 401, 427.
103. *Ibid.,* 401.
104. *Ibid.,* 440.

It is significant that these hybrid beings belong to a common iconographic realm and often appear together: birds with bipeds[105] or quadrupeds,[106] bipeds with quadrupeds,[107] or all three together.[108] George E. Mendenhall suggests[109] that the cherubim cart belongs to the first combination.

Other features of the biblical descriptions of the cherubim also merit iconographic study.[110] The figures on the walls of Ezekiel's temple have two faces; those in his vision have four. In our survey, we have noted two-headed monsters (the lions of Zinjirli and Carchemish); but the biblical texts do not refer to such creatures with two heads and two necks, since only their faces are mentioned. There are figures with two faces: the Levantine human figure with two canine heads, probably reflecting Hittite influence;[111] a Hittite two-headed eagle;[112] an early dynastic two-headed goat;[113] and a two-headed man (Janus type) in attendance on Ea.[114] These are only partially relevant, since the two heads are always identical. The same is true of the figures with four faces: they are uncommon, and the four faces are identical.[115] The multifaced cherubim in Ezekiel thus appear to be unparalleled in the ancient Near East. The omnipresent eyes of the vision are attested elsewhere only with reference to the Egyptian pygmy god Bes.[116]

Among the representations mentioned here, there are several that might be identified as cherubim. When de Vaux says that the winged sphinx "appears to correspond better than the others to the description and functions of the biblical cherub,"[117] he overlooks the fact that there is no single persuasive identification of the cherubim.

IV. Concluding Remarks. Heb. *kᵉrûḇ* is a technical term for a class of hybrid beings associated with God, either directly as part of his chariot throne or indirectly as inhabitants of sacral vegetation. These beings are associated with the obscure term *śᵉrāp̱îm* (Isa. 6), which clearly denotes another class of hybrid creature; if etymology is a reliable clue to meaning, the *śᵉrāp̱îm* resemble dragons or serpents.[118] The two words would then be categorized as follows: *kᵉrûḇîm* denotes beings that resemble birds, bipeds, and quadrupeds; *śᵉrāp̱îm* denotes beings resembling serpents.

The relationship between these creatures and other beings associated with the deity remains obscure. Possibly they occupy an intermediate position between Yahweh's

105. *ANEP,* 705, 829, 855, 653.
106. *ANEP,* 534, 650, 332.
107. *ANEP,* 192, 651.
108. *ANEP,* 658, 857.
109. P. 39.
110. On the sex of the cherubim, see de Vaux, *MUSJ,* 116.
111. Frankfort, 274.
112. *Ibid.,* 261.
113. *Ibid.,* 82A.
114. *ANEP,* 685, 687.
115. Cf. Eichrodt, 56f., n. 2; Zimmerli, 125f.
116. Cooke, *Ezekiel,* 116.
117. P. 98.
118. → שׂרף *śārap̱.*

primordial enemies and the angels or messengers[119] of Yahweh's heavenly court. Ezekiel, who mentions the cherubim frequently, is also familiar with the *mayim rabbîm,* where the primordial monsters dwell, as well as two of the most distinctive angels of the Bible: the man clothed in linen (Ezk. 9) and the man of gleaming bronze (ch. 40). Later developments do nothing to clarify the evidence.

Outside the Hebrew Bible, only Sir. 49:8 (praising Ezekiel) speaks of cherubim. In the Enoch texts, they have taken over the seraphim's function of praise. In the NT, they appear in a quotation in Heb. 9:5; Revelation speaks of hybrid creatures, but their specific role is unknown, and the great *zṓa* have no function except praising God (Rev. 4:6-11; 5:6-14; 6:1-7; 7:11; 14:3; 15:7; 19:4). Ultimately the wingless messengers coalesce with the hybrid creatures to form a single category of angels; this development, however, is a process as complicated as the complexity of the original figures.

Freedman — O'Connor

119. → מלאך *mālʼaḵ.*

כֶּרֶם *kerem;* כֹּרֵם *kōrem;* כַּרְמֶל *karmel*

Contents: I. Semantics: 1. Semitic **karmu*; 2. Egyptian; 3. Hebrew Derivatives. II. Viticulture: 1. History; 2. Negative Appraisal; 3. Positive Appraisal. III. 1. Work; 2. Vineyard Rituals. IV. Metaphorical Usage: 1. Erotic Language; 2. Religious Symbolism. V. LXX, Dead Sea Scrolls.

I. Semantics.

1. *Semitic *karmu.* The Proto-Semitic primary noun **karmu* means "vineyard" in Ugaritic, Hebrew, Aramaic, and Syriac; in Arabic and Ethiopic, it denotes the produce of the vineyard: Arab. *karm^{un},* "grape, vine," Eth. *kĕrm/karm,* "vine." In Akkadian, the two groups of meanings have become associated with different forms: in *karmu* II, "dry, barren land,"[1] what was originally a topographical term has taken on negative overtones,

kerem. G. Dalman, *AuS,* IV (1935), 319-335; M. Delcor, "De l'origine de quelques termes relatifs au vin en hébreu biblique et dans les langues voisines," *ACLingSémCham,* 223-233 = *Études bibliques et orientales de religions comparées* (Leiden, 1979), 346-356; M. Fraenkel, "Drei verkannte Flüssigkeitsbenennungen im Hebräischen," *Sef,* 27 (1967), 3-11; J. S. Licht, "כֶּרֶם," *EMiqr,* IV (1962), 318-322; J. F. Ross, "Vine, Vineyard," *IDB,* IV, 784-86; L. Rost, "Noah der Weinbauer," *Geschichte und AT. Festschrift A. Alt. BHTh,* 16 (1953), 169-178 = *Das kleine Credo* (Heidelberg, 1965), 44-53; S. Yeivin, "Philological Notes, VIII," *Lešonénu,* 24 (1959/1960), 40-46 [Heb.]; V. Zapletal, *Der Wein in der Bibel. BSt,* 20/1 (1920), 23-30; → גֶּפֶן *gep̱en;* → יַיִן *yayin.*

1. *AHw,* I (1965), 449.

possibly because the viticulture the Mesopotamians knew from Syria did not involve irrigation; *karānu(m)*, "grapevine, wine," on the other hand, refers to the produce of the vineyard. Only at Ugarit, obviously on account of Canaanite influence, does Akk. *karānu* also mean "vineyard." Here, too, we find the compound *kirî*, "garden," + *karāni.*[2] The fluidity of the Semitic terminology for viticulture is illustrated by Old South Arabic's use of the nominal root *wyn,* elsewhere reserved for "wine," for "vineyard."[3]

Metonymy is involved when Heb. (and Ugar.) *kerem* (*krm*) is used in the general sense of "planting" — possibly in *kerem zayiṯ,* "olive orchard" (Jgs. 15:5 [textually problematic]),[4] and with more likelihood in the diminutive *karmel* I, "orchard."[5]

2. *Egyptian.* The Egyptian noun *k3n.w,* found as early as the Pyramid texts, and its later equivalent *k3m* originally meant "garden," grapes being only one of several possibilities. Whether these words have any connection with Sem. **karmu*[6] may remain an open question. The noun *ḥsp* is also used for "vineyard"; it likewise has as its primary meaning the general sense of "land covered with plants, garden plot."[7]

3. *Hebrew Derivatives.* Being a primary noun, **karmu* cannot be derived from a verbal root. It is not related either to Arab. *karuma,* "be magnanimous, generous," or to Akk. *karāmu(m)*, "hold (back)." On the other hand, the ptcp. *kōrem,* "wine-grower," is a denominative from *kerem,*[8] as are the probable diminutive *karmel* I, "orchard,"[9] and the Middle Hebrew verb *krm,* "amass, accumulate," obviously used by metonymy for the typical activity in a vineyard.

II. Viticulture.

1. *History.* Although for Canaanite cities like Shechem (Jgs. 9:27) and Shiloh (21:20f.), as well as for the Philistines in Timnah (14:5), vineyards are mentioned at an early date (cf. Nu. 13:24f.; 20:17; 21:22), it is clear that the Israelites adopted viticulture only gradually. Gen. 9:20(-27) makes Noah the first to plant a vineyard; it is hard to date this statement and to determine to whom it originally referred. Gen. 9:21ff. (unlike v. 20; cf. 5:29) takes a negative view of this achievement: it is the cause of Canaan's servitude.

It is still exclusively a royal prerogative for Saul to give his followers "fields and vineyards"; he argues that the upstart David cannot do the same (1 S. 22:7; cf. 8:14f.;

---

2. *PRU,* IV, 167, 15; *Syr,* 18 (1937), 251, 8.
3. W.W. Müller, "Altsüdarabische Beiträge zum hebräischen Lexicon," *ZAW,* 75 (1963), 310.
4. Cf. *UT,* no. 1306.
5. See I.3 below; → כרמל *karmel.*
6. As suggested by *WbÄS,* V, 106, and Delcor, *ACLingSémCham,* 232.
7. *WbÄS,* III, 162.
8. Cf. H. Gese, "Kleine Beiträge zum Verstandnis des Amosbuches," *VT,* 12 (1962), 417-438, esp. 432-36.
9. See I.1 above.

1 Ch. 27:27). It is probably not by accident that Isa. 3:14 uses the expression *bā'ēr hakkerem,* "devour the vineyard," to describe the conduct of the Jerusalem aristocracy (cf. Jer. 12:10). Large-scale profitable viticulture does not seem to have begun in the northern kingdom until the Omride period, the end of which is marked by the Rechabite reaction (2 K. 10:15). The Samaria ostraca speak of a *krm htl* (?), "vineyard of the mound [?],"[10] and a "vineyard of *yḥw'ly*"[11] as sources of wine; in the same context,[12] they mention *šmn rḥs,* "refined [?]/cosmetic [?] oil," which also appears by itself. Whatever the purpose and legal status of the shipments may have been,[13] we are dealing with deliveries to the court, around which highly developed agriculture still tends to concentrate. The juxtaposition of wine and oil recalls the frequent association of *k*ᵉ*rāmîm* and *zêṯîm,* "olive trees" (Dt. 6:11; Josh. 24:13; 1 S. 8:14; Neh. 5:11; 9:25; also 2 K. 5:26; Am. 4:9). As a parallel to the mention of vineyards in the Samaria ostraca, see the common appearance of Aram. *krm'* in the formally and functionally similar ostraca from Nisa (Turkmenistan, Arsacid Parthia), dating from the first century B.C.[14]

Among the kings of Judah, Uzziah is said to have been devoted to agriculture; in his service he had farmers (*'ikkārîm*) and vinedressers (*kōr*ᵉ*mîm*) "upon the hills and *bakkarmel*" (2 Ch. 26:10). The Arad ostraca also presuppose that the fortresses held supplies of wine (cf. the *'ōṣ*ᵉ*rôṯ hayyayin* of David [1 Ch. 27:27]), oil (cf. 2 Ch. 11:11), and grain (2 Ch. 32:28).[15]

The exilic and postexilic periods brought radical changes in the ownership of such properties. The Babylonian commissary Nebuzaradan distributed "vineyards and fields [?]" to some of the poor people left in the land, thus putting them in the place of the former aristocracy (Jer. 39:10; 52:16; 2 K. 25:12). In the postexilic period, however, newly impoverished Judahites had to mortgage property like vineyards and olive orchards to raise the cash necessary to pay the taxes imposed by the Persian king (Neh. 5:3,5). It is clear that the cancellation of debts subsequently decreed by Nehemiah (vv. 10f.) was able to restore relative equality only for a short period. While Eccl. 2:4 declares that the planting of vineyards is a luxury granted to the rich,[16] Job 24:18 curses the fields and vineyards of the same ruling class.

With reference to vineyards, the NT speaks of property owners and tenants obligated to pay rent in kind (Mk. 12:1-11 par.) as well as day laborers (Mt. 20:1-15).

---

10. Samaria ostraca, 20, 5; 53, 2; 54, 1/2; 58, 2; 61, 1.
11. *Ibid.,* 55, 1/2; 60, 1.
12. *Ibid.,* 20, 3; 53, 3; 54, 2/3; 55, 3.
13. Cf. *KAI,* II, 183-85; A. Lemaire, *Inscriptions hébraïques,* I. *LAPO,* 9 (1977), 73-81.
14. For text, transl., and comm., see M. Sznycer, "Ostraca d'époque parthe trouvés à Nisa (U.R.S.S.)," *Sem,* 5 (1955), 65-98.
15. Also found at Ebla: G. Pettinato, "Il Calendario di Ebla al Tempo del Re Ibbi-Sipis sulla base di TM.75 G.427," *Festschrift E. Weidner. AfO,* 25 (1974/77), 1ff.; cf. *idem, et al.,* "Catalogo dei testi cuneiformi di Tell Mardikh-Ebla." MEE, I (1979), no. 230. See also K. Galling, "Wein und Weinbereitum," *BRL*³, 362.
16. Cf. Ahikar 40.

2. *Negative Appraisal.* From the earliest period after the occupation, the Nazirites abstained from wine. The antiquity of this group is indicated by the association of abstinence from wine with the archaic custom of letting the hair grow uncut (Jgs. 13:5,7): both are magical practices to increase prowess, as in the case of Samson (Jgs. 16:17ff.) and probably also of Absalom (2 S. 14:26). An early date is also suggested by the use of *n^ezîr 'eḥāyw* for the warlike tribe of Joseph in Gen. 49:26; Dt. 33:16; we are, however, in no position to say anything concerning the relationship between an individual and a tribe described as a Nazirite. By contrast, the Rechabites' abstinence from wine, which is associated with a repristinative rejection of agriculture and permanent dwellings, represents a later criticism of developed civilization.[17]

The analogous words of the early prophets likewise represent reactionary criticism. Am. 4:9 already looks back on the destruction of gardens and vineyards as the result of Yahweh's judgment. Am. 5:11 proclaims judgment against "houses of hewn stones" and "pleasant vineyards" (cf. Zeph. 1:13); they will become places of lamentation for the dead (Am. 5:16f.; cf. Joel 1:11). In Mic. 1:6, the disapproval seems so extreme that "planting vineyards" symbolizes the desolate world left after the fall of Samaria.

3. *Positive Appraisal.* On the other hand, some early prophetic texts also speak positively of vineyards. Hos. 2:17(Eng. v. 15) mentions vineyards in an oracle of salvation for the time after God's judgment. Later, *nṭ'* ("plant") + *k^erāmîm* became a commonplace in oracles of salvation, whether short term (Isa. 37:30 par. 2 K. 19:29; cf. Sennacherib's offer of peace in Isa. 36:17 par. 2 K. 18:32) or looking toward the distant future (Jer. 31:5 [cf. 32:15]; Ezk. 28:26; Isa. 65:21; Am. 9:14). In Jer. 31:5 — in contrast to Mic. 1:6 — the phrase *b^ehārê šōm^erôn* suggests the resumption of wine production around the old capital as attested in the Samaria ostraca. In Nu. 16:14a (date?), Moses is attacked for not having given his followers a *naḥ^alâ* of "fields and vineyards."

Late texts like Isa. 65:8; Ps. 107:37 associate wine and vineyards with blessing; in Josh. 24:13; Neh. 9:25, vineyards are listed as a matter of course among the rewards bestowed by Yahweh. On the other hand, the curse on houses and vineyards in Dt. 28:30,39 uses words that echo Am. 5:11. Isa. 16:10, an eschatological prophecy of disaster, states that joy shall be taken away from "fruitful field" and "vineyards."

III. 1. *Work.* The demanding labor required to maintain a vineyard is detailed in Isa. 5:1-6.[18] Viticulture has its own specialized vocabulary.[19] The verb *zmr* II (Lev.

---

17. Cf. F. Stolz, "Rausch, Religion und Realität in Israel und seiner Umwelt," *VT,* 26 (1976), 170-186, esp. 182ff.; contrast F. S. Frick, "The Rechabites Reconsidered," *JBL,* 90 (1971), 279-287.

18. See the comms.

19. See A. von Selms, "The Etymology of *yayin,* 'Wine,'" *JNSL,* 3 (1974), 76-84, esp. 76f.; cf. the chart of Egyptian, Sumerian, Akkadian, and Hebrew nomenclature in R. J. Forbes, *Studies in Ancient Technology,* III (Leiden, [2]1965), 77.

25:3; Isa. 5:6) denotes the pruning of the vines (*zᵉmôrâ*) with a pruning knife (*mazmērâ*) in the spring (*ʿēṯ hazzāmîr* [Cant. 2:12 (?)]);[20] the agricultural calendar from Gezer[21] may use *zmr* for the harvest; *zimraṯ hāʾāreṣ,* "the produce of the land," in Gen. 43:11 is a possible parallel. Gustaf Dalman[22] and many others, however, are probably correct in interpreting this to mean a second pruning of the vines, which the position of *zmr* in the calendar would suggest took place in June or July. The verb *bṣr* I can be used to denote the actual grape harvest.

2. *Vineyard Rituals.* In addition, a variety of rituals and rules of conduct incorporated viticulture — like all forms of agriculture — into a religious and social system.

The prohibition against mixing things that do not belong together includes sowing (*zrʿ*) two kinds of seed in a vineyard. If this prohibition is ignored, "the whole yield becomes holy" (Dt. 22:9; cf. Lev. 19:19) and must be withdrawn from secular use because of the danger it represents. But vineyards are also sacred by nature: to enjoy (*ḥll* I, originally "profane") the first harvest (Dt. 20:6; 28:30; Jer. 31:5) is a profanation; between the planting of a new vineyard and the first harvest, its owner is in a state of increased numinous vulnerability, which prevents him from taking part in battle. Dt. 20:6 represents a labored attempt to explain this prohibition on social grounds. Finally, when Isa. 17:10 speaks of the Israelites as planting rapidly growing "plants of the pleasant [deity]" or "slips of an alien [deity]," the sacredness of the soil appears to be embodied in a god similar to Adonis.[23] The festivals of Dionysus likewise employ rapidly growing vines, just as stalks of grain are associated with the mysteries of Demeter.[24] It is clear that the prohibition against stripping a vineyard bare (Lev. 19:10; Dt. 24:21), now given an ethical basis, originally involved a sacrifice to the powers associated with the soil; the poor and the "beasts of the field" who benefit from the fallow year (which includes vineyards) may likewise be a rationalizing substitute for numinous figures. Other instances such as Samson's prank in Jgs. 15:5 may be compared to apotropaic rites protecting against demons.[25] The high point of the festivities associated with viticulture are the *hillûlîm* at harvest, which bring the participants to eat and drink in the temple (Jgs. 9:27). The vineyards themselves are the site of singing (Isa. 5:1; cf. *ʿnh,* "sing antiphonally" [27:2ff.]) and rejoicing (Isa. 16:10).[26] Jgs. 21:19ff. (date of the tradition) speaks of maidens dancing at a festival; their rape has a well-known parallel in the rape of the Sabine women.[27]

---

20. Cf. the citations of analogous Middle Hebrew texts in I. Löw, *Die Flora der Juden,* I (Vienna, 1926), 71.

21. *KAI,* 182, 6.

22. Pp. 330f.

23. W. Baumgartner, "Das Nachleben der Adonisgärten auf Sardinien und im übrigen Mittelmeergebiet," *Zum AT und seiner Umwelt* (Leiden, 1959), 247-273.

24. W. F. Otto, "Der Sinn der eleusinischen Mysterien," *ErJb,* 7 (1939), 102.

25. F. Schwally, *Semitische Kriegsaltertümer,* 1: *Der heilige Krieg im alten Israel* (Leipzig, 1901), 81ff., esp. 88.

26. See II.3 above.

27. Livy *Hist.* i.9f.

IV. Metaphorical Usage.

1. *Erotic Language.* The use of *kerem* in erotic language also derives from nature worship.

Cant. 1:6; 8:11f. are based on a pun involving the literal and metaphorical meaning of the word: on the one hand, "vineyard" denotes the plot of ground that needs to be guarded or yields its fruit; on the other, it denotes the female body and its sexual charms. The metaphor is related to the poetic disguise of the actors as gardeners or royal figures. In 2:15, the stock metaphor includes the motif of (little) foxes as notorious destroyers of vineyards — obviously with some unexplained double meaning. In 1:14; 7:13(12), localization of the beloved or the setting of love *in* a vineyard serves to create a poetic atmosphere.

The metaphorical usage of *kerem* to denote the female body is thus a particular instance of the common identification of women with fields and soil. Two probable parallels from Ugaritic mythology relate to this context. In one text, the moon-god Yariḫ seeks through sexual intercourse to make the goddess Nikkal's "field a vineyard [vineyards? *kř̌m*[*m*]], the field of her love [*šd ddə*] an orchard [? *ḥrnq*[*m*]]."[28] In another, "a field of the gods" ([*wšd.*] *šd.ɜlm*) appears to be identified as "the field of [the double goddess] *'at̠rt wrḥm*[*y*]."[29] The metaphorical use of "vineyard" has a counterpart in the use of "garden" to symbolize the bride in Cant. 4:12–5:1; 6:2,11; 7:13(12).

2. *Religious Symbolism.* Only against this background can we fully appreciate the description of Israel as Yahweh's vineyard in Isa. 5:1-7; 27:2f.; Jer. 12:10: Israel takes on the mythological role of the deity's female partner. This is attested for the name Yahu in the Elephantine papyri (*'ntyhw*), for Yah in the PN *'nttyh* (1 Ch. 8:24), and for Yahweh probably in inscription 3[30] from Khirbet al-Qom (*brk.'ryhw. lYHWH. w . . . l'šrth,* "blessed by 'RYHW through Yahweh and through his Asherah")[31] and certainly in two jug inscriptions from Kuntillat 'Ajrud in Wadi Quraiya (Sinai) (. . . *brkt 'tkm lYHWH. šmrn. wl'šrth,* ". . . I bless you through Yahweh, who protects us, and through his Asherah"; . . . *brktk lYHWH . . . wl'šrth,* ". . . I bless you through Yahweh . . . and through his Asherah").[32] Now when Isa. 5:1 calls Yahweh *yād̠îd̠* and *dôd̠,* and both "with respect to his vineyard" (*lᵉk̠armô*), we are dealing with a mythological transfer of erotic language to Yahweh; on the other hand, the motif of

28. *KTU,* 1.24, 22f. A different translation is proposed by A. Caquot/M. Sznycer, and A. Herdner, *Textes Ougaritiques,* 1: *Mythes et légendes. LAPO,* 7 (1974), 393.

29. *KTU,* 1.23, 13, 28. Cf. H.-P. Müller, "Die lyrische Reproduction des Mythischen im Hohenlied," *ZThK,* 73 (1976), 23-41, esp. 33ff.

30. IDAM, 72, 169.

31. A. Lemaire, "Les Inscriptions de Khirbet El-Qôm et l'Ashérah de YHWH," *RB,* 84 (1977), 595-608, esp. 599; contra G. Garbini, "Su un'inscrizione ebraica da khirbet el-Kom," *AION,* 38 (1978), 191-93.

32. Z. Meshel, *Kuntillet 'Ajrud. Exhibition Catalog of the Israel Museum,* 175 (Jerusalem, 1978); cf. F. Stolz, "Monotheismus in Israel," in O. Keel, ed., *Monotheismus im AT und seiner Umwelt. BibB,* 14 (1980), 167-174.

love between deities is neutralized by the suffixes of *y^e^ḏîḏî* and *dôḏî,* which refer to the prophet (v. 1), and by the shift of the vineyard metaphor to symbolize Israel (v. 7). The erotic nature of the imagery is preserved almost intact, however, in the characterization of the "men of Judah" (par. "house of Israel") as *n^e^ṭaʿ šaʿ^a^šûʿāyw,* "his [Yahweh's] planting of delight" (v. 7). The parallelism of "vineyard" and "field" as metaphorical terms for a woman is suggested, finally, by the substitution of *ḥelqāṯî* and *ḥelqaṯ ḥemdāṯî* (with suffixes referring to Yahweh), "field of my delight," for *karmî* in Jer. 12:10. Because the metaphorical expressions *yāḏîḏ, dôḏ, kerem, šaʿ^a^šûʿîm,* and *ḥelqaṯ ḥemdāṯî* already have mythological connotations in the symbolic realm, they can be used to describe the way Yahweh actually treats Israel; the mythological atmosphere that envelops them allows them to serve as metaphors. Conversely, the realm from which the symbols associated with *kerem* are drawn takes on a kind of sacral aura from the realm symbolized. If a fragment of traditional nature mythology can serve as a metaphor for Yahweh's acts, it becomes impossible to surrender the realm of nature to banal secularity.

V. LXX, Dead Sea Scrolls. Almost without exception, the LXX uses *ampelṓn* (79 times) or *ámpelos* (4 times) to translate *kerem.* In a few passages it uses a more general word (*ktḗma, chōríon* [twice each]). The equivalent of *kōrem* is *ampelourgós* (4 times).

In the Dead Sea scrolls, *kerem* appears 4 times (1Q25 8; 3Q15 10, 5 [*bêṯ-hakkerem,* a toponym], 1QapGen 12:13, and 11QT 57:21). In the latter passage, which discusses the king's being subject to the general law, the Tenth Commandment of the Decalog is adapted to the special temptations the monarch faces: he is not to covet fields, vineyards, possessions, houses, or valuables.

H.-P. Müller

כַּרְמֶל *karmel*

Contents: I. 1. Etymology; 2. Occurrences (Other than Mt. Carmel). II. 1. Geography and Political Control; 2. The "Holy Mountain" in General; 3. Elijah and Elisha; 4. Elsewhere in the OT.

---

karmel. F.-M. Able, *Géographie de la Palestine,* I (Paris, 1933), 350-53; Y. Aharoni, "Mount Carmel as Border," *Archäologie und AT. Festschrift K. Galling* (Tübingen, 1970), 1-7; L. Heidet, "Carmel," *DB,* II (1899), 288-302; A. Jepsen, "Karmel, eine vergessene Landschaft?" *ZDPV,* 75 (1959), 74f.; P. Joüon, "Les deux termes d'agriculture: יער et כרמל," *JA,* 10/8 (1906), 371-78; Z. Kallai-Kleinmann, "כַּרְמֶל," 1, 3, *EMiqr,* IV (1962), 323f., 324-29; C. Kopp, "Karmel," *LThK*², V (1960), 1365f.; J. S. Licht, "כַּרְמֶל," 2, *EMiqr,* IV, 324; E. Lipiński, "Note de topographie historique," *RB,* 78 (1971), 84-92; E. Graf von Mülinen, "Beiträge zur Kenntnis des Karmels," *ZDPV,* 30 (1907), 117-207; 31 (1908), 1-258.

I. 1. *Etymology.* Besides its use as a geographical term denoting a range of foothills along the Palestinian coast and a site west of the Dead Sea, the word *karmel* appears with two meanings in the OT: "new grain" and "orchard." Some recent lexica[1] list them separately; others[2] lump them together. The word is generally derived from → כרם *kerem* with the addition of an *l* suffix.[3] Opinions differ, however, as to the meaning of the suffix. F. H. W. Gesenius[4] early on suggested treating it as signifying a diminutive; many have followed his lead. Rudolf Ružička[5] showed that *karmel* represents a progressive dissimilation from *n* through *m* to *l (karmel < karmen < kerem* + postformative *n*). Ludwig Koehler proposed that two different words are involved: one with an epenthetic *l* ("garden"),[6] the other with consonantal dissimilation of *mm* > *rm*;[7]

Selected bibliog. for II.1-3: A. Alt, "Das Gottesurteil auf dem Karmel," *Festschrift Georg Beer* (Stuttgart, 1935), 1-18 = *KlSchr,* II (1953), 135-149; D. R. Ap-Thomas, "Elijah on Mount Carmel," *PEQ,* 92 (1960), 146-155; M. Avi-Yonah, "Mount Carmel and the God of Baalbek," *IEJ,* 2 (1952), 118-124; O. Eissfeldt, *Der Gott Karmel. SDAW,* 1953/1; G. Fohrer, *Elia. AThANT,* 53 (²1968); E. Friedman, "The Antiquities of el-Muhraqa and 1 Kings 18,31," *Ephemerides Carmeliticae,* 22 (1971), 95-104; K. Galling, "Der Gott Karmel und die Ächtung der fremden Götter," *Geschichte und AT. Festschrift A. Alt. BHTh,* 16 (1953), 105-125; T. H. Gaster, *Myth, Legend, and Custom in the OT* (New York, 1969), 504-511; H. Gunkel, *Elijah, Yahweh and Baal* (Eng. trans. 1951); G. Hentschel, *Die Elijaerzählungen. ErfThSt,* 33 (1977); R. Hillmann, *Wasser und Berg* (Halle, 1965), 95-103; A. Jepsen, "Elia und das Gottesurteil," in H. Goedicke, ed., *Near Eastern Studies in Honor of W. F. Albright* (Baltimore, 1971), 291-306; H. Junker, "Der Graben um den Altar des Elias," *TrThZ,* 69 (1960), 65-74; C. Kopp, *Elias und Christentum auf dem Karmel. Collectanea Hierosolymitana,* 3 (Paderborn, 1929); E. Lipiński, "La fête de l'ensevelissement et de la résurrection de Melqart," *Actes de la XVIIe Rencontre Assyriologique Internationale, Bruxelles, 1969* (Ham-sur-Heure, 1970), 30-58; M. J. Mulder, *Ba'al in het OT* (Hague, 1962), 30-44; *idem, De naam van de afwezige god op de Karmel* (Leiden, 1979); H. D. Preuss, *Verspottung fremder Religionen im AT. BWANT,* 92[5/12] (1971), 80-100; W. Röllig, "Baal-Karmelos," *WbMyth,* I/1 (1961), 272; E. Rössler, *Jahwe und die Götter im Pentateuch und im deuteronomistischen Geschichtswerk* (diss., Bonn, 1966), 103-113; H. H. Rowley, "Elijah on Mount Carmel," *BJRL,* 43 (1960/61), 190-219; H. Seebass, "Elia und Ahab auf dem Karmel," *ZThK,* 70 (1973), 121-136; O. H. Steck, *Überlieferung und Zeitgeschichte in den Elia-Erzählungen. WMANT,* 26 (1968); N. J. Tromp, "Water and Fire on Mount Carmel," *Bibl,* 56 (1975), 480-502; F. Vattioni, "Aspetti del culto del Signore dei cieli, II," *Aug,* 13 (1973), 57-73; R. de Vaux, *Élie le prophéte, I. Études carméelitaines* (Paris, 1956), 53-64; *idem,* "Les prophètes de Baal sur le Mont Carmel," *BMB,* 5 (1941), 7-20; E. Würthwein, "Die Erzählung vom Gottesurteil auf dem Karmel," *ZThK,* 59 (1962), 131-144.

1. E.g., *KBL*[1,3]; cf. Jepsen, *ZDPV,* 75 (1959), 74.
2. *GesB, BDB,* König; Zorell accidentally omits the second meaning.
3. J. Olshausen, *Lehrbuch der hebräischen Sprache* (Braunschweig, 1861), § 216b; *GK,* § 85s; *BLe,* 503i; Kallai-Kleinmann, *EMiqr,* IV, 329.
4. *GesTh,* 713.
5. R. Ružička, *Konsonantische Dissimilation in den semitischen Sprachen. BASS,* 6/4 (1909), 104.
6. L. Köhler, "Problems in the Study of the Language of the OT," *JSS,* 1 (1956), 19.
7. *Ibid.,* 18; cf. also *idem,* "Vom hebräischen Lexikon," *OTS,* 8 (1950), 151f.; M. Fraenkel, "Bemerkungen zum hebräischen Wortschatz," *HUCA,* 31 (1960), 85f.; *KBL*³, *s.v.* כרמל IV.

such dissimilation, however, occurs only in Aramaic. According to this latter etymology, ***kāmmal* derives from **kāmal,* related to Arab. *kamala,* "be complete"; the later homonyms meaning "new grain" and "orchard" do not come from a common root. Although this hypothesis has much in its favor, it is impossible to determine whether the name of the mountain and the city is connected etymologically with one of the two roots[8] or with both.

Etymologies (popular?) for the name of the mountain were suggested at an early date. Origen, followed by Jerome and others, proposes *Kármēl, epígnōsis peritomḗs* (*Carmel, cognitio circumcisionis*).[9] This etymology indicates a connection between *krh* and *mûl.*[10] The notion that the name of the mountain is connected with the word *karmel,* "orchard," is nevertheless reasonable.[11] In the first place, it is not always possible to distinguish the two meanings in texts of the OT itself, and the ancient versions often vacillate between the two meanings.[12] Furthermore, other mountains and villages are named for their characteristic features (e.g., Lebanon). The frequent use of the definite article with Carmel also suggests a proper name.[13] Mt. Carmel was probably known as a cultic site in the ancient Near East at an early date.[14] The word *karmel* in the sense of "new grain" or "orchard" has not yet been found in other Semitic languages.

2. *Occurrences (Other than Mt. Carmel).*

a. *City in Judah.* The toponym *karmel* appears in Josh. 15:55; 1 S. 15:12; 25:2 (twice),5,7,40; and possibly 2 Ch. 26:10.[15] The name probably denotes a city in Judah located about 12 kilometers (7.5 mi.) southeast of Hebron (modern *el-Kermil*).[16] It is already mentioned by Eusebius,[17] and Jerome notes that there were two mountains named Carmel, of which one was the workplace of *Nabal Carmelius,* the other a mountain *iuxta Ptolemaidem.*[18] According to 1 S. 15:12, Saul set up a monument in Carmel after his victory over the Amalekites. Primarily, however, this city was known for its association with the story of David and Abigail, whose husband Nabal lived in Maon but sheared his sheep in Carmel (1 S. 25).

In addition to the name of the city, the gentilic forms *karm^{e}lî* (masc.: 1 S. 30:5; 2 S. 2:2; 3:3; 23:35; 1 Ch. 11:37) and *karm^{e}lîṯ* (fem.: 1 S. 27:3; 1 Ch. 3:1) are found.

---

8. Cf. *KBL.*
9. *MPL,* 23, 1231f.; cf. 803f., 820.
10. Cf. also Heidet, 291.
11. Cf. also Jepsen, *ZDPV,* 75 (1959), 74.
12. See I.2.c below.
13. Cf. Kallai-Kleinmann, *EMiqr,* IV, 329.
14. See II.2 below.
15. See also Kallai-Kleinmann, *EMiqr,* IV, 323f.; Jepsen, *ZDPV,* 75 (1959), 74.
16. Cf. *GTTOT,* 149.
17. *Onomasticon* (ed. E. Klostermann [1904, repr. Hildesheim, 1966]) 92, 20; 118, 5ff.
18. *Comm. on Am. 1:2. MPL,* 25, 993.

In the LXX, the name of the city appears also in 1 S. 25:4; 30:29. In the MT of the first passage, the name does not appear; in the second, we find the reading *b^e rākāl.*[19]

The Carmel in these passages has not always been identified solely with a city southeast of Hebron. In Josh. 12:22; 15:55, L. Heidet[20] interprets Carmel as a city in the territory of Judah; but he thinks there was also a region bearing the same name in this territory.[21] Alfred Jepsen, too, has pointed out the likelihood of this theory.[22] The region in question lies between Maon to the west and the desert to the east; it is here that Nabal sheared his sheep. According to Jepsen, the "Carmel" mentioned in 2 Ch. 26:10 likewise denotes the region on the eastern slope of the mountains of Judah.[23] Jepsen even theorizes that in the early period there was only a single region called Carmel in Judah; its primary city was Maon Carmel (Josh. 15:55). Not until the Roman period, he suggests, did a new town take its name from the ancient region and eliminate all recollection of the latter. This extreme theory, however, seems to be disproved by 1 S. 15:12.

b. *New Grain.* In 2 K. 4:42, *karmel* ("new grain") constitutes part of the provisions brought to Elisha by a man from Baal-shalishah. Lev. 23:14 prohibits the eating of *karmel* and certain other foods from the new harvest until the day when the first sheaf is presented before Yahweh. When a cereal offering of firstfruits is offered, Lev. 2:14 requires that the new grain (*gereś karmel*) be roasted in the fire. Since 2 K. 4:42 also mentions *leḥem bikkûrîm,* we see that the word *karmel* is associated closely with the offering of firstfruits and is intended to denote fresh, unmilled grain. As early as the Babylonian Talmud,[24] word play divides *karmel* into *rak̲ ûmal* ("soft and easy to grind") or *kar mālē'* ("a bag full"), thus "explaining" it. Today the word is often translated (correctly) as "new grain" or "new corn."[25] Rabbinic literature already interpreted *gereś karmel* as "grains of newly ripe wheat"[26] or "scattered grains of wheat." In 2 K. 4:42, the LXX translated *karmel* as *paláthē,* the usual translation of *d^e b̲ēlâ,* "fig cake" (1 S. 25:18; 30:12; 2 K. 20:7; Isa. 38:21; 1 Ch. 12:41[40]).

c. *Orchard.* Sometimes it is hard to determine whether *karmel* refers to Mt. Carmel or an "orchard." There are thus cases in which modern lexica and commentaries differ as to the translation of the word. The following passages are involved: 2 K. 19:23 (par. Isa. 37:24); Isa. 10:18; 16:10; 29:17 (twice); 32:15 (twice),16; Jer. 2:7; 4:26; 48:33; Mic. 7:14. In all these passages, the Vulg. uses the geographical proper noun *Carmel(us)*

19. Cf. W. Caspari, "Eine Dodekapolis in I. Sam. 30, 27-30," *OLZ,* 19 (1916), 174; contra H. J. Stoebe, *Das erste Buch Samuelis. KAT,* VIII/1 (1973), 509, who prefers to retain the MT.

20. P. 288.

21. *Ibid.,* 290.

22. Pp. 74f.

23. Cf. also Heidet, 290; K. Galling, *Die Bücher der Chronik. ATD,* XII (1959), *in loc.*

24. Bab. *Menaḥ.* 66b.

25. See, e.g., *AuS,* I/2 (1928), 452; K. Elliger, *Leviticus. HAT,* IV (1966), 47, 315; *KBL*[3], *s.v.*

26. Targ. Onqelos: *pêrûk̲ān r^e k̲ik̲ān* (cf. Targ. Jonathan I and II: *pêrûk̲ān*; T. Neofiti [in error?]: *pryḥyn*); LXX: *chídra eriktá,* "soft grains of wheat"; *AuS,* III (1933), 266f.

or *Chermel*; the LXX differs in Isa. 10:18; 16:10; Jer. 48:33(LXX 31:33). Elsewhere, however, the LXX speaks of Mt. Carmel, sometimes quite clearly (e.g., Isa. 29:17: *tó hóros tó Chérmēl* [twice]). The Syr. uniformly reads *krml'*. The Targ., however, vacillates between the name of the mountain and the metaphorical expression *mašrîṯā'*, "camp" (2 K. 19:23 par. Isa. 37:24; Isa. 10:18).

In Mic. 7:14, the lexica[27] generally translate *karmel* as "orchard" or the like; *BDB*, however, finds here the geographical term Carmel. This interpretation has been supported by such scholars as Otto Eissfeldt[28] and, more recently, A. S. van der Woude,[29] who proposes an emendation, reading *śukkennû* (from *śkk* = *skk*, "protect") for *šōḵᵉnî*, and translating: "Protect the people in safety in the forest on Carmel." In this passage there is much to recommend the interpretation of *karmel* as referring to the well-known mountain, since the immediate context also mentions Bashan and Gilead.

The contexts of some of the other passages listed likewise mention the names of mountains (e.g., 2 K. 19:23 par. Isa. 37:24; Isa. 29:17 [Lebanon]) or other geographical features (e.g., Jer. 48:33 [*'ereṣ mô'āḇ,* not mentioned in Isa. 16:10]; Jer. 2:7 [*'ereṣ hakkarmel*]), which might indicate that *karmel* is the name of a mountain. On the other hand, there are 3 occurrences of *karmillô,* i.e., *karmel* with a pronominal suffix, which suggest a meaning other than "the Carmel mountains" (2 K. 19:23 par. Isa. 37:24; Isa. 10:18).

In a short lexicographical note on the words *karmel* and *ya'ar,* Paul Joüon once tried to interpret *ya'ar* in some texts as meaning "orchard" and *karmel* in all the texts in which it cannot be a toponym meaning "field." He notes a kind of antithesis *ya'ar/karmel* in Isa. 10:18; 29:17; 32:15; 37:24 (par. 2 K. 19:23); Mic. 7:14, but is forced to resort to textual emendation in some passages. Quite apart from the question of emendation, this proposal must be rejected as being unjustified both etymologically and contextually not only for → יער *ya'ar* but also for *karmel.* No one has since followed Joüon's lead.

Of course there is sometimes a kind of antithesis between *ya'ar* and *karmel,* but the difference is of another sort. In Isa. 37:24 (par. 2 K. 19:23), the close association of the two words is not an antithesis at all,[30] and suggests that the passage reflects the notion of the "garden of God." In other cases, "orchard" is possible, above all in Isa. 10:18 (*kᵉḇôḏ ya'ᵉrô wᵉḵarmillô*); 29:17; 32:15f., but also in 16:10; Jer. 48:33. Even here, of course, it is possible to vacillate, as does Otto Kaiser[31] in the case of Isa. 29:17, translating the first occurrence of *karmel* as "garden" and leaving the second untranslated ("and Carmel shall be regarded as a forest?"). It is clear, however, that it is often better to translate *karmel* as "garden" or the like in these passages than to treat it as meaning Mt. Carmel.

---

27. *GesB, LexHebAram, KBL*[1,3].
28. "Ein Psalm aus Nord-Israel, Micha 7, 7-20," *KlSchr,* IV (1968), 63, 66; cf. *Der Gott Karmel,* 7, n. 3.
29. *Micha. PredOT* (1976), 259ff.
30. → יער *ya'ar,* IV.
31. *Isaiah 13–39. OTL* (Eng. trans. 1974), 277.

The situation is more complex in Jer. 2:7; 4:26. The former uses a construct phrase (*'ereṣ hakkarmel*) that is usually translated "fruitful land." Although the context mentions the fruits and good things of the land of Israel, and the semantic nuance of "orchard" would be quite appropriate, it is not entirely out of the question that *karmel* stands by synecdoche for all Israel; the verse would then allude to the fertility of the Mt. Carmel region in particular and to that of the land in general. A similar usage appears in 4:26, which speaks of *hakkarmel hammiḏbār,* all of whose cities were laid in ruins before Yahweh. Orchards can turn to desert, and this meaning chimes with the vision of chaos[32] that serves as a kind of antithesis to creation (4:23ff.). Here, too, however, it is possible to think of Mt. Carmel as the acme of fertility and delight in the land of Israel.

In 2 Ch. 26:10, we find *haššᵉp̄ēlâ, hammîšôr, hehārîm,* and *hakkarmel* side by side. The word *karmel* in this passage is often understood as "fertile land" or the like;[33] more likely, however, it is a toponym.[34]

II. 1. *Geography and Political Control.* A ridge with an altitude of about 550 meters (1800 ft.) stretches northwest from the mountains of Samaria to the Mediterranean Sea, reaching the coastal plain just south of Acco.[35] This spur drops steeply to the northeast; to the southwest, it descends gently to the Plain of Sharon. It rises steeply from the Mediterranean (cf. Jer. 46:18). It is still debatable whether the OT name Carmel refers to the entire ridge northwest of Samaria or denotes just the highest portion of the promontory south and southeast of modern Haifa.[36] In any case, the Elijah episode is set somewhere on the latter, with its many caves and ravines.[37] Springs at the foot of the mountain supply the Kishon (*Nahr el-Muqaṭṭaʿ*) with a perennial flow;[38] this brook finds its way through a narrow outlet and empties into the sea east of Haifa (cf. also Jgs. 4:7,13; 5:21; Ps. 83:10[9]; 1 K. 18:40).

Ample precipitation and the nature of the soil give the mountainous region of Carmel abundant vegetation.[39] It is not unsuitable for human settlement: there is evidence of human habitation dating from the Stone Age, especially in the caves.[40]

At the time of the Israelite "occupation," Carmel was already settled by Canaanites or Phoenicians, as we can see from a list of the vanquished kings: Josh. 12:22 mentions the king of Jokneam in Carmel. Possibly the region of Carmel should be considered an independent territory. In the distribution of the land outlined elsewhere in the book of Joshua, Carmel constitutes a kind of buffer between the tribes of Asher, Manasseh,

---

32. A. Weiser, *Das Buch Jeremia 1–25,14. ATD,* XX (⁶1969), 46f.
33. See the lexica.
34. See I.2.a above.
35. *GTTOT,* § 47.
36. Kallai-Kleinmann, *EMiqr,* IV, 329.
37. See II.3 below.
38. Kopp, *Elias und Christentum,* 50f.
39. → יַעַר *yaʿar.*
40. Cf. D. A. E. Garrod, *CAH*³, I/1, 83f.; see esp. T. Noy, "Carmel Caves," *EAEHL,* 290-98, with bibliog.

Issachar, and Zebulun (Josh. 19:11,26; 17:11).[41] Which tribe received the mountain itself is disputed.[42] In any case, it is clear that Carmel was not part of Israelite territory until the monarchy and that even then non-Israelites constituted the majority of the population (cf. Jgs. 1:27,31), although the Israelites may have intermarried with the original population. The list of Israel's administrative districts in the time of Solomon assigns the entire hill country of Dor to one of Solomon's officials (1 K. 4:11);[43] Mt. Carmel may have been included.[44] Albrecht Alt proposed the theory that Carmel passed from Israelite to Tyrian jurisdiction as early as the time of Solomon. The story of the contest on Mt. Carmel[45] shows that it had reverted to Israel by the time of King Ahab.[46] Many scholars have accepted Alt's theory;[47] others have made their voices heard in opposition.[48]

In the time of Tiglath-pileser III, when the Assyrian king established the districts of Gilead, Megiddo, and Dor, Israel totally lost its sovereignty over the region of Carmel. For administrative purposes, the mountain was probably included in the province of Dor. In ancient times, Jewish influence made itself felt once more in this territory during the Maccabean period: according to Josephus,[49] Alexander Jannaeus took possession of Carmel and many other places.[50]

2. *The "Holy Mountain" in General.* Like many other mountains in the ancient Near East, Carmel was often considered a "holy mountain." Since time immemorial, this mountain that rises so majestically from sea and plain was thought of as the habitation of various deities to whom cultic worship should be offered.[51] There are several documents outside the OT that may occasionally suggest the "holiness" of Carmel. The mention of an "antelope nose" in an Egyptian monumental text from the middle of the third millennium[52] and of a *rú-š(a) qad-š* or *rú-ʾu-š qad-š* ("sacred headland") in city lists of Thutmose III (*ca.* 1490-1426) and later pharaohs[53] hardly constitutes proof. Even if this mention of the "sacred height" does refer to Carmel, it leaves unanswered the question of what deity was worshipped there.[54]

---

41. See also Josephus *Ant.* v.1.22 (84ff.).

42. Cf. Alt, *KlSchr,* II, 140, n. 3: "the purely theoretical assignment to Asher of all Carmel"; Kallai-Kleinmann, *EMiqr,* IV, 327; see also Aharoni, 3f.

43. Cf. Josephus *Ant.* viii.2.3 (37): *Saphátēs dé tó Itavýrion hóros kaí Karmḗlion . . .*

44. But cf. Fohrer, 66.

45. See II.3 below.

46. Alt, *KlSchr,* II, 140-46; *idem,* "Der Stadtstaat Samaria," *BSAW,* 101/5 (1954) = *KlSchr,* III (1959), 258-302.

47. E.g., Fohrer, 66.

48. Kallai-Kleinmann, *EMiqr,* IV, 327; cf. also Würthwein, 143f.; Rössler, 107-110.

49. *Ant.* xiii.15.4 (396).

50. For further details, see Kopp, *Elias und Christentum,* 42.

51. → הַר *har,* V.

52. *ANET,* 228; W. Helck, *Die Beziehungen Ägyptens zu Vorderasien im 3. und 2. Jahrtausand v. Chr. ÄgAbh,* 5 (^{2}1971), 18; Eissfeldt, 6.

53. Helck, 127, 220; see also Galling, 106, n. 7; Aharoni, 2 and n. 8.

54. On the location of the "sacred headland" (Râš en-Nāqūra) in the time of Shalmaneser III, see Lipiński, "Note de topographie historique," *RB,* 78 (1971), 84-92.

From a much later period we have a statement of Pseudo-Scylax (4th or 5th century B.C.)[55] referring to Carmel as the "holy mountain of Zeus." In the context of the optimistic promises given Vespasian in the year A.D. 69, Tacitus describes the god and the mountain as follows: "Carmel — as they call both the mountain and the god — lies between Judea and Syria; it has neither the image of a god nor a temple (so most say) but an altar and a place of reverence."[56] With reference to the same Vespasian, Suetonius says: "When he consulted the oracle of the god Carmel in Judea, the lots confirmed that whatever he planned or desired to do, however great, they promised it would take place."[57] Tacitus and Suetonius thus refer to the god of Carmel as "the god Carmel" (= *ba'al karmel*), probably a "relatively autonomous"[58] deity. The Neo-Platonist Iamblichus (*ca.* A.D. 300) tells how Pythagoras, brought to Mt. Carmel by Egyptian seamen, frequently stayed alone in a shrine there.[59] In this context, he also speaks of "the highest peak of Carmel, considered the most sacred of all mountains, inaccessible to many." This passage thus mentions a holy place on Carmel, but not the god of Carmel.[60] Orosius can speak of Carmel as the site of an oracle: ". . . misled by certain oracles on Mt. Carmel."[61]

It is not so easy to decide where the cultic site — there is no mention of any temple — of the god (of) Carmel was located — at the northwest tip of the spur or on the Muḥraqa peak (514 m. [1686 ft.]) at the southeast end of Carmel.[62] Most likely the deity had several places of worship that changed with the passage of time.[63] In 1952, Michael Avi-Yonah described a marble right foot, twice life size, kept in the Monastery of Elijah on the northwest side of Carmel; on its plinth, the following inscription can be read: ΔΙΙ ΗΛΙΟΠΟΛΕΙΤΗ ΚΑΡΜΗΛΩ/Γ. ΙΟΥΛ ΕΥΤΥΧΑΣ/ΚΟΛ>ΚΑΙΣΑΡΕΥΣ.[64] This foot should be dated *ca.* A.D. 200, which probably means that at the time it was consecrated the northwest portion of Carmel was considered a site sacred to the god Carmel, identified with Zeus Heliopoleites.[65] This Zeus Heliopoleites is closely related to the Semitic weather- and fertility-god Ba'al (or Hadad).[66] Furthermore, many of the passages cited above show that the god Carmel had universal as well as local significance, at least in the late period.

3. *Elijah and Elisha.* The decision as to whether the "contest on Mt. Carmel" (1 K. 18) is an independent narrative affects the identification of the deity engaged

---

55. *Periplus* civ; C. Müller, *GGM,* I, 79, albeit with *Kármēlos* supplied by the editor.
56. *Hist.* ii.78.3.
57. *De vita Caesarum* viii.6.
58. Eissfeldt, 10.
59. *De vita Pythagorica* iii.15.
60. Cf. Eissfeldt, 10f.
61. *Hist. adversus paganos* vii.9
62. See also Friedman.
63. Eissfeldt, 14.
64. Avi-Yonah, 118.
65. Mulder, *Ba'al in het OT,* 42f.
66. Eissfeldt, 22.

in the struggle with Yahweh upon the mountain; some scholars see in this deity a local numen, some the Tyrian god Melqart (Heracles), some Baʿal himself or Baʿal-shamem. Verse 27 in particular provides some important information about the nature of this god,[67] which has led many — above all Roland de Vaux — to identify the Baʿal of the Carmel episode with the Tyrian Melqart (Heracles).[68] This seems all the more reasonable because the context makes it clear that Ahab's wife Jezebel, the daughter of Ethbaal of Sidon, was fanatically devoted to her native god (1 K. 16:31f.; 18:4,13,18f.; 19:1f.),[69] while her husband, although playing no role in 18:21-40,[70] sought to establish political peace not only between the worshippers of Baʿal and Yahweh but also between the Canaanites and Israelites through a policy of neutrality and parity.[71]

It has nevertheless been asked whether the story of the contest, which can hardly be called an "ordeal" in the usual sense,[72] in the present Elijah cycle is part of a larger literary unit including the other elements[73] or whether the whole must be analyzed more on the basis of the formerly independent elements it now comprises. The latter view was already espoused by Hermann Gunkel[74] and above all by Alt; many other scholars also support the independence of the contest narrative.[75] According to Alt, Yahweh — whose altar built in the time of David had been thrown down (v. 30) — is engaged in a struggle not primarily with a Tyrian Baʿal but with the ancient Baʿal of Carmel. Eissfeldt, by contrast, from his perspective that the Elijah stories constitute a cohesive whole, defends the theory that the Baʿal of Carmel is primarily neither a local deity nor the Tyrian Melqart but Baʿal-shamem,[76] "who is clearly not the god of a political group but of the universe and also of the individual."[77] The universal character of the Baʿal worshipped on Carmel is also defended by other scholars, not all of whom, however, identify him with Baʿal-shamem.[78]

It is possible to claim that the story of the contest in its present form is a sanctuary or cult legend,[79] a prophetic legend, or even a mixture of all three,[80] intended to support the claims of an Israelite minority to the Carmel sanctuary of Yahweh established in

---

67. Gunkel, 17; Preuss, 82, 86ff.; Seebass, 125.
68. De Vaux, *BMB,* 5 (1941), 7-20; *idem,* Élie le prophéte, I, 61f.; W. F. Albright, *From the Stone Age to Christianity* (Garden City, N.Y., 1957), 307.
69. See, e.g., Hillmann, 96, n. 1.
70. Tromp, 498.
71. Fohrer, 77; Seebass, 122ff.
72. E. Kutsch, "Gottesurteil. II. In Israel," *RGG*^{3}, II, 1809; Rössler, 104f.
73. Eissfeldt, 33; cf. also Fohrer, 33ff.; J. Gray, *I and II Kings.* OTL (^{2}1970), 383ff.
74. P. 13.
75. E.g., Fohrer, 36f.; Würthwein, 131ff.; Steck, 132; Jepsen, *Festschrift W. F. Albright,* 297ff.; Seebass,134f.; Tromp, 490; Mulder, *Naam,* 7ff.
76. Cf. also Hillmann, 99ff.; J. A. Montgomery and H. S. Gehman, *The Books of Kings. ICC* (1951), 308.
77. "Baʿalšamēm und Jahwe," *KlSchr,* II (1963), 187.
78. Junker, 66, n. 3; Preuss, 87f.; cf. also Galling, 121; Ap-Thomas, 150; Vattioni, 72f.
79. Cf. Würthwein, 135; also Seebass, 125; contra Rowley,199, etc.; cf. Steck, 17, n. 2.
80. Rössler, 110f.

the time of David.[81] It is undeniable, however, that the description of the contest between Yahweh and Baʿal, despite all the local features of the god of Carmel,[82] includes universalistic motifs of the one Baʿal par excellence.[83] What was at stake on Carmel was more than a local decision between Yahweh and worshippers of Baʿal, without any fundamental significance for all Israel (cf. the secondary material in vv. 19f. and 31f.). The Baʿal of Carmel, besides his local features, clearly has characteristics typical of Baʿal in general. Some attributes of the Tyrian Melqart (Heracles) associated by de Vaux with Baʿal Carmel are also associated with the Baʿal of the Ugaritic texts. A god — in this case Baʿal, although René Dussaud thinks in terms of Hadad[84] — who suffers defeat on his own home territory, Carmel, cannot be considered god anywhere in Israel, not to mention Carmel, or stand alongside Yahweh, the victor.[85]

The narrative itself is clearly a literary composition[86] with scant evidence as to what actually took place; it contains few geographic, cultic, or other details.[87] Possibly a story concerning Yahweh has been reshaped deliberately as an attack on Baʿal.[88] It is also uncertain where the contest on Carmel should be pictured as taking place — on the headland near the Carmelite monastery[89] or at the southeast end of the spur (*el-Muḥraqa*) not far from the Kishon, where Elijah is said to have slain the prophets of Baʿal[90] and where he later went up to pray on the top of Carmel.[91] The LXX reads only: *epí tón Kármēlon* (v. 42).

Mt. Carmel played an even more important role as a sacred site in the life of Elijah's successor Elisha, who is said to have stayed there on several occasions. We are told in 2 K. 2:25 that, after forty-two children were killed by bears near Bethel, the prophet went to Mt. Carmel before returning to Samaria (if this is not a redactional addition[92]). When the Shunammite woman needed the man of God to help her son, she knew precisely that Elisha was dwelling on Mt. Carmel (2 K. 4:25). It is significant in this context that the boy's father asked his wife why she wanted to go to Elisha at that particular time, since it was neither new moon nor Sabbath (v. 23). We may conclude from his words that on such days Mt. Carmel was a holy place much frequented by the prophet and the people. Possibly the prophet's disciples also assembled here. In

---

81. Gray, 399f.
82. Steck.
83. → בעל *baʿal,* III.2; Mulder, *Baʿal in het OT,* 43f.; Fohrer, 98 ("a rain- and fertility-god"); Seebass, 135; cf. Gray, 393, etc.
84. R. Dussaud, *Syr,* 29 (1952), 385; *idem, Syr,* 31 (1954), 148.
85. Preuss, 91f.; cf. Fohrer, 65.
86. Cf. Tromp, 488-494.
87. Rössler, 105; Jepsen, *Festschrift W. F. Albright,* 296ff.; also Mulder, *Naam,* 15-18.
88. Preuss, 93; also G. von Rad, *OT Theology,* II (Eng. trans., New York, 1965), 24f.; Steck, 76.
89. Alt, *KlSchr,* II, 139; Galling, 123.
90. E.g., Kopp, *Elias und Christentum,* 49-54; de Vaux, *Élie le prophéte,* I, 59; Gray, 402; cf. Friedman, 95ff.; Vattioni, 68f.; Seebass, 125, n. 7; 128, n. 21.
91. Alt, *KlSchr,* II, 135ff.; Fohrer, 81ff., 93f.
92. See H.-C. Schmitt, *Elisa* (Gütersloh, 1972), 76f.

addition, the mention of a ruined altar of Yahweh in 1 K. 18:30 suggests that Carmel was a sacred site consecrated to the God of Israel at an early date, even if the cult of Yahweh displaced the cult of Baʿal only from time to time.[93]

4. *Elsewhere in the OT.* The other OT passages that mention Mt. Carmel (Cant. 7:6[5]; Isa. 33:9; 35:2; Jer. 46:18; 50:19; Am. 1:2; 9:3; Mic. 7:14; Nah. 1:4)[94] do not speak explicitly of any particular cultic tradition associated with the mountain, although there may be overtones of such, especially in Am. 9:3; Jer. 46:18.[95] Am. 9:3 records a prophetic vision in which Yahweh stands beside an altar and proclaims a catastrophe to the people. This passage speaks not only of descending into the underworld and ascending to the heavens (v. 2), but also of trying to hide on the top of Carmel or at the bottom of the sea, where Yahweh would send a biting serpent. Here Carmel may represent the heights; its situation adjacent to the Mediterranean also plays a role, and its thick forests made it a good hiding place.[96] The sea serpent, however, is a mythological motif (cf. Job 26:13; Ps. 74:13f.; 89:11[10]; Isa. 27:1; 51:9) alluding to ideas found in the Ugaritic texts, so that in mentioning Carmel the prophet may have been thinking of the cult of the god of Carmel practiced there.[97] A cultic or mythological allusion is much less clear in Jer. 46:18, where both Mt. Tabor and Mt. Carmel are compared to an unidentified person who "comes."[98] Here it makes more sense to think of Carmel as being mentioned on account of its prominent situation by the sea. This striking situation is also emphasized in Cant. 7:6(5), which uses Carmel as an image for a proudly carried head.[99]

Carmel frequently appears in combination with other geographical names to symbolize mourning or drought in the land (Isa. 33:9 [with Lebanon, Sharon, and Bashan]; Nah. 1:4 [with Bashan and Lebanon]) or to depict rejoicing, with the glory and majesty of the mountain being extolled (Isa. 35:2 [with Lebanon and Sharon]). Jer. 50:19 promises that Israel will pasture on Carmel and in Bashan and be satisfied on the hills of Ephraim and in Gilead. As we have seen,[100] the word *karmel* in Mic. 7:14 probably refers to Mt. Carmel. Here again the context mentions Bashan and Gilead. Eissfeldt has suggested translating the hemistich thus: "[Yahweh], who dwellest alone in the forest on Carmel."[101] This proposal has been rejected by van der Woude.[102] It is quite conceivable, however, that the prophet is alluding to a sanctuary of Yahweh on Carmel,

93. See Seebass, 133, n. 39; 135.
94. See I.2.c above for 2 Ch. 26:10.
95. Galling, *Festschrift A. Alt,* 119, n. 3.
96. W. Rudolph, *Amos. KAT,* XIII/2 (1971), 246.
97. H. W. Wolff, *Joel and Amos. Herm* (Eng. trans. 1977), 340f.
98. W. Rudolph, *Jeremia. HAT,* XII (^{3}1968),232; *BHS, in loc.,* reads "enemy."
99. K. Budde, *Das fünf Megillot: Das Hohelied. KHC,* XVII (1898), 39; W. Rudolph, *Das Hohelied. KAT,* XVII/2 (1966), 173; contra *KBL*^{3}, 474: "crimson."
100. See I.2.c above.
101. *KlSchr,* IV, 63, 66; *Der Gott Karmel,* 7, n. 3.
102. See above.

although the context suggests rather that the mountain symbolizes the fertility of the land.

Am. 1:2a uses a metaphor (*YHWH miṣṣiyyôn yišʾāg ûmîrûšālayim yittēn qôlô*) that appears also (with some variation) in Joel 4:16(3:16); Jer. 25:30.[103] It may allude to a cultic theophany,[104] in which case Am. 1:2b describes the results of this theophany: the pastures of the shepherds mourn and the top of Carmel withers (probably better than the reading *w^eyēḇôš* proposed by Bernard Duhm and others). Here, too, Carmel should be understood as representing by synecdoche the generally luxuriant countryside and the forests of the mountain, without any cultic associations. But this drought that causes the top of Carmel and the pastures to die is of "eschatological dimensions."[105] Here Carmel has moved into a world fraught with theological and eschatological significance. Carmel, a fertile, mountainous site emerging from the depths of the sea, thus becomes as it were an image of God's promised salvation and disaster.

Mulder†

---

103. See M. Weiss, "In the Footsteps of One Biblical Metaphor," *Tarbiz,* 34 (1964/65), 107-128 [Heb.], I-II [Eng. summary].

104. C. van Leeuwen, "Amos 1:2: Epigraphe du livre entier ou introduction aux aracles des chapitres 1-2?" *Verkenningen in een Stroomgebied. Festschrift M. A. Beek* (Amsterdam, 1974), 93-101.

105. Wolff, 125.

כָּרַע *kāraʿ*

Contents: I. Occurrences. II. General. III. Prayer. IV. Significance. V. LXX. VI. Dead Sea Scrolls.

I. Occurrences. The verb *kāraʿ* occurs 30 times in the OT in the qal and 5 in the hiphil. It is attested in Ugaritic,[1] Jewish Aramaic, Samaritan,[2] Arab. *rakaʿa,* "bow,"

---

kāraʿ. D. R. Ap-Thomas, "Notes on Some Terms Relating to Prayer," *VT,* 6 (1956), 225-241; E. Brunner-Traut, "Gesten," *LexÄg,* II (1977), 573-585; M. Falkner, "Gebetsgebärden und Gebetsgesten," *RLA,* III (1971), 175-77; A. Greiff, *Das Gebet im AT. AVA,* 5/3 (1915); F. Heiler, "Die Körperhaltung beim Gebet," *Orientalische Studien. Festschrift F. Hommel,* II. *MVÄG,* 22 (1917), 168-177; E. Kutsch, *"Trauerbräuche" und "Selbstminderungsbräuche" im AT. ThSt,* 78 (1965), 25-42; S. Langdon, "Gesture in Sumerian and Babylonian Prayer," *JRAS,* 1919, 531-556; F. Nötscher, *Biblische Altertumskunde. HSAT,* sup. 3 (1940), 345-350; R. de Vaux, *AncIsr,* 458f.

1. *WUS,* no. 1389.

2. Z. Ben-Hayyim, *The Literary and Oral Tradition of Hebrew and Aramaic amongst the Samaritans* (Jerusalem, 1957-1961) [Heb.].

and in the Targumim.[3] Some scholars[4] think the verb is a denominative from the corresponding noun *k^e^ra'*, "shank," which appears in P passages (Ex. 12:9; Lev. 1:9; etc.) as well as Am. 3:12. The noun is used only of animals' limbs, whereas the verb (except in Job 39:3; Isa. 46:2) always refers to human actions.

II. General. Even when *kāra'* stands by itself and one would expect to find its literal meaning, it probably refers to an act that goes beyond simple kneeling. In Job 31:10, it is used of a male in sexual intercourse. Struck by Jehu's arrow, King Joram sinks in his chariot (2 K. 9:24). In Isa. 46:1, the very gods Bel and Nebo are forced to their knees, as are the animals that bear their images in v. 2. In both verses, our verb is amplified by *qāras,* "stoop"; the two "deliberately harsh and grating verbs are placed chiastically at the beginning of each verse and for emphasis. . . . Gods like these cannot save or uphold."[5] In Isa. 10:4, *kāra'* is used of prisoners who fall slain.[6] In Isa. 65:12, finally, the people must kneel to be slaughtered. The hiphil expresses the idea of forcing people to their knees (2 S. 22:40 par. Ps. 18:40[Eng. v. 39]; Ps. 17:13). Ps. 78:31 speaks of this happening to the picked men of Israel. Jephthah's emotional desolation is also expressed by *kāra'*, reinforced by its infinitive absolute (Jgs. 11:35).

More frequently, we find *kāra'* in sequence with other verbs: a lion kneels and couches (*rāḇaṣ:* Gen. 49:9; *šāḵaḇ*: Nu. 24:9). Sisera sinks to his knees (Jgs. 5:27), which leads to *nāpal* (also in Isa. 10:4; Ps. 20:9[8]) and *šāḵaḇ* (cf. also Isa. 10:4). Kneeling before giving birth is similar (1 S. 4:19; cf. Job 39:3). For the most part, then, the verb *kāra'* indicates that someone is suffering violence (Jgs. 11:35; 2 K. 9:24; Job 4:4; 31:10; Ps. 20:9[8]; Isa. 46:1f.; 65:12); but it can also express such an everyday act as the kneeling of Gideon's army to drink water (Jgs. 7:5f.).

III. Prayer. One important use of *kāra'* is to express subservience. One individual may kneel before another (2 K. 1:13; Est. 3:2 [twice], 5), but kneeling is especially appropriate in prayer before God (1 K. 8:54; 19:18; 2 Ch. 7:3; 29:29; Ps. 72:9; 95:6; Isa. 45:23). Do such passages denote kneeling from an erect position? This conclusion is suggested by the frequent use of *kāra'* with *bereḵ* (Jgs. 7:3 [twice]; 1 K. 8:54; 19:18; 2 K. 1:13; Ezr. 9:5; Job 4:4; Isa. 45:23); there is also Ps. 95:6a, with the verb *bāraḵ* in v. 6b. Here, too, belongs 1 K. 8:54, even though v. 22 states that Solomon stood to pray. Ernst Würthwein suggests that v. 54 represents a later addition, when kneeling was considered the only appropriate posture of prayer.[7] The description of the same event in 2 Ch. 6:13 combines standing and kneeling in the same verse. D. R. Ap-Thomas,[8] however, denies that standing was the real posture of prayer in the OT. He

3. Cf. St.-B, II (1924), 259-262.
4. Ap-Thomas, 228; *KBL*[3], 475.
5. H. D. Preuss, *Verspottung fremder Religionen im AT. BWANT,* 92[5/12] (1971), 219.
6. Cf. H. Wildberger, *Isaiah 1/-12* (Eng. trans., Minneapolis, 1991), 190, 194, 216.
7. E. Würthwein, *Die Bücher der Könige. ATD,* XI/1 (1976), 94, 100.
8. P. 226, contra J. Herrmann, "εὔχομαι," *TDNT,* II, 788f.

argues, for example, that *'āmaḏ* in 1 K. 8:22 merely expresses Solomon's presence before the altar, while v. 54 describes his kneeling in prayer. He cites Neh. 9, where the Israelites stand to read scripture (v. 3a) and prostrate themselves to confess their sins (v. 3b), after which the Levites say, "Stand up and bless the Lord" (v. 5). There is a similar sequence of liturgical actions in Ezr. 9:3,5; 10:1,4. Ap-Thomas explains the sequence of standing and kneeling as reflecting cultic rubrics, maintaining that, at least for confession and petition, the proper posture of prayer was kneeling.[9]

Some passages with *kāra'* show that kneeling could also lead to prostration. Ps. 72:9 states that Yahweh's foes are not only to fall to their knees before him but also to lick the dust (cf. also 1 K. 19:18). The passages that use *hištaḥ^{a}wâ* along with *kāra'* are quite unambiguous. Three occurrences speak of homage to a human being (Est. 3:2 [twice],5), but 5 speak of homage to God (Ps. 22:30[29]; 72:9; 95:6; 2 Ch. 7:3; 29:29).[10] When Ps. 22:30(29); 95:6 mention prostration before kneeling, they are probably amplifying the general description of the act by adding its introduction.

The use of *kāra'* before prostration probably indicates that prostration involved bending over forwards. This is also suggested by licking the dust in Ps. 72:9 and kissing Ba'al in 1 K. 19:18. The posture is described explicitly in 2 Ch. 7:3. There are also passages that speak of prostration following a deep bow, expressed by *qāḏaḏ* (Nu. 22:31; 1 S. 24:9[8]; 1 K. 1:31; etc.). Not so clear are the passages that speak of falling down (*nāpal*) before prostration (Josh. 5:14; 2 S. 9:6; 14:4; 2 Ch. 20:18; Job 1:20). There is probably no OT passage, however, that provides clear evidence for prostration on one's back, as is found elsewhere.[11]

IV. Significance. By kneeling, possibly even bowing down to the ground, one expresses a humble awareness of being an inferior, dependent on an exalted lord. A petitioner kneels to do homage (Est. 3:2,5; 2 K. 1:13). Kneeling before God also represents a confession of faith (Isa. 45:23); Israelites are therefore forbidden to kneel before any foreign god (1 K. 19:18). Kneeling before Yahweh is a special confession of faith: he is our God, we are his people (Ps. 95:6). Because this confession of the covenant faith takes place "before Yahweh" (Ps. 95:6b), we must think in terms of a cultic observance. Ezra, for example, kneels for a penitential ritual at the time of the evening sacrifice, spreads his hands, and pronounces a confession of sin (Ezr. 9:4f.). In 2 Ch. 7:3, we are told how a miraculous fire consumes the burnt offering in a cultic theophany, while the congregation kneels and gives thanks to God (cf. also 1 K. 8:54). In 2 Ch. 29:29, Hezekiah's sacrifice concludes with a prayer of thanksgiving during which the king and the worshippers kneel and prostrate themselves. In the intertestamental period, too, kneeling (*kāra'*) for prayer was customary, although in the NT and Talmudic period standing appears to be the appropriate posture (Mt. 6:5; Mk. 11:25;

9. Cf. also *AncIsr,* 459.

10. For iconographic evidence, see H. J. Boecker and W. Schmauch, "Gebet," *BHHW,* I (1962), 522; O. Keel, *The Symbolism of the Biblical World* (Eng. trans., New York, 1978), figs. 312f., pls. XXIIIf.

11. EA 318f.; *AOB,* fig. 87.

Lk. 18:9-14).[12] Although *kāra'* is used in the sense of "kneel," it can also mean simply "bow down."[13]

Eising†

V. LXX. The LXX uses a series of verbs to translate *kāra'* (*kámptein* [9 times], *píptein* [8], *klínein* [6], *proskyneín,* and *sympodízein* [3 each]). The variety suggests that it does not understand *kāra'* as a clearly defined term denoting a form of devotion and proskynesis.

VI. Dead Sea Scrolls. In the Dead Sea scrolls, the verb *kāra'* appears only in 1QM 11:13, which refers to the Essenes at Qumran as *kôrᵉ'ê 'āpār,* "those who kneel in the dust," into whose power God will deliver the enemy at the eschaton. In the Temple scroll, we find the noun *kr'ym* denoting the "shanks" of a sacrificial animal (11QT 16:12; 24:4; 34:11; cf. 48:5).

Fabry

---

12. Cf. Ap-Thomas, 226.
13. E.g., see St.-B., II, 260.

כָּרַת *kāraṯ;* כְּרֻתוֹת *kᵉruṯôṯ;* כְּרִיתֻת *kᵉrîṯuṯ*

Contents: I. Ancient Near East: 1. Sumerian; 2. Akkadian; 3. West Semitic. II. 1. Etymology; 2. Statistics; 3. Distribution; 4. LXX; 5. Semantically Related Terms; 6. Basic Meaning. III. Religio-theological Usages: 1. Prophetic Writings; 2. Psalms and Proverbs; 3. Historical Literature. IV. Formula-like Phrases: 1. Extermination and Nonextermination Formulas. 2. Covenant-making Formulas. V. Dead Sea Scrolls.

---

kāraṯ. A. Ahuvya, "תוקתו ובריתו אשר כרת," *BethM,* 13/2 (1968), 87-114; J. Barr, "Some Semantic Notes on the Covenant," *Beiträge zur alttestamentliche Theologie. Festschrift W. Zimmerli* (Göttingen, 1977), 23-38; E. Bikerman, " 'Couper une Alliance'," *AHDO* 5 (1950/51), 133-156; E. Kutsch, "כרת *krt* abschneiden," *THAT,* I, 857-860; *idem,* "*Karăt Bᵉrît* 'Eine Verpflichtung festsetzen,' " *Wort und Geschichte. Festschrift K. Elliger. AOAT,* 18 (1973), 121-27; *idem, Verheissung und Gesetz. BZAW,* 131 (1973); S. E. Loewenstamm, "Zur Traditionsgeschichte des Bundes zwischen den Stücken," *VT,* 18 (1968), 500-506; D. J. McCarthy, *Treaty and Covenant. AnBibl,* 21A (²1978); M. Noth, "OT Covenant-making in the Light of a Text from Mari," *The Laws in the Pentateuch* (Eng. trans. 1966, repr. London, 1984), 108-117; F. Sierksma, "Quelques remarques sur la circoncision en Israel," *OTS,* 9 (1951), 136-169; J. A. Soggin, "Akkadisch TAR *BERÎTI* und Hebräisch כרת ברית," *VT,* 18 (1968), 210-15; H. Yalon, "כריתות, כָּרַת, הכרת," *Lešonénu la-'Am,* 18 (1967), 259-261; W. Zimmerli, "Die Eigenart der prophetischen Rede des Ezekiel," *ZAW,* 66 (1954), 1-26 = *Gottes Offenbarung. Gesammelte Aufsätze,* 1. *ThB,* 19 (²1969), 148-177.

I. Ancient Near East.

1. *Sumerian.* The words *kur*$_5$*/kud* and *sil.ḫaš,* written with the Sumerian logogram TAR, provide such meanings as "separate, divide, cut."[1] The logogram appears frequently in Neo-Sumerian legal documents with the object *nam-erím* "evil" > "curse," in the phrase *nam-erím*-TAR, " 'cut' a curse,"[2] in the sense of "swear to an assertion."[3] In royal legal proceedings TAR means literally "cut an oath" or "swear an oath";[4] figuratively it can also mean "decide" a court case.[5] The logogram TAR is generally equated with the Akkadian verb *parāsu,* "separate, decide,"[6] or *parā'u,* "cut."[7]

2. *Akkadian.* In Akkadian, the verb *karātu*[8] is used literally for "cutting off" a tail[9] or hands[10] or "breaking off" horns.[11] It exhibits a similarity to the range of meanings in Hebrew. In ritual texts, *karātu* has the meaning "cut"[12] or "break" (clay figurines with sticks of ash wood).[13] The verbal adj. *kartu*[14] is used in connection with a "cut-up reed"[15] which is to be burned.

3. *West Semitic.* The root *krt* (meaning?) has been found in Ugaritic only in the name "Keret," the hero of the epic of Keret.[16] The root *gzr,* "cut off, separate,"[17] is represented by the nouns *gzr,* "piece, portion,"[18] and *'gzrt,* "one cut or pinched off" > "image."[19]

---

1. *ŠL,* II, 45; III, 205.
2. A. Falkenstein, *Die neusumerischen Gerichtsurkunden,* I. *ABAW,* N.S. 39 (1956), 64; *idem,* III. *ABAW,* N.S. 44 (1957), 144f., 165; cf. D. O. Edzard, *Sumerische Rechtsurkunden des III. Jahrtausends aus der Zeit von der III. Dynastie von Ur. ABAW,* N.S. 67 (1968), 223.
3. Falkenstein, I, 64, 67; III, 144f.; Edzard, 152, no. 96, vo. ll. 3′-4′.
4. A. Gamper, *Gott als Richter in Mesopotamien und im AT* (Innsbruck, 1966), 16-21.
5. Falkenstein, II, 226f.
6. *AHw,* II (1972), 830-32.
7. *ŠL,* III, 205; R. Borger, *Assyrisch-babylonische Zeichenliste. AOAT,* 33 (1978), 59, no. 12.
8. *AHw,* I (1965), 448; *CAD,* VIII (1971), 215.
9. *KAR,* 307, r. 14.
10. Ash, §68, III, 24.
11. *KAR,* 307, r. 13.
12. G. van Driel, *The Cult of Aššur. SSN,* 13 (1969), 194, l. 3; context not clear.
13. Maqlû, IX, 159, 181; *CAD,* VIII, 215.
14. *AHw,* I, 451; *CAD,* VIII, 226.
15. E. Reiner, *Šurpu. BAfO,* 11 (1958), I, 2; *KAR,* 90, r. 1; cf. E. Ebeling, *Tod und Leben nach den Vorstellungen der Babylonier* (Berlin, 1931), 118.
16. *UT,* no. 1314; *PNU,* 152.
17. M. Dietrich and O. Loretz, "GZR 'Abschneiden, Abkneifen' im Ugar. und Hebr.," *UF,* 9 (1977), 51-16; cf. *UT,* no. 570; *WUS,* nos. 642f.
18. *KTU,* 1.23, 63.
19. *KTU,* 1.13, 29f.; 1.23, 58, 61.

The Mesha inscription (*ca.* 840-830 B.C.) contains the much-debated clause *w'nk krty hmkrtt l,*[20] usually translated: "and I cut beams."[21] This translation derives from the Moabite perf. *krty* and the noun *mkrtt*[22] from the root *krt.*[23] The Moabite forms have also been associated with the root *krh,* "dig."[24] The proposed association of *krty* with *krt* in the sense of making a covenant,[25] equating Moab. *krt mkrtt l* with Heb. *kāraṯ b^e^rîṯ l^e^* meaning "he cut the 'thing in between' in behalf of"[26] or simply "and I made a covenant for,"[27] is hardly supportable, because the Moabite expression has no philological or syntactic equivalent in Hebrew; furthermore, the context of the Mesha inscription speaks of building activities, which have nothing to do with making a covenant. The forms *krty* and *mkrtt* can be assigned to the root *krt* with some assurance.[28]

A Phoenician incantation text from Arslan Tash (7th century B.C.) contains the expressions *kr[r]t ln 'lt,*[29] "cut (make) a covenant with us,"[30] and *'šr krt ln,*[31] often translated elliptically as "Ashur made [a covenant] with us"[32] or "he has made out a bond for us."[33] The phrase *krt 'lt* is generally taken as equivalent to *krt 'ālâ* (Dt. 29:11,13[12,14])[34] and thus *krt b^e^rîṯ* (cf. Isa. 61:8; Jer. 32:40), but the linguistic parallel is not absolute. The Hebrew expression *krt 'ālâ* is not attested independently,[35] because *krt* refers to both *b^e^rîṯ* and *'ālâ* (Dt. 29:11,13[12,14]).

The Punic noun *krt* is an uncertain reading in the clause "the vow that ʿZMLK the

---

20. L. 25.

21. Cf. *ANET*³, 320; A. H. van Zyl, *The Moabites. POS,* 3 (1960); *DISO,* 127; *LidzNE,* 299; A. Lemaire, "'House of David' Restored in Moabite Inscription," *BAR* 20/3 (1994), 33; etc.

22. *KBL*³, 477; M. Noth, *Könige 1–16. BK,* IX/1 (1968), 102.

23. For the verb, cf. R. S. Tomback, *A Comparative Semitic Lexicon of the Phoenician and Punic Languages. SBL Diss.,* 32 (Missoula, 1978), 149.

24. S. Segert, "Die Sprache der moabitischen Königsinschriften," *ArOr,* 29 (1961), 242; followed by *KAI,* II, 178; J. C. L. Gibson, *Textbook of Syrian Semitic Inscriptions,* I (Oxford, ²1973), 77, 82.

25. F. I. Anderson, "Moabite Syntax," *Or,* 35 (1966), 107.

26. E. Lipiński, "Etymological and Exegetical Notes on the Mešaʿ Inscription," *Or,* 40 (1971), 337.

27. E. Lipiński in W. Beyerlin, ed., *Near Eastern Religious Texts Relating to the OT. OTL* (Eng. trans. 1978), 239, l. 25.

28. Contra E. Kutsch, *THAT,* I, 857.

29. *KAI,* 27, 8f., with dittography; cf. F. M. Cross, *Canaanite Myth and Hebrew Epic* (Cambridge, Mass., 1973), 17f.; A. Caquot, "Observations sur la Première Tablette Magique d'Arslan Tash," *Festschrift T. H. Gaster. JANES,* 5 (1973), 48.

30. Cf. W. Röllig in R. Degen, W. W. Müller, and Röllig, *Neue Ephemeris für Semitische Epigraphik,* II (Wiesbaden, 1928), 21; *KAI,* 27; J. Friedrich, *Phönizisch-Punische Grammatik. AnOr,* 46 (²1970), 131; *DISO,* 127.

31. *KAI,* 27, 10f.

32. Röllig, *Neue Ephemeris,* II, 18; Z. Zevit, "A Phoenician Inscription and Biblical Covenant Theology," *IEJ,* 27 (1977), 112; *ANET*³, 658.

33. Lipiński, *Near Eastern Religious Texts,* 248.

34. Cf. T. H. Gaster, "A Canaanite Magical Text," *Or,* 11 (1942), 65.

35. *KBL*³, 476, is inexact; cf. Barr, 28, n. 5.

stonecutter [?; *hkrt*] took."[36] The meaning of the verb *krt* is also uncertain in a Neo-Punic text: "[upon] its ruins he cut (*hykrt*) the foundation."[37]

The Hadad statue of Panammuwa I (mid-8th century B.C.) contains two lines in which *krt* has been restored.[38] The first reads: "he cut [(*hkr*)*t*] sword and tongue from the house of my father."[39] The subject is Hadad, who put an end to the revolutionary disturbances.[40] The restoration in line 11 is more secure: "and he made a treaty."[41] The meaning "make [lit., 'cut'] a treaty" for *'mn kr*[*t*][42] is supported by Neh. 10:1[Eng. 9:38] and may be considered certain.[43]

Mandaic employs *kruta* with the uncertain meaning "cutting off, mutilation" and has the uncertain root *krt*.[44] In Syriac, *krt* has a wide range of uses.[45]

In Tigre we find *karta,* "take an end,"[46] and *kärtäta,* "bite off,"[47] and in Tigriña, *kärāta,* "cut."[48]

II. 1. *Etymology.* The Hebrew root *krt* is of Common Semitic origin and has its correspondences in Akkadian[49] and West Semitic.[50] Note should also be taken of parallel expressions in Sumerian[51] and in Aramaic in the form *gzr,* "cut" > "cut off, cut up, cut apart," abstractly "decide, determine."[52]

The root *krt* appears in five Hebrew verbal forms: qal, niphal, pual, hiphil, and hophal. Occasionally niphal forms (Josh. 3:13,16; 4:7 [twice]; Job 14:7; Sir. 44:18) and both pual forms (Jgs. 6:28; Ezk. 16:4) represent the passive of the qal. The niphal is usually used intensively in the sense of "exterminate."[53] This extended meaning is also attested twice for the qal (Jer. 11:19; 50:16; emendation is not necessary).[54]

---

36. Tomback, 150; *DISO,* 127.
37. *KAR,* 12 (1963/64), 50; Tomback, 150.
38. *KAI,* 214, 9, 11.
39. The restoration proposed by H. D. Müller, "Die altsemitischen Inschriften von Sendschirli," *WZKM,* 7 (1893), 33-70, 113-140, has been accepted by many, including Gibson, *Textbook of Syrian Semitic Inscriptions,* II (Oxford, 1975), 71, l. 9.
40. Cf. *KAI,* II, 218.
41. Cf. Gibson, II, 67, 11: "and a sure covenant struck."
42. Cf. S. A. Cook, *A Glossary of the Aramaic Inscriptions* (Cambridge, 1898), 66.
43. Cf. J. J. Koopmans, *Aramäische Chrestomathie* (Leiden, 1962), II, nos. 9, 11; cf. *KAI,* 214, restored as *k*(*'t*).
44. *MdD,* 223.
45. *LexSyr,* 583f.
46. *TigrWB.*
47. Leslau, *Contributions,* 27.
48. *Ibid.*; cf. W. Leslau, *Etymological Dictionary of Hariri* (Berkeley, 1963), 130.
49. See I.2 above.
50. See I.3 above.
51. See I.1 above.
52. Cf. Z. W. Falk, "Hebrew Legal Terms: III," *JSS,* 14 (1969), 43f.; for biblical usage, see II.5 below.
53. See III.2; IV below.
54. Cf. *BHK*/*BHS*; W. Rudolph, *Jeremia. HAT,* XII ([3]1968), 302.

The verbal noun k^e*ruṯôṯ* (a fem. pl. derived from the qal pass. ptcp.), literally, "cut off pieces," is found only in 1 K. 6:36; 7:2,12 in the sense of dressed and trimmed "beams,"[55] possibly more exactly "sections (of cedar trunks) trimmed shorter in contrast to timbers."[56]

The verbal noun k^e*rîṯuṯ,* "divorce, separation,"[57] also derives from the root *krt* (Dt. 24:1,3; Isa. 50:1; Jer. 3:8); this resembles the meaning of *krt,* "separate [a marriage], divorce," in Middle Hebrew.[58]

It is a matter of debate whether the name of the brook Cherith (1 K. 17:3,5) derives from *krt*[59] or *krh,* "dig, make a hole."[60]

2. *Statistics.* Derivatives of the root *krt* occur 295 times in the OT. The verb appears 288 times: 134 times in the qal, 73 in the niphal,[61] 78 in the hiphil, twice in the pual, and once in the hophal. The nouns appear 7 times: k^e*rîṯuṯ*[62] 4 times and k^e*ruṯôṯ*[63] 3 times. These numbers do not include the 2 occurrences of k^e*rîṯ*.[64]

3. *Distribution.* Verbs and nouns deriving from *krt* appear in 33 books of the OT — all but Jonah, Habakkuk, Song of Songs, Ecclesiastes, Lamentations, and Esther. The Pentateuch uses 69 verbal forms (31 qal, 28 niphal, 10 hiphil), the prophetic books 100 (33 qal, including 16 in Jeremiah and 8 in Isaiah; 22 niphal, including 6 in Isaiah and 4 in Jeremiah; 43 hiphil, including 14 in Ezekiel, 7 in Jeremiah, and 4 in Isaiah; 1 pual [Ezk. 16:4]; and 1 hophal [Joel 1:6]), the historical books 96 (64 qal, including 18 in 1-2 Samuel, 16 in 1-2 Kings, and 6 each in Joshua and Judges; 11 niphal, including 5 in Joshua; 20 hiphil, including 8 in 1-2 Kings and 6 in 1-2 Samuel; 1 pual [Jgs. 6:28]), the Psalms 14 (4 qal, 5 each niphal and hiphil), and Wisdom Literature 7 (4 niphal in Ecclesiastes, 2 qal and 1 niphal in Job). A niphal occurs in Dnl. 9:26; Ruth 4:10. The distribution of these occurrences throughout the entire OT from the earliest texts to the latest books bears witness to the extensive range of the root's literal and extended semantic spheres of meaning.

4. *LXX.* The LXX uses a great variety of Greek words to translate the Hebrew verbal forms. The verb *exolethreúein* appears 77 times (42 times translating a hiphil, 31 times a niphal, and 4 times a qal); the related *olethreúein* appears 4 times (twice translating a qal,

---

55. *KBL*³, 477.

56. Noth, *BK,* IX/1, 102, 135, rejecting the LXX reading *kōṯārôṯ,* "capitals," in 7:2.

57. *KBL*³, 473; E. Neufeld, *Ancient Hebrew Marriage Laws* (London, 1944), 180, n. 2.

58. Jastrow, 674; *WTM,* II, 418f.

59. *KBL*³, 477; *BLe,* 471s.

60. *KBL*³, 473; *BLe,* 504m; A. W. Schwarzenbach, *Die geographische Terminologie im Hebräischen des ATs* (Leiden, 1954), 203; Kutsch, *THAT,* I, 857.

61. Lisowsky, 702a, cites Nu. 15:31 only once and therefore has only 72 occurrences of the niphal.

62. See II.1 above.

63. See II.1 above.

64. See II.1 above.

once each a hiphil and pual).[65] Almost as common is *diatithénai,* with 74 occurrences, of which 68 are in the significant phrase *diatíthesthai diathḗkēn,* which usually translates *kārat̲ b^erît̲.*[66] The related *tithénai* appears only 5 times. The verb *kóptein* and its compounds appear 34 times, including 14 occurrences of *ekkóptein* and 2 of *apokóptein.*[67] The following verbs also deserve mention: *exaírein* (20 times), *apolýein/apolýnai* (14 times), *ekleípein* (11 times), *aphaírein* (9 times), *ektríbein* (6 times), *aphanízein* and *poíein* (3 times), *aphistán* and *syntélein* (twice). There are 20 other verbal forms that appear once. The use of these 36 Greek words and their distribution shows that the Hebrew verbal forms embody a variety of semantic nuances. The LXX does not exhibit any consistent approach to translation, not even in the phrase *diatíthesthai diathḗkēn,* which also represents the verbs *hēqîm* (Gen. 9:17) and *ṣiwwâ* (Josh. 7:11) with *b^erît̲* as object.

5. *Semantically Related Terms.* Semantically close to the niphal of *krt* with the meaning "exterminate, destroy" is the Hebrew verb → שׁמד *šmd* niphal, "exterminate, destroy" (Isa. 48:19; Ps. 37:38). The hiphil of this verb also resembles the hiphil of *krt* in the sense of "annihilate" (Lev. 26:30; 1 S. 24:22[21]; Isa. 10:7; Ezk. 25:7). In the "extermination formula,"[68] the hiphil of *krt* can be used interchangeably with the hiphil of *šmd* (Dt. 4:3; Ezk. 14:8f.) and the hiphil of → אבד *'āb̲ad̲* (Lev. 23:30).[69] In parallelism with the niphal of *krt* we find *dmh* III, "be destroyed" (Zeph. 1:11).[70] There appears to be a mimetic and figurative semantic relation to *krt* in the general Semitic root *ḥrṣ,*[71] found in Hebrew in verbal forms with the figurative meaning "threaten, determine"[72] and in the noun forms *ḥārûṣ* and *ḥārîṣ* I.[73] The Hebrew verb → גזר *gzr* with the literal meaning "cut (apart)" and the figurative meaning "decide"[74] exhibits a number of spheres of meaning identical with *krt.* Finally, we must note the hapax legomenon *ḥtk,* "cut off, determine" (Dnl. 9:24),[75] which has reflexes in Akkadian,[76] Ugaritic,[77] and Arabic.[78]

6. *Basic Meaning.* The basic meaning of the verb *kārat̲* can be defined with relative

---

65. Cf. J. Schneider, "ὀλεθρεύω," *TDNT,* V, 167, 171.
66. Cf. J. Behm and G. Quell, "διατίθημι," *TDNT,* II, 104-134.
67. Cf. G. Stählin, "ἀποκόπτω," *TDNT,* III, 852-60.
68. See IV.1 below.
69. Cf. K. Elliger, *Leviticus. HAT,* IV (1966), 310, 319, n. 24; E. Jenni, "אבד *'bd* zugrunde gehen," *THAT,* I, 19.
70. Cf. *KBL*³, 216.
71. *AHw,* I, 326; *UT,* no. 900; *DISO,* 96.
72. *KBL*³, 341.
73. *KBL*³, 338f.
74. *KBL*³, 179f.
75. Cf. J. L. Palache, *Semantic Notes on the Hebrew Lexicon* (Eng. trans., Leiden, 1959), 19; J. Doukhan, "The Seventy Weeks of Daniel 9: An Exegetical Study," *AUSS,* 17 (1979), 6 and n. 11.
76. *AHw,* I, 335.
77. *UT,* no. 911: in the context of a father-son relationship, where the son is a "chip" off the father.
78. Lane, I/2, 510, col. 3: "walk with short steps, and quickly; scrape up, dig up, hollow out."

certainty as "cut" (Isa. 18:5);[79] this meaning is supported by the usage of other Semitic languages (Akkadian, Moabite, Old Aramaic, Neo-Punic). The meanings "chop down, cut off"[80] or simply "cut off"[81] do not need to be considered primary; like various other nuances, they result from the use of the verb with different objects: "cutting off" branches (Nu. 13:23), grapes (v. 24), the corner of a garment (1 S. 24:5,6,12[4,5,11]), parts of the body such as the foreskin (Ex. 4:25), testicles (Lev. 22:24), or the male member (Dt. 23:2[1]); "cutting off" > "chopping off" a head (1 S. 17:51; 31:9; 2 S. 20:22), head and hands (1 S. 5:4), or a branch (Jgs. 9:48) or limb (v. 49); "cutting away" a garment (2 S. 10:4 par. 1 Ch. 19:4); "cutting off" > "breaking down" asherahs (Ex. 34:13; Jgs. 6:25,26,30; 2 K. 18:4; 23:14) and abominable images (1 K. 15:13 par. 2 Ch. 15:16);[82] "cutting" > "felling" trees (Dt. 19:5; 20:19,20; Jer. 6:6; 10:3; 11:19; 1 K. 5:20[6]; 2 Ch. 2:7,9,15[8,10,16]), cedars (Isa. 44:14; Ezk. 31:12), cedars and cypresses (Isa. 37:24), or forests (Jer. 46:23). The qal of *krt* is used figuratively in the sense of "annihilate" with reference to a prophet (Jer. 11:19) or sower and reaper (50:16). In the other stems, the figurative meaning predominates.

III. Religio-theological Usages.

1. *Prophetic Writings.* a. *Israel and the Remnant.* In the book of Joel, a natural catastrophe in which the food supply is destroyed (*krt* niphal: Joel 1:16) is a harbinger of the day of Yahweh; this destruction calls a halt even to worship. The details of the "day of Yahweh" include the threat that the money-changers (synecdoche for the financiers and their financial system; Zeph. 1:11) and idolaters (v. 4) will be "cut off" or destroyed (cf. Zec. 13:2; Ezk. 14:8,13,17,19,21; 17:17). Because the destruction of the nations has not served as an example for the people of God and their leaders (Zeph. 3:6,7),[83] Yahweh comes to judge the world, "cutting off" everything that lives (Zeph. 1:3; cf. Gen. 9:11). It is prophesied that Israel's "head and tail" will be cut off (Isa. 9:13[14]) and that God's judgment of total annihilation will strike Judah (Jer. 44:7,8,11). God's eschatological annihilation will destroy horses (Mic. 5:9[10]), the cities of the land (v. 10[11]), sorceries (v. 11[12]; cf. Dt. 18:10f.; Lev. 19:26; Jer. 27:9), idols and asherahs (Mic. 5:12[13]), and bows (synecdoche for weapons; Zec. 9:10) — everything that gives a false sense of security; but a purified remnant will emerge (Zec. 13:9). It is promised that those who are left will not be destroyed (Zec. 14:2; cf. Gen. 9:11).

Apocalyptic literature includes predictions of the destruction of the *māšîaḥ* (Dnl. 9:26), identified primarily with Onias II of the Maccabean period[84] or Christ.[85]

---

79. Cf. *GesB,* 364.
80. Kutsch, *Verheissung und Gesetz,* 40.
81. Kutsch, *THAT,* I, 858.
82. Cf. Noth, *BK,* IX/1, 324.
83. Cf. K. Elliger, *Das Buch der zwölf kleinen Propheten, II: Zephanja. ATD,* XXV (^{7}1975), 76f.
84. Cf., among others, L. F. Hartman and A. A. DiLella, *The Book of Daniel. AB,* XXIII (1978), 252; A. Lacocque, *The Book of Daniel* (Eng. trans., Atlanta, 1979), 196.
85. Cf., among others, B. K. Waltke, "The Date of the Book of Daniel," *BS,* 133 (1976), 329; J. G. Baldwin, *Daniel. TOTC* (1978), 175-78.

b. *Oracles against the Nations.* The term "cut off" or "destroy" (*krt* hiphil) is a common expression of divine judgment in the oracles against the nations of the major (Isa. 14:22; Jer. 47:4; 48:2; 51:62; Ezk. 21:8,9[3,4]; 25:7,13,16; 29:8; 30:15; 35:7) and minor prophets (Am. 1:5,8; 2:3; Ob. 14 [cf. 9,10]; Zec. 9:6). In this destruction, Yahweh proves himself the lord of history, demonstrating his ultimate superiority by destroying the idols and gods of the Gentiles (Nah. 1:14; 2:1,14[1:15; 2:13]; 3:15). In his punishment, Yahweh includes the empire of Assyria, which overstepped its commission by destroying many nations (Isa. 10:7), and the empire of Babylon (14:22),[86] which experiences total destruction of name and remnant, offspring and posterity. This general destruction carried out by God in the prophetic oracles against the nations takes on universal scope in OT apocalypticism.

2. *Psalms and Proverbs.* In the Psalms, the notion of destruction frequently refers to the hostile powers that appear as enemies of the righteous.[87] In his acute distress, he appeals to Yahweh to destroy those who are wicked and evil, to blot out their memory (Ps. 34:17[16]; 109:15) and cut off their posterity (37:28; 109:13). The wicked[88] plots against the righteous, who remains faithful to the covenant relationship with Yahweh (37:12); he lies in wait for him and seeks to slay him (v. 32; 94:21). God, however, does not abandon the righteous; God sees that he is not condemned when brought to trial (37:33) and assures him that he will see the destruction of the wicked (vv. 9,34,38). God's justice finds expression in the divine anathema that cuts off all who are cursed (37:22) and in the divine judgment that destroys all lying lips and boasting tongues (12:4[3]). Also noteworthy is the duty of the king in Jerusalem to enforce justice by cutting off all evildoers (cf. 5:6[5]; 6:9[8]; 14:4f.; 28:3)[89] from the city of God (101:8).

Israelite proverbs speak of cutting off the wicked from the land (Prov. 2:22; 10:31), while the devout continue to dwell in it through Yahweh's grace.[90]

3. *Historical Literature.* The historical books also commonly use the hiphil of *krt* to mean "exterminate." In the context of the wars of Yahweh, we are told that Joshua wiped out the Elamites (Josh. 11:21) and all the nations (23:4). From the period of the judges, we have the statement that the Israelites destroyed Jabin king of Canaan (Jgs. 4:24). In the period of the monarchy, we are told that Yahweh exterminated the enemies of David (1 S. 20:15; 2 S. 7:9 par. 1 Ch. 17:8), that Saul cut off the mediums and wizards (1 S. 28:9), that Joab destroyed every male in Edom (1 K. 11:16), that Jehu cut off the house of Jeroboam (14:10,14), and that Jezebel cut off the prophets of Yahweh (18:4).

Yahweh will show himself as Destroyer of every male descendant of Ahab (1 K.

86. Cf. G. F. Hasel, *The Remnant. AUM,* 5 (^{2}1974), 359-364.

87. → צדק *ṣaddîq.*

88. → רשע *rāšāʿ.*

89. → און *'āwen ('āven),* I, 146; H.-J. Kraus, *The Theology of the Psalms* (Eng. trans., Minneapolis, 1986), 152.

90. Cf. W. L. McKane, *Proverbs. OTL* (1970), 288.

21:21; 2 K. 9:8; cf. 2 Ch. 22:7). If Israel turns aside from Yahweh, it will be cut off (1 K. 9:7), just as Yahweh cut off the nations from before Israel (cf. Dt. 12:29; 19:1).

In the covenant of friendship between David and Jonathan (1 S. 20:8),[91] Jonathan asks David to promise never to cut off his covenant loyalty (v. 15).[92]

IV. Formula-like Phrases.

1. *Extermination and Nonextermination Formulas.* A formulaic idiom appears in the judicial sentence *w^enik̲r^et̲â hannep̲eš hahîʾ,* which combines the basic meaning of the verb with the basic meaning of the subject *nep̲eš,* literally, "the throat shall be cut (through)." This formula should probably be translated: "and the person in question shall be cut out."[93] It is commonly called an "extermination formula" or (following one interpretation) "excommunication formula."[94] The niphal is found 24 times (Gen. 17:14; Ex. 12:15,19; 30:33,38; 31:14; Lev. 7:20,21,25,27; 17:4,9,14; 18:29; 19:8; 20:17,18; 22:3; 23:29; Nu. 9:13; 15:30,31; 19:13,20) and the hiphil 5 times with God as subject (Lev. 17:10; 20:3,5,6; Ezk. 14:8; cf. Lev. 26:30; Ezk. 14:13,17,19,21) in connection with this formula.[95] Added emphasis is lent by separative expressions such as *min* (13 times: Gen. 17:14; Ex. 12:15,19; 30:33,38; Lev. 7:20ff.; etc.), *miqqereb̲,* "from among" (5 times: Ex. 31:14; Lev. 18:29; 20:18; 23:30; Nu. 15:30; cf. Dt. 4:3 with *šmd*), *mittôk̲,* "from the midst" (Nu. 19:20), and "before the eyes" (Lev. 20:17), which reflect extirpation in the sense of being cut off from a center or a circle in which the offender lives. This circle from which the offender is removed is defined more particularly as *ʿammîm,* "[own] people, family" (12 times: Gen. 17:14; Ex. 30:33,38; 31:14; Lev. 7:20ff.; Nu. 9:13; etc.), *ʿam,* "people," in the sense of "covenant community"[96] or even more narrowly in the sense of "clan,"[97] "Israel" (Ex. 12:15; Nu. 19:13), "assembly of Israel" in the sense of "cultic community" (Ex. 12:19), or "assembly" (Nu. 19:20). Originally, the circle from which the offender was cut off appears to have been the larger family; it was then extended to the cultic community and all Israel as the covenant people.

Offenses of the perpetrator that break the covenant include refusal to be circumcised (Gen. 17:14), transgression of the Passover ordinance (Ex. 12:15,19; Nu. 9:13), failure to fast on the Day of Atonement (Lev. 23:29), profanation of the Sabbath (Ex. 31:14), consuming sacrificial fat (Lev. 7:25) or blood (v. 27), eating sacrificial flesh while

91. H. J. Stoebe, "חֶסֶד \ud\aaœs\aaœd Güte," *THAT,* I, 608f.

92. Cf. D. W. Thomas, "A Consideration of Some Unusual Ways of Expressing the Superlative in Hebrew," *VT,* 3 (1953), 209-224.

93. Cf. R. Meyer, *Hebräische Grammatik,* I (Berlin, ^{3}1969), § 31.4.

94. Zimmerli, *ZAW,* 66 (1954), 19; also D. Vetter, "שׁמד *šmd* hi. vertilgen," *THAT,* II, 964; A. R. Hulst, "עם/גוי *ʿam/goj* Volk," *THAT,* II, 297; G. von Rad, *OT Theology,* I (Eng. trans., New York, 1962), 264, n. 182.

95. W. Zimmerli, *Ezekiel I. Herm* (Eng. trans. 1979), 310ff.

96. Zimmerli, *ZAW,* 66 (1954), 17; cf. *Ezekiel* I, 313.

97. Hulst, *THAT,* II, 297f.

unclean (vv. 20,21) or on the third day (19:8), unauthorized use of anointing oil or incense (Ex. 30:33,38), transgression of sexual ordinances (Lev. 20:18f.), various regulations governing uncleanness (Lev. 22:3; Nu. 19:13,20), idolatry (Lev. 20:3,5,6; Ezk. 14:8f.; cf. Lev. 26:30), or despising the word or commandment of Yahweh (Nu. 15:30,31). This list shows that the offenses are against religion, morality, or sacral law (Walther Zimmerli's restriction to the latter[98] can hardly be maintained).

Various proposals have been made as to how the sentence of "cutting off" was executed.[99] It is certain that the final goal of the sentence was the premature death of the offender (Ex. 31:14; Lev. 20:2-6),[100] as is also clear in later talmudic law.[101] Two passages speak of execution carried out by the offender's own people: for profanation of the Sabbath (Ex. 31:14; cf. Nu. 15:32-36) and for sacrificing children to Molech (Lev. 20:2). These passages show clearly that an institutional judgment convicts the offender and sentences him to death; the offender is "cut off" when the sentence is executed. If the offender is not executed, Yahweh himself will "cut off" the offender and his kin (Lev. 20:4ff.). The "cutting off" formula therefore does not appear to refer solely to human execution of the death penalty. In the majority of offenses, "cutting off" means a "cutting out" which leads to "banishment"[102] or "excommunication"[103] from the cultic community and the covenant people (compare Lev. 20:17 with CH §154, which also speaks of banishment), except for offenses that can hardly come to public notice (cf. Ex. 30:38; Lev. 7:20f.; Nu. 15:30f.), which cannot be punished by human agency. In the case of offenses that lead to exclusion from one's own clan (cf. Gen. 17:14) and from the covenant community, as in the case of secret sins that cannot be punished institutionally, the ultimate end of the punishment, the premature death of the offender, is in God's hands (cf. *krt* hiphil in Lev. 17:10; 20:3,5,6; Ezk. 14:8-14).

These observations show that the "extermination" formula as such does not denote banishment or excommunication in every instance; it should therefore not be called an "excommunication" formula. Neither does it simply denote the premature death the offender suffers when the sentence is executed by human agents. On the contrary, it expresses the fact that the ultimate punishment is in God's hands; only in certain cases has God designated human agents to carry it out (Lev. 20:2; cf. Ex. 31:14). In other cases, the cultic community or the clan can "cut off" the offender (to the extent that his offense is known) from life in God's presence through exclusion. The one so cut off is then left to God as the ultimate agent of final punishment.

A formula of "nonextermination," conditional upon keeping the covenant with

98. *ZAW,* 66 (1954), 15.

99. See J. L. Saalschütz, *Das mosaische Recht* (Wiesbaden, ^{2}1853, repr. 1974), 476ff.; Elliger, *HAT,* IV, 101; G. J. Wenham, *The Book of Leviticus. NICOT* (1979), 241f.

100. J. Morgenstern, "Addenda to 'The Book of the Covenant, Part III — The *Ḥuqqim,*'" *HUCA,* 8f. (1931/32), 46-48 and 43, n. 51; Zimmerli, *ZAW,* 66 (1954), 18f.

101. M. Tsevat, "Studies in the Book of Samuel. I: Interpretation of I Sam. 2:22-36," *HUCA,* 32 (1961), 197-201.

102. Zimmerli, *ZAW,* 66 (1954), 19.

103. Morgenstern, *HUCA,* 8f. (1931/32), 33-58.

David (2 Sam. 7), appears in the statement "there shall not fail (lit., 'not be cut off') you a man/successor on the throne of Israel" (1 K. 2:4; 8:25 par. 2 Ch. 6:16; 1 K. 9:5 par. 2 Ch. 7:18). The promise to David that his descendants would continue upon the throne of Israel is repeated in these statements in conjunction with various conditions (cf. Ps. 132:12) and is confirmed by Yahweh (Jer. 33:17). The formula of "nonextermination" is also used of the levitical priests (Jer. 33:18) and Jonadab the son of Rechab (35:19). The Jeremiah texts say nothing of any condition on which Yahweh's act depends. The same usage appears in the statement of the nonextermination of someone's name (Isa. 48:19; 56:5; Ruth 4:10), which insures the continuance of a person, family, and group (cf. Josh. 7:9; Isa. 14:22; Zeph. 1:4). The "nonextermination" formula can also promise the continuance of a family (Nu. 4:18; 1 S. 24:22[21]; cf. 2:33) or of Israel (Isa. 48:9). Yahweh promises that faithfulness (Jer. 7:28) and a sign (Isa. 55:13) will not be cut off.

2. *Covenant Making Formula.* The theologically important phrase *kāraṯ bᵉrîṯ* appears frequently (80 usages). It does not mean: (a) "to slaughter a covenant sacrifice";[104] (b) "cut off food";[105] (c) "knot a net";[106] (d) "make a covenant through an oath" in the sense of an "oath sworn by God";[107] or (e) "stipulate a requirement or obligation."[108] The phrase means literally "cut a covenant,"[109] like the Sumerian expression *nam-erím*-TAR, "cut a curse,"[110] in which TAR literally means "cut." In the Hebrew phrase, the verb *kāraṯ* has an idiomatic meaning[111] that can be derived from the literal meaning "cut." The direct object is no longer expressed in *kāraṯ bᵉrîṯ,* but can be reconstructed from an animal ritual that accompanies covenant-making. A different object (*bᵉrîṯ*), which denotes the purpose of the action, has replaced it.[112] The idiomatic meaning of *kāraṯ* appears in synonymous expressions with *dāḇār* (Hag. 2:5; Ps. 105:8f. [par. 1 Ch. 16:15f.][113]), *'ᵃmānâ* (Neh. 10:1[9:38]), and *'ālâ* (Dt. 29:11,13[12,14]),[114] as well as in absolute usage without an object, in the sense of "cut > make a covenant" (Isa. 57:8; 1 S. 20:16; 22:8; 1 K. 8:9 par. 2 Ch. 5:10; 2 Ch. 7:18[115]); in 1 S. 11:2, *kāraṯ* is used absolutely but the object is clear from v. 1.

---

104. J. Fürst, *A Hebrew and Chaldee Lexicon to the OT* (Eng. trans., Leipzig, ⁴1871), 702; similarly E. König, *Hebräisches und aramäisches Wörterbuch* (Leipzig, ⁷1936), 189.

105. L. Koehler, "Problems in the Study of the Language of the OT," *JSS,* 1 (1956), 7.

106. M. Fraenkel, "Karat bᵉrit = Einen Bund schliessen," *International Anthropological and Linguistic Review,* 3 (1957/58), 37-46.

107. N. Lohfink, *Die Landverheissung als Eid. SBS,* 28 (1967), 107f.

108. Kutsch, *Festschrift K. Elliger,* 127; opposed by McCarthy, 92f., n. 25.

109. Cf. M. Weinfeld, "ברית *bᵉrîṯ* (*bᵉrîth*)," II, 259f.

110. See I.1 above.

111. Barr, 28.

112. Quell, *TDNT,* II, 108f., with bibliog.

113. See M. Dahood, *Psalms III. AB,* XVIIA (1970), 53f.

114. See I.3 above for similar usage in Phoenician.

115. See W. Rudolph, *Chronikbücher. HAT,* XXI (1955), 211; see I.3 above for the identical usage in Phoenician.

The idiomatic meaning of the formula *kāraṯ bᵉrîṯ,* "make a covenant," appears to derive from a ritual associated with the covenant. In Jer. 34:18, *kāraṯ* in the sense of "cut apart" is used of a heifer between the separated parts of which the subordinate parties to the covenant pass (v. 19). Although the textual problem of Jer. 34:18f. is almost insoluble,[116] there seems to be a parallel in the substitutionary ritual of a vassal treaty of Ashurnirari V (8th century): "This spring lamb was not brought from its flock to be sacrificed. . . . It was brought to sanction the treaty between Ashurnirari and Mati'ilu. . . . This is not the head of the lamb, it is the head of Mati'ilu. . . . Just as this lamb's head is cut off . . . , so may be head of Mati'ilu be cut off."[117] This symbolic action is a ritual of self-cursing, representing the fate of an offending vassal.[118]

The meaning of the animal ceremony in Gen. 15:9f.,17 differs from that in Jer. 34:18f.[119] Gen. 15:10 uses the verb *btr,* "cut in half, cut into two parts," for the cutting up of sacrificial animals (cf. the tradition of the 3rd millennium that describes the slaying of animals and doves in the treaty between Naram-Sin and the Elamites[120] and the treaty between Lagash and Umma[121]). In Gen. 15:18, however, *kāraṯ bᵉrîṯ* summarizes what has taken place; here the emphasis is on the animal ceremony as an act of covenant-making. In Gen. 15:17, unlike Jer. 34:18f., Yahweh himself passes through the divided animals. Abraham, as the other party to the covenant, takes no part in this ceremony. The ritual does not signify the agreement of the covenanting parties,[122] the appropriation of the vital force of either animal or deity,[123] or the self-cursing of the party passing between the halves.[124] The latter explanation assumes that the self-cursing of the subordinate party in Jer. 34:18f. is transferred to God; but

116. See J. G. Janzen, *Studies in the Text of Jeremiah. HSM,* 6 (1973), 104f., 225f.; J. Bright, *Jeremiah. AB,* XXI (1965), 220.

117. See *ANET*³, 532; E. F. Weidner, "Der Staatsvertrag Aššurnirâris VI. von Assyrien mit Mati'ilu von Bît-Agusi," *AfO,* 8 (1932/33), 18f.

118. Cf. similar rituals in the Sefire treaty I A, ll. 37-40; *ANET*³, 660a, and D. J. Wiseman, *The Vassal-Treaties of Esarhaddon. Iraq,* 20 (1958), Z, 551-54; *ANET*³, 539, no. 70.

119. See M. Weinfeld, "The Covenant of Grant in the OT and in the Ancient Near East," *JAOS,* 90 (1970), 199; D. J. McCarthy, *OT Covenant* (Oxford, ²1972), 61; R. Kilian, *Die vorpriesterlichen Abrahams-Überlieferungen. BBB,* 24 (1966), 36-73, 295-99.

120. W. Hinz, "Elams Vertrag mit Narām-Sîn von Akkade," *ZA,* N.S. 24[58] (1967), 66-96.

121. S. N. Kramer, *The Sumerians* (Chicago, 1963), 311; *CAD,* II (1966), 266.

122. C. F. Keil, *Genesis und Exodus. KD,* 184; B. Duhm, *Das Buch Jeremia. KHC,* IX (1901), 284; J. Henninger, "Was bedeutet die rituelle Teilung eines Tieres in zwei Hälften?" *Bibl,* 34 (1953), 352f.; for the arguments against this interpretation, see J. J. P. Valeton, "Das Wort *bᵉrīt* in den jehovistischen und deuteronomischen Stücken des Hexateuchs, sowie in den historischen Bücher," *ZAW,* 12 (1892), 227.

123. W. R. Smith, *Lectures on the Religion of the Semites* (New York, ³1927, repr. 1969), 480f.; Bikerman; F. Horst, "Der Eid im AT," *EvTh,* 17 (1957), 380; opposed by H. H. Rowley, *Worship in Ancient Israel* (Philadelphia, 1967), 30f.; McCarthy, *Treaty and Covenant,* 94-99.

124. Kutsch, *THAT,* I, 859; *idem, Verheissung und Gesetz,* 44; Loewenstamm, 503; W. Zimmerli, *1. Mose 12–25: Abraham. ZBK,* I/2 (1976), 55; C. Westermann, *Genesis 12–36* (Eng. trans., Minneapolis, 1985), 228.

the different parties and contexts rule out such a transfer, which conflicts with the Israelite image of God. In a covenant between human parties, divine punishment can be invoked for transgressions (Jer. 34:18f.), but the notion of a punishment imposed on God himself overtaxes the OT image of God.[125] Neither does Gen. 15:10,17 record a ritual oath reinforcing the promise of the land.[126] It describes a ritual ratification of the covenant, in which Yahweh ratifies the covenant by passing through the divided animals, thus guaranteeing his promise irrevocably. The formula *kāraṯ b^eriṯ* proves to be a covenant-making formula, as suggested by its original meaning (Gen. 15:18). The original direct object of *kāraṯ* was an animal or several animals, cut up or cut in half (*ktr*/*btr*).[127]

This interpretation of *kāraṯ* in the formula is reinforced by the earliest parallels in the treaty literature of the ancient Near East, which differ sharply from those of the later Neo-Assyrian period. There is an obvious parallel in content between *kāraṯ b^eriṯ* and the idiom *ḫayarum qatālum* (lit., "kill an ass") of the Mari texts,[128] which means "cut > make a treaty."[129] There is no oath or cursing ritual here; killing the animal is part of the treaty ratification.[130] There is a parallel in a treaty (17th century) between Abba-AN and Yarim-Lim of Alalakh: "Abba-AN is bound by oath to Yarim-Lim and has also cut the throat of a sheep. [He swore:] I will not take back what I have given you."[131] We notice first that in this treaty the oath and the killing of the animal are independent,[132] because the conjunction *u* is used;[133] the killing therefore does not necessarily include an oath. The cutting of the throat represents a ratification ceremony[134] symbolizing an enduring bond.

The formula *kāraṯ b^eriṯ*, "cut > make a covenant," thus derives from the literal "cutting" of one animal or several animals. The noun *b^eriṯ* expresses the purpose of the act: ratification of the covenant. The development of the idiomatic meaning of *kāraṯ*

---

125. Cf. Rowley, 30, n. 2.

126. Lohfink, 117, followed by Westermann, 228.

127. Cf. G. F. Hasel, "The Meaning of the Animal Rite in Genesis 15," *JSOT*, 19 (1981), 61-68.

128. C.-F. Jean, *Lettres diverses. ARM*, II (1959, repr. 1978), 37, 6-8; G. Dossin, "Les archives épistolaires du palais de Mari," *Syr*, 19 (1938), 108, l. 19; 108, l. 23; *idem*, "Benjaminites dans les textes de Mari," *Mélanges syriens offerts à Monsieur René Dussaud*, II (Paris, 1939), 986, l. 12.

129. Cf. W. F. Albright in *ANET*^{3}, 482, n. 4; Noth, *The Laws in the Pentateuch*, 111f.; J. M. Munn-Rankin, "Diplomacy in Western Asia in the Early Second Millennium B.C.," *Iraq*, 18 (1956), 90f.; McCarthy, *Treaty and Covenant*, 91.

130. Cf. R. Frankena, "The Vassal-Treaties of Esarhaddon and the Dating of Deuteronomy," כה *1940-1965. OTS*, 14 (1965), 139.

131. D. J. Wiseman, "Abban and Alalaḫ," *JCS*, 12 (1958), 126, 129; A. Draffkorn, "Was King Abba-AN of Yamḫad a Vizier for the King of Hattuša?" *JCS*, 13 (1959), 94-97; McCarthy, *Treaty and Covenant*, 307.

132. Cf. G. Wallis, "Eine Parallele zu Richter $19_{29ff.}$ und 1. Sam. $11_{5ff.}$ aus dem Briefarchiv von Mari," *ZAW*, 64 (1952), 60; McCarthy, *Treaty and Covenant*, 93.

133. Cf. *GaG*, §117b.

134. Cf. Wiseman, *JCS*, 12 (1958), 124; Noth, *The Laws in the Pentateuch*, 110ff.

b^e^rîṯ begins with actual "cutting" in an animal ritual or ratification ceremony, which establishes the binding nature of the covenant relationship and thus of the covenant itself.

V. Dead Sea Scrolls.

The Dead Sea scrolls contain various forms of the root more or less corresponding to the usage in Biblical Hebrew. The qal is used in the sense of "digging" a well[135] and 6 times in the technical idiom *kāraṯ b^e^rîṯ,*[136] always with reference to Israel's past history.[137] For those who enter into the covenant, instead of *kāraṯ b^e^rîṯ* the Qumran community uses the phrases *ʿāḇar babb^e^rîṯ* (cf. Dt. 29:11), "pass into the covenant" (1QS 1:16,18,20,24; 2:10; etc.), and *bōʾ babb^e^rîṯ* (cf. Jer. 34:10; Ezk. 16:8; 2 Ch. 15:12), "enter into the covenant" (1QS 2:12,18,25f.; CD 3:10; 8:1; 15:5; etc.).

The passive use of the niphal appears in the figurative meaning "extirpate," used to describe God's punishment of human beings in the past (CD 3:1,6,9) and in his future (eschatological) judgment (1QS 2:16; CD 18:49 [83 in Haberman]; 20:26; 4QpPs^a^ 2:4; 3:12; 4:18; 1Q25 13[15]:2 [? fragmentary]; the Temple scroll [11QT 25:12; 27:7] decrees *krt* as the punishment for those who profane the Day of Atonement). The niphal appears also in an apocryphal text that speaks of (messianic) hope and promises that the enthroned (king) of Davidic descent "will [not] be cut off" (4QPB 2).[138] In 11QT 59:17, the obedient king is promised in general terms that his descendants will not be "cut off" from the throne (cf. Dt. 17:20; 11QT 59:15).

The hiphil has also been found in the sense of "exterminate" as God's punishment in his future judgment on those who practice deception and break their word (1QH 4:20,26) and on the horn of Belial (1QM 1:4). In 1QH 6:34, *krtw* appears without context. The verb is used twice in parallel with *šmd* (1QM 1:4; 4QpPs^a^ 3:12).[139] In every case where God is the explicit or logical subject who does the punishing, extermination means irrevocable exclusion from (eschatological) salvation.

Hasel†

---

135. CD 6:9.

136. 1QM 13:7; CD 15:8,20 (reconstructed; cf. A. M. Habermann, *The Scrolls from the Judean Desert* [Tel Aviv, 1959], 88 [Heb.]); 11QT 2:4,12; 29:10 (alluding to an otherwise unknown covenant with Jacob at Bethel).

137. Barr, 28f.

138. See J. M. Allegro, "Further Messianic References in Qumran Literature," *JBL,* 75 (1956), 174.

139. See II.5 above.

כָּשַׁל *kāšal*; מִכְשׁוֹל *mikšôl*; כִּשָּׁלוֹן *kiššālôn*; מַכְשֵׁלָה *makšēlâ*

Contents: I. Root: 1. Distribution; 2. Meaning; 3. Versions; 4. Occurrences. II. Verb: 1. Semantic Field; 2. Verbal Stems; 3. Genres; 4. "Proper" and "Improper" Usage. III. The Noun *mikšôl*: 1. Occurrences; 2. Genres; 3. Constructions; 4. Meaning; 5. *mikšôl lēb*.

I. Root.

1. *Distribution.* The root *kšl* is unique to Hebrew and several Aramaic dialects; it is not found in Akkadian, Ugaritic, or Arabic. Its appearance in dialects of Aramaic, both Western (Samaritan, Christian Palestinian) and Eastern (Syriac, Mandaic, Jewish Aramaic[1]), might be explained as a borrowing from Biblical Hebrew. The origin of its use in Ethiopic and Tigre is also obscure.[2] For *kšl,* the Targumim use the synonymous but probably unrelated *tql.*[3]

2. *Meaning.* The large number of notions involved makes it hard to define the basic meaning of *kšl.* At first glance, the root — like → נפל *nāpal*[4], often found in parallel with it — appears simply to denote the "falling (down)" of someone while walking. In contrast to *npl,* however, *kšl* often refers also to the "staggering" or "stumbling" that precedes falling. Frequently the idea of striking an obstacle that causes the stumbling and falling is also present. The meaning of the root, therefore, can be dominated by the idea of striking, stumbling, or falling; but it can also combine two or even all three of these ideas. The notion of "disaster on the way" probably comes closest to representing all three aspects.

3. *Versions.* The range of meanings of the root is reflected in the variety of its translations in the ancient versions. The LXX usually uses *astheneín* to render the verb *kāšal,* less often *adynateín, kopiázein,* or *apollýnai.* Possibly[5] it is following the lead of the Targumim, whose use of *tql*[6] likewise emphasizes the notion of "stumbling" or

---

kāšal. H. A. Brongers, "Darum, wer fest zu stehen meint, der sehe zu, dass er nicht falle," *Symbolae biblicae et mesopotamicae. Festschrift F. M. T. de Liagre Böhl. StFS,* 4 (1973), 56-70; G. Stählin, "ἀσθενής," *TDNT,* I, 490; *idem,* "προσκόπτω," *TDNT,* VI, 748-751; *idem,* "σκάνδαλον," *TDNT,* VII, 340-44; W. Zimmerli, *Ezekiel I. Herm* (Eng. trans. 1979), 146.

1. Cf. *KBL*³ and E. Y. Kutscher, "Mittelhebräisch und Jüdisch-Aramäisch im neuen Köhler-Baumgartner," *Hebräische Wortforschung. Festschrift W. Baumgartner. SVT,* 16 (1967), 168.
2. See *KBL*³.
3. See *ChW,* 551f.
4. See II.1.d below.
5. Stählin.
6. See I.1 above.

"being weak." The Vulg. yields a more differentiated picture: in 35 of 60 comparable passages the notion of "collapsing" or "falling" is dominant (*corruere, ruere, cadere, ruina*); in 12, the notion of "being weak" (*infirmare, debilitare, vacillare*); and in 11, that of "striking" (*impingere, offendere*). In the case of the derived noun *mikšôl,* the notions of a "stumbling block" (*skándalon, skō̃lon, próskomma, offendiculum,* etc.), "weakness" (*asthéneia*), and "collapse" (*ptō̃ma, ruina*), or "punishment" (*básanos, kólasis*) are represented about equally.

4. *Occurrences.* Statistics of the root's usage show 63 occurrences of the verb and 16 of the derived nouns. There is only a single occurrence of the root in the Pentateuch (Lev. 26:37); there are 50 in the Prophets (verb: 36) and 28 in the Hagiographa (verb: 26). It does not necessarily follow that in *kāšal* we are dealing with "a term associated with prophecy and Wisdom."[7] It is true that the root is especially common in certain prophetic books (Hosea [6 occurrences], Proto-Isaiah [8], Jeremiah [12], Ezekiel [11], Nahum [2]); but its use in Wisdom Literature is relatively infrequent (6 occurrences in Proverbs, 1 in Job) in comparison to Psalms (8 occurrences), Lamentations (2), Nehemiah and 2 Chronicles (5), and Daniel (6).

There are numerous occurrences of the root in the Dead Sea scrolls: 15 of *kāšal,* 10 of *mikšôl,* and 1 of *kiššālôn.*[8] Walter Grundmann has published a study of the semantic field.[9]

II. Verb.

1. *Semantic Field.* The meaning and function of *kāšal* can best be determined by observing the context in which it appears. This context involves statements having to do with "walking" or "going" on a "way" (→ דרך *derek*).

a. Many passages say explicitly that "walking" (*hlk:* Hos. 14:10[Eng. v. 9]; Isa. 28:13; Jer. 31:9; Prov. 4:12) or "running" (*rwṣ*: Isa. 40:30f.; Prov. 4:12) in a "way" (*derek*: Hos. 14:10[9]; Jer. 18:15; 31:9; Prov. 4:19) in a literal or figurative sense[10] is involved. This usage is also illustrated by the fact that the context of *kāšal* and its synonyms frequently speaks of feet (*raglayim*: Dt. 32:35; Ps. 38:17[16]; 66:9; 121:3; 91:12; 94:18), knees (*birkayim*: Ps. 109:24; Isa. 35:3; Job 4:4), and steps (*ṣaʿad*: Prov. 4:12; *paʿam*: Ps. 17:5; 140:5[4]).

b. When *kāšal* refers primarily to "striking" or "stumbling over" something, the idea is expressed by naming the obstacle or an appropriate parallel. People may "stumble over" or "strike against" a stone (Isa. 8:15), bodies (Nah. 3:3), "one another" (Lev. 26:37; Jer. 46:12), or (abstractly) "guilt" (*ʿāwôn*: Hos. 5:5; 14:2[1]) or "wickedness" (Ezk. 33:12). The construction always uses *b^e*. As parallels to *kāšal* in this sense

7. Brongers, 65; see II.3 below.

8. Kuhn.

9. W. Grundmann, "Stehen und Fallen im qumranischen und neutestamentlichen Schrifttum," in H. Bardtke, ed., *Qumran-Probleme. DAWB,* 42 (1963), 147-166.

10. See II.4 below.

we find *ngp* and *dḥh,* "strike against" (*ngp*: Jer. 13:16; Prov. 3:23; the "stumbling stone" in Isa. 8:14; Ps. 91:12; *dḥh* or *deḥî*: Ps. 56:14[13]; 116:8; 118:13; 140:5[4]).

c. The meaning "stagger, totter" is suggested by association of *kāšal* with verbs like → מוט *mûṭ* (with *regel*: Dt. 32:35; Ps. 38:17[16]; 66:9; 121:3; cf. 1QS 11:12), → מוג *mûg* (Nah. 2:6f.[5f.]; Ezk. 21:20[15]; cf. 1QM 14:5f.), and *pwq* (1 S. 25:31; Isa. 28:7; Nah. 2:11[10]), as well as *šgh,* "stumble," and *tʿh,* "stagger" (Isa. 28:7; CD 2:17).[11]

A "staggering" or "tottering" gait goes hand in hand with the notion of "fatigue" or "weakness," which became the dominant interpretation of *kāšal* in the LXX (*astheneín*). There are many illustrations in the semantic field. We find the synonyms → יגע *ygʿ* and → יעף *yʿp,* "be tired, exhausted" (Isa. 5:27; 40:30f.; 1QH 8:36) as well as → רפה *rāpâ,* "be feeble" (Isa. 35:3; Job 4:3), and the antonyms → כח *koaḥ,* "strength" (Ps. 31:11[10]; Isa. 40:29; Lam. 1:14; Neh. 4:4[10]; Dnl. 11:14f.; 1QH 5:36) and → חיל *ḥayil* (1 S. 2:4; CD 2:17). We also find expressions with *lō'-yāḵōl* (Jer. 20:11; Isa. 59:14; Lam. 1:14; Neh. 4:4[10]; 1QH 9:27; 15:13,21). Typical contrastive words include verbs of "strengthening" such as → אמץ *'mṣ,* → חזק *ḥzq* (Isa. 35:3; Job 4:3; 1QH 5:28; 1QM 14:5; 1QSa 2:7), and → כון *kwn* hiphil (Jer. 10:23; Prov. 16:9). This cluster of ideas also includes persecution (→ רדף *rāḏap*: Jer. 20:11; Ps. 31:16[15]; Lev. 26:36f.) and flight (→ נוס *nûs*: Jer. 46:5f.; Lev. 26:36f.).

d. The meaning "fall (down)" is echoed by the verb *nāpal,* which is especially common in this semantic field. The stereotyped phrase *kāšal wᵉnāpal* can be interpreted as denoting the sequence of "stumbling" and "falling" (Isa. 8:15; Jer. 46:6,12,16; 50:32; Ps. 27:2; Dnl. 11:19); in other cases, however, the two verbs should be taken as synonyms, so that *kāšal* should be translated as "fall" or the like (Isa. 3:8; 31:3; Jer. 6:15; 8:12; Lev. 26:36f.; Prov. 24:16f.). The derived noun *maḵšēlâ,* "heap of ruins," in Isa. 3:6 reflects this sense of the root. That "fall" is the correct translation in many other cases is shown by such parallels as → אבד *'āḇaḏ,* "perish" (Jer. 6:21; Ps. 9:4[3]), → כלה *kālâ,* "vanish away" (Isa. 31:3; Ps. 31:11[10]; 1QH 5:36), and → שׁבר *šbr,* "break" (Isa. 8:15; 28:13; Jer. 48:4,17,25; 50:23; 51:8,30; Prov. 16:18; Dnl. 11:20), as well as by the antonym → קום *qûm,* "rise up" (Lev. 26:37; Jer. 50:32; Job 4:4; Prov. 24:16; Lam. 1:14). This same interpretation is suggested when *kāšal* is expanded by the addition of the image "into the trap/snare" (Isa. 8:14f.; 28:13).

2. *Verbal Stems.* Of the verbal stems, the qal is most frequent (29 occurrences, 5 in the Dead Sea scrolls). It is always used intransitively. Depending on the context, it may mean "strike against," "stumble," or "fall." The ptcp. *kôšēl* (5 occurrences) denotes someone who cannot walk because he has fallen or is exhausted (Isa. 5:27; Ps. 105:37; Job 4:4; 2 Ch. 28:15); it can also refer to someone weak with age (Sir. 42:8; 1QSa 2:7).

The niphal occurs 23 times (also CD 2:17). Its meaning is fundamentally passive ("be caused to trip/stumble/fall"), but it is never absolutely certain that a second party is involved who brings about the "stumbling." There the qal and niphal are practically synonymous.

---

11. On *mʿd,* "totter," see Brongers, 61.

The hiphil (10 occurrences, 5 in the Dead Sea scrolls), however, presupposes the work of an enemy ("cause to stumble," etc.). To the list of occurrences should be added Zeph. 1:3; Job 18:7.[12] In Lam. 1:14; 2 Ch. 25:8; Zeph. 1:3 (conj.); Jer. 18:15 (conj.[13]]), the enemy in question is God. The hophal participle is found only in Jer. 18:23 (reading *miḵšôlām?*); cf., however, Ezk. 21:20(15) (reading *hammuḵšālîm*).

The two piel forms in Ezk. 36:14f. are irrelevant, since they must be errors for *t^ešakk^elî*. According to E. Y. Kutscher,[14] in Middle Hebrew the factitive piel replaces the causative hiphil.[15]

3. *Genres*. The occurrences of *kāšal,* with few exceptions, are associated with certain literary genres.

a. The prophetic threat is represented no less than 16 times: Hos. 4:5; 5:5 (in the threats 4:4-6; 5:1-7; redaction has applied both passages to Judah); Isa. 3:8 (in vv. 1-11); 5:27 (in vv. 27-30); 8:15 (in vv. 11-15); 28:13 (in vv. 7-13); 31:3 (in vv. 1-3); Jer. 6:15 (in vv. 10-15); 6:21 (in vv. 16-21); 8:12 (in vv. 10-12, borrowed from 6:13-15); 18:15 (in vv. 13-17); 46:6,12 (in vv. 3-12); 46:16 (in vv. 14-26); 50:32 (in vv. 29-32); Nah. 3:3 (in vv. 1-7); Mal. 2:8 (in 1:6–2:9). The catastrophe denoted by *kāšal* is usually predicted for the near future. In Isa. 3:8; Jer. 46:6,12, the prophetic perfect also anticipates what is to come. As a rule, the threats are addressed to Israel, Judah, Jerusalem, or their leaders, such as priests and prophets. Jer. 46 is addressed to the Egyptian army, Jer. 50:32; Nah. 3:3 to Babylon.

b. Other prophetic genres are equally common. The verb *kāšaltā* in Hos. 14:2(1) presupposes that catastrophe has befallen the northern kingdom; it appears in the context of a "call to repent" (vv. 2-9[1-8]). Jer. 6:15 has the form of a threat, but stands in the context of one of Jeremiah's typical prophetic monologues (vv. 10-15). Jer. 20:11 is likewise formally a threat, but belongs to a prophetic "meditation" (vv. 7-13), where it marks the turning point from lament to assurance of salvation that is characteristic of individual laments. Jer. 31:9 stands in the context of an oracle of salvation concerning the return of the deported Israelites (vv. 7-9), which belongs in turn to the collection of salvation oracles in 30:1–31:40; with respect to the promise *lō' yikkāšēlû* addressed to those who return, cf. Ezk. 33:12; Isa. 63:13; also 40:30; Ps. 105:37. The mention of young men who stumble in Isa. 40:30 has reminded some scholars of a communal lament (cf. Lam. 1:14; 5:13), but it is only the contrasting background for an assurance of salvation within the framework of a disputation (Isa. 40:27-31). The salvation oracle Ezk. 33:12 is part of the didactic discourse vv. 12-16 within the framework of vv. 1-20. Zec. 12:8 comes in an oracle of salvation (vv. 7f.) that belongs to a collection of eschatological promises (12:1–13:6). The postexilic conclusion of Hosea (Hos. 14:10[9]) is discussed in II.3.d below.

---

12. See *BHS* and the comms.
13. W. Rudolph, *Jeremia. HAT,* XII (^{3}1968), *in loc.*
14. See *KBL*^{3}.
15. Cf. *WTM,* II, 421f.

c. The language of psalmody also uses *kāšal*. There are 4 instances of an individual lament (Ps. 27:2; 31:11[10]; 64:9[8]; 109:24). Pss. 31,109 lament the psalmist's own stumbling; Pss. 27,64 express assurance that the psalmist's enemies will stumble and fall (cf. Jer. 20:11). The same assurance is expressed in Ps. 9:4(3) (in the context of an Individual Hymn of Thanksgiving [Ps. 9/10]). V. 12 of Ps. 107, a thanksgiving liturgy, recalls the hopeless situation of those in prison (*kāšᵉlû wᵉʾên ʿōzēr*), while 1 S. 2:4 (in an individual hymn [vv. 1-10]) extols the uprightness of those who are weak and defenseless (*wᵉnik̲šālîm ʾāzᵉrû ḥāyil*). The verb *kāšal* also has a traditional place in communal laments (Lam. 1:14; 5:13; cf. Isa. 63:13 in 63:7–64:11[12]). Isa. 59:10,14; Neh. 4:4(10) appear to cite such hymns (Isa. 59:9-11,12-14) or at least to imitate them. There are at least 5 occurrences in the Thanksgiving scroll from Qumran.

d. In the realm of Wisdom Literature, ch. 4 of Proverbs (generally considered late) is especially important. There are 3 occurrences of *kāšal* in the group of proverbs in vv. 10-19, devoted significantly to the theme of "the way of wisdom." Those who walk in this way will neither stumble nor fall (*lōʾ tikkāšēl*: v. 12; cf. Hos. 14:10[9]). Conversely, Prov. 4:16 says that the godless cannot rest "unless they have made some one stumble" (*yak̲šîlû*) — only to fall themselves without knowing why (*lōʾ yād̲ᵉʿû bammeh yikkāšēlû*: v. 19). Prov. 24:16 expresses the same theme: the righteous man falls seven times and rises again, but the wicked "are overthrown by calamity" (*yikkāšᵉlû b̲ᵉrāʿâ*). Prov. 16:18 uses the derived noun *kiššālôn* to express the familiar warning that "a haughty spirit goes before a fall." Job 18:7 says that the wicked man is cast down by his own schemes (*tak̲šîlēhû* [conj.]). Those who are wise do not rejoice when their enemy stumbles (Prov. 24:17); instead, they know how to help those who are weak and stumble (*kôšēl*) (Job 4:3f.).

e. The use of *kāšal* in other genres can be summarized rapidly. The 3 hiphil forms in 2 Ch. 25:8 (twice); 28:23 seem to show that *kāšal* found its way into narrative literature late in the biblical period, but 2 Ch. 25:7f. clearly borrows the style of prophetic oracles (as does 28:23). Only *kôšēl* in 2 Ch. 28:15 is a colloquial term for someone who is unable to walk.[16] Lev. 26:36f. indicates that *kāšal* was used in "levitical" preaching of the law; here, too, however, prophetic influence (Jer. 46:12) is unmistakable. The plethora of niphal forms in Dnl. 11:14,19,33-35,41 shows that the apocalyptic writer treats *kāšal* as a key motif: he considers the "stumbling and falling" not only of foreign kings but also of Israel and its sages to be evidence of the purifying eschatological judgment (→ צרף *ṣrp* and its synonyms in v. 35; cf. *mṣrp* at Qumran).

4. *"Proper" and "Improper" Usage*. The categories of modern Western thought would require a distinction between a "proper" literal usage of *kāšal* and an "improper" metaphorical usage. In the sense of this distinction, the "proper" usage is illustrated by only a few occurrences, which describe "real" tripping, stumbling, or falling "on the ground": for example, Isa. 5:27; Nah. 3:3 (the Assyrian army); Jer. 31:9 (the

16. See II.2 above.

returning Israelites); 46:12 (the Babylonian and Egyptian armies); Lam. 5:13; Isa. 40:30 (exiled Jews); Ps. 105:37 (Israel during the exodus). The mass of other occurrences would have to be considered "improper" metaphorical usage.

But the application of such categories to the usage of *kāšal* is highly dubious. The attempt to establish a schematic distinction between "literal" and "figurative" usage[17] is questionable from the outset because it implies an insufficiently grounded appraisal ("superior" or "inferior") of the usage in question. "Figurative" usage is the poetic application of a basically inappropriate word to a situation that would normally be described in other terms. In "literal" usage, the basic meaning corresponds precisely to what is actually being communicated. It is clear that this distinction ventures a momentous judgment with respect to the reality conveyed by either usage.

The attempt to operate with the "literal" meaning of *kāšal* also raises serious problems. The frequent mention of ways and stones, feet and knees,[18] in the semantic field seems to point clearly enough to "stumbling and falling on the road." But how is one to know that this is the primary and proper meaning and usage of *kāšal?* There is no more certainty here than in the case of the root *drk,*[19] where little besides convention supports the assumption that *dereḵ* originally meant a "road through the countryside" and *dāraḵ* "walking on such a road." If there is no clear definition of the basic meaning and "proper" usage of *kāšal,* the project of distinguishing and delimiting its "improper," "figurative," or "metaphorical" usage is suspect. In the present state of our knowledge, we can start with the assurance that the word expresses a notion with three aspects and symbolizes a "drastic disaster on the way."[20] Lexicographical analysis of its varied usage will then make it possible to distinguish a "narrower" usage ("disaster on the road") and a "wider" usage ("disaster in life"). The dualism of a "proper" and "improper" meaning becomes unnecessary when the various usages are seen as ontologically equal concretions of a single symbol.

III. The Noun *miḵšôl.* Besides *kiššālôn*[21] and *maḵšēlâ,*[22] the noun *miḵšôl* is derived from *kšl.* It is also attested in the Dead Sea scrolls and in Middle Hebrew.

1. *Occurrences.* There are 14 occurrences of *miḵšôl* in the OT: 1 in the Pentateuch (Lev. 19:14), 12 in the Prophets, and 1 in the Hagiographa (Ps. 119:165). Of these, we may disregard Ezk. 21:20, where the hophal participle should be read with the versions. On the other hand, we may include Jer. 18:23 as an additional occurrence.[23] The book

17. Brongers, 65.
18. See II.1.a-b above.
19. See II.1 above.
20. See I.2 above.
21. See II.3.d above.
22. See II.1.d above.
23. See II.2 above.

of Ezekiel has a remarkable concentration of occurrences (8 or 7). There are numerous occurrences in the Dead Sea scrolls.

2. *Genres.* The noun *mik̲šôl* appears most often in prophetic genres. It occurs 3 times in threats: Isa. 8:14 (in vv. 11-15); Jer. 6:21 (in vv. 16-21); Ezk. 44:12 (in vv. 10-14, which resembles a threat); cf. 7:19c (a secondary addition to vv. 1-27). Ezekiel has a fondness for using *mik̲šôl* in disputations that culminate in a call to repent: Ezk. 3:20 (in vv. 16b-20); 14:3,4,7 (in vv. 1-11); 18:30 (in vv. 1-32). Like *kāšal,*[24] when negated it finds a place in oracles of salvation: Isa. 57:14 (in vv. 14-21).

There is a single occurrence in narrative prose (1 S. 25:31).[25] The noun also appears once in sacral law and once in cultic poetry: Lev. 19:14 (in vv. 11-18, a series of prohibitions) and Ps. 119:165. Most of the occurrences in the Dead Sea scrolls are in the Thanksgiving scroll.

3. *Constructions.* The usage of *mik̲šôl* exhibits a series of characteristic forms. We frequently find the expression *nāṯan mik̲šôl* (Jer. 6:21; Ezk. 3:20; 14:3; Lev. 19:14), often with *lip̄nê* added (e.g., Lev. 19:14). Another typical expression is *hāyâ lᵉmik̲šôl* (1 S. 25:31; Isa. 8:14; Ezk. 18:30; 44:12; cf. 7:19), which in both form and meaning recalls the Deuteronomistic expression *hāyâ lᵉmôqēš* (Ex. 23:33; 34:12; Josh. 23:13; Jgs. 2:3; 8:27; Ps. 106:36; etc.). It appears in *figura etymologica* with *kāšal* in Isa. 8:14f. (where v. 15a is probably secondary[26]); Jer. 6:21. The important construct phrases are *ṣûr mik̲šôl* (Isa. 8:14), *mik̲šôl ʿᵃwôn,*[27] and *mik̲šôl lēḇ.*[28]

4. *Meaning.* After the analogy of *kāšal, mik̲šôl* could mean "stumbling block," "stumbling," or "fall." Most of the occurrences, however, involve the meaning "stumbling block." The word normally denotes an "obstacle," concrete or otherwise, struck by an unsuspecting traveler, which causes him to stumble and finally to fall. The prohibition in Lev. 19:14 clearly refers to an obstacle "in the road."[29] This may also be the primary meaning in Isa. 57:14; here, however, obstacles of quite a different sort are also suggested. Ezk. 7:19 calls gold and silver stumbling blocks, and 14:3,4,7 treat idols the same way. Transgressions[30] (Ezk. 18:30) or the idolatrous Levites collectively (Ezk. 44:12) can be a stumbling block. The stumbling blocks that Yahweh himself "places" (*nāṯan*) in Jer. 6:21; Ezk. 3:20 are obscure.

Only in Ezekiel do we find the formula *mik̲šôl ʿᵃwôn* (Ezk. 7:19; 14:3,4,7; 18:30; 44:12; cf. 1QS 2:12,17; 1QH 4:15). It calls actions, events, objects, and persons

---

24. See II.3.b above.
25. See III.5 above.
26. Cf. T. Lescow, "Jesajas Denkschrift aus der Zeit des syrisch-ephraimitischen Krieges," *ZAW,* 85 (1973), 324, n. 46.
27. See III.4 below.
28. See III.5 below.
29. See II.4 above.
30. → פשע *pāšaʿ.*

"stumbling blocks" that lead to sin, guilt, and catastrophe (cf. already Hos. 14:2[1]). In translating these passages in his commentary,[31] Walther Zimmerli uses the German word *Anstoss,* "stumbling block," in another of its senses, "incentive, goad," expressing — however imperfectly — the irresistibility of the catastrophe that is unleashed.

A few passages may involve the meaning "stumbling" or "fall" instead of "stumbling block." The parallelism in Isa. 8:14, for example, suggests that *ṣûr mik̠šôl* may best be translated "stone of stumbling." Ps. 119:165 is often translated "no stumbling," but the antithetical parallelism with *šālôm* suggests instead the meaning "no fall," i.e., "no disaster" (cf. 1QH 10:18).

5. *mik̠šôl lēḇ.* The usage in 1 S. 25:31 requires special attention. The independent construct phrase *mik̠šôl lēḇ* (par. *pûqâ,* "staggering") is translated "pangs of conscience" by the RSV; *KBL*[3] [32] suggests "remorse of conscience." This interpretation is unsatisfactory, although *lēḇ* can mean "conscience" (1 S. 24:6[5]). An "uneasy conscience" is far too weak an expression for what David would have to expect in consequence of murdering Nabal on the day of his exaltation. He is threatened with much more: a "stumbling of heart" (Martin Buber), an inward staggering and breakdown, the ruin of his identity as Yahweh's anointed. This catastrophe — as Abigail rightly sees — David cannot desire under any circumstances.

Barth

31. Zimmerli, 146, 211, 306.
32. P. 551b.

כָּשַׁף *kāšap̱*; כֶּשֶׁף *kešep̱*; כַּשָּׁף *kaššāp̱*; אַשָּׁף *'aššāp̱*; יִדְּעֹנִי *yidd[e]'ōnî*; לָחַשׁ *lāḥaš*; לַחַשׁ *laḥaš*; נָחַשׁ *nāḥaš* I; נַחַשׁ *naḥaš*; עָנַן *'ānan* II; שָׁחַר *šāḥar* I

Contents: I. 1. Etymology, Semantic Field; 2. Occurrences; 3. LXX. II. Ancient Near East: 1. Egypt; 2. Mesopotamia; 3. Western Semites. III. Israel: 1. Negative Assessment; 2. Alien Origin; 3. At Court. IV. Positive Assessment. V. 1. Magic; 2. Divination; 3. Astrology.

kāšap̱. J. F. Borghouts, "Magie," *LexÄg,* III (1980), 1137-1151; G. Contenau, *La magie chez les Assyriens et les Babyloniens* (Paris, 1947); É. P. Dhorme, *Les religions de Babylonie et d'Assyrie. Mana,* I/1 (Paris, [2]1949), 258-298; M. Jastrow, *Die Religion Babyloniens und Assyriens,* II/1-2 (Giessen, 1912); R. Largement, A. Massart, and A. Lefèvre, "Magie," *DBS,* V (1957), 705-739; W. Mayer, *Untersuchungen zur Formsprache der babylonischen "Gebetsbeschwörungen." StPohl,* Ser. maior, 5/16 (1976); B. Meissner, *BuA,* II, 198-282; H. Ringgren, *Die Religionen des Alten Orients. ATDSond* (1979), 45f., 98ff., 150-160, 236f.; J. Wellhausen, *Reste arabischen Heidentums* (Berlin, [2]1897, repr. 1927).

I. 1. *Etymology, Semantic Field.* In the OT, the root *kšp,* "practice magic," usually appears with other terms denoting various forms of magic and divination. The precise meaning of these terms is unknown; etymological evidence helps in some cases, but only as a rough approximation.

Heb. *kšp* is cognate with Akk. *kašāpu, kuššupu,* "bewitch, enchant,"[1] and its nominal derivatives *kišpu,* "magic, witchcraft,"[2] and *kaššāpu/kaššaptu,* "magician, witch."[3] Arab. *kasafa* can mean both "grow dark" and "cut apart";[4] the latter meaning is connected with Eth. *kasaba* and Tigre *kašaba,* "circumcise," and possibly Syr. *kšp* ethpael, "ask, pray" (possibly a reference to self-mutilation to appease the deity[5]). Cf. also Mand. *kšp* aphel or pael, "enchant, bewitch," and Ugar. *kṯpm,* found in a text that speaks of oil to anoint *kṯpm.*[6] The intial aleph indicates that *'aššāp̱,* Biblical Aram. *'āšap̱,* "conjurer," is an Akkadian loanword.[7]

The root *lḥš,* usually translated "whisper (a spell)," is cognate with Ugar. *lḥšt,* "whispering" (three times in the phrase *lḥšt 'bn,* "whispering of the stone"[8]), *mlḥš,* "snake charmer,"[9] Akk. *laḫāšu,* "whisper,"[10] Syr. and Mand. *lḥš,* "enchant," and Eth. *'lḥōsasa,* "whisper."

Some scholars connect *nḥš,* "practice divination, seek omens," with *nāḥāš,* "serpent," interpreting it as "snake charming." More likely, however, it is connected with Arab. *nḥs,* which originally probably meant "omen" in general but came to be understood as an unfavorable or negative omen.[11] Other Semitic languages use the possible cognate *lḥš.*[12]

The polel form *'ônēn* has been explained variously.[13] There is only 1 occurrence of *šḥr,* which is cognate with Arab. *siḥr,* "magic,"[14] and Akk. *sāḫiru,* "enchanter";[15] cf. OSA *shr,* "magical protection."

The noun *yidd^e'ōnî* always appears in the context of necromancy. It is derived from → ידע *yāḏa',* "know," and characterizes the shade as "wise."

The semantic field also includes → אוב *'ôḇ,* "shade"; → דרש *dāraš (*'el*),* "inquire"; → חבר *ḥāḇar* II, "practice magic"; → חכם *ḥāḵam,* "be wise"; → חלם *ḥālam,*

1. *AHw,* I (1965), 461; *CAD,* VIII (1971), 284f.
2. *AHw,* I, 491.
3. *AHw,* I, 463.
4. *WKAS,* I, 190ff.
5. Wellhausen, 126, n. 5, following W. R. Smith.
6. *KTU,* 1.107, 23; see below.
7. From *āšipu* (*CAD,* I/2 [1968], 431), root *wšp*; cf. *šiptu,* "incantation."
8. *KTU,* 1.3 III, 23; IV, 14f.; 1.7, 31.
9. See below.
10. *AHw,* I, 528.
11. Wellhausen, 201 and nn. 1f.
12. See above.
13. *GesB, s.v.* *'nn* II.
14. Wellhausen, 159.
15. *AHw,* I, 1009.

"dream"; → חרטם *ḥarṭōm,* "incantation priest"; *kaśdîm,* "Chaldeans"; and → קסם *qsm,* "practice divination by arrows."

2. *Occurrences.* There are 8 occurrences of *'aššāp̄*/Aram. *'āšap̄,* all in Daniel. The piel of *kšp* appears 6 times, *kešep̄* 6 times, and *kaššāp̄* once; the hithpael appears twice with the meaning "whisper together." There are 9 occurrences of *nḥš* in the piel, 2 of the noun *naḥaš.* There are 2 occurrences of *'ônēn.* There is only 1 certain occurrence of *šḥr* in the sense of "practice magic" (Isa. 47:11; also v. 15 conj.); in Job 30:30, it probably means "turn black."

3. *LXX.* The LXX always uses *mágos* to translate *'aššāp̄.* For *yiddᵉ'ōnî* it uses *gnṓstēs* (4 times), *gnōristḗs* (once), *epaoidós* (4 times), *engastrímythos* (twice), and *teratoskópos* (once). The group of *kšp, kešep̄,* and *kaššāp̄* are represented by *pharmakeúein, phármakos,* and *pharmakeía.* The piel and hithpael of *lḥš* are translated by *psithyrízein* (once by *epaoídein*), *laḥaš* by *epaoídein, epilaleín,* or *akroatḗs.* The piel of *nḥš* is translated by *oiōnízesthai, oiōnismós,* or *pharmakeúein, naḥaš* by *oiōnismós* or *oíōnos.* The polel of *'nn* is represented by *apophthéngesthai, blépein, klēdonízesthai, klēdonismós, klēdṓn, oiṓnisma,* and *ornithoskopeín.* The phrase *bᵉnê 'ōnᵉnâ* in Isa. 57:3 is rendered as *huioí ánomoi.* In Isa. 47:11, the LXX reads the piel of *šḥr* as something else. The variety of translations shows that the precise meaning of the terms was not known.

II. Ancient Near East.

1. *Egypt.* Egyp. *ḥk3,* usually translated "magic,"[16] properly denotes a supernatural power that enables the gods to perform miracles. The purpose of charms and spells is to activate this power. Magical texts therefore invoke the gods, and charms are based on divine myths. Images of Horus standing triumphant on a crocodile serve as protection against disease; the accompanying spell expresses the prayer, for example, that someone stung by a scorpion or bitten by a snake be healed as Horus was healed by the magical words of the gods.[17] A charm against scorpions calls on the cat goddess Bastet, said to have been healed by Re; interestingly, Re replies with an "oracle of salvation": "Fear not."[18] Against crocodiles, one invokes Osiris, who was himself saved from the water. "The charm is intended to imbue the events of the myth with new reality; the healing of the deity takes place once again ('today') in the person of the devotee."[19]

---

16. *WbÄS,* III, 175f.
17. See, e.g., the so-called Metternich stela in G. Roeder, *Urkunden zur Religion des alten Ägypten* (Jena, ²1923), 82ff.
18. *Ibid.,* 84.
19. Ringgren, 46.

2. *Mesopotamia.* Akkadian texts distinguish witchcraft (*kišpu*), which is proscribed as a capital offense, and magic, which is recognized officially by kings and priests. The latter is used to resist the former.

A sorcerer or witch (*kaššāpu/kaššaptu*) may be responsible for the evil that befalls a person: *kaššāptu takšipanni,* "a witch has bewitched me";[20] ". . . whoever has inflicted this evil upon me, whether sorcerer or witch (*lû kaššāpu lû kaššāptu*). . . ."[21] Exorcism takes place at night. After recitation of a long litany, the afflicted person turns to the gods through the exorcist, praying that they will lift (*paṭāru*) the curses (*mamîtu*). He states that he has made images of the sorcerers (*ṣalmu annûti ša kaššāpia u kaššaptia*),"[22] and continues: *qumi kaššāpī û kaššaptī,* "burn my sorcerer and my witch."[23] The exorcist, an *ašipu* priest, pronounces a formula (*šiptu*), e.g., "Fire-god, O mighty one, exalted among the gods, who dost vanquish the wicked and the enemy, vanquish them [the witches] lest I be destroyed. Thou art my god, thou art my lord, thou art my judge, thou art my helper, thou art my avenger."[24] *Laḫāšu, liḫšu,* and *mulaḫḫišu* are mentioned in conjunction with exorcisms, but are not linked explicitly with witchcraft.

3. *Western Semites.* There are four interesting magical texts from the West Semitic area. Two, from Ras Shamra, are charms against snakebite.[25] In *KTU* 1.100, Paḥlat, the daughter of the sun-goddess, asks her mother's aid in the charm. Other deities are also invoked. It is of interest that one passage calls the sorcerer *mlḥš.*[26] A damaged passage speaks of anointing *kṯpm* (= Heb. *kšp*).[27] The term *mnt* is also used for a magical rite.[28]

The Ugaritic text Ras Ibn Hani 78/20 contains an incantation against distress brought about by sorcerers, who are called *kšpm* (with *š!*), *dbbm* ("enemies"?), *ḥbrm,* and *dʿtm.* These terms recall Dt. 18:10f., which mentions *mᵉkaššēp̱, ḥōḇēr ḥeḇer,* and *yiddeʿōnî.*[29]

The Phoenician text, from Arslan Tash, appears on an amulet with pictures.[30] Here a female demon, called "the flying lady" and "the slayer of the lamb," is adjured to keep away, since the owner has the support of all the gods.[31]

---

20. Maqlû, I, 127.
21. E. Ebeling, *Literarische Keilschrifttexte aus Assur* (Berlin, 1953), 115, 11.
22. *KAR,* 80, r. 25.
23. Maqlû, II, 15.
24. *Ibid.,* 85-90.
25. *KTU,* 1.100; 1.107; cf. E. Lipiński, "La légende sacrée de la conjuration des morsures de serpents," *UF,* 6 (1974), 169-174; M. Dietrich, O. Loretz, and J. Sanmartín, "Bemerkungen zur Schlangenbeschwörung RS 24.244 = Ug. 5, S. 564ff. Nr. 7," *UF,* 7 (1975), 121-25; *idem,* "Einzelbemerkungen zu RS 24.251 = Ug. 5, S. 574-578 Nr. 8," *UF,* 7 (1975), 127-131.
26. Ll. 5, 59.
27. *KTU,* 1.107, 23.
28. *KTU,* 1.107, 4, 9.
29. Y. Avishur, "The Ghost-Expelling Incantation from Ugarit (Ras Ibn Hani 78/20)," *UF,* 13 (1981), 13-25, esp. 22.
30. *KAI,* 27.
31. Cf. M. Astour, "Two Ugaritic Serpent Charms," *JNES,* 27 (1968), 32.

III. Israel.

1. *Negative Assessment.* The OT usually uses the various terms for magic, divination, and the like in combinations of two or more words.

The most detailed list appears in Dt. 18:10f.: "There shall not be found among you anyone who causes his son and his daughter to go through fire (*heʿeḇîr bāʾēš*),[32] anyone who practices divination,[33] a soothsayer, or an augur (*meʿônēn*), or a sorcerer (*menaḥēš*), or a charmer (*mekaššēp*), or a medium,[34] or one who inquires (*šʾl*) of a shade,[35] or a wizard (*yiddeʿônî*), or a necromancer." This list, which obviously aims to be comprehensive, clearly reflects the situation of the late monarchy.[36] Especially important is the reason: all these practices are an abomination (*tôʿēḇâ*) to Yahweh (v. 12), the abominable practices of the Gentiles (v. 9); they are detrimental to the proper relationship with God (cf. v. 13: "You shall be blameless [*tāmîm*] before Yahweh your God"). V. 14 speaks once more of *meʿônenîm* and *qōsemîm,* differentiating them from the true prophets of Yahweh; this contrast shows that the terms refer to divination.

A similar list is found in 2 K. 21:6, which records that Manasseh "caused his son to go through fire, practiced soothsaying and augury (*ônēn weniḥēš*; 2 Ch. 33:6 adds *kšp*), and dealt with mediums and wizards (*ʿāśâ ʾôḇ weyiddeʿōnîm),*" all of which was evil in the eyes (*raʿ beʿênê*) of Yahweh and provoked him to anger (*hikʿîs*). V. 2 describes Manasseh's actions as "the abominable practices (*tôʿaḇōṯ*) of the nations whom Yahweh drove out before the people of Israel," that is, pagan abominations. Lev. 20:1-6 mentions only Molech worship (vv. 1-5) and *ʾōḇōṯ* and *yiddeʿōnîm* (v. 6). Ex. 22:17(Eng. v. 18) decrees capital punishment for *mekaššēpâ.*

Idolatry and *kšp* are treated as synonymous by 2 K. 9:22; "sons of the *ʿōnenâ,* offspring of of the adulterer and the harlot," are called "children of transgression" and "offspring of deceit" by Isa. 57:3f.

The roots *kšp* and *ʿnn* also appear in other lists of sinful phenomena that Yahweh will destroy: horses, chariots, cities, strongholds, *kešāpîm* and *meʿônenîm,* images, pillars, and asherahs (Mic. 5:9-13[10-14]). In Mal. 3:5, *kšp* introduces a list of transgressors whose offenses are primarily social, showing that they do not fear God: *mekaššepîm,* adulterers, those who swear falsely, and those who oppress day laborers, widows, and orphans and thrust aside the sojourner. In Jer. 27:9, "prophets" lead a list of false prophets who should not be listened to: *neḇîʾēḵem, ḥalōmōṯēḵem* (vss.: *ḥōlemêḵem*), *ʿōnenêḵem, kaššāpêḵem.*

2. *Alien Origin.* The various kinds of magicians and augurs are often characterized

32. → מלך *mōleḵ.*
33. → קסם *qsm.*
34. → חבר *ḥbr.*
35. → אוב *ʾôḇ* (*ʾôbh*).
36. See G. von Rad, *Deuteronomy. OTL* (Eng. trans. 1966), *in loc.*

as alien. The *ḥakāmîm* and *mekaššepîm* of Pharaoh are Egyptian *ḥarṭummîm* (Ex. 7:11). In Babylon there were *ḥarṭummîm, 'aššāpîm, mekaššepîm, kaśdîm, ḥakāmîm,* and *gāzerîn* (Isa. 47:9,12; Dnl. 1:20; 2:2,10,27; 4:4,6[7,9]; 5:7,11,15). Nineveh is a beautiful harlot who consorts with *kešāpîm* (Nah. 3:4). Jezebel introduced *kešāpîm* into Israel (2 K. 9:22). The Philistines and foreigners practice *'nn,* an activity described as "eastern (? [*qeḏem*])" (Isa. 2:6).[37]

3. *At Court.* Magicians and soothsayers often appear at court: with Pharaoh (Ex. 7:11; cf. Gen. 44:15), Nebuchadnezzar (Dnl. 2), Manasseh (2 K. 21:6 par. 2 Ch. 33:6), and Jezebel (2 K. 9:22). Together with mighty men, soldiers, judges, prophets, elders, captains, men of rank, and counselors, they represent the upper stratum of society (Isa. 3:2f.). Saul had driven the *'ōḇôṯ* and *yidde'ōnîm* out of the land (1 S. 28:3); but when he was in peril and Yahweh did not answer by dreams or Urim or prophets, he sought out a *ba'alaṯ-'ôḇ* at En-dor (v. 7).

Prophecies often deal with the fate of an entire nation: Egypt (Ex. 7), Assyria (Nah. 3), Judah (Jer. 27), Babylon (Isa. 47; Dnl. 2), Saul's kingdom (1 S. 28), Israel (Nu. 24).

IV. Positive Assessment. One term is occasionally treated positively: *nḥš.* Laban says to Jacob: "I divine (*niḥaštî*) that Yahweh has blessed me because of you" (Gen. 30:27). Joseph divines (*naḥēš, yenaḥēš*) with the silver cup found in Benjamin's sack (Gen. 44:5,15); the use of cups for divination was common in Mesopotamia[38] but is a late phenomenon in Egypt.[39] When Ben-hadad's men asked Ahab to have mercy on their king, they interpreted his answer as a good omen (*yenaḥašû*: 1 K. 20:33). In Nu. 24:1, the summary phrase *liqra'ṯ neḥāšîm* refers to the fact that Yahweh spoke to Balaam and came to him (22:8-12,19,38), that Balaam knew (*yāḏa'*) what Yahweh said (22:19), and that Yahweh met (*qārâ*) him and spoke with him (23:3-5).

V. The precise meaning of the various terms is hard to distinguish, but they can be categorized in three groups: magic, divination, and astrology.

1. *Magic.* Magic includes *'aššāp, kšp, lḥš,* and *šḥr.*

The noun *'aššāp* or *'āšap* is cognate with Akk. *āšipu*; it denotes the kind of magic assessed positively in Assyria and Babylonia. Only Dnl. 2 mentions *'aššāpîm.*

The *mekaššepîm* and *ḥarṭummîm* of Pharaoh imitate the miracles performed by Moses and Aaron (Ex. 7:11). In Isa. 47:9,12, *kešāpîm* and *ḥaḇārîm* refer to the magical arts that the Babylonians thought could avert disasters but are impotent against the power of Yahweh. In Jer. 27:9 and several passages in Daniel (e.g., 2:2), however, the

---

37. This reading is disputed on cogent grounds by O. Kaiser (*Isaiah 1–12. OTL* [Eng. trans. [2]1983], 56) and H. Wildberger (*Isaiah 1–12.* [Eng. trans., Minneapolis, 1991], 99). The latter reads *qōsemîm miqqeḏem.*

38. J. Hunger, *Becherwahrsagung bei den Babyloniern. LSS,* 1 (1903); E. Ebeling, "Becherwahrsagung," *RLA,* I (1932), 467.

39. J. Vergote, *Joseph en Égypte. OrBibLov,* 3 (1959), 172ff.; → כוס *kôs.*

same words are lumped together with others denoting soothsayers of various kinds in obviously stereotyped lists.

The piel of *lḥš,* referring to magic, is found only in Ps. 58:6(5), where it describes snake charmers, also called *ḥôḇēr ḥaḇārîm.* Both expressions are used in a metaphor describing the wicked as serpents that will not hear the voice of the charmer. The passage does not condemn *lḥš* as such. Eccl. 10:11 also uses *lāḥaš* in a totally neutral sense: if a serpent bites before it is charmed, the charmer's art is of no advantage. Jer. 8:17 speaks similarly of serpents that cannot be charmed; once again, the charming is accepted without comment. Isa. 3:20 probably refers to amulets; Isa. 26:16 is very obscure. The best translation of *laḥaš* is probably "whispered prayer."[40]

The verb *šḥr* appears only in Isa. 47:11, in a description of the disaster about to overwhelm Babylon: "You will not be able to exorcise it." In Isa. 47:15, *sōḥarayiḵ* ("those with whom you have traded") should possibly be emended to *šōḥarayiḵ,* "your magicians"; this reading would fit well with v. 11 and the astrologers in v. 13.

2. *Divination.* The divination category includes *ʿnn, nḥš, qsm, ʾôḇ,* and *yiddeʿōnî.*

The root *ʿnn* is shown by Dt. 18:14 to denote some kind of mantic practice.[41] Lev. 19:26, which prohibits both *nḥš* and *ʿnn,* points in the same direction. Jgs. 9:37 mentions an "Augurs' Oak" (*ʾēlôn meʿônenîm*) near Shechem. The relation between this tree and the "Oak of the Seer" (*ʾēlôn môreh*)[42] in Gen. 12:6 is obscure. The other occurrences are ambiguous.

The root *nḥš* has already been discussed. *qsm* is cognate with Arab. *istiqsām,* "arrow oracle," and clearly denotes a similar procedure. See also → אוב *ʾôḇ* and the discussion of *yiddeʿōnî* above.

3. *Astrology.* The *gāzerîn* in Dnl. 2:27; 4:4(7); 5:7,11 are probably astrologers, as the *ḥōḇerê šāmayim* and *haḥōzîm bakkôḵāḇîm* of Isa. 47:13 clearly are. Significantly, they are all Babylonians.

André

40. G. André, *Determining the Destiny: PQD in the OT. CB,* 16 (1980), 134.
41. See above.
42. → ירה *yārâ.*

כָּשֵׁר *kāšēr*; כִּשְׁרוֹן *kišrôn*

Contents: I. 1. Etymology; 2. Occurrences. II. Meaning and Usage. III. *kôšārôṯ* (Ps. 68:7). IV. *kîšôr* (Prov. 31:19). V. **kaššîr* (Ezk. 33:32).

I. 1. *Etymology.* Comparison of Heb. *kšr* with Akk. *kašāru,*[1] Ugar. *kṯr,*[2] and Arab. *kaṯura*[3] shows that the *š* in the root *kšr* (firmly established in Aramaic) demands explanation, since phonetic laws would predict *ktr.* It has therefore been proposed that Aram. *kšr* is a Canaanite or Akkadian loanword[4] and that the existence of an Aramaic root *ktr* meaning "wait for" helped preserve the *š* to avoid homonymy.

We note, however, that *kšr* is common throughout the domain of Aramaic: Jewish Aramaic,[5] Christian Palestinian Aramaic,[6] Syriac,[7] and Mandaic;[8] cf. also Samaritan Aramaic[9] and Palmyrene.[10] This observation casts doubt on the proposed etymology. This doubt is strengthened by the fact that Akk. *kašāru* has a wide range of meanings: "rebuild, repair, pursue, complete, restore."[11] Furthermore, Arab. *kaṯara,* "surpass (in number)," and *kaṯura,* "be numerous,"[12] exhibit no semantic association with Heb.-Aram. *kšr.* Finally, we note that in Ugaritic — apart from *kṯr,* the craftsman-god, and *kṯrt,* the goddesses who aid childbirth — the root *kṯr* appears only twice: once in the form *mkṯr*[13] and once in the form *kṯrm.*[14] The interpretation of both passages is debated. It is therefore reasonable to ignore the dubious Akkadian, Ugaritic, and Arabic cognates and treat *kšr* as an Aramaic root and the rare Heb. *kšr* as an Aramaic loanword.[15] This

---

kāšēr. A. van Selms, "The Root *k-ṯ-r* and its Derivatives in Ugaritic Literature," *Festschrift C. F. A. Schaeffer. UF,* 11 (1979), 739-744.

1. *AHw,* I (1965), 461f.
2. *WUS,* no. 1417.
3. *WKAS,* I, 60-69; cf. A. Guillaume, "Hebrew and Arabic Lexicography: A Comprehensive Study II," *Abr Nahrain,* 2 (1960/61, repr. Leiden, 1965), 19.
4. With E. Y. Kutscher in *KBL*³ and W. McKane, review of *KBL*³, I-II, *JTS,* N.S. 27 (1976), 151.
5. *ChW,* 392a-93a; *WTM,* II, 424a-27a.
6. F. Schulthess, *Lexicon Syropalaestinum* (Berlin, 1903), 98b.
7. R. P. Smith, *Thesaurus Syriacus,* I (Oxford, 1879), cols. 1847-49; *LexSyr,* 350b-51a.
8. *MdD,* 225a; R. Macuch, *Handbook of Classical and Modern Mandaic* (Berlin, 1965), 21, 36.
9. S. Ben Ḥayyim, *The Literary and Oral Tradition of Hebrew and Aramaic amongst the Samaritans,* II. *Mekharim,* 1 (Jerusalem, 1957-1961), 484a.
10. *kšyr* for Gk. *krátistos* in a tax schedule; cf. *DISO,* 127.
11. *CAD,* VIII (1971), 285f., and esp. A. K. Grayson, "Akkadian *ksr* and *kšr,*" *Assur,* 1/4 (1975), 3-7.
12. *WKAS,* I, 60-69.
13. *KTU,* 1.4 II, 30.
14. *KTU,* 1.14 I, 16.
15. Following E. F. Kautzsch, *Die Aramaismen im AT* (Halle, 1902), 44; M. Wagner, *Die*

proposal is hardly problematic, since *kšr* appears in the OT only in the late books of Esther and Ecclesiastes, as well as Sirach, where an aramaism is not surprising.

The LXX uses *euthḗs, stoicheín,* and *chrēsimeúein* to translate *kāšēr,* and *andreía* to translate *kišrôn* (3 times).

2. *Occurrences.* A basic meaning "be proper" can account for the various nuances the context requires for both the verbal forms and the abstract noun *kišrôn* (formed with the suf. *-ôn*), "excellence, success, skill." The OT uses *kāšēr* once as a predicate adjective (Est. 8:5). The parallel structure of the two clauses 5aβ and 5aγ appended by *w* to the second conditional clause introduced by *wᵉʾim* shows that *kāšēr* is not a 3rd person masculine singular qal perfect, as the lexica state, but an adjective. Qal imperfects appear only in Eccl. 11:6; Sir. 13:4. The Masoretic pointing indicates a hiphil in Eccl. 10:10. The noun *kišrôn* appears in Eccl. 2:21; 4:4; 5:10(Eng. v. 11). We shall discuss below the derivation of *kôšārôṯ* in Ps. 68:7(6) and *kîšôr* in Prov. 31:19 from *kšr,* as well as the emendation **kaššîr* for *kᵉšîr* in Ezk. 33:32.

The root *kšr* has not been found in the Dead Sea scrolls, not even in the Temple scroll, which still uses the biblical root → טהר *ṭhr* for "cultically clean."[16] Only in the Mishnah and later Jewish literature, in discussions of what is ritually permissible under religious and civil law, do we find *kāšēr* used as a technical term for whatever religious law approves for use and consumption. In modern usage, "kosher" appears almost exclusively in the context of the dietary laws.

II. Meaning and Usage. In Est. 8:5, *kāšēr* appears as a predicate adjective in Esther's appeal to the king. Four conditional clauses with formulas of courtesy reinforce the queen's request; the clauses *wᵉḵāšēr haddāḇār lipnê hammeleḵ* and *wᵉṭôḇâ ʾănî bᵉʿênāyw,* introduced by *w,* are explicative of *wᵉʾim māṣāʾṯî ḥēn lᵉpānāyw.* The purpose is to make the matter appear right to the king and in his own interests.

Eccl. 2:21 provides the best insight into the meaning of *kišrôn.* In conjunction with *daʿaṯ,* knowledge of how to do something, *kišrôn* is the skill to translate this knowledge into success. Both together, *daʿaṯ* and *kišrôn,* are called *ḥoḵmâ.* Thus Koheleth can say: "Sometimes someone who has toiled with wisdom — that is, with knowledge and skill — must leave it all to someone who did not toil for it." In Eccl. 4:4, similarly, *kišrôn* is skill in work that leads to success (*ʿāmāl,* as in 2:21[17]). Eccl. 5:10(11) should also be read against the background of 2:21: "When goods increase, they increase who eat them; and what skill (*kišrôn*) that brings success does their owner then have but to watch them go?" The warning to the poor in Sir. 13:4 is similar: "If you seem skilled (*tkšr*) to (the rich man), he will only exploit you."

---

lexikalischen und grammatikalischen Aramaismen im alttestamentlichen Hebräisch. BZAW, 96 (1966), 68; F. Rosenthal, *Die aramaistische Forschung seit Th. Nöldeke's Veröffentlichungen* (Leiden, 1939), 42f.

16. Cf. esp. G. W. Buchanan, "The Role of Purity in the Structure of the Essene Sect," *RevQ,* 4 (1963-64), 397-406.

17. The meaning is discussed by H. Gese, *Vom Sinai zum Zion. BEvTh,* 64 (1974), 168, n. 1.

Eccl. 10:10 is one of the most difficult verses in the entire book.[18] The tripartite (or more likely bipartite; v. 10aβ appears to be a gloss) protasis illustrates the fact that failure to heed wisdom has its drawbacks:[19] when one lets an iron (tool) get dull or uses one that is already dull, the work takes incomparably more effort. The apodosis (v. 10b) draws a general conclusion from the example. Following Franz Delitzsch,[20] we might translate the MT: "The advantage given by the provision of proper tools is wisdom." This interpretation takes *haḵšēr* as a hiphil infinitive absolute. The ancient versions are little help; each tries in its own way to cope with the text. H. W. Hertzberg and Kurt Galling emend the text to read *kišrôn,* translating: "Is there then profit or advantage in wisdom?" If the hiphil pointing is correct, "make fit" probably means "repair"; Delitzsch states that the Mishnah regularly uses *haḵšēr* for arranging something according to order.[21] But the banal statement that care and repair of tools demonstrates wisdom because it provides a benefit is probably the result of an attempt to restore a corrupt text.[22]

Eccl. 11:6 also creates interpretative problems that depend on the exegete's perspective. Some translations would have a nuance allowing "a glimmer of hope,"[23] since there seems to be "a chance of success." Friedrich Ellermeier,[24] however, argues persuasively that 11:6 must be understood as concessive: "Though you sow your seed in the morning, and though you do not withhold your hand at evening, you still do not know what will prosper (*yiḵšar*), this or that, or whether both alike will be good."

III. *kôšārôṯ* (Ps. 68:7). The noun *kôšārôṯ* is found only in Ps. 68:7(6). The Hebrew lexica associate this word with *kšr.* Ever since the discovery of the term *kṯrt* in Ugaritic mythological texts, referring to the goddesses who aid childbirth, many scholars have interpreted Ps. 68:7(6) as a reference to these Kotarat as bringers of joy.[25] The same term may also occur at Ebla.[26] Ps. 68:7(6) says that Yahweh gives the desolate a home in which to dwell, that he leads out the prisoners *bakkôšārôṯ,* and that only the rebellious continue to dwell in a parched land. Since the translation "songs of joy" for *kôšārôṯ*

---

18. See discussion in H. W. Hertzberg, *Der Prediger. KAT,* XVII/4 (1963), 191; A. Lauha, *Kohelet. BK,* XIX (1978), 188f.
19. K. Galling, *Der Prediger. HAT,* XVIII (^{2}1969), 117.
20. *Ecclesiastes. KD,* VI, 381.
21. *Ibid.,* 193.
22. Cf. also N. Lohfink, *Kohelet. NEB* (1980), 76.
23. Lauha, 203.
24. F. Ellermeier, *Qohelet,* I (Herzberg am Jarz, 1967), 253-268.
25. J. P. Brown, "Kothar, Kinyras, and Kythereia," *JSS,* 10 (1965), 215f.; E. Lipiński, "Les conceptions et couches merveilleuses de ʿAnath," *Syr,* 42 (1965), 65ff.; *idem,* "Psalm 68:7 and the Role of the Košarot," *AION,* N.S. 21[31] (1971), 532-37; W. Herrmann, *Yariḫ und Nikkal und der Preis der Kuṯarāt-Göttinnen. BZAW,* 106 (1968), 35, 46; J. Vlaardingerbroek, *Psalm 68* (diss., Amsterdam, 1973), 27f., 197f., 201; B. Margolis, "The *Kôšārôt/Kṯrt*: Patroness-saints of Women," *JANES,* 4 (1971/72), 52-61; *idem,* "Of Brides and Birds," *JANES,* 4 (1971/72), 113-17; M. H. Lichtenstein, "Psalm 68:7 Revisited," *JANES,* 4 (1971/72), 97-112.
26. M. Dahood, "Ebla, Ugarit, and the OT," *Congress Volume, Göttingen 1977. SVT,* 29 (1978), 86.

can be derived only indirectly through comparison with Ugar. *kṯrt,* Manfred Dietrich and Otto Loretz,[27] citing Akk. *kušartu/kušāru/kušru,*[28] have suggested interpreting Heb. *kwšrwt* as some kind of metal objects like chains. This proposal, which best reflects the context, should not be rejected out of hand. The translation would then be: "He brings forth the prisoners from (*bᵉ* in the sense of *min*) their iron [chains]." In any case, no connection can be established between *kôšārôṯ* in Ps. 68:7(6) and the Aramaic/Hebrew root *kšr,* "be proper."

IV. *kîšôr* (Prov. 31:19). In the poem extolling the good housewife (Prov. 31:10-31), v. 19 uses the hapax legomenon *kîšôr.* The Syr. (*kšyrwtʾ*), followed by the Targ. (*kwšrʾ* > *kwnšrʾ*) associated this word with the root *kšr,* Older commentaries[29] therefore translated *kîšôr* as "distaff," i.e., "the rod that goes straight up."[30] The parallel *peleḵ,* however, shows that William F. Albright's translation[31] "spinning whorl" is correct: *kîšôr* is probably a loanword related to Akk./Sum. *giš-sur,* having nothing to do with the root *kšr.*

V. *kaššîr (Ezk. 33:32). In Ezk. 33:32, Mitchell Dahood has proposed[32] repointing *kᵉšîr* (conj. *kᵉšār*) *ʿᵃgāḇîm,* "like a love song"/"like a singer of love songs"[33] as *kaššîr ʿûgāḇîm,* "a skillful flutist." Since this suggestion has already been accepted by *KBL*³,[34] it must at least be mentioned here. The absence of the comparative particle *kᵉ* is awkward, however; it is therefore better, with Walther Zimmerli, to accept the image of an itinerant singer and retain the MT.

Kellermann

---

27. M. Dietrich and O. Loretz, "Zur Ugaritischen Lexikographie (II)," *OLZ,* 62 (1967), 541.
28. *AHw,* I, 516f.
29. H. L. Strack, *SZ*; G. Wildeboer, *Die Sprüche. KHC,* XV (1897).
30. Strack, 103.
31. W. F. Albright, *Archaeology and the Religion of Israel* (Garden City, ⁵1968), 218, n. 68; cf. A. Boissier, "A Sumerian Word in the Bible," *PSBA,* 35 (1913), 159f.; S. Landersdorfer, *Sumerisches Sprachgut im AT. BWAT,* 21 (1913), 45.
32. M. Dahood, "An Allusion to Koshar in Ezekiel 33,32," *Bibl,* 44 (1963), 531f.
33. W. Zimmerli, *Ezekiel 2. Herm* (Eng. trans. 1983), 197, 201.
34. P. 478a; cf. M. Dahood, "Hebrew Lexicography: A Review of W. Baumgartner's *Lexikon,* Volume II," *Or,* 45 (1976), 341.

כָּתַב kāṯaḇ; כְּתָב keṯāḇ; מִכְתָּב miḵtāḇ; כְּתֹבֶת keṯōḇeṯ

Contents: I. 1. Occurrences; 2. Meaning. II. 1. Materials; 2. Implements. III. Ancient Near East: 1. Biblical Evidence; 2. Archaeology. IV. Secular Texts: 1. Letters; 2. Contracts; 3. Historical Events; 4. Royal Decrees; 5. Official Documents; 6. Instruction; 7. Legal Documents. V. Religious Texts: 1. Prophecy; 2. The Law of Yahweh Given through Moses; 3. Heavenly Books. VI. Dead Sea Scrolls: 1. Scriptural Quotations; 2. Lists; 3. Inscribed Weapons; 4. Sacred and Heavenly Documents. VII. Nouns: 1. *keṯāḇ*; 2. *miḵtāḇ*; 3. *keṯōḇeṯ*. VIII. Aramaic: 1. *keṯaḇ*; 2. *keṯāḇ*.

I. 1. *Occurrences.*

a. *West Semitic.* Hardly any root is as widespread in West Semitic as *ktb*; by contrast, it does not appear at all in the Semitic cuneiform languages, which instead use *šaṭāru,*

---

kāṯaḇ. H. Bauer, *Der Ursprung des Alphabets* (Leipzig, 1937); A. Bertholet, *Die Macht der Schrift in Glauben und Aberglauben. ADAW,* 1948/1; H. Brunner, "Ägyptisches Schreibmaterial," *Ägyptologie. HO,* I/1, 1 (1959); M. S. R. Cohen, *La grande invention de l'écriture et son évolution,* 2 vols. (Paris, 1958); F. M. Cross, "The Development of the Jewish Scripts," *The Bible and the Ancient Near East. Festschrift W. F. Albright* (Garden City, 1961), 133-202; D. Diringer, *L'Alfabeto nella storia della civiltà* (Florence, 1937); *idem, The Alphabet,* 2 vols. (New York, [3]1968); *idem, Writing* (New York, 1962); G. R. Driver, *Semitic Writing from Pictograph to Alphabet* (London, [3]1976); O. Eissfeldt, *The OT: An Intro.* (Eng. trans., New York, 1965), 669-678; J.-G. Février, *Histoire de l'écriture* (Paris, [2]1959); J. Friedrich, *Geschichte der Schrift* (Heidelberg, 1966); F. Funke, *Buchkunde* (Leipzig, [3]1969); K. Galling, "Tafel, Buch und Blatt," *Near Eastern Studies in Honor of W. F. Albright* (Baltimore, 1971), 207-223; I. J. Gelb, *A Study of Writing* (Chicago, [3]1969); H. Haag, "Die Buchwerdung des Wortes Gottes in der Heiligen Schrift," in J. Feiner and M. Löhrer, eds., *Mysterium Salutis,* I (Einsiedeln, 1965), 289-406; W. Herrmann, "Das Buch des Lebens," *Das Altertum,* 20 (1974), 3-10; L. Koep, *Das himmlische Buch in Antike und Christentum. Theophaneia,* 8 (Bonn, 1952); *idem,* "Buch IV (himmlisch)," *RAC,* II, 664-731; J. Kühlewein, "סֵפֶר *sēfær* Buch," *THAT,* II, 162-173; B. Lang, "Schule und Unterricht im alten Israel," in M. Gilbert, ed., *La Sagesse de l'AT. BETL,* 51 (1979), 186-201; A. Lemaire, "Abécédaires et exercises d'écolier en épigraphie nord-ouest sémitique," *JA,* 266 (1978), 221-235; P. K. McCarter, "The Early Diffusion of the Alphabet," *BA,* 37 (1974), 54-68; A. R. Millard, "The Practice of Writing in Ancient Israel," *BA,* 35 (1972), 98-111; *idem,* "The Ugaritic and Canaanite Alphabets — Some Notes," *Festschrift C. F. A. Schaeffer. UF,* 11 (1979), 613-16; L. Perlitt, *Bundestheologie im AT. WMANT,* 36 (1969); O. Procksch, "Der hebräische Schreiber und sein Buch," *Von Büchern und Bibliotheken. Festschrift E. Kuhnert* (Berlin, 1928), 1-15; W. Röllig, "Die Alphabetschrift," *Handbuch der Archäologie* (Munich, 1969), 289-302; H. P. Rüger, "Schreibmaterial, Buch und Schrift," *BRL*[2], 289-292; G. Schrenk, "βίβλος," *TDNT,* I, 615-620; *idem,* "γράφω," *TDNT,* I, 742-773; K. Sethe, *Vom Bilde zum Buchstaben* (1939); M. Sznycer, "L'Origine de l'alphabet sémitique," *L'Espace et la lettre. Cahiers Jussieu,* 3 (Paris, 1977), 79-123; S. Warner, "The alphabet: an innovation and its diffusion," *VT,* 30 (1980), 81-90; C. Wendel, *Die griechisch-römische Buchbeschreibung verglichen mit der des Vorderen Orients* (Halle, 1949); E. Würthwein, *The Text of the OT* (Eng. trans., Grand Rapids, 1979).

"write"[1] (cf. Heb. *šōṭēr*, "registrar"), and *šapāru*, "send, write"[2] (cf. Heb. *spr*, discussed below). In West Semitic, we may cite Ugar. *ktb*[3] and various inscriptions.[4]

In modern literary Arabic, the root appears in many expressions, e.g., *kitāb*, "letter, document"; *al-kitāb*, "Koran, Bible"; *kitāba*, "writing"; *maktab*, "office"; and *kātib*, "scribe, secretary."

Egyptian goes its own way. As a verb, *sš* (etymology unknown) means "write," but also "paint," "draw lines," and even "register recruits." As a noun, it means "writing," "painting," "illustration," "picture," "drawing," "book," etc., but also "writer (= official)," and often even "writing material, papyrus."[5]

b. *Hebrew and Aramaic*. The verb *ktb* is common throughout most of the OT, with 222 occurrences (none in Genesis, only 6 in Psalms). It appears 17 times in the niphal and twice in the piel (Isa. 10:1); the other occurrences are all in the qal. The active participle appears only 3 times (Neh. 10:1[Eng. 9:38]; Jer. 32:12; 36:18). The professional "scribe" is not called *kōṯēḇ* but → סֹפֵר *sōp̄ēr* (beginning with Ezra "the scribe").[6] There are 17 occurrences of the noun *keṯāḇ*, "document, list," and 8 of *miḵtāḇ*, "writing, document"; *keṯōḇeṯ*, "tattoo," occurs once (Lev. 19:28). The Aramaic verb *keṯaḇ* occurs 8 times, the noun *keṯāḇ* 12 times.

c. *LXX*. When representing the MT, the LXX regularly uses *gráphein* to translate *ktb*. Exceptions: *epigráphein* (Nu. 17:17f.[2f.]; Isa. 44:5; Prov. 7:3), *diagráphein* (Josh. 18:4; Ezk. 43:11), *katagráphein* (Ex. 17:14; Nu. 11:26; 1 Ch. 9:1; Hos. 8:12; Job 13:26), *engráphein* (Ps. 149:9), *merízein* (Josh. 18:6), *chōrobateín* (Josh. 18:8), *katachōrízein* (Est. 2:23), *dogmatízein* (Est. 3:9), and paraphrastic constructions with *graphḗ* (Ps. 87[LXX 86]:6; 2 Ch. 30:5,18) and *syngraphḗ* (Job 31:35).

2. *Meaning*. The basic meaning of *ktb* (like that of *gráphein*) is undoubtedly "incise, inscribe." This is shown above all by its use in parallel with *ḥrš*, "engrave" (Jer. 17:1: on the horns of the altar [stone] and the tablet of the heart [metaphorically of stone]); *ḥqq*, "engrave" (Isa. 30:8, which speaks curiously of "writing" on a tablet and "engraving" on a *sēp̄er*[7]); *ḥṣb*, "carve out" (Job 19:24: with an iron stylus on rock[8]); *b'r*, "carve" (Dt. 27:8; Hab. 2:2); *ptḥ*, "engrave" (Ex. 28:36: on gold; cf.

---

1. *AHw*, II (1972), 1203.
2. *AHw*, II, 1170f.
3. *WUS*, no. 1400; *UT*, no. 1320.
4. See *DISO*, 128f.; *KAI*, 12, 35. For other dialects, see *KBL*[3], *s.v.* The double root *ktb/kdb* in Mandaic is discussed by F. Altheim and R. Stiehl, *Die Araber in der alten Welt* IV (Berlin, 1967), 172f.; *MdD*, 225a.
5. *WbÄS*, III, 475ff.
6. Cf. H. H. Schaeder, *Esra de Schreiber. BHTh*, 5 (1930), 39-42.
7. For a discussion of the passage, see H. Wildberger, *Jesaja. BK*, X/3 (1982), 1166-69; Wildberger suggests that *sēp̄er* here means "bronze." In Job 19:23, too, *sēp̄er* probably means "bronze"; see, e.g., É. P. Dhorme, *A Comm. on the Book of Job* (Eng. trans. 1967, repr. Nashville, 1984), 281f.
8. See the comms.; also J. J. Stamm, "Versuch zur Erklärung von Hiob 19,24," *ThZ*, 4 (1948),

39:30). God's own writing is "engraved" (*ḥrt*) on tablets of stone (Ex. 32:16). These passages speak of the earliest writing materials used in Syria and Palestine: stone and metal.[9] At first ostraca, too, were incised — for example, the ostracon from Izbet Sartah (12th century B.C.), discussed below.

More generally, *ktb* means "write upon" (Ex. 31:18; 32:15; Dt. 9:10), "write down" (Ex. 17:14), "write" (e.g., letters[10]), "sign" (Jer. 32:12), "list" (Nu. 11:26; etc.), "sketch" (Ezk. 43:11); figuratively, it can mean "prescribe, enjoin."[11]

The most important antonym of *ktb* is → מחה *māḥâ,* "wipe out" (cf. Nu. 5:23).

II. 1. *Materials.* The basic meaning of *ktb* suggests the incising of characters on stone or metal;[12] normally, however, people used materials that could be written on with less cost and effort. The OT uses the word *sēp̱er,* literally "document," for such material. This Hebrew word should not be translated invariably as "book"; it can denote a wide variety of documents, as well as the writing surface itself.[13] The most obvious choice would be clay tablets, which were written upon with a stylus while still moist; but they were suitable only for a script like Akkadian and Ugaritic cuneiform, which consisted of impressible straight lines. For Hebrew script, with its cursive ductus, the most readily available materials were potsherds, written upon with ink (or sometimes incised[14]). As elsewhere in the ancient Near East, short texts were undoubtedly written on flat pieces of wood covered with wax, usually bound together with leather hinges (such wooden "tablets" may be mentioned in Isa. 30:8; Hab. 2:2).

Sheets of papyrus were introduced from Egypt. The writing was done in columns on leaves that could be glued together to form a scroll, as Jer. 36:23 probably assumes. In Palestine, leather was an especially common writing material. It was more durable than papyrus and therefore more suitable for heavily used documents that had to have a long life-span. Leather is prescribed for copies of the Torah.[15] Most of the scrolls and fragments discovered at Qumran are leather, with writing only on the hair side. The scroll described in Ezk. 2:9f., contrary to normal usage, has writing on both sides, possibly to suggest the terrible overabundance of the divine message.

2. *Implements.* A stylus (made of iron: Jer. 17:1 [with a diamond point]; Job 19:24)

331-38); *idem,* "Zu Hiob 19_{24}," *ZAW,* 65 (1953), 302; K. Galling, "Die Grabinschrift Hiobs," *WO,* 2 (1954/59), 3-6.

9. Rüger, 289f.
10. See below.
11. See V.2.b below.
12. See I.2 above.
13. Cf. Kühlewein, 165-67.
14. See above.
15. Ep.Arist. 176; Josephus *Ant. xii.*89f.

could serve as a writing implement for incising characters on hard materials. As a rule, however, the writer used a pen made of reed or (as in Egypt) rush to write with ink on potsherds, papyrus, or leather (Jer. 36:18).

III. Ancient Near East.

1. *Biblical Evidence.* The root *ktb* (*ca.* 220 occurrences[16]) appears substantially less often than *'mr* (*ca.* 5,280 occurrences[17]) and *dbr* (*ca.* 1,100 occurrences); this observation by itself indicates that in Israel the spoken word played an incomparably more important role than the written word as a medium of both human communication and divine revelation. It cannot be accidental that Genesis never mentions writing. The first person the Bible associates with the act of writing is Moses (Ex. 17:14; 24:4; 34:27f.; Nu. 33:2; Dt. 31:9,22,24). Indeed, Yahweh himself is described as "writing" in contexts involving Moses (Ex. 24:12; 31:18; 32:15f.; 34:1; Dt. 4:13; 5:22; 9:10; 10:2,4). Joshua writes (Josh. 8:32; 24:26), and the miracle of sun that was granted him is written in "the Book of the Upright" (Josh. 10:13). The representatives sent by Joshua to describe the land can also write (Josh. 18:2-9). In the "period of the Judges," writing is assumed to be relatively common (Jgs. 8:14). Samuel writes down the law concerning kingship (1 S. 10:25), and the Chronicler characterizes not only Samuel but also Nathan and Gad as writing prophets (1 Ch. 29:29). David is assumed to be able to write as a matter of course (2 S. 11:14f.); in his administration, he employs a *mazkîr* and a *sôpēr* (2 S. 8:16f.), Solomon two *sôp^e^rîm* and a *mazkîr* (1 K. 4:3). Deuteronomy assumes that the father of a family is able to write the words of the law on the doorposts of his house (Dt. 6:9; 11:20). Isa. 10:19 can represent the postexilic period.

In the Hebrew Bible it is presupposed that one ordinarily writes in the Hebrew language. Documents written in Aramaic are mentioned explicitly in Dnl. 2:4; Ezr. 4:7. The edict of Xerxes regarding the Jews was communicated in the "script and language" of the Jews (Est. 8:9), undoubtedly in Aramaic, while the decrees of the great king were communicated to the other subjects "in all the scripts and languages of the Persian empire" (Est. 3:12; 8:9).

2. *Archaeology.* Scholars today generally agree that writing was widespread in Canaan at an early date. During the second millennium, five writing systems were in use: Egyptian hieroglyphics; Akkadian cuneiform; the pseudo-hieroglyphic script of Byblos, which used 114 signs; the cuneiform alphabet of Ugarit; and the linear Phoenician-Canaanite alphabet. Vestiges of other scripts are also found.[18] Mesopotamian cuneiform in particular was taught in all the Canaanite city-states during the Middle and Late Bronze Age.[19]

---

16. See I.1.b above.
17. *KBL*³.
18. See Rüger, 291f.
19. See H. Tadmor, "A Lexicographical Text from Hazor," *IEJ*, 27 (1977), 98-102.

It is becoming increasingly clear that the alphabet originated in the Palestinian region, "where the cuneiform and hieroglyphic spheres of influence met."[20] The earliest alphabetic cuneiform tablet found at Ugarit dates from *ca.* 1360 B.C.;[21] the script itself is earlier. The earliest known evidence for Israel's adoption of the Phoenician-Canaanite alphabet of twenty-two consonants is a twelfth-century ostracon from Izbet Ṣarṭah, near Aphek ("the period of the judges"[22]). Schooling in Israel dates from a similarly early period. According to Bernhard Lang,[23] the alphabet fragments from Lachish[24] "make it reasonable to assume that there was formal school instruction" as early as the ninth or eighth century. The earliest extended Hebrew text outside the Bible, however, is still the Siloam inscription (*ca.* 700).

IV. Secular Texts. In the ancient Near East, writing was used for interpersonal communication ("letters"), songs (work songs, laments, victory songs, love songs), binding agreements (bills of sale, leases, labor contracts, marriage contracts, wills, vassal treaties, and international treaties), preserving events for posterity (annals, chronicles, inscriptions), laws and other public statements (proclamations of the sovereign), administrative documents, didactic works (including Egyptian autobiographies), epics, stories and tales, scholarly texts (medicine, mathematics, astronomy, jurisprudence), myths, magical texts, sacrificial rituals, hymns, and prayers. The Hebrew Bible explicitly mentions the use of writing for the following types of documents:

1. *Letters.* Letters are written by David to Joab (2 S. 11:14f. [*sēp̱er*]), Jezebel to the elders and nobles of Jezreel (1 K. 21:8f.,11 [*sᵉp̱ārîm*]), Jehu to the rulers of Samaria (2 K. 10:1,6 [*sᵉp̱ārîm*]), Hezekiah to the tribes of Ephraim and Manasseh (2 Ch. 30:1 [*'iggᵉrôṯ*]), Sennacherib to Hezekiah (2 Ch. 32:17 [*sᵉp̱ārîm*]), Mordecai and Esther to the Jews throughout the Persian Empire (Est. 9:20,29 [*sᵉp̱ārîm, 'iggereṯ*]),[25] the Samaritans to Xerxes (Ezr. 4:6 [*śiṭnâ*]) and Artaxerxes (Ezr. 4:7f. [*ništᵉwān, 'iggᵉrâ*]), and Sanballat to Nehemiah (Neh. 6:5 [*'iggereṯ pᵉṯûḥâ*]).

2. *Contracts.* The bill of divorce (*sēp̱er kᵉrîṯuṯ*) mentioned in Dt. 24:1,3 is written, as is the deed for the field purchased by Jeremiah (Jer. 32:10; cf. v. 44); here *ktb* also denotes the act of signing by witnesses (Jer. 32:12). Also written down are the agreement between king and people at the inception of the monarchy (1 S. 10:25 [*mišpaṭ hammᵉlūḵâ*]) and the obligation imposed upon the community by Nehemiah (Neh. 10:1[9:38] [*'mānâ*]).

---

20. Röllig, 295.
21. Millard, *UF,* 11 (1979), 613.
22. J. Naveh, "Some Considerations on the Ostracon from ʿIzbet Ṣarṭah," *IEJ,* 28 (1978), 31-35.
23. P. 119.
24. Cf. Lemaire.
25. See IV.4 below.

3. *Historical Events.* Historical events are recorded in writing: the battle with the Amalekites (Ex. 17:14 [in a *sēp̄er*]) and (in poetic form in the "Book of the Upright") the battles at Gibeon and on the mountains of Gilboa (Josh. 10:13; 2 S. 1:18). The text refers to several historical writings: the "Book of the Acts of Solomon" (*sēp̄er diḇrê šᵉlōmōh*: 1 K. 11:41), the "Book of the Chronicles of the Kings of Israel" (*sēp̄er diḇrê hayyāmîm lᵉmalḵê yiśrāʾēl*: 1 K. 14:19; 15:31; 16:5,14,20,27; 22:39; 2 K. 1:18; 13:8,12; 14:15,28; 15:11,15,21,26,31), the "Book of the Chronicles of the Kings of Judah" (*sēp̄er diḇrê hayyāmîm lᵉmalḵê yᵉhûḏâ*: 1 K. 14:29; 15:7,23; 22:46; 2 K. 8:23; 12:20[19]; 14:18; 15:6,36; 16:19; 20:20; 21:17,25; 23:28; 24:5), the "Book of the Kings of Israel" (*sēp̄er malḵê yiśrāʾēl*: 1 Ch. 9:1; 2 Ch. 20:34), the "Book of the Kings of Judah and Israel" (*sēp̄er hammᵉlāḵîm lîhûḏâ weyiśrāʾēl*: 2 Ch. 16:11; *sēp̄er malḵê-yᵉhûḏâ wᵉyiśrāʾēl*: 2 Ch. 25:26; 28:26; 32:32), the "Book of the Kings of Israel and Judah" (*sēp̄er malḵê-yiśrāʾēl wîhûḏâ*: 2 Ch. 27:7; 35:27; 36:8), the "Midrash of the Book of the Kings" (*miḏraš sēp̄er hammᵉlāḵîm*: 2 Ch. 24:27), and the "History of the Kings of Israel" (*diḇrê malḵê yiśrāʾēl,* without *ktb*: 2 Ch. 33:18).

The following should also be listed as historical works: the "Words of Shemaiah the Prophet and Iddo the Seer" (2 Ch. 12:15), the "Midrash of Iddo the Prophet" (2 Ch. 13:22), the "Words of Jehu the Son of Hanani" (2 Ch. 20:34), the "Acts of Uzziah" written by Isaiah the son of Amoz (2 Ch. 26:22), the "Vision of Isaiah the Prophet in the Book of the Kings of Judah and Israel" (2 Ch. 32:32), and the "Annals of Xerxes" (Est. 2:23; 6:1) or the "Annals of the Kings of Media and Persia" (Est. 10:2).

4. *Royal Decrees.* Written royal decrees appear primarily in Esther. The king's command to depose Vashti is to be written among the laws of the Medes and Persians (Est. 1:19). Also written are Xerxes' decree to destroy the Jews (3:9,12), the counter-order to save them (8:5,8,10), and the Purim letters of Mordecai (9:20-22) and Esther (vv. 29-32).

5. *Official Documents.* Official documents or lists are mentioned frequently. Nu. 33:1-49, whose present late form probably conceals an earlier document,[26] is based on a list of stages in the desert. Nu. 11:26 mentions a register of the seventy or seventy-two elders who are to relieve Moses of some of his burdens. Lists of towns in Benjamin, Simeon, Zebulun, Issachar, Asher, Naphtali, and Dan are "recorded" in Josh. 18:11–19:48 (cf. *ktb* in 18:4,6,8 [twice],9). Gideon has a young man write down the names of the seventy-seven officials and elders of Succoth (Jgs. 8:14). In Nu. 17:16-18(1-3), the names of the tribes are written on twelve rods — possibly an allusion to Egyptian scepters, which often bore the name of the owner.[27] Ezk. 37:16,20 probably reflects the same practice (with *ʿēṣ* instead of *maṭṭeh*). Jer. 22:30 alludes to a list of the Davidic

---

26. M. Noth, "Der Wallfahrtsweg zum Sinai (Nu 33)," *PJ,* 36 (1940), 5-28 = *Aufsätze zur biblischen Landes- und Altertumskunde* (Neukirchen-Vluyn, 1971), I, 55-74; J. Koening, "La localisation du Sinäi et les traditions des scribes," *RHPR,* 43 (1963), 2-31; 44 (1964), 200-235.

27. Cf. A. Erman and H. Ranke, *Ägypten und ägyptisches Leben im Altertum* (1928 repr. Hildesheim, 1984), 256, n. 5.

kings (or a list of the citizens of Jerusalem, a kind of "city register"[28]). A list of the heads of the Simeonite families who helped their people find new territory in the time of Hezekiah appears in 1 Ch. 4:34-37 (cf. v. 41: "registered by name"). A list of the twenty-four courses of priests, ostensibly written in the time of David but probably Maccabean, is found in 1 Ch. 24:6-19. A list found by Nehemiah in Jerusalem contains the names of the first exiles to return (Neh. 7:5ff.). The Chronicler cites a list, contained in the Book of the Chronicles, of the heads of the priestly and levitical families (Neh. 12:22ff.). A record of the contribution to the temple brought by Ezra is mentioned in Ezr. 8:34. The date when the siege of Jerusalem began is written down (Ezk. 24:2), as is the plan of the temple (Ezk. 43:11).[29] The practice of tattooing with an owner's name is reflected by Isa. 44:5. The engraving of *qōḏeš leYHWH* on the diadem of the high priest is denoted by *pth* in Ex. 28:36 and by *ktb* in 39:30.[30]

6. *Instruction.* In Prov. 22:20, the wisdom instructor notes that he has written down his teaching for his student. Koheleth is likewise said to have composed and written astute and true sayings (Eccl. 12:10).

7. *Legal Documents.* Job 31:35 speaks of an indictment written by an adversary. On the other hand, Job wants his defense to be written down permanently for posterity (Job 19:23f.).

V. Religious Texts. In religious contexts, *ktb* is used for three major types of written documents.

1. *Prophecy.* Yahweh commands Isaiah and Habakkuk to write inflammatory words for everyone to read (Isa. 8:1; 30:8; Hab. 2:2). Jeremiah is the first prophet to have his words written down on a large scale at his own behest (Jer. 36; cf. 25:13; 30:2; 45:1; 51:60). The prophet's message, rejected by his listeners, is preserved in writing for the future; it retains its significance beyond the moment of its oral proclamation. But the written scroll suffers the same fate as the spoken word: the two are therefore identical. Nevertheless, the word of Yahweh cannot be destroyed; it comes forth once more, and will not be denied (Jer. 36). This lays the foundation for the notion that the written word speaks, a familiar concept in rabbinical exegesis (*hakkāṯûḇ 'ômēr*) and the NT (*légei hē graphḗ*).[31] The written word always remains a spoken word. Postbiblical Judaism came to prefer the term *hammiqrā'*, "what is read" (cf. Neh. 8:8), to *hakkāṯûḇ*, "what is written."[32] The Islamic "Koran" is based on the same

28. W. Rudolph, *Jeremia. HAT,* XII (^{3}1968).

29. W. Zimmerli, *Ezekiel 2. Herm* (Eng. trans. 1983), 419: "draw."

30. Cf. I.2 above.

31. Cf. W. Bacher, *Die exegetische Terminologie der jüdischen Traditionsliteratur,* 2 vols. (1899-1905, repr. Darmstadt, 1965), *s.v. 'mr*; J. Bonsirven, *Exégèse rabbinique et exégèse paulinienne* (Paris, 1939), 29-32, 339-345.

32. See V.2.b below.

root.[33] Ezk. 2:9f. presupposes that the prophetic word has become a book. The speaker of Ps. 102 also wishes to record his trust and deliverance as a prophetic message for the future (v. 19[18]). The redactor of Dt. 31:16-22 sees in the Song of Moses (Dt. 32) a testimony against Israel written down by Moses for later ages, should Israel break its covenant with Yahweh (16:19,22).

The Chronicler ascribes historiographical writing to the prophets Samuel, Nathan, Gad, Ahijah the Shilonite, and Iddo (1 Ch. 29:29; 2 Ch. 9:29). A lament for Josiah sung by Jeremiah and included with other laments in the book of "Laments" is noted in 2 Ch. 35:25.

Although writing was undoubtedly a major function of the priesthood, the scribal work of priests is mentioned only once (Nu. 5:23: writing a curse for jealousy trial). Here we find an almost magical conception of the power inherent in the written word (cf. also Jer. 51:63f.).

2. *The Law of Yahweh Given through Moses.*

a. *d^eḇārîm.* In line with the Deuteronomic and Deuteronomistic conception of a written covenant document, Moses writes (or is commanded to write) "all the words of Yahweh" (Ex. 24:4), "these words" (Ex. 34:27), or "all the words of this law in a *sēp̱er*" (Dt. 31:24). Similarly, Israel is to write "these words which I command you this day" (Dt. 6:6) or "these words of mine" (Dt. 11:18) on its doorposts (Dt. 6:9; 11:20), and "all the words of this law" on twelve stones (Dt. 27:3,8). Thus "(all) the words of the (this) law" (Dt. 28:58; 2 K. 23:3) or "the (this) covenant" (2 K. 23:3; 2 Ch. 34:31) are written in "a (this) book." Ex. 24:4 refers to the Decalog;[34] 34:27 probably refers to vv. 12-26. The other passages have in mind the Deuteronomic law in the broader or narrower sense. The word of Yahweh written "in this book" includes curses (2 Ch. 34:21,24).

Alongside the tradition that Moses wrote the words of Yahweh in a *sēp̱er,* we find the Deuteronomic and Deuteronomistic notion (probably later[35]) that Yahweh himself used his finger (Ex. 31:18; Dt. 9:10) to write his words on two stone tablets (Ex. 31:18; 32:15 [without object]; 34:1; Dt. 10:2 ["the words"]; 5:22 ["these words" = the Decalog]; 9:10 ["all the words that Yahweh spoke out of the midst of the fire"]; 4:13; 10:4 ["the ten words"]; Ex. 34:28 ["the words of the covenant, the ten words"]; 24:12 [*hattôrâ w^ehammiṣwâ*]). Jer. 17:1 speaks figuratively of "the tablet of the heart" (on which the sin of Judah is written), as do Prov. 3:3; 7:3 (writing *ḥeseḏ* and *'^emeṯ* or the *tôrâ* and *miṣwôṯ* of Yahweh on it).

b. *tôrâ.* Although the Deuteronomistic tradition and the Chronicler's history associate the *tôrâ* with the name of Yahweh and Moses, the text rarely says that Yahweh or Moses wrote the *tôrâ.* Jer. 31:33 says figuratively that in the new covenant Yahweh

---

33. Cf. R. Paret, *Mohammed und der Koran* (Stuttgart, ⁴1976), 53-55.

34. See H. Haag, "Das 'Buch des Bundes' (Ex 24,7)," *Wort Gottes in der Zeit. Festschrift K. H. Schelkle* (Düsseldorf, 1973), 23f.

35. Contra Perlitt, 211.

will write his *tôrâ* on the human heart. Referring to the Deuteronomic law, Dt. 31:9 says: "Moses wrote this law, and gave it to the priests the sons of Levi, who carried the ark of the covenant of Yahweh, and to all the elders of Israel." Josh. 8:32 says that Joshua made a copy (*mišneh*) of the law of Moses, which he had written. We are also told that Joshua wrote the text of the Shechem covenant in the "book of the law of God" (Josh. 24:26). Finally, the king is instructed to write a copy (*mišneh*) of "this law" in a *sēp̱er* (Dt. 17:18). This passage already thinks of Deuteronomy as a "literary document."[36]

In fact, most of the relevant passages say nothing about the process through which the written Torah came into being, but think of it as "written" (*kāṯûḇ*), a complete (Dt. 4:2; 13:1[12:32]) and authoritative document. Israel is bound by what is written in the "law" (Neh. 8:14: "that Yahweh commanded by Moses"), "the book of the law" (*sēp̱er hattôrâ*: Josh. 8:34), "this book of the law" (*sēp̱er hattôrâ hazzeh*: Dt. 29:20[21]; Josh. 1:8; *hazzō'ṯ*: Dt. 28:61), "the law of Yahweh" (*tôraṯ YHWH*: 1 Ch. 16:40), "the law of Moses" (*tôraṯ mōšeh*: Josh. 8:32; Dnl. 9:11), "the book of Moses" (*sēp̱er mōšeh*: Neh. 13:1), "the book" (*hassēp̱er*: 2 K. 23:24), "this book" (*hassēp̱er hazzeh*: Dt. 29:19,26[20,27]; 2 K. 22:13; 23:3), "the book of the law of Moses" (*sēp̱er tôraṯ mōšeh*: Josh. 23:6), or "the book of the law of God" (*sēp̱er tôraṯ 'ᵉlōhîm*: Josh. 24:26). In rabbinic literature, *kāṯûḇ* comes to mean an individual passage from scripture, *hakkāṯûḇ* the entire Bible (a usage superseded in turn by *hammiqrā'*[37]). The pl. *kᵉṯûḇîm* can also refer to the scriptures as a whole, but more commonly it denotes the writings constituting the third division of the canon.

All activities, but especially the celebration of festivals and the performance of the temple cult, must be done according to "what is written" (*kakkāṯûḇ*; Dnl. 9:13: *ka'ᵃšer kāṯûḇ*) in "the law" (*tôrâ*: Neh. 10:35,37), "the law of Yahweh" (*tôraṯ YHWH*: 2 Ch. 31:3; 35:26), "the law of Moses" (*tôraṯ mōšeh*: 1 K. 2:3; Ezr. 3:2; 2 Ch. 23:18; Dnl. 9:13), "the book of the law of Moses" (*sēp̱er tôraṯ mōšeh*: 2 K. 14:6; 2 Ch. 25:4 conj.), "the book of Moses" (*sēp̱er mōšeh*: 2 Ch. 35:12), or "this book of the covenant" (*sēp̱er habbᵉrîṯ hazzeh*: 2 K. 23:21). The absolute expression *kakkāṯûḇ,* "as it is written," "according to what is prescribed," which lies behind the NT idiom *hōs/hṓsper/kathṓs/katháper gégraptai,*[38] conceives of the Torah as a single normative entity (2 Ch. 30:5,18; Ezr. 3:4; Neh. 8:15). In Ps. 40:8(7), the supplicant is aware of this notion: what he must do is written in the scroll of the book (*mᵉgillaṯ-sēp̱er*: v. 8[7]). The "psalms of the law" as a group, and especially Ps. 1, assume that the worshipper has the written Torah before him.

Therefore *ktb* in the sense of "express one's will" can sometimes mean "prescribe" or "ordain." Yahweh prescribed for Israel *haḥuqqîm wᵉeṯ-hammišpāṭîm wᵉhattôrâ wᵉhammiṣwâ* (2 K. 17:37, par. *ṣwh* in v. 34) and *tôrāṯî* (Hos. 8:12). Yahweh ordained "bitterness" (*mᵉrōrôṯ*) for Job (Job 13:26). Isaiah castigates the legal capriciousness

---

36. G. von Rad, *Deuteronomy. OTL* (Eng. trans. 1966), 119.
37. See V.1 above.
38. See "γράφω," *TDNT,* I, 747-49.

of the royal officials, "overzealous scribes" (*m^e^ḵatt^e^ḇîm*) who ordain oppression (Isa. 10:1). The root is used similarly in Arabic: *kutiba,* "it is prescribed" (Koran 2:183); *kataba ʿalā nafsihi,* "he has pledged himself" (Koran 6:12).

3. *Heavenly Books.* Heavenly books in which the fates of individuals and nations are recorded constitute a third complex of the written word of Yahweh. In Ps. 69:29(28), the supplicant prays that his enemies "may be blotted out of the book of the living" and "not be enrolled among the righteous." In a similar vein, Moses prays that Yahweh — if he will not forgive the sinful people — will blot him "out of thy book which thou hast written" (Ex. 32:32); Yahweh replies that he blots only sinners out of his book (v. 33). It is thought that the names of all those living on the earth are entered by God in his book; to be blotted out of this book means death. The devout psalmist even believes that every one of his days has been written providentially in God's book (Ps. 139:16). Isa. 4:3 defines the sacred remnant in Zion as "every one who has been recorded for life in Jerusalem." These are the elect, chosen to live and set apart for eschatological salvation.[39] The same idea is taken up in Dnl. 12:1. On the other hand, those who forsake Yahweh are "written in the earth" (Jer. 17:13). Ezk. 13:9 threatens that the false prophets "shall not be enrolled in the register of the house of Israel, nor shall they enter the land of Israel." Here the notion of lists of tribes and returning exiles coalesces with the idea of a heavenly book. Nations as well as individuals are registered in the book of Yahweh (Ps. 87:6). According to Erich Zenger,[40] the notion of heavenly tablets containing lists of citizens and the living was also the source of the tablet tradition.[41]

Somewhat different is the notion that good and evil deeds are recorded so that those who do them may be rewarded and punished. Nehemiah, for example, prays that God will not wipe out his good deeds (Neh. 13:14). Because evil deeds are recorded by God, his judgment is "written judgment" (*mišpāṭ kāṯûḇ*: Ps. 149:9). It will come without fail, even if not at once (Isa. 65:6). Mal. 3:16 comforts the faithful with the notion that their sufferings are recorded in a "book of remembrance."

VI. Dead Sea Scrolls. The verb *ktb* appears 61 times in the Dead Sea scrolls: once in 1QpHab, 12 times in 1QS, 34 times in 1QM, once in 1QSa, once in 1Q34, 4 times in 4QFlor, 16 times in CD, and twice in 4QDibHam. The occurrences fall into three basic groups:

1. *Scriptural Quotations.* Scriptural quotations are limited to 1QS, CD, and — predictably — 4QFlor. Quotations are introduced by *haddāḇār ʾ^a^šer kāṯûḇ* (CD 7:10; 19:7), *kî kēn kāṯûḇ* (1QS 5:15; CD 11:18), *kî kāṯûḇ* (CD 11:20), *ʾ^a^šer kāṯûḇ* (4QFlor

---

39. H. Wildberger, *Isaiah 1–12* (Eng. trans., Minneapolis, 1991), 168-170.

40. E. Zenger, "Ps 87, 6 und die Tafeln von Sinai," *Wort, Lied und Gottessprach. Festschrift J. Ziegler,* II. FzB, 2 (1972), 97-103.

41. See V.2.a above.

1:15f.), *'ᵃšer hāyâ kāṯûḇ* (CD 1:13), or, most commonly — as in the canonical scriptures[42] — by *ka'ᵃšer kāṯûḇ* (1QS 5:17; 8:14; 4QFlor 1:2,12; CD 7:19) or abs. *kāṯûḇ* (CD 5:1,10; 9:5). An interesting passage is CD 19:1, which uses *kk* as an abbreviation for *ka'ᵃšer kāṯûḇ* or *kakkāṯûḇ*; this shows how common the citation formula was.

2. *Lists.* The verb *ktb* is used in 1QS, 1QSa, and CD for the listing of aspirants and community members in hierarchies, registers, and divisions (1QS 5:23, etc.; 1QSa 1:21; CD 13:12; 14:4; 19:35). Specialized meanings include "charge to someone's account" (CD 6:20) and "record a criticism" (by the *mᵉḇaqqēr*; 9:18).

3. *Inscribed Weapons.* The War scroll uses *ktb* 34 times for inscriptions on trumpets, standards, shields, and lances (1QM 3:2ff.).

4. *Sacred and Heavenly Documents.* A prophetic word written down at God's command is mentioned in 1QpHab 7:1; the Decalog is referred to by 1Q34 3:2,7, addressed to God: "Thy right hand hath written." In 4QDibHam 3:12f., the author cites "what Moses and thy servants the prophets have written" (cf. Lk. 16:29; 24:27; Acts 26:22); in 4QDibHam 6:14, the words "all that is written in the book of life" clearly refer to the Mosaic law.[43] But when CD 3:3 states that Isaac and Jacob are recorded "as friends of God and his allies forever," the author is probably thinking of a heavenly book; the same is true of CD 20:19, which says that a "book of remembrance" (*sēp̄er zikkārôn*) will be written "for those who fear God and honor his name."

Strangely enough, the Dead Sea scrolls never mention their own writing.

VII. Nouns.

1. *kᵉṯāḇ.* The noun *kᵉṯāḇ* is found only in postexilic texts, especially Esther. In 8 passages (Est. 3:14; 4:8; 8:8,13; 9:27; Dnl. 10:21; 1 Ch. 28:19; Ezr. 4:7) it means "document," always of an official nature. In Est. 3:13, it refers to a document distributed in *sᵉp̄ārîm*; in 4:8, it describes a "legal document" (*kᵉṯāḇ-haddāṯ*); in 9:27, it denotes the Purim ordinance; in Ezr. 4:7, it is the Hebrew translation of Pers. *ništᵉwān,* "document, letter." Only twice does it have a theological meaning: in Dnl. 10:21, it presumably refers to the canonical book of Jeremiah; in 1 Ch. 28:19, it denotes the description of the temple from the hand of Yahweh.[44]

In 3 passages, *kᵉṯāḇ* means "register." Ezr. 2:62 (par. Neh. 7:64) speaks of registers of priestly genealogies. Ezk. 13:9 has already been discussed.[45] In Ps. 87:6, the proposed

42. See V.2.b above.

43. M. Baillet, "Un recueil liturgique de Qumrân, Grotte 4: 'Les paroles des luminaires,' " *RB*, 68 (1961), 232.

44. Contra W. Rudolph, *Chronikbücher. HAT,* XXI (1955), 188.

45. See V.3 above.

emendation of *biḵtōḇ* to *biḵtāḇ* is not persuasive.[46] Finally, on 4 occasions (Est. 1:22; 3:12; 8:9 [twice]) *kᵉṯāḇ* means the script used in writing (as distinct from *lāšôn,* "language"). The expression *biḵtāḇ* can mean either "in writing" (2 Ch. 2:10[11]) or "as prescribed" (35:4).

2. *miḵtāḇ*. The noun *miḵtāḇ* does not appear to differ in meaning from *kᵉṯāḇ*. It can refer to a document (Isa. 38:9: Hezekiah's thanksgiving; 2 Ch. 21:12: Elijah's letter to Joram) or written instructions (2 Ch. 35:4: Solomon's directions, par. *kᵉṯāḇ*[47]), the written text (Dt. 10:4), as well as the script used in writing (Ex. 32:16; 39:30). Twice in the *dᵉḇārîm* tablet tradition (Ex. 32:16; Dt. 10:4)[48] it refers to Yahweh's writing. The expression *bᵉmiḵtāḇ* (like *biḵtāḇ*) means "in writing" (2 Ch. 36:22 par. Ezr. 1:1; antonym: *qôl*).

3. *kᵉṯōḇeṯ*. The hapax legomenon *kᵉṯōḇeṯ* in Lev. 19:28 refers to a tattoo for protection against the spirits of the dead.

VIII. Aramaic.

1. *kᵉṯaḇ*. The Aramaic verb *kᵉṯaḇ* (only in the peal) is used primarily with secular documents: the letter sent by the ringleaders of the Samarian opposition (Ezr. 4:8) to thwart the rebuilding of the wall; Tattennai's letter to Darius (5:7,10); the edict of Cyrus (6:2); a proclamation of Darius (Dnl. 6:26[25]). Two texts have theological significance: in Dnl. 7:1, Daniel writes down his dream (writing is the preferred medium for apocalypticism!); in 5:5, God himself writes upon the plaster wall of the palace. Interpretation of what God has written is the function and privilege of the Jewish sages!

2. *kᵉṯāḇ*. In Dnl. 5:7,8,15,16,17, the noun *kᵉṯāḇ* refers to God's writing on the wall; in 6:9,10,11(8,9,10), it refers to Darius's decree. According to Ezr. 6:18, the service of God in the temple was restored "according to the prescription (*kîḵᵉṯāḇ*) of the book of Moses." In Ezr. 7:22, "without prescription" means "as much as one likes."

H. Haag

46. Cf. *BHK*³ and *BHS*; see V.3 above.
47. See above.
48. See V.2.a above.

כֻּתֹּנֶת *kuttōnet*

Contents: I. 1. Etymology, Distribution; 2. LXX. II. OT Usage: 1. Paradise; 2. *k^etōnet passîm*; 3. Priestly Vestments; 4. Other Texts.

I. 1. *Etymology, Distribution.* The word *kuttōnet* is the Hebrew equivalent of one of the most common terms in the civilized world.

In Mesopotamia, we find Sum. *gada* and Akk. *kitû*, "flax, linen."[1] It is unclear whether the Akkadian word derives from the Sumerian[2] or vice versa.[3] There is also *kitītu*, "linen garment,"[4] probably a by-form. In Ugaritic inventories we find *ktn*, "(linen) tunic."[5] There is a single occurrence in Phoenician,[6] where it is distinguished from *bṣ*, "byssus." Most of the occurrences in Imperial Aramaic are found at Elephantine; the word means both a kind of material and a garment.[7] In later Aramaic dialects the predominant meaning is "linen cloth," but in a few cases it denotes a garment: Jewish Aram. *kittānā'*, "flax, linen"; *kittûnā'*, "tunic"; Mand. *kitana*, "linen"; *kituna*, "tunic"; Syr. *kettānā, kuttînā*, "linen."

In Arabic, we find *kattān/kittān*, "flax, linen";[8] in Ethiopic, *k^etān*, "linen."

In Mycenaean Linear B, the word appears as *ki-to*, pl. *ki-to-ne*,[9] which corresponds to Gk. *chitṓn* (Ionian *kithṓn*), which in Homer denotes a short tunic for men.

---

kuttōnet. F. C. Fensham, "A Cappadocian Parallel to Hebrew *kuttōnet*," *VT*, 12 (1962), 196-98; E. Y. Kutscher, "Contemporary Studies in North-western Semitic," *JSS*, 10 (1965), 21-51; A. L. Oppenheim, "Essay on Overland Trade in the First Millennium B.C.," *Festschrift A. Goetze. JCS*, 21 (1967), 236-254; *idem*, "The Golden Garments of the Gods," *JNES*, 8 (1949), 172-193; K. R. Veenhof, *Aspects of Old Assyrian Trade and its Terminology. StDI*, 10 (1972).

1. *AHw*, I (1965), 495.

2. S. Landersdorfer, *Sumerisches Sprachgut im AT. BWAT*, 21 (1916); M. Ellenbogen, *Foreign Words in the OT* (London, 1962), 96.

3. D. O. Edzard, "Sumerische Komposita mit dem 'Nominalpräfix' nu-," *ZA*, N.S. 21 (1962), 94, n. 15.

4. *AHw*, I, 493.

5. *WUS*, no. 1406. The most interesting passage is *KTU*, 3.1, with the addition of the Akkadian text RS 17.227; on the reading, see M. Dietrich and O. Loretz, "Die Vertrag zwischen Šuppiliuma und Niqmandu," *WO*, 3 (1966), 227-233; also B. Landsberger, "Über Farben im Sumerisch-akkadischen," *Festschrift A. Goetze. JCS*, 21 (1967), 158, n. 102.

6. *KAI*, 24, 12.

7. *DISO*, 129; cf. G. R. Driver, "The Aramaic *Papyri* from Egypt," *JRAS*, 59 (1932), 78f.

8. *WKAS*, I, 54f.

9. M. Ventris and J. Chadwick, *Documents in Mycenaean Greek* (Cambridge, 1963), 319f., 397; cf. L. R. Palmer, *The Interpretation of Mycenaean Greek Texts* (Oxford, 1956), 294f., 428f.; and esp. É. Masson, *Recherches sur les plus anciens emprunts sémitiques en grec. Études et commentaires*, 67 (1967), 27-29.

Sappho first uses it for a woman's garment.[10] Lat. *tunica* (< **ktunica*) is probably also related.

Three other words are less certain. Arabic *quṭ(u)n,* "cotton," is probably related. Akk. *q/kutānu,* "fine sheer cloth,"[11] could also be derived from *qṭn,* "be small, thin"; it appears primarily in Old Assyrian economic texts.[12] A Neo-Babylonian word *kid/tinnu,* a kind of cloth, is associated by A. Leo Oppenheim[13] with *kitû*; according to Wolfram von Soden, it is of unknown origin.[14]

The range of forms shows that a direct line cannot be traced from Sumerian through Akkadian, Aramaic, and Canaanite to Europe. It is typical of loanwords to exhibit a variety of forms and not to follow the usual linguistic patterns.

2. *LXX.* The usual LXX translation is *chitṓn*; sometimes other translations are found, such as *himátion, stolḗ,* or *podḗrēs.*

II. OT Usage. In the OT, *kuttōneṯ* is used for two different garments: the archaic *kᵉṯōneṯ passîm* and the simple *kuttōneṯ,* an undergarment or tunic.

1. *Paradise.* The primeval history provides a special case. When the first human beings discovered their nakedness, they made themselves aprons (*ḥᵃgōrōṯ*) out of fig leaves (Gen. 3:7); later, after Yahweh punished their transgressions, he added "garments of skin" (*koṯnōṯ ʿôr*) to their clothing (v. 21). It is usually assumed on the basis of this statement that a *kuttōneṯ* could be made out of skin. Closer examination of the text, however, shows that *ʿôr* is qualified by a variety of plays on words and roots.

		Word	Root	Meaning
A.	2:25	*ʿarûmmîm*	*ʿwr*	naked
B.	3:1	*ʿārûm*	*ʿrm*	cunning
C.	3:7	*ʿêrummim*	*ʿwr*	naked
	3:10	*ʿêrōm*	*ʿwr*	naked
	3:11	*ʿêrōm*	*ʿwr*	naked
D.	3:21	*ʿôr*	*ʿwr*	skin

Here we see a chiastic structure. The cunning of the serpent (B) leads to knowledge of nakedness (C); God's intervention (D) ends the nakedness (A). If this is the case, the passage cannot be used to reconstruct the physical world of the Bible. Only one other passage, 2 K. 1:8, associates *ʿôr* with clothing; here it describes Elijah's leather girdle, which is also unusual, since an *ʾēzôr* is usually made of linen. A parallel in the

10. For a further etymological discussion, see also S. Levin, "Grassman's 'Law' in the Early Semitic Loan-word χιτων, χιθων," *SMEA,* 8 (1969), 66-75.

11. *AHw,* II (1972), 930.

12. Landsberger, *JCS,* 21 (1967), 158, n. 102; Oppenheim, *JCS,* 21 (1967), 251, n. 82.

13. Oppenheim, *JCS,* 21 (1967), 250f.

14. Cf. Landsberger, *JCS,* 21 (1967), 158, n. 2.

Gilgamesh epic may be cited: when Enkidu becomes human through intercourse with a harlot, she divides her two pieces of clothing so that each receives one.[15] In the Genesis account, each person receives two pieces. Since the stories exhibit other common features, the relationship between the two texts deserves closer study.

2. *k^{e}ṯōneṯ passîm.* In the story of Amnon's rape of Tamar, we are told that she was wearing a *k^{e}ṯōneṯ passîm,* "for thus were the daughters of the king clothed while they were virgins" (2 S. 13:18). The following word, *m^{e}ʿîlîm* ("overgarment"), is often emended to *mēʿôlām* ("of old"),[16] on the grounds that in Ex. 28:4 *m^{e}ʿîl* and *kuttōneṯ* are different garments. Since the Exodus passage refers to an ordinary *kuttōneṯ,* however, this argument is hardly persuasive. The noun *m^{e}ʿîlîm* is then either an explanatory gloss or an adverbial accusative ("as a garment"). It is probably safe to assume that a *k^{e}ṯōneṯ passîm* was more like a *m^{e}ʿîl* than an ordinary *kuttōneṯ*.

The second context where *k^{e}ṯōneṯ passîm* occurs is the Joseph story (Gen. 37:3,23,31-33): Joseph's *k^{e}ṯōneṯ passîm* arouses the envy of his brothers. The precise nature of this garment is obscure, since the word *pas* is found only here and at 2 S. 23:18. There are three traditional interpretations. The Targumim, LXX, and Vulg. have "coat of many colors." Others prefer the midrashic translation "coat with long sleeves," on the basis of a supposed *pas* meaning "flat of the hand or foot"; but there is little evidence for this meaning outside the Aramaic dialects.[17] A third translation, "brocade," is suggested by Saadia Gaon.[18] Ludwig Köhler derives *pas* as a part of the body from a more general meaning "flat," citing Pun. *ps,* "tablet,"[19] and Jewish Aram. *pas,* "spade";[20] from this sense he derives the translation "brightly colored robe put together out of separate pieces of fabric."[21] He also cites a proposal to derive *pas* from *'epes,* "end," dual "ankles" (Ezk. 47:3), which yields the meaning "ankle-length robe." These explanations are inadequate.

E. A. Speiser has put forward an important explanation, citing the term *kitû pišannu* found in Mesopotamian temple documents.[22] (Oppenheim[23] and von Soden, however, read ^{gada}*pišannu,* with *gada* as a determinative, indicating that *pišannu* is an article of clothing. According to von Soden, it is "a pouch or the like used in the cult of goddesses."[24]) Speiser says: "The article so described was a ceremonial robe which could be draped about statues of goddesses, and had various gold ornaments sewed onto it." The word *passîm* would then be a variant of Akk. *pišannu,* "a technical term denoting appliqué ornaments on costly vests and bodices."[25]

---

15. Old Bab. version II, II.26-30; *ANET,* 77.
16. *BHK*^{3}, *KBL*^{2}, but not *BHS.*
17. For Ugaritic, see G. E. Mendenhall, *The Tenth Generation* (Baltimore, 1973), 54f.
18. See *AuS,* V (1937), 215.
19. *DISO,* 230.
20. *KBL*^{2}, 1113.
21. *KBL*^{2}, 768.
22. E. A. Speiser, *Genesis. AB,* I (1964), 290.
23. *JNES,* 8 (1949), 177f.
24. *AHw,* II, 868.
25. Speiser, 290.

If von Soden is right in distinguishing the *pišannu* associated with a goddess from the other occurrences, we face another problem: the former is attested only in Late Babylonian texts, and can therefore hardly be cited to explain ancient Israelite traditions. The Sumerian loanword *pišannu,* "chest," is attested earlier, but would seem to be irrelevant here; we may note, however, that such a chest was used for garments at Ugarit.

In short, Speiser's explanation is not certain, but is much better than earlier explanations.

The context shows only that the *k^{e}ṯōneṯ passîm* was old-fashioned in the period when 2 Samuel was written and that it was an outer garment, visible from a long distance. It may well have had long sleeves or many colors, but this cannot be proved.

3. *Priestly Vestments.* The regulations of Exodus and Leviticus stipulate robes made in different ways for the high priest and the ordinary priests. The *k^{e}ṯōneṯ tašbēṣ* in Ex. 28:4 was probably checkered or interwoven, with gold, blue, purple, and scarlet threads running through the fine linen. The making of the high priest's robe is commanded in Ex. 28:39 (carried out in 39:27), but the making of the robes for the ordinary priests is not mentioned (cf. 28:40; 39:27). There does not seem to have been anything unusual about the form of the garment; but at some time the robe itself must have had a particular significance, as we see from the ordination ritual in Ex. 29: the high priest is ordained with investiture and anointing (v. 5), while the ordinary priests are ordained with investiture only (v. 8). There is no point in speculating over the significance of the investiture; the robes worn by the king have probably influenced the tradition.[26] As Martin Noth remarks, Ex. 29:5-8 represents an earlier tradition than the ordination itself, in which all are anointed (Ex. 40:15; Lev. 8:7,13, two texts that belong together but have been separated by Lev. 1–7:27). Lev. 8:7 may record the actual ceremony of investiture; but aside from the fact that the *m^{e}ʿîl* is placed over the *kuttōneṯ,* the passage ...es not help us reconstruct the appearance and position of the other garments.

Lev. 10:5 says that Nadab and Abihu were buried in their coats, which seems to ...gest that the coat was an appropriate burial garment. Noth points out that their coats ...ld in fact have been destroyed when God's fire devoured them; the text may be ...ed to emphasize "the removal of their garb from the holy place, in order that it ... never again be used."[28]

... mention of Aaron's coat in the ritual for the Day of Atonement (Lev. 16:4) is ... it may indicate "that Aaron was not to wear the full regalia in the once-a-year ... n the 'holy place', but only a more modest dress."[29] It is hardly noteworthy ... stexilic priests wore coats, which are mentioned only as offerings (Ezr. 2:69; ... 1[70,72]; the sequence of the offerings is of no importance).

... *Exodus. OTL* (Eng. trans. 1962), 230.

... *viticus. OTL* (Eng. trans. 1965), 86.

The vesting of Aaron is described in detail in Sirach's praise of famous men, where it occupies six of the seventeen verses devoted to Aaron. The coat is mentioned in Sir. 45:8c. This emphasis on Aaron's vestments can be viewed as a first step leading to the Christian tradition of Jesus' seamless robe.

Although Isaiah's oracle against the arrogant Shebna mentions the latter's *kuttōneṯ* (Isa. 22:21), there is no reason to assume that it was out of the ordinary, except perhaps for being especially luxurious. It is also possible that it was made of special cloth, like a priestly *kuttōneṯ*.

4. *Other Texts.* There is little to say about other passages. In 2 S. 15:32, the *kuttōneṯ* is the garment that Hushai tears out of desperation over the political situation. In Cant. 5:3, it is the garment the beloved has put off, so that she does not rise to open the door for her lover. Job. 30:18 mentions a *kuttōneṯ*, but the verse is so difficult that many interpreters leave it untranslated;[30] the passage therefore has nothing to contribute to our discussion.

Freedman—O'Connor

In the Dead Sea scrolls, the Aaronic priests are clothed with *ktwnt bd,* "linen garments," according to 1QM 7:10. Line 11, however, shows that these are not part of their regular vestments; they belong to the *bigdê milḥāmâ,* "garments of war." In 4QOrd 2:1–4:7, *ktnt* represents MT *śimlaṯ 'iššâ* (Dt. 22:5). In 11QtgJob, it represents the *mᵉʿîl* of Job 29:14. This evidence may indicate that in the intertestamental period *kuttōneṯ* became an inclusive term for "outer garment."

Fabry

30. M. Pope, *Job. AB,* XV (³1979), 223.

כָּתֵף *kāṯēp*

Contents: I. 1. Occurrences; 2. Meaning. II. 1. Part of the Body; 2. Part of a Building; 3. Part of an Object; 4. Part of a Hill. III. Religious Usage.

kāṯēp. É. P. Dhorme, "L'Emploi métaphorique de noms de parties du corps en hébreu et en akkadien," *RB,* 31 (1922), 215-233; H. Donner, "Ugaritismen in der Psalmenforschung," *ZAW,* 79 (1967), 322-350; Z. Kallai, "Kateph — כתף," *IEJ,* 15 (1965), 177-79; Y. Komlosh, "מוּעָף — וְעָפוּ," *Bar-Ilan,* 4f. (1967), 42-49 [Heb.], xxii-xxiii [Eng. summary]; A. Schwarzenbach, *Die geographische Terminologie im Hebräischen des ATs* (Leiden, 1954); L. A. Snijders, "L'Orientation du temple de Jérusalem," *OTS,* 14 (1965), 214-234.

I. 1. *Occurrences.* The noun *kāṯēp* occurs 67 times in the OT, 4 times in Ugaritic, and once in a Hebrew inscription.[1] It is also found in Jewish Aramaic, Syriac, Mandaic, Arabic, Tigriña, and Ethiopic; Akk. *katappātu* is problematic.[2]

2. *Meaning.* In Ugaritic, *ktp* denotes the part of the body best suited to bearing burdens, the shoulder, together with the upper portion of the chest. Aliyan Baʿal raised *špš,* the lamp of El, "upon the shoulder of ʿAnat" (*lktp ʿnt*).[3] Another text[4] describes a messenger as taking the word of his lord upon his shoulders (*ml'k bm ktpm rgm bʿlh*). In the battle between Baʿal and Yam, Baʿal's club struck "the shoulder of prince Yam, the breast of the ruler of the flood" (*ktp zbl ym/bn ydm ṯpṭ nhr*).[5] The parallelism between *ktp* and *bn ydm* suggests that *ktp* means not so much the back of the shoulder as the front, including the collarbone — in other words, the upper portion of the chest.[6]

One text[7] probably uses *ktp* to denote a kind of weapon.

Syr. *katpā,* Arab. *katif/katf/kitf,* Tigr. *maktaf,* and Eth. *matkaft* all mean "shoulder." Akk. *katappātu* probably means the breast of an animal. An inscription from Silwan in the Kidron valley contains the phrase *ḥdr bktp hṣr,* "chamber in the shoulder of the rock," probably referring to a rocky mountain slope.[8] In the OT, besides the "shoulder" of a human being or animals, *ktp* can denote an analogous landform, as well as a part of a building or tool. As a consquence, the LXX uses a variety of translations: *nṓtos* (17 times), *ṓmos* (15), *ōmía* (12), *epōmís* (8), and *klítos* (6). In 9 passages, the LXX does not provide a suitable equivalent.

II. 1. *Part of the Body.* The OT uses *ktp* twice to denote part of an animal's body. Ezk. 24:4 lists the thigh (*yārēḵ*) and shoulder (*kāṯēp*) as choice pieces of meat. Isa. 30:6 describes the transportation (*nś'*) of goods in the Negeb "on the shoulders of asses" (*ʿal-keṯep ʿᵃyārîm*) and "on the humps of camels."

In an animal metaphor, Ezk. 34:21 uses our word to describe heedless human conduct. Zec. 7:11; Neh. 9:29 use it similarly to represent stubbornness.

The specific meaning of *kāṯēp* with respect to the human body is clear from Job 31:22; Isa. 49:22. Cursing himself, Job cries out: "Let my *kāṯēp* fall from its shoulder (*miššiḵmâ*)." The *kāṯēp* is thus part of the shoulder area, probably the "shoulder blade."[9] Deutero-Isaiah promises that Israel's daughters "shall be carried (*nś'* hiphil) on the *kāṯēp,*" Israel's sons "in the bosom" (*bᵉḥōṣen*). The parallelism between *kāṯēp* and *ḥōṣen* recalls the association of *ktp* and *bn ydm* in Ugaritic, suggesting that here,

1. N. Avigad, "The Second Tomb-Inscription of the Royal Steward," *IEJ,* 5 (1955), 165f.
2. *KBL*³, 481; P. Fronzaroli, "Studi sul lessico comune semitico. II: Anatomia e Fisiologia," *AANLR,* 19 (1964), 257, 271, 278.
3. *KTU,* 1.6 I, 14f.
4. *KTU,* 1.2 I, 42.
5. *KTU,* 1.2 IV, 14-17.
6. Cf. *WUS,* no. 1407.
7. *KTU,* 1.6 V, 2; cf. *WUS,* no. 1408, supported by Donner, 348.
8. *KBL*³.
9. A. Dillmann, *Hiob. KEHAT,* II (⁴1891), 268.

too, *kāṯēp* denotes the part of the body around the collarbone, roughly the chest. We read how Samson puts (*śym*) the doors of the city gates on his shoulders and carries them away (Jgs. 16:3), how Ezekiel lifts (*nś'*) the exiles' baggage upon his shoulders as a sign that even the prince will do the same (Ezk. 12:6,7,12 [reading *'al* instead of *'el*[10]]), how the wicked will likewise lift (*nś'*) their idols upon their shoulders (Isa. 46:7), and how Goliath carries a bronze *kîḏôn* between his shoulders (1 S. 17:6).[11] In his description of Nebuchadrezzar's laboring army, Ezekiel speaks of heads made bald and shoulders rubbed bare (Ezk. 29:18).[12] The sons of Kohath had to carry (*nś'*) the holy things upon their shoulders (Nu. 7:9). The "sons" of the Levites carried (*nś'*) the ark of God upon their shoulders with poles (1 Ch. 15:15); after it was lodged in the temple, however, they no longer had to carry (*maśśā'*) it upon their shoulders (2 Ch. 35:3).

In Ezk. 29:7, "you tore all their shoulders," many scholars emend *kāṯēp*[13] to *kap*.[14]

2. *Part of a Building*. The most frequent use of *kāṯēp* is to denote a part of a building.[15] The "right side of the house (= the temple)" (*keṯep habbayiṯ hayyᵉmānîṯ*) is mentioned in 1 K. 6:8; 7:39; 2 K. 11:11; Ezk. 47:1(,2); 2 Ch. 4:10 (conj.); 23:10 (cf. 1 K. 7:39), the left side (. . . *haśśᵉmā'lîṯ*) in 2 K. 11:11; 2 Ch. 23:10 (cf. 1 K. 7:39), the "side of the gates" of the temple (*keṯep haššᵉʿārîm*) in Ezk. 40:18 (sg.: 46:19; 40:44 [twice]), the "sidewalls of the entrance" (*kiṯpôṯ happeṯaḥ*) in Ezk. 41:2 and of the vestibule (*hā'ûlām*) in v. 26. Ezk. 40:40 mentions the "side" twice without further qualification. Similarly, the law of the tabernacle speaks of curtains on both "shoulders" or "sides" (Ex. 27:14,15; 38:14,15), referring to "the two side pieces of the system of hangings to the right and left of the opening on the front side."[16] In these passages, *kāṯēp* denotes the side of a structure, like the Eng. "flank."[17]

3. *Part of an Object.* In 1 K. 7:30,34, we read of four "side pieces" of a metal stand used in the temple,[18] which L. A. Snijders[19] interprets as "brackets." The ephod that is part of the priestly vestments has two "shoulder-pieces"[20] (Ex. 28:7; 39:4) decorated

---

10. *BHS.*

11. Cf. W. Caspari, *Die Samuelbücher. KAT,* VII (1926), 299: "hardly . . . 'over his shoulder' "; RSV and H. J. Stoebe, *Das erste Buch Samuelis. KAT,* VIII/1 (1973), 316: "slung between his shoulders"; H. W. Hertzberg, *I & II Samuel. OTL* (Eng. trans. 1964), 142, n. c: "literally, 'between the shoulder blades'; he thus carried it lightly."

12. See W. Zimmerli, *Ezekiel 2. Herm* (Eng. trans. 1983), 117, 119.

13. Interpreted by G. R. Driver, "Ezekiel: Linguistic and Textual Problems," *Bibl,* 35 (1954), 299, in the sense of "arm-pit."

14. First suggested by C. von Orelli, *Das Buch Ezechiel und die zwölf kleinen Propheten. SZ* (^{2}1896), 120, on the basis of the LXX and Syr.; most recently, Zimmerli, 119.

15. See Snijders, 220f.

16. M. Noth, *Exodus. OTL* (Eng. trans. 1962), 217.

17. M. Noth, *Könige 1–16, BK,* IX/1 (1968), 116; *DISO,* 129.

18. Noth, *Könige 1–16,* 158f.

19. P. 220.

20. *Idem*: epaulettes.

with stones (28:12; 39:7) and furnished with golden cords (28:25; 39:18) and golden rings (28:27; 39:20).

4. *Part of a Hill.* Finally, *kāṯēp* can denote a specific landform. The description of the borders of Judah and Benjamin speaks of the shoulder of "the Jebusite" (Josh. 15:8; 18:16), "Mount Jearim" (15:10), "Ekron" (15:11), "Jericho" (18:12), "Luz" (18:13), "Beth-arabah" (18:18),[21] and "Beth-hoglah" (18:19). Nu. 34:11 speaks of "the shoulder of the sea of Chinnereth," Ezk. 25:9 of "the shoulder of Moab," and Isa. 11:14 (conj.) of "the shoulder of the Philistines."[22]

This is not the place to discuss the geographical problems raised by these texts. They clearly refer to a specific landform associated with mountains or hills; what is not clear is whether *kāṯēp,* which literally means "shoulder," refers to a ridge,[23] or — as in the case of animals, human beings, and buildings — to a side or slope. The Silwan inscription mentioned above suggests that *kāṯēp* means "a sloping hillside," because the tomb referred to is located on the hillside opposite Jerusalem.[24] Even if this interpretation is correct, it is still debatable whether the border runs along the foot of the hill on which the city is situated or along the edge of a hill opposite.[25]

III. Religious Usage. We are clearly dealing with religious usage when *kāṯēp* is associated with Yahweh, as in the tribal oracle concerning Benjamin (Dt. 33:12). Scholars differ as to whether Yahweh (or Elyon[26]) is the subject of the final stich ("The beloved of Yahweh, he dwells in safety by him; Elyon encompasses him all the day long, and makes his dwelling between his [Benjamin's] shoulders") or Benjamin is to be construed as the subject, so that the shoulders must belong to Yahweh or Elyon.[27]

---

21. Cf. M. Noth, *Das Buch Josua. HAT,* VII (^{3}1971), 108; H. W. Hertzberg, *Das Bücher Josua, Richter und Ruth. ATD,* IX (^{5}1974), 105.

22. The textual problem is discussed by Komlosh, 42-49.

23. Snijders, 220.

24. Y. Aharoni, *The Land of the Bible* (Eng. trans., Philadelphia, ^{2}1979), 283, n. 185.

25. See esp. the discussion in Kallai.

26. See *BHS.*

27. Among the scholars who prefer the first interpretation are K. H. Graf, *Der Segen Mose's* (Leipzig, 1857), 39f.; A. Dillmann, *Numeri, Deuteronomium und Josua. KEHAT* (^{2}1886), 425; S. R. Driver, *ICC* (^{3}1902, repr. 1978), 404; E. Sellin, "Das Zelt Jahwes," *Alttestamentliche Studien Rudolf Kittel. BWANT,* 13 (1913), 184-86; E. Koenig, *Das Deuteronomium. KAT,* III (1917), 226; G. Dalman, "Stammeszugehörigkeit der Stadt Jerusalem und des Tempels," *Abhandlungen zur semitischen Religionskunde und Sprachwissenschaft. Festschrift W. W. G. von Baudissin. BZAW,* 33 (1918), 111; C. Steuernagel, *Das Deuteronomium. HKAT,* I/3 (^{2}1923), 178; A. Welch, *Deuteronomy* (London, 1932), 122; R. Tournay, "Le Psaume et les bénédictions de Moïse," *RB,* 65 (1958), 196; also F. Delitzsch in O. Eissfeldt, *Franz Delitzsch und Wolf Graf Baudissin. SSAW,* Phil.-hist. Kl. 112/2 (1966), 12. The other side includes C. F. Keil, *KD,* I/3, 503f.; E. Meyer, *Die Israeliten und ihre Nachbarstämme* (1906, repr. Darmstadt, 1967), 522; K. Budde, *Der Segen Mose's* (Tübingen, 1922), 34; T. H. Gaster, "Deuteronomy xxxiii.12," *ExpT,* 46 (1934/35), 334; E. Sellin, *Einleitung in das AT* (^{7}Leipzig, 1935), 24; H. Junker, *Das Buch Deuteronomium. HS,* II/2 (1933, repr. Darmstadt, 1952), 132; F. M. Cross and D. N. Freedman, "The Blessing of Moses," *JBL,* 67 (1948), 194 and 205, n. 40; G. von Rad, *Deuteronomy, OTL* (Eng. trans. 1966), 207.

Hans-Jürgen Zobel[28] argues for the latter view on the basis of the structure of the verse: the second and third stichs develop the statement of the first. He also points out (as have others) that the two occurrences of *škn* in the verse cannot have different subjects, first Benjamin and then Yahweh or Elyon. Finally, he suggests that *kāṯēp* may mean "hillside." Read thus, the oracle states that Benjamin, beloved of Yahweh, dwells secure: El Elyon — to whom other passages of the OT also attribute protection (cf. Gen. 14:20; Ps. 18:14[Eng. v. 13]; 21:8[7]; etc.) — encompasses him all the day long, for the tribe has settled in a hilly territory especially protected by Elyon. Cf. Ps. 46:5(4): there are other "habitations of Elyon" besides Jerusalem.

The metaphorical phrase *kāṯēp sōrāreṯ* in Zec. 7:11; Neh. 9:29 also belongs in the religious realm. Zechariah's sermon attacks the Judeans' confidence that their fasting, lamentation, and sacrifices have fulfilled all that Yahweh requires (Zec. 7:4-6). He reminds them of Yahweh's words spoken through the former prophets, to whom their ancestors refused to hearken, so that the pleasant land was made desolate (vv. 1,11-14). The text uses several idioms to describe the previous generations' rejection of the prophets' message: they refused to hearken, they turned stubborn shoulders and stopped their ears (v. 11), they made their hearts like adamant so as not to hear the Torah and the words of Yahweh (v. 12).

In Neh. 9, this phrase appears in a long prayer that describes Yahweh's mercies to his people from Abraham on, at each stage contrasting them with Israel's rejection. Verse 29 in particular says that Yahweh warned the Israelites — through his prophets, of course — in order to bring them back to his Torah; but they acted presumptuously, refused to obey the commandments, sinned, turned a stubborn shoulder, stiffened their necks, and would not obey. Commenting on the passage, Conrad von Orelli notes: "The image is of a stubborn ox that refuses to wear the yoke (to which the law of God is likened)."[29] He cites Hos. 4:16, which uses *srr* in its original meaning.

"The picture of history that we find here reflects the views of the Deuteronomic school."[30] Because the phrase is identical in both passages, we may see in it a stylistic device of postexilic preaching — if Neh. 9 did not borrow the expression from Zec. 7.

We come finally to Ezk. 34:21, which also uses an animal metaphor. The prophet proclaims deliverance for the Israelites in exile: Yahweh will favor the lean sheep over the fat and strong, because the latter have pushed the weak and feeble sheep away with side and shoulder and thrust at them with their horns, scattering them abroad.

Thus *kāṯēp* is a metaphor for strength and power. The shoulder bears burdens; it guards and protects. The word also came to express stubborn, sustained, vigorous resistance to Yahweh and his commandment, as well as the unequal contest between the enemy and God's weak people, who would be vanquished if Yahweh did not intervene to save them. We receive a general impression that *kāṯēp* is used metaphorically in religious language to express human rebellion against Yahweh and the opposi-

---

28. H.-J. Zobel, *Stammesspruch und Geschichte. BZAW,* 95 (1965), 34f.
29. Von Orelli, 189.
30. W. Rudolph, *Esra und Nehemia. HAT,* XX (1949), 161.

tion of the nations to the people of God. This impression must be qualified, however, by Isa. 49:22, where Deutero-Isaiah states in an oracle of salvation that the nations will bring the exiles home "in their bosom" and "on their shoulders."

Zobel

כתת *ktt*; כָּתִית *kāṯîṯ*

Contents: I. 1. Etymology; 2. Occurrences. II. 1. Basic Meaning; 2. Specialized Usage; 3: Objects; 4. *kāṯîṯ*.

I. 1. *Etymology.* Outside the OT, the verb appears with the same meaning in the Dead Sea scrolls (qal: 1QpHab 3:1; hophal: 1QM 18:2), as well as Middle Hebrew (piel) and Jewish Aramaic, both Galilean (pael) and Babylonian. Cognates of *ktt* include Syr. *kettā'*, "fine dust," and Mand. *kita,* "lump." In Tigre, the cognate verb means "make small incisions" and in Tigriña, "grind up." Akk. *katātu,* "vibrate (?),"[1] differs markedly in meaning (cf. Arab. *ktt,* "seethe[2]).

Warmuth

For this reason, Heb. and Akk. *ktt* should be considered different roots, despite their consonantal identity.

Von Soden

Ugar. *ktt*[3] may denote a kind of metalworking ("beaten" copper); this parallel may be relevant to the interpretation of Isa. 2:4 par. Mic. 4:3; Joel 4:10(Eng. 3:10).

2. *Occurrences.* The verb *ktt* appears 17 times in the OT: 5 times in the qal, 5 times in the piel, once in the pual, twice in the hiphil, and 4 times in the hophal. Its nominal derivatives are *kāṯîṯ* (5 occurrences) and *meḵittâ* (1 occurrence).

In Jgs. 20:43, some scholars propose emending *kitterû* to a form of *ktt* on the basis of the LXX; Hans-Joachim Kraus proposes inserting *kitteṯû* in Ps. 74:6.[4] Because the

---

ktt. B. Halper, "The Participial Formations of the Geminate Verbs," *ZAW,* 30 (1910), 125; E. Jenni, *Das hebräische Pi'el* (Zurich, 1968), 185f.; Jörg Jeremias, "Die Deutung der Gerichtsworte Michas in der Exilszeit," *ZAW,* 83 (1971), 330-354, esp. 336; W. Rudolph, *Micha — Nahum — Habakuk — Zephanja. KAT,* XIII/3 (1975); H. Wildberger, *Isaiah 1–12* (Eng. trans., Minneapolis, 1991).

1. *AHw,* I (1965), 465a; *CAD,* VIII (1971), 304: "be low or short."
2. For a different view, see A. Guillaume, "Hebrew and Arabic Lexicography," *Abr Nahrain,* 2 (1960/61, repr. Leiden, 1965), 10.
3. *UT,* no. 1327.
4. H.-J. Kraus, *Psalms 60–150* (Eng. trans., Minneapolis, 1989), 95.

arguments for these emendations are not persuasive (although *ktt* would be appropriate in both contexts), we shall ignore these passages. In Isa. 30:14, the MT reads the qal passive participle. The two hiphil forms (Nu. 14:45; Dt. 1:44) exhibit aramaizing features (gemination of the initial consonant).

The LXX uses a variety of verbs to translate *ktt*; the most frequent is *synkóptein* or *katakóptein* (Dt. 9:21; Ps. 89:24[23][LXX 88:24]; 2 Ch. 34:7; Zec. 11:6; Nu. 14:45; Mic. 1:7; also Joel 4:10[3:10] and Isa. 2:4 par. Mic. 4:3, which supports the interpretation of these passages in the same way as the other occurrences). In a few passages, the specific sense of *ktt* does not find expression (2 Ch. 15:6; Job 4:20; Isa. 24:12).

II. 1. *Basic Meaning*. Ignoring for a moment the specialized use of *ktt* in Mic. 4:3 par. Isa. 2:4; Joel 4:10(3:10), we find everywhere a basic meaning "break (into small pieces), crush, grind." Of the passages using qal forms (Dt. 9:21; Isa. 30:14; Ps. 89:24[23]; Lev. 22:24), the first two are especially vivid. Dt. 9:21 says that Yahweh burned the golden calf and crushed it; two infinitives absolute (*ḥêṭēḇ* and *ṭāḥôn*, "pulverize") make the description more precise: "into powder." The purpose and result are further emphasized: "until it was ground (*dqq*) as fine as dust."

In Isa. 30:14, the breaking (*šbr*) of a potter's vessel serves as an image of destruction; the extent of the breakage is defined more precisely by *kāṯûṯ lō' yaḥmōl*, "ruthlessly smashed." As a result of this breaking (the only occurrence of the nominal derivative *m^e^ḵittâ*), not a sherd will be found with which one might take fire from a hearth or dip water from a cistern.

In Ps. 89:24(23), the object of *ktt* is personal ("his foes"). From the parallelism (*ngp*: "and strike down [or 'smash to pieces'] those who hate him"), we may conclude that *ktt* still retains its basic meaning "crush, smash" when human beings are the object.

According to Lev. 22:24, animals with injured testicles must not be sacrificed to Yahweh. Four types of injury are named: bruising (*mā'ûḵ*), crushing (*kāṯûṯ*), tearing (*nāṯûq*), and cutting (*kārûṯ*). The crushing of testicles was considered one possible method of castration.

The piel (2 K. 18:4; 2 Ch. 34:7; Zec. 11:6) is used in narrative and in prophetic oracles to emphasize the result of the action. In 2 K. 18:4, it describes by itself the smashing of the bronze serpent. In 2 Ch. 34:7 it describes the smashing of the Asherim and idols; the purpose is stated by *l^e^* plus the infinitive construct of *dqq*: "to pulverize." In Zec. 11:6, the extent of the object demands a somewhat figurative translation: the shepherds and kings shall devastate (*ktt*) the earth.

The single pual form (2 Ch. 15:6) also conveys the same basic meaning and emphasizes the result (one nation broken by another).

The two hiphil forms (Nu. 14:45; Dt. 1:44) appear in very similar clauses with the same construction (acc. + *'aḏ*). The enemy defeated and dispersed (*ktt* hiphil) the Israelites — that is, the cohesive formation dissolved into separate groups, scattering in flight. The image of *ktt* is clearly visible. The hiphil may have been chosen for its causative aspect.

The hophal forms function as passive equivalents to the qal.[5] The meaning is again "be crushed (to pieces)" in Mic. 1:7 (idols); Isa. 24:12 (city gate); Job 4:20 (human beings). In Jer. 46:5, however, the meaning corresponds to the hiphil ("their warriors are scattered").

2. *Specialized Usage.* In contrast to these passages, Joel 4:10 (qal); Mic. 4:3 par. Isa. 2:4 (piel) use the verb as a technical term (with the acc. + *l*[e]) for the transformation of one kind of implement into another by a metalworker; in these texts, it is often translated "(re)forge." The basic meaning, however, is still very much present, since the process implies total destruction of the old object. Either one stage has come to represent the entire process, denoted now by *ktt,* or the word refers only to the destruction of the original implement — for example, the breaking of weapons to pieces — and only the prep. *l*[e] extends the basic meaning by indicating the purpose of the destruction: "Break up your weapons — for plows" (i.e., in order to make plows). In any case, even if the verb is translated "reforge," the emphasis is on the necessary destruction. Two different purposes are expressed by the qal (Joel 4:10: plowshares into swords) and the piel (Isa. 2:4 par. Mic. 4:3: swords into plowshares). "In Joel, the emphasis is on the imminent act of mobilization; in Isaiah, it is on the permanent condition resulting from the action."[6]

3. *Objects.* Most frequently, *ktt* refers to the destruction of idols (Dt. 9:21; Mic. 1:7 [in the context of a polemic against idols[7]]; 2 K. 18:4; 2 Ch. 34:7) and enemies (Nu. 14:45; Dt. 1:44; Jer. 46:5; 2 Ch. 15:6; Ps. 89:24[23]). Once (Job 4:20) it refers to people in general and once to the earth with its inhabitants (Zec. 11:6). Single passages refer to the crushing or breaking of a vessel (Isa. 30:14), a gate (Isa. 24:12), and the testicles of an animal (Lev. 22:24).

The problems involved in trying to date the individual texts make it impossible to associate the verb with a particular period. Jörg Jeremias[8] considers *ktt,* "smash (idols)," to be a term characteristic of Hosea and Deuteronomy.

4. *kāṯîṯ.* The derived noun *kāṯîṯ* always denotes oil[9] of the highest quality. It is made by crushing olives in a mortar. The oil released before or at least at the time of the first pressing was particularly esteemed: it was used for the sacred lamp (Ex. 27:20; Lev. 24:2), for sacrifice (Ex. 29:40; Nu. 28:5; 11QT 21:15). It was also exported by Solomon to the court of Hiram (1 K. 5:25[11]).[10]

Warmuth

---

5. *GK,* §53u; *BLe,* §38m; for the suggestion of an aramaizing hophal, see *GK,* 67y.
6. Jenni, 186.
7. See H. D. Preuss, *Verspottung fremder Religionen im AT. BWANT,* 92[5/12] (1971), 133f.
8. P. 336.
9. → שמן *šemen.*
10. *AuS,* IV (1935, repr. 1964), 238ff.; D. Kellermann, "Öl und Ölbereitung," *BRL*², 238-240, with bibliog.; E. Segelberg, "Öl," *BHHW,* II, 1336f.; H. Frehen, "Öl," *BL*², 1257f.

לָאָה *lā'â*

Contents: 1. Etymology; 2. OT Usage; 3. LXX.

1. *Etymology.* Heb. *lā'â* is cognate etymologically with Ugar. *lʿy,* "tire,"[1] Jewish Aram. *l^e'â,* "labor, tire," Syr. "exert oneself." In Arabic, we find *la'ā,* "be sluggish,"[2] and in Akkadian, *la'û,* "be weak."[3] A different root is reflected in Ugar. *l'y,* "be strong,"[4] and Akk. *le'û,* "be competent";[5] it appears also in Phoenician personal names.[6] This latter root may be represented in Hebrew by the personal name Leah (*lē'â*). The two roots may be ultimately related, since both refer to strength or expenditure of strength.[7]

2. *OT Usage.* In the OT, the verb *lā'â* appears 3 times in the qal (besides Sir. 43:30), 10 in the niphal, and 5 (or 6) in the hiphil. All the texts have more to do with mental and spiritual exhaustion than with physical fatigue; the word refers to the will and the emotions. It can often be translated "be unable to bear," "be tired of," or "dislike." We may note that it never occurs in conjunction with → יגע *yāgaʿ* or → יעף *yāʿēp̄.* In the qal, the emotional aspect is especially clear in Job 4:2,5: "You 'dislike' having someone speak to you"; "now it [misfortune] has come to you, and you 'cannot bear it' (i.e., 'you are impatient,' par. 'dismayed' [*bhl* niphal])." Gen. 19:11 is a little different: the men of Sodom, struck with blindness, "wore themselves out" groping for the door.

The same nuance is also very clear in two occurrences of the niphal in Jeremiah, where the verb is associated with forms of the verb *kwl.* In Jer. 6:11, the prophet says: "I am so full of the wrath of Yahweh that I cannot hold it in (*nil'êṯî hāḵîl*)"; he must let all feel Yahweh's wrath. In Jer. 20:9, in the context of one of his "confessions," he says that he tried to keep silent, but the message was like a burning fire within him: "I wearied myself trying to hold it in (*nil'êṯî kalkēl*), but I could (*ykl*) not." In a similar vein, Yahweh says in Isa. 1:14 that he hates the people's festivals: "They have become a burden to me, I cannot bear them (*nil'êṯî n^{e}śô'*)." Jer. 15:6 also belongs in this category: "I have stretched out my hand against you and destroyed you — I was tired of relenting (*nil'êṯî hinnāḥēm*)."

The emotional aspect also appears in Prov. 26:15: "The sluggard buries his hand in

1. *WUS,* no. 1429.
2. *WKAS,* II, 72f.
3. *AHw,* I (1965), 540.
4. *WUS,* no. 1430.
5. *AHw,* I, 547.
6. Benz, 336f.
7. On the problem of antithetical words, see D. Cohen, "*Aḍdād* et ambiguïté linguistique en arabe," *Arabica,* 8 (1961), 1-29.

the dish and 'is too lazy' to bring it back to his mouth" — in other words, he has no desire to do so. Ex. 7:18 is similar: "The Egyptians 'could' not drink the [putrid] water of the Nile" — it disgusted them.

Jer. 9:4(Eng. v. 5) comes closer to the idea of wearing oneself out: "They have taught their tongue to speak lies; they weary themselves with committing iniquity (*haʿᵃwēh nilʾû*)." The MT is difficult; Josef Schreiner[8] includes the following *šûḇ*: "They are too lazy to repent." Isa. 47:13 may also belong here: "You 'have wearied yourself' with your many counsels." As the context shows, this refers to consulting astrologers. The text of Isa. 16:12 may be corrupt: "When Moab presents himself (*nir'â*; a doublet of *nil'â*?), when he 'wearies himself' upon the *bāmâ* and enters his sanctuary to pray, he will not succeed." Moab's many prayers and laments are in vain and of no avail.[9]

A different nuance is present in Ps. 68:10(9): "Thy heritage [i.e., the land], which was 'exhausted' [by drought], thou [God] didst restore [with rain]." There is no evidence to support Mitchell Dahood's theory[10] that this text uses *lā'â,* "gain the upper hand."

In the hiphil, the emotional aspect is once again clear in Isa. 7:13: "Is it too little for you to 'weary' mortals, that you 'weary' my God also?" — in other words, God's patience is exhausted. The other three passages have more to do with physical fatigue. Jer. 12:5: "If you have raced with foot-runners and have 'exhausted yourself,' . . . how will you compete with horses?" — that is, as the parallel implies: "If you have failed in easy tasks, what will you do when hard ones come?"[11] Job 16:7: "Now he [God] has 'worn me out'; thou hast made desolate all my company [family?]." The text is probably corrupt, but the meaning of *lā'â* hiphil is clear: Job is at the end of his rope; he can endure no more. In Mic. 6:3, in an accusation against Israel, Yahweh says: "O my people, what have I done to you? In what have I 'wearied' you?" God has given his people every blessing, but they act as though he had laid heavy burdens upon them.

Ezk. 24:12 is probably corrupt: *tᵉʾunîm hel'āṯ* is probably a dittography of *tittum ḥel'āṯâ,* "its rust is consumed," in the preceding verse.

3. *LXX.* The LXX uses a variety of translations: qal: *paralýesthai* (Job 4:2,5 [paraphrase]); niphal: *epéchein, astheneín, dúnasthai, kopián, pariénai*; hiphil: *agṓn, eklýein, katákopos, lypeín, parenochleín, paréchein, poieín.*

Ringgren

8. J. Schreiner, *Jer. 1–25,14. NEB,* 69.
9. O. Kaiser, *Isaiah 13–39. OTL* (Eng. trans. 1974), 74, considers the verse secondary.
10. M. Dahood, "Hebrew-Ugaritic Lexicography IV," *Bibl,* 47 (1966), 408.
11. W. Rudolph, *Jeremia. HAT,* XII (^{3}1968), 75.

לְאֹם l^e'ōm

Contents: I. Etymology, Distribution, Semantic Field, Meaning. II. Usage.

I. Etymology, Distribution, Semantic Field, Meaning. The noun l^e'ōm (only in Prov. 11:26: l^e'ôm; cf. Isa. 51:4?) is usually considered an archaic or archaizing[1] word for "people" (cf. Prov. 11:26: "people"; Gen. 25:3: "tribe, clan"; cf. the other occurrences in Proverbs). It usually appears in the plural, rarely in the singular;[2] it is limited to poetic texts, which include Gen. 25:23; 27:29.

In the Semitic languages, we find an analogous *lɜm* or *l'm,* "people, host" (sg. and pl.), in Ugaritic[3] and Akkadian (*līmu,* "thousand").[4] The root appears also in Arabic (*lamma* VIII: "come together").[5]

The LXX usually translates l^e'ōm (or its pl.) as *éthnē,* sometimes *laoí* (or its sg.); but it also uses *árchontes* (Gen. 27:29; Isa. 34:1; 41:1; 43:4,9) or *basileís* (Isa. 51:4; cf. Ps. 148:11; 7:8[6]). Once it uses *phylḗ* (Prov. 14:34).[7]

In later Hebrew, l^e'ōm is replaced by *'ummâ* (probably the correct reading in Isa. 55:4, but cf. Ps. 117:1).

The semantic field includes above all → עם *'am* and → גוי *gôy.*[8] Scholars generally make a clear distinction between the latter two terms, but only rarely try to define l^e'ōm more precisely.[9]

It must be noted first that the sg. l^e'ōm is found in only 4 OT passages (Gen. 25:23 [twice];[10] also Prov. 11:26; 14:28; probably pl. in Isa. 51:4). In all these passages, the translation "people" or "nation" is appropriate.

---

l^e'ōm. → גוי *gôy.* Also: C. de Jong, *De Volken bij Jeremia* (diss., Kampen, 1978); A. R. Hulst, "גוי/עם *'am/goj* Volk," *THAT,* II, 290-325; R. Martin-Achard, *Israël et les nations. CahTh,* 42 (1959); H. Schmidt, *Israel, Zion und die Völker* (Marburg, 1968).

1. *KBL*³, 488a.

2. See below.

3. *UT,* no. 1346; *WUS,* no. 1433; *CML*², 149.

4. *AHw,* I (1965), 553b; cf. *KAI,* 236, vo. 1; see also *DISO,* 134 (Imperial Aramaic); also J. Barr, *Comparative Philology and the Text of the OT* (1968, repr. Winona Lake, 1987), 133, 172, 254, 329: "governor, official, ruler," citing Gen. 27:29; Isa. 34:1; 41:1; 43:4,9; 51:4 LXX.

5. See also *KAI,* 224, 23-26: people of *tl'm*; according to H. Cazelles, "Israël du nord et arche d'alliance (Jér. III 16)," *VT,* 18 (1968), 150, n. 3, not a toponym.

6. On both, see Barr.

7. See also the discussion in G. Bertram, "ἔθνος," *TDNT,* II, 364-69; H. Strathmann, "λαός," *TDNT,* IV, 32-37.

8. See Hulst, 315ff., with bibliog.

9. *KBL*³: archaic or archaizing; K. Elliger, *Deuterojesaja. BK,* XI/1 (1971), 118: "rarer" or "more sonorous" — but on what evidence?

10. The passage and its close relationship with Gen. 27:29 are discussed by L. Schmidt, "Überlegungen zum Jahwisten," *EvTh,* 37 (1977), 237, who argues that l^e'ōm was used for Israel only in the period of the Davidic empire.

Most texts (34 to 36) use the plural: Ps. 2:1; 7:8[Eng. v. 7]; 9:9[8]; 44:3,15[2,14]; 47:4[3]; 57:10[9]; 65:8[7]; 67:5[4][twice]; 105:44; 108:4[3]; 148:11; 149:7; Prov. 14:34; 24:24; Isa. 17:12,13; 34:1; 41:1; 43:4,9; 49:1; 51:4; 55:4 [twice?]; 60:2; Jer. 51:58; Hab. 2:13.

It is noteworthy that the plural is never used in isolation (on Isa. 17:13, cf. v. 12) but always appears in poetic parallelism, where it is used as a synonymous variation. The pl. *l^{e}'ummîm* is used with *gôyîm* in Gen. 25:23; Ps. 2:1; 44:3,15(2,14); 105:44; 149:7; Isa. 34:1; 43:9; also Ps. 117:1 (conj.). It is used with *'ammîm* in Gen. 27:29; Isa. 17:12f.; 55:4 (read *l^{e}'ammîm* once?); Ps. 47:4(3); 57:10(9); 67:5(4); 108:4(3); Prov. 24:24; Jer. 51:58; Hab. 2:13. The plural appears also with *tēḇēl* (Ps. 9:9[8]), the "circle of the earth" (Ps. 148:11; Isa. 60:2), the "islands" (Isa. 41:1; 49:1), the "ends of the earth" (Isa. 41:5 [cf. 41:1]; also 43:4?), the "kings of the earth" (Ps. 148:11; cf. 2:1f.), and the "sea" (Ps. 65:8[7]; Isa. 17:12; Hab. 2:13f.).[11] In Isa. 43:4, it is not necessary to change *'āḏām* to *'ᵃḏāmôṯ.*[12] In Prov. 14:28, the sg. *l^{e}'ōm* appears with the sg. *'am* (cf. Isa. 51:4?).

Both the singular and the plural are rarely used for "people" in general. The reference is usually to foreign nations; the word is used for Israel only in Gen. 25:23. The poetically inclusive language makes either "people" or "nation" an acceptable translation, with no further attempt at precision. The word is used only to extend the term with which it appears in synonymous parallelism, making its meaning more inclusive.

II. Usage. A distinction is made between Israel and the "nations" (Ps. 44:3[2]; 47:4[3]; 105:44; 149:7; cf. Isa. 43:9f.); above all, however, both salvation oracles and prayers, scenes of judgment and promises declare that Yahweh is ruler of the nations. It is therefore in vain that these nations rise up like the powers of chaos against him, his city (the Zion tradition with its theme of the nations!), or his people (cf. the synonym pairs cited above): ultimately they cannot prevail and will fall victim to destruction as objects of divine judgment (Isa. 17:12f.; Ps. 65:8[7]; cf. Isa. 34:1; 49:1; 51:4; Ps. 7:8[7]; 9:9[8]; Jer. 51:58; Hab. 2:13; Ps. 2:1; 44:3[2]; 44:15[14]; 47:4[3]; 105:44). Yahweh gives nations in exchange for his people (Isa. 43:4). Thus the peoples and foreign nations are described as standing within Yahweh's rule and sway (hymnic expansion). The promises are then extended to these peoples (Isa. 55:4; 60:2f.); the worshipper will sing the praises of the God of the nations (Zion tradition!) among the peoples (Ps. 57:10[9]; 108:4[3]; cf. also 117:1 conj.; 148:11), since Yahweh also guides the nations (65:8[7]).

We conclude that *l^{e}'ōm* (and its pl.) has its locus in poetic texts, where it is used in poetic extension to show that Yahweh's power extends beyond the borders of Israel, that his judgment and salvation include other peoples and nations.

The texts in the Dead Sea scrolls (only sg.) stay within the usage we have noted for the OT (1QH 6:12; 1Q27 1:9; uncertain text in 1QSb 3:18; 5:28).

Preuss

11. Cf. *KTU,* 1.3 II, 7.
12. Cf. again *KTU,* 1.3 II, 7f.

לֵב *lēḇ*; לֵבָב *lēḇāḇ*

Contents: I. Etymology and Distribution. II. Ancient Near East: 1. Egypt; 2. Mesopotamia; 3. Ugarit; 4. Aramaic. III. OT Usage: 1. Distribution; 2. Syntax; 3. LXX; 4. Sirach. IV. Meaning: 1. General, "Chest"; 2. Plants; 3. Animals; 4. "Midst." V. The Human Heart: 1. Personal Identity; 2. Vital Center; 3. Affective Center; 4. Noetic Center; 5. Voluntative Center; 6. Religious and Ethical Realm. VI. Idols. VII. Yahweh. VIII. Dead Sea Scrolls

---

lēḇ. J. B. Bauer, "De 'Cordis' Notione Biblica et Iudaica," *VD* 40 (1962), 27-32; F. Baumgärtel and J. Behm, "καρδία," *TDNT,* III, 606-611; J. H. Becker, "Het begrip 'hart' in het OT," *GThT,* 50 (1950), 10-16; C. A. Briggs, "A Study of the Use of לב and לבב in the OT," *Semitic Studies in Memory of A. Kohut* (Berlin, 1897), 95-105; H. Brunner, "Das Herz als Sitz des Lebensgeheimnisses," *AfO,* 17 (1954-56), 140f. = *Das hörende Herz. OBO,* 80 (1988), 6f.; *idem, Das Herz im Umkreis des Glaubens* (Biberach, 1965), 81-106 = *OBO,* 80 (1988), 8-41; *idem,* "Das hörende Herz," *ThLZ,* 79 (1954), 697-700 = *OBO,* 80 (1988), 3-5; É. P. Dhorme, "L'emploi métaphorique des noms de parties du corps en hébreu et en akkadien, VI," *RB,* 31 (1922), 489-517; M. Dijkstra, "A Ugaritic Pendant of the Biblical Expression 'Pure in Heart' (Ps 24:4; 73:1)," *UF,* 8 (1976), 440; J. Doresse, "Le coeur et les anciens Égyptiens," *Le Coeur. Études carmélitaines,* 29 (1950), 82-97; K. Galling, *Das Bild vom Menschen in biblischer Sicht. Mainzer Universitäts-Reden,* 3 (1947); B. de Geradon, "Le coeur, la bouche, les mains," *BVC,* 1 (1953), 7-24; A. Guillaumont, "Les sens noms du coeur dans l'Antiquité," *Le Coeur. Études carmélitaines,* 29 (1950), 41-81; A. Hermann, "Das steinharte Herz," *JAC,* 4 (1961), 77-107; F. Hintze, "Zu den Wörten für 'Herz' und 'Magen' im Altägyptischen," *Ägyptologische Studien. Festschrift H. Grapow. DAWB,* 29 (1955), 140ff.; E. Jacob, "ψυχή," B.4, *TDNT,* IX, 626ff.; A. R. Johnson, *The Vitality of the Individual in the Thought of Ancient Israel* (Cardiff, [2]1964); P. Joüon, "Locutions Hébraïques avec la préposition עַל devant לֵבָב, לֵב," *Bibl,* 5 (1924), 49-53; A. Kammenhuber, "Die hethitischen Vorstellungen von Seele und Leib, Herz und Leibesinnerem, Kopf und Person, 2," *ZA,* N.S. 23[57] (1965), 177-222; L. Köhler, *Hebrew Man* (Eng. trans., Nashville, 1956); H. Kornfeld, "Herz und Gehirn in altbiblischer Auffassung," *Jahrbücher für jüdische Geschichte und Literatur,* 12 (1909), 81ff.; P. Lacau, *Les noms des parties du corps en Ëgyptien et en Sémitique* (Paris, 1970); F. H. van Meyenfeldt, *Het Haart (LEB, LEBAB) in het OT* (Leiden, 1950) [Eng. summary]; F. Nötscher, *Gotteswege und Menschenwege in der Bibel und in Qumran. BBB,* 15 (1958), *s.v.* Herz; J. Oelsner, *Benennung und Funktion der Körperteile im hebräischen AT* (diss., Leipzig, 1961); W. O. E. Oesterley, *The Book of Proverbs* (New York, 1929), Excursus IX: "The Connotation of Lêb ('Heart') in Proverbs," lxxvii-lxxx; J. Pedersen, *ILP,* I, 99-181, esp. 103f.; A. Piankoff, *Le "Coeur" dans les textes égyptiens depuis l'Ancien jusqu'à la fin du Nouvel Empire* (Paris, 1930); J. Pidoux, *L'homme dan l'AT. CahTh,* 32 (1953); F. Popitz, *Die Symbolik des meschlichen Leibes* (Stuttgart, 1956); M. Z. Qaddari, "בלשון המקרא הצירופים השמניים של 'לב (לבב)'," *Bar-Ilan,* 4f. (1969), 352-390 [Heb.]; H. W. Robinson, "Hebrew Psychology," in A. S. Peake, ed., *The People and the Book* (Oxford, 1925), 353-382, esp. 363ff.; A. Rupp, *Vergehen und Bleiben. FARG,* 2 (1976); H. Rusche, "Das menschliche Herz nach biblischen Verständnis," *BiLe,* 3 (1962), 201-6; J. Scharbert, *Fleisch, Geist und Seele im Pentateuch. SBS,* 19 ([2]1967); *idem, Der Schmerz im AT. BBB,* 8 (1955); W. H. Schmidt, "Anthropologische Begriffe im AT," *EvTh,* 24 (1964), 374-388; E. Schmitt, *Leben in den Weisheitsbüchern Job, Sprüche und Jesus Sirach. FreibThSt,* 66 (1954); J. Schreiner, "Persönliche Entscheidung vor Gott nach biblischen Zeug-

I. Etymology and Distribution. Heb. *lēḇ/lēḇāḇ* comes from a common Semitic root **libb.*[1] Jakob Barth[2] derives the noun (originally *libāb*) from an intransitive verb, for which Ludwig Koehler[3] gives the meaning "throb." The verb itself, however, is not attested. The derivation, according to Barth, is analogous to that of *db,* "bear," from *dbb,* so that he takes *lēḇāḇ* as a "word extension."

Whether this root is present in Akk. *labābu,* "rage (verb),"[4] *libbatu,* "rage (noun),"[5] is not clear.[6] Heb. *lbb* I (niphal: "be made intelligent"; piel: "take the heart away, enchant")[7] is a denominative verb from *lēḇ.*

The nominal form[8] is found in all Semitic languages: Akk. *libbu,* "body, interior, heart";[9] Ugar. *lb,* "heart."[10] It is probable, therefore, that *lēḇ* is a primary noun. Other cognates include Old Aram. *lbb,* "heart"; Phoen., Pun., and Aram. *lb,* "heart, center of personal action";[11] Jewish Aram. *lēḇ/lēḇāḇ,* "heart, thought, mind,"[12] and *libbā'/lîbbā'/liḇᵉḇā',* "heart, disposition, thought";[13] Syr. *lebbā',* "heart, interior of the body, etc.";[14] South Semitic: Arab. *lubbun,* "heart, mind, intelligence, interior, core," *labbatun,* "upper portion of the chest, throat,"[15] with its derivatives *labābun,* "understanding, intelligence," *labibun,* "clever, wise," *labba,* "be intelligent," etc.;[16] OSA *lb,* "heart";[17] Eth. *lᵉb,* "heart, mind, reason, intellect";[18] Tigre, Ge'ez, and

nis," *BiLe,* 6 (1965), 107-121; F. Stolz, "לֵב *lēb* Herz," *THAT,* I, 861-67; H. W. Wolff, *Anthropology of the OT* (Eng. trans., Philadelphia, 1974); *idem, Menschliches. Kaiser Traktate,* 5 (1980); W. Zimmerli, *Das Menschenbild des ATs. ThEH,* N.S. 14 (1949).

1. Cf. P. Kahle, *Der masoretische Text des ATs* (1902, repr. Hildesheim, 1967), 68: *lbb.*
2. J. Barth, *Die Nominalbildung in den semitischen Sprachen* (²1894, repr. Hildesheim, 1967), 107.
3. L. Köhler, "Problems in the Study of the Language of the OT," *JSS,* 1 (1956), 3-24, esp. 15.
4. *Ahw,* I (1965), 521.
5. *Ibid.,* 548.
6. See G. R. Driver, "Some Hebrew Words," *JTS,* 29 (1927/28), 393; *idem,* "Studies in the Vocabulary of the OT. III," *JTS,* 32 (1931), 366; *KBL*³, *s.v.* לבב I. For the contrary view, see G. Rinaldi, "Nota: *libbâ,*" *BeO,* 17 (1975), 172.
7. *KBL*³, 490; A. Cohen, "Studies in Hebrew Lexicography," *AJSL,* 40 (1923/24), 174f.
8. Cf. G. Bergsträsser, *Introduction to the Semitic Languages* (Eng. trans., Winona Lake, 1983), 214f.; P. Fronzaroli, "Studi sul lessico comune semitico. II: Anatomia e Fisiologia," *AANLR,* 19 (1964), 272.
9. *AHw,* I, 549-551; *CAD,* IX (1973), 164-176.
10. *WUS,* no. 1434; *UT,* no. 1348.
11. *DISO,* 134.
12. *WTM,* II, 463.
13. *Ibid.,* 464.
14. *LexSyr,* 345f.
15. *WKAS,* II/2, 77-92.
16. On Tham. *lb*(*b*), "hither," see H. Grimme, "Die thamudische Präposition לב (לבב) 'her–zu,'" *ZDMG,* 95 (1941), 359-366.
17. ContiRossini, 171.
18. *LexLingAeth,* 41f.

Amhar. *l*ᵉ*b,* "heart, mind,"[19] *l*ᵉ*bbam,* "intelligent," *l*ᵉ*bonna,* "intelligence";[20] Libyan *ul.*[21]

Whether Egyp. *ỉb,*[22] "heart, mind, thought," is etymologically cognate with Sem. *lbb* is uncertain.[23]

II. Ancient Near East.

1. *Egypt.* In Egyptian, both *ỉb*[24] and *ḥ3.ty,*[25] "heart," are represented by the hieroglyph for an animal heart, a popular sacrifice even in the early period.[26] The difference between *ḥ3.ty,* occurring first in the Pyramid texts, and the ancient and much more common *ỉb* is not clear.[27] When used in parallel, they sometimes denote the same part of the body, sometimes different parts; *ḥ3.ty* appears to include a larger region. Egyptian medicine thinks of the breath as flowing to the heart, from which symmetrical "vessels" pervaded the body. In these vessels the heart "speaks" (the pulse?).[28] The heart is the focus of the individual — body, spirit, soul, and will — the center of the entire personality and its relationship with God. But the heart as the vital center (the *ka* being at work in each person's heart[29]) is not identical to the individual; it can forsake its owner, enter into dialogue with him, but also forsake him.[30] Here dwell the individual's attributes and feelings — trust ("openness of heart"), love, concern, pity, mercy, joy ("bigheartedness"), and fear ("palpitation"). Pharaoh gives his confidant a precious heart amulet.[31] "Swallow one's heart" is an idiom encompassing both discretion and hardness of heart.[32] To be self-controlled is to keep one's heart firmly in hand, so that it does not flutter, bound, or skip;[33] a brave warrior is "stouthearted" (*wmt-ỉb*).[34] Pride and arrogance have their seat in

---

19. *TigrWb,* 39.
20. W. Leslau, *Hebrew Cognates in Amharic* (Wiesbaden, 1969), 50.
21. *KBL*³, 488. On **lub *lubbu,* see O. Rössler, "Der semitische Charakter der libyschen Sprache," *ZA,* N.S. 16[50] (1952), 134f.
22. *WbÄS,* I, 59f.
23. Lacau, 92f.; Sem. *l* < *ỉ* under the influence of the following *b,* as in *ỉby,* "thirsty"; cf. Arab. *l'b.*
24. *WbÄS,* I, 59f.; cf. E. S. Meltzer, " 'Heart': *'Ib* or **'Inb* in Egyptian?" *JNES,* 36 (1977), 149-151.
25. *WbÄS,* III, 26f.
26. Lacau, 91.
27. Cf. *WbÄS,* III, 27.
28. Cf. H. Brunner, "Herz," *LexÄg,* II (1972), 1159.
29. *Ibid.,* 1163.
30. Cf. Rupp, 160f.; Hermann, 101-4.
31. *Urk.,* IV, 1427f.; K. Lange and M. Hirmer, *Egypt: Architecture, Sculpture and Painting in Three Thousand Years* (Eng. trans., London, ⁴1968), pl. 23f.
32. Brunner, 1160.
33. Papyrus Anastasi IV.2.5.
34. Cf. Piankoff, 37.

the heart, as do longing and homesickness. Greed (*ʿwn-ib*) is considered a disease, and anger makes the heart foul. When the Egyptians castigate a fool as "heartless,"[35] they are thinking of the heart as the seat of intellect, judgment, and "memory."[36] God speaks to mortals through the heart, but the heart is also where God can be known and God's will recognized.[37] God can even dwell personally "in the human heart";[38] according to Hellmut Brunner,[39] this represents an early stage in the idea of conscience. The heart is the locus of an individual's ethical competence; it is therefore weighed in the judgment of the dead ("the straits of the heart"). Finally, the heart is associated intimately with the tongue in determining sincerity. In old age, the heart grows weary (cf. Osiris's epithet "weary of heart") but continues to be an essential element of the individual; rituals guarantee that it will not be removed after death, a matter of great concern.[40] In deities, too, the heart is the seat of activity, especially in creation (in Memphite theology)[41] and in testing and sustaining the world. In a daily morning ritual at the awakening of the deity, its heart is offered to its image in the temple.[42]

2. *Mesopotamia.* From Old Akkadian on, the word *libbu*[43] is very common. It covers a broader range of meanings than Heb. *lēḇ/lēḇāḇ*. Its semantic range makes it more difficult to distinguish from such synonyms as *ṣurru,* "interior, heart"; *kabattu,* "liver, belly, interior, disposition, mind" (Heb. *kāḇēḏ*); *karšu,* "stomach, interior of the body, disposition, mind, intellect" (Heb. *kārēś* [Jer. 51:34; Sir. 36:23]); and *qerbu,* "interior, midst" (Heb. *qereḇ*).[44] Old Babylonian lists associate *libbu* with *irtu,* "breast," *qātu,* "hand," and *šēpu,* "foot";[45] it probably denotes the whole lower half of the torso (*CAD:* "abdomen"). A person feels sick when his *libbu* ("stomach") refuses food;[46] when his "liver" is damaged, he spits gall.[47] It can mean "womb"[48] and "fetus," especially in the Code of Hammurabi[49] and the Assyrian laws. Then, too, it can refer

35. H. Brunner, *Altägyptische Erziehung* (Wiesbaden, 1957), 110ff.
36. De Buck, VII. *OIP,* 87 (1961), 464d.
37. S. Morenz, *Egyptian Religion* (Eng. trans., Ithaca, N.Y., 1973), 63f.
38. *RÄR,* 297.
39. *ThLZ,* 79 (1954), 697-700, esp. 699.
40. See esp. E. Feucht, "Herzskarabäus," *LexÄg,* II, 1168-1170.
41. D. Müller, "Die Zeugung durch dad Herz in Religion und Medizin der Ägypter," *Or,* 35 (1966), 247-274; H. Kees, *StudGen,* 19 (1966), 124ff.
42. A. Moret, *Le rituel du culte divin journalier. BdÉ,* 14 (1902), 63.
43. *AHw,* I, 549-551; *CAD,* IX, 164-176.
44. *AHw,* II (1972), 914f.; Dhorme, 109ff.
45. F. Köcher and A. L. Oppenheim, "The Old-Babylonian Omen Text VAT 7525," *AfO,* 18 (1957), 66, III, 9.
46. F. Küchler, *Beiträge zur Kenntnis der assyrisch-babylonischen Medizin. Assyriologische Bibliothek,* 18 (1904), 26, III, 6.
47. Atraḫasis, 92, III, ii.47.
48. A. Poebel, *Historical and Grammatical Texts. PBS,* 5 (1914), 100, I, 5.
49. §209.29.

to the "viscera" in general.[50] Finally, *libbu* means "heart," whose beating is a sign of life, whose stoppage is proof of death: "He touched his heart, but it had ceased to beat."[51] A stab in the *libbu* can end a life.[52] Nevertheless, the *libbu* was hardly thought of as the seat or source of life.[53] There are many phrases using *libbu*: *dur libbi,* "diaphragm"; *elītu libbi,* "top"; *išdu libbi,* "bottom"; *kubšu libbi,* "viscera"; *rēš libbi,* "epigastrium"; *šamnu libbi,* "belly fat"; etc. Their variety shows that *libbu* does not denote a specifically identifiable part of the body. The *libbu* can suffer from many symptoms and diseases.[54]

At an early date, *libbu* came to be used figuratively for the "interior" of something in general: the eye (iris?[55]), the ear,[56] the nose. Soon it was extended to the "inside" of houses, regions, cities, rivers, the heavens, pots,[57] plants (e.g., *qanê,* "reed pith"; *iṣṣi,* "heart of palm"[58]), even oil. We may therefore suspect that *libbu* came to denote the essential core of something, its being, value, and purpose.

Animal hearts were of minor importance. They were sacrificed to the gods of the underworld.[59] They were more important in augury: "Thou, Šamaš, hast inscribed thine oracle on the *libbu* of the sheep."[60] The omen priest observes whether the heart is *šalim* ("sound"), *ḫaniq,* ("compressed"), or *tarik* ("dark").[61]

While the *kabattu* was thought of more as the seat of the blind passions, the *libbu* is the locus of the emotions that are more subject to the will (desire, love, friendship, mercy, faithfulness, etc.), of consciousness, wisdom, and understanding. This meaning probably derives from the experience of loss of consciousness (*ramān-šu ul īde*) and return to consciousness (*libba-šu ēr,* "his heart is awake"[62]). The heart devises good and evil;[63] from it spring both loyalty[64] and intrigue.[65] Although respect for Marduk dwells in the heart,[66] it was hardly the center of human religiosity (cf. *kabattu*).[67]

---

50. C. J. Gadd and S. N. Kramer, *Literary Texts. UET,* VI/1, 410, 12.
51. Gilg., VIII, II, 16.
52. EA 154, 44.
53. R. Labat, "Herz," *RLA,* IV (1972-75), 366f.
54. See *CAD,* IX, 167.
55. Küchler, 54, III, 4.
56. *RAcc,* 26, I, 17.
57. For citations, see *CAD,* IX, 168.
58. See *AHw.*
59. *RAcc,* 14, II, 16; *KAR,* 60, 15.
60. *STT,* 60, 15.
61. G. Dossin, *Correspondance de Šamši-Addu et du ses fils (suite). ARM,* IV (1951), 54, 10; cf. F. Blome, *Die Opfermaterie in Babylonien und Israel,* I. *SSAOI,* 4 (1934), 173ff., 182ff.
62. Labat, 367.
63. *VAS,* 1, 57, III, 2.
64. E. G. Klauber, *Politisch-religiöse Texte aus der Sargonidenzeit* (Leipzig, 1913), 139, r. 10.
65. Ashurbanipal annals, 28, III, 81.
66. *VAB,* 4, 116, II, 26.
67. See Dhorme, 128ff.

The enormous semantic field reveals the range of meanings. Our noun is used with verbs meaning "appease, reconcile," "rejoice," "be angry," "be alert," "be worried" (cf. the PN *Libbi-ilim-li-im-ra-aṣ*[68]), "fear" (cf. Late Bab. *libbi paliḫ,* "heart full of fear [of the gods]"[69]), "wish," "encourage," "discourage," "return," "be faithful," and many more.[70] Associated adjectives include "angry, wrathful," "wild," "distant, inscrutable," "beautiful, good, useful," "evil," "pure," "dark, troubled," "wise," "proud," "heavy, respected," "sound, healthy," "sick," and "whole" (*ina libbi gamri,* "[do something] with a whole heart";[71]; cf. Heb. *bᵉlēḇ šālēm*).[72] In noun phrases, (*libbu* only as *nomen rectum*) we find "health," "nourishment, healing," "nausea (?),"[73] "terror,"[74] "joy,"[75] "care, sadness,"[76] "burning,"[77] "agitation,"[78] "understanding,"[79] "hardness, anger,"[80] "oath, fidelity,"[81] "desire, longing"[82] (cf. esp. *nīš libbi,* "sexual potency," in incantation texts[83]), "stomach ache, vexation,"[84] "favorite of the heart" (often in conjunction with royal names),[85] and finally "peace of heart."[86]

Only seldom does a text mention the *libbu* of a deity, referring to what proceeds from this divine *libbu*: desire, pleasure, plan, decree. Formulas expressing divine pleasure are clearly analogous to the idiom *šumma libbi bēliya,* "as it pleases my heart":[87] cf. the PNs *Šumma-libbi-Aššur* and *Šumma-li-ib-ilī.*[88] The will of the gods

68. *AHw,* II, 609.
69. *VAB,* II, 262, 4.
70. For citations, see *AHw,* I, 549f.; *CAD,* IX, 172.
71. Cf. F. Thureau-Dangin, *Tablettes d'Uruk. TCL,* 6 (1922), 2, vo. 18; C.-F. Jean, *Lettres diverses. ARM,* II (1959, repr. 1978), 35, 27.
72. *AHw,* I, 279f.; other citations: *CAD,* IX, 172.
73. *AHw,* I, 242.
74. *CAD,* VI (1956), 150f.
75. *BER,* IV, 150, 10.
76. *AHw,* I, 564.
77. A. Goetze, *Old Babylonian Omen Texts. YOSBT,* 10 (1947), 54, vo. 13.
78. W. G. Lambert, "Three Literary Prayers of the Babylonians," *AfO,* 19 (1959-1960), 64, 90.
79. D. J. Wiseman, "A New Stela of Aššur-naṣir-pal II," *Iraq,* 14 (1952), 33, 22.
80. Goetze, 42, I, 54, etc.
81. A. Falkenstein, *Literarische Keilschrifttexte aus Uruk* (Berlin, 1931), 33, vo. 8.
82. T. G. Pinches and J. N. Strassmaier, *Late Babylonian Astronomical and Related Texts* (Providence, 1955), 1571 a, r. 17.
83. R. D. Biggs, *ŠÀ.ZI.GA: Ancient Mesopotamian Potency Incantations. TCS,* 2 (1967), 2; W. Heimpel, review of Biggs, *ZDMG,* 120 (1970), 189f.
84. *AHw,* II, 676.
85. *Syr,* 32 (1955), 16, 16.
86. Biggs, 15, 31f. On *libbu* in omens, see A. L. Oppenheim, *The Interpretation of Dreams in the Ancient Near East. TAPhS,* N.S. 46/3 (1956), 319.
87. Jean, 133, 14.
88. F. J. Stephens, *Personal Names from Cuneiform Inscriptions of Cappadocia. YOSR,* 13/1 (1928, repr. 1980), 66f.

(*libbi ilāni*) played an especially important role at the accession of a king, above all if he reigned *kî la libbi ilāni,* "contrary to the will of the gods."[89]

3. *Ugarit.* The word *lb,* "heart,"[90] occurs some 30 times in Ugaritic texts.[91] It is sometimes confused with *klb,* "dog," or *lb',* "lion."[92] In mythological texts, the heart of the deity (together with the kidneys [*klyt*][93]) is the seat of feelings and emotions. The liver (*kbd*) swells with joy and the heart is filled with laughter;[94] Pǵt weeps in her heart.[95] El and ʿAnat furrow their breasts (*'p lb,* "the region of the heart") in mourning for the death of Baʿal.[96] The heart is the locus of motherly instinct and desire for the beloved: "As the heart of the cow longs for her calf, as the heart of the ewe longs for her lamb, so the heart of ʿAnat longed for Baʿal."[97] ʿAnat devises evil in her *lb* (par. *kdb* and *qrb*).[98] The *lb* can be likened to a serpent (*bṯn*).[99] Textually problematical is the phrase *mgr lb* (cf. Akk. *migir libbi*), "subjection of heart, obedience," that the lesser gods must show to El.[100]

In Ugaritic epistolary texts we find the formulaic request "not to take to heart" (*b lb 'l št*),[101] that is, not to worry about them (cf. *ina libbika lâ išakin*[102]), not to be anxious.[103] One text[104] contains the unique expression *brt lb,* "be pure of heart"; Meindert Dijkstra[105] claims that the phrase refers to morality. The phrase *lb mlk,* "heart of the king,"[106] a nickname of Niqmepa, has connotations of endearment. We also find *lb* in sacrificial tariffs.[107]

4. *Aramaic.* Already in Old Aramaic *lbb* appears in the Sefire inscription as a term for the place where a party to the treaty frames his secret intent. This "thinking in the heart" (*ʿst blbb*)[108] concerning loyalty to the treaty or letting the idea of breaking the

---

89. *CAD,* IX, 172.
90. *UT,* no. 1348; *WUS,* no. 1434.
91. Whitaker, 395.
92. See esp. *KTU,* 1.19 I, 10, 13; 1.24, 30; 1.114 I, 12; H. M. Barstad, "Festmahl und Übersättigung: Der 'Sitz im Leben' von RS 24.258," *AcOr,* 39 (1978), 23-30.
93. *KTU,* 1.82, 3.
94. *KTU,* 1.3 II, 26; 1.7 I, 7; 1.12 I, 13; 1.17 IV, 41.
95. *KTU,* 1.19 I, 34.
96. *KTU,* 1.5 VI, 21; 1.6 I, 5; cf. the similar *b lb tqb* [] in 1.15 V, 15.
97. *KTU,* 1.6 II, 6-8, 28f.
98. *KTU,* 1.17 VI, 41; 1.18 I, 17.
99. *KTU,* 1.19 IV, 61.
100. *KTU,* 1.114 I, 12.
101. *KTU,* 2.30, 23; 2.38, 27.
102. EA 35, 12, 15.
103. Cf. *KTU,* 2.25, 3.
104. *KTU,* 2.8, 4; possibly also 2.3, 5.
105. P. 440.
106. *KTU,* 7.63, 8.
107. *KTU,* 1.39, 8; 1.41, 17; 1.87.19.
108. *KAI,* 223B, 5; cf. Zec. 7:10.

treaty "come to the heart" (*ysq ʿl lbb*)[109] is included in the formulation of the treaty itself.[110] In Imperial and Egyptian Aramaic,[111] *lb/lbb* represents the individual and the center of his being; it is the seat of emotion, reflection, purpose, and will.[112] It is difficult to bring someone "from under the heart" (*mn tḥt lbb*)[113] of a person, i.e., to remove him from that person's influence.

The proverbs of Ahikar illustrate the whole anthropological range of the word's meaning. Reticence ("hardening one's heart"; different in meaning from Ex. 8:11,28[Eng. vv. 15,32])[114] adorns those who keep someone's words in their *lb* as in an intact vessel (cf. Sir. 21:14; 27:19).[115] "Turn one's *lb*" means "turn one's attention."[116] The prudent person does not allow the heart to "leap" (*yḥd*; cf. Sir. 16:1)[117] nor pervert the *lb* by heaping up riches (*šg*ʾ; cf. Sir. 8:2b).[118] The word of the king is nourishment for the heart;[119] it must never be discussed with an angry heart.[120]

A "good heart" (*lbb ṭb*) and an "outstanding character" (*špyr middh*)[121] are ideal qualities.[122] But a person's heart, character, and intentions cannot be perceived from without.[123] The degree to which the *lb* represents the entire person and his self-sacrificing work is illustrated by the sage's lament over a stupid disciple: "My eyes which I fastened on you and my *lb* which I gave you in wisdom you have rejected, and you have used my name for trivialities."[124]

In the concluding clauses of treaties and protocols, the combination of *ṭb*[125] with *lbb* constitutes the so-called *ṭb-lbby* formula, which Y. Muffs interprets as having legal force:[126] it documents the claim of the contracting party to appropriate damages together with a definitive resignation of further claims on the part of the person satisfied. The formula is found in two forms: *ṭyb lbby,* "my heart is satisfied,"[127] and *hwṭbh libby,*

---

109. *KAI,* 224, 14, 15.

110. For the parallel Akkadian terminology, see R. A. Brauner, *A Comparative Lexicon of Old Aramaic* (Philadelphia, 1974), 299f.

111. *DISO,* 134.

112. *AP,* 40, 3; 71, 6; Hermopolis papyrus IV, 5; *KAI,* 264, 8f.

113. *BMAP,* 2, 14.

114. Ahikar 98.

115. Ahikar 109.

116. Ahikar 65.

117. Ahikar 106.

118. Ahikar 137.

119. Ahikar 100; text possibly corrupt.

120. Ahikar 104. On proper respect for the words of the king, cf. also Instruction of Ptah-hotep 147ff.; *ANET*³, 413a.

121. Ahikar 195; text possibly corrupt.

122. Cf. *KAI,* 26A, I, 13.

123. Ahikar 163.

124. Ahikar 169.

125. → טוב *tôḇ,* V, 302.

126. Y. Muffs, *Studies in the Aramaic Legal Papyri from Elephantine. StDI,* 8 (1969; repr. New York, 1973).

127. *AP,* 2, 9; 14, 5; 15, 5 (*ṭb*); 15, 15; 20, 9; 43, 7; *BMAP,* 1, 4; 3, 6; 12, 6; 14, 26.

"you have satisfied my heart."[128] Muffs compares the formula to Akk. *libbašu ṭāb,*[129] Egyp. *m-ỉb-hr,* "with a satisfied heart,"[130] and Demotic *dy.k-mty ḥ3ty(ỉ).*[131] This formula, in which *lbb* stands by synecdoche for the person, was probably first used in a "quitclaim" explicitly documenting the resolution of a legal action by confirming that the necessary conditions had been met.[132]

There are also 5 occurrences of *lb*/*lbb* in the Aramaic texts from Deir ʿallā.[133] "Speak in the heart,"[134] "the sighing in the heart of one who is blind" (*nqr blbbh n'nḥ*),[135] and the rhetorical question whether the *lbb* of one who is blind can be firm (*kwn*)[136] are recognizable idioms.

III. OT Usage.

1. *Distribution.* The noun *lēḇ*/*lēḇāḇ* occurs 853 times in the OT. In the Hebrew OT, *lēḇ* is found 596 times,[137] *lēḇāḇ* 249 times.[138] In the Aramaic portions, *lēḇ* occurs once, *leḇaḇ* 7 times. The word appears in all the books of the OT except Micah and Habakkuk. It is most common in Psalms (137 occurrences), Proverbs (98), Jeremiah (66), Deuteronomy (51), Ezekiel (47), Exodus (45), 2 Chronicles (44), and Ecclesiastes (41). In the Pentateuch, only Deuteronomy (like the Deuteronomistic history) and the Holiness Code exhibit a clear preference for *lēḇāḇ*. Deuteronomy uses *lēḇ* (at least in Dt. 4:11) only for the sake of a play on words,[139] whereas JEP use *lēḇ* almost exclusively; indeed, *lēḇāḇ* does not appear to occur at all in J. E also uses *lēḇ* (Gen. 31:20; 45:26[140]). Proto-Isaiah prefers *lēḇāḇ,* while Deutero-Isaiah, Trito-Isaiah, Jeremiah, and Ezekiel prefer *lēḇ.* Of the Minor Prophets, Hosea, Amos, Obadiah, Zechariah, and Malachi use *lēḇ,* while Joel, Haggai, and Jonah use *lēḇāḇ*. Wisdom Literature generally prefers *lēḇ*; Daniel and the Chronicler's history show the opposite preference.

It appears that *lēḇ* was used more in the early period and *lēḇāḇ* later, especially in Deuteronomic and Deuteronomistic circles and in the Chronicler's history. There is no discernible semantic difference; on the contrary, *lēḇ* and *lēḇāḇ* appear to be totally synonymous and interchangeable (cf. 1 S. 6:6a,b; 1 Ch. 12:39a,b[38a,b]; Gen. 31:20

---

128. *AP,* 6, 12; 20, 8.
129. Pp. 63-141.
130. *Ibid.,* 142-49.
131. *Ibid.,* 150-172.
132. *Ibid.,* 107.
133. See J. Hoftijzer and G. van der Kooij, *Aramaic Texts from Deir ʿAllah. DMOA,* 19 (1976), 250f.
134. II, 12.
135. II, 12; cf. Ps. 13:3(2); *KTU,* 1, 19 I, 34.
136. II, 14.
137. A. Even-Shoshan, ed., *A New Concordance of the OT* (Grand Rapids, ²1989), gives 599.
138. *Ibid.*: 252.
139. Cf. G. Braulik, *Die Mittel deuteronomischer Rhetorik. AnBibl,* 68 (1978), 99, 126.
140. Contra Stolz, 861.

par. 26; Ezk. 28:2c par. 6; 2 Ch. 12:14 par. 19:3; Jgs. 19:5 par. 8, 6 par. 9 [in Jgs. 19, the difference may be significant for literary analysis]).

2. *Syntax.* a. The noun *lēḇ* is used absolutely 210 times (primarily in Proverbs, Psalms, Exodus, and the Deuteronomistic history); it is also used with the particles *b*ᵉ (70 times), *min* (12 times), and *k*ᵉ (8 times), and with almost all the pronominal suffixes (except the 2nd person fem. pl.). The pl. *libbôṯ* appears 7 times. The abs. *lēḇāḇ* appears 32 times (primarily in Psalms, the Chronicler's history, and Job); the construct without a suffix appears 22 times. It is used 46 times with *b*ᵉ, 6 with *k*ᵉ, and twice with *l*ᵉ, and is also found with almost all the suffixes (except the 2nd person fem. pl.). The pl. *l*ᵉ*ḇāḇôṯ* appears only in 1 Ch. 28:9. While *lēḇ* is used primarily with suffixes of the 1st person (104 times) and 3rd person (160 times) (in statements, narratives, etc.), *lēḇāḇ* appears surprisingly often (96 times) with suffixes of the 2nd person (in parenesis, etc.).

b. As *nomen regens* in a construct phrase, *lēḇ* appears with *marpēh,* "calmness"; *'eḇen,* "stone"; *bāśār,* "flesh"; *da'aṯ,* "sense of knowledge"; *'aryēh,* "courage of a lion"; *gibbôrîm,* "courage of warriors"; *'ayin,* "without understanding'; *'awlâ,* "perversity"; *niḏkā'îm,* "defeat"; *nāḇāl* and *k*ᵉ*sîlîm,* "fool(s)"; *ḥāḵām,* "sage"; and *r*ᵉ*šā'îm,* "wicked." All these expressions have clear ethical connotations. It is used figuratively in the phrases *lēḇ-yam*/*yammîm,* "the midst of the sea" (cf. Akk. *ina libbi tāmti*), and *lēḇ-haššāmayim,* "into the very heavens." It also appears in construct phrases with *'îš,* "man"; *'iššâ,* "woman"; *'āḇôṯ,* "fathers"; *bānîm,* "sons"; *na'ar,* "young man"; *'almâ,* "young woman"; *meleḵ* and *par'ōh,* "king"; *śārîm,* "princes"; *hā'ām,* "people"; *rā'šê,* "leaders" (of the *'am-hā'āreṣ*); *'ᵃḇāḏîm,* "servants"; *'ammîm rabbîm,* "many nations"; and *b*ᵉ*nê 'āḏām,* "people." The text also speaks of the *lēḇ* of the Israelites, the Egyptians, Jerusalem, Adam, Laban, Aaron, Ammon, Absalom, David, Solomon, Joash, and all the Levites. Finally, even enemies (and idols; *šiqqûṣîm,* Ezk. 11:21 [MT?]) have *lēḇ*.

c. Much more frequent are construct phrases with *lēḇ* as *nomen rectum.* The anthropological sphere is represented by *qereḇ,* "bottom of the heart "; *tôḵ,* "midst"; *qîrôṯ,* "walls"; *sēṯer,* "concealment"; *ta'ᵃlumôṯ,* "secrets"; *n*ᵉ*ṣurâ,* "inmost thoughts"; *ra'yôn,* "zeal"; *kôaḥ,* "strength"; and *dereḵ,* "way." Many phrases speak of the heart as the seat of the emotions: "gladness" (Cant. 3:11; Eccl. 5:19[20]), "joy" (Lam. 5:15), "desires" (Ps. 37:4), "sorrow" (Prov. 15:13), and "pain" (Isa. 65:14). Others associate the heart with noetic activity: "largeness" (1 K. 5:9[4:29]), "simplicity (RSV: 'integrity')" (Gen. 20:5f.), "intelligence" (Ex. 36:1,2,8), "imagination" (Gen. 8:21), "meditation" (Ps. 19:15[14]), and *ḥiq*ᵉ*qê-lēḇ,* "searchings of heart" (Jgs. 5:15; corrected to *ḥiqrê* on the basis of v. 16). The *lēḇ* represents the ethical center in conjunction with "arrogance" (Prov. 16:5; Ob. 3), "dullness" (Lam. 3:65, Hos. 13:8), "lack" (Prov. 6:32; 7:7),[141] "heartlessness" and its opposite, *š*ᵉ*rirûṯ lēḇ* (Dt. 29:18[19]), contrite "brokenheartedness."[142] In combination with *mûsār,* "discipline," *q*ᵉ*rāḇ,* "struggle,"

141. → חצר *ḥāṣēr.*

142. For a different interpretation, see L. Kopf, "Arabische Etymologien und Parallelen zum Bibelwörterbuch," *VT,* 9 (1959), 283: "secret thoughts."

and *mikšôl,* "pangs," *lēḇ* means "conscience." The "godless" are *ḥanpê lēḇ* (Job 36:13). Other phrases include *lûaḥ lēḇ,* "tablet of the heart" (Jer. 17:1; Prov. 3:3; 7:3),[143] and *ḥᵃzôn lēḇ,* "vision of the heart." The latter expression, like *nᵉḇîʾê millibbām,* "self-called prophets," denotes false prophecy (Ezk. 13:17).

d. Since *lēḇāḇ* has a suffix in most of its occurrences, it almost never appears as *nomen regens*; cf. *lēḇ* and *lēḇāḇ ḥoḵmâ,* "wise heart" (Ps. 90:12).

As *nomen rectum, lēḇāḇ* (cf. *lēḇ*) is found with *ʾîš,* "intelligent man"; *maśkîṯ,* "imagination"; *paḥaḏ,* "terror"; *ṣûr,* "solace"; *yišrâ,* "uprightness"; *gōḏel,* "arrogance"; *ʿorlâ,* "foreskin of the heart"; and *negaʿ,* "remorse."[144]

e. Many adjectives modify *lēḇ.* They may be categorized as anthropological: "strong" (Isa. 46:12), "powerful" (Ezk. 2:4), "faint" (Ps. 61:3[2]), "tranquil" (Prov. 14:30), "full" (Eccl. 8:11), "deluded" (Isa. 44:20); emotional: "cheerful" (Prov. 17:22), "willing" (Ex. 35:22); noetic: "understanding" (1 K. 3:12), "knowing" (Prov. 14:10), "wise" (Prov. 16:23), "senseless" (Prov. 15:21), "inscrutable" (Ps. 64:7[6]); and ethical: "good" (Eccl. 9:7), "evil" (Prov. 26:23), "clean" (Ps. 51:12[10]), "righteous" (Ezk. 13:22), "hearkening" (1 K. 3:9), "upright" (Ps. 36:11[10]), "harmonious" (2 Ch. 30:12; Isa. 38:3), "stout" (Am. 2:16), "awake" (Cant. 5:2), "stubborn" (Ezk. 3:7), "perverse" (Prov. 12:8), "stubborn and rebellious" (Jer. 5:23), "proud" (Prov. 21:4), "hard" (Ex. 7:14), "godless" (Prov. 14:14), "uncircumcised" (Lev. 26:41), "fearful" (Isa. 35:4), "broken" (Ps. 34:19[18]), "new" (Ezk. 36:26).

f. The nouns *lēḇ* and *lēḇāḇ* function as subject of many verbs. Those with anthropological meaning include "be deep, inscrutable" (Ps. 64:7[6]), "fail" (Ps. 73:26), "be large" (Isa. 60:5), and verbs meaning "be firm" (Ex. 7:13,22; etc.). We also find "be pierced" (Ps. 109:22), "wither" (Ps. 102:5[4]), "go out" (Gen. 42:28), "be distant" (Isa. 29:13), and finally "die" (1 S. 25:37). In the emotional sphere, we find (intransitive) "tremble" (Job 37:1), "be amazed" (Ps. 45:2[1]), "dread" (1 S. 28:5), "rejoice" (Ps. 105:3), "grow warm" (Ps. 39:4[3]), "be inclined" (Ps. 119:112), "be willing" (Ex. 25:2), and (transitive) "cry" (Lam. 2:18), "say" (Ps. 27:8), "rejoice over" (Ps. 84:3[2]), and "seize" (Hos. 4:11). In the noetic sphere, we find (intransitive) "ponder" (Prov. 15:28), "be occupied (with wisdom)" (Eccl. 2:3), but also "be dull" (Ps. 119:70) and "fail" (Jer. 4:9), and (transitive) "consider" (Isa. 10:7), "see" (Eccl. 1:16; 2:1), and "know" (Eccl. 8:5). In the ethical sphere, *lēḇ* is the subject of intransitive verbs meaning "repent," "trust" (Prov. 31:11), and "be stubborn" (Ex. 7:14; etc.), as well as "be haughty" (Prov. 18:12), "turn away" (Dt. 30:17), "turn aside" (Jer. 17:5), "be unfaithful" (Prov. 14:14), "go astray" (Isa. 21:4), "go after idols" (Ezk. 20:16; cf. Job 31:7), "fall" (1 S. 17:32), and "be false" (Hos. 10:2). Transitively, we find "reproach" (Job 27:6), "desert" (Ps. 40:13[12]), "delude" (Dt. 11:16), and "rule" (Neh. 5:7).

g. In the anthropological sphere, *lēḇ/lēḇāḇ* can be the object of verbs meaning "make, prepare" (Eccl. 1:13,17; etc.), "make sick, healthy, or pure" (Prov. 13:12),

---

143. See A. Schenker, "Die Tafel des Herzens," *Vierteljahresschrift für Heilpädagogik und ihre Nachbargebiete,* 48 (1979), 236-250.

144. See Even-Shoshan, 1092.

"revive" (Isa. 57:15), "see, test" (Jer. 12:3; etc.), and "hide" (Job 17:4). In the emotional sphere, we find "make fearful/courageous" (Job 23:16; 37:1; etc.), "satisfy" (Jgs. 19:22), "rejoice" (Prov. 15:30), "stir up" (Dnl. 11:25), "cause to rejoice" (Job 29:13), "search" (1 Ch. 28:9), and "seize" (Hos. 4:11). In the noetic sphere, we find "set one's mind" (2 S. 13:33), "incline" (2 S. 19:15[14]), "turn to/from" (Mal. 3:24[4:6]), "tell" (Jgs. 16:17f.), and "cause to understand" (Prov. 8:5). In the ethical sphere, we find "turn" (Ps. 105:25; etc.), "direct in the right/wrong way" (Prov. 23:19), "harden,"[145] "circumcise" (Dt. 30:6), "(lift up, make presumptious, and then) humiliate" (Ps. 69:21[20]), "deceive" (Gen. 31:20),[146] and the unique expression *yaḥēḏ lᵉḇāḇî* (Ps. 86:11), "unite my heart."[147]

h. We also find several idiomatic expressions. Anthropological: *hēšîḇ 'el-lēḇ,* "call to mind" (Lam. 3:21; etc.); "say in one's heart (i.e., to oneself)" (Gen. 27:41); "write something on the tablet of one's heart" (Prov. 3:3; 7:3); "put something into someone's heart" (Ezr. 7:27). Affective: "touch someone's heart" (1 S. 10:26); "beat one's breast (lit., 'heart')" (Nah. 2:8[7]); "bind to one's heart" (Prov. 22:15); "be glad in one's heart" (Ex. 4:14); "grieve in one's heart" (Gen. 6:6); "hate in one's heart" (Lev. 19:17); "despise in one's heart" (2 S. 6:16); "speak to someone's heart" (Gen. 34:3); verb + *bᵉlēḇ šālēm,* "do something with a whole heart" (1 Ch. 28:9; etc.). Noetic: *ʿālâ ʿal-lēḇ,* "come to mind" (Isa. 65:17); *yāḏaʿ ʿim-lᵉḇāḇ,* "know in one's heart" (Dt. 8:5). Ethical: "return with all one's heart" (Jer. 24:7); "test God in one's heart" (Ps. 78:18); *hālaḵ bᵉḏereḵ libbô,* "walk in the ways of one's own heart," i.e., "be self-willed" (Eccl. 11:9); *dibber bᵉlēḇ wālēḇ,* "speak with a double tongue (lit., 'heart')" (Ps. 12:3[2]); the opposite *bᵉlō'-lēḇ-wālēḇ,* "with singleness of purpose" (1 Ch. 12:34[33]).

3. *LXX.* The LXX generally uses *kardía* to render *lēḇ/lēḇāḇ* (718 times). Other translations are *diánoia* (51; esp. common in Genesis[148]), *psyché̄* (27), *noús* (12), *phrḗn* (7), *stḗthos* (3), and *phrónēsis* (2). Once each we find *éndeia* (*ḥᵃsar lēḇ*), *epithymía, euphrosýnē* (*ṭôḇ lēḇ*), and *homónoia.* Adjectives include *akárdios* (*'ên lēḇ*), *thrasykárdios* (*sûg/rᵉḥaḇ lēḇ*), *sklērokárdios* (*ʿiqqēš/qᵉšēh-lēḇ*), *áphrōn* (*ḥᵃsar lēḇ,* elsewhere for *'ᵉwîl*), *ekousíōs, hēdéōs, nōthrokárdios, prothýmōs, stereokárdios, hypsēlokárdios,* and *phrónimos.* For *ʿorlaṯ-lᵉḇāḇ* it uses *sklērokardía.* Verbal translations include *boúlesthai* (*nāśā'/śîm lēḇ*), *dianoeísthai* (*ʿāsaḇ 'el-lēḇ*), *epaírein* (*gîl lēḇ*), *epérchesthai, esthíein* (*sāʿaḏ lēḇ*), *euphraínein, gígnesthai* (*ṭôḇ lēḇ*), *katanoeín, proséchein* (*śîm ʿal-lēḇ*), *pontoporeín,* and *tolmán* (*mālē' lēḇ*).

4. *Sirach.* In Sirach we find *lēḇ* 58 times and *lēḇāḇ* 10 times; the usage is similar to Ahikar and Proverbs. The Greek text uses *kardía* (46 times), *psyché̄* (11), along with

145. See V.6.c below and *šāman* hiphil, lit. "cover with fat."

146. Kopf, 250f.

147. According to H.-J. Kraus, *Psalms 60–150* (Eng. trans., Minneapolis, 1989), 182, an idiom denoting "concentration on obedience and fear of God."

148. See A. Schmitt, "Interpretation der Genesis aus hellenistichem Geist," *ZAW,* 86 (1974), 153f.

synetós and *anḗr* (once each). Phrases include *ḥ^a^sar lēḇ* (*akárdios*; Sir. 6:20), *lēḇ nāḇāl* (*splánchna*; 36:5), *bal ʿal-lēḇ* (*anyponóētos*; 11:5), and *z^e^ḏôn lēḇ* (*sklērokardía*; 16:11).

IV. Meaning. It is generally assumed that the primary meaning of *lēḇ* is the organ we call the heart,[149] but this cannot be proved. The anatomical reference of *lēḇ* is quite vague in all the Semitic languages.

1. *General, "Chest."* The OT scarcely ever uses *lēḇ* for the "heart" as a physical organ. In 2 S. 18:14; 2 K. 9:24; Ps. 37:15; 45:6(5), it denotes a part of the body that can, for example, be pierced by arrows[150] without necessarily causing the death of the individual in question (cf. esp. 2 S. 18:14). Often *lēḇ* serves in the absence of a Hebrew word for "breast" or "chest" (cf. *šaḏ*). In Hos. 13:8, *s^e^ḡôr lēḇ,* "enclosure of the heart," refers to the thoracic cage. Ex. 28:29f. says that Aaron wears the breastpiece (*ḥōšen*) "upon his *lēḇ*"; v. 30 plays on the figurative meaning "devote special attention to" (cf. Cant. 8:6). Mourning includes "beating [*tpp* polel] one's *lēḇ*" (Nah. 2:8[7]). According to Ernst Kutsch,[151] this action expresses a sense of diminution; according to others,[152] it is an act of self-abasement to influence the deity. It may also involve a ritual act of pointing backwards, found in Egypt as a gesture of rejoicing (*hnw*) and lamentation.[153] It is quite uncertain that the "heart attack" in 1 S. 25:37 (Fritz Stolz — although the passage only says in general terms that Nabal's *lēḇ* "died" [*mûṯ*] and that he himself died ten days later!) or the "throbbing" of the heart in Ps. 38:11(10) (expressing intense emotion) can be interpreted with anatomical precision. The passages in the prophets that speak of "heart attacks" (Jer. 4:19: "raging of the *lēḇ,*" interpreted by H. W. Wolff as arrhythmia;[154] Jer. 23:9; etc.) or "faintness of heart" (Isa. 1:5; 57:15) are more expressions of excitement or sickness than physiologically accurate descriptions. It is therefore wrong to interpret *lēḇ* literally as "heart"[155] or "throat."[156]

In our search for the primary meaning of *lēḇ,* the absence of a specific anatomical reference must not lead us into un-Semitic abstraction, so that we define *lēḇ* as "the fixed point, the central point . . . the nucleus of something, in the sense of the most important constituent in which something is completely represented,"[157] although such metonymy is found in early East Semitic usage, where the noun can denote the

149. Scharbert, 94; E. Schmitt, 36; Stolz, 861.

150. C. Conroy, *Absalom, Absalom!: Narrative and Language in 2 Sam 13–20. AnBibl,* 81 (1978), 44, 154: "chest."

151. E. Kutsch, *"Trauerbräche" und "Selbstminderungsbräuche" im AT. ThSt,* 78 (1965), 26, 34.

152. W. Frankenberg, "Israelitische und altarabische Trauerbräuche," *PJ,* 2 (1906), 73; A. Dihle, "Demut," *RAC,* III (1957), 747.

153. E. Brunner-Traut, "Gesten," *LexÄg,* II (1977), 580.

154. *Anthropology of the OT,* 42.

155. Joüon, 49ff.

156. H. L. Ginsberg, "Lexicographical Notes," *Hebräische Wortforschung. Festschrift W. Baumgartner. SVT,* 16 (1967), 80.

157. Meyenfeldt, 221.

"interior" (of the body or an object), hidden from view but externally operative and thus verifiable.

2. *Plants.* After the analogy of the "heart of the palm tree,"[158] 2 S. 18:14 speaks of the *lēḇ* of the oak in which Absalom's hair was caught (cf. par. in v. 9: *bā'ēlâ*). The word undoubtedly refers to the branches of the treetop, the vague "interior" of the observed surface.

3. *Animals.* The notion of an animal's *lēḇ* is largely unknown to the OT. According to Job 41:16(24), the *lēḇ* of Leviathan is hard as stone. The reference is to his belly, which is impervious to spears, swords, and arrows (v. 18[26]). The *lēḇ* of a lion is a metaphor for his courage (2 S. 17:10). The Aramaic occurrences in Daniel likewise are not anatomically specific: Nebuchadnezzar is punished by being given a *l^eḇaḇ ḥêwā'*, a "bestial nature" (Dnl. 4:13[16]; cf. 5:21); conversely, the apocalyptic lion is given a *l^eḇaḇ '^enāš,* a "human nature" (Dnl. 7:4).

4. *"Midst."* The impossibility of finding a fixed referent for *lēḇ* is particularly clear when it means simply the "midst" of something. The *lēḇ* of the sea is the great unknown stretch of the high seas extending beyond the visible horizon (Ex. 15:8; Jon. 2:4[3]; Ps. 46:3[2]; Prov. 23:34; 30:19; cf. 4Q158 14 I:7. Ezekiel says that the city of Tyre lies on a neck of land *b^elēḇ yammîm* (Ezk. 27:4,25ff.; 28:2,8; cf. the mythological concept of the divine throne in the midst of the sea[159]). Equally vague is the remnant of naive cosmology that pictures the volcanic eruptions associated with the Horeb theophany as reaching to the *lēḇ* of heaven (Dt. 4:11). Finally, the OT speaks of the *lēḇ* of the people (Jer. 30:21; etc.), from which, for example, the ruler will come forth.

V. The Human Heart.

1. *Personal Identity.* The *lēḇ* functions in all dimensions of human existence and is used as a term for all the aspects of a person: vital, affective, noetic, and voluntative. The prescientific anthropology of the OT does in fact view the human person as composite,[160] although the analysis is not everywhere the same. This analysis is never the primary focus, since the OT texts seek to know men and women only as they stand before God (cf. Ps. 8:5[4]; 144:3; Job 7:17).[161] Even the Yahwistic Creation Story reveals the composite nature of the individual when J describes the human person as being made up of *'āpār* and *nišmaṯ ḥayyîm* (Gen. 2:7), while P speaks of *'āḏām* created *b^eṣelem '^elōhîm* (Gen. 1:27). The primary point of both texts is the relationship of the

---

158. *AHw,* I, 550.

159. → כסא *kissē'*; also O. Loretz, "Der Sturz das Fürsten von Tyrus (Ez 28, 1-19)," *UF,* 8 (1976), 456-580.

160. Cf. L. Köhler, *OT Theology* (Eng. trans., Philadelphia, 1957), 135-147; W. Eichrodt, *Man in the OT. SBT,* 4 (Eng. trans. 1951); Pidoux.

161. Köhler, 129-131, 160-66.

human individual to God the creator rather than the structure of the person. It is nonetheless surprising that the *lēḇ* is not such an essential element of the person that it should be mentioned in the Creation Story.

The OT sense of a composite personality appears in several merismic phrases, which are dominated by *lēḇ*: *šeʾēr* and *lēḇāḇ* (Ps. 73:26), *bāśār* and *lēḇ* (Prov. 14:30; Eccl. 2:3; cf. 11QtgJob 36:9), *lēḇ* and *ʿaṣāmôṯ* (Isa. 66:14; cf. Prov. 15:30), *bāśār* and *rûaḥ* (Gen. 6:17; 7:15), *lēḇ, ʿênayim,* and *nep̄eš* (Dt. 28:65), *lēḇ, rûaḥ, nešāmâ,* and *bāśār* (Job 34:15), *lēḇ, kāḇôḏ,* and *bāśār* (Ps. 16:9).[162] Cf. also *nep̄eš* and *bāśār* (Ps. 63:2[1]) and *ʿāp̄ār* and *rûaḥ* (Ps. 104:29; 146:4).

Different from these merisms are sequences that denote specific aspects of the person: "Heart and kidneys [RSV: 'mind']" (Ps. 7:10[9]; 26:2; Jer. 11:20; 12:2f.; 17:10; 20:12) stands for the inmost nature of the individual, known only to God and tested by him.[163] "Heart and lips" (Prov. 23:16f.; cf. 26:25) contrasts interior and exterior, which should be in harmony in an upright person (cf. "heart and eyes" in Job 31:7). Because this harmony cannot be assumed (cf. Prov. 27:19), the *lēḇ* is hidden from human sight; it is "deep" (*ʿāmōq*: Ps. 64:7[6]; cf. Ahikar 163), "deceitful" (*ʿāqōḇ*: Jer. 17:9 [text?]), and "unsearchable" (*ʾên ḥēqer*: Prov. 25:3). Since *lēḇ* denotes the fundamental nature of a person, can stand for the person (Ezk. 13:22; Ps. 22:15[14]; 27:3; Prov. 18:2; etc.), or even substitute for a personal pronoun (Gen. 18:5; Ex. 9:14), it is in many respects identical with → נפשׁ *nep̄eš*.[164]

2. *Vital Center.* Even the early wisdom of Proverbs knows the central importance of *lēḇ*: "Keep your *lēḇ* with all vigilance; for from it flow the springs of life" (Prov. 4:23; cf. 25:13). In it is concentrated the vital physical nature of the individual: if one is to live, the *lēḇ* must be refreshed (*sāʿaḏ,* "strengthen": Jgs. 19:5,8,22), usually with bread. Wine rejoices the *lēḇ* (Ps. 104:15). Food and drink can revive the afflicted (Ps. 22:27[26]), but assurance of a favorable hearing also revives the *lēḇ* (Ps. 69:33[32]). This vital aspect of the personality gives rise to most of the images and ideas common to laments. People lament because they feel afflicted to the very core of their being. The *lēḇ* throbs (Ps. 38:11[10]), beats wildly in anguish (Jer. 4:19), is pricked in the kidneys (Ps. 73:21). The *lēḇ* faints (Ps. 61:3[2]; 102:5[4]) so that one cannot eat. The sufferer is poured out like water, his bones are out of joint, his heart grows soft as wax and melts (Ps. 22:15[14]); his throat is like a dry potsherd (v. 16[15]). The *lēḇ* trembles (1 S. 28:5) and with it falls the whole person (Ezk. 21:20[15]), or it is hot as fire (Ps. 39:4[3]). The *lēḇ* is sick (*raʿ*: 1 S. 1:8; → חלה *ḥālâ*: Prov. 13:12; *dawwāy*: Isa. 1:5; Jer. 8:18; Lam. 1:22; 5:17);[165] because the cause can be apostasy, sin, or misfortune, sickness of the *lēḇ* can have ethical overtones. The *lēḇ* can be appalled (Ps. 143:4), break (Jer. 23:9), and die (1 S. 25:37).

---

162. Cf. F. Nötscher, "Heisst *kāḇōd* auch 'Seele,' " *VT,* 2 (1952), 358-362 = *Vom Alten zum NT. BBB,* 17 (1962), 237ff.

163. See V.6.a below.

164. Cf. esp. Köhler, *Hebrew Man,* 97-105; Wolff, 10ff.

165. See also Lachish ostracon III, 6f. (*KAI,* 193); cf. P. Humbert, "Maladie et médicine dans l'AT," *RHPR,* 44 (1964), 1-29.

Finally, the *lēḇ* is the center not only of the vital processes of life and nourishment, but also of sexual desire (cf. esp. Prov. 6:25; Ezk. 16:30); according to Hos. 4:11; Job 31:9, this desire itself deludes the heart.[166] The OT extends statements about the vital aspect of the personality from the individual to groups: Abraham's visitors refresh their *lēḇ* with bread (Gen. 18:5), and the *lēḇ* of the people melts like water (Josh. 7:5).[167]

3. *Affective Center.* The notion of the *lēḇ* as the seat of human emotions emerged gradually from that of the vital *lēḇ*. This development is especially clear in the commonplace language of the lament, which often uses the vital functions of the body to describe emotional reactions: pounding, fluttering, or convulsions of the heart symbolize excitement, fear, and apprehension;[168] the heart skips with joy. The prayer of the afflicted "Relieve the straits of my *lēḇ*" (Ps. 25:17) still shows the connection. According to Wolff,[169] distress of body and mind are here one and the same, but the purely vital aspect (as in Ps. 119:32; cf. esp. Isa. 60:5) is already transcended.[170] Prov. 14:30 ("A tranquil *lēḇ* gives life to the body"), too, still speaks of *lēḇ* in terms of its vital function. But this usage soon vanishes from sight entirely, and *lēḇ* becomes totally the seat of the emotions. Here are rooted both bitterness and joy (Prov. 14:10), which are only revealed outwardly by the countenance (Prov. 15:13; Eccl. 7:4; Sir. 13:25). According to Eccl. 11:9, one should use the joyous excitement of the heart to enjoy life (cf. Job 31:7).

a. *Elemental Emotions.* The "fundamental emotions of human existence"[171] are rooted in the *lēḇ*: despair, grief, and sadness are mentioned more than 80 times, outweighing the positive emotions of joy and pleasure (some 50 times). The OT describes the *lēḇ* in quite general terms as being "bad" (*ra'*) when someone is upset (Dt. 15:10). Reasons for the *lēḇ* to grieve are many: childlessness (1 S. 1:8), bad news (1 S. 25:37), the destruction of Jerusalem (Lam. 2:19; Neh. 2:2[1]), the vanity (*heḇel*) of everything (Eccl. 2:23), sickness (Ps. 38:9[8]), threats of the enemy (Ps. 13:3[2]), and sin (Sir. 14:1b). Outward signs of a grieving *lēḇ* include refusal to eat (1 S. 1:8), rigidity (1 S. 25:37), tears (Lam. 2:19), disquiet (Eccl. 2:23), and a sad countenance (Neh. 2:2). It weighs one down (Prov. 12:25) and finally leads to death (Sir. 38:18). It is important to strike the right note in social intercourse with those who grieve (Prov. 25:20), especially because people often conceal the inward mood of the *lēḇ* (Prov. 14:13). Late wisdom is agreed that sadness prevents one from giving full attention to true values (Eccl. 11:10; Sir. 38:20).[172]

---

166. Contra Stolz.

167. For a discussion of corporate personality, see H. W. Robinson, "The Hebrew Conception of Corporate Personality," *Werden und Wesen des ATs. BZAW,* 66 (1936), 49-62; J. R. Porter, "The Legal Aspects of the Concept of 'Corporate Personality' in the OT," *VT,* 15 (1965), 361-380.

168. Scharbert, 93-97.

169. P. 44.

170. H.-J. Kraus, *Psalms 1–59* (Eng. trans., Minneapolis, 1988), 322.

171. Lersch, 230.

172. → אבל *'āḇal* (*'ābhal*).

Joy and pleasure, rapture and delight likewise have their locus in the human *lēḇ*. Many reasons are named: expectation of a friend (Ex. 4:14; Prov. 27:9 [MT]), eating and drinking (Jgs. 19:6,9; Ruth 3:7; 1 S. 25:36; 1 K. 21:7), bread and wine (2 S. 13:28; Est. 1:10; Ps. 4:8[7]; 104:15; Eccl. 9:7; Sir. 31:28; 40:20; cf. Zec. 10:7), victory or the defeat of the enemy (Jgs. 16:25; Isa. 30:29; Prov. 24:17 [a warning against gloating]), the marriage and coronation of the king (Cant. 3:11), and an invitation (Est. 5:9). Wisdom Literature names wisdom (Sir. 51:15), the arts (Sir. 40:20), the wisdom of one's son (Prov. 27:11), wealth, toil, and the fulfillment of desires (Eccl. 2:10), the freshness of youth (Eccl. 11:9), shining eyes (Prov. 15:30), and the rare, shining splendor of snow (Sir. 43:18).

From early times, however, there were theological motivations for the *lēḇ* to rejoice: appointment as a priest (Jgs. 18:20), Yahweh's help (1 S. 2:1), his mighty acts (1 K. 8:66; 2 Ch. 7:10), his word (Jer. 15:16), his law (Ps. 19:9[8]; 119:111), and hope for his effectual presence (Ps. 16:9; 33:21). A central cause for rejoicing of the *lēḇ* is the return from exile (Zec. 10:7), eschatologically the dawn of the age of salvation (Zeph. 3:14), in which Yahweh's deliverance of Israel will be manifest (Isa. 60:5; 66:14). Contrariwise, the destruction of Jerusalem (Lam. 5:15) and the fall of the city (Isa. 24:7) make an abrupt end to the rejoicing of the heart. A joyous *lēḇ* is considered a cause of long life (Sir. 30:22f.); a cheerful *lēḇ* is thus the best medicine (Prov. 17:22) and the highest good (Sir. 30:16). Because it is God's gift (Ps. 4:8[7]; Eccl. 5:19[20]; Sir. 50:23), it provides security (Ps. 16:9) and strengthens trust in God (Ps. 33:21). The outward signs of a joyous *lēḇ* are shining eyes (Ps. 19:9[8]) and a glowing countenance (Ps. 104:15; Prov. 15:13; Isa. 60:5; Sir. 13:26; 26:4). A collective *lēḇ* as the subject of joy appears in 1 K. 8:66; 2 Ch. 7:10; Isa. 30:29; 60:5; 66:14; Zec. 10:7 (the people of Israel or the inhabitants of Jerusalem); Isa. 24:7 (inhabitants of the city); Jgs. 16:25 (the Philistines).

b. *Individual Emotions.* The emotions associated with individual life include fear, terror, and despair. They are especially destructive of the *lēḇ*. The *lēḇ* is most vulnerable to fear, as when one faces an enemy known to be superior (Nu. 32:7,9; Dt. 1:28; Josh. 7:5; 1 S. 17:32; 28:5; Isa. 7:2,4; Jer. 4:19; 49:22), when siege and battle threaten (Ps. 27:3; 112:8; Jer. 48:41), when the call to arms is heard (Dt. 20:3,8).[173] Fear is the normal reaction of the *lēḇ* in the face of rumored disaster (Jer. 51:46), a threat (1 S. 21:13[12]), hostility (Ps. 143:4), or a hostile environment (2 Ch. 13:7). But defamation (Ps. 55:5[4]), a putative crime (Gen. 42:28), or lengthy separation (Ps. 61:3[2]) can also fill the *lēḇ* with fear. Danger (Ps. 25:17), poverty (Ps. 109:16,22), insult (Ps. 69:21[20]), and discouragement (Isa. 65:14) cause the *lēḇ* to despair. Yahweh can also be a source of fear: God (Job 23:16), his threats (Dt. 28:65), his curse (Lev. 26:36; Dt. 28:67), and above all his power as manifested in history (Josh. 2:11; 5:1; Job 37:1; Isa. 19:1; Jer. 23:9) and his judgment (Isa. 13:7; 21:4; Jer. 4:9; Lam. 1:20; Ezk. 21:12,20[7,15]; Nah. 2:11[10]). When someone is afraid, his *lēḇ* trembles (Isa. 21:3f.; Jer. 48:41; 49:22; Sir. 48:19) like that of a woman in labor. It rages (2 K. 6:11), trembles

173. See also below.

(Job 37:1), faints (Ps. 61:3[2]), is wrung (Lam. 1:20), stiffens (Ps. 143:4; Jer. 4:9), breaks (Ps. 69:21[20]; Jer. 23:9), and finally fails (Ps. 40:13[12]). The outward signs are many: the person affected may tremble (1 S. 28:5; Job 37:1; Ps. 55:5[4]; Isa. 7:2,4; Jer. 23:9) or become agitated (1 S. 21:13[12]) and confused (Job 41:16[24]); he writhes because his loins are filled with anguish (Isa. 21:4) and tremble (Nah. 2:11[10]). His breast (Lam. 1:20) and face (Nah. 2:11[10]) are aglow, his eyes fail (Dt. 28:65), his knees grow weak (Ezk. 21:12[7]; Nah. 2:11[10]), his hands grow feeble (Isa. 13:7; Ezk. 21:12[7]), he sighs (Ezk. 21:12[7]), his days drag on (Dt. 28:67). Finally he forgets to breathe (Josh. 2:11; 5:1) and collapses into a coma (1 S. 25:37; Ps. 55:5[4]). The *nep̱eš* is also affected: it rages (Jer. 4:19) and languishes (Dt. 28:65).

In the face of enemy superiority, the *lēḇ* of the people can melt like water (Josh. 7:5; 14:8) or shake like a tree (Isa. 7:2); Yahweh's mighty acts cause the *lēḇ* of the Egyptians to melt (Isa. 19:1) and trouble the *lēḇ* of many peoples (Ezk. 32:9).

The frailty of the *lēḇ* documents the creatural vulnerability of mortals and the omnipotence of God. The psalmist, therefore, associates the motif of faintness of heart with God's intervention (Ps. 61:3[2]; cf. 25:17; 55:5[4]). Lamentation begins with the heart: it cries out (Isa. 15:5), it laments (Jer. 48:36), it cries to Yahweh (Lam. 2:18). The growing understanding of God's righteousness gave rise to the theologoumenon that the righteous and those who are faithful to Yahweh have nothing to fear, that their *lēḇ* can be full of courage in the face of all assaults (Ps. 27:3; 112:8). This knowledge finds linguistic expression in the formula *'al-yēraḵ lēḇāḇ,* "Let not the heart faint," as a parallel to the *'al-tîrā'* formula;[174] it appears in the context of the holy war (Dt. 20:3; Isa. 7:4; Jer. 51:46; cf. 1 S. 17:32). Exilic texts, especially passages echoing Isaiah, emphasize reassurance of those whose hearts are fearful (*nimhᵃrê-lēḇ*: Isa. 35:4; cf. 1QH 2:9; *'ᵃḇîrê lēḇ*: Isa. 46:12 [reading *'ōḇᵉḏê lēḇ* with *BHS*]) and broken (*nišbᵉrê-lēḇ* [Isa. 61:1]). These passages mark the transition from the emotional to the ethico-theological understanding of *lēḇ* (cf. Isa. 57:15).

c. *Wrath.* Semitic thought associates anger and wrath primarily with the nose[175] and the liver (Akk. *kabattu*);[176] some passages, however, involve the *lēḇ*. The *lēḇ* of the avenger of blood is "hot" (*ḥmm*: Dt. 19:6; in Ps. 39:4[3], however, *ḥam-libbî* has nothing to do with anger, as suggested by A. R. Johnson,[177] representing instead the urgent power of the psalmist's inmost impulses); the *lēḇ* of the king of Syria "rages" (*sʿr*: 2 K. 6:11) because his plans have been betrayed. Anger can also be directed against God: the man whose own folly brings him to ruin blames Yahweh rather than himself and his *lēḇ* rages against Yahweh (Prov. 19:3).[178] Similarly, Eliphaz indirectly accuses Job of folly because he lets his *lēḇ* carry him away and turn him against God (Job 15:12f.).

d. *Love, Hate, Gratitude.* In the OT, the extensive realm of "transitive emotions"

---

174. → ירא *yārē'* V.
175. → אנף *'ānap* (*'ānaph*).
176. Labat, *RLA,* IV, 367; → כבד *kāḇēḏ.*
177. P. 76.
178. → זעף *zāʿap.*

involving others is dominated by sympathy and love, antipathy and hate. These, too, are seated in the *lēḇ*. Sympathy and love[179] are often understood as activities of the *lēḇ,* without any sexual connotations.[180] They represent affection and trust (Jgs. 16:15,17,18; Prov. 31:11; Cant. 5:2; but cf. Sir. 9:9), for instance between father and son (2 S. 14:1; Sir. 48:10). Willingness to follow a commander can be based on affection (*lēḇ lᵉ*), as illustrated first by the Song of Deborah (Jgs. 5:9). Absalom gained such affection through fraud (*gānaḇ*: 2 S. 15:6). The same expression can describe the relationship between commander and soldiers (1 Ch. 12:18,39[17,38]), teacher and disciples (Prov. 23:26; Sir. 37:12), people and king (or claimant) (Jgs. 9:3; 2 S. 15:13; 19:15[14]; 1 K. 12:27; 1 Ch. 12:39[38]). This affection of the *lēḇ* is the basis of the later acclamation of the people at the enthronement of a king.

Deuteronomistic parenesis also uses *lēḇ* terminology, in conjunction with *'āhaḇ,* to express the love of the people for Yahweh — albeit now in an ethico-theological sense.[181]

A common idiom for wooing affection is *dibber 'al-lēḇ,* "speak to someone's heart." According to Gen. 34:3 (J), the *nep̱eš* of Shechem "is drawn to" (*dbq*) Dinah; he loves (*'āhaḇ*) her and therefore speaks to her.[182] Cf. also the descriptions of how the Levite goes after his concubine (Jgs. 19:3) and Boaz woos Ruth (Ruth 2:13). Joseph also "speaks to the heart" of his brothers to comfort them (Gen. 50:21, par. *niḥam*). There is no consensus as to the source stratum of this verse.[183] According to Lothar Ruppert,[184] Gen. 50:21 concludes the Joseph narrative of J; Joseph's friendly words to his apprehensive brothers demonstrate the family focus of the whole story, in which the motif of care and support takes precedence over that of deliverance, despite the latter's historical and theological significance. According to Horst Seebass,[185] however, the passage belongs to E; its purpose is to emphasize the centrality of Joseph after the death of his father and the solidarity of all the brothers as the ancestors of the future Israel.[186]

"Speaking to the heart" to comfort and cheer is by no means restricted to the circle of the family. In this same seductive way, David speaks to his troops (2 S. 19:8[7]) and Hezekiah addresses the Levites (2 Ch. 30:22) and the commanders of Jerusalem (2 Ch. 32:6).

---

179. → אהב *'āhaḇ* (*'āhabh*).

180. → אהב *'āhaḇ* (*'āhabh*), III.1; → ידע *yāḏa'*, III.1.f.

181. See V.6.d below.

182. Cf. A. Neher, "Le symbolisme conjugal," *RHPR*, 34 (1954), 30-49, esp. 32.

183. Cf. D. B. Redford, *A Study of the Biblical Story of Joseph (Genesis 37–50). SVT,* 20 (1970); A. Meinhold, "Die Gattung der Josephsgeschichte und des Estherbuches: Diasporanovelle I," *ZAW,* 87 (1975), 306-324; contra H. Donner, *Die literarische Gestalt der alttestamentlichen Josephsgeschichte. SHAW,* 1976/2. See now H.-C. Schmitt, *Die nichpriesterliche Josephgeschichte. BZAW,* 154 (1980), 191; L. Ruppert, *Die Josepherzählung der Genesis. StANT,* 11 (1965); H. Seebass, *Geschichtliche Zeit und theonome Tradition in der Joseph-Erzählung* (Gütersloh, 1978).

184. Pp. 191f.

185. Pp. 94f.

186. Cf. Schmitt, 78, 81.

The locus classicus, however, is Hos. 2:16(14): Yahweh will entice Israel, bring her back to the wilderness, and there "speak to her heart." Within the kerygmatic unit Hos. 2:4-17(2-15) (a "lawsuit charging infidelity"[187] or a "pedagogical tribunal"[188]), this verse describes return to the wilderness as Yahweh's final effort, which Israel refuses to enter into freely. Yahweh will therefore employ enticement (*pāṯâ* implies the possibility of cunning and deception; cf. Ex. 22:15[16]; 2 S. 3:25; also Jer. 20:7,10[189]) and seductive persuasion (*dibber ʿal-lēḇ* as the mode of speech used by lovers). But this approach, aiming to restore the unbroken bond between Israel and Yahweh, demonstrates that Yahweh's unconditional love is the only requirement for the healing of faithlessness and shows his punishment to be an act of love.

The function of *dibber ʿal-lēḇ* in providing comfort appears in Deutero-Isaiah's formulation of his prophetic commission; he introduces his message of deliverance from exile with the cry: "Comfort, comfort my people, speak to the heart of Jerusalem" (Isa. 40:1f.). He underlines the importance of his message of comfort, using the most effective means of proclaiming it.

Only rarely are contempt (→ בזה *bāzâ* [*bāzāh*]) and hatred (→ שׂנא *śānēʾ*) seated in the heart. In 2 S. 6:16 (Deuteronomistic) and its parallel 1 Ch. 15:29, Michal contemns David as he dances before the ark *beliббāh*. In the Holiness Code, Lev. 19:17 reads: "You shall not hate your brother in your heart, but you shall reason with your neighbor, lest you bear sin because of him." This may be an expanded[190] negative form of the commandment to love one's neighbor (v. 18b),[191] paralleling the prohibition of vengeance in v. 18a. Here *lēḇ* as the locus of hatred might be an echo of pre-juridical emotionalism. The prohibition of hatred *belēḇ* might also be a deliberate contrast to judicial settlement of disputes in the public forum of the *qāhāl*. Henning Graf Reventlow,[192] finally, sees hatred *belēḇ* as endangering just administration of the law.

The OT does not speak of the *lēḇ* as the seat of human gratitude (→ ידה *ydh*) toward others. Postexilic individual hymns of thanksgiving speak of thanking Yahweh *beḵol-lēḇ*. The "todah formula"[193] appears 5 times with the addition *beḵol-lēḇ* (Ps. 9:2[1]; 86:12; 111:1; 138:1) or *beyōšer lēḇāḇ* (Ps. 119:7). The psalmist thanks Yahweh for his help (Pss. 9, 86), his mighty acts (covenant, faithfulness) in history (Ps. 111), his Torah

187. Wolff.

188. D. Kinet, *Ba'al und Jahwe: Ein Beitrag zur Theologie des Hoseabuches. EH,* 23/87 (1977), 178-190.

189. M. Saebø, "פתה *pth* verleitbar sein," *THAT,* II, 495-98.

190. Cf. A. Chowlewinski, *Heiligkeitsgesetz und Deuteronomium. AnBibl,* 66 (1976), 44ff., 131ff.

191. → אהב *'āhaḇ* (*'āhabh*), I, 111; also J. Fichtner, *Gottes Weisheit. Gesammelte Studien zum AT. ArbT,* 2/3 (1965), 88-114, esp. 102f.

192. *Das Heiligkeitsgesetz formgeschichtlich untersucht. WMANT,* 6 (1961), 72.

193. F. Crüsemann, *Studien zur Formgeschichte von Hymnus und Danklied in Israel. WMANT,* 32 (1969), 267-278. Because it appears frequently in 1QH — with *beḵol-lēḇ* and always (except in 1QH 14:26) in exactly the same form — J. M. Robinson calls it the "hodayot formula" ("Die Hodajot-Formel in Gebet und Hymnus des Frühchristentums," *Apophoreta. Festschrift E. Haenchen. BZNW,* 30 [1964], 194, 198).

(Ps. 119), and recovery from severe illness (? Ps. 138), as well as for the gift of knowledge (1QH 14:26). Claus Westermann has pointed out the confessional witness of the voluntative introduction "I will give thanks to Thee,"[194] to which the phrase *bᵉkol-lēḇ,* reflecting Deuteronomistic parenesis (cf. Dt. 6:5),[195] lends special warmth and intensity.

Independently of this formulaic language, the *lēḇ* also sings praises (*rnn*) to the living God (Ps. 84:3[2]; Sir. 39:35). The heart rejoices (*gîl*) in God's salvation (Ps. 13:6[5]), overflows (*rāḥaš*) with gracious words (Ps. 45:2[1]), sings (*šîr*) and makes music (*zāmar*) to the Lord (Ps. 57:8[7]; 108:2[1]); Sir. 47:8). All these terms belong to the standard vocabulary of the individual hymn of thanksgiving. In combination with *lēḇ,* they express the joy of the devout over the existential experience of salvation (cf. Ps. 105:3 par. 1 Ch. 16:10; 1 S. 2:1; Zeph. 3:14).

4. *Noetic Center.* The documents of the OT look on the human *lēḇ* as the noetic seat of a wide range of activities. While the senses engage in "sense perception" (the expression "the generous heart savors" [Sir. 31:13] is unique), within the *lēḇ* take place intellectual visualization (cognition and memory), thought, understanding, and attention. Finally, wisdom is pictured as residing in the heart.

a. *Cognition.* Initially, cognition[196] in the *lēḇ* is related to sense perception: it is prior to seeing with the eyes and hearing with the ears, because it initiates the operation of the senses (Dt. 29:3[4]; Eccl. 7:21; Ezk. 3:10; frequently with ethically negative meaning in "hardness of heart," as in Ex. 7:22; Jer. 5:21[197]). Then it comes to mean the preservation and internalization of what the senses perceive (Prov. 22:17; Eccl. 7:2; Isa. 32:4; Ezk. 40:4; 44:5; Mal. 2:2; Sir. 16:24) for the purpose of making judgments and decisions. Thus cognition in the *lēḇ* is always understood as a compact whole, in that it denotes the total noetic ability of an individual (cf. Dt. 8:5). Its opposite, therefore, is not a failure of sensory perception, but inattention, heedlessness, and confusion to the point of ethically negative duplicity. Perception and cognition in the *lēḇ* are directed accordingly: initially toward concrete objects like the land of Canaan (Josh. 14:7), parental instruction (Prov. 6:21), the words of the wise (Prov. 4:21; 7:3; 22:17; cf. also Job 22:22; Sir. 16:24); then increasingly (esp. in the context of Deuteronomy) toward theological objects like Torah (Dt. 6:6),[198] God's promise (Josh. 23:14), or signs and wonders (Dt. 29:3[4]; Isa. 42:25; cf. Ps. 48:14[13]; Sir. 16:20). In prophetic contexts, the object may be a vision (Ezk. 40:4; 44:5), the word of God (Isa. 9:8[9]; Ezk. 3:10; Mal. 2:2), or his grace and mercy (Lam. 3:21). In Wisdom Literature, objects include wisdom (Prov. 15:14; Eccl. 7:25; 8:16; Sir. 6:32; 14:21; 50:28), love and faithfulness (Prov. 3:3), the fate that may be discerned in human life (Eccl. 7:2; 9:1), and the

194. C. Westermann, *Praise and Lament in the Psalms* (Eng. trans., Atlanta, 1981), 102.
195. See V.6.d below.
196. → ידע *yāḏaʿ* III.1.c.
197. See V.6.c below.
198. See V.6.d below.

movement transcending history that may be deduced from the historical conduct of the human race (Eccl. 8:9; cf. Isa. 46:8).

Only rarely does this attention of the *lēḇ* have the nature of worry about something: sheep (Prov. 27:23), asses (1 S. 9:20), rape (2 S. 13:20), soldiers (2 S. 18:3), ploughing (Sir. 38:26). In some cases, the word signals a special intensity: writing or binding something upon one's heart (Dt. 6:6; Prov. 3:3; 6:21; 7:3), keeping something in one's heart (Josh. 14:7; Jer. 51:50).

Eccl. 3:11b is very difficult: *gam 'eṯ-hā'ōlām nāṯan b^e^libbām.* God has made everything beautiful in its time; "eternity, too, he has put into their [= men and women's] hearts."[199] This statement is easily misunderstood as suggesting that humanity is made in God's image.[200] There is no reason to emend or repoint the MT; the proposals assume too narrow a meaning for both *lēḇ* and → עולם *'ôlām.* The many suggested interpretations fall into a few major classes: (1) *lēḇ* is interpreted indefinitely as "midst" and associated with *hakkōl,* despite the disagreement of number of the suffix: "he has put eternity into everything."[201] Against this interpretation are the suffix and the fact that *b^e^lēḇ* is locative: "in the midst of," not "into the midst of." (2) *lēḇ* is interpreted as the human heart, but a different meaning is suggested for *'ôlām*: "love of the world,"[202] "enigma,"[203] "endurance,"[204] striving "for enduring reputation and fame,"[205] "endless continuance and subjection to the passage of time,"[206] "distant future."[207] James Barr[208] interprets the phrase as referring to the past: "the consciousness of memory, the awareness of past events." Rainer Braun[209] suggests "lifetime, life-span," which limits the extent of human knowledge. (3) *lēḇ* is understood as the noetic and voluntative[210] center of the individual and *'ôlām* (vv. 11b, 14) in the literal sense of "eternity." Franz Delitzsch[211] already sees Eccl. 3:11 as expressing the human yearning for eternity. A "sense of eternity"[212] is inherent in human nature; people have the gift and need

---

199. F. Nötscher, *Kohelet, Ekklesiastes, oder Prediger. EB* (1948); W. Zimmerli, *Das Buch des Predigers Salomo. ATD,* XVI/1 (^{3}1980), 80.

200. H. W. Hertzberg, G. Wildeboer, W. Eichrodt.

201. N. Lohfink, *Kohelet. NEB* (1980), 32f.: eternity "in the sense of perpetual recurrence"; similarly Lauha, *Kohelet. BK,* XIX (1978), 61, 68f.; F. Ellermeier, *Untersuchungen zur Buche Qohelet,* I (Herzberg am Harz, 1967), 321: "endlessness"; cf. G. Gerleman, "Die sperrende Grenze: Die Wurzel 'lm im Hebräischen," *ZAW,* 91 (1979), 341f.: in the midst of the world there is a boundary (*'ōlām*) to human knowledge.

202. R. Gordis, *Koheleth — The Man and His World* (New York, ^{2}1968), 232.

203. R. B. Y. Scott, *Proverbs–Ecclesiastes. AB,* XVIII (1965), 220.

204. E. Jenni, "Das Wort *'ôlām* im AT, III," *ZAW,* 65 (1953), 26.

205. O. Loretz, *Qohelet und der alte Orient* (Freiburg, 1964), 281-84.

206. Lauha, 69.

207. G. von Rad, *Wisdom in Israel* (Eng. trans., Nashville, 1972), 230, n. 55.

208. J. Barr, *Biblical Words for Time. SBT,* 33 (^{2}1969), 118, n. 4.

209. R. Braun, *Kohelet und die frühhellenistische Popularphilosophie. BZAW,* 130 (1973), 114.

210. See V.5 below.

211. F. Delitzsch, *KD,* VI, 261.

212. A. Strobel, *Das Buch Prediger (Kohelet). KHS,* 9 (1967), 55f.; similarly C. W. Reines, "Kohelet on Wisdom and Wealth," *JJS,* 5 (1954), 80.

"to look beyond the present hour and ask about the past and future."[213] The verse does not suggest a human striving to be like God but rather a striving of individuals to transcend themselves in the face of their real limitations (cf. esp. the contrast in Ps. 90:12). Thus *lēḇ* here denotes in a unique way the existential nature of humanity. Svend Holm-Nielsen[214] renders the sense roughly as: "He has made human beings cognizant of their existence (life-span)."

b. *Memory.* "As the seat of memory, the heart makes it possible to incorporate particular apperceptions into a larger realm of experience."[215] Phrases like *śîm 'al-lēḇ* are used in the same semantic constructs as → זכר *zāḵar.*[216] The similarity is seen first in synthetic and synonymous parallelisms with *zāḵar* in Isa. 46:8; 47:7; 57:11; 65:17; Jer. 3:16; 17:1f.; 44:21; 51:50); these passages suggest an alert and fervent act of recollection. The wider semantic range of *lēḇ,* however, forbids reducing this observation to a simple formula.[217] The motif of "recalling a situation in order to find a motive for a certain action"[218] is common in Wisdom Literature as a "piece of advice"[219] or an "empirical rule."[220] It appears in many forms: failure to consider the consequences of a misdeed (Isa. 47:7), constant remembrance of death (Eccl. 7:2; purpose: a new attitude toward life) or of the futility of idols (Isa. 46:8; purpose: a new understanding of God). In Hag. 1:5,7; 2:15,18, recollection of how the people have fared is to spur them on to rebuild the temple. Just as *zāḵar* can express involved participation (Jer. 17:1f.),[221] failure to remember can express the opposite: when the ark does not come to mind (*lō' 'ālâ 'al-lēḇ*), the people are indifferent to this ancient religious institution (Jer. 3:16).[222] In interpersonal relationships, similarly, to let someone slip out of mind (Ps. 31:13[12];[223] cf. 88:6[5]) terminates not just a mental relationship but a personal bond. To be casually forgotten is tantamount to death. The exiles are to hold Jerusalem *'al-lēḇ* (Jer. 51:50, par. *zāḵar 'eṯ-YHWH*), a demand that keeps the melancholy situation of the occupied city before their eyes (cf. Ps. 137:1f.,5f.). Not to take guilt to heart (2 S. 19:20[19]) means to rehabilitate the offender (even apart from a forensic context[224]). Recollection of God's mighty acts and his Torah provides a motive for obedience to the Torah (Dt. 4:9); remembrance of sacred history serves as a signal to set forth from exile (Jer. 31:21). When the age of salvation dawns, people will no longer

213. Zimmerli, *ATD,* XVI/1 (^{3}1980), 172.

214. S. Holm-Nielsen, ". . . Han har och lagt evigheten i människornas hjärten . . .," *SEÅ,* 41f. (1976-77), 107-119.

215. G. J. Botterweck, "ידע *yāḏa',*" *TDOT,* V, 462.

216. II.1,2.

217. W. Schottroff, *"Gedenken" im alten Orient und im AT. WMANT,* 15 (^{2}1967), 116.

218. *Ibid.,* 136f.

219. *Ibid.,* 139.

220. G. von Rad, *OT Theology,* I (Eng. trans., New York, 1962), 430ff.

221. Schottroff, 144ff.

222. → ארון *'ᵃrôn,* I, 371.

223. Cf. J. J. M. Roberts, "NIŠKAḤTÎ . . . MILLĒB, Ps. xxxi 13," *VT,* 25 (1975), 797-800.

224. Cf. Schottroff, 115ff.; contra H. J. Boecker, *Redeformen des Rechtslebens im AT. WMANT,* 14 (^{2}1970), 108-115.

remember the terrors of the past (Isa. 33:18 [a late, post-Isaianic protoapocalypse[225]]; cf. 65:17).

c. *Wisdom.* Like wisdom itself,[226] the *lēḇ* as the seat of wisdom has a wide range of meanings. With few exceptions, the relevant passages are concentrated in Wisdom Literature. Wisdom — bestowed by Yahweh (Prov. 2:6; 1 K. 10:24; 2 Ch. 9:23; Sir. 45:26) — enters into the human *lēḇ* (Prov. 2:10), giving it an ethical aspect: *daʿaṯ* is the joy of those who possess it (Prov. 2:10; Sir. 51:20), their attention is focused on the Torah (Prov. 2:2; 10:8), their ears are open to knowledge (Prov. 18:15; Sir. 3:29), and their words are well chosen (Prov. 15:28; 16:21,23; Job 33:3; Isa. 32:4).[227] Such a *lēḇ* should be the goal of all (Prov. 19:8; cf. Dnl. 10:12), especially kings (*lēḇ šōmēaʿ/ḥāḵām*: 1 K. 3:9,12; 5:9[4:29]; 10:24; 2 Ch. 1:11; 9:23).

Siegfried Herrmann[228] saw the prayer for a "listening heart" as issuing from the very core of the Israelite spirit. Hellmut Brunner,[229] however, has cited the Egyptian Instruction of Ptahhotep, which deems the human heart to be the organ that heeds the will of God;[230] he concludes that the notion of the "listening heart" is probably Egyptian in origin.[231] The "hearing heart" comprehends the "fullness of all world phenomena,"[232] thus becoming a "spacious heart" (*rōḥaḇ lēḇ*): 1 K. 5:9-14[4:29-34]), i.e., "wide intelligence,"[233] "a feeling for the truth which emanates from the world and addresses man,"[234] "a dimension of experience informed by the utmost degree of subtlety."[235]

For Ecclesiastes, this endeavor is ultimately a striving after wind (*raʿyôn rûaḥ*, → הבל *heḇel*; Eccl. 1:17), although he, too, concedes certain advantages to a wise heart (8:5; 10:2). Wisdom in the *lēḇ* makes the sage superior to the fool (Prov. 11:29; cf. 14:33; Eccl. 10:3; Job 9:4). In the book of Job, *lēḇ/lēḇāḇ* appears in various contexts in the sense of "wisdom." Job states sardonically that wisdom will perish with his friends (Job 12:2); he wishes that his understanding (*lēḇāḇ*) were the equal of theirs (v. 3). For Elihu, the wise man (*ʾîš lēḇāḇ*) is the one who acknowledges God's righteousness and divinity (Job 34:10,34; 37:24). The extravagant claims to wisdom put forward by the book of Sirach are signalized by its colophon: "Jesus, son of Sirach, son of Eleazar, of Jerusalem, from whose *lēḇ* wisdom poured forth like rain" (Sir. 50:27). P sees in *ḥᵃḵam-lēḇ* the sacral expertise of those charged with fashioning the

225. H. Wildberger, *Jesaja 28–39. BK,* X/3 (1982), *in loc.*

226. → חכם *ḥāḵām.*

227. Cf. von Rad, *Wisdom in Israel,* 117.

228. S. Herrmann, "Die Königsnovelle in Ägypten und in Israel," *Festschrift A. Alt. WZ* Leipzig, 3 (1953/54), 51-62.

229. Brunner, *ThLZ,* 79 (1954), 697-700.

230. *ANET*³, 414.

231. Cf. C. Kayatz, *Studien zu Proverbien 1–9.* WMANT, 22 (1966), 46f.

232. Wolff, 47.

233. E. Power, "A Study of the Hebrew Expression 'Wide of Heart,' " *Bibl,* 1 (1920), 59-75.

234. Von Rad, *Wisdom in Israel,* 296f.

235. H. Timm, " 'Das Weite Herz': Religiöses Philosophieren in Israel," *ZThK,* 74 (1977), 224-237, esp. 228.

priestly vestments (Ex. 28:3) and constructing the tabernacle (31:6; 35:25,35; 36:1,2,8). Ex. 35:34 uses the same terminology for those divinely inspired to teach.[236]

d. *Confusion and Folly.* If the *lēḇ* lacks wisdom, it is in the grip of "folly." Folly shows itself as heedlessness (Ex. 9:21; Hos. 7:2), willfulness (Ex. 7:23), and failure to see the larger picture (Jer. 12:11; Isa. 44:19; Sir. 16:23). For the redactor of Ecclesiastes,[237] wickedness and folly are so fundamental to the *lēḇ* ("human nature") that they are the cause of human mortality (Eccl. 9:3; cf. Prov. 10:21). Folly as the absence of *lēḇ* (*'ên lēḇ*) leads to disorientation (*pāṯâ*: Hos. 7:11) and senselessness (Prov. 10:13; 17:16,18; 24:30), adultery (Prov. 6:32), and contempt for one's neighbor (Prov. 11:12); in a youth, "lack of heart" (*ḥ^a^sar lēḇ*) manifests itself in stupidity (Prov. 7:7; cf. 22:15), pleasure in worthless pursuits (12:11), and delight in foolishness (15:21). The *lēḇ* of the fool (*k^e^sîl*) loses control over the tongue (Prov. 10:20; 12:23; 15:7; cf. 23:33) and even goes so far as to deny God (Ps. 14:1; 53:2[1]). Sir. 36:5a[238] likens the fool to a blockhead.

The *lēḇ* is deluded by wine (Hos. 4:11;[239] Prov. 23:29ff.), women (Job 31:9 [cf. 11QtgJob 18:2]; Prov. 6:25; 7:10; 9:4,16; Sir. 19:2), worldly goods (Ps. 62:11[10]), gain (Jer. 22:17; Ezk. 33:31), temptations (Job 31:7), idolatry (Job 31:27 [cf. 11QtgJob 19:1]), wicked words (Ps. 141:4), and corruption (Eccl. 7:7). But it can also deceive itself (Isa. 44:20); Nu. 15:39 commands the Israelites to let the tassels on their garments constantly remind them of the danger of being misled by the *lēḇ*. A particularly extreme and dangerous form of deception by the *lēḇ* is the phenomenon of false prophets, who prophesy out of their own *lēḇ* and not as commanded by Yahweh (Ezk. 13:2f.); they follow their own *rûaḥ* (v. 3), prophesy lies (Jer. 14:14; 23:26[240]) and the visions of their own *lēḇ* (23:16), thus leading the people astray. When Moses (Nu. 16:28) and Balaam (24:13) insist that they are not speaking *millibbî,* "from my own heart," we see that this idiom is ideally suited to express the authentic sending of a prophet by God.[241] Confusion of *lēḇ,* like hardness of *lēḇ,* is often ascribed to Yahweh (Dt. 28:28; Job 12:24; 17:4).

5. *Voluntative Center.* The line between the rational function of the *lēḇ* and the activity of the will is blurred, because it is impossible pragmatically to distinguish between theory and praxis.[242] The *lēḇ* functions as the driving force behind the voluntative endeavors of the individual; it engages in performative conceiving and planning; it is the seat of courage and enterprise.

---

236. → חכם *ḥāḵām,* IV, 378f.

237. Lauha, 167.

238. Barthélemy.

239. Cf. F. Stolz, "Rausch, Religion und Realität in Israel und seiner Umwelt," *VT,* 26 (1976), 170-186.

240. On the textual problems, see I. Meyer, *Jeremia und die falschen Propheten. OBO,* 13 (1977), 134f.

241. W. Gross, *Bileam. StANT,* 38 (1974), 316.

242. Wolff, 51.

a. *Driving Force.* Jeremiah feels within himself the driving force of his *lēḇ,* which burns like fire when he tries to refrain from proclaiming the troubling word of Yahweh (Jer. 20:9; cf. 23:29). The suffering psalmist, too, is incited to pray by the burning of his heart (Ps. 39:4[3]). Balaam must subordinate himself (*lēḇ*) totally to the will of Yahweh (Nu. 24:13).[243] Almost all the other passages date from the later period of the OT: the use of *lēḇ* with *ndb,* "be willing," serves to describe the human heart as initiating voluntary contributions or offerings (Ex. 25:2; 35:5,21,22,29 [P]; 1 Ch. 29:9; cf. 2 K. 12:5[4] [*ʿālâ ʿal lēḇ*]) and sacrifices (2 Ch. 29:31; cf. 2 Ch. 11:16 [*nāṯan ʾeṯ-lēḇ*]). The phrase *nāśāʾ lēḇ* (Ex. 35:26; 36:2), describing eager participation in constructing the tabernacle, has a similar function (cf. Neh. 3:38[4:6]).

b. *Conceiving and Planning.* The voluntative activity of the *lēḇ* includes the realm of conceiving and planning up to the point of action, but not the act itself. We may note a gradual differentiation of particular aspects.

In Ps. 19:15(14), the postexilic[244] psalmist dedicates to Yahweh the words of his mouth (*ʾimrê-pî*) and the meditations of his heart (*hegyôn lēḇ*), a comprehensive expression for all his intentions and plans, which he devoutly subjects to Yahweh's will expressed in the Torah. For Ecclesiastes, contrariwise, "all the toil and striving of his heart" (*kol-ʿamālô ûḇraʿyôn libbô*) is pointless and brings no gain (Eccl. 2:22). These contrasting passages illustrate the wide range of this notion.

The first stage of the voluntative process is "thinking to oneself" (expressed in a nominal clause). A particular idea becomes cystallized as an intention *beléḇ* (1 S. 14:7; 2 S. 7:3; 1 Ch. 17:2; always deliberately left vague) or *ʿim-lēḇāḇ* (2 Ch. 29:10: to make a *berîṯ*). The plan to build the temple took concrete form in the *lēḇ* (verbal clause) (*hāyâ ʿim-lēḇāḇ*: 1 K. 8:17,18; 1 Ch. 22:7; 28:2 [text?; cf. LXX]; 2 Ch. 6:7,8; 24:4; cf. 7:11 [with *bôʾ*]). The queen of Sheba, too, had in her *lēḇ* a list of questions to ask Solomon (1 K. 10:2; 2 Ch. 9:1).

Other verbal formulations in the voluntative realm are found only sporadically: *bāḏāʾ millēḇ* (1 K. 12:33: Jeroboam plans his own feast at Bethel; cf. Neh. 6:8); *tûr belēḇ* (Eccl. 2:3: Ecclesiastes plans a rational, hedonistic way of life); *śîm ʿal-lēḇ* (Dnl. 1:8: Daniel's tactics against Nebuchadnezzar); and the hapax legomenon *mālaḵ* (cf. Akk. *malāku*[245]) *lēḇ ʿal* (Neh. 5:7: a political plan to attack poverty). The phrase *ḥiqrê-lēḇ* in Jgs. 5:16 (conj. v. 15) probably also denotes political plans.

An intention becomes a desire when one cannot accomplish it by oneself (cf. Job 17:11; Ps. 20:5[4]; 21:3[2]). The psalmist praises Yahweh, who fulfills these desires of the heart (Ps. 37:4). A plan already has clear contours when the text uses the phrase "speak in the heart" (*ʾāmar belēḇ,* less often *dibber belēḇ*). But the semantic range of this expression is also very broad, from moving the lips during prayer (1 S. 1:13) through rational calculation (Gen. 17:17; 24:45; Eccl. 1:16; 2:15; 3:17,18) and analytic questioning (Dt. 18:21; Jer. 13:22; Est. 6:6 [political]) to planning (Gen. 27:41 [murder];

243. See above.
244. Kraus, *Psalms 1–59,* 269.
245. *AHw,* I, 593f.; → יעץ *yāʿaṣ,* III, 791.

1 S. 27:1 [flight]; 1 K. 12:26 [succession to the throne]; Eccl. 2:1 [a hedonistic way of life]) and strong desire (Zec. 12:5). This voluntative function of the *lēḇ* aims at a variety of goals: battle and destruction (Ps. 55:22[21]; 74:8; 140:3[2]), wickedness and evil (Gen. 6:5; 8:21; Ps. 58:3[2]; Prov. 24:2; Eccl. 8:11), political intrigue (Ezk. 38:10; Dnl. 8:25; 11:27), machinations (Prov. 6:18; 12:20), conspiracy (Hos. 7:6; Ps. 83:6[5]), treachery (Prov. 6:14), antisocial behavior (Zec. 7:10; 8:17), and godlessness (2 Ch. 12:14). Particularly despised is a difference between *lēḇ* and tongue (Sir. 12:16; 37:17); people are therefore cautioned against enemies who hide their true plans (Isa. 10:7; 2 Ch. 32:31; Ps. 55:22[21]). For the psalmist, this discrepancy between a malicious heart and a hypocritical tongue is practically the definition of the *reša'* (Ps. 28:3; 41:7[6]). Deuteronomy places great value on keeping an upright *lēḇāḇ* in dealing with one's brother (Dt. 15:9) and acting accordingly.

c. *Courage.* Like *rûaḥ, lēḇ* can also denote the human "courage" that makes possible acts of military valor (1 S. 10:26; 2 S. 17:10; 1 Ch. 12:34[33]; Dnl. 11:25), resistance to the king (Est. 7:5), and religious reform (2 Ch. 17:6). This courage vanishes, however, in the face of Yahweh's mighty acts (Ezk. 22:14; Am. 2:16; Ps. 76:6[5]).

6. *Religious and Ethical Realm.* Texts referring to the religious and ethical realm of the relationship between human beings and God make frequent use of *lēḇ*.

a. *The Locus of God's Influence.* Here the primary axiom is: "He who fashioned the heart of them all knows all their deeds" (Ps. 33:15). The creator of the *lēḇ* is also the universal lord and judge. Whatever plans mortals may conceive, in the view of early proverbial wisdom it is ultimately Yahweh who governs the heart (cf. Prov. 16:1,9; 19:21; 20:5; 21:1). Yahweh knows the *lēḇ* of all (*yāḏa'*: 1 K. 8:39 [twice] par. 2 Ch. 6:30 [twice]; Ps. 44:22[21]; 139:23); therefore he is expected to take just vengeance (Jer. 20:12; Prov. 24:12). He sees through outward appearances (1 S. 16:7), for the *lēḇ* lies open to him (Prov. 15:11). Already in Ps. 7:10(9) (a very early text), we find as an epithet of Yahweh the "hymnic"[246] formula *bōḥēn libbôṯ ûḵᵉlāyôṯ,* "who triest the heart and the reins," which uniquely expresses God's knowledge of mortals (cf. Ps. 17:3; 26:2; Jer. 11:20; 12:3; 17:10; cf. also Prov. 17:3; 21:2; 1 Ch. 29:17; Sir. 42:18). Yahweh can bow the heart (*kāna'*: Ps. 107:12; cf. Sir. 10:13) or strengthen it (*kûn* hiphil, expressing a sense of existential exaltation: Ps. 10:17). Yahweh can change the heart in a negative direction (Ps. 105:25: toward hostility) or a positive direction (Jer. 32:39: toward fear of God). He takes away a heart of stone (*lēḇ 'eḇen*: according to 1 S. 25:37, a dead *lēḇ*) and gives a "new heart,"[247] a new and authentic life in relationship to Yahweh (Ezk. 11:19; the MT reads *lēḇ 'eḥāḏ* [cf. Jer. 32:39], but the LXX presupposes *lēḇ 'aḥēr*; possibly the text should be emended to read *lēḇ ḥāḏāš* as in Ezk. 18:31; 36:26; cf. 1 S. 10:9). This new creation revives those who have been turned to stone, fills them with a new *rûaḥ,* and reestablishes

---

246. Kraus.

247. On the opposite process in the funeral liturgy of the Egyptian pharaoh, see Hermann, 105.

the lost reality of the covenant,[248] as the beneficiaries cast aside their sins (Ezk. 18:31) and obey God's will (36:26).

Late texts use the phrase *nāṯan bᵉlēḇ,* "put something into someone's heart," to describe Yahweh's influence on the human heart: the restoration of the temple (Ezr. 7:27), Nehemiah's inspection of the city walls (Neh. 2:12), his census (7:5), and Yahweh's gift of *ʿôlām* (Eccl. 3:11).[249] As the vital core of each individual, the heart is thus the point where Yahweh impinges on human existence.

b. *Conscience.* The OT does not have a special word meaning "conscience."[250] At an early date, however, the "self-consciousness that makes ethical judgments"[251] was felt to be a personal authority within the individual. The Egyptians believed that the human heart (conscience) should be in harmony with the norm (*maʿat*).[252] This harmony demands knowledge[253] of *maʿat.* In Israel,[254] the Israelites were commanded constantly to follow the Torah and shape their *lēḇ* in obedience to God's word (Dt. 30:14,17; Jer. 31:33; Ezk. 36:26f.). The *lēḇ* as the organ of knowledge[255] notes deviations from God's will. The OT (almost exclusvely in the Deuteronomistic history) makes this function transparently clear by constrasting God's word to the "beating" of the *lēḇ* in reaction to a misdeed (1 S. 24:6[5]; cf. v. 13[12]; 25:31; 2 S. 24:10; cf. v. 3). The *lēḇ* also reacts to a breach of oath (1 K. 2:44).

In the Deuteronomistic prayer of dedication of the temple (1 K. 8:23-53), which demonstrates the importance of the temple for the people, v. 37 provides that the temple is to be the Israelites' chosen house of prayer when beset by any kind of affliction (*negaʿ*). Using this catchword, in v. 38b a later redactor introduces *negaʿ lēḇāḇ* ("affliction of heart," i.e., "pangs of conscience") as the motivation for praying in the temple.

Although Wisdom Literature does not address conscience as a theme, its role can be seen in Job's reaction to the accusations of his friends. The fact that his *lēḇ* has never reproached him (Job 27:6) demonstrates his *ṣᵉḏāqâ.* Sir. 37:13 urges unqualified attention to the voice of conscience, since the conscience can tell one more than seven watchmen on watch (v. 14). That person is happy who need suffer no pangs of conscience (Sir. 14:1f.). Wisd. 17:11 cautions against a bad conscience, because it confuses the mind.

c. *Vices.* The *lēḇ* is seen as the seat of all human vices: a wicked *lēḇ,* often disguised by a dissembling tongue, is the mark of the *rešaʿ* (Ps. 28:3; 41:7[6]). Proverbial wisdom likens such a person to glazed earthenware that is fundamentally worthless (Prov. 26:23). This wickedness of *lēḇ* detroys one's relationship to God and to one's neighbors

248. Zimmerli.
249. See V.4.a above.
250. C. Maurer, "σύνοιδα." *TDNT,* VII, 908.
251. E. Schick, "Gewissen," *LThK*², IV (1960), 860.
252. Morenz, 131.
253. → ידע *yāḏaʿ,* II.1.
254. Cf. Schreiner, 110f.
255. See V.4.a above.

(Isa. 32:6); therefore the king must renounce it so that he can judge justly (Ps. 101:4). For Jeremiah, it is the grounds for Yahweh's judgment (Jer. 4:14,18); therefore he exhorts Jerusalem urgently to wash its heart (v. 14). Ecclesiastes sees in this wickedness the true grounds for human mortality (Eccl. 9:3).

Even in the preexilic period (Hos. 13:6), prophecy sees the *lēḇ* as the seat of hubris.[256] It is the result of Israel's surfeit and unrestrained self-aggrandizement (Isa. 9:8[9]). Isaiah calls this arrogance *gōḏel lēḇāḇ* (a phrase applied to Assyria by a glossator in 10:12), possibly drawing on wisdom vocabulary (cf. *g^eḇah-lēḇ*: Prov. 16:5;[257] *r^eḥaḇ-lēḇ*: Prov. 21:4; Ps. 101:5; cf. Dt. 17:20). This particular terminology does not need to be present; direct discourse (*'āmar b^elēḇ*) often signals clearly the presence of hubris (Ps. 10:6,11; 35:25; Isa. 14:13; 47:8,10; Jer. 49:16; Ob. 3; Zeph. 1:12; 2:15).[258] Arrogance of *lēḇ*, already morally condemned by early proverbial wisdom as *tô'ēḇaṯ YHWH* (Prov. 16:5), is a frequent theme of prophetic denunciation. This condemnation is probably grounded in Deuteronomic and Deuteronomistic parenesis, which cautions against arrogance in conjunction with the gift of the land (Dt. 8:14,17; 9:4; interpreted secondarily as forgetting Yahweh and failing to keep the law [8:11b][259]).

The warning against arrogance is addressed primarily to the foreign nations: Edom (Jer. 49:16; Ob. 3), Moab (Jer. 48:29), Tyre (Ezk. 28:2,5,6,17[260]), Egypt (Ezk. 31:10), Assyria (Zeph. 2:15), Babylon (Isa. 47:8,10), Nebuchadnezzar (Dnl. 5:20), the "king of the south" (Dnl. 11:12), and the apocalyptic ruler of the world (Isa. 14:13), but also to the inhabitants of Jerusalem (Zeph. 1:12). The arrogance of several kings of Judah is mentioned in 2 K. 14:10 par. 2 Ch. 25:19 (Amaziah); 2 Ch. 26:16 (Uzziah); 2 Ch. 32:26 (Hezekiah). In individual laments, the wicked are characteristically described as arrogant (Ps. 10:2-4,6,11; 35:25).

Human obduracy ("hardness of heart") is particularly associated with the *lēḇ*. The terminology is vivid: → כבד *kāḇēḏ*, "be heavy" (chiefly J); → חזק *ḥāzāq*,[261] "be hard" (preferred by E and P); → קשה *qāšâ* hiphil, "harden" (Ex. 7:3 [P]; Dt. 2:30; Ps. 95:8; Prov. 28:14); *qāšaḥ* hiphil, "harden" (Isa. 63:17; cf. Sir. 30:12); → אמץ *'āmaṣ* piel,[262] "make strong"; *šāman* hiphil, "cover with fat" (Isa. 6:10; cf. Ps. 119:70); also *š^erirûṯ lēḇ*, "hardness of heart" (following Dt. 29:18, chiefly in the Jeremiah tradition) and *m^eginnaṯ-lēḇ*, "dullness of heart" (Lam. 3:65).[263] Obduracy is manifested in hardening of the neck (*'ōrep̱*: Dt. 10:16; etc.), face (Jer. 5:3), and forehead (Ezk. 3:7), uncircum-

---

256. → גאה *gā'â*; → גבה *gāḇâ*.

257. For a discussion of the semantic field, see → גבה *gāḇâ*, II, 357f.

258. For a discussion of the terminology, see G. Bertram, " 'Hochmut' und verwandte Begriffe im griechischen und hebräischen AT," *WO*, 3 (1964/66), 32-43; *idem*, "ὕβρις," *TDNT*, VIII, 295-307.

259. G. Seitz, *Redaktionsgeschichtlichen Studien zum Deuteronomium. BWANT*, 93[5/13] (1971), 79.

260. See Loretz, *UF*, 8 (1976), 457f.

261. IV, 308.

262. I, 326.

263. For a discussion of the terminology, see J. L. Ska, "La sortie d'Égypte (Ex 7–14) dans le récit sacerdotale (P^g) et la tradition prophétique," *Bibl*, 60 (1979), 191-215, esp. 198-205.

cised lips (Ex. 6:12,30) and ears (Jer. 6:10), as well as hardening or fattening of the *lēḇ*; according to Franz Hesse,[264] this obduracy infects the religious and ethical character of its possessor.

All the Pentateuchal sources associate the motif of hardness of *lēḇ* with the exodus and occupation traditions: Pharaoh's treatment of the Israelites reflects the political event of an attempted emigration by a group of foreign laborers and the reaction of the national bureaucracy.[265] J conceives "obduracy" actively as a "making heavy" (*kāḇēḏ* hiphil) of the *lēḇ,* whether the agent is Pharaoh himself (Ex. 8:11,28[15,32]; 9:7,34)[266] or Yahweh (Ex. 10:1). Only once, using the verbal adj. *kāḇēḏ,* does J interpret obduracy as a condition (Ex. 7:14). Ex. 4:21, a latter addition to J or JE,[267] uses *ḥāzāq* piel, "make hard," to describe the hardening of the *lēḇ*. This is the terminology used by P, who restricts the action to Yahweh: Yahweh hardens Pharaoh's *lēḇ* (Ex. 9:12; 10:20,27; 14:4,8,17; cf. *qšh* hiphil in 7:3), whereas the preceding narrative of the plagues[268] uses the qal of *ḥāzāq,* "be hard," to express the same idea passively (Ex. 7:13,22; 8:15[19]; 9:35). The narratives of J and P thus progress from Pharaoh's inherent hardness of heart to Yahweh's active hardening of Pharaoh's heart. Exegetes have therefore accused Yahweh of injustice,[269] especially since Ex. 14:4 uses the recognition formula to describe the theological purpose of the hardening of the Egyptians' hearts: they are to know[270] "that I am Yahweh" (cf. Sir. 16:15). In 1 S. 6:6, Pharaoh's obduracy is called a "malicious sport" (*hiṯʿallēl*). It finds expression in his inability, in the face of all the evidence, to recognize the meaning of the plagues and act accordingly. This clear purpose of Pharaoh's obduracy makes it unlikely that the notion of "hardening the heart" is of military origin (preparation for battle).[271] Jean-Louis Ska,[272] comparing P^G with Ezk. 2:4; 3:7, is more likely correct in identifying the context as "judgment in the prophetic tradition."

Obduracy is dissolved by understanding (Ex. 9:21), confession, and prayer for forgiveness (Ex. 10:16f.) in the face of the overwhelming manifestation of Yahweh's power in history. This theme is developed extensively in textual additions (cf. Ex. 9:29; etc.);[273] for the period of the occupation, the Deuteronomistic history also associates it with Sihon (Dt. 2:30) and the Canaanite kings (Josh. 11:20).

While the obduracy of Yahweh's enemies ultimately serves to demonstrate his power

---

264. F. Hesse, *Das Verstockungsproblem im AT. BZAW,* 74 (1955), 4.
265. Hermann, 94.
266. On the Egyptian wisdom principle of the "firm heart" (*dns ỉb = lāḇ kāḇēḏ*), see *ibid.,* 103f.
267. M. Noth, *Exodus. OTL* (Eng. trans. 1962), 47.
268. See E. Otto, "Erwägungen zum überlieferungsgeschichtlichen Ursprung und 'Sitz im Leben' des jahwistischen Plagenzyklus," *VT,* 26 (1976), 3-27.
269. For citations, see Hermann, 25f.
270. → ידע *yāḏaʿ,* V, 471.
271. P. Weimar, *Untersuchungen zur priesterschriftlichen Exodusgeschichte. FzB,* 9 (1972), 209-212.
272. Pp. 202f.
273. Otto, 25.

in history, the obduracy of Israel associated with the Massah and Meribah tradition (Ps. 95:8; cf. Ex. 17:1ff.;[274] also Jer. 11:8) is construed as apostasy (Ps. 81:13[12]). The prophetic tradition interprets this obduracy itself as Yahweh's judgment.[275] The polarity implicit in Yahweh's authorship of Israel's obduracy and hardness of *lēḇ* is clear in Isa. 6:10, where Isaiah receives a "command for hardening."[276] This command is the primary reason why M. M. Kaplan and O. H. Steck do not consider Isa. 6 a call vision.[277] The LXX avoided the theological problem by having the heart of the people harden itself. In his message of obduracy, the prophet envisions the actual conduct of Israelites: faced with Yahweh's acts of judgment, they shut themselves off more and more from God,[278] and continue to do so (cf. Isa. 57:17).[279] Obduracy as rejection of the call to repent (cf. Jer. 5:23; 18:12; Ezk. 2:4; 3:7) goes hand in hand with self-deluding idolatry (Jer. 9:13[14]; 13:10). Trito-Isaiah, too, ascribes Israel's obduracy to Yahweh, but on the grounds that Yahweh is the universal cause of all things (Isa. 63:17). For prophetic lament over Israel's obduracy, see Jer. 16:12; 23:17; Isa. 44:18; for obduracy as antisocial conduct, see Dt. 15:7; Ps. 73:7; Zec. 7:12. Proverbial wisdom associates obduracy with suffering and disaster (Prov. 28:14; Sir. 3:26f.)

According to Hos. 10:2, the human *lēḇ* is inclined to apostasy and idolatry. This view is adopted by Jeremiah (Jer. 7:24; 17:5) and restated in cultically provocative language: "on the tablet of their heart, and on the horns of their altars" (17:1). Deuteronomy warns repeatedly against the tendency toward idolatry of the *lēḇāḇ* (Dt. 11:16; 29:17,18[18,19]; 30:17; cf. 1 K. 15:3; 2 Ch. 20:33; 25:2) and, in the law of the king, requires the king to be exemplary in this regard (Dt. 17:17; cf. 1 K. 11:2,4,9). Ezekiel speaks of a "wanton heart" (*lēḇ hazzōneh*: Ezk. 6:9), of "taking idols into the heart" (14:3,4,7), of "estrangement" (*zûr*) from Yahweh, which Yahweh counters by "laying hold of the heart" (14:5). The desert generation of Israel is characterized by the inclination of the heart to go after idols, manifest in neglect of the Torah and the Sabbath (Ezk. 20:16). The psalmist raises the question of theodicy by noting that the wicked prosper even though their *lēḇ* is inclined to apostasy (Ps. 10:13; 36:2[1]). Drawing on the motif of Israel's obduracy, he describes apostasy as *nsh* (piel) *bilḇaḇ*, "testing [God] in the heart" (Ps. 78:18; cf. v. 37). Proverbial wisdom, too, warns against an erring heart (Prov. 7:25; 14:14; Sir. 10:12; 46:11).

d. *Virtues*. On the other hand, the *lēḇ* is also the seat of human virtues. In it

---

274. H. F. Fuhs, "Kadesch in Geschichte und Überlieferung," *BN*, 9 (1979), 45-70.

275. Cf. Ska, 205.

276. H. Wildberger, *Isaiah 1–12* (Eng. trans., Minneapolis, 1991), 272; J. Gnilka, *Die Verstockung Israels. StANT*, 3 (1961); Chung Hsin Chi, *The Concept of "Hardening the Heart"* (diss., South East Asia Graduate School of Theology, 1974).

277. M. M. Kaplan, "Isaiah 6_{1-11}," *JBL*, 45 (1976), 251-59; O. H. Steck, "Bemerkungen zu Jesaja 6," *BZ*, N.S. 16 (1972), 188-206; cf. *idem*, "Rettung und Verstockung: Exegetisch Bemerkungen zu Jesaja 7,3-9,"*EvTh*, 33 (1973), 77-90.

278. Wildberger, *Isaiah 1–12*, 273.

279. For the arguments against Hesse's "retrojection" theory, see R. Kilian, "Der Verstockungsauftrag Jesajas," *Bausteine biblischer Theologie. Festschrift G. J. Botterweck. BBB*, 50 (1977), 209-225.

uprightness dwells (associated with wisdom in Prov. 23:19). The "upright in heart" (*yišrê-lēḇ*)[280] are mentioned primarily in the Psalms. Psalmists include themselves among the upright of heart as grounds for God to hear their prayer (Ps. 7:11[10]; 11:2; 36:11[10]; cf. 66:18; 125:4). With uprightness of heart come confidence (Ps. 94:15; 97:11) and joy (32:11; 64:11[10]). For the concrete expression of this uprightness, see Ps. 15:2; 2 K. 10:15; 2 Ch. 19:9; 29:34; 31:21; for warnings against duplicity, see Prov. 11:10; 17:20; Ps. 12:3[2]).

Proverbial wisdom calls for the *lēḇ* to be open to instruction (*mûsār*: Prov. 23:12; cf. 5:12; 15:32). Finally, Sir. 7:35 suggests that a positive inclination of the *lēḇ* has a social dimension: visiting and caring for the sick.

The semantic field "purity of heart" includes *tom-lēḇ*. The word *tōm* denotes "integrity of an act" or "absence of guile."[281] In this connection, we may note especially Abimelech's asseverations of innocence (Gen. 20:5,6 [E]) and the parallels to Solomon's "uprightness" (*yōšer*) and observance of the Torah (1 K. 9:4; cf. also Ps. 78:72; 101:2; Dt. 9:5). Ritual purifications and ablutions give rise to the metaphor of "washing" (*kibbes*) the heart (Jer. 4:14). The primary meaning of the metaphor is ethical, however, as we see especially in the use of → זכה *zāḵâ* piel,[282] "keep the heart clean" (Ps. 73:13; Prov. 20:9; cf. Sir. 38:10) and its parallels.[283] Also figurative is the phrase *bar lēḇāḇ*, "pure in heart" (Ps. 73:1),[284] parallel to *nᵉqî kappayim*, "clean hands" (24:4). In "entrance liturgies," these two phrases serve to describe the cultic requirements of inward and outward purity, that is, purity of thoughts and acts. Even the use of the levitical term *ṭāhôr* with *lēḇ* (Ps. 51:12[10]; Prov. 22:11) shows no trace of its ritual background. No ritual can purify the heart; a "pure heart" and a "steadfast spirit" are the gift of Yahweh alone.

Affliction (*ʿᵃnāwâ*), the opposite of *gāḇāh lēḇ* (Prov. 18:12; Ps. 131:1), is likewise seated in the heart and is described anthropologically as "brokenness"[285] of heart. This expression itself shows that affliction implies not only physical liability (cf. Jer. 23:9) but also a failure of self-confidence: the afflicted must set all their hopes on God. To them in particular the promises of God's presence are addressed (Ps. 34:19[18]; 147:3), and the prophet knows that he is sent above all to them (Isa. 61:1). The knowledge that God is with the afflicted (cf. 2 K. 22:19; 2 Ch. 34:27) inspires the worshipper to offer himself to Yahweh as *raḵ-lēḇāḇ*.

Hosea already bewails the absence of sincere religiosity. People perform religious rituals for a variety of reasons, but no one cries out to Yahweh *bᵉlēḇ* (Hos. 7:14). Jer. 29:13 likewise emphasizes the necessity of seeking Yahweh *bᵉḵol-lēḇāḇ*. As Dt. 4:29

---

280. → ישר *yāšar.*

281. K. Koch, "תמם *tmm* vollständig sein," *THAT,* II, 1047.

282. IV, 63.

283. See the attempt by L. R. Fisher, "An Amarna Age Prodigal," *JSS,* 3 (1958), 115, to interpret *zāḵâ* in the legal sense as "not guilty."

284. → ברר *bārar,* II, 310f.

285. → שבר *šāḇar*; cf. O. Garcia de la Fuente, "Sobre la idea de contrición en el AT," *Sacra Pagina,* I. *BETL,* 12f. (1959), 559-579, esp. 572-75.

shows, this prophetic demand is the foundation for the Deuteronomic commandment to love God and worship him *bᵉkol-lᵉḇāḇᵉḵā ûbᵉḵol-napšᵉḵā* (Dt. 6:5; 10:12; 11:13; 13:4[3]; cf. 28:47), an idiom expressing complete and total devotion; half-heartedness and indifference indicate grudging commitment to Yahweh. The Deuteronomistic history and later the Chronicler's history repeatedly cite this primary commandment and describe obedience to it: paradigmatically (1 K. 15:14; 2 K. 10:31; 23:3; 2 Ch. 15:12,15,17; 19:3; 22:9; 34:31; Isa. 38:3; cf. Sir. 49:3), as realized admonition (Josh. 22:5; 1 S. 7:3 [in conjunction with polemic against idols]; 12:20,24; 1 K. 14:8; 1 Ch. 22:19; 28:9; 2 Ch. 16:9), as a reminiscence of ancient promises (1 K. 2:4; 8:23; 2 K. 20:3; 2 Ch. 6:14), in thanksgiving for assistance (1 K. 3:6), and in prayer to God (1 Ch. 29:18f.; 2 Ch. 30:19).

The Psalms and proverbial wisdom agree that patient endurance (Ps. 27:14; 31:25[24]), trusting in Yahweh (Ps. 28:7; 62:9[8]; 112:7; Prov. 3:5) and following him *bᵉlēḇāḇ* (Ps. 84:6[5]) result in Yahweh's favor and assistance (cf. also Job 11:13f.).

Deuteronomy links observance of the Torah[286] directly with the commandment to love God (Dt. 6:5f.) and interprets such observance as obedience to the commandment (10:12f.; cf. 11:13; 13:4f.[3f.]). According to Jer. 17:1; 31:33, the Torah is written on the human heart and is thus directly present in the human center of decision (cf. Dt. 30:14; Ps. 37:31; Isa. 51:7).[287] The totality of human life is concentrated in observance of the Torah. This is emphasized by the parenetic conclusion of the Deuteronomic history in Dt. 26:16,17-19. This fundamental demand of Deuteronomic and Deuteronomistic parenesis (cf. Dt. 11:18; 30:1; 32:46 [expanded into a command to teach subsequent generations]) is frequently restated, with some variation, by DtrN.[288] It appears also at a homiletic climax in the parenetic prayer of blessing over the people at the end of the prayer of dedication of the temple (1 K. 8). Yahweh inclines (*hṭh*) the *lēḇāḇ* of the people to him, enabling them to obey the commandments (1 K. 8:58). Echoing this prayer, 1 K. 8:61 demands that the people let their *lēḇāḇ* be "wholly true" (*šālēm*) to Yahweh and keep his commandments. In 2 K. 23:3, the same terminology serves to describe wholehearted fidelity to the *bᵉrîṯ*.[289]

Jeremiah considers Torah observance impossible in the present and hopes that it will come in the future (Jer. 31:31ff.; 32:38ff.). There — in the new → ברית *bᵉrîṯ*[290] — the ultimate spiritualization is attained, since the stage of volition based on sensory experience is skipped: *bᵉrîṯ* and Torah observance are written on the heart itself.[291] Even here, however (as in 1 K. 8:58), the emphasis is on Yahweh's initiative (cf. Ezk. 2:4; 3:7; 2 Ch. 30:12).

In both the Deuteronomistic history and the Chronicler's history, the postulated relationship between love of God, observance of the law, and fidelity to the *bᵉrîṯ* is

286. → שמע *šāmaʿ*.
287. Cf. Schenker.
288. R. Smend, *Die Entstehung des ATs. Theologische Wissenschaft,* 1 (Stuttgart, 1978), 115.
289. For a discussion of *bᵉrît* terminology, → ברית *bᵉrîṯ* (*bᵉrîth*), II, 261 (M. Weinfeld).
290. II, 277.
291. Cf. von Rad, *OT Theology,* II (Eng. trans., New York, 1965), 270.

described as *bᵉlēḇ* or *bᵉlēḇ šālēm.*[292] Walter Eisenbeis has compared the Deuteronomistic passages with those from the Chronicler and analyzed the formulaic expression *hāyâ lēḇāb šālēm ʿim YHWH* (1 K. 11:4; 15:3,12,14);[293] he proposes a nuanced distinction. In the Deuteronomistic history, he claims, *lēḇ*(*āḇ*) *šālēm* denotes absolute obedience with all one's being and willing as the response to an absolute demand made by God. The Chronicler understands obedience primarily in relationship to specific demands, which can be fulfilled with "extraordinary effort" if one's will is correct. F. L. Schults,[294] however, accepts Friedrich Baumgärtel's interpretation,[295] distinguishing "conformity to the terms of the covenant" (Deuteronomistic history), "existence of right relationship between God and man," and "balance between man's *capacity* to will and the *extent* of his willingness" (Chronicler's history). Finally, Gillis Gerleman[296] would put more emphasis on what he takes to be the basic meaning, seeing in *lēḇ*(*āḇ*) *šālēm* a "paying" heart, i.e., one that is willing and submissive.

The intensity of devotion to the Torah *bᵉḵol-lēḇ* — less an immanent qualification of the devout than a gift from Yahweh — is the primary theme of Ps. 119.

Knowledge of God as "a practical, religio-ethical relationship"[297] between individuals and Yahweh is also seated in the *lēḇ*. Its primary concern is Yahweh, the covenant God who delivers Israel; but it is also directed against other gods. This polarity appears in the scattered texts that use *lēḇ* to describe a more intense knowledge of God (cf. esp. Dt. 4:39; 8:5). Jer. 24:7 states that this *lēḇ* that knows God — and therefore also the knowledge of God — is a gift from Yahweh.

The fear of God is also understood to be seated in the *lēḇ*. The use of *lēḇ* with *rkk,* "be soft," to express discouragement[298] and with *mss* niphal, "melt,"[299] denotes emotional terror, but this usage does not touch the ethical dimension of fear of God (cf. *yārēʾ* in Jer. 5:24). This is clearly the case, however, in Dt. 5:29, where Yahweh expresses the wish that the human *lēḇāḇ* were so fashioned as to fear[300] him always. Jer. 32:39 states that Yahweh will give the Israelites a *lēḇ ʾeḥāḏ* as the requisite for fearing God. According to Joachim Becker,[301] this statement is intended to undergird the integrity of worship of Yahweh (cf. also Ps. 86:11). Proverbial wisdom also counsels the *lēḇ* to be zealous in fearing Yahweh (Prov. 23:17; Sir. 7:29; 40:26; 45:23).

---

292. For a synopsis of the terminology, see M. Weinfeld, *Deuteronomy and the Deuteronomic School* (Oxford, 1972), 334f.

293. W. Eisenbeis, *Die Wurzel* שלם *im AT. BZAW,* 113 (1969), 338-348.

294. F. L. Shults, שלם *and* תמם *in Biblical Hebrew* (diss., Univ. of Texas at Austin, 1974), 84-94.

295. P. 607.

296. G. Gerleman, "שלם *šlm* genug haben," *THAT,* II, 919-935, esp. 927.

297. → ידע *yāḏaʿ,* V, 469.

298. J. Becker, *Gottesfurcht im AT. AnBibl,* 25 (1965), 17.

299. *Ibid.,* 18.

300. → ירא *yārēʾ,* VI.1, i.e., "venerate" in the sense of fidelity to the covenant God in a staunch and perfect habit of the will (Becker, *Gottesfurcht im AT,* 97; Weinfeld, *Deuteronomy and the Deuteronomic School,* 274, thinks rather of "a meaning of general morality").

301. P. 166; the triad *ʾeḥāḏ/lēḇ/dereḵ* is described on p. 168.

Finally (albeit not in preexilic texts), penitent return[302] is seated in the *lēḇ*. To emphasize the radical nature of this demand, the OT writers use the metaphor of circumcising the *lēḇ*. While historical events (Isa. 46:8; 49:21) and the hubris of Babylon (47:7) lead Deutero-Isaiah to speak of "knowing" (lit., "laying to heart" with repentance as the end; cf. also 57:1,11), Jeremiah and Deuteronomy use the word *šûḇ* in similar contexts. Jer. 24:7, an early exilic text,[303] emphasizes the close connection between knowledge of God, the covenant, and penitent return to Yahweh — the latter underscored by the Deuteronomistic *beḵol-lēḇ*. Yahweh brings about (*nāṯan lēḇ*) knowledge and return (cf. Ezk. 11:19; Dt. 29:3[4]; on Yahweh as the initiator of repentance and return, see 1 K. 18:37). Jeremiah demands this return as total conversion to Yahweh, because false penitence only increases culpability (Jer. 3:10; cf. 23:26). In Dt. 30:2,10, we find the kerygmatic "culmination" of the Deuteronomic history[304] in the association of return *beḵol-lēḇāḇ* with observance of the Torah (cf. also 1 K. 8:47f.; King Josiah as paradigm in 2 K. 23:25). DtrN[305] exemplifies this postulate in 1 S. 7:3 in linking return to Yahweh, destruction of idols, and serving Yahweh. Echoing such passages as Am. 4:6ff.; Hos. 3:5, the Deuteronomist also interprets return with all one's heart as the salvific effect of Yahweh's judgment and as part of the promise. Joel attacks all empty ritualism when he rejects rituals of mourning and penance in favor of radical inward conversion. Citing the well-known ritual of rending one's clothing, he interprets repentance as *qāraʿ lēḇāḇ* (par. *šûḇ ʾel-YHWH* [Joel 2:12f.]), "rending the heart."

The meaning of the phrase *mûl ʾeṯ ʿorlaṯ lēḇāḇ*, "circumcise the foreskin of the heart," is closely tied to the meaning of the rite of circumcision[306] itself: a purification ritual,[307] a sacrifice (for redemption),[308] an act of consecration,[309] or a sign of the covenant.[310]

Dt. 10:16 is probably the earliest text[311] that calls on the people to circumise the foreskin (*ʿorlâ*) of their hearts and to put aside hardness of heart (*ʿōrep̱*: alliteration). If Gottfried Seitz and Hans-Jürgen Hermisson[312] are correct in connecting v. 16 with the preceding verses,[313] there is a surprising parallelism between the association of Israel's election with circumcising the heart and P's association of the *beriṯ* with circumcision (Gen. 17). Just as circumcision is a mark of the covenant, so circumcision

---

302. → שׁוב *šûḇ*.

303. Cf. K.-F. Pohlman, *Studien zum Jeremiabuch. FRLANT,* 118 (1978), 20f., 22f.

304. G. von Rad, *Deuteronomy. OTL* (Eng. trans. 1966), 183; H. W. Wolff, "Das Kerygma des deuteronomistischen Geschichtswerkes," *ZAW,* 73 (1961), 180ff. (= *GSAT. ThB,* 22 [[2]1973], 318ff,), suggests a different hand — DtrN?

305. T. Veijola, *Die ewige Dynastie. AnAcScFen,* 193 (1975).

306. → מול *mûl,* ערלה *ʿorlâ.*

307. C. von Orelli, C. Steuernagel, and the LXX on Dt. 30:6.

308. Meyer, Eichrodt; cf. Lev. 19:23f.

309. H.-J. Hermisson, *Sprache und Ritus im altisraelitischen Kult. WMANT,* 19 (1965).

310. → אות *ʾôṯ* (*ʾôth*), Gen. 17:11 (P).

311. Seitz, 81, claims that vv. 14-22 are a later passage dependent on Jeremiah.

312. P. 72.

313. Contra Steuernagel.

of the heart is a mark of election. Roger Le Déaut[314] sees a direct reference to the commandment to fear and love Yahweh *bᵉkol-lēḇāḇ* in v. 12.

Jer. 4:1-4, Yahweh's response to the people's hymn of contrition (3:22-25), is a compendium of radical repentance moving toward the climax of v. 4: put away idols, swear by Yahweh, circumcise yourselves *laYHWH,* remove the foreskin of your heart (cf. also Ezk. 44:7,9). According to Dt. 30:6 (late exilic), it is Yahweh himself who circumcises the heart of the people. The echo of Yahweh's gift of a new heart in Jer. 31:31ff.[315] is unmistakable.[316] Just as circumcision is associated with the divine gift of the covenant as a sign of submission,[317] so circumcision of the heart stands for this submission itself.[318] Outward circumcision presupposes circumcision of the heart (not the reverse); otherwise it brings condemnation (Jer. 9:25). For the Holiness Code and later texts, humbling of the people's uncircumcised heart is the *sine qua non* for existence of the covenant (Lev. 26:41).

VI. Idols. The OT never speaks of idols having hearts: they are powerless and dead.[319] The MT of Ezk. 11:21 (supported by the LXX, Aquila, Symmachus, and Theodotion) does speak of those remaining in Jerusalem as setting their hearts on the *lēḇ* of their abominations, but the Vulg. already treated this reading as an error. Following the Vulg., Carl Heinrich Cornill proposed the emendation *wᵉʼēlleh ʼaḥᵃrê šiqqûṣêhem* . . . ; this reading, which has a parallel in Ezk. 20:16, has been generally accepted.[320] In fact, however, the emendation is based on a theological argument.

In Job 1:8; 2:3, Yahweh asks Satan whether he has turned his *lēḇ* to Job; the idiomatic phrase has no bearing on the nature of Satan.

VII. Yahweh. The texts that speak of Yahweh's *lēḇ* (26 times: 8 in Jeremiah, 5 in the Deuteronomistic history, 4 in Job) probably trace their origin to J's fondness of anthropomorphisms. The introduction to the Deluge Story states that human wickedness grieved Yahweh to his heart (Gen. 6:6). The conclusion records Yahweh's determination never again to curse the earth, a decision seated in his heart (Gen. 8:21). For Yahweh, as for human beings, the heart is the center of decision. Here arise Yahweh's compassion for Israel (Hos. 11:8) and his might on behalf of the righteous (Job 36:5); his *lēḇ* is the source of his revelatory will (2 S. 7:21; 1 Ch. 17:19). To speak of God's *lēḇ* is to express

---

314. R. le Déaut, "Le thème de la circoncision du coeur (Dt. XXX 6; Jer. IV 4) dans les versions anciennes (LXX et Targum) et à Qumrân," *Congress Volume, Vienna 1980. SVT,* 32 (1982).

315. Hermisson, le Déaut.

316. Cf. J. H. Tigay, " 'Heavy of Mouth' and 'Heavy of Tongue': On Moses' Speech Difficulty," *BASOR,* 231 (1978), 57-67, esp. 57.

317. Hermisson, 76.

318. Le Déaut.

319. Cf. H. D. Preuss, *Verspottung fremder Religionen im AT. BWANT,* 92[5/12] (1971), 111f.

320. *BHK, BHS*; A. Bertholet, *Hesekiel. HAT,* XIII (1936), 40; W. Eichrodt, *Ezekiel. OTL* (Eng. trans. 1970), 112; H. Graf Reventlow, *Wächter über Israel. BZAW,* 82 (1962), 54; W. Zimmerli, *Ezekiel 1. Herm* (Eng. trans. 1979), 230.

the "fervour of his kindness" toward mortals.[321] Thus God's plan for judgment cannot ultimately be characteristic of his *lēḇ,* as Lam. 3:33 (exilic) states, using the formula of self-exoneration (cf. Nu. 16:28). God's *lēḇ* thus becomes a term for his nature, which rejects cruelty.

The *lēḇ* of Yahweh as the seat of his will functions as a norm for human conduct. A faithful priest acts according to Yahweh's heart (1 S. 2:35); the king is in accord with Yahweh's *lēḇ* when he keeps Yahweh's commandments (1 S. 13:14). The endurance of the royal line is grounded in agreement with the *lēḇ* of Yahweh (2 K. 10:30; cf. 1QH 4:21), as are the leadership qualities of the shepherds (Jer. 3:15): knowledge (*yd'*) and understanding (*śkl*). Everything associated with idolatry is contrary to the *lēḇ* of Yahweh (Jer. 7:31; 19:5; 32:35). In Yahweh's *lēḇ* is concentrated God's firm purpose (Ps. 33:11; cf. 1QH 4:13,21; Job 10:13). While Job is prepared to think of the plan in Yahweh's *lēḇ* as blind fateful determination, for Jeremiah the thoughts of Yahweh's heart are correlated with the acts of the wicked (Jer. 23:20; 30:24). What Yahweh will do in the future is already determined in his *lēḇ*: for some it brings a "day of vengeance" (Isa. 63:4), for others a return to the promised land (Jer. 32:41).

The expression *bᵉḵōl-lēḇ ûḇᵉḵōl-nep̱eš* is rooted in Deuteronomic and Deuteronomistic parenesis, where it used in divine discourse as a formula of emphasis, affirming the absolute reliability of the promise. Despite God's omniscience, the *lēḇ* of Yahweh has a noetic function, which emerges clearly in polemic against idolatry. Jer. 44:21 states that the worship of the queen of heaven has "gone to the heart" (*'ālâ 'al-lēḇ*) of Yahweh. Yahweh remembers idolatry, but the charge that he has not cared for Israel touches his *lēḇ*. In the context of Deutero-Isaiah's polemic against idolatry, Yahweh summons the idols to court: they must prove their divinity (their power to shape history) so convincingly that Yahweh can "take to heart" (*śîm lēḇ*) their existence (Isa. 41:22). This serves to establish the key assertion of Deutero-Isaiah's polemic: "You are nothing, and your work is nought" (Isa. 41:24).[322]

God's attention also proceeds from his *lēḇ*. In amazement, Job takes up the psalmist's question: "What is man that thou art mindful of him" (Ps. 8:5[4]; 144:3); but he conceives of God's interest much more intensively in his expansion of the question: ". . . and that thou dost set thy *lēḇ* upon him" (Job 7:17). In his own case, Job finds this attention on God's part extremely burdensome; it is responsible for his wretched situation. The narrator, however, is well aware of the creative, nurturing power at work when God sets his *lēḇ* on the world and those who dwell in it (Job 34:14; cf. Ps. 104:29f.; Eccl. 12:7; → רוח *rûaḥ*).

Finally, there is the unparalleled statement that Yahweh's eyes and *lēḇ* dwell (*hāyâ*) in the Jerusalem temple (1 K. 9:3; 2 Ch. 7:16). A late Deuteronomistic interpreter has extended the notion that Yahweh's name[323] dwells in the temple by speaking of the presence of God's invocability (*šēm*) and attention (*'ênayim*) (cf. 1 K. 8:29) together

321. Wolff, *Anthropology of the OT,* 56.
322. Cf. Preuss, 197f., 203-6.
323. → שׁם *šēm*; cf. esp. A. S. van der Woude, "שֵׁם *šēm* Name," *THAT,* II, 954f.

with God's deepest favor in "sympathy" and "favour" (cf. Ps. 78:72).[324] Finally, though, the statement that Yahweh's *lēḇ* dwells in the temple is an unsurpassable expression of Israel's election.

VII. Dead Sea Scrolls. The nouns *lēḇ* and *lēḇāḇ* occur about 140 times in the Dead Sea scrolls; they are most common in the markedly anthropological 1QH (56 times), followed by 1QS (24 times), CD (16 times), 1QM (13 times), 11QT (10 times) 4QDibHam (5 times), and the Aramaic 4QapGen (5 times). It comes as no surprise that none of these texts refers to the anatomical organ. Emotions of the *lēḇ* are mentioned (1QH 5:31; 6:2; 10:30,33; 14:26; CD 20:33; 4Q185 1f.II.12; 11QPs^a 21:12), but the predominant interest is anthropological. In the *lēḇ* are concentrated human frailty and weakness. The Qumran Essenes localize their failings in the *lēḇ*. It is depraved (1QS 11:9; 1QH 7:27; 17:19), obdurate (1QH 18:26f.), confused (1QH fr. 4:13), appalled (1QH 7:3), broken (1QH 2:9; 11QPs^a 24:16). It melts like wax (1QH 2:6,28; 4:33; 8:32; 1QH fr. 4:14; 4QpIs^a 3:4) and grows weak with fear (1QM 1:14; 8:10; 10:6; 11QT 62:3f.). It trembles (1QH 7:5) and threatens to fail (1QM 10:3; 11:9; 14:6; 15:8). But God tests (1QM 16:15) and strengthens (1QH 7:13; 1QM 16:14) the individual. When 1QH 18:24 describes the human heart as a *lēḇ ʿāpār,* we see clearly the sense of creaturely weakness felt by the Qumran Essene, who is totally dependent on God.[325]

It is typical of the attitude of these Essenes to state repeatedly that the understanding God bestows as a mark of election[326] is situated in the *lēḇ* (1QS 2:3; 4:23; 10:24; 11:16; 1QH 1:37; 2:18: 5:9,33; 10:31; 12:34; 14:8; 1QH fr. 4:12; 11QPs^a 18:5; 26:12; 11QT 61:2). The *lēḇ* is the locus of the internalized Torah (1QS 2:13; 1QH 4:10; 6QCD 5:5); but long experience with this postulate has taught the Essenes that the *lēḇ* is very often the seat not of the Torah but of arrogance (1QpHab 8:10; 1QS 4:9; 1Q22 2:4; 4Q184 1:2) and obduracy (1QS 1:6; 2:14,26; 3:3; 5:4; 7:19,24; 9:10; 1QH 4:15; CD 2:18; 3:5,12; 8:8,19; 19:20,33; 4QM^a 5; 11QtgJob 27:7; the ethical components of this semantic element are already evident from its frequent mention in the texts dealing with the Community Rule).

The phrase *š^{e}rirûṯ lēḇ* occurs 8 times in 1QS and 6 times in CD. As an expression of the individual's essential being, it emphasizes the personal nature of sin.[327] The noun *lēḇ* takes on a totally new semantic function when it is understood as the locus of idolatry (1QS 2:11; CD 20:9f.: "powers hostile to God are introjected into the heart"[328]). The *lēḇ* of Belial is called the source of all evil (1QS 6:21, possibly corrupt).[329] A later interpretation shifts the conflict between the spirit of wickedness and the spirit of truth (1QS 4:15ff.) to the human *lēḇāḇ* (4:23); cf. the subsequent

324. Wolff, *Anthropology of the OT,* 57; M. Noth, *Könige 1–16. BK,* IX/1 (1968), 197.
325. Cf. H.-W. Kuhn, *Enderwartung und gegenwärtiges Heil. StUNT,* 4 (1966), 106.
326. Nötscher, *Gotteswege und Menschenwege,* 85.
327. See J. Becker, *Das Heil Gottes. StUNT,* 3 (1964), 184; H. Bardtke, "Acedia in Qumrān," *Qumran-Probleme. DAWB,* 42 (1963), 37f.
328. Stolz, *THAT,* I, 863; but cf. the similar polemic in Ezk. 14:3,4,7.
329. → יעץ *yāʿaṣ,* III, 750.

development of *yēṣer* in rabbinic literature.[330] In an act of renunciation, the penitent declares that he has driven Belial from his *lēḇāḇ* (1QS 10:2) and desires to banish all wickedness (1QS 10:21). Like the false prophets in the OT, the wicked in the Dead Sea scrolls act after their own hearts to their ruin (1QH 5:26); they feign devotion and seek Yahweh, but only *beḷēḇ wālēḇ* (1QH 4:14).

The *lēḇ* of Yahweh as a guideline for the faithful is mentioned in 1QH 4:13,18,21,24; 6:7. According to CD 1:11, it is the function of the Teacher of Righteousness to provide guidance in religious and ethical questions,[331] i.e., to give instruction in this *lēḇ*. It finds realization in seeking after God (CD 1:10), love of God (1QH 15:10), worship of God (1QH 16:7; 11QT 54:13), return to God (1QH 16:17; 11QT 59:10), and — characteristic of Qumran — return to the Torah of Moses (CD 15:9; cf. 16:1,4; 1QS 5:8) *bekol-lēḇ,* which establishes the new community of the Qumran Essenes.[332]

The motif of circumcising the foreskin of the heart undergoes a characteristic development (1QpHab 11:13; the orthography that represents *ʿōrlaṯ* as two words [*ʿwr lat*] has not been explained satisfactorily[333]). The author capitalizes on the uncertainty of the MT in Hab. 2:16, where the LXX suggests *hērāʿēl* instead of *hēʿārēl*; he cites the text used by the LXX, but uses the MT variant as the basis for his interpretation, which he develops with the help of Dt. 10:16. Refusal to circumcise the foreskin of the heart is a token of the wicked priest's depravity. In 1QS 5:5 (stratum 3, *ca.* 110 B.C.), *lēḇ* is replaced by *yēṣer*: "they (the *'anšê hayyaḥaḏ*) are to circumcise the foreskin of 'desire' in the community."

The noun *yēṣer*[334] is thus understood as denoting an activity of the *lēḇ,*[335] but with pejorative implications (cf. the par. "stiffneckedness").

In "uncircumcision of the heart" is concentrated all hostility to the ideals of Qumran (cf. 4Q184); "circumcision of the heart" denotes the attitude of the devout who conform to the *yaḥaḏ,* true worship at the end of days (4Q177).[336]

Fabry

330. St.-B., IV (1928), 466f.

331. Nötscher, *Gotteswege und Menschenwege,* 75.

332. Cf. H.-J. Fabry, *Die Wurzel ŠûB in der Qumran-Literatur. BBB,* 46 (1975), 28-32.

333. Cf. W. H. Brownlee, *The Midrash Pesher of Habakkuk. SBL Mon.,* 24 (1979), 191f.

334. → יצר, VI, 264f.

335. Cf. R. E. Murphy, "*Yēṣer* in the Qumran Literature," *Bibl,* 39 (1958), 343.

336. Cf. also D. Simeone, *Il "cuore" negli scritti di Qumran* (diss., Univ. of Rome, 1979). For later developments in rabbinic literature, see St.-B., III (1926), 126; IV, 467; comms. on Rom. 2:29; le Déaut, *passim.*

לבן *lbn*; לְבֵנָה *l^e^bēnâ*; לָבַן *lāḇān*; לְבָנָה *l^e^ḇānâ*

Contents: I. Roots, Etymology. II. OT Usage: 1. Bricks; 2. White; 3. Moon. III. LXX.

I. Roots, Etymology. There are two different roots *lbn* in Hebrew.[1] The first, *lbn* I, "be white," is related to Ugar. *lbn,*[2] Phoen. *lbn,*[3] Jewish Aram. *l^e^ḇān,* "white," and Arab. *laban,* "milk." The second appears in *l^e^ḇānâ,* "brick," and the denominative verb *lāḇan,* "make bricks." Heb. *l^e^ḇēnâ* is related to Akk. *libittu* (<*libintu*),[4] Ugar. *lbnt,* the Canaanite gloss *labinat* in the Amarna letters, Egyptian Aram. *lbnh,* Jewish Aram. *l^e^ḇentā',* Syr. *l^e^ḇentā'/l^e^ḇettā',* Mand. *lbyn', lbyt',* OSA *lbn*[5] and *lbt,*[6] Eth. *l^e^bn,*[7] and Arab. *labinah* (verb *lbn* II: "make bricks").

II. OT Usage.

1. *Bricks.* Brickmaking is associated primarily with the tower of Babel (Gen. 11:3) and the slave labor of the Israelites in Egypt (Ex. 1:14; 5:7f.,14,16,18f.). The bricks in question were air-dried rather than being baked; according to Ex. 5:7,18, they were made with straw and reeds,[8] unlike baked bricks (Akk. *agurru*).[9] To symbolize the arrogance of the inhabitants of Samaria, Isa. 9:9 (Eng. v. 10) contrasts fallen brick walls to new walls built of dressed stones. Ezk. 4:1 speaks of a brick used as a tablet, on which the prophet is to sketch the city of Jerusalem. Ex. 24:10 describes the throne of God as resting on a *l^e^ḇēnâ* (probably a slab or paving stone) of sapphire.[10]

Isa. 65:3 speaks of offering incense on bricks. Whether the text refers to brick altars, the pavement of the sacrificial area, or clay vessels[11] is disputed. The word may well be a garbled form of *l^e^ḇônâ,* "incense." Mitchell Dahood[12] defends the translation

---

lbn. D. Conrad, "Zu Jes 65_{3b}," *ZAW,* 80 (1968), 232-34; K. Galling, "Ziegel," *BRL*², 364; R. Gradwohl, *Die Farben im AT. BZAW,* 83 (1963); A. Salonen, *Die Ziegeleien im alten Mesopotamien. AnAcScFen,* B/171 (1972).

1. Contra Gradwohl, 34ff., and G. Rinaldi, "Nota: *lbnh,*" *BeO,* 10 (1968), 38.
2. *WUS,* no. 1438.
3. *DISO,* 134.
4. *AHw,* I (1965), 551, from *labānu,* "rub," *AHw,* I, 522; II (1972), 1570.
5. ContiRossini, 172.
6. W. W. Müller, "Altsüdarabische Beiträge zum hebräischen Lexicon," *ZAW,* 75 (1963), 311.
7. Leslau, *Contributions,* 31.
8. See Galling; *BuA,* I, 257f.
9. *AHw,* I, 17; cf. Galling.
10. For a recent discussion of this passage, see E. Ruprecht, "Exodus 24,9-11 als Beispiel lebendiger Erzähltradition aus der Zeit des babylonischen Exils," *Worden und Wirken des ATs. Festschrift C. Westermann* (Göttingen, 1980), 138-173.
11. Conrad, 232f.
12. M. Dahood, "Textual Problems in Isaiah," *CBQ,* 22 (1960), 406-8, citing *KTU,* 1.4 IV, 61f.

"brick" and suggests a connection with the goddess Asherah as a maker of bricks. If so, the passage would contain an allusion to the cult of Asherah. In any case, the cult in question is objectionable. The text of 1QIs[a] in the Dead Sea scrolls offers a totally different reading: *wynqw ydym ʿl ʾbnym,* in which *yāḏ* probably means "penis" and *ʾoḇnayim* the female genitalia, suggesting some kind of sexual cult.

2. *White.* The adj. *lāḇān,* "white," appears 20 times in Lev. 13 describing the white spots considered symptoms of leprosy. In a similar vein, Gen. 30:35, 37 speak of the white color of the goats and of the peeled strips on rods Jacob places in front of the copulating animals so that the kids will be spotted.[13] The manna[14] in Ex. 16:31 is also white. Zec. 1:8 sees white horses along with red and sorrel horses behind the red horse whose rider reports peace on the earth. In Zec. 6:3,6, white horses draw one of the four chariots representing the four winds of heaven. Wilhelm Rudolph[15] has shown that there is no evidence for the theory that the colors were associated with particular points of the compass.[16] Jacob's blessing of Judah (Gen. 49:12) says that Jacob's eyes are red with wine and his teeth white with milk — obviously an allusion to the abundance of his riches. The parallelism makes the translation "whiter than milk" less likely.

In Eccl. 9:8, white garments (par. oil on the head) are a mark of joy. It is worth noting that white garments do not appear in Israel until late (Est. 8:15 [which does not use *lāḇān*]; Jth. 10:3), whereas they are an ancient Egyptian custom.[17] There is also a passage in Gilgamesh that reads: "Fill your body, rejoice day and night. . . . Let your garments be clean, your head washed, be bathed in water."[18]

Of much greater interest are the occurrences of the verb (4 times in the hiphil, once in the hithpael); with a single exception, they have a figurative sense referring to forgiveness of sins and purification. We find here the same association of whiteness with purity that is seen in → טהר *ṭhr* and → זכה *zāḵâ.* The author of Ps. 51 prays in v. 9(7) that God will wash (*kbs* piel) him and make him whiter than snow; the parallel terms are *ḥṭʾ* piel, "purge," and *ṭhr,* "be clean." The outward act of washing, which is actually meant to effect ritual purity, is here applied to the removal of sin. In this context, "white" and "pure" are more or less synonymous. The same imagery appears also in Isa. 1:18. As antonyms of "white" we find two terms for "red" (*šānî* and *tôlāʿ*),[19] and as an additional symbol of whiteness we find *ṣemer,* "(white) wool." The question is whether the text is to be taken as a promise of forgiveness (conditional upon

13. → לח *laḥ.*

14. → מן *man.*

15. *Sacharaja 1–8. KAT,* XIII/4 (1976), 124.

16. Cf. the "system of the winds" postulated by H. Gese, "Anfang und Ende der Apokalyptik, dargestellt am Sacharjabuch," *ZThK,* 70 (1973), 33f.

17. P. Humbert, *Recherches sur les sources égyptiennes de la littérature sapientiale d'Israel* (Neuchâtel, 1929), 98.

18. *AOT,* 194; cf. W. Zimmerli, *Das Buch des Predigers Salomo. ATD,* XVI/1 (^{3}1980), 226f.

19. Cf. Gradwohl, 73ff.

repentance) or as a denial of this possibility, stated in the form of a question. An unconditional promise would not fit the context; but the passage cannot be deleted as a late addition, since v. 18a requires a continuation. Since the interpretation of the text as a question (without an interrogative particle) expecting a negative answer presumes that the author wrote with almost deliberate obscurity, the interpretation as a conditional promise may be preferable.[20]

A similar figurative usage appears twice in Daniel. According to Dnl. 11:35, the tribulations under Antiochus Epiphanes are intended to refine (*ṣrp*) and cleanse (*brr*) the wise and "make them white" (pointed by the MT as a hiphil without *h,* but probably to be read as a piel: *l^elabbēn*). The same series of verbs appears again in 12:10, but with the hithpael of *brr* and *lbn* and the niphal of *ṣrp*.

The hiphil in Joel 1:7, however, is used literally to describe the vines eaten bare by the locusts: only the exposed white of their branches is left.

3. *Moon.* From *lāḇān* is derived *l^eḇānâ,* "the white lady," a term for the moon. The word appears 3 times in poetic texts (at least 2 of which are postexilic), always in conjunction with *ḥammâ,* "the hot lady," meaning the sun. Isa. 24:23 says: "The moon will be confounded (*ḥpr*), and the sun ashamed (*bôš*), for Yahweh has become king on Mount Zion." The *kāḇôḏ* of the divine king is so glorious that the light of the sun and the moon seems pale; they are ashamed that they can no longer serve as sources of light. Isa. 30:26 speaks of a day in the future when Yahweh will bind up the hurt of his people, and the sun and moon will increase in brilliance: "The light of the moon (*l^eḇānâ*) will be as the light of the sun, and the light of the sun will be sevenfold [stronger]." This notion contradicts Isa. 24:23, but both belong to the apocalyptic tradition.[21] Finally, Cant. 6:10 likens the beauty of the beloved to the moon and her purity to the sun.

Whether the personal name Laban (*lāḇān*; 52 occurrences in Genesis) is also based on an ancient epithet of the moon is disputed. According to Julius Lewy,[22] a divine name *La-ba-an* is found in Old Assyrian and Amorite personal names, but Herbert Huffmon[23] cites no such name. Lewy[24] also sees in *māt Laban*[25] a term for Lebanon; he sees in Laban a West Semitic deity worshipped in the land of Lebanon. All this remains hypothetical. Benjamin Mazar[26] considers Laban the eponymous ancestor of the Arameans. But it is also quite possible that "Laban" simply means "the white man."

In 1QapGen 20:4, *lbnh'* is used to describe the beauty of the matriarch Sarai, i.e., the "whiteness" of her skin.

---

20. O. Kaiser, *Isaiah 1–12. OTL* (Eng. trans. ²1983), 38.
21. Cf. O. Kaiser, *Isaiah 13–39. OTL* (Eng. trans. 1974), 195.
22. J. Lewy, "The Old West Semitic Sun-God Ḥammu," *HUCA,* 18 (1943/44), 434, n. 39.
23. *APNM.*
24. J. Lewy, "Le textes paléoassyriens et l'AT," *RHR,* 110 (1934), 44f.
25. *KAH,* I, 2 IV, 14.
26. B. Mazar, "The Aramean Empire and its Relations with Israel," *BA,* 25 (1962), 99.

III. LXX. The LXX generally uses forms of *leukós* or *leukaínein* to translate *lbn.* For *l^eḇēnâ,* it uses *plínthos, plintheía,* and *plinthourgía.*[27] For *l^eḇānâ,* it uses *selḗnē, leukótēs,* or the transliteration *Labaná.*

Ringgren

---

27. Cf. esp. J. P. Brown, "Literary Contexts of the Common Hebrew-Greek Vocabulary," *JSS,* 13 (1968), 182-84.

לְבֹנָה *l^eḇōnâ*

Contents: I.1. Etymology; Ancient Near East; 2. Occurrences. II. Frankincense in OT Sacrifice: 1. Incense Offering; 2. Other Offerings. III. Dead Sea Scrolls. IV. Medicinal Use. V. Toponyms. VI. Metaphorical Usage.

I. 1. *Etymology; Ancient Near East.* The Hebrew term *l^eḇōnâ* for frankincense, the resin of the tree *Boswellia carterii* Birdwood,[1] is a loanword deriving from OSA **libān,* "incense." W. W. Müller was able to determine "that in the dialects spoken today in the South Arabian *regio̧ turifera* a word in the form *libān* . . . is used for incense."[2] The various forms in the South Semitic and Cushitic languages[3] provide evidence, according to Müller, for an OSA noun vocalized as **libān,* meaning "incense." Contrary to *KBL*[3],[4] there is no evidence for an OSA *lbnt,* "incense." The form cited[5] is a toponym; since the region referred to in the text is far from the

---

l^eḇōnâ. E. G. C. F. Atchley, *A History of the Use of Incense in Divine Worship* (London, 1909); G. W. van Beek, "Frankincense and Myrrh," *BA,* 23 (1960), 70-95; *idem,* "Frankincense and Myrrh in Ancient South Arabia," *JAOS,* 78 (1958), 141-151; H. Bonnet, "Die Bedeutung der Räucherungen im ägyptischen Kult," *ZÄS,* 67 (1931), 20-28; H. von Fritze, *Die Rauchopfer bei den Griechen* (Berlin, 1894); K. Galling, "Incense Altar," *IDB,* II, 699f.; M. Haran, "The Uses of Incense in the Ancient Israelite Ritual," *VT,* 10 (1960), 113-129; F. N. Hepper, "Arabian and African Frankincense Trees," *JEA,* 55 (1969), 66-72; M. Löhr, *Das Räucheropfer im AT. SKG.G,* 4/4 (1927), 155-191; W. Michaelis, "λίβανος," *TDNT,* IV, 267f.; W. W. Müller, "Alt-Südarabien als Weihrauchland," *ThQ,* 149 (1969), 350-368; *idem,* "Weihrauch," *PWSup,* XV (1978), 700-777; *idem,* "Zur Herkunft von λίβανος und λιβανωτός," *Glotta,* 52 (1974), 53-59; E. Neufeld, "Hygiene Conditions in Ancient Israel (Iron Age)," *BA,* 34 (1971), 42-66, esp. 57-62; E. Pax, "Weihrauch," *LThK*[2], X (1965), 990-92; A. Vincent, *La Religion des Judéo-Araméens d'Éléphantine* (Paris, 1937), 212-223.

1. *BRL*[2], 138.
2. *Glotta,* 52 (1974), 55f.
3. Cited *ibid.*
4. P. 493a.
5. From *RÉS,* 3945, 11.

territories where the incense tree grows, the name probably derives from the color of a striking geological formation.[6] The noun **libān* derives from the common Semitic root *lbn,* "white, be white"; it probably means "milky incense resin" and is associated with the appearance of the incense grains rather than having anything to do with the appearance and color of the smoke that rises from the incense. Like Heb. *l^eḇōnâ,* the terms in other Semitic languages derive directly or indirectly from OSA **libān.*

Incense played an important role in Mesopotamian religious rituals.[7] Herodotus reports that a thousand talents worth of incense was offered each year in Babylonia; to further impress the reader, he adds that all the incense was offered at a single festival.[8] The word for incense (*labanātu, lub(b)unītu;*[9] also *lubbunū*[10]) nevertheless appears only in a few Late Babylonian and Neo-Babylonian texts, the reading of which is not entirely certain.

No Ugaritic cognate has yet been found; the noun *lbnt*[11] means "bricks" (but cf. *qṭr*).

The single instance in Punic occurs in a lost sacrificial tariff from Carthage,[12] containing the sequence *wqṭrt lbnt dqt.* The noun *qṭrt* can be interpreted as incense made from a mixture of ingredients; "powdered frankincense" (cf. Ex. 30:36: *šāḥaqtā . . . hāḏēq*) is mentioned separately.

The Imperial Aramaic occurrences[13] are found in the Elephantine papyri.[14] The context in each case is the sacrificial cult in the temple of the Jewish military colony at Elephantine. In all the passages, *lbwnh/lbwnt'* is closely associated with *mnḥh/mnḥt'.* It is therefore highly unlikely that there was a separate incense offering: instead, *mnḥh* is to be understood specifically as a "cereal offering" (cf. Lev. 2), and frankincense is the memorial (*'azkārâ*) portion burned as required by Lev. 2. The Syriac word for frankincense, *lḇottā'* (written *lbwnt'*),[15] is a Hebrew loanword. In Arabic, we find the form *luban,*[16] with regressive labialization of the first vowel.[17] Tigre *luban* (found only

---

6. Müller, *Glotta,* 52 (1974), 56f. The form *lbnhn* in *CIH,* 338, 8, probably means "two incense containers" (*ibid.*; *ThQ,* 149 [1969], 357f.).

7. See *BuA,* II, 75ff., 87ff., and *passim*; *qatāru*: *AHw,* II (1972), 907f.; *qutāru, qutrēnu*: *ibid.,* 930f.

8. *Hist.* i.183.

9. *AHw,* I (1965), 522; E. Ebeling, "Mittelassyrische Rezepte zur Bereitung von wohlreichenden Salben," *Or,* 17 (1948), 137.

10. *AHw,* I, 560.

11. *KTU,* 1.4 IV, 62; V, 11; VI, 35.

12. *KAI,* 76 B, 6.

13. Cf. Vincent.

14. *AP,* 30, 21, 25; 31, 21; 32, 9; 33, 11.

15. *LexSyr,* 357a.

16. *WKAS,* II, 172f.

17. Müller, *Glotta,* 52 (1974), 53-59.

in the dialect of Massaua, heavily influenced by Arabic)[18] and Mand. *lubānā*[19] derive from the Arabic form. The form *lbnt* in an inscription on the altar found at Tell ed-Duweir probably means "incense altar."[20]

Incense probably played an even more significant role in the Egyptian cult than in Mesopotamia. Its importance is illustrated by the word itself, *śnṯr,* which either derives from *śty-nṯr,* "divine fragrance,"[21] or employs the causative preformative, meaning "that which qualifies for intercourse with the deity."[22] Incense played an important role in the cult and in daily life as a means of purification and ornament. We also find the notion of incense as "perspiration of the deity falling to earth,"[23] endowed with quickening power. One who has died "lives on through incense," for burning incense imparts the strength of eternity and paves the way to the gods.[24] It is therefore easy to understand why both Hatshepsut (whose expedition to Punt, described in both word and picture [Deir el-Bahri], brought back thirty-one live incense trees in tubs) and Rameses III tried to transplant incense trees in Egypt, obviously with little success.[25]

All earlier attempts to derive the Semitic loanwords *líbanos,* "incense, incense tree," and *libanōtós,* "incense gum," NT "censer," from Heb. *l^eḇōnâ* or a similar Phoenician or Punic form suffered from the impossibility of ascribing the vocalization to any known phonetic laws. Secondary influences therefore had to be invoked, making the derivation unconvincing. Müller[26] was the first to solve the riddle, showing that *líbanos* was borrowed directly from OSA **libān.*

2. *Occurrences.* The noun *l^eḇōnâ* occurs 21 times in the OT: 9 times in P (Ex. 30:34; 7 times in Leviticus; Nu. 5:15); 3 each in the book of Isaiah (once in Deutero-Isaiah, twice in Trito-Isaiah), Jeremiah, and Song of Songs; Neh. 13:5,9; 1 Ch. 9:29; also Sir. 24:15; 39:14; 50:9. The relative paucity of occurrences cannot obscure the importance of incense in Palestine as well as throughout the ancient world. Pure, genuine frankincense was imported (from Sheba: Jer. 6:20; Isa. 60:6) and therefore both valuable and expensive (cf. Isa. 43:23). It is therefore quite likely that censing for cultic worship or for cosmetic or deodorizing purposes, attested archaeologically by the multitude of

---

18. *TigrWB,* 40a.
19. *MdD,* 232b.
20. Cf. R. Degen, "Der Raucheraltar aus Lachisch," *Neue Ephemeris für Semitische Epigraphik,* I (Wiesbaden, 1972), 39-48; A. Lemaire, "Un nouveau roi arabe de Qedar dans l'inscription de l'autel à encens de Lakish," *RB,* 81 (1974), 63-72; also W. F. Albright, "The Lachish Cosmetic Burner and Esther 2:12," *A Light unto My Feet. Festschrift J. M. Myers* (Philadelphia, 1974), 25-32.
21. *RÄR,* 625.
22. Löhr, 190.
23. *RÄR,* 625.
24. Cf. Bonnet; *RÄR,* 624-26.
25. See also D. M. Dixon, "The Transplantation of Punt Incense Trees in Egypt," *JEA,* 55 (1969), 55-65.
26. *Glotta,* 52 (1974), 53-59.

incense altars of various forms that have been discovered,[27] involved not pure frankincense but a mixture of aromatics[28] including frankincense or various surrogates. The use of incense was probably brought by Israel from Egypt.[29]

II. Frankincense in OT Sacrifice.

1. *Incense Offering.* Frankincense is one component of the aromatic mixture *qᵉṭōreṯ* used for the daily incense offering. The formula is given in Ex. 30:34-38: equal parts of *nāṭāp̄* (LXX and Vulg.), "stacte," the exudate of the shrub *Pistacia lentiscus*;[30] *šᵉḥēleṯ*, "incense claw," "onycha," made from the crushed operculum of the strombus conch; *ḥelbᵉnâ*, "galbanum," the resinous gum of an umbelliferous plant (*Ferula galbaniflua*); and pure frankincense (*lᵉḇōnâ zakkâ*; also Lev. 24:7) pulverized and mixed with salt. Every morning and evening (Ex. 30:7f.) the officiating priest is to offer some of this mixture on the incense altar by scattering it over glowing charcoal. Archaeological evidence indicates that the private use of incense (cf. Cant. 3:6, which mentions it as part of a festal procession) was common; it is even presupposed in Ex. 30:34ff., where the formula (cf. Sir. 24:15) is explicitly protected against profanation by the prohibition in Ex. 30:38: "Whoever makes any like it to use as perfume shall be cut off from his people." Later, up to twelve additional ingredients were added to the four required by Ex. 30:34.[31] According to Bab. *Yoma* 38a, the preparation of this substantially more extravagant mixture was a proprietary secret of the priestly family of Abṭīna.

2. *Other Offerings.* Frankincense in its raw form was required as part of the cereal offering.[32] It was put on top of the flour over which oil has been poured (Lev. 2:1). At the offering of firstfruits, oil and frankincense were also added to the parched new grain, as in the normal cereal offering (Lev. 2:15). The exact quantity is not stated. Probably the person offering the sacrifice could decide how much he wanted to add. Neh, 13:5,9 mention temple chambers where frankincense was stored; according to 1 Ch. 9:29, the Levites were in charge of the frankincense. We may conclude that the incense to be added could be purchased at the temple if the pilgrims coming to present their offerings did not bring any along, as described in Jer. 41:5; CD 11:19. The Talmud[33] states that only "oily priests" (*qmṣy šmyny*) may remove the measure of the

27. N. Glueck, "Incense Altars," *Translating and Understanding the OT. Festschrift H. G. May* (Nashville, 1970), 325-341; J. B. Pritchard, "An Incense Burner from Tell es-Saʿidiyeh, Jordan Valley," *Studies on the Ancient Palestinian World. Festschrift F. V. Winnett* (Toronto, 1970), 3-17; L. F. De Vries, *Incense Altars from the Period of the Judges and Their Significance* (diss., Southern Baptist Theological Seminary, 1975).

28. → קטרת *qᵉṭōreṯ*.

29. See above.

30. But cf. J. Feliks, "Stakte," *BHHW*, III (1966), 1851.

31. Cf. Bab. *Ker.* 6a,b.

32. K. Elliger, *Leviticus. HAT*, IV (1966), 38ff.

33. Bab. *Yoma* 47b.

cereal offering to be burned: the fingers of the priest who removes the handful must be pressed together to prevent grains of incense from falling through. This shows that even in the Roman period incense was not to be wasted. In a cereal offering, the incense is part of the *'azkārâ*[34] and is burned on the altar as *rêaḥ nîḥōaḥ* (Lev. 2:2,16; 6:8). Isa. 66:3, which speaks of offering incense as a memorial in parallel with blessing an idol, is obscure.[35] When *l^e^bōnâ* is mentioned together with *minḥâ,* we may assume that *minḥâ* is being used in the specialized sense of a cereal offering in its raw form, as in Jer. 17:26; Isa. 43:23, in contrast to *'ôlâ* and *zeḇaḥ*; and also Isa. 1:13, which uses the general term *q^e^ṭōreṯ,* "incense," instead of *l^e^ḇōnâ*; and finally Jer. 41:5; Neh. 13:5,9, where no animal sacrifices are mentioned.[36]

When a poor man offers a cereal offering as a sin offering because he cannot afford two doves, a tenth of an ephah of fine flour is required, without the additional oil and incense which Lev. 2 specifies for a cereal offering (5:11ff.). This exception may be considered an accommodation to prevent the need for incense from turning a concession to poverty into its opposite. In the cereal offering for jealousy (Nu. 5:15),[37] too, incense is not added to the woman's offering. This shows that this offering of the suspect woman was not a normal cereal offering, as is already clear from the fact that it consists of barley flour rather than wheat flour. It also shows that in a trial by ordeal, intended to determine guilt, no cathartic elements like incense could be employed.

The bread of the Presence was set out in two stacks, each containing six cakes. As in the cereal offering of Lev. 2, pure frankincense was put on top of each pile (Lev. 24:7). Again, the quantity is not stated; it probably depended on the current level of prosperity. Later the incense was kept in two golden bowls[38] until being burned as an *'azkārâ* to Yahweh (with the addition of salt according to the LXX) when the bread was replaced on the Sabbath.[39] A possible parallel to this association of bread and incense may be found in the phrase *lḥm qṭrt* in the Carthaginian sacrificial tariff;[40] its interpretation, however, is disputed.

Bar. 1:10 reports that the Jews in Babylon took up a collection for the temple cult in Jerusalem so that burnt offerings, sin offerings, and incense could be purchased; an addendum (text emended) adds cereal offerings. The latter was probably occasioned by the mention of incense, because Lev. 2 requires incense as part of the cereal offering. The list of sacrifices reflects their relative importance in the late period. This hierarchy, observable in P, is dominant in the Mishnah. The inclusion of incense also bears witness to its costliness.

---

34. H. Eising, → זכר *zāḵar* (*zākhar*), IV, 79ff.
35. See the discussion by G. J. Botterweck, → חזיר *ḥ^a^zîr* (*ch^a^zîr*), 297-99.
36. Cf. R. Rendtorff, *Studien zur Geschichte des Opfers im alten Israel. WMANT,* 24 (1967), 191.
37. Cf. D. Kellermann, *Die Priesterschrift von Numeri 1_1 bis 10_{10}. BZAW,* 120 (1970), 70ff.
38. Bab. *Menaḥ.* 96a.
39. Elliger, 328f.
40. *KAI,* 76 B, 3; see also M. Haran, *Temples and Temple-Service in Ancient Israel* (Oxford, 1978), 230-245.

III. Dead Sea Scrolls. The Damascus document mentions *lbwnh* twice (CD 11:4,19), in different contexts. CD 11:19 prohibits having a burnt offering, a cereal offering, incense, or wood brought to the altar by someone who is unclean. The pairing of cereal offering and incense shows that incense is a necessary part of the cereal offering, so that Lev. 2 is in the background. Unless we assume that Qumran had its own altar at some point in time, we can only conclude that 11:19 enshrines an earlier regulation whose practical application was not open to debate, or else dates from a time when the members of the Qumran community still participated in the sacrificial cult at Jerusalem or at least sent offerings to the temple. CD 11:4 includes among the rules governing the Sabbath the statement that dirty garments or garments stored in a chamber may be worn only after having been washed with water or scoured (*šwpym*) with incense. The latter probably refers to a bit of apotropaic magic,[41] in which a piece of incense gum was rubbed over the garment. Possibly, however, the text represents a misunderstanding of an original requirement that the garment be hung in the smoke of burning incense.

The Temple scroll diverges from rabbinic tradition when it speaks[42] of the ritual of putting incense on the bread of the Presence (cf. Lev. 24:7).[43] 11QT 20:10 mentions a cereal offering at the vintage festival. As in the OT offering of firstfruits (Lev. 2:15), the inclusion of incense is required. 11QT 38:8 is obscure.

IV. Medicinal Use. The medicinal use of incense is attested in many formulas given by Hippocrates, Galen, Celsus, Dioscurides, etc.[44] It is also recorded in Bab. *Sanh.* 43a: wine mixed with incense is used as a narcotic for someone being led to execution. Wine mixed with incense was assumed to have an intoxicating effect on the elephants that were to trample the Jews in the stadium at Alexandria (3 Mc. 5:2,10,45).

V. Toponyms. The word for incense is also found in the toponym $l^e\underline{b}\bar{o}n\hat{a}$ (Jgs. 21:19).[45] The desert camp *libnâ* (so vocalized by the MT in Nu. 33:20f.) reappears in Dt. 1:1 as *lāḇān*.[46] The Samaritan Pentateuch and LXX^A, as well as the "Libona"[47] that may be identified with the Syrian "incense monastery" Deir da-Lbotta,[48] suggest that the name may refer to a stopping place on the incense route or a common transshipment point for this costly substance.

41. Cf. O. Keel, "Kanaanäische Sühneriten auf ägyptischen Tempelreliefs," *VT,* 25 (1975), 413-469, esp. 424-436.
42. 11QT 8:10,12.
43. Cf. also 2Q24 fr. 4:8,14.
44. W. W. Müller, *Deutsche Apotheker-Zeitung,* 117 (1977), 174.
45. G. Kampffmeyer, "Alte Namen im heutigen Palästina und Syrien, Theil II — Vorbemerkungen," *ZDPV,* 16 (1893), 47f.; for a different interpretation, see H. Bauer, "Die hebräischen Eigennamen als sprachliche Erkenntnisquelle," *ZAW,* 48 (1930), 74.
46. See S. Mittmann, *Deuteronomium* 1_1–6_3. *BZAW,* 139 (1975), 8ff., 17.
47. *Notitia dignitatum* 80, 27.
48. Müller, *Glotta,* 52 (1974), 58.

VI. Metaphorical Usage. In Cant. 4:6, the mountain of myrrh and hill of frankincense (*giḇʿaṯ hallᵉḇônâ*) may represent the breasts of the bride, if they do not stand for topographical entities[49] or even the temple mount.[50] According to Mt. 2:11, gold, frankincense, and myrrh were the tribute brought by the Magi.[51]

Sir. 24:15 compares wisdom to various aromatics, concluding with the "odor of incense in the tabernacle" (NRSV); in other words, wisdom takes part in the cult. The comparison of the prayers of the faithful to incense whose perfume rises up before God (Ps. 141:2; Rev. 5:8; 8:3) is found also in Sir. 39:14, where the command "Praise Yahweh" probably stands in parallel with "send forth fragrance like incense" (*wklbwnh ttnw ryḥ*). The image continues on in Paul Gerhardt's poetry: "hymns of praise are incense and rams."

Kellermann

49. G. Gerleman, *Das Hohelied. BK,* XVIII (1965), 150.
50. Pax.
51. Cf. G. Ryckmans, "De l'or(?), de l'encens et de la myrrhe," *RB,* 58 (1951), 372-76; citing OSA *ḏhb,* a type of incense, Ryckmans identifies the gifts as three types of aromatic.

לְבָנוֹן *lᵉḇānôn*

Contents: I. Location, Extrabiblical Usage, Etymology. II. OT: 1. Linguistic Usage; 2. Geography; 3. Economic Significance; 4. Literary and Theological Significance. III. Late Jewish Tradition.

lᵉḇānôn. F.-M. Abel, *Géographie de la Palestine,* I (Paris, 1933), 340-44; Y. Aharoni, "לְבָנוֹן," *EMiqr,* IV (1962), 425-430; T. Bauer, "Ein viertes altbabylonisches Fragment des Gilgameš-Epos," *JNES,* 16 (1957), 254-262; J. P. Brown, *The Lebanon and Phoenicia,* I: *The Physical Setting and the Forest* (Beirut, 1969); H. Donner, *Einführung in die biblische Landes- und Altertumskunde* (Darmstadt, 1976); W. B. Fisher, *The Middle East* (London, ⁶1971), 381-84, 403-6; R. Giveon, "Libanon," *LexÄg,* III (1980), 1013f.; A. Gustavs, "Die syrischen Berge Šá-ri-ja-na und Bi-i-šá-i-šá in den Boghazköi-Texten," *ZAW,* 42 (1924), 154f.; H. Guthe, "Libanon," *RE,* XI, 433-38; W. Helck, *Die Beziehungen Ägyptens zu Vorderasien im 3. und 2. Jahrtausend v. Chr. ÄgAbh,* 5 (1962), col. 277; P. K. Hitti, *History of Syria including Lebanon and Palestine* (New York, 1951); E. Honigmann, "Libanos," *PW,* XIII/1 (1926), 1-11; H. Klengel, "Der Libanon und seine Zedern in der Geschichte des Alten Vorderen Orients," *Das Altertum,* 13 (1967), 67-76; E. Lipiński, " 'Garden of abundance, image of Lebanon,' " *ZAW,* 85 (1973), 358f.; F. Stolz, "Die Bäume des Gottesgartens auf dem Libanon," *ZAW,* 84 (1972), 141-156; H. Treidler, "Libanos," *KlPauly,* III (1969), 615f.; G. Vermès, " 'Car le Liban c'est le conseil de communauté,' " *Mélanges Bibliques. Festschrift A. Robert. Travaux de l'Institut Catholique de Paris,* 4 (1957), 316-325; *idem, Scripture and Tradition in Judaism. StPb,* 4 (1961), esp. 26-39; *idem,* "The Symbolic Interpretation of *Lebanon* in the Targums," *JTS,* N.S. 9 (1958), 1-12.

I. Location, Extrabiblical Usage, Etymology. The western mountain range in what is today the Republic of Lebanon is about 160 kilometers (100 mi.) long and rises more than 3,000 meters (9,800 ft.) above sea level.[1] This range was already called "Lebanon" in antiquity,[2] although it is not always clear whether the term included the Anti-Lebanon range to the east together with the Beqaʿ valley in between, and also whether it included Mount Hermon. As late as the Roman period, some geographers were misinformed about the length and orientation of the Lebanon range, as we see in Strabo's statement[3] that the Lebanon and Anti-Lebanon are parallel ranges, with the Lebanon beginning at Theouprosopon, not far from Tripoli, and the Anti-Lebanon at Sidon.[4] On the other hand, written evidence from Israel and its environs shows that the Lebanon was often distinguished clearly from the Anti-Lebanon and Hermon. The Ugaritic texts, for example, like Ps. 29:6 later, speak of *lbnn* and *šryn* together.[5] Although opinions differ as to whether *šryn* refers to the Anti-Lebanon (possibly including Hermon[6]) or to Hermon alone, *lbnn* is probably to be thought of as denoting the portion of the central Syrian mountains still referred to today by the same name.[7] This interpretation is confirmed by a cuneiform text from Boghazköy, in which a treaty names as witnesses $^{HUR.SAG}$*la-ab-la-ni*, $^{HUR.SAG}$*ša-ri-ya-na*, and $^{HUR.SAG}$*bi-i-šá-i-šá*.[8] A similar passage occurs in a Hittite translation of another treaty.[9] The reference is undoubtedly to the mountains Lebanon and Sirion. An Old Babylonian fragment of the Gilgamesh epic published by Theo Bauer contains the names Saria and Labnana together.[10]

Referring to the Lebanon, besides Hitt. *niblani/a* and *lablani/a*,[11] Akk. *labnānu/i/a* (esp. in the royal inscriptions),[12] Ugar. *lbnn* (cf. Syr. *lbnn* and Old Pers. *la-b-na-a-na*[13]), and Gk. *Líbanos óros*,[14] we find Egyp. *rmnn*,[15] written once *r-bꜣ-n-ꜣ* in the story of Wen-amon. The texts from the third and second millennia as well as the later texts of the Babylonians and Assyrians show that the Lebanon was a major source of wood for

---

1. For further description, see Aharoni, 425f.; Fisher; Hitti, 32-37; cf. Treidler.
2. Cf. Eusebius *Onomasticon* 122, 27: *Líbanos óros Phoiníkēs epiphanés.*
3. *Geography* xvi.2.16ff.
4. Cf. Honigmann, 7; Brown, 28-32.
5. *KTU*, 1.4 VI, 18ff.
6. See II.2 below.
7. In the Ugaritic texts, *lbnn* also appears in *KTU*, 1.17 VI, 21; 1.22 I, 20, 25; 4.65, 4.
8. Gustavs, 154.
9. *Ibid., in loc.*
10. Bauer, 256; cf. 260.
11. Cf. also Honigmann, 1; A. Jirku, "Der Baʿal Lebanon in den keilschrifturkunden von Boghazköj," *OLZ*, 26 (1923), 4f.; O. Eissfeldt, "Der Gott des Tabor und seine Verbreitung," *KlSchr*, II (1963), 48f.
12. *ARAB*, *passim*; *ANET*, index; S. Parpola, *Neo-Assyrian Toponyms*. *AOAT*, 6 (1970), 221f.
13. F. W. König, *Der Burgbau zu Susa*. *MVÄG*, 35/1 (1930), 32.
14. E. Honigmann, "Historische Topographie von Nordsyrien im Altertum," *ZDPV*, 47 (1924), 11.
15. *WbÄS*, II, 421; R. O. Faulkner, *A Concise Dictionary of Middle Egyptian* (Oxford, 1962), 149; A. Gardiner, *Ancient Egyptian onomastica*, I (Oxford, 1947), 172*f.

temples, ships, etc.[16] Even in prehistoric Egyptian tombs archaeologists have found coniferous wood that may have come from the Lebanon. Egyptian texts frequently mention *mrw* and above all *'š* wood, although the precise identification of these kinds of wood is still problematical.[17] Scholars generally agree that *rmnn* (from the period of the eighteenth-twentieth dynasties) is a Semitic loanword for *lᵉḇānôn,* comparable to the *rbrn* or *la-bí-ra-na* of the story of Wen-amon.[18]

The most commonly accepted etymology of *lᵉḇānôn* associates it with the root *lbn,* "white,"[19] with the suf. *-ānu* > *-ôn.*[20] Julius Lewy, however, is of the opinion that in the word we find an epithet of the moon-god Laban, with *labnânu* deriving by syncope from *laban* + *ân(um).*[21] A euhemeristic legend derives the name of the mountains from that of a giant.[22] There is more support for the first of these etymologies than for the second, because the "white snow" (cf. Jer. 18:14; Tacitus[23]) can be thought of as suggesting the name; cf. "Mont Blanc" or the "White Mountains."[24] The rock of this range, however, cannot be called white.[25]

Another possible etymology may possibly be found in the Hittite and Hurrian group of languages. Hitt. $^{ḪUR.SAG}$*lablana,* "Lebanon Mountains," is identical with Hurr. *lablaḫḫi*[26] and *laḫlaḫḫi.*[27] The appearance of these words in parallel with the words for "cypress" and "juniper" suggests that they likewise refer primarily to some kind of tree.[28] If so, the only reasonable candidate is the cedar.

II. OT.

1. *Linguistic Usage.* The noun *lᵉḇānôn* occurs 71 times in the OT: Dt. 1:7; 3:25; 11:24; Josh. 1:4; 9:1; 11:17; 12:7; 13:5f.; Jgs. 3:3; 9:15; 1 K. 5:13,20,23,28(Eng. 4:33;

---

16. Honigmann, 2; Klengel.

17. See, e.g., H. A. Ducros, "L'arbre *ash* des anciens Égyptiens," *ASAE,* 14 (1914), 1-12; V. Loret, "Quelques notes sur l'arbre *âch,*" *ASAE,* 16 (1916), 33-51; Helck, 28ff.; B. Couroyer, "La terre du Dieu," *RB,* 78 (1971), 69f.; *idem,* "Sapin vrai et sapin nouveau," *Or,* 42 (1973), 339-356.

18. Jirku, 5; *WbÄS,* II, 414; Gardiner, I, 172*f.; etc. G. Daressy, "Lieu d'origine de l'arbre *âch,*" *ASAE,* 25-28, suggests that *rmnn* should be identified with Hermil, the northern part of the Lebanon in the valley of the Orontes.

19. See the lexica; Honigmann, 4; Abel, 340; Brown, 88; etc.

20. See, e.g., Gardiner, *in loc.*; W. Borée, *Die alten Ortsnamen Palästinas* (Leipzig, ²1968), 59.

21. J. Lewy, "The Old West Semitic Sun-God Ḥammu," *HUCA,* 18 (1943/44), 455f.; *idem,* "Zur Amoriterfrage," *ZA,* N.S. 4[38] (1929), 266f.

22. Cf. Philo Byblius as cited by Eusebius *Praep. ev.* i.10.9 (K. Mras ed., 45); Honigmann, 8.

23. *Hist.* v.7.

24. Brown, xxxv.

25. An etymology still proposed by S. Schulz (in *GesTh, s.v.* לבנון).

26. *KBo,* XX, 126, r. 11, 2f.

27. *Ibid.,* 129, r. 11, 4.

28. Cf. V. Haas and H. J. Thiel, "Ein Beitrag zum hurritischen Wörterbuch," *Festschrift C. F. A. Schaeffer. UF,* 11 (1979), 343f.

5:6,9,14)(twice); 7:2; 9:19; 10:17,21; 2 K. 14:9(3 times); 19:23; 2 Ch. 2:7(8)(twice),15(16); 8:6; 9:16,20; 25:18(3 times); Ezr. 3:7; Ps. 29:5f.; 72:16; 92:13(12); 104:16; Cant. 3:9; 4:8(twice),11,15; 5:15; 7:5(4); Isa. 2:13; 10:34; 14:8; 29:17; 33:9; 35:2; 37:24; 40:16; 60:13; Jer. 18:14; 22:6,20,23; Ezk. 17:3; 27:5; 31:3,15f.; Hos. 14:6-8(5-7); Nah. 1:4; Hab. 2:17; Zec. 10:10; 11:1. There are also 2 occurrences in the Hebrew text of Sirach (Sir. 50:8,12). Only once (Dt. 3:25) is it written with defective orthography.[29] In the historical books it almost always appears with the article (exception: 2 Ch. 2:7[8]); the article sometimes appears in the poetic and prophetic books (compare Isa. 14:8 with Ps. 29:5). Only once is *l^eḇānônâ* found (1 K. 5:28). The name appears frequently in the construct as *nomen rectum* or is introduced by a preposition. It is rarely used as the subject of a clause (e.g., Isa. 29:17) or as a vocative (Zec. 11:1).

2. *Geography.* The geopolitical importance of the Lebanon for Israel is especially clear in the historical books. Occasionally — particularly in idealizing sections (Dt. 1:7; 3:25; 11:24; Josh. 1:4; 11:17; etc.) — it is described as belonging to the land of Israel or at least constituting its northern boundary. One passage (1 K. 9:19 par. 2 Ch. 8:6; cf. also Cant. 7:5[4]) even suggests that King Solomon built there. This statement can be compared to the LXX text of 3 K. 2:46c, which says that Solomon *ḗrxato dianoígein tà dynasteúmata toú Libánou.*[30] The expression *tà dynasteúmata* may refer to mines.[31] At the least, these texts stress that Solomon, like his father before him (2 S. 5:11), maintained close relationships with Hiram, the king of Tyre, for help in his building program (1 K. 5:20,23,28[6,9,14]; 2 Ch. 2:7,15[8,16]). Even in the postexilic period, wood from the Lebanon for the temple was still transported along the coast on Tyrian rafts (Ezr. 3:7), as was the practice in the time of Solomon.[32] Other rulers in the ancient Near East did the same.[33] In Jerusalem, we are told, Solomon built the "House of the Forest of Lebanon" (1 K. 7:2f.; 10:17,21 par. 2 Ch. 9:16,20; cf. also Isa. 22:8; Jer. 22:23), possibly made entirely of cedar. At first it probably served as a royal reception hall; later it was used as an arsenal.[34]

The economic importance[35] of the fertile and well-watered Lebanon as a source of wood and minerals (copper and iron[36]) attracted the great powers of the ancient Near East, making the Phoenician coast an international battlefield; it also induced the Israel of the monarchy to expand by sending expeditions to the north. We get the impression from 1 K. 9:19 par. 2 Ch. 8:6 that Solomon exercised de facto power in the Lebanon,

---

29. But see the apparatus of *BHK, in loc.*; also *LexHebAram, s.v.* לבנון on Isa. 2:13.

30. Cf. Guthe, 436; Aharoni, 429; etc.

31. But see Brown, 87.

32. Klengel, 75f.

33. Honigmann, 3f.

34. See M. J. Mulder, "Einige Bemerkungen zur Beschreibung des Libanonwaldhauses in 1 Reg $7_{2f.}$," *ZAW,* 88 (1976), 99-105.

35. See II.3 below.

36. Honigmann, 4; and esp. Brown, 87-104.

and from the Deuteronomistic texts that in Solomon's time Israel put forward a de jure claim to the mountains. It is not clear, however, how the biblical writers defined the Lebanon. Dt. 1:7 would suggest that it was roughly equivalent to the modern state of Lebanon, possibly minus the Phoenician coastal plain.[37] Here and in Dt. 3:25; 11:24; Josh 1:4; 9:11, the LXX reads "Antilebanon" (distinguished from the Lebanon in Jth. 1:7). The book of Joshua uses the phrase *biqʿaṯ hallᵉḇānôn* (cf. Dt. 8:7),[38] which J. J. Simons claims can refer only to the southern part of the Beqaʿ, the Merj ʿAyūn,[39] along with other names: *hāhār heḥālāq* (Josh. 11:17; 12:7) in the south (Jebel Ḥalāq, "the bald mountain"[40]), and Baal-gad (cf. 13:5) "below Mount Hermon" (11:17; 13:5), which Simons identifies with Tell Ḥauš. The *har baʿal ḥermôn* of Jgs. 3:3 is occasionally identified with Baal-gad.[41] The same verse speaks of the Lebanon mountains as the dwelling place of the Hivites.[42]

In Josh. 13:5, *kol-hallᵉḇānôn* "in the east" (or: "toward the sunrising") probably means not just the Antilebanon but the entire Lebanon range, including Hermon and the Antilebanon (cf. v. 6). In this and a few other OT texts (cf. also LXX Sir. 24:13), "Lebanon" is thus a general term encompassing the whole mountainous area, the various parts of which we commonly call by different names today. Whenever the OT uses the term *lᵉḇānôn,* we have to determine whether it refers to the mountain in the narrow sense or the whole central Syrian range. Cant. 4:8, a poetic verse that describes the enticing descent of the bride from Lebanon, speaks of Lebanon twice in conjunction with Hermon, Amana, and Senir. Does *lᵉḇānôn* here refer to the entire range, of which Amana, Senir, and Hermon are individual crests? The noun *ʾᵃmānâ* might denote the southern slope of the Taurus range[43] or Jebel Zebedāni in the Antilebanon,[44] where one of the rivers of Damascus mentioned in the OT has its source (2 K. 5:12). Here and in 1 Ch. 5:23, *śᵉnîr* (Dt. 3:9; 1 Ch. 5:23; Ezk. 27:5) is distinguished from Hermon; it may denote the Antilebanon,[45] although Dt. 3:9 says that the Amorites identified it with Hermon.[46] In Ezk. 27:5, *śᵉnîr* is clearly distinguished from the Lebanon; as in Akkadian inscriptions, it refers to the northern portion of the Antilebanon.[47] According to Dt. 3:9, finally, *ḥermôn* (Dt. 3:8f.; 4:48; Josh. 11:3,17; 12:1,5; 13:5,11; 1 Ch. 5:23; Ps. 42:7[6] [pl.]; 89:13[12]; 133:3) was also called *śiryōn* (Ugar. *šryn;* Hitt. *ša-ri-ia-na*) by the Phoenicians (cf. Ps. 29:6). Here we may be dealing with a variant name for the southern part of the Anti-

---

37. *GTTOT,* §275.
38. Cf. Brown, 60, n. 2; also Guthe, 437.
39. *GTTOT,* §509.
40. *GTTOT.*
41. See M. J. Mulder, *Baʿal in het OT* (Hague, 1962), 149.
42. See, however, G. F. Moore, *Judges. ICC* (1895), 79, 81; cf. also Josh. 11:3.
43. O. Loretz, *Studien zur althebräischen Poesie,* I: *Das althebräische Liebeslied. AOAT,* 14/1 (1971), 29, n. 7.
44. *GTTOT,* §9; Abel, 347; cf. Brown, 22, n. 3.
45. *GTTOT,* §228: *Jebel eš-Šerqi*; cf. Abel, 344ff.
46. Cf. also H. Bauer, "Al-Muštarī," *OLZ,* 38 (1935), 477.
47. Guthe, 438.

lebanon,[48] not necessarily identical with Hermon.[49] Such texts as Ps. 29:6; Cant. 4:8; Ezk. 27:5 make it clear that the literature of the OT occasionally uses *l^eb̲ānôn* in its narrower sense.

3. *Economic Significance.* The wealth and power of the Phoenician cities derived from the forests of the Lebanon (cf. Ezk. 27:5). In particular, the timber used in building temples, palaces, etc., gave the Lebanon its economic importance.[50] The wood transported from the Lebanon by the Egyptians, Assyrians,[51] Israelites, etc., was not just — or even primarily — cedar, but included such species as fir and pine. Although the word *'erez,* which the OT often associates with the Lebanon, is usually translated "cedar," it more likely refers generically to the conifers of the diverse Lebanon flora than specifically to the Lebanon cedar.[52] Ezk. 31, for example, mentions other species of trees in the Lebanon. In the garden of God, besides "cedars" (*'^arāzîm*) we find junipers (*b^erôšîm*)[53] and plane trees (*'armōnîm*) (Ezk. 31:8; cf. vv. 3, 15f.). Only the cedars, however, are described as "cedars of Lebanon";[54] they even take on cosmic dimensions.[55] The juniper, frequently mentioned in the OT (almost always in conjunction with *'^arāzîm*[56]) is also found in the Lebanon (2 K. 19:23 par. Isa. 37:24; Isa. 14:8; 60:13; Zec. 11:2; cf. 1 K. 5:24[10]; Ps. 104:17[? *b^erôšîm*]; Hos. 14:9[8]; etc.); it, too, was used in construction (1 K. 5:22,24[8,10]; 6:15,34; etc.). In Isa. 60:13, it is not the *'^arāzîm* that are singled out as *k^eb̲ôd̲ hall^eb̲ānôn* (cf. 35:2), but the *b^erôš, tid̲hār* (only here and 41:19), and *t^e'aššûr* (only here and 41:19; Ezk. 27:6 conj.; 31:3 conj.). The identity of these trees is not entirely clear. Possibly *tid̲hār* is a conifer, perhaps a fir or pine, and *t^e'aššûr* a box-tree or cypress.[57] In 2 Ch. 2:7(8), an elaboration of 1 K. 5:20(6), Solomon asks the king of Tyre to send him *'^aṣê '^arāzîm* from the Lebanon; the text then specifies *b^erôšîm* and *'algûmmîm.* The latter word, also written *'almuggîm* (1 K. 10:11f.; also 2 Ch. 9:10f.; Cant. 3:10 conj.), refers to a kind of timber imported from Ophir.[58] Some scholars have suggested sandalwood, but it was not native to the Lebanon.[59] Instead of *'^aṣê '^arāzîm,* etc., 1 K. 5:20(6) reads simply *'^arāzîm,* which the LXX translates as *xýla.*[60] The immense economic significance of the Lebanon for Israelite construction during the time of Solomon is illustrated, for example, by 1 K. 5:29(15):

48. See, e.g., Abel, 345, n. 5.
49. *GTTOT,* §108: *Jebel eṭ-Ṭelǵ* or *Jebel eš-Šeiḫ.*
50. Klengel; H. Mayer, "Das Bauholz des Tempels Salomos," *BZ,* N.S. 11 (1967), 53-66.
51. A. Salonen, "Holz," *RLA,* IV (1972-75), 453f.
52. See the lexica. *s.v.*; "אֶרוּסִין," *EMiqr,* I (1955), 553-55: *cedrus libani.*
53. Loretz, 11, n. 7.
54. Cf. Stolz, Lipiński.
55. See II.4 below.
56. K. Elliger, *Deuterojesaja. BK,* XI/3 (1971), 167.
57. See W. Zimmerli, *Ezekiel 2. Herm* (Eng. trans. 1983), 141f.
58. See also M. Noth, *Könige 1–16. BK,* IX/1 (1968), 227.
59. *KBL*[3], 56; cf. J. Feliks, "Sandelholz," *BHHW,* III (1960), 1667f.
60. J. W. Wevers, "Exegetical Principles underlying the Septuagint Text of 1 Kings 11 12–xxi 43," *OTS,* 8 (1950), 302, calls this translation a "rationalization."

besides many thousands of burden-bearers and overseers, Solomon sent eighty thousand (!) woodcutters to the Lebanon. As later when the postexilic temple was being built in Jerusalem (Ezr. 3:7; cf. LXX 1 Esd. 4:48; 5:53), the Phoenicians were richly compensated. Probably the single word *'ᵃrāzîm* sometimes referred generally to the abundant conifers of the Lebanon. An even more general term for the flora is *'ᵃṣê hallᵉḇānôn* (Cant. 3:9), which may have included thorny scrub such as *ḥôaḥ* (2 K. 14:9).

The Lebanon mountains were famous in Israel not only for their timber but also for their wine (Hos. 14:8[7]).[61]

4. *Literary and Theological Significance.* Occasionally an unmistakable Canaanite-Phoenician substratum appears in prophetic and poetic texts (like Ps. 29) that use the name "Lebanon." It is mentioned above all in connection with nature — the trees, animals, and plants of the mountains — especially in metaphors and similes. This usage suggests that the Lebanon either made a deep impression on the ancient Israelites or encouraged them to draw on common Canaanite idioms for their metaphors. The "cedars" of the Lebanon were especially popular in fables and similes, as we see from Jgs. 9:15;[62] 2 K. 14:9 par. 2 Ch. 25:18;[63] Ezk. 17:3. A simile in Jer. 18:14 speaks of the snow of the Lebanon; 22:6 compares the king to its summit. In the latter chapter, the Lebanon already clearly symbolizes the king's palace of cedar (v. 23).[64] One tradition (1 K. 5:13[4:33]) records that some of Solomon's poetry described the Lebanon trees. In some of the fables mentioned above, these trees are personified and speak. Some scholars explain these passages as reflecting a primitive animism.[65] This theory is mistaken: we are dealing instead with a literary commonplace. The cosmic Lebanon cedar envied by all the trees of Eden (Ezk. 31:9,16,18) is a different matter: it is probably rooted in Canaanite mythology, and can be used to symbolize the (fallen) power of the Egyptian king.[66]

Not just the cedars of the Lebanon but the mountains themselves can represent creation in Canaanite tradition. In Ps. 104, "Lebanon" is the only geographical name (v. 16); it points to Phoenicia as the psalm's place of origin or as a link between Israel and Egypt.[67] Here the LXX translates *'ᵃṣê YHWH* as *tá xýla toú pedíou,* possibly reflecting an original text with the divine name *šaddai.*[68] This psalm combines motifs from Phoenician mythology with images from Akhenaten's hymn to the sun. Similarly, the Assyrian king Sennacherib boasts: "With my many chariots I have gone up the

---

61. On libations of wine in the region, see J. C. de Moor, *The Seasonal Patterns in the Ugaritic Myth of Ba'lu. AOAT,* 16 (1971), 79; also Fisher, 405.

62. Cf. Josephus *Ant.* vii.2 (236ff.).

63. On this parable, see also E. Jenni, "Distel und Zeder: Hermeneutische Überlegungen zu 2 Kö 14:8-14," *Studia Biblica et Semitica. Festschrift T. C. Vriezen* (Wageningen, 1966), 165-175.

64. See II.2 above.

65. See W. Robertson Smith, *Lectures on the Religion of the Semites* (New York, [3]1927, repr. 1969), 133; Brown, 164.

66. See Stolz; Brown, 167-172.

67. Smith, 103; Brown, 23-27.

68. Brown, 27, n. 6.

heights of the mountains, to the far recesses of the Lebanon; I felled its tallest cedars, its choicest cypresses" (2 K. 19:23 par. Isa. 37:24).[69] His words impugn God's power over the Lebanon, the symbol of his creation.

The notion of a Lebanon cedar as a "cosmic tree" or "tree of paradise," which can be identified with the "king of the universe," is be associated with rulers other than Pharaoh (Ezk. 31).[70] In Isa. 10:28-34, the prophet depicts the destruction of the Assyrians in words describing the felling of the gigantic trees of the Lebanon: *w*^e*hall*^e*ḇānôn b*^e*'addîr yippôl.* (We shall ignore the problem of the mysterious *'addîr.*[71]) Using language only slightly different, Zec. 11:1-3 also describes the destruction of the world powers. Here the Lebanon is summoned to open its doors — i.e., its passes[72] — that fire may devour its cedars, while "the pride of Assyria" is laid low and "the scepter of Egypt" must depart (10:11). In describing the felling of the Lebanon cedars, the prophets were probably not still thinking consciously of a "cosmic tree"; their language, however, bears a mythological stamp.

The trees of the Lebanon often symbolize all kinds of pride and arrogance, which God attacks to bring down (Isa. 2:13; 10:34). This applies especially to the Israelite kings, who built palaces of Lebanon cedar and lived in them like nests (Jer. 22:6,20,23). Other metaphors can speak of such trees as rejoicing — for example, because the Assyrian emperor has fallen and the world can dwell in peace and safety (Isa. 14:8). This image recalls the Old Babylonian fragment of Gilgamesh, which tells how Enkidu and Gilgamesh slay the guardian of the cedar forests of the Lebanon, bringing peace to the Lebanon and Antilebanon.[73] The lively interest of the Assyrians in the Lebanon and its forests is illustrated clearly by 2 K. 19:23 (par. Isa. 37:24), discussed above. Hab. 2:17 suggests that under Nebuchadnezzar the Babylonians, too, harvested cedars and possibly massacred wildlife in the Lebanon.[74]

Isa. 33:9; Nah. 1:4f. illustrate the devastation that humans or the forces of nature could inflict on the beauty of the Lebanon mountains. The latter text may refer to the destruction caused by an earthquake.[75] An earthquake (together with other natural phenomena) is often a sign of a theophany.[76] This is clear also in Ps. 29, where the geographical names are all Syro-Phoenician.[77] Here God is manifested in full glory, so

---

69. → יער *ya'ar,* IV.

70. See also H. Gressmann, *Der Messias. FRLANT,* N.S. 26[43] (1929), 266f.

71. See also III below.

72. Brown, 165, n. 1.

73. See Bauer; also H. P. Müller, "Gilgameschs Trauergesang um Enkidu und die Gattung der Totenklage," *ZA,* N.S. 34[68] (1978), 245f.

74. For a different interpretation, see W. Rudolph, *Habakuk. KAT,* XIII/3 (1975), 228.

75. On earthquakes in this area, see Brown, 113-139.

76. See also D. L. Christensen, "The Acrostic of Nahum Reconsidered," *ZAW,* 87 (1975), 21ff.

77. Besides the comms., see N. H. Ridderbos, "Enkele aspecten van Psalm 29," *GThT,* 60 (1960), 64-69; P. C. Craigie, "Psalm XXIX in the Hebrew poetic tradition," *VT,* 22 (1972), 143-151; A. Fitzgerald, "A Note on Psalm 29," *BASOR,* 215 (1974), 61-63; for structural analysis, see D. N. Freedman and C. Franke-Hyland, "Psalm 29," *HThR,* 66 (1973), 237-256;

that "the voice of Yahweh . . . breaks the cedars of the Lebanon. He makes the Lebanon to skip like a calf, and Sirion like a young wild ox" (Ps. 29:5f.).

A different manifestation of God is described in Ezk. 31:15: when Pharaoh descends to the realm of the dead, God restrains the rivers so that the Lebanon mourns and all its vegetation withers. Yahweh — not some Baʿal of the Lebanon — governs the forces of nature that rule the Lebanon. Even its cedars were planted by Yahweh (Ps. 104:16; cf. 80:11[10]). And when Mount Zion mourns, the Lebanon, too, is wretched (*'umlal*: Isa. 33:9; Nah. 1:4).[78] The description of Zion's future glory as *k^e^bôd hall^e^bānôn* shows that Zion continued to be associated with the Lebanon in prophetic discourse (Isa. 60:13; cf. 35:2).[79]

The Lebanon and its cedars — as symbols of majesty and power — appear in descriptions not only of kings and empires, but also of individuals. Ps. 92:13(12) states that the righteous will grow "like a cedar upon the Lebanon"; Ps. 37:35 describes the wicked as overbearing, "towering like a cedar." The LXX adds "in the Lebanon"; the concordance of Hatch and Redpath inadvertently omits this verse under *Líbanos*. Sir. 50:8 (likewise omitted by the concordance) compares the high priest Simon to "the flowers of the Lebanon in the days of summer" (cf. Nah. 1:4); "a garland of sons surrounded him like young cedars upon the Lebanon" (Sir. 50:12: Heb. *š^e^tîlê hall^e^bānôn* [cf. Ps. 128:3]; Gk. *blástēma kédrōn*). Sir. 24:13 sings the praises of personified Wisdom: "like a cedar upon the Lebanon I grew tall, like a cypress upon Mount Hermon."

In the Song of Solomon, the Lebanon plays a special role in the amorous interplay between the bride and bridegroom. Solomon, we are told, made himself a palanquin from Lebanon wood (Cant. 3:9). The delights of the mountains are also cited in other ways: the appearance of the bridegroom is like that of the Lebanon (5:15); the bride's nose is like a Lebanon tower (7:5[4]). In the fourth chapter, which may comprise "a series of poems brought together by the catchword *l^e^bānôn*,"[80] the bride is called upon to leave the Lebanon and join her friend (Cant. 4:8; also vv. 6, 14 in the LXX). The scent of the woman's garments is compared to the scent of the Lebanon (4:11; cf. also Hos. 14:6[5][81]), and her beauty is described as a well of living water, flowing streams from the Lebanon (Cant. 4:15). The relationship between the bride and bridegroom in the Song of Solomon, which Jewish tradition interprets as an allegory of the love between Yahweh and his people,[82] appears similarly in the promise of salvation to come at the end of the book of Hosea (Hos. 14:5-9[4-8]). Hos. 14:6-8(5-7) recalls the words

---

also Brown, 115f.; cf. G. C. Macholz, "Psalm 29 und 1. Könige 19: Jahwes und Baals Theophanie," *Werden und Wirken des ATs. Festschrift C. Westermann* (Göttingen, 1980), 325-333); K. Seybold, "Die Geschichte des 29. Psalms und ihre theologische Bedeutung," *ThZ,* 36 (1980), 208-219.

78. → כרמל *karmel,* II.4.

79. See also Lipiński.

80. G. Gerleman, *Das Hohelied. BK,* XVIII (²1981), 151.

81. Discussed below.

82. See also M. J. Mulder, *De Targum op het Hooglied* (Amsterdam, 1975).

of the Song of Songs: Yahweh will be to Israel like the dew, so that Israel will blossom like a lily and strike root like the Lebanon (often read *liḇneh,* "poplar").[83] The fragrance of Israel will likewise be like the fragrance of the Lebanon, and Israel will be praised like the wine of the Lebanon (Hos. 14:7f.[6f.]).

In other passages, too, these mountains on the northern border of the "promised land," mysterious to many Israelites, play an important role in the eschatological day of salvation. When God summons his people to lead them into battle for the last time, he will "bring them home from the land of Egypt, and gather them from Assyria; . . . and bring them to the land of Gilead and to the Lebanon" (Zec. 10:10). When the prince of peace comes, the land will have an abundance[84] of grain; it will wave on the tops of the mountains, and its fruit will be like the Lebanon (Ps. 72:16; cf. 104:16). The Lebanon mountains also play a role in the eschatological oracles of the prophets (Isa. 35:2;[85] 60:13), because, like the other tall mountains often mentioned in the same context, they reflect the glory of God. But they are no more than a reflection, for "the Lebanon would not suffice for fuel, nor are its beasts enough for a burnt offering," to express Yahweh's preeminence over worthless idols (Isa. 40:16).

III. Late Jewish Tradition. There is no clear cultic tradition in the OT of a sanctuary on the Lebanon, nor do we find the divine name "Baʿal of the Lebanon" attested elsewhere.[86] Only a few poetic and prophetic texts suggest in their background a Canaanite Phoenician cult or sanctuary in the Lebanon.[87]

In later Jewish tradition, however, the Lebanon took on a specialized symbolic meaning that appears also in the Aramaic translations of the OT and is probably rooted in the OT itself. This interpretation identifies *l^eḇānôn* with the temple and similar entities.[88] The Targumim in particular translate *l^eḇānôn* as "temple" or "sanctuary" (Targ. Onqelos: Dt. 3:25; Targ. Jonathan and Targ. Neofiti: Dt. 1:7; 3:25; 11:24; also 2 K. 19:23 [par. Isa. 37:24]; Jer. 22:6,20,23; Hos. 14:8[7]; Hab. 2:17; Zec. 10:10; Cant. 4:8,15 [cf. 3:9; 5:15]). We also find "king" (of the house of David: 1 K. 5:13[4:33]); "the rich" (Isa. 14:8; Ezk. 31:16); "nations" (Isa. 2:13; 10:34 [attacking Israel]; Zec. 11:1); and "Zion" (Cant. 7:5[4]). The "House of the Forest of Lebanon" (1 K. 7:2; 10:17; etc.) is called a "cool summer palace of the king."

In the Dead Sea scrolls we already find similar symbolic interpretations of the word. In 1QpHab 12:3f. (on Hab. 2:17), "Lebanon" stands for the "community council"

83. See *KBL*³; but cf. H. W. Wolff, *Hosea. Herm* (Eng. trans. 1974), 235f.; W. Rudolph, *Hosea. KAT,* XIII/1 (1966), 248, 252.

84. See G. R. Driver, "Hebrew Notes," *VT,* 1 (1951), 249.

85. → יער *yaʿar,* IV.

86. See, e.g., *KAI,* 31, 1f.; M. J. Lagrange, *Études sur les religions sémitiques. ÉtB* (²1905), 91, 190; Eissfeldt, *KlSchr,* II, 48f.; T. Klauser, "Baal," *RAC,* I, 1077; on "high places" in the Lebanon, see Honigmann, 8.

87. See II.4 above.

88. See Vermès.

(*ʿᵃṣaṯ hayyaḥaḏ*);[89] in 4Q169 1–2:7f. (on Nah. 1:4),[90] it stands for "the men of the council" ([*'anšê ʿᵃṣā*]*ṯām*).[91] In 4Q161 8–10:8f. (on Isa. 10:34),[92] the "Kittim" are handed over "to the power of a great man." This passage interprets "Lebanon" as meaning the "nations," as does the Targum to this verse.

In later Tannaitic and other Jewish literature, the symbolic usage of "Lebanon" in the sense of "temple" is very common.[93] The OT itself, however, includes texts that support this symbolism: in Jer. 22:23, for example (cf. also vv. 6, 20), "Lebanon" stands for the royal palace. It is also reasonable to assume that the use of Lebanon cedar to build both temples contributed a necessary element to this symbolism. The OT occasionally uses "Lebanon" and "temple" in the same context (e.g., Ps. 92:13f.[12f.]; Isa. 40:16). In this manner, too, these timbered mountains, whose height and eternal snow evoked fear and awe, left a deep mark on the literature, theology, and symbolism of Israel.

Mulder†

89. Vermès, *Festschrift A. Robert,* 316-325.
90. J. M. Allegro, *Qumran Cave 4. DJD,* V (1968), 37.
91. A. Weiser, πιστεύω," *TDNT,* VI, 185.
92. See Allegro, 13f.
93. Vermès, *Scripture and Tradition in Judaism,* 33ff.

לָבֵשׁ *lāḇēš*

Contents: I. Ancient Near East: 1. Archaeology and Iconography; 2. Distribution. II. OT Occurrences: 1. Morphology and Syntax; 2. Semantic Field; 3. Extended and Figurative Meanings. III. Theological Usage: 1. Human Dignity; 2. God; 3. Sources of Salvation; 4. Cult; 5. Eschatology; 6. Idioms. IV. Summary. V. Dead Sea Scrolls.

lāḇēš. J. P. Brown, "The Sacrificial Cult and its Critique in Greek and Hebrew," *JSS,* 24 (1979), 159-173; 25 (1980), 1-21; G. Brunet, "Y eut-il un manteau de prophète?" *RSO,* 43 (1968), 145-162; M. Dahood, " 'To pawn one's cloak'," *Bibl,* 42 (1961) 359-366; É. P. Dhorme, *L'emploi métaphorique des noms de parties du corps en hébreu et en akkadien* (Paris, 1923, repr. 1963); R. Eisler, *Weltenmantel und Himmelszelt,* I (Leipzig, 1910); I. Eitan, "A Contribution to Isaiah Exegesis," *HUCA,* 12/13 (1937-38), 55-88; K. Galling, "Das vierte Nachtgesicht des Propheten Sacharja," *ZMR,* 46 (1931), 193-208; M. Görg, "Zum sogenannten priesterlichen Obergewand," *BZ,* N.S. 20 (1976), 242-46; H. Grapow, *Vergleiche und andere bildliche Ausdrücke im Ägyptischen. AO,* 21/1f. (1920); M. Haran, "מלבושי כהונה," *EMiqr,* IV (1962), 1045-49; E. Haulotte, *Symbolique du vêtement selon la Bible. Théologie,* 65 (Paris, 1966); H. W. Hönig, *Die Bekleidung des Hebräers* (Zurich, 1957); E. Jenni, "לבש *lbš* sich bekleiden," *THAT,* I, 867-870; A. Jirku, "Zur magischen Bedeutung der Kleidung in Israel," *ZAW,* 37 (1917/18), 109-125; P. Joüon, "Le costume d'Elie et celui de Jean Baptiste," *Bibl,* 16 (1935), 74-81; *idem,* "Notes de lexicographie Hébraïque," *MUSJ,* 6 (1913), 160-183;

I. Ancient Near East.

1. *Archaeology and Iconography.* In the cultures of the ancient Near East, both literary and iconographic[1] evidence shows that people (and deities) were normally clothed, at least minimally. Only in exceptional situations were human beings (enemies, prisoners, impaled malefactors, military casualties, laborers, children, female dancers [often adorned with jewelry]) and many deities[2] naked. It is not always clear whether some representations (even genre scenes[3]) are meant to be realistic or symbolic, as in the case of deities (especially female),[4] or both, as in the case of (male) cultic personnel[5] depicted without clothing or jewelry.[6] Many examples will be found in *RLA.*[7]

2. *Distribution.* The root *lbš,* with the basic meaning "garment," is found throughout the Semitic realm, including Ethiopic and Tigre,[8] with the exception of Phoenician and Punic.[9] In Akkadian, the primary association with human clothing has been widely extended[10] and applied to deities (clothing for them or their images[11]), the

---

C. le Comte de Landberg, *Études sur les dialectes de l'Arabie méridionale,* II (Leiden, 1913); *idem, Glossaire daṯînois,* I (Leiden, 1920); J. W. McKay, "My Glory — a Mantle of Praise," *SJT,* 31 (1978), 167-172; W. Magass, "Texte und Textilien," *LB,* 34 (1975), 23-36; R. North, "Flesh, Covering, and Response, Ex. xxi 10," *VT,* 5 (1955), 204-6; J. L. Palache, *Semantic Notes on the Hebrew Lexicon* (Eng. trans., Leiden, 1959); E. Peterson, "Theologie des Kleides," *Benediktinische Monatsschrift,* 16 (1934), 347-356 = *Marginalien zur Theologie* (1956), 41-55; H. Petschow, "Gewand(saum) im Recht," *RLA,* III (1957-1971), 318-322; J. Reider, "Miscellanea hebraica," *JJS,* 3 (1952), 78-86; J. Ruppert, *Le costume juif depuis des temps patriachaux jusqu'à la dispersion* (Paris, 1939); S. Schreiner, "Mischehen — Ehebruch — Ehescheidung," *ZAW,* 91 (1979), 207-228; A. Tosato, "Il ripudio: delitto e pena (Mal 2,10-16)," *Bibl,* 59 (1978), 548-553; R. von Ungern-Sternberg, *Redeweisen der Bibel. BSt,* 54 (1968); E. Vogt, *LexLingAram*; Z. Weisman, "Elijah's Mantle and Consecration of Elisha," *ShnatMikr,* 2 (1977), 93-99; G. Widengren, *Psalm 110 och det sakrala kungadömet i Israel. UUÅ,* 1941/7:1, 3-26, repr. "Psalm 110 und das sakrale Königtum in Israel," in P. H. A. Neumann, ed., *Zur neueren Psalmenforschung. WdF,* 192 (1976), 185-216; S. Yeivin, "מַלְבּוּשִׁים," EMiqr, IV (1962), 1034-45.

1. See *ANEP, passim.*
2. E.g., Gilg. I, II, 38; *ANET,* 74.
3. E.g., *ANEP,* 195, 208.
4. See the many examples in *ANEP,* 465-479, 542, 543.
5. *Ibid.,* 299, 502, 597, 600.
6. Cf. H. Ringgren, "Nacktheit," *BHHW,* II (1964), 1277; W. Jannasch, "Kleidung," *RGG*[3], III (1959), 1646-48; C. A. Schmitz, "Nacktheit," *RGG,* IV (1960), 1294.
7. H. Waetzold, "Kleidung: A. Philologisch," *RLA,* VI (1980-83), 18-31; E. Strommenger, "Kleidung: B. Archäologisch," *ibid.,* 31-38.
8. *KBL*[3], 493.
9. Cf. Jenni, 867.
10. Cf. *AHw,* I (1965), 523f., with references to derivatives.
11. *Ibid.,* I, 561; *CAD,* IX (1973), 235, 4.

cult, the cosmos (the mantle of heaven, a cloak of clouds[12]), ethical and religious values, both positive and negative,[13] and disguise.[14] In contrast to these, usages of a more technical nature are not found in the OT: e.g., paneling,[15] the outer leaf of new grain, unshorn sheep.[16] Two Ugaritic examples are noteworthy with regard to the OT: *lpš* with *ksy* for the loincloth worn by a mourner,[17] and repeated *lbš* for the attire of a female figure: female garments over male garments, with armor between (?) them.[18] At Elephantine, both noun and verb are common in daily life, the cult, and literature.[19] Probably unique is the meaning "my shroud" (*lbšy*) found at Nerab.[20]

We find a striking semantic bifurcation, morphologically signaled: Arab. *labisa,* "clothe," *labasa,* "conceal, deceive"; also Arab. *baǵada,* "dupe," *biǵād,* "striped garment"; Heb. *bgd,* as a verb meaning only "deal treacherously"; *beg̱eḏ,* usually "garment" in general, but also "treachery."[21] Probably the distinction depends on the possible intent, whether to conceal something or someone or to bring about an error in connection with a person.[22]

II. OT Occurrences. The same basic range of possibilities is found in the OT.

1. *Morphology and Syntax.* Heb. *lbš* occurs primarily in the qal (finite forms and pass. ptcp.) and hiphil; there are 4 occurrences of the pual participle, and a single occurrence of the hithpael in Sir. 50:11b. Nominal forms include the common *lᵉḇûš* and the rarer *malbûš*; only in Isa. 59:17 do we find *tilbōšeṯ* (cf. Akk. *talbuštu*).[23] The constructions are those common to verbs meaning "put on," with minor variations.[24] The qal appears once with *bᵉ* (Est. 6:8), once absolutely (Hag. 1:6), and once with the adv. *kēn* (2 S. 13:18). The hiphil twice uses *ʿal* with the person and the accusative of the thing (Gen. 27:16; Lev. 6:3[Eng. 6:10]). In the Aramaic parts of the OT, the qal is used as in Hebrew (Dnl. 5:7,16); the only haphel, however, uses *lᵉ* (v. 29; similarly at Elephantine and Hermopolis).[25] The LXX generally uses *endýein/en-*

---

12. *Aw,* II (1972), 724; cf. Widengren, 205, 209.
13. *CAD,* IX, 18, 3′, etc.
14. *AHw,* III (1981), 1310.
15. *CAD,* IX, 21f., etc.
16. *AHw,* I, 560f.
17. *KTU,* 1.5 VI, 16f.
18. *KTU,* 1.19 IV, 46ff.; cf. *CML*², 73, 121; *WUS,* no. 1476, 1444.
19. Cf. Vogt, 94.
20. *KAI,* 226, 7; cf. *DISO,* 135; *CAD,* IX, 236, ic.
21. *KBL*³, 104, 493.
22. Landberg, *Études,* II, 364-67; *idem, Glossaire Daṯînois,* I, 135; Joüon, *MUSJ,* 4 (1913), 171; Palache, 10-12.
23. *AHw,* III, 1310. For a statistical summary, see Jenni, 868.
24. Cf. Jenni, 867-870; Joüon, *A Grammar of Biblical Hebrew,* §125d.
25. Cf. Vogt, 94.

dýnein to translate *lāḇēš* (about 90 times),[26] but occasionally *peribállein* (13 times) or *stolízein* (8 times).

2. *Semantic Field.* a. The primary meaning of the verb is clear from the various functional articles of clothing it can have as its material object. In decreasing frequency, such clothing or individual garments[27] include: *beged* (23 times), *kuttōneṯ/keṯōneṯ* (6), *śaq* (5), *maḏ* (2 or 3: Lev. 6:3[10]; 1 S. 17:38; cf. Ps. 109:18), *širyôn* (2 or 3: 1 S. 17:5,38; cf. Isa. 59:17), *śimlâ* (2: Dt. 22:5; Isa. 4:1), *meʿîl* (2: Ex. 29:5; Lev. 8:7), *siryôn* (Jer. 46:4), *'addereṯ* (Zec. 13:4), *maḥalāṣôṯ* (Zec. 3:4), *miḵnās* pl. const. (Lev. 6:3[10]), and *malbûš* (Zeph. 1:8). Materials or fabrics include: *baddîm* (19 times in the abs., only in Ezekiel and Daniel), *šānî* (abs. only in 2 S. 1:24; Jer. 4:30; Prov. 31:21), *šaʿaṭnēz* (Dt. 22:11), *ṣemer* (Ezk. 34:3), and *šēš* (Prov. 31:22; Ezk. 16:13 [*Q*], with *mešî*). The nouns *malbûš* and *leḇûš* also refer to physical articles of clothing. Moving in the direction of figurative usage is the simile *kalleḇûš* (Ps. 102:27[26]; 104:6; cf. the more common *kabbegeḏ* with the same meaning). Verbs used in parallel with *lbš* or with the same objects include: *ksh, ʿṭh, ʿṭp, ḥbš, ntn ʿal, hyh ʿal, ʿlh ʿal, ʿdh,* and *ʿnd*; in metaphorical use only we also find *ʿṭr, 'zr,* and *ḥgr*.

b. The subject of the verb is always a "wearer," a person or personification, never an object as such. This usage distinguishes *lbš* from many other verbs meaning "cover." It refers to the uniquely human need for some kind of covering — not merely for physical protection, but to make the wearer "socially acceptable." It can serve a wide range of special purposes, including total concealment, as when Rebekah "clothes" Jacob's hands and neck with skins to simulate his brother (Gen. 27:16; the unusual construction *lbš* hiphil *ʿal* has probably been influenced by another verb, possibly *ksh*; compare Lev. 6:3[10] with Ex. 28:42). Deliberate disguise is expressed naturally by *lbš* (1 S. 28:8; 2 S. 14:2; 1 K. 22:30 par. 2 Ch. 18:29); other verbs are used when the element of disguise is absent (1 S. 19:13; 2 S. 20:12). It may be more than chance that *lbš* is used for foreign fashions that are attacked but followed (Zeph. 1:8), but not for ridiculous frippery (Isa. 3:17-24). The derogatory statement that drowsiness clothes the sloven in rags (Prov. 23:21) emphasizes its subject's social decline (cf. Job 7:5; Zec. 3:3-5; cf. also Job 9:31).

c. The occurrences of *lbš* in the OT are distributed unevenly. Earlier documents use only the literal sense, even in theological contexts: J in the narratives of Eden (Gen. 3:21), Jacob (27:15f.; 28:20), Tamar (38:19), and Joseph (41:42); the early material of Deuteronomy (Dt. 22:5,11) and the Deuteronomistic history (Jgs. 6:34; 1 S. 17:5,38; 28:8; 2 S. 1:24; 13:18; 14:2; 20:8; 1 K. 10:5; 22:10,30; 2 K. 10:22); and prophetic texts in Isa. 4:1; 22:21; Zeph. 1:8. This interest reappears later (Hag. 1:6; Zec. 3:3-5; 13:4), and enjoys a renaissance in Esther, P (and Ezk. 42:14; 44:17,19), and Proverbs (Prov. 31:21f.,25; cf. 23:21). Later authors may use either the literal or the figurative meaning (cf. already Gen. 49:11; also Isa. 63:1-6) as they please. The documents in question

26. See A. Oepke, "δύω," *TDNT,* II, 318-321; H. Paulsen, "ἐνδύω *endyo* put on, dress," *EDNT,* I (1990), 451f.

27. Haulotte, 343.

are Jeremiah, Ezekiel, Deutero-Isaiah, Trito-Isaiah, Psalms, and Job; the most important texts will be discussed below. If the evidence is not totally misleading, forms of *lbš* referring to clothing usually occur in key passages.

3. *Extended and Figurative Meanings.* As we approach theological contexts, we find three apparently important themes.

a. Without clothing, the individual would be helpless. "Naked" is used to describe the newborn and the dying (e.g., Job 1:21; Eccl. 5:14[15]), those defeated in battle and taken prisoner (e.g, 2 Ch. 28:15), the totally helpless (Job 1:21; 24:7,10; 31:19; Dt. 28:48; Am. 2:16). People rend their garments (usually *qr*ʿ + *b*ᵉ*gāḏîm*) to symbolize that something of fundamental importance to their being has been destroyed (cf. 2 S. 13:18f.). To exploit the weak is to "strip the naked of their clothing" (Job 22:6: *biḡdê ʿᵃrûmmîm*). Garments given in pledge are therefore subject to special protection (Ex. 22:25f.[26f.]),[28] for clothing is one of the necessities of life (Gen. 28:20; Dt. 10:18) and a charitable gift to those in need (Ezk. 18:7,16; Job 31:19f.). Clothing and jewelry were esteemed as gifts (Gen. 24:53; 45:22; Jgs. 14:12; 2 S. 1:24; 2 K. 5:5,22,23,26) and booty (Josh. 22:8; Jgs. 5:30; 14:19). "Nakedness" usually does not have sexual connotations.[29]

b. Clothing expresses and establishes the structure of society by assigning all their place: men and women (cf. Dt. 22:5), prophets (1 K. 11:29f.; 19:19; 2 K. 1:7f.; 2:8,12-14; Zec. 13:4),[30] kings, dignitaries, warriors (1 K. 22:10,30; Est. 5:1; 6:8; 8:15; cf. Dnl. 10:5; Job 38:3; 40:7; Isa. 22:21; Zec. 3:3-5; Gen. 41:42), and princesses (2 S. 13:18), but also slaves (Dt. 21:13), mourners (e.g., 2 S. 14:2; 1 K. 20:31f.; Isa. 58:5; cf. Jth. 4:12; 9:1), participants in a wedding (e.g., Ps. 45:14[13]), widows (Gen. 38:19; cf. v. 14), and priests (especially in P). It does not have to be proved that clothing commonly serves as an important criterion by which both individuals and entire groups are recognized, even with respect to their spirituality (Zeph. 1:8; cf. Isa. 3:16-24). Departure from customary usage would normally risk one's identity.

c. Clothing can express close personal ties, e.g., between Jacob and Joseph (Gen. 37:3; cf. vv. 31-34), David and Jonathan (1 S. 18:1,3f.; cf. Ps. 35:13f.; 1 S. 17:38f.). Israel's closeness to God is represented by the image of a waistcloth (Jer. 13:11; cf. the image of a ring in 22:24; Hag. 2:23; Cant. 8:6). Parental instruction is to be worn (in writing?) near one's heart (Prov. 6:21). Job would lay his indictment on his shoulders and bind it on as a crown (Job 31:36). Jewelry commonly takes on symbolic meaning, especially in the cult: the Urim and Thummim in the *ḥōšen* on Aaron's breast (Ex. 28:29f.), the *ṣîṣ* on his forehead (Ex. 28:36), tassels (Nu. 15:38-41; cf. Dt. 22:12), the *ṭôṭāpôṯ* (Ex. 13:16; Dt. 6:8; 11:18) as a "continual" (Ex. 28:29f.,38) "remembrance" (Ex. 28:29; cf. Zec. 6:9-15), a "sign" (Ex. 13:9,16; Dt. 6:8; 11:18) "for acceptance" (Ex. 28:38). Many of these texts probably reflect secondary interpretations of traditional customs no longer understood spontaneously (cf. the apotropaic interpretation of the bells in Ex. 28:35).

---

28. Cf. *KAI,* 200.

29. Cf. A.-M. Dubarle, *The Biblical Doctrine of Original Sin* (Eng. trans., New York, 1965), 73ff.

30. Cf. Brunet.

III. Theological Usage. Such nontheological ideas may be used to make theological statements — with increasing frequency, it seems, as time goes on.

1. *Human Dignity.* The imagery of clothing was among the means used by the Israelites to express awe, bafflement, or bewilderment when faced with the works of God.

a. The "nakedness" of "the man and his wife" (Gen. 2:25) in the Yahwist's primeval history has nothing to do with a primal "natural state" (but cf. Enkidu[31]). Using several symbolic means, the Yahwist illuminates the difference in the relationship between God and humanity before and after the Fall. Despite the *ḥᵃgōrōṯ* the man and the woman have sewed together (Gen. 3:7), they remain "naked" before God (vv. 8-11). God fashions "garments of skin" and "clothes" (*wayyalbišēm*) them (Gen. 3:21), making life worth living in spite of their sin (cf. v. 20; cf. "garments made of rushes" as a curse in a treaty of Ashurnirari V[32]). For the Yahwist, human integrity and dignity would not be preserved in the actual experience of being without clothing. Ham violates his father's dignity by uncovering his nakedness (Gen. 9:21-24; cf. Ezk. 16:22,39; 23:26,29; Hab. 2:15f.; Lam. 4:21f.; 1 S. 19:24; 2 S. 10:4f.). The victorious Israelites preserve this dignity when they decide to treat their captured Judahite brethren humanely: *wᵉḵol-maʿᵃrummêhem hilbîšû* (2 Ch. 28:15). In a recreation of the dawn of history, Ezekiel describes the king of Tyre "in Eden, the garden of God," clothed in a garment of gold and jewels (Ezk. 28:13-15). Jerusalem began her days as a naked foundling, rescued by God and clothed in splendid raiment (Ezk. 16:4-14, esp. 10, 13). When she grows up and proves faithless, God threatens to "strip her naked and make her as in the day she was born" (Hos. 2:5[3]; cf. Am. 2:16). Nakedness and clothing are complementary elements signifying extreme situations: beginning and end, depth and height, deliverance and disaster.

b. Job reflects that at his creation God clothed him with skin and flesh (*ʿôr ûḇāśār talbîšēnî*: Job 10:11a; cf. vv. 9f.; Ps. 139:13-16; Ezk. 37:6,8), an act that remains incomprehensible (cf. Eccl. 11:5; 2 Mc. 7:22).[33] God in turn seeks to confound Job by the impossible demand that he clothe himself with glory and splendor (*wᵉhôḏ wᵉhāḏār tilbāš*: Job 40:10b; cf. Prov. 31:25). The psalmist is awed at the "crown" of humanity: *wᵉḵāḇôḏ wᵉhāḏār tᵉʿaṭṭᵉrēhû* (Ps. 8:6[5]; on *ʿṭr,* cf. 21:4[3]; 103:4).

c. A human being can no more "strip off" the outer layer (*pᵉnê lᵉḇûšô*) of a crocodile's hide (Job 41:5[13]; cf. LXX) than clothe (*lbš* hiphil) a horse's neck with a mane (Job 39:19) or a meadow with flocks (Ps. 65:14[13] [*lbš* qal];[34] Isa. 60:6). Such metaphors and images illustrate how the work of God surpasses all the accomplishments of much admired human skill. Late wisdom is even freer in combining such metaphors to commend itself (e.g., Sir. 6:30: 27:8 [Heb.]).

d. On the other hand, Job laments: *lāḇaš bᵉśārî rimmâ wᵉgîš ʿāp̄ār* (Job 7:5).[35] The

31. Gilg. II, IIf., esp. III, 26f.; *ANET*³, 77; *AOT,* 188.
32. *ANET*³, 533.
33. Dhorme, 4f.; R. Schweizer, "σῶμα," *TDNT,* VII, 1048.
34. Cf. *CAD,* IX 22, 5c.2′.
35. Cf. *BHS.*

wicked shall "put on" (*lbš* qal: Job 8:22; Ps. 35:26; 109:29) or "be covered with" (→ *ksh* piel or pual: Jer. 3:25; 51:51; Ps. 44:16[15]; 69:8[7]; Ob. 10; Mic. 7:10) *bōšeṯ* (Ps. 35:26; 44:16[15]; Job 8:22; cf. 1 Mc. 1:28), *bûšâ* (Ob. 10; Mic. 7:10), *kᵉlimmâ* (Ps. 35:26; 69:8[7]; 109:29; Jer. 3:25; 51:51), and *qᵉlālâ* (Ps. 109:18a). God threatens David's enemies: *'albîš bōšeṯ*; on David, however, "his crown will shed its luster" (Ps. 132:18). The notion of the lex talionis is more or less clearly present: the enemy *ye'ᵉhaḇ qᵉlālâ,* therefore *yilbaš qᵉlālâ kᵉmaddô* (Ps. 109:17a,18a). With its parallels, *lbš* shows that (retaliatory) disaster strikes all aspects of its victim and is ineluctable.

e. Garments also can symbolize impermanence (Josh. 9:13; Job 13:28). It is a sign of God's special providence that during the long journey through the wilderness the clothing (*śᵉmālôṯ, śalmôṯ*) of the people did not wear out (Dt. 8:4; 29:4[5]; Neh. 9:21). God alone "stands" unchanged; creatures *kabbegeḏ yiḇlû; kallᵉḇûš taḥᵃlîpēm wᵉyaḥᵃlōpû* (Ps. 102:27[26]; cf. Isa. 50:9; 51:6).

2. *God.* Although garments are a necessary element of anthropomorphic conceptions of God, God's garments are rarely mentioned. In Isaiah's call vision, probably the earliest relevant text, God's "fringe" or "train" alone fills the temple (Isa. 6:1). The hymnic invocation of the God who is manifested in the cosmos (Ps. 104) speaks of splendid apparel (*hôḏ wᵉhāḏār lāḇaštā*: v. 1c, probably an adverbial construction; cf. Ps. 93:1) with related elements (surrounding light like a garment, the heavens like a tent: Ps. 104:2), along with references to the works of creation that draw primarily on the technical language of craftsmanship (vv. 3ff.). The important thing is not the garment itself, but a conceptual contrast: what protects the ultimate privacy of human individuals, while also accentuating their finiteness, is spread out by God over the entire cosmos, transcending and effacing all boundaries (cf. esp. Ps. 104:6: *tᵉhôm kallᵉḇûš*; the textual uncertainty of the suffix may be a symptom of "imprecise" thought[36]). In addition, God naturally and effortlessly "wears" the wonders of creation, before which mortals can only stand in awe. Recollection of Yahweh's creation and history and observation of his work in human history find expression in a poetic apostrophe to the "arm of Yahweh": *'ûrî 'ûrî liḇšî-'ōz zᵉrôa' YHWH* (Isa. 51:9a); there follow four mythological descriptions of the primordial chaos that Yahweh vanquished (vv. 9c-10). Isa. 59:17 develops the image of Yahweh the warrior (cf. Ex. 15:3; Isa. 42:13; 52:10) armed with a series of abstractions: *wayyilbaš ṣᵉḏāqâ kašširyān wᵉkôḇa' yᵉšû'â bᵉrō'šô wayyilbaš bigḏê nāqām tilbōšeṯ wayya'aṭ kammᵉ'îl qin'â* (cf. Wis. 5:17-23; Eph. 6:14-17; 1 Th. 5:8).[37] Sometimes abstract nouns form the girdle (*'ēzôr*) of Yahweh: *ṣeḏeq* and *'ᵉmûnâ* (Isa. 11:5), *gᵉḇûrâ* (Ps. 65:7b[6b]). The imagery uses the terminology of salvation, affirming God's readiness (cf. Ex. 12:11) and combining will, power, execution, and success (cf. esp. Isa. 59:18-20).

3. *Sources of Salvation.* Poetic language uses similar images and metaphors to characterize those who bring and obstruct salvation.

---

36. See O. Keel, *The Symbolism of the Biblical World* (Eng. trans., New York, 1973), 43.
37. *CAD,* IX, 18, 1c.3′.

a. For Zion, Yahweh declares: *wᵉḵōhᵃnêhā 'albîš yēšaʿ* (Ps. 132:16a); its priests *yilbᵉšû-ṣeḏeq* (v. 9a), to the joy of the devout (vv. 9b, 16b). In a bold personification, Deutero-Isaiah calls on redeemed Jerusalem to appear in an appropriate state: *liḇšî ʿuzzēḵ . . . liḇšî bigḏê tip'artēḵ* (Isa. 52:1). Zion, God swears, will put on all those returning like jewelry (! — cf. *BHS) kullām kaʿᵃḏî ṯilbāšî* (Isa. 49:18; cf. 14:19), while according to Jer. 4:30 the harlot Jerusalem will not be saved by all her clothing and makeup. Ezk. 16:13 (cf. Job 29:14; Bar. 5:1-3) uses similar language.

The anonymous figure in Trito-Isaiah describes himself as clothed by God with the garments of salvation and covered with a robe of righteousness, reflecting the joy of a marriage or a blossoming garden (Isa. 61:10f.). He knows he is sent to bring to those who mourn in Zion "a [garment of] splendor [RSV "a garland"] instead of [a garment of] ashes, the oil of gladness [a festal garment?] instead of mourning [garments?], a mantle of praise instead of a faint spirit" (v. 3).[38]

In other passages, representatives of the powers of wickedness are dressed in the consequences of their total failure. The "prince" of Jerusalem *yilbaš šᵉmāmâ* instead of his robes (Ezk. 7:27; cf. v. 18; Ps. 55:6[5]; Job 21:6). The princes of Tyre step down from their thrones, strip off their finery, *ḥᵃrāḏôṯ yilbāšû,* and perform the rituals of mourning (Ezk. 26:16; cf. Isa. 32:11). In contrast to the kings of the nations, who lie in state, the king of Babylon is "cast out" and *lᵉḇûš hᵃrugîm* (Isa. 14:18f.; cf. 49:18) — in other words, he lies under a pile of those slain in battle (cf. Ezk. 31:17f.; 32:20-32).[39] The perversely negative use of *lbš* highlights the sense of degradation.

b. Despite the unusual construction, the problematic *wᵉrûaḥ YHWH lāḇᵉšâ 'eṯ-giḏʿôn* (Jgs. 6:34; cf. 1 Ch. 12:19[18]; 2 Ch. 24:20) probably has an analogous positive sense: the power of God envelops Gideon, "clothing" him with this very power. The influence of related verbs like *ml'* and *ksh* may account for the unusual construction. The point is the special bond between the spirit and the person,[40] not the intensity of the experience (as in Ezk. 36:27; cf. Jgs. 3:10; 11:29; 13:25; 14:6,19; 15:14; Isa. 61:1; Nu. 11:17,25f.).

c. Clothing in the literal sense plays a certain theological role in the symbolic actions of both the early (1 K. 11:29-39; 19:13,19; 2 K. 2:8,13f.) and the classical prophets (Isa. 20:1-6; Jer. 13:1-11; Ezk. 24:15-24). The meaning and interpretation of these actions depends on the context in which they are performed. A garment probably emphasizes personal involvement (cf. also Jer. 27f.), whatever the cultural and religious presuppositions may be.[41] A late polemic against idolatrous prophets declares: *wᵉlô' yilbᵉšû 'addereṯ śēʿār lᵉmaʿan kaḥēš* (Zec. 13:4). Nowhere else is *lbš* used with *'addereṯ*; the text may reflect the seductive solemnity of the deceptive garment.[42]

4. *Cult.* In the cult, the context itself is "theological," although not all the elements are always consciously accorded a theological interpretation.

38. Cf. *BHS*; McKay.
39. *CAD,* IX, 181.
40. Cf. Reider, 79.
41. Cf. G. Fohrer, *Die Symbolische Handlungen der Propheten. AThANT,* 54 (^{2}1968), *in loc.*
42. Cf. Joüon, *Bibl,* 16 (1935), 76-78; Brunet, 159-162.

a. It goes without saying that the presence of God, however it may come to pass or be perceived, requires deportment distinct from everyday life. This has to include clothing in the widest sense. In the presence of a "holy place," one removes one's shoes (Ex. 3:5; Josh. 5:15; cf. Ps. Sol. 2:2). One sign of submission to God's wrath is demonstrative neglect of the usual attention to one's clothing and person, summarized in the psalmic phrase *hlk qōḏēr* (Ps. 38:7[6]; 42:10[9]; 43:2; cf. 2 S. 12:20; 15:30; 19:25[24]; Jer. 4:28; 8:21; 14:2; Mal. 3:14; 1QH 5:32 [*qdrwt lbšty*]), the frequent *śaq* (e.g., Isa. 20:2), in "dust and ashes" (e.g., Isa. 58:5) — whether these expressions are literal, symbolic, or merely cliches.

In a different context, taking off shoes (Ruth 4:7f.; cf. Dt. 25:7-10)[43] and covering with the corner of a garment (Ruth 3:9; Ezk. 16:8) are formalities associated with family law. Even in passages where the biblical authors acknowledge certain changes (Ruth 4:7), they do not feel any need for further inquiry. The problems are matters less of theology than of cultural history or psychology (e.g., Gen. 41:14; Est. 4:2,4; 1 S. 15:27; 24:5f.[4f.]).[44]

Formal codification is at least suggested when all the people are required to wash (Ex. 19:10,14) or change (Gen. 35:2) their garments before a meeting with God. In Ex. 19:10,14 (J), the piel of *qdš* associates this ritual so closely with the people that other texts can use the piel of *kbs* with a personal direct object to express deliverance from evil and guilt (Ps. 51:4,9[2,7]; Jer. 2:22; 4:14; cf. Gen. 35:2 and "spiritualization" in texts like Joel 2:12f.; Mal. 3:2).

b. P records detailed regulations governing the clothing of the official cultic personnel,[45] seeking at all costs to be exhaustive.[46] Only the breeches (*miḵnās*) have a practical purpose: prevention of exposure (Lev. 6:3[10]: *lbš* qal with *ʿal*; similar regulations appear in Ex. 28:42; Lev. 16:4; a different approach is found in Ex. 20;26). P is no less interested in the rituals involving these vestments than in their form. The installation of Aaron and his sons in their office includes investiture (frequently characterized by the hiphil of *lbš* and *beḡāḏîm*: Ex. 29:5f.,8f.; 40:12-14; Lev. 8:13). The installation of his successors includes transference of materially identical vestments: they are taken off the father predecessor and put on the son successor (Ex. 29:29f.; Nu. 20:26,28; cf. Isa. 22:20-23). The exchange of clothing is extremely ritualized and stylized (cf. Gen. 35:2; 41:14; 2 S. 12:20; 2 K. 10:22).[47]

In (late) strata of P in Lev. 6, 16,[48] the (perpetual) burnt offering, certain propitiatory rites on the great Day of Atonement, etc. are set apart by special vestments and special ceremonies involving them. When performing these functions in the most holy place, Aaron wears only linen (*bāḏ*: 5 occurrences in Lev. 16:4,23 alone; but cf., e.g., 8:7-9). He leaves these simple archaic garments in the most holy place and changes into

43. Jirku, 119, 125.
44. *Ibid.*, 115-19, 125.
45. Cf. *BRL*^{3}, 256f.
46. Cf. *AncIsr*, 349-351.
47. Haulotte, 76-79.
48. Cf. K. Elliger, *Leviticus. HAT*, IV (1966), *in loc.*

"other" garments (6:4[11]) or "his garments" (16:24) for ceremonies in the outer precincts. On the Day of Atonement, a bath (not the washing of garments) is also required (16:4,24). Lev. 6, 16 recognize this distinction between areas with different degrees of holiness only on these occasions; no explanation is offered. Ezekiel describes it as a permanent arrangement, explaining that it protects the people from being "infected" with holiness (Ezk. 44:19; cf. 42:14; 46:20,24; Ex. 29:37; 30:29; a different view is recorded in Hag. 2:11-13).

P speaks of two further rituals involving vestments: the sprinkling of Aaron, his sons, and all their garments (*bᵉḡāḏîm*) with a mixture of blood and oil (Ex. 29:21; Lev. 8:30; cf. Ezk. 36:25: sprinkling with pure water for purification [*ṭhr*]) and washing (*kbs* piel with *bᵉḡāḏîm*: Nu. 8:7,21, in conjunction with other rituals, to set apart the Levites).

c. The regulations governing ritual purity, which were extended eventually to their entire populace,[49] use a standard formula for the washing of garments to restore their cleanness, i.e., their acceptability for the cult: *wᵉḵibbes bᵉḡāḏāyw* (*wᵉṭāhēr*) (e.g., Lev. 13:6; cf. Lev. 11 *passim*; 13f.,15,17). The ritual and its formula are so fixed and autonomous that they can also be used for uncleanness contracted through eating, when contact with a garment can hardly be a cause (Lev. 11:40; 17:15f.). The notion is sometimes quite concrete and physical (as when clothing made unclean by "leprosy" must be ritually washed twice [Lev. 13:58]); the language, however, betrays the presence of other ideas as well: not the garments but those who wear them are restored to holiness or cleanness (*ṭhr*).[50] Two other P passages, probably secondary, speak of garments themselves as being "sanctified" by sprinkling (*qdš*: Ex. 29:21 qal; Lev. 8:30 piel). But the two dozen or so occurrences of the construct phrase *biḡḏê* (*haq*)*qōḏeš* in Ex. 28–40 and Lev. 16 probably refer exclusively to use in an exclusively "holy" setting, namely the cult (cf. the construct phrase *šeqel haqqōḏeš,* which is twice as common).

In P's codification and perhaps partial reshaping of the cult, with emphasis on ritual purity, clothing plays an important role only in the sense that (like water) it must always be present; there can be no question of nakedness. The vestments are not singled out for association with the Sinai event; this association applies to the entire law governing the cult. Besides the passages mentioned above (Ex. 28:30,35,38), a single text, probably secondary,[51] alludes to the vestments collectively: the "glory and beauty" of Aaron (Ex. 28:2; cf. Sir. 50:11), the holiness of the priesthood as such: *lᵉqaddᵉšô lᵉḵahᵃnô-lî* (Ex. 28:3; cf. v. 4; 40:13). But this expression is a commonplace, referring to more than vestments (e.g., Ex. 29:1; 40:13). The verb *lbš,* qal or hiphil, usually stands alone or at the beginning of a series; it has as its material object either the collective regalia (*bᵉḡāḏîm*: Ex. 29:5,30; 40:13; Lev. 21:10; Nu. 20:26,28; cf. Ezk. 42:14; 44:17,19) or a prominent component (*kuttōneṯ*: Ex. 28:41; 29:5,8; 40:14; Lev. 8:13; 16:4; *mᵉʿîl*: Lev.

49. Cf. *AncIsr,* 460-64.
50. Cf. H. Ringgren, → טהר *ṭāhar,* V, 287-296.
51. M. Noth, *Exodus. OTL* (Eng. trans. 1962), 217-19.

8:7). The root *lbš* does not occur at all in the laws governing cleanness. Except for Lev. 6,16 and Ezekiel, it appears only in rites of initiation, possibly its natural and original context. This observation may confirm the theory that P is always thinking of all the cultic regalia and that *lbš* itself connotes the totality.

5. *Eschatology.* Figures in eschatological and apocalyptic visions are clothed in linen. The phrase *lāḇûš (hab)baddîm* (Ezk. 9:2,3,11; 10:2,6,7; Dnl. 10:5; 12:6f.) is like a title or term of office. These are priestly figures,[52] already set outside the limits of earthly reality by the external framework and associated by their vesture with the unique and final end (cf. Lev. 6:4[11]; 16:23f.; also the priests in 1QM 7:9).

6. *Idioms.* Some texts that cannot be assigned to any of these categories may reflect a fluid, nonstandardized usage that has left little literary deposit.

In spite of a variety of proposed emendations, Job 30:18 reads: "With all his might he [Yahweh] grasps my garment, like the collar of my tunic he surrounds me."[53] The expression "my garment" (*l^eḇûšî*) is preceded by *rûaḥ n^eḏiḇāṯî, napšî,* and *'^aṣāmay* (vv. 15-17), which the context suggests are all anthropological terms, as are the following *ḥōmer, 'āpār,* and *'ēper* (v. 19). It is possible, therefore, that *l^eḇûšî* functions as a surrogate for the pronoun "me" (cf. Isa. 22:17-19). In all proposed syntactic analyses of Job 9:31, the speaker uses a figure of speech in which he stands apart from his own personified clothes (*śalmôṯay*; only here).

Using visionary language with poetic affinities, Zec. 3:3-5 includes natural, spontaneous symbolism in the scene alongside standard cultic and forensic stylization. In v. 4b, what is signified is the removal of the iniquity defiling the high priest Joshua; in vv. 6f., it is his rehabilitation in office or ministry.[54] Both the filthy garments (*lāḇuš b^egāḏîm ṣô'îm*: v. 3; cf. v. 4) and the rich (*maḥ^alāṣôṯ*: v. 4) and clean (*ṭāhôr*: v. 5) garments are effective as well as symbolic (cf. Gilg. VI, 3; XII, 13, 33[55]). Too neat a distinction between symbol and reality would not do justice to the visionary context.

Lam. 4:14 expresses revulsion that even people's garments (*l^eḇûšîm*) are defiled with blood (cf. Isa. 9:4[5]; Jer. 2:34), which should not even be seen on the ground (Gen. 4:10; Hos. 4:2; Ezk. 24:7-9; Job 16:18; Lev. 6:20[27]; cf. the expression in 1 K. 2:5 and blood like a garment (*lbš, lpš*) and tunic in *KTU,* 1.12 II, 46ff.).

The attack on easy divorce in Mal. 2:13-16 concludes — possibly with a faint allusion to the practice of covering a woman with the edge of one's garment as a token of marriage (Ruth 3:9; Ezk. 16:8) — by suggesting an image: violence, the belief that might makes right, is like a cloak, an outward "second nature," so malicious that the weak have no chance.[56]

---

52. Cf. W. Zimmerli, *Ezekiel 1. Herm* (Eng. trans. 1979), 248f.

53. G. Fohrer, *Das Buch Hiob. KAT,* XVI (1963), *in loc.,* following the LXX. Cf. *KTU,* 1.6 II, 9-11; Ahikar 171; *AP,* 218.

54. Cf. Galling.

55. *ANET*[3], 83, 97, 98.

56. Cf. K. Rudolph, *Maleachi. KAT,* XIII/4 (1976), *in loc.*; also Ps. 73:6; 50:17-20.

IV. Summary.

The "theology" of clothing is not so much explicit as implicit in many theological statements. The root *lbš,* because of its inclusiveness and its originally anthropological connotations, has special — although not exclusive — significance. The OT data may be summarized roughly as follows:

a. Human beings have an inherent need for clothing; the wearing of clothing is inescapable and a matter of course. Mortals, God, deities, intermediate beings (divine messengers, apocalyptic figures) are thought of clothed. Mythical figures that appear without attire are naturally clothed in hair; their appearance is described in terms of clothing: "clothed like the god Sumuqan" (i.e., naked and covered with hair; Gilg. I, II, 38).[57]

b. The distinction between abstract humanity and the concrete individual is not common in the OT, but it is not entirely unknown (cf. Gen. 2:18). Clothing is intrinsic to the latter. It makes possible and establishes basic interpersonal communication. The plasticity inherent within the context of anonymous social structures and constraints lends itself to the intentional use of clothing for a variety of contacts that cannot be comprehended adequately in conceptual language. If clothing does not establish the identity of an individual in human society, at least it plays an indispensable role in signalizing this identity unmistakably.

c. Therefore metaphors, images, and allegories draw on the rich language of clothing in many portions of the OT, especially the later strata.

d. The functional purpose of real garments can virtually vanish from sight in favor of their ultimate symbolic meaning, especially in the cult (P), although few texts detail this meaning.

Gamberoni

V. Dead Sea Scrolls.

The root *lbš* is infrequent in the Dead Sea scrolls. It is used metaphorically in 1QH 5:31: the oppressed supplicant feels "clothed in darkness" (*qdrwt lbšty*). Elsewhere the scrolls use *lbš* only in cultic contexts. The clothing of the sons of Aaron is described in 1QM 7:10. Several passages in the Temple scroll emphasize the need for ritually correct vesture when taking part in the cult (cf. 11QT 35:6; 32:10ff.; 33:1-7); others prohibit those wearing priestly garments from going out into the outer courts (40:1); the biblical basis for these strictures is found in Lev. 6:2ff.(9ff.). 11QT aludes to the investiture of the high priest.

Usage in the Targum, Talmud, and Midrash is discussed elsewhere.[58]

Fabry

---

57. *ANET*³, 74.

58. *WTM,* II, 471ff.; L. Prijs, "Ergänzungen zum talmudisch-hebräischen Wörterbuch," *ZDMG,* 120 (1970), 6-29, esp. 18.

לַהַב *lahab*; לֶהָבָה *lehāḇâ*; שַׁלְהֶבֶת *šalhebet*

Contents: I. 1. Occurrences; 2. LXX; 3. Ancient Near East. II. Usage: 1. Secular; 2. Theological.

I. 1. *Occurrences.* Heb. *lahaḇ* and its variant *lehāḇâ* (according to Diethelm Michel,[1] the former a collective noun and the latter denoting an individual instance) are used in two ways: in the sense of "flame," usually in conjunction with *'ēš* (26 times: Ex. 3:2; Nu. 21:28; Jgs. 13:20 [twice]; Job 41:13[Eng. v. 21]; Ps. 29:7; 83:15[14]; 105:32; 106:18; Isa. 4:5; 5:24; 10:17; 13:8; 29:6; 30:30; 43:2; 47:14; 66:15; Jer. 48:45; Lam. 2:3; Dnl. 11:33; Hos. 7:6; Joel 1:19; 2:3,5; Ob. 18); and, in the context of weapons, in the sense of "blade, lance" (5 times: Jgs. 3:22 [twice]; 1 S. 17:7; Job 39:23; also figuratively in Nah. 3:3). The Aramaic form[2] appears only in the sense of "flame" (3 times: Job 15:30; Cant. 8:6; Ezk. 21:3[20:47]). The relationship between the two senses is discussed below.

The Dead Sea scrolls also use the noun in both senses: *l^ehôḇ* (flame) in 1QH 2:26 (figuratively for the flashing of a lance [cf. Nah. 3:3]); 1QH 3:30; *lahaḇ* in 1QM 5:10 (weapon); CD 2:5 (flame); *lôhaḇ* in 1QM 5:7,10; 6:2 (weapon). Sirach uses the term in 16:6(7);[3] 43:21 (only in ms. B), in the Greek text only in 45:19 — always in the sense of "flame."

2. *LXX.* The LXX usually uses *phlóx* to translate the noun in the sense of "flame"; *lehāḇâ* is also translated by *pýr* with an additional qualifier (Ps. 105:32[LXX 104:32]: + *kataphlégein*; Hos. 7:6 + *phéngos*; Ex. 3:2; Isa. 10:17: + *kaíein*). As translations of *lahaḇ* in the sense of a weapon we find *ozysthenḗs* (*máchaira*) (Job 39:23); *phléx* or *phléps* (Jgs. 3:22), *stilboúsēs* (*hromphaías*) (Nah. 3:3), and *lónchē* (1 S. 17:7).

3. *Ancient Near East.* Precise etymological equivalents to Heb. *lahaḇ* are not found

---

lahaḇ. T. Fahd, ed., *Le feu dans le Proche-Orient antique. Travaux du Centre de Recherche sur la Proche Orient et la Grèce antique,* 1 (Leiden, 1973); J. Jeremias, *Theophanie. WMANT,* 10 (^{2}1977); O. Keel, *The Symbolism of the Biblical World* (Eng. trans., New York, 1978); *idem,* "Wer zerstörte Sodom?" *ThZ,* 35 (1979), 10-17; J. C. H. Laughlin, *A Study of the Motif of Holy Fire in the OT* (diss., Southern Baptist Theological Seminary, 1975); E. Lipiński, *Le royauté de Yahwé dans la poésie et le culte de l'ancien Israël. VVAW.L,* 27/55 (1965), 220-226; A. Ohler, *Mythologische Element im AT. KBANT* (1969); → אֵשׁ *'ēš* (*'ēsh*).

1. D. Michel, *Grundlegung einer hebräischen Syntax* (Neukirchen-Vluyn, 1977), 66f.

2. See M. Wagner, *Die lexicalischen und grammatikalischen Aramaismen im alttestamentlichen Hebräisch. BZAW,* 96 (1966), no. 305.

3. T. Middendorp, *Die Stellung Jesu Ben Siras zwischen Judentum und Hellenismus* (Leiden, 1973), 41.

in the other languages of the ancient Near East (Akk. *la'bu* = "fever"[4]). A flame (or lamp[5]) can symbolize the Sumerian and Akkadian fire-god Nusku, as on the symbol socle of the Assyrian king Tukulti-Ninurta I.[6] The use of flames as a mark of the fire-god shows that in Akkadian, too, the notion of flames is inherent in the context of fire, which can be destructive as well as purifying.[7]

In Egypt, the protective aspect of flames is emphasized.[8] The tutelary deities Bes and Thoeris, who assist at births, are represented with serpents upon their heads;[9] like the blazing flame in the form of the eye of Horus, these are intended to drive away demons.[10] The protective function of flames is sought not only at birth but also in the other extreme situation of human life: in ch. 137 of the Book of the Dead, the ritual kindling of a flame serves to protect the dead. Here we already see a transition to the destructive aspect of flames. Flames provide protection by serving as a weapon to drive away what is evil.[11] Their destructive effect is embodied above all in the uraeus serpent, which has the shape of a blazing flame. In the cult of the dead, the "isle of flames" is actually the site of the dawn, the place of justification and of triumph over hostile powers.[12]

In Punic, *lhbh* may occur once in the form *lhb't*;[13] the uncertain context, however, makes interpretation difficult.[14]

No direct equivalent is found in Ugaritic. For the extended semantic field *'kl/b'r,* one text[15] may suggest a new stichometry for Lam. 2:3, with *lahab̲* and *'ēš* as syntactic equivalents.[16]

With respect to the relationship between the two aspects of *lahab̲,* we may cite the warlike god Resheph,[17] whose name means "flame," as well as the iconographic material of the ancient Near East, in which lightning is represented in the form of a lance.[18]

In Hebrew, then, *lahab̲* does not have two meanings but rather appears in two usages,

---

4. *AHw,* I (1965), 526b.

5. *WbMyth,* I, 116f.

6. E. Unger, "Flamme," *RLA,* III (1957-1971), 82; on the association of Nusku with flames, see also J. Bottéro in Fahd, 11.

7. E. Ebeling, "Feuer," *RLA,* III, 55f.

8. For the numerous equivalents, see *WbÄS,* VI, 53.

9. *RÄR,* 190.

10. I. Grumach-Shirun, "Feuerbohrer," *LexÄg,* II (1977), 206; M. Lurker, *The Gods and Symbols of Ancient Egypt* (Eng. trans., New York, 1980), 50.

11. *RÄR,* 191; Lurker, 50.

12. *RÄR,* 194.

13. Cherchell, II, 7; according to *KBL*[3], equivalent to a Hebrew construct.

14. *DISO,* 135; *KAI,* 161, 7.

15. *KTU,* 2.61, 8f.

16. M. Dahood and T. Penar, "Ugaritic-Hebrew Parallel Pairs," *RSP,* I, 107, no. 24.

17. See H. Gese, *Die Religionen Altsyriens, Altarabiens und der Mandäer. RdM,* 10/2 (1970), 141-45; Keel, *The Symbolism of the Biblical World,* 219-222.

18. Keel, *The Symbolism of the Biblical World,* 216f.; on the association of lightning, flame, lance, and dagger, see also E. F. Weidner and E. Unger, "Blitz," *RLA,* II (1938), 54-57.

each of which reflects a different aspect (lance/flame) of what was perceived as a single phenomenon (cf. the representation of the flame of lightning by a lance).

II. Usage.

1. *Secular.* In the Dead Sea scrolls, the sense of "weapon" is as common as the sense of "flame." The OT, by contrast, uses the noun only 5 times to denote a weapon. In Jgs. 3:22; 1 S. 17:7, this weapon serves as a means of destroying an enemy; Job 39:32 (cf. the similar usage in 1 S. 17:7) emphasizes instead the bravery and spirit of a horse when attacked by weapons, while not losing sight of their destructive nature. Dnl. 11:33 describes how in the last days the wise (i.e., the devout) will suffer the consequences of war. Here *lahab̲* is to be understood as a weapon, like the *ḥereb̲* mentioned in the same passage. The construction of such a weapon[19] as well as iconographic evidence[20] establishes the connection between the two usages, flame and lance: the flashing point of a metal lance or spear suggests comparison to a lightning flash or flame (cf. Nah. 3:3).

The noun appears 4 times in secular usage in the sense of "flame." In Job 41:13(21) (a text with mythological overtones[21]); Hos. 7:6 (as a simile [*kᵉ*] for the sudden rage of conspirators), the emphasis is on destructive power. Another figurative usage is found in the much debated text Cant. 8:6. Regardless of whether *šlhbtyh* is interpreted as "flame of Yahweh" (= lightning)[22] or an intensive form,[23] the word is used to express the great intensity of love. In Isa. 13:8, *lᵉhāb̲îm* describes the expression on the faces of the inhabitants of Babylon when they experience Yahweh's judgment (cf. Joel 2:6; Nah. 2:11 as a consequence of the day of Yahweh).

2. *Theological.* It is noteworthy that *lahab̲* is rarely used alone (Jgs. 13:20; Job 15:30); it usually appears in combination with fire[24] and associated verbs (*bʿr, lhṭ, ʾkl*). Both aspects — positive in the sense of protection, negative in the sense of destruction — are involved. In this usage, *lahab̲* may appear as an element of *ʾēš* (Ex. 3:2; Ps. 29:7; etc.) or especially (in parallelism) as its syntactic equivalent (Job 15:30; Lam. 2:3; etc.). Theological usage is concentrated in the prophetic writings and their supplementary material from the exilic and postexilic period, as well as in late Psalm texts, with the exception of the early text Ps. 29:7, which is influenced most strongly by ancient Near Eastern mythology.

---

19. H. Weippert, "Dolch und Schwert," *BRL*², 57-62; *idem,* "Lanze," *BRL*², 201f.; on the iron lance in 1 S. 17:7, see A. Alt as cited by S. Herrmann, *A History of Israel in OT Times* (Eng. trans., Philadelphia, ²1981), 144, n. 29.

20. See above.

21. Ohler, 52ff.

22. W. Rudolph, *Das Hohelied. KAT,* XVII/2 (1966), 180; K. Budde, *Das Hohelied. KHC,* XVII (1898), 45.

23. G. Gerleman, *Das Hohelied. BK,* XVIII (²1981), 217.

24. → אֵשׁ *ʾēš* (*ʾēsh*).

a. The concentration of occurrences in texts from the period of the exile and reconstruction helps explain the usage of *lahaḇ* and *lehāḇâ* in oracles of judgment — frequently against the nations, less often against Israel — as an attempt to interpret history. Ezk. 21:3(20:47) proclaims the total destruction of Israel/Judah after repeated apostasy, heightened by the doubled *laheḇeṯ šalheḇeṯ*. Lam. 2:3 is already dealing with the experience of God's wrath against his own people, which has been as devastating as a devouring flame of fire. The three texts in Joel are likewise directed against Israel. Joel 1:19 is part of a lament occasioned by the experience of the day of Yahweh. Joel 2:3,5, on the other hand, describe and threaten the events of this day, to be understood against the background of the theophany traditions (cf. Ps. 97:3) with echoes of apocalyptic ideas (esp. Joel 2:5).

This is also the setting of the phrase *lahaḇ 'ēš 'ôḵēlâ* in Isa. 29:6; 30:30, two texts directed against the enemies of Jerusalem. Elements of the (storm) theophany tradition, with many ancient Near Eastern parallels,[25] are used to describe Yahweh's coming to destroy the enemy.[26] In Ps. 105:32 (postexilic), the flames are a means of punishing the Egyptians and making the exodus of the Israelites possible (cf. Ex. 9:23). Isa. 47:14 refers to the wise counselors of Babylon, who fall victim to God's judgment. Nu. 21:28; Jer. 48:45 are closely related texts, threatening Moab in almost identical terms. Nu. 21:28 belongs to a taunt song (of the Ammonites), in which *'ēš* and *lahaḇ* are not described explicitly as instruments of Yahweh's judgment; the setting of Jer. 48:45, however, is a judgment oracle of Yahweh, which clearly describes both as being Yahweh's instruments.

Isa. 10:17 breaks the pattern. Here Yahweh does not make use of fire and flame, but rather as light of Israel (cf. Ps. 27:1; 36:10[9]) and Israel's Holy One becomes both *'ēš* and *lahaḇ*. This text does not think of Yahweh as a personified force of nature, but presents Yahweh as a being characterized by "fire" and "flame" and describes how he acts.

The noun *lahaḇ* is also used to describe Yahweh's punishment of the godless and wicked. Ps. 106:18 describes the punishment of those who followed Abiram or Korah. Isa. 5:24 threatens divine judgment upon those who despise Yahweh in their actions; Job 15:30 depicts Yahweh's judgment upon the wicked as total annihilation of the fruits of their lives. Isa. 43:2 also involves the aspect of judgment and destruction, but promises that the flame will not touch the people. The presence of Yahweh, now beneficent, breaks the power of the forces of nature.

b. The oracles of judgment against Israel or against the enemies of Israel or Yahweh show that the language of fire and flame is ambivalent. Destruction of the enemy (negative aspect) means deliverance for Israel (positive aspect); this is quite clear in Ps. 105:32; Isa. 29:6. In Ob. 18, Israel itself is fire and flame, an instrument in Yahweh's hand to destroy Edom. The aspect of protection is virtually explicit in Isa. 4:5, drawing on Ex. 13:21: the verse describes the presence of Yahweh as protector and guide.

---

25. Jeremias, 90.

26. *Ibid.*, 71f.; for the dating of these texts, see the comms.

c. We often find *lahab̲* in texts with theophanic elements or in actual theophanies. A storm theophany is implied in Isa. 29:6; 30:30 (which also exhibits affinities to descriptions of Yahweh as warrior); 66:15; Ps. 29:7; according to Jörg Jeremias,[27] only the last of these can be considered a true theophany. Elements of ancient Near Eastern storm-god worship are transferred to Yahweh; *lahᵃb̲ôt̲ 'ēš* once more suggests lightning. In Ps. 29:7, however, the combination *ḥṣb* + *lahᵃb̲ôt̲ 'ēš* is not original, but points to a parallel stich that has been lost.[28] In this text, the theophany serves to extol the glory of Yahweh; Ps. 83:15; Isa. 29:6; 30:30, however, use theophanic elements to describe Yahweh's intervention as judge against the enemy or (Isa. 66:15) the wicked within the Israelite community (v. 17).[29] Ex. 3:2; Jgs. 13:20 speak of flames in connection with the *mal'ak̲ YHWH.* The combination of the two elements likewise expresses the *mysterium tremendum et fascinosum* in the presence of Yahweh.

Flames and fire are thus understood as the instrument or sign of Yahweh's presence, of his judgment and protection; he is not, however, embodied in them.

Hausmann

27. Pp. 71f.
28. *Ibid.,* 30, n. 6.
29. See *ibid.,* 160, 178.

לָהַט *lāhaṭ*; לַהַט *lahaṭ*

The root *lhṭ* appears in the OT as a verb in the qal (Ps. 57:5[Eng. v. 4]; 104:4) and the piel (Dt. 32:22; Job 41:13[21]; Ps. 83:15[14]; 97:3; 106:18; Isa. 42:25; Joel 1:19; 2:3; Mal. 3:19[4:1]) and as a noun (Gen. 3:24). It is also found in 1QH 8:12 (noun) and Sir. 3:30 (qal); 9:9 (piel). The LXX translates *lhṭ* with verbs derived from the nouns used for *lhb*(*h*). There are no cognates in other languages, with the possible exception of Ps. 57:5(4): if *lhṭ* is to be read in this verse,[1] there may be a parallel in Arab. *lahaṭa* or Akk. *la'ātu,* "swallow." Because this is the only text that speaks of human oppression, there may be grounds for postulating a *lhṭ* II meaning "act greedily."

The other texts (except for Job 41:13(21); Ps. 104:4) connect *lhṭ* with God's actions. The verb (often in the setting of a theophany) describes an act of divine judgment associated with the day of Yahweh (Joel 1:19; 2:3; Mal. 3:19[4:1]) or of divine punish-

lāhaṭ. E. Lipiński, *La royauté de Yahwé dans la poésie et le culte de l'ancien Israël. VVAW.L,* 27/55 (1965), 20-26; N. J. Tromp, *Primitive Conceptions of Death and the Nether World in the OT. BietOr,* 21 (1969). → להב *lahab̲.*

1. *KBL*³, 495.

ment of enemies (Ps. 83:15[14]; 97:3) or apostate Israel (Dt. 32:22; Ps. 106:18; Isa. 42:25). This punishment is annihilating, for *lhṭ* is often used in conjunction with → אשׁ *'ēš,* which wreaks devastation in judgment. In Ps. 83:15(14); 106:18; Joel 1:19; 2:3, *lhṭ* serves as the predicate of *lehāḇâ,*[2] which may therefore be cited for the semantics of *lhṭ*. The verb denotes the action of flames or fire in general, parallel to → בער *b'r* (Ps. 83:15[14]; 106:18) or → אכל *'kl* (Joel 1:19; 2:3): "devour, consume." There is not enough evidence to support Edward Lipiński's proposed *lhṭ* II, which is not identical with the *lhṭ* II of *KBL*[3] cited above.

The nature of the burning is illustrated by Ps. 97:3. The verb *sāḇîḇ* suggests being "surrounded" by flames. Lipiński[3] reinforces this interpretation with his derivation of *lhṭ* from *lûṭ* with an epenthetic *h.* The element of "surrounding" also appears in Isa. 42:25, where *sāḇîḇ* appears once more. This text, however, uses *lhṭ* figuratively to describe battle and Yahweh's wrath.

In describing the terrifying Leviathan, Job 41:13(21) uses *lhṭ* with its menacing overtones.

The verb appears in a totally different context in Ps. 104:4, which praises God's creation. In conjunction with *'ēš,* it and the wind are described as God's messengers. Hans-Joachim Kraus[4] proposes emending the ungrammatical attributive phrase *'ēš lahaṭ* to *'ēš w^{e}lahaṭ,* interpreting both *'ēš* and *lahaṭ* as repudiated deities. This personification, however, is not found anywhere else in the OT, nor is such a deity known elsewhere in the ancient Near East. The attributive phrase, even though ungrammatical, should therefore be retained.

In Gen. 3:24, the construct phrase *lahaṭ hahereḇ* stands as an independent entity alongside the cherubim, guarding the way to the tree of life. Here *lhṭ* (like *lhb*) may possibly be associated with the phenomenon of the flashing sword.[5] Gen. 3:24 probably lies behind 1QH 8:32, where *lhṭ* likewise performs a guarding function, together with *'ēš* protecting the source of life.

Sir. 3:30 compares atonement for sin by almsgiving to the extinguishing of a blazing fire by water. In Sir. 9:8, *lhṭ* describes passion for a woman, which is condemned.

Besides its figurative use, then, *lhṭ* is used primarily to describe an act of divine punishment; it is also used to describe God's protection of something. The similarity to *lhb* in both meaning and usage is clear.

Hausmann

---

2. → להב *lahaḇ.*
3. P. 224.
4. H.-J. Kraus, *Psalms 60–150* (Eng. trans., Minneapolis, 1989), 297.
5. For further discussion, see C. Westermann, *Genesis 1–11* (Eng. trans., Minneapolis, 1974), 275.

לָוָה *lāwâ* I

Contents: I. 1. Etymology; 2. Occurrences. II. OT Usage: 1. Qal; 2. Niphal.

I. 1. *Etymology.* For Biblical Hebrew, we should probably postulate three distinct roots *lwh* with different meanings: *lāwâ* I, "accompany"; *lāwâ* II, "lend"; and *lāwâ* III, "twist, turn." The three Hebrew verbs may possibly derive from a common root *lwy,* which at an early date developed differently in the various Semitic languages, with semantic nuances traceable to a basic meaning "twist, turn." This meaning is found in Arab. *lawā(y),* Eth. *lawaya,*[1] Tigriña *läwäyä,* "bend, braid," and Tigre *läwya,* "bent," to which we should add Arab. *liwā',* "(act of) twisting," and OSA *lw'm,* probably "valley bend," the name of a palm grove.[2] In Hebrew, this meaning appears only in the two nouns *liwyâ,* "wreath" (Prov. 1:9; 4:9; 14:24 conj.; possibly also 1 K. 7:29), and → לויתן *liwyāṯān*; probably also in *lulā'ōṯ,* "loops" (Ex. 26:4f.,10f.; 36:11f.,17), and possibly in the technical architectural term *lûlîm* (1 K. 6:8).

Outside of Biblical Hebrew, the meaning "accompany, adhere to" is found in Middle Hebrew,[3] Egyptian Aramaic,[4] Jewish Aramaic, Syriac,[5] and Mandaic.[6] To trace the development from the basic meaning "twist, turn," we only note Akk. *lawû/lamû,*[7] "surround, besiege." Several personal names probably also derive from a verb *lwy* meaning "accompany": Lihyanic *lwyn* and Thamudic *lwy,*[8] OSA (Hadramautic) *tlwy,*[9] and Old Sabaean *lwyḥy.*[10] We may also cite Arab. *waliya,* "be near, be adjacent, be next to,"[11] if we assume that *waliya* is a metathesized form of the root *lwy.*[12] The Ugaritic occurrence of *lʒ'* < *lwy* with the meaning "accompany"[13] is more easily derived from *l'y,* "tire."[14] It is also true that the text *nhmmt šnt tlʒnn*[15] is difficult to interpret.

---

1. *LexLingAeth,* 54.
2. Cf. M. Höfner, "Die sabäischen Inschriften der südarabischen Expedition im Kunsthistorischen Museum in Wien (I)," *WZKM,* 40 (1933), 23.
3. *WTM,* II, 483f.
4. *DISO,* 136.
5. *LexSyr,* 360b.
6. *MdD,* 232a.
7. *AHw,* I (1965), 541.
8. G. L. Harding, *An Index and Concordance of Pre-Islamic Arabian Names and Inscriptions* (Toronto, 1971), 522.
9. *RÉS,* 4068, no. 58; cf. W. W. Müller, *Die Wurzeln Mediae und Teriae Y/W im Altsüdarabischen* (diss., Tübingen, 1962), 100.
10. Gl, 1699, 1; cf. A. G. Lundin, *Die Eponymenliste von Saba. SAW,* 248, 1 (1965), 40.
11. L. Kopf, "Arabisch Etymologien und Parallelen zum Bibelwörterbuch," *VT,* 8 (1958), 181f. = *Studies in Arabic and Hebrew Lexicography* (Jerusalem, 1976).
12. Cf. *VG,* I, 275.
13. Still proposed by G. R. Driver in *CML,* 28f., 158.
14. f. *WUS,* no. 1429; but now see J. C. L. Gibson, *CML*², 83, 149, who derives the form from *l'y,* "was strong, victorious, prevailed."
15. *KTU,* 1.14 I, 33.

2. *Occurrences.* The qal of *lāwâ* I in the sense of "adhere to, accompany" appears in the OT only in Eccl. 8:15, as well as Sir. 41:12. The niphal is found 11 times: Gen. 29:34; Nu. 18:2,4; Ps. 83:9(Eng. v. 8); Isa. 14:1; 56:3,6; Jer. 50:5; Zec. 2:15(11); Dnl. 11:34; also Est. 9:27. The meaning ranges from "join" in the sense of "ally oneself with" to the specialized usage "attach oneself to (Israel as a proselyte)."

II. OT Usage.

1. *Qal.* The qal of *lāwâ* I is found in Eccl. 8:15, where Qoheleth speaks of pleasure accompanying toil all one's days. Sir. 41:12 uses the verb in a similar sense: take thought for your good name, because it will attend you better than wealth by the thousands.

2. *Niphal.* The 11 texts using the niphal can be classified into three groups.

a. In Gen. 29:34, describing the birth of Levi, Leah's third son, the narrator interprets the name in a play on the root *lwh.* Like similar OT explanations of names on the basis of nothing more than a vague assonance, this etymology has little value. When her third son is born, Leah says: *ʿattâ happaʿam yillāweh ʾîšî ʾēlay,* "Now this time my husband will surely be joined to me," i.e., "devoted to me" (contra G. R. Driver,[16] who translates: "now my husband has joined himself with me again"). Probably the narrator's only purpose is to address the notion of the "unloved" wife, without any special interest in explaining the position or office of Levi or the Levites. The situation is different in Nu. 18:2,4, likewise a play on words; here we read that the Levites are to join Aaron, meaning that they attend (*wîšārᵉṯûḵā*) him (i.e., the priests) in a special role.

b. The verb is used in a negative sense in Ps. 83:9(8), where it describes the hostile alliance of Israel's enemies that Assyria has joined. Dnl. 11:34 speaks in a similar vein of those who hypocritically join any group that seems to offer help and support.

c. The other passages are very different. Here the niphal of *lāwâ* refers either to alien proselytes who join Yahweh (Isa. 56:3,6), the many nations who join the community of Yahweh (Zec. 2:15[11]), or aliens who join the community of Israel by adopting its faith (Isa. 14:1). Thus the proselytes in Est. 9:27 (*kol-hannilwîm ʿᵃlêhem,* "all who joined them [the Jews]") are required to celebrate the festival of Purim. In Jer. 50:5, finally, the niphal of *lāwâ* with *ʾel-YHWH* can be taken as equivalent to "believe in." The Israelites returning from exile, we are told, will say to each other: "Come, 'let us'[17] join ourselves to Yahweh in an everlasting *bᵉrîṯ* which will never be forgotten." The call to be joined to Yahweh, i.e., not to forsake belief in Yahweh, is here called *bᵉrîṯ ʿôlām,* "a perpetual and therefore unforgettable obligation — on the part of the Israelites alone."[18]

Kellermann

---

16. G. R. Driver, *Problems of the Hebrew Verbal System. OT Studies,* II (Edinburgh, 1936), 143.

17. Reading *wᵉnillāweh* instead of *wᵉnilwû,* with Syr.

18. E. Kutsch, *Verheissung und Gesetz. BZAW,* 131 (1973), 18.

לָוָה II *lāwâ* II

Contents: I. Etymology and Occurrences. II. OT Usage.

I. Etymology and Occurrences. The qal of the verb appears in both Biblical and Middle Hebrew with the meaning "borrow"; the hiphil means "lend." The qal denotes "acceptance of a loan in return for the debtor's promise to repay," whereas → נשׁא *nš'* refers to the rights of the creditor.[1] Arab. *lawā(y)*, "put off a creditor, delay payment, fail to pay a debt," first cited by Jakob Barth,[2] suggests that the basic meaning of the root *lwy,* "twist, turn," may well be the point of departure for the meaning of the Arabic verb and that Heb. *lāwâ* II is likewise just a special development of this root *lwy.* We arrive at the same conclusion if we follow Jacob Levy[3] in understanding *lāwâ,* "borrow," in the sense of "as if it were attached to or by, *nexum esse.*" The concrete sense of "borrow" is also attested by *lw'n,* "person as temple security," found only in North Minaean,[4] and possibly by *lw'm,*[5] the name of a Sabaean palm grove mentioned under *lāwâ* I.[6]

The qal of *lāwâ* II, "borrow," appears 5 times (Dt. 28:12; Isa. 24:2; Ps. 37:21; Prov. 22:7; Neh. 5:4) and the hiphil, "lend," 9 times (Ex. 22:24[Eng. v. 25]; Dt. 28:12,44[twice]; Ps. 37:26; 112:5; Isa. 24:2; Prov. 19:17; 22:7; also Sir. 8:12[twice] and ms. B of Sir. 32:12 as a marginal interpolation from Prov. 19:17). There is no observable pattern in the distribution of the verb.

II. OT Usage. In Ex. 22:24(25), the Covenant Code prohibits loans with interest (*nešek̲*) in Israel (cf. Lev. 25:35-38; Dt. 23:20f.[19f.], with different terminology). This prohibition presupposes an economically undeveloped society in which loans aided the poor and the hungry. The restriction to loans within Israel ("any of my people with you who is poor" [Ex. 22:24(25), expanded in Dt. 23:20(19)]) is due to God's requirement of justice, which made the Israelites responsible for each other. An Israelite who was poor and therefore had to borrow found support within the clan or tribe. To have mercy on the needy and lend to them is therefore a mark of the *ṣaddîq* (Ps. 37:26; 112:5).

---

lāwâ II. R. K. Sikkema, *De Lening in het OT* (Hague, 1957); cf. J. W. Wevers, review of Sikkema, *BiOr,* 18 (1961), 96f.; H. Gamoran, "The Biblical Law Against Loans on Interest," *JNES,* 30 (1971), 127-134.

1. Cf. F. Horst, "Brachjahr und Schuldverhältnisse: 15, 1-18," *Gottes Recht. GSAT. ThB,* 12 (1961), 84f.
2. J. Barth, *Etymologische Studien zum Semitischen* (Leipzig, 1893), 12.
3. *WTM,* II, 483a.
4. *RÉS,* 3351, 2; 3603, 3; fem. *lw'tn*: 3357, 2; 3697, 3; with 3rd person masc. suf. *lw'ths*: 3357, 1.
5. *RÉS,* 4194, 4.
6. → לוי *lēwî.*

The OT envisions two dangers associated with borrowing and lending. The rich can come to rule the poor by lending (Prov. 22:7). Social unrest like that described in Neh. 5:1ff. is traced to the necessity of mortgaging fields and vineyards to pay the royal tax, so that the people lament: "Our fields and vineyards now belong to others" (NRSV). On the other hand, Ps. 37:21 deplores unethical conduct on the part of debtors: to borrow without repaying is a mark of the *rāšāʿ*. According to Dt. 28:12, being able to lend without having to borrow is among the blessings of Yahweh. But having to borrow from a stranger without being in a position to lend to him (Dt. 28:44: *hûʾ yalwᵉḵā wᵉʾattâ lōʾ talwennû*) creates the danger that the creditor will gain control over the debtor. The warning of Sir. 8:12 is similar: do not lend to someone more powerful than you; if you do, consider the loan a loss. Isa. 24:2 uses creditor (*malweh*) and debtor (*lōweh*) as antonyms in a warning that the coming judgment will strike all and that all social differences will be abolished.

Wis. 15:16 calls human life a loan from God (*to pneúma dedaneisménos,* "one whose breath has been loaned"). On the other hand, Prov. 19:17 and the marginal note of Sir. 32:12 (ms. B) say that one who is kind to the poor lends to God. We even read in 4 Mc. 2:8 that one who walks according to the law will lend to the needy without interest, even though well aware that in the year of release (cf. Dt. 15:1ff.) the principal itself will be lost.

The LXX regularly uses forms of *daneízō* to translate *lāwâ* II, except in Ps. 112:5(LXX 111:5) (*kichráō*).

The NT expressly demands lending without interest (Mt. 5:42; Lk. 6:34; 11:5) as expressing love of one's neighbor.

Kellermann

לוז *lûz*; לָזוּת *lāzûṯ*

Contents: 1. Etymology; 2. Occurrences; LXX; 3. Usage.

1. *Etymology.* Apart from Middle Hebrew (niphal: "be perverse"; hiphil: "pervert," "speak evil"), the root *lwz* is attested only in Arab. *lāḏa,* "turn aside."[1] The noun *lûz,* "almond tree" (Gen. 30:37), is a different word.

2. *Occurrences; LXX.* The qal and hiphil occur once each with the meaning "lose from sight"; the niphal occurs 4 times with the meaning "be perverse." There is also a single occurrence of the abstract noun *lāzûṯ*. All the occurrences are in wisdom texts or texts influenced by wisdom (Isa. 30:12).

---

lûz. M. G. Glenn, "The Word לוז in Gen 28.19 in the LXX and in Midrash," *JQR,* N.S. 59 (1968/69), 73-75.

1. For a different view, see W. von Soden, "*n* als Wurzelaugment im Semitischen," *Studia orientalia. Festschrift C. Brockelmann. WZ Halle-Wittenberg,* 17, 2/3 (1968), 181.

The LXX translates the qal in Prov. 3:21 with *pararréō,* and the hiphil in Prov. 4:21 with *ekleípō*. Each of the niphals is translated differently. In Isa. 30:12, *beʿōšeq wenālôz* is translated *epí pseúdei kaí hóti egóngysas*; the participle is translated by *kámpylos* ("crooked": Prov. 2:5), *paránomos* (3:32), and *skoliázō* (14:2).

3. *Usage.* The qal appears only in Prov. 3:21: "Let them not escape (*'al-yāluzû*) from your sight; keep sound wisdom (*tušiyyâ*) and discretion (*mezimmâ*)." The context of the verse is a discourse on the value of wisdom. The verb *lûz* has no subject; we would expect something like "the words of wisdom or the wise." It is possible that vv. 21-26 stood originally in a different context, in which the subject was expressed.[2] In any case, the verse declares that one must never lose sight of wisdom in her various manifestations, but rather seek and preserve her with zeal, for she bestows life and happiness. In Prov. 4:21, the hiphil appears in a long passage praising wisdom; the verse is very similar to 3:21: "Let [my words] not escape from your sight; keep them within your heart." The preceding verse makes it clear that the verb refers to "my words" and "my sayings"; the same is probably true for v. 21.

The niphal in Prov. 14:2 appears in the phrase *nelôz derāḵāyw,* "one who is devious in his ways," in contrast to *hōlēḵ beyošrô*: "One who fears Yahweh walks in uprightness, but one who despises him goes by devious ways." The point is clearly religious. The fear of God and right conduct go hand in hand; saying "one who fears God walks in uprightness" is the same as saying "one who walks in uprightness fears God." Despising God likewise goes hand in hand with devious ways. Ways are also mentioned in Prov. 2:15, where *nālôz* appears in combination with *maʿgālâ,* "path," and in parallel with *ʿiqqēš,* "crooked": ". . . whose paths are crooked, and who are devious in their ways." Wisdom will protect her disciple from those who are devious in their ways.

Prov. 3:32 also uses *nālôz* and *yāšār* as antonyms: "The perverse man is an abomination to Yahweh, but the upright are in his company (*sôḏ*)." The verse speaks of perverse conduct, which separates people from fellowship with God.

Isa. 30:12 deals with the consequences of rejecting the prophet's message: "Because you despise this word, and trust in oppression (*ʿōšeq*) and perverseness . . . ," punishment will come upon you. It is tempting to conjecture something like *ʿiqqēš,* "crooked," instead of *ʿōšeq,*[3] since *lûz* is often used with *ʿqš*. Failure to trust in Yahweh is condemned as religious perverseness; it must bring catastrophe.

The situation is a bit different in Sir. 31/34:8 "Happy is the man[4] who is found guiltless, and who does not go astray after riches (*māmôn*)." Here *nālôz 'aḥar* means "turn aside from the right way to pursue [riches]."

The noun *lāzûṯ* occurs only in Prov. 4:24, which warns against crookedness (*ʿiqqešûṯ*) of the mouth and perverseness of the lips.

Ringgren

2. See below.
3. Cf. *BHK*[3].
4. The LXX and Syr. read "the rich man."

לוּחַ *lûaḥ*

Contents: I. 1. Etymology, Ancient Near East; 2. Meaning and Occurrences; 3. Archaeology. II. Original Meaning. III. Writing Tablets. IV. Figurative Usage. V. Tables of the Law.

I. 1. *Etymology, Ancient Near East.* The noun *lûaḥ* is a primary noun, found in almost all Semitic languages: Akk. *lē'u* (or *lēyu*),[1] Ugar. *lḥ,*[2] Neo-Punic *lḥ,*[3] Jewish Aram. and Syr. *lûḥā,* Egyp. Aram. *lwḥ,*[4] Arab. *lauḥ,* Eth. *lawḥ.* Amh. *lûk,* "sheet of paper," is probably also cognate.[5] The proper noun *lûḥîṯ*[6] (Isa. 15:5; Jer. 48:5) may reflect a topographical phenomenon. In most languages, *lûaḥ* is masculine; in Ugaritic, Egyptian Aramaic, and Syriac it is also feminine.

2. *Meaning and Occurrences.* In all the Semitic languages, *lûaḥ* is a technical term for flat objects (boards, planks, plates) of various materials (wood, metal, or stone), especially writing tablets.

The noun occurs 43 times in the OT (45 if we accept the LXX reading in 1 K. 8:9 par. 2 Ch. 5:10; but Prov. 3:3 is probably an addition from Prov. 7:3). The occurrences are clearly concentrated in certain books: 17 in Exodus and 16 in Deuteronomy, referring to the tables of the law;[7] 1 K. 8:9 par. 2 Ch. 5:10 belong to the same context, as do 4 other occurrences. The other 8 are distributed among the prophets (Isa. 30:8; Jer. 17:1; Ezk. 27:5; Hab. 2:2), Proverbs (Prov. 3:3; 7:3), Kings (1 K. 7:36), and the Song of Songs (Cant. 8:9). This distribution shows clearly how the meaning "tables of the law" dominates in the OT, an emphasis that probably does not reflect normal usage.

The dual of *lûaḥ* appears in Ezk. 27:5, unless we accept the reading *lûḥôṯāyik.*[8]

The LXX regularly uses *pláx* to translate *lûaḥ* in the sense of "table of the law," except in Ex. 24:12, which uses *pyxíon*; the latter appears also in Isa. 30:8; Hab. 2:2. Proverbs uses *plátos,* Cant. 8:9; Ezk. 27:5 *sanís,* and Ex. 27:8 *sanidōtós,* a hapax legomenon.

---

lûaḥ. K. Galling, "Tafel, Buch und Blatt," *Near Eastern Studies in Honor of W. F. Albright* (Baltimore, 1971), 207-223; → דלת *deleṯ* (*deleth*) I.2.

1. *AHw,* I (1965), 546f.

2. *WUS,* no. 1449; cf. also C. Virolleaud, "Notes de lexicographie ougaritiques," *GLECS,* 8 (1957-59), 90-95; A. van Selms, "A Forgotten God: *Laḥ,*" *Studia Biblica et Semitica. Festschrift T. C. Vriezen* (Wageningen, 1966), 318-326.

3. *KAI,* 145, 8.

4. *DISO,* 136.

5. W. Leslau, *Hebrew Cognates in Amharic* (Wiesbaden, 1969), 96.

6. See W. Schottroff, "Horonaim, Nimrim, Luhith und der Westrand des 'Landes Ataroth,' " *ZDPV,* 82 (1966), 163-208.

7. See V below.

8. See Galling, 208.

3. *Archaeology.* Stone was used as a writing material from an early date (inscriptions on rock, statues, and stelae). Distinctly different are portable writing tablets, sometimes meant expressly for writing practice or official scribes. The most familiar example from Israel is the agricultural calendar from Gezer (10th century B.C.),[9] of which probably only the top half is extant (6.7-11.1 cm. [2.6-4.4 in.] high, 7.2 cm. [2.8 in.] wide). The writing is incised on the soft limestone. The conjunction of a writing tablet with a calendar is interesting, since "calendar" is a common meaning for *lûaḥ* in Postbiblical Hebrew.

Plates of lead or precious metal were commonly used for writing in the ancient Near East, but not in Syria-Palestine. The same is true of clay tablets, the preferred material for cuneiform.

Wooden tablets, however, were convenient for both cuneiform (covered with a layer of wax) and for cursive scripts like Hebrew (for which they were often covered with lime or whitewash). A diptych comprising two tablets hinged together was the notebook preferred by scribes. Many illustrations from the eighth century onward depict one scribe sitting behind another recording lists (of booty, for example); the first uses a tablet of clay or waxed wood for cuneiform, the second a piece of leather or papyrus (or a wooden tablet) for cursive Aramaic.[10] Such a tool had to be compact; several tablets could be joined together (cf. the folding book of twenty-three ivory and wood tablets measuring 33.8 × 15.6 cm. [13.3 × 6.1 in.] found at Nimrud[11]). The two leaves of a diptych joined by hinges worked like the leaves of a door (cf. Jer. 36:23, where → דלת *delet̲*, "wing of a door," is used for the "columns" of a papyrus scroll).[12]

II. Original Meaning. Originally, *lûaḥ* probably denoted any kind of flat object without regard for its use. Thus we find it referring to wooden boards and planks (cedar [Cant. 8:9], acacia [Ex. 27:1,8], juniper [Ezk. 27:5]) used to bar a door (Cant. 8:9),[13] to build an altar (Ex. 27:8), or to build a ship (Ezk. 27:5; the dual form, if not emended, may refer to the two sides of the ship or to a special type of construction — double planks to guarantee watertightness[14]). The size and shape of the boards seem to have varied, but all seem to have been rectangular.

The OT does not mention uninscribed stone slabs, but cf. the proper noun *lûḥît̲*. Metal plates are mentioned in 1 K. 7:36; the fact that they were engraved makes them similar to writing tablets.

III. Writing Tablets. OT usage provides some information about writing tablets: clay tablets are never mentioned. When *lûaḥ* appears without qualification, wooden tablets, especially diptychs, are probably meant.[15] Isa. 30:8, for example, may well

---

9. *KAI,* 182.
10. Galling, 210ff.; H. P. Rüger, "Schreibmaterial, Buch und Schrift," *BRL*^{2}, 290f.
11. Galling, 207, n. 3.
12. Cf. *KAI,* 194; *TGI,* 45, 4.
13. → דלת *delet̲* (*deleth*) IV.
14. See I.3 above.
15. See I.3 above.

refer to a diptych covered with wax, so that the writing could be inscribed. Hab. 2:2, also, probably has a diptych in mind. In Cant. 8:9, the LXX pictures a writing tablet, as the translation shows.

Tablets of stone had to be specifically identified as such (Ex. 24:12; 31:18; 34:1; etc.). Such tablets were probably rare in later periods. The frequent emphasis on the two tables of the law (Ex. 31:18; 34:1; Dt. 4:13; 9:11; 10:1; 1 K. 8:9; etc.) may indicate that they were thought of after the analogy of (rectangular!) wooden diptychs. The depiction of the tables of the law with rounded tops, normal in Jewish and Christian iconography, may be due to the analogy of (mortuary?) stelae. Ex. 34:1,4 presupposes that the tablets were carved out of larger blocks, so that the surface was as flat as possible. Writing on both sides (Ex. 32:15) is attested elsewhere in the ancient Near East; it makes it possible to keep the dimensions as small as possible. Furthermore, the Decalog probably did not require much space.[16] Moses could easily have carried such tablets of stone down from the mountain of God. The inscribed texts cited in Isa. 30:8; Hab. 2:2 are even shorter (Isa. 30:9-14; Hab. 2:3f.).

Writing implements included pens of iron with diamond points (Jer. 17:1; cf. Job 19:24). Writing with ink is denoted by *ktb* (Exodus and Deuteronomy; also Hab. 2:2; Prov. 3:3; 7:3), more rarely by *ḥqq* (Isa. 30:8; cf. Job 19:23f.) or *ḥrš* (Jer. 17:1). Furthermore, only Ex. 32:16 uses *ḥrt,* "incise," to describe the writing on tables of the law; other texts use *ktb,* "write upon," which probably presupposes that the stone was first whitened with lime (cf. Dt. 27:8).

The purpose of writing is always to record a spoken utterance for later ages (Isa. 30:8; cf. Job 19:23f.), so that it can be read once more at any time (Hab. 2:2).

IV. Figurative Usage. This brings us close to the figurative usage of *lûaḥ* as the "tablet of the heart" (Jer. 17:1; Prov. 3:3; 7:3).[17] In such contexts, it represents an imperishable "recording" of both transgressions and wisdom instruction. When used in this sense, *lûaḥ* becomes a metaphor for memory.

V. Tables of the Law. The OT uses *lûaḥ* in a special sense to refer to the tables Moses brought down from the mountain of God. While the noun always serves to denote these particular tablets with the writing upon them, their significance is defined by various explanatory qualifications. The original expression probably referred only to the "two tables" (Ex. 31:18; 34:1,4,29; Dt. 4:13; 5:22; 9:11,15,17; 10:1,3; 1 K. 8:9 par. 2 Ch. 5:10) or the (two) "stone tables" (Ex. 24:12; 31:18; 34:1,4; Dt. 4:13; 5:22; 9:9,10,11; 10:1; 1 K. 8:9) or simply "the tables" (Ex. 32:19; 34:1,28; Dt. 10:2,4). They are important because God gave them to Moses (Ex. 24:12) and also because the writing upon them was the work of God (Ex. 32:16) or God's own writing (Dt. 10:2,4) or was even done by God's own finger (Ex. 31:18; Dt. 9:10). In this context, the substance of what was written on the

---

16. U. Cassuto, discussing Ex. 32:15, suggests a height of some 30 cm. (12 in.); *A Comm. on the Book of Exodus* (Eng. trans., Jerusalem, 1967), *in loc.* Cf. I.3 above.

17. → לב *lēḇ.*

tables is stated more precisely: not simply words of God in general but very specific words, the "ten words" of the Decalog (Ex. 34:28; Dt. 4:13; 10:4).

Two traditions must be noted that associate the tables of the law very closely with the ark:[18] the Deuteronomic and Deuteronomistic tradition calls the tables "tables of the covenant"[19] (Dt. 9:9,11; cf. Ex. 34:28; Dt. 4:13; 1 K. 8:9 conj. par. 2 Ch. 5:10 conj.). In this tradition, the ark appears as the receptacle for the tables (Dt. 10:1,3,5; 1 K. 8:9 par. 2 Ch. 5:10). The Priestly tradition refers to them as "tables of the testimony"[20] (Ex. 31:18; 32:15; 34:29), a phrase intended to express the relationship between the ark, the Decalog, and the ensuing covenant commitment.

It is important that the tradition of the tables speaks of their being broken and restored. More is involved than just a physical process. The restoration of the tables (and their preservation in the ark) is visible testimony that it is God's will to maintain his covenant. Clearly, in ancient times, the symbolism of a written text was especially pregnant: the writing represented something binding and enduring. We see this already in Job 19:23f.; Isa. 30:8; Hab. 2:2. Jer. 36:27ff. makes it clear that human attempts to destroy what has been written cannot deflect the will of God: the burned scroll declaring imminent judgment is rewritten. Through the ages, however, the two tables of the law have been the most powerful symbol of God's unchanging demands on his people as well as God's unchanging love for his people.

Baumann

---

18. → ארון *'ªrôn*.
19. → ברית *b^e^rîṯ* (*b^e^rîth*).
20. → עוד *'wd* IV.1.

לֵוִי *lēwî*; לְוִיִּם *l^e^wîyîm*

Contents: I. 1. Occurrences, Statistics; 2. Etymology. II. Secular Tribe: 1. Gen. 49:5-7; 34; 2. Levi among the Twelve Tribes. III. Priestly Tribe. IV. The Levitical Cities. V. Levi in the Individual Sources: 1. Deuteronomy; 2. Ezekiel; 3. P; 4. Chronicler's History. VI. 1. Age; 2. Support; 3. Redemption of the First-born; 4. Consecration; 5. *b^e^rîṯ* with Levi. VII. Dead Sea Scrolls and Postbiblical Literature.

---

lēwî. R. Abba, "Priests and Levites," *IDB,* III, 876-889; *idem,* "Priests and Levites in Deuteronomy," *VT,* 27 (1977), 257-267; *idem,* "Priests and Levites in Ezekiel," *VT,* 28 (1978), 1-9; M. W. T. Allan, *The Priesthood in Ancient Israel with Special Reference to the Status and Function of the Levites* (diss., Glasgow, 1971); N. Allan, "Some Levitical Traditions Considered with Reference to the Status of Levites in Pre-exilic Israel," *HeyJ,* 21 (1980),

1-13; W. W. Graf Baudissin, "Priests and Levites," *HDB,* IV, 67-97; I. Ben-Zvi, "The Levites among Arabian Tribes," *In the Time of Harvest. Festschrift A. H. Silver* (New York, 1963), 129-135; cf. *Molad,* 20 (1962), 166f., 241-44; G. R. Berry, "Priests and Levites," *JBL,* 42 (1923), 227-238; A. Caquot, " 'Siméon et Lévi sont frères . . .' (Genèse 49,5)," *De la Tôrah au Messie. Festschrift H. Cazelles* (Paris, 1981), 113-19; A. Cody, "Priesthood in the OT," *Studia missionalia,* 22 (1973), 309-329; S. A. Cook, "Simeon and Levi," *AJT,* 13 (1909), 370-388; S. I. Curtiss, *The Levitical Priests* (Edinburgh, 1877); A. Eberharter, "Der israelitische Levitismus in der vorexilischen Zeit," *ZKTh,* 52 (1928), 492-518; J.-M. Fenasse, "Lévi, Lévites," *Catholicisme,* VII, 506f., 516-521; G. Fohrer, "Levi und Leviten," *RGG*[3], IV (1960), 336f.; T. H. Gaster, "The Name לֵוִי," *JTS,* 38 (1937), 250f.; M. Gertner, "The Masorah and the Levites," *VT,* 10 (1960), 241-272; C. H. J. de Geus, *The Tribes of Israel. SSN,* 18 (1976), 97-108; J. Goettsberger, "Das alttestamentliche Priestertum und Ezechiel," *Festschrift Kardinal Faulhaber* (Munich, 1949), 1-19; H. Graetz, "Eine Strafmassregel gegen die Leviten," *MGWJ,* 35 (1886), 97-108; K. H. Graf, "Zur Geschichte des Stammes Levi," *Zur Geschichte des Stämmes Levi. AWEAT,* 1 (1867/69), 68-106, 208-236; M. Greenberg, "A New Approach to the History of the Israelite Priesthood," *JAOS,* 70 (1950), 41-47; P. Grelot, "Sprritualité lévitique et spiritualité cléricale," *Catholic Historical Review,* 9 (1962), 291-305; H. Grimme, "Der südarabische Levitismus und sein Verhältnis zum Levitisimus in Israel," *Mus,* 37 (1924), 169-199; B. Halpern, "Levitic Participation in the Reform Cult of Jeroboam I," *JBL,* 95 (1976), 31-42; M. Haran, *Temples and Temple-Service in Ancient Israel* (Oxford, 1978), 58-131; C. Hauret, "Aux origines du sacerdoce danite," *Mélanges Bibliques. Festschrift A. Robert. Travaux de l'Institut Catholique de Paris,* 4 (1957), 105-113; G. Hölscher, "Levi," *PW,* XII/2 (1925), 2155-2208; A. van Hoonacker, "Ezekiel's Priests and Levites: A Disclaimer," *ExpT,* 12 (1900/01), 383, 494-98; *idem,* "Les prêtres et les lévites dans le livre d'Ezéchiel," *RB,* 8 (1899), 177-205; *idem, La sacerdoce lévitique dans la loi et dans l'histoire des Hébreux* (London, 1899); A. Jepsen, "Mose und die Leviten," *VT,* 31 (1981), 318-323; D. R. Jones, "Priests and Levites," *DB* (1963), 793-97; M. de Jonge, "Levi, the sons of Levi and the Law, in *Testament Levi* X, XIV-XV and XVI," *Festschrift H. Cazelles,* 513-523; E. Kautzsch, review of W. W. Graf Baudissin, *Die Geschichte des alttestamentlichen Priesterthums* (Leipzig, 1889; repr. Osnabrück, 1967), *ThStKr,* 1890/1, 767-786; J. Kelly, *The Function of the Priests in the OT* (diss., Jerusalem, 1973); J. Köberle, *Die Tempelsänger im AT* (Erlanger, 1899); E. König, "The Priests and Levites in Ezekiel xliv. 7-15," *ExpT,* 12 (1900/01), 300-303; C. Lattey, "The Tribe of Levi," *CBQ,* 12 (1950), 277-291; A. Lefèvre, "Lévitique (organisation)," *DBS,* V (1957), 389-397; *idem,* "Notes d'exégèse sur les généalogies des Qehatites," *RScR,* 37 (1950), 287-292; A. Legendre, "Lévi," "Lévi (tribu de)," *DB,* IV (1908), 200-213; S. Lehmig, "Zur Überlieferungsgeschichte von Gen 34," *ZAW,* 70 (1958), 228-250; J. S. Licht, "לֵוִי, לְוִיִּם," *EMiqr,* IV (1962), 460-478; J. Liver, *Chapters in the History of the Priests and Levites* (Jerusalem, 1968) [Heb.]; *idem,* "Korah, Dathan and Abiram," *ScrHier,* 8 (1961), 189-217; S. E. Loewenstamm, "The Investiture of Levi," *ErIsr,* 10 (1971), 169-172 [Heb.], XIVf. [Eng. summary]; O. Loretz, "Aharon der Levit (Ex 4, 14)," *UF,* 8 (1976), 454; J. Maier, "Zur Geschichte des Bundesgedankens und zur Rolle der Leviten in der politischen und religiösen Geschichte des alten Israel," *Jud,* 25 (1969), 222-257; J. A. Maynard, "The Rights and Revenues of the Tribe of Levi," *JSOR,* 14 (1930), 11-17; T. J. Meek, "Aaronites and Zadokites," *ASJL,* 45 (1928/29), 149-166; *idem,* "Moses and the Levites," *ASJL,* 56 (1939), 113-120; A. Menes, *Die vorexilischen Gesetze Israels im Zusammenhang seiner kulturgeschichtlichen Entwicklung. BZAW,* 50 (1928), 1-19; E. Meyer, *Die Israeliten und ihre Nachbarstämme* (1906, repr. Darmstadt, 1967), 78-89, 118-120; *idem,* "Die Mosesagen und die Leviten," *SDAW,* 1905, 640-652 = *KlSchr,* I (Halle, 1910), 315-332; R. Meyer, "Levitische Emanzipationsbestrebungen in nachexilischer Zeit," *OLZ,* 41 (1938), 721-28; W. Michaelis, "Λευ(ε)ίτης," *TDNT,* IV,

245-47; J. Milgrom, "The Levitical ʿABOḎĀ," *JQR,* 61 (1970/71), 132-154; K. Möhlenbrink, "Die levitischen Überlieferungen des ATs," *ZAW,* 52 (1934), 184-231; S. Mowinckel, "Levi und Leviten," *RGG*^{2}, III, 1601-1603; E. Nielsen, "The Levites in Ancient Israel," *ASTI,* 3 (1964), 16-27; *idem, Shechem* (Copenhagen, ^{2}1959), 264-286; F. S. North, "Aaron's Rise in Prestige," *ZAW,* 68 (1954), 191-99; B. Pîpal, "Sčítání bojovníků a Lévitů," *Theologická příloha,* 34 (1967), 49-52; G. von Rad, *Das Geschichtsbild des chronistischen Werkes. BWANT,* 54[4/3] (1930); *idem,* "Die levitische Predigt in den Büchern der Chronik," *Festschrift O. Procksch* (Leipzig, 1934), 113-124; M. D. Rehm, *Studies in the History of the Pre-Exilic Levites* (diss., Harvard, 1967); R. B. Robinson, "The Levites in the Pre-monarchic Period," *StBTh,* 8 (1978), 3-24; J. P. Ross, *The "Cities of the Levites" in Joshua XXI and 1 Chronicles VI* (diss., Edinburgh, 1973); H. H. Rowley, "Early Levite History and the Question of the Exodus," *JNES,* 3 (1944), 73-78; W. H. Schmidt, "Mose als Levit," *Exodus. BK,* II (1977), 65-67 (excursus); W. Schottroff, *Der altisraelitische Fluchspruch. WMANT,* 30 (1969), 134-142; J. Schreiner, "Levi," *LThK*^{2}, VI (1961), 993-95; E. Seydl, "Der Simeon-Levi-Spruch (Gen. 49,5-7)," *Der Katholik,* 80 (1900 [I]), 548-556; G. H. Skipwith, "The Name of Levi," *JQR,* 11 (1899), 264f.; W. R. Smith, "The Deuteronomic Code and the Levitical Law," *The OT in the Jewish Church* (Edinburgh, ^{2}1892), 343-387; *idem* and A. Bertholet, "Levites," *EncBib,* III, 2770-76; F. Spadafora, "Ilsacerdozio in Israele," *Palestra del Clero,* 54 (1975), 711-724; J. J. Stähelin, "Versuch einer Geschichte der Verhältnisse des Stammes Levi," *ZDMG,* 9 (1855), 704-730; L. Steinberger, *Der Bedeutungswechsel des wortes Levit* (Berlin, 1936); H. Strathmann, "Λευ(ε)ί," *TDNT,* IV, 234-39; H. Strauss, *Untersuchungen zu den Überlieferungen der vorexilischen Leviten* (diss., Bonn, 1959); R. de Vaux, " 'Lévites' minéens et lévites Israélites," *Lex tua veritas. Festschrift H. Junker* (Trier, 1961), 265-273; H. Vogelstein, *Der Kampf zwischen Priestern und Leviten seit den Tagen Ezechiels* (Stettin, 1889); H. C. M. Vogt, *Studie zur nachexilischen Gemeinde in Esra-Nehemia* (Werl, 1966), 123-135; L. Waterman, "Moses the Pseudo Levite," *JBL,* 59 (1940), 397-404; *idem,* "Some Determining Factors in the Northward Progress of Levi," *JAOS,* 57 (1937), 375-380; *idem,* "Some Repercussions from Late Levitical Genealogical Accretions in P and the Chronicler," *AJSL,* 58 (1941), 49-56; M. Weber, *Ancient Judaism* (Eng. trans., New York, 1952), 169-187; A. C. Welch, *The Code of Deuteronomy* (London, 1924); *idem, The Work of the Chronicler* (London, 1939), 55-80; J. Wellhausen, *Prolegomena to the History of Israel* (Eng. trans. 1885, repr. Cleveland, 1957), 121-167; G. Westphal, "Aaron und die Aaroniden," *ZAW,* 26 (1906), 201-230; G. E. Wright, "The Levites in Deuteronomy," *VT,* 4 (1954), 325-330; S. Yeivin, "לֵוִי," *EMiqr,* IV (1962), 450-460; W. Zimmerli, "Erstgeborene und Leviten," *Near Eastern Studies in Honor of W. F. Albright* (Baltimore, 1971), 459-469 = *Studien zur alttestamentlichen Theologie und Prophetie. Gesammelte Aufsätze,* II. *ThB,* 51 (1974), 235-246; H. J. Zobel, *Stammesspruch und Geschichte. BZAW,* 95 (1965), 67-72; → כֹּהֵן *kōhēn.*

IV: Y. Aharoni, *The Land of the Bible* (Eng. trans., Philadelphia, ^{2}1979), 301-5; W. F. Albright, "The List of Levitic Cities," *L. Ginzberg Jubilee Volume* (New York, 1945), 49-73; A. Alt, "Bemerkungen zu einigen judäischen Ortslisten des ATs," *BBLAK,* 68 (1951), 193-210 = *KlSchr,* II (1959), 289-305; *idem,* "Festungen und Levitenorte im Lande Juda" (1952) = *KlSchr,* II, 306-315; A. G. Auld, "The 'Levitical Cities': Texts and History," *ZAW,* 91 (1979), 194-206; A. Cody, "Levitical Cities and the Israelite Settlement," *Homenaje a J. Prado* (Madrid, 1975), 179-189; G. H. Davies, "Levitical Cities," *IDB,* III, 116f.; M. Greenberg, "Idealism and Practicality in Numbers 35:4-5 and Ezekiel 48," *Essays in Memory of E. A. Speiser. JAOS,* 88 (1968), 59-66; *idem,* "Levitical Cities," *EncJud,* XI, 136-38; M. Haran, "The Levitical Cities: Utopia and Historical Reality," *Tarbiz,* 27 (1957/58), 421-439 [Heb.], I-II [Eng. summary]; *idem,* "Studies in the Account of the Levitical Cities, 1: Preliminary Considerations," *JBL,* 80 (1961), 45-54; *idem,* "Studies in

I. 1. *Occurrences, Statistics.* According to the concordances,[1] the forms *lēwî* and *halᵉwîyîm* occur 354 times in the OT. The distribution of these occurrences among the individual books is as follows: Genesis, 6; Exodus, 11; Leviticus, 4; Numbers, 75; Deuteronomy, 26; Joshua, 17; Judges, 10; 1 Samuel, 1; 2 Samuel, 1; 1 Kings, 2; Isaiah, 1; Jeremiah, 3; Ezekiel, 10; Zechariah, 1; Malachi, 3; Psalms, 1; Ezra, 24; Nehemiah, 45; 1 Chronicles, 48; 2 Chronicles, 65. Levi is not mentioned in the Minor Prophets (except for Zechariah and Malachi), Job, Proverbs, the Five Scrolls, and Daniel. It is noteworthy that the book of Leviticus, whose common title suggests that it deals with matters of special concern to the priests and Levites, mentions the Levites explicitly in only two verses (Lev. 25:32,33 [twice each]).

The sg. *lēwî* appears 98 times, 38 of which have the definite article; the other 250 occurrences involve the pl. *halᵉwîyîm* (with or without a prep., but always with the art.) or the Aramaic form *lēwāyē'* (Ezr. 6:16,18; 7:13,24). Only one text uses a suffixed form (*lᵉwîyēnû*: Neh. 10:1), in sharp contrast to *kōhēn,* "priest," which appears frequently with suffixes. We also find *lwy* in Sir. 45:6. In two additional texts (Dt. 33:8; 2 Ch. 23:18), textual evidence may suggest emendations restoring *lēwî* or *halᵉwîyîm.*

Besides the 26 occurrences in Deuteronomy, there are two major groups of texts in which Levi plays a prominent role: P, with 66 occurrences, and the Chronicler's history, with 182.

2. *Etymology.* The numerous attempts to explain the etymology of *lēwî* illustrate the uncertainty that reigns over the question. The proposals of various scholars are often linked to their theories about the origin of the levitical priesthood and ancient Israelite religion.

If we could assume that *lēwî* was originally an appellative, the etymology could provide important information about the original duties and functions of the Levites. Without claiming to be exhaustive, the following paragraphs will mention the proposed etymologies of the Hebrew noun *lēwî,* most of which involve one of the three semantically distinct Hebrew roots *lāwâ.*

---

the Account of the Levitical Cities, 2: Utopia and Historical Reality," *JBL,* 80 (1961), 156-165; Z. Kallai, "The System of Levitic Cities," *Zion,* 45 (1980), 13-34 [Heb.], I-II [Eng. summary]; Y. Kauffmann, *The Biblical Account of the Conquest of Palestine* (Eng. trans., Jerusalem, 1953), esp. 40ff.; *idem, Sefer Yehoshuʿa* (Jerusalem, 1959), 270-282; S. Klein, "Cities of the Priests and Levites and Cities of Refuge," *Qobeṣ JPES,* 1935, 81-107 [Heb.]; A. Legendre, "Lévitiques (villes)," *DB,* IV (1908), 216-221; B. Mazar, "The Cities of the Priests and the Levites," *Congress Volume, Oxford 1959. SVT,* 7 (1960), 193-205; *idem,* "ערי הלויים והכהנים," *EMiqr,* IV (1962), 478-485; Y. Tsafrir, "The Levitic City of Beth-Shemesh in Juda or in Naphtali?" *N. Glueck Memorial Volume. ErIsr,* 12 (1975), 44f. [Heb.], 119* [Eng. summary]; J. Wellhausen, *Prolegomena to the History of Israel,* 159-164.

1. Mandelkern and Lisowsky agree.

In the story of the birth of Levi, Leah's third son, Gen. 29:34 explains his name by citing Leah's words: *ʿattâ happaʿam yillāweh ʾîšî ʾēlay,* "Now this time my husband will be joined (→ לוה *lāwâ* I) to me"; but this free play on words does not provide any clue as to the meaning of the name. The same pun appears in Nu. 18:2,4, which says that the Levites will join Aaron. This text also emphasizes that they stand in a special relationship to the priests, a statement we would expect from P. It must be confessed, however, that these passages show at most how later ages interpreted the name *lēwî*; they have nothing to say about the original meaning.

Ex. 32:26 has also been cited as proof that the Levites, in contrast to the other Israelites, were supporters of Moses, his adherents in a special sense, although this text uses the niphal of *ʾsp,* not *lāwâ.* Karl Budde,[2] for example, accepts this theory, interpreting Ex. 32:26b (*wayyēʾāsᵉpû ʾēlāyw kol-bᵉnê lēwî,* "then all the sons of Levi gathered themselves together to him") as referring to "all those who are now called Levites."

Paul A. de Lagarde[3] thought that "the Levites were those Egyptians that had joined the Semites returning to Asia from the Nile region." The *ʿereḇ raḇ* (Ex. 12:38) that departed from Egypt with the Israelites, like the *hāʾsapsup* of Nu. 11:4, could refer specifically to the Levites, and the name interpreted as meaning "those who join(ed)" could be based on these accounts.

W. W. Graf Baudissin[4] prefers an abstract or collective noun *lēw,* "attendants, retinue," from which *lēwî* was derived — first as an adjective, then as a name. He therefore theorizes that the original function of the Levites was to provide a military escort for the ark as the Israelites traveled. "The Levites constituted the bodyguard, as it were, of Israel's divine warlord, the God of Hosts, present in the sacred ark."[5]

It is interesting that according to Jub. 31:16 Jacob himself interprets the name of his son as meaning "joined to God," citing the name given him by his mother, although differing from Gen. 29:34. The text reads:[6] "Your mother called you Levi by name, and in truth she named you thus: you shall be joined to God and (shall be) a comrade of all the sons of Jacob."

A contrary theory starts from the fact that it is God who chooses a person to join with; explanation appears in the Midrash (*Ex. Rab.* i.5), which interprets the name *lēwî* by the statement that God joined himself to the Levites (*šeniṯhabbēr lāhem*).

It was G. H. Skipwith who associated the name *lēwî* with *liwyāṯān,* proposing that the tribe of Levi took its name from a serpent-god. The statement of 2 K. 18:4 that Hezekiah had the bronze serpent → נחשתן *nᵉḥuštān* destroyed, Nu. 21:8, and above all the name of the *nāśîʾ* of the tribe of Judah in Nu. 1:7 (*naḥšôn ben-ʿammînāḏāḇ*)

---

2. K. Budde, *Die altisraelitische Religion* (Giessen, ³1912), 46.
3. P. A. Lagarde, *Orientalia* (Göttingen, 1880), II, 20.
4. P. 72.
5. *Ibid.,* 73.
6. Translation based on A. Dillmann.

lend credence to this theory. Since 1 Ch. 2:10; Ruth 4:20 list this *naḥšôn ben-ʿammînāḏāḇ* among the ancestors of David, and Ex. 6:23 indicates that the same man was Aaron's brother-in-law, at least in theory there must have been a connection between Levi and the tribe of Judah. In this context, we may also note that the Levite in Judg. 17:7 is said to come from Judah.

Bernhard Luther and Eduard Meyer[7] likewise derive the name *lēwî* from the same root as *liwyāṯān,* concluding that "among the Levites, the cult of Yahweh was originally inseparable from the serpent cult." They also interpret the name *lē'â* as "divine serpent," and conclude: "Eve, the primordial mother of all, is ultimately identical with Leah, the mother of Simeon and Levi."[8]

Theophile J. Meek[9] in particular attempts to develop this theory, citing additional serpent names of Levites (like *šuppîm* in 1 Ch. 26:16) as well as archaeological evidence of serpent worship in Palestine. The fact that the traces are not clearer may be due to their having been largely eradicated in the interests of orthodoxy.[10]

Sigmund Mowinckel[11] cites the same root *lāwâ,* "twist, turn," and suggests that the ecstatic ritual dance of the Levites gave rise to their name. Édouard P. Dhorme's theory[12] deserves attention because it takes as its point of departure the designation of the Levites as *bᵉnê lēwî* (25 times, plus 6 occurrences of *bēn lēwî* and 1 of *baṯ lēwî*). After the analogy of *bᵉnê hannᵉḇî'îm* (1 K. 20:35, etc.) and Palmyrene *bny kmr'* Dhorme sees here a phrase denoting membership in a class or professional group and suggests that original meaning may have been "cult associate."

Morris E. Jastrow[13] connects *lēwî* with Heb. *lāḇî',* "lion," so that *bᵉnê lēwî* would designate the members of the "lion clan," like the *banū 'asad* of the Arabs. Jastrow's further arguments, which cite the well-known Lab'aya of Shechem mentioned in the Amarna letters, cannot be followed without falling into the temptation of seeing in this Lab'ayu the ancestor of the Levites.

Thomas K. Cheyne,[14] finally, citing possible ethnic relationships, dissociates *lēwî* from Leah, explaining the name instead by the venturesome sequence *lwyn* = *lbyn* = *lmyn* = *rm'l* = *yrḥm'l,* opening the way once more to southern Palestinian Levi traditions.

Ever since Julius Wellhausen,[15] many scholars have preferred to interpret the name *lēwî* as a gentilic form of the matriarchal name *lē'â.* Jastrow was the first to

7. *Die Israeliten und ihre Nachbarstämme,* 426f.

8. *Ibid.,* 427, n. 1.

9. T. J. Meek, *Hebrew Origins* (^{2}1950, repr. New York, 1960), 119ff. 122ff.

10. Cf. Ross, 8.

11. S. Mowinckel, "Kadesj, Sinai og Jahvë," *Norsk Geografisk Tidskrift,* 9 (1942), 23.

12. É. P. Dhorme, *La religion des hébreux nomades* (Brussels, 1937), 226f.

13. M. E. Jastrow, "Hebrew Proper Names compounded with יה and יהו," *JBL,* 11 (1892), 120f.

14. T. K. Cheyne, "Levi," *EncBib,* III, 2769.

15. P. 145.

point out the problem that the gentilic form of *lē'â* should not be *lēwî* but rather *l^e'ēyî lē'î.*

Paul Haupt, comparing Arab. *'alwā* (< *lwy* III) with Heb. *hôrâ* and consequently *lēwî* (< **lāwî*) with *môreh,* concluded that "the Levites were Edomite priests."[16] This audacious and totally hypothetical argument has been cited frequently, but should finally be rejected.[17] The meaning of Arab. *'alwā,* "turned aside, shifted,"[18] has nothing to do with Heb. *hôrâ.* The only explanation must be that Haupt was suggesting a possible alternation between *l* and *r,* but there is absolutely no evidence for such alternation in this specific case.

Late Babylonian and Neo-Babylonian *lamūtānu/lawūtānu,* "attendant, servant," and *lātānu,* "maidservants,"[19] are loanwords from Aramaic and therefore cannot contribute anything to illuminate the etymology of *lēwî.*

In 1884, Julius Euting found and transcribed several inscriptions in the Minaean language and script at el-ʿUlā, biblical Dedan,[20] about 230 kilometers (145 mi.) south of Elath or 375 kilometers (235 mi.) from Kadesh-barnea. Three fragmentary inscriptions[21] use the word *lw'* with suf. *lw'n* and *lw'nhn* and the fem. *lw't* with suf. *lw'thn.* D. H. Müller, who published the inscriptions,[22] already translated *lw'* and *lw't* as "priest" and "priestess"; when F. Hommel[23] thereupon identified the terms with Heb. *lēwî,* he saw "new and hitherto unsuspected religio-historical perspectives" opening up. In 1908/1909 and 1910, A. Jaussen and R. Savignac[24] were able to add three more inscriptions with the word *lw'.*[25]

In 1924, in his critical analysis of the inscriptions, Hubert Grimme determined that the persons called *lw'/lw't* in these dedicatory inscriptions were probably personal pledges, who became devotees of a sanctuary for goods or money owed. Now it cannot be denied that ancient South Arabia knew the institution of personal service of a devotee, "who performed some kind of labor for the temple to pay a debt incurred by a clan through its failure to perform some obligation."[26] The terminology varies,

---

16. P. Haupt, "Hobab = Schweigervater," *OLZ,* 12 (1909), 163; similarly *idem,* "Midian und Sinai," *ZDMG,* 63 (1909), 522.

17. Cf. also A. Cody, *A History of OT Priesthood. AnBibl,* 35 (1969), 30, n. 99, who puts his finger on the extension of this theory through Mowinckel's additional theory that the linguistic parallel refers to oracle priests.

18. G. W. F. Freytag, *Lexicon arabica-latinum* (Halle, 1830): "in latus inflexit, motitavit."

19. *AHw,* I (1965), 534, 540; *CAD,* IX (1973), 77f.

20. Cf. W. F. Albright, "Dedan," *Geschichte und AT. Festschrift A. Alt. BHTh,* 16 (1953), 1-12.

21. *RÉS,* 3351, 2; 3356, 3; 3357, 1, 2.

22. *DAW,* Phil.-hist. Kl., 37 (1889).

23. *Aufsätze und Abhandlungen arabitisch-semitologischen Inhalts* (Munich, 1892), 11.

24. *Mission archéologique en Arabie (Mars-Mai 1907),* II (Paris, 1914).

25. *RÉS,* 3697, 3, 9: *lw'tm*; 3698, 2: *lw'nhn*; also 3603, 3, from Medain-Salih: *lw'n.*

26. M. Höfner in H. Gese, Höfner, and K. Rudolph, *Die Religionen Altsyriens, Altarabiens und der Mandäer. RdM,* 10/2 (1970), 333f.

however; inscriptional evidence for the word *lw'* is exclusively North Minaean. Roland de Vaux[27] was able to show that the inscriptions, however they may be interpreted in detail, cannot possibly demonstrate the origin of the Israelite Levites in Dedan. We know that el-ʿUlā had a Jewish population by the first century A.D. at the latest, which had probably settled there in the time of Nabonidus during the sixth century B.C.; it therefore makes more sense to assume that Heb. *lēwî* influenced Minaean *lw'* than the reverse.

Eduard Nielsen,[28] following Johannes Pedersen and William F. Albright, proposed translating *lēwî* as "devotee of the Lord = one who is given away, or has given himself away, for the service of the Lord." This proposal probably represents an attempt to incorporate what had been learned from the Minaean inscriptions and comes closest to the probable meaning of the word *lēwî*; for the most likely interpretation is that *lēwî* should be considered a hypochoristic personal name meaning "adherent, client, worshipper of the god N."[29] This interpretation is supported above all by the Amorite PNs *lawi-(la)-(DN)*, already recognized as parallels by Martin Noth.[30]

A different interpretation has been proposed by Albrecht Goetze,[31] who explains *lawi* on the basis of a verbal form *la-yawi,* the meaning of which Goetze is unable to define. In this explanation, the *e* sound in Hebrew would have developed from the diphthon *ay* according to regular phonetic laws.[32]

Here we should also mention a toponym preserved in Egyptian as *ra-wi-'i-ri* = **lawi'ili,* "client of the the god El." It is no. 111 in the city list of Rameses III, which according to H. Wolfgang Helck[33] derives from a lost list possibly originating with Thutmose I.[34] No. 74 in Shishak's list is a toponym that may be read *ngb r(l)wy*;[35] this would be evidence for the name Levi in southern Palestine.[36]

---

27. *Festschrift H. Junker,* 265-273.

28. *Ibid.,* 26, n. 25.

29. Cf. M. Weippert, *The Settlement of the Israelite Tribes in Palestine. SBT,* ser. 2, 21 (Eng. trans. 1971), 43, n. 139.

30. "Remarks on the Sixth Volume of Mari Texts," *JSS,* 1 (1956), 327 (= *Aufsätze zur biblischen Landes- und Altertumskunde* [Neukirchen-Vluyn, 1971], II, 238f. [Ger.]); cf. *APNM,* 50, 225f.

31. A. Goetze, "Remarks on Some Names Occurring in the Execration Texts," *BASOR,* 151 (1958), 31f.; cf. W. L. Moran, "Das bildhethitische Siegel des Br-Rkb von Sam'al," *Or,* 26 (1957), 342f.

32. Cf. also Cody, *A History of OT Priesthood,* 32f., n. 111.

33. H. W. Helck, *Die Beziehungen Ägyptens zu Vorderasien im 3. und 2. Jahrtausend v. Chr. ÄgAbh,* 5 (^{2}1971), 238.

34. Cf. also W. F. Albright, *The Vocalization of the Egyptian Syllabic Orthography. AOS,* 5 (1934), 8.

35. Cf. S. Yeivin, "The Exodus," *Tarbiz,* 30 (1960/61), 1-7 [Heb.], I [Eng. summary].

36. But see J. Simons, *Handbook for the Study of Egyptian Topographical Lists Relating to Western Asia* (Leiden, 1937), 180, 184.

II. Secular Tribe. Ever since Wellhausen, scholars have attempted to arrange the OT texts concerning Levi on the basis of their literary affinities so as to yield an historical picture of the origin and development of a secular or religious tribe. The results have been extremely mixed. Opinions differ as to whether there was ever a secular tribe of Levi and, if so, what its relationship might have been to the levitical priesthood. Some assume the existence of such a tribe, which then perished in a catastrophe reflected in the narrative of Gen. 34, to be resurrected, as it were, as a unique group of Yahweh worshippers especially qualified to carry out the cult. Others assume that from the very beginning the Levites were a group of individuals or families who devoted themselves particularly and exclusively to extending and performing the cult of Yahweh. It remains unanswered whether there was any connection between the two entities — the secular tribe and the priestly tribe — so that the remnants of the former were incorporated into the latter, or the accidental identity or similarity in name led to their later identification. Apart from general considerations, the arguments in favor of a secular tribe are based on conclusions drawn from Gen. 49:5-7 in conjunction with Gen. 34, together with the appearance of Levi in lists of the twelve tribes.

1. *Gen. 49:5-7; 34.* Hans-Jürgen Zobel[37] considers Gen. 49:5-7 a prophetic curse oracle. He summarizes his conclusions as follows: "After a temporary settlement and violent conflict in central Palestine, Simeon and Levi traveled south. On the way, however, they were overtaken by some fate involving them both, in consequence of which the remnants of Simeon were absorbed into Judah, while the surviving Levites went on to Kadesh, where they became priests around the middle of the fourteenth century B.C. A substantial portion if not all of them joined the Israelite groups moving into Egypt in search of food. At the end of the thirteenth century, they took part in the exodus and occupation along with these groups. Finally, toward the end of the period of the judges, thanks to their increasing influence, they came forward as a priesthood of the land, revering Moses as their most prominent ancestor and thus tracing their origins to him." In this synthesis we see once again the theory proposed by Wellhausen and since him, with modifications, by many others.

The discrepancies between the two texts (Gen. 34, e.g., says nothing about "hamstringing oxen" [49:6]) have led Sigo Lehming[38] to conclude that Gen. 49:5-7 refers to an otherwise unknown incident and that the mentions of Jacob's sons Simeon and Levi in Gen. 34:25,30 presuppose the Simeon-Levi text in Gen. 49, seeking to set it in a concrete historical context.

If one maintains that we have no information about the location of a secular tribe

---

37. *Stammesspruch und Geschichte,* 60.
38. *ZAW,* 70 (1958), 228-250.

of Levi[39] — in contrast, say, to Simeon — and no information about the secular history of such a tribe (e.g., the Song of Deborah in Jgs. 5 does not mention Levi), the question arises whether Gen. 49:5-7 has not confused two discrepant entities, a tribe of Simeon and a tribe of Levi. This question has led scholars like Nielsen[40] to see in Gen. 34 a tradition that originally mentioned only Simeon and was later expanded by the addition of Levi. A. H. J. Gunneweg[41] takes the opposite approach, seeing in Gen. 49:5-7 a text that spoke originally only of Levi, reflecting the conflicts between the Levites and their opponents.

It must be admitted that Gen. 34; 49:5-7 by themselves provide insufficient evidence for the existence of a secular tribe of Levi.

2. *Levi among the Twelve Tribes.* Levi also appears in the followings lists of the tribal eponyms: Gen. 29:31–30:24; 35:16-18; 35:23-26; 46:8-25; 49:3-27; Ex. 1:2-4; Dt. 27:12f.; 33:6-25; 1 Ch. 2:1f.; Ezk. 48:31-35. Ever since Noth's study of the twelve tribe system,[42] scholars have distinguished these lists, which include Levi, from another system in which Levi does not appear. The latter system reaches the total of twelve by dividing the tribe of Joseph into Ephraim and Manasseh: Nu. 1:5-15,20-43; 2:3-31; 7:12-83; 10:14-28; 13:4-15; 26:5-51; Josh. 13–19; 21:4-7,9-39. The evidence seems to suggest that there was a secular tribe of Levi that belonged to a group of six comprising Reuben, Simeon, Levi, Judah, Zebulun, and Issachar. After this secular tribe of Levi perished, the fortuitous identity of names made it possible to identify the priestly tribe of Levi with the secular tribe. P singled out this tribe for theological reasons and gave it a special position.[43] Gunneweg is probably correct in saying: "Between the system with Levi and the system without Levi there does not lie the destruction of the secular tribe of Levi, but rather the difference between a purely amphictyonic organization and a tribal list put together on the basis of geographical, historical, and genealogical data, adapted more or less awkwardly to the former."[44] K. Namiki's studies[45] yield even more radical results. He shows that both systems are highly artificial constructs that must be used with the utmost caution for historical reconstruction.[46]

---

39. The levitical cities are discussed in IV below.

40. *Shechem,* 279-283.

41. *Leviten und Priester. FRLANT,* N.S. 71[89] (1965), 45-51.

42. M. Noth, *Das System der zwölf Stämme Israels. BWANT,* 52[4/1] (^{2}1966).

43. Cf. D. Kellermann, *Die Priesterschrift von Numeri 1_1 bis 10_{10}. BZAW,* 120 (1970), 10f.

44. P. 63.

45. K. Namiki, "Reconsideration of the Twelve-Tribe System of Israel," *AJBI,* 2 (1976), 29-59.

46. See also H. Weippert, "Das geographische System der Stämme Israels," *VT,* 23 (1973), 76-89; de Geus, 97-108, who likewise concludes that a secular tribe of Levi never existed.

III. Priestly Tribe. We can discuss Ex. 32:25-29; Dt. 33:8-11 together, because Ex. 32 speaks of the Levites' special devotion to Yahweh and Dt. 33 quite clearly deals with their priestly functions. Many scholars have associated the two texts,[47] seeing the sacrificial act of religious fidelity in Ex. 32:25-29 reflected in the Blessing of Moses in Dt. 33. But we must agree with Gunneweg[48] that Ex. 32:25-29 crystalized around the "levitical law" of v. 29, *'îš bibnô ûbᵉ'āḥîw,* which states that "a Levite is a Levite only at the cost of sacrificing his closest family ties."[49] Since we are dealing primarily with self-evaluations on the part of the Levites, we can also add that the texts support a claim to be the true priesthood of Yahweh in opposition to an Aaronic priesthood.

If we accept Zobel's interpretation[50] of the Levi passage in the Blessing of Moses (Dt. 33:8-11), vv. 8f. look back to the past while v. 10 envisions the situation when the text was composed. V. 11 embodies "the hopes of the Levites for the future." The difficulty of the passage lies in the first line. The LXX reads *dóte Leui*; the recently discovered 4Q175 (Testimonia) reads in l. 14 *hbw lwy.* Following this lead, many scholars add *tēn lᵉlēwî* ("give Levi")[51] or *nāṯattā lᵉlēwî* ("thou hast given Levi"),[52] although both the LXX and 4Q175 have a plural rather than a singular. In addition, exegetes have been quick to emend *lᵉ'îš ḥᵃsîḏeḵā* to *ḥasdeḵā,*[53] although 4Q175 clearly supports the MT. The present MT is in fact clear and translatable: "May thy Thummim and thy Urim belong to the men of thy godly one." The phrase *'îš ḥᵃsîḏᵉḵā* as a designation for the tribe of Levi has been interpreted in many different ways. As vv. 9f. show, the 2nd person singular masculine suffix must refer to Yahweh; in the present context, this reference is also supported by v. 7, in which Yahweh is addressed. Stade's attempt[54] to interpret "the man of thy godly one" as meaning "the man of thy God," taking *ḥāsîḏ* as an epithet for Yahweh, is off the mark. Scholars generally agree that *'îš* is to be taken collectively, but the identitity of the *ḥāsîḏ* remains an open question. It might seem reasonable to suppose that the word denotes Levi, the patriarch, as an individual;[55] but there is no evidence for such an interpretation. Since Ex. 32:4ff. rules out Aaron as bearer of this title of honor, *ḥᵃsîḏeḵā* (= *ḥāsîḏ* of Yahweh) probably refers to Moses. Gunneweg, for example, concludes: "Moses and Levi seen together, related so closely that it is difficult to decide which the text is actually speaking of."[56] We may note that the designation of Moses as *ḥāsîḏ* has its counterpart in the description of Moses as *'ānāw mᵉ'ōḏ* in Nu. 12:3, which has always attracted attention.

---

47. R. Kittel, *Die Religion des Volkes Israel* (Leipzig, 1921), 39, 44; Budde, *Die altisraelitische Religion,* 46; E. König, *Geschichte der alttestamentlichen Religion* (Gütersloh, ³,⁴1924), 269f.

48. Pp. 29-37.

49. *Ibid.,* 32.

50. Pp. 29ff.

51. C. Steuernagel, *Das Deuteronomium. HKAT,* I/3/1 (²1923), 176.

52. Zobel.

53. E.g., *ibid.,* 26.

54. B. Stade, *Geschichte des Volkes Israel,* I (Berlin, 1887), 156.

55. Cf. K. Marti, *Das fünfte Buch Mose oder Deuteronomium. HSAT,* I (³1909), 324, who suggests Levi, Moses, or Aaron.

56. Pp. 41-43.

Dt. 33:8b is also very difficult, since extant traditions make no special mention of the tribe of Levi at either Massa (Ex. 17:2,7) or Meriba (v. 7; Nu. 20:13). Following Otto Eissfeldt,[57] we may translate *nissîṯô* as "thou didst strengthen him" instead of "thou didst test him" and *tᵉrîḇēhû* as "thou didst teach him to contend" instead of the usual "thou didst contend for him" (definitely not "thou didst contend with him," which is linguistically possible); but this interpretation still does not clarify the situation reflected in these lines. We may theorize with Zobel[58] that the words suggest "some kind of military training of the newly formed priestly band, localized in or at least near Kadesh," without necessarily agreeing with Leo Steinberger, who sees in the tribe of Levi a "militia" that later became a priestly caste.[59] It is undeniable, however, that in describing the duties of the Levites P still uses terminology derived from military language (*šmr, mišmereṯ, ṣāḇā', śar*).

Scholars vary widely in their dating of Dt. 33:8-11. Zobel would locate the events lying behind this tradition "long before the occupation of Canaan by the central Palestinian tribes."[60] Nielsen[61] is much more cautious, ascribing the observations of Dt. 33:8-11 to the period before the destruction of Samaria or possibly even the premonarchic period.

We may state four conclusions concerning the Levites: they must have been priests associated with sanctuaries; they must have administered sacral law and pronounced *tôrâ* in matters of cultic law; they must have been authorized to offer sacrifice; and they had enemies or competitors.[62]

IV. The Levitical Cities. A much debated and still puzzling institution is that of the levitical cities. Josh. 21:1-42 assigns the Levites forty-eight cities together with the immediately surrounding land as pasturage (*migrāš*). This list reappears with some variations, especially in its names, in 1 Ch. 6:39-66(Eng. vv. 54-81). The assignment of the levitical cities totally contradicts the so-called "levitical law" that the Levites are to own no property. Thus the notion of levitical cities seems to be an idealized embodiment of idealized claims, a purely utopian scheme dating from a later period.[63] It is hard to imagine that forty-eight cities, theoretically four per tribe, were to be inhabited exclusively by Levites. Even the schematic description of the territory belonging to the cities as measuring 2,000 cubits (*ca.* 1 km. [.6 mi.]) from the city in each direction (Nu. 35:5), which clearly treats the city and its wall as a single point, shows that this definition cannot be based on a law governing pasturage, which would not ignore the natural features of the land. The list of levitical cities includes six cities of refuge (Nu. 35:6): Hebron, Shechem, Golan, Kedesh, Bezer, and Ramoth-Gilead.

57. O. Eissfeldt, "Zwei verkannte militärtechnische Termini im AT," *VT,* 5 (1955), 235-38 = *KlSchr,* III (1966), 356-58.
58. P. 30.
59. *Der Bedeutungswechsel des wortes Levit.*
60. Zobel, 70.
61. *ASTI,* 3 (1964), 16-27.
62. Cf. Zobel, 67f.
63. Wellhausen and Kaufmann.

Although there can be no doubt that the institution of the cities of refuge has an ancient nucleus, the relationship between the cities of refuge and the levitical cities is secondary.

The schema further divides the Levites into three subgroups: the Kohathites, the Gershonites, and the Merarites; the Kohathites include a further subgroup, the Aaronites. Scholars such as Albrecht Alt consider this subdivision secondary, but Aelred Cody[64] finds in it the key to understanding the list. He maintains that we see here "a certain regional solidarity which had gradually grown up among the Levites once they had progressed from the stage of wandering *gērîm* to that of settled *gērîm* scattered throughout the Land."

We must also note that, according to OT evidence, several of these cities were not Israelite in the earlier period: Gibeon, Shechem, Gezer, Aijalon, Taanach, and Nahalal. This observation has led to the theory that the list of levitical cities might reflect an institution dating from the end of David's reign or that of Solomon.[65] When all forty-eight cities are located on a map,[66] two areas are seen to be without Levites: the central section of Judah south of Jerusalem, and the center of the kingdom of Israel (apart from Shechem). Several scholars[67] have suggested an explanation based on the reform of Josiah, who brought all the priests of the Judahite cities to Jerusalem (2 K. 23:8) and had the priests of the high places in the cities of Samaria slain (vv. 19f.). This theory merely suggests a date and explains the gaps in geographical distribution without explaining this list of the levitical cities as a whole, while the first hypothesis cannot explain the gaps.

The hypothesis that the historical basis of the list is merely that the cities named were cultic centers with well-known shrines served by the Levites is unconvincing. J. P. Ross suggests the interesting theory that the list of levitical cities does not refer to cities of or for Levites in the usual technical sense at all, but rather to cities that came to belong to Israel not through conquest but through alliance, so that the word *lēwî* here has an original meaning of "alliance, coalition." The original meaning of the caption would thus have been "cities of the Levite allies," which developed into "cities of the Levite priests."[68]

Ross also asks[69] whether the phrase *ʿārê halᵉwîyîm* may not represent textual corruption. The territory occupied by the so-called levitical cities appears to be largely coextensive with a territory occupied by Hivites or Hurrians. According to Ross, the list may therefore designate cities that came to belong to Israel during the second millennium by alliance rather than by conquest; its original caption was *ʿrm lḥwy,* which became *ʿry hlwy.* De Vaux thinks the cities were inhabited by Levites without dependable revenue, so that "the list originally represented the dispersal of the Levite population after the foundation of the Temple and after the organization of the official cult at Bethel. The foundation of the Temple would explain why no other Levites are

64. *A History of OT Priesthood,* 160f.
65. Albright.
66. Most recently Haran, *Temples and Temple Service,* 86.
67. E.g., Alt.
68. P. 275.
69. *Ibid.,* 280.

mentioned in the immediate environs of Jerusalem, and the foundation at Bethel would explain why there were no Levitical cities in the centre of Israel either."[70] Even if the riddle of the list has not been solved completely, its utopian and realistic elements can be recognized and defined.

V. Levi in the Individual Sources. The following sections will examine the treatment of the Levites in Deuteronomy, Ezekiel, P, and the Chronicler's history.

1. *Deuteronomy.* Following Gunneweg,[71] we can distinguish four stages in the treatment of the Levites by Deuteronomy.

a. In Dt. 12:12,18; 14:27,29; 16:11,14; 26:11,12,13, "the Levite within your gates" (*hallēwî ʾªšer bišʿārêḵā*) or some similar expression denotes a special kind of alien, like the classic examples in Jgs. 17f.,19f. The person so designated owns no land and is therefore commended to the loving support of Israel, along with the widow, orphan, and sojourner (*gēr*). He is explicitly allowed to participate in the festivals of Yahweh (Dt. 12:12,18; 14:27,29) and must receive his portion of the regular tithes and the tithes of the third year (26:12f.). The Levite is invited to celebrate the Feast of Weeks (16:11), the Feast of Booths (16:14), and the Festival of Firstfruits (26:11), along with the sojourner (*gēr*), orphan, and widow.

b. "The Levite within your gates" has the same rights as the Levite at the central sanctuary. This equality is total with respect to cultic ministry (*ʿāmaḏ, šērēṯ*), standing before Yahweh to minister to him (*laʿªmōḏ lipnê YHWH lᵉšārᵉṯô*: Dt. 10:8), and blessing in his name (*ûlᵉḇārēḵ bišmô*). Dt. 18:6-8 insists that "all Levites, whether already resident at the ideal central shrine or coming to it as pilgrims, are equally entitled to priestly ministry (*šrt*) there."[72]

c. A balance is established between priests and Levites by the identity formula *hakōhªnîm halᵉwîyîm.* Both have the same function. This view of a gradual development toward identical treatment of priests and Levites also resolves the conflict between George E. Wright, who espoused the theory that Deuteronomy reflects a difference between altar priests with full rights and auxiliary cultic ministers,[73] and J. A. Emerton, who shows that the centralization of the cult at Jerusalem created the class of auxiliary Levites.

A key to understanding the identity formula appears in Dt. 18:1. The expression *lakkōhªnîm halᵉwîyîm kol-šēḇeṭ lēwî* is not to be interpreted as distinguishing Levites who are priests from other Levites who are not (in other words, levitical priests from the rest of the tribe of Levi); *kol-šēḇeṭ lēwî* stands in apposition, so that the formula must be translated: "the levitical priests, that is, the whole tribe of Levi." According to the Talmud,[74] the identity formula priest-Levites = priestly Levites or levitical priests

70. *AncIsr,* 367.
71. Pp. 126ff.
72. *Ibid.,* 129.
73. Cf. also Abba, *VT,* 27 (1977), 257-267.
74. Bab. *Yebam.* 86f.; Bab. *Ḥul.* 24b; Bab. *Bek.* 4a; Bab. *Tamid* 27a.

occurs twenty-four times, including Ezk. 44:15. Unfortunately there is no list of dubious passages, and concordances as well as the Masoretic lists[75] yield a smaller number. It is therefore likely that some passages now having a copula between the two words were interpreted either like the identity formula or as if they did not yet have the copula.[76] The identity formula in Deuteronomy does not imply, however, that from the very beginning all Levites were priests and all priests Levites; it "proclaims the theoretical principle of the Levites' claim to minister as priests of Yahweh at a sanctuary of Yahweh: only Levites can and must be priests."[77]

d. The identification of priest and Levite makes it possible to say that the whole tribe of Levi (*kol-šēḇeṭ lēwî*: Dt. 18:1; similarly *bᵉnê lēwî*: 21:5; 31:9) is called to cultic service of Yahweh.

2. *Ezekiel.* In Ezekiel's plan for the restored temple (Ezk. 40–48),[78] the levitical priests, the sons of Zadok (*hakkōhᵃnîm halᵉwîyîm bᵉnê ṣāḏôq*: 44:15; cf. 40:46: *bᵉnê ṣāḏôq* are also *bᵉnê lēwî*; 43:19: *hakkōhᵃnîm halᵉwîyîm* are *mizzeraʿ ṣāḏōq*) — i.e., the priesthood of Jerusalem — are distinguished from the Levites proper, who have a subordinate position. According to Ezk. 44:6-16,[79] the Israelites sinned by allowing uncircumcised men to minister in the temple. These men are now to be replaced by Levites. For the Levites, this service is a punishment for assisting Israel's idolatry. The Levites are punished by exclusion from the strictly priestly functions, being required to serve as "gatekeepers, police, butchers, and general handymen."[80] Scholars have suggested that the Levites in question had been in charge of minor sanctuaries before the reform of the cult and were now degraded to menial service. More likely, however, these directives primarily represent claims, in part polemically tinged, countering the Zadokite program of the autochthonous Jerusalemite priesthood. In Ezr. 2:42 par. Neh. 7:45, for example, the gatekeepers (*šōʿᵃrîm*) are listed separately from the Levites, whereas in 1 Ch. 15:18; 2 Ch. 23:4 they are clearly included among the Levites.

Ezk. 44:11 requires the Levites to slay the animals for the burnt offerings and sacrifices of the people (*yišḥᵃṭû ʾeṯ-hāʿōlâ wᵉʾeṯ-hazzeḇaḥ lāʿām*); but this directive, too, was not enforced.[81] We must remember that the texts in Ezekiel dealing with the Levites exhibit several strata, revealing change and development with respect to the theoretical and/or practical conflict between the Jerusalem priesthood and the non-Jerusalem Levites during a period of affliction and oppression.[82]

---

75. Mm 1188, 1199, 2451 in G. E. Weil, *Massorah Gedolah Iuxta Codicem Leningradensem, 1: Catalog* (Rome, 1971).

76. Cf. Curtiss, who makes every effort to recover the missing passages by text-critical methods — without clear results.

77. Gunneweg, 77.

78. Cf. the traditio-historical analysis by H. Gese, *Der Verfassungsentwurf des Ezechiel (Kap. 40-48) traditionsgeschichtlich untersucht. BHTh,* 25 (1957).

79. Cf. W. Zimmerli, *Ezekiel 2. Herm* (Eng. trans. 1983), 456-59.

80. G. Hölscher, *Hesekiel, der Dichter und das Buch. BZAW,* 39 (1924), 197.

81. Cf. Zimmerli, *Ezekiel 2,* 455f.

82. Cf. Cody, *A History of OT Priesthood,* 168, who attempts to build on these observations.

3. *P.* P, also, makes a clear distinction between priests and Levites. The true priestly office is a privilege reserved to all Aaronites, including above all the Zadokites (traced through Eleazar in 1 Ch. 5:34[6:8]; cf. the preeminent position of Eleazar in P: Nu. 3:32; 4:16 or 17:2,4[16:37,39]; 19:3,4; 20:25ff.; etc.). The other temple functions are assigned to all non-Aaronite descendants of Levi, i.e., the Levites proper, whose subgroups (Gershonites, Kohathites, Merarites) are probably meant to reflect the official organization of the postexilic temple. Gunneweg sums up: "Aaronites and Levites together constitute the tribe of Levi; the Aaronites are the priests, to whom the Levites are subordinate as minor clergy. The rank and duties of each class are defined precisely."[83]

The complex nature of the P materials reveals a power struggle still underway between the Aaronite (and Zadokite) priests and the Levites on the one hand and among the individual groups of Levites on the other. Nu. 3:5-10, for example, emphasizes that the Levites are subordinate to the priests, while underlining their significance for the community, for whom they minister vicariously as they carry out their duties at the sanctuary.[84] There was obviously recurring rivalry among the individual Levite families, as we can see in Nu. 4, where the genealogical sequence of Gershon, Kohath, and Merari (Nu. 3:17; etc.) is changed to give precedence to Kohath. Probably the Kohath group is based on the same clan that lies behind the name Korah.[85] Thus Nu. 16–18 with its various strata reveals conflicts, shifts of emphasis, and attempts to voice or realize the special hopes of individual groups.

The duties of the priestly ministry in P can be clearly recognized and described — to offer sacrifice in the burnt offering (Lev. 1:7,9,12f.), the cereal offering (2:2f.,9f.), the peace offering (3:5,8,11,16), etc.; to perform blood rituals (Lev. 1:5,11,15), etc.; to burn incense (Ex. 30:7f.); to keep the lamps burning (Lev. 24:1-4; Nu. 8:2); to set out the showbread (Lev. 24:8f.). It is difficult, however, to define precisely the functions and duties of the Levites. Cody, for example, can say: "On the duties of the Levites, P has not much to tell us that is realistically concrete."[86] Because P strictly maintains the fiction of the desert sanctuary, it is difficult to determine the specific duties in the postexilic Jerusalem temple that lie behind the functions prescribed for the desert sanctuary. In particular, the directives for taking down, transporting, and erecting the desert sanctuary have no direct parallels to functions in the Jerusalem temple. Jacob Milgrom has shown that *ʿᵃḇōḏâ* or *ʿāḇaḏ* in the context of the Levites' duties never denotes a priestly function; it always refers to physical labor. The phrase *šāmar mišmereṯ,* used frequently by P in connection with the duties of the Levites, especially when followed by an objective genitive such as *miškan hāʿēḏûṯ* (Nu. 1:53) or *miškan YHWH* (Nu. 31:30,47) or *haqqōḏeš* (Nu. 3:28,32,38 conj.; 18:5), must be understood similarly. It never denotes cultic ministry, but refers concretely to guard duty.[87] This

83. P. 185.
84. Cf. Kellermann, 45f.
85. Cf. Gunneweg, 171-188.
86. *A History of OT Priesthood,* 185.
87. Cf. Haran, *Temples and Temple Service,* 60f.

function is expressed metaphorically by the assignment of the Levites to the innermost circle of the desert encampment, where they guard the sanctuary.

4. *Chronicler's History.* The books of Samuel and Kings display an interest only in the Jerusalem priesthood. Even the statement (1 K. 12:31; cf. 13:33) that Jeroboam I appointed priests who were not Levites from among the entire population for his royal sanctuary at Bethel turns out to be Judahite polemic (cf. 2 K. 23:9, which clearly refers to levitical priests).[88] Hos. 6:9 may also suggest conflicts with Levites.[89] Elsewhere Levites are mentioned in connection with the ark only in 1 S. 6:15; 2 S. 15:24; 1 K. 8:4; it is easy to see that these texts are later additions intended to bolster the rights of the Levites.

The Chronicler's history, on the other hand, ascribes astonishing importance to the Levites. The texts reveal that the cultic life of the postexilic period was agitated and full of conflict. As an example of competing claims, we may cite the regulations governing the showbread: according to 2 Ch. 13:11 (like Lev. 24:8 [P]), only the Aaronites (i.e., priests) were in charge of setting out the showbread; 1 Ch. 9:32, however, reports that some of the Kohathite Levites were allowed to perform this task. The identity formula still appears (1 Ch. 9:2; 2 Ch. 5:5; 23:18; 30:27); more often, however, the formula "priests and Levites" (1 Ch. 13:2; 15:14; 23:2; 24:6,31; 2 Ch. 8:15; 11:13; 19:8; 23:4; 24:5; 30:15,25; 31:2,4; 35:8,18) marks the distinction between priests and minor clergy. Throughout Chronicles, the Levites are second-class cult personnel. The program of turning the cultic personnel into Levites has been completed; with the help of genealogical constructs, the singers (*hammᵉšōrᵉrîm*) and gatekeepers (*haššōʿᵃrîm*) have been incorporated into the Levites (but not yet in Ezr. 2:42,70; 7:24; 10:24; Neh. 7:45; 10:29[28]; 11:19), as have even the bakers who made the baked goods needed for the temple cult in the form of flat cakes (*haḥᵃḇittîm* [1 Ch. 9:31], probably for the *minḥâ* of the high priest [Lev. 6:14(21)]) and showbread (*leḥem hammaʿᵃreḵeṯ*: 1 Ch. 9:32). The Levites took part in cultic ministrations (*mᵉleʾḵeṯ hāʿᵃḇôḏâ*: 1 Ch. 9:19), took care of the utensils (*kᵉlê hāʿᵃḇôḏâ*: 1 Ch. 9:28), and did the work necessary for the service of the house of Yahweh (*ʿōśēh hammᵉlāʾḵâ laʿᵃḇōḏaṯ bêṯ YHWH*: 1 Ch. 23:24). The word "Levite" was now "a collective term including very heterogeneous elements." " 'Levi' has become the embodiment of everything, whatever its function, that mediates between Yahweh and the laity of Israel."[90]

It is undeniable that the phenomenon of levitism is hard to grasp.[91] We see a certain kinship with prophecy in 2 Ch. 20:14-17, where God's answer to the lament of the people or of the king speaking on behalf of the people is pronounced by the Levite

88. See also H. W. Wolff, "Hoseas geistige Heimat," *ThLZ,* 81 (1956), 83-94 = *GSAT. ThB,* 22 (²1973), 232-250, who espouses the theory that Hosea had close associations with levitical circles in the northern kingdom.

89. See H. W. Wolff, *Hosea. Herm* (Eng. trans. 1974), 122.

90. Gunneweg, 212.

91. But see A. Neher, *The Prophetic Existence* (Eng. trans., South Brunswick, N.J., 1969), 166-176.

Jahaziel (*yaḥ^{a}zî'ēl*), upon whom the Spirit of Yahweh came (*hāy^{e}ṯâ ʿālāyw rûaḥ YHWH*). This passage pictures Jahaziel as a charismatic, who has taken over the functions and heritage of the preexilic cult prophets. In 1 Ch. 25:1-3, the activity of the singers is described by the niphal of *nb'*, which elsewhere denotes prophetic proclamation. More is meant than ecstatic playing of instruments.

Even though an individual Levite may be a *sôp̄ēr* (1 Ch. 24:6) and levitical *sôp̄^{e}rîm* are mentioned alongside *šōṭ^{e}rîm* (2 Ch. 34:13), the technical work of a scribe is probably not envisioned; we have here the first evidence for "scribes" in the later sense. This is also suggested by the words of 2 Ch. 35:3 concerning the teaching function of the Levites (*lal^{e}wîyîm hamm^{e}ḇînîm l^{e}ḵol-yiśrā'ēl*) and by 2 Ch. 17:7ff., where this function is described as *l^{e}lammēḏ b^{e}ʿārê y^{e}hûḏâ* (cf. also 1 Ch. 25:8).

VI. 1. *Age.* The evidence varies as to the age at which the Levites began their ministry. P states that they are to serve from the age of thirty to the age of fifty (Nu. 4:3,23,30,35,39,43,47; the same age is given for the overseer of all the storehouses in CD 14:8f.); 1 Ch. 23:3 also mentions the age of thirty. A later stratum in P reduces the starting age of service to twenty-five (Nu. 8:23-26). According to Ezr. 3:8 par. 1 Esd. 5:58; and 1 Ch. 23:24,27; 2 Ch. 31:17, Levites began their service at the age of twenty. The lists of returnees show that very few Levites returned from exile (74 according to Ezr. 2:40 par. Neh. 7:45; cf. also Ezr. 8:15-19), in contrast to the large number of priests (4,289 according to Ezr. 2:36-39 par. Neh. 7:39-42); the age of service may have been lowered to make up for a scarcity of levitical cultic personnel.[92] Against this theory is the presence of a postexilic Levite colony at Keilah (Khirbet Qîlā) in Judah (Neh. 3:17f.). Since at least the family of Henadad (*ḥēnāḏāḏ*: Neh. 3:18) is not listed among the returnees in Ezr. 2:40, we may conclude that many Levites remained behind during the exile, possibly because, unlike the priests, they did not belong to the aristocratic upper class of Judah. Possibly the differing ages reflect suitability for different tasks based on age and therefore experience; the rabbinic sources, for example, presuppose a five-year training period.[93]

2. *Support.* The support of the Levites was secured through the tithe (*ma^{ʿa}śēr*), primarily of grain, wine or must, and oil (Dt. 14:23; Neh. 13:5; Nu. 18:30 ["produce of the threshing floor and produce of the wine press"]; cf. the detailed list of tithes in Neh. 10:36-38[35-37]). Lev. 27:30-33 extends the tithe to cattle, but this extension was never more than theory; the allusion to it in 2 Ch. 31:6 is an interpolation based on Lev. 27:30-33. The tithe presented by the Israelites to Yahweh as an offering (*'^{a}šer yārîmû l^{e}YHWH t^{e}rûmâ*: Nu. 18:24) was given to the Levites by Yahweh for an inheritance (*naḥ^{a}lâ*). That this provision for the support of the Levites was not without problems is shown by Neh. 13:10ff. When Nehemiah learns that the Levites have deserted the temple because their only fixed revenue, the tithe, has not been paid, he

92. Cf. Kellermann, 121f.
93. Cf. F. Hüttenmeister, *Der Toseftatraktat Schekalim* (1970), iii.26, 158.

appoints a commission charged with supervising the storehouses (Neh. 13:13) and distributing the tithe. In the postbiblical period, too, there is evidence that the revenue of the Levites from the tithe was controverted.[94]

Disregarding the ancient rule that Levites should not possess land, over the course of time they did come to own real estate, as is clear from the Levite colony at Keilah mentioned above and the statement in Neh. 13:10 that each Levite fled to his own field (*'îš-leśāḏēhû*).

In the law of the Sabbatical Year and Jubilee Year (Lev. 25), the regulations concerning real property and debtors are followed by special provision for Levites (vv. 32-34) that also provides an insight into their ownership rights. It appears that a Levite had an unlimited right to redeem his house in the city at any time and that the house, if sold, was returned to him in the Jubilee Year if it had not been redeemed for any reason whatsoever.[95] Martin Noth,[96] however, thinks that the passage deals with a house that a Levite has purchased from another Israelite. In the Jubilee Year, it would be returned "not to the original owner but to the Levites, who in the meanwhile had entered by purchase into the possession." In any case, we are dealing with a special privilege of the Levites, which exempts their ownership of city houses from the general law concerning such houses (vv. 29f.). V. 34 then adds the special requirement that the Levites must under no circumstances sell any of the pasture land (*migrāš*) belonging to the levitical cities. A similar law prohibiting the sale of land by the Levites is found in Ezk. 48:14, which deals with the Levites' portion of the land contributed to Yahweh (*terûmâ*). Here, too, we see how the levitical rule prohibiting ownership of land occasioned consideration of ways to enhance the social status of the Levites through special privileges. It is even possible that the addition to the law in Lev. 25 was made by a Levite, putting forward claims that may or may not ever have been realized.

3. *Redemption of the First-born.* According to Ex. 13:11-16, all firstlings have belonged to Yahweh since the day on which Yahweh slew all the first-born of Egypt (Ex. 12:29). Ex. 13:2 contains a commandment of Yahweh transmitted to all Israel through Moses, stated in imperative form: "Consecrate to me all the first-born" (*qaddeš-lî kol-beḵôr*); Nu. 3:12, by contrast, states the requirement in personal terms: "Behold, I have taken the Levites from among the people of Israel instead of every first-born," as does Nu. 3:13: "I consecrated for his own all the first-born in Israel (*hiqdaštî lî kol-beḵôr beyiśrā'ēl*), . . . they shall be mine (*lî yihyû*)." Here we have a clear expression of "the elective initiative of God."[97] The fact that the entire tribe of Levi is thought of as representing each first-born individual in Israel makes it possible for a whole individual to be given to God. In this fashion the commandment is remarkably fulfilled through vicarious human action. "One might speak of an absolute

94. Graetz.
95. Cf. K. Elliger, *Leviticus. HAT,* IV (1966), 356.
96. M. Noth, *Leviticus. OTL* (Eng. trans. 1965), 191.
97. Zimmerli, *Festschrift W. F. Albright,* 468.

spiritual rehabilitation of the Levites."[98] This perspective is clouded, however, by the census that concludes the muster of the Levites (Nu. 3:40,42f.). The 273 first-born Israelites over and above the number of Levites are redeemed for just five shekels each, a sum that suggests a certain deprecation of the minor clergy.[99]

4. *Consecration.* Nu. 8:5-22 describes a consecration of Levites analogous to the consecration of priests in Lev. 8 par. Ex. 29.[100] The preparations, consisting of a special purification ritual and a sacrificial offering, are followed by the actual consecration before the assembled congregation through laying on of hands (*s^emîḵâ*) and a wave offering (*t^enûpâ*), together with a sin offering and a burnt offering. It is particularly important to note the statement that the Levites make atonement for the Israelites (*l^eḵappēr ʿal-b^enê yiśrāʾēl*: Nu. 8:19).[101]

5. *b^erîṯ with Levi.* The esteem and special importance of the Levites lead certain relatively late texts in the OT to speak of a *b^erîṯ* of Yahweh with Levi, the levitical priests (Jer. 33:21; Mal. 2:4f.,8; Neh. 13:29), or the Aaronites (Nu. 25:12f.).[102] Jer. 33 says that Yahweh's *b^erîṯ* "with the Levites, the priests, my servants," which stands in parallel to the *b^erîṯ* with David, can be broken only if the *b^erîṯ* of Yahweh with respect to day and night can be broken, so that they cease to come at their appointed time. Since this is impossible, the argument runs, by analogy there must always be a levitical priest exercising the priestly office in the temple of Yahweh, making it possible to offer sacrifice (burnt offering, cereal offering, and peace offering being mentioned specifically).

The difficult text of Mal. 2:1ff. (a threat discourse) contains in v. 4 a clear reference to a Yahweh *b^erîṯ* with Levi;[103] this verse is problematic, however, because the words of the MT seem to suggest that punishment is being sent in order to restore Yahweh's *b^erîṯ* with Levi. With this *b^erîṯ,* Yahweh has given Levi life and peace (*ḥayyîm* and *šālôm*: v. 5). By giving Levi awe of his name, Yahweh bestowed blessings on him, enabling him to walk[104] in peace and uprightness before Yahweh and to protect the people from sin and harm (*w^erabbîm hēšîḇ mēʿāwōn,* "he caused many to turn from iniquity") by true instruction (*tôraṯ ʾ^emeṯ*: v. 6).

VII. Dead Sea Scrolls and Postbiblical Literature. That the Qumran community was established by Zadokites "who had been robbed of their position in the temple by

98. *Ibid.,* 469.

99. Cf. Kellermann, 42, 44, 48.

100. *Ibid.,* 115-124.

101. See B. Janowski, *Sühne als Heilsgeschehen. WMANT,* 55 (1982), 202, n. 91; 151, n. 232.

102. See E. Kutsch, *Verheissung und Gesetz. BZAW,* 131 (1973), 118-121.

103. Cf. G. J. Botterweck, "Ideal und Wirklichkeit der Jerusalemer Priester," *BiLe,* 1 (1960), 107-9.

104. → הלך *hālaḵ* (*hālakh*), III, 394f.

the 'late levitical' Hasmonean zealots" is "an irony of history."[105] The Qumran community appears to have been divided into three groups: priests, Levites, and laity (1QS 2:19ff.; also 1QM 15:4). This division is not always strictly maintained: 1QS 6:8f. speaks of elders instead of Levites, and CD 14:3ff. divides the community into four groups: priests, Levites, Israelites, and proselytes. That 1QSa 1:23f., a rather difficult text, shows the Levites to have been subordinate to the heads of families (*r'šy 'bwt*), having to act according to their instructions, as Johann Maier concludes,[106] is not entirely clear. Members of the tribes of Levi, Judah, and Benjamin appear among the sons of light (1QM 1:1f.; cf. also T.Lev. 4:3: "Levi shall shine as the light of wisdom"). The Temple scroll has the tribe of Levi incorporated once more in the schema of the twelve tribes — in contrast to the system of P. As a priestly tribe, it is listed first, before Judah, in the regulations governing the order of sacrifices (11QT 23/24); this position is also represented by the east gate of the temple, which is named for Levi and Judah (11QT 39/40).[107] That the assignment of offices to priests or Levites remained a matter of controversy is shown by the addition of Aaron in CD 10:5, which says that four of the ten men constituting the college of judges of the community must come from the tribe of Levi and Aaron. CD 4:1f. explains who are priests and Levites by saying: "The priests are the converts of Israel who withdrew from the land of Judah and 'the Levites are those'[108] who followed them." Whether this text supports the notion of a universal priesthood is an open question.[109]

The special position of Levi in Jubilees and the Testaments of the Twelve Patriarchs must be understood in the context of the Hasmonean and Maccabean wars. Levi is priest, prince, and prophet (Jub. 31:14f.). God has given dominion to Levi (T.Reu. 6:5) and singled out Levi before all the other tribes (T.Nap. 5:3f.). The appointment of Levi to the priesthood is described in T.Lev. 8.[110] The political position of the Hasmoneans and Maccabeans, who belonged to the tribe of Levi, produced many passages in the Testaments of the Twelve Patriarchs that picture all the other tribes as being dependent on Levi, so that all attempts to rebel against Levi are doomed to failure (T.Jud. 21:1ff.).

Kellermann

105. Maier, 256.
106. J. Maier, *Die Texte vom Toten Meer,* 2: *Anmerkungen* (Munich, 1960), 157.
107. J. Maier, *The Temple Scroll. JSOTSup,* 34 (1985), 102.
108. Restored text; cf. C. Rabin, *The Zadokite Documents* (Oxford, ^{2}1958), 14f.
109. Cf. König, *Geschichte der alttestamentlichen Religion,* 593f.
110. See A. Caquot, "La double investiture de Lévi," *Ex Orbe Religionum. Festschrift G. Widengren,* I. *SNumen,* 21 (1972), 156-161.

לִוְיָתָן *liwyāṯān*

Contents: 1. Name; 2. Hebrew Tradition; 3. Parallels; 4. Theological Function.

1. *Name.* The name "Leviathan" appears 6 times in the Bible, only in poetic passages (Job 3:8; 40:25[Eng. 41:1]; Ps. 74:14; 104:26; Isa. 27:1 [twice]). Like *n*ᵉ*ḥuštān, liwyāṯān* is a substantive of the fem. *qiṭlat-ān* type. It is derived from the root *lwy* (Arab. *lawiya*), "twist, coil," and means "the sinuous one," designating a kind of serpent. Since it does not exhibit the regular phonetic development *-ān* > *-ôn,* it may represent a loanword in Hebrew,[1] where it is also treated as masculine. Nevertheless, the word appears as *lywytwn* in the talmudic period,[2] a form reflecting the phonetic change. The book of Enoch speaks of a female Leviathan: ". . . a female monster named Leviathan, appointed to dwell in the depths of the sea over the sources of the waters" (1 [Eth.]En. 60:7). This description of Leviathan might come from the Aramaic Book of the Giants,[3] part of the original Enoch corpus, fragments of which have been found at Qumran. In any case, a Parthian fragment of the Manichaean version of this work speaks of the dragon Leviathan (*lwy'tyn,* a form also found in

---

liwyāṯān. A. Caquot, "Léviathan et Behémoth dans la troisième 'parabole' d'*Hénoch,*" *Sem,* 25 (1975), 111-122; G. R. Driver, "Leviathan and Behemoth," *VT,* 1 (1951), 314; *idem,* "Mythical Monsters in the OT," *Studi orientalistici. Festschrift G. Levi della Vida,* I (Rome, 1956), 234-249; C. H. Gordon, "Leviathan: Symbol of Evil," *STLI,* 3 (1966), 1-9 = A. Altmann, ed., *Biblical Motifs* (Cambridge, Mass., 1966), 1-9; H. Gunkel, *Schöpfung und Chaos in Urzeit und Endzeit* (Göttingen, 1895, ²1921), 61ff.; J. Guttmann, "Leviathan, Behemoth, and Ziz: Jewish Messianic Symbols in Art," *HUCA,* 39 (1968), 219-230; A. Heidel, *The Babylonian Genesis* (Chicago, ²1963), 105-114; E. Herthlein, "Rahab," *ZAW,* 38 (1919/1920), 113-154, esp. 146ff.; P. Humbert, "A propos du 'serpent' (bšn) du mythe de Môt et Aleïn," *AfO,* 11 (1936), 235-37; O. Keel, *Jahwes Entgegnung an Ijob. FRLANT,* 121 (1978); N. K. Kiessling, "Antecedents of the Medieval Dragon in Sacred History," *JBL,* 89 (1970), 167-177; J. V. Kinnier Wilson, "A Return to the Problems of Behemoth and Leviathan," *VT,* 25 (1975), 1-14; G. R. Levy, "The Oriental Origin of Herakles," *JHS,* 54 (1934), 40-53; S. Loewenstamm, "The Ugaritic Myth of the Sea and its Biblical Counterpart," *Festschrift W. F. Albright. ErIsr,* 9 (1969), 96-101 [Heb.], 136 [Eng. summary]; S. I. L. Norin, *Er spaltete das Meer. CB,* 9 (Ger. trans. 1977); P. Reissing, *Lewiathan im AT* (diss., Würzburg, 1966); J. Schirmann, "The Battle between Behemoth and Leviathan According to an Ancient Hebrew Piyyuṭ," *PIASH,* 4/13 (1970), 327-369; A. Schoors, "Literary Phrases," *RSP,* I (1972) 33-36; H. Wallace, "Leviathan and the Beast in Revelation," *BA,* 11 (1948), 61-68 = *BA Reader,* I, 290-98; → בהמה *b*ᵉ*hēmâ* (*b*ᵉ*hēmāh*); → מבול *mabbûl.*

1. Cf. M. Wagner, *Die lexikalischen und grammatikalischen Aramaismen im alttestamentlichen Hebräisch. BZAW,* 96 (1966), 127.

2. C. D. Isbell, *Corpus of the Aramaic Incantation Bowls. SBL Diss,* 17 (Missoula, 1975), no. 7.

3. J. T. Milik, ed., *The Books of Enoch* (Oxford, 1976), 91.

Mandaic[4]), which did battle with the giant Ohya (*'why'*) or his brother Ahya (*'hy'*).[5] Since the Book of the Giants was probably composed around the end of the second century B.C.,[6] the tradition envisioning Leviathan as a female monster may be quite ancient and possibly original.

Stig Norin[7] proposes an entirely different etymology, interpreting *liwyāṯān* as a translation loanword from Egyp. *mḥn* ("the coiling one"), an epithet of the Apophis serpent.

2. *Hebrew Tradition.* The most extensive biblical text in which Leviathan appears is Job 40:25–41:26(41:1-34). These verses are part of the discourse in which Yahweh emphasizes his power. They contain a description of the monster suggesting that he dwells in the sea; he breathes fire, and the mere sight of him is terrifying. No human weapon can touch him, and the waters boil when he swims through the sea. The author of Job may have included some of the features of the crocodile in the description of Leviathan,[8] but these features are undoubtedly incidental to the mythical creature being described.

A second passage mentioning Leviathan appears in Job 3:8, where *ym (yām),* "sea," should be read for *ywm (yôm),* "day," as first proposed by Hermann Gunkel.[9] This reading is supported by an Aramaic incantation text: "I shall deliver you with great magic from Leviathan, the sea monster."[10] The enchanter goes on to threaten the demons: "I shall bring upon you the fate, the verdict, and the curse inflicted upon Mt. Hermon and upon the sea monster Leviathan, upon Sodom and Gomorrah."[11] Another incantation text differs somewhat: "I shall bring down upon you the verdict of heaven and the curse that you have brought upon yourselves (*'ytyty*) and upon Mt. Hermon and upon the sea monster Leviathan."[12] Since the curse on Mt. Hermon referred to by these texts most likely comes from the Book of the Giants,[13] the curse on Leviathan could also come from this source. Thus a connection between Job 3:8 and the Jewish Aramaic incantation texts seems more credible. The reading *yām* yields the translation: "Let those curse it [the day of Job's birth] who curse the sea, who are skilled to rouse up Leviathan." As is often true in mythological poetry, the sea represents the rebellious waters and stands in parallel with Leviathan. The basic conception is typologically

---

4. *MdD,* 236.
5. W. B. Henning, "The Book of the Giants," *BSOAS,* 11 (1943/46), 71f.; Milik, 299.
6. Milik, 57f.
7. Pp. 67-70.
8. E. Rupprecht, "Das Nilpferd im Hiobbuch," *VT,* 21 (1971), 209-231.
9. Cf. G. R. Driver, "Problems in the Hebrew Text of Job," *Wisdom in Israel and in the Ancient Near East. Festschrift H. H. Rowley. SVT,* 3 (1955), 72.
10. Isbell, nos. 2, 3f.; 6, 8; 7, 6f.
11. *Ibid.,* 2, 6; 6, 9f.
12. *Ibid.,* 7, 9.
13. Milik, 335-39.

earlier than the Ugaritic myth in which the sea is personified as the eldest son of El;[14] but it is clearly related to an even earlier stratum of the myth preserved elsewhere,[15] which speaks of the sea in parallel with the sea monster *tnn.* It has been pointed out that the anonymous enchanters Job calls upon to curse the day of his birth are enemies of God.[16] This suggests the giants Ohya (*'why'lh*) and Ahya (*'hyh*), who battled Leviathan before they were themselves destroyed by the Deluge. If so, Job 3:8 would allude to a mythological tradition that later found literary expression in the Book of the Giants.

Further allusions to Leviathan appear in Job 7:12; 26:12f. (cf. also 9:13; 38:8-11). Here Leviathan is pictured as a sea monster subjugated by Yahweh after a long battle. This conception also lies behind Ps. 74:13f., which alludes to the primordial battle between Yahweh and the monster personifying the waters of chaos. This text also shows that Leviathan was pictured as a many-headed dragon.

Ps. 104:26, whose text has been unjustifiably questioned, expresses (like Gen. 1:21) the idea that the sea monsters were created by Yahweh. According to 2 Esd. 6:49; 2 Apoc.Bar. 29:4; *Gen. Rab.* vii.4; Targ. Ps.-J. on Gen. 1:21, God created the two great monsters Leviathan and Behemoth on the fifth day. 1 (Eth.)En. 60:7f. appears to know a different tradition, according to which they were created on the third day (cf. Gen. 1:9f.). Both traditions assign the watery depths to Leviathan (1 [Eth.]En. 60:7; 2 Esd. 6:52).

Isa. 27:1 is the final and perhaps most important passage in the OT dealing with Leviathan. Here Leviathan personifies the evil powers that will be destroyed on the day of Yahweh: "In that day Yahweh with his hard and great and strong sword will punish Leviathan the agile serpent, Leviathan the twisting serpent, and he will slay the monster of the sea." The author of this verse, who probably lived in the Persian period, adapted an ancient mythological text to express the notion that Yahweh will ultimately triumph over all.

3. *Parallels.* There is in fact a striking similarity between Isa. 27:1 and the Ugaritic Baʿal epic. Mot sends a message to Baʿal, reminding him of his victorious battle with Leviathan (written *ltn*; probably from the name **liwyatānu* > **līyatānu* > **lītānu,* although the standard vocalization "Lotan" is generally accepted). Mot says to Baʿal: "If you slay Leviathan (*ltn*), the agile (*brḥ*) serpent and kill the twisting (*ʿqltn*) serpent, the tyrant with the seven heads. . . ."[17] Both Isa. 27:1 and this Ugaritic text describe Leviathan as *brḥ* ("agile") and *ʿqltn,* "twisting."

Undoubtedly, then, the biblical Leviathan is borrowed from Canaanite mythology, in which the seven-headed serpent is vanquished by the young warrior Baʿal or his consort ʿAnat, who describes the victory herself: "I have slain the twisting serpent, the tyrant with seven heads."[18] The uncertainty as to whether it was Baʿal or ʿAnat who

---

14. *KTU,* 1, 2.
15. The small tablet *KTU,* 1.83, and *KTU,* 1.3 III, 38-42.
16. G. Fohrer, *Das Buch Hiob, KAT,* XVI (1963), 110.
17. *KTU,* 1.5 I, 1-3, 27-30.
18. *KTU,* 1.3 III, 41f. (cf. 1.83).

slew Leviathan shows that the epics discovered at Ras Shamra contain allusions to earlier material that clearly was never integrated consistently into the mainstream of mythological tradition. The Hebrew allusions are clearly independent of Ugaritic literature, as can be seen from the form of the sea monster's name.[19] The Hebrew Leviathan motif is most likely borrowed from the South Canaanite tradition, with its divine hero quite logically replaced by Yahweh. The Hebrew tradition may have achieved its literary form as part of the story of Yahweh's battle with Rahab and other sea monsters; it is also referred to in certain biblical and postbiblical texts.[20]

The possible antiquity of the Leviathan motif suggests an identical motif in Mesopotamia, where a seven-headed serpent already appears in literary and pictorial works in the Early Dynastic Period III and in the Old Akkadian period. The "seven-tongued" serpent mentioned in the lexical series ḪAR-ra = ḫubullu, XIV, 17[21] and the omen series Šumma ālu[22] may be another name for the "seven-headed" serpent.[23] We also encounter this creature in the mythological tradition of Sumerian poetry, where it is called *muš-sag-imin,* "seven-headed serpent." The Sumerian Lugal epic alludes to its death at the hands of the warrior-god Ninurta,[24] as does the text called An-gim.[25] Ninurta was replaced by Nabû in a Sumerian litany with Akkadian translation for the cult of Nabû in the temple of Ezida at Borsippa. This litany, probably a compilation dating from the early first millennium, has incorporated some earlier Ninurta litanies[26] that mentioned the slaying of the seven-headed serpent by the deity. Although no extant narrative recounts this episode, a pictorial representation of a god slaying a seven-headed monster gives an idea of the scene. The earliest known illustration of a battle with a seven-headed serpent appears as part of an early clay impression from the temple of Abu at Eshnunna (Tell Asmar). The impression dates from the Early Dynastic Period III.[27] It shows the victor kneeling and holding two serpent heads in his hands; the remaining five heads are intact. A further reference to a seven-headed serpent appears in the decoration of a Sumerian scepter pommel.[28] The battle of a deity with a seven-headed dragon is the only scene on a basin from the Old Akkadian period.[29] The god is kneeling in front of a dragon, one of whose heads is already slain although the others

---

19. Cf. also Loewenstamm.

20. See E. Lipiński, *La royauté de Yahwé dans la poésie et le culte de l'ancien Israël. VVAW.L,* 27/55 (1965), 126ff.; also Loewenstamm.

21. B. Landsberger, *The Fauna of Ancient Mesopotamia,* 2: *Tablets XIV and XVIII. MSL,* VIII/2 (1962), 8.

22. *CT,* 40, pl. 23, K. 3674, 34 par. pl. 24, K. 6294, 5.

23. Cf. *CT,* 40, pl. 23, K. 3674, 33 par. pl. 24, K. 6294, 4.

24. E. Chiera, *Sumerian Epics and Myths. OIP,* 15 (1934), no. 44, obv. 13 = no. 45, obv. 11.

25. Published by J. S. Cooper, *The Return of Ninurta to Nippur: An-gim dim-ma. AnOr,* 52 (1978), 62ff.

26. See W. G. Lambert, "The Converse Tablet: A Litany with Musical Instructions," *Near Eastern Studies in Honor of W. F. Albright* (Baltimore, 1971), 335-353, esp. 340 and 345, l. 16.

27. H. Frankfort, *Stratified Cylinder Seals from the Diyala Region. OIP,* 72 (1955), no. 497.

28. H. Frankfort, "Early Dynastic Sculptured Maceheads," *AnOr,* 12 (1935), 107.

29. *ANEP,* 671.

are still alive. A similar scene is found on an Old Akkadian seal from the temple of Abu IV at Eshnunna.[30] This seal depicts two gods using a spear to slay a seven-headed monster. Four heads are already hanging down dead; three are still alive, with their forked tongues hanging out. Both scenes depict flames rising from the back of the monsters, whose bodies are serpentine and are supported by four legs with claws. This image might suggest the notion of a serpent with four legs before it was condemned to crawl upon its belly (Gen. 3:14).

Later scenes of a battle between the warrior-god and a serpentlike creature do not include any clear instances of a many-headed dragon, although many representations of such a battle have been found in Northern Syria, Anatolia, and Mesopotamia from the period 1600-1500 B.C.[31] The Neo-Hittite relief from Malatya[32] (1st millennium) may represent an exception, but the critical part of the relief is not extant and only the lowest dead head of the great serpent is visible. The relief depicts two armed deities, one of whom is engaged in battle with the serpent while heavenly beings hurl balls of fire or stones at the monster (cf. Josh. 10:11). Without real evidence, this scene has often been connected with the Hittite myth of Illuyankas.[33]

The absence of any clear illustrations of many-headed dragons after the Old Akkadian period may indicate that the seven-headed serpent mentioned in the Ugaritic texts and alluded to in Ps. 74 (vv. 13f.) belongs to the third millennium. The many-headed Greek hydra and the story of its destruction by Hercules (Heracles) with the help of Iolaus obviously derive from an ancient Near Eastern prototype.[34] Especially striking are the similarities between the Greek version of Hercules's victory and the scene depicted on the Old Akkadian seal. Here a deity helps the protagonist, just as Iolaus helps Hercules; and the flames rising from the back of the seven-headed dragon recall the fact that Hercules finally had to pass through fire. Nevertheless, the association with the Malatya relief would be even stronger if the great serpent in it were really represented as a many-headed creature like the Greek hydra.

The differing representations show that several traditions of this sort existed in the Near East or that an evolutionary development lies behind the different dragon conceptions. When it was believed that Leviathan dwelt in the sea while the hydra dwelt in the marshes of Ledra near Argos, there is apparently no reason to connect the four-legged Old Akkadian monster with water. Furthermore, the Leviathan of Ps. 74:13f. has multiple heads, while the Leviathan of Job 41 clearly has only a single head, since the poet speaks of the head only in the singular (40:31[41:7]). Nevertheless, both are called Leviathan, just like the monster battled by Ohya and/or Ahya in the Book of the Giants.

Direct contacts between Mesopotamia and the Western Semitic world — now amply documented by the Ebla discoveries for the period just before the first appearance of the seven-headed dragon in Mesopotamia — could well suggest that the same funda-

30. Frankfort, *Stratified Cylinder Seals,* no. 478 = *ANEP,* 671.
31. Cf. W. Orthmann, "Hydra," *RLA,* IV (1972-75), 537.
32. L. J. Delaporte, *Malatya: Arslantepe,* I (Paris, 1940), 34f. and pl. xxii, 2 = *ANEP,* 670.
33. *ANET*^{3}, 125f.
34. Cf. Levy.

mental myth spread throughout the two regions. But this conclusion does not demonstrate either a Canaanite or a Sumerian priority.

4. *Theological Function.* In summary, we may say that Leviathan is to be thought of as part of a mythopoetic motif whose original purpose was to glorify the warrior God of Israel. Although the connection between the seven-headed Sumerian serpent and the Canaanite Leviathan remains uncertain, the close relationship of the biblical Leviathan to the Canaanite Leviathan of the Ugaritic texts has been attested clearly. They spring from the same roots, although the Ugaritic *ltn* cannot be seen as the prototype of the Hebrew Leviathan. After the traditions of Leviathan and other sea monsters became known in Israel, major changes were made in the traditions themselves: the polytheistic elements of the original myths were removed (Ps. 74:13f.; Job 3:8; 7:12; 9:13; 26:12f.; 38:8-11; 40:25–41:26[41:1-34]), and new ideas were introduced, especially later in the postbiblical period. One innovation was the rejection of Leviathan and other sea monsters as mythical opponents of Yahweh; they were now thought of simply as creatures formed by the Creator at the proper time and in their proper place (Ps. 104:26; cf. Gen. 1:21; 1 [Eth.]En. 60:7; 2 Esd. 6:49; 2 Apoc.Bar. 29:4; *Gen. Rab.* vii.4; Targ. Ps.-J. on Gen. 1:21). The second major innovation was the fact that among the Israelites these monsters came to symbolize all the powers of evil, while God's victory over them represents his ultimate victory at the end of days (cf. esp. Isa. 27:1, but also Rev. 11:7; 13:1-10; 17:3,7-17). The "beast that ascends from the bottomless pit" (Rev. 11:7) and the "beast rising out of the sea, with ten horns and seven heads" (Rev. 13:1) derive in part from the ancient Leviathan motif. The "sea monster with seven heads" (Bab. *Qidd.* 29b; Odes Sol. 22:5) is also a symbol of depravity. A later form of this Leviathan tradition, based on Ps. 74:14, appears in the notion of the eschatological banquet, at which the flesh of Leviathan will be devoured by the righteous and the elect (Bab. *B. Bat.* 74b-75a; Jer. *Meg.* i.7b; iii.74a; Jer. *Sanh.* x.29c; Targ. Ps.-J. on Gen. 1:21; *Tanḥ. B.* 34b; *Midr. Ps.* on Ps. 23:7; 2 Apoc.Bar. 29:4; 2 Esd. 6:52; cf. *Lev. Rab.* xiii, xxii).

Lipiński

לון *lûn*; תְּלֻנּוֹת *t^elunnôṯ*

Contents: I. 1. Etymology, Occurrences; 2. Meaning. II. OT Usage: 1. Against Other Human Beings; 2. Against God. III. Theological Usage: 1. Historical Basis; 2. Reinterpretation.

---

lûn. G. W. Coats, *Rebellion in the Wilderness* (Nashville, 1968); S. Herrmann, "Bemerkungen zur Inschrift des Königs Kilamuwa von Senğirli," *OLZ,* 48 (1953), 295-97; P. Joüon, "Études de morphologie hébraïque," *Bibl,* 1 (1920), 353-371, esp. § 6, 361f.; R. Knierim, "לון *lūn* rebellieren," *THAT,* I, 870-72; F. de Luna, *Estudios para una teología bíblica de la murmuracion* (Lic., Fribourg, 1971); T. Nöldeke, *Beiträge zur semitischen Sprachwissenschaft* (Strasbourg, 1904), 42; K. H. Rengstorf, "γογγύζω," *TDNT,* I, 728-737.

I. 1. *Etymology, Occurrences.* Outside of Hebrew, the root *lûn* is attested only in the Phoenician inscription of Kilamuwa from Zinjirli.[1] A connection with Arab. *lwn,* "be undecided,"[2] or Arab. *lwm,* "chastise,"[3] is unlikely. In the OT, the root appears 15 times as a verb and 8 times as a noun. The verb appears only in the niphal and hiphil (5 times and 10 times, respectively, using the *qere* readings). In the Tiberian punctuation, the hiphil forms tend to double the first radical; several passages accordingly vacillate in orthography and punctuation between niphal and hiphil (Ex. 16:2,7; Nu. 14:36; 16:11). The frequent use of defective orthography (Ex. 15:24; Nu. 14:2; 17:6[Eng. 16:41]; Josh. 9:18; Kilamuwa 10) and in particular the gemination of the *nûn* in the noun, a feminine abstract with a *t*-preformative, suggest derivation from a root *lnn.*[4] It is noteworthy that — apart from Josh. 9:18; Ps. 59:16(15) (emended) — the root is used only in narratives describing events during Israel's wandering in the desert, i.e., only within Ex. 15–17; Nu. 14–17.

Outside the OT, the verb also appears in the Dead Sea scrolls (1QS 7:17; 1QH 5:25). The Kilamuwa inscription from Zinjirli probably contains a hithpolel form defectively written.[5]

2. *Meaning.* The OT texts indicate that the basic meaning of the root is "murmur, grumble." The context may suggest the stronger sense of "rebel" (Josh. 9:18)[6] or, in metaphorical comparison to dogs, the specialized meaning "growl" (Ps. 59:16[15] emended).[7] The Dead Sea scrolls passages, which describe the behavior of opponents, and the Kilamuwa inscription, which also uses the metaphor of growling dogs, agree with these meanings. Semantically, the root is closely related to → מרד *mrd,* "revolt," and → מרה *mrh,* "rebel."

The LXX regularly uses *(dia)gongýzein* to translate the root; this verb appears accordingly in 1 Cor. 10:10.

II. OT Usage. In all the texts that use the root *lûn,* the act of murmuring or growling is ascribed solely to creatures of Yahweh. In Nu. 16:11 it is the Korahites who rebel against Aaron; in all the other passages in Ex. 15–17; Nu. 14–17 as well as Josh. 9:18, the subject is the Israelites, the congregation of the Israelites, or the people. In Ps. 59:16(15) emended (and the Kilamuwa inscription), similarly, it is dogs that murmur or growl.

1. *Against Other Human Beings.* In the OT, the range of persons against whom others murmur is severely limited. The majority of texts speak of murmuring against

---

1. *KAI,* 24, 10; cf. Herrmann.
2. *KBL*[3], 498b.
3. *GesB,* 382b; *KBL*[2], 477b.
4. Nöldeke, 41; Joüon, 361f.
5. Herrmann, 295f.; *KAI,* II, 33.
6. Knierim, 870.
7. H. Gunkel, *Die Psalmen. HKAT,* II/2 ([5]1968), 252; Herrmann, 296.

Moses and Aaron (Ex. 16:2,7; Nu. 14:2; 17:6,20[16:41; 17:5]); all these passages belong to P. Moses appears alone just 3 times as the object of murmuring on the part of the people (Ex. 15:24; 17:3) or the congregation (Nu. 14:36). Ex. 15:24; 17:3 are also the only occurrences of the root in Ex. 15–17; Nu. 14–17 that do not come from P. Only once is Aaron alone the object of murmuring (Nu. 16:11). Once the congregation murmurs against unspecified leaders of the congregation (Josh. 9:18). Besides these clear references, finally, we have the metaphor that likens human enemies (Ps. 59:15f.[14f.]) or a subject population (Kilamuwa 10) to growling dogs.

The reasons people murmur against others include primarily lack of food and water in the desert (Ex. 15:24; 16:2,7; 17:3) and fear of the inhabitants of Canaan (Nu. 14:2,36), but also the leadership of Moses and Aaron (Nu. 16:11) as well as a hasty and unnecessary treaty with elements of the Canaanite population (Josh. 9:18).

2. *Against God.* In the OT, people murmur against Yahweh as well as against others. Such statements are limited to narratives of events during the desert period and are associated with P. A distinction must be made between a mere statement that the congregation murmured against Yahweh (Ex. 16:7,8; Nu. 14:27,29; also Nu. 17:25[10]) and Yahweh's explicit hearing of this murmuring against him (Ex. 16:8,9,12; Nu. 14:27).

The people murmur against Yahweh for the same major reasons they murmur against their leaders during the desert period, namely lack of food and water and fear of the Canaanites (cf. Ex. 16:7-9,12; Nu. 14:27,29). This murmuring against Yahweh represents the high point in the murmuring of the Israelites.

III. Theological Usage.

1. *Historical Basis.* All the texts in the Hexateuch that describe the people or the congregation of the Israelites as murmuring against their leaders or against Yahweh bear the stamp of theological reflection. The starting point for the use of the concept as well as for the development of the individual murmuring narratives is probably to be found in the historically trustworthy tradition of the Korahites' rebellion against the leadership of Moses and Aaron and the priestly privilege of Aaron during the desert period (Nu. 16:2-11).[8] This tradition probably comprises two versions (vv. 2-7a, 7b-11) that were combined and later incorporated by P.[9] Subsequently, just as the exodus, desert, and occupation tradition was extended to include all Israel, this tradition of a rebellious group within the Moses band was extended to the whole people or congregation of the Israelites. The object of the rebellion was similarly shifted from Moses and Aaron to the exodus, desert wandering, and occupation as a whole (cf. Ex. 17:3; 16:2-12; Nu. 14:2-38). This process, which includes the tradition of Josh. 9:18, is reflected in all the source strata of the Hexateuch and therefore was probably completed during the preexilic period.

---

8. Knierim, 871.
9. M. Noth, *Numbers. OTL* (Eng. trans. 1968), 124f.

2. *Reinterpretation.* Within the complexes of Ex. 15–17; Nu. 14–17 (with the exception of Nu. 16:11), the people rebel against Moses and Aaron as well as against Yahweh because they have been brought out of Egypt into the desert to die there (cf. Ex. 16:2f.; 17:3; Nu. 14:3). They therefore demand to return to Egypt (cf. Nu. 14:3f.) instead of going forward into the land of Canaan (cf. Nu. 14:2,36). The people's rebellion is thus based on a total misunderstanding of the history of deliverance as a history of perdition; its aim is to reverse the course of history.[10] As a result, Moses, Aaron, and even Yahweh are looked upon not as deliverers but as bringers of affliction and death. Yahweh, the God of the congregation of Israel, is the true agent of this situation and is therefore the ultimate object of the rebellion.[11]

By failing to understand events during their time of wandering in the desert between the exodus from Egypt (deliverance) and the occupation of Canaan (consummation of deliverance) and by distrusting Yahweh their God, the people of Israel reject the history of deliverance designed by Yahweh and thus also reject their own salutary future. Viewed theologically, the rebellion of the people is a manifestation of sin. It therefore provokes an appropriate reaction on the part of Yahweh and impugns the future well-being of the whole people of Israel. For the actual rebels, this rebellion results in death (cf. Nu. 14:27ff.).

Josh. 9:18 comports with the theological understanding exhibited in Ex. 15–17; Nu. 14–17: again the whole congregation of Israel rebels, this time against their leaders during the occupation of Canaan. And again this rebellion must be called sin, although it is right in attacking a transgression of the sacral tradition of the ban, since it impugns a treaty sworn in the presence of Yahweh (cf. Josh. 9:15-20).

Schunck

10. Knierim, 871.
11. Cf. II.2.

לַח *laḥ*; לֵחַ *lēaḥ*

Contents: I. Etymology and Extrabiblical Occurrences: 1. Ugaritic; 2. Akkadian; 3. Aramaic, Middle Hebrew. II. OT: 1. Occurrences; 2. Usage. III. Dead Sea Scrolls.

I. Etymology and Extrabiblical Occurrences. The root *lḥ*, a *qall* form in Hebrew, ends by nature with a double consonant.[1] The verbal root *lḥḥ*[2] is attested in pure form

laḥ. A. van Selms, "A Forgotten God: *Laḥ,*" *Studia Biblica et Semitica. Festschrift T. C. Vriezen* (Wageningen, 1966), 318-326.

1. *BLe,* §453y.
2. *KBL*³, 499; van Selms, 320f.

only in the Ethiopic verb *'lḥaḥa,* "moisten."[3] All occurrences of the root are concentrated in West and South Semitic.

1. *Ugaritic.* The evidence for the root in Ugaritic is highly problematic. Of the four lexemes *lḥ* (I: *lwḥ,* "writing tablet"; II: *lḥw,* "offend"; III: *lḥy,* "cheeks"; IV: *lwḥ,* "glisten"),[4] none seems to be connected with our root. The occurrences cited by Richard E. Whitaker[5] (placed under *lḥm* by Andrée Herdner) are not confirmed by *KTU,* 4.34. Scholars have associated a variety of formatives with *lḥ*(*ḥ*):

In *KTU,* 1.17, I, 28f., William F. Albright[6] interprets *ṭbq.lḥt.nȝṣh* as "who smothers the life-force of his detractors."[7] Here a son wishes that his father may gain power over the vital force of his detractors.[8]

In *KTU,* 1.17 VI, 28, Albright interprets *'šlḥk* as a causative from *lḥḥ,* "be moist, fresh, vigorous," and translates: "I will give thee life-force," i.e., "sexual power." Probably, however, we are dealing with a form of *šlḥ,* "send,"[9] which must be distinguished from *šlḥ,* "become fluid, melt."[10]

In *KTU,* 1.3 I, 6-8, the *mlḥt* of *b ḥrb mlḥt* is often connected with *mlyḥ,* "good,"[11] and the phrase translated "with a good sword." Mitchell Dahood[12] proposes "a succulent sword" (from *lḥḥ*). More likely, however, are etymologies citing Arab. *lāḥa,* "gleam,"[13] and especially *mlḥ,* "salt."[14]

In *KTU,* 1.6 I, 20, Adrianus van Selms[15] interprets the divine name *ydʿ ylḥn* as a

---

3. *LexLingAeth,* 30.

4. *WUS,* no. 1449-1452.

5. *CTA,* 134, 2, 3, 4, 6, 9; Whitaker, 397.

6. W. F. Albright, "The 'Natural Force' of Moses in the Light of Ugaritic," *BASOR,* 94 (1944), 35.

7. Also G. R. Driver and van Selms; understood differently by *UT*; J. Gray, *The Legacy of Canaan. SVT,* 5 (²1965) (< *lwḥ,* "plates"); *WUS*; L. Delekat, "Zum ugaritischen Verbum," *UF,* 4 (1972), 23; M. Dijkstra and J. C. de Moor, "Problematical Passages in the Legend of Aqhâtu," *UF,* 7 (1975), 176 (< *lḥy,* "abuse").

8. → דבה *dibbâ* (*dibbāh*).

9. H. L. Ginsberg, "The North-Canaanite Myth of Anath and Aqhat," *BASOR,* 98 (1945), 17ff.; W. J. Horwitz, "A Study of Ugaritic Scribal Practices and Prosody in *CTA* 2:4," *UF,* 5 (1973), 172; Y. Avishur, "Studies of Stylistic Features Common to the Phoenician Inscriptions and the Bible," *UF,* 8 (1976), 4; D. W. Young, "With Snakes and Dates: A Sacred Marriage Drama at Ugarit," *UF,* 9 (1977), 298; *WUS,* no. 2610; *UT,* no. 2419.

10. M. Dietrich and O. Loretz, "Die sieben Kunstwerke des Schmiedegottes in KTU 1.4 I 23-43," *UF,* 10 (1978), 59; T. H. Gaster, "The Conflict of 'Aleyân-Baʿal and Mōt," *JRAS,* 1935, 10f., already notes Heb. *šlḥ,* "water conduit" (*GesB,* 833).

11. *UT,* no. 1482; Gray, 38; J. Blau and S. E. Loewenstamm, "Zur Frage der scriptio plena im Ugaritischen und Verwandtes," *UF,* 2 (1970), 21, n. 9.

12. M. Dahood, "Ugaritic Lexicography," *Mélanges E. Tisserant,* I. *StT,* 231 (1964), 92f.

13. *WUS*; E. Lipiński, "Banquet en l'honneur de Baal: CTA 3 (V A), A, 4-22," *UF,* 2 (1970), 79.

14. E. Ullendorff, "Ugaritic Marginalia II," *JSS,* 7 (1962), 344f.; M. Dietrich, O. Loretz, and J. Sanmartín, "Zur ugaritischen Lexicographie (XII)," *UF,* 6 (1974), 40.

15. Pp. 325f.

reference to the deity's "vital vigour." J. C. de Moor[16] interprets it as an epithet describing ʿAthtar as "god 'who is able to moisten.'" G. R. Driver and Frank M. Cross[17] are more likely correct in suggesting the root *lḥn,* "be intelligent."

In *KTU,* 1.85, 3, de Moor interprets *ymsś.hm.b.mskt.dlḥt* as referring to a "mixture of saps."

The evidence for the existence of Laḥ, a god of vital force, is thus very scant. The theophorous elements in the personal names cited by van Selms are better derived from the divine name *šlḥ,* the god of the river of the underworld.[18]

2. *Akkadian.* In Akkadian, *lāḫu* appears only as a West Semitic loanword, synonymous with *perḫu,* "shoot."[19] It is uncertain whether our word with the meaning "moist, wet" appears in Hurr. *laḫlaḫḫi,*[20] the name of a mountain range (= *lablanḫi,* "Lebanon range").[21]

3. *Aramaic, Middle Hebrew.* The occasional lengthening of the root in the first syllable does not permit identification with *lwḥ.*[22] The verb *lawwaḥa,* "begin to ripen" (of grapes), found in the colloquial Syrian dialect of Arabic, as well as *talāwīḥ,* "fruit that is beginning to ripen,"[23] may be associated with our root. Cf. Aram. *laḥlaḥ,* "moisten, cause to flow";[24] Christian Palestinian *lêḥa',* "moisture";[25] Talmudic *laḥ,* "moist, fresh,"[26] often used metaphorically on the basis of Dt. 34:7. The male semen is the "sap of life" par excellence; its degeneration shows the total corruption of the individual (*lēḥâ sᵉrûḥā*: *Cant. Rab.* vii.9).

II. OT.

1. *Occurrences.* The adj. *laḥ* occurs 6 times in the OT (Gen. 30:37; Nu. 6:3; Jgs. 16:7,8; Ezk. 17:24; 21:3[Eng. 20:47]). The noun *lēaḥ* is found only in Dt. 34:7 and Jer. 11:19 conj.[27]

---

16. J. C. de Moor, *The Seasonal Pattern in the Ugaritic Myth of Baʿlu. AOAT,* 16 (1971), 202f.

17. *CML*², 150; F. M. Cross, "Epigraphic Notes on the Ammān Citadel Inscription," *BASOR,* 193 (1969), 18, n. 12.

18. Cf. M. Tsevat, "The Canaanite God Šälaḥ," *VT,* 4 (1954), 41-49; O. Loretz, "Der Gott *ŠLḤ*, HE. *ŠLḤ* I und *ŠLḤ* II," *UF* (1975), 584f.

19. *CAD,* IX (1973), 45; *AHw,* I (1965), 528.

20. *KBo,* XX, 129, obv. II, 24.

21. P. Haas and H. J. Thiel, "Ein Beitrage zum hurritischen Wörterbuch," *Festschrift C. F. A. Schaeffer. UF,* 11 (1979), 343f.

22. Van Selms, 320f.

23. J. B. Belot, *Vocabulaire arabe-français* (Beirut, ¹¹1920), cited in van Selms, 311.

24. G. H. Dalman, *Aramäisch-neuhebräisches Handwörterbuch zu Targum, Talmud und Midrasch* (1938, repr. Hildesheim 1967), 216.

25. F. Schulthess, *Grammatik des christlich-palästinischen Aramäisch* (Tübingen, 1924), §24, 3b.

26. *WTM,* II, 491f., 494.

27. See M. Dahood, "Hebrew-Ugaritic Lexicography IV," *Bibl,* 47 (1966), 409; *BHS, in loc.*

a. The adj. *laḥ* and its pl. *laḥîm* (3 occurrences of each) are used in the botanical realm of *maqqēl,* "branch," *ʿanāḇîm,* "grapes," and *ʿēṣ* "tree." Its antonyms are *yāḇēš* and *ḥāraḇ*. Note also *ṭārāp,* "fresh" (Ezk. 17:9; cf. v. 24). The suffix with *lēaḥ* in Dt. 34:7 is ambiguous. The MT reads *lēḥōh* (*kethibh*: *lēḥâ,* referring to *ʿênô,* "the moisture of his eyes";[28] *qere*: "his [vital] sap"[29]); but cf. several LXX traditions. The Vulg. reads *šinnayw,* "his teeth." Sir. 34(31):13 is obviously based on Dt. 34:7.

b. The LXX translates *laḥ* with *chlōrós* (3 times), *hyrós* (twice), and *prósphatos* (once); it renders *lēaḥ* by *tá chelýnia* and accurately paraphrases Sir. 31:13 with *dakrýein.*

c. In addition to Jer. 11:19 conj. (*belēḥô* for *belaḥmô,* against the LXX[30]), emendations have also been proposed for Job 5:26 (*beḵelaḥ*); 30:2 (*kālaḥ*). The unknown etymology[31] of *klḥ* (Aram. *kalaḥa,* "look sternly,"[32] does not help) led even Jerome to emendation: *omnis vita* = *kl ḥyym.* In Job 30:2, following Dt. 34:7, Karl Budde conjectured *kol-lēaḥ.*[33] Adalbert Merx and Thomas K. Cheyne similarly proposed *belēaḥ* in Job 5:26. Dahood[34] sees in *klḥ* a "congeneric assimilation" (*kōaḥ,* "strength" + *lēaḥ,* "freshness") with the meaning "ripeness,"[35] but this meaning is inappropriate in the context of Job 5:26.[36] Following the Rabbis, we should probably read a form of *klh,* "bring to completion."

2. *Usage.* a. The earliest occurrences of *laḥ* in the OT are found in Gen. 30:37 (J); Jgs. 16:7f. The pre-J Jacob tradition already recounted Jacob's cunning in making plain goats mate while looking at fresh (*laḥ*) peeled rods of wood so that their offspring would be speckled. To explain this stratagem, Hermann Gunkel,[37] Gerhard von Rad,[38] and Claus Westermann[39] point out the well-known "oversight" of female animals,[40] probably a popular term for the influence of the environment on embryonic development. Possibly, however, the placing of rods before the mating animals may be related to mythological notions.[41] Illustrations on Mesopotamian cylinder seals[42] also suggest

---

28. *GesB,* 382.
29. *KBL*³, 499.
30. Cf. W. Rudolph, *Jeremia. HAT,* XII (³1968); *BHS*; contra van Selms. See II.1.
31. F. Horst, *Hiob. BK,* XVI/1 (1968), 89.
32. *KBL*³, 455; S. R. Driver and G. B. Gray, *Job. ICC* (²1927, repr. 1977), 33f.
33. See also M. H. Pope, *Job. AB,* XV (²1973), 219.
34. M. Dahood, "Northwest Semitic Philology and Job," *The Bible in Current Catholic Thought. M. J. Gruenthaner Memorial Volume. St. Mary's Theology Studies,* 1 (New York, 1962), 56f.; *idem,* "Hebrew-Ugaritic Lexicography XI," *Bibl,* 54 (1973), 358; cf. A. C. M. Blommerde, *Northwest Semitic Grammar and Job. BietOr,* 22 (1969), 12, 26, 112.
35. *KBL*³, 455.
36. Cf. G. Fohrer, *Das Buch Hiob. KAT,* XVI (1963), 129, 156.
37. H. Gunkel, *Genesis. HKAT,* I/1 (⁹1977), 339.
38. G. von Rad, *Genesis. OTL* (Eng. trans. 1961), 296f.
39. C. Westermann, *Genesis 12–36* (Eng. trans., Minneapolis, 1985), 483.
40. Cf. already S. Borchart, *Hierozoicon,* I, 619f.
41. → כבשׂ *keḇeś.*
42. Cited by I. Seibert, *Hirt, Herde, König. DAWB,* 53 (1969), 58f.

a possible allusion to the tree of life motif in the context of fertility magic. The binding of Samson with seven "fresh" (still moist) bowstrings (Jgs. 16:7f.) is also viewed as a magical act, since these strings were thought to be still "full of mysterious life."[43] The parallel attempts to bind him with "new" ropes (*ʿaḇōṯîm ḥ^adāšîm*: Jgs. 16:11; cf. 15:12f.) and to weave the seven locks of his hair with the *masseḵeṯ,* the warp threads of the horizontal loom,[44] lend credence to the magical background. By way of explanation, Robert G. Boling[45] cites the curse ritual of the oath taken by Hittite soldiers,[46] in which "tearing apart of the soul" represents the death of the forsworn soldier. A. G. van Daalen[47] views the story of Samson as being based on the myth of a solar deity, recounting the vain attempts of mortals to bind the sun.

Nu. 6:3 states that a Nazirite is not permitted to drink wine, strong drink, or grape juice; neither may he eat dry (*yāḇēš*) or fresh (*laḥ*) grapes. According to E. Zuckschwerdt,[48] a later redactor has here expanded on the prohibition of wine.[49]

b. Dt. 34:7 reports that Moses died at the age of 120 years. Despite his great age, his eyes were not dim and his *lēaḥ,* "sap of life" (syn. *ʿalûmîm*: Job 20:11; etc.), was unabated. The text-critical problems of this text are discussed above. Rabbinic legend (Sifre on Dt. 34:7) reinterprets it: from Moses' body water flowed in all directions (cf. the noncanonical scriptural quotation in Jn. 7:37f.).[50]

Jer. 11:19 uses a tree full of sap as a vivid metaphor to represent Jeremiah in his full vigor, exposed unsuspectingly to the persecutions of his friends. The parallel metaphor of the lamb that is led to the slaughter has resulted in a wealth of christological interpretations clustering around this verse.[51]

Ezk. 17:24 uses the green tree and the dry tree as a merism for all of nature, in which Yahweh reveals his works.

In an oracle of judgment against the "land of the south," Ezk. 21:3(20:47) proclaims that every green tree and every dry tree will be burned, again a merism revealing Yahweh's sovereignty over all the earth (cf. the association with the recognition formula in 21:4,10[20:48; 21:5]).

In rabbinic literature, the argument from the burning of green wood to the much easier burning of dry wood is a favorite metaphor for the inevitability of divine judgment.[52]

---

43. H. W. Hertzberg, *Das Bücher Josua, Richter und Ruth. ATD,* IX ([4]1969), 234.
44. *AuS,* V (1937), 101; K. Galling, "Weben und Weberei," *BRL*[2], 360.
45. R. G. Boling, *Judges. AB,* VI A (1965), 249.
46. *ANET*[3], 553f.
47. A. G. van Daalen, *Simson. SSN,* 8 (1966), 107-114.
48. E. Zuckschwerdt, "Zur literarischen Vorgeschichte des priesterlichen Nazir-Gesetzes (Num $6_{1\text{-}8}$)," *ZAW,* 88 (1976), 196.
49. Cf. also D. Kellermann, *Die Priesterschrift von Numeri 1_1 bis 10_{a0}. BZAW,* 120 (1970), 87.
50. On the metaphor of the "spring of the living water," see R. Schnackenburg, *The Gospel according to St. John,* 2. *HTC* (Eng. trans. 1980), 152ff.
51. Cf. O. Michel, "σφαγή,"" *TDNT,* VII, 935-38; A. Feuillet, "Les martyrs de l'humanité et l'Agneau égorgé," *NRTh,* 99 (1977), 190-207.
52. See St.-B., II (1924), 263; Lk. 23:31; J. Schneider, "ξύλον," *TDNT,* V, 37.

III. Dead Sea Scrolls. Three occurrences of *laḥ* have been found in the Dead Sea scrolls. In 1QH 3:29, it is related to Ezekiel. In apocalyptic tones, the hymnic confession of faith describes the growth of Belial like a devouring fire that destroys *kol ʿēṣ laḥ* *wᵉyāḇēš.* The text of 1QH 8:19 (possibly corrupt) marks an antithesis to 3:29: the "elect"[53] "who were hidden in secret" (*mᵉḥûbbāʾîm bassēṯer*) will become a spring of water (?) for green and dry — i.e., all — trees. In this metaphor is concentrated the sense of election and mission shared by the Essenes of Qumran.

In 11QT 49:12, the Temple scroll prescribes how the house of someone who has died is to be cleansed,[54] incorporating and elaborating on the regulations of Nu. 19:11-22. The "water of purification" (*mê niddâ*)[55] of Nu. 19:13[56] is now specified as comprising oil (*šmn*), wine (*yyn*), and moisture of water (*lḥt mym*); the house must be cleansed with it on the first and third day after a death.

Fabry

53. A. Dupont-Sommer, *The Essene Writings from Qumran* (Eng. trans. 1961, repr. Gloucester, Mass., 1973), 228.

54. Cf. Y. Yadin, *Mᵉgillat hammiqdaš* (Jerusalem, 1977), I, 251-57; II, 151 [Heb.].

55. Cf. J. Bowman, "Did the Qumran Sect Burn the Red Heifer?" *RevQ,* 1 (1958), 73-84; J. M. Baumgarten, *Studies in Qumran Law. StJLA,* 24 (1977), 95.

56. → טמא *ṭāmē',* V, 333f., 341f.; cf. J. Neusner, *The Idea of Purity in Ancient Judaism. StJLA,* 1 (1973), 23.

לְחִי *lᵉḥî*

Contents: 1. Etymology; 2. Occurrences, LXX; 3. OT Usage.

1. *Etymology.* Heb. *lᵉḥî* "jaw, cheek," corresponds to Jewish Aram. *liḥyā'* and *lᵉḥāyṯā';* Arab. *laḥy,* "jaw" (cf. *liḥyah,* "beard"; also Soq. *laḥyeh*[1]); and Tigre *lᵉḥē,* "cheek."[2] Ugaritic has a form *lḥm*[3] that appears with *dqn,* "beard," in *KTU,* 1.6 I, 3 and 1.5 VI, 19 and may be interpreted as a dual of **lḥy*: "pair of jaws." Cyrus H. Gordon[4] points out the possibility that, like Arab. *liḥyāh,* it may mean "beard." In Akkadian we find *laḫû,* "jaw,"[5] which may be related to *lᵉḥî* (in spite of having *ḫ*

lᵉḥî. A. van Selms, "A Forgotten God: *Laḥ,*" *Studia Biblica et Semitica. Festschrift T. C. Vriezen* (Wageningen, 1966), 318-326.

1. Leslau, *Contributions,* 28.

2. Cf. P. Fronzaroli, "Studi sul lessico comune semitico. II: Anatomia e Fisiologia," *AANLR,* 19 (1964), 270.

3. *WUS,* no. 1451.

4. *UT,* no. 1366.

5. *AHw,* I (1965), 528f.

instead of *ḥ*). Akkadian also has a word *lêtu,* "cheek,"[6] which Wolfram von Soden associates with the Aramaic by-form *lô'aḥ/lû'â.* Since *l^eḥî,* as Ugaritic and Arabic show, has *ḥ* rather than *ḫ, lêtu* might also be related to *l^eḥî.*[7]

2. *Occurrences, LXX.* The word appears 21 times in the OT, 4 of which are in Jgs. 15:15-17. The LXX usually translates it with *siagṓn,* sometimes with *siagónion* or *cheílos.*

3. *OT Usage.* The noun *l^eḥî* is used first of all in its literal sense, as in the 4 occurrences in Jgs. 15, which recounts Samson's heroic slaying of a thousand men with the jawbone of an ass.[8] The story ends with the statement that the place was called Ramath-lehi ("jawbone heights"). There follows an account of how a spring opened, named "caller spring," which is still "at Lehi." Here the toponym Lehi or Ramath-lehi also serves as the point of departure for an etymology. Adrianus van Selms considers this popular etymology to be erroneous and interprets the place name as evidence for the worship of Laḥ, a Canaanite god of life force.[9]

Dt. 18:3 decrees that the jaws and stomach of a sacrificed ox or sheep shall belong to the levitical priest.

Job 40:25f.(Eng. 41:1f.) describes the invulnerability of the crocodile as follows: "Can you draw him out with a fishhook . . . ? Can you put a rope through his nose, or pierce his jaw with a hook?" Of course the answer is "No."

This literal usage leads to metaphorical usage in the language of the prophets. Ezekiel addresses Pharaoh as a monstrous dragon: "I will puts hooks in your jaws . . . and draw you up out of [the Nile]" (Ezk. 29:4). Herodotus describes how crocodiles were captured with hooks; in like manner, Pharaoh will be captured by Yahweh and drawn from his true element. The same image is addressed to Gog: "I will entice you, and put hooks into your jaws" (Ezk. 38:4).

Isa. 30:28 described a punitive theophany. Yahweh appears and "sways the nations by the bridle of destruction, and places on the jaws of the people a cord that leads astray." Just as one controls stubborn horses, mules, and asses by means of bridle and halter, so God will mislead the nations "into their certain ruin."[10]

The situation is quite different in Hos. 11:4, a difficult passage. Yahweh describes how he cared for his people, whom he delivered out of Egypt: he led them with cords of love; according to the MT, he eased the yoke from their jaws and fed them. Normally, of course, a yoke does not rest on the jaws. Furthermore, the abrupt shift of imagery is disturbing: the rest of the passage describes Israel as a son or a child. It is therefore reasonable to read *'ûl,* "suckling," instead of *'ōl,* "yoke." This emendation preserves the image throughout the entire passage: Yahweh is like a father who lifts his child to his cheeks.

---

6. *Ibid.,* 546.
7. Cf. van Selms, 321.
8. → חמור *ḥ^amôr* (*ch^amôr*).
9. Pp. 323ff.; → לח *laḥ.*
10. O. Kaiser, *Isaiah 13–39. OTL* (Eng. trans. 1974), 307.

Two descriptive poems in the Song of Solomon mention cheeks: the bride's cheeks are comely with their ornaments (Cant. 1:10; the next element is her neck); the bridegroom's cheeks are like beds of spices (5:13; the next element is his lips). Lam. 1:2 speaks of tears on the cheeks of Jerusalem, described as a woman in mourning.

To strike someone on the cheek was considered a disgraceful act. The court prophet Zedekiah strikes Micaiah ben Imlah on the cheek when the latter calls him a false prophet (1 K. 22:24 par. 2 Ch. 18:23). Job relates in Job 16:10 how his former friends have gaped at him with their mouths and struck him insolently (*b^eḥerpâ*) upon the cheek. Mic. 4:14(5:1) (probably from the period before 587[11]) speaks of the destruction of Jerusalem, saying that "with a rod (*šēḇeṭ*) they strike upon the cheek the judge (*šōpēṭ*) of Israel," insolent treatment of the king, the anointed of Yahweh.[12]

Lam. 3:30 calls upon the Israelites to bear their present humiliation and "give (their) cheek to the smiter," since God will not cast off forever and will have compassion.

Finally, the third Servant Song says that the Servant gave his back to the smiters and his cheeks to those who pulled out the beard (Isa. 50:6); the next words speak of shame and disgrace. Similar treatment is inflicted on the king in the Babylonian *akītu* festival: the priest strikes him on the cheek and plucks at his beard. Since other royal features appear in the Servant Songs,[13] it is reasonable to see dependence on the royal cult. It is equally likely, however, that both the Servant passage and the royal cult make use of a general expression of insolence.[14]

In an imprecatory prayer, the author of Ps. 3 expresses the wish that God will smite his enemies on the cheek (v. 8[7], par. "break their teeth"). Here, too, we are dealing with a kind of insolent treatment, although the destruction of the enemies is implied more clearly.

Ringgren

---

11. Cf. H. W. Wolff, *Micah* (Eng. trans., Minneapolis, 1990), 137ff.

12. Cf. Z. Ilan, " 'Gedud' and 'Leḥi' in the Book of Micah," *BethM*, 20/2 (1975), 209-218 [Heb.], 311 [Eng. summary].

13. O. Kaiser, *Der königliche Knecht. FRLANT*, N.S. 52[70] (1959).

14. For a discussion of the issue, see H. Ringgren, "König und Messias," *ZAW*, 64 (1952), 141; Kaiser, *Isaiah 13–39*, 88.

לָחַךְ *lāḥaḵ*

Contents: 1. Etymology; 2. Occurrences, LXX; 3. OT Usage.

1. *Etymology.* The root *lḥk* is found in all the Semitic languages except Ethiopic: Akk. *lêku*;[1] Ugar. *lḥk*;[2] various Aramaic dialects, including Syr. *l^eḥaḵ*; Arab. *laḥika,* all meaning "lick." The only occurrence in Ugaritic[3] speaks of a female being who "licks the heavens with her tongue, singes the sea with her tail, and puts a gag in the mouth of Tannin" — obviously the work of a triumphant deity.

2. *Occurrences, LXX.* The verb *lāḥaḵ* occurs 7 times in the OT, once in the qal and 6 times in the piel. The LXX translates with *leíchein* or *ekleíchein.*

3. *OT Usage.* The only occurrence of the qal is in Nu. 22:4, which speaks of oxen licking up (i.e., devouring) the grass (*yereq*) of the field to describe the devastation that Balak fears the Israelites will wreak in Moab. The beginning of the verse uses the piel with the same meaning: "this horde will now lick up all that is round about us." "The metaphor describes the oxen during the act of eating, while the Moabites' fear is concerned with the result."[4] The piel has a similar meaning in 1 K. 18:38 (Elijah on Mt. Carmel): the fire of Yahweh falls from heaven, devouring the burnt offering, the wood, the stones, and the earth, and licking up the water in the trench so that nothing remains.

The other occurrences speak of licking the dust as a sign of subjection or humiliation. Mic. 7:17 describes the enemy nations as "licking the dust like a serpent, like the crawling things of the earth," an image of defeat and humiliation. According to Isa. 49:23, kings and princes will bow down (*hištaḥ^awâ*) before Israel and lick the dust of Israel's feet. The enemies are like subjects licking the feet of their sovereign; Israel is triumphant, for the kings will realize "that I am Yahweh."

Ps. 72:9 speaks of those who dwell in the wilderness bowing down (*kāraʿ*) before the king and his enemies licking the dust. Whether this text refers to kissing the feet as an act of homage or humiliation of the king's enemies is not quite clear; possibly both are involved. Kissing the sovereign's feet as an act of homage is amply attested in Mesopotamia; the action is described as *šēpē našāqu,* "kissing the feet," or *qaqqara našāqu,* "kissing the ground."[5] This act of homage is mentioned in Ps. 2:12, especially if the common emendation *naššᵉqû bᵉraglāyw* is accepted.

Ringgren

---

1. *AHw,* I (1965), 542.
2. *WUS,* no. 1453.
3. *KTU,* 1.83, 5.
4. E. Jenni, *Das hebräische Piʿel* (Zurich, 1968), 146.
5. *CAD,* XI/2 (1980), 58f.; cf. *AHw,* II (1972), 759.

לחם *lḥm* → מִלְחָמָה *milḥāmâ*

לֶחֶם *leḥem*

Contents: I. Etymology and LXX. II. Secular Usage: 1. Baking; 2. Meals; 3. Bread = Food; 4. Phrases; 5. Idioms; 6. Manna. III. Cultic Usage: 1. Showbread; 2. Offerings and Feasts. IV. Dead Sea Scrolls.

I. Etymology and LXX. The noun *leḥem,* "bread, food, grain," occurs some 300 times in the OT. The same meaning is found in Ugaritic, Phoenician, Aramaic Syriac, and Mandaic. The original meaning appears to have been "solid food." Arab. *laḥm* means "meat"; in the South Arabic dialect of the island Soqoṭra, *leḥem* means "fish." According to Edward Ullendorff,[1] the Semitic root means merely "primary food," so that the specific sense can vary from region to region. For the verbal root, the meaning "eat" is found, especially in Hebrew and Ugaritic poetry. Other derivatives of the root *lḥm,* such as Heb. *nilḥam*[2] and Moab. *ltḥm,* "fight," Syr. *laḥḥem,* "join," and Arab. *laḥḥama,* "solder, weld," *luḥma,* "weft," "relationship," suggest the basic idea of

---

leḥem. C. W. Atkinson, "The Ordinances of Passover-Unleavened Bread," *ATR,* 44 (1962), 70-85; J. Behm, "ἄρτος," *TNDT,* I, 477f.; M. Bič, "La folie de David," *RHPR,* 37 (1957), 156-162; F. Blome, *Die Opfermaterie in Babylonien und Israel,* I. *SSAOI,* 4 (1934); P. A. H. de Boer, "An Aspect of Sacrifice, I: Divine Bread," *Studies in the Religion of Ancient Israel. SVT,* 23 (1972), 27-36; M. Haran, "The Complex of Ritual Acts Performed Inside the Tabernacle," *Studies in the Religion of the Bible. ScrHier,* 8 (1961), 272-302; W. Herrmann, "Götterspeise und Göttertrank in Ugarit und Israel," *ZAW,* 72 (1960), 205-216; F. Hrozny, *Das Getreide im alten Babylonien* (Vienna, 1913); L. Koehler, "Alttestamentliche Wortforschung: Loch- und Ringbrot," *ThZ,* 4 (1948), 154; G. Krotkoff, "*Laḥm* 'Fleisch' und *leḥem* 'Brot'," *WZKM,* 62 (1969), 76-82; F. Nötscher, "Sakrale Mahlzeiten vor Qumran," *Lex tua veritas. Festschrift H. Junker* (Trier, 1961), 145-174 = *Vom Alten zum NT. BBB,* 17 (1962), 83-111; A. Pelletier, "Une particularité du rituel des 'pains d'oblation' conservée par la Septante," *VT,* 17 (1967), 364-67; R. Rendtorff, *Studien zur Geschichte des Opfers im Alten Israel. WMANT,* 24 (1967); L. Rost, *Studien zum Opfer im Alten Israel. BWANT,* 113 (1981); *idem,* "Zu den Festopfervorschriften von Numeri 28 und 29," *ThLZ,* 83 (1958), 329-334; J. Schoneveld, "Het breken van de staf des broods," *NedThT,* 27 (1973), 132-145; H. Schult, "Marginale zum 'Stab des Brotes,' " *ZDPV,* 87 (1971), 206-8; Å. V. Ström, "Abendmahl. I," *TRE,* I (1977), 43-47; E. Ullendorff, "The Contribution of South Semitics to Hebrew Lexicography," *VT,* 6 (1956), 190-98 = *Is Biblical Hebrew a Language?* (Wiesbaden, 1977), 189-197; R. de Vaux, *Studies in OT Sacrifice* (Cardiff, 1964); M. Währen, *Brot und Gebäck im Leben und Glauben des alten Orient* (Bern, 1967).

1. P. 192.
2. → מלחמה *milḥāmâ.*

"coming together" (in close combat, contact with food, or joining together for a meal). Flesh and bread share the characteristic of being a soft, adhesive mass. Flesh sticks to the bones and binds them together. The bread denoted by *leḥem* was initially eaten raw or only partially baked because fuel was scarce.[3]

The LXX usually translates with *ártos* (about 250 times), but sometimes with *sítos, dōrón, trophḗ,* or *trápeza*.

II. Secular Usage.

1. *Baking*. Along with water, bread was the primary food in the ancient Near East (Sir. 29:21). In the OT, the most important grain used for bread was wheat, but barley, spelt, and millet are also mentioned. The making of flour and bread was part of a housewife's daily work (Prov. 31:15; Jer. 7:18). Since the period of the monarchy, there were also professional bakers (Hos. 7:4; Jer. 37:21: "bakers' street"). The grain was ground in mortars or between millstones; in later periods, hand-mills were also used. Larger quantities were ground in basalt mills consisting of one round flat stone set upon another and turned by animals. Flour and water were made into dough and combined with a little salt and leaven (sourdough). The dough was allowed to rise and then shaped into round flat cakes (*kikkar-leḥem*: Jgs. 8:5; 1 S. 2:36), from 2 millimeters to 1 centimeter (0.1 to 0.4 in.) thick and 20 to 50 centimeters (8 to 20 in.) in diameter. Less common were round loaves with a hole in the middle (*ḥallaṯ leḥem*: 2 S. 6:19). Since barley dough is less elastic than wheat dough, it was made into oblong loaves. If a guest had to be fed speedily, the dough was kneaded without leaven. The cakes were usually baked on a round metal plate 35 to 50 centimeters (14 to 20 in.) in diameter, set on stones surrounding a fire. An even simpler way of baking was to dig a small pit, fill it with stones, and light a fire on top of them. When they were hot, the fire was cleared away and the dough was placed on the hot stones and covered with glowing coals. According to 1 K. 19:6, Elijah found such a "cake baked on hot stones" (*ʿugaṯ reṣāpîm*). The stones could also be covered with a thick clay pot heated externally with hot coals. An actual oven (*tannûr*) could also be used:[4] a two-tiered clay cylinder, narrower at the top than at the bottom, some 60 cemtimeters (24 in.) high and 80 centimeters (32 in.) across; the fire burned in the bottom section while the cakes or loaves baked above. The fuel consisted of dry wood, briars, and animal dung mixed with stubble or dry grass. The hot bread (*leḥem ḥām*: Josh. 9:12) was placed in baskets; a "bread staff" (*maṭṭēh-leḥem*: Lev. 26:26; Ezk. 4:16; etc.)[5] could be used to store ring-shaped loaves. A piece of bread was called *paṯ*-or *peṯôṯê leḥem* (1 K. 17:11; Ezk. 13:19).

---

3. Krotkoff, 79ff.
4. Cf. W. Röllig, "Babylon," *BRL*², 29.
5. → מטה *maṭṭeh*.

2. *Meals.* Bread and water were constituted the major meal for prisoners and the poorer classes (Ex. 23:25; 2 K. 6:22; Job 22:7; Ezk. 12:18f.). Among the wealthy, bread was a side-dish at banquets. The soldiers who made David king used draft animals to bring bread to Hebron for three days of feasting, together with meal, cakes of figs and raisins, wine and oil, oxen and sheep (1 Ch. 12:41[Eng. v. 40]). Sweet cakes and honey might accompany bread; the wife of Jeroboam I set out with these foods to visit the prophet Ahijah (1 K. 14:3). Indispensable accompaniments also included onions, leeks, and garlic (Nu. 11:5); various kinds of fruit, either fresh or dried, were also eaten with bread (2 S. 16:1f.). Bread was the heart of any banquet, and *leḥem* itself can even mean "banquet" (Eccl. 10:19).

In Judaism, a meal begins with a benediction over the bread: "Blessed be Yahweh our God, who brings forth bread from the earth."[6] After the guests respond "Amen," the host breaks the bread and gives some to each of the guests. This benediction exempts everything else eaten with the bread during the meal (meat, fish, or eggs) from needing a further blessing. As long as pieces of bread are on the table, everyone knows that another dish is coming. But as soon as these pieces are cleared away and a whole loaf with legumes is served as dessert, the meal concludes.

3. *Bread = Food.* Besides meaning "bread grain" (Isa. 28:28; often in Gen. 41–47), *leḥem* can also mean "food" or "provisions." Dt. 8:3 says that one does not live by bread alone, i.e., by earthly food, but by everything that proceeds out of the mouth of Yahweh (cf. Am. 8:11). Even the wild beasts receive their "food" from Yahweh (Ps. 147:9); during the summer, the ant secures its "sustenance" for the winter (Prov. 6:8; 30:25); the wicked becomes "fodder" for vultures (Job 15:23); and dust is the serpent's "food" (Isa. 65:25). A prudent owner of livestock sees that there is always enough goats' milk for his "food" (Prov. 27:27), and the diligent housewife brings her "food" from afar (Prov. 31:14). The children of the righteous will never need to beg for "food" (Ps. 37:25), and proper fasting includes, among other things, sharing "food" with the hungry (Isa. 58:7). Solomon's daily "provisions" are listed in 1 K. 5:2f.(4:22f.).

Very often *leḥem* occurs in conjunction with → אכל *'āḵal.* David showed Meribaal special favor by letting him live at court: "You shall eat at my table always" (2 S. 9:7). Jehoiachin was granted the same privilege at the Babylonian court after his pardon: "Every day of his life he dined regularly at the king's table" (Jer. 52:33). The generous Nehemiah did not lay claim to the food allowance of a governor, the "bread of the *peḥâ*" (Neh. 5:14). Amaziah ordered the prophet Amos to flee to Judah and eat bread there, i.e., earn his support there (Am. 7:12).

Quite generally, "eat bread" means "have a meal" (Gen. 31:54; 37:25; 43:32; Ex. 2:20; 1 S. 20:24; Jer. 41:1), "eat no bread" means "eat nothing" (1 S. 20:34; 28:20; 1 K. 13:8f.). "Eat food" can also be expressed by *bārâ* or *ṭāʿam leḥem* (2 S. 12:17; 3:35); *nāṯan leḥem* (1 K. 5:23[9]; 11:18) means "provide food." One can have "a surfeit of food" (*śāḇaʿ leḥem*: Prov. 30:22) but also "a lack of food" (*ḥāsēr leḥem*:

6. *Ber.* vi.1.

Am. 4:6). During a period of mourning, Daniel ate no "delicacies" (*leḥem ḥ^{a}mudôt*: Dnl. 10:3).

4. *Phrases.* The significance of bread also finds expression in biblical phrases. The phrase "bread and wine" (Gen. 14:18; Neh. 5:15; etc.) means more than just "food and drink": it refers to an abundant banquet like that prepared, for example, by hospitable wisdom (Prov. 9:5) and to the blessing that proceeds from the word of God (Isa. 55:1f.). The fertility of the land can also be suggested by phrases like "bread and vineyards" (2 K. 18:32; Isa. 36:17). "Bread and water," on the other hand, denotes minimal sustenance (1 K. 18:4,13; 2 K. 6:22; Isa. 21:14; Ezk. 4:17). Ahab orders that the imprisoned prophet Micaiah be fed with "the bread of adversity and the water of affliction," i.e., short rations, as during a siege (1 K. 22:27; cf. Isa. 30:20). "To eat no bread and drink no water" means having nothing at all to eat or drink (1 S. 30:12; Dt. 9:9,18; Ezr. 10:6). Fugitives are offered at least bread and water (Dt. 23:5[4]; Isa. 21:14). Abraham gives Hagar "bread and a skin of water" to take with her (Gen. 21:14). Esau sells his birthright to Jacob for "bread and pottage of lentils" (Gen. 25:34), and Joseph supplies his brothers with "grain, bread, and provision" (Gen. 45:23). God feeds his people with "bread and meat" in the wilderness, as he did in Egypt (Ps. 78:20; Ex. 16:3); and, at God's command, ravens supply the prophet Elijah with "bread in the morning, and meat in the evening" (1 K. 17:6). "Bread and clothing" are often mentioned together as the necessities of life; everyone needs them, and they are given to the needy (Gen. 28:20; Isa. 4:1; Ezk. 18:16).

5. *Idioms.* Many situations — some pleasant and some not so pleasant — are associated with bread. "To eat bread with someone" means to be a friend and confidant (Ps. 41:10[9]). In Ob. 7, "men of your bread" (RSV "your trusted friends") denotes the confederates who have set traps for Edom; in Sir. 9:16, it refers to proper company at table. Hospitality is considered a sacred obligation; it turns one's own bread into bread for the stranger (Gen. 18:5). It is a splendid expression of love to give one's bread to the hungry (Ezk. 18:7; Prov. 22:9); the wicked, however, do not deserve help: they should be refused bread (Sir. 12:5). Joshua and Caleb admonish the Israelites not to fear the Canaanites, "for they are bread for us," i.e., we can easily overcome them (Nu. 14:9). According to Ps. 14:4, the wicked eat up Yahweh's people as callously as though they were eating bread. Abundance or lack of bread has symbolic value: abundance signifies God's blessing (Ps. 132:15; Prov. 12:11), wealth, prosperity, and security (Gen. 49:20; Jer. 44:17; Lev. 26:5); a lack signifies God's punishment for sin (Jer. 5:17; Ezk. 4:16) and grinding poverty (2 K. 25:3; Lam. 1:11). Those who were full will suffer extreme want and have to hire themselves out for bread (1 S. 2:5). Equally poor are those who stayed behind in Palestine after the year 586: they can keep body and soul together only by begging bread from their enemies (Lam. 5:6).

Various interpretations have been proposed for Eccl. 11:1: "Cast your bread upon the waters, for you will find it after many days." This text is not an exhortation to selfless charity or eager daring, but a statement that even an unwise action can have a good ending, so that one never knows how a particular event will turn out. One would normally think that throwing bread on the water would result in the bread's being lost. It is possible, however, for a light, dry, piece of bread that absorbs only a little water to stay afloat and be washed ashore by the waves.[7] In a *figura etymologica* in Prov. 9:5, wisdom calls on the simple to eat her bread. What she offers as food for spiritual life is the "bread of understanding" and the "water of wisdom" (Sir. 15:3). In interpreting Prov. 9:5, Judaism treats the Torah figuratively as "bread" or speaks of the "bread of the world of souls," referring to eternal bliss.[8] Finally, rich and plenteous bread is the most noble gift of the eschatological age (Isa. 30:23).

"Bread of tears" (*leḥem dimʿâ*: Ps. 80:6[5]) suggests a long period of constant disaster for the people of God (cf. Ps. 42:4[3]). Job 3:24 transforms this image: Job's "sighing" comes before his "bread" (i.e., food) and is more important. The wicked eat the "bread of wickedness" (*leḥem rešaʿ*: Prov. 4:17), and the "bread of lies" (*leḥem šeqer*: Prov. 20:17; *leḥem keẓābîm:* 23:3) at first it tastes good to them. The sin of unchastity to which Dame Folly entices is called "stolen water" and "secret bread" (*leḥem seṯārîm*: Prov. 9:17). The diligent housewife does not eat the "bread of idleness" (*leḥem ʿaṣlûṯ*: Prov. 31:27). One should not long for the "bread of the envious" (*leḥem raʿ ʿayin*: Prov. 23:6), but be satisfied with the "needful bread" (*leḥem ḥuqqî*: Prov. 30:8) given by God. Because Yahweh is the giver of all that is good, agonizing labor, the "bread of anxious toil" (*leḥem hāʿaṣāḇîm*: Ps. 127:2) is considered worthless. It is an expression of profound anguish to loathe bread (Job 33:20; cf. Ps. 102:10[9]) or simply forget to eat bread (Ps. 102:5[4]). According to Ezk. 24:17,22, eating the "bread of mortals" (*leḥem ʾanāšîm* or better *leḥem ʾônîm* = "bread of mourners") is one of the standard elements of mourning in which the prophet is not to engage (cf. Hos. 9:4).

6. *Manna.* The food the Israelites ate while wandering in the desert is call *mān*. When the people murmur, Yahweh promises to rain bread from heaven, bread in abundance (Ex. 16:4,8). The later hymnody of Israel therefore calls manna "bread of heaven" (*leḥem šāmayim*: Ps. 105:40) or "bread from heaven" (*leḥem miššāmayim*: Neh. 9:15). The historical Ps. 78:25 speaks of the "bread of the mighty one," probably referring to heavenly beings; it is a food that comes from the dwelling place of the angels. The people, who are sick and tired of wandering in the desert, loathe his "worthless bread" (*leḥem haqqelōqēl*: Nu. 21:5).

III. Cultic Usage.

1. *Showbread.* Several Hebrew phrases are translated by the traditional (and erroneous) term "showbread." The original expression was the collective phrase *leḥem pānîm,* "face bread(s)"; it appears in Ex. 25:30, where Yahweh gives Moses a brief commandment concerning this bread: "You shall set face bread on the table, continually before my face." Nu. 4:7 therefore speaks of *leḥem hattāmîḏ* in the sense of a permanent

---

7. H. W. Hertzberg, *Der Prediger. KAT,* XVII/4f. (1963), 200f.
8. St.-B., II, 482ff.

offering. More frequently we find the variant with the article: *leḥem happānîm* (Ex. 35:13; 39:36; 1 S. 21:7[6]; 1 K. 7:48; 2 Ch. 4:19). In 1 S. 21:5ff.(4ff.), this bread is identified as *leḥem qōḏeš,* "holy bread," in contrast to *leḥem ḥōl,* "common bread." Ex. 40:23 speaks of *ʿēreḵ leḥem,* "arrangement of bread," while Ex. 40:4 speaks simply of setting out the *ʿēreḵ*. From the root *ʿrk* ("arrange") come also the phrases *maʿareḵeṯ leḥem* (2 Ch. 13:11) or *leḥem hammaʿareḵeṯ* (Neh. 10:34[33]; 1 Ch. 9:32; 23:29), meaning "arrangement of bread" or "bread of the arrangement"; we also find simply *maʿareḵeṯ* (1 Ch. 28:16; 2 Ch. 29:18). The *leḥem hattāmîḏ* of Nu. 4:7 is represented in 2 Ch. 2:3(4) by *maʿareḵeṯ tāmîḏ*. The LXX prefers *ártoi tḗs prothéseōs,* the Vulg. *panes propositionis*.

In the Second Temple, the preparation of the showbread was the duty of the Kohathite Levites (1 Ch. 9:32);[9] in particular, they supervised the measurements (1 Ch. 23:29). More detailed regulations are found in Lev. 24:5-8. Twelve cakes were always baked; each used two tenths of an ephah (*ca.* 4-8 l. [1-2 qts.]) of the finest wheat flour (*sōleṯ*). The term *ḥallôṯ* suggests rather thick round loaves with a hole in the middle (ring bread) or loaves in which holes are made with the fingers before being baked.[10] In the sanctuary, the loaves were arranged in two piles of six loaves each on the gilded table described in Ex. 25:23-30. Incense was placed on each pile, and possibly salt as well (Lev. 24:7 LXX). The loaves were changed weekly on the Sabbath, when the incense and salt were burned as a "memorial portion" for Yahweh. The old loaves, being extremely holy, were given to the priests and could be eaten only by them. Josephus notes also that the bread was made without leaven.[11]

According to Mishnah *Menaḥ.* xi, the dough was kneaded and formed into a loaf ten spans (hand's breadths) long and five spans wide. To make all the loaves the same size, special baking forms were used. The four corners were extended in points seven fingers' breadths long. These corners ("horns") were to prevent the loaves from lying tightly atop each other. Since each loaf touched only the "horns" of the loaf above it, air could pass between them. To lessen the pressure of the loaves, tubes were placed between the layers of bread to prevent the loaves from breaking; they overhung the front and back of the table by two spans. These tubes themselves — twenty-eight in all — were supported by four pedestals or columns in front and in back of each pile. On each pile of loaves were placed two golden bowls of incense. The loaves themselves were replaced in a solemn ceremony early on the morning of the Sabbath. First two priests took away the old incense from the two piles, to be burned later during the morning *tāmîḏ* offering. Two other priests removed the old piles of bread, while fresh loaves were inserted from the other side of the table. In this manner the requirement of *tāmîḏ* ("continuous") was fulfilled. Finally, two bowls with fresh incense were placed on top. The old bread was distributed to the priests: the retiring division and the division assigned to the new week each received six loaves; the further distribution

9. → לוי *lēwî*.
10. Cf. *AuS,* IV (1935), 119, 114.
11. *Ant.* iii.6.6.

to the individual priests was performed within each division. The loaves were eaten in the inner court.

The earliest biblical reference to the showbread is 1 S. 21:2-7(1-6). Ahimelech, the priest at the sanctuary of Nob, gave five of these sacred loaves to David and his followers, who were fugitives but had kept themselves from women and were therefore ritually clean; the loaves had just been replaced by fresh bread and would normally have been eaten only by the priests and members of their families. Saul had the priests of Nob slain for thus supporting David. The priest Abiathar, a son of Ahimelech, escaped the bloodbath; David installed him as priest in Jerusalem, and we may assume that the use of showbread came to Jerusalem with him. The tradition in 1 K. 7:48, which says that Solomon made a golden table for the showbread, is therefore probably in error. For the postexilic temple, the showbread is attested by Neh. 10:34(33); 1 Mc. 1:22; 2 Mc. 1:8. A representation on the arch of Titus shows that a showbread table was still part of the inventory of the Herodian temple.[12]

The practice of setting bread before the deity "to eat" was common to ancient Near Eastern civilization. The Egyptians practiced the custom of placing bread that had been censed and sprinkled with wine on mats and platters before the deity as a guarantee that the sacrificial offerings would endure forever.[13] Babylonian ritual texts speak of placing bread offerings on tables; they also mention the number twelve. This bread, however, was removed with the other gifts after the offering rather than being left continuously before the deity.[14] Bel (LXX Add.Dnl. 14:)3,8,11,14 also mentions the practice of setting food for the Babylonian deity Bel on a table in the temple.

The showbread represents a food offering in its original form: food for God. It is a relic of a meal of bread and wine offered to the deity. The wine is suggested by the bowls and flagons mentioned in Ex. 25:29; 37:16; Nu. 4:7. People offered food and drink to feed and thus gain favor with the deity. The custom of placing bread before the "face" of God is simply an ancient tradition that was retained with a different meaning. From the staff of life, the bread of its table, Israel makes an offering to Yahweh, and Yahweh permits all Israel (the number twelve), represented by the priests, to share his table. This continuous offering acknowledges Yahweh as the giver of food and life; it gives thanks to him as the giver of all good things. It signifies that God's table fellowship with his people will endure. Dt. 26:10 with its offering of firstfruits may be seen as a parallel. To further underline the sacrificial meaning of the custom, later practice turned the showbread into a "fire offering" by burning at least the incense.[15]

2. *Offerings and Feasts.* P frequently refers to the offering quite anthropomorphically as the "food of God" (*leḥem *ᵉ*lōhîm*). A priest with a physical deformity, for example, must not approach to offer "the food of his God"; he may only eat of it (Lev. 21:17,22).

12. *AOB,* 509.
13. *RÄR,* 557ff.
14. Blome, 247-250.
15. K. Elliger, *Leviticus. HAT,* IV (1966), 328.

Israel must not offer blemished animals as the "food of God" (Lev. 22:25); it must honor its priests because they offer the "food of [its] God" (Lev. 21:8). Lev. 21:6,21 use *leḥem ᵉlōhîm* synonymously with a fire offering to Yahweh (*'iššê YHWH*). Other passages also closely associate *leḥem* and *'iššeh.*[16] Thus the priests are to burn the fat with the *šᵉlāmîm* offering on the altar as "fire offering food" for Yahweh (Lev. 3:11,16). According to Nu. 28:2,24, both the burnt offering and the cereal offering are "fire offering food" for Yahweh. In Ezekiel's plan for the temple (Ezk. 44:7), the sacrificial fat and blood are called Yahweh's "food"; and Mal. 1:7 accuses the priests of offering polluted "food," i.e., inferior offerings, upon the altar.

The ritual for the ordination of priests (Ex. 29; Lev. 8) includes bread. According to Ex. 29:2, in addition to a young bull and two rams without blemish three kinds of bread are needed: unleavened breads, unleavened cakes mixed with oil, and unleavened flat bread spread with oil. For the actual ordination offering, the "filling of hands," a *kikkar leḥem* (loaf of bread), a *ḥallaṯ leḥem* (cake of bread) with oil, and a loaf of flat bread are given to the priests, waved before Yahweh, and then consumed by fire with the burnt offering upon the altar (Ex. 29:23ff.). Instead of the *kikkar leḥem* of Ex. 29:23, Lev. 8:26 has the less appropriate *ḥallaṯ maṣṣâ.* Later the priests consume the "bread" along with the flesh of the ram. Anything that remains must be burned, because it is holy. What this ritual signifies is induction into office: in the future, the priests will receive the fat and the cereal offerings to be burned. There is also, however, an economic element: part of the offerings goes to support the priests.

The word *leḥem* is never used in connection with the cereal offering proper, the → מנחה *minḥâ,* which according to P consists of unleavened cakes and flour. Only Lev. 7:13, in the context of the *šᵉlāmîm* offering of thanksgiving, mentions the earlier practice of offering leavened bread (*ḥallōṯ leḥem ḥāmēṣ*), probably as a discretionary provision. There may have been a notion that at sacrificial meals, which in practice constituted the only relatively infrequent occasions when Israelites ate meat, people might not be satisfied with unleavened bread. Am. 4:5 also attests to the use of leavened bread for a thank-offering.[17]

The sacred offerings that Israel gives to Yahweh, which then are distributed to the priests, are also called *leḥem.* They are subject to special regulations: an unclean priest may not partake of them, nor may his day laborer, a sojourner living with him, or a priest's daughter who has married a man who is not a priest (Lev. 22:7,12,13).

The phrase "eat bread" (*'ᵉḵol-leḥem*) before God (Ex. 18:12) also suggests "share a sacrificial meal."

The offerings of the Feast of Weeks included two loaves of firstfruits bread (*leḥem habbikkûrîm*), made of two tenths of an ephah of flour with leaven. Every Israelite family was thus to thank God for the gift of bread and, by sacrificing the first bread of the new harvest, have free use, as it were, of the rest of the grain for ordinary

16. But cf. J. Hoftijzer, "Das sogenannte Feueropfer," *Hebräische Wortforschung. Festschrift F. Baumgartner. SVT,* 16 (1967), 114-134, who understands *'iššeh* as an offering to the deity.

17. → חמץ *ḥmṣ,* IV, 490.

purposes. After being waved before Yahweh, these loaves were given to the priest (Lev. 23:17-20; Nu. 15:19; cf. 2 K. 4:42). The beginning of the barley harvest was celebrated by the eating of unleavened bread (*maṣṣôṯ*) for seven days. This bread was made entirely from new grain and without leaven, because leaven had to come from the previous harvest. In the story of sacred history, this festival was associated with Israel's hasty escape from Egyptian slavery, when only unleavened dough could be brought along. The unleavened bread is therefore also called *leḥem ʿōnî,* "bread of affliction" (Dt. 16:3).[18]

Dommershausen

IV. Dead Sea Scrolls. The Dead Sea scrolls mention *leḥem* in many contexts. The priest, for example, blesses bread and new wine (1QS 6:5f.; cf. 1QSa 2:19ff.). In the disciplinary regulations governing the Qumran Essenes, 1QS 6:25 speaks of stopping a quarter of a member's rations (*leḥem*). In the laments of 1QH, the poet complains that even his closest friends, those "who ate my bread," have turned against him (1QH 5:23); he himself eats the *leḥem ʾᵃnāḥâ,* "bread of sighs" (5:33), and he laments that his bread has been transformed into strife (5:35). The Temple scroll mentions *leḥem* only in cultic contexts: showbread (11QT 8:10-13), *tᵉnûpâ* bread at celebration of priestly ordination (?) (15:3,10,12), and bread made from the firstfruits of the crop at the Feast of Unleavened Bread (18:14; 19:6,7,12). The fragmentary Aramaic text 2Q24 (= 2QJN ar [New Jerusalem])[19] likewise mentions showbread, its display on the "table before Yahweh" (cf. Ezk. 41:22), and an otherwise unattested ritual of distributing the bread, with cosmological overtones (cf. also 11QJN ar [New Jerusalem] 5). The *lḥm* of 4QpIs*ᵃ* 5–6:11 and 4QpIs*ᵉ* 5:6 is probably from *lḥm* I, "fight."

Fabry

---

18. Cf. B. N. Wambacq, "Les Maṣṣôt," *Bibl,* 61 (1980), 31-54.

19. Cf. M. Baillet, J. T. Milik, and R. de Vaux, *Les 'petites grottes' de Qumrân. DJD,* III (1962), 84-89.

לָחַץ *lāḥaṣ;* לַחַץ *laḥaṣ*

Contents: I. Extrabiblical Evidence. II. OT: 1. Verb; 2. Noun; 3. Versions; 4. Conjectural Emendations. III. Meaning: 1. Literal; 2. Figurative. IV. Theological Aspects.

I. Extrabiblical Evidence. Outside of Hebrew, the root *lḥṣ* is found only in Arabic and the West Semitic dialects. It does not appear in Biblical Aramaic; but Samaritan, Jewish Aramaic, and Christian Palestinian all use *lḥṣ* with the same meanings as Hebrew. The root is not found in the other Semitic languages, with the exception of Ethiopic. In the East Aramaic dialects, its semantic function is performed by the root *ʾlṣ,* found in Hebrew only in Jgs. 16:16 (piel), where the context suggests the meaning "importune." The meanings cited by Carl Brockelmann[1] for *'lṣ* ("press, oppress") are largely identical with those of Heb. *lḥṣ*. The root *'lṣ* is also attested in Mandaic,[2] where it appears alongside *hlṣ*,[3] which should therefore probably be considered a variant of *'lṣ* rather than *lḥṣ*.[4] More precise differentiation is needed for the *ḥlṣ* of the East Syrian dialects: some of the meanings cited by A. J. Maclean[5] are related to *'lṣ* (nos. 1-5), others to the common Semitic → חלץ *ḥlṣ* (nos. 6-8). Apparently the originally distinct roots *'lṣ* and *ḥlṣ* became phonetically assimilated and confused in the vernacular dialects.

II. OT.

1. *Verb.* In Biblical Hebrew, the root *lḥṣ* appears almost exclusively in the qal (18 occurrences); only in Nu. 22:25 do we find the niphal, with reflexive meaning. No passive usage is attested. The action denoted by the qal always has an object; even in Isa. 19:20, where no direct object appears with the ptcp. *lōḥᵃṣîm,* the verb is not used absolutely, but refers to those who oppress Egypt. On the rare occasions when the verb is used literally, the object can be any person or thing (Nu. 22:25; 2 K. 6:32). In the much more common figurative usage (except for Ps. 56:2[Eng. v. 1], where the object is the psalmist), the object is always a group of persons or an entire nation (usually Israel; Egypt in Isa. 19:20). In Ex. 22:20(21); 23:9, the sg. *gēr* represents a social group, not an individual.[6] The subject of *lḥṣ* is always a group or nation (Egypt, the Amorites, unspecified nations, the enemies of the psalmist) or, in the singular, their representative (Jgs. 4:3: Sisera; 2 K. 13:4,22: Hazael; Ex. 22:20[21]; 23:9: the Israelite addressed by the Covenant Code). In its predominant figurative usage, therefore, *lḥṣ* serves to denote an action or mode of conduct in the relationship between political or social groups.

2. *Noun.* The situation is rather different in the case of the noun *laḥaṣ* (12 occurrences). As a segholate form from **laḥs,*[7] the noun is an abstract denoting the result of the action expressed by the root. In Ex. 3:9; 2 K. 13:4, this relationship is underlined by the appearance of the verb *lāḥaṣ* with the noun *laḥaṣ* (in Ex. 3:9 even as the inner object in a relative clause). In these passages as well as Dt. 26:7; Ps. 44:25(24); 106:42, *laḥaṣ* (like the verb) is done by foreign enemies and affects the nation as a whole. Unlike the verb, however, the noun can be used absolutely (Job 36:15); this is also true when *laḥaṣ* appears in apposition with *mayim* (Jer. 30:20; 1 K. 22:27 par. 2 Ch. 18:26) or *leḥem* (1 K. 22:27 par. 2 Ch. 18:26). Here the apposition brings out the distinguishing feature;[8] the theory

1. *LexSyr,* 22b2, 23a.
2. *MdD,* 21a.
3. *Ibid.,* 149a.
4. Contra *KBL*³, 501a.
5. *A Dictionary of the Dialects of Vernacular Syriac* (Oxford, 1901).
6. Cf. M. Schwantes, *Das Recht der Armen. BET,* 4(1977), 44, n. 6.
7. *GK,* §84aa.
8. *Synt,* 62g; *GK,* §131c.

that we are dealing in these cases with a double accusative depending on *nāṯan* or *'kl* hiphil is therefore wrong. The meaning is rather "water [or bread] appropriate to [a time of] distress," i.e., "short rations" (RSV "scant fare"; cf. the Syr. of 1 K. 22:27). As in the case of the verb, the use of the noun in individual laments is exceptional: in Ps. 42:10(9); 43:2, *laḥaṣ 'ôyēḇ* denotes the situation of the psalmist in his personal plight.

3. *Versions.* Among the ancient versions, the LXX is the most consistent, always using a form of the root *thlib-*to translate *lāḥaṣ* or *laḥaṣ* (*thlíbein*; *ek-, apo-, para-, prosthlíbein*; *thlimmós*; *thlípsis*); only in Jgs. 2:18 does it use *poliorkeín.* Job 36:15 (*kríma dé praéōn ekthýsei*) obviously reflects a different text. The Syr. prefers *'lṣ* or its derivatives, but uses other verbs in 12 passages (e.g., *'wq* aphel in Ex. 22:20[21]; 23:9; *'bd* shaphel in Jgs. 4:3; *dḥq* in Am. 6:14). The Vulg. translates without any recognizable principle, but often uses the very general *affligo*.

4. *Conjectural Emendations.* In 2 texts, *BHS* arrives at *lāḥaṣ* by emendation. In Nu. 24:8b it reads *w^{e}lōḥ^{a}ṣāyw yimḥaṣ* instead of *w^{e}ḥiṣṣāyw*; not only may the part of the verse in question be secondary, but the emendation would be at odds with the figurative language of v. 8bα,β.[9] Emendation is likewise unnecessary in Ps. 7:5b(4b) if the full semantic range of *ḥlṣ* is taken into account. The LXX has been cited erroneously in support of emendation to *w^{e}'elḥ^{a}ṣâ*: it never uses *apopíptein* to translate *lāḥaṣ,* but almost always (*ek*)*thlíbein.* In spite of the Syr. and Targ., we also reject the emendation proposed by Jacob Leveen,[10] since it presupposes an unnecessary emendation of the following word.

III. Meaning.

1. *Literal.* The literal sense of the verb *lāḥaṣ* appears only rarely, of the noun *laḥaṣ* never. The few texts in question, however, clearly exhibit the basic meaning "press, exert pressure." Semantic nuances depend on the varying reaction of the object to this pressure. If the object cannot escape the pressure, it is forced, squeezed, or driven into a corner. This nuance appears in Nu. 22:25: *lāḥaṣ* is used twice in the episode of the Balaam narratives where the ass proves wiser than the "blind" seer. At the second encounter with the *mal'āḵ,* the ass cannot turn aside as at the first encounter, but still sees a way out: she can "push" by the angel by pressing (*lḥṣ* niphal) close to the wall; in doing so, however, she squeezes (*lḥṣ* qal) her rider's leg. Arab. *laḥaṣa* II, "drive into a corner," exhibits a similar meaning; the nominal form *laḥaṣ,* "narrow valley," cited by *KBL*[3] for the South Arabic dialect of Soqoṭra is probably related to this sense.[11]

---

9. On the translation of the MT, see J. de Vaux, *Les Nombres. SB* (1972), 286.
10. J. Leveen, "The Textual Problems of Psalm VII," *VT,* 16 (1966), 440.
11. On OSA *ḥlṣ,* "oppress," see A. Jamme, "Les antiquités sud-arabes du Musæe Borély a Marseille," *CahB,* 8 (1958/59), 159.

When the object can escape the pressure, there is a different semantic nuance. We see it in 2 K. 6:32: Elisha, sitting in his house with the elders, seeks to prevent the king's messenger from entering. He therefore commands: "Shut the door, *ûlᵉḥaṣtem 'ōṯô baddeleṯ.*" In this situation, the clause can only mean: push him back with the door, brace yourselves against the door and keep him out. The same meaning appears in Jgs. 1:34 (missed by *KBL*³). The Amorites prevent the Danites from occupying the plain by "pressing them back into the hill country" (*wayyilḥᵃṣû . . . hehārâ*).

2. *Figurative.* The figurative meaning of *lāḥaṣ* derives from the first situation: with an individual or group as its object, "press" means "put in a bind, rob of mobility, oppress, repress." Examination of the subjects and objects of *lāḥaṣ* has already suggested what we shall now show clearly, namely that the verb denotes repressive treatment of one social or political group by another. Two types of oppression can be denoted by *lāḥaṣ*. Only in the Covenant Code does the verb refer to the "oppression" of a socially weaker person, the *gēr* (Ex. 22:20[21]; 23:9). The first text links the hiphil of *ynh* and the piel of *'nh*;[12] Ex. 23:9 prohibits oppressing the *gēr* in the context (perhaps secondary) of rules of judicial conduct. This may indicate that *lāḥaṣ* aims at antisocial exploitation of the *gēr*'s inferior legal position.

Much more often, however, *lāḥaṣ* means the subjugation of one people or nation by another. As we have just seen, Jgs. 1:34 does not represent this usage; but there are no less than 14 other texts that use *lāḥaṣ* in this sense, in 13 of which it is Israel that is oppressed. Ex. 3:9; Dt. 26:7 refer to the oppression in Egypt, Jgs. 2:18; 4:3; 6:9; 10:12; 1 S. 10:18; Ps. 106:42 to the period of the judges; 2 K. 13:4,22 tells of the situation in the time of Hazael; Am. 6:14 threatens the northern kingdom with "oppression" by a foreign nation; Ps. 44:25(24) refers to an unknown situation; Jer. 30:20 probably refers not only to the Assyrians who have subjugated "Jacob," but to potential future enemies as well. The actual circumstances envisioned can vary: the military superiority of an enemy, the exile of the northern kingdom, a specific conflict between the Canaanites and the tribes looking for land, or enslavement in Egypt.

In far fewer passages, *lāḥaṣ* refers to the distress of an individual psalmist (Ps. 42:10[9]; 43:2; 56:2[1]). Here the language of lament has borrowed the common idiom and "individualized" a concept applied to Israel.

IV. Theological Aspects. The root *lḥṣ* is not a religious term, but it is far from being theologically neutral. Yahweh is opposed to all "oppression," even when imposed as a judgment (Am. 6:14). In the Covenant Code, God expressly prohibits oppressing the *gēr.* When Israel calls out in its oppression, God intervenes to deliver. The psalmist hopes that God will put an end to oppression and the oppressors.

A special theological nuance appears when *lāḥaṣ* represents one of the key concepts for Israel's fate in Egypt (Dt. 26:7). In E's version of the call of Moses, *laḥaṣ* is even the key word.

---

12. Cf. Schwantes, 43f.

One might conjecture that *laḥaṣ* acquired this usage from Ex. 22:20(21); 23:9, where the prohibition against oppressing the *gēr* is motivated by the statement that Israel itself was a *gēr* in Egypt. Even apart from the date of the motivation clauses,[13] however, the key word *laḥaṣ* does not occur in them. Furthermore, the pre-Deuteronomistic tradition does not use *gēr* to interpret Israel's condition in Egypt. In fact, Deuteronomistic influence on this usage is clear. The root *lḥṣ* belongs to the semantic field of the Deuteronomistic deliverer schema, with *ṣʿq, yšʿ* hiphil, *nṣl* hiphil, *yṣ'* hiphil, and the complementary phrases "out of/into the hand of NN." It appears frequently in Deuteronomistic texts or texts influenced by Deuteronomistic theology (Dt. 26:7; Jgs. 2:18; 4:3; 6:9; 10:12; 1 S. 10:18; 2 K. 13:4; Ps. 106:42; Jer. 30:20).

The mention of *laḥaṣ* expresses the liberating aspect of God's work, God's deliverance of those oppressed by a foreign power. The key word does not refer solely to the past. Jer. 30:20 announces the punishment of the *lōḥᵃṣîm* as an event in the future. The third expansion of Isaiah's oracle against Egypt (Isa. 19:19-22), which exhibits Deuteronomistic influence, speaks of eschatological salvation. On the day when Egypt comes to worship Yahweh, it will experience the same liberating power of God already experienced by Israel, which Egypt oppressed: "When they cry to Yahweh because of oppressors he will send them a savior (*môšîᵃʿ*)." In a repetition and reversal of history, Yahweh's salvation will deliver the former oppressor nation.

Reindl

13. See H. Rücker, *Die Begründung der Weisungen Jahwes im Pentateuch. ErfThST,* 30 (1973).

לַיְלָה/לַיִל layil/laylâ

Contents: I. 1. Etymology; 2. Statistics; 3. Syntax. II. General Usage: 1. Darkness; 2. Domain of the Moon; 3. Division of Time; 4. Period of Time; 5. Time for Certain Activities. III. Theological Contexts: 1. Creation; 2. God's Presence; 3. Deliverance; 4. Passover; 5. Judgment; 6. Revelation; 7. Israel's Response. IV. Dead Sea Scrolls.

laylâ. G. Dalman, *AuS,* I (1928), 630-642; P. Joüon, "Études de sémantique hébraïque," *Bibl,* 2 (1921), 336-342; S. Krauss, "Der richtige Sinn von 'Schrecken in der Nacht' Hl III,8," *Occident and Orient. Festschrift M. Gaster* (London, 1936), 323-330; H.-M. Lutz, *Jahwe, Jerusalem und die Völker. WMANT,* 27 (1968); H.-P. Müller, *Ursprünge und Strukturen alttestamentlicher Eschatologie. BZAW,* 109 (1969); E. Otto, "Erwägungen zum überlieferungsgeschichtliche Ursprung und 'Sitz im Leben' des jahwistischen Plagenzyklus," *VT,* 26 (1976), 3-27; W. Rordorf, "Nacht und Tag," *BHHW,* II, 1275f.; G. Sauer, "שׁמר *šmr* hüten," *THAT,* II, 982-87; O. H. Steck, *Der Schöpfungsbericht der Priesterschrift. FRLANT,*

I. 1. *Etymology.* The Heb. noun *layil* or *laylâ,* which represents a common Semitic root,[1] is probably a primary noun. *KBL*³ suggests **lailai* as the basis of Heb. *laylâ.* The form *lêl,* shortened from *lẹlḗ,*[2] prevailed over equivalent forms with endings; the *ẹ* is a contraction of *ay,* and *ḗ* represents a raising of the accented final *î.* According to *GK,*[3] the long form *laylâ* comes from a reduplicated form *lyly* (cf. West Aram. *lêlyā'* and Syr. *lîlyā*); Rudolf Mayer,[4] however, considers *laylâ* an adverbial accusative strengthened by the deictic particle *-hā (laylâ < *laylā < *lêlā < *lêlah < *lêlahā),* usually translated as a noun ("night") but not infrequently as an adjective ("at night").[5]

2. *Statistics.* The word group, which includes the noun *lîlîṯ* and possibly the verb → לין *lyn,*[6] is represented 7 times in the OT by the short form *layil* or *lêl* and 225 times by the long form *laylâ,* if Isa. 38:13 is omitted as dittography. There are also 5 occurrences of Aram. *lêlyā'* and 44 occurrences of Gk. *nýx* in the deuterocanonical books. The distribution of the 215 occurrences of Heb. *laylâ* in the singular varies widely: Psalms: 25 + 3 plurals; Genesis: 25; 1-2 Samuel: 21 + 1; Exodus: 18; Isaiah: 16 + 1; Job: 15 + 2; Judges: 12; Jeremiah: 12; 1-2 Kings: 11; Numbers, Deuteronomy, and Nehemiah: 9; Joshua and 1-2 Chronicles: 7; Ruth: 4; Proverbs and Lamentations: 3; Jonah: 2 + 1; Song of Solomon: 1 + 2; Leviticus, Esther, Ecclesiastes, Hosea, and Zechariah: 2; Amos, Obadiah, and Micah: 1.

As the list shows, our word is especially common in the Psalms, in the narrative literature of the OT, and in the books of Isaiah, Job, and Jeremiah.

3. *Syntax.* Syntactically, *laylâ* serves 12 times as subject and 4 times as object.[7] It is associated 26 times with the adverbial *yômām,* a combination that gives *laylâ* itself the adverbial sense of "at/by night." The word (both normal and short form) appears 61 times with prepositions, of which *b*ᵉ (53 occurrences) is by far the most common. It appears 3 times with *k*ᵉ, twice each with *ʿaḏ* and *min,* and once each with *l*ᵉ and *bên.*[8] The construct is found only in Isa. 15:1; Ex. 12:42, an observation that is significant for the semantics of *layil/laylâ.* We may note its use with *kōl* (20 times), which emphasizes the aspect of duration, as well as the phrases *ballaylâ hahûʾ* (19 times), *kōl hallaylâ hahûʾ* (2 S. 2:29), and *hallaylâ hahûʾ* (Job 3:6,7), which specifically

---

115 (²1981); *idem, World and Environment* (Eng. trans., Nashville, 1978); R. de Vaux, *AncIsr,* 180-83; → יום *yôm;* → חשך *ḥāšaḵ.*

1. Cf. *KBL*³, 502.
2. Cf. K. Beyer, *Althebräische Grammatik* (Göttingen, 1969), 43, n. 1.
3. §90f.
4. R. Meyer, *Hebräische Grammatik,* I (Berlin, ³1966), §45, 3c.
5. Cf. *BLe,* §65s; Joüon, *A Grammar of Biblical Hebrew,* §93.
6. Cf. *GesB, s.v.*
7. Cf. Lisowsky.
8. Cf. S. Mandelkern, *Veteris Testamenti Concordantiae Hebraicae atque Chaldicae* (New York, ²1955), and *KBL*³.

associate the statement of time with the immediate context. Also important are the phrases referring to Passover: *ballaylâ hazzeh* (Ex. 12:8,12) and *hû' hallaylâ hazzeh* (Ex. 12:42). The meaning "midnight" is conveyed by *ha^a^ṣōṯ hallaylâ* (Ex. 11:4; Job 34:20; Ps. 119:62) and *ḥ^a^ṣî hallalâ* (Ex. 12:29; Jgs. 16:3; Ruth 3:8).

II. General Usage.

1. *Darkness.* The physical phenomenon reflected in the term *laylâ* is the constant alternation of light[9] and darkness[10] as a fundamental fact of the created world, as P explicitly states in Gen. 1:3-5, where *laylâ* is identified with the darkness "separated" in the realm of creation. This association accounts for the usage of *laylâ,* whose primary semantic component is "darkness." In Ex. 14:20aβ, for example, *laylâ* is the darkness that has to be lit up (cf. Jer. 31:35). God illuminates the night (Ps. 105:39), but God can also turn day into night (Am. 5:8); therefore the darkness of night cannot hide anyone from God (Ps. 139:11f.). The difficult text Zec. 14:7 probably also uses *laylâ* to denote darkness: on the "day of Yahweh,"[11] light and darkness will no longer alternate in the rhythm of day and night.[12] The aspect of darkness is also emphasized in Wis. 7:30; 17:20.

Metaphorical use of *laylâ* draws on this note of "darkness," as when Job laments (Job 17:12) — depending on how one interprets the text — that night has become his day and his light comes from the darkness[13] or that his friends are trying to convince him that night is day.[14] Here *laylâ* means "suffering, disaster." Mic. 3:6 also uses the morpheme *laylâ* for the notion of "darkness": the prophet speaks of night without vision and darkness without divination to proclaim the absence of prophetic enlightenment because no revelation comes from God.[15]

2. *Domain of the Moon.* Gen. 1:16,18; Ps. 136:9 think of *laylâ,* the separate realm of darkness in the created world, as the domain of its associated luminary, the moon. This dominion is not absolute, however: Ps. 121:6 expresses Yahweh's protection by saying that the moon will not smite (*nkh* hiphil) the devout by night.

3. *Division of Time.* As the separate realm of darkness in the created world, *laylâ* is essentially a "temporal quantity." It is determined by the stars (Gen. 1:14) and defines the passage of time through continual alternation with day (Gen. 8:22). It can be personified and, like day, speak the praises of its creator to its "companion," the following night (Ps. 19:3[Eng. v. 2]). The morpheme *laylâ* appears most commonly in

---

9. → אור *'ôr.*
10. → חשך *ḥōšeḵ.*
11. → יום *yôm.*
12. W. Rudolph, *Sacharja 9–14. KAT,* XIII/4 (1976), *in loc.*
13. F. Horst, *Hiob. BK,* XVI/1 (⁴1983), *in loc.*
14. H. Junker, *Job. EB* (1959), *in loc.*; G. Fohrer, *Das Buch Hiob. KAT,* XVI (1963), *in loc.*
15. W. Rudolph, *Micha. KAT,* XIII/3 (1975), *in loc.*

statements of time, where it is first of all an integral part of the Israelite day, which is based on the solar day. Throughout much of Israel's history, days were calculated from morning to morning (as in Egypt); this reckoning is especially clear in the meristic formula *yômām wālaylâ* (Nu. 9:21; 1 K. 8:59; Ps. 1:2; etc.).[16] In the postexilic literature of the OT, the elements of this formula often appear in reverse order (1 K. 8:29; Isa. 27:3; 34:10; Est. 4:16; Jth. 11:17; Sir. 38:27; etc.; cf. Ps. 55:18[17]; Dnl. 8:14), which probably means that in the exilic and postexilic period it became customary to reckon days from evening to evening, especially since this method was standard in Mesopotamia. According to Roland de Vaux,[17] the change took place between the end of the monarchy and the epoch of Nehemiah. This reckoning seems to be reflected in many cultic regulations (e.g., Lev. 11:24; 15:5; 23:5f., 32; Ex. 12:18).[18] Since the opposite reckoning also appears in cultic ordinances (Lev. 7:15; 22:30),[19] however, certainty is hardly possible.

Nights were divided into "watches" (*'ašmûrâ/ᵃšmōreṯ*): Lam. 2:19 mentions a first watch (*lᵉrō'š 'ašmurôṯ*), Jgs. 7:19 a middle watch (*hā'ašmōreṯ hattîḵônâ*), and Ex. 14:24; 1 S. 11:11 a morning watch (*'ašmōreṯ habbōqer*).[20] This division of the night into three parts was also standard in Mesopotamia.

4. *Period of Time.* In 52 passages, *laylâ* is an integral part of a "durative statement of time" in the merism "day and night"; the aspect of duration is underlined either by numbers preceding the parts of merism ("forty days and forty nights": Gen. 7:4,12; Ex. 24:18; 34:28; Dt. 9:9,11,18,25; 10:10; 1 K. 19:8; "three days and three nights": 1 S. 30:12; Jon. 2:1[1:17]; "seven days and seven nights": Job 2:13) or by the use of *kōl* (Ex. 10:13; Nu. 11:32; 1 S. 19:24; 28:20; Isa. 62:6; cf. also Isa. 21:8, with *tāmîḏ yômām* instead of *kol-hayyôm*).[21] The durative aspect of the "day and night" polarity appears not only in the meristic formula but also in parallelistic statements like Ps. 77:3(2): "In the day of my trouble (*bᵉyôm ṣārāṯî*) I seek the Lord; in the night (*laylâ*) my hand is stretched out . . ." (cf. Ps. 88:2[1]; 2 S. 21:10).

But *laylâ* by itself can also express duration when the text states that some condition, action, or event extends through the night, especially when *kōl* is added for emphasis (Ex. 14:20,21; Lev. 6:2[9]; Nu. 22:19; Jgs. 16:2; 19:25; 20:5; 1 S. 14:36; 2 S. 2:29,32; 4:7; 17:16; 19:8[7]; Ps. 78:14; 90:4; Hos. 7:6). To express the terminus of a period of time, 2 Ch. 35:14 uses *laylâ* with the prep. *'aḏ*: "until night" (cf. 2 S. 19:8[7]).

5. *Time for Certain Activities.* Most texts use *laylâ* to describe some event as taking place "during the night." This usage results in a certain semantic expansion of the

16. Cf. *AncIsr,* 1181.
17. *Ibid.,* 182.
18. Rordorf, 1275.
19. *AncIsr,* 182.
20. Sauer, 984.
21. For a discussion of the merism, see J. Krašovec, *Des Merismus im Biblisch-Hebräischen und Nordwestsemitischen. BietOr,* 33 (1977), 116.

morpheme *laylâ,* especially when a particular event appears to be inherently associated with the night. The following paragraphs will attempt to classify several ways in which *laylâ* is so used.

a. First, simple statements of time may use *laylâ* to emphasize that an event takes place during a particular (*hû'*) night, without establishing any semantic association between this event and *laylâ* (cf. Gen. 32:23[22]; Jgs. 16:3; 1 S. 28:25; 2 S. 2:29; Ruth 3:8; Est. 6:1f.; Tob. 6:13 [Syr.]; 7:11; Jth. 11:5; 1 Mc. 4:5; 13:22).

b. Several texts use *laylâ* to denote a period of relaxation, of rest from labor (Ruth 3:13), of sleep (1 K. 3:19; Est. 6:1; Tob. 2:9; 6:1; Sir. 40:5), or of respite for the Israelites while entering Canaan (Josh. 4:3) or engaged in hostilities (Josh. 8:9,13). To work at night is a sign of particular zeal (Prov. 31:15,18). Inability to rest at night — for example, out of worry over possessions — is an alarming symptom (Eccl. 2:23). When certain tasks have to be performed at night, especially in the military (Josh. 10:9; 1 S. 14:34; 31:12; 2 K. 7:12; 1 Mc. 5:29) but also in everyday life (1 S. 19:11), it is a sign of particular urgency.

As a time of rest and sleep, *laylâ* has special significance in sexual life (Gen. 19:33-35; 30:15f.; Ruth 1:12; Dt. 23:11[10]). According to Tob. 6:14,16; 8:9, it is the time when the newly married come together; at night one yearns for one's beloved (Cant. 3:1). Job, however, in his lament curses night precisely because it is the time when life is conceived (Job 3:3,6f.).

As the time of rest and sleep, *laylâ* is also the time of dreaming, a process that identifies night as the time when people become aware of things that are otherwise hidden (Gen. 40:5; 41:11).[22]

c. When people must go without sleep, night becomes a time of agony — for example, when someone is afflicted with a severe illness (cf. Job 30:17). Job laments that nights of hardship (*'āmāl*) have come to be his lot (Job 7:3); he can hardly wait for them to pass. Sickness and affliction turn night into a time one floods one's bed with tears (Ps. 6:7[6]). In the riddling oracle Isa. 21:11f.,[23] *laylâ* probably suggests night as such a time of suffering and affliction, metaphorically representing the period of foreign domination.

d. Many occurrences of *laylâ* emphasize that night is a "time of darkness," for example when Yahweh goes before the Israelites as a pillar of fire by night (Ex. 13:21a,22; Nu. 14:14; Dt. 1:33; Neh. 9:12,19; Ps. 78:14; Wis. 10:17) or is present above the wilderness tabernacle as a fire by night (Ex. 40:38; Nu. 9:16). This aspect is also present when the figurative language of Job 5:14 uses *laylâ.* As a time of darkness, night presents special dangers, making it necessary to keep watch (Neh. 4:16[22]; Jth. 7:5); the night is therefore divided into watches. Those standing under God's protection need not fear the "terror of the night" (*paḥaḏ laylâ*: Ps. 91:5). Here *paḥaḏ* probably means not just danger in general,[24] but danger from demons and other creatures that

---

22. See III.6 below; also → חלם *ḥālam.*

23. See H. Wildberger, *Jesaja 13–27. BK,* X/2 (1978), *in loc.*; O. Kaiser, *Isaiah 13–39. OTL* (Eng. trans. 1974), *in loc.*

24. Joüon, *Bibl,* 2 (1921), 338.

are especially likely to strike by night (cf. Ex. 12:12,29). Such danger seems also to be alluded to by Cant. 3:8, which speaks of sixty mighty men at arms who accompany the bride's palanquin to protect it against "alarms by night," defending against the evil beings held by popular opinion to threaten the wedding night.[25] In the form of a fairy tale, Tobit describes how the newlyweds are threatened on their wedding night by the demon Asmodeus, who loves the bride and slays every rival, until he is himself overcome with divine aid (Tob. 3:8; 6:15ff.; 8:2f.).

Because of its darkness, *laylâ* is the best time for military operations intended to have an element of surprise: assaults on the enemy camp and army (Gen. 14:15; 2 S. 17:1; 2 K. 8:21; 2 Ch. 21:9; Jer. 6:5; 1 Mc. 4:1; 12:26; 2 Mc. 8:7; 12:9), setting up an ambush (Josh. 8:3; Jgs. 9:32,34), stealthily surrounding a city (2 K. 6:14), infiltration (Josh. 2:2; 1 S. 26:7), and secret flight (2 K. 25:4; Jer. 39:4; 52:7; Jth. 8:33).

Quite generally, night is the time for actions one does not dare expose to the light of day. Gideon tears down his father's Baʿal altar and cuts down its Asherah (Jgs. 6:27) at night because he is afraid of his family and the people of the city. According to 1 S. 28:8, Saul visits the necromancer at Endor at night, both because such transactions usually take place at night (cf. Isa. 65:4)[26] and because he wants to conceal his identity from both the woman and the Philistines. According to 1 S. 28:3, Saul had himself sought to suppress these magical practices. Now — as *laylâ* emphasizes — he is acting contrary to his own views and conscience.

This brings us to a further element typical of *laylâ*: as the time of darkness, it is also the time of villainy, when all who shun the light do their deeds (Job 24:13-15), including thieves (Jer. 49:9b; Ob. 5) and rapists (Jgs. 19:25; cf. Gen. 19:4-11); murders are carried out (Jgs. 20:5; 1 S. 19:10f.); deceivers do their work (1 K. 3:20); the strange woman entices the foolish young man so that he runs to his destruction (Prov. 7:6-23).

e. As a sign of darkness, *laylâ* is the time of the cold (*qeraḥ*) which anyone who must spend the night without protection suffers (Gen. 31:40) and to which the dead are exposed if they have to lie unburied (Jer. 36:30). The latter can also be a gruesome sign that Yahweh's prophetic word is being fulfilled (Bar. 2:25).

As a time of chill, night is also the time when dew falls, which Nu. 11:9 associates with the falling of manna (cf. Ex. 16:13-26). The "drops of the night" (*reṣîsê laylâ*) of Cant. 5:2 are not so much a reference to nighttime storms[27] as a symbol of fertility, blessing, and the renewal of life.[28]

III. Theological Contexts.

1. *Creation.* In discussing the theological aspects associated with the morpheme *laylâ,* we start with the observation that in the order of creation it represents "separated darkness," as P describes in some detail (Gen. 1:3-5). According to this text, night

---

25. *AuS,* I, 638f.; Krauss.
26. → אוב *ʾôḇ.*
27. E. Würthwein, *Die fünf Megilloth: Das Hohelied. HAT,* XVIII (²1969), *in loc.*
28. G. Gerleman, *Das Hohelied. BK,* XVIII (²1981), *in loc.*

results from several stages in God's creative work. In the beginning, darkness reigns; at God's creative word, light comes into being (v. 3a) and is approved by God (v. 4a); then God separates the light from the darkness (v. 4b) and names the entities that bring light and darkness to the created realm *yôm* and *laylâ* (v. 5a). Thus *laylâ* is "darkness" characterized as a reality created by God's magisterial act,[29] demonstrating God's power over the primordial chaos. It is devalued by P because of P's one-sided tendency to emphasize light.[30]

In the interpretation of the cosmos presented by Ps. 104, *laylâ* appears as a manifestation of God's love, which shows itself in all aspects of the world (cf. Ps. 104:20): night is the time assigned by the Creator to the beasts of the forest and the young lions, when they carry out their activities and receive their food from the Creator (Ps. 104:20f.).[31] Because night is an expression of God's love for his creation, the immutable alternation of day and night may be called a *b^e^rîṯ* of God, in the sense that God has established the alternation in an irrevocable ordinance (Jer. 33:25), a sign of God's irrevocable love (Gen. 8:21f.). As recipients of God's statutes and ordinances (Jer. 33:20a,25), day and night are shown to be realms of God's dominion. This notion also finds expression in Gen. 1:14-18; Ps. 74:16, where God assigns an appropriate luminary (*mā'ôr*) to the domain of darkness. Because night is an entity taken by God into his service, it likewise serves the praise of God without language in the realm of creation (Ps. 19:3b[2b]).

2. *God's Presence.* In sacred history, night is associated with God's acts as the temporal setting for his coming to bring salvation and judgment. At night God's care for his pilgrim people is realized in the provision of manna (Nu. 11:9). While Yahweh's people wander through the desert, he leads them by his presence in the pillar of fire, so that a region totally unsuited to the pilgrim people becomes through Yahweh's presence a realm of active life (Ex. 13:21a,22; Nu. 14:14; Dt. 1:33; Neh. 9:12,19; Ps. 78:14; Wis. 10:17). God's appearance by night in the fire (*'ēš*: Ex. 40:38; Nu. 9:16) above the desert tabernacle turns the desert years into a time of God's gracious presence. Isa. 4:5 associates the notion of Yahweh's presence in the cloud (*'ānān*) by day and in the smoke and fire of a flashing flame (*'āšān w^e^nōgâ 'ēš lehāḇâ*) by night with Zion: the people of Zion, made a "holy remnant" through the *rûaḥ* of "judgment" and "burning," experience the creative (*br'*) presence of Yahweh day and night on Zion, so that God's gracious work of restoring the escaped of Israel achieves its purpose.[32] Thus the signs of Yahweh's presence become an expression of the absolute protection that encompasses the entire milieu of the Zion congregation.

3. *Deliverance.* Beleaguered Jerusalem was delivered by the mighty hand of Yahweh during the night (2 K. 19:35; Isa. 37:36). Closely associated with this event is the pre-P

29. → בדל *bdl*; → קרא *qr'*.
30. Steck, *Der Schöpfungsbericht der Priesterschrift,* 167, n. 710.
31. Cf. Steck, *World and Environment,* 85-89.
32. Cf. H. Wildberger, *Isaiah 1–12* (Eng. trans., Minneapolis, 1991), *in loc.*

statement that the deliverance of Israel at the sea took place during the morning watch (*bᵉʾašmōreṯ habbōqer*: Ex. 14:24a). It is most unlikely that this statement can be equated with the notion of "help in the morning" (Ps. 30:6[5]; 90:14; 143:8; Lam. 3:22f.),[33] quite apart from the fact that the variety of language makes it difficult to speak of a consistent motif of "help in the morning." More closely related to Ex. 14:24a is Ps. 46:6(5), which says that Yahweh's intervention to deliver Zion comes *lipnôṯ bōqer,* "before the morning," i.e., before military aid is possible. Thus Yahweh intervenes to deliver Zion during the "night" (cf. Isa. 17:14; Jth. 13:14) as an expression of his unconditional and sovereign commitment to his "holy mountain" (Ps. 2:6). We will not discuss in detail the connection between the motif of "Yahweh's help in the night" and the Zion ideology, but will say only that the language describing Yahweh's deliverance of Zion includes the motif of "deliverance by Yahweh at night." It is impossible to say whether the inhabitants of Jerusalem performed a cultic representation of Yahweh's intervention to deliver his people "before the dawn," i.e., during the night,[34] of a specific day of the year — Passover, for instance.[35] That this notion of "Yahweh's help for Zion at night" did not spring from the deliverance of Jerusalem in 701 B.C., when the city was besieged by Sennacherib, is clear from the observation "that this quite unsupernatural event needed an existing tradition in order to be interpreted as a miraculous deliverance."[36] But the theological interpretation of this event through the notion of "Yahweh's help for Zion at night," the elements of which most likely go back to pre-Israelite Jerusalem, probably led to a retelling of the deliverance of Israel at the sea, in which Yahweh's deliverance during the night (Ex. 14:21,24a) became the central element.

4. *Passover.* We have explicit information from OT Israel concerning only one night of the greatest theological and liturgical significance: the "night of deliverance from Egypt," set traditio-historically in the context of two festival traditions. As the "night of the final plague, when the first-born of Egypt were slain" (Ex. 11:4f.; 12:29), it belongs in the context of the Feast of Unleavened Bread;[37] as the "night in which the *mašḥîṯ* passes through Egypt to inflict disaster," it has its traditio-historical roots in Passover. The association of the Passover ritual with the Feast of Unleavened Bread, which probably took place under Deuteronomistic auspices, turned Passover into the night when the first-born were slain (cf. the *laylâ* added almost as an afterthought to Dt. 16:1 and the statements concerning Passover in Dt. 16:1aβ,5-7, which interrupt the narrative). The mention of "night" belongs properly to the Passover ritual, which was a noctural ceremony from the very beginning — whether among a group of nomadic herdsmen or later in the setting of the Israelite family. In this context, *laylâ* was originally the time when the *mašḥîṯ* wrought its destruction (and thus a concretion of

---

33. Cf. Lutz, 50, n. 1; Wildberger, *BK,* X/2, 675; for a different view, → בקר *bōqer.*
34. Cf. Müller, 43f.
35. *Ibid.,* 93f.
36. *Ibid.,* 45, n. 78.
37. Otto.

the general sense that night is the time when the powers of evil are at work), to be warded off by a blood ritual. The association of Passover with Yahweh turned this night into a setting for the revelation of Yahweh's intervention to deliver Israel (Ex. 12:13,23,27). The association of Passover with the Feast of Unleavened Bread uses the slaying of the Egyptian first-born to illustrate this deliverance (Ex. 12:12,29; 13:15; Wis. 18:6,14-16). The later tradition of Israel therefore interprets this night as *lêl šimmurîm* for Yahweh (Ex. 12:42), a night of Yahweh's care for his people manifested in watching over the integrity of the faithful. This term probably refers to the "watching" of the Israelites during the night of Passover (Ex. 12:42b), to recall Yahweh's loving care for his people revealed during this night.[38]

5. *Judgment.* The OT also mentions *laylâ* in connection with God's judgment; Isa. 15:1 alludes to this association. Job 27:19f. likewise pictures judgment as a noctural event; the mention of *laylâ* seeks to indicate the sudden and unpredictable nature of God's judgment, before which mortals are helpless despite their prowess (cf. Job 34:20,25). In the late OT period, *laylâ* was used as a metaphor for this judgment, as when the author of the Elihu speeches calls the judgment upon the nations *hallāylâ laʿᵃlôṯ ʿammîm taḥtām* (Job 36:20; cf. Wis. 17:2,5,13,20). As Jon. 4:10 emphasizes, when God's actions are described, *laylâ* is the element that signifies God's absolute sovereignty and seeks to express the impossibility of trying to influence him.

6. *Revelation.* Above all, *laylâ* is the time when God reveals himself in dreams:[39] Yahweh appears (*r'h* niphal) in the night *baḥᵃlôm* (1 K. 3:5); Yahweh comes and speaks *baḥᵃlôm hallaylâ* (Gen. 20:3; 31:24). Semantically related are *bᵉmar'ōṯ hallahlâ* (Gen. 46:2); *ḥezyôn laylâ* (Job 4:13; 20:8; 33:15 [par. *ḥᵃlôm*]); *ḥᵃzôn laylâ* (Isa. 29:7 [par. *ḥᵃlôm*]); cf. Aram. *ḥezwê (dî-) lêlyā'* (Dnl. 2:19; 7:7,13); *r'h hallaylâ* with the prophet as subject (Zech. 1:8). A noctural vision is a dream vision. When the OT speaks of *laylâ* in connection with revelation, God is the subject of several verbs: *r'h* niphal (Gen. 26:24; 2 Ch. 1:7; 7:12); *bw'* (Nu. 22:20); *'mr* (Gen. 26:24; Nu. 22:19f.; Jgs. 6:25; 7:9; 1 S. 15:16). In 2 S. 7:4; 1 Ch. 17:3, *laylâ* appears with the word-event formula. That night should be the time of revelation is probably connected with the fact that it is the time of dreaming, when dreams rise up from the human subconscious, revealing to general consciousness realities that lie beyond all human manipulation and thus exhibit a special affinity to the divine. A related phenomenon is the practice of incubation, which seems to be reflected in Gen. 46:1aβ-5a; 1 K. 3:4-15. Sleeping the night at a sanctuary brought the sleeper especially close to the deity. As criticism mounted in Israel against the practice of seeking to elicit a revelation from God through sacrifice and incubation, and thus against dreams themselves as a vehicle of revelation (cf. Jer. 23:25ff.; Dt. 13:2ff.[1ff.]), the statement that God revealed himself in a dream is replaced increasingly by the statement that God appeared, spoke, or came during the

---

38. Cf. M. Noth, *Exodus. OTL* (Eng. trans. 1962), *in loc.*
39. → חלם *ḥālam.*

night. In passages that talk about the God who reveals himself, *laylâ* thus shows that all God's speaking, appearing, and coming to human beings is entirely God's own initiative (cf. Jgs. 6:40).

7. *Israel's Response.* The morpheme *laylâ* also plays a role in contexts dealing with the relationship of the faithful Israelites to their God. For both the people (Nu. 14:1; Lam. 1:2) and the individual, night is a time of particularly moving lament (1 S. 15:11) or lamenting meditation (Ps. 77:7[6]) over the incomprehensible actions of Yahweh. Night is also a time that underlines the intensity and fervor of petitions (Jth. 6:21; 11:17). But just as night can be a time of anxious yearning after God (Isa. 26:9), experience of God's help can transform it into a time of thankful and joyous remembrance (Ps. 119:55). It becomes a time of rejoicing, when God shows his loving mercy to the individual (Ps. 42:9[8] [MT]; Ps. 119:62), so that Elihu can call God *nōṯēn zᵉmirôṯ ballāylâ* (Job 35:10). But night can also be a time of praise for the whole congregation of the faithful (Ps. 134:1; Isa. 30:29). Such texts probably reflect liturgical reality, since traces of hymns used in these nocturnal celebrations are still extant — in Ps. 8:4ff.(3ff.), for example. The only explicit mention of a nocturnal celebration in the OT has to do with Passover; the statement in Isa. 30:29 about "the night when a holy feast is kept" cannot be explained unambiguously.

IV. Dead Sea Scrolls. The occurrences of *laylâ* in the Dead Sea scrolls do not exhibit any new usages. In 1QH 12:6f., night appears as the domain of darkness; in 1QS 6:6; 1QH 8:29; 10:15; 11QT 57:10, it is an integral element of the durative expression "day and night"; in 1QM 19:9, night is a time of rest; in 1QS 6:7; 10:10; 1QM 14:13, it is a time for special praise of God and study of his instruction.

Stiglmair

The other texts think of night primarily as a time for dreams and visions (1QapGen 19:14; 21:8; 4QEnGiants*ᵇ* 2:16; 11QtgJob 22:9), for performing one's many obligations (11QtgJob 26:6), but also for particularly fervent prayer (1QapGen 20:12). The Temple scroll uses *laylâ* in its restoration of the OT cultic regulations (11QT 17:8, eating the Passover at night [cf. Ex. 12:8]; 11QT 45:7, cultic uncleanness caused by noctural emission [cf. Dt. 23:10ff.]). Finally, 4Q184:1,4,6 — a fragment about the "Wiles of the Wicked Woman" — sees the "coming of night" (*b'yšny lylh*)[40] as the time this woman prefers for her deceits.

Fabry

---

40. J. Strugnell, "Notes en marge du volume V des 'Discoveries in the Judaean Desert of Jordan,' " *RevQ,* 7 (1969), 265.

לִין *lîn*; מָלוֹן *mālôn*; מְלוּנָה *m^elûnâ*

Contents: I. 1. Etymology; 2. Occurrences; 3. LXX. II. Syntactic Combinations. III. Semantic Combinations. IV. Meaning and OT Usage: 1. Semantic Elements; 2. Primary and Secondary Meanings.

I. 1. *Etymology.* The root *lyn* and its by-form *lwn* (in derivatives), "spend the night," is found only in Hebrew (including Middle Hebrew) and Ugaritic.[1] According to Carl Brockelmann,[2] it comes from *lyl,* "night," by dissimilation; but its appearance in Ugaritic casts doubt on this etymology. The Phoenician hithpael form *ytlnn,*[3] often taken to mean "spend the night," is more likely associated with *lwn,* "growl, murmur."[4]

2. *Occurrences.* The root appears 80 times in the OT (13 in Judges, 11 in Genesis, 8 in Job, 7 in Isaiah; the rest widely scattered), 70 times as a verb (68 times in the qal, twice in the hithpael). Its derivatives are *mālôn,* "night's lodging" (8 occurrences), and *m^elûnâ,* "watchman's hut" (2 occurrences).

3. *LXX.* The LXX usually translates with *aulízein, koimán,* or *katalýein*; also found are translations such as *katapaúein, méenein, hypárchein,* and *hypnoún.*

II. Syntactic Combinations. As the subject of *lîn,* we find: (a) groups: "all the people of Israel" (Josh. 3:1); "merchants and sellers" (Neh. 13:20; cf. v. 21); (b) individuals: "Joshua" (Josh. 8:9); "I and my concubine" (Jgs. 20:4); "a man of war" (2 S. 17:8); "the sojourner" (Job 31:32; cf. Gen. 32:22[Eng. v. 21]; 2 S. 19:8[7]; Ps. 91:1); (c) corpses: "his body shall not remain all night upon the tree" (Dt. 21:23); (d) animals: "bitterns [?] and owls" (Zeph. 2:14); (e) things, including parts of the body: "an ear that listens will lodge among the wise" (Prov. 15:31; belongs semantically with [b] above, because the meaning is "the one whose ear heeds"); "the dew spends the night" (Job 29:19); "the fat of my feast shall not remain until the morning" (Ex. 23:18; cf. 34:25 [sacrifice of the Feast of Passover] and Dt. 16:4 [Passover lamb]); "the wages of a hired servant shall not remain with you all night until the [next] morning" (Lev. 19:13); (f) conditions: "my error remains with myself," i.e., "I have erred, I have sinned" (Job 19:4); "weeping may tarry for the night" (Ps. 30:6[5]); "righteousness lodged in her [Jerusalem]" (Isa. 1:21); "strength" (Job 41:14[22]); "his soul" (Ps. 25:13).

As temporal adverbs, we find: (a) *bōqer,* "morning," with *l^e* or *'aḏ,* "until" (e.g., Ex. 34:25; Dt. 16:4; Ex. 23:18); (b) *laylâ,* "night" (Gen. 32:14,22[13,21]; Nu. 22:8;

1. *WUS,* no. 1470.
2. *VG,* I, 228.
3. *KAI,* 24, 10.
4. *DISO,* 136.

Josh. 4:3; 8:9,13; Ruth 3:13; 2 S. 17:16; 19:8[7]); (c) *'ereḇ*, "evening" (Ps. 30:6[5]; Isa. 21:13).

The place of lodging is often a house or other enclosure: "the house" (Jgs. 19:15; cf. Zec. 5:4), "the house of Micah" (Jgs. 18:2), "the chamber" (Ezr. 10:6), "with Balaam" (Nu. 22:8), "the camp" (Gen. 32:22[21]; Josh. 6:11), "with you" (Lev. 19:13; cf. 2 S. 19:8[7]), "with me" (Job 19:4), "at your crib" (Job 39:9), "in a cave" (1 K. 19:9), *bannᵉṣûrîm*, "in secret places [caves ?]" (Isa. 65:4). One may also spend the night in the open: "at the fords of the wilderness" (2 S. 17:16; cf. Ps. 55:8[7]: "in the wilderness"), "on the mountain" (Gen. 31:54), "in (*bᵉṯôḵ*) Jerusalem" (Neh. 4:16[22]; cf. Jer. 4:14: *bᵉqirbēḵ*; Prov. 15:31: "among [*bᵉqereḇ*] the wise"), "round about the house of God" (1 Ch. 9:27), "in a cucumber field" (Isa. 1:8), "outside Jerusalem" (Neh. 13:20; cf. Job 31:32: "[outside] in the street"), "upon the ground" (2 S. 12:16), "in the square" (Gen. 19:2; Jgs. 19:20), "in the villages" (Cant. 7:12[11]), "on the steppe" (Isa. 21:13), "in Zion" (Isa. 1:21), "before the wall" (Neh. 13:21).

Other locations, some metaphorical, are also found: "between my breasts" (Cant. 1:13), "in prosperity" (Ps. 25:13), "in the shadow" (Ps. 91:1), "on my branches" (Job 29:19),[5] "in his neck" (Job 41:14[22]), "upon the tree" (Dt. 21:23), "on the rock . . . and in the fastness of the rocky crag" (Job 39:28), "there" (Gen. 28:11; Josh. 3:1; Jgs. 18:2; 1 K. 19:9; Ezr. 10:6), "here" (Nu. 22:8; Jgs. 19:9).

The place may also be specified as a "night's lodging" (*mālôn*: Gen. 42:27; 43:21; Ex. 4:24; Josh. 4:3,8; 2 K. 19:23), Gibeah (Jgs. 20:4), Geba (Isa. 10:29 [text corrupt]), room (*māqôm*: Gen. 24:23,25). It may also be indefinite: "wherever" (Ruth 1:16).

III. Semantic Combinations. The root *lîn* is sometimes associated semantically with other words that further define its meaning. Four such combinations occur in the OT: (1) *lîn* and *rāḇaṣ*. Zeph. 2:14 ("herds shall lie down [*rāḇaṣ*] in the midst of her [Nineveh], . . . bitterns and owls shall spend the night in her capitals") uses *lîn* and *rāḇaṣ* in parallelism to express lodging by day (*rāḇaṣ*) and by night (*lîn*). (2) *lîn* and *yāraš*. Ps. 25:13 ("his soul [= he] shall abide [*lîn*] in prosperity, and his descendants shall inherit [*yāraš*] the land") uses progressive parallelism: the one who fears Yahweh will live a happy life, and his descendants will enjoy the prosperity of the promised land. Present and future happiness are expressed by the verbs *lîn* and *yāraš*. (3) *lîn* and *yāšaḇ*. Ps. 91:1 ("whoever dwells [*yāšaḇ*] in the shelter of the Most High, who abides [*yiṯlônān*] in the shadow of Shaddai . . .") uses the verbs *yāšaḇ* and *lîn* almost as synonyms to describe life under God's protection. (4) *lîn* and *šāḵaḇ*. In Gen. 19:2,4, *šāḵaḇ* represents the final phase of *lîn*. V. 2: "Turn aside . . . to your servant's house and spend the night." V. 4: "Before they lay down to sleep (*šāḵaḇ*). . . ." The various elements included in the general concept of *lîn* (washing of feet, eating and drinking) precede the primary element: lying down to sleep. The men of Sodom came before the angels lay down in bed, and *lîn* was not completed.

---

5. See A. Weiser, *Das Buch Hiob. ATD,* XIII ([7]1980), 202.

IV. Meaning and OT Usage.

1. *Semantic Elements.* In the literal sense, *lîn* begins in the evening and ends in the morning (Gen. 19:1; 24:54; 32:1[31:55]; Jgs. 19:6f.,11; Ruth 3:13; Ps. 30:6[5]; Jer. 14:8). It presupposes that a traveler interrupts his journey, either because he is tired or because he has reached his destination. This is the case, for example, with the arrival of the two angels at Sodom in the evening (Gen. 19:2) and the arrival of Abraham's oldest servant in the city of Nahor (Gen. 24:23-25). The prophet Jeremiah describes the situation clearly: "Why are you like a stranger (*gēr*) in the land, like a wayfarer (*'ōrēaḥ*) who only stays the night?" (Jer. 14:8; cf. Jgs. 19:15; Job 31:32). The question *'ānâ ṯēlēḵ ûmē'yin tāḇô'*, "Where are you going, and whence do you come?" (Jgs. 19:17), illustrates the temporary nature of the activity expressed by *lîn.* The association with traveling distinguishes the root from *yāšēn,* "sleep," and *šāḵaḇ,* "lie down." A journey is presupposed by *lîn,* while *yāšēn* and *šāḵaḇ* presuppose a fixed dwelling. The situation described in Ezr. 10:6 appropriately uses *lîn,* because Ezra and his companions are returning "wayfarers."

The activity denoted by *lîn* requires a place, which can be an open square, a field, or a house. The two angels spend the night (*lîn*) in the house of Lot (Gen. 19:5), Abraham's servant in the house of Bethuel (Gen. 24:23-25,54), the five Danites in the house of Micah (Jgs. 18:2), the Levite in the house of his father-in-law in Bethlehem (Jgs. 19:4f.) and in Gibeah (Jgs. 20:4). Some places are appropriate for *lîn* and some are not: in any case, one should not spend the night outside in the street (Job 31:32). Nevertheless, it was common to spend the night in the open: Elijah lodges in a cave (*meʿārâ*: 1 K. 19:9), Jacob upon the mountain (Gen. 31:54; cf. 32:14[13]), in a camp (*maḥaneh*: Gen. 32:21f.[20f.]), and at a (holy) place (*māqôm*: Gen. 28:11), Joshua and the Israelites on the east bank of the Jordan (Josh. 3:1) and in a camp at Gilgal (Josh. 6:11). The five thousand mighty men encamped between Bethel and Ai (Josh. 8:9; cf. vv. 12f.); David cannot spend the night with his army at the fords of the wilderness (2 S. 17:16, reading *beʿaḇrôṯ hammiḏbār* instead of MT *beʿarḇôṯ*; cf. Ps. 55:8[7]; Isa. 10:29; 21:13; Jer. 9:1[2]).

The nuance of temporariness — i.e., lodging for only one night, or at most a few — is maintained in military situations (Josh. 8:9,13; 2 S. 17:8). Cant. 7:12(11) speaks of spending the night in the villages (*kep̄ārîm*; emendation to *kerāmîm,* "vineyards," is unnecessary[6]). The four chief gatekeepers lodge round about the house of God (1 Ch. 9:26f.). Ezra spends the night in the chamber of Jehohanan (Ezr. 10:6). Nehemiah commands the people to spend the night in the midst of Jerusalem (Neh. 4:16[22]), and forbids the merchants and sellers to spend the night before the wall of Jerusalem (Neh. 13:20f.). Isa. 65:4 speaks of *neṣurîm* (secret places? caves?) as a place to spend the night. David spends the night in his house (2 S. 12:16); the elders of the Moabites and Midianites lodge with Balaam, probably for only a single night (Nu. 22:8,13).

The place where one spends the night is a *mālôn* ("lodging, shelter"). Josh. 4:3 defines a *mālôn*: ". . . in the shelter where you spend the night" (*bammālôn 'ašer-tālînû bô hallāylâ*; cf. v. 8). A *mālôn* may also be nothing more than a resting place in a dense

---

6. G. Gerleman, *Das Hohelied. BK,* XVIII (²1981), 207.

forest (2 K. 19:23). Moses experienced a perilous theophany at a *mālôn* (Ex. 4:24). In practice, a *mālôn* was the place where travelers could rest, wash their feet, eat, and drink (Gen. 19:2; 31:54; cf. Jgs. 19:4,6; Ezr. 10:6; and Prov. 19:23: "lodge satisfied"), and where the animals could be fed (Gen. 24:23,25; 42:27; 43:21).

The outdoor shelter where watchmen could spend the night was called a *m*^e*lûnâ*. It was a structure made of strong branches (LXX *opōrophylákion*),[7] set high above the fields to guarantee an unbroken field of view (Isa. 1:8; 24:20).

Having a suitable place to spend the night presupposes hospitality. The OT often mentions invitations to spend the night. We see the form of such an invitation in Gen. 19:2: "My lords, turn aside, I pray you, to your servant's house and spend the night." Balaam invites the elders of Moab and Midian (Nu. 22:8); similarly, the father-in-law of the Levite from Ephraim offers him an invitation (Jgs. 19:9). Absent such an invitation, one would have to spend the night outdoors (Jgs. 19:15). Job underscores his hospitality by saying: "No stranger has had to lodge in the street," i.e., he invited them all to spend the night in his house (Job 31:32). An erotic invitation to spend the night is recorded in Cant. 7:12(11). Ruth 3:7,13 records a "forced" invitation. Abraham's oldest servant makes an indirect request for lodging (Gen. 24:23-25).

2. *Primary and Secondary Meanings.* Of the 80 occurrences of *lîn,* 50 belong to the semantic category "lodge, spend the night." This meaning is found 37 times in the historical books (Gen. 19:2; 24:23,25,54; 28:11; 31:54; 32:14,22[13,21]; Nu. 22:8; Josh. 3:1; 4:3; 6:11; 8:9,13; Jgs. 18:2; 19:4-15 [9 times],20; 20:4; Ruth 1:16; 3:13; 2 S. 12:16; 17:8,16; 19:8[7]; 1 K. 19:9; 1 Ch. 9:27; Ezr. 10:6; Neh. 4:16[22]; 13:20). The other 13 occurrences speak of spending the night for a particular purpose or use *lîn* metaphorically.

a. Marital dependence of a woman on her husband (and his family) is denoted by *lîn* (Ruth 1:16), as is fidelity in general (2 S. 19:8[7]). The dependence and obedience of an animal are described metaphorically in terms of spending the night at its owner's crib (Job 39:9).

b. Since for a woman to spend the night with a man has overtones of sexual intercourse, *lîn* can also refer to (sacral) marriage (Cant. 1:13; 7:12[11]).

c. Although *lîn* has a temporal aspect, it can also be used without temporal limitation to underline the permanent nature of a characteristic. Thus the strength of Leviathan "lodges" in his neck, where it "resides" (Job 41:14[22]).[8] In a similar vein, Isa. 1:21 describes the former righteousness of Zion as "lodging" in her. Some texts convey a nuance of "establishing oneself," as Karl Elliger notes with respect to Zec. 5:4.[9]

d. Isa. 65:4 describes the rebellious people as spending the night in caves. According to such exegetes as Claus Westermann,[10] *lîn* here refers to ritual incubation, an interpretation supported by the explanatory addition of the LXX: *di' enýpnia,* "for dream oracles."

Oikonomou

---

7. *AuS,* II (1932), 61, nn. 12f.
8. G. Fohrer, *Das Buch Hiob. KAT,* XVI (1963), 530.
9. K. Elliger, *Das Buch der zwölf kleinen Propheten, II: Sacharja. ATD,* XXV (^{7}1975), 106.
10. C. Westermann, *Isaiah 40–66. OTL* (Eng. trans. 1969), 401.

ליץ *lyṣ; ליץ lîṣ; לֵץ lēṣ; לָצוֹן lāṣôn; מֵלִיץ mēlîṣ

Contents: I. 1. Root; 2. Etymology; 3. Occurrences. II. 1. *lîṣ/lûṣ*; 2. *lēṣ, lāṣôn.* III. *mēlîṣ*: 1. Epigraphic Evidence; 2. Biblical Usage; 3. Postbiblical Usage.

I. 1. *Root.* The root *lyṣ* is represented by the verb *lîṣ* or *lûṣ,* the verbal subst. *lēṣ* (possibly a qal ptcp.), the noun *lāṣôn,* and rarely by *mēlîṣ* (hiphil ptcp.). As a rule, the etymology of *mēlîṣ* is treated separately; if it is interpreted as a hiphil participle, one must posit an independent root *lyṣ* II.[1] The noun *m*ᵉ*lîṣâ* is best assigned to the root *mlṣ.*[2] The root *lyṣ* I appears to be unique to Hebrew; any connection with Akk. *lâṣu,* "mock (?)," the reading of which is uncertain,[3] is extremely dubious. Neither has any convincing Arabic reflex been found (cf. *lyṣ,* "deflect, avert";[4] *lwṣ,* "peer through a crack in the door"[5]). From Biblical Hebrew are derived both Middle Heb. *lîṣ/lûṣ* and Middle Heb./Jewish Aram. *lîṣān, lîṣānûṯ,* and *lēṣûṯ.*[6]

2. *Etymology.* Ever since Frantz Buhl's study, attempts have been made to correct the traditional translation[7] "scoff(er), mock(er)(y)" and arrive at the "basic meaning" of the root — if possible, including *mēlîṣ* and *m*ᵉ*lîṣâ* in the discussion. Several basic meanings have been proposed: "be arrogant,"[8] "be foolish,"[9] "repeat (in a different form),"[10] "talk big, brag."[11] The juxtaposition of such widely diverse meanings as "be foolish," "talk big," "mock," and "interpret" under a single lemma[12] reflects the confusion of Hebrew lexicography.

---

lyṣ J. Behm, "παράκλητος," *TDNT,* V, 806-812; G. Bertram, "ὕβρις," *TDNT,* VIII, 299-305; F. Buhl, "Die Bedeutung des Stammes לוץ oder ליץ im Hebräischen," *Studien zur semitischen Philologie und Religionsgeschichte. Festschrift J. Wellhausen. BZAW,* 27 (1914), 79-86; P. A. H. de Boer, *De voorbede in het OT. OTS,* 3 (1943), 165f.; S. A. Mandry, *There is No God: A Study of the Fool in the OT* (diss., Rome, 1972); H. N. Richardson, "Some Notes on ליץ and its Derivatives," *VT,* 5 (1955), 163-179; *idem,* "Two Addenda . . . ," *VT,* 5 (1955), 434-36; C. Schedl, "Tᵉšûbâh und melîṣ: Über die wahre Busse und den Fürsprecher," *Bibl,* 43 (1962), 168-179.

1. *GesB,* 386; *LexHebAram,* 394f.
2. Richardson, *VT,* 5 (1955), 178.
3. *AHw,* II (1972), 1162a.
4. Gaster, *KBL*².
5. *KBL*³.
6. *WTM,* 504, 521.
7. E.g., *BDB.*
8. Buhl, *GesB, LexHebAram.*
9. Joüon.
10. De Boer.
11. M. A. Canney, "The Hebrew מֵלִיץ," *AJSL,* 40 (1924), 135-37, followed by Richardson; cf. *KBL*³.
12. *KBL*³.

3. *Occurrences.* The verb *lîṣ* (or *lûṣ*) occurs 7 times in the Hebrew Bible (Ps. 119:51; Prov. 3:34; 9:12; 14:9; 19:28; Isa. 28:22; Hos. 7:5). The noun *lēṣ* is especially frequent in Proverbs (14 occurrences); it also appears in Ps. 1:1; Isa. 29:20. The word *mēlîṣ* is found 5 times (Gen. 42:23; 2 Ch. 32:31; Job 16:20; 33:23; Isa. 43:27), *meliṣâ* only twice (Prov. 1:6; Hab. 2:6).

This survey shows clearly that the word group *lîṣ/lēṣ/lāṣôn* is rooted in Wisdom Literature. The 2 occurrences in Isaiah (Isa. 28:14,22) confirm the ties between this prophet and the language and thought of the sages.[13] Sirach (8 occurrences of *lēṣ*) and the Dead Sea scrolls (1 occurrence of *lēṣ,* 4 occurrences of *lāṣôn*) continue this usage.

II. 1. *lîṣ/lûṣ.* Interpretation of the verbal forms of *lyṣ* I is difficult: *welaṣtā* (Prov. 9:12, the only clear qal form); *helîṣunî* (Ps. 119:51, hiphil); *yālîṣ* (Prov. 3:34; 14:9; 19:28, qal or hiphil); *lōṣeṣîm* (Hos. 7:5, probably polel); *tiṯlôṣāṣû* (Isa. 28:22, hithpolel). The traditional translation of all stems of the verb has been "scoff" or "mock." In all these texts, however, the LXX provides a different translation, never using a word that means "scoff." In fact, the LXX translations do not denote any kind of speaking, but refer mostly to some negative attitude or conduct: "be evil, act illegally" (Prov. 9:12; Hos. 7:5; Ps. 119:51), "be arrogant" (Prov. 19:28). Isa. 28:22 is a mistranslation; Prov. 14:9 probably represents a variant text. The meaning "scoff" makes its appearance rarely in the Syr. (Isa. 28:22), more often in the Targ. (Ps. 119:51; Prov. 9:12; 19:28). This meaning also appears in the later Greek versions (cf. Prov. 14:9 in Aquila, Symmachus, and Theodotion), and becomes dominant in the Vulg. (*inludere, deludere, deridere*; only in Ps. 119:51 iuxta LXX do we find *inique agere*).

In Prov. 9:12, parallelism with *ḥāḵamtā* makes it likely that the qal form *welaṣtā* denotes foolish and wicked behavior, not a type of speech.[14] Textual problems complicate the interpretation of all 3 passages where *yālîṣ* occurs. In Prov. 3:34, the meaning "babble" is inappropriate (the subject is Yahweh, from v. 33!); H. Neil Richardson[15] thinks the text is corrupt, but the MT makes sense with a different meaning. The antithesis *ʿaniyyîm* (*ʿanāwîm* [*Q*]) / *lēṣîm* in v. 34 suggests the meaning "arrogant" for the latter. The hiphil *yālîṣ* would then mean "act arrogantly." Ps. 18:26f.(Eng. vv. 25f.) admits the translation: "God meets the arrogant with arrogance." The text of Prov. 14:9 is clearly corrupt and has so far eluded interpretation. In Prov. 19:28, the subject of *yālîṣ* is "a worthless witness"; the object is *mišpāṭ*. Does the witness "mock" the law (metaphorically[16]) or "babble" of the law?[17] If the MT of the parallel stich (v. 28b) is correct (*yeḇallaʿ-'āwen,* "spreads iniquity," from *blʿ* II[18]), a translation along the lines proposed by Martin Buber (". . . outbrazens the law") is possible. Also unclear is the

---

13. Cf. J. Fichtner, "Jesaja unter den Weisen," *ThLZ,* 74 (1949), 75-80 = *Gottes Weisheit. ArbT,* 2/3 (1965), 18-26.

14. Contra Richardson, *VT,* 5 (1955), 164; → חכם *ḥāḵam* (*chākham*), IV, 372f.

15. *VT,* 5 (1955), 166.

16. *KBL*³, 503a.

17. Richardson, *VT,* 5 (1955), 166.

18. *KBL*³, 129b.

exact meaning of the lament in Ps. 119:51a. For *zēḏîm hᵉlîṣunî* the LXX has *hyperéphanoi parēnómoun,* without translating the personal suffix. If one rejects the transitive meaning "treat arrogantly, insolently," which would be appropriate for the hiphil, there remains the possibility of reading *'illᵉṣunî,* "they [the insolent] oppress me," following the Syr. The meaning of *lōṣᵉṣîm* in Hos. 7:5 can only be conjectured.[19] For the admonition *'al-tiṯlôṣāṣû* in Isa. 28:22, the subject matter of 28:7-13,14 has led Richardson[20] to propose the translation "do not babble"; but this misses the nuance of the hithpolel ("behave in the manner of something"[21]). Furthermore, Isa. 28:14-22 more likely attacks the rulers of Jerusalem for their arrogance and self-confidence than for their "babbling."

2. *lēṣ, lāṣôn.* The versions use many different words to translate *lēṣ,* often with widely different meanings. They all understand *lēṣ* to denote a reprehensible person, but differ in their interpretation of the specific fault. The LXX treats it as arrogance (*hyperéphanos* [2]), wickedness (*loimós* [5], *kakós* [3]), licentiousness (*akólastos* [3]), or folly (*áphrōn* [1]) — nothing suggesting speech. The Greek text of Sirach often connects *lēṣ* with "arrogance" (*hyperéphanos* [5]; *hybristḗs* [1]). The Syr. usually suggests wickedness (*bîšā'* [9]), but sometimes finds the meaning "scoffer" (4 times); this became the regular translation of the Targ. Through the later Greek versions and the Vulg. (*inlusor, derisor*), it became the generally accepted interpretation of the word. The noun *lāṣôn* exhibits a parallel development; in Prov. 1:22 it is translated "arrogance" by the LXX, but "mockery" by the Syr. and Targ.

An attempt to determine the meaning of the word from its context must be more aware than has generally been the case that the meanings of *lēṣ* and *lāṣôn* probably shifted within the biblical period itself. Of the 14 occurrences of *lēṣ* in Proverbs, 10 occur in the preexilic collections 10:1–22:16; 22:17–24:22; 28f.; the later introductory collection 1–9 (which includes earlier material) contains 4 others.

a. The antithesis *lēṣ/ḥāḵām*[22] is one of the commonplaces of early wisdom (cf. Prov. 9:8,12; 13:1; 15:12; 20:1; 21:11). As a synonym of *ḥāḵām,* we frequently find *nāḇôn* (Prov. 14:6; 19:25). As synonyms of *lēṣ* we find such words as *kᵉsîl,* "fool" (Prov. 1:22; 3:35; 14:7f.; 19:29); *'ᵉwîl,* "fool" (24:9 conj.; 29:9); *peṯî,* "simple" (1:22), *zēḏ,* "proud," and *yāhîr,* "haughty" (21:24). It is characteristic of a *lēṣ* — as of a *zēḏ*[23] — to be incapable of learning from the admonitions, reproof, or punishment of someone who knows better (Prov. 9:7f.; 13:1; 14:6; 15:12; 19:25). In a crisis, Isaiah calls the rulers of Jerusalem *'anšê lāṣôn* (Isa. 28:14), although and in fact precisely because they consider themselves *ḥᵃḵāmîm* and *nᵉḇônîm* (Isa. 29:14). The difference between *zēḏ/zāḏôn* and *lēṣ/lāṣôn* may be that the former refers more to presumptuous arrogance toward others, while the latter puts more emphasis on foolish self-aggrandizement. The

19. See the comms.
20. *VT,* 5 (1955), 167, 177f.
21. Cf. Duhm, *in loc.*
22. → חכם.
23. → חכם *ḥāḵam* (*chākham*), IV, 48f.

lēṣ is a typical manifestation of what it means to be "unwise" in one's plans, words, and actions — presumptuous, arrogant, and conceited.

b. In postexilic wisdom and related genres, *lēṣ* seems to have taken on more theological overtones. The discourses and poems praising "Dame Wisdom" in Prov. 1–9 still emphasize the antithesis between wisdom and folly, but now with an explicit criterion to distinguish them: Yahweh and his commandment. Wisdom is understood increasingly as "fear of God," folly as "godlessness." In Prov. 1:22; 9:7f., the use of *lēṣ, lāṣôn,* and *lîṣ* still appears to reflect the old meaning; but theological elements in the context (1:28; 9:10) clearly voice the new understanding, to which 3:34 gives pregnant expression in the antithesis *lēṣîm*/*ʿᵃniyyim* or *ʿᵃnāwîm.*[24] The same is true in Ps. 1:1f., where the *lēṣîm* (par. *rᵉšāʿîm* and *ḥaṭṭāʾîm*), contrasted with the one who delights in the Torah, must be understood as arrogant scorners of the Torah.

c. Isa. 29:20 represents a still later stage in the semantic development of *lēṣ*: "The *ʿārîṣ* shall come to naught and the *lēṣ* cease, / and all who watch to do evil shall be cut off." The verse belongs to an oracle of salvation (29:17-24) that was not included in the collection of Isa. 28–32 until the second century B.C.[25] Here the *lēṣ* is once more the enemy of the devout (*ʿᵃnāwîm, ʾebyônîm*: 29:19; *ṣaddîq*: v. 21). Since the wrongdoing consists primarily in calumny and false accusation (v. 21), this passage appears to understand *lēṣ* (also found with *ʿārîṣ* in 1QH 2:10f.) as denoting an enemy of the faithful whose offense is specifically verbal. The Dead Sea scrolls also connect *lēṣ* and *lāṣôn* with verbal attacks on the faithful. What is involved is not so much "mockery" as the spreading of "lies."[26] The *ʾᵃnšê lāṣôn* of 4Q162 2:6,10; CD 1:14; 20:11 and the *ʾîš kāzāḇ* of 1QpHab 2:2; 5:11; CD 20:15 must belong to the same group of enemies. There is no great distance separating this usage from Middle Heb. *lîṣān* and Jewish Aram. *lîṣānûṯāʾ*, which refer primarily to blasphemy and mockery of what is holy.[27]

III. *mēlîṣ*.

1. *Epigraphic Evidence.* Northwest Semitic epigraphy has contributed greatly to our understanding of the biblical and postbiblical noun *mēlîṣ* (a hiphil ptcp.?), but its meaning is not yet entirely clear. In some texts, the Phoenician and Punic noun *mlṣ* means "interpreter"; for other texts such meanings as "boaster," "rebel," "counselor," "dignitary," and "demigod" have been proposed.[28]

Citing Gen. 42:23, G. A. Cooke[29] understood the *mlṣ hkrsym* of *CIS,* I, 44 and 88 as "interpreter of thrones." The graffiti left by Phoenician and Aramaic travelers visiting the temple of Osiris at Abydus include a name followed by the occupational title *hmlṣ.*[30]

---

24. → עני *ʿānî.*
25. O. Kaiser, *Isaiah 13–39. OTL* (Eng. trans. 1974), *in loc.*
26. → כזב *kzb.*
27. Buhl, 81f.
28. Cf. *DISO,* 138.
29. G. A. Cooke, *A Textbook of North-Semitic Inscriptions* (Oxford, 1903), 60, 73.
30. *KAI,* 49, 17.

Herbert Donner and W. Röllig are likely correct in translating it "the interpreter." Heb. *mēlîṣ,* "interpreter," is clearly associated with *mlṣ* in this sense.

The meaning of *mlṣ* in an inscription of King Azitawadda of Karatepe (*ca.* 720 B.C.)[31] is disputed. The immediately following statement about eradicating (?) "all the evil that was in the land" suggests that *wšbrt mlṣm* must mean "and I shattered the rebels." Donner and Röllig arrive at this translation of *mlṣ* by citing Heb. *lîṣ,* "talk big." This interpretation is more convincing if the basic meaning of *lîṣ* (*GesB, LexHebAram*: *lîṣ* I) is taken as "be arrogant, impudent."

2. *Biblical Usage.* In one of the biblical texts containing *mēlîṣ,* it clearly refers to a professional "interpreter" (Gen. 42:23). Three other texts seem to involve related professions: "envoy" (2 Ch. 32:31), "advocate" (Job 16:20; 33:23). Only in Isa. 43:27 is it more reasonable to translate *mlṣ* "rebel," as in Phoenician.

a. That Gen. 42:23 refers to an official interpreter (LXX: *hermēneutḗs*; Vulg.: *interpres*) is assured by the use of *šmʿ* (v. 23a) in the sense of "understand (a language)." In 2 Ch. 32:31, the *melîṣê śar*[32] *baḇel* also come to Hezekiah on an official mission; in this case, however, they are not interpreters but "intermediaries" or "envoys" (LXX: *presbeuteís*; Vulg.: *legatio*).

b. Job 16:20 ("My *melîṣîm* [are] my friends/to God my eye constantly [looks]"; text corrupt?) already caused problems for the ancient versions. The LXX rewrote the entire stich freely; the Targ. has *peraqlîṭay,* "my advocates."[33] The Vulg., however, has *verbosi,* which might constitute late evidence in favor of "talk big" as the alleged basic meaning of *lyṣ*. Friedrich Horst[34] insists that the solution must give the verse a meaningful function between vv. 19 and 21 and finds such a solution in the Targ.'s *mēlîṣ* in the sense of "advocate": "If my advocate is my friend/my eye remains open to God without sleep." Horst derives this meaning for *mēlîṣ* from "bigmouth" > "spokesperson" > "advocate," but it would seem better to begin with the etymologically independent *mēlîṣ* = "interpreter" > "intermediary" > "advocate."

Closely related is the use of *mēlîṣ* in the first discourse of Elihu (Job 33:23): "If there be for him an angel/of the thousand a single *mēlîṣ* . . . ." The LXX misinterprets the text, but the Targ. reads: "an advocate among a thousand accusers." The Vulg. translates freely: *si fuerit pro eo angelus loquens unum de milibus.* This is the earliest passage to ascribe to an angel the role of mediator.[35]

c. Especially difficult is the interpretation of *melîṣeyḵā* in Isa. 43:27.[36] The statement "your first father sinned,/and [or 'but'] your *melîṣîm* transgressed against me" appears in the context of a judgment oracle (Isa. 43:22-28), where it explains why, after a long

---

31. *KAI,* 26A, I, 8.
32. *BHS.*
33. Cf. Behm.
34. F. Horst, *Hiob. BK,* XVI/1 (^{4}1983), 240-42, 252-55.
35. Cf. Behm, 809f.
36. For a full discussion of the problem, see K. Elliger, *Deuterojesaja. BK,* XI/1 (1978), 361f., 381-86, with bibliog.

history trying Yahweh's patience, Jacob/Israel was finally delivered to destruction (v. 28). In parallel with the "first father" (Jacob), the *m*ᵉ*ṣîlîm* can only be important representatives of the people — kings, priests, prophets, or the leadership as a whole. The LXX (*árchontes*) and Syr. (*š*ᵉ*lîṭānē'*) think primarily of judges and kings, but this isolated translation is probably influenced by the *śārê* of v. 28. Aquila, Symmachus (*hermēneutaí*) and the Vulg. (*interpretes*) follow the usage of Gen. 42:23; ever since Jerome, exegetical tradition has understood the *m*ᵉ*lîṣîm* as prophets. Karl Elliger[37] and many recent exegetes derive the meaning "spokesman" (NEB "your spokesmen") or "speaker" from the basic meaning of *lyṣ* (according to Maurice A. Canney/Richardson). In the light of Phoen. *mlṣm,*[38] it might be better to treat the word as a hiphil participle of *lyṣ* I, "be arrogant," and translate with "your arrogant ones" or "your rebels." For similar characterizations of the leaders responsible for the catastrophe, cf. Isa. 1:23; Jer. 2:8; 6:28; Hos. 9:15; also Isa. 48:8.

3. *Postbiblical Usage.* In the deuterocanonical books and related literature of later Israel, *mēlîṣ* seldom occurs; only the Dead Sea scrolls constitute an exception.

Sir. 10:2: "As the ruler (*šôp̄ēṭ*) of a people, so are his *m*ᵉ*lîṣîm*;/and as the head of a city, so are its inhabitants." The parallelism of the two stichs indicates that the *m*ᵉ*lîṣîm* must be royal officials. The LXX and Syr. translate freely with "servants," possibly under the influence of the similar aphorism in Prov. 29:12. Since the negative element of "arrogance" found in the wisdom tradition is absent here, we should posit an extended meaning of *mēlîṣ*: "interpreter" > "intermediary" > "official."

In the Hebrew text of T.Nap. 9:2, God himself (or the archangel Michael[39]) is called *m*ᵉ*lîṣ*ᵉ*ḵem bammārôm,* "your *mēlîṣ* on high." This text comes from the circles associated with the Qumran community. As in Job 16:20; 33:23, the most likely meaning is "advocate."

In the Dead Sea scrolls, there are 8 certain occurrences of *mlyṣ,* all in Hodayoth. In most cases, the best translation is "interpreter" or "intermediary" in the nontechnical sense. Someone who conveys a message or teaching is a *mlyṣ,* The *mlyṣ d't brzy pl'* in 1QH 2:13 (cf. 8:11) recalls the "Teacher of Righteousness," but cf. the plural in 1QH fr. 2:6. The teachers of error are accordingly called *mlyṣy t'wt* (1QH 2:14), *mlyṣy kzb* (2:31; 4:9f.), or *mlyṣy rmyh* (4:7). Only in 6:13 is the meaning of the word obscure, since the legible text breaks off immediately after *w'yn mlyṣ bnym.* Johann Maier's restoration *lq*[*dwšykh*] would yield the translation: "No mediating interpreter is needed by thy holy ones"; the notion of revelation without a mediator, however, is alien to the Hodayoth. The possiblity exists of understanding *mlyṣ* in its other sense: "No arrogant rebel is in between."

Barth

37. *Ibid.,* 382f.
38. *KAI,* 26A, I, 8.
39. Behm.